The Second Empire
Art in France under Napoleon III

*This exhibition is supported in part by
a grant from the National Endowment for the
Arts, a Federal agency, and by a Federal
indemnity from the Federal Council on the
Arts and the Humanities*

*This exhibition is sponsored at
The Detroit Institute of Arts
by the Eleanor and Edsel Ford Exhibitions Fund,
Founders Society Detroit Institute of Arts,
and by a generous grant from the State of Michigan*

*This catalogue is sponsored at the Philadelphia
Museum of Art by the Women's Committee of the
Philadelphia Museum of Art*

Philadelphia Museum of Art
October 1 — November 26, 1978

The Detroit Institute of Arts
January 15 — March 18, 1979

Grand Palais, Paris
April 24 — July 2, 1979

# The Second Empire 1852–1870

# Art in France under Napoleon III

Philadelphia Museum of Art
1978

This exhibition was organized by Victor Beyer,
Conservateur en Chef Chargé de l'Inspection Générale
des Musées Classés et Contrôlés, Musée du Louvre;
Kathryn B. Hiesinger, Curator of European Decorative
Arts after 1700, Philadelphia Museum of Art;
Jean-Marie Moulin, Conservateur en Chef du Musée
National du Château de Compiègne; and Joseph
Rishel, Curator of European Painting before 1900,
Philadelphia Museum of Art.
The objects in this exhibition were selected by the
organizers and by Daniel Alcouffe, Conservateur au
Département des Objets d'Art, Musée du Louvre;
Eugenia P. Janis, Associate Professor, Department of
Art, Wellesley College; Geneviève Lacambre,
Conservateur au Département des Peintures, Musée du
Louvre; Anne Pingeot, Conservateur au Département
des Sculptures, Musée du Louvre; Colombe
Samoyault-Verlet, Conservateur au Musée National du
Château de Fontainebleau; Arlette Sérullaz,
Conservateur au Cabinet des Dessins, Musée du
Louvre; and David Van Zanten, Associate Professor,
Department of the History of Art, University of
Pennsylvania.

Cover:
Detail of *The Garden of Armida*, 1854 (no. II-16)

Distributed by Wayne State University Press
Detroit, Michigan 48202

# Contents

# Lenders to the Exhibition

## Canada

Ottawa
  The National Gallery of Canada

## France

Private Collections (7)
Alençon
  Musées d'Alençon
Amiens
  Chapitre, Cathedral of Amiens
  Musée de Picardie
Angers
  Musée des Beaux-Arts
Arras
  Musée des Beaux-Arts
Auxerre
  Musées de la Ville d'Auxerre
Bagnères-de-Bigorre
  Musée Salles
Besançon
  Musée des Beaux-Arts
Bordeaux
  Musée des Beaux-Arts
Boulogne-sur-Seine
  Private Collection
Bourg-en-Bresse
  Musée de l'Ain
Caen
  Musée des Beaux-Arts
Châlons-sur-Marne
  Musées de Châlons-sur-Marne
Cléry
  Basilica of Notre Dame
Compiègne
  Musée National du Château
Eure-et-Loir
  Château de Maintenon
Fontainebleau
  Musée National du Château
  Palais de Fontainebleau,
    Direction de l'Architecture

Gimouille (Nevers)
  Collection Comte Henri de Martimprey
Gironde
  Collection Mlle de Baritault, Château de
    Roquetaillade
Le Havre
  Musée des Beaux-Arts "André Malraux"
Le Mée sur Seine
  Musée Municipal Henri Chapu
Lille
  Archives Historiques du Diocèse de Lille
  Musée des Beaux-Arts
Limoges
  Haviland
  Musée National Adrien-Dubouché
Lunéville
  Musée Municipal
Lyons
  Musée des Beaux-Arts
  Musée Historique des Tissus
Lyons-Paris
  Prelle S.A.
Marseilles
  Musée des Beaux-Arts
Montauban
  Musée Ingres
Montpellier
  Musée Fabre
Nantes
  Musée des Beaux-Arts
Neuilly
  Fonds Viollet-le-Duc
Paris
  Archives de Paris
  Archives Nationales
  Baccarat
  Bibliothèque des Arts Décoratifs
  Bibliothèque Historique de la Ville de Paris
  Bibliothèque Nationale, Cabinet des
    Estampes, Département de la Musique,
    Bibliothèque et Musée de l'Opéra
  Centre de Recherches sur les Monuments
    Historiques, Ministère de la Culture et de
    la Communication

  Comédie Française
  Collection Devinat
  Ecole Nationale Supérieure des Beaux-Arts
  MM. Fabius
  Collection Pierre Fabius
  Institut de France—Musée Frédéric
    Masson
  Collection André Jammes
  Collection Comtesse Napoléon Lepic
  Collection Gérard-Lévy
  Ministère de la Culture et de la
    Communication—Musée de Notre Dame
    de Paris, Trésor de Notre Dame de Paris
  Mobilier National
  Musée Carnavalet
  Musée de l'Armée
  Musée des Arts Décoratifs
  Musée du Louvre, Cabinet des Dessins,
    Département des Objets d'Art,
    Département des Peintures,
    Département des Sculptures,
    Galerie du Jeu de Paume
  Musée du Petit Palais
  Musée Hébert
  Musée National des Techniques—C.N.A.M.
  Musée Rodin
  Palais National du Louvre, Direction de
    l'Architecture
  Collection S.A.I. Prince Napoléon
  Collection S.A.I. Princesse Marie-Clotilde
    Napoléon, Comtesse de Witt
  Société Française de Photographie
  Tassinari & Chatel, S.A.R.L.
  Collection Vaudoyer
Poitiers
  Abbaye Ste. Croix
  Musée des Beaux-Arts
Pontoise
  Musée Tavet-Delacour
Quimper
  Musée Municipal des Beaux-Arts
Reims
  Association Diocésaine de Reims
Roanne
  Musée Joseph Déchelette (Musée
    Municipal)

Rouen
  Musée des Beaux-Arts
Saint-Etienne
  Musée d'Art et d'Industrie
Saint-Louis
  Compagnie des Cristalleries
Saint-Omer
  Musée de l'Hôtel Sandelin
Sèvres
  Musée National de Céramique
Thann
  City of Thann
Toulouse
  Musée Paul Dupuy
Tours
  Musée des Beaux-Arts
Troyes
  Musées des Beaux-Arts
Verdun
  Musée de la Princerie
Versailles
  Musée National du Château
Villeneuve-sur-Lot
  Musée Gaston Rapin
Vincennes
  Musée Kodak-Pathé

## Germany

Bremen
  Kunsthalle
Cologne
  Wallraf-Richartz-Museum und
    Museum Ludwig

## Great Britain

Collection Peter Rose and
  Albert Gallichan
Barnard Castle
  The Bowes Museum

London
  Bethnal Green Museum
  Collection Walter Godny
  Victoria and Albert Museum
Oxford
  The Visitors of the Ashmolean Museum
Southampton
  Southampton Art Gallery

## Mexico

Mexico City
  Museo Nacional de Historia, Castillo
    de Chapultepec

## The Netherlands

Amsterdam
  The Citroen Collection

## Norway

Oslo
  Nasjonalgalleriet

## United States

Baltimore
  The Walters Art Gallery
Boston
  Museum of Fine Arts
Brooklyn
  The Brooklyn Museum
Cambridge
  Fogg Art Museum, Harvard University
Chicago
  The Art Institute of Chicago

Cleveland
  The Cleveland Museum of Art
Detroit
  The Detroit Institute of Arts
Hartford
  Wadsworth Atheneum
Houston
  Collection Mr. and Mrs. T.C. Morrow
Los Angeles
  Los Angeles County Museum of Art
Minneapolis
  The Minneapolis Institute of Arts
New Haven
  Yale University Art Gallery
New York
  Private Collection
  The *Forbes* Magazine Collection
  The Metropolitan Museum of Art
  Estate of Germain Seligman
  Shepherd Gallery, Associates
  Collection Samuel Wagstaff, Jr.
Norfolk
  Chrysler Museum
Northampton, Massachusetts
  Smith College Museum of Art
Oberlin
  Allen Memorial Art Museum
Old Westbury, New York
  Collection Mr. and Mrs. Harry Glass
Philadelphia
  John G. Johnson Collection
  Philadelphia Museum of Art
Rochester
  International Museum of Photography at
    George Eastman House
Saint Louis
  Washington University Gallery of Art
Toledo
  The Toledo Museum of Art
Washington, D.C.
  Lunn Gallery/Graphics International Ltd.
  National Gallery of Art
Williamstown, Massachusetts
  Sterling and Francine Clark Art Institute
Worcester, Massachusetts
  Dr. and Mrs. Lambi Adams

# Contributing Authors

D.A.  Daniel Alcouffe
Conservateur au Département des Objets d'Art,
Musée du Louvre

B.C.  Bernard Chevallier
Conservateur au Musée National du Château de
Fontainebleau

N.D.  Nancy Davenport
Instructor, Philadelphia College of Art

B.E.  Betty Elzea
Research Assistant, Department of European
Decorative Arts after 1700, Philadelphia Museum of
Art

K.B.H.  Kathryn B. Hiesinger
Curator of European Decorative Arts after 1700,
Philadelphia Museum of Art

E.P.J.  Eugenia P. Janis
Associate Professor, Department of Art, Wellesley
College

G.L.  Geneviève Lacambre
Conservateur au Département des Peintures, Musée
du Louvre

J.-M.L.  J.-M. Leniaud

S.G.L.  Suzanne G. Lindsay
Research Assistant, Department of European
Painting before 1900, Philadelphia Museum of Art

D.F.M.  Dewey F. Mosby
Curator of European Art, The Detroit Institute of
Arts

J.-M.M.  Jean-Marie Moulin
Conservateur en Chef du Musée National du
Château de Compiègne

M.N.  Monique Nonne

O.N.  Odile Nouvel
Conservateur au Musée des Arts Décoratifs

A.P.  Anne Pingeot
Conservateur au Département des Sculptures, Musée
du Louvre

L.-A.P.  Louis-Antoine Prat
Chargé de Mission au Cabinet des Dessins, Musée
du Louvre

J.R.  Joseph Rishel
Curator of European Painting before 1900,
Philadelphia Museum of Art

D.R.  Donald Rosenthal
Assistant Curator, Department of European Painting
before 1900, Philadelphia Museum of Art

J.-P.S.  Jean-Pierre Samoyault
Conservateur du Musée National du Château de
Fontainebleau

C.S.-V.  Colombe Samoyault-Verlet
Conservateur au Musée National du Château de
Fontainebleau

O.S.  Odile Sebastiani*
Conservateur au Musée National du Château de
Compiègne

A.S.  Arlette Sérullaz
Conservateur au Cabinet des Dessins, Musée du
Louvre

D.V.Z.  David Van Zanten
Associate Professor, Department of the History of
Art, University of Pennsylvania

*Deceased

# Preface

*The Second Empire: Art in France under Napoleon III* marks a continuation of a series of large undertakings sponsored jointly by French and American museums. This exhibition was initiated in 1974 under the direction of Jean Chatelain and Evan H. Turner, former directors, respectively, of the Musées de France and the Philadelphia Museum of Art. Shortly thereafter, the project was joined by The Detroit Institute of Arts, thereby assuring the success of the exhibition. The Second Empire (1852-1870) has remained a neglected and misunderstood period in French history. It has been prejudged as an era of bourgeois and commercial profusion in the arts, wherein the State patronized a preferred clique and ignored a large group of artists, including some of the most progressive, while the applied arts were left to proliferate without artistic direction. The Second Empire, in fact, is revealed in this exhibition as an immensely rich and innovative period of artistic creation. An ambitious undertaking, *The Second Empire* presents the entire range artistic production of the period: architectural drawings, decorative arts, sculpture, paintings, drawings, and photography. Many of the 372 works included in the exhibition are lent for the first time. It is due to the generosity of our lenders that this monumental exhibition has been possible, permitting an entirely new and more accurate appraisal of the character and importance of this period.

Arnold Jolles
Acting Director, Philadelphia Museum of Art

Frederick J. Cummings
Director, The Detroit Institute of Arts

Hubert Landais
Directeur des Musées de France

# Notes for Use
# of the Catalogue

This catalogue is arranged in eight sections according to medium, each designated by a Roman numeral. Biographies precede the major representation of each artist's and maker's work; consult index if biography does not immediately precede catalogue entry, and for cross references (q.v.), which indicate the inclusion of a biography in the catalogue.

An asterisk (*) following the name of an artist or maker indicates that biographical information is to be found in the entry and that no separate biography is included.

In listing dimensions, height precedes width precedes depth.

Citations of bibliography and exhibitions have been abbreviated. Complete references are provided in the list of Publications and Exhibitions Cited in Abbreviated Form beginning on page 436.

The following abbreviations have been used in the text and references:

| | |
|---|---|
| anon. | anonymous |
| bibl. | bibliography |
| c. | circa |
| cat. | catalogue |
| col. | column |
| coll. | collection |
| ed. | editor/edition |
| enl. | enlarged |
| fig. | figure |
| ff. | following |
| h. | height |
| inv. | inventory |
| l. | length |
| n.d. | no date |
| n.l. | no location |
| no., nos. | number, numbers |
| n.p. | no page |
| n.s. | new series |
| p., pp. | page, pages |
| pl. | plate |
| pseud. | pseudonym |
| q.v., q.q.v. | *quod (quae) vide,* which see |
| r | recto |
| repro. | reproduced |
| rev. | revised |
| s. | series |
| v | verso |
| vol. | volume |

| | |
|---|---|
| Arch. nat. | Paris, Archives nationales |
| Arch. de la Garantie | Paris, Archives de la Direction de la Garantie |
| Bib. nat. | Paris, Bibliothèque nationale |
| Compiègne | Compiègne, Musée National du Château |
| Fontainebleau | Fontainebleau, Musée National du Château |
| Louvre | Paris, Musée National du Louvre |

# The Second Empire: Art and Society

Only rarely do periods of art coincide with political regimes. The Second Empire is no exception. That such a phenomenon as a "Napoleon III style" exists is generally accepted, but this is more a matter of sentiment than of reason. It is not easy to discern this style nor to describe it. One of the purposes of this exhibition is to achieve a definition of the style, and it is for this reason that its organizers have selected only works that can be firmly dated between 1852 and 1870. The vagueness that, even today, clouds the notion of "Second Empire art" has made this restriction necessary.

Still, it would be wrong to believe that a specific style of art was born, developed, and died in the course of this nineteen-year period during which France knew its last absolute regime. Why then have we nonetheless chosen these dates? Because this is a period that has been ignored—one might almost say erased—by French art historians, who have considered it insignificant, if not monstrous. The impetus for initiating such an exhibition had to come from without, in this instance our colleagues in Philadelphia. Had it been proposed in France by Frenchmen it would have had great difficulty seeing the light of day. Those who have had the experience of working on the Second Empire in the area of the arts have felt the scorn (sometimes tinged with indulgence) that has surrounded the period, even—and perhaps especially—among the specialist and the knowledgeable layman. The causes of this ostracism, sometimes even fury (only recently, important ensembles created by the Second Empire have been destroyed or disfigured) are deeper than one would think. One must recognize that even a hundred years later, passions are still burning.

In the aftermath of the fall of the Second Empire, France woke up stunned. For several centuries this ancient nation had witnessed both reversals and victories. Yet it was the first time perhaps that the French felt responsible for a defeat in the sense that they had a vague awareness of having suffered it not as subjects but as directly involved citizens. As always happens in such cases, however, scapegoats were sought. The fallen sovereigns and their entourage were foreordained. Because the regime had been so brilliant, the French were less able to forgive it. The splendor of the reign, the technical advances that accompanied it, had given the French, even those who did not

benefit directly from it but were merely spectators astounded before a dazzling display that made them forget their misery, a sense of total self-confidence, confirming the belief, naturally common to all peoples, that they were the best and the strongest.

The surrender of Napoleon III to the Germans at Sedan and the ensuing defeat, despite an attempt at resistance by the newly proclaimed Third Republic, came as a violent trauma which the country's rapid economic recovery could not overcome. The loss of Alsace-Lorraine was felt by each Frenchman as a personal mutilation. From 1871 on the French kept their eyes fixed on what would later be called "the blue line of the Vosges." Whatever the injustices and mistakes of the regime, they would have been excused if the provinces had not been lost. Forgotten were the economic developments and the past glories of the Second Empire, which were dearly bought but greatly praised, such as the annexation of Savoy and Nice. The nascent and very fragile Third Republic needed this foil—it needed to affirm itself, to create its own identity, to live and exist *against* the Second Empire, and in opposition to it. It did its best to achieve this goal. For three generations of schoolchildren, the defeat was a humiliation, and Napoleon III, the man responsible for it, could not be absolved. Among politicians and intellectuals there were not enough terms of contempt to criticize the previous regime. For decades, French historians were unable to be impartial—it was all too immediate, too alive, too painful. It has only been recently, long after English and German historians, that French historians have been able to step back and take a more detached view.

But all this is, understandably, the concern of specialists—in the depth of public feeling nothing has changed. Even today there are many Frenchmen who consider the reign of Louis XIV, which ended catastrophically, to have been a brilliant era; that of Louis XV, with indulgence; that of Louis XVI, with compassion; and that of Napoleon as a glorious period despite Waterloo, a defeat that is looked upon as an unlucky and almost unjust turn of fortune. Yet in spite of the time elapsed, and in spite of the lost provinces regained, Napoleon III has still not been forgiven for his capitulation at Sedan. References to absolute power, despotism, and social injustices, always

excuses advanced to condemn the regime, seem only to mask a deeper feeling—a sense of collective guilt for having made one man alone responsible. From this stems the tendency to make of the Second Empire a kind of parenthesis within the nineteenth century, a period apart, despised politically as well as artistically, even though, on the latter score at least, it fits in with a steady line of development. The style of the Second Empire, or of Napoleon III, actually began under Louis Philippe and continued until the end of the century.

Yet in the artistic domain, just as in the political domain, we find ourselves faced with the contradictions of a society which either refused to acknowledge its errors or else felt them so deeply that it blamed itself for them. The class that dominated the entire nineteenth century was the bourgeoisie. After having felt much remorse on a political level for its enthusiastic support of a regime that had come to a disastrous end (it must be remembered that the electoral body, which was essentially bourgeois, had by plebiscite voted Napoleon III into power three times with overwhelming majorities, the last time only four months before the proclamation of the Republic), this same bourgeoisie would later find that it had reasons to feel a sense of guilt on the artistic level as well.

The bourgeoisie of the Third Republic and among them, the art historians, who either emerged from it or belonged to it, were unwilling to forgive their predecessors for having "missed" the Impressionist movement, for having recognized neither its birth during the Second Empire nor its development in the years following, and for having abandoned themselves from 1840 to the end of the century to the pleasures of a style of art which was apparently easier and more readily accessible. The motivating force behind this was not always perfectly pure. To the remorse of disinterested art historians for having failed to recognize an art so glorious was joined that of the public at large, a regret, more prosaically bourgeois, of having failed to profit materially from this art. One of the consequences of this was in art history, where Romanticism led into Impressionism with only a brief mention, in passing, of "official art." Once again, it seemed easy to throw the blame for a certain bourgeois bad taste onto the Second Empire, which had witnessed the triumph of an art that an educated and active society had hailed and which had reached a peak between 1852 and 1870, precisely because of the regime's splendor.

If one is to search for the *raison d'être* as well as the explanation for Second Empire art it is certainly within the relationship between art and society that one has the chance of finding it. All the artistic activity of the period appears to have been dominated by the tastes of the bourgeois class, whose importance had been growing since the French Revolution of 1789, reaching its highest point at this time. The life of the court itself simply concealed a bourgeois society, while the mixed aristocracy that surrounded the sovereigns had the same tastes as the bourgeoisie.

It would be difficult to discern any genuine concerted, directed, or coherent exercise of imperial power in the domain of the arts. The Emperor never hid the fact that he had little appreciation for the arts in any form whatsoever. His visits to the Salons were merely official formalities, during which he most often refrained from expressing personal preferences. He cared more about the subjects portrayed than their treatment. If the personal taste of Napoleon III did occasionally appear, it was for paintings or statues portraying well-developed, plump women. This, one would imagine, is more an indication of his own temperament than of a particular artistic penchant. His authorization of the Salon des Refusés in 1863 did not come about from artistic conviction but rather from liberalism. The purchases of works of art from his own pocket were often only the result of recommendations, or more often, made because they allowed the Emperor to come to the aid of artists whose struggles had been brought to his attention. In any case, he trusted the officials in charge of purchasing and never acted decisively in this realm. While he appreciated Carpeaux (q.v.)—remembering, perhaps, his relief portraying Abd-el-Kader's reception at Saint-Cloud—he could not in all honesty impose him because he did not trust his own judgment. For Napelon III, exercising power in the artistic domain was but one aspect of social action.

At the beginning of his reign, he was perfectly content to live in the imperial palaces—the Tuileries, Saint-Cloud, Fontainebleau, and Compiègne—with the décor and furnishings inherited from the first Empire, and which had survived the previous reigns without major modifications. If he decided, around 1860, to have the palaces completely refurnished, it was mainly because the first Empire furnishings, already half a century old, were by then thoroughly out of fashion. No doubt he also saw in this the opportunity to provide work for

an entire sector of the economy—namely craftsmen in silk, trimmings, and cabinetry. Redecorating the palaces would assure work for several thousand craftsmen in the artistic trades. He exercised his influence indirectly, not through his personal taste but through his interest in technical innovations. If he encouraged Christofle (q.v.) and gave him major commissions, it was because electroforming and the process of galvanic silver plating seemed to him to hold great promise for the future. In so doing the Emperor expressed the idea, dear to the period, that artistic creations be accessible to all purses. By the same token he was particularly interested in the possible artistic applications of a new metal, aluminum (*see* no. III-23).

Unlike the Emperor, the Empress Eugénie had some pretensions to taste. Periodically she tried her hand at watercolors. She submitted to the competition for a new Opéra (*see* nos. I-10, I-30) a sketch, which was touched up by Garnier (q.v.). Her passion for decorating was well known and occasionally was affectionately mocked by her entourage. "If you were to tell her she was beautiful, witty, or charitable, she probably wouldn't even answer…. But if you swore to her that there wasn't a decorator around who could choose furniture, match fabrics, and decorate a drawing room the way she could…." "Would she perhaps decorate me too?" This is the dialogue of two characters in a revue composed by the duc de Morny and Prosper Mérimée, *La Corde sensible ou les Dadas favoris,* which was performed by the guests at one of the series at Compiègne in 1862.

Fortuné de Fournier's watercolors (*see* nos. II-2, II-3) provide a good visual account of the suites of furniture arranged, for the most part, by the Empress at Saint-Cloud. With surprising eclecticism, the Empress mixed authentic eighteenth-century pieces and those of the first Empire, both with contemporary pieces which were pastiches of earlier styles and more "modern" pieces (tufted chairs, seats made of English-type leather). These ensembles were judged to be in perfect taste, and not solely for flattery. Even after the fall of the Empire, they were still being marvelled over. The introduction of eighteenth-century elements in these ensembles often stemmed from the peculiar fascination which the memory of Marie Antoinette held for the Empress. Yet this was not incompatible with the emphasis on comfort which was common to the whole period. For example, this desire for comfort led her to have the seats of the royal furniture tufted—and what is more, in colors which were typically those of the Second Empire and not those of the eighteenth century. Thus, in a drawing room at

Compiègne, the Empress used Louis XVI chairs from Saint-Cloud which she arranged to have tufted and covered with dark gray-green silk. Certainly this decorating activity was a diversion for the Empress, yet it was also a means for her to participate in the Emperor's politics regarding the artistic crafts. This, perhaps, was the most important aspect of the Empress's activity. For it would be wrong to believe that in decoration she was responsible for creating fashion—she was merely following the ideas in vogue.

The same holds true for painting or for sculpture. In these areas, the taste of the imperial couple conformed absolutely to that of its time. One gets a clear idea of this from the list of artists who took part in the "series" at Compiègne. There, during each week-long series, the court brought together guests it wished to honor. Only a few invitations were extended to the artistic world, and it seemed that they were intended more to acknowledge success than to encourage budding talents. Among architects, since Viollet-le-Duc (q.v.) was working nearby on the château of Pierrefonds, he was practically an integral part of these series, and must be considered apart. He acted as guide for the obligatory tours to Pierrefonds, which were among the standard forms of entertainment offered at each of the series. In addition, he made himself indispensable in Compiègne's amateur theater, in which he acted both as designer and prompter. His only architect colleagues invited to Compiègne were Lefuel (q.v.; 1864), Hittorff (q.v.; 1865), and Garnier (1866). Among sculptors, only five were invited: Cavelier (q.v.; 1862), Carpeaux (1864), Schoenewerke (q.v.; 1864), Dubois (q.v.; 1865), and Bartholdi (1868). As for the duchesse de Castiglione-Colonna (Marcello, q.v.) invited in 1864, 1865, and 1866, there is reason to believe that she was there more because of her social standing than her status as a sculptress. There were far more painters: Cabanel (q.v.) was invited three times (1861, 1864, 1868); others twice: Baudry (q.v.; 1861, 1865), Meissonier (q.v.; 1861, 1864), and Doré (q.v.; 1864, 1868). Most of the painters, however, were invited only once: Winterhalter (q.v.; 1853—even before the institution of the series), Isabey (1856), H. Vernet (1856), Couture (q.v.; 1856), Delacroix (q.v.; 1858), Gudin (1858), Yvon (1859), Flandrin (q.v.; 1861), Bida (q.v.; 1861), Hébert (q.v.; 1862), Gérôme (q.v.; 1862), Jadin (1862), Pils (1863), Cogniet (1863), Boulanger (q.v.; 1864), Amaury-Duval (q.v.; 1864), Fromentin (q.v.; 1864), Protais (1864), T. Rousseau (q.v.; 1865), J. N. Robert-Fleury (1865), and Lami (q.v.; 1865). Although the name of Ingres (q.v.) figures on the list of guests invited in 1856, he did not attend the series. Penguilly-L'Haridon (q.v.), who came in 1865 and 1866, was invited, not as a painter but rather, described by the title of commander, as the curator of the Musée de l'Artillerie. Furthermore, one must note that the artists invited during a given year were not all part of the same series; they were distributed among all the series for that year. If one takes account of the fact that each series comprised about one hundred guests, and that generally there were four each year—though sometimes five, and in 1861, six—one sees clearly that the place reserved for the artistic world was not very great, even with musicians included. In any case, it is clear that the artists selected were those who were widely recognized at the time of their invitation.

In any discussion of artistic activity during the Second Empire, one must mention the role that Princess Mathilde played. There is no doubt in the least that she genuinely loved painting. At her death sale held in 1904, no less than one hundred modern paintings dating from the Second Empire, not counting watercolors, pastels, and drawings, were listed. She herself painted watercolors with great diligence and also tried her hand at pastels from time to time. Her work was exhibited in seven different Salons between 1859 and 1867, and in 1865 she was even awarded a medal—though its bestowal was undoubtedly due, at least in part, to flattery. Certainly her liaison with Nieuwerkerke, director of museums and subsequently Superintendent of Fine Arts, enabled her to exert an influence behind the scenes whose extent is difficult to determine. In addition to her literary salon at the rue de Courcelles (see no. II-4), she also held an artistic salon. Among the guests she received there were, notably, Carpeaux, Marcello, Gavarni, Lami, Doré, Meissonier, J. Lefebvre, Carolus-Duran (q.v.), Gervex, Flameng, the two Robert-Fleurys, Boulanger, Gérôme, Bouguereau (q.v.), and Hébert. Charles Giraud (q.v.) and above all Eugène Giraud, whose student Mathilde called herself, were the favorites of the house. The Princess prided herself at having been the first to buy works of Bonnat (q.v.), Roybet, Jacquet, and Detaille (q.v.)—painters who would enjoy their greatest renown during the Third Republic. In reality her tastes very closely embraced those of her time; thus, her role as initiator is far from evident. Her position appears rather ambiguous—a combination of a true taste for painting and the sense of obligation she felt, because of her rank, to receive artists and writers. She may have perceived her responsibility all the more strongly since she was aware of playing a role neglected by the Tuileries.

Princess Mathilde helped artists; she did not give artistic direction to her time.

The role of her brother, Prince Napoleon, less generally known, may actually have been more important, though limited. His force was felt only within a very specific domain—that of the revival of the Pompeian style. Actually, it was the influence of Rachel (see no. VI-1), the great tragedienne, that, through the intermediary of the Prince, was decisive—she gave him a certain taste for Classical antiquity, and it was for her that, in 1855, he asked Hittorff to build a large model reconstructing the Temple of Empedocles. After Rachel's death it was, in a way, out of loyalty to her memory that the Prince had the famous "Maison Pompéienne" constructed on the avenue Montaigne (see no. I-22)—a house furnished in the Classical style, where he gave theatrical performances also in the Classical style (see no. VI-12). This house created a sensation with the result that the Prince played a significant role in the artistic development of his time. Yet, changeable, he soon tired of the Pompeian fantasy.

Like that of the imperial family, the taste of the court and of the financial powers was the same as that of the official organizations—the Institut de France and the Ecole des Beaux-Arts— which was confirmed in the policies of art purchases and commissions pursued by those supervising the responsible agencies, the Ministère de la Maison de l'Empereur and the Ministry of State. It is enough to say that their choices went either to recognized artists or to artists whose work did not shock accepted visual tastes. Yet it would be difficult to define a deliberate policy from this. One gets the general impression that purchases and commissions were made either somewhat by chance or as a function of prevailing taste. It seems these ministries felt the necessity of giving work to artists while taking care not to impose biases. As a result, the available funds were distributed among the greatest possible number of artists. The list of official commissions and acquisitions is impressive—although an exhaustive survey has not yet been undertaken, its publication would surely fill a large volume. It would reveal that few periods have been as favorable to the development of the arts insofar as they could depend on existing institutions.

Should Second Empire officialdom then be reproached for not having determined any real artistic direction? In the highly complex relationships between artist and State, what more can the artist request of the State than it give him the opportunity to express himself as he wishes, without imposing a direction on him? In this respect one can maintain that the Second Empire was exemplary. That today our

choices would be different is another matter entirely, one which reflects changes in the history of taste.

Hence it is not in the official milieus that we should look for an influence exerted upon the artistic world. Rather it is in the taste of the predominating class, the class which represented the nation's most vital economic force—the bourgeoisie. The Second Empire marks the ultimate development of the bourgeois taste which emerged under Louis Philippe. It is natural that art shaped by and designed for a social class presents the essential characteristics particular to that class.

The consequences of the arrival of the bourgeoisie are very important. Before this time it had rather passively witnessed the rise and subsequent flowering of Romanticism, a movement it certainly had neither approved of nor understood. During the Restoration and at the beginning of the July Monarchy, the bourgeoisie, with a few individual exceptions from the top of its hierarchy, did not represent an effective force in the realm of the arts. It was too busy establishing the material foundations of its power to take a genuine interest, as a class, in the artistic domain.

Everything changed after the Revolution of 1848. The seizure of power by the Prince-President and his creation of the Empire, coinciding with an economic prosperity that favored it, brought the bourgeoisie to its height. Freed from its most material anxieties, it began to think about the "superfluous," to become interested in the "Fine Arts," to visit the Salon, to buy paintings and objects, and to wish to show off at last after having established itself in the preceding decades.

A new clientele, the bourgeoisie necessarily imposed its tastes. Established materially, positively, it had a constant point of reference—a standard of moderation—and anything which deviated from this norm was dismissed. It is because of this that Romanticism, an art of excess, scarcely survived the Revolution of 1848. It is also why the bourgeoisie rejected Naturalism and Realism, both movements which borrowed their subjects—peasants, laborers, and people on the fringes of society—from outside the bourgeoisie and which, in any case, produced images that were not beautified. For even if this bourgeois society lacked imagination, had a taste for the commonplace, and wanted art which was its own reflection, in truth, it would accept only a glossy, restrained, and idealized version of reality. The reason for this is simple—already it was not content with its station and entertained higher aspirations. Having become the nation's active force, the bourgeoisie now wanted to be considered its true aristocracy.

Actually, these aspirations were encouraged by the fact that at the same moment, the aristocratic class had fallen prey to material preoccupations and desired to enrich itself, no longer by its traditional and quasi-historic means, land, but by new means—commerce and speculation—and, thus, through this materialism inclined also toward bourgeois taste. The two classes, each moving a bit toward the other, came together, and the art they both desired was a middle ground, that of the *juste milieu*, which would be either an idealized reflection of society or a very measured idealism. This is why the society of the Second Empire did not understand Realism any better than it understood Impressionism, and for the same reasons: Realism seemed to lack idealization, and Impressionism seemed to lack reality.

This art of the *juste milieu* was that of most of the artists of the Second Empire and, as such, appears as the exact reflection of the society of its time. Daumier (q.v.), who for many years had been directing his sarcastic attacks at the bourgeoisie, presented on several different occasions during the Second Empire their very characteristic reactions to art. Faced with Realism, a few very ugly bourgeois before a Courbet, remark: "This Monsieur Courbet paints faces that are much too vulgar; there is no one in the world as ugly as that" (1855). Faced with idealism, a group of bourgeois at the Salon comment: "This year, still more Venuses, always Venuses, as if there were actually women built like that" (1864). Artistically inclined, a bourgeois, accompanied by his family, stands before his portrait bust: "To think that I will soon be exhibited and that all Paris will see me…. How flattering for me, my wife" (1859).

The bourgeois is tempted, but troubled. Taking up art, commissioning his bust, happy to be seen, he is nevertheless uneasy with certain of the conventions which remove him from the everyday world. He wants to see himself, but in a favorable light. He wants especially to be "recognizable." Daumier always insisted upon this point. In 1852 he also had portrayed a bourgeois and his family before his bust: "This bust is very well lit; it is quite striking. I regret only that the artist didn't think to put my hat on my head—it would have added much more to the likeness." In 1859 the wife of the same bourgeois who had earlier rejoiced at being seen by all Paris, answers him: "My dear, I am troubled by one thing… it is that you are portrayed without your cravat; it's really quite careless. So if there is still time, ask the sculptor to add at least a detachable collar." In 1864 another bourgeois, standing in front of his bust,

regrets that the artist had neglected to show him with his spectacles. Painting does not require these idealizations, and that is why the bourgeoisie leaned more toward it than toward sculpture.

The result of these pressures which were exerted upon art was a reassuring vision of the world, for this new clientele likewise needed reassurance. Much later the "enlightened" sector of the same bourgeoisie, confident in its own continuity, called this art "pretentious" *(pompier)* and "official," and willingly ridiculed it, forgetting that this art sprung from within its own ranks. The Second Empire was the naïve phase of bourgeois art.

The confirmation of the bourgeoisie had still more profound consequences in the areas of architecture and the decorative arts. Like all materially based societies, the Second Empire had a taste for eclectism and, therefore, a taste for imitation. This phenomenon is one of the least well understood, and above all, the least accepted by our more complex era—and perhaps the one which spurred the most obstinate condemnations of the Second Empire. We are still surprised by those Second Empire pseudo-Gothic, Renaissance, Louis XIV, Louis XV, and Louis XVI buildings and objects. This taste for imitation was by no means a phenomenon which began under the Second Empire—it originated under Louis Philippe and its explanation is at least twofold.

In the first place, it may be seen as one of the consequences of Romanticism, one of its vestiges which, revived by the bourgeoisie, survived at a time when Romanticism was dead. In the eighteenth century, for example, and even during the first Empire, anything old was considered old-fashioned—and thus both ugly and of little value. Appraisals in furniture inventories, for example, appraisals of Louis XV furniture during the reign of Louis XVI, can be revealing in this respect. Once furniture had gone out of style, it was appraised at a very low value, without any regard for its original worth—no matter how great this had been. Today we have a certain respect for the past and have acquired a taste for earlier styles. This change in the orientation of taste took place with Romanticism, which, in one of its aspects, turned toward the past.

In the initial phase which one could call "primitive," past styles were copied because in other respects there was a taste for the new, the solid, a taste which was essentially bourgeois. And it was here that, in spite of itself, the bourgeoisie took up where Romanticism had left off. The pastiches that had originated under Louis Philippe reached the height of their popularity during the Second Empire and contin-

ued until the end of the century and indeed for the lower classes who had only lately moved into the bourgeoisie, until the First World War and after. Appreciation for true antiques appeared only in a more advanced phase. It emerged during the Second Empire, but only among a very limited number of intellectually refined individuals who furnished their homes with genuine antiques, rather than imitations (for example, the Goncourts); the majority of those who bought furniture and other objects, however, were not yet at this point. The illusion of age was enough to satisfy them.

In the second place, this constant reference to the past may appear as another means of bourgeois self-reassurance. A class which had only recently "arrived," it did not yet have the audacity to initiate a new style. That was possible only for established society, those who were confident, rightly or wrongly, in their continuity and especially in themselves, because they had been so long dominant. The style of the first Empire was able to assert itself on the strength that it had acquired at the end of the *ancien régime* and also because, in spite of the Revolution, there had not been any truly profound modifications in the structure of society or in the patronage of the arts, which remained basically the same as before. The bourgeoisie, newcomers as art patrons, turned toward a past which reassured them.

Here again the bourgeoisie concurred in its taste with the aristocratic society, which also turned toward the past in order to reassure itself, but for different reasons. One class wished to affirm its wealth, its power, to be sure that it did not err; the other was motivated by an insecurity whose causes were contradictory. In many respects the imperial court and the aristocratic society which revolved around it appeared as an artificial institution, a survival of a past form of government in a nation which now had other aspirations. This society was, however, vaguely aware of its own artificiality. It felt doomed and it feared for its future. One frequently receives the impression that Napoleon III doubted whether his son would ever reign. The most clear-sighted persons in his entourage, such as Morny, knew the fragility of the regime; others sensed it. The new aristocracy as well turned determinedly toward the past to find points of reference, feeling the need to link itself with former regimes in order to establish its legitimacy. As for the old-guard aristocracy when it rallied, it had the same fears; yet when it did not, it sought refuge in the past—a way of displaying a certain loyalty to its traditions. Here again, in this idolatry of the past, there was a convergence of the ruling bourgeoisie and the landed aristocracy, whose passion for antiquated styles often produced the most bizarre results, which surprise us still.

Yet the copies made of earlier styles were not simply replicas. One never has the slightest doubt of the real origin of a piece of "Louis XV" furniture executed during the Second Empire. The period had sufficient vital energy—demonstrated primarily in the economic domain—and sufficient ingenuity as well, to believe that it was possible to improve upon former styles and, since its artists and artisans were equipped with better tools and had new techniques at their disposal, that they could do better than their distant predecessors. The belief in the idea of progress was one of the great constants of the entire nineteenth century, and especially of the Second Empire.

The notion of progress in the arts may appear odd today; at the time, it was perfectly natural. All the reports of the Expositions Universelles stressed this view. For example, marquetry decorations made by contemporary cabinetmakers were considered to be superior to their earlier models because of their absolute precision. New techniques acquired an importance in themselves, as, for example, in silverwork. In the accounts of each exposition—besides the Expositions Universelles, there was a proliferation of exhibitions of "industrial art" (the juxtaposition of the terms is significant)—the press explained how and why electroforming and the use of silver-plated metal offered every possible advantage: making available to nearly everyone products that when made of solid silver had been intended for the very wealthy alone. In 1867 Ducuing wrote about Christofle's work: "I have said that in our day, art has been obliged to become industrialized. Consequently, taste and luxury are now the patrimony of the classes which are the least well to do. Art loses nothing by popularizing itself in this way—it can even gain immeasurably, as it already has, by putting science to work for it...."[1] Indeed, electroforming was by no means thought to be a makeshift, a substitute, or an inferior technique: by eliminating risks and uncertainties, it permitted achievements which heretofore could only have been accomplished with great difficulty. Above all, with electroforming it was possible to duplicate works with perfect regularity. One tried to persuade oneself that silver-plated metal was so similar in appearance to solid silver that solid silver became superfluous, if not immoral. "Elkington and Christofle have replaced the sixty-pound table services of our fathers with ours of *six francs* — and it looks the same, sounds the same, and has the same function.... No one complains about this; on the contrary, everyone admires it.... There are still too many of us who do not know how to read and who must eat brown bread in our society, to allow capital to remain unexploited and to dwindle away without issue. No matter what is said, that which is superfluous has absolutely no right to take precedence over that which is necessary. In place of diamonds, glass; in place of velvet, paper; in place of bronze, plaster; in place of marble, cardboard; in place of silver, tin; in place of gold, whatever can be found, what does it matter! It is the outside that glitters, not what is within—and have we not Art, that Prometheus, eternal thief of the Olympian spark? At least that which Art has *created* can remain."[2] The material was of little importance since it was the art alone that mattered.

Specifically, it was not only to technology that the notion of progress applied. The period was convinced that progress could also be relevant to the plastic arts. It was recognized that certain artists of the past had attained heights which were difficult to match, Raphael, for example. But progress was considered possible throughout the entire realm of artistic production, in both painting and sculpture. People were not far from believing that with the advancement of civilization it would be conceivable to surpass even the most established values: perfection would no longer be exceptional, it would be general. The idea of progress was so well anchored in peoples' minds that it was even applied to forms of expression which had nothing to do with technology: in 1868 there appeared under the auspices of the Ministry of Public Instruction a *Rapport sur le progrès des Lettres.*[3] The idea was not a totally new one. Already in 1816, M.-J. Chénier had published a *Tableau historique de l'état et des progrès de la littérature française depuis 1789.*[4] The eighteenth century, which had generally believed in the progress of humanity, had not yet dared to believe in progress in literature and the arts. The idea originated around the time of the Revolution, precisely with the rise of the bourgeoisie. It made headway during the early nineteenth century. Under the Second Empire the notion of progress in letters, as well as in the arts, became a kind of credo: every form of expression naturally and constantly was to evolve toward perfection. It would thus be wrong to think that the taste for imitation, that the repeated reference to the past, was only a sign of conservatism. It was also, and perhaps more important, a dynamic, the past being utilized like elements of vocabulary which, when combined, improved, and perfected, yielded a contemporary language both more advanced and thus more perfect. In this respect it is absurd to think of Viollet-le-Duc's work at Pierrefonds (*see* no. I-29) as a "restoration." Pierrefonds was, in actuality, his own creation.

In contrast, this notion of perfecting led the period to strange aberrations. Side by side with true faïence, Sèvres (q.v.) manufactured vases which had all the appearances of faïence, but executed in porcelain, a more "noble" material, technically more "perfect." In this way, the taste for a return to the past was reconciled with the bourgeois taste for "solidity." Moreover, as a general trend, one loved to give things the appearance of what they were not, passing one material off for another, for instance, silver-plated metal for solid silver. Carton pierre was invented in order to produce false sculptural decorations; "zinc sculptures" were given bronze patinas. More than ever, tapestries became false paintings. Auguste Luchet's text quoted above is quite revealing in this regard—his series of "in place of" points to one of the great constants of the Second Empire.

This taste for false pretense was sometimes carried quite far, as with the creation of "photopainting." The article-advertisements of Disdéri, who laid claim to this process in the newspapers of the time, are perfectly explicit—the process involved, quite simply, enlarging a photograph on canvas and then painting it. The result was guaranteed—the portrait would have all the appearances of a real oil painting, yet a more faithful likeness could be achieved and at a much lower price: "You simply go to pose in Disdéri's studios. We shoot your picture.... Once the print is obtained, using standard methods, we enlarge it on canvas, up to the size the customer desires—life-size, half lifesize, bust-size, etc.... It's merely a question of price. Once the canvas has been prepared in this manner, it is delivered to a skilled artist. Working from a sketch of mathematical precision in which life has been captured in its rapid and fleeting expression, he needs only one visit of his model to produce in ten or twelve days a portrait whose likeness is, naturally, guaranteed—no matter what its size. An ordinary painter would require three weeks to a month's time at least for a portrait such as this, and would be unable to promise anything more than an approximate likeness...."[5] We would bet that there are many family portraits today passing as honest paintings but which in reality are photo-paintings. It was with the same spirit that photographs were watercolored in order to give them the appearance of miniatures.

In yet another domain Villème created photo-sculpture. The combination of a series of photographic negatives with a pantograph connected to an etching-needle permitted the production of busts and statuettes in stearic plaster. Théophile Gautier, who was responsible for promoting this technique, had some revealing thoughts on the subject: "The century is at once prodigal and parsimonious. It finds art expensive. With the aplomb of a parvenu, it sometimes dares haggle over old masters. It is frightened by marble and bronze, finding them too timeless for fleeting likenesses. Photosculpture is not the *grande dame* that statuary is.... It knows its limitations and is perfectly content with a shelf for a pedestal, happy to have faithfully reproduced a beloved countenance, the head of a pretty child, a young girl clasping roses to her bosom, a young woman dressed for a dance, a successful financier, celebrated artists, or a man of the world, with their modern elegance.... It does not scorn overcoats; crinolines do not bother it: it accepts nature and fashion as they are...."[6]

This search for inexpensive "art" was another aspect of the period and suited bourgeois taste, which recoiled from spending money and was readily satisfied with appearances. Yet this at least was necessary; as we have mentioned, one of the traits of the period was the desire to be seen. At the court as well as with the bourgeoisie, everyone was obsessed with the need to be seen to his best advantage, but secretly wishing at the same time that this be un-

der the least expensive circumstances. One wonders whether the good intentions so widely professed—that art be made available to all—were not rather ambiguous and did not constitute also a convenient means once again of justifying consciences. In any case the facts stand. We frequently come across brilliant interiors which were achieved at little expense. As one descends the social ladder, this passionate sense of economy naturally becomes more apparent because it becomes more necessary.

This suffices to explain the proliferation of "cheap" objects which have not stood the test of time, which the passing years have stripped of their original showiness. Necessarily, in the overall artistic production of the period, these objects were, and remain, the most numerous. Their predominance is responsible for giving a false impression of the Second Empire, masking by their abundance the inevitably rarer objects of high quality and painstaking execution by artists who sought perfection.

The present exhibition has brought together a great number of those highly crafted objects. The exhibition has been realized without accommodation; yet likewise without scorn. Its organizers have not by any means attempted to favor the Second Empire, but rather, to show, artistically speaking, that it did

exist, and that, far from being a parenthesis in the development of the nineteenth century, as we have too often been led to believe, it was in fact a key period in it. On the artistic level, as on the social level, the Second Empire emerges as a period traversed from one end to the other by every current and drift, a crossroads exposed to every wind. In the heart of the nineteenth century, it was the meeting point, where all the tendencies of the century crossed, came to fruition, or found their start.

Paradoxically, the image left by the Second Empire is of an era of worldly brilliance but not a period favorable to the arts. This is the case, perhaps, because it succeeded only too well in leaving us with the image it wished us to have of it—the one it had striven to show and not one which reflected its deeper values. That it was from the historical point of view a crucial period is certain; whether it should be judged favorably or not from the artistic point of view is a matter of personal taste. In any event, it did exist, and indeed, with a singular liveliness. The purpose of this exhibition is to present the Second Empire. It is not up to museums to judge, but rather to make known.

J.-M.M.

*Notes*

1. Ducuing, 1868, vol. II, p. 227.

2. A. Luchet, writing about the International Exhibition in London (*Le Monde Illustré*, July 12, 1862).

3. Ministère de l'Instruction Publique, *Rapport sur le progrès des Lettres par MM. S. de Sacy, P. Féval, Th. Gautier, Ed. Thierry.* Paris, 1868.

4. M.-J. Chénier. *Tableau historique de l'état et des progrès de la littérature française depuis 1789.* Paris, 1816.

5. *Le Monde Illustré*, September 2, 1865.

6. *Le Monde Illustré*, December 17, 1864.

Oscar-Claude Monet.
*Spring Flowers,* 1864.
The Cleveland Museum of Art (no. VI-88)

Gustave Baugrand.
*Clock*, 1867.
The Walters Art Gallery,
Baltimore (no. III-17)

Claudius Popelin.
*Napoleon III*, 1865.
Institut de France—
Musée Frédéric Masson,
Paris (no. III-31)

Eugène Lami.
*Supper Given by the Emperor Napoleon III for Queen Victoria of England in the Theater of Versailles, August 25, 1855,* 1855.
Musée National du Château, Versailles (no. VII-43)

Gustave-Clarence-Rodolphe Boulanger.
*Rehearsal of "The Flute Player" in the Atrium of the House of H.I.H. the Prince Napoleon,* 1861.
Musée National du Château, Versailles (no. VI-12)

Charles-Henri-Joseph Cordier
*Negro in Algerian Costume,*
1856–57.
Musée du Louvre, Paris
(no. V-16)

Auguste Rodin.
*Young Girl with Roses
on Her Hat,* c. 1865–70.
Musée Rodin, Paris
(no. V-32)

Alexandre Cabanel.
*The Triumph of Flora*, 1869.
Cabinet des Dessins, Musée du Louvre, Paris (no. VII-10)

Franz-Xaver Winterhalter.
*The Empress Eugénie Surrounded by Her Ladies-in-Waiting,* 1855.
Musée National du Château, Compiègne (no. VI-110)

Jean-Auguste-Dominique Ingres.
*Joan of Arc,* 1854.
Musée du Louvre, Paris (no. VI-70)

Albert-Ernest Carrier-Belleuse.
*Torchères,* c. 1862.
The Minneapolis Institute of Arts
(no. V-10)

Edouard Manet.
*The Battle of the Kearsage and the Alabama,* 1864.
John G. Johnson Collection, Philadelphia (no. VI-80)

# Art and Its Critics: A Crisis of Principle

"The ideas which have made humanity live for many centuries are slow to vanish," observed Théophile Gautier in 1853, "even when their reign has ended, for paganism, despite the arrival of a new religion and a new civilization, still lives in our arts, our customs, our habits, and the names of the abolished gods continue to designate our months and days. Today art has at its disposal only dead ideas, and formulas which no longer correspond to its needs. From this comes this uneasiness, this vagueness, this diffusion, this facility for passing from one extreme to another, this eclecticism, and this cosmopolitanism, this traveling in all possible worlds which leads from the Byzantine to the daguerreotype, from a far-fetched mannerism to a deliberate brutality. It is well known that something must be done,—but what?"[1]

What was done—or rather what happened during the next two decades—is the subject of this exhibition. While few objects presented here immediately reflect, when individually regarded, the disintegration of old values in the face of modern complexity or the presumed absence of forceful new principles to replace them, Gautier's sense of apprehension and disquietude is central to an understanding of the aesthetic tenor of the period and the critical context within which these works were created.

One, and possibly the primary, cause of the problem was the sheer volume of art created and seen during the Second Empire, much of it brought about as a result of the direct involvement of the State: "In France, perhaps no other government has shown a greater interest in the arts than that of the present. Within the space of a dozen years more buildings have been constructed than since the time of Louis XIV. Painting has been able to create one of the greatest chapters of its history; sculpture has become exalted; our museums have been further enriched; our libraries made still more vast and capable of receiving the ever-increasing number of users. The discoveries of exploratory expeditions have thus been passed on to artists and scholars immediately. And to add to our good fortune, photography has placed in our hands the master-works of all periods and all cultures, just as the great exhibitions of London and Paris have brought to light a vast quantity of art normally hidden in private collections.... [Further] the railroad has allowed us to see more monuments within a

week than it would previously have been possible to visit in a month."[2]

While Viollet-le-Duc (q.v.) intended to flatter with this assessment, the statistics support his claims. For example, the money spent on the rebuilding of Paris from 1851 until 1869 under the direct supervision of the Emperor and his Prefect of the Seine, Baron Haussmann, totaled some 2,500,000,000 francs, a sum whose vastness can be better understood in comparison with the 55,000,000 francs which was the average annual expenditure for the entire city during this period. [3]

Add to this the large urban building projects in the provinces (Marseilles being the single most extensive), the state's support of the Salons (where works shown in all mediums except the decorative arts increased from 1,757 in 1852 to 5,434 in 1870), the two huge Expositions Universelles in 1855 and 1867, as well as the frequent government purchases and commissions, and Viollet's seemingly exaggerated claims for the Second Empire no longer sound grossly inflated. Certainly, the State can take only partial credit for this flourishing of the arts, since—quite apart from any official act—the Second Empire was a period of great economic prosperity and material growth. From its very beginnings, however, the regime quite conciously linked its destiny with these progressive and abundant artistic developments. Even while Louis Napoleon was still Prince-President in 1852, the comte de Persigny, in a highly charged speech praising the munificent enlightenment of the State, promised those gathered at the awards ceremony which closed the Salon "that the arts will not be forgotten and the government will prepare for you a great era of prosperity."[4] In the same year the comte de Nieuwerkerke spoke in a similar tone at the behest of the Prince-President: "He commands me to give you assurance of his concern for one of the most precious glories of our country. He wishes to be among the first to applaud your successes. More than any other, he comprehends that France has always been renowned for the genius of its artists, whose works have sustained the honor of the French throughout the nations of the world."[5] So flowed the official rhetoric, yet the union of art and State was a reality and had real benefits, as the frequent quality of work brought about through the encouragement of the State confirms.

However, such optimism rarely went beyond official pronouncements and even these, as time developed, expressed certain dissatisfactions and doubts.[6] Despite what seems to us a particular vitality, characterized by an increasing spirit of invention and innovation, nearly all those who spoke to the general issue of the state of the arts shared, in some fashion, Gautier's troubled opinion. They found it progressively more difficult to discern any positive order in the extremely complex variety of art presented to them, and were still more perplexed as artistic activity continued to diversify, not only in terms of style, but also in technique and subject. "When one enters our exhibitions it is no longer nature which jumps to the eyes, but rather a conflict of ideas... tumult and confusion."[7] Or more specifically from Viollet-le-Duc: "We had come to a new 'Temple of Babel.'" The painters, the architects, and the sculptors speak, each in their own way, a quite different language."[8] One critical response to this profusion, during what was a period of unprecedented quantity of writing on the arts, was to choose one clear path through the confusion and to champion a single cause to the exclusion of nearly all else. Almost every definable style (or, for that matter, handling of any given genre or medium) had its advocates, some of whom—Champfleury for Courbet (q.v.), Zola for Manet (q.v.), Baudelaire for Delacroix (q.v.), for example— have been instrumental in forming our ideas as to the truly important aspects of the period. However, even among these "progressive" critics there are few unifying themes or basic points of agreement. There did appear, however, one persistent idea which was, perhaps, more fundamental to understanding the critical frustration of the period than any other: the desire that art address itself fully to the present. Already eloquently formulated by Baudelaire in his "Salon of 1846," in which he called for the "Painter of Modern Life," it may be traced back to the beginning of the century in the writing of Stendhal. By the 1850s and 1860s it had appeared with such a variety of applications—what was required was a painter "of the bourgeoisie just as we have painters of the peasants,"[9] an artist who will present "familiar scenes of our time"[10]— furthered by the desire for formation of a "Napoleon III style"[11] that it contained its own form of fragmentation. The fact that with the clear (and often over-simplified) perspective of the twentieth century we now see that artists who might have fulfilled this desire were indeed present—be it Manet in painting, Labrouste (q.v.) in architecture, Carpeaux (q.v., particularly in portraits), and the very art of photography itself—still does not clarify the contextual situation or explain why the great majority of the public as well as the critics and the official administration did not find a satisfactory resolution in any of these figures. The inverse and inevitable conservative response was a defense of the inherited and immutable principles of "high art," which alone could provide one sustaining set of values required to prevent increasing diffusion within the arts. "Poetry, morality, religion, and history; these are the divine sources; do not be dissuaded by the promise of success into lesser forms...."[12]

In painting this implied a defense of the art of David, and of Classicism and the Antique as the only true guides and sources for sculpture and architecture. However, even in the award speeches at the Salon during the 1850s, which frequently hark back to these treasured values, the references to Classical principles became more and more vague, and by the 1860s rarely occur. Further, with the steady erosion of the independent power of the Académie des Beaux-Arts, particularly after 1863, this emphasis which, at least in theory, had sustained the unity of French art at its greatest, disappeared. Even before this time, the actual application of Classical principles as they were understood earlier in the century had withdrawn some distance from reality. It seems to have struck no one as ironic that "Père" Schnitz, the director of the Académie Française in Rome during most of the Second Empire, was a charming, but hardly Davidian, painter of rustic peasant subjects drawn from the Italian countryside. The presence of Meissonier (q.v.), arguably one of the artists whose public success with subjects of historical genre contributed most to the decline of traditional history painting,[13] on the jury of the Salon of 1867 along with Cabanel (q.v.), Français (q.v.), and Pils indicates the degree to which the Classicists' position had been eroded.

Yet the desire on the part of certain figures in the official administration to create some substantial order within the arts did continue, even with the knowledge of a critical fragmentation which disallowed an effective new aesthetic, and the limited relevance of inherited conservative values. This is perhaps most clearly exemplified by the attempt, beginning with the formation of an investigatory commission in March 1862, to examine the possible reform of art instruction as it was given at the Ecole des Beaux-Arts and at the French

Académie in Rome. [14] Viollet-le-Duc, whose series of articles of 1863 had particularly influenced the decree as finally presented by Nieuwerkerke in that same year, defined the problem: "The ancient gathering of the arts has lost its bonds; what remains is scattered to infinity."[15] The solution? A restructuring of the faculty, under the direct authority of the State, with one head, a professor of aesthetics and history (Viollet-le-Duc himself, as it happened) who would supervise instruction within a rigorously standardized curriculum. The students demanded, insisted Viollet-le-Duc, "one direction, not several."[16] However, neither in his essay nor in the final declaration are the guiding aesthetic values clearly defined, beyond the assurance of encouragement of subjects other than the Antique and a welcoming of a broader range of contemporary experience. The reform met with limited success, and while the professorship created by it and important changes concerning the length of time a Prix de Rome winner could stay at the Villa Medici were retained, Viollet-le-Duc himself was ousted by the students and few of his theories put into practice. The reform of the Ecole failed to inspire unity among the teaching faculty, nor did there appear to be a marked improvement in the quality of student work, which was quite high even before 1863, despite the protest of Viollet-le-Duc.

However, it has been observed[17] that this fundamental desire of the State to liberalize through centralization is also reflected in the creation that same year of the Salon des Refusés, which helped to broaden the quantity, diversity, and quality of art seen by the public, while offering the previously excluded artists a place within the traditional, State supported institution of the Salon. The reform of the Salon jury the following year, which removed members of the Académie from any direct power in the selection and awarding of prizes, is still another example of the assumption of further democratic responsibility by the official art administration for decisions previously made by a body outside their control. From the early 1860s until the collapse of the regime, the State ran a race against time, trying by a series of acts to accommodate as much of the new as possible. This inevitably strained the fundamental principles that had formerly guided such decisions. The results were striking, as we know from the fury and perplexity of the conservative critics and the general public on the acceptance of Manet's Olympia at the Salon of 1865 by the reformed jury.[18] For many this decision represented a complete abandonment of standards, and the organizing committee was eventually persuaded to remove the picture to

a much less conspicuous site in the exhibition.

The dilemma of how to accommodate the new while maintaining a set of governing principles is nowhere more evident than in the applied arts, where an attempt was made to join the principles of fine arts with modern methods of industry. The expression "fine arts applied to industry" ("beaux-arts appliqués à l'industrie") was first generally adopted (although it did not originate) during the Second Empire by manufacturers, artists, and critics who, faced with growing competition from abroad and the apparent decline of aesthetic standards at home, sought to raise the quality of French industrial design through application of teaching methods and principles traditional in the fine arts. However, such principles often seemed incompatible with modern industrial processes, and within industry there was disagreement of a social as well as an artistic nature as to who should set the standards and provide industrial designs: whether craftsmen and designers trained by apprenticeship or in special trade and design schools, or painters, sculptors, and architects educated at the Ecole des Beaux-Arts and the French Académie in Rome. Despite these problems, which were never adequately resolved, the applied arts of the Second Empire enjoyed unparalleled activity, and at their best displayed mastery of new industrial techniques as well as an extraordinarily high level of craftsmanship, making them in general the most sought-after and frequently exported luxury products in Europe. It was because in industry's unremitting efforts at self-improvement—chiefly through attempts to apply "art" to manufactures by improving the education of its designers—that the applied arts met their new and serious challenges most successfully during the Second Empire.

The government, however, provided little direct legislative aid to applied art education, although the Emperor paid frequent lip service to the need for improvement in industrial design, voicing the progressive opinion that the problems of art and industry were parallel, and suggesting that education in fine and applied arts should be combined. As early as 1853 the Emperor ruled against the traditional separation of fine art and industrial exhibitions, stating that since "improvements in industry are closely tied to those in fine arts," and because "exhibitions are one of the most effective means of contributing to progress in the arts," the annual Salon exhibition should be held for the first time in conjunction with an international industrial exhibition—that scheduled for Paris in 1855.[19]

A decade later, in 1863, Nieuwerkerke's report on the government's reform of the Ecole des Beaux-Arts and the Académie maintained that "in improving the education of the artists, our industry would be assured a superiority which is beginning to be disputed,"[20] a view bitterly opposed by Académie conservatives, who feared that an association with industry would debase fine art. However, the ateliers of painting, sculpture, architecture, and engraving established at the Ecole by the 1863 decree—while emphasizing métier and technical procedures in a manner similar to apprenticeship in crafts and industry—were designed to educate painters, sculptors, and architects in the nature of their materials, not in manufacturing skills, nor were they intended to instruct craftsmen in the fine arts of composition and design. Only in 1873 was a *Cours supérieur d'art décoratif* offered at the Ecole, and even this was aimed primarily at architects, who were taught various techniques for applying architectural ornament.

In the state manufactories of Sèvres (q.v.), Gobelins (q.v.), and Beauvais, the fine arts were, however, linked with industry at government expense by the many Ecole-trained painters, sculptors, and architects who provided them with artistic direction and working designs. The Second Republic, which defended the national manufactories as experimental "schools" for industry, and sources of models and technical innovations,[21] established in 1848 the Conseil Supérieur de Perfectionnement des Manufactures Nationales, which examined the three manufactories "in their dual artistic and industrial aspects"[22] and dealt with many of the same problems that persisted during the Second Empire concerning the role of fine artists as industrial designers. Between 1848 and 1851, Conseil members included the painter Delaroche, the sculptor Klagmann; the architects Séchan and Feuchère; Badin, *administrateur* of Gobelins and Beauvais; Ebelmen, *administrateur* of Sèvres; Diéterle (q.v.); Chevreul, *directeur des travaux de teinture* at Gobelins and Beauvais; Ingres (q.v.); Labrouste; the critic de Lasteyrie; Viollet-le-Duc; the critic and collector the duc de Luynes; Lacordaire, also *administrateur* of Gobelins; Cornu; Nieuwerkerke; Scheffer; Duban (q.v.); and Flandrin (q.v.).

One of the Conseil's accomplishments was sponsorship of an exhibition of the products of the national manufactories which was held in April–May, 1850, at the Palais National, and preceded by visits of the Conseil to Sèvres and Gobelins. Séchan's report from Gobelins advised that compositions, cartoons, and painted models for tapestries be commissioned from "the most notable" artists, and that there be additional means for the State to encourage the arts and to procure from artists "serious and considerable" work.[23] Lasteyrie's review of the 1850 exhibition pointed out that the national manufactories, as "model" for private industry, were "in a better position than industry to obtain the assistance of eminent artists, of first-rate minds... to open new avenues to industry, and to influence even the public taste by the artistic purity with which each of their works must be stamped."[24]

The role of fine artists in providing industry (as well as the state manufactories) with the best in design as specified by the Conseil was stressed repeatedly at the international exhibitions held in London in 1851 and 1862, and in Paris in 1855 and 1867. In 1851 and 1855 Richard Redgrave, Henry Cole's art superintendent in the Department of Practical Art at South Kensington, made special reports on design in which he credited the success of France's national manufactories to the employment of "the best painters, sculptors, and designers,"[25] and Sèvres's "acknowledged reputation" to the "ablest artists and most skillful workmen in the world," adding that "in pictorial art of a high class on porcelain... Sèvres is without rival. Many of the subjects are designed for this material by artists of great reputation [including] Hamon [q.v.] and... Gérôme [q.v.]."[26] French critics, too, in reports on "the application of art to industry" insisted on the importance of proper artistic direction in industry. In 1867 the architect-decorator Guichard blamed what he considered to be lack of taste in French applied arts on "art too often directed, not by artists, but by blind fashion,... [by] an often ignorant clientele, and by the necessity of selling ,"[27] and in 1862 Mérimée had maintained that only "an artist of high quality will always be for industry a cause of durable reputation and even of assured profit."[28]

If, indeed, established painters, sculptors, and architects were meant to provide industry with leadership, their designs only rarely satisfied critics. In 1850 Lasteyrie complained that a monumental porcelain vase by Ferdinand Régnier unsuitably imitated decorative effects traditional in earthenware;[29] that Sèvres's illusionistic paintings on porcelain by Fragonard, Hamon, and André were "inappropriate to use," masking the quality and form of the material;[30] that certain "bizarrely" decorated table services abandoned good taste to public fashion;[31] that a woven carpet from Gobelins lacked "originality" of design;[32] and that the tapestry coverings woven at Beauvais for furniture suffered from a lack of decorative unity.[33] These ideas of the appropriateness of ornament and material to use, and of a style over-ornamented and lacking in unity were echoed in Redgrave's reports of 1851 and 1855 and developed by Mérimée in 1862. Mérimée charged that French design as a whole lacked originality, that designers imitated past styles "with critical impartiality": "Beside a sculpted cabinet which could be taken for the work of a sixteenth-century Venetian, we see another which looks as though it had been made for Mme du Barry. They come from the same workshops; they were made by the same hands.... Fashion commands, art obeys without protest, because it no longer seems to have conviction."[34] According to Mérimée, several acknowledged styles were often inappropriately combined within the same work and ornamental details incorrectly applied to their forms: "This year's exhibition offers strange combinations of different styles brought together by accident which denote on the part of their authors nothing but an absence of ideas and a lack of reasoning. Between the general form of an object and its details there is a correct and natural relationship which cannot be disturbed with impunity."[35] On grounds of originality and suitability of materials, Mérimée also criticized the practice of reproducing old master paintings in porcelain and tapestry[36]—a practice criticized earlier by the Conseil de Perfectionnement but defended by Ingres as a means of preserving masterpieces "in permanent materials" for posterity.[37] If during the Second Empire French artists were considered "superior" in matters of taste to their European rivals[38] (in 1861 the Prince Napoleon remarked that "good taste" gave French products an "inimitable cachet"[39]), by 1867 Guichard warned that "taste alone does not suffice."[40]

While French design was being attacked for its lack of purpose and principle, it was at the same time being defended as the hapless victim of industrial progress and commercialism. Burty complained that the "tyranny of public taste" drove designers to "lock themselves into an established style and period," sacrificing utility to style, and that machine production was responsible for the destruction of hand craftsmanship: "The perfection of the chisel and font are conditions of the craft which have fought, often unequally, against the introduction of the machine and chemical processes."[41] Barbedienne (q.v.) blamed the loss of quality in modern metalwork design on division of labor: "Formerly, the artist cast and chased his work himself, whereas today the artist's work must pass through the hands of the workman, and however skillful the latter may be, he can achieve a product equal to that of the master only with difficulty."[42]

If artists trained at the Ecole appeared indifferent, and incompetent to improve the standards of industrial design, many critics and manufacturers found a solution in educating workers and craftsmen. In his monumental criticism of French design at the 1851 exhibition (published in 1856), Léon de Laborde declared that "industry should recruit its artists from within itself,"[43] and that only "the general teaching of design [to apprentices and workers] in the primary schools, continued through apprenticeship, would render to industry its true place in the realm of art."[44] De Laborde pointed out that fine artists often conceived designs in ignorance of technical processes, "following art theory completely abstractly and in no way taking into account the obligations imposed on industry by materials, processes of manufacture, and usage," while craftsmen, "being masters of all the processes, knowing their tools and their material perfectly,"[45] were uniquely qualified to be educated as industrial designers. A decade later, Michel Chevalier, the noted economist, reiterated that "the necessity of spreading the teaching of fine arts among the working population is certainly in the interest of French civilization.... It is essential that at least one segment of the workers in the manufactories be initiated in the arts of form, design, and color, by the appropriate courses."[46]

The imperial government further endorsed this remedy, seeking popular favor by posing as a friend to the working man. At the exposition of 1855, the Prince Napoleon, president of the imperial commission, encouraged the "working classes" to visit the exhibition because "the spectacle of the progress achieved by industry in every part of the globe, and the comparative study of the improvements in techniques and methods are in effect a powerful means of professional education,"[47] and for the first time, as an "innovation... based on our concern for the working class," awarded medals to *coopérateurs*, "the foremen and workers recognized for services rendered to the industry."[48] In 1862 the imperial commission (of which Prince Napoleon was also president) aided nearly 1,000 workers and craftsmen from various French cities in visiting the international exhibition held in London, awarding 47,885 francs toward their transportation expenses.[49]

The idea that the State should bear responsibility for educating the working classes as a means of improving industrial design was anticipated by de Laborde, who advocated government support of existing schools of design, with a curriculum that emphasized drawing and composition; the establishment of more *écoles supérieures* for applied art; and

greater state patronage of the arts in the form of commissions, publications, public monuments, and urban planning.[50] Yet, over a decade later, Mérimée complained that the government had failed to sufficiently "protect and encourage the alliance of art and industry" and to exercise its patronage. Evoking, like de Laborde, the specter of English rivalry, Mérimée pointed out that the Department of Practical Art at the South Kensington Museum, founded in 1852, had accounted for enormous progress in English applied art, and although Mérimée felt that industrial reform would come about in France only through an improvement in educating fine artists (at the Ecole and Académie), he also pointed out the inadequacies of the secondary schools of design, which he considered overcrowded and under-financed.[51] During the 1860s other critics deplored the inadequacy of state schools and the government's failure to encourage industrial art through educational reform. In 1863, Adalbert de Beaumont stated the urgent need "for the complete reform of teaching industrial art" in France, pointing out that French art schools "lacked proper direction."[52] In 1864 Emile Reiber (q.v.), editor of *L'Art pour Tous*, protested that "official encouragements" of the industrial arts were "notoriously insufficient" and that only "private art education, having the Science of decoration as its base and production as its end" would guarantee artists "an honorable future."[53] In 1867 Guichard advocated the establishment of new schools of design in provincial manufacturing centers and improvements of existing applied-art teaching.[54]

Since the State never assumed full responsibility for problems of industrial design and education, reform, of necessity, came from private enterprise during the Second Empire, and in fact, owed a great part of its success to its independence from government. In 1864 Reiber claimed that the imperial government was incompetent to effect improvements in industrial design and that such a task was better assigned to industry itself: "An artistic revival, springing not from the accidental or ephemeral protection of princes and the wealth of courts, but from the urgent needs of commercial exchange... far be it from us to consider entrusting this task to official teaching: the answer lies with the past, [and] with private initiative; already we see some praiseworthy efforts."[55] Among the praiseworthy efforts cited by Reiber were the establishment of the Société du Progrès de l'Art Industriel in 1858, and more importantly, the Union Centrale des Beaux-Arts Appliqués à l'Industrie in 1864.

The Union Centrale was born from two exhibitions of "fine arts applied to industry"

held in Paris in 1861 and 1863, sponsored and promoted by the private Caisse de Secours des Inventeurs et Artistes Industriels founded by Baron Taylor, and organized by a separate committee of manufacturers, critics, and artists, of which Guichard was president. The idea to hold such exhibitions had been proposed during the Second Republic by Jules Klagmann, who suggested in 1850 to the Conseil de Perfectionnement and in 1852[56] to the Prince-President, Louis Napoleon, that a public exhibition, a museum, and a central school of fine arts applied to industry were "necessary for the progress of art, industry, and more rational teaching"[57]—as the combined museum and school at South Kensington, only just established, was soon to demonstrate.

The exhibitions of 1861 and 1863 earned Taylor's Caisse de Secours 4,577 and 25,000 francs respectively. Immediately following the 1863 exhibition, members of its organizing committee—including Guichard; the silversmith Mourey; the manufacturers of bronzes, Lerolle; lace, Lefébure; wallpapers, Turquetil; carpets, Chocqueel; furniture, Mazaroz; and metalwork, Veyrat—established the Union Centrale des Beaux-Arts Appliqués à l'Industrie. The Union Centrale was to sponsor, for a general membership subscribed in categories of 100 and 36 francs, a museum, a library, special courses and lectures, competitions "among French artists and among the various schools of design and sculpture," and general exhibitions of "fine arts applied to industry."[58] The proceeds from subscriptions and exhibitions were to fund acquisitions for the museum and library as well as the non-profit activities of the Union. Given official authorization in July and August, 1864, the Union Centrale held major exhibitions in 1865 and 1869, with profits of more than 35,000 francs from each exhibition benefiting the Union directly for the first time.

In all contemporary reports concerning the foundation of the Union and the four exhibitions held during the 1860s, the theme of private enterprise is resoundingly dominant. Moreover, it was echoed and encouraged by the imperial government as a means of achieving industrial reform without cost to the State. The Emperor had made clear his support of private enterprise when he stated at the prize ceremony following the 1862 international exhibition: "In private enterprises, where individual initiative is exercised with tireless energy, the government is relieved of being the sole promoter of a nation's vital forces; also, instead of regulating everything, it leaves to the individual the responsibility for his own actions."[59] In 1863 Guichard reported that the

Emperor (who visited the Union's exhibition twice) had sponsored five gold prize medals, and the Empress another five, thereby "sanction[ing] private endeavors in the name of the State." Also, according to Guichard, it was decided that Armand Béhic, Minister of Agriculture, Commerce, and Public Works, should not preside at the 1863 awards ceremony, in order to "allow individual initiative to come to the fore."[60] In 1865 Guichard viewed the Emperor's loan of arms to the Union's "Musée Retrospectif"[61] as a demonstration both of official sanction and private liberality: "Napoleon III knew that behind the amateur in him, one would always see the sovereign, and that one could believe that the elite of our collectors could do nothing but follow his example.... His Majesty's very presence among us was the most vivid example, and the supreme sanction of the work of the Union Centrale."[62] In September 1864, when the Union Centrale first opened its museum and library, *Le Moniteur* officially praised "this institution... due entirely to private initiative... that men of good will, in realizing [this] eminently useful idea, created at their own risk, with their own money, and which they direct and administer completely without charge"[63]—a sentiment dutifully repeated by numerous government officials who visited the institution.[64]

Aside from demonstrating the capabilities of private enterprise, the Union's museum, library, and education programs were viewed as instruments of social change, providing the public with moral and commercial benefits through access to superior examples of art and manufactures. The historical objects displayed in the Union's museum and at the "retrospective museums" in the 1863 and 1865 exhibitions opened for the education of craftsmen and workers the hitherto closed art collections of privileged connoisseurs, as the Union's letter, sent to collectors in April 1865, made clear: "To assemble these collections and these precious objects, to exhibit them temporarily in the public in a manner both fitting and useful for all, to foster by their gathering the study of the past and the development of the industries dependent upon art; such has been the goal proposed by the Union Centrale.... The results will apply to the education of our workers and to the improvement of our industrial professions."[65] Even the location of the Union on the place Royale was praised by Burty for its accessibility to Parisian industry: "The place was judiciously chosen to bring the numerous and intelligent workers of the Marais within reach."[66]

However, the most important aspects of the Union's efforts to educate workers and craftsmen as designers for industry were the separate competitions among the schools of design held in conjunction with the exhibitions of 1863, 1865, and 1869,[67] and the professional design competitions held in 1865 and 1869. In 1862 Félix Aubry asked the rhetorical question of how French industry could best meet growing foreign competition; the answer, according to Aubry (and as de Laborde had earlier replied), lay in improving and multiplying the schools of design: "What are the means of sustaining the struggle which is beginning? The Ecole Centrale supplies engineers to all the large firms; the schools of design furnish artists to all our factories.... Schools of design certainly exist in our large cities, but how many manufacturing centers are deprived of them! How few [of the schools] apply the study of art to designs for manufacture, and how many are lacking in special courses!"[68] In 1863, fifty-two schools specializing in or including design participated in the first competition, which was won by the Ecole des Beaux-Arts de Toulouse (its gold medal sponsored by the imperial family) for teaching "by a method almost exclusively based on the imitation of models in relief"[69]—an improvement over the traditional practice of drawing strictly from drawings, which the German architect Gottfried Semper had earlier advocated for South Kensington. By 1869, the competition program included drawings from life, as well as from three-dimensional models, adding a variety which one critic described as "new and instructive."[70]

In 1865, the Union held a separate professional competition for the "composition" and "execution" of industrial products; it included designs in two different programs: one for an earthenware table service, the other for bedroom furnishings of moderate price which the organizing committee hoped would improve the taste and quality of the popular market. The bedroom designs were to be judged in separate categories of "creation" and "execution," which according to the competition rules could be entered by single contestants, "or by groups of artists and manufacturers united, with some creating the models and others executing [them]."[71] However, by 1869 critics were already aware that such separation of design from processes of manufacture was inimical not only to the best teaching of applied art, but to the very purposes of the Union Centrale. According to the Commission Consultative which reported on the 1865 competition: "In these first efforts there was not sufficient relationship between the requirements of the forms of art and those of the physical processes of execution. The aim of the Union Centrale is, above all, to promote the search for qualities which cause an artistic idea to pass from the realm of conception to that of reality.... The Commission has therefore thought it advisable to compel in some way the artist dedicated to industry to face the difficulties of rationally bringing these aspects together."[72] The Commission therefore proposed that the 1869 competition be restricted to "designs for products [actually] manufactured."[73]

The Union's education of workers and craftsmen, competitions among the design schools, and recognition of the integral relation between the "fine arts" of aesthetic form and the working processes of industry were among the most important institutional advances in industrial reform that occurred during the Second Empire. In addition, the beginnings of a studio movement among craftsmen in industries such as those of ceramics and glass (*see* Avisseau and Brocard) encouraged a general concern for handcraft that was reflected in the commercial manufactories. In 1867, giving voice to the problems brought about by the modern division of labor, Barbedienne, like de Laborde before him, proclaimed the necessity of educating a new class of artist-craftsmen to effect a production integrated from design through manufacture: "This state of affairs urgently requires us to mold artist-workers.... It is absolutely necessary to introduce design [and] modeling, to shape the new generation of workers which the bronze industry can no longer do without."[74] It is this basic understanding that the material processes of manufacture should govern design, and conversely that design should respect technical processes, that best demonstrates progress made in the design of applied arts during the Second Empire. From this insight came the widespread development of studio crafts as well as acceptance of certain handicraft standards in commercial production that characterized the modern reform of European industrial design at the end of the nineteenth century.

If within the applied arts private enterprise must be credited with establishing the fundamental principles and institutions of industry's self-improvement, it was given every encouragement by the official arts administration of the Second Empire. As a matter of policy the State accommodated as much individuality and diversity as its peculiar blend of liberalism and authoritarianism would allow. In 1853 the Prince Napoleon remarked that "a vast field of art has been opened through the prosperity of the present regime. But... neither the protection of an enlightened Prince nor his munificence can create a masterpiece."[75] De Laborde similarly advised that one should commission only "self-respect" from artists, and that by allowing "free inspiration," one would "rejuvenate art through liberty."[76] While the State's position may be viewed by critics as indecisive, weak, and potentially corrupt, it was not unavailing to the greater good, permitting in all the arts the vast diversity and complexity which this exhibition so richly illustrates. Innovative and diverse both in its techniques and aesthetic references, art in France during the Second Empire achieved in its brilliance a degree of international prestige and influence unknown since the reign of the first Napoleon.

K.B.H./J.R.

*Notes*

1. T. Gautier [1853], quoted in Sloane, 1951, p. 21.

2. Viollet-le-Duc, 1862, vol. XIII, p. 254.

3. Pinkney, 1958, p. 174.

4. 1853, Paris, Salon, p. 9.

5. 1853, Paris, Salon, p. 14.

6. *See particularly,* Nieuwerkerke, in 1864, Paris, Salon, pp. xii-xiv.

7. About, 1858, p. 37.

8. Viollet-le-Duc, 1862, vol. XII, p. 394.

9. Jean-Aubry, 1968, p. 72.

10. Viollet-le-Duc, 1862, vol. XII, p. 529.

11. *See above,* "The Second Empire: Art and Society."

12. A. Fould, in 1858, Paris, Salon, p. x.

13. Stranahan, 1888.

14. Boime, 1977.

15. Viollet-le-Duc, 1862, vol. XII, p. 394.

16. Viollet-le-Duc, 1862, vol. XII, p. 399.

17. *See* Boime, 1969, "Salon des Refusés."

18. *See* Hamilton, 1954, pp. 67–80.

19. Decree of June 22, 1853, in *Catalogue 1855,* p. iii.

20. Nieuwerkerke, 1863, p. 565.

21. *Le Moniteur,* July 2, 1850.

22. Decree of March 30, 1848, in Vaisse, 1974, p. 153.

23. Vaisse, 1974, p. 161.

24. De Lasteyrie, 1850, p. 137.

25. In *Reports 1851,* class 30, p. 711.

26. *Reports 1855,* part 3, p. 380.

27. *Rapports 1867,* vol. III, p. 6.

28. In *Rapports 1862,* vol. VI, p. 252.

29. "Aimed too closely at the imitation of certain earthenwares of the past... without even recognizing the difference in hardness, in solidity, or luster which exists between these two materials, a difference which would never permit the eye, however untrained, to confuse them (de Lasteyrie, 1850, p. 140).

30. De Lasteyrie, 1850, pp. 141–42.

31. De Lasteyrie, 1850, p. 145.

32. De Lasteyrie, 1850, p. 149.

33. "The number, the unhappy disposition of ornaments of questionable taste, overwhelmed the flowers to which they should have been only an accessory (de Lasteyrie, 1850, p. 150).

34. In *Rapports 1862,* vol. VI, p. 250.

35. P. Mérimée, in *Rapports 1862,* vol. VI, p. 251.

36. P. Mérimée, in *Rapports 1862,* vol. VI, pp. 254–55.

37. Vaisse, 1974, pp. 156–57.

38. R. Redgrave, in *Reports 1855,* part 3, p. 320.

39. *Recueil de documents 1862,* no. 4.

40. In *Rapports 1867,* vol. III, p. 13.

41. In *Union Centrale 1865,* p. 400.

42. In *Rapports 1867,* vol. III, p. 284.

43. De Laborde, 1856, vol. II, p. 244.

44. De Laborde, 1856, vol. II, p. 234.

45. De Laborde, 1856, vol. II, pp. 231, 232.

46. In *Rapports 1867,* vol. III, p. 13.

47. In *Rapports 1855,* p. 83.

48. In *Rapports 1855,* p. 92, although there were occasional exceptional medals awarded to foremen and workers at the 1849 Paris exposition.

49. *Commission Rapport 1862,* pp. 42, 55, and table XIV "Dépenses Ordonnancées," p. 104.

50. De Laborde, 1856, vol. II, pp. 31, 255 ff.

51. In *Rapports 1862,* vol. VI, pp. 257, 262.

52. De Beaumont, 1863, pp. 986–87, 988.

53. In *L'Art pour Tous,* 4th year, 1864, introduction, n.p.

54. In *Rapports 1867,* vol. III, p. 14.

55. In *L'Art pour Tous,* 4th year, 1864, introduction, n.p.

56. With Clerget and Chabal-Dussurgey (q.v.), among twenty-six signatories.

57. Véron, n.d., p. 11.

58. Véron, n.d., p. 23.

59. In *Commission Rapport 1862,* p. 58.

60. *Rapports 1863,* p. viii.

61. The Emperor had previously lent the Alesia cup, known as the "Vase of Caesar," in 1863; *see* no. III-2.

62. *Catalogue 1869,* p. 54.

63. *Le Moniteur,* September 30, 1864, in *Rapports 1865,* p. 33.

64. *Rapports 1865,* pp. 39–40.

65. *Rapports 1865,* p. 83.

66. *Rapports 1865,* p. 31.

67. Similar competitions were also included in the international exhibitions of 1862 (class 29) and 1867 (class 8), but in the former, emphasis was on primary schools, and in the latter, the French chose to exhibit designs from established applied artists rather than from design-school students.

68. In *Union Centrale 1865,* p. 7.

69. *Rapports 1863,* p. 92.

70. Grandgedor, 1869, p. 426.

71. *Union Centrale 1865,* p. 307.

72. *Catalogue 1869,* pp. 124–25.

73. *Catalogue 1869,* p. 125.

74. In *Rapports 1867,* vol. III, p. 284.

75. In 1853, Paris, Salon, p. xliv.

76. De Laborde, 1856, vol. II, pp. 534–35.

# Architecture

The architectural profession in France had just emerged from a profound crisis when Louis Napoleon Bonaparte proclaimed the Second Empire on December 2, 1852. Many among a group of academic Neoclassicist architects who had been firmly established as the favored instrument of official design and teaching doctrine by Quatremère de Quincy upon the reorganization of the Académie des Beaux-Arts and the Ecole des Beaux-Arts during the years 1816–19 had died.[1] In their places there now stood a younger generation of architects and theorists calling themselves "Romantics," no less tightly knit for having battled the Neoclassicists during most of the July Monarchy. Like their contemporaries in the Romantic movement, they at first saw the Revolution of 1848 as the beginning of a new age in which they could freely achieve their ideals, and some continued to believe this possible as the new imperial government slowly emerged. However, while Félix Duban (q.v.), Louis Duc, Henri Labrouste (q.v.), and Léon Vaudoyer (q.v.) set to work on the great government buildings that henceforth were to testify to their talents, and while Viollet-le-Duc (q.v.) and Constant-Dufeux (q.v.) enjoyed the protection of the imperial family, a still younger generation of designers appeared purveying a less cerebral and more brilliant—some said merely more popular—style, most notably Hector Lefuel (q.v.) and Charles Garnier (q.v.). The success of the Romantics was spoiled and the public acceptance that they thought they had finally achieved was partially withdrawn as they found themselves paired with these "Eclectics." Nonetheless the Second Empire was a brilliant moment in the history of French architecture: the extravagance of the Emperor and of his Prefect of the Seine, Baron Georges Haussmann, created vast opportunities for architects of all persuasions and degrees of talent finally to make buildings of their ideas. Even the struggle of the Romantics and the Eclectics produced an atmosphere of choice that spawned a newer generation of designers, students at the Ecole des Beaux-Arts during the 1860s—Julien Guadet, Jean-Louis Pascal, Emile Bénard, Henri Mayeux (q.v.)—who were to evolve a rich, supple style that during the Third Republic made Paris the capital of world architecture and the Ecole des Beaux-Arts the world's architectural school.

Romanticism appeared in French official architecture as various forms of rationalism.[2] Architecture was conceived as the necessary product of certain facts, as opposed to being the embodiment in stone of traditional, allegorical fictions. The forms of the Orders, which early nineteenth-century Neoclassicism venerated as eternal symbolic forms, were held by the Romantics to have been merely the most efficient structural shapes—that is, to have been merely facts.[3]

There were, however, a number of distinct families of architectural facts perceived by the Romantic Rationalists, and a series of different interpretations evolved from them. The forms of past styles of architecture could be taken as facts and a new, French, nineteenth-century style created by a meaningful combination of these forms. The dictates of physical structure might be accepted as facts—the building might be seen as a sort of vertebrate organism—and a new, French, nineteenth-century architectural style be permitted to impose itself by constructing with modern materials (especially iron) and according to modern mathematical calculations. Or, finally, it could be proposed that behind the various specific forms of art throughout history there lay a single, abstract vocabulary—a universal, natural language—which could be rediscovered by scientific analysis and become the language of a new architecture. Regardless of differences in system, all of these schools of thought valued principle over form[4] and sought to bring about a new architecture according to some evolutionary law.

The generation of a Romantic architecture from the combination of historical forms—eclecticism, as it was at first called[5]—was addressed by Duban and Vaudoyer. Duban, the oldest of the Romantic group, had been named architect of the Ecole des Beaux-Arts in 1832 and between that date and 1840 completed the main building and its double forecourt on the rue Bonaparte using a compendium of Late Gothic and Early Renaissance forms, both copied in his facades and present in reality in the architectural fragments composing the courts. His nineteenth-century facade is literally seen through the skeletal remains of the tradition Duban called upon to engender it, creating a tableau of the history of architecture like that Duban's friend Paul Delaroche painted around the walls of the Salle des Prix inside.[6] Vaudoyer, beginning in 1852, created a truly vast encyclopedic building in his Marseilles cathedral (nos. I-23–I-27), embracing the whole history of Christian architecture.

Structural rationalism was the central idea of Labrouste's early work, especially of his Bibliothèque Sainte Geneviève (1838–50).[7] Here was the first monumental use of the new, nineteenth-century material, iron, producing an expansive, single interior space, its ceiling held aloft by slim metal columns supporting openwork arches. To protect this fragile interior organism from the elements, Labrouste wrapped it in a masonry envelope, itself reduced to a structural skeleton consisting of a cage of deep, narrow stone buttresses defining unbroken files of arched openings partially filled with thin curtain walls, like flesh stretched between buttress-bones. The building otherwise is a narrow box, the direct expression of its structural system, decorated only with motifs scratched lightly into its surface, all in no immediately identifiable style.

Viollet-le-Duc, thirteen years younger than Labrouste, combined this structural rationalism with his conception of historical style. He perceived a steady progress in structural efficiency from Greek to Roman to Gothic, which had been deflected by the copyism of the Renaissance. He proposed that the nineteenth century, with its new materials, should go back to where the Gothic left off, conceptually leaping over the Renaissance, and commence the slow evolution of a post-Gothic, structurally rationalist architecture.[8] He also saw the Gothic period as a socially superior one, worthy of emulation, as did his mentor the Labrouste student Jean-Baptiste Lassus (q.v.), who, however, unlike his anticlerical friend, wished to revive medieval religious faith as well.

The structural rationalists influenced the eclectic rationalists in turn: although the structural organism of Duban's earliest work at the Ecole des Beaux-Arts is concealed, Vaudoyer's cathedral is made up of volumetric units with membranelike walls and buttressed, bony edges. By the time Duban erected the quai Malaquais wing of the Ecole (1858–62, with its exposed iron ceilings) the volumes, too, had come to push out the exterior wall-veil of his buildings, restrained by a skeletal system of buttresses, while the pilasters disappeared into the surfaces of the stone facades.

The third group of Romantic Rationalists, those seeking a universal language of form, was led by Constant-Dufeux and the architectural journalist César Daly. Their ideas (with help from Labrouste) eventually inspired a fashion called the "Néo-Grec." Beginning with Constant-Dufeux's tomb of Dumont d'Urville (1842–44) and culminating in the theoretical essays introducing Daly's *Motifs historiques* (1869) and *Architecture funéraire contemporaine* (1871), the two men developed the idea that both the specific nature of a single monument and the general world view of a civilization could be communicated in the underlying geometry of their architectural forms. Thus the rectilinearity of Egyptian architecture expressed that culture's fixation upon death while the aspiring lines of Gothic architecture expressed the medieval belief in eternal life. They proposed that the characteristic form of the future might be the mathematically complex elliptical arc, reflecting the scientific sophistication of modern society. Similarly, both men proposed that the geometric abstraction of ornament rendered it expressive of the material from which it was made and communicative of ideas.[9]

Romantic Rationalism, despite its admirable principles and its striking decorative forms, was too cerebral. Napoleon III had a whole nation to win over to his side and to remake: his imperial gestures had to be sweeping, rapid, gorgeous, and immediately comprehensible. Romantic Rationalism was intricate and laborious. While Louis Napoleon, as Prince-President, was pursuing his campaign to reestablish the Empire, Duban was commencing the restoration of the Louvre. The Prince-President increasingly bridled at the architect's slowness and professional arrogance, until on March 12, 1852, three months after the coup d'etat, he appointed Visconti (q.v.) architect for the great work of the union of the Louvre and the Tuileries in preference to Duban.[10] Visconti, in turn, was followed by the even more expeditious and pliable Lefuel. The latter, named *architecte de l'Empereur* in 1855, swiftly established himself as the domestic architect of the Second Empire, building or rebuilding houses for the Minister of Fine Arts, Achille Fould; the director of the museums of the Louvre, the comte de Nieuwerkerke; and for the Princess Mathilde. In these designs Lefuel combined Renaissance forms from many historical sources. He did not adhere to a principle like that embodied in Vaudoyer's Marseilles cathedral, but rather produced compositions of forms beautiful in themselves,[11] leading the younger, post-Romantic generation in a return to form. But although his art sometimes was called "classical,"[12] this was not the classical form of Percier and Quatremère—ascetic, controlled by the rules of harmonic proportions. Rather it was an intuitive, extravagant demonstration of architectural virtu, borrowing widely, essentially eclectic. This art was convincing only if Lefuel could make it seem so, producing an appropriate setting for a man who was Emperor only if he could make his nation believe it. And Lefuel made it even more appropriate by seeking beauty and force in richness, elaboration, and *coups de théâtre* like the treatment of the topmost pediment of his project for the Pavillon de l'Horloge (no. I-19).

In spite of Napoleon III's impatience with Duban—impatience Philippe de Chennevières says the Emperor later blamed on his minister Fould and regretted[13]—two of the most radical of the Romantic Rationalists, Constant-Dufeux and Viollet-le-Duc, were welcome at court, having been introduced by Eugénie's friend Prosper Mérimée. Constant-Dufeux's "Néo-Grec" (nos. I-5, I-6) was appropriately elaborate for the reconversion of Soufflot's Panthéon. Viollet-le-Duc's Gothic pleased all the more at Pierrefonds (no. I-29) for being something more substantial than the Strawberry Hill Gothic of the July Monarchy. What Viollet-le-Duc intended as archaeological correctness became exquisite fantasy when viewed in the spirit of the "Maison Pompéienne." Nonetheless, this part of the story also ended in a disaster for Romantic Rationalism. Viollet-le-Duc's very serious (and un-Gothic) project for the Paris Opéra competition of 1860–61 (nos. I-30, I-31), in spite of the lobbying of the Empress, was passed over for the design of an unknown young architect, Charles Garnier (no. I-10).

Garnier, like Lefuel, provided a setting, but now an interior setting, one constructed around movement through the building. In 1871 he published a 415-page description of a walk through his building entitled *Le Théâtre*. He escorts his readers up to the porte-cochere under the dome on the east facade, and into the round, rococo vestibule for subscribers, up the double staircase to the Grand Stair Hall where the subscribers join the ticket holders who entered on foot through the facade arches, and up the famous Grand Staircase to the broad foyers of the *piano nobile* and to their seats. From the tiers of balconies on three sides of the Grand Stair Hall the ticket holders watch the gorgeously attired subscribers' entrance and exit. Garnier's friend Théophile Gautier described the scene: "A graciously flaring ramp whose steps are almost unnoticeable leads to a landing beyond which continue two other ramps which reach the main floor by gradual slopes. The structure embracing the staircase is supported by paired columns of the Ionic Order, in veined marble, upon which rest immense arches, and which are connected from story to story by balconies with richly ornamented balusters where the curious may lean as in a painting by Paolo Veronese—spectators and spectacle at the same time—in order to witness this marvel of modern civilization that one calls a *sortie d'Opéra*, namely this cascade of diamonds, pearls, feathers, flowers, white shoulders, satins, velvets, moirés, gauzes, laces, which here tumbles down their white marble steps amid the sparkle of vivid light, enclosed in a fairy architecture."[14]

Impressive as the Louvre, Pierrefonds, and the Opéra are as settings, Napoleon III's greatest accomplishment was making the whole of Paris an imperial stage set.[15] The Emperor and his prefect, Haussmann, used the existing city of Paris as raw material out of which to carve a network of avenues and squares, defined by uniform walls of newly built stone apartment houses. These great cuts were led back and forth across the face of the city, punctuated by public buildings—either new or recently restored—so that all Paris became like the experience of Garnier's Opéra vastly multiplied: a setting unfolding as one moved through it by carriage, smoothly connected, uniform in background to set off significant variations in foreground motif: the characteristic arch of the Gare de l'Est, the crownlike dome of the Opéra, the tower of La Trinité. It is appropriate that one of the most celebrated publications documenting Second Empire Paris was an illustrated carriage ride around the boulevards, *Paris dans sa splendeur* (1863), the urbanistic equivalent of Garnier's *Le Théâtre*.

The physical size of this project reduced to triviality the professional architects' bickering—Duban's eclectic rationalism against Lefuel's classical eclecticism; Viollet-le-Duc's structural rationalism against Garnier's *mise en scène*. One did not have time, one was not close enough, to perceive the distinctions. Instead, Napoleon III's new Paris posed the architect elementary problems of pure architectural composition: the selection of a meaningful form and its elaboration at the new urban scale. All architects, regardless of their personal principles, were equals: Duc's Palais de Justice—riding the Ile de la Cité like the superstructure of a battleship, vast in scale and deep in relief—is the real brother of Garnier's Opéra; Baltard's Halles Centrales (nos. I-2–I-4), Hittorff's Gare du Nord (nos. I-12, I-13), and Hector Horeau's projects all compete virtually on the same level.

Although Haussmann in his *Mémoires* takes much credit to himself and gives very little to his architects,[16]—they did, in fact, rise to the occasion. Their buildings do succeed in the elementary compositional senses that were the

terms of this huge project. That it was precisely at this moment that the Ecole des Beaux-Arts emerged as the most respected architectural school in the world, teaching exactly these elementary principles of formal composition that the experience of Second Empire Paris proved valuable, is proof of their success. It had been assumed since the eighteenth century that architectural design consisted, first of all, of the setting out of significative tableaux in carefully paced sequence.[17] During the Second Empire this simple idea was elaborated into a method of architectural thinking at the Ecole, with the development of graphic techniques for spatial analysis. The reason why the 1863 reform of the Ecole failed remains unclear,[18] but one reason why Viollet-le-Duc's lectures were shouted down by the architecture students may have been that they seemed irrelevant: the students were there to learn composition.[19] Immediately after that abortive reform a series of magisterial compositions were produced in the competition for the Grand Prix de Rome, which set the standard for academic composition until 1920: Julien Guadet's of 1864, Jean-Louis Pascal's of 1866, Emile Bénard's and Henri Mayeux's of 1867.[20] All but Mayeux had worked for Garnier on the Opéra and it was his refinement of processional composition, translated into the terms of school projects, that inspired the vigorous play of pavilions in Guadet's project, the double-hinged plan in Pascal's, and the squeezing vertical volumes in Mayeux's. And all but Guadet's design are clothed in Lefuel's and Garnier's extravagant, eclectic detailing.

Nevertheless, during the 1860s, just when Second Empire theatricality had arrived at unabashed maturity, Labrouste was erecting the last and most impressive work of Romantic Rationalism, the Reading Room of the Bibliothèque Nationale (no. I-14). Like the Reading Room of his earlier Bibliothèque Sainte Geneviève, it is a fragile cage of exposed iron, but now treated suggestively so that it becomes a poetic tableau exploring the visual and philosophical nature of such construction.

In the small vestibule of the Bibliothèque Sainte Geneviève a series of stone piers intrude into the space, bearing a grid of thin openwork iron beams. Their fragility in comparison to the piers and thus their apparent inability to support the ceiling was responded to by Labrouste's painting the ceiling sky blue. The illusion continues down the side walls, with treetops appearing against the sky, behind an order of pilasters.[21] Similarly, in the Reading Room of the Bibliothèque Nationale, a series of

piers intrude into the space. Here, however, the illusion begins at the floor: these piers are thin iron members whose apparent inability to bear a ceiling is resolved by the superposition of a seemingly weightless roof structure. The iron crosspieces of the ceiling bow upward in smooth semicircular arches enframing nine ceramic-tile domes; their color and texture make them seem made of fabric and their billowing forms imply that the function of the piers is less to hold them up than to tie them down. These domes suggest a breeze gusting across the chamber and, in fact, on the side walls, the lunettes described by the iron arches are painted away as vistas of blue sky and trees, while on the back (north) side they are glass windows opening to views of real sky and (originally) real treetops.

Labrouste himself explained the first level of his conceit: "When I was at lycée, I used to go and study in the Luxembourg gardens, especially in the nursery, before or after class. There, where nothing distracted me, my eyes as well as my mind found pleasant repose amid the beautiful and luxuriant greenery that surrounded me. I thought that in a place of study the representation of what had so much charm for me would, in the library, be an unpretentious decoration that might also offer an opportunity for repose to the minds of the readers using the room."[22]

This would not seem to be all there is to the matter: Labrouste's obviously Pompeian detailing implies some historical allusion; his peculiar gridding and illusionistic extension of space reflect a search for a particular visual effect; and his treatment of iron and tile suggests complex thoughts about the nature of modern industrial materials. (A glance at such practical iron roofs as that of Hittorff's Gare du Nord makes it obvious that Labrouste's ceiling is not simply an efficient, minimal form.[23]

It was believed that the Pompeian wall paintings represented a real architecture—a light structural cage filled out with awnings set amid gardens, like the *zotheca* described in Pliny's letters—and that modern industrial materials could finally reproduce it. "The author has attempted in this composition,"wrote Hector Horeau about 1855, "to present a specimen of modern industry, which today permits one at little cost to build the dreams of the Pompeian painters."[24] Across the garden facade of the"Maison Pompéienne," Normand erected a *jardin d'hiver* of slim iron columns and awnings—weatherproofed with glass sheets all around. Numerous other examples existed during the Second Empire, but only Labrouste monumentalized the conceit in ceramic domes and painted garden vistas, and only he applied it to a public space—thus rendering that space private and intimate: each reader can look up and imagine that he is Pliny in his *zotheca*.

This sense of reverie, of permitting the mind to wander, is furthermore addressed by the nine equal domes defining the space. Contrary to academic compositional practice, there is no axis, no point to which the eye is inevitably drawn, except for the exedra beyond the room itself (and the axis there draws the eye to a void, the door into the bookstacks). It is a labyrinth, like those of Piranesi's "Carceri" with their cat-walks and arches and files of columns.

Shortly before this a series of literary works had appeared evoking Piranesi's "Carceri" as symbols of the mind in contemplation.[25] But almost every author interpreted these labyrinths as closed and restraining, expressive of the mind entrapped. Labrouse, on the contrary, imbued his labyrinth with lightness and openness. If there is an intended reference to Piranesi here, it is to show his reputed nightmare banished. Labrouste dematerialized Piranesi's stones and brought light, breezes, and foliage into deep, interior spaces. And the instruments that permitted Labrouste to conquer the Piranesian labyrinth were the new industrial materials of iron and gas lighting, implying that the instrument that would enable the human mind to flee the nightmare of unfulfillment was the new science made available to the general public in the books in the Bib-

liothèque Nationale. Stone is ignorance, iron knowledge; stone confines, iron sets free. The whole Reading Room, then, is a symbol—one composed of space and materials, of illusions and allusions—the most complete and powerful architectural symbol produced by the nineteenth century.

The world by 1860 was very different from what it had been only a few decades earlier. Labrouste tried to comprehend how; he tried to explore it philosophically in a work of architectural art. But it is both frustrating and inevitable that the most devastating changes for architecture were not ones of ideas, but ones of means—the technical developments and liberal financial policy that made Napoleon III's transformation of Paris possible. These changes carried less cerebral architects out of their restricted professional ranges and into vast new worlds which they could not dominate and in which they could survive only by returning to the most elemental tricks of their craft. Labrouse, with his characteristic "fixité,"[26] remained true to his private ideal, ruminating upon it in his design of the Reading Room. Garnier, willing to confront problems imposed by circumstances, pleased to see what could be done with the new Second Empire world of wealth and industry, found a way to make architecture function as a part of it, as the mirror of its pretenses.

D.V.Z.

*Notes*

1. L.-P. Baltard, professor of theory at the Ecole, and A.-L.-T. Vaudoyer, master of one of the most influential ateliers, had both died in 1846. Quatremère himself had retired in 1839 and died in 1849. This fact was pointed out to me by Neil Levine.

2. Immediately after 1830 there was a noisy group practicing an intuitive, fantastic architecture—led by Aimé Chenavard, Bruno Galbacio, and Alfred Pommier, among others—but it soon faded away, in part because architecture is a practical art, in part because it was constituted of not very profound artists.

3. *See* F.-L. Reynaud, "Colonne," in *Encyclopédie nouvelle*, 1836–39, vol. III, pp. 686–88; Viollet-le-Duc, 1863–72, vol. I, chap. 2.

4. Léon Vaudoyer, in a letter to his father A.-L.-T. Vaudoyer of January 29, 1832 (in the collection of the family), quotes his friend Louis Duc summarizing a conversation with the classicist J.-N. Huyot: "They parted in agreeing that Duc was a partisan of that which was produced by necessity and by reason and that Huyot was a partisan of that which pleased the eyes regardless of these two considerations."

5. Blouet, 1838; Vaudoyer, 1847, vol. II, col. 2195.

6. As Peisse (1841) observed.

7. *See* Levine, 1975. I am deeply indebted to Professor Levine's ideas in this entire essay although we often disagree. *See also* his essay, "The Romantic Idea of Architectural Legibility: Henri Labrouste and the Neo-Grec," in Drexler (ed.), 1977.

8. Viollet-le-Duc, 1863–72, vol. II, chap. 12.

9. This paragraph was contributed by my wife, Ann Van Zanten, based on material in her doctoral dissertation for Harvard University (in preparation).

10. Mlle Katherine Marmoz, writing a thesis on Duban, has kindly informed me that Duban actually executed a project for the reunion of the palaces, and that the drawings had already been discovered to be missing in 1852.

11. Rouyer, 1867, states Lefuel's intentions in his introduction.

12. An adjective insisted upon by Pascal, 1881.

13. Chennevières, 1883–89, vol. II, pp. 10–11.

14. *Le Moniteur*, May 20, 1863. He is picturing the effect from Garnier's drawings.

15. Pinkney, 1958.

16. Haussmann, 1890–93, vol. I, p. x.

17. I have developed these ideas further in "Architectural Composition from Charles Percier to Charles Garnier," in Drexler (ed.), 1977.

18. *See* R. Chafee, "The Teaching of Architecture at the Ecole des Beaux-Arts," in Drexler (ed.), 1977.

19. This was particularly true of the American students after 1870 who, as shown by their Ecole records, most frequently entered the competitions in architectural composition, to the almost complete exclusion of construction, mathematics, or perspective.

20. Drexler (ed.), 1977, repro. pp. 236–37, 240–41, 255–57.

21. On the reading of these spaces, *see* Beutler, n.d.; *see* N. Levine, in Drexler (ed.), 1977.

22. Quoted in Bailly, 1876.

23. As is often asserted; *see* S. Giedion, *Space, Time and Architecture* (Cambridge, Mass., 5th ed., 1973), pp. 222–28.

24. Quoted from a broadsheet publishing his project for a system for construction of international exposition pavilions (British Museum Library 4°1701.6.1 [11]).

25. *See* Keller, 1966.

26. Delaborde, 1878, p. 1.

## Gabriel-Auguste Ancelet
*Paris 1829–1895 Paris*

*Ancelet was one of the most successful architecture students at the Ecole des Beaux-Arts during the revolutionary years of the late 1840s and won the Grand Prix de Rome in 1851, when he was only twenty-one years old. The studies of ancient Roman architectural details that he executed during his stay in Italy were among the most celebrated and often reproduced of their genre.*

*The son of a minor architect, he entered the Ecole des Beaux-Arts as a student of Baltard (q.v.) in 1845, after spending four years at the Ecole des Arts Industriels. At the Ecole des Beaux-Arts he distinguished himself by his designs in the "Néo-Grec" style (Drexler [ed.], 1977, pp. 200–201, 404, 412). During his years as a pensionnaire in Rome he traveled to Sicily, Smyrna, Constantinople, and Athens, but in the end found the decorative remains of Pompeii and Rome most to his taste.*

*Returning to Paris early due to illness, he was appointed* inspecteur *under Théodore Labrouste (brother of Henri Labrouste, q.v.) at the Bibliothèque de l'Arsenal and again* inspecteur *under H. Janniard at the Archives Nationales. Then, in 1858, after the death of Couvrechef (q.v.), he was appointed architect of the medieval imperial château at Pau and the new imperial villa at Biarritz. These required the small-scale, decorative embellishments for which his talent seemed suited. He added an arched entranceway at Pau, in the style of Francis I, and a wing and outbuildings at Biarritz lightly "Néo-Grec" to harmonize with the first part of the villa designed by Hippolyte Durand (1854–55). He also continued Couvrechef's restoration of the château at Arteaga near Bilbao in Spain for the Empress Eugénie. In 1864 he was appointed ar-chitect of the château at Compiègne, restoring the theater (begun in 1867) on the model of that at Versailles.*

*With the fall of Napoleon III, Ancelet became a government institutional architect. He was appointed architect at the Conservatoire des Arts et Métiers in 1872 and erected the wing along the rue Saint Martin. In 1873 he was made professor of ornamental design at the Ecole des Beaux-Arts and in 1892 he was elected to the Académie des Beaux-Arts.*

D.V.Z.

Bibliography:
Nénot, 1896

Gabriel-Auguste Ancelet

## I-1
## Portion of the Via Appia, Rome: Present State and Reconstruction

1856
Signed and dated, lower right: A. Ancelet. Roma. 1856
Ink wash and watercolor on heavy paper, backed
100 × 330 cm

Provenance:
Ecole Impériale des Beaux-Arts; Ecole Nationale Supérieure des Beaux-Arts (inv. no. 2267)

Before 1867 an architect's education at the Ecole des Beaux-Arts did not terminate with the receipt of a diploma but culminated instead with the opportunity to compete for the Grand Prix de Rome (R. Chafee, in Drexler [ed.], 1977, pp. 61–109). This prize, awarded to one architect each year, bestowed a five-year *pension* at the Académie de France à Rome with the requirement that each year a set of drawings, or *envoi*, be produced so that the *pensionnaire's* work could be judged by the Académie des Beaux-Arts in Paris. The *envois* of the first three years were analytical studies of ancient architecture; that of the fourth year, an archaeological reconstruction; and that of the fifth year, a modern design on a program of the *pensionnaire's* own devising.

The *envois* were put on public display in both Rome and Paris and were analyzed in a report at the public meeting of the Académie des Beaux-Arts; they were a means for a young architect to make a reputation, and a great deal of effort was put into them. They were almost always executed in the traditional architects' medium of ink wash mixed with watercolor, and as the century progressed, their technique became increasingly subtle and complex (*see*, for example, Drexler [ed.], 1977, pp. 143, 145, 165, 167, 320). While around 1830 the *envois* had been used to make points about the history and theory of architecture, by the Second Empire they had become displays of virtuoso technique.

Ink wash involved the "floating" of successive layers of thin ink washes, usually a half dozen in number, over heavy paper, put on between alternate washings of the sheet. The washes themselves could be colored with pigments and graded from light to dark; they could be made to overlap (usually in the background) or kept apart by a thin stripe of white paper (usually in the foreground and in architectural features). The effect sought was a luminous, planar quality, which quickly became a convention (Magonigle, 1922, pp. 46–47).

In the fourth-year drawing by Ancelet shown here, one sees how the medium could

I-1

be made to produce piquant landscape effects, like a watercolor. But it had been originally developed most particularly for the depiction of shadows on light stone surfaces, that is, for the study of the cut-stone ornament that was a basic element of Classical architecture, and it was for this reason that a hard, airless luminosity became a standard of quality.

Although the elaborateness of this procedure has come to seem an affectation—especially because of the twentieth century's insensitivity to moldings and rendered forms—it is clear that the ink-wash medium was one particular form in which the general sophistication of technique in Second Empire art expressed itself in architecture.

D.V.Z.

Ecole Nationale Supérieure des Beaux-Arts, Paris

---

## Victor Baltard

### Paris 1805–1874 Paris

*Baltard remains the most puzzling (and, evidently, puzzled) architect of the Second Empire. He was the son of the archconservative architect Louis-Pierre Baltard, yet one of the first outsiders to adopt the "Néo-Grec" fashion in the 1840s; he was thoroughly committed to the tradition of masonry architecture, yet by the force of events became the author of the vastest iron-and-glass building of the period, the Halles Centrales; and when afterward his design was touted the greatest monument of the Second Empire, his authorship was disputed by a crowd of administrators, engineers, and architects who pictured him as a mere executant or plagiarist.*

*Winning the Grand Prix de Rome in 1833 in the steps of the Romantic phalanx, this clever but dutiful son of the Neoclassicist professor of theory at the Ecole des Beaux-Arts was the leader in Rome of the reaction against the innovations of Labrouste (q.v.). He rose rapidly in the government architectural service upon his return to Paris in 1839, being appointed in-*specteur *at the Ecole Normale Supérieure in 1841; adjunct professor of the theory of architecture (under his father) at the Ecole des Beaux-Arts and* inspecteur des Beaux-Arts *for the City of Paris in 1842;* architecte en chef de la première section des travaux *for the City of Paris and diocesan architect of the Department of the Seine in 1848; and finally Haussmann's director of architectural services in his reorganization of the administration of Paris. In these posts he carried out a large number of church restorations (most notably, perhaps, those of Saint*

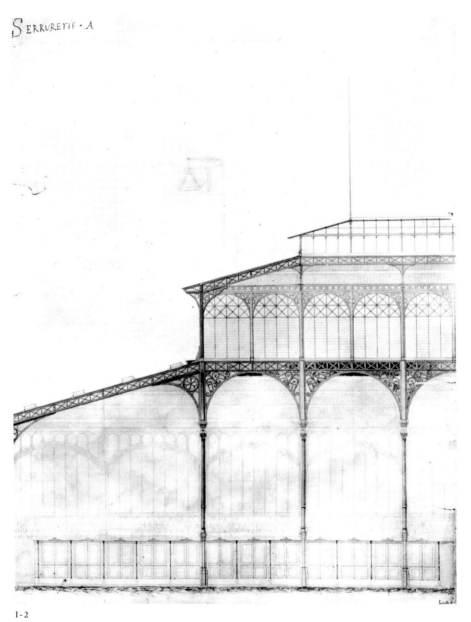

I-2

*Germain des Prés and Saint Eustache) and city projects, including alterations to the old Hôtel de Ville and many fete decorations (see also no. II–7). He was elected to the Académie des Beaux-Arts in 1863.*

*Baltard erected three major monuments on his own account: the Hôtel du Timbre (1846–50, taking over from Paul Lelong); the Halles Centrales (1851–66); and the Church of Saint Augustin (1862–68). All three used iron extensively and were* characterized by a particularly dry "Néo-Grec" ornament. All three confused critics and in each case it has been suggested that Baltard was not entirely responsible for the design.

D.V.Z.

Bibliography:
Delaborde, 1874; C. Garnier, 1874; Sédille, 1874; Haussmann, 1890–93, vol. III, pp. 478–89

Office of Victor Baltard

## I-2
## Halles Centrales, Paris: Structural Section of a Typical Pavilion (Final Project)

c. 1853–54
Ink wash on paper
68.7 × 54 cm

Provenance:
Archives de Paris (cartes et plans 552, dessin no. 25)

Office of Victor Baltard

## I-3
## Halles Centrales, Paris: Detail of Ironwork (Construction Drawing)

c. 1853–54
Ink wash on tracing paper
162 × 72 cm

Provenance:
Archives de Paris (cartes et plans 552, dessin no. 31)

The outcry accompanying the recent demolition of Les Halles reminds one again that these vast iron-and-glass sheds were so extraordinary that they had been quickly accepted on their own terms and had taken their place among the celebrated landmarks of Paris. They were admired by both artists and the public upon their construction: when the Grand Prix de l'Empereur for the best work of art produced by a French artist during the years 1864 to 1869 was awarded to Louis Duc's Palais de Justice, there were strident protests that the Halles Centrales alone were worthy of the honor (*Le Figaro*, August 8, 14, 15, 1869). They established a building type repeated over and over again throughout the nineteenth-century world, becoming an integral part of the period's cityscape.

A public market had existed in the Marais since medieval times, scattered among a number of open spaces just south of Saint Eustache. It had been improved periodically by the City, culminating in a competition project of 1748 to rebuild the quarter, and in 1763 with the construction of the large circular Halle au Blé (Boudon et al., 1977, vol. I, pp. 17–20). In 1811 Napoleon I had decreed the erection of a market building beside the Halle au Blé, but this

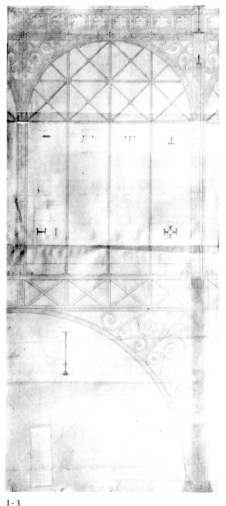

I-3

was never begun. The comte de Rambuteau, Louis Philippe's Prefect of the Seine, instituted a commission to study the problem of a central market in 1842 and in 1845 asked for a detailed project from Baltard and Félix-Emmanuel Callet. Since 1842 Hector Horeau had pressed a scheme of his own to move the market to the bank of the Seine (for ease of communication) and to erect vast gas-lit iron-and-glass pavilions above underground warehouses provided with railways (Horeau, 1845; Arch. nat. F²¹ 1463). Baltard traveled to Germany, Holland, Belgium, and England to study public markets and in 1847 submitted a design in which he divided the space into a series of stone pavilions with iron roof structures (Baltard and Callet, 1863, pl. 3; Hautecœur, 1957, p. 310). Construction was begun September 15, 1851, but upon the completion of the first pavilion in June 1853,

ventilation proved poor and access, difficult. It was dubbed the "Fort de la Halle," punning on the popular name of the burly market porters, the *forts des halles*. When the Emperor visited the site he stopped work on Baltard's project, and then opened an informal competition for a better scheme.

Baltard and Callet—like Viel and Desjardins in the contemporaneous Palais de l'Industrie (*see* no. I-11)—were reluctant to give up masonry forms, but they may have been helped out of their dilemma by a series of suggestions from nonacademic quarters. In his *Mémoires*, Baron Haussmann wrote that the Emperor explained to him "'I need vast umbrellas, nothing more!'... sketching with a few pencil lines the form he had in mind" (1890–93, vol. III, p. 479). Haussmann then claimed to have developed this scheme in a drawing of his own, "giving him [Baltard] the general plan and elevation of this very modern building conceived by my August Master.... Yes, the Prefect of the Seine was both an administrator and an artist!" (1890–93, vol. I, pp. xi-xii). "'Make me a sketch following these suggestions as quickly as possible,'" he remembered telling Baltard, as the architect showed the prefect scheme after scheme. "'Du fer, du fer, rien que du fer!'" ("'Iron, iron, nothing but iron'") (1890–93, vol. III, p. 480). As a result Baltard's revised final project held its own against the iron-and-glass projects of other competitors—among them the engineers Eugène Flachat and Alfred Armand and the architect Joseph Nicolle (q.v.)—so that Haussmann managed Baltard's retention as architect. Horeau, the first to suggest an iron structure for the Halles Centrales, believed himself plagiarized (*Le Figaro*, August 15, 1867) as did Flachat (*L'Architecture*, vol. IV, 1890, pp. 576–77). Construction of Baltard's sheds was commenced in 1854, the Pavillon de l'Est was completed in 1857, and the whole original ensemble was finished in 1866. (Callet died in 1854; his contribution to the design also remains unclear.)

In spite of the rival claims of authorship, the beauty and success of Les Halles lay in its obviousness and anonymity as well as in the direct way it satisfied the requirements of a market structure. It must be big and open to permit the movement of crowds and the admission of light and air. Light wooden pavilions had been used since medieval times; after iron became available in long elements around the turn of the nineteenth century, it was applied to markets, most impressively in London at the Hungerford Fish Market (1835) and in Paris at the Marché de la Madeleine (1824). In 1811–13 Bélanger had erected an iron dome over the courtyard of

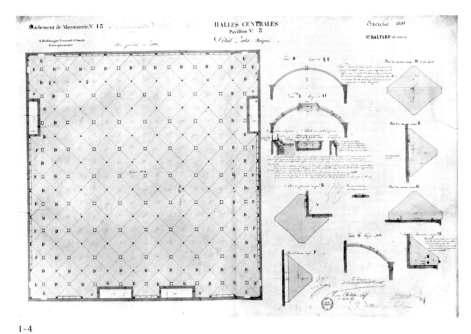

I-4

1859
Signed, lower right, by architect, contractors, and government officials
Ink, ink wash, and watercolor on heavy paper
67 × 101 cm

Provenance:
Archives de Paris (cartes et plans 551, dessin no. 36)

This is an especially elegant example of the technical drawings produced around the middle of the century. Signed by the architect, the contractor, and the government officials concerned, it was a kind of contract demonstrating that everyone agreed to the execution of the work in just this way. It should have been produced by the architect's office although the contractor's signature is so placed as to suggest that his draftsmen might have been responsible for it. The colors are conventions: blue for metal, gray for cut stone, pink for brick.

The reflected plan of the whole pavilion is rendered on the left side of the sheet and detail drawings of typical bays in plan and section occupy the right part. The structural system is a light, modern one composed of an iron skeleton of columns and vault ribs bearing brick vault webs. In contemporary, efficient materials it reproduces the Gothic vault as it had been explained by Viollet-le-Duc (q.v.) during the 1840s with its ribs and webbing constructed separately and working in elastic combination.

D.V.Z.

Archives de Paris

---

*Simon-Claude Constant-Dufeux*
*Paris 1801–1871 Paris*

*Constant-Dufeux shared with Labrouste (q.v.) the position of the most radical of the Romantic Rationalist designers and chefs d'atelier. He never had the opportunities to build that Labrouste did, however, and is remembered chiefly for his teaching and his perfection of the "Néo-Grec" fashion in decoration.*

*The grandson of Simon Dufeux, a celebrated stonecutter of the late eighteenth century who worked on Soufflot's Sainte Geneviève (The Panthéon), he was a student engineer at the Ecole Polytechnique before passing on to the Ecole des Beaux-Arts in 1819 as a student of François Debret and winning the Grand Prix de Rome in 1829. During this time he*

the old Halle au Blé next to Baltard's site. Baltard claimed originality chiefly in dividing the total area into pavilions devoted to separate functions and linking them by covered "streets" (*Le Figaro,* August 14, 1869); Haussmann, however, claimed that even this was his idea (1890–93, vol. III, p. 480). The simplicity and anonymity of Baltard's conception, in fact, contrast to the more insistently "modern" scheme of some of his rivals in the Emperor's informal competition. Nicolle had proposed a slightly sloped roof stretching in five sections from the Hôtel de Ville to the west facade of the Louvre supported by widely spaced iron caryatids holding brackets of flowers, while Flachat had suggested covering most of the old site with a huge iron "box," its roof opening in a series of stepped clerestories for light and ventilation (*Revue Générale de l'Architecture,* vol. XII, 1854, pls. 1–5).

These drawings for the Halles Centrales are from a volume of studies and construction drawings by Baltard and his office. They show the project after he had settled upon the form of the ironwork and while he was working out the details. After having reduced the masonry walls of his earlier projects to the diaphanous open-work panels seen here, he tried to impose some sort of decorative form upon it. The left-hand spandrels of the section of a pavilion are filled with Gothic tracery, the right-hand spandrels

with Classical volutes. In the background the less classifiable and more successful exterior elevation is indicated with its segmental arches surmounted by tall, arched open panels. Baltard's handling of ironwork should be compared to that of Labrouste at the Bibliothèque Sainte Geneviève and that of Hittorff at the Gare du Nord (no. I-13). In the upper left of this drawing Baltard sketched in a view of the exterior of the pavilion together with a diagram of a bell activated by a rope and pulley. The second sheet is a detail construction drawing showing how the decorative and structural members of the main interior arcade were to be jointed and dimensioned.

D.V.Z.

Archives de Paris

Office of Victor Baltard (with A. Dallemagne, Vernaud & Cousté, Entrepreneurs*)

## I-4
## Halles Centrales, Paris: Plan and Details of Basement Ceiling Structure of Pavilion Three (Construction Drawing)

also worked on his own, for other architects—Visconti (q.v.), for one, on the Fontaine Gaillon—and for the Administration des Ponts et Chaussées (1817–25). Arriving in Rome immediately after the departure of Duban (q.v.) and Labrouste, he established himself as the leader of a group continuing their Romantic experiments on a more exaggerated scale. He drew the sternest warnings from the Académie des Beaux-Arts for his envois, especially his fifth-year project for a parliament building (Drexler [ed.], 1977, pp. 178–79). Indeed, such was his reputation for obstreperousness that he was excluded initially from the cursus honorum of Grand Prix winners, returning to Paris in 1836 but receiving a government position only in 1838, when the sympathetic Emile Gilbert took him on as inspecteur (together with Théodore Labrouste) at the asylum at Charenton. Still no major appointments were forthcoming and he had to make his reputation

during the July Monarchy with the rebuilding of the tiny Ecole Gratuite de Dessin (1841–44) and the tomb of Admiral Dumont d'Urville (1842–44) in the Montparnasse cemetery.

Constant-Dufeux had more success as a teacher. In 1836 he opened an atelier which attracted a number of brilliant students, and in 1845 was appointed professor of perspective at the Ecole des Beaux-Arts, where he propounded his elaborate theory of art. With the reorganization of the Ecole in 1863 by the comte de Nieuwerkerke he was made patron of one of the three ateliers officiels (along with Alexis Paccard and Jean-Charles Laisné).

During the Second Empire he enjoyed the personal favor of the Empress Eugénie (through the intermediacy of Prosper Mérimée), but although he was appointed architect of the Bois de Vincennes (1858–59) and the churches of Saint Laurent (1862–66) and Sainte Geneviève (1850–71), he

never received the opportunity to erect a single large government building, nor gained election to the Académie des Beaux-Arts.

D.V.Z.

Bibliography:
Féraud, 1872; Lance, 1872

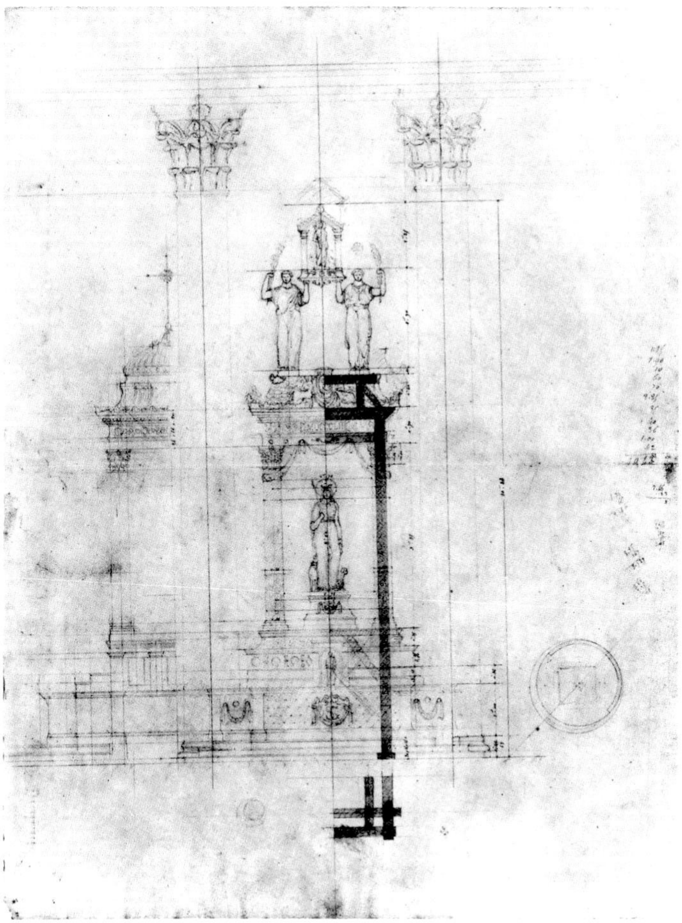

Simon-Claude Constant-Dufeux

## I-5
## Church of Sainte Geneviève (The Panthéon), Paris: Front Elevation of the Altar of Saint Genevieve and Side Elevation of the Altar of the Virgin (Studies)

1852
Dated on frieze of Altar of Saint Genevieve: MDCCCLII
Pencil on heavy paper
69.5 × 52.5 cm

Provenance:
Archives Nationales, Versement d'Architecture (XVI-100)

On December 6, 1851, immediately after his coup d'etat, Napoleon III announced that the Panthéon, whose dome dominated Paris from the top of the Montagne Sainte Geneviève, would be transformed into a church dedicated to that saint. This indeed was the purpose for which it had been erected by J.-G. Soufflot during the years 1756–80, the fulfillment of a vow by Louis XV. During the Revolution it had been made by Quatremère de Quincy into a pantheon for the tombs of the great men of France, its exterior windows blocked up, its towers cut down to the cornice line, and a great statue of the French Republic designed for the apse. After the restoration of the Bourbon monarchy in 1814, it served again as a church—with the addition of suitable altars, paintings, and carvings—but upon that dynasty's fall in 1830 it became once more a pantheon, with a new west pediment carved by David d'Angers. In April 1848, at the beginning of the Second Republic, Ledru-Rollin, the Minister of the Interior, authorized Paul Chenavard to decorate the interior with an ambitious symbolic history of all religions told in mosaics, paintings, and sculpture (Sloane, 1962, pp. 40–65). Support for the project di-

I-5

minished with the evaporation of the ideals of the Republic, and upon the reestablishment of the cult of Saint Genevieve, Chenavard's work was halted.

Considering the importance attributed to the building by the previous regime, Napoleon III's act of December 6 was a decisive statement of his rapprochement with the Pope. Constant-Dufeux, the architect who carried out the transformation, was a sincere supporter of the new government: already at the time of the coup d'etat he had barricaded the Panthéon against republican demonstrators on his own initiative (an action he carefully detailed in a report to the Minister of Public Works; Arch. nat. F²¹ 845).

Constant-Dufeux had been appointed architect of the Panthéon in 1850, upon the death of the former architect L.-N.-M. Destouches, but previously had been concerned with upkeep and the casting of four bronze doors for the transept entrances. In December 1851 he set to work designing three huge altars scaled to Soufflot's building—that of Saint Genevieve reaching to the necking of the giant order— two pulpits, confessionals, and an organ case (Arch. nat., Versement d'Architecture, XVI). Most of the work was finished by the end of 1852. In the drawing of the Altar of Saint Genevieve, the image of the shepherdess-saint, distaff in hand, a sheep and sheep dog at her feet, stands within a baldachin on top of which two palm-bearing angels support a reliquary.

A subsequent project for the florid decoration of the exterior of the dome, which was circulated as a lithographic plate by A. Joilly (examples exist in the Free Library of Philadelphia, A720.C76, and the Bibliothèque Doucet Paris, fol. 226), was never executed, to Constant-Dufeux's chagrin, for this could have been his great work.

D.V.Z.

Archives Nationales, Paris

Simon-Claude Constant-Dufeux

## I-6
## Church of Sainte Geneviève (The Panthéon), Paris: Front and Side Elevations, Section, and Plan of a Pulpit (Study)

c. 1852
Pencil on heavy paper
52 × 71.7 cm

Provenance:
Archives Nationales, Versement d'Architecture (XVI-104)

Constant-Dufeux had established himself during the 1840s as the master (along with Labrouste) of the strange decorative mode called the "Néo-Grec." His designs for the furniture for the Church of Sainte Geneviève gave him an opportunity to demonstrate this style. The pulpits, especially, being small, could be treated in this new manner, there being less need for them to harmonize with their eighteenth-century architectural surroundings.

The "Néo-Grec" style was Greek in principle, not in form. Indeed, the term began to be applied only in the 1860s, the simple adjective "Romantic" having previously been sufficient. The principle of the "Néo-Grec" was that decorative embellishment should derive from, and articulate, the structural facts of the object ornamented and should communicate its function by an abstract language of form and line (N. Levine, in Drexler [ed.], 1977, pp. 325–416). In 1861 an American observer, the architect Henry Van Brunt, stated its objective: "Like the gestures of pantomime, which constitute an instinctive and universal language, these abstract lines, coming out of our humanity and rendered elegant by the idealization of study, are, it is hoped, restoring to architecture its highest capacity of conveying thought in a monumental manner" (Van

Brunt, 1861, vol. VIII, p. 87). In addition to Labrouste's Bibliothèque Sainte Geneviève he cites as an example Constant-Dufeux's tomb of Admiral Dumont d'Urville: "Probably the most remarkable indication of this capacity [of architectural lines to constitute a language] as yet shown.... This structure contains in its outlines a symbolic expression of human life, death, and immortality, and in its details an architectural version of the character and public services of the distinguished deceased" (Van Brunt, 1861, vol. VIII, p. 86). Constant-Dufeux himself had explained the monument in 1844. He had made it in three superimposed parts: a low, plinthlike tomb slab symbolizing death; above, a cylinder carved with the events of the admiral's life in diagrams and inscriptions; and crowning it all, a red-painted parabolic cippus, carved and gilded with a scene of the admiral's death in a flaming train wreck, he and his wife and son floating upward from the disaster, symbolizing his immortality (*Revue Générale de l'Architecture,* vol. VIII, 1849, cols. 437–40). In the case of the pulpit design shown here, the mass of the pedestal of the reading desk has been left in its elementary rectangular form except for light carving of the side profile where it brackets out. The resulting silhouette does not follow a historical model but expresses the implied upward and downward thrusts at the front and back. Each surface bears an engraved abstract floral motif, reinforcing these mo-

I-6

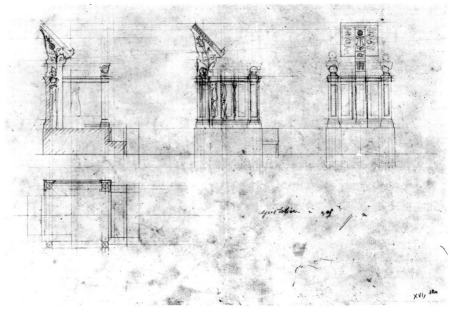

ments in the structural form. The pedestal seems to rise like a living thing and bend to support the reading board.

Constant-Dufeux's work at Sainte Geneviève came at a moment when the "Néo-Grec" had just been perfected in the decorative designs of the older Romantic Rationalists—Labrouste's Bibliothèque Sainte Geneviève; Duban's Salle des Sept Cheminées in the Louvre (upon which Constant-Dufeux worked as *inspecteur*)—and was being adopted enthusiastically by a younger generation. The fashion spread rapidly throughout Europe and to the United States in the 1850s and 1860s, sometimes merely as a decorative style mixing with other vocabularies and declining into a kind of abstracted Baroque, but also sometimes as the basis of a rational, organic style with great novelty and power (as was the case with the French-trained Richard Morris Hunt and his students—among them Van Brunt—in America).

D.V.Z.

Archives Nationales, Paris

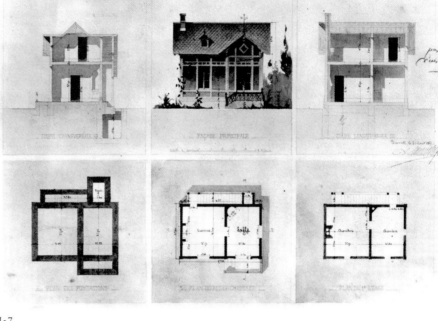

I-7

---

## Auguste-Déodat Couvrechef

*Mathieu (Calvados) 1827–1857 Arteaga (Spain)*

*Couvrechef was the favored architect of the estates that Napoleon III developed in the region of the Pyrenees immediately after his marriage with the Spanish countess, Eugénie de Montijo, on January 29, 1853. Born at Mathieu, near Caen, he is said to have worked at first as a stonecutter. On December 1, 1848, he was admitted to the second class of the Ecole des Beaux-Arts as a student of Constant-Dufeux (q.v.), entering the first class on April 4, 1851 (Arch. nat. Aj 52 361). Unlike most of his successful contemporaries, he did not pursue his education further. In 1854 he appeared as* inspecteur *under Hippolyte Durand at the Villa Eugénie in Biarritz. When Durand was dismissed as architect of that project in late May or early June, 1855, Couvrechef became his replacement at the unusually young age of twenty-seven (Arch. nat. F²¹ 1349). During the following two years he passed from being* inspecteur chargé de l'achèvement des travaux *to full architect of the imperial residences at Pau and Biarritz and restorer of Eugénie's Spanish château at Arteaga. His promising career was cut short, however, by his death at the age of thirty in 1857, while on a visit to Arteaga. He was replaced in these functions by another brilliant young designer, Gabriel-Auguste Ancelet (q.v.). In 1860 the imperial family had his*

*body ceremoniously transported back to his birthplace, Mathieu, for reinterment.*

D.V.Z.

Bibliography:
*Le Moniteur,* June 6, 1860

Auguste-Déodat Couvrechef

## I-7
## Villa Eugénie, Biarritz: Elevation, Plans, and Sections of the Gardener's Cottage (Presentation Drawing)

1855
Signed and dated, center right: Biarritz, le 21 août 1855. A. Couvrechef
Pencil, ink, ink wash, and watercolor on heavy paper
33.8 × 44 cm

Provenance:
Archives Nationales, Versement d'Architecture (portefeuille 164, no. 17)

Auguste-Déodat Couvrechef

## I-8
## Villa Eugénie, Biarritz: Elevations and Plan of an Ornamental Sentry Box on the Cliffs (Presentation Drawing)

1855
Signed and dated, lower right: Biarritz le 25 août 1855. A. Couvrechef
Pencil, ink, ink wash, and watercolor on heavy paper
31 × 27 cm

Provenance:
Archives Nationales, Versement d'Architecture (portefeuille 164, no. 18)

On July 21, 1854, Napoleon III and Eugénie arrived at the medieval city of Bayonne, where the Pyrenees touch the coast just north of the Spanish border, and proceeded to the château de Gramont at the small fishing village of Biarritz (*Le Moniteur,* July 22, 1854). Eugénie had loved the scenic stretch of coast since she had first visited it in 1833, and it was at her insist-

I-8

ence that they had come. The Emperor stayed thirty-nine days and the Empress somewhat longer. Before leaving she had purchased a parcel of land at the extremity of what was to become the Grande Plage. She asked the architect of the department of the Basses-Pyrénées, Hippolyte Durand, to draw up plans for an imperial villa, and by August 7 he had a project ready. The contractor's bid was approved by the Ministre d'Etat de la Maison de l'Empereur on October 12, and work was begun at once (Arch. nat. F²¹ 1349).

Although from 1844 to 1847 Durand had been the architect of Alexandre Dumas's fanciful Gothic house, Monte Cristo, in Bougival (Hautecœur, 1955, pp. 316–19), the design he produced for the Villa Eugénie was a strikingly undistinguished piece of Louis Philippe classicism. Either for aesthetic or for other reasons he was abruptly removed from his position and paid his outstanding fees in 1855, and Couvrechef was employed to complete the villa and to erect what came to be an extensive series of outbuildings on the grounds.

Couvrechef, unlike Durand but like Lefuel (q.v.), understood that the imperial couple would appreciate his work the more for its being presented in picturesque and carefully finished drawings. The style of his designs is in harmony with their rendering: he used a colorful combination of red brick and yellow limestone for the walls of both the sentry box (guérite) and the gardener's cottage, and arranged their silhouettes for pictorial effect. Two flaps on the drawing of the guérite show an alternative treatment of the crowning.

Here, at the commencement of the Second Empire, began the evolution of a colorful, picturesque style of informal architecture that was to culminate in the buildings of the Bois de Boulogne and of numerous country estates. Around the imperial villa itself there soon developed a colony of expensive villas erected by the *haut monde*, and Biarritz joined the duc de Morny's contemporaneous Deauville in Normandy as a new sort of informal meeting place of the very rich established within a new sort of architectural setting.

D.V.Z.

Archives Nationales, Paris

## Jacques-Félix Duban
*Paris 1797–1870 Bordeaux*

*Duban had established his reputation as a leader of the Romantic Rationalist "revolution" during the 1830s, but by the time of the Second Empire had become one of the old masters of Parisian architecture.*

*The son of a Parisian ironmonger, he entered the architectural profession when the architect François Debret married his older sister and accepted him as a student in his atelier. In 1823 Duban won the Grand Prix de Rome with a celebrated design for a customs house, thereafter becoming the eldest of the group of Romantic Rationalists. In 1829 his fifth-year* envoi, *a "Protestant Temple," arrived in Paris, becoming, together with a reconstruction of the temples at Paestum by Labrouste (q.v.), one of the earliest examples of French Romantic architecture put before the public. Upon his return to Paris that year, Duban became an influential* chef d'atelier, *temporarily taking over the studio of Abel Blouet, then, in 1831, opening his own studio. From 1832 to 1840 he designed and erected the first structures of the Ecole des Beaux-Arts, from 1835 to 1839 he was architect of the Hôtel Pourtalès on the rue Tronchet, and from 1839 to 1841 he designed several rooms for the duc de Luynes in the château at Dampierre, including the Salle d'Honneur (containing Ingres's uncompleted murals).*

*By the beginning of the Second Empire, Duban was an established government architect: he was in charge of the restoration of the Louvre (voted in 1848) and had been elected to the Académie des Beaux-Arts in 1854. His relations with the Emperor were not good, however. Because of his painstaking slowness in redesigning the Salon Carré and the Salle des Sept Cheminées, Louis Napoleon in 1852 turned to Visconti (q.v.) for further work on the Louvre (Hautecœur, 1928, p. 96). The Emperor is said to have remarked that he had to deal with Duban "de puissance à puissance"—"as one diplomatic power with another" (Pascal, 1881, col. 263). Nonetheless, from 1858 to 1862 Duban was able to continue work at the Ecole des Beaux-Arts by erecting the vast Salle de Melpomène and its facade on the quai Malaquais. Later, in 1863, he covered the inner courtyard of the old Ecole building with an iron-and-glass roof. Still, his failure with the Emperor is said to have broken his spirit, causing him to become reclusive and misanthropic, so that when the Prussians approached Paris in 1870 he fled to Bordeaux a sick man and died soon after.*

D.V.Z.

Bibliography:
Vaudoyer, 1871; Baltard, 1872; Beulé, 1872; Questel, 1872; Blanc, 1876, pp. 1–22

Jacques-Félix Duban

## I-9
## Pompeian Architectural Fantasy

1856
Signed at left, on column: FELIX DUBAN; on amphora: Félix Duban, 1856
Watercolor and pencil on paper
38 × 48 cm

Provenance:
André Varenne; sale, Paris, Hôtel Drouot, November 26, 1965; private coll., Boulogne-sur-Seine
Bibliography:
D'Espouy, 1900, vol. I, pl. 28

This watercolor shows what Normand actually tried to build as the Prince Napoleon's "Maison Pompéienne" (no. I-22) and clarifies what wishes of the Second Empire artists such dwellings fulfilled. Duban's exquisite Pompeian architecture, embellished with an even more exquisite and graceful polychromy, incorporates a series of household furnishings shaped, carved, painted, and embroidered in excruciatingly refined taste. (The figure in the wall painting was copied from a panel found at Herculaneum [Roux and Barré, 1870–75, vol. IX, pl. 49] thought to represent Pomona or Chastity.) Colorful, exotic fruit and flowers are scattered about, and a view opens out into a

fountained garden and forested hills beyond. Duban's composition is a study of the constituents of perfect taste in domestic environment, imagined in terms of ancient Pompeii and so suggesting that the Pompeian way of domestic life was a model of sensual sophistication.

The tradition of architects creating elaborate architectural fantasies had begun in the eighteenth century, spurred by Piranesi's "Carceri" prints, and culminated in France in Ledoux's fantastic elaboration of the city of Chaux of 1804. Charles Percier refined the type (and jettisoned Ledoux's symbolic ballast) in such highly finished works as his conceptual drawing of a "Museum in the Style of Those Erected in the Sixteenth Century" (1972, Paris, Louvre, pl. 14), nostalgic, lyrical, and decorative. Around 1830 Duban and Labrouste had signaled their Romantic "revolution" with a series of compositions of ancient and Renaissance architecture (Van Zanten, 1977, pp. 36–47, pls. C, E, F), which these young architects, as yet unable to build, used to make a statement about the history of architecture.

As their professional careers prospered, Duban and Labrouste ceased to devote their time and labor to such drawings. During the 1850s, however, after his failure at the Louvre, Duban returned to them, producing a series that was nostalgic and private, like Percier's in their intent, but rich and complicated in touch. They

seem internalizations of the evolution in his art that had produced the ceilings of the Salle des Sept Cheminées and the Salon Carré. Duban, like some other Romantic Rationalists of his generation, proved himself to be at least as interested in beauty of form as he was in dogmatic principle during the Second Empire.

Series of Duban's compositions were exhibited at the Exposition Universelle of 1855 and again, after his death, at the Ecole des Beaux-Arts in 1872 (Baltard, 1872; Blanc, 1876, pp. 1–22). Charles Blanc, writing of the latter exhibition, began by observing that "the truth is that he mixed into architecture a dose of poetry, which should have destroyed the equilibrium between sentiment and reason that is absolutely necessary in that great art," but he concluded, "it is especially in reference to the works of Duban that we can say: architecture, in the most noble sense, is not a construction that one decorates, but rather a decoration that one constructs" (1876, pp. 2, 22). Second Empire architecture was the art of creating settings, of architectural tableaux: Duban's compositions were taken seriously (perhaps even more so than he had intended) because they presented an opportunity to conceive and refine pieces of architectural theater.

D.V.Z.

Private Collection, Boulogne-sur-Seine

I-9

Jean-Louis-Charles Garnier
Paris 1825–1898 Paris

The reputations of Lefuel (q.v.) and Garnier were made during the Second Empire and were intimately linked to that epoch's particular pretenses. Lefuel, however, was a man of the 1850s who looked back to the "Style Troubadour" of the previous reign; Garnier was a man of the 1860s who took account of the newer ideas of the Romantics and created a distinctly Second Empire synthesis.

Born of a poor family on the rue Mouffetard, Garnier slowly worked his way up from humbler schools to the Ecole des Beaux-Arts and the venerable classicist atelier of Hippolyte Lebas. He supported himself in part by working as a draftsman for Viollet-le-Duc (q.v.). In 1848 he won the Grand Prix de Rome and during his five-year pension executed a controversial study of the architectural polychromy of the Temple of Jupiter at Aegina (published in 1884) after a trip to Greece and Turkey, during which he met the writer Théophile Gautier.

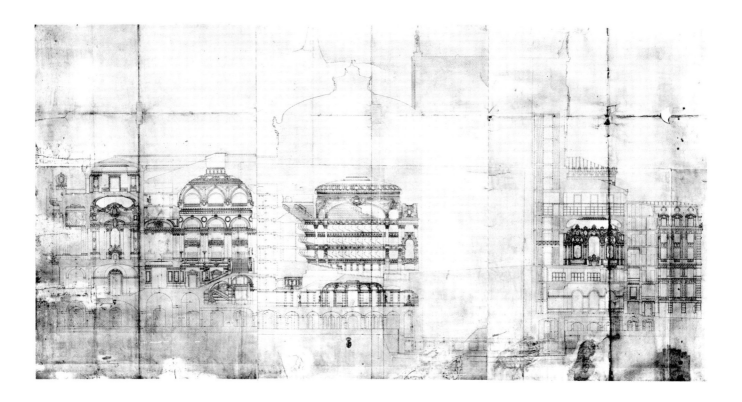

Upon his return to Paris in 1854 Garnier became sous-inspecteur *of the restoration work at the Tour Saint Jacques (under Théodore Ballu) and* inspecteur des travaux *at the Ecole des Mines, designed an apartment building on the new boulevard de Sébastopol, and finally became architect of the City of Paris for the Vth and VIth arrondissements. A real opportunity, however, came only with the competition for the Opéra during the winter of 1860–61. After winning it, Garnier set to work organizing the execution of the most elaborate building of the age, completed only in 1875. He explained this work in two books:* Le Théâtre *(1871) and* Le Nouvel Opéra de Paris *(1878–81).*

*After the completion of the Opéra, Garnier refined his style in the Observatory in Nice (1880–88), which he felt his next-best design, and in the casinos at Vittel (1885) and Monte Carlo (1878–81). He built a villa for himself (1872–73) at Bordighera on the Italian Riviera and subsequently erected the Villa Bischoffsheim, the church (1883–85), the public school (1874), and the Hôtel du Belvédère (1886) there. In Paris he was the architect of the Dépot des Décors for the Opéra (1872); the Cercle de la* Librairie *(1878–79), 195, boulevard Saint Germain, for Hachette (1880–81); and the Panoramas Marigny (1883–84) and Valentino (1882–83; now destroyed).*

D.V.Z.

Bibliography:
Guadet, 1899; Larroumet, 1904; L. Garnier, 1925

Jean-Louis-Charles Garnier

## I-10
## Académie Impériale de Musique (Opéra), Paris

### A. Longitudinal Section (Study)
1861–62
Ink line and pencil on paper, backed
150 × 360 cm

Provenance:
Descended in architect's family; gift to the Bibliothèque et Musée de l'Opéra (plan d'architecture L)

*(Shown in Philadelphia only)*

### B. Longitudinal Section of the Auditorium (Structural Study)
1861–62
Ink line and pencil on paper, backed
190 × 136 cm

Provenance:
Descended in architect's family; gift to the Bibliothèque et Musée de l'Opéra (plan d'architecture M)

*(Shown in Detroit only)*

NOUVEL OPERA

I-10 B

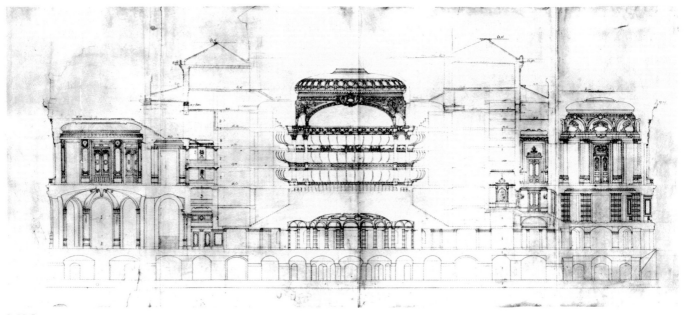

I-10 C

## C. Lateral Section at the Auditorium (Study)

1861–62
Ink line and pencil on paper, backed
157 × 300 cm

Provenance:
Descended in architect's family; gift to the Bibliothèque et Musée de l'Opéra (plan d'architecture K)

*(Shown in Paris only)*

The Opéra, crowning Haussmann's Paris at the crossing of six boulevards, was intended to be, and remains, the great monument of the Second Empire transformation of that city. Contemporaries at court and in the architectural profession considered it a brilliant but bizarre work, however, and only some younger students at the Ecole des Beaux-Arts and a few critics, notably Théophile Gautier, appreciated Garnier's design from its inception in 1861.

When a project produced by the architect of the old Opéra, Charles Rohault de Fleury, proved unsatisfactory (Steinhauser, 1969, pl. 56), an open competition was announced on December 29, 1860, and by January 31 the following year, 171 entries had been received. The submission of Léon Ginain was judged the best, that of Garnier placing fifth, and that of Viollet-le-Duc not placing at all (see nos. I-30, I-31). The authors of the five best projects were then asked to submit more detailed designs, and from them Garnier's was selected for

execution on May 29, 1861, to the lifelong chagrin of Ginain. During the remainder of 1861 and the spring of 1862, Garnier refined his project and simultaneously commenced its execution, beginning excavation on August 27, 1861, and supervising the laying of the first stone on July 21, 1862. The masonry shell was completed rapidly and the scaffolding was removed from the elaborately carved facade on August 15, 1867. The completion of the interior and its ornamentation (see nos. V-8, VII-4), however, took longer and the Opéra was not opened until January 5, 1875.

These three cross sections are part of a series of huge studies for the building in which Garnier can be seen determining the shapes of the spaces and coordinating and elaborating their decorative details. Here one witnesses him experimenting with various solutions in pencil and then choosing to finalize certain of them in ink. These drawings would have followed preliminary plan studies (see, for example, Steinhauser, 1969, pl. 124) and served as the basis for the study of individual details in large-scale drawings rendered by Garnier in ink wash (see, for example, Drexler [ed.], 1977, pp. 265, 271). They would then have been transferred into pencil working drawings by his draftsmen (see, for example, Drexler [ed.], 1977, p. 273).

The longitudinal section must date from early in Garnier's study of the design because it includes a large chamber over the Grand Foyer

that was early suppressed and a treatment of the ceiling of the Grand Stair Hall all-too-obviously derived from Duban's decoration of the Salle des Sept Cheminées in the Louvre. The lateral section demonstrates the spatial and mass relationships of the porte-cochere and the Emperor's Pavilion to the Auditorium. The section of the Auditorium shows the structural and ventilation systems and demonstrates that the hall was merely a fragile plaster box supended in a vast iron cage beneath a massive air chamber. The form and the decoration of the space, however, give no hint of the elaborate technological organism that embraces it and provides for its occupants' safety and comfort.

D.V.Z.

Bibliothèque Nationale, Département de la Musique, Bibliothèque et Musée de l'Opéra, Paris

---

## Jacques-Ignace Hittorff

*Cologne 1792–1867 Paris*

*Together with Baltard (q.v.), Hittorff was Baron Haussmann's principal executant and like Baltard he was conservative in taste but experimental in technique.*

*The son of a Cologne tinsmith who had prospered after the French absorption of the Rhineland in 1794, Hittorff went to Paris and entered the atelier of Charles Percier in 1810. He won the admiration of Percier, which—together with his work as François-Joseph Bélanger's assistant on the dome of the Halle au Blé (1811–13)—led to a prosperous practice in house and theater design during the Restoration as well as to the appointment in 1818 (upon Bélanger's death)* as architecte du Roi pour les fêtes et cérémonies *(in partnership with his friend Joseph Lecointe). In the atelier of Percier, he had also become a close friend of the scholar-architect François-Christian Gau with whom he frequented the salon of the painter Baron Gérard. From 1822 to 1824 Hittorff visited Rome and Sicily and returned with a series of reconstructions of the polychrome decoration of the ancient Greek temples that embroiled him in an archaeological controversy that lasted until the publication of his massive* De l'architecture polychrome chez les Grecs *in 1851.*

*Under the July Monarchy, he was appointed architect for the completion of the Church of Saint Vincent de Paul (1831–44, begun by his father-in-law Jean-Baptiste Lepère) and for the planning and decoration of the Champs Elysées (1834–40) and the place de la Concorde (1832–40). Then, after the coup d'etat, he received a series of government commissions—among them the Mairie of the Ist arrondissement (1855–61), the facades around the place de l'Etoile (1852ff), and the Institut Eugène-Napoléon (1853–55)—as well as the request for a project for the "Maison Pompéienne" (see no. I-22) from the Prince Napoleon and the commission to execute, together with his friend Ingres (q.v.), a tiny Temple of the Muses (1854–55). It was a private commission, however, the new Gare du Nord (1859–66), that was his most magisterial production. He was elected to the Académie des Beaux-Arts in 1853, but was unsuccessful in his attempt to obtain the important post of secrétaire perpétuel of the Académie des Beaux-Arts in 1854.*

D.V.Z.

Bibliography:
Hammer, 1968; Schneider, 1977

Office of Jacques-Ignace Hittorff

# I-11
# Palais de l'Industrie, Exposition Universelle of 1855, Paris: Lateral Section at Transept (Project)

1853?
Ink line and ink wash on tracing paper, backed
58 × 57 cm

Provenance:
Descended in architect's family; gift to the Wallraf-Richartz-Museum, 1898 (inv. no. CH 459)

Bibliography:
Hammer, 1968, pp. 236–37

The stories of the design and erection of the first two great iron-and-glass international exposition buildings are complex and intertwined. Prince Albert and several of his friends conceived the idea of the London Universal Exhibition of the Works of Industry of All Nations in 1849 while visiting the quinquennial Exposition des Produits de l'Industrie in Paris. A competition for suggestions for the London structure was announced and on May 9, 1850, Hector Horeau's project was proclaimed the best. He proposed a long, low, sloping structure entirely of iron and glass, like his Halles Centrales scheme of 1845 and his *jardin d'hiver* on the Champs Elysées of 1847. A counter project was put forward by the English building committee, but, proving too costly and time-consuming, it was replaced at the last moment with the scheme of Joseph Paxton—the huge iron-and-glass Crystal Palace, in scale and purity of construction like Horeau's dreams but in detail like the greenhouses Paxton had erected as the Duke of Devonshire's gardener.

The London exhibition challenged Napoleon III to respond, and in 1853 he created an imperial commission for a universal exposition in Paris. The commission contracted for a monumental exhibition building on the Champs Elysées from a joint-stock company, the Compagnie du Palais de l'Industrie. This company retained the architects Jean-Marie-Victor Viel and Antoine Desjardins, who presented a project in which a large iron-roofed central space was ringed by paired galleries, with masonry walls on the ground floor and ornamented iron panels above (Barrault and Bridel, 1857, pl. 1; Hautecœur, 1957, p. 317, seems to have misread their text). York and Company contracted to build the structure, but solicited a new project from the engineer Alexis Barrault and the architect François-Alexis Cendrier because of the excessive cost of Viel and Desjardins's scheme (Barrault and Bridel, 1857, pl. 2). The contract for this project—an iron gallery ringing a larger, central iron-roofed space—was signed in December 1852. On May 1, 1854, after the masonry envelope was up but before it was cut, Cendrier resigned his post and Viel was placed in charge, executing the ornamentation (Desjardins had resigned earlier). The structure was inaugurated on May 15, 1855.

Because Hittorff was the architect of the Champs Elysées (having built a series of fountains and restaurants in that capacity during the

I-11

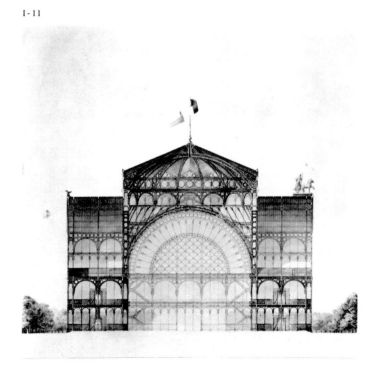

1830s), it is not surprising that he worked up a project for the exposition building to be erected there. There is no mention, however, of this project in his correspondence and exactly when and to what end he made the eight drawings composing this series is unclear (Hammer, 1968, pp. 236–37, pl. 128).

The building consists of a nave and a central transept intersecting at a dome. The vocabulary—the open columnar skeleton, the arched and circular stiffeners, the ridged glass roofs—is Paxton's (Hittorff had visited the London exhibition in 1851). In his use of this vocabulary, however, Hittorff composed and proportioned the volumes according to the conventions of academic taste, multiplied the curving forms to set up continuous, decorative rhythms, and placed ornamental gilded cornices along the roof lines and a gilded-metal quadriga on the principal gable peak (suggesting what its proportions imply, that it is a pediment). The compactness of Hittorff's composition deceives one as to its size. In a drawing in Hittorff's series showing it side-by-side with Paxton's Crystal Palace and Perrault's east facade of the Louvre one sees that Hittorff's structure would have been twice as high as the former and half again as long and twice as high as the latter. Had it indeed been erected where the Petit Palais now stands, its dome, sixty-eight meters above the ground, would have loomed over Second Empire Paris as an ethereal predecessor of the Eiffel Tower.

D.V.Z.

Wallraf-Richartz-Museum und Museum Ludwig, Cologne

I-12

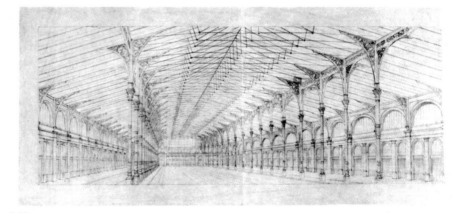

I-13

Office of Jacques-Ignace Hittorff

## I-12
## Gare du Nord, Paris: Exterior View from Southwest

1861 or 1864
Pencil on heavy paper
34.9 × 47.1 cm

Provenance:
Descended in architect's family; gift to the Wallraf-Richartz-Museum, 1898 (inv. no. GN 279)

Bibliography:
Hammer, 1968, p. 211, pl. 136; Schneider, 1977, pp. 647–48, pl. 375

Office of Jacques-Ignace Hittorff

## I-13
## Gare du Nord, Paris: Perspective Study of Interior of Train Shed, Looking South (Final Project)

1862–63
Pencil on tracing paper, backed
33 × 77.5 cm

Provenance:
Descended in architect's family; gift to the Wallraf-Richartz-Museum, 1898 (inv. no. GN 264)

Bibliography:
Hammer, 1968, p. 211, pl. 138; Schneider, 1977, pp. 632–39, pl. 366

Paris lies in a shallow basin defined by low hills. Between the slopes of Montmartre and the Buttes Chaumont is a narrow depression leading from the slowly rising ground of the Faubourg Poissonnière out northward to Saint-Denis and on into the plains of Picardy. This small valley was the city's corridor to the north and northeast: for centuries one of the busiest roads out of Paris has passed through it, paralleled since the eighteenth century by the canal de l'Ourcq. With the rapid exploitation of Belgian, Rhenish, and northeast French coal and iron after the turn of the nineteenth century, this busy but unprepossessing defile was perceived as the necessary route of a great railroad line. Already in 1832 Michel Chevalier had broached the scheme (*Le Globe*, February 5, 12, 1832); in 1837 a detailed project was submitted to the Chamber of Deputies (but rejected by the opponents of railroad development); and in 1842, with the passage of the "Code des Chemins de Fer," two of the six lines to be built to the borders of France went out from Paris through this corridor (Clozier, 1940). Two stations were erected during the July Monarchy at the southern end of the depression where the rue La Fayette led down to the heart of Paris: the Gare de l'Est (François-Alexandre Duquesney, architect, 1847–50) and the Gare du Nord (Léonce Reynaud, architect, 1843–47).

Capitalism and industrialization had passed from a tentative to a full-blown, self-confident state with the establishment of the Second Empire. First among the new centralized industries were iron and railroads, and the Compagnie de Chemin de Fer du Nord (dominated by James de Rothschild), which linked Paris to the iron and coal lands of the north, experienced vast expansion and prosperity. In 1857, within a decade after the inauguration of its first Paris terminus, the company authorized the erection of another much-enlarged structure. In 1859 Hittorff was appointed architect of the project and Léonce Reynaud, engineer. Government approval was received in October 1861, and the building was open for use on April 18, 1864, although it was not completely finished until 1866 (Hammer, 1968, pp. 206–16; Schneider, 1977, pp. 619, 624, 649–51).

The architectural problem faced in the Gare du Nord was to what extent a railroad station is a monument and to what extent a shed; as a monument, just what should it express, and how, as a shed, could it be made to express it. During the years 1840–60 a variety of solutions had been presented in the earliest Parisian stations. The Gare de Lyon (1847–52), by the Saint-Simonian François-Alexis Cendrier, was a naked, double iron-and-glass shed resting on a masonry base, articulated by tall, carved stelae at its front and back; that is, an industrial artifact accepted for itself like Joseph Paxton's Crystal Palace in London with primitive signs of entry placed about it—"Néo-Grec" equivalents of Hardwick's Euston Arch in London. The offices and waiting rooms were constructed of masonry and attached at various points on the shed's sides (*Revue Générale de l'Architecture*, vol. XVII, 1859, pls. 12–22). The Gare de l'Est had an iron train shed concealed behind two blocks of offices and halls facing a monumental court. The masonry facade acknowledged the shed and transformed it into an expression of entry by stating its lines in a broad masonry gable punctured by a huge arched window.

Appropriately, one entered the Gare de l'Est under this arch, but approached the Gare de Lyon from either side (as one originally did in Hittorff's Gare du Nord).

Hittorff's solution (chosen from an extraordinary number of his variants; Hammer, 1968, pls. 130–35; Schneider, 1977, pp. 642–46) was to make the volume of his building that of the shed itself, like Cendrier's station, and to clothe it in masonry, like Duquesney's. Continuing this idea of combination, he transformed the masonry shell into an impossibly thin grid of primitive Greek Doric columns which revealed the new structural properties of the iron shed they sheathed—its openness and the strength of its individual members—but in the Neoclassical vocabulary. Hittorff converted Cendrier's stelae to Hardwick's "arch" (Hittorff had made a trip to England in 1859 immediately after receiving the commission)—now literally an arch—but on the two ends of the facade, marking the pavilions there for the *arrivées* and *départs*. On the interior, instead of giving the space a closed, geometric form like the arched space of the Gare de l'Est, Hittorff left the sloping roof in its simple technical shape: straight with two rows of thin intermediate supports—the system Hector Horeau had proposed in his Crystal Palace scheme of 1850, as Schneider points out.

With an English rather than French bluntness and naïveté of combination, Hittorff merely ornamented the individual parts of his technical artifact, like the contemporaneous engineers who supported the walking beams of their engines on pairs of cast-iron Doric columns. Hittorff was attacked by both classicists and rationalists for his inconsistency in combining the forms of the lithic Greek Orders with the spacing and composition of the nineteenth-century iron shed (*Gazette des Architectes et du Bâtiment*, vol. I, 1863, pp. 190–92; see Schneider, 1977, pp. 660–72). Today, however, we are less moved by the nineteenth century's preoccupation with the Classical Orders and its search for a new order, and have come to admire the blunt juxtapositions of the Gare du Nord—as also that of the archless Euston Arch.

The drawing of the exterior of the Gare du Nord is a miniature pencil rendering of the project as it was executed, which Hammer and Schneider date to 1861, when, in a letter of May 4, Hittorff presented his final project (Hammer, 1968, p. 211 n. 19; Schneider, 1977, pp. 647–48). However, we would suggest that it could as easily be a drawing executed after the fact for the purpose of engraving. It falsifies the experience of the station by depicting an unlimited space in front (Hittorff himself laid out the narrow square the station actually faces

upon) and by showing trees to its east (an area that was already built up).

The interior perspective is a study of the train shed in its final form (arrived at in 1862–63), although the detailing of the iron ceiling trusses was simplified in execution. Here one can see the original southern termination of the space, today much encumbered. The low Doric colonnade of the facade carries through into the interior to define the waiting rooms. Above them is a terrace permitting the great arched opening of the facade to light the shed. The Doric colonnade continues down the side of the shed defining the halls and baggage rooms to the right and left. (Today everything below the entablature has been removed to permit the lateral expansion of the track space.) The middle story, marked on the facade by caryatids, continues around its shed as a clerestory. Thus, the interwoven orders stated on the facade originally reflected the layout of the interior and these spaces were once clearly defined—small-scale, closed spaces for the public within a large, open space for the trains.

D.V.Z.

Wallraf-Richartz-Museum und Museum Ludwig, Cologne

## Pierre-François-Henri Labrouste
### Paris 1801–1875 Fontainebleau

*Labrouste was the founder of the Romantic Rationalist school of French architecture, and his work and teaching during the July Monarchy set the stage for the great combat between Viollet-le-Duc (q.v.) and Charles Garnier (q.v.) that was to occur during the Second Empire. His most impressive work, the Reading Room in the Bibliothèque Nationale, was itself a Second Empire undertaking.*

*The son of an important functionary in the Ministry of Finance, Labrouste was educated at the Collège Sainte Barbe before entering the Ecole des Beaux-Arts in 1819 as a student of Antoine-Louis-Thomas Vaudoyer and Hippolyte Lebas. He won the Grand Prix de Rome in 1824 at the early age of twenty-three, and became, together with Duban (q.v.), the leader of the Romantic pensionnaires in Rome. In 1829 his fourth-year envoi, a reconstruction of the temples at Paestum, was sharply criticized by Quatremère de Quincy, secrétaire perpétuel of the Académie des Beaux-Arts, leading to a furious controversy marking the appearance of Romanticism in official French architecture. Upon his return to*

*Paris in June 1830, a group of dissidents in the atelier of Vaudoyer and Lebas persuaded Labrouste to open a new atelier for them. Despite the discrimination of the Ecole against his students in competitions, he continued the atelier until 1856, when, after its closing, his students dispersed, some to Viollet-le-Duc and others to Jules André. His many notable students included Lassus (q.v.), Bossan (q.v.), Juste Lisch, Eugène Millet, Anatole de Baudot, and Julien Guadet.*

*Buttressing his achievement as a teacher were two great works: the Bibliothèque Sainte Geneviève (1838–50), the masterwork of the July Monarchy and the first building to use iron monumentally, and the rebuilding and expansion of the Bibliothèque Nationale (1854–75). Labrouste also executed a number of minor commissions, aiding Duban in 1833 at the Ecole des Beaux-Arts, presenting schemes in 1836–40 for the decoration of the Pont de la Concorde (together with his brother Théodore), erecting a seminary at Rennes (1854–74), a city house of the Minister of Fine Arts Achille Fould (1856–58), the Thouret villa in Neuilly (1860), the administration building of the Paris-Lyon-Méditerranée railroad (1862), and the Hôtel Villgruy (1865). He was elected to the Académie des Beaux-Arts in 1867.*

D.V.Z.

Bibliography:
Delaborde, 1878; Millet, 1882; *Souvenirs de Labrouste*, 1928; Levine, 1975; N. Levine, in Drexler (ed.), 1977, pp. 325–93

Pierre-François-Henri Labrouste

# I-14
# Bibliothèque Impériale
# (Bibliothèque Nationale), Paris

### A. Study for the Decoration of a Heater
1865
Ink wash and pencil on heavy paper, backed
105.8 × 67.3 cm

Provenance:
Descended in architect's family; gift to the Bibliothèque Nationale, Cabinet des Estampes

Exhibition:
1976, Paris, Hôtel de Béthune Sully, no. 230

(*Shown in Philadelphia only*)

### B. Section and Elevations
### (Preliminary Project)
1859
Signed and dated: H. Labrouste 1859
Ink line and ink wash on heavy paper, backed
67.8 × 102.3 cm

I - 14 A

Provenance:
Descended in architect's family; gift to the Bibliothèque Nationale, Cabinet des Estampes

Exhibition:
1976, Paris, Hôtel de Béthune Sully, no. 217

(*Shown in Detroit only*)

### C. Study for a Carved Lamp Motif
1865
Signed, dated, and inscribed: Bibliothèque Nationale: Deux candélabres en pierre de… le 12 décembre, 1865, H. Labrouste, grandeur de l'exécution.

Ink wash and pencil on heavy paper, backed
201 × 40.5 cm

Provenance:
Descended in architect's family; gift to the Bibliothèque Nationale, Cabinet des Estampes

Exhibition:
1976, Paris, Hôtel de Béthune Sully, no. 232

(*Shown in Paris only*)

Henri Labrouste was appointed architect of the Bibliothèque Impériale in 1854 after the death of its architect Visconti (q.v.). On December 19, 1857, a commission, led by Prosper

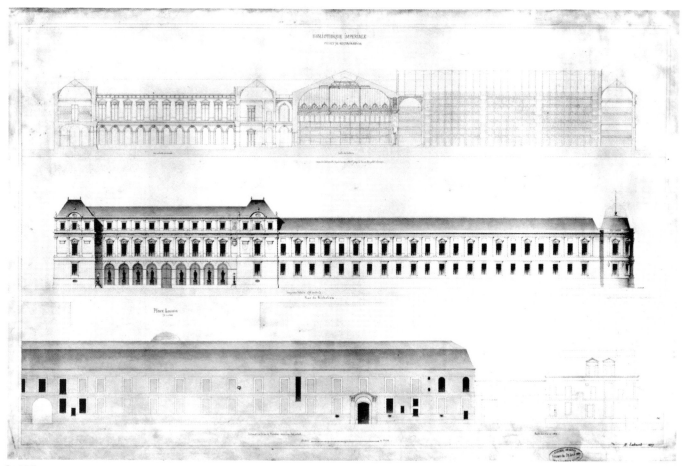

BIBLIOTHÈQUE IMPÉRIALE

I - 14 B

Mérimée, was appointed to study the reorganization and rebuilding of the library, located in the Hôtel Mazarin. Labrouste drew up several proposals. The commission published its report on August 20, 1858 (*Le Moniteur,* August 20, 1858), and on April 7, 1859, Labrouste submitted a definitive design to the Conseil des Bâtiments Civils, who approved it on April 27. Construction was commenced on June 1 of that year at the corner of the rue de Richelieu and the rue des Petits Champs. Labrouste, however, continued to study the design of the most important part, the Reading Room, into the 1860s, signing the contract for the faïence domes forming its ceiling only on March 8, 1864 (Arch. nat. F²¹ 1361). The room was essentially complete by the end of 1866 and work moved on to the wing facing the rue de Richelieu, which was constructed and decorated from 1867 to Labrouste's death in 1875 (Labrouste, 1885).

The sheet bearing the section and elevations (the lowest showing the building in its original state) is one of the set of drawings prepared for official approval in 1859. The basic layout of the building is set here: the placement of the Reading Room on the location of the *corps de logis* of the old Hôtel Mazarin, the retention of the *cour d'honneur,* and the establishment of the stacks in the former garden. It is a less radical scheme than an alternative project submitted to the commission of 1857–58 in which Labrouste proposed to demolish all the buildings on the site and to erect a new structure around a vast iron-and-glass reading room (Mérimée, 1941–61, vol. VIII, pp. 625–27; *Le Moniteur,* August 20, 1858). In the project exhibited, the Reading Room had not yet achieved its final form, being a square version of Smirke and Panizzi's British Museum Reading Room: a closed geometric volume under a simple iron-and-glass ceiling, the readers' desks arranged

concentrically around the librarian's counter (at Mérimée's suggestion Labrouste visited Panizzi at the British Museum in 1857). Although in subsequent studies Labrouste was able to transform this psychologically oppressive scheme into the room one sees today, he did have to bow to the administration's wish that the arcade opening the *cour d'honneur* to the square Louvois be closed and that an exedra (proposed later) embracing the whole southern side of that court—echoing the exedra he added on the southern side of the Reading Room—be omitted.

The two designs for decorative details shown here are full-scale studies from Labrouste's hand for one of the twenty cast-iron heaters of the Reading Room and for one of the lamps carved into the masonry of the jambs of the arched entrance to the bookstacks. The contract for the heaters was signed on November 4, 1865, and the payment of 11,200

I - 14 C

francs was made after delivery on June 28, 1866 (Arch. nat. F²¹ 1361). They are particularly magnificent examples of Labrouste's late "Néo-Grec" decorative style with their energized abstraction of archaic classical forms. In the study for the heater, one witnesses Labrouste in the process of working up the design in pencil and then fixing and articulating it in ink line and wash.

D.V.Z.

Bibliothèque Nationale, Cabinet des Estampes, Paris

## Jean-Baptiste-Antoine Lassus

Paris 1807–1857 Vichy

*As one of the leaders of the nine students who seceded from the atelier of Vaudoyer and Lebas and on July 6, 1830, petitioned Labrouste (q.v.) to found his atelier for them, Lassus might very well have become the chief Romantic Rationalist architect of the younger generation during the Second Empire had he not died at a relatively early age in 1857 (see biography preceding no. III-15). During his lifetime he produced a series of Gothic churches in which he refined a rational, systematized vision of medieval architecture.*

*Achieving no academic success at the Ecole des Beaux-Arts (because he was a student of Labrouste, it was suspected), he turned his attention to archaeological studies of old Parisian buildings, winning recognition in the Salon of 1833 for his drawings of the Tuileries and in 1835 for his project to restore the Sainte Chapelle. In 1836 he was appointed* inspecteur *under Duban (q.v.) for the reconstruction of the Sainte Chapelle; the following year he was appointed, together with another student of Labrouste, Adolphe-Gabriel Gréterin, to rebuild the facade of Saint Séverin and made* inspecteur *under Hippolyte Godde for the restoration of the Church of Saint Germain l'Auxerrois. In 1843 he received the commission to redesign the large parish church of Saint Nicolas in Nantes (begun by Louis-Alexandre Piel in 1841), producing a carefully correct composite of High Gothic forms, a systematized and scaled-down cathedral. In 1844, together with Viollet-le-Duc (q.v.), he won the competition for the restoration of the Cathedral of Notre Dame in Paris, a project on which he worked until his death. In 1848 he was appointed diocesan architect of Chartres, Le Mans, and Moulins, restoring the cathedrals in the first two cities and laying the foundations of the nave for the cathedral in Moulins (after his death redesigned and executed by Eugène Millet),*

*as well as building the Church of the Sacré Cœur there. In 1848 he also erected a Gothic house for Prince Alexis Soltykoff on the avenue Montaigne in Paris. In 1853 he erected the parish church of Saint Pierre in Dijon and in 1854–57 that of Saint Jean Baptiste in the district of Belleville in Paris. The year before his death, 1856, saw his best design and the quintessential statement of systematized Gothic, the competition project for the huge Church of Notre Dame de la Treille in Lille.*

D.V.Z.

Bibliography:
Troche, 1857: Lance, 1872; Leniaud, 1976

Jean-Baptiste-Antoine Lassus

## I - 15
## Church of Notre Dame de la Treille, Lille: Plan (Competition Project)

1856
Inscribed and dated, lower right: L'Eclectisme est la plaie de l'art—1856
Ink wash on paper
97 × 66 cm

I - 15

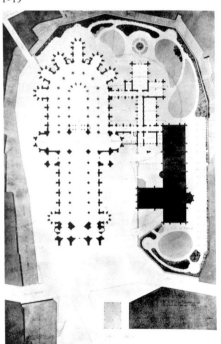

Provenance:
Archives de l'Œuvre Notre Dame de la Treille;
Archives Historiques du Diocèse de Lille, 1913 (Fonds
de la Treille, dossier concours, projet XIX, 1)

Bibliography:
*Notre-Dame-de-la-Treille*, 1856

Jean-Baptiste-Antoine Lassus

## I-16
## Church of Notre Dame de la Treille, Lille: West Elevation (Competition Project)

1856
Inscribed and dated, upper left: L'Eclectisme
est la plaie de l'art—1856
Ink and ink wash on paper
98 × 67 cm

Provenance:
Archives de l'Œuvre Notre Dame de la Treille;
Archives Historiques du Diocèse de Lille, 1913 (Fonds
de la Treille, dossier concours, projet XIX, 3)

Bibliography:
*Notre-Dame-de-la-Treille*, 1856

Jean-Baptiste-Antoine Lassus

## I-17
## Church of Notre Dame de la Treille, Lille: Interior Perspective (Competition Project)

1856
Inscribed and dated: L'Eclectisme est la plaie de
l'art—1856
Ink and ink wash on paper
101 × 70 cm

Provenance:
Archives de l'Œuvre Notre Dame de la Treille;
Archives Historiques du Diocèse de Lille, 1913 (Fonds
de la Treille, dossier concours, projet XIX, 15)

Bibliography:
*Notre-Dame-de-la-Treille*, 1856

Jean-Baptiste-Antoine Lassus

## I-18
## Church of Notre Dame de la Treille, Lille: Longitudinal Section (Competition Project)

I-16

1856
Inscribed and dated, upper left: L'Eclectisme
est la plaie de l'art—1856
Ink wash on paper
93 × 127 cm

Provenance:
Archives de l'Œuvre Notre Dame de la Treille;
Archives Historiques du Diocèse de Lille, 1913 (Fonds
de la Treille, dossier concours, projet XIX, 18)

Bibliography:
*Notre-Dame-de-la-Treille*, 1856

Lille was one of the fastest growing and richest industrial cities of Second Empire France. It harbored a miraculous image of the Virgin, but one that had not been housed in a suitable edifice since 1793, when the church in which it was kept, Saint Pierre, had been demolished. In 1852 a commission was founded to solicit contributions for the erection of a "monumental church," and in late 1854 a competition for its design was announced, with the deadline for submissions established as December 1, 1855 (the date was later postponed to March 1, 1856). The Gothic style was specified in the program and the jury was packed with ecclesiological archaeologists to enforce it—Adolphe-Napoléon Didron, Arcisse de Caumont, August Reichensperger, and Arthur Martin. The size specified was adequate for a cathedral, and indeed later in the century the episcopal seat moved there from Cambrai. On March 25, 1855, after a mass before the

I-17

When analyzed for itself or in the context of contemporaneous French architecture—the cathedrals of Marseilles (nos. I-23–I-27) and Clermont-Ferrand (no. I-32), for example—Lassus's project reveals subtle variations and adjustments that lead one to conclude, admiringly, that he had adapted a simple vocabulary in order to express some very complex and beautiful architectural sentiments. The same is true of the three other large churches he designed earlier in his career, Saint Nicolas at Nantes, the Sacré Cœur at Moulins, and Saint Jean in Belleville. All, upon first glance, appear to be almost the same design, and all, upon closer examination, prove to create distinct architectural experiences appropriate to their individual sites and functions. This indeed was Lassus's conscious aim, stated in a series of articles in Didron's *Annales Archéologiques* in 1844–45: he observed that Gothic architecture had a system, an "order," that made it as subtle a means of expression as Greco-Roman architecture with its Orders. The implication was that the traditional French sense of composed tableaux could be exercised in the Gothic just as it could in the Greco-Roman vocabulary, and one should read the project for Notre Dame de la Treille as a French compositional exercise rather than as an English picturesque design—or as a Gothic cathedral.

All the forms Lassus utilized in his design are to be found in French Early Gothic architecture, but they are drawn from a variety of monuments, no one of which contains this whole series of motifs and no one of which was composed in this manner. For example, Lassus's nave bays are the four-storied ones of Noyon, while his choir bays have the tall nave arcade and double ambulatory of Bourges or Le Mans; his transepts are shallow, aisleless, and dominated by rose windows like those of Notre Dame in Paris, but they have apsidal terminations somewhat like those at Noyon; his chevet has the deep, projecting chapels of Le Mans and his facade the triple-buttressed towers and triple portal of Noyon. The end to which Lassus picked and combined these forms is evident if one walks, in one's mind, through the projected building. Upon entering, one sees that the darker, closer volume of the nave is set off against the lighter, more open space of the chevet—the two separated just sufficiently by the vestigial transept, carefully de-emphasized so as not to confuse the tableau. Arriving at the chevet, one finds a similar construction in space and light: the tall nave arcade with its clerestory contrasts with the lower inner aisle, unlit and squat, which in turn is silhouetted in front of the bright, windowed outer aisle—beyond which protude the deep chapels, six of the

miraculous image of the Virgin "in order to invoke the blessings of the Lord for the deliberations" (*Notre-Dame-de-la-Treille*, 1856, p. 9), the jury commenced their work. On Sunday, April 13, they read their decision in a lengthy public ceremony punctuated by the singing of hymns and pronouncement of laudatory remarks on medieval architecture.

Among the nineteen premiated projects, only four were by French architects (eight being by Englishmen and three by Germans). The first and second prizes were won by William Burges in partnership with Henry Clutton and by George Edmund Street, the third prize going to Lassus. On the grounds of religion and nationality, however, Lassus was preferred for the

erection of the church, which provoked much controversy and bitterness. Construction was begun at once (indeed the first stone of the yet undesigned church had been laid on July 1, 1854) and building proceeded for a few years before faltering and ceasing altogether, leaving the monstrous relic of ambitious intentions that still stands in Lille. The design had been modified by the commission, however, and because of Lassus's death in 1857, execution was entrusted to Charles Leroy.

It is a cliché oft repeated by historians of nineteenth-century art that Lassus's project is boring—and so it seems when put beside the squat, polychromed, consciously primitive designs of the Englishmen Street and Burges.

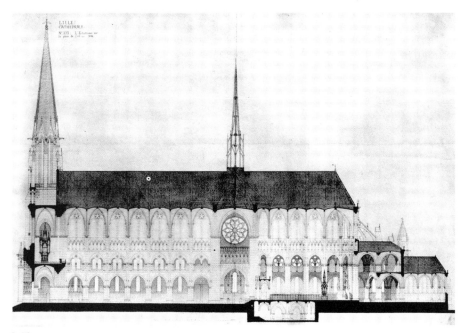

I-18

seven with blank, dark inner bays and windowed outer bays. As a French spatial composition, Lassus's project is of the same family as Vaudoyer's Marseilles cathedral or even Garnier's Opéra (no. I-10), although distinct in mood and use of historical sources.

Lassus set out to prove that such an effective, subtle spatial composition could be carried out in the Gothic vocabulary. To him this was a point of historical necessity and of moral principle, as he explained in his articles in the *Annales Archéologiques*. The many similarities found in Gothic cathedrals prove that they were ordered—all they lacked were the Orders: Doric, Ionic, and Corinthian columns. Studying this Gothic ordering, Lassus defined its systems of proportion, decoration, and construction (the last Viollet-le-Duc treated more fully in contemporaneous articles in the *Annales Archéologiques*), finding the first to be based on a human rather than an absolute measure, the second on variety of motif within the unity of composition, the third on vaulted construction in small, "elastic" materials. This, Lassus asserted, was a different and more sophisticated understanding of the elements of architectural order requiring that Gothic architecture be seen as "an obvious advance over ancient art" (Lassus, 1845, p. 201). The French Renaissance, in abandoning this progressive system and going back to the Greco-Roman

Orders, had surrendered a French, modern ideal for an Italian, Antique one: practicing eclecticism, it had valued sentimental beauty of form over the necessary progress of principle. Thus, for Lassus, eclecticism was "la plaie de l'art" ("the scourge of art"), to quote the motto of his competition submission. He encouraged French architects to evolve instead a system of modern architecture out of the Gothic, the last systematic style to exist in France.

D.V.Z.

Archives Historiques du Diocèse de Lille

---

## Hector-Martin Lefuel
### Versailles 1810–1880 Paris

As architect for the New Louvre succeeding Visconti (q.v.) and subsequently architecte de l'Empereur, Lefuel emerged as the court architect of the Second Empire. He introduced a new mode in which the old Neoclassical respect for form was infused into a Neo-Renaissance style to produce a theatrical, nationalistic setting for the Empire.

Lefuel entered the atelier of Jean-Nicolas Huyot in 1829 and won the Grand Prix de Rome in 1839.

Upon returning to Paris in 1845 he was appointed successively inspecteur des travaux for the house of the president of the Chamber of Deputies, then architect of the château at Meudon (1848), and finally architect of the château at Fontainebleau (1853).

At the commencement of the Second Empire, while Duban (q.v.) was laboriously and contentiously restoring the Louvre, Lefuel was expeditiously repairing Fontainebleau and designing its Rococo theater (see no. II-27). There he demonstrated the practical knowledge gained when he conducted his family's contracting business after his father's death in 1833. With Duban's fall from favor and Visconti's death, Lefuel was asked to carry on the work at the New Louvre in 1854, which he did with such success that on May 19, 1855, he was named architecte de l'Empereur. He worked on the Louvre, in stages, for the rest of his career. Concurrently, he refurbished the hôtel of the Princess Mathilde and built a house for Achille Fould and one for the comte de Nieuwerkerke. For the Exposition Universelle of 1855 he designed the fine arts building on the avenue Montaigne in the French Renaissance style. In 1869 came the commission from Prince Henckel von Donnersmarck for an immense villa at Neudeck in Silesia, a project he worked on until 1876, despite intimations of a lack of patriotism (Chennevières, 1883–89, vol. II, p. 15). Then in 1855, after three Romantic Rationalists in succession had been elected to the Académie des Beaux-Arts, Lefuel turned the tide, winning election over Louis Duc (the runner-up) and Labrouste (q.v.), who was supported by Mérimée. Nonetheless, Lefuel never won the respect of his most incisive contemporaries: Viel-Castel and Mérimée felt him fawning and tasteless (Viel-Castel, 1883–84, vol. III, p. 250, vol. IV, pp. 65, 75, 116); Delacroix, "mediocre" (1932, vol. II, p. 77). Jean-Louis Pascal, however, a young admirer, described him as an "arranger" (arrangeur)—"broad, correct, traditional, and distinguished" (1881, col. 261).

D.V.Z.

Bibliography:
Pascal, 1881; Questel, 1881; Delaborde, 1882; Ginain, 1882

Hector-Martin Lefuel

## I-19
## New Louvre, Paris: West Elevation of the Pavillon de l'Horloge (Study)

c. 1854
Ink wash on tracing paper
58 × 38 cm

Office of Hector-Martin Lefuel

## I-20
## New Louvre, Paris: South
## Elevation of the "Guichets"

Before 1870
Ink wash on paper
61 × 170 cm

Upon taking over Visconti's post as architect of the Louvre and Tuileries early in 1854, Lefuel enriched the detailing, elaborated the silhouette of the building, and added the narrow third floor. In this drawing of the new west facade that Lefuel erected on the back of Jacques Lemercier's seventeenth-century Pavillon de l'Horloge to harmonize it with the six new pavilions on the Cour Napoléon, sculptural groups—large in scale and vigorously posed—invade the pediments and cornices. The roof lines bear thick, contorted moldings that animate the architectural masses, as do the tall "Francis I" chimneys that flank the square dome. The style has become more insistently French Renaissance than it had been in Visconti's project (*see* no. I-33). Lefuel's drawing style—using three-dimensional washes in-

I-20

I-19

stead of flat lines—makes these changes even more emphatic. Indeed, Lefuel's decorative imagination was tightly constrained by the fact that all the masonry up to the second-story cornice had been laid before Visconti's death; below that level all Lefuel could do was carve the already existing blocks in a more florid style (Vitet, 1866, p. 63; Hautecœur, 1928, pp. 98–106; Aulanier, 1953, p. 15).

The basic composition of Lefuel's elevation follows that of Lemercier's original eastern facade, but the carving and the treatment of the silhouette are Lefuel's. In this drawing he experimented with an unprecedented arrangement in the broken pediment where the fragment of raking cornice that should have capped it has been suppressed to permit a monumental sculptural group to rise up beyond the pediment field, resting elegantly on a piece of entablature below and enframed by bits of projecting cornice on either side. In execution, however, Lefuel reestablished the integrity of the pediment, following Lemercier.

Lefuel's work for Napoleon III at the Louvre culminated in his rebuilding of the Grand Gallery and the erection of a broad road passageway (the so-called guichets) below the new Salle des Etats. After the inauguration of the building in 1857, Lefuel had worked on decoration of the interiors, including a suite of private apartments for the Empress begun in 1858 (Rouyer, 1867). In 1861 a commission of architects recommended the repair of the dilapidated Grand Gallery, which Lefuel undertook with characteristic vigor and completed in 1869.

Little of the structure and less of the form of the old Grand Gallery survived. To the west of the old Pavillon de Lesdiguières the guichets were opened and made the center of a composition completed by the symmetrical repetition of the existing pavilion and the block further west. The south facades of the western half of the gallery proper were stripped of their giant pilaster orders and given the more decorative, layered treatment of the eastern half, now serving as wings in the single, centralized composition of the masses pyramiding at the guichets. In order to sustain the weight of attention attracted to them in this way, Lefuel put aside a preliminary scheme in which the openings were conventionally proportioned in favor of the broad arches seen here springing just above the carriage tops in the mighty rolling gesture later reproduced by Victor Laloux at the Gare du Quai d'Orsay across the Seine (1898–1900). François Jouffroy's gesticulating sculptural groups, *Naval Power* and *Marine Commerce*, respond to the majesty of their situation, breasting the flow of traffic on the two

intermediate piers. This drawing of the south elevation was probably done after the completion of the building since both the architecture and sculpture appear as they were executed (including Barye's equestrian relief of Napoleon III, which was taken down in 1870, giving *a terminus ante quem* as well).

Lefuel's raising of roofs and spreading of portals, his erasure of pilasters and multiplication of pediments, seem imbued with a sense of new-found power over both the brute structural masses of building and its aesthetic forms. The size of his spans and the range of his eclecticism seem to have a positive beauty for him: the exercise of structural and formal power appears an end in itself. In 1867 the architect and publisher Eugène Rouyer wrote thus in introducing his publication of Lefuel's Tuileries apartments for the Empress Eugénie:

"One will note the original style of all this decoration without it being pointed out. We do not fear to say 'original'; indeed, in spite of received opinion, any impartial judge will accept our view in this matter. If the style of the PRIVATE APARTMENTS is not an entirely new creation, this is because man, no more than nature, cannot create something out of nothing. Just as the art of Louis XV proceeds from the art of Louis XIV, and that art from the art of the Renaissance with the modifications caused by the individual genius of the artists and by the evolution of society, so the art, the beautiful productions of which we publish here, is a prolongation, so to speak, and an adaptation of earlier styles to the needs and the very sophisticated methods of fabrication of the second half of our century.

"Someday one will surely recognize in the architectural works of our times what we hesitate to recognize today: the STYLE NAPOLEON III.

"...If we consider the whole ensemble of our great modern monuments, so different in individual appearance, these vast boulevards with their magnificent borders of houses, one will recognize with us that all these immense works truly constitute a style particular to our period" (Rouyer, 1867, p. 10).

To Ludovic Vitet, writing a scathing review of the building in 1866, Lefuel's Louvre was but a giant confection imposed upon, not derived from, the structure's function and meaning. A modern palace is a habitation, he asserted, and, "Today, because of modern requirements in habitation, one says to the architect: 'These niches, these statues serve no purpose; windows are what is needed. Eliminate the niches and put in windows!...

"At least, addressing the problem [of rebuilding the Louvre], one must accept also the consequences, one must give a building thus

pierced with windows its true physiognomy, admit that you have rebuilt it, that it is something modern, half barracks, half palace, and one must create for it a whole system of ornamentation, less coy, less rich, more simple and restrained, permitting here and there a glimpse of the smooth, naked stone surface....

"Try, then, to speak this language in this time of ornamental frenzy! Cut out the sculptures, omit the borders! Be less elegant, less rich than our fathers! It is the opposite that one wishes and one does. In sacrificing these somewhat bourgeois necessities, one has redoubled luxury and princely airs. Such is the spirit of our epoch, the confusion and amalgamation of things that are mutually exclusive, the union of opposites...." (Vitet, 1866, pp. 79–81).

Vitet, an Orleanist and a supporter of the Romantic Rationalists of 1830, clearly preferred Duban's compact, thin-shelled, wide-windowed facade of the Ecole des Beaux-Arts of 1858–62 on the quai Malaquais within sight of Lefuel's Louvre.

D.V.Z.

Palais National du Louvre, Direction de l'Architecture, Paris

---

## Pierre-Henri Mayeux
### Paris 1845–1927 Paris

*Mayeux was one of the most brilliant and fanciful of the architecture students at the Ecole des Beaux-Arts during the fertile years of the 1860s. Entering the Ecole in 1862 as a student of François-Jean-Baptiste Guénepin, he shifted in 1865 to the atelier officiel of Alexis Paccard, where he studied alongside Léon Labrouste (the doctrinaire son of Henri Labrouste, q.v.), Emile Bénard (a brilliant but impractical amateur), and Edmond-Jean-Baptiste Paulin (a strict rationalist and later a successful* chef d'atelier). *Paccard's doctrine was such that Léon Labrouste later included him among the Romantic Rationalists beside his father and Viollet-le-Duc (q.v.), although Mayeux and Bénard also gained from this experience a sense of powerfully molded form and elaborately eclectic details, as is evident in their student designs (Drexler [ed.], 1977, pp. 240–41). Upon Paccard's death in 1867, the atelier was combined with that of Jules André. As a student of André, Mayeux placed second in the competition for the Grand Prix de Rome in 1867 and 1868, but never won that coveted honor. He received his diploma in 1869, competed for the Grand Prix for a last time in 1870, and won the Prix Achille Leclère in 1872.*

*In 1868 Mayeux had been named sous-inspecteur under André, working on the latter's design for the Muséum d'Histoire Naturelle. In 1873 he was appointed inspecteur at the Ecole Polytechnique, then, in 1883, named architect of that building, erecting the chemistry lecture hall. In 1876 he won the Prix de Sèvres for the design of a monumental vase. From 1893 to 1900 he designed and erected the Ecole Nationale and Musée des Arts Décoratifs in Limoges.*

*Mayeux also had a distinguished career as a teacher of ornamental design at various écoles professionnelles in Paris, beginning in 1876, and at the Ecole des Beaux-Arts (1893–1927). In 1885 he published the manual* La Composition décorative *and during the 1890s two volumes of his own sketches,* Fantaisies architecturales *and* Dessins et croquis décoratifs.

D.V.Z.

Pierre-Henri Mayeux

## I-21
## Church Facade

1868
Inscribed on reverse by school authorities: Mayeux, 1868
Ink and wash on heavy paper
140.5 × 102 cm

Provenance:
Ecole Impériale des Beaux-Arts: Ecole Nationale Supérieure des Beaux-Arts (inv. no. 2256)

This strange design for a church facade, the elevation of a rendered project for the *concours d'emulation,* was drawn with all the care the students at the Ecole des Beaux-Arts customarily bestowed, and was awarded the second medal (Paul Blondel won the first; Drexler [ed.], 1977, p. 289). The building represented escapes the banality that often plagued student conceptions. The style of the design is a mixture of Late Gothic and French Early Renaissance, an historically possible mixture as seen in the Church of Saint Eustache (restored by Baltard, q.v., in 1853). But Mayeux has seen these sources through the eyes of the great Second Empire architects. For example, the corbeled balconies of the facade towers are copied from Duban's Porte Jean Goujon in the restored Louvre while the porch gables are distant descendants of Auguste Vaudremer's Saint Pierre de Montrouge.

Overdone as Mayeux's design seems, a glance at the premiated projects in the competition of 1874 for the Sacré Cœur shows that it was an accurate harbinger of late-nineteenth-

I-21

century church design, while mention of the great Second Empire churches, Baltard's Saint Augustin (1862–68) and Théodore Ballu's La Trinité (1861–67), suggests that it was the natural outcome of the evolution of academic design during the 1860s.

Comparing Mayeux's facade to two designed in the previous decade, Lassus's at Lille (no. I-16) and Viollet-le-Duc's at Clermont-Ferrand (no. I-32), one sees that in Mayeux's scheme the decorative details have sunk back into the surfaces while the faceted architectural volumes have inflated and drawn the whole into a taut, large-scale mass composition. The buttresses and flyers that are so important in the Gothicist projects are the most fragile, secondary episodes in Mayeux's design. Two corner turrets have expanded to become octagonal masses seeming to draw the facade

plane to each side in a broad arch, leaving the profile of the nave apparent as a membrane of tracery and glass. From the bottom of the central cavity projects an octagonal porch, restating the geometric motif of the towers.

This is precisely what Garnier had accomplished in his designs for the Opéra of 1861–62 (*see* no. I-10) and what pushed Parisian architecture to the monumental eclectic form it suddenly took on in the 1860s. Ballu's La Trinité, commissioned in 1861, demonstrates the possibility of exploding the dimensions of French Early Renaissance detailing to produce an architecture that combined a decorative, eclectic surface with Baroque girth in its members and masses. It proved that the Louis Philippe "Style Troubadour" could be monumental as well as picturesque. Baltard at Saint Augustin, begun the following year, reduced the depth of his detailing and concentrated attention upon the church's complex composition of volumes—its over-scaled dome tightly held between four towers, crowded about by apses and fronted by a wedge-shaped nave. A series of brilliant students emerged at the Ecole des Beaux-Arts at the middle of the decade practicing this same sort of volumetric composition. Only Mayeux, however, used it with such determination (as is seen in his Grand Prix project of 1867, Guérinet, 1900, pls. 92–96) and combined it with fiercely eclectic detailing. The result is close to what Gustave Raulin and Albert Dillon, Constant Moyaux, or even Jean-Louis Pascal prepared for the Sacré Cœur five years later (Duc, 1874).

D.V.Z.

Ecole Nationale Supérieure des Beaux-Arts, Paris

---

## Alfred-Nicolas Normand

### Paris 1822–1909 Paris

*Normand had two careers: that of the brilliant young designer of the Prince Napoleon's "Maison Pompéienne" and that of the dutiful pillar of the profession, an authority on prison design and president of the Institut de France. His experience is an extreme instance of the combination of the sublime and the banal that characterized the life of the Second Empire architect.*

*Normand's grandfather had been architect of the House of Orléans before the Revolution, his father, architecte de la Couronne during the Restoration. After studying first at the Ecole des Arts Décoratifs then at the Ecole des Beaux-Arts under his father and A.-M.-F. Jaÿ, he won the Grand Prix de Rome in 1846 at the age of twenty-four. Upon his return to Paris he was immediately gathered into the burgeoning government architectural administration, being appointed inspecteur des travaux for the City of Paris (under Baltard, q.v.) and inspecteur de la sixième circonscription in 1852, auditeur of the Conseil des Bâtiments Civils in 1854, and inspecteur général of penal buildings in 1861. During the years 1854–58 he worked on a publication of model prison plans with Edmond-Jean-Louis Grillon; from 1875 to 1877 on a second in collaboration with Auguste Vaudremer; and from 1867 to 1876 he erected the penologically ideal prison at Rennes. In 1855 he designed a large tenement, the cité ouvrière, in Belleville. He also held a variety of other posts, including that of editor of the journal Moniteur des Architectes. He was elected to the Académie des Beaux-Arts in 1890.*

I-22

*In the midst of all this Normand found the time from 1856 to 1860 to design and erect the elaborately detailed "Maison Pompéienne" to the exaggerated taste of the Prince Napoleon. Contemporaneously, during the Second Empire, he designed two large châteaux, that at Liancourt and that of La Madeleine near Vernon; erected the iron-and-glass market in the Grenelle quarter of Paris; built a number of apartment buildings for the Société Immobilière (1863–64); and put up several monuments, including that to the Prince's father Jérôme Bonaparte and his family in the Dôme des Invalides.*

D.V.Z.

Bibliography:
Yvon, 1911; Laloux, 1916

Alfred-Nicolas Normand

## I-22
## "Maison Pompéienne," Paris: Section of Atrium Looking Inward (Study)

1856
Dated, at top: 10 Février 1856
Pencil, ink, ink wash, and watercolor on heavy paper
64 × 51.1 cm

Provenance:
Descended in architect's family; gift to the Musée Carnavalet, 1938 (Topographie GC XXXIV)

The monumental pavilion that Lefuel (q.v.) built for the fine arts section of the Exposition

Universelle of 1855 stood on the east side of the avenue Montaigne. Upon its demolition, the Prince Napoleon, president of the commission for the exposition, purchased a portion of the lot, where he was to erect a house commensurate with his pretenses. He wanted it to be Pompeian and commissioned Auguste-Joseph Rougevin, the son of his architect friend Auguste Rougevin, to go to Pompeii to make studies for it. The younger Rougevin died there in 1856, however, and the Prince turned for advice to Hittorff (q.v.), who, while making a project himself (Hammer, 1968, pp. 126–27, pls. 235–36), suggested—perhaps after a disagreement with the Prince—the recently returned *pensionnaire* Normand (Laloux, 1916, p.9). Normand set to work at once, producing a vast number of exquisite "Néo-Grec" drawings (now in the Musée Carnavalet, the Musée des Arts Décoratifs, and the Bibliothèque Nationale). He succeeded in having the building up and decorated for a ball on February 14, 1860. Like so many of the most elaborate monuments of the Second Empire, its life was short: in 1866 it was sold, and after passing through a number of hands and serving a variety of purposes, it was demolished in 1891 (Dejean de la Bâtie, 1976; de Gary, 1978).

What Normand provided the Prince and his friends as a setting was a free copy of a Pompeian dwelling, like the Villa of Diomedes or the houses of Pansa or the Tragic Poet (Gautier, Houssaye, and Coligny, 1866, p. 10), with the principal rooms opening off an atrium, complete with impluvium and compluvium (*see* no. VII-12). The walls were decorated in the illusionistic Pompeian "Third Style," with a series of symbolic groups painted by Sébastien Cornu in the panels. Busts of the Bonaparte family were ranged around the basin and a statue of the first Emperor stood opposite the door. An iron-and-glass *jardin d'hiver* faced out into the garden at the back, in the corner of which stood a "Turkish bath," partly "Néo-Grec," partly Islamic, in decoration. Next door, in striking constrast, stood the polychromed-brick Gothic house of Prince Soltykoff by Lassus (q.v.).

The colors were rich (red and black predominating on the walls); the ornamentation heavy and curling—everything the more intense for the diminutive size of the dwelling. In it the Prince and his friends sometimes dressed in Roman togas and sought to feel themselves cut off from the banalities of everyday Paris, in a "dream," to use Gautier's word for the house, like the dream house he had conjured up in 1832 in *Mlle de Maupin:* "I picture to myself supreme happiness like this. It is a great square building without windows on the outside; a great courtyard surrounded by a colonnade of white marble, having a crystal fountain in the center with a quicksilver stream after the Arabian fashion, and groves of orange trees and pomegranates, placed alternately, stands beneath the bluest of blue sky in the very yellow sunlight...."

The atrium was altered in execution from what is shown in this drawing. A glass roof was placed over the courtyard at the second-story cornice, transforming the first-story roof into a terrace accessible by doors in place of the windows on axis. The columns and the entablature, however, are close to their final form.

D.V.Z.

Musée Carnavalet, Paris

---

## Léon Vaudoyer

*Paris 1803–1872 Paris*

*Vaudoyer established his reputation during the Second Empire with his majestic design of the cathedral of Marseilles, after having been a minor Romantic Rationalist architect during the reign of Louis Philippe. This work raised him in the opinion of his contemporaries to the stature of Duban (q.v.) and Labrouste (q.v.), as the Palais de Justice did for Louis Duc.*

*Vaudoyer belonged to a dynasty of artists and architects. His father was the architect Antoine-Louis-Thomas Vaudoyer, secretary of the Ecole des Beaux-Arts and member of the Académie des Beaux-Arts; his maternal grandfather was the painter Jean-Jacques Lagrenée. His son, the architect Alfred Vaudoyer, married the daughter of the architect Bouwens van der Boijen; his daughter married the painter Adolphe Viollet-le-Duc, brother of the architect.*

*Like his friend Henri Labrouste, Vaudoyer studied at the Collège Sainte Barbe (1810–18), then entered the Ecole (1818) as a student of his father and Hippolyte Lebas (his cousin). Winning the Grand Prix de Rome in 1826, he enthusiastically joined the Romantic* pensionnaires, *traveling extensively with Duban, Duc, and the Labrouste brothers.*

*In 1839, after serving under Jacques Lacornée as* inspecteur *at the Conseil d'Etat and Cour des Comptes (1833–40), he was appointed architect of the Conservatoire des Arts et Métiers (1839), which he rebuilt in stages until his death in 1872, producing an interesting but not profound rationalist building.*

I-23

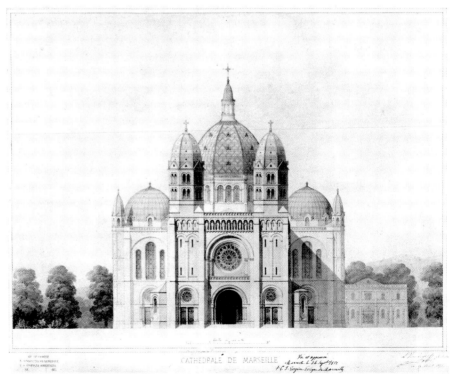

CATHÉDRALE DE MARSEILLE

His project of 1852–53 for the rebuilding of the Sor-
bonne might be described similarly. More important
at this time was his work as a chef d'atelier and his
writing. A theorist like his father, he contributed to
the Encyclopédie nouvelle (1836–39). He wrote a
serialized history of French architecture for the
Magasin Pittoresque, which was awarded the Prix
Bordin in 1857, and an essay on the same topic for
the encyclopedic volume Patria (1847). He knew the
Pugins, father and son, and traveled extensively: in
1836 he visited Italy again; in 1837, England; in
1839, Algeria; and in 1840 he traveled throughout
Germany with the critic Hippolyte Fortoul.

The two decades of the Second Empire saw his
complete devotion to the erection of the cathedral of
Marseilles, which was commissioned in 1845, but
designed only in 1852–55 and commenced in 1856.
He was elected to the Académie des Beaux-Arts in
1868.

D.V.Z.

Bibliography:
Ballu, 1873; Davioud, 1873; Blanc, 1876

I-24

I-25

Office of Léon Vaudoyer

## I-23
## Cathedral of Sainte Marie Majeure, Marseilles: East Facade (Preliminary Project)

1852
Signed and dated, lower right: L. Vaudoyer architecte le 15 août 1852.
Ink wash and watercolor on paper
51 × 65 cm

Provenance:
Descended in architect's family
Bibliography:
Hautecœur, 1955, p. 268, fig. 229

Ink wash and watercolor on paper
51 × 92 cm

Provenance:
Descended in architect's family
Bibliography:
Hautecœur, 1955, p. 269, fig. 231

Office of Léon Vaudoyer

## I-24
## Cathedral of Sainte Marie Majeure, Marseilles: North Elevation (Preliminary Project)

1852
Signed, lower right: L. Vaudoyer architecte

Office of Léon Vaudoyer

## I-25
## Cathedral of Sainte Marie Majeure, Marseilles: Longitudinal Section (Preliminary Project)

1852
Signed and dated, lower right: L. Vaudoyer architecte le 15 août 1852
Ink wash on paper
51 × 92.7 cm

Provenance:
Descended in architect's family
Bibliography:
Hautecœur, 1955, p. 269, fig. 230

Léon Vaudoyer was commissioned to execute a project for a new cathedral in Marseilles by the Minister of Public Worship on March 14, 1845. He visited the city in August of that year to participate in the selection of its site, refusing to study the design until that had been decided. When in 1851 it was settled that the building would rise on a terrace over the new port just constructed behind jetties on the seashore west of the old, natural harbor, Vaudoyer set to work, producing by August 15 of the following year a first project embodied in part in these three drawings. This project was approved by the bishop of Marseilles on September 24, 1852, and the first stone ceremoniously laid two days later on September 26 by Louis Napoleon, still Prince-President. (He laid the first stone of the bourse there on the same day.) This project was not Vaudoyer's last thought nor had it passed all the stages of government approval (it was approved by the *inspecteur général* of diocesan buildings only on April 24, 1854); and it was greatly refined in detail before its formal promulgation in 1855. Even after that date Vaudoyer constantly made small alterations that were worked out on a large plaster model in the cathedral *agence*. (Photographs of the model are in the possession of the architect's family.) Work on the foundations was begun in 1856 and by the time of Vaudoyer's death in 1872 the masonry was in place (although not cut) for everything except the central dome. After 1872 the work was carried on by Henri Espérandieu, then Henri-Antoine Révoil, and finally by Vaudoyer's son Alfred, with no significant alterations to the project as it stood in 1872. The cathedral was dedicated in 1893.

These three drawings are typical of the small, carefully executed presentation sheets drawn by Second Empire architects to communicate their basic schemes to the various committees and officials whose approval was required. They are of the same sort as Labrouste's 1859 drawing for the Bibliothèque Nationale (no. I-14 B), and like it, show a project quite different from the executed building, which was the product of great refinement while construction was under way. Here, although the basic plan and massing appear as they were finally executed, the proportions, the modeling of the masses, and the "style" (Romanesque rather than Byzantine) are different. The project seems of the 1840s, resembling Charles-Auguste Questel's Church of

Saint Paul nearby in Nîmes, designed in 1835 and completed in 1849. Between the time of the conception of this project and the promulgation of the definitive design, Vaudoyer became a Second Empire architect as his design simultaneously became more tightly knit, more forceful, and more richly ornamented. The change parallels that which one witnesses between Visconti's and Lefuel's studies for the Louvre (*compare* no. I-33 and no. I-19).

D.V.Z.

Collection Vaudoyer, Paris

Office of Léon Vaudoyer

## I-26
## Cathedral of Sainte Marie Majeure, Marseilles: Plan (Final Project)

1860
Signed and dated, lower right: L. Vaudoyer architecte 1860.
Ink wash on paper
97 × 64.5 cm

Provenance:
Descended in architect's family

Office of Léon Vaudoyer

## I-27
## Cathedral of Sainte Marie Majeure, Marseilles: South Elevation (Final Project)

1857 or later
Ink wash on paper
46 × 79.4 cm

Provenance:
Descended in architect's family

Upon being commissioned to design the new cathedral of Marseilles, Vaudoyer wrote his friend the critic Hippolyte Fortoul: "One must grapple with the celebrated problem of the Catholic church type in 1845. Alas, it is not easy and I tremble..." (Arch. nat. 246 A.P. 14 [May 15, 1845]). He had been thinking about this problem much of his career, however, and

by 1855 had evolved a building that was historicizing in the subtlest sense and powerful in form.

The building is composed of a three-bay Roman thermal hall forming the nave; a domed Greek cross attached to it to make the crossing, transepts, and choir; a French Romanesque two-towered facade as well as chapeled chevet; and finally, a Florentine Gothic polychrome-marble-banded exterior, unexpectedly made to seem Cairene by six minarets on the corners of the three western arms. That there was an intellectual purpose in this conglomeration becomes evident if one reads a series of historical studies Vaudoyer and his friends Léonce Reynaud and Hippolyte Fortoul published between 1836 and 1852 in the *Encyclopédie nouvelle,* the *Magasin Pittoresque,* and elsewhere (*see* Drexler [ed.], 1977, pp. 223–31). There, the cathedral of Florence and its first architect, Arnolfo di Cambio, are presented as the source of modern Western architecture. The cathedral is described as a combination of the Roman thermal hall and the centralized domical Byzantine church, that is, a summation of Italian and Christian architecture understood in terms of characteristic volumes. These volumes are seen to have been coordinated by Arnolfo and clothed in a light,

I-26

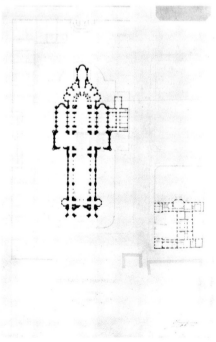

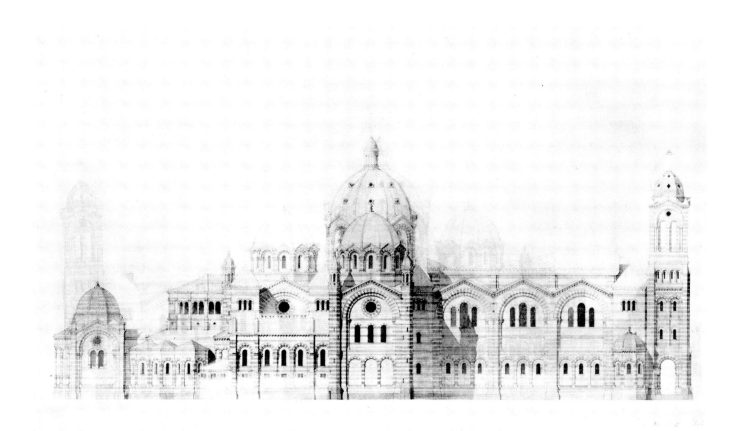

I-27

decorative skin, "a strange drapery, a rich and diaphanous veil, which decorates without concealing anything" (F.-L. Reynaud, in *Encyclopédie nouvelle*, 1836–39, vol. I, p. 777). This was the real Renaissance, which declined into formalism when Bramante promiscuously placed the Pantheon on top of the Basilica of Constantine to produce Saint Peter's (F.-L. Reynaud, in *Encyclopédie nouvelle*, 1836–39, vol. II, p. 75).

This was an admittedly eclectic attitude, but one operating according to strict principles, in which the communication of an idea was the objective, rather than the production of intrinsically beautiful compound forms. In the case of Vaudoyer's Marseilles cathedral, one perceives that the core of the composition is Arnolfo's cathedral reduced to its original components—the thermal hall and the domed Greek cross. Set in front and behind are French accretions, the towers and the chapels, nationalistic branches on an Italian Renaissance trunk, in turn a compound of the Western and Eastern antique traditions. Layered over these volumes without encumbering and blurring their lines is

a revetment of colored marble—simultaneously Italian and Islamic—that suggests Marseilles's function as France's portal to the Mediterranean; this harmonizes the building with the brilliant light and color of the Côte d'Azur and relates it to the naked cliffs surrounding the city, from whose quarries its materials came.

These two drawings are part of a series of large ink-wash studies dating from 1855 to 1860 as Vaudoyer refined the final project. In the south elevation, which must date from 1857 or later, when the projected east facade was advanced a bay, Vaudoyer sketched alternative profiles of the masses on the finished drawing executed by one of his draftsmen. The plan shows the cathedral as executed, together with its massive vaulted base above the quays of the new port and the bishop's palace, which Vaudoyer contemporaneously rebuilt.

D.V.Z.

Collection Vaudoyer, Paris

*Eugène-Emmanuel Viollet-le-Duc*

*Paris 1814–1879 Lausanne*

*Almost a generation younger than Labrouste (q.v.) and Duban (q.v.), Viollet-le-Duc became the leader of the Romantic Rationalists during the Second Empire, and indeed his numerous writings make him today the most lucid exponent of that architectural philosophy. He moved in the imperial circle, where he worked to counterbalance the influence first of Lefuel (q.v.) and later of Garnier (q.v.).*

*He was the son of a minor government functionary with important architectural connections (the architects Jean-Jacques Huvé, Charles-Edouard Isabelle, and Pierre-François Fontaine were all relations). The early tutelage of his uncle, the painter and critic Etienne-Jean Delécluze, helped to mature his artistic ideas. Although a student in the atelier of Achille Leclère during the years 1830–32, he refused to enter the Ecole des Beaux-Arts (virtually the only architect—radical or conservative—of the period to do so) and instead traveled to Italy on his own*

*(1836–37). In 1839 he received the fortuitous opportunity to restore the abbey church at Vézelay for the newly constituted Commission des Monuments Historiques. Laboring and studying for several years there and in other Gothic towns of Burgundy, he gained a profound knowledge of medieval construction and his particular understanding of architectural rationalism. From 1844 to 1847 he produced a series of articles on the construction of religious buildings in France for Didron's* Annales Archéologiques, *followed in 1854 by the first of ten volumes of his* Dictionnaire raisonné de l'architecture française… *(1854–68) and in 1858 the first of six volumes of his* Dictionnaire raisonné du mobilier français *(1858–75). In 1863 he published the first of two volumes of his* Entretiens sur l'architecture *(1863–72).*

*His work for the Commission des Monuments Historiques rapidly expanded in these years: in 1844 he (together with Lassus, q.v.) won the competition to restore Notre Dame in Paris, simultaneously beginning work on the restoration of the city of Carcassonne; in 1858 he commenced the rebuilding of the château of Pierrefonds; and in 1864 began erecting the facade and towers of the cathedral of Clermont-Ferrand—to mention only a few of his projects. At the same time he executed a number of original designs, including the new sacristy at Notre Dame (with Lassus, 1844), an apartment building on the rue de Liège (1846–48), the Church of Saint Gimer in Carcassonne (1852), the parish church at Aillant-sur-Tholon (1865–67), his house on the rue Condorcet (1862), and the tomb of the duc de Morny in Père Lachaise cemetery (1865–66). Both in his restorations and in his original designs he executed decorations and furnishings of high quality, harmonizing with the architecture in style and workmanship (see nos. II-1, II-30, II-31, III-3).*

D.V.Z.

Bibliography:
Gout, 1880; Sauvageot, 1880; 1965, Paris, Hôtel de Béthune Sully; Viollet-le-Duc, 1971

Eugène-Emmanuel Viollet-le-Duc (possibly with assistants)

## I-28
## Porte Narbonnaise, Carcassonne: Restored Exterior Elevation

1852–55
Marked, lower right: seal of Viollet-le-Duc
Ink wash and watercolor on paper
30.8 × 24.3 cm

Provenance:
Descended in architect's family

Exhibitions:
1964, Carcassonne, no. 22; 1965, Paris, Hôtel de Béthune Sully, pp. 69–71, no. 184

Viollet-le-Duc's lifelong work at the medieval city of Carcassonne was one of most massive pieces of archaeological rebuilding of the mid-nineteenth century.

Carcassone occupies a promontory over the river Aude where it makes a passage between Aquitaine and the Mediterranean coastal plain forty miles southeastward. Its strategic location made it an important town by Roman times, and it remained so after the Visigothic conquest and throughout the Middle Ages. The Cathedral of Saint Nazaire was constructed in stages beginning in 1096, and a massive ring of fortifications was erected by Saint Louis in the thirteenth century (Viollet-le-Duc, 1858).

Falling into decline in the seventeenth century, the town and its cathedral remained little changed until after the foundation of the Commission des Monuments Historiques in 1837. In a report of January 10, 1841, Prosper Mérimée recommended that the commission supervise the restoration of the cathedral and on April 19, 1844, Viollet-le-Duc was appointed architect (Commission des Monuments Historiques Archives, Carcassonne dossier). The work at first was slow because of very small annual allocations, but in the years 1850–53 it sped up and in 1855 was expanded to include the rebuilding of the medieval enceinte. The restoration of the cathedral was completed in 1860, while that of the fortifications continued beyond Viollet-le-Duc's lifetime, carried on after him by Emile Boeswillwald.

The drawing of the Porte Narbonnaise is one of a series of carefully rendered studies of the fortifications executed by Viollet-le-Duc and his assistants during the years 1852–55. Some were exhibited in the Salon of 1875 as

I-28

well as at the Exposition Universelle of 1878 and have since been considered among the most exquisite examples of ink-wash technique.

D.V.Z.

Fonds Viollet-le-Duc, Neuilly

Eugène-Emmanuel Viollet-le-Duc

## I-29
## Château of Pierrefonds: Reconstructed View

c. 1857
Ink line and pencil on heavy paper, backed
50.9 × 88.2 cm

Provenance:
Descended in architect's family; gift to the Centre de Recherches sur les Monuments Historiques (338 C.R.M.H.)

During the fourteenth century, the Carolingian seat at Pierrefonds was rebuilt by Louis d'Orléans, achieving its impressive form by the time of his assassination in 1407. It was burned in the early seventeenth century and thenceforth remained an awesome ruin hidden at the back of what became the royal forest of Compiègne (Viollet-le-Duc, 1857; Harmand, 1959; Grodecki, 1965).

In August 1832, to celebrate the marriage of his daughter to Leopold I of Belgium, Louis Philippe held a grand banquet amid the ruins.

In 1850 Louis Napoleon visited the château for the first time, and later, when he adopted the palace at Compiègne as a regular retreat where he entertained artists and intellectuals— prominent among them Viollet-le-Duc— it became the object of increasing attention. In 1857 Viollet-le-Duc, upon the imperial family's request, worked out a project for the restoration of the donjon as a lodge in the ruin itself (executed 1858–61), and in 1861 he began work to restore the whole structure as an imperial residence (executed 1862–66). The completion of many details, however, stretched on after the fall of Napoleon III in 1870 and after Viollet-le-Duc's death in 1879, to remain unfinished to this day.

This drawing is in Viollet-le-Duc's personal pen-and-ink style that is familiar from the illustrations in his many books. His facility with perspective (here so much more comfortable than that of his office assistants in the Opéra perspective, no. I-30), with the minimal delineation of volumes, and with the quick setting down of a figure (the knight galloping across the bailey, for example) is extraordinary. His pencil sketches of Carcassonne (1965, Paris, Hôtel de Béthune Sully, pl. 40) are equally summary and evocative. With this technique he produced remarkably clear expositions of the architectural organisms he was delineating, reflecting his analytical mind and serving his pedagogical ends. Despite the fact that skill in light-line sketching was an accomplishment expected of all nineteenth-century French architects, few equaled Viollet-le-Duc. The great

draftsmen of the Second Empire used the more formal mediums of watercolor (Duban, see no. I-9), brush and ink (Garnier—although Viollet-le-Duc rivaled him in this medium), or ink wash (Mayeux, see no. I-21). These techniques, moreover, were practiced because they permitted the study of effects of light and shade, of moldings and silhouettes, seen in elevation. To Viollet-le-Duc, the rationalistic elegance of molded form was secondary to structural function and this function was most clearly caught by line drawing in perspective. In 1863–64 it was a point of dispute between Viollet-le-Duc and the professors at the Ecole des Beaux-Arts whether or not perspective drawings should be required from the students, and during his short hegemony there perspectives were required for the only time in the competition for the Grand Prix de Rome (Drexler [ed.], 1977, p. 249).

D.V.Z.

Centre de Recherches sur les Monuments Historiques, Ministère de la Culture et de la Communication, Paris

Office of Eugène-Emmanuel Viollet-le-Duc

## I-30
## Académie Impériale de Musique (Opéra), Paris: Perspective View (Competition Project)

1860–61
Inscribed, upper left: Aedificare diu cogitare oportet; marked (later): seal of Viollet-le-Duc
Ink line, ink wash, and watercolor on paper, backed
65 × 91.3 cm

Provenance:
Descended in architect's family; gift to the Centre de Recherches sur les Monuments Historiques (1366 C.R.M.H.)

Exhibitions:
1965, Paris, Hôtel de Béthune Sully, no. 263; 1975, New York, Museum of Modern Art

Bibliography:
Viollet-le-Duc, 1884, pls. 75–76; Steinhauser, 1969, pl. 76; Drexler (ed.), 1977, repro. p. 285

The 1860–61 competition for the design of the Opéra (see no. I-10) was the great architectural opportunity of the Second Empire: for once a major commission was awarded on the basis of merit rather than by appointment. A Romantic Rationalist, Louis Duc, placed fourth, but Viollet-le-Duc, supported by the Empress

I-29

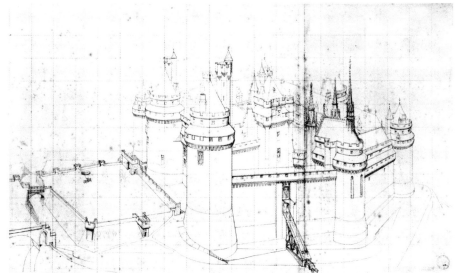

ACADÉMIE IMPÉRIALE DE MUSIQUE

I-30

Eugénie, received no recognition at all from the jury, which included Hittorff (q.v.), Duban (q.v.), Emile Gilbert, Hippolyte Lebas, Lefuel (q.v.), and Constant-Dufeux (q.v.).

The virtues and defects of Viollet-le-Duc's scheme have been debated ever since (Steinhauser, 1969, pp. 60–67). The wall system that he wrapped around his mass is a paradigmatic example of rationalist articulation: the facade plane is a thin, smooth surface, cut into by two tiers of arches revealing the interior spaces, and stiffened by a row of projecting buttresses. These buttresses diminish from capitaled piers to three-quarter columns to caryatids as they rise, a kind of superimposition of "orders" expressive of the lessening load borne. The arches of the facade plane are open in the first story to create a porte-cochere and

closed above by a diaphragm of stone members and glass. The cornice line runs unbroken around the various parts of the building and is articulated by the greater or lesser openness of the bays and, at the front, by a kind of pediment.

The project fails, however, when considered in terms of space and volume. Inside there is no single, clear circulation system, but rather a maze of corridors and narrow stairs (Steinhauser, 1969, pls. 68–70). Outside, although the constituent volumes—the fly loft, the auditorium, the side entrances—are visible, they have not been proportioned and molded into an effective mass composition. Garnier's crownlike expression of the auditorium, his angular, utilitarian rendering of the fly lofts, and his tall pavilioned treatment of

the wings are both more expressive of function and more visually satisfying.

The vocabulary of Viollet-le-Duc's project is one of the most eclectic of the entire Second Empire, with Greek, Roman, Gothic, and Baroque elements all appearing. It is evident that he, like Vaudoyer (q.v.), accepted each historical detail as a sign in a comprehensive system, although here the message is structural rather than historical. Viollet-le-Duc's designs of the late 1860s and 1870s were to carry this further. His old mentor Lassus, whose 1856 competition project (nos. I-15–I-18) bore the motto "Eclecticism is the scourge of art," saw historical style quite differently. Viollet-le-Duc's motto on his Opéra project was "Aedificare diu cogitare oportet"—"To build one must think."

This thinking in terms of parts is, in fact,

paralleled by Viollet-le-Duc's whole treatment of his project, and the key to its failure. It is an architecture of parts, of a single deeply pondered bay repeated around the building with insufficient inflection to satisfy the great variety of situations or to produce a cohesive, large-scale design. It is the same problem that appears in his facade of the Clermont-Ferrand cathedral (no. I-32), and seems to make him, as an architect, second to both Lassus and Garnier.

D.V.Z.

Centre de Recherches sur les Monuments Historiques, Ministère de la Culture et de la Communication, Paris

Eugène-Emmanuel Viollet-le-Duc

## I-31
## Académie Impériale de Musique (Opéra), Paris: Detail of Loges in Auditorium (Competition Project)

1860–61
Inscribed, lower left: Aedificare diu cogitare oportet; marked (later), lower right: seal of Viollet-le-Duc
Pencil, watercolor, and gilding on paper, backed
29.2 × 40.3 cm

Provenance:
Descended in architect's family; gift to the Centre de Recherches sur les Monuments Historiques (1367 C.R.M.H.)
Bibliography:
Steinhauser, 1969, pl. 73; Drexler (ed.), 1977, repro. p. 284

The criticisms that can be voiced of the exterior and plan of Viollet-le-Duc's Opéra project do not extend to his ornamentation of the interiors. The auditorium was to resemble that of the old Opéra, and he accomplished this by molding his forms into decorative, curvilinear shapes that are as much Art Nouveau as they are Gothic or Classical (particularly the openwork brackets, presumably to be executed in iron). The designer sought a *fin-de-siècle* richness of color and ornament appropriate to the social ceremonies of the building.

The design makes Viollet-le-Duc appear more like a court decorator-architect than his stern writings prepare one to believe. But contemporary diaries and reminiscences paint just such a picture of the part he played in the imperial circles. He was frequently at Com-

piègne and was celebrated for his contributions to games of charades. Philippe de Chennevières called him the Emperor's "most personal instrument and closest crony" in his military and archaeological pursuits. "The Emperor could not get along without him even in the simplest amusements at Compiègne, and he himself said gaily to those of his friends who sometimes would try to detain him: 'Papa is waiting, I am going to Papa'; of all the imperial household he was heaped with the most coddling attentions" (1883–89, vol. II, p. 14). Through such reminiscences, we are made to imagine Viollet-le-Duc as an all too charming, dutiful courtier.

D.V.Z.

Centre de Recherches sur les Monuments Historiques, Ministère de la Culture et de la Communication, Paris

Office of Eugène-Emmanuel Viollet-le-Duc

## I-32
## Cathedral of Notre Dame, Clermont-Ferrand: Facade (Final Project)

1864
Signed and dated: Dressé par l'architecte soussigné le décembre, 1864 — E. Viollet-le-Duc
Ink line and ink wash on paper, backed
102 × 65.5 cm

Provenance:
Descended in architect's family; gift to the Centre de Recherches sur les Monuments Historiques (1833 C.R.M.H.)
Exhibitions:
1880, Paris, Cluny; 1965, Paris, Hôtel de Béthune Sully, no. 51
Bibliography:
Viollet-le-Duc, 1884, pl. 1

The High Gothic cathedral of Clermont-Ferrand crowns the hill occupied by that ancient city nestled against the volcanic mountains of Puy-de-Dôme. Construction had been begun on the chevet in 1248 and by the fourteenth century work had progressed as far as the three easternmost bays of the nave, stopping against a pair of Romanesque towers. Between 1850 and 1853 this termination and the area in front of it were cleared and in 1855 a project for the completion of the cathedral was requested from Viollet-le-Duc. In September of that year he submitted a preliminary project (Centre de Recherches sur les Monuments Historiques, 874–75). Between then and 1864 he carried out a series of minor tasks: the excavation of the Carolingian crypt (1855), the execution of an episcopal throne and a grille to close the choir (1856), the consolidation of the

I-31

ÆDIFICARE DIV COGITARE OPORTET

DETAIL DES RANGS DE LOGES

Projet D'OPERA

I-32

foundation (1862), and the repair of the bell tower on the north transept. In 1864 Viollet-le-Duc was asked to submit a final project for the completion of the nave and the erection of a west facade. He submitted that project (including the facade drawing shown here) on April 10, 1865, it was approved on June 3 of that year, and the new nave was consecrated on Christmas, 1874. It adheres to the basic disposition of the 1855 project and was executed without major changes. Viollet-le-Duc added three bays to the three existing Gothic bays and erected two tall, spired towers facing a very narrow parvis (even more narrow in feeling; the ground slopes pronouncedly downward to the west).

This facade should be compared with that of Notre Dame de la Treille (no. I-16). Lassus's facade is clearly a combination of the facades of Reims, Noyon, and Chartres (especially the southern tower of Chartres). The emphatic entrance surrounds and Gallery of Kings, below and above an elaborate rose window, follow the example of Reims; the treatment of the towers and their median buttresses is from Chartres. However, Lassus carried certain hints in his models further—the incipient diagonal axes of the Chartres tower result in the faces of Lassus's bell stage being set at an angle—and articulated them sharply so that his facade seems more successful aesthetically than Viollet-le-Duc's despite the latter's greater originality in arrangement. Viollet-le-Duc's elevation is too even in emphasis, too broken up in parts, and too decorative to have the cohesion and power, as an image, possessed by Lassus's more archaeological project.

D.V.Z.

Centre de Recherches sur les Monuments Historiques, Ministère de la Culture et de la Communication, Paris

## Louis-Tullius-Joachim Visconti

Rome 1791–1853 Paris

*Visconti, together with his contemporary Hittorff (q.v.), looked back to the formalist Neoclassicism of the eighteenth century across the Romantic Rationalism of the reign of Louis Philippe. Nonetheless, the work he commenced at the Louvre and the Tuileries months before his death—continued and elaborated by Lefuel (q.v.)—was the first intimation of what was to become the characteristic style of the Second Empire.*

*Visconti was brought to Paris in 1798 when his father, the distinguished antiquary Ennio-Quirinio Visconti, fled there from Italy. Ten years later he entered the Ecole Spéciale d'Architecture (the predecessor of the Ecole des Beaux-Arts) as a student of Charles Percier. His contemporaries in the atelier were Hittorff, François Debret, Hippolyte Lebas, Paul-Marie Letarouilly, and the other members of the "Ecole de Percier," which was to oppose the Romantics during the July Monarchy. Visconti won the second Grand Prix in 1817, but failing to win the first prize and the consequent five-year pension in Rome, he accepted a series of minor government architectural posts that led, in 1825, to his being appointed architect of the Bibliothèque du Roi. From this date until his death in 1853 he produced a vast number of projects for this building (the modern Bibliothèque Nationale) in which his interest in the decorative application of French Early Renaissance architecture became evident. At the same time, in the late 1820s, he erected a number of important city houses in a similar style, most notably the Hôtel Collot on the quai d'Orsay and the Hôtel Pontalba on the rue du Faubourg Saint Honoré.*

*During the July Monarchy, Visconti was occupied with small decorative commissions—houses, theater interiors, tombs, public street decorations—as well as public fountains and, from 1841, the erection of Napoleon's tomb under the dome of the Invalides. Among the fountains he designed were the Fontaine Gaillon (1828), the Fontaine Louvois (1839), the Fontaine Molière (1844), and the Fontaine des Quatre Evêques in front of Saint Sulpice (1844). The increasing scale and richness of French Renaissance detailing in these fountains and in his successive studies for Napoleon's tomb distinguished them from the work of Duban (q.v.), Labrouste (q.v.), and the younger, official architects of the 1830s and 1840s and presaged the design for the New Louvre that Visconti was to present to the Emperor on February 29, 1852. He was elected to the Académie des Beaux-Arts in 1853, immediately before his death.*

D.V.Z.

Bibliography:
Lance, 1872

Office of Louis-Tullius-Joachim Visconti

## I-33
## New Louvre, Paris: Typical Facade of an Axial Pavilion on the Cour Napoléon (Preliminary Project)

1852 or 1853
Signed, upper right: M Visconti architecte
Ink on paper
97 × 66 cm

Provenance:
Palais National du Louvre, Direction de l'Architecture
(inv. no. 121)

I-33

The palaces of the Louvre and the Tuileries had lain roughly on axis a quarter mile apart since the sixteenth century, and a series of great French monarchs had attempted to join them to produce a single huge royal residence. Catherine de Médicis conceived the idea in 1565 and Henry IV made the first attempt to carry it out in 1595, when he commenced the Grand Gallery along the Seine. Projects to erect a similar wing to the north and to develop the interior space thus defined were put forward during the reign of Louis XIV. Napoleon I had Percier and Fontaine erect part of the northern gallery and situate the Arc de Triomphe du Carrousel (1810–12) in the partially cleared court. Other projects were proposed during the Restoration and the July Monarchy, but only in 1852 did Louis Napoleon, soon to proclaim himself Emperor, actually get work underway.

This was the first of Napoleon III's great building projects and it was typical of what followed. Huge in scale, it was completed in five years (first stone laid July 25, 1852; inaugurated August 14, 1857) at unprecedented expense and effort. The new wings did not contain reception halls and royal chambers; instead, they housed the machinery of nineteenth-century centralized government, a telegraph office, a printing office, two ministries, museum spaces, and a stable.

In his design (Pfnor, 1853), Visconti rendered imperceptible the fact that the responding facades of the Louvre and the Tuileries were at a slight angle to each other by leaving the space between them entirely open except for two "palaces" enframing the west facade of the Louvre. These were given a scale sufficient to assert themselves in this broad space by the placement of taller pavilions on their principal axes and at their corners. These forms also had the advantage of picking up the similar pavilions on the east-west axis of both the Louvre and the Tuileries, making by this insistent re-petition what formerly had been a secondary motif in the complex its characteristic form. Thus in spite of his insistence that he "religiously followed the architecture of the Old Louvre" (Visconti, 1853), Visconti turned his back on Perrault's colonnade and on the long, low pilastered wings of Métezeau and Percier, instead establishing as the style of the Emperor's residence something tall-roofed, picturesque—"classical" in the terms of the French Renaissance, not of academic classicism refined from Perrault to Percier.

The drawing of a typical pavilion, however, shows how difficult Visconti found the aban-donment of Percier's Neoclassicism. The thin, linear drawing style is entirely that of the first Empire. The silhouette of the roofs is simple, the sculptural decoration discrete and small-scaled, the pattern of forms even and unemphatic (more so in this drawing, in fact, than it would have been when executed).

D.V.Z.

Palais National du Louvre, Direction de l'Architecture, Paris

# Furnishings

Mention of the furnishings of the Second Empire usually evokes the standard generalizations that the Second Empire introduced two novelties, comfortable armchairs and lacquer furniture with mother-of-pearl inlay, but otherwise was content to imitate earlier styles, notably that of Louis XVI (the famous "Louis XVI Empress style," inspired by the Empress Eugénie's passion for the furnishings of Marie Antoinette). In fact, this is not true, for neither of these characteristics dates from the Second Empire.

Furniture in lacquer and papier-mâché, with mother-of-pearl inlay, enhanced with gold and floral motifs, developed under the reign of Louis Philippe. Specialists in this style—Goudel, Osmont, Mainfroy—exhibited as early as 1834. The remote antecedent of these pieces was obviously the Far East, but the closer source, in particular for the technique of applying lacquers to papier-mâché, was England, which was then inundating all of Europe with its products. Some illustrious examples—the bedroom of Lamartine, the furniture of Louis Philippe in the château of Neuilly—attest to the vogue of this style in France between 1840 and 1850. The small standard pieces of this type made during the Second Empire, gueridons and chairs, were survivals from the previous reign. The manufacturers (the widow Osmont, Mainfroy, Salomon Périer, Drugeon) continued to exhibit in 1855 but did not appear in subsequent expositions.

With regard to comfortable armchairs, the problem is more complex, for although their origin was likewise earlier, they did not disappear under the Second Empire. Quite the contrary, they left such a strong mark that they have justly been seen as the very symbol of the furnishings of this period. One should, however, distinguish two aspects with respect to these chairs—on the one hand, the type of piece, a seat whose wood is completely covered, on the other, the method of covering, tufting.

The "pommier" of the first Empire, the four-sided divans ordered by the duchesse de Berry for the Tuileries in 1821, the large circular ottoman of the Royal Pavilion at Brighton standing out so visibly in John Nash's watercolor of 1826—all are seats in which no wood is seen, and they all derive from the same principle, a particularly comfortable seat with no upright to hit the back or arms. But the real creator of the comfortable armchair seems to have been Derville, a Parisian upholsterer in the rue Saint Guillaume, who as early as 1837 was described in the *Almanach du Commerce* as "Inventor of chairs and armchairs with framework in iron and other pieces known as *confortables.*" This statement agrees moreover with the one in Deville's *Dictionnaire du tapissier,* which forty years later attributed to the same Dervillé (misspelled Dervilliers) the creation of these comfortable armchairs, while dating the first examples from 1838 and specifying that until 1840 they had an iron framework, later replaced by a frame of beechwood, but keeping the same elastic upholstery. Palace inventories—notably that of Fontainebleau—prove that pieces of this type were ordered under the reign of Louis Philippe.

To make these pieces even more comfortable, it became customary to tuft them. Tufting was not an innovation of the Second Empire either (Havard, in his *Dictionnaire de l'ameublement...,* mentions a tufted armchair in the Versailles inventory of 1708!), but this very soft stuffing made with floss silk (the tufting itself) held by small knots likewise stuffed was generally reserved for the armchairs of invalids. The upholsterers of the nineteenth century adopted it, with wool padding and buttons replacing the knots of silk, for its comfort and its shimmering appearance: silks treated in this manner catch the light particularly well. From the *confortable,* this method of upholstery soon extended to all seats.

The imitation of older styles also began before the Second Empire. For the Gothic style this is an acknowledged fact. A few examples taken from within the royal family, and thus accurately dated, should be sufficient to indicate that after 1835–40 the styles of various periods were more or less freely copied. In 1834 Jacob Desmalter executed a Boulle piece for the concert hall of the Tuileries, and in 1836 gilded-wood chairs in the Louis XIV style for the apartment of Mme de Maintenon at Fontainebleau. The Louis XV style—that style so misunderstood by the first Empire—reappeared at the Tuileries. "Louis XV-style" seats of gilded wood were delivered in 1845 for the duchesse de Nemours, and two years later the drawing room of the duc de Nemours received similar furnishings. As for the Louis XVI style, it is found in the furnishings of the duchesse d'Aumale: Monbro Aîné (q.v.) delivered two rosewood pieces with plaques of Sèvres porcelain for her boudoir, then a table and a large rosewood piece, respectively in 1845 and 1847, while several purchases were made from Grohé (q.v.) for Chantilly, in particular a desk with shelves and a Louis XVI table.

What was new under the Second Empire was that the imitation of earlier styles became the only source of inspiration. The Louis Philippe style, this bourgeois style despised by later generations, with its softly curving mahogany and palisander pieces, its large, flat, unadorned surfaces, without bronzes, and barely set off by a few simple moldings, a few holly inlays, which was itself a corrupt derivation from the Empire and Restoration styles, produced no offspring, as though the evolution had stopped short, exhausted.

This lack of creativity is even harder to explain, since all the conditions seem to have been present for the blossoming of a new style. Thanks in particular to increased building activity, there was a great demand for furniture, both in France and abroad. French superiority in the arts of furnishing was overwhelmingly demonstrated at all the international exhibitions. England, in search of inspiration, bought French objects at the exhibitions, and Graham and Jackson, the most important firm of cabinetmakers in London, hired French designers (Eugène Prignot and later Alfred Lormier). The architect Séchan had furniture for Abdul Medjid, sultan of Constantinople, executed in Paris, while the bronze manufacturer Denière (q.v.) worked for the viceroy of Egypt, Saïd Pasha. Many such examples could be enumerated, and furniture exports, which amounted to some 1,457,000 francs in 1826, rose to 6,899,000 francs in 1860.

In France itself the demand increased rapidly and workshops took on proportions hitherto unknown (the home craftsman, peddling his own wares from a cart, practically disappeared under the Second Empire). Very revealing of this expansion was the model displayed at the 1867 Exposition Universelle by the firm of Racault-Krieger, showing the transformations of the workshops in the faubourg Saint Antoine, from the home workshop set up by Antoine Krieger around 1845 to the vast factory employing over five hundred workmen some twenty years later. How revealing it would be to have such models for the Fourdinois (q.v.), Jeanselme (q.v.), Grohé, or Mazaroz firms!

The critics at the various expositions—and they were always chosen from among the keenest minds, Léon de Laborde, Prosper Mérimée, Adalbert de Beaumont, Paul Dalloz—were in agreement in recognizing not only the growing prosperity but also the technical progress that was achieved between 1851 and 1867. The demand in fact encouraged investments for the purchase of materials and the installation of machines facilitating or improving the work of craftsmen: ribbon saws to cut grooves with precision, blades to permit thinner and thinner inlays, steam planes to shape moldings—all these for cabinetmaking. In the field of bronze wall fittings and bronze furnishings one should cite the development of galvanoplasty, as well as improvements in casting techniques.

The numerous well-trained and well-equipped craftsmen were from the artistic standpoint also generally well directed. Architects at all times have been interested in the problem of furnishing (it is enough to mention at random the names of Du Cerceau, Bélanger, or Percier), but under the Second Empire the custom of ordering a completely built and furnished house became common. It was thus no accident that Viollet-le-Duc (q.v.) and Manguin (q.v.) were rewarded as *coopérateurs* in the twenty-fourth class (furnishing and decoration) at the 1855 Exposition Universelle. Nor was it by accident that the principle of stylistic unity prevailed so strongly at this time: the interior decoration of a room and its furnishings were to be strictly in the same style. In imitation of these architects, the foreman might have been an upholsterer (who in the reign of Louis Philippe began to be called decorator) like Fournier (q.v.), or a cabinetmaker like Henri Fourdinois, who provided Lyons with designs for silks and Aubusson with designs for carpets (but Fourdinois had been a pupil of the architect Duban). Sculptors—Carrier-Belleuse (q.v.) being the most famous example—also frequently executed designs for furnishings.

By looking closely at what would seem to be the elements of success for the blossoming of an original style of the Second Empire—an improved technique guided by good artistic advisors and supported by a large clientele—one can perhaps better discern the causes of a development that is at first sight disconcerting, and one is tempted to conclude that facility does not necessarily promote creativity.

In the technical area, modernization was transforming the spirit of work. It is difficult nowadays, when the handmade appears as the height of luxury, to imagine the fascination once exercised by mechanization, even in so craftsmanlike a field as furnishings. For exam-

ple, the mathematical precision of the machine in the shaping of moldings became an ideal, and the craftsmen working by hand would have felt dishonored if he had not achieved something as rigorous and, we might add, as cold as the machine.[1]

The desire for profit, due both to the investments in machinery and the large number of workmen, brought about a division of labor reinforcing this anonymity of the finished product. These drawbacks might have passed unseen if a new style had emerged from these new working conditions. But the flaws became evident as soon as they tried to reproduce by modern, and thus repetitive, means those models that had been conceived with flexibility in order to meet the needs or desires of a customer.

At the customer's level, the view changed as well. The time had passed when one went to a carpenter or cabinetmaker to order a piece of furniture of one's choosing. The workshop was distinct from the store. The customer bought a finished product, and thus he no longer had any control over its workmanship. Mechanization lowered prices and multiplied the number of objects for sale; exhibitions and department stores displayed the latest styles. Objects of furnishing became, like clothing, accessible to a greater number of pocketbooks. They thus lost some of their value. There was less concern for their beauty, for their durability. It was only in the country that people on getting married still bought the furniture and the Sunday clothes that would remain with them until their death. This lowering of standards was felt in all classes of society. Simple buyers, dazzled by the products of the expositions, were content with the imitations that were offered them: seats carved by machine and gilded with water paint; marquetry pieces with veneer as thin as cigarette paper, embellished with fittings of gilded zinc; clocks and candelabra likewise in zinc.

The *nouveaux riches*—and the Second Empire saw many of them in the world of business and industry (and, one might add, in the demimonde)—lacked confidence in their own judgment and entrusted themselves entirely to an intermediary in deciding how to furnish their homes, giving up all personal opinions. When the work was put in the hands of a Manguin, one got the Hôtel de Païva, which was brought off quite well. The easy solution for decorators of lesser talent was to let themselves be carried along by the prevailing taste, to propose, in certainty of pleasing, a large Louis XV or Louis XVI drawing room in gilded wood, upholstered in red damask; a Renaissance dining room with a monumental buffet in carved oak; a library-study for the master of

the house in black wood set off by brass in the style of Boulle; and a boudoir for Madame, in the Louis XVI style, evoking the charm of Marie Antoinette.

But it was among enlightened connoisseurs that the absence of criticism was most strongly felt. Let us not forget that the middle of the nineteenth century was the period that witnessed the formation of the finest collections of seventeenth- and eighteenth-century *objets d'art*. Sales during the Revolution had put into commercial circulation pieces of antique furniture of high artistic quality, which in other countries, and under other political conditions, would have remained with the families. What a temptation for people of taste, both French and foreign, to buy up the remains of these furnishings and to accelerate by their choice the process of a return to the past! These pieces were bought for use and not only as objects in a collection. The Empress set the example; the Rothschilds, the Pereires, and John Bowes in England utilized their antique pieces, better still they completed them with modern works in the same style, since at that time there was no fetishism over originals, no phobia about copies. But it must be admitted that this state of mind would hardly encourage the development of a new art.

What now appears to us as an obstacle to creation was not felt as such by critics of the time. They did not so much denounce the imitation of previous styles as the lack of overall composition in the objects, particularly exhibition pieces, which often borrowed disparate elements from several periods and which accumulated details, well executed in themselves, perhaps even too well executed, to the detriment of the general impression. Taking as a point of comparison England and the progress achieved by its furnishing industry between 1850 and 1860, they thought they had found a solution—especially after the London International Exhibition of 1862—in a reform of the teaching of industrial design and in the creation of an institution similar to the South Kensington Museum. Their judgment was sound since these reforms, brought about after the Second Empire, contributed to a renewal of the decorative arts.

One should not, however, conclude from these observations that the style of furnishings under the Second Empire was simply a lack of style. Except for a few literal copies—certain commodes by Riesener, specific seats, candelabra, and clocks—the designers created new objects, strongly inspired by the work of their predecessors, to be sure, but in which their individuality entered into the choice of forms, the arrangement of motifs, and the purpose of the pieces.

The Second Empire style was also a way of life. Comfort—it is for good reason that the most characteristic piece of this period was called a *confortable*—became an end in itself. The seats of a salon might be Louis XV or Louis XVI, but they would be tufted, and they would be accompanied by a great number of *confortables*, ottomans, *confidantes* (settees), and *chauffeuses* (low armchairs); they would be grouped around lamps in the evening, around the fireplace in winter. The lighting fixtures would be Renaissance or Louis XVI, but they would be mounted with mechanical lamps to ensure regular and brilliant lighting. Only interior views or engravings in the illustrated weeklies of the time can evoke for us these over-stuffed rooms with their draperies and tufted furniture. These representations also bring home to us how much this furniture, in which the formal was combined with the comfortable, was truly in the spirit of a society in which social life played an important part in all milieux and in which receptions were frequent.

The Second Empire style also embodied the idea, new at the time, that the furniture and décor of everyday life could contribute to the improvement and education of the lower classes. Hence the importance, often mentioned by theorists, of the choice of models, especially for the bronzes repeated in innumerable copies or for the "zincs d'art" that most often replace them: "The more vulgar the material," wrote Longpérier in 1867, for example, "the more appeal it has for many buyers, and the more important it is that only excellent works, capable of elevating the mind and providing a useful lesson, be popularized."[2]

Finally, the style of the Second Empire was not simply a parenthesis in the evolution of furniture. Careful study of works of the past, by drawing attention to antique objects, certainly contributed to saving many of them. Craftsmen, obliged to take their inspiration from these models, had to rediscover certain techniques well known in the eighteenth century but which were already beginning to be lost. It was not by pushing his plane forever over Louis Philippe moldings that the wood carver refined his technique; it was not two-toned damasks or plain velvets that heightened the reputation of Lyons silk. On the contrary, the variety of achievements under the Second Empire led the head of workshops to train qualified workers in all fields: in the field of weaving, for example, for the reproduction of the great Louis XVI brocades or the imitation of Italian velvets, in the field of embroidery for the renewal of liturgical vestments, in the field of marquetry and of sculpture in solid wood.

This mastery of traditional techniques was one of the most positive aspects of the arts of furnishing under the Second Empire. In this way the future was prepared. The natural woods of Art Nouveau have their origin in the oak carvings of "Gothic" buffets, while one could not imagine the work of a Ruhlmann had the art of veneer been lost.

C.S.-V.

*Notes*

1. The fabrication of wallpaper underwent a fairly similar evolution. The first experiments with machine fabrication, which sought to increase production speed and cut sale costs, paralleled the gradual dawning of new aesthetic necessities. At the same time panoramic decoration became something apart, a luxury and ultimately a work of art — a "masterpiece" as the manufacturers liked to say. The artists designated for these compositions specialized, often copying the masters of The Académie. The printers were carefully selected — so much so that the impression from the plate took on the noble character of established tradition. Tasks became more and more specialized in order to produce the perfect object which could rival great art and conceal its industrial origin. [O.N.]
2. Longpérier, in *Rapports 1862.* vol. VI, p. 350.

# Interior Views

## Edmond-Clément-Marie-Louis Duthoit
### Amiens 1837–1889 Amiens

*Born into a family of artists in Amiens, Duthoit, a student of Viollet-le-Duc (q.v.), exhibited architectural drawings at the Salon from 1863 to 1879. He first became known through his participation in the expedition to Syria of the comte de Vogüé in 1863–64 and from his collaboration on Vogüé's* Architecture civile et religieuse du Ier au VIIième siècle en Syrie. *He collaborated with his teacher Viollet-le-Duc on several restorations, in particular, that of the château of Roquetaillade (Salon of 1868), and executed various works in churches of the Oise (Notre Dame, Senlis; the church of Mogneville) and the Somme (chapel of the château of Souverain-Moulin) (Roquetaillade Archives).*

C.S.-V.

Edmond-Clément-Marie-Louis Duthoit

## II-1
## The Rose Room of the Château of Roquetaillade (Preparatory Drawing for the Decoration)

1868
Watercolor
68 × 88 cm

Provenance:
Château of Roquetaillade

When in 1866 the marquis Lodoïs de Mauvesin decided to restore his medieval château of Roquetaillade in the Gironde, he turned to the undisputed master in this field, Viollet-le-Duc (q.v.). The famous architect both inspired these works and was responsible for carrying them out. He made several trips to Roquetaillade—at least three in 1868, one in August 1869, and one in 1870 (Roquetaillade Archives, letter from Viollet-le-Duc of February 1, 1868, statement of July 29, 1871). Though unfortunately not dated, notes taken by the marquise de Mauvesin during one of these visits show how he worked, going through the château room by room, giving ideas, changing a design. These trips could have happened only rarely, usually on the occasion of visits to other work sites (Saint Sernin in Toulouse, for instance). Thus the work had to be supervised more closely by another architect, and Viollet-le-Duc designated for this job the man he called "my young aide-de-camp" (Roquetaillade Archives, letter of January 26, 1867), his pupil Edmond Duthoit. All the statements from contractors and suppliers, from 1869 to 1870, and later from 1872 to 1875, were certified by Duthoit, who also made arrangements with the marquis for Viollet-le-Duc's fees and travel expenses, showing the close collaboration in which the two architects worked.

A number of watercolors, designs for the decoration and furnishing of the main rooms of the château, as well as the ensembles that were executed and are very fortunately preserved, attest to the activity of the two architects (two watercolors, for the Great Hall and a room that was not carried out, are reproduced in Jullian, 1971, pp. 88, 93). Inspired by Viollet-le-Duc, these watercolors, painted with extreme care, are by Duthoit, who exhibited some of them at the Salon of 1868 (1868, Paris, Salon, pp. 513–14). They are by no means an austere and cold archaeological reconstruction: figures, familiar objects, books, and flowers bring them to life. They show that although in the designs for certain pieces of furniture (*see* nos. II-30, II-31) Viollet-le-Duc was inspired by models from the Middle Ages published in his own *Dictionnaire du mobilier,* this château is not a museum but a family dwelling endowed with modern comfort (he altered the pump to bring water to the rooms, installed a bathroom and a laundry room, etc.; Roquetaillade Archives, undated notes by the marquise de Mauvesin) in which the furniture, upholstered and functional, was adapted to modern life. Duthoit's very precise watercolor conveys well the cheerful and comfortable, though solemn, aspect of the Rose Room, which was executed almost as shown (except for altering the painting of the furniture, a simplification of the armrests of the armchairs, and the placing of a fine, early Madonna and Child on the mantelpiece of the fireplace). The furniture is likewise perfectly described in the statements of the cabinetmakers and upholsterers Tricot et Jeancourt (q.v.), who in September 1869 delivered all the furnishings for this room, up to and including the spring mattress, "everything in accordance with drawings and plans" (Roquetaillade Archives, statement certified by Duthoit, October 28, 1869).

C.S.-V.

Collection Mlle de Baritault, Château de Roquetaillade (Gironde)

II-1

## Jean-Baptiste-Fortuné de Fournier

*Ajaccio 1798–1864 Paris*

*A painter of watercolors and miniatures and an engraver, Fournier specialized in views of interiors, some of which were shown at the Salons of 1843, 1852, 1855, 1857, and 1863. Those depicting the imperial palaces—Saint-Cloud, the Tuileries, Fontainebleau (British Royal Collections, museums of Compiègne and Fontainebleau, private collections)—are important documents, especially for the history of the first two, the former having been destroyed in 1870, the latter in 1871. Unfortunately, the whereabouts of views of certain rooms in the grand apartments of the Tuileries, executed several times by the artist and bought by the Emperor for his private collection (Louvre Archives 2 DD 20) are unknown. At the Salons of 1859 and 1861 Fournier showed his portrait of Napoleon III in miniature and, at the Salon of 1863, plans for decorative panels.*

J.-P.S.

Jean-Baptiste-Fortuné de Fournier

## II-2
## Dressing Room of the Empress Eugénie at Saint-Cloud

1860
Signed and dated, lower right: F. de Fournier
Paris 1860
Watercolor
31 × 45.5 cm

Provenance:
Firmin Rainbeaux, equerry of Napoleon III; Félix Rainbeaux; Rainbeaux estate sale, Paris, Hôtel Drouot, October 21–23, 1936, no. 88; purchased by the State; deposited at the Musée National du Château, Compiègne, 1972 (inv. no. C 72 D 4)

Bibliography:
Clouzot, 1925, pp. 186–88, pl. 19

The Empress's dressing room at Saint-Cloud was depicted twice by Fournier, first in 1855 in a watercolor in the British Royal Collections in which Queen Victoria appears (*see Journal*, 1961, repro. p. 80; Hayward, 1964, repro. p. 229; de Bellaigue, 1975, p. 38; copy at Compiègne, formerly Fould-Springer coll.; Terrier, 1959, pl. 26; Demoraine, 1961, repro. p. 76). The watercolor exhibited, dated 1860, is Fournier's second view (a copy, dated 1863, was formerly with Fabius Frères; Praz, 1964, repro. p. 354). These views become even more interesting when studied with the 1855 Saint-Cloud inventory (Arch. nat. AJ[19] 1155; Louvre Archives 37 DD 36) and the records of the Mobilier de la Couronne (despite gaps in those

in the Archives Nationales; *see* Arch. nat. AJ[19] 684, 1047).

Situated in the left wing of the palace, this corner dressing room had been an inner chamber of Louis XVI and then the bedroom of the Empress Josephine; later it became the study of Marie Amélie. Like the rest of Eugénie's apartment (*see* no. II-3), it was occupied by Queen Victoria when she visited France in August 1855. The wall decoration was restored for the occasion in July 1855, the ceiling embellished with carton-pierre ornaments (Huber Frères), and a marquetry floor laid (Seiler, Muhlemann et Cie). The furnishings seen in the watercolors represent both changes made by the Empress as early as 1854 and arrangements carried out for Queen Victoria's visit. The objective was to achieve harmony with the Louis XVI-style décor, while answering the needs of a dressing room, and comfort, as understood under the Second Empire.

The color scheme is white and blue: white taffeta curtains bordered in light-blue satin, blue damask upholstery patterned in white. The furniture shows no homogeneity. A Louis XVI ensemble of gilded wood, itself disparate, stands side by side with modern pieces: comfortable armchairs, a matching dressing-table chair, and light Chiavari chairs.

The toilet objects were redone for the queen of England; a sumptuous mahogany *psyché* by Fourdinois (no. II-24) was installed as well as a

marble-top dressing table and mirror, painted white and set off with gold, also by Fourdinois (identical versions at Fontainebleau), and a flounced "Pompadour" dressing table. On this table stood two gilded-bronze candelabra "rocaille style," and a gilded-wood mirror. The toilet objects are different in 1860, Queen Victoria having been invited to take those she had used: "The toilette of the finest *point d'Angleterre*, with choice ornaments, beautiful modern Sèvres china, with my initials on the washing-stand, gold and glass tumblers and bottles, which they insisted on my taking with me" (August 27, 1855; *Journal*, 1961, p. 141).

The other furniture and objects were also mostly installed in 1855: the richly inlaid Riesener writing table (1771; Petit Trianon); two low rosewood cabinets between the windows with "doors adorned with groups of children and baskets of fruit in medallions" by Wassmus in the style of Riesener; two small rosewood jardinieres, "stands with rams' heads, vase in porcelain light-blue background with medallion...," purchased from Grohé (q.v.). The fireplace garniture includes a gilded-bronze Lenoir clock, adorned with cupids, and two candelabra, Minerva and Victory, by Cauvet, in this room by 1833 (Louvre).

Although some objects and small pieces of furniture were removed between 1855 and 1860 (Louis XVI candleholders with satyrs' heads; the table where Queen Victoria wrote), added by 1860 were a composite octagonal-top

II-2

gueridon bearing the monograms of the dauphin Louis (XVI) and Marie Antoinette (Versailles) and two "Greek-style candelabra on tripods," cast by Barbedienne (q.v.) after the Antique and bought by the Empress in 1855 at the Exposition Universelle.

This characteristic setting, where the modern stands side by side with the old in an atmosphere of comfortable intimacy, reveals the Empress's artistic preferences, which are inseparable from the cult she devoted to the martyred Marie Antoinette.

J.-P.S.

Musée National du Château, Compiègne

Jean-Baptiste-Fortuné de Fournier

## II-3
## Study of the Empress Eugénie at Saint-Cloud

1860
Signed and dated, lower right: F. de Fournier
Paris 1860
Watercolor
30.5 × 45 cm

Provenance:
Firmin Rainbeaux, equerry of Napoleon III; Félix Rainbeaux; Rainbeaux estate sale, Paris, Hôtel Drouot, October 21–23, 1936, no. 88; purchased by the State; deposited at the Musée National du Château, Compiègne, 1972 (inv. no. C 72 D 5)

Bibliography:
Clouzot, 1925, pp. 185–86, pl. 16

Two artists depicted the Empress's study at Saint-Cloud: Jean-Baptiste Van Moer (whose signature in initials has been mistaken for that of Bénédict Masson) in 1855, and Fournier in 1960. Of the work of the first, there exist several watercolors (British Royal Collections; Compiègne, Terrier, 1959, pl. 24; Lemmermann coll., Rome, Praz, 1964, repro. p. 352) and a painting in the Musée des Arts Décoratifs. By Fournier, in addition to the watercolor shown here, a replica formerly in the Fabius collection, dated 1863, is known (Praz, 1964, repro. p. 353).

Adjacent to the dressing room (no. II-2), the study had been the bedroom of Marie Amélie. Eugénie transformed it into a study and in 1853–54 had its Louis XVI-style decoration restored. A new wainscoting was installed, with carton-pierre ornaments by the sculpteurs Huber Frères, in keeping with the earlier decoration surrounding the windows. The crown monogram EN was added above the door, and the ceiling was painted with a "clouded, azure-blue sky" by Nolau et Rubé (Arch. nat. F²¹ 3425ᴮ). The following year,

prior to the arrival of Queen Victoria, an inlaid parquet was put down by Seiler, Muhlemann et Cie (Arch. nat. F²¹ 1629).

Judging from the watercolors, the palace inventory, and the archives of the Mobilier de la Couronne, the furnishings, installed in 1854 after the first restoration work, were sumptuous. Clearly the Empress wanted to be surrounded by renowned pieces of furniture. The most important was the Louis XV desk from the Pavillon de Marsan at the Tuileries (Versailles museum). Without being concerned over a clash of materials or a disparity of styles, she placed it in the midst of pieces in black lacquer: a fine commode by M. Carlin, at Saint-Cloud since the Consulate (Louvre), and (not visible here) the rich commode of Mesdames (the daughters of Louis XV) from Bellevue by Carlin, removed from Fontainebleau as early as 1853 (Louvre). The gilded wood chairs were likewise chosen for their quality: two bergères (back of one behind desk) and six chairs (two at far right) from the "Turkish" boudoir of the comte d'Artois at the Temple (Mobilier National; Versailles); four armchairs and six chairs from the inner chamber of Marie Antoinette at Saint-Cloud (Louvre); and a sofa from Fontainebleau (stamped by Foliot; Mobilier National). Transitional in style, it was supposed to harmonize with the Louis XV desk. The earlier seats were recovered in a tufted green-damask watered silk that pleased Queen Vic-

toria (Journal, 1961, p. 141).

Alongside these fine pieces stood armchairs and confortables upholstered in the same green damask, Chiavari chairs, and two small tables brought at the time of Queen Victoria's visit, one, Louis XVI by Riesener (Louvre), the other, in the style of Louis XV by Wassmus (in front of the sofa). As elsewhere in the suite, there are no rugs (except for a small sofa rug), so as not to hide the beautiful parquet (Queen Victoria noted in her diary: "Parquets in all the rooms"). The Empress later added the small revolving bookcase, nest of tables, and another Louis XV table, on which books can be seen. The bronze lights, apart from the chandelier, are new, made by Marquis in 1854, after celebrated earlier models. Fine Sèvres vases highlight the furnishings, as well as several objets d'art: two bathers in Sèvres biscuit, after Falconet and Boizot (1853), and the candelabrum of American Independence (Versailles). The pictures, different from those of 1855, belong to the Empress: floral medallions in pastel (identified by Terrier [1959] as by Mme Sturel-Paigné); a reduction of Winterhalter's official standing portrait of Napoleon III; and on the easel, an emblazoned frame that appears to contain the portrait of Leopold I of Belgium, presented by the duc de Brabant on his visit to Saint-Cloud in 1855.

J.-P.S.

Musée National du Château, Compiègne

II-3

## Sébastien-Charles Giraud

*Paris 1819–1892 Sannois (Val-d'Oise)*

At first a pupil of his brother, the painter Eugène Giraud (1806–1881), Charles Giraud entered the Ecole des Beaux-Arts in 1835 and submitted to the Salon as early as 1839. Two long trips inspired a portion of his œuvre: he accompanied the French expedition to Tahiti in 1846–47 as dessinateur de la marine, then in 1853–55 was part of a scientific voyage to the Arctic organized by Prince Napoleon. Eugène, having been introduced to Princess Mathilde in 1847 and becoming one of the habitués of her salon, presented his brother to her, and Charles Giraud came to specialize under the Second Empire in the representation of interiors of the homes of Parisian notables (Princess Mathilde, Nieuwerkerke), of the galleries of museums (Louvre, Cluny), and of scenes in Brittany, which he continued to paint after 1870. Thanks to the patronage of the princess, the State acquired many works by the Giraud brothers, which are preserved in various museums.

D.A.

Bibliography:
Thieme and Becker, 1907–50, vol. XIV, p. 173; de Mirimonde, 1969, pp. 135–51; 1974, Paris, Grand Palais, p. 84

Sébastien-Charles Giraud

## II-4
## Salon of the Princess Mathilde

1859
Signed and dated, lower right: Ch. GIRAUD. 1859
Oil on canvas
63 × 100 cm

Provenance:
Prince Napoleon; Prangins sale, 1950 (no. 370); Musée National du Château, Compiègne, 1951 (inv. no. 51.030)

Exhibitions:
1859, Paris, Salon; 1953, Compiègne, no. 111; 1953–54, Paris, Bibliothèque Nationale, no. 409; 1959, Florence, no. 114; 1974, Paris, Bibliothèque Nationale, no. 459; 1976–77, Paris, Archives Nationales, no. 640

Bibliography:
Cantrel, 1859, p. 131; Cantrel, 1863, p. 200; *L'Illustration,* March 30, 1867, p. 197; "Napoléon III," 1954, repro. p. 37; Terrier, 1959, p. 47; *Le Journal de la France,* no. 56, 1970, pp. 1554–55; Richardson, 1971, p. 223; de Gaigneron, 1977, pp. 98–99

Charles Giraud executed for the Princess Mathilde several views of the interior of her hôtel in the rue de Courcelles (now destroyed, the site of the present numbers 24–28), which

II-4

had been granted to her by the Emperor at the end of 1852. She soon created there a brilliant salon. With the advice of her friends Nieuwerkerke, Chennevières, *inspecteur* of the provincial museums, and Reiset, curator at the Louvre, she assembled a collection of both old and contemporary paintings. None is shown here in the rotunda drawing room, the most informal space in the ground-floor suite, which included a salon, a dining room with garden setting, a *jardin d'hiver,* etc., known from Giraud's paintings and from a "reportage" appearing in *L'Illustration,* where Auguste Anastasi's faithful drawings pictured them on the evening of a reception.

Despite the forty-five years that separate this painting from the auction held after the princess's death (May 17–21, 1904), it seems that one can identify a certain number of objects with the help of the sale catalogue, in particular, the Chinese screen in carved wood "decorated with flowering branches" (no. 446); on the mantel the two three-branched candelabra in gilded bronze with lights held by a mermaid (no. 433); on the round table, the "vase in old Chinese porcelain, *famille rose,* mounted in bronze as a lamp" (no. 317?). The lamps in turquoise-blue celadon (nos. 328, 329) mounted in bronze might correspond to the vases mounted as lamps, one of which can be seen at the edge of the rotunda. Like all the lamps in the room these are mechanical, a type widely used at the time, and with the fire help create a comfortable atmosphere.

The red tones of the salon, which add to this impression of warmth, were frequent during the Second Empire, while white-and-gold walls and crimson damask were customary for drawing rooms. The eclecticism of the furniture is likewise quite characteristic. The seats are a mixture of Louis XV copies in gilded wood—armchairs, chairs, and sofas—and of distinctly modern ones, such as a light chair, a *confortable,* and a *confidante* (two-seat S-shape sofa). ("The princess is convinced that our present-day craftsmen have more taste and do better work than those of all the past centuries," observed Viel-Castel [1942; June 24, 1861].) On the other hand, the large Chinese vases, *famille verte,* and the Louis XVI clock with cupids and candelabra on the mantel call the collector to mind. A few details are also particularly suggestive: the open piano for musical soirées, the gilded wood valances with the crowned monogram M, the green plants in jardinieres and vases, and the celebrated round table which, along with the princess's sofa, is mentioned in all the accounts of evenings at the rue de Courcelles.

The innumerable reports suffice to enliven the setting: Viel-Castel, habitué of the "Princess's Wednesdays" (probably the bald individual bending over the table); Mme Octave Feuillet, who speaks of the Chinese vases from which rise gigantic palms; the Goncourts, who note the red silks and engraved mirrors (these last do not appear in this painting, but in *L'Illustration*). One can almost hear the princess, seated in a white gown on her sofa, questioning the guest sitting before her, while Mme de Fly, her reader, sits in a corner silently embroidering.

Criticism was not unanimous when this painting was exhibited. "M. Charles Giraud is a master and a great master... but he should never portray a figure in his large views of interiors. See... the interior of the salon of Madame the Princess Mathilde" (Cantrel, 1863, p. 200). And there is no need to quote Viel-Castel's spiteful remarks on the favor enjoyed by Giraud with Princess Mathilde and Nieuwerkerke! But it is not the pictorial qualities of this work that capture our attention: better than any description, it evokes the atmosphere of a great salon under the Second Empire.

C.S.-V.

Musée National du Château, Compiègne

Sébastien-Charles Giraud

## II-5
## A Salon at Monsieur P.'s

1866
Signed, lower right: Ch. Giraud/1866; Salon label on frame: 823
Oil on canvas
62 × 100 cm

Provenance:
Executed for Basile-Joseph Parent (1807–1866); daughter, Marie-Jeannette-Mathilde Parent (1841–1915), married 1861, to Ernest-Gabriel, vicomte, comte (1868), then marquis (1871) des Roys (1836–1903), auditor of the Conseil d'Etat (1858–67); private coll.

Exhibition:
1866, Paris, Salon, no. 823

Bibliography:
Jahyer, 1866, p. 131

After Claude Baudard de Vaudésir, baron de Sainte-James, acquired the mansion situated at number 5 (now 12), place Vendôme in 1777, he had it decorated by Bélanger in 1779: "This house is remarkable for a magnificent salon, whose ceiling and overdoors have been painted by M. la Grenée the younger, *peintre du Roi.* This salon is very richly decorated from designs by M. Bellanger" (Thiéry, 1787, vol. I, p. 128). Indeed, at the Salon of 1781, Jean-Jacques Lagrenée (1739–1821) exhibited sketches for the ceiling and the four overdoors of this salon, situated on the main floor with two windows on the square. This view shows the south half

of the room during the Second Empire, when the house was bought by Basile Parent, a Pereire rival of Belgian origin, founder of a railroad construction company, *administrateur* of the Compagnie du Chemin de Fer de Lyon à la Méditerranée, and chevalier of the Legion of Honor. Other railroad companies were already installed in the place Vendôme when Parent settled there in 1856 at number 12, which became the headquarters of his company as well as the family residence. Parent carried out some remodeling, but while certain adjoining rooms were completely decorated at that time, the Louis XVI atmosphere of the salon was respected and appreciated, as is shown by this view, which was exhibited at the Salon of 1866 on May 1, shortly before Parent's death on June 2. Lagrenée's overdoors were retained, as were the mirror panels occupying the centers of the four walls, the sixteen Corinthian columns, and the four doors carved with gilded reliefs situated to north and south. Lagrenée's ceiling had been replaced nevertheless by a modern, unsigned composition in the allegorical taste of the eighteenth century, in which a woman holding a triangle (Euterpe?) appears, surrounded by cupids playing music. Another innovation, the Louis XVI-style fireplace in white marble (existing today), is adorned with fine gilded bronzes: two caryatids, and a medallion in the center of the lintel representing the profile of a woman, which is signed VP under a closed crown. This is probably the work of the bronze manufacturer Victor Paillard, established in Paris at 8, rue Saint Claude *(Almanach du Commerce,* 1855), then at 105, boulevard Beaumarchais *(Almanach du Commerce,* 1860). After being awarded a medal at the 1851 exhibition, Paillard was a member of the juries of the international exhibitions of 1855 (his collaborators Piat, Willms, and Rambert, q.q.v., were awarded) and 1862, and received a gold medal in 1867 *(Rapports 1855,* pp. 891, 920, 925–26; *Catalogue 1862,* p. 204; Waring, 1863, vol. I, pl. 92; *Récompensés 1867,* group III, p. 40). This salon (presently occupied by the Chaumet firm) later underwent some alterations before 1913, including the moving of the fireplace to the middle of the north wall (Vacquier, 1913, pls. 47–48, showing its present state).

Although the painted view puts more emphasis on the decoration than on the furniture, the latter nevertheless reveals Parent's wealth. The consoles may have been created by Bélanger and been part of the room's original furnishings; the screen and the andirons appear to be Louis XVI, while the armchairs are of the Empire period. However, the bronzes, the tufted seats, and the curtains represent contemporary decorative art. A large rug covers the inlaid parquet decorated in the center by a compass rose. (See *Almanach du Commerce;* Cain, 1908, appendix, pp. 7–8; Vacquier, 1913, pp. 26–27, pls. 47–50.)

D.A.

Private Collection

II-5

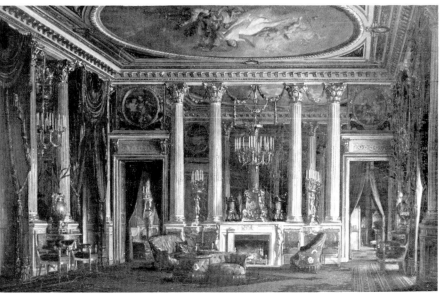

## Jean Sorieul

*Rouen 1824–1871 Rouen*

*A pupil of Hippolyte Bellangé and Léon Cogniet, Sorieul exhibited at the Salon between 1847 and 1853. He specialized in military subjects, either those from the past* (Passage of the Army of the Vendée at Saint-Florent, Engagement at Quiberon, Battle of Le Mans, Passage of the Ponary, Pass during the Russian Campaign) *or present* (The Camp at Compiègne, Review on the Champs-de-Mars in Honor of Queen Victoria in 1855, Capture of Sebastopol, Battle of Traktir). *For the duc de Morny, he executed three watercolors showing ceremonies at the coronation of Czar Alexander II of Russia (1856), which Morny as Napoleon III's ambassador extraordinary had witnessed (Salons of 1857 and 1859).*

J.-P.S.

Jean Sorieul

II-6

## II-6
## Bedroom of the Duc de Morny in the Palace of the President of the Corps Législatif (Hôtel de Lassay)

1866
Signed, lower left: J. SORIEUL 1866
Watercolor
36 × 60.5 cm

Provenance:
Duc de Morny; Pierre Fabius
Exhibition:
1953, Compiègne, p. 29, no. 238
Bibliography:
Praz, 1964, p. 345, fig. 346

Dated 1866, this watercolor was executed after the death of Napoleon III's famous half-brother on March 10, 1865, probably commissioned by the duchesse de Morny to preserve the memory of the room in which her husband died. The estate inventory drawn up after Morny's death by the notary Dufour, beginning in March 1865 (supplied by E. Dufour), enables us to identify it as Morny's room, not on the Champs Elysées, but in the palace of the President of the Corps Législatif. This is not explicit at first, since Mme de Morny had removed her husband's furnishings from the palace as early as March 1865 and the inventory for his bedroom lists only four objects, a chronometer, a barometer and thermometer, and an iron chest. However, the first three are indeed seen here,

the chronometer to the right of the fireplace, the barometer and thermometer on either side of the window. Many of the room's furnishings may be traced through the same inventory from the pieces reassembled by Mme de Morny in the rue Fortin and from the Morny sale catalogue. The rapid removal of the furnishings suggests that Sorieul worked from his own earlier sketches and not directly on the spot.

The most striking feature is that this room is both a bedroom and a study—which should not be surprising, for Alphonse Daudet, who modeled the duc de Mora in *Le Nabab* after Morny, places Mora's private interviews in his bedroom, "where so many ambitions have felt their wings expand, where so many hopes and disappointments fluttered. . . ."

The room is rather simple, and the furniture not luxurious but functional and comfortable. Unity is created by the red tones of the silk hangings and upholstery on the comfortable sofa, tufted armchair, Louis XV–Louis Philippe armchair and chair, and the light chair in blackened wood. Other seats are the ottoman, Empire desk chair, leather Brougham armchair, and a stool. The mahogany cabinetry with ebony fillets—the boat-shaped bed, three bookcases, the tall bookcase, the writing

stand—seems to be Louis Philippe rather than Second Empire. The large writing table, probably part of the same ensemble, is lengthened on one side by a card table with folding leaves. Before the sofa is the only old piece (besides the desk chair), an eighteenth-century kidney-shaped table.

A private room, and not an art gallery, this chamber contains none of the pictures that made Morny's collection famous, but only family portraits (the duchesse by Winterhalter, two children by Hugues Merle, q.v.). Nevertheless, it is still the room of a collector with various *objets d'art*, including bronzes (*Tiger Devouring a Gavial* by Barye, q.v.; race horses), terra-cottas (*Bacchante Carrying a Child* by Marin, for instance), malachite boxes, etc. And on the chair is a small landscape that seems to be awaiting the examination of the master of the house.

Here then is a comely interior; it is not only the room where Morny died, it is also a place where his presence is felt. Here one grasps his informal side, perceiving more than one aspect of his personality, which is what makes this watercolor an exceptional document.

J.-P.S.

Collection Pierre Fabius, Paris

# Textiles

Maison Biais

## Maison Biais

*Active Paris from c. 1827*

*Maison Biais, 76, place Saint Sulpice, then Biais et Rondelet, specialized in church vestments, particularly in Gothic embroideries. It worked closely with many architects, and made a number of celebrated embroidered vestments, including those for the cathedral in Lima, Peru. Paris (with Hubert-Ménage and Biais) was then rivaling Lyons and Brussels in the embroidery of church vestments.*

*Biais exhibited successfully at the Expositions Universelles.*

C.S.-V.

Bibliography:
De Farcy, 1890, pp. 111–13, pl. 142

## II-7
## Cope

1856
Gold cloth, with embroidery in gold thread and satin-stitch embroidery in polychrome silk
138 × 300 cm

Provenance:
Gift of the Minister of Public Worship to Monseigneur Boudinet, bishop of Amiens, 1856; gift to the Treasury of the Cathedral

Bibliography:
Durand, 1901, vol. III, p. 135

It was the practice for each new bishop to present to the chapter of the Amiens cathedral a cope in golden cloth. Monseigneur Jacques-Antoine Boudinet, named bishop of Amiens in 1856, was obligated to observe this custom, but, lacking the necessary financial means, addressed himself to the Minister of Public Worship, Fortoul. He furnished the sum of 2,000 francs to the chasuble maker Biais for a "cope *en drap d'or* richly embroidered in gold, twisted fringe," an amount that was accepted (Arch. nat. F¹⁹3821). The files of the Minister of Public Worship abound in donations of this sort, but it seems nevertheless that the cathedral of Amiens was especially favored. The cathedral received, among other things, an altar cloth for the Chapel of Saint Theudosie (restored by Viollet-le-Duc, q.v., thanks to the Empress), another cope, and in 1867, a large pontifical vestment in gold cloth.

This cope is well within the tradition of the revival of liturgical vestments under the impetus of such archaeologists as Viollet-le-Duc, Lassus (q.v.), Didron, and Father Martin (*see* no. III-16). This fashion was launched in France by another bishop of Amiens, Monseigneur Mioland, who in 1847 had ordered a vestment in the style of the Middle Ages (de Farcy, 1890, p. 111).

The best-known makers specializing in vestments under the Second Empire were

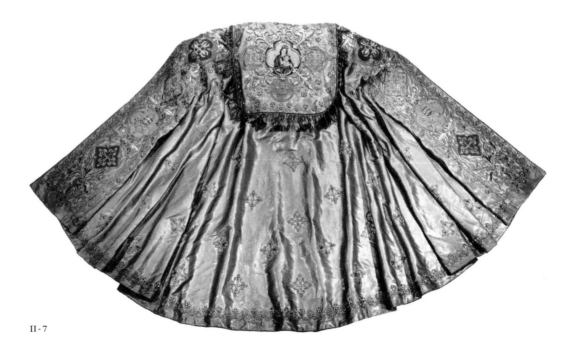

II-7

Hubert-Ménage and Biais; and the names of architects who supplied the designs for several vestments are known. Almost all the important cathedrals and churches sought new vestments, which went hand in hand with the restoration of the buildings and decorations within and led to a renaissance in gold-thread embroidery and needlepoint whose consequences were felt until recent times.

Monseigneur Boudinet's cope is proof of the high quality of such embroidery.

C.S.-V.

Chapitre, Cathedral of Amiens

Furnion Père & Fils*; designed by Auguste Malpertuy*

## II-8
## Napoleon III
## (Medallion of Left Profile)

1855
Signed and dated, lower left: FURNION Père & Fils Aîné LYON 1855.; lower right: A. MAL PERTUY.D.
Velvet ciselé
67 × 42 cm

Provenance:
Made for the Exposition Universelle of 1855; Tarbes museum; deposited in the Musée d'Art et d'Industrie, Saint-Etienne (inv. no. 856.10.1)

Exhibition:
1855, Paris, Exposition Universelle, no. 7007

The firm of Furnion, which produced this panel with a pendant representing Napoleon I for the 1855 Exposition Universelle, specialized in raised and figured velvets most often designed for clothing.

This profile of the Emperor, executed in a short-napped woven velvet, is a type of exhibition piece that did not represent an ordinary demand of its clientele but was made to demonstrate the technical virtuosity of the company. The enframement, very strongly shaded, is woven: a torus of laurel encircling the profile, the branches of oak and laurel, the large garland of fruits, the cross of the Legion of Honor, the imperial crown, the star surmounting the profile—everything accentuates the very official aspect of the piece.

Furnion Père et Fils received a Medal of Honor for their entire presentation at the exposition, with mention for a two-sided, reversible plush velvet and the two woven portraits (*Rapports 1855*, p. 1055). Auguste Mal-

II-8

pertuy, the designer attached to this firm, was awarded a second-class medal for "his skill and upright morality" (*Rapports 1855*, p. 1065).

C.S.-V.

Musée d'Art et d'Industrie, Saint-Etienne, on deposit from the Musée de Tarbes

---

## Jules-Pierre-Michel Diéterle
*Paris 1811–1889 Paris*

*At an early age Diéterle worked with Cicéri, director of the decoration studio at the Opéra, where he collaborated on the décor for Robert le Diable (1831). Diéterle left with three other students to establish Séchan, Feuchères et Cie, later Séchan, Diéterle et Despléchin (1841–48). They created stage sets (La Juive, Opéra, 1835) and decorated theaters in France and other countries.*

*On March 24, 1848, Diéterle entered the Sèvres factory as artiste en chef, a newly created post. He renovated Sèvres's forms by creating new models for vases, some inspired by historical styles ("Louis XV Balaster" vase, 1848; "Rimini" vase, 1849, see no. IV-6) and some without earlier precedent ("Diéterle" vase, 1851, see no. IV-4; "Venice" coupe, 1849), his compositions covering the entire surface of the object with floral or geometric motifs*

accompanied by figures. Diéterle, who became chef des travaux d'art in 1852, left Sèvres in 1855.

*About 1851, when Séchan's daughters married Diéterle and the decorator Haumont, Séchan and his sons-in-law undertook work for Sultan Abdul Medjid. From Constantinople, Séchan suggested ideas to Diéterle, who made the drawings in Paris; they furnished projects for the Sultan's bedroom in the Dolma-Bahçe Palace, in an adapted Louis XIV style (1851), a Louis XIII dining room (1853), and a splendid theater (1858). In 1853 the three artists decorated the salons in the Conversationshaus in Baden-Baden, each in a different style (Renaissance, Louis XIV, Louis XV). This association ended in 1861. In addition, Diéterle painted the ceiling of the grand dining room of the Palais Royal in 1852, and supplied designs for a dessert service for Christofle (q.v.).*

*Diéterle also worked at Gobelins, where his first known works date from 1861 (décor for the ladies' salon in the Elysée palace). His major undertaking there was the design of the tapestry suite, "The Five Senses," his principal work in textiles. He also designed for the Savonnerie manufactory, with Chabal-Dussurgey, carpets for the three new salons of the Empress in the Tuileries, inspired by the eighteenth-century, and carpets of the bedchamber (1878) and salon (1882) of the Pope's apartment at Fontainebleau, in seventeenth-century style. In 1877 Diéterle became administrator of the manufactory of Beauvais.*

B.C.

Bibliography:
Sèvres Archives Ob 4, R 47, R 51, R 57; Guiffrey, n.d., nos. 138–42; Fenaille, 1903–23, vol. V, pp. 130–42, 332, 335, 337; Doin, 1925, pp. 344–60; Ratouis de Limay, 1937, pp. 157–79; Vaisse, 1974, pp. 153–71.

---

## Pierre-Adrien Chabal-Dussurgey
*Charlieu (Loire) 1819–1902 Nice*

*A student at the Ecole des Beaux-Arts in Lyons, Chabal-Dussurgey specialized very early in drawing flowers and ornaments. As a designer he entered the firm of Cinier, a manufacturer of church vestments; he exhibited at the Salon of Lyons (beginning in 1839), and then moved to Paris, at the request of Braun (q.v.) to collaborate on his publications of floral designs. In 1844, thanks to Duban (q.v.), the duc de Luynes entrusted him with decorative works at the château of Dampierre and commissioned flower paintings in gouache (Salon of 1845). In the following years, and under the Second Empire, he continued to send flower paintings to the Salon, usually in gouache, some of which are in museums (Saint-Quentin, Lyons).*

In 1849 he was engaged by the national man-factories, where his chief role was to provide designs of floral compositions for seat coverings in tapestry or savonnerie carpet (for example, at Compiègne, those of the family drawing room, and, in 1863 the bor-ders of those in the Salon des Cartes). He participated besides in larger projects, designing with Diéterle cartoons for the three carpets in the Empress's new salons in the Tuileries as well as for the Gobelins "Five Senses" tapestries (1862–65). At the same time, he was entrusted with several mural decorations: fourteen panels (vases of flowers) for the foyer of the Théâtre Français (1864); the hemicycle of the small salon in the Empress's private hôtel, rue de l'Elysée (1866); two salons in the palace of Biarritz; and similar works in the hôtels Pourtalès and Galliera.

No less important were his publications of litho-graphed designs for the use of industrial designers and his Etudes et compositions de fleurs et de fruits (1867). He was particularly interested in teaching; under the Third Republic, while contin-uing his works and exhibiting at the Salons, he became an inspecteur de l'enseignement and, having retired to Nice, helped to establish there in 1881 a national school of decorative arts, which he directed until 1892.                                J.-P.S.

Bibliography:
Chabal-Dussurgey, 1903, p. 25; Guiffrey, n.d., pls. 127–31, 138–42

Manufacture Impériale des Gobelins; designed and coordinated by Jules-Pierre-Michel Dié-terle, with figures by Paul Baudry, flowers by Pierre-Adrien Chabal-Dussurgey, and ani-mals by Eugène Lambert,* and woven under the supervision of Pierre Munier*

## II-9
## Touch

1864–67
Tapestry, wool and silk; high-warp weaving
359 × 160 m

Provenance:
One of a series of thirteen tapestries (five large and six small panels, two overdoors) commissioned in 1861 for the Grand Salon of the Empress in the Elysée palace; remained unfinished in 1870 and never in-stalled; burned in the Gobelins fire of May 24, 1871, with only this panel and an overdoor (Spring and Summer) saved; assigned to the Gobelins manufac-tory by decree of June 9, 1887 (inv. no. 230)

Exhibitions:
1960, Nice, no. 263; 1966, Paris, Mobilier National, no. 36

Bibliography:
Guiffrey, 1886, p. 463; Gerspach, 1887–88, p. 364;

II-9

II   Furnishings

Gerspach, 1893, p. 208,; Fenaille, 1903–23, vol. V, pp. 135–44; Calmettes, 1912, pp. 205–18

The tapestries for the Grand Salon of the Empress in the Elysée palace constituted, along with the portraits of artists and sovereigns for the Galerie d'Apollon of the Louvre, the only original creations of the Gobelins manufactory during the Second Empire. At the Empress's request, the administrator of the factory, Jules Badin, was entrusted in 1861 with the preparation of a general decoration for the four rooms of the main floor of the Elysée palace—the ladies' reception room, the dining room, the Salon des Glaces, and the Grand Salon.

The parts to be decorated in the Grand Salon were, in addition to two overdoor panels and three for between the windows, three large panels opposite the windows and two on the side walls. The fact that there were to be five large panels led Badin to suggest to the Empress the theme of the "Five Senses," which was accepted. In order to ensure the greatest success of his project, Badin proposed to employ for the cartoons Paul Baudry (q.v.) to paint the figures, Pierre Chabal-Dussurgey for the flowers, and Eugène Lambert for the animals, while the ensemble of the composition would be designed and coordinated by Jules Diéterle.

In September 1862 Diéterle's sketches were approved; a sample panel painted by Baudry was presented in June 1863 and in October 1864 the first tapestry was put on the loom. The weaving remained unfinished in 1870, and what had been completed as well as what was still being woven perished in the fire of May 24, 1871. Only this panel representing Touch (begun October 1, 1864, and finished February 22, 1867), an overdoor, and some sketches were preserved, but they suffice to give an idea of the series.

Diéterle, obliged to take into account the wood paneling of the Grand Salon, which dated from the beginning of the eighteenth century, was strongly inspired by a tapestry of the same period, the series of "Portieres of the Gods" by Claude Audran, in which gods and goddesses were portrayed under colonnaded porticoes and surrounded by flowers and animals.

The accusation of pastiche hurled at Diéterle by his contemporaries was partly justified, but the artist deserves credit on two counts: first, in adapting his tapestries perfectly to the height of the panels by combining two motifs, the figures under arcades and the ovals with the games of love, which provided the necessary height while avoiding excessive elongation of the figures; second, for having surrounded himself with excellent collaborators, in particular, the painter Baudry, whose figure of Touch has considerable charm. Indeed, by taking his inspiration for this series from earlier examples, was not Diéterle merely applying to tapestry what his contemporaries were doing in the other decorative arts?

C.S.-V.

Mobilier National, Paris

---

## Lamy et Giraud
*Lyons, established 1855*

*Alexander Giraud (died 1868) founded at Lyons a silk-weaving factory, which was revived by his sons, A. and E. Giraud, who entered into partnership with A. Lamy in 1855. The factory was later successively at 1, rue Romarin, then 3, quai de Retz.*

*Giraud alone won an honorable mention at the Exposition Universelle of 1855 for "good material, uniform and well-fashioned." The firm of Lamy et Giraud was awarded a "prize medal" at the London International Exhibition in 1862 and a silver medal in Paris in 1867. Four of its* chefs d'ateliers *and master craftsmen, and an embroiderer, Mme Leroudier, also won prizes as* coopérateurs.

*This firm combined, according to the eighteenth-century custom which continued often into the nineteenth, the manufacturing of silks for clothing and for furnishings. Little by little this practice was abandoned in the course of the Second Empire because the demands of fashion (in particular seasonal collections) were so different from those of furnishings. Factories were compelled to specialize, and that of Lamy et Giraud devoted itself entirely to silk goods for furnishings. The contribution of designers of talent, in particular Chabal-Dussurgey (q.v.), together with a great technical mastery, earned this factory a wide reputation during the Second Empire.*

C.S.-V.

Lamy et Giraud

## II-10
## Panel

1865
Three-ply velvet
156 × 75 cm

Provenance:
Ordered by the architect Pierre Manguin for the Hôtel de Païva; model remained with Prelle S.A. (inv. no. p. 4862)

Bibliography:
Maison Prelle Archives

II-10

As he did with every object used in the construction and decoration of the Hôtel de Païva (see nos. II-15, II-23), Pierre Manguin (q.v.) carefully supervised the execution of this velvet, as indicated by the customers' book of the present Maison Prelle, successor to Lamy et Giraud. This three-ply velvet, in a Renaissance-style design, was ordered "with modifications by M. Manguin for the residence of the Comtesse [sic] de Païva on the Champs Elysées," the design being a variation of another sample, itself taken from a Moorish design. (It is amusing to note in passing that it took only a few modifications to make a Renaissance fabric out of a Moorish motif.)

The room for which the velvet was intended is unfortunately not mentioned in the order book, but it seems that it can be recognized in the photographs of the portieres of the large dining room (Houssaye, 1896, pp. 19, 21), the room dominated by the monumental fireplace by Dalou (q.v.), with its young girl with grapes and the two hieratical lionesses by Jacquemart (q.v.).

This velvet, in three harmonizing chamois tones, is a fine technical achievement, much more advanced than (although inspired by) cut velvets of the seventeenth century. The design is actually in cut velvet, and uncut velvet serves only to outline the contours.

C.S.-V.

Prelle S.A., Lyons-Paris

Lamy et Giraud

## II-11
## Decorative Panel

1867
Brocaded lampas, polychrome silks, gold and silver thread
370 × 182 cm

Provenance:
Gift of the manufacturers to the Musée Historique des Tissus, Lyons, 1900 (inv. no. 26.877)

Exhibition:
1867, Paris, Exposition Universelle

The overall composition of this silk fabric in the style of Bérain suggests a tapestry, in particular, the small structure with lambrequins. It should in fact be noted that the adaptation of so-called Bérain decoration to silk fabrics was an invention of the Second Empire (Cox, 1902, p. 100). Compositions at the beginning of the eighteenth century did not employ such large designs but consisted of repeated motifs based on flowers, foliage, fruit, and small architectural structures, thus corresponding more closely to the actual spirit of weaving. A panel such as this one is a technical feat because of the number of cartoons necessary for the weaving of a single pattern. It demonstrates—and such was its purpose in view of the impending Exposition Universelle—the skill of the weavers of Lyons (two *chefs d'atelier*, Bichet and Buret, and two master craftsmen, Bois and Gonin, of the firm of Lamy et Giraud, received awards at the exposition of 1867). In the end, it would have seemed more economical, especially for a single specimen, to have had it executed in embroidery. Under the Empire, Bony, the predecessor of Lamy et Giraud, had adopted this formula with considerable success, and when one recalls that Mme Leroudier, one of the most famous Lyons embroiderers of the period, was employed by this firm, one would think that the experiment might easily have been tried.

II-11

Be that as it may, the panel's composition (attributed to Chabal-Dussurgey, q.v.) is elegant. The hanging garlands of flowers and the large central bouquet show an animation in the iridescent colors of the silk that delights and soothes the eye. The enframement, which imitates Louis XV paneling, clearly indicates the purpose of the piece—it is not a portiere, as has sometimes been incorrectly stated, but a panel to be stretched on a wall.

C.S.-V.

Musée Historique des Tissus, Lyons

---

## Henri Mathevon and Eugène Bouvard
*Lyons, established 1811*

*This firm of silk manufacturers, which was founded in Lyons in 1811 and located on the place Tholozan, specialized in fabrics for interior furnishings. The manufacturer's research was directed to the imitation of embroidery effects by means of weaving. Its creation of wall and door hangings, where stitched brocades were combined with velvet and silver and gold threads, was very well known. As a result of this skill in the use of metallic threads, this factory also made gold and silver fabrics for church vestments.*

*The manufacturer won a Medal of Honor at the Exposition Universelle of 1855, and a silver medal and the Legion of Honor in 1867.*

C.S.-V.

Bibliography:
*Rapports 1855*, pp. 382, 1035; *Catalogue 1862*, p. 134

Henri Mathevon and Eugène Bouvard

## II-12
## Poetry

c. 1867
Silk lampas with raised and lancé decoration
290 × 160 cm

Provenance:
Gift of the manufacturers to the Musée Historique des Tissus, Lyons, 1976 (inv. no. 36.815)

Exhibitions:
1867, Paris, Exposition Universelle; 1934, Paris, Salomon de Rothschild, no. 44

Bibliography:
*Etoffes merveilleuses*, 1976, vol. II, pl. 46

II-12

This panel gives somewhat the appearance of a Louis XVI woodwork: arabesque scrolls, a small antique bas-relief, bucranium, antique medallion, and torus of laurel. At the same time, there are reminders of the style of the early eighteenth century, especially in the lambrequins. The central figure, Poetry, in a symmetrical enframement of vases filled with flowers and lambrequins, evokes to some degree the hanging woven at the Gobelins factory for the Elysée palace (no. II-9). It is probably because of this that, without documentation, this design has been attributed to Chabal-Dus- surgey (q.v.). One cannot help mentioning a contemporary reaction to this factory's contribution to the Exposition Universelle of 1867: "Sumptuous materials in Algerian silk were shown by MM. Mathevon and Bouvard. Their Pompeian designs were a little weak" (Dognée, 1869, p. 127).

Whatever might be said about this design, in which there is an obvious disparity between the lower part, crammed with ornamentation, and the upper parts, where empty spaces assume too much importance, the weaving shows great skill, especially in the use of

ows to create the impression of a relief.
finally, is it not strange to reduce a silk
c, in full color moreover, a sumptuous
rial full of decorative possibilities, to the
of a *trompe l'œil* bas-relief?

C.S.-V

sée Historique des Tissus, Lyons

---

ultz (Eugène) et Béraud

ns, established 1825

This firm of silkmakers, founded in Lyons,
rue du Griffon, in 1825 was first called Schultz
ères, then Schultz et Béraud, and then Schultz et
ourdon. The firm specialized in silks and figured
lvets for dress fabrics and silk shawls and exhibited
ith great success at the international exhibitions
nd had the honor of making the Empress's court
obes (Rapports 1855, p. 1054). Its reputation was
lso built on the wealth of its imagination, due in
art to its imitation of Chinese embroideries. Its warp
rinting (chinés), a delicate technique inherited
rom the eighteenth century, was also highly regarded. This house seems to have been especially
eager to attract female clientele with the quality of its
fabrics and the variety of its designs.

C.S.-V.

Eugène Schultz et Cie

## II-13
## Court Robe

1853?
"Gandin" ciselé velvet with silk and gold thread
360 × 190 cm

Provenance:
Gift of the manufacturers to the Musée Historique des
Tissus, Lyons (inv. no. 23840)

Bibliography:
Cox, 1902, p. 241; Catalogue, Lyons, Musée Historique des Tissus, 1929, p. 106, no. 655; d'Hennezel,
1930, p. 156, fig. 232; Schwartz and de Micheaux,
1964, pl. 29

Should this fabric, intended for a court robe,
be identified with the mantle given by the City
of Lyons to the Empress in 1853 and woven by
the firm of Schultz (*Rapports 1855*, p. 1054)?
This robe was designed by the Mulhouse designers Georges Zipélius and Joseph Fuchs,
whose designs manufacturers in Paris,
Beauvais, Lyons, Tours, and even England

II-13

were scrambling to buy up (*L'Industrie de Mulhouse,* 1902, p. 638). Supporting this idea is the fact that Joseph Fuchs specialized in floral designs and that the composition of this sumptuous velvet is based on flowers, roses, Hortensias, and fritillarias ("crown imperials"), the last two, symbolic flowers, definitely showing that this cloth was intended for the Empress.

There is, however, nothing to suggest that this piece was ever delivered. It remains exactly as it was when taken from the loom and was a gift from the manufacturers to the museum in Lyons. It is rose-colored cut velvet, a "velours gandin," i.e., with a base of gold thread. This piece shows that this technique, of which there are so many fine examples in furnishing velvets under the Empire or the Restoration, was still prized.

C.S.-V.

Musée Historique des Tissus, Lyons

Schultz et Béraud

## II-14
## Birds of the Antilles

Before 1862?
Satin brocaded with polychromed silks
160 × 68 cm

Provenance:
Gift of the manufacturers to the Musée Historique des Tissus, Lyons, 1866 (inv. no. 18.788)

Exhibitions:
1862, London; 1864, Oporto; 1934, Paris, Salomon de Rothschild

Bibliography:
Schwartz and de Micheaux, 1964, pl. 28

The composition of this white satin woven with polychrome silks is of exotic inspiration. Birds of the Antilles, lyre birds, birds of paradise, and hummingbirds, play amidst bamboo and orchids. The design is very free, much more airy than certain contemporary compositions with heavy garlands of flowers. It reveals a search for original sources of inspiration, so apparent in the fashion for reproductions of earlier fabrics, and is reminiscent of embroideries from the Far East, especially from China.

This is believed to have been a model for dress fabric bought by Queen Victoria, but the first known mention of it is at the London Exhibition of 1862. It is highly unlikely that it could have been bought at that date by the

II-14

Queen for she was then in mourning for Prince Albert, who had died the preceding year. One might, therefore, date it prior to 1862.

C.S.-V.

Musée Historique des Tissus, Lyons

## Tassinari (Cléto) et Chatel (Louis)
*Lyons, established 1762*

*Successors to Camille Pernon and after him the Grand Frères, Tassinari et Chatel took over this ancient and illustrious Lyonnaise firm of silk manufacturers on the place Croix Paquet in 1864. Under the Second Empire, this firm benefited from its long tradition and its very important collection of earlier samples, which gave it a preeminent position at a time when reproductions and imitations of seventeenth- and eighteenth-century fabrics were much sought after.*

*After the crisis of 1848, which had severe repercussions on the Lyonnaise silkmakers, business began to pick up and the house received official commissions: the Salle des Maréchaux in the Tuileries, copies of Louis XVI silks for the Empress Eugénie. The sovereigns even visited Paul Grand's workshops in the Croix Rousse in 1860 (Le Moniteur, August 27, 1860).*

*The firm of Grand, later Tassinari et Chatel, also worked for foreign courts (Portugal, Egypt, Turkey) and in France received famous commissions such as that for the Hotel de Paiva and the Ministère d'Etat (today the Ministère des Finances).*

C.S.-V.

Bibliography:
Jardel, 1962

## Pierre Manguin
*Paris 1815–1869 Paris*

*A student of Lebas, Pierre Manguin began his career as designer for the Commission Historique. Between 1837 and 1858 he showed architectural drawings regularly at the Salon and undertook a number of restorations, among them the churches of La Ferté-Bernard and Bourg-Saint-Andéol and the château de Pontchartrain.*

*He is known mainly for the construction and the interior decoration of the hôtel of the marquise de Païva on the Champs Elysées, which he directed from 1856 to 1866. The rest of his career remains obscure*

*to the point that Champier remarked around 1901: "The dearth of information about him is already so great that one could easily mistake him for a fifteenth-century artist."*

C.S.-V.

Bibliography:
Champier, 1901

Tassinari et Chatel; designed by Avisse,* supervised by Pierre Manguin

## II-15
## Panel

1865
Mark printed on lining: GRAND FRERES
Border of blue, green, gold, and silver brocade on a violet *cannetille* background; violet satin curtain
300 × 200 cm

Provenance:
Model for the brocade executed in 1865 for the Hôtel de Païva; retained by Tassinari & Chatel

Bibliography:
Houssaye, 1896; Champier, 1901, p. 256; Jardel, 1962

The archives of Tassinari et Chatel, which succeeded the Grand Frères in 1864, noted on April 10, 1865, in the order book: "Ordered by M. Manguin for the Hôtel de Païva, silks for the bedroom of the marquise: plain satin in dark lilac, gros de Tours, and matching borders." This order also included the wall hangings for the grand salon, entrance hall, boudoir, library, small dining room, and the bedroom and small salon of "M. le Comte."

The borders of the marquise de Païva's room—"woven background, in the Renaissance style, brocaded in gold and silver, design given by M. Avisse"—appear in the order book for the month of May 1865.

The border was woven on a violet background for the bedroom and on a China rose background for the grand salon. In both

II-15 (detail)

cases, the order included a wide border, a narrow border harmonizing with the wide one, a medallion in the middle of the wide border, and braid on each side of the border.

The design of this silk fabric is attributed to a certain Avisse, but no designer of this name appears in the Lyonnais manufacturer's books. It could perhaps have been the decorator Alexandre-Paul Avisse (died 1886), a decorative painter at the Sèvres works from 1850 to 1885, when he retired (Sèvres Archives, Ob[1]).

Knowing with what care the architect Pierre Manguin directed the construction and the decoration of the Hôtel de Païva (*see* nos. II-10, II-22), it is not surprising that he wanted to see the design for these borders worked out in his presence instead of confining them to a designer in Lyons. Le Senne (1910, p. 20) went so far as to state that "the walls are hung with a brocaded satin designed by Manguin himself."

The border is composed of large palmettes in gold and silver and small flowers and wheat spikes entwined with baguettes. This motif is said to be in the Renaissance style although the form of the palmettes and the lines of the scrolls are more reminiscent of Persian motifs. Unfortunately, there is no example of this fabric *in situ*. While photographs published in 1896 show the wide border in the grand salon (Houssaye, 1896, pp. 5, 7, 11, 13) and the small border with the same rose background in the adjacent music room (Houssaye, 1896, p. 15),

the bedroom no longer had the silks ordered in 1865. The date of the renovation is unknown. Perhaps the passage in *Nana* describing the Hôtel de Païva should be taken literally ; "Twice she redecorated her bedroom ; the first time, in mauve satin, the second, in lace appliqued on a blue background..." (E. Zola, *Nana,* quoted in Rheims, 1972, p. 239).

C.S.-V.

Collection Tassinari & Chatel, S.A.R.L., Paris

# Wallpaper

## Manufacture Jules Desfossé

*Active Paris after c. 1851*

*Nothing is presently known about the origins or the personality of Jules Desfossé (died 1889). The factory that bears his name appeared in 1851 at the time of the purchase of the stock of plates and decorations of the Mader firm. The importance that the Desfossé factory quickly acquired under the Second Empire can be explained by its policy of buying up printing materials during a period of fifteen years ; in 1863 Jules Desfossé became a partner of his brother-in-law Hippolyte Karth, himself the successor of the Dauptain, Brière, Clerc, and Margeridon factories. In 1865, buying the printing plates from the firm of Kob et Pick, Desfossé inherited the prestigious stock of Dufour, one of the most famous manufacturers of panoramic décors at the beginning of the nineteenth century. Desfossé thus built a veritable empire in the art of wallpaper, which enabled him to reprint some of the most beautiful landscapes conceived by his predecessors.*

*In addition the factory was also very creative. Jules Desfossé called upon recognized artists, such as Muller, Wagner, Poterlet, Cron, Fuchs, and Dumont, which gave his collections a rare quality and helped open up the numerous possibilities for expression of the style of Napoleon III. Between 1852 and 1861 Desfossé created panoramic decorations which earned him the unanimous admiration of his contemporaries : The Dream of Happiness composed by Dunand in 1852 ; The Jardin d'Hiver, The Garden of Armida, and The Gallery of Flora, designed by Muller between 1853 and 1857 ; The*

*Monuments of Paris in 1858 ; and finally The Garden of Eden, painted by Fuchs in 1861, a veritable technical tour de force requiring more than 3,600 printing plates.*

*Together with Etienne Delicourt, his principal competitor, Jules Desfossé revived the art of panoramic wallpapers and helped to give it its masterful dimension.*

O.N.

## Edouard Muller (called Rosenmuller)

*Glarus 1823 (or Mulhouse 1825)–1876 Nogent-sur-Marne*

*Muller, a student of Henri Lebert, was a painter and designer for the textile and wallpaper industries. In 1845 he moved to Paris, where he first became associated with Ladveze, but then, in 1854, began to work alone. In addition to his creations for the textile industries in Mulhouse and Lyons, Muller distinguished himself with his compositions for wallpaper, notably The Jardin d'Hiver (1853), The Garden of Armida (1854), and The Gallery of Flora (1856–57), all three done for the Manufacture Desfossé. He also executed decorative panels for the Manufacture Zuber.*

*A nearly forgotten artist today, Muller had a distinctive and exceptionally adept style of rendering flowers naturalistically. Extremely knowledgeable about printing techniques and* trompe l'œil, *Muller specialized in compositions where veg-*

*etation was combined with other materials for contrast. In this refined juxtaposition of materials, the softness of the flowers was always rendered with an especially fine sensitivity. A great colorist, Muller always knew how to illuminate his compositions with a soft light to enhance the liveliness of the vegetable dyes and to heighten their contrast with the deliberately pale colors of stone.*

O.N.

Bibliography :
Bellier and Auvray, 1882–87, vol. II, p. 142 ; Brun, 1917, p. 323 ; *L'Industrie de Mulhouse,* 1902, p. 431 ; Thieme and Becker, 1907–50, vol. XXV, p. 223 ; Bénézit, 1948–54, vol. VI, p. 259

Manufacture Jules Desfossé ; designed by Edouard Muller (called Rosenmuller)

## II-16
## The Garden of Armida

1854
Block-printed wallpaper
389 × 337 cm

Provenance :
Gift of the Manufacture Hoock et Desfossé to the Union Centrale des Arts Décoratifs, 1882 ; Musée des Arts Décoratifs (inv. no. 29810)

Exhibitions :
1855, Paris, Exposition Universelle ; 1967, Paris, Musée des Arts Décoratifs, no. 103

II-16

Bibliography:
*L'Illustration*, vol. XXVI, 1855, p. 261 (repro.); *Rapports 1855*, p. 1146; Desfossé, 1855; *Revue Générale de l'Architecture et des Travaux Publics*, vol. XIII, 1855, col. 461; Maison Maigret et Cie, *Album de références*, n.d., nos. 2302 ff.; McClelland, 1924, p. 330 (repro.); Clouzot and Follot, 1935, p. 219, repro. p. 223; Catalogue, Paris, Musée des Arts Décoratifs, 1967, p. 40, repro. p. 103; Olligs (ed.), 1969–70, vol. II, p. 230

*See* Cover

Edouard Muller conceived *The Garden of Armida* as an ensemble of three tableaux framed by a border and surmounted by a frieze. Only the central panel is shown here; in the other panels at its sides are two semicircular colonnades topped by a glass dome; two enormous basins suspended by chains from the ceiling overflow with multicolored flowers. Above the three tableaux is a motif of eight putti repeated in a frieze.

Awarded a first-class medal at the Exposition Universelle of 1855, *The Garden of Armida* stimulated new trends in the art of panoramas. The main innovation was its goal of creating masterpieces rivaling "great painting" rather than just wallpaper. Desfossé discussed this point: "If one could give this piece the attention it deserves, one would be struck by the enormous distance between this work, this truly artistic study, and all similar articles the industry has produced so far.... By associating with my industrial productions illustrious names from the fine arts, like those of Messrs. Couture [q.v.], Clésinger [q.v.], Muller, I know I have paved new paths for progress and have drawn our industry closer to art, the source of so much of its brilliance" (Desfossé, 1855).

The decoration develops around the statue of Flora, depicted in the central panel. The title given to the work places it in the mysterious world of the magician Armida. In Tasso's *Jerusalem Delivered*, Armida lures the knight Rinaldo into her palace garden, with the intention of killing him. But the scents, the brilliance of the flowers, the beauty of the landscape, and the ornamental statuary lend Rinaldo seductive powers, and Armida falls in love with him.

Muller conceived this décor with a discipline that is masked by the floral abundance and the romantic atmosphere. The meaning of *The Garden of Armida* becomes apparent through the examination of its three horizontal parts. The socle, treated as a stage, elevates the work into another world and creates a distance between the spectator and the unnatural garden. Above is the garden itself over which Flora, a cold and expressionless statue, reigns. The architecture and the statue in neutral tones are counterpoints to the luxuriant vegetation. The distribution of light, too, enhances the many-colored flowers, the only sign of life in this mysterious universe. Above, the frieze of putti, disporting themselves, full of spontaneity, seems to be the realization of the promises of happiness suggested by the seductions of Flora. Indeed, the progression of the forms of life depicted can hardly be accidental: the base of stone, an inert, unalterable element; the garden, a living world; paradise finally reached, where man appears in the innocence of childhood.

The statue of Flora is the vertical axis around which the whole composition revolves. Only a stretch of water suggested to the right of the statue breaks the absolute symmetry of the work. The frieze, whose motif extends the width of the central panel, obeys the same strict rule in the arrangement of the putti in groups. In addition, Flora belongs to the three worlds depicted here: she is made of stone, like the socle; has a human face; and symbolizes the flowers from which she seems to rise.

Muller's style is characterized by the intimacy he created between architecture and floral composition. In contrast with the techniques of perpective traditionally used in panoramic decorations, in which the surface was punctuated by distant motifs, Muller conceived his foregound as a nearly opaque screen. He brought the colored masses into the foreground and gave the diaphanous luminosity of the background the task of suggesting mystery, thereby heightening the emotional intensity. Instead of a slow progression toward a distant horizon line following the laws of classical perspective, which would allow the eye gradually to adjust to the décor, Muller, in *The Garden of Armida*, relied on the initial shock to unleash sensitivity. By this means Muller helped to introduce Romanticism into the industry.

Developing the experiments done by the Manufacture Zuber in *Isola Bella*, *Chinese Décor*, and *Eldorado*, which do not depend on literary or anecdotal support, Muller executed in 1853 *The Jardin d'Hiver* which already gave less importance to the narrative theme than to the Romantic feeling for nature.

O.N.

Musée des Arts Décoratifs, Paris

# Furniture

## Pierre-Charles Simart

Troyes 1806–1857 Paris

For Simart, who had won the Prix de Rome in 1833, the Second Empire corresponded to the age of honors. His career ended brutally in an accident at the age of fifty-one. Elected to the Institut de France in 1852, succeeding Pradier, he was able to promise his vote the following year to Nieuwerkerke (Louvre Archives S 30 [October 8, 1853]), which made their relationship somewhat different than usual between the Directeur Général des Musées and an artist.

After finishing one of the large commissions undertaken in a spirit of reconciliation during the reign of Louis Philippe (statue of Napoleon I and bas-reliefs surrounding his tomb in the Invalides), Simart was asked to work on all the major imperial construction projects: the New Louvre owes to him the caryatids of the Pavillon de l'Horloge and the pediment of the Pavillon Denon (Awakening of the Arts and Industry on the Accession of Napoleon III, the only image of the Emperor visible outdoors today in Paris), and the Sénat, one of the groups in the throne room (Art Taking Inspiration from Poetry).

His native city of Troyes, which granted him a pension in 1823 when he had "gone up to Paris," has collected in the Musée des Beaux-Arts a great many of his models—donated, in particular, by Gabriel de Vendeuvre (1872), the duc de Luynes, and Simart's widow.

Simart's devotion to his "good master" Ingres (see the warm and moving letter of February 29, 1840, in the Bibliothèque Doucet) increased his admiration for antiquity. He owed to this the eulogy: "You have revived Greek art" (Duguet, 1897, p. 8). Thus was he proclaimed "savior of good principles" by the opponents of Romanticism, which put Théophile Gautier in a delicate position when writing his obituary. In it, Gautier described Simart as a victim of the conservative movement, "appreciated by the Romanticists who loved Greek art very much, although they hated academic art." It is questionable whether Simart really freed himself from the latter tendency, although his chryselephantine Minerva (1846–51) executed for the duc de Luynes (château of Dampierre) is a rather "disturbingly bizarre creation" (T. Gautier, L'Artiste, vol. LIX, 1857, pp. 169–71).

Within the Louvre can be seen his astonishing decoration on the ceiling of the Salon Carré (1849–51), restored in 1971. The department of sculpture has four medallions, two statuettes, and a marble Venus from 1842, which was bequeathed by the son of his first patron, M. Marcotte-Genlis.

A.P.

Bibliography:
T. Gautier, L'Artiste, vol. LIX, 1857, pp. 169–71; Duguet, 1897; Lami, 1914–21, vol. IV, pp. 257–62; Catalogue, Troyes, Musée, 1931, pp. 79–96

## Henri-Marie-Alfred Jacquemart

Paris 1824–1896 Paris

Entering the Ecole des Beaux-Arts in 1845, exhibiting at the Salon from 1847 to 1879, Jacquemart, in his correspondence, reveals himself a skillful courtier. Nieuwerkerke favored him. His letter of December 4, 1868, to the viceroy of Egypt (Louvre Archives N 00) robbed Charles Cordier (q.v.), who was executing the monument to Ibrahim Pasha, of orders for Alexandria and Cairo.

Through its symbols the Second Empire gave work to animaliers, born, oddly enough, for the most part in Paris (Barye, Cain, Frémiet, q.q.v., Mêne, Rouillard, q.v.). Nieuwerkerke wanted Jacquemart to execute the eagle for the Montmirail column, but he demanded such a high price that the committee had to make do with a current model from the Val d'Osne foundry (Louvre Archives N 00 [June 1866]).

The Louvre has no examples of the sculptor's work other than three capitals in the Salle de Manège (models reproduced by Aulanier, 1953, nos. 70–72), but his animals abound all over Paris: two lions on top of the niche of a fountain in the Jardin des Plantes (the yawning lion is the one from the Salon of 1857); four stone sphinxes on the Châtelet fountain (1858); two bronze dragons on the Fontaine Saint Michel (1860), which were called "stupid" by the Goncourts: they evoke "the creative genius of Chinese and Japanese monsters.... What an imagination for the monstrous!... But also, why ask for chimeras from members of the Institut [which Jacquemart was not]..." (1956, vol. I [November 1, 1862]); lionesses and a hunting relief on the fireplace of the dining room of the Hôtel de Païva (1864); bronze eagles on the rostral columns on the west facade of the Opéra; eight lions for the Château d'Eau fountain (1874), today on the place Félix Eboué (damaged during the Commune, they were restored by the firm of Thiébaut which had originally cast them); Jacquemart also executed the bust of Victor-Charles-Antoine Thiébaut [1849–1908] in 1874); the gilded, cast-iron rhinoceros (1878) from the Trocadéro (today on the place de la Porte de Saint Cloud); and two seated lions for the east facade of the Hôtel de Ville.

Jacquemart's sculptures were perhaps edited in bronze by Goupil (one is led to believe this by his undated letter to Barbedienne; Arch. nat. AP 368-1) and then by Barbedienne (animals appear in the catalogues of 1875, 1880, 1884, and 1900, where, in addition, a Bonaparte in Egypt is also listed).

A.P.

Bibliography:
Lami, 1914–21, vol. III, pp. 191–94

Designed by Victor Baltard; cabinetry by Guillaume Grohé, silverwork by Fannière Frères and P.-H. Emile Froment-Meurice after Pierre-Charles Simart (figure of Paris, genii) and Henri-Marie-Alfred Jacquemart (eagle), and enamels by the Manufacture Impériale de Sèvres (Alfred-Thompson Gobert and Jean-Baptiste-César Philip) after Hippolyte-Jean Flandrin

## II-17
## Cradle

1856
Rosewood, gilded silver, silver, painted enamels
Height 53 cm, width 125 cm, depth 25.5 cm; figure height 110 cm, width 40 cm

Provenance:
Presented by the City of Paris on March 15, 1856; restored to the Empress Eugénie and given by her to the City of Paris, 1904; Musée Carnavalet (inv. no. NB 249)

Exhibitions:
1867, Paris, Exposition Universelle; 1901, Paris, Petit Palais; 1922, Paris, Musée des Arts Décoratifs, no. 531; 1949, Arenenberg, no. 147

Bibliography:
Magne, 1856, pp. 199–200; Le Moniteur, March 13, 1856; Fêtes et cérémonies, 1860; M. Chevalier, in Rapports 1867, vol. III, p. 263; Mesnard, 1867, vol. II, p. 226; Sédille, 1874, p. 490; Vever, 1906–8, vol. II, p. 131; Bouilhet, 1908–12, vol. III, pp. 31–32; Filon, 1912, p. 272, pl. 2; Christ, 1949, p. 128, no. 167; Wilhelm, 1956, p. 2; Ledoux-Lebard, 1965, p. 217; Baccheschi, 1966, p. 83; González-Palacios, 1969, p. 62, no. 85

With the official announcement of the Empress's pregnancy, the City of Paris, as it had done for the king of Rome and the comte de Paris, asked the Emperor's permission to prepare the cradle of the imperial infant. Haussmann, Prefect of the Seine, had obtained from the Municipal Council on December 14, 1855, an unlimited credit "to have the imperial cradle made by the most skillful artists and employing the most precious materials" (*Fêtes et cérémonies*, 1860, p. 1). For the conception, Haussmann naturally turned to the architect of the City of Paris, Baltard (q.v.), who with his Neoclassical and eclectic taste, incorporated a multiplicity of symbols: the cradle itself is in the form of a boat, evoking the arms of Paris; at its bow is a silver eaglet with outspread wings; while on the poop, a silver statue of the City, flanked by two genii, holds a crown. Four enamel medallions in *grisaille* on the sides represent four cardinal virtues. At the stern are two silver-gilt mermaids holding garlands.

Baltard asked his nephew by marriage, Simart, to model the figure of the City and the two genii, which were cast and chased by the Fannière Frères (q.v.), while Jacquemart provided the model for the eaglet. All the ornamental silverwork was entrusted to the firm of Froment-Meurice at the request of the Emperor himself, apparently to lessen the blow that the premature death of François-Désiré Froment-Meurice (q.v.) on the eve of the 1855 Exposition Universelle had brought to the firm.

To complete such a work in less than three months was a challenge. It was finished the night of March 12, and on March 13, at the Emperor's request, it was displayed to the public in the throne room of the Hôtel de Ville, "where everyone will be admitted without ticket from 10 a.m. to 2 p.m." (*Le Moniteur*, March 13, 1856). In two days 25,000 people had admired it, and the display was extended until the sixteenth, when the Municipal Council was to have solemnly handed it over to the sovereigns after Mass. Events moved swiftly, however; on the fifteenth the cradle was transported without ceremony to the Tuileries and the Prince was born on the morning of the sixteenth.

The gift had cost the City 161, 751.45 francs: art sculpture, 6,000 (Simart, Jacquemart, Fannière); enamel cartoons, 2,000 (Flandrin, q.v.); execution of enamels at Sèvres, 2,080 (done by Gobert, q.v., assisted by Philip, q.v.; Sèvres Archives Pb 13, Vj' 62, Vq' 6); cabinetry and carving of ornaments, 12,985 (Grohé, q.v.); silverwork, 63,322.95 (Froment-Meurice); lace, 68,250 (the netting dotted with bouquets of violets and the imperial arms, pillow, and eiderdown, now lost, had been executed in Alençon stitch, gauze stitch, and

II-17

needlepoint by the well-known Lefébure firm in Paris); furnishings, 1,662 (probably the tufted blue-satin lining); various expenses, 1,451.50; fee for the direction of the work, 4,000 (Baltard).

The haste of the execution of the cradle made it necessary to return it to the artists, particularly to finish the ornamental sculptures and the chasing and to replace the silvered-bronze eagle with one of oxidized silver (Meeting of the Municipal Council, Paris, March 28, 1856; *Fêtes et cérémonies*, 1860, p. 25).

This cradle was received with unanimous praise for the quality of execution and the beauty of Simart's figure. But the allegories seemed obscure (the critics do not even agree on their meaning) and especially too pagan for "the godson of a pope, the son of a Spanish lady, and the grandnephew of the author of the Concordat" (Magne, 1856, p. 200). But its sumptuousness, adapted to its purpose, appeared so representative of the art of the period that it was shown in 1867 in the pavilion of imperial manufactures.

In the presence of this gift made for a prince whose fate was to be so tragic, one cannot help quoting Théophile Gautier's verses: "As a cradle for its newborn babe,/Paris with maternal delicacy,/Has lent its boat.../Then sail, strong in memory,/In thy cradle now a bark/On the ocean of the future" (*Le Moniteur*, March 17, 1856). (*See also* no. V-12.)

C.S.-V.

Musée Carnavalet, Paris

---

### Louis-Auguste-Alfred Beurdeley

*Paris 1808–1882 Paris*

*Beurdeley's activities parallel those of Monbro (q.v.). His father, Jean Beurdeley (1772–1853), born in the Côte-d'Or, established an antique and furniture shop in Paris during the first Empire. The Beurdeley shop was located at 355, rue Saint Honoré (Almanach du Commerce, 1818 — the first year it was listed — and 1819), then at 364, rue Saint Honoré (Almanach du Commerce, 1820–39). Alfred bought the Pavillon de Hanovre at 32–34, rue Louis le Grand, at the corner of the boulevard des Italiens, where he moved his father's business (Almanach du Commerce, 1840). He added a workshop for furniture restoration, which led to his manufacturing business. Beurdeley specialized in interpreting eighteenth-century furniture, especially Louis XVI, and because of the fine quality of his*

*work became the most famous cabinetmaker of this kind during the Second Empire, supplying furniture notably to the Garde Meuble Impérial.*

*At the Exposition Universelle of 1855, where his furniture was shown in the "Empress's boudoir," he won a bronze medal. He did not exhibit in 1862. In 1867 he showed a series of Louis XVI pieces including, besides this bookcase, a table inspired by Carlin and Weisweiler, decorated with lacquer panels and mother-of-pearl, copper, and silver marquetry, and a sideboard in lemon wood with marquetry designed by Brandely (q.v.). He also exhibited porphyry, rose granite, and green antique marble vases mounted in the style of Louis XVI, as well as coupes of jasper and rock crystal with enameled gold mounts, executed by the goldsmith Duron, winning a gold medal for the furniture and the vases.*

*His son Alfred, Jr. (1847–1919) directed the firm's activity toward exact reproductions of antique furniture and copied all the famous pieces of the Mobilier National. He retired in 1893 in order to enrich his own collections and sold off his stock at fifteen auctions held from 1895 to 1901.*

D.A.

Bibliography:
*Rapports 1855*, p. 1124; *Récompensés 1867*, group III, p. 2; Ducuing, 1868, vol. I, pp. 132–34; *Rapports des délégations 1867*, vol. I, "Bijoutiers," p. 1, "Découpeurs marqueteurs," p. 11, "Dessinateurs d'ameublement," pp. 48–50; sale, Paris, Galerie Georges Petit, May 6–7, 1920, pp. v–xviii; Demoriane, 1961, pp. 78–82; Ledoux-Lebard, 1965, pp. 46–48; Baccheschi, 1966, pp. 31–44

Louis-Auguste-Alfred Beurdeley

## II-18
## Bookcase

c. 1867

Stamp: A. BEURDELEY A PARIS

Ebony, gilded bronze, lapis lazuli, jasper, marble

Height 290 cm; width 220 cm; depth 65 cm

Provenance:
Second Beurdeley sale, Paris, Galerie Georges Petit, May 27–June 1, 1895, p. 78, no. 565; Mr. and Mrs. T.C. Morrow, 1969

Exhibition:
1867, Paris, Exposition Universelle

Bibliography:
Ducuing, 1868, vol. I, pp. 132–34 (repro.); Burty, 1868, "Le Mobilier moderne," p. 40; *Rapports des délégations 1867*, vol. I, "Dessinateurs d'ameublement," p. 48 (repro.); Dognée, 1869, pp. 262–63; Demoriane, 1961, p. 84, repro. p. 85; Ledoux-Lebard, 1965, p. 47, pl. 17

In contrast to many of Beurdeley's works, this is not a pastiche, but an original creation. Although its architectural construction evokes

the Renaissance, one can see in the composition and proportions of the upper part the influence of cabinets made after that period: French seventeenth-century ebony cabinets, which might well have suggested the use of this wood (one appeared in the second sale after Beurdeley's death; Paris, Hôtel Drouot, April 23–25, 1883, room 8, no. 306); the jewel cabinet of Marie Antoinette (261 × 202 × 67 cm), then on exhibit at the Louvre (Catalogue, Paris, Louvre, Musée des Souverains, 1868, no. 144 bis); the jewel cabinet of Josephine (278 × 203 × 64 cm), flanked, like the bookcase, by six columns, at that time in the palace of Fontainebleau (Louvre).

Riesener's commodes, on the other hand, inspired the division of the lower part into three rectangular compartments, with shaped corners on the center one. The form and the material are in contrast to the decoration. The use of plaques of hard stones and marble was borrowed from Renaissance furniture. The bronzes "are all, or just about all, molded from old pieces, which may be seen in the imperial palaces such as at Saint-Cloud, etc." (*Rapports des délégations 1867*). Whether or not this is so, Beurdeley did use authentic Louis XVI sources.

The four upper panels are decorated in Pompeian style, used in the time of Louis XVI for murals like those in the Salon des Jeux and the boudoir of Marie Antoinette at Fontainebleau, and in furniture, on large painted-glass panels decorating such exceptional pieces as the queen's jewel cabinet mentioned above. Replacing the geometric cartouches decorated in the manner of cameos with plaques of hard stones, Beurdeley transposed this decoration into bronze. The eagle on the lower part of the left door, for instance, is found on the walls of the Salon des Jeux, while the sphinxes in the left center panel and the woman holding two lamps in the center right panel appear in the boudoir. Similar Pompeian taste was found in English furniture in 1867 (see Burty, 1868, "Le Mobilier moderne," pp. 31, 33, 35). One can compare other motifs with Louis XVI bronzes. The two little satyrs playing trumpets, on the left upper door, is a frequent motif in Louis XVI friezes like the one that decorates a commode then in Saint-Cloud (Williamson, 1883–85, vol. II, pl. 88; now at Compiègne); the motif supporting the satyrs is related to Louis XVI candelabra bases (see Williamson, 1883–85, vol. II, pl. 94). The reliefs with the basket are reminiscent of the handles of Marie Antoinette's cylinder desk from the Tuileries, then kept at Saint-Cloud (Williamson, 1883–85, vol. II, pl. 81; Louvre); the garland of the bottom central panel was without a doubt inspired by the pair of commodes in Marie Antoinette's

II-18

Salon des Jeux at Compiègne in which the queen's monogram was designed in flowers (at that time in the Empress's bedroom at Saint-Cloud; *see* Praz, 1964, pp. 350–51); on both sides the two foliated scrolls ending in rosettes seem to be adapted from the ones on a regulator by Riesener (Williamson, 1883–85, vol. II, pl. 61; Louvre), which was then at the Tuileries.

D.A.

Collection Mr. and Mrs. T. C. Morrow, Houston, Texas

---

## Braquenié Frères

### Alexandre Braquenié
*Born Tournai–1879 Paris*

### Henri-Charles Braquenié
*Tournai c. 1815–1897 Paris*

*The carpet dealer Demy-Doineau, who was established in Paris at 8, rue de Buci (Almanach du Commerce, 1833), then at 16, rue Vivienne and 10, rue de Buci (Almanach du Commerce, 1834–44), took Alexandre Braquenié as a partner, remaining at 16, rue Vivienne (Almanach du Commerce, 1845–51). The firm's name became Braquenié et Cie (Almanach du Commerce, 1852), then Braquenié Frères on May 8, 1857 (see Almanach du Commerce, 1858). Such was the origin of the Braquenié carpet and tapestry manufacture, still located today at 16, rue Vivienne, and in Aubusson. The firm received a medal in London in 1851, then a gold medal in Paris in 1855. Following an agreement with the comte Descantons de Montblanc, baron of Ingelmunster (Belgium), the Braqueniés established a workshop there from 1855 to 1869. In 1862 they participated in the decoration of the headquarters of the Commission Impériale at the London exhibition and received a medal. In 1867 they received a gold medal in Aubusson and a silver one in Ingelmunster, while five of their employees received awards, including the designer Jules Leblanc. After the Ingelmunster factory closed, they set up another in Mechelen. Their production was partly inspired by the past (Henri collected antique tapestries), but designs were also furnished by such artists as Pierre-Victor Galland and Alexis-Joseph Mazerolle, collaborators at Gobelins; the designer Eugène Adan (silver medal as coopérateur, 1867); and, after 1870, Fernand Thesmar. The firm's archives contain watercolor designs that sometimes give clients' names. The Braqueniés received commissions from the Garde Meuble and supplied a large French and foreign clientele, executing carpets for the dining room of the Dolma-Bahçe palace in Constantinople*

II-19

*(c. 1856), for Prince Soltykoff, Princess Bacciochi, and the Ministère d'Etat (the present Ministère des Finances). Among their tapestries were Mazerolle's* Sleeping Beauty *(exhibited 1862);* Perrault's Tales, *after Gustave-Adolphe Jundt (1866); and those presented in 1867: Mazerolle's* Industry, *Galland's* War *and* Peace, *a Louis XVI set by Adan, a Louis XVI set representing the* Fables of La Fontaine, *reproductions of paintings, and a screen copying the Gobelins* Grotesque Months.

D.A.

Bibliography:
Braquenié Archives; Arch. nat. F¹² 3042 [Exposition Universelle of 1867]; *L'Art du Dix-Neuvième Siècle*, vols. I–VI (1856–61); *Rapports 1855*, pp. 1081, 1086; *Catalogue 1862*, p. 151; Darcel, 1863, p. 83; *Récompensés 1867*, group III, pp. 25–26, 29–30; *Rapports 1867*, vol. III, p. 188; *Rapports des délégations 1867*, vol. III, "Peintres décorateurs," pp. 3–4; Luchet, 1868, pp. 268–69; Dussieux, 1876, p. 388; Champier, 1896, p. 375; sale, H. Braquenié, Paris, Hôtel Drouot, May 18, 1897, rooms 5, 6; sale, Mme H. Braquenié, Paris, Hôtel Drouot, December 15–16, 1902, room 1

Attributed to Braquenié Frères

## II-19
## Sofa

c. 1860
Monogram CPDB under ducal crown on back; monogram CPB on sides
Waxed oak, tapestry
Height 110 cm; width 220 cm; depth 70 cm

Provenance:
Part of a suite of furniture executed for Charles-

Jérôme, comte and later first duc Pozzo di Borgo (1791–1879), cavalry colonel, and his wife Victurnienne-Louise-Valentine des Balbes Berton de Crillon (1813–1890), daughter of the last duc de Crillon, who were married in 1832; made for the grand salon of the château of Montretout at Saint-Cloud (Hauts-de-Seine); private coll.

The château of Montretout, which already existed in the seventeenth century and was later restored, was acquired by the future duc Pozzo di Borgo in 1841. After the fighting in 1870–71, it was once more restored in 1871, then re-erected at Dangu (Eure) in 1896 by the nephew and successor of the first duc (Marie, 1966, pp. 92–94). The furnishings still accompanying the sofa consist of a second similar sofa, ten armchairs, eight chairs, and eight pairs of curtains designed for the three rectangular windows and five arched windows of the salon that occupies the whole right side of the château. Originally there may have been additional seats, including two other sofas. Few ensembles of this kind, though numerous then, seem to remain today. For seating, Louis XV forms had reappeared at the time of Louis Philippe. Under the Second Empire in general, the earlier models were more respected, as is shown by the form and the carved decoration of the sofa. These Louis XV seats could be gilded or painted in black, but it is well known that in spite of the taste of the period for richness of appearance, natural wood was also appreciated, sometimes to the point of scraping the gilding off old seats. Unlike those of the eighteenth century, the sofa is upholstered on all its sides. On this ensemble, the flower basket suspended from a ribbon on the back of the sofa, like the bouquet of flowers tied with a ribbon that adorns all the seats, is in harmony with the wood and evokes, by their rather Louis XVI inspiration, certain furnishings created by Chabal-Dussurgey (q.v.) for the Beauvais factory (see Williamson, 1883–85, vol. II, pls. 68, 82). The monogram formed of flowers and foliage, frequent in the eighteenth century, also appears under the ducal crown at the center of the curtains and on the backs of the armchairs and chairs. An undulating ribbon around which wind flowers and foliage separates the central motifs from the red background.

Charles-Jérôme Pozzo di Borgo probably ordered this furniture in the years following the granting of the ducal title by letters patent of the king of Naples on November 29, 1852. Braquenié seems to have worked a great deal for the several residences of the duke. Two watercolor designs preserved in the factory archives allow us to attribute the execution of this furniture to him. Each represents a covering for a sofa with Louis XV lines, whose back displays

in the center the Pozzo di Borgo and Crillon arms under the ducal crown and on both sides a cartouche enclosing the monogram PC under the same crown. In one of the designs, bearing the notation "Duc Pozzo," the back and the seat, with green background, are decorated also with Louis XIV floral scrolls. The sofa with the yellow background of the other design, the execution of which was ordered in June 1856, was intended to have no wood showing; the decoration, more Louis XVI and close to that of the present sofa, consists of flowers on the back, between the arms and the monograms, as well as on the seat, both being surrounded also by a ribbon and intertwined flowers.

D.A.

Private Collection

## Emile-Auguste Reiber
### 1826–1893

*Of Alsatian origin, Reiber began his architectural studies in Paris with Blouet. In 1850 he won the Grand Prix. He became more and more involved in industrial design and together with his fellow Alsatian, the ceramist Deck (q.v.) he founded the magazine L'Art pour Tous, which specialized in the applications of art to industry. Christofle (q.v.) named him chef des dessinateurs of its workshops, and it was in this capacity that he furnished a large quantity of designs, some of which were put into production (drawings and designs in the Christofle Archives).*

*Reiber was distinguished for the rapidity with which he was able to find an inexhaustible source of inspiration in the various styles he studied. One after the other he used the German Renaissance, Louis XVI, and the Antique, and from 1869 on, Japanese art was for him a remarkable discovery. His work contributed greatly to the revival of silverwork forms and is a fine example of the role architects played in the evolution of the decorative arts under the Second Empire.*

C.S.-V

Bibliography:
Ménard, 1876, pp. 186–89; Bouilhet, 1908–12, vol. III, pp. 105–14

## Gustave-Joseph Chéret
### Paris 1838–1894 Paris

*Gustave-Joseph Chéret, older brother by two years of the designer and graphic artist Jules Chéret, was apprenticed to the ornamentalist Gallois, then to Carrier-Belleuse (q.v.) in about 1860. The sculptor's exuberant personality was to dominate Chéret's life; moreover, in 1868, he married Marie, one of Carrier's five daughters. The bust Carrier-Belleuse did of her when she was seven is now in the Louvre (RF 2502). In 1887 Chéret succeeded Carrier-Belleuse for a few months as chef des travaux d'art at the Sèvres factory. (He had competed for the Prix de Sèvres since 1875, and finally won it in 1879.)*

*Chéret worked for Derville, Guérin, Huillard, Menier, Pereire (mantels for Godillot, Gravier, Zamoïsky) but received very few official commissions. However, his designs were widely distributed by his atelier as well as by Baccarat (q.v.), Christofle (q.v.), Delpy, Royer, and E. Soleau. Some of his models are still featured in the Sèvres catalogue.*

*His work was exhibited in the Salon (only twice during the Second Empire; Flowers in 1863 and a medallion of the Empress in 1865) and then in the Société Nationale des Beaux-Arts. He was named chevalier of the Legion of Honor in 1894 on the occasion of the Chicago World's Columbian exhibition.*

A.P.

Bibliography:
Sale, Paris, Hôtel Drouot, December 26–29, 1894; Morin, 1894; Lami, 1914–21, vol. I, pp. 371–75

Paul Christofle and Henri Bouilhet; designed by Emile-Auguste Reiber, modeled by Albert-Ernest Carrier-Belleuse and Gustave-Joseph Chéret

## II-20
## Dressing Table

1867
Signed on top of drawer: P. Christofle & H. Bouilhet orfèvres/E. Reiber dessinateur, Paris 1867/Carrier Belleuse & J. Chéret sculpt
Silver, gilded silver, gold, lapis lazuli, jasper
Height 70 cm; width 95 cm; depth 62 cm

Provenance:
Purchased from the Exposition Universelle of 1867 by Mme Isaac Pereire; Messrs. A. and J. Pereire; gift to the Musée des Arts Décoratifs, 1938 (inv. no. 33777)

Exhibitions:
1867, Paris, Exposition Universelle; 1900, Paris, Exposition Universelle Centennaire; 1964, Paris, Musée

des Arts Décoratifs; 1965, Paris, Bibliothèque Nationale (not in catalogue)

Bibliography:
*L'Illustration,* October 5, 1867, p. 217, repro. p. 216; Mesnard, 1867, vol. I, p. 93; M. Chevalier, in *Rapports 1867,* vol. III, p. 277; Burty, 1868, p. 40; Bouilhet, 1908–12, vol. III, pp. 70–73, repro. p. 79; Demoriane, 1961, repro. p. 78, no. 5; Keim, 1930, vol. IV, p. 6, no. 5

The focal point of Christofle's display in 1867 was a masterful piece, a silver dressing table fitted with accessories and surmounted by a mirror. The official reports on the exposition do not describe this table because, as a member of the jury, Christofle was excluded from competition, but all unofficial accounts mention this exceptional piece, which displayed the skills of the chasers of the ateliers and the new investigations that had been made in different metals. The front legs are formed of two caryatids in gilded bronze, carrying baskets of flowers on their heads. The back legs, both fluted, have Ionic capitals. The legs are linked together by a curved ebony stretcher which is laced with a garland of bronze flowers in two shades, red and yellow. In the center, a base of acanthus leaves supports a red jasper sphere on which rests a bronze cupid holding a bow and a crown of flowers. The apron is in lapis, covered with scrolls and garlands of lilacs and jasmine in gilded bronze, with two cupids in the center, holding a crown above an urn overflowing with strings of pearls. The top is red jasper from Mont Blanc, with a border of Persian lapis, encrusted with silver-gilt fretwork and daisies.

The design for the table is by Emile Reiber, then *chef des dessinateurs* for Christofle, who asked Carrier-Belleuse to model the caryatids and Chéret, the ornaments. The table was originally surmounted by an oval mirror attributed to the sculptor Charles Gumery: two female figures, Art and Nature, flanking the mirror, leaned against candelabra with three scrolled branches. (Another dressing table by Christofle, much simpler but surmounted by a similar mirror, was shown in Paris in 1892 and in 1922 (1922, Paris, Musée des Arts Décoratifs, no. 556.) This piece was completed by the toilet accessories, a water jar, pommade jars, and a ring holder with cupids, ribbons, and flowers, which also have disappeared.

This very well preserved table displays a strong Louis XVI influence. One cannot help but compare it to the little writing table executed by Weisweiler for Marie Antoinette and purchased by the Empress Eugénie in 1865 at the prince de Beauvau's sale, which has the same legs with caryatids, the same richly chased bronzes. But Reiber put his personal stamp on it, especially the cupid on the base

II-20

which evokes a carved wooden rocaille console, thus displaying the eclecticism so dear to the ornamentalists of the period.

C.S.-V.

Musée des Arts Décoratifs, Paris

---

## Michel-Victor Cruchet

*Active Paris from c. 1836*

*Established by 1836, Cruchet worked for the Mobilier de la Couronne during the reign of Louis Philippe. In June 1845 he furnished for the grand salon of the duc de Nemours in the Tuileries a model for an andiron in the style of Louis XIV copied from an engraving by Bérain and executed by the founder Chaumont (preserved at Fontainebleau; Arch. nat. AJ[19] 652), and in 1847, a set of wooden Louis XV-style chairs for the audience chamber of the duc de Nemours at the Tuileries (Arch. nat. AJ[19] 652; sent to Fontainebleau under Napoléon III for the Council Hall).*

*Under the Second Empire no less prestigious orders came to Cruchet as a result of his skill and his reputation. When richly carved chairs or consoles based on ancient models or on modern designs were needed, it was to him that the administration came. Among the orders listed by Ledoux-Lebard, it should be noted that the sofa, six chairs, and three stools delivered on November 10, 1857, were intended for the salon in apartment A in the palace of Compiègne, and that the console and bed canopy in the Louis XVI style, executed for Fontainebleau in 1860, were accompanied by a screen, two armchairs, and four chairs, made to match the bed and two earlier armchairs from Louis XVI's bedroom at Saint-Cloud (installed in the bedroom of the "Louis XV" apartment at Fontainebleau, where they remain today). In addition, Cruchet executed in 1855 a luxurious salon ensemble in the style of Louis XVI, inspired by Georges Jacob, which was upholstered in Beauvais tapestry and installed at Saint-Cloud (Mobilier National). Finally, one of Cruchet's most notable works was the decoration in 1856 of the small salon of the Emperor facing the orangerie at Saint-Cloud (Arch. nat. F[21] 3425B). The creator of the carton-pierre ceiling ornaments, the carved woodwork, and the marble mantelpiece, all in the Louis XVI style, Cruchet displayed a dazzling virtuosity in this room, known today only from a few stereoscopic views.*

J.-P.S.

Bibliography:
Williamson, 1883–85, vol. I, pl. 82; Ledoux-Lebard, 1965, p. 118

Michel-Victor Cruchet

## II-21
## Table

1858
Carved and gilded wood, red cloth inset
Height 88 cm; width 198 cm; depth 158 cm

Provenance:
Delivered in 1858 for the salon of apartment A, château of Compiègne; transferred to the Musée du Second Empire (inv. no. C 536 C)

Bibliography:
*Palais de Compiègne,* n.d., vol. I, pl. 89

This oval center table entered Compiègne October 18, 1858, for the salon of apartment A, reserved for important guests. It was part of a large order for carvings given to Cruchet to furnish this room, formerly the salon of Marie Antoinette, in a style in keeping with its wall decoration. Inspired by a gilded wooden armchair by Georges Jacob, richly carved with garlands of laurel leaves (one of a set of eight sent from the château of Fontainebleau), Cruchet made new wooden seat frames: a sofa, six chairs, and three stools, then another sofa and four small settees, the last having been gilded by the *doreur* Mars (Fontainebleau Archives; Arch. nat. 0⁵ 1681, AJ¹⁹ 1027, AJ¹⁹ 1028). At the same time, Cruchet and Mars delivered for this room two large consoles in the Louis XVI style to be set under the large mirrors, three small consoles in the same style to go between the windows, and this "large center table, six legs, four turned and carved, two as consoles, a scrollwork frieze with cast central motifs, stretcher below with a vase of fruits, etc..., all carved and gilded, 2 m by 60 c. 1,650 fr, on top a purplish cloth 32,30 fr, total 1,682,30 fr" (Arch. nat. AJ¹⁹ 692, fol. 30 [March 23, 1859]). The entry slip for the consoles and table at Compiègne specifies that they were in carved wood, painted white and varnished, which might lead one to suppose that a change of design took place during their execution. However, one can

be sure they graced the salon ungilded for more than ten years, because on May 15, 1869, they were sent to the Garde Meuble with these instructions: "In accordance with the wishes of the Empress, these pieces of furniture are to be gilded." They were returned to Compiègne on November 18, 1869 (Compiègne Archives).

This history is interesting from several points of view. In 1858 the consoles and the table were viewed as harmonizing with the woodwork of the salon, most of which was white (only the mirror frames and certain parts of the high relief carving were then gilded). By 1869 a discord was felt between the woodwork and the seating, gilded from the first. The modifications of 1869 again underscore the Empress's role in furnishing the palace, aside from that of her own living quarters.

The center table itself was designed by Cruchet to go with his consoles. It has the appearance of having been made up of two large consoles joined together, which explains the rather surprising volutes at the long ends of the oval; six similar legs would be more usual so that the table could be viewed in the same way from any angle. The carving is fine, almost too fine, a reminder that Cruchet was a specialist in carton-pierre ornaments and thus accustomed to great ease in rendering details.

C.S.-V.

Musée National du Château, Compiègne

II-21

## Aimé-Jules Dalou
*Paris 1838–1902 Paris*

Son of a Paris glover with strong Republican sympathies, Dalou followed the advice of Carpeaux (q.v.) and enrolled at the Petit Ecole in 1852. In 1854 he entered the Ecole des Beaux-Arts, in the atelier of Duret. Yet, despite these connections, he failed four times to win the Prix de Rome.

Dalou began to exhibit at the Salon in 1861, but it was only in 1869 that his group Daphnis and Chloë, *singled out for attention by Thoré and Gautier and bought by the State, was commissioned to be edited in marble. The* Embroiderer *also was well received at the following Salon, the last of the Second Empire, but neither commission was to be executed.*

When Dalou, whose outlook was akin to that of Courbet (q.v.) and Millet (q.v.) (Roujon, in Dreyfous, 1903, p. 111), embarked on his career, he had worked for bronze manufacturers, silversmiths, and in the rich Second Empire society, in a style quite alien to his own nature (caryatids in the rue Lafayette, winged figures in the rue de la Paix, the Hôtel de Païva, Hôtel Menier, Hôtel André). He was unusually sensitive to his environment, and during his exile in England, produced works depicting everyday occupations, beginning with The Embroiderer—*the descendent of* The Winder *by Salmson (no. V-33). On his return to France he worked on the large didactic compositions celebrating the men and ideals of the Third Republic. However, it was through his sketches, especially the studies made for the* Monument to the Workers, *that Dalou most clearly expressed, in a modern sense, his artistic personality, another aspect of which is revealed in the letter he wrote to the director of the Arts Orphanage (Bibliothèque Doucet ms 37, sculp.) in order to settle his estate and the inheritance of his daughter Georgette, which was to pave the way for the many posthumous editions of his works.*

A.P.

Bibliography:
Dreyfous, 1903; Caillaux, 1935; Hunisak, 1977

Aimé-Jules Dalou; supervised by Albert-Ernest Carrier-Belleuse

## II-22
## Console

1864–65
Bronze, gilded bronze, colored marbles
Height 110 cm; width 161 cm; depth 58 cm

Provenance:
Executed with three other identical consoles in 1864–65 for the Hôtel de Païva on the Champs Elysées; remained in the hôtel in 1902 after the dispersal of the furnishings; sold, apparently, before 1904, the date the hôtel was acquired by the Travellers Club; John Guille Millais, England; Raoul Millais; sale, London, Christies, November 24, 1960, no. 59 (repro.); purchased with funds bequeathed by Florence Scott Libbey by the Toledo Museum of Art (inv. no. 60.32)

Exhibition:
Possibly 1922, Paris, Musée des Arts Décoratifs, no. 541 (as collection of Sir Georges Donaldson)

Bibliography:
Houssaye, 1896, pls. 5, 11, 13; Champier, 1901, pp. 224, 256; Dreyfous, 1903, p. 20; Le Senne, 1910, p. 20; Clouzot, 1939, pl. 17; Verlet, 1972, vol. II, p. 193; Olander, 1974; Hargrove, 1977, pp. 152–55; Hunisak, 1977, pp. 44–47

The construction and decoration of the hôtel of the marquise de Païva on the Champs Elysées was an important achievement in the history of decorative arts under the Second Empire. This hôtel, built in the Renaissance style under the direction of the architect Pierre Manguin (q.v.), stands as a monument to what an architect can accomplish with complete financial freedom (the millions of Count Henckel von Donnersmarck), limited only by its "commissioner's" view of its construction as a manifestation of power and social ascendancy rather than as a display of aesthetics or good taste. The systematic use of colored marbles, malachite, and gilded, patinated, and silvered bronze, betrays the origin and career of the mistress of the house, but the architect's role was certainly the decisive one. How could the

director of such a project fail to become excited by the new possibilities open to him? He brought together sculptors (Carrier-Belleuse, Legrain, Delaplanche, Dalou), painters (Baudry, q.v., Barrias, Thirion, Picou, Ranvier), cabinetmakers (Kneib), bronze manufacturers (Barbedienne, q.v.), forming ateliers that worked right before his eyes, perfecting all of the decorative details of each piece. He achieved a great homogeneity in the overall decoration and a luxury of detail that only an architect constantly in attendance and solely occupied with this endeavor could obtain.

Carrier-Belleuse (q.v.) was in charge of the many sculptures whose heroic figures abound on fireplaces and ceilings. He was already an established artist and his sculptures for the hôtel in 1865—the Venus and Cupid fountain, the two silvered caryatids on the bedroom fireplace, and his sculptures for the *jardin d'hiver*—are all done in his mannerist style. Carrier-Belleuse enlisted the help of younger sculptors, especially Dalou, to whom Manguin entrusted a certain number of prestigious works in 1864 and 1865: the large fireplace in the dining room and the Diana in the center of the ceiling, the library fireplace and various reliefs for this room. Lami (1914–21, vol. IV, p. 6) credited him also with the atlantes supporting the four consoles in the grand salon, and since then all catalogues and monographs list them under his name, although older monographs, especially Champier's well-documented article, attribute them to Carrier-Belleuse. Perhaps, as Dreyfous

suggests (more recently Hunisak, 1977, and Hargrove, 1977), the work could be by Carrier-Belleuse, with certain details simply retouched by Dalou before being cast by Barbedienne.

Whoever the artist, these superb consoles, with their majestic proportions, are arresting. The idea of atlantes bearing a table top was not new. It was obviously taken from Italian seventeenth-century consoles and cabinets.

These consoles, part of the architecture of the room, were not taken to Silesia by the Henckels von Donnersmarck after the Franco-Prussian War along with most the furnishings of the hôtel. Because of their material and their size they would hardly have been considered furniture. They are entirely of bronze: the base, in gilded bronze, rests on five feet and has a ring in the center to hold a vase; the atlantes are of "Florentine bronze," young Ephebes with curly hair and sweet expressions (very Italianate, but also close to Carpeaux, q.v.); the top and border are of colored marble framed with gilded bronze.

The consoles, however exceptional they may be, are by virtue of their similarity with the rest of the décor of the hôtel, especially the caryatids found in most of the pieces, an example of the search for unity of decorative style under the Second Empire, a unity fostered here, as in most instances, by the dominant role played by the architects.

C.S.-V.

The Toledo Museum of Art, Gift of Florence Scott Libbey

II-22

## Charles-Guillaume Diehl

*Steinbach (Hesse) 1811– c.1885*

*Settling in Paris in 1840, Diehl founded a factory, which was located on rue Michel le Comte at number 16 (Almanach du Commerce, 1850, the first year it was listed), later at 21 (Almanach du Commerce, 1851–52), then at 19 (Almanach du Commerce, 1853–55). In his large workshops 600 workers were employed in 1870. Diehl simultaneously provided all kinds of coffrets (necessaries, liquor cabinets, game boxes, tea caddies, boxes for gloves, shawls, pins, and jewels) as well as small furnishings ("Boule-style, rosewood, and thuja pieces, fancy items with bronzes and porcelain, drawing-room tables, ladies' work tables and dressing tables, novelties in small furnishings and meubles de mariage, faïence cachepots mounted on legs"). His production included both ordinary pieces and deluxe objects, among them those executed especially for the expositions and which in 1855 won him a bronze medal. In 1867 he was awarded a silver medal in the category of tabletterie (fancy goods), thanks to his coffrets of all styles and materials, the most original at the exposition, while his master cabinetmaker, Kowalewski, was awarded an honorable mention also in the same category as coopérateur. However, for his deluxe furniture he won only a bronze medal, which he refused. Diehl was later to receive a Medal of Honor at the Union Centrale exhibition in 1869, and a Medal of Progress in Vienna in 1873. Becoming a French citizen in 1872, he was by 1878* hors concours.

D.A.

Bibliography:
Arch. nat. F[12] 5129 [Legion of Honor]; *Rapports 1855*, pp. 1124, 1205; *Récompensés 1867*, group III, pp. 5, 63, 68; Mesnard, 1867, vol. I, pp. 178–83, vol. II, pp. 129–35, 148–51; *Rapports 1867*, vol. III, pp. 446–47; Luchet, 1868, pp. 105–7, 114, 241–43, 248; Ledoux-Lebard, 1965, pp. 140–41

## E. Brandely

*Active Paris*

*An industrial designer, well acquainted with manufacturing, "a bold, strange artist, an enterprising man with spontaneity" (Luchet), Brandely provided plans for furniture and designs for marquetry. At the Exposition Universelle of 1855 his designs won a silver medal, while thanks to the inlaid furniture executed from his plans and exhibited by various cabinetmakers and* tabletiers *(makers of fancy work)—Cremer, Giroux, Lemoine, Tahan—he received a bronze medal as a* coopérateur *in the category of furnishings. For the 1867 exposition, where he himself received no*

II-23

*award, he worked in collaboration with Diehl, Beurdeley (q.v.), and Tahan, whose small pieces won a gold medal. In 1867 he lived at 230, rue du Faubourg Saint Antoine (Almanach du Commerce).*

D.A.

Bibliography:
*Rapports 1855*, pp. 1155, 1225–26; Luchet, 1868, pp. 241–45

Charles-Guillaume Diehl; designed by E. Brandely; bas-reliefs by Emmanuel Frémiet

## II-23
## Medal Cabinet

1867
Signed on central bas-relief, lower left: E. FRE-MIET, beneath the lower edge: BRANDELY DIEHL FREMIET; inscribed on the door hinge: Exposition Universelle/1867/Exposition de Vienne/1873/DIEHL/19, rue Michel-le-Comte/PARIS
Oak; veneer of cedar, walnut, ebony, and ivory; silvered bronze
Height 238 cm; width 151 cm; depth 60 cm; central bas-relief 102.5 × 67 cm

Provenance:
Executed for the Exposition Universelle of 1867; purchased in Paris by the opera singer Nicolas-Marie Simon, known as Simon-Max (1848–1923); daughter, Mme René Martin; sale, Paris, Hôtel Drouot, April 9, 1973, room 6, no. 40 (repro.); acquired by the Louvre (inv. no. OA 10440)
Exhibitions:
1867, Paris, Exposition Universelle; 1873, Vienna
Bibliography:
*The Art Journal*, 1867, p. 151 (repro.); Mesnard, 1867, vol. I, pp. 178–81 (repro.), vol. II, p. 132; Luchet, 1868, pp. 105–6; *Rapports des délégations 1867*, vol. I, "Découpeurs marqueteurs," p. 12 (repro.), "Dessinateurs d'ameublement," pp. 33–34 (repro.); Vitry, 1898, pp. 67–68 (repro.)

Brandely designed the form, inlays, and bronzes of this medal cabinet, which was exhibited at the 1867 Exposition Universelle and described there as "Merovingian in style" (Mesnard, 1867), "a Gaulish piece" (Luchet, 1868), "a large Gaulish piece in Romanesque style" (*Rapports des délégations 1867*). Its architectural design did not make use of a Classical vocabulary: capitals, bases, and pediments are replaced by original motifs. Most of the exterior displays a cedar veneer interrupted in the frames either by a walnut veneer with applied walnut reliefs, or a marquetry decoration, Diehl's specialty. This marquetry was highly praised in the "Rapport des Découpeurs marqueteurs," one of whose three authors, Au-

guste Levallois, worked on the piece, making the door frame, while Jules Labarre, Georges Lévy, and other craftsmen executed the marquetry on the sides, the inside of the door, and the drawers.

But it is in the "old silver" bronze decoration imitating oxydized silver, on this, the only piece of furniture on which Frémiet collaborated, that the significance of the object lies. The central bas-relief—following the traditional iconography for a triumph—represents the Frankish King Mérovée, who with the Roman general Aetius, defeated Attila at the Catalaunian Plains near Châlons-sur-Marne in 451. The bronzes of the frame amplify the central subject: at top center, before the sarcophagus of the Frankish leader, is a trophy of the Frankish weapons intertwined with mistletoe, which includes a horn hung with medals to evoke, as on eighteenth-century medal cabinets, the purpose of the piece. On the front uprights, above two ox hooves, appear two thistles, whose meaning is unclear. The door, with inlaid ebony thistles on the interior, "closes in a completely new fashion" (Mesnard, 1867), the hinges entering the piece by sliding. The interior displays two rows of twenty-five drawers each in solid walnut with handles front and back, the front inlaid with two thistles.

By turning to an official sculptor and exhibiting at the same time a large marble chest adorned in gilded bronze with the profiles of the sovereigns and imperial emblems (Mesnard, 1867, vol. II, repro. p. 131), Diehl hoped, according to Vitry, to sell this piece to the Emperor. The French theme may indeed have pleased Napoleon III, who in founding the Musée des Souverains in 1852 created a section for Merovingian antiquities. The inspiration, completely new, evokes the history of the past, but not its art. Brandely and Diehl created a new style in 1867 with this piece and three others in the Greek style. They were considered the most innovative at the exposition and aroused the enthusiasm of the critics. However, they do not seem to have had any influence.

Another version of the cabinet, probably executed at the same time, was kept by Diehl in his country house in Lagny until his death, when it was sold—according to Albert Dubosc, collector of works by Frémiet, who owned it in 1910 in Sainte-Adresse (de Biez, 1910, pp. 268, 280, repro. facing p. 252).

D.A.

Musée du Louvre, Paris

## Fourdinois

*Paris, established 1835*

*Fourdinois is the greatest name in Parisian cabinetmaking under the Second Empire. Alexandre-Georges Fourdinois founded the firm in 1835 and was in partnership with Fossey until 1848. He won a silver medal at the industrial expositions of 1844 and 1849, a Council Medal at the London Universal Exhibition of 1851, and the Grand Medal of Honor at the Exposition Universelle of 1855. His son Henri-Auguste (born 1830) studied with Duban (q.v.) and then worked with Morel (q.v.) and the bronze manufacturer Paillard (see no. II-5) before joining his father in 1860. At the London International Exhibition of 1862 the elder Fourdinois won two medals for excellence in composition and execution, and was made officer of the Legion of Honor. According to the 1863 trade directory, the factory had added upholstery to its activities, enabling it to execute "complete furnishings, simple, and rich." This expansion was probably due to the son, who brought the firm to its pinnacle at the Exposition Universelle of 1867, winning the Grand Prix in two classes, while five collaborators received medals or mentions.*

*In addition to its usual production, Fourdinois's ateliers also turned out grand pieces for expositions, its principal client, the Mobilier de la Couronne, and wealthy private clients (the bankers Pereire and Hottinguer, the Parisian businessman J.-F. Cail) and aristocrats taken with the past (comte de Saint-Laumer, comte de Cholet à Beauregard, vicomte de Boisgelin).*

*Even more than the Louis XVI style, from which he often took inspiration—sometimes brilliantly, as in the Empress's cheval glass for Saint-Cloud—Fourdinois's specialty seems to have been carved furniture in the Renaissance manner, the style of their masterpieces: the monumental marble, bronze, and carved-wood fireplace exhibited by the father in 1855 and in 1862; a carved ebony double-bodied cabinet by the younger Fourdinois, exhibited in London in 1862 ("one of the most superb furnishings that has ever been made"), and a stately cabinet on a columned base, shown in Paris in 1867, in which ebony is combined with hard stones and various woods in a veritable embroidery of sculptures (Bethnal Green Museum). Though less spectacular, the furnishings (1860) of the large bedroom of the apartment of Louis XIII in the château of Fontainebleau, in the same style, attest to the Fourdinoises' talents.*

J.-P.S.

Bibliography:
*Rapports 1855*, p. 1117; P. Merimée and E. du Sommerard, in *Rapports 1862*, vol. VI, pp. 266–67; *Magasin Pittoresque*, 1862, pp. 393–94; Waring, 1863, vol. I, pl. 47; Dalloz, 1867; J.-P.-M. Diéterle and J.-H. Pollen, in *Rapports 1867*, vol. III, p. 21; Reybaud, 1867, p. 957; Burty, 1868, "Le Mobilier moderne," pp. 34–36; *Magasin Pittoresque*, 1868, pp. 41–42, 369–70; Ledoux-Lebard, 1965, pp. 180–83

II - 24

Alexandre-Georges Fourdinois

## II-24
## Cheval Glass

1855
Mahogany and gilded bronze
Height 232 cm; width 127 cm; depth 66 cm

Provenance:
Entered dressing room of the Empress at Saint-Cloud,
1855; Mobilier National, 1875; Musée National du
Château, Compiègne, 1928 (inv. no. C 28.054)
Exhibition:
1922, Paris, Musée des Arts Décoratifs, no. 607
Bibliography:
Dumonthier, 1923, pl. 45; Demoraine, 1961, p. 81

This sumptuous cheval glass, or *psyché*, deposited by the Mobilier National in the château of Compiègne, had lacked a provenance. Mistaken even at the time of its entrance into the Mobilier Impérial for another and simpler *psyché* produced by Fourdinois in painted wood, it did not bear the Saint-Cloud inventory marks, which would have made it possible to identify it with certainty as the one depicted in the watercolors of Fortuné de Fournier showing the dressing room of the Empress at Saint-Cloud (one dated 1855, belonging to H.M. the Queen of England; Hayward, 1964, p. 229, pl. 4; the other, no. II-2, dated 1860, at Compiègne) and in a number of stereoscopic views of the same period (Bib. nat.; Bibliothèque Forney).

On April 20, 1855, Fourdinois delivered to the Garde Meuble, without a precise destination, "a Louis XVI-style *psyché* in varnished mahogany with richly chased bronzes, gilded with a mat finish, escutcheon at top with the monograms of Their Majesties in painted enamel on emerald green background; holders for two lights at each column with mirrors, double casters with rollers," valued at 8,000 francs (Arch. nat. Aj[19] 687). And this same *psyché* is found in the entry register of Saint-Cloud for 1855 listed in the Empress's dressing room (Louvre Archives 37 DD 36). Placed there before Queen Victoria's visit in August 1855, it escaped the fire in 1870, since its reentry in the Garde Meuble was recorded on December 31, 1875 (Arch. nat. Aj[19] 1057).

This *psyché* is closely related to a number of earlier examples. The rectangular framing, fluted columns, and vases at the corners can also be found on certain Louis XVI *psychés*, at the very beginning of the production of this type of piece. The similarities with certain screens of the same period are equally striking. The oval mirror, conceived by Percier, made its appearance under the Empire, and the best-known example is an oval *psyché* at Compiègne. Fourdinois's combination of an oval mirror with a rectangular frame (with, it is true, a rounded top, as in even the simplest *psychés* designed by this cabinetmaker) has something illogical about it. But one hardly notices it, so striking is the richness of the bronzes. The whole Louis XVI decorative repertoire—Vitruvian scrolls, branches of roses tied by a ribbon, foliated scrolls, tiny flowers in the fluting, Ionic capitals, doves at the top—are all combined in a well-ordered sumptuosity. A piece of furniture of this kind designed for a palace or the grand pieces made for the Expositions Universelles were the most spectacular aspect of Fourdinois's work. But it should not be forgotten that most of the activity of his workshops—and the countless designs by him and his son preserved in the Bibliothèque Forney are proof of it—was directed toward a much simpler production for private clients and the ministries.

C.S.-V.
Musée National du Château, Compiègne

Alexandre-Georges Fourdinois

## II-25
## Cabinet

1855
Carved walnut
Height 297 cm; width 122 cm; depth 61 cm

Provenance:
Purchased from the manufacturer at the Exposition
Universelle of 1855, Paris, by the South Kensington
Museum (now Victoria and Albert Museum) (inv. no.
2692-1856)
Bibliography:
*Rapports 1855*, p. 1117

In 1851 at the close of the Universal Exhibition in London, the English government bought numerous objects that would constitute at the South Kensington Museum an illustration of the best of what was being done in the industrial arts abroad, as much from a purely technical point of view as from an artistic one. Such a policy was continued at the time of the Exposition Universelle of 1855 (when Queen Victoria and Prince Albert went to Paris especially to visit the exposition and bought several pieces of furniture there; *see* no. II-29). Thus it was that Alexandre-Georges Fourdinois, whose contribution in 1851 had been already well recognized, saw the South Kensington Museum buy this double-bodied cabinet in the sixteenth-century style. In 1867 the same museum would also buy a magnificent carved ebony cabinet, inlaid with various woods, by his son Henri Fourdinois.

The work shown here was directly inspired by the so-called Ile-de-France cabinets. Highly architectural in feeling, with caryatids in the lower parts, columns and a broken pediment on the upper part, it is a manifestation of the taste for the Renaissance that swept France from the time of the reign of Louis Philippe.

The most remarkable aspect of this cabinet is its carved decoration: scrolls in very low relief on the sides, motifs in higher relief on the front. In the upper part candelabra and arabesques surround oval medallions; below are niches from which putti emerge. The medallions represent allegorical figures in a complex iconography symbolizing day and night, and are very close to certain oval medallions found on Renaissance cabinets. The same type of sculpture is found in later works by Henri Fourdinois, for example, the low cabinets in the bedroom of the apartment of Louis XIII at Fontainebleau (1860) or the pieces delivered to each of the Pereire brothers (Bibliothèque Forney, recueils de dessins Fourdinois, 5914, I, III).

The lower part is carved in very high relief.

The two putti in the niches are not quite Renaissance in style; rather they seem more like eighteenth-century cupids (and moreover, they are out of proportion with their niches). In addition, the caryatids seem to be inspired more by certain Italian engravings than by the sculptures of Goujon.

This piece attracted the attention of the critics at the exposition of 1855 where Fourdinois won a Grand Medal of Honor. It was described as a "veritable masterpiece in execution, evoking the most stunning production of the sixteenth century" (*Rapports 1855*, p. 1117). The especially beautiful quality of the sculpture is what truly sets this piece apart from innumerable Henri II buffets that would be the pride of French dining rooms until the end of the century.

C.S.-V.

Victoria and Albert Museum, London

## Guillaume Grohé

*Wintersheim 1808–1885 Neuilly-sur-Seine*

*Born in Hesse-Darmstadt, Grohé worked as a cabinetmaker in Paris, and, in 1829, with his brother Jean-Michel, created under Louis Philippe the firm known as Grohé Frères. Jean-Michel retired in 1861, but Guillaume continued until 1884.*

*Grohé won an honorable mention at the Exposition des Produits de l'Industrie Française in 1834, a silver medal in 1839, and gold medals in 1844 and 1849, the Medal of Honor at the Exposition Universelle of 1855, and a Medal of Excellence at the London International Exhibition of 1862. As a member of the jury he was hors concours at the Exposition Universelle of 1867, but several of his employees won awards.*

*Grohé's production was as voluminous as it was eclectic; he seems to have readily adapted to shifts in fashion even if he himself did not initiate them. In 1834 he showed two ensembles, one Gothic, the other Egyptian; in 1839, among other things, a salon dresser in the Renaissance style, in 1844 an extraordinary Renaissance carved ebony double-bodied cabinet, decorated with bronze figures, which was exhibited again in 1855 and bought by Queen Victoria (Osborne House). The same year he showed furnishings in the sixteenth-century and Louis XVI styles. In fact, from the Louis Philippe period, Grohé began to take inspiration from seventeenth- and eighteenth-century styles (Chantilly), continuing under the Second Empire, "reproducing styles from every period" (Catalogue 1862, "Renseignements," p. 854).*

The orders he delivered to the Mobilier de la Couronne for the imperial palaces reveal his diversity. He did not limit himself to cabinetmaking; he also made consoles and carved wooden seats. The Administration ordered quality furnishings in the most diverse styles, dictating most of the designs and ideas: for instance, in the Louis XVI style, two consoles and two bedside tables (one at Fontainebleau) delivered for Saint-Cloud in 1855 and a cheval glass for the Empress's dressing room at the Tuileries in 1858 (Mobilier National); in the Neo-Empire style, an Amboyna gueridon (1858) and a mahogany console (1861); and in the Renaissance style, two sets of carved walnut seats and tables after designs by Ruprich-Robert (1860–63), all for Fontainebleau.

J.-P.S.

Bibliography:
Keim, 1930, vol. III; Ledoux-Lebard, 1965, pp. 215–18; Verlet, 1972, vol. II, p. 170; de Bellaigue, 1975

## Victor-Marie-Charles Ruprich-Robert
### Paris 1820–1887 Cannes

A student of Constant-Dufeux (q.v.), consequently on the fringe of the formal education of the Ecole des Beaux-Arts, Ruprich-Robert was marked throughout his life by this teaching. As inspecteur of historical monuments he took part in the restoration of numerous religious buildings (in Normandy and Haute-Garonne, for which he left many drawings and plans). His role in the evolution of ornamental design and decoration in France was particularly important. A teacher with Viollet-le-Duc (q.v.) at the Ecole Speciale de Dessin from 1843 (he was named professor in 1851), he developed there his theories on the history of French architecture and the study of ornament. They were presented in the numerous articles he published in the Revue de l'Architecture, and especially in his important Flore ornementale (Paris, 1866–76), in which he advocated a return to the study of nature. His theories, directly opposed to the academic doctrine of the imitation of the Antique, paved the way for the new movement that at the end of the century would lead to Art Nouveau.

Named architecte-dessinateur to the Mobilier de la Couronne, he furnished from 1856 on many projects for the decoration of the various imperial palaces (some of which have been preserved). Strong in its design, his furniture reflects well the archaeological taste of the Second Empire, being inspired by earlier styles, from the Renaissance to Louis XVI. It appears that the execution of the furniture

II-26

designed by Ruprich-Robert had by preference been entrusted to Guillaume Grohé.

C.S.-V.

Bibliography:
Dassy, 1887

Guillaume Grohé; designed by Victor-Marie-Charles Ruprich-Robert

## II-26
## Armchair

1860–63
Stamped under the belt and on the pediment
Walnut, carved and waxed; upholstered in red velvet
Height 148 cm; width 101 cm; depth 84 cm

Provenance:
Commissioned for the Gallery of Francis I in the château of Fontainebleau (inv. no. F 459 C)

Bibliography:
Lionnard de Lens, 1956, p. 38; Ledoux-Lebard, 1965, pp. 216–17

This armchair was commissioned in 1860 as part of a program for refurnishing the Gallery of

Francis I and the vestibule of the chapel of the château of Fontainebleau. Designs were requested from the architect Ruprich-Robert (the drawings are preserved in a private collection), and the execution of the furniture (one armchair and one table for each of the two rooms) was entrusted to Guillaume Grohé. The work was delayed, for in June 1862 it had not yet been completed. "It is acknowledged that the furniture for the vestibule of the reception hall, as well as the table and armchair for the Gallery of Francis I, will not be ready in time for the stay, and it will therefore be necessary to put everything back in place as in previous years. This fellow Grohé doesn't keep his word. Since we haven't had much to do this year in the palace, it is too bad that an arrangement that would have earned us some gratitude should have been postponed" (letter from Lafontinelle, inspecteur of the Mobilier Impérial, to Lamy, steward of the château, June 3, 1862, Fontainebleau Archives). The chair was finally delivered on March 13, 1863 (letter from Lafontinelle to Lamy, Fontainebleau Archives).

Of large proportions, this piece was a kind of guard's armchair, designed for the ushers on guard in the gallery. The back has a rounded pediment, surmounted by a scrolled strapwork cartouche. The arms are straight, supported by two large winged lions, the legs square in section. The general ornamentation consists chiefly of scrolled strapwork, acanthus leaves, and interlaced moldings.

There can be no doubt that Ruprich-Robert, in designing this Renaissance-style seat, took his inspiration from the woodwork in the Francis I Gallery, in particular the benches, which also have winged lions. The garlands of fruit on the pediment are likewise a clear reminder of the decoration of the gallery. Moreover, Ruprich-Robert had also supplied another design for this armchair, which was surmounted by a standing cupid, similarly close to some of the stuccoes in the gallery.

This armchair illustrates particularly well the desire, so characteristic of the period of the Second Empire, to adapt furniture to the decoration of the room for which it was made.

C.S.-V.

Musée National du Château, Fontainebleau

Guillaume Grohé; designed by Victor-Marie-Charles Ruprich-Robert

## II-27
## Table

1860–63
Walnut, carved and waxed
Height 74.5 cm; width 185 cm; depth 103 cm

Provenance:
Commissioned for the Gallery of Francis I in the château of Fontainebleau (inv. no. F 462 C)

Bibliography:
Lionnard de Lens, 1956, p. 38; Ledoux-Lebard, 1965, pp. 216–17

Like Grohé's armchair (no. II-26), this usher's table was commissioned from Grohé in 1860 and entered Fontainebleau on March 13, 1863 (Fontainebleau Archives). Some of the motifs are similar on both pieces, but their conception is very different. The chair aspires to be Renaissance in style by the motifs of its ornamentation, the importance of the back (perhaps a reminder of the high-backed chairs of the sixteenth century), and the use of carved natural wood—marking in the nineteenth century a return to the old traditions—but its general form is not copied from any earlier piece of furniture. The same cannot be said for the table. It represents a faithful transposition of the "fan-shaped" table, in which the legs consist of two symmetrical motifs forming consoles, this double motif being narrower at the base and expanding toward the top. Many tables of this type were engraved by Jacques Androuet du Cerceau in *Les Meubles* (c. 1560) (*see* Jervis, 1974, pls. 78–84).

Ruprich-Robert was content to adapt this model to the decoration of the Gallery of Francis I. The consoles consist of the lions in the form of winged chimeras taken from the benches, combined, in the center, with a cascade of fruits borrowed directly from the stuccoes of the gallery (frame of the fresco of *Lost Youth*). One might note that the knot of ribbon holding the fruit has a slight, and unexpected, Louis XVI appearance among the acanthus scrolls.

C.S.-V.

Musée National du Château, Fontainebleau

II-27

## Joseph-Pierre-François Jeanselme
*Died c. 1860*

## Charles-Joseph-Marie Jeanselme
*Born Paris 1827*

The firm of Jeanselme, created in 1824, is one of the great names of nineteenth-century Parisian cabinetry. Its name changed several times: Jeanselme Frères (1824–40); Jeanselme (1840–54); Jeanselme Père et Fils (1854–62); Jeanselme Fils, Godin et Cie (from 1862). At first a chair joinery, Jeanselme prospered and acquired the stock of the firm of Jacob-Desmalter in 1847, which led to the decision to make all kinds of furniture. Jeanselme participated in various expositions, winning in 1849 a silver medal; in 1851 a prize medal at the Universal Exposition in London; in 1855 a first-class medal and the Legion of Honor; and in 1867 a silver medal. In 1855, besides gilded-wood salon chairs, the firm exhibited an armoire in carved oak forming an arms rack, a dining room buffet in black wood highlighted by gilded bronzes, and a small bookcase "in the style of the reign of Henri II." By then, the manufactory was employing more than 300 workers. In 1863–64, the company extended its activities to upholstery.

A supplier to the Mobilier de la Couronne since the reign of Louis Philippe, Jeanselme usually received orders for chairs from the Administration (exceptionally, in 1853, he delivered a suite of furniture for the Palais Royal). In the 1840s they had already made seats inspired by earlier styles (Louis XIV, Renaissance). During the Second Empire the company shared with Quignon, Meynard, sometimes Grohé (q.v.), and the widow of Fossey the majority of orders for common wooden seating for the imperial palaces, and more than its competitors seems to have been specialists in sofas, armchairs, and confortables in which exposed woodwork was reduced to a minimum. One of Jeanselme's most important deliveries at that time was the furnishings in the Louis XVI style for the theater at Fontainebleau. Other works by the firm were without much originality, such as the seats for the family salon at Compiègne or copies of chairs made in 1774 for the clock room at Versailles.

This firm should not be confused with Jeanselme jeune, the upholsterer Ternisien's son-in-law, who in 1853 furnished the bed of the Empress at the Tuileries and who, at the exposition of 1855, exhibited rich furnishings in the style of Boulle.

J.-P.S.

Bibliography:
*Rapports 1855*, p. 1119; P. Mérimée and E. du Sommerard, in *Rapports 1862*, vol. VI, p. 267; J.-P.-M. Diéterle and J.-H. Pollen, in *Rapports 1867*, vol. III, p. 23; Ledoux-Lebard, 1965, pp. 298–304

Joseph-Pierre-François Jeanselme and Charles-Joseph-Marie Jeanselme

## II-28
## Armchair

1854–55
Gilded wood; upholstered in yellow damask
Height 109 cm; width 63 cm; depth 61 cm

II-28

Provenance:
Entered Fontainebleau, February 11, 1855, as part of the ensemble of theater seats for the château (inv. no. F 1883 C)

Exhibition:
1922, Paris, Musée des Arts Décoratifs, no. 581

Bibliography:
Demoriane, 1961, p. 81; Samoyault-Verlet, 1975, vol. I, p. 292

In 1854 the architect Hector Lefuel (q.v.) was put in charge of fitting out a court theater in the Louis XV wing of the château of Fontainebleau. This small auditorium (slightly less than four hundred seats) consists of an orchestra; a first balcony whose balustrade, painted with a trellis of flowers, is a play on the word *corbeille,* which in French can mean both "basket of flowers" and "first balcony"; and two levels of boxes, one of them decorated with latticework. The walls are adorned with carved and painted ornaments in the Louis XVI style and partly covered with yellow damask, as is the Emperor's salon, while the salons of the foyers are in blue damask. The stage machinery and a small orchestra pit complete this theater, which evokes by an atmosphere that is at the same time precious and informal the visits of the court to Fontainebleau. For the furnishing, which was accomplished rapidly, the Mobilier de la Couronne called on several suppliers: Marquis for the lights; Fourdinois (q.v.) for the woodwork of the *confortable* armchairs and di-

vans in the foyers; and the firm of Jeanselme, Père et Fils, for that of the armchairs, chairs, stools, and benches in the theater (Arch. nat., AJ[19] 687). However, the upholstering was entrusted to its own workshops.

Four armchairs and four more elaborately carved chairs were made for the center of the first balcony, which took the place of an imperial box. They all have the same curved back surmounted by flowers tied with a ribbon (although variations exist in the carving), the same legs with scroll-shaped consoles adorned with acanthus. This model was not the creation of Jeanselme; rather, the chairs are faithful reproductions (except for the garland of flowers) of a number of chairs by Georges Jacob, four of which were then and still are at Fontainebleau. The design of armchairs with their arms supported by receding brackets is an interpretation based on the chair.

This armchair is even more interesting for its upholstery than for its form. Its original tufted damask, the material used for all the theater seats and wall hangings, has been preserved. Tufting is, for good reason, one of the characteristics of the Second Empire style. At first it seems to have been limited to the upholstering of "comfortable" *(confortable)* seats. *Confortables* themselves first appeared under Louis Philippe, and from the start they would have been mounted on elastic and upholstered with tufting: "In this way it was possible to give the upholstery more flexibility and a more shimmering appearance" (Deville, 1878–80, p. 21). After 1850, *confortables,* at first reserved for fireside, occupy all parts of the salon and are made in the most diverse forms. Tufted upholstery thereby came to be used more frequently and little by little spread to all seats covered in such soft fabrics as damask, Indian silk, lampas, chintz, etc. Its use was so common that one no longer saw how anachronistic tufted upholstery was for a piece so deliberately Louis XVI as this theater seat.

C.S.-V.

Musée National du Château, Fontainebleau

---

## Edouard Kreisser

*Active Paris 1843–63*

*From his shop on the rue neuve du Luxembourg in 1843, the boulevard de la Madeleine in 1845, and the rue basse du Rempart in 1847, Kreisser sold "bronzes and objets d'art, curiosities, marquetry and rosewood furniture, Vieux Sèvres porcelain" (An-*

*nuaire général du commerce, 1854). He exhibited at the Exposition Universelle of 1855 and received an honorable mention "for his furniture in the style of the reign of Louis XVI, with painted porcelain and enamel appliqués, and for his 'incrustations' of mosaic in relief" (Rapports 1855, p. 1128). In 1862 his shop was at 54, faubourg Saint Honoré, but it closed the following year.*

*The only extant works known to have come from his firm are the two beautiful pieces bought by Queen Victoria at the 1855 exposition, a writing table (Victoria and Albert Museum) and a cabinet (Kensington Palace).*

J.-P.S.

Bibliography:
*Rapports 1855,* p. 1128; Hayward, 1964; Ledoux-Lebard, 1965, p. 318; de Bellaigue, 1975

---

Edouard Kreisser

## II-29
## Writing Table

1855
Signed in marquetry top: E. Kreisser à Paris, 52 rue Basse-du-Rempart Exposition Universelle de Paris 1855
Marquetry, silvered metal, gilded bronze, porcelain plaques
Height 83 cm; width 119 cm; depth 61 cm

Provenance:
Purchased by Queen Victoria during her trip to Paris, 1855; gift to Prince Albert, Christmas 1855; withdrawn from royal collections at an unknown date; George Farrow; gift to Victoria and Albert Museum, 1964 (inv. no. W9-1964)

Exhibition:
1855, Paris, Exposition Universelle

Bibliography:
Hayward, 1964; Ledoux-Lebard, 1965, p. 318; de Bellaigue, 1975

When Queen Victoria and Prince Albert went to Paris in August 1855, one of the purposes of their voyage was to visit the Exposition Universelle. From Saint-Cloud, where they stayed (*see* nos. II-2, II-3), the Queen made three trips to the exposition, and Prince Albert returned alone another time (*Journal,* 1961). Undoubtedly it was during one of these visits that the Queen noticed the furnishings shown by the cabinetmaker and bronze founder Kreisser, whose work is little known except for his contribution to the Exposition Universelle. None of his furniture is specifically cited in either the official report or the various accounts of the exposition, but two pieces, the writing table shown here and a cabinet ornamented with porcelain plaques, seem to have caught the Queen's eye, and she purchased them. Their entry into the royal collections was traced by Bellaigue through the Royal Archives (1975, p. 38). The Queen paid 10,575 francs for them out of her own purse (2,500 for the table, 8,000 for the cabinet, plus transport) as presents for Prince Albert, the table for Christmas 1855, the desk for the Prince's birthday the following August 26.

The cabinet, preserved today in Kensington Palace, is a curious piece of furniture, richly decorated with sixty porcelain plaques and ornamented with bronzes in the style of Louis XVI. The writing table carries the pastiche even further, and it gives the impression of déjà vu : the oval medallions and background of lozenges on the marquetry top, the gilded-bronze garlands of naturalistic flowers and bas-reliefs of cherubs on the sides, the fluted legs in which the use of silvered metal evokes steel are all strongly reminiscent of Riesener. However, Kreisser did not copy any table in particular. One can compare it with certain earlier pieces, for example, a table that belonged to Marie

Antoinette, which was then in England (now at Waddesdon Manor, *see* Bellaigue, 1974, vol. II, pp. 520–27) but which Kreisser had surely never seen. Among their similarities are garlands of flowers and festooned draperies tied back with tasseled ropes. These reminiscences do not deny the originality of Kreisser's work, which he signed prominently in the marquetry top. To satisfy the order from the Queen, he enriched his table with the monogram of Victoria and Albert and the royal arms of England on porcelain plaques (which indicates that the work was altered after the exposition). Kreisser combined the bronze elements, such ornaments as the Ionic capitals, and the singularly proportioned legs according to his own taste. Although the quality of these bronzes may lack a certain refinement and the garlands on the sides may be too repetitive, Kreisser proved himself highly accomplished in the art of marquetry by his adroit combination of various woods (rosewood, *bois gris*, sycamore, greendyed wood) in extremely fine motifs.

C.S.-V.

Victoria and Albert Museum, London

II-29

## Monbro Aîné (or Monbro Fils Aîné)
*Died 1884*

*Under the name of Monbro Aîné (Monbro the Elder) or Monbro Fils Aîné (Monbro the Elder Son), Monbro's establishment was at first only a curiosity shop, founded in Paris on the rue Basse du Rempart (at the site of the boulevard des Capucines), at numbers 32–34 (Almanach du Commerce, 1838, the first year the name of Monbro was listed); then at numbers 14 and 18, opposite the rue de la Paix (Almanach du Commerce, 1840). Monbro's activities soon extended to the production of furnishings and bronzes in imitation of earlier styles (Almanach du Commerce, 1841). Monbro made carved and gilded furnishings, cabinetry, and also had workshops for repairs. The Garde Meuble de la Couronne, under Louis Philippe and Napoleon III, was among the clients of this fashionable supplier, as was the writer Eugène Sue, while Mme de Girardin (1855) mentioned him with regard to an antique clock: "I saw one yesterday in the same style at Monbro's." At the beginning of the Second Empire, Monbro opened a branch in London, at 370 Oxford Street, then at 2 Frith Street, Soho Square (Almanach du Commerce, 1861), which disappeared after 1870. Following the expropriation of the rue Basse du Rempart, Monbro held a sale of ancient and contemporary furnishings and objects on December 12–17, 1859, and moved to 19, rue de Helder (Almanach du Commerce, 1860–68), then to 56, rue de l'Arcade (Almanach du Commerce, 1869–70), and organized other sales in Paris and London from 1862 to 1870. He moved his shop to 82, boulevard Haussmann (Almanach du Commerce, 1871–76), where, having become expert in furnishings and objets d'art (Almanach du Commerce, 1877–84), he remained. A sale of objects from his estate took place on February 19–21, 1885. A clock in gilded bronze, signed Monbro aîné, is in the royal palace of Ajuda in Lisbon, and a clock signed Monbro fils aîné is in the Musée d'Ennery in Paris.*

D.A.

Bibliography:
De Girardin, 1855, p. 25; Burty, 1883, p. 19; Lugt, 1938–64, vols. II, III; Ledoux-Lebard, 1965, pp. 412–13

Attributed to Monbro Aîné

## II-30
## Mirrored Wardrobe

c. 1855
Various woods, ivory, copper, mother-of-pearl, gilded bronze
Height 293 cm; width 189 cm; depth 66 cm

Provenance:
Acquired in Paris by John Bowes (1811–1885), son of the tenth Count of Strathmore, and his wife, née Josephine-Benoîte Coffin-Chevalier (1825–1874), Countess of Montalbo (in 1868); given by John Bowes to the Bowes Museum

Bibliography:
Watson, 1963, p. 468, repro. p. 470

Many borrowings from the furniture of the seventeenth and eighteenth centuries contributed to the creation of this mirrored wardrobe, a form of furniture that appeared at the beginning of the nineteenth century. While the pediment on the central part evokes provincial or foreign eighteenth-century pieces, the flanking corner cabinets, which ensure the balance of the piece, are reproductions of corner cabinets with shelves executed under Louis XV by Parisian cabi-

II-30

netmakers, like the famous one by Jacques Dubois (*Ebénistes*, 1963, repro. pp. 100–101), but on their sides, mirrors replace the veneered panels of the models. The marquetry compartments on a background of thuja reflect in their subjects—flowers and birds—the influence of Louis XIV wooden marquetry and Louis XVI décor. The Boulle technique of marquetry, one of Monbro's specialties, was not used here, but it suggested the use of different materials: copper scrolls mixed with wooden marquetry in an original manner, mother-of-pearl used for the birds' heads, green-tinted ivory for the latticework cartouches. Bronze ornamentation in a completely rocaille style is distributed over the corner sections in the same way as on eighteenth-century pieces and evokes around the central mirror the carved frames of certain Louis XV boiserie panels.

The affluent John Bowes, having been a member of Parliament from South Durham from 1832 to 1847, gave up political life to take up residence in Paris. In 1852 he married a former actress and in the same year bought her the château of Mme du Barry in Louveciennes, selling it in 1862. In Paris the Bowes lived at 7, cité d'Antin, then, in a large house at 7, rue de Berlin (today rue de Liège), which still exists. The Bowes decided in 1859 to found a museum and bought for it antique and contemporary works of all kinds. In 1864 they decided to create the museum at Barnard Castle (Durham), where they built a French Renaissance-style château to house it, on plans by the French architect Jules Pellechet. In 1892 the museum opened, housing besides the Boweses' collections, the contemporary furnishings bought, mainly between 1854 and 1856, for Louveciennes and the rue de Berlin (Hardy, 1970). Their supplier was Monbro, whose invoices (preserved in the museum's archives) list certain deliveries which are extant: furniture in Boulle marquetry (bookcase, pair of cabinets, piano-harmonium), furniture in the Louis XV style (pair of sideboards in carved oak, seats), Louis XV- or Louis XVI-style bronzes (clocks, mounted porcelains).

This armoire has been tentatively identified with one described in Monbro's April 1856 invoice for a "large armoire with mirror and three doors, palisander, with carved pediment and arms," sold for 1,400 francs for Mrs. Bowes's bedroom in the house on the rue de Berlin. The description does not completely fit this armoire, although the price would be right for it. It can also be compared to certain other pieces of furniture in the museum: the Boweses' gilded-wood bed, also in a rocaille style, and a game table delivered by Monbro in 1855 and also decorated with a marquetry of flowers and trellises and Louis XV bronzes. In 1859 Monbro sold "two lovely Louis XV corner cupboards with two arched doors, with a marquetry in colored woods of flowers and birds, decorated with gilded rocaille bronze" (no. 324), possible sources of inspiration for this piece of furniture. Its attribution to Monbro is quite possible, and it was, in any case, among the purchases the Boweses made in France at the beginning of the Second Empire. Without this certainty, it would be impossible to date, since the use of the Louis XV style on spectacular furniture of this type lasted from Louis Philippe's reign until the end of the nineteenth century.

D.A.

The Bowes Museum, Barnard Castle

*Julien-Nicolas Rivart*
See no. II-39

*Tricot et Jeancourt*
*Active Paris*

The cabinetmakers and upholsterers Tricot et Jeancourt, "sculptors, decorators... manufacturers of seats, chairs, and armchairs," 32, rue de la Contrescarpe in Paris, are listed in the trade directory beginning in 1868 (Annuaire-almanach, 1868, pp. 542, 1240; 1869, pp. 549, 894, 1256, 1265). They were the successors to Charles Gasc, who is listed at the same address until 1867 (Annuaire-almanach, 1867, p. 1212) and who executed, from designs by Rossigneux, the vitrines in the Galerie d'Apollon in the Louvre (Barbet de Jouy, 1867, p. xx).

Tricot received an honorable mention at the exposition of 1855 as a woodcarver in the employ of the cabinetmaker Jules Fossey (Rapports 1855, p. 1155).

C.S.-V.

Tricot et Jeancourt; designed by Eugène-Emmanuel Viollet-le-Duc and Edmond-Clément-Marie-Louis Duthoit

## II-31
## Hanging Armoire

1869
Painted wood
Height 195 cm; width 127 cm; depth 42 cm

Provenance:
Created for the Rose Room of the château of Roquetaillade

Bibliography:
Jullian, 1971

The two large, double rooms created at Roquetaillade in 1869, the Green Room and the Rose Room (see no. II-1), have similar furnishings: two double beds with canopies held by rods with crook-shaped ends, six chairs, two armchairs (see no. II-32), two night tables, a writing table, tufted sofas in each of the rooms, a large cupboard and three upholstered benches in the Green Room, two hanging armoires and six benches in the Rose Room. The decoration of these two large rooms is also quite similar: each has a large central arch and the same painted wall decoration and coffered ceiling.

All the furniture, both the woodwork and the upholstery, was made by the cabinetmakers Tricot et Jeancourt from extremely precise

II-31

drawings supplied by the architect Edmond Duthoit (q.v.). The hanging armoires, inspired in their form—especially their crenellations and sloping top—by the armoire from Noyon illustrated in Viollet-le-Duc's *Dictionnaire du mobilier* (Viollet-le-Duc, 1858–75, vol. I, pl. 1, p. 10), were a little late in being delivered because the lacquer was slow to dry: "We still have to deliver to you the... white armoires. This work must be allowed to dry after each coat of varnish. It is going to take us another two weeks," they wrote to the marquis de Mauvesin on June 28, 1869, when sending him the rest of the furniture (Roquetaillade Archives). The price of each armoire was 300 francs: "Two large hanging armoires, double doors secured by bascule locks, inside shelves, built and carved according to drawings and plans. White and gold lacquered wood, carvings and moldings in several shades of color, decoration and letters [the monogram of the Mauvesin family] on the four doors according to the drawing, 300 each" (Roquetaillade Ar-

chives, statement certified October 28, 1869).

The originality of this piece resides above all in its painted decoration, and one cannot help comparing it to English furniture of the same period. At the London International Exhibition of 1862, for example, there was exhibited a painted cabinet in the form of a roofed building in the Gothic style by Harland and Fisher of London, designed by the architect William Burges, with reference being made to the *Dictionnaire du mobilier* (Waring, 1863, vol. II, pl. 155). And a few years later, William Morris, in making painted furniture, no longer concealed the influence that the writings and teachings of Viollet-le-Duc had had on him.

Even in France, where carved "Gothic" pieces of furniture are numerous, only a few painted ones are known. The furniture of Roquetaillade, produced under the supervision of Viollet-le-Duc from the drawings of one of his pupils and very close collaborators, is thus particularly interesting. It goes beyond the simple whim of a Legitimist manor owner in love with the Middle Ages; it corresponds to the movement that the lessons of the great architect were to give to the decorative arts in England.

C.S.-V.

Collection Mlle de Baritault, Château de Roquetaillade (Gironde)

Tricot et Jeancourt; designed by Eugène-Emmanuel Viollet-le-Duc and Edmond-Clément-Marie-Louis Duthoit

## II-32
## Armchair

1869
Pear wood, blackened and waxed; upholstered in green wool moquette
Height 128 cm; width 72 cm; depth 60 cm

Provenance:
Created for the Green Room of the château of Roquetaillade
Bibliography:
Jullian, 1971

II-32

This large armchair, like the rest of the furniture in the château of Roquetaillade (*see* nos. II-1, II-31), is a rare, fully documented and perfectly preserved example of the ideas of Viollet-le-Duc (q.v.) in the field of furniture and interior decoration. Looking at it, one cannot help but recall Prosper Mérimée's review in *Le Moniteur* of February 14, 1859, in which he hailed the publication of the first volume of Viollet-le-Duc's *Dictionnaire du mobilier:* "Our modern manufacturers would assuredly make very poor use of the *Dictionnaire du mobilier* if they were to limit themselves to taking the author's charming drawings as models, without profiting by the excellent lessons that accompany them. One should not copy the throne of a Capetian king in order to make an armchair for a stockbroker, nor the reading desk of a thirteenth-century monk for the writing table of a nineteenth-century journalist.... In employing the same materials that served our ancestors, we must adapt them to our modern needs and uses." This is exactly what Viollet-le-Duc does here: the greyhounds on the arms of the chair are, in fact, to be found in the drawing of the throne of Charles V under the entry *fauteuil* ("armchair") (Viollet-le-Duc, 1858–75, vol. I, p. 113), while the cresting of the back is borrowed from figure 14 under *chaise* ("chair") (Viollet-le-Duc, 1858–75, vol. I, p. 53). However, there is nothing Gothic about the structure. The armchair is comfortably up-

holstered, and has casters so that it may be easily moved. It is a modern piece in the Gothic style, and could, if required, be transformed simply by a change of decorative elements into a Renaissance, Louis XIII, or Louis XIV chair.

This armchair was executed by the firm of Tricot et Jeancourt, which in 1869 produced all the furniture for the Rose and Green rooms of the château, including "two large carved armchairs in blackened and waxed pear wood, gold and red threads in accordance with the drawing, 120 francs each" (Roquetaillade Archives, statement certified October 28, 1869).

C.S.-V.

Collection Mlle de Baritault, Château de Roquetaillade (Gironde)

## II-33
## Armchair

c. 1856
Gilded wood; upholstered in tapestry
Height 120 cm; width 70 cm; depth 50 cm

Provenance:
Executed for the Grand Gallery of the château of Maintenon

The château of Maintenon, the estate of Madame de Maintenon, has been in the Noailles family since her niece, Françoise d'Aubigné, married Adrien-Maurice de Noailles. In the nineteenth century the château was restored by the duc Paul de Noailles (1802–1885). The duke, mentioned frequently in the letters of the duchesse de Dino and those of the princesse de Liéven, retired from political life after 1848 and devoted himself to literature. Among the important restorations that he undertook at Maintenon was the refurbishment of the wing connecting the château with the chapel, and especially the decoration of the Grand Gallery. The gallery housed portraits of members of the Noailles family from the Crusades to the nineteenth century and pictures of the illustrious events in which they took part.

The gallery is decorated with a coffered ceiling, carved and painted wainscoting, the portraits richly framed with armorial crests and broken scrolled pediments, all in a kind of Renaissance style. The furniture, on the contrary, is deliberately in the Louis XIV style, undoubtedly in accordance with the wishes of the duke himself, who had become familiar with the period through his studies of Madame de Maintenon.

Two gilded wood consoles under the portraits of Madame de Maintenon and her niece

II-33

on one side, and the cardinal de Noailles on the other, mark the middle of the gallery. Four bookcases in the style of Boulle, made of ebony and gilded bronze, set off the four historical scenes. The rest of the gallery is rigidly laid out with four sofas, twelve armchairs, and eight stools in gilded wood. These pieces are upholstered in tapestry with a red background, ornamented with roses and white lilies. The same fabric appears around the twelve windows, simulating draped curtains.

The architect who designed the gallery and its furnishings is still unknown, but one might suggest that it was done in 1856, the date that appears on two of the four historical paintings, by Alexander Hesse, Hippolyte Bellangé, and Eugène Bataille.

The chairs do not bear a signature. They were apparently inspired by an original model of the mid-seventeenth century with a high back, console armrests, an H-shaped stretcher joining the legs, and an additional stretcher between the front legs. The furniture in this gallery is a good example, fortunately very well preserved, of the archaeological taste which governed the renovation of many châteaux during this period and whose importance the order books of Fourdinois (q.v.), for example, suggest.

C.S.-V.

Château de Maintenon (Eure-et-Loir)

# Bronze Furnishings

## Compagnie des Marbres Onyx d'Algérie (Société Alphonse Pallu et Cie)

Established 1858

*Algerian onyx marble appeared with success under the Second Empire. Delmonte, a marble dealer from Carrara, had undertaken to find the transparent marbles used in antiquity and having searched in vain in southern Europe, Asia Minor, and Egypt, began prospecting in Algeria around 1843. In 1849, as a result of road construction operations between Oran and Tlemcen, he discovered at Aïn-Tembalek in the province of Oran a quarry that had been once exploited by the Romans and which produced what has come to be called Algerian onyx marble: a translucent material, somewhere between marble and alabaster, existing in different colors (white, yellow, red, green). Delmonte obtained the concession for this quarry, but was unable to exploit it successfully owing to his lack of means. After exhibiting the material, both uncut and worked, in 1855, he ceded his rights in 1858 to the Compagnie des Marbres Onyx d'Algérie, founded by the Société Alphonse Pallu et Cie. Until that time only small pieces had been produced in onyx marble. The wealthy company set up a factory in Paris, at 29, rue Popincourt; there the raw material, arriving from Algeria, was processed with mechanical saws and lathes, and transformed into slabs, columns, fireplaces, vases, clocks, and sculptures, the forms for which were provided by the sculptor Eugène Cornu (died 1875). The establishment included a bronze studio which executed the mounts.*

*The vogue for Algerian onyx marble was confirmed in the exposition of products from Algeria at the Palais de l'Industrie in 1860, then at the 1862 London International Exposition, where the company, which had a branch in London and exhibited among other things, a* coupe *mounted in gilded bronze by Carrier-Belleuse (q.v.: Bethnal Green Museum, London), was awarded a medal. Later, G. Viot, who worked for the company, took it over from the Société Pallu and won a gold medal in 1867. The material was also worked by Béghé, a marble dealer in Blida, who exhibited mounted bowls in London in 1862 (L'Algérie, vol. II, 1863, p. 155), and by Donnadieu, 20, rue des Vosges (now rue de Birague) in Paris, who in the Algerian section at the Exposition Universelle of 1867, exhibited all kinds of onyx marble objects (Catalogue 1867, vol. III, p. 70). The Hôtel de Païva (now Travellers Club) in Paris remains as evidence of the use of Algerian onyx marble in interior decoration of the period.*

D.A.

Bibliography:
*Catalogue 1855*, p. 206; Durant, 1860, "L'Algérie," pp. 166–67; *Catalogue 1862*, p. 232, "Renseignements," pp. 152–53; *L'Algérie*, 1863, vol. II, pp. 144, 159; Waring, 1863, vol. II, pl. 164; *Récompenses 1867*, group III, pp. 10–11; Luchet, 1868, pp. 226–27; de Champeaux, 1886, p. 323

Ferdinand Barbedienne; designed by Louis-Constant Sévin, onyx marble probably furnished by Compagnie des Marbres Onyx d'Algérie

### II-34
## "Oriental Style" Footed Bowl

c. 1862
Algerian onyx marble, gilded and enameled bronze
Height 42 cm; width 70 cm; depth 33 cm

Provenance:
Acquired by Thomas Couture (q.v.) from Barbedienne, December 17, 1862 (Compiègne Archives); gift of Mme Camille Grodet-Moatti, Couture's granddaughter, to the Musée National du Château, Compiègne, 1971 (inv. no. C71.122)

Exhibition:
1862, London

Bibliography:
Barbedienne, 1862, p. 52; Luchet, 1862, "Barbedienne," pp. 92–94 (repro.)

This work consists of two pieces of onyx marble, probably supplied by the Compagnie des Marbres Onyx d'Algérie: a thick twelve-sided bowl and a square base. Executed by Barbedienne, the mount includes twelve similar plaques encircling the belly, four identical palmettes adorning the two handles, and a ring surrounding the foot, all decorated with opaque enamels—yellow, red, white, green (two tones), and blue (two tones). The bowl corresponds to an object described in Barbedienne's 1862 catalogue under the heading "Opaque Cloisonné Enamels Flattened in the Manner of the Ancients": "A large *coupe*, Oriental style, in Algerian onyx marble, dodecagonal, decorated with gilded and enameled bronze, fine mounts (can be used as a jardiniere or centerpiece)." In the same year Barbedienne exhibited in London a *coupe*, reproduced by Luchet, which—as J.-M. Moulin has observed—exactly resembles the *coupe* shown here, except that it rests on a base of bronze instead of onyx marble. However, these are probably the same bowl, which is known to have passed from Barbedienne to his friend Couture at the end of the year. In exchange for works by the painter, the founder customarily gave Couture art objects, which led Bar-

II-34

bedienne to set up a series of statements of account between them, in which this *coupe* figures: for 1,600 francs on July 30, 1865; for 1,400 francs only on January 12, 1866, when the *coupe* is described more specifically: "1 onyx marble *coupe*, dodecagonal in shape, encircled with opaque, cloisonné and flattened enamels, on foot of onyx and gilded bronze."

The conception of the *coupe* is that of Constant Sévin (Luchet). Greek art is "the basis of his beliefs and the first rule of his studies," stated his employer. But although the overall form, the handles, and the decoration on the foot are derived from the "Néo-Grec" style abundantly represented by Barbedienne in 1862 (see no. III-2), the enamel decoration (interlacings, palmettes, stylized foliage) was of Oriental inspiration. Sévin greatly enjoyed creating designs for enamels (Champier, 1888–89, p. 173). Enamel and onyx marble were recent ventures in 1862 for Barbedienne, always an enterprising innovator. Although he applied the term "cloisonné" to his enamels—and they have rather the appearance of champlevé—they do not constitute true cloisonné work, the cloisons having been obtained by casting.

Beginning in this period Barbedienne's enamel workshop produced bronze objects decorated with enamels in medieval and Oriental styles (chandeliers, clocks, candelabra, etc.), as well as such completely enameled objects as the large vase exhibited at the 1862 International Exhibition in London and now in the Bethnal Green Museum. The same museum owns two small *coupes* in onyx

mounted in enameled bronze, also displayed by Barbedienne in 1862. The combination of the two materials, which the Compagnie des Marbres Onyx also used at the same time in its own creations, would continue to be used by both establishments. The 1862 exhibition, where Barbedienne received three medals, including one for bronze—particularly the fortunate combination of bronze, enamel, and onyx—(Sévin also received a medal), witnessed the triumph of the founder, who in 1863 was decorated and had settled his debts. Later he also became interested in painted enamels, and gave commissions to Popelin (q.v.) and Gobert (q.v.) in 1867, before hiring his own enameler, Alfred Serre (Falize, 1893–94, vol. X, pp. 62–63, 479, 488, vol. XI, pp. 138–40).

D.A.

Musée National du Château, Compiègne

Antoine-Louis Barye

## II-35
## Candelabra

1858–61
Patinated bronze, red marble base
Height 112 cm; width 60 cm; depth 27 cm

Provenance:
Ordered in 1858 from Barye by Isaac Pereire and placed in the château of Armainvilliers (Seine-et-Marne); Fabius coll.

Exhibitions:
1889, Paris, Ecole des Beaux-Arts, no. 353; 1957, Paris, Musée Jacquemart-André (not in catalogue)

Bibliography:
Mantz, 1867, "Barye," p. 124; "Barye," 1888–89, p. 371; Ballu, 1890, pp. 122–23; Huyghe (ed.), 1957–61, vol. III, p. 364

Among the many decorative bronzes executed by Barye, several particularly important commissions are worthy of mention. Under the July Monarchy, the duc d'Orleans ordered from him in 1834 a large centerpiece, which was never finished, and the duc de Montpensier, a mantelpiece garniture (the group on the clock of Roger and Angelica mounted on a hippogriff, and two candelabra). Under the Second Empire, Isaac Pereire ordered a mantelpiece garniture in two sets, one in gilded bronze for his hôtel at 35, rue du Faubourg Saint Honoré, the other in patinated bronze for his château of Armainvilliers. The molds would have been broken after casting, which explains why this model does not appear in any of Barye's sales catalogues.

These two sets, executed entirely by Barye himself, from the casting to the mounting, between 1858 and 1861, consisted of an ornamental clock (Apollo standing in his chariot, the horses held by the Hours) and two candelabra. This clock, little known by contemporaries since the only two examples were in a private collection, evoked the admiration of critics invited to see it, especially at the time of the retrospective exhibition of Barye's work in 1889. The fan-shaped composition was very skillful: the horses drew apart, and the perspective was so well thought out that the group had amazing depth. All traces of the clocks seem to have disappeared (known only from illustrations, for example, Bibliothèque des Arts Décoratifs, recueil Maciet, 237 [44]; Ballu, 1890, p. 124; the original models of Apollo and one of the women leading the chariot are in the Louvre); on the other hand, the Armainvilliers candelabra are preserved. Each consists of the figure of a woman emerging from a stand of reeds and leaning on a tree whose foliage ends in nine bobeches. The feet of the woman, supported on a base of red marble ornamented with bronze, are hidden by a winged dragon. The two candelabra are not identical, and the two women are not symmetrically opposed, but both have the same backward movement of withdrawal, seeming to shield themselves from the sunlight with a hand. This suggests that they might symbolize night vanishing on the arrival of the chariot of the sun, the winged dragons then being their phantasms.

These candelabra, although they do not equal the beauty of the clock, are nevertheless remarkable. The branches, rocaille in inspiration, lack a little detail, but it is mainly the figures that capture the attention. There are very few figures of women in Barye's works: the Three Graces and the seated goddesses in the candelabrum of the duc de Montpensier (Beaulieu, 1975, pp. 272–74) and Angelica mounted on the hippogriff on the clock. "All these women are sisters. They have elegance of line and power of design and, with that, such lustrous skin, such soft complexions as to suggest that in modeling them with his chisel, M. Barye remembered the huntresses and sirens of Rubens." This quote from Mantz (1867, p. 117) is equally applicable to the figures on these candelabra: they have the same full-blown beauty, the same tranquil serenity. (A model in plaster and wax, for the figure raising her left arm, signed, 43 centimeters high, figured in the Barye exhibition of 1889 and was part of the J. Zoubaloff sale in 1929.)

The work is valuable, too, for what it reveals about Barye's ideas on the decorative arts. It was not only for reason of profit that the cel-ebrated sculptor turned to the creation of flam-beaux, candelabra, clocks, fireplace fenders, and even inkwells. Under the Second Empire his renown as a sculptor of animals and the casting of his reductions would have been sufficient to earn him a good living. But he thought that beauty could be allied with utility and that through the expedient of the industrial arts (if inspired by true artists like himself and not junk dealers), great art could take its place in interior design. This explains the long listing of bronze furnishings in his sales catalogue (see Pivar, 1974, pp. 46–48).

It is probably no accident that this preoccu-pation of Barye's met with the patronage of Pereire, the financier formed by the school of Saint-Simon, which encouraged all aspects of the beautiful, seeing in it moral progress for all of society.

C.S.-V.

MM. Fabius, Paris

## Charles Crozatier

### Le Puy 1795–1855 Paris

Born into a poor family in the Velay, Crozatier began his apprenticeship with a Parisian engraver and then succeeded in entering the Ecole des Beaux-Arts, where he was a student of Cartellier. On his return from a trip to Italy he brought back more than fifty cases of casts of works by Ghiberti, Michelangelo, Cellini, Bernini, and others. His reputation as a founder came from the deftness with which he could tastefully assemble pieces of various origins to create such works as candelabra, torchères, and clocks. He is recorded as having delivered many clocks and candelabra to the Garde Meuble de la Couronne; during the July Monarchy there were many such deliveries, which continued under the Second Empire until 1854. In 1852, for example, he delivered for the Tuileries two fireplace garnitures, one with a large clock with children holding the portrait of Louis XIV, and candelabra and bouquets; the other including a clock entitled The Elements, with children carrying a globe, and candelabra with women and children after a model by Clodion. In 1854 he supplied, also for the Tuileries, two pair of large candelabra in the Louis XVI style, one with children and the second with women (Arch. nat. AJ[19] 1099). It might be said that Crozatier was one of the initiators of a return to the art of the eighteenth century during the reign of Louis Philippe.

But his activity as manufacturer of bronze objects should not make one overlook the large casts he made for various sculptors, and his discovery of several different processes for the improvement of the molds. His most famous pieces were the group crowning the Arc de Triomphe du Carrousel, by Bozio, and the statue of Louis XIV in the cour d'honneur at Versailles, by Petitot and Cartellier.

Crozatier was completely caught up in his trade and had large workshops on the rue du Parc Royal where he encouraged the original ideas and talent of young workers. Death kept him from accomplishing his dream of presenting to the city of his birth a colossal statue of the Virgin.

C.S.-V.

Bibliography:
Mandet, 1855; de Champeaux, 1886; Viel-Castel, 1942, vol. I, p. 213

II-35

Charles Crozatier

## II-36
## Candelabra

1854
Gilded and patinated bronze
Height 138 cm; diameter 60 cm

Provenance:
Entered the Garde Meuble, September 2, 1854; installed in the Salon d'Apollon in the Tuileries (Arch. nat. Aj[19] 684); escaped the fire and entered the Garde Meuble, 1874 (Arch. nat. Aj[19] 1099); sent to Fontainebleau, 1883; exhibited in the Salle des Colonnes (inv. no. F 979 C)

II-36

These large-scale candelabra were delivered for the Tuileries by the founder Charles Crozatier and were in the Salon d'Apollon during the inventory of 1855. They had been ordered from the 1853 budget and Crozatier was paid 3,600 francs for them. They were among the last works Crozatier delivered to the Garde Meuble (he was to die February 8, 1855).

The two candelabra, though a pair, are not identical. The girandoles, thirteen branches with typically Louis XVI acanthus scrolls, are the same, but the lower parts are different. One seems to symbolize marine life: three putti of "Florentine" bronze stand on a rock where reeds grow and dolphins and shells are found, these elements being of gilded bronze. One of the putti with both hands upraised seems to support the overhanging foliage; the second, seated on the dolphin's head, blows on a shell; and the third, a little girl with her hair tied with a ribbon, holds a net.

The other candelabrum seems to represent the riches of land. Again, there are three children in patinated bronze, but they are somewhat larger (about 52 centimeters high as opposed to 43 centimeters in the other candelabrum) and somewhat older. One, in front of some reeds, bends toward a duck waddling through his legs (representing fresh-water fishing?); the second, a sort of child-Bacchus, dances at the foot of a grapevine (harvesting?), while the third, leaning against a tree trunk, has a fox pelt over his shoulder (hunting?).

However, despite stylistic reminiscences, bronzes, especially of this quality, cannot be discussed without raising the question of models. Crozatier was a founder for some of the most famous sculptors, but he also worked alone from casts collected during his travels, notably in Italy. His reputation was in large part based on his facility for making harmonious combinations of elements from diverse origins. Thus one should not be surprised by the presence of children in different styles. Some of them, especially the trumpeter, evoke Bouchardon; others, more slender, are closer to seventeenth-century Italian models, and they all are united with Louis XVI garlands and boughs.

These candelabra have the general appearance of the Louis XVI style, and it should be noted that Crozatier delivered two other pairs of candelabra in this style to the Tuileries at the same time as these.

C.S.-V.

Musée National du Château, Fontainebleau

## Guillaume Denière
*Active Paris from 1844*

*The son of a bronze manufacturer who had been in business in Paris since 1804 and who had done work for the palace of the landgrave of Kassel in 1825 and for the prince of Orange in 1828, Denière succeeded his father in 1844. He manufactured bronze furnishings, candelabra, lights, and flambeaux, as well as clocks with subjects, centerpieces in gilded bronze, and "artistic" bronzes, taken from earlier models (Clodion, Pigalle) or modern ones (including Carrier-Belleuse, q.v., Fratin, Prouha).*

*His consignments to the Mobilier de la Couronne under the July Monarchy and the Second Empire were very important: in 1852 for the Tuileries, several clocks (Genius of the Arts; Woman Reading; Dog, after Christophe Fratin), chandeliers, and Louis XVI candelabra with a vase and bouquets or with children (Arch. nat. AJ¹⁹ 681); in 1854 again for the Tuileries, a series of clocks, Sappho, Hagar and Ishmael, Child with Pipe, Woman Reading, and several pair of flambeaux and rich candelabra with children; in 1857, matching clocks and candelabra; and in 1861, a clock (Arch. nat., AJ¹⁹ 683, 689, 694). At the Exposition Universelle of 1867 the Emperor purchased a chimney garniture, "figures in white marble," for 7,500 francs (Arch. nat. AJ¹⁹ 954). He also received many orders from abroad. The most spectacular among them were a large gilded-bronze centerpiece for Kisselef, the Russian ambassador, in 1854 (sculptures by P.-B. Prouha and P.-A. Gagné, exhibited at the Exposition Universelle of 1855); several bronze furnishings for the viceroy of Egypt, Said Pasha, among which were decorations for a gallery after designs by Carrier-Belleuse, in 1862; and somewhat later the grille of the throne room of the king of Cambodia, Norodom I, after a design by Ducrot.*

*His contributions to the international exhibitions, always eagerly awaited and appreciated, were the equal of those of Barbedienne (q.v.).*

C.S.-V.

Bibliography:
*Rapports 1855,* p. 921; *Catalogue 1862,* p. 163; Lanoue, 1874, p. 524; Dussieux, 1876, pp. 345, 393, 572; de Champeaux, n.d., vol. III

II-37

---

Guillaume Denière; *biscuit* plaque by Gille Jeune*

## II-37
## Clock

1857 or 1861
Signed on face: DENIERE Fᵗ DE BRONZES A PARIS; on movement: Bᵗ DENIERE A PARIS 2872
Gilded bronze, *biscuit* plaque
Height 71.5 cm; width 68 cm; depth 24 cm

Provenance:
Entered the château of Fontainebleau, May 8, 1861 (Fontainebleau Archives, feuille d'entrée no. 189); installed in the corner room of the apartment of Louis XV (inv. no. F 3854)

Exhibitions:
1900, Paris, Exposition Universelle Centennale; 1922, Paris, Musée des Arts Décoratifs, no. 649

Bibliography:
Keim, 1930, vol. III, pl. 7, no. 7

Although the entry of this clock in the château of Fontainebleau was noted in 1861, the incompleteness of the entry and exit records of the Mobilier de la Couronne in the Archives Nationales precludes an exact determination of the date of its delivery by Denière. Among the clocks delivered by Denière, there are two that could be identified with the one shown here: "A richly ornamented clock with children and clouds in mat gold and ormolu," delivered in 1857 (Arch. nat. AJ¹⁹ 687), and "a clock in the style of Louis XVI in mat gilded bronze, group of children, spirits of Spring," delivered in 1861 (Arch. nat. AJ9 694 [objects acquired by the Emperor]). However, this clock is more likely the one delivered in 1861 rather than the first (allegory of Spring, with five cherubs instead of the four shown here), which it seems was also sent to Fontainebleau.

This clock was inspired by Louis XVI pieces with cherubs (it should be compared, for example, with the crowning of Riesener's large clock in the Louvre), but its interpretation is very personal. The cherubs are treated freely, especially the two below, who seem to be running away, trailing garlands of flowers behind them. The one on top, seated, with raised arms, is much closer to Louis XVI examples.

The base, which combines a fluted frieze, acanthus leaves, and ribbons, is characteristic of the way in which the bronze manufacturers of the period found their sources of inspiration, combining various elements of the decorative vocabulary. The *biscuit* plaque in the spirit of Louis XVI, depicting cherubs gathered around a vase, is by Gille Jeune, a Parisian porcelain manufacturer.

An identical clock was in the Hôtel de Païva at the end of the nineteenth century (Bibliothèque des Arts Décoratifs, recueil Maciet, 234 [44]).

C.S.-V.

Musée National du Château, Fontainebleau

## Léon Marchand

*Active Paris*

As director of a Parisian bronze factory founded in 1820 by his uncle and continued by his father, Marchand was established at 57, rue de Richelieu, then at 43, boulevard du Temple from 1860, and after the Exposition Universelle of 1867, at 8, rue du Grand Chantier (now rue des Archives) (Almanach du Commerce). His production included sculptures by earlier artists (Pigalle's Mercury, Houdon's Voltaire) and by contemporaries (Bosio, Schoenewerk, q.v.), as well as bronze furnishings (lights, clocks, vases). He was awarded a medal in London in 1851, and a silver medal in 1855 where his most important pieces were torchères supported by female figures by Klagmann. In 1862 he received two medals, one for his bronzes, the other for the fireplace by Piat. He received a gold medal in 1867.

D.A.

Bibliography:
Catalogue 1855, p. 117; Rapports 1855, p. 921; Durant, 1860, "Mouvement artistique," p. 228; Catalogue 1862, p. 203, "Renseignements," p. 157; Luchet, 1862, "Marchand," pp. 219, 221; Waring, 1863, vol. I, pl. 31, vol. III, pl. 213; Catalogue 1867, vol. III, p. 45; Récompensés 1867, group III, p. 40; Luchet, 1868, pp. 324–25

## Frédéric-Eugène Piat

*Montfey (Aube) 1827–1903 Paris*

The son of a carpenter who settled in Paris in 1833, Piat received but cursory training in the workshops of designers (Martin, who worked mainly for bronze manufacturers, Didier, and Protat), as well as in the studio of the sculptor Gossin. From 1845 on, he worked on his own, and it is to his own imagination that he owed his rapid fame. He provided designs and sculpted models for lights, clocks, and so forth, or for more unusual objects intended for the international exhibitions. His projects executed in bronze, zinc, cast iron, wrought iron, and silver plate, were made for the largest Parisian manufacturers of the Second Empire: Denière (q.v.), Graux-Marly, Boy, Paillard (see no. II-5), Marchand, Gagneau, and others. In 1855, recognized by Paillard, he received an honorable mention as coopérateur, and he and Lebeau (see below) received in 1867 a silver medal as Marchand's coopérateurs. Piat and his friends Sévin (q.v.) and Carrier-Belleuse (q.v., who did his bust in 1859) were the most inventive decorative sculptors of the Second Empire. Continuing his successes at the Expositions Universelles of 1878, 1889, and 1900, Piat

by the end of his life had earned the nickname, the "king of bronze." In Troyes he established a decorative arts museum (it opened on May 31, 1894, as the Musée Piat), donating, notably, some of his models. Both he and his widow later were to enrich it still further. Those of his works preserved in Troyes, although they have not been on exhibit since the war, were made the subject of an exhibition in that city in 1975–76.

D.A.

Bibliography:
Rapports 1855, p. 926; Récompensés 1867, group III, p. 44; Catalogues, Troyes, Musée, 1897, 1905; Sainte-Marie, 1975

## Bernard-Alfred Meyer

*Paris 1832–1904 Paris*

The son of a fabric designer and the student of the painter Picot, Meyer at first did various kinds of commercial painting, and then, on Picot's recommendation, was hired by the Sèvres (q.v.) factory on April 1, 1858. In addition to his work at Sèvres, Meyer, connected with Apoil and his wife, both painters at Sèvres, made, like them, imitations of painted Limoges enamels for antique dealers. Acquiring an excellent technique in this field, which he continued to improve, he left Sèvres in 1862 to teach enameling to Popelin (q.v.), then returned to Sèvres on April 1, 1863, as a permanent decorator, retiring on April 1, 1871.

The Sèvres Archives has a number of his designs for the decoration of porcelain in the Renaissance style. After having met Popelin, he directed his work as an enameler toward more artistic use. Encouraged by Popelin's success, and aided by his friend the painter Emile Lévy, who made the designs for him, Meyer exhibited enamel panels at the Salons beginning in 1864, notably, in 1864, Dante, after Raphael; in 1865, Apollo Driving the Chariot of the Sun, a clock face ordered by Count Aguado; in 1866, when he won a medal, Renée of France (Victoria and Albert Museum, London), and Julius Caesar, after Lévy (themes treated by Popelin in 1863 and 1864); in 1867, the Condottiere, after A. de Messine.

At the 1867 exposition, he showed, among other things, ornaments for a clock made for the château of Anet. After 1870, making his own designs, he continued to exhibit at the Salon. He took part in the first Impressionist exhibition at Nadar's (q.v.) in 1874. In addition, from the end of the Second Empire he executed small enamels with Renaissance subjects or imitating cameos to decorate jewelry, used notably by Baugrand at the 1867 exposition and by Boucheron.

Meyer became a teacher at the Ecole Bernard

Palissy and published L'Art de l'émail de Limoges ancien et moderne in 1895 (second edition 1896).

D.A.

Bibliography:
Sèvres Archives Y11, fol. 121 v; Sèvres Archives Ob[8]; Darcel, 1868, p. 79; Bellier and Auvray, 1882–87, vol. II, p. 81; Falize, 1893–94, passim; Vever, 1906–8, vol. III, pp. 373, 496; Thieme and Becker, 1907–50, vol. XXIV, p. 462; 1974, Paris, Grand Palais, "Impressionisme," p. 241

Léon Marchand; designed by Frédéric-Eugène Piat and enameled by Bernard-Alfred Meyer

## II-38
## Fountain for Perfumed Water

1867
Signed, on reverse of enamel, with monogram of A. Meyer in gold letters
Silvered bronze, painted enamel, veneer of blackened pear wood
Height 196 cm; width 62 cm (270 × 80 cm including support)

Provenance:
Created by Piat for the firm of Marchand (unique piece); exhibited by Marchand, 1867; retained by Piat; gift to the Musée Piat, 1894; Musée des Beaux-Arts, Troyes (inv. no. 894.15.20)

Exhibition:
1867, Paris, Exposition Universelle

Bibliography:
Luchet, 1868, p. 320; Champier, 1894–95, "Piat," p. 27 (repro.); Catalogue, Troyes, Musée, 1897, pp. 11–12, 36–37, no. 26

This wall fountain is composed of a Gothic pinnacle incorporating three Renaissance aedicule on which is mounted the reservoir and a lobed basin, from which the water flows through a pierced motif in the form of a fleur-de-lis. The silvered metal is set off by plaques of painted enamel, flat and concave. The white motifs on a blue background, heightened by gold, are borrowed from the grotesques decorating certain Italian Renaissance majolica pieces. The top spire of the pinnacle and the enameled shields held by the lions are missing.

Marchand's success was largely due to Piat, who decorated his new shop in 1860. For the 1862 exhibition, Marchand assured himself of success by contracting for Piat's exclusive collaboration. There they showed creations in the Greek style, including the sculptor's most celebrated work, made especially for this occasion: a fireplace about six meters high, a sort of homage to Minerva, in which the marble was enhanced by figures and ornaments in green and gilded bronze. After being exhibited again in 1867, it was lost in a shipwreck.

"Countless" works by Piat appeared in 1867 in various styles—medieval, Louis XIII, Louis XVI, Chinese—and for many firms: the Val-d'Osne foundry, Boy, Lefèvre, Bion, Morizot, Wagner, Paillard (for whom he also created a large fountain in red marble and bronze). But he was once again particularly conspicuous at Marchand's, where his main work was this fountain, the chasing of which was done by the foreman Pierre Lebeau (A. Luchet). Intended to illustrate the transition between the fifteenth and sixteenth centuries, it is characteristic of Piat, who used all styles with originality and, being more at ease than Sévin in large pieces, designed structured forms with frequent architectural elements. The fountain is also representative of the attempts to employ painted enamel in the decoration of large-size objects. The cradle of the Prince Imperial (no. II–17) from 1856 is an earlier exam-

ple. Subsequently, Fourdinois adorned a bookcase with enamels by Gobert (q.v.; now Musée des Arts Décoratifs) and Popelin (q.v.) executed enamel for two pieces of furniture by Mazaroz-Ribaillier in 1863 (Falize, 1893–94, vol. IX, p. 510, vol. X, p. 63), two pieces by Sauvrezy in 1867 (Luchet, 1868, p. 108), and a fireplace by Barbedienne (q.v.) in 1868 (Burty, 1868, "L'Email," p. 592). The heraldic lions of the fountain recall two erect lions adorning a pair of nineteenth-century French andirons in gilded bronze preserved at Waddesdon Manor (de Bellaigue, 1974, vol. II, pp. 728–29). In the faïence torchères in the form of lions that Gallé was to create several years later (one in the Musée du Conservatoire National des Arts et Métiers in Paris), one should perhaps also see an example of Piat's strong influence on the decorative arts of his time.

D.A.

Musées des Beaux-Arts, Troyes

II - 38

## Julien-Nicolas Rivart

*Died Paris 1867*

*Rivart began his career decorating porcelain in Paris and was established successively at 76, rue du Faubourg Saint Martin (Almanach du Commerce, 1835–36); 6, rue Samson (Almanach du Commerce, 1837–39); and 16, rue de la Folie Méricourt (Almanach du Commerce, 1840–50). To the decoration of porcelain Rivart added the manufacture or sale of bronzes, first in partnership with Dumont (Almanach du Commerce, 1847–48), then alone. Afterward he turned to the production of "fancy" furniture. Rivart invented the technique of porcelain marquetry, with floral, fruit, and other designs inlaid in wood, marble, velvet, and leather; he obtained a patent for this process which he exercised after 1849 in furniture and objects such as clocks, inkstands, desk furnishings, and wallets. He exhibited for the first time in London in 1851 where he received a medal. He established himself at 1, rue de Normandie (Almanach du Commerce, 1851–59) in partnership with Andrieux (Almanach du Commerce, 1852–54), and having perfected his technique, won a silver medal at the*

*Paris Exposition Universelle in 1855. Later he was established at 26, boulevard Beaumarchais (Almanach du Commerce, 1860–65).*

*At the London exhibition of 1862 he did part of the furnishings for the headquarters of the French Imperial Commission and showed furniture decorated with porcelain marquetry. At that time 50 percent of his work was made for export. He also worked for other furniture makers, probably supplying them only with marquetry panels; in 1862 the cabinetmaker Frédéric Roux exhibited pieces of "furniture called Rivart, with bouquets of porcelain set in wood, which surpassed everything in effect and taste" (Le Monde Illustré, vol. XI, July–December 1862, p. 238).*

*In 1867, established at 61, rue Sedaine, he intended to show marble panels inlaid with porcelain at the Exposition Universelle, but he died on February 17. Roux, however, did again exhibit furniture decorated by Rivart.*

D.A.

Bibliography:
Archives de Paris, Etat civil; *Rapports 1855*, pp. 1120–21; *Catalogue 1862*, p. 195; *Catalogue 1867*, vol. III, p. 9; Luchet, 1868, pp. 128–29; Ledoux-Lebard, 1965, p. 482

Julien-Nicolas Rivart

## II-39
## Table

c. 1861

Signed in engraving on lock: Rivart B^te^/B^art^ Baumarchais. 26; Manneville and Benoist coats of arms engraved in copper in center of top under count's crown and surmounting the Benoist device: BENE. FACIENTES. BENEDICTI.

Oak with palisander veneer, porcelain marquetry, gilded bronze, and engraved copper

Height 78 cm; width 144 cm; depth 104 cm

Provenance:

Made for Charles-André, comte de Manneville, and Marie-Félicité Benoist, daughter of Prosper-Désiré, comte Benoist, lieutenant-colonel in the cavalry, granddaughter of Pierre-Vincent Benoist, Minister of State, comte (1828), and of Mme Benoist, née Marie-Wilhelmine Le Roux de la Ville, a painter; purchased by the Musée National de Céramique, 1977 (inv. no. 24600)

This table, carefully crafted so that even the inside of the drawer is veneered, seems at first to be very much influenced by Louis XV furniture, notably in the form of the legs and in the bronze ornamentation set off by the veneer, which in the disposition and choice of motifs and the style is also reminiscent of the writing desks of this period.

But while the form of the top is very characteristic of the Second Empire, the porcelain marquetry which adorns it represents—as was already noted by 1851—"one of the major innovations in decoration for pieces of furniture" (*Rapports 1855*, p. 1120).

However, it was around 1760 that the idea had first been conceived of decorating luxury furniture with porcelain in the form of plaques fixed onto furniture with a bronze enframement. This type of ornamentation was still practiced in the Second Empire as can be seen in the Kreisser cabinet bought by Queen Victoria (*see* no. II-29) or the jewel cabinet of the Empress (Compiègne).

Although furniture of this type might have encouraged Rivart to adapt porcelain to furniture ornamentation, the use he made of it was quite different, being integrated into the veneer like wood marquetry. "This system is quite simple: once the design which one wants to represent is set, M. Rivart makes a model of it in wood and produces it in porcelain; the paste is then replaned on the face with high precision; then, the cutting faults are corrected by sanding, it goes for enameling, and the porcelain, once painted and finished, is encrusted in the wood or marble" (*Rapports 1855*, pp. 1120–21).

Although the motif—garlands of flowers tied by ribbons—is reminiscent of Florentine hard-stone mosaics, the naturalistic style is related, as H.-P. Fourest pointed out, to the decoration of certain porcelain pieces made by Jacob Petit under Louis Philippe (*see* de Plinval de Guillebon, 1972, pp. 223, 227, 229).

Since the comte and comtesse de Manneville were married in Paris on February 5, 1861, when Rivart was in fact working at the boulevard Beaumarchais, the table must have been made around this time. The same technique is found again in a jewel case in the Louis XVI style which belonged to the Empress Eugénie and is decorated on the top and four sides with porcelain flowers similar to the ones on the table and like them encrusted in a kingwood veneer ("Serre-Bijoux," 1957, p. 85, repro.; Ledoux-Lebard, 1965, p. 96, pl. 26). One of the branches of flowers bears the signature of Guérou, a flower painter at the Manufacture de Sèvres (q.v.) in 1847–48 (Brunet, 1953, p. 45). The *Almanach du Commerce* of 1867 lists P.-J. Guérou, artist designer, 16, rue du Pont aux Choux. Although this piece has on the lock the signature of the cabinetmakers Charon Frères, *fournisseurs de l'Empereur*, 2, rue de Braque in Paris, it is most likely that Rivart employed Guérou and supplied the porcelain marquetry.

This process disappeared after the death of Rivart, as Luchet pointed out in 1867: "The exposition at Roux's has shown us some marvelous panels on which Rivart was working when he died while trying to make even more beautiful than the most beautiful for that great rendezvous of universal magnificence. Never again will what he did be done: now the merchant wants things fast and cheap. May the touching memory of this dear hard-working man draw the attention of the jury for a moment! Plaques bearing his name will be worth a great deal of money some day" (Luchet, 1868, pp. 128–29).

D.A.

Musée National de Céramique, Sèvres

II-39

# Fine Metalwork and Hard Stones

It has been customary to attribute all composite objects produced in the nineteenth century to the Second Empire, although they often were made earlier or later. Is it possible to distinguish in the field of fine metalwork—silverwork, goldwork, jewelry, enamels—and hard stones those traits that are particular to this period, which, after slandering itself ("our period, which is still anything but original";[1] "modern art... powerless to create a style of its own in silverwork and goldwork"[2]) continued to be so discredited since the end of the nineteenth century? In pursuing this goal one must lean heavily on texts of the period—records still only partly known, criticisms that often repeat each other—and on dated objects, which are difficult to find, especially in the ephemeral realm of goldwork and jewelry. Around the turn of the century Falize[3] and Vever[4] had already noted the disappearance of a number of Second Empire objects, and since then the destruction of objects or the obscurity into which they have fallen has increased even more.

In fact, there has rarely been such a deliberate effort for innovation of forms and ornamentation, techniques and materials, as occurred during the Second Empire in reaction against the symptoms of decadence for which previous periods were held responsible: "The nineteenth century began... with thirty years of the most disheartening sterility."[5] "What was then [c. 1840] manufactured was monstrous.... Table settings were copper ware made of silver."[6] With increased production earlier techniques had been sacrificed, while merchants, under the influence of the growing taste of the public for antiquities, preferred, under Louis Philippe, to manufacture objects inspired by the past.

The very causes of the decline partly account for the revival. New creations had to be constantly offered to a large clientele, who, coming from a newly prosperous class, demanded large numbers of luxury objects. Besides, the attempt to imitate or counterfeit antique objects led to the rediscovery of abandoned techniques. Already under Louis Philippe, certain precursors—Fauconnier (1776–1839), the Prussian Charles Wagner (see Rudolphi), François-Désiré Froment-Meurice (q.v.), Morel (q.v.), Duponchel (see Morel), Jean-Baptiste Fossin (see Fossin)—whose production was generally inspired by the Renaissance, were improving their techniques.

They began to restore enamel to a place of honor. Wagner, familiar with the technique of niello, brought it back into fashion at the Exposition des Produits de l'Industrie of 1834. Since the first Empire silversmiths had ceased to practice repoussé and chasing, techniques that were, however, preserved by the Strasbourg silversmith Kirstein, who exhibited bas-reliefs in repoussé silver at the Salon between 1810 and 1834, and by Fauconnier, who under Louis Philippe had founded a school of chasing, which ceased to function after his death. Antoine Vechte (1799–1868), who had worked for Fauconnier, was to salvage definitively these techniques by making imitation Renaissance pieces that certain dealers sold as authentic.[7] Employed by Froment-Meurice as early as 1839, he brought about the reestablishment of brilliant chasers under the Second Empire.

A concern to improve training and production was revealed by the founding of the Société d'Art Industriel in 1845. It became the Société pour l'Encouragement et le Développement de l'Art Industriel en France (1855), and later the Société du Progrès de l'Art Industriel (1858), whose members included the silversmith Wièse, the chasers Honoré, Dalberge, Fannière (q.q.v.), and the gilder Mourey (see no. III-23). In 1863 it became known as the Union Centrale des Beaux-Arts Appliqués à l'Industrie, and its activities included publications, lectures, and exhibitions (1861, 1863, 1865, 1869).

Science came to the aid of fine metalwork by presenting new materials. Thanks to gold and silver plating, practiced by Christofle (q.v.) from 1842, the appearance of silverwork could be given to objects of cheap metal (brass, nickel silver), which made it possible to undertake even the boldest enterprises. "In our time, galvanoplasty [or electroforming] has come to offer stiff competition to silversmith's work in solid metal. Now, when wealth is almost always based on one's holdings in silver, why tie up several hundred thousand francs? You can get the same appearance with a few tens of thousands of francs."[8] Napoleon III revolutionized the practice of the courts by commissioning from Christofle a table service in silver plate. Aluminum also offered new possibilities (see no. III-23).

Another element in the revival of fine metalwork was the interest taken in it by painters and sculptors, who in this way felt they were imitating the artists of the Renaissance. While sculptors took an interest in silver- and goldwork, the rebirth of painted enamel was brought about by such painters as Delaroche, Gobert (q.v.), and Popelin (q.v.). "The cooperation of distinguished, learned & able artists will wrest these arts from the hacks & protect them from the influences of the manufacturer."[9]

Thus different factors came together to rescue these crafts from the routine, after they had been interrupted by the Revolution of 1848, which, by causing considerable emigration and a temporary reduction in sales, compelled them to make a fresh start. The London Universal Exhibition of 1851, and those that came after, stimulated inventiveness, and on these occasions the manufacturers respected the ideas of the designers, sparing no expense, in particular from fear of English competition, an obsession expressed by the press in patriotic terms throughout the Second Empire.

It is often difficult to discover the authors of these innovations. Dealers exhibiting at the international exhibitions were not always the manufacturers. "In general and with very rare exceptions, Parisian dealers sell what the various makers deliver; they are strangers to the manufacture of the work."[10] Thus, whereas the architect Duponchel dabbled in silverwork, Lemonnier (q.v.) sold pieces executed by the jewelers Maheu and Massin, while the first pieces of cloisonné enamel jewelry by Falize (q.v.) were offered for sale by Martz (see no. III-20). Manufacturers in Paris were concentrated in the Marais, while the jewelry shops were distributed around the Palais Royal, the boulevards, and the rue de la Paix. Heads of certain firms belonged to families working in these branches of the arts since the beginning of the nineteenth century, or even, in the case of the Odiots, since the *ancien régime.* The role of foreigners—Rudolphi (q.v.), Wièse, Massin from Liège—was also important. While the firm of Christofle took social measures for the benefit of its employees, the union of goldsmiths, jewelers, and silversmiths, whose first president was Alexis Falize, was founded in 1864, and the Ecole Professionnelle de Dessin et de Modelage was established in 1868. In the provinces, Lyons made a unique name for itself thanks to Armand-Calliat (q.v.), the only one of the twenty-five silversmiths exhibiting in 1867 who was not established in Paris.

The activity of silversmiths *(orfèvres),*

goldsmiths (bijoutiers), and jewelers (joailliers) was not distinctly separate, each of them often practicing the various kinds of work. Although the three crafts were in the same class at the Exposition Universelle of 1855 in Paris and at the London International Exhibition of 1862, silversmiths were separated from goldsmiths and jewelers at the 1867 Exposition Universelle, where nevertheless one could see jewelry with P.-H. Emile Froment-Meurice (q.v.), who was classed among the silversmiths, and silverwork with Wièse, who exhibited with the jewelers.

The head of the firm no longer had the time to do work himself, but relied on collaborators, who sometimes, as in the case of chasers, enamelers, and engravers on semiprecious stones, worked independently outside the firm. As a result of the Revolution of 1848, and beginning with the Exposition des Produits de l'Industrie of 1849, collaborators, whether outside or not, were specified and given awards like the manufacturers, the most important of whom ended up receiving the Legion of Honor.

A number of them have been designated "artist-manufacturers"[11] because of the personal part they took in the creation of pieces, notably Froment-Meurice, Morel, Falize. An exceptional case, the Fannières both conceived their works and executed them. The actual designer, however, was generally the artist who provided the model: an architect (Baltard, q.v.; Rossigneux; the diocesan architects for ecclesiastical silverwork); a sculptor; most of the time, an "industrial artist" trained as a draftsman or sculptor—Piat, Rambert, Reiber, Sévin (q.q.v.)—whose role passed unnoticed by the public. The wish to create a style inspired these industrial artists, such as Piat: "He is one of the few men with the noble idea that a period should have its own art, which would represent it, explain it, and one day serve to characterize it."[12]

The past—better known thanks to the progress of archaeology, to the museums, private collections, and retrospective exhibitions (the first organized by the Union Centrale in 1865; another attached to the 1867 Exposition Universelle)—still furnished a great part of the inspiration for forms and decoration. The trends that emerged under Louis Philippe persisted during the Second Empire, judging by the reports of the Expositions Universelles. The Middle Ages inspired only ecclesiastical silverwork. Father Martin, under Louis Philippe, was the first to have liturgical objects executed by the silversmith Cahier in medieval style (see Poussielgue-Rusand), the only style tolerated for them under the Second Empire: "The archaeologist is no longer satisfied to be a scholar,

he thinks himself an artist,"[13] and he creates his own models. Thus the originality of Armand-Calliat was applauded in 1867. The influence of the Renaissance, diminishing in 1862, would still remain strong among such silversmiths as P.-H. Emile Froment-Meurice and the Fannières. In 1862 Darcel noted that "after having blindly followed the Rococo style, whose errors it naturally exaggerated,"[14] silver tableware had become more sober; the Louis XV style would reappear in this area after the Second Empire. "In bronzes and silverwork, the exposition of 1855 had nothing to show us but the Louis XVI style,"[15] a trend that persisted.

A creation of the Second Empire, the "Néo-Grec" style, seemingly foreshadowed by Duponchel's chryselephantine Minerva (1846–51) and the figures and decoration of the bases of Christofle's centerpiece for Napoleon III (1855), developed in the following years and dominated in 1862. This fashion in goldwork, launched in Rome by the goldsmith Castellani, grew more marked in France after the unveiling of the Campana collection, acquired in 1861 in Rome by Napoleon III. Exhibited at the Palais de l'Industrie in 1862 under the name "Musée Napoleon III," and then at the Louvre in 1863, it comprised notably 1,200 Greek, Etruscan, and Roman pieces of jewelry,[16] and aroused the enthusiasm of such goldsmiths as Fontenay (q.v.). In 1867, with the progress of work on the Suez Canal, Egyptian art also penetrated the art of silversmiths and goldsmiths, for example, Baugrand (q.v.).

To the influence of the past was added that of exoticism, thanks to trade, politics, lithographic and photographic reproductions, and the specialization of certain Parisian silversmiths and goldsmiths (Fontenay, Crouzet, Viette) in the manufacture of Oriental-style pieces for export to the Middle East. The China expedition (1860) and the opening up of Japan, whose works were discovered in the last years of the Second Empire, notably at the Union Centrale exhibition of 1869, again supplied new themes (see no. III-20).

In decoration, certain motifs seem particularly frequent: cartouches surrounded by Renaissance strapwork whose use in goldwork was launched by Marchand Aîné around 1840,[17] or polylobate cartouches in the Muslim style; interlacings in which Turkish, Persian, or Indian influence is blended with that of Moresque decorations of the Renaissance; antique-style or Oriental palmettes; other motifs from Classical antiquity (rinceaux), treated with all the variations that later periods had given them.

If the designers were crippled by their admiration for the decorative arts of the past, their

goal was not to imitate them, but to find therein suggestions for use in their compositions, which, however, they hoped would be completely new. It is often difficult to uncover their sources: nothing was ever the exact replica of a previous formula. "[Piat] is indeed the copyist of the past, the times demand it; but he is not the copyist of any artist of the past."[18] "'I search constantly,' said Sévin, 'and if I borrow from the styles of the past.... I always interpret them.'"[19] They mixed different currents, amassed diverse materials for the same object, used the forms and decorations in one technique that previously were restricted to another. In addition, they borrowed from architecture specific elements (pediments) and from painting and sculpture a taste for subject matter.

The decorative arts were at times intellectual and pedantic, this being a period when literature took an interest in them. François-Désiré Froment-Meurice had been celebrated by Victor Hugo (q.v.), and Popelin inspired sonnets by Théophile Gautier, Théodore de Banville, François Coppée, and José Maria de Heredia. The object often illustrated a theme which was emphasized by emblems and inscriptions as in the Renaissance.

For the implementation of the subject sculptors were requested to model the figures planned by designers (allegories inspired by antiquity or the Renaissance, putti in the manner of the eighteenth century, animals) which stood on each side of a central motif, flanked the base, served as handles or feet, or surmounted the object. The example of Pradier and Feuchère who, under Louis Philippe, were the first sculptors to work for silversmiths, was followed by Klagmann, Cavelier (q.v.), Geoffroy-Dechaume, as well as Rouillard (q.v.), Schoenewerk (q.v.), Gilbert, Diébolt, Carrier-Belleuse (q.v.), Gumery, Mathurin Moreau (q.v.), Millet, Maillet (q.v.), and Thomas. Their work was sometimes so overwhelming that Darcel reproached Christofle for executing "sculpture and architecture in silver"[20] (see nos. III-3–III-7). This participation by sculptors constituted, however, an original contribution; also new was the naturalism that sometimes appeared in vegetable ornament, in subjects of some agricultural contest trophies, and in such figures as the workers shown on the centerpiece of the manufacturer Pétin, exhibited by Odiot in 1867.[21]

Designers overshot their goal by pursuing it too far: the juxtaposition of sources, materials, and of collaborators interfered with their homogeneity. The execution "exceeds"[22] as one can see by examining the production of the various crafts.

In silverwork, Froment-Meurice, Christofle, Morel, Duponchel, Rudolphi, Wièse, Gueyton, Odiot, Aucoc (specialist in necessaries), and the Fannière Frères attracted the most attention. To the manufacture of useful objects, the silversmiths added, largely under English influence, that of numerous "art pieces," which were generally offered for commemorative purposes: cups, prizes for sports competitions (see no. III-6) and agricultural contests (see nos. III-5, III-7), dress swords (see no. III-27), shields. Ecclesiastical silverwork thrived especially under Napoleon III, who presented countless churches with pieces furnished by Bachelet, Thiéry, Trioullier, and above all Poussielgue-Rusand (q.v.). Silversmiths on occasion manufactured centerpieces and sacred objects in bronze (see no. III-15). The Fannières chased iron and steel, while a few attempts at chryselephantine work appeared (see no. III-11). Henri Dufresne revived damascening.[23] An interest in coloring silverwork led Bouilhet (q.v.), at Christofle, to plate golds of different colors, for example on the centerpiece of the Hôtel de Ville (1862), and to exhibit in 1867 the first objects in bronze inlaid with gold and silver obtained by "damascene plating" in imitation of Chinese and Japanese work.

Most of the great silversmiths (Froment-Meurice, Rudolphi, Wièse, Gueyton) also excelled in goldwork, along with such goldsmith-jewelers as Baugrand, Mellerio, Rouvenat, Oscar Massin, and Frédéric Boucheron—these last two exhibiting for the first time in 1867. The most characteristic jewels were bracelets (a variety may be seen on the arms of the ladies of the court in Winterhalter's painting; see no. VI-110); oval lockets; earrings, especially in the second half of the reign, after the disappearance of the long spiral curls known as anglaises; and, beginning in 1865, aigrettes, invented by Massin. Jewelry in gold and silver was rivaled by jewelry in steel (140 manufacturers in Paris in 1864) and cast iron, and by imitation goldwork made of copper to which a thin sheet of gold was soldered (Murat, who exhibited for the first time in 1855; Savard), and of gilded copper. Familiar themes (animals, domestic objects), endlessly varied, inspired so-called sporting and horse-racing pieces, and those representing mechanical objects, and it was against this that "Néo-Grec" jewelry reacted.

Jewelry set with precious stones, banal at the beginning of the Second Empire—"pointed foliage, round flowers, and bezels"[24]—was profoundly transformed, thanks especially to the designer and manufacturer Massin. The lowering of the price of stones, which allowed the use of larger ones, led him to lighten the

gold or silver mounts, while beginning in 1861, he undertook to reproduce his jewelry flowers and branches in a highly naturalistic manner. The masterpiece in this style was Rouvenat's spray of lilacs, exhibited in 1867.[25]

To the credit of the Second Empire must go the revival of enamelwork, in combination with silverwork—for the first time since the seventeenth century—goldwork, and jewelry, which became again an art in itself. It had survived under only two forms: translucent enamel on a ground of flinqué or guilloché gold, employed in goldwork (see no. III-18); and miniatures on enamel, known at the time as "Toutin," "Petitot," or "Geneva" enamels, devoted to the reproduction of paintings. The needs of restorers and forgers account partly for the rediscovery of almost all other techniques. Thus Legost (q.v.) revived champlevé enamel while doing restorations, before putting it again to the service of religious silverwork in 1853. Rather than by hollowing out the metal, the champlevé technique was soon achieved more readily by either using stamped grounds (see no. III-16) or by casting the "cloisons," following the example of Barbedienne (q.v.), whose enamels were improperly called "cloisonné" (see no. II-34). True cloisonné did not reappear until the Exposition Universelle of 1867 with Tard (q.v.), under the name of "émail à cloisons rapportées." In the field of painted enamels ("émail des peintres" or "Limoges" enamels, as it was called at the time), attempts initiated around 1840 by Wagner and Froment-Meurice received official recognition by the creation of the enamel workshop at Sèvres (q.v.) in 1845. Gobert, Meyer (who trained Popelin), and Frédéric de Courcy had connections with Sèvres. Charles Lepec, working independently, made innovations by using gold as a ground and covering it with translucent colors. His masterpiece was a nef exhibited in 1867 (acquired in 1976 by the Badisches Landes museum, Karlsruhe). Under Louis Philippe, Lefournier, thanks also to restoration work, succeeded in reviving enameling on three-dimensional figures in repoussé gold (see no. III-33). On the occasion of the 1867 exposition, Riffault, anticipating Thesmar, executed enamels without metallic grounds (émaux à jour) for Boucheron, while P.-H. Emile Froment-Meurice tried to imitate enamels on glass (émail en résille sur verre) by inlaying a rock crystal ewer with enamel.[26]

Hard stones were among the fine materials in which the Second Empire was interested. Following François-Désiré Froment-Meurice ("Vintage" cup, exhibited in 1844) and Morel (see no. III-33), many silversmiths attempted the execution of vases mounted with silver-

work, as was done in the Renaissance and the seventeenth century. Duron, in particular, exhibited in 1867 pieces imitating those in the Louvre. The glyptic art lay dormant, however, enslaved to the production of engraved gems designed for jewelry, the fashion for which never abated and in fact increased under the influence of "Néo-Grec" taste. A sincere wish to revive this art led to the commissioning of the cameo (no. III-32) by David.

Such is how the various aspects of the French arts of hard stones and fine metalwork appeared under the Second Empire, insofar as one can give an account of them in a brief examination. It was a time when they undeniably reacquired in the eyes of foreigners the prestige they had had in the eighteenth century. Whereas English silverwork was being revived from 1848 on by the French craftsman Vechte and his disciple Morel-Ladeuil, in fact numerous purchases were made in France by foreign collectors. Thus a good number of the objects assembled here come from foreign museums whose forward-looking attitude they demonstrate.

D.A.

Notes

1. Labourieu, 1857, p. 56.
2. Mantz, 1863, "Orfèvrerie," p. 549.
3. Falize, 1893–94, vol. X, p. 483.
4. Vever, 1906–8, vol. II, pp. 184–85.
5. Honoré, 1859, pp. 149–50.
6. Darcel, 1862, p. 320.
7. Mantz, 1863, "Orfèvrerie," p. 544.
8. Burty, 1866, Chefs-d'œuvre, p. 555.
9. Popelin, 1866, p. 28.
10. Mesnard, 1867, vol. II, p. 192.
11. Champier, 1888–89, p. 164.
12. Luchet, 1868, p. 320.
13. Chertier, 1859, p. 114.
14. Darcel, 1862, p. 320.
15. Deville, 1856, p. 80.
16. See Clément, 1862.
17. Fontenay, 1887, p. 367.
18. Labourieu, 1857, p. 56.
19. Champier, 1888–89, pp. 173–74.
20. Darcel, 1862, p. 318.
21. Bouilhet, 1908–12, vol. III, p. 67, repro. pp. 70, 73.
22. Luchet, 1868, p. 310.
23. Waring, 1863, vol. I, pl. 14.
24. Vever, 1906–8, vol. II, p. 91.
25. Ducuing, 1868, vol. II, p. 462, repro. p. 463.
26. Bouilhet, 1908–12, vol. III, p. 40.

# Silverwork (Secular)

## Ferdinand Barbedienne

*Saint-Martin-de-Fresnay (Calvados) 1810–1892 Paris*

*France's leading manufacturer of artistic bronzes during the second half of the nineteenth century, Barbedienne made casts of historical and contemporary sculpture and produced original decorative bronzes designed in the firm's studios. Apprenticed at twelve to a Parisian papermaker, Barbedienne was by 1834 a successful manufacturer of wallpapers. In 1838 he began a new career as a fondeur in partnership with Achille Collas, inventor of a system for making reductions of sculptures: the firm, under the name Collas and Barbedienne, specialized in antique reproductions and developed new chemical processes for patinations and colored bronzes. At the London exhibition of 1851 the firm, listed as Barbedienne, was awarded two Council Medals. At the Exposition Universelle of 1855 the firm won a Grand Medal of Honor and eleven lesser medals for the work of its chasers and mounters; its exhibit included bronze reductions of sculptures by Michelangelo and Clésinger (q.v.) as well as furniture, vases, coupes, candelabra, and other ornaments (Catalogue 1855, p. 116, no. 5144), and pieces in innovative "Néo-Grec" styles. Barbedienne's success at international exhibitions led to many official commissions: between 1850 and 1854 the firm provided Renaissance-style furnishings for the Hôtel de Ville, Paris; after 1855 they designed "Néo-Grec" ornaments for Prince Napoleon's "Maison Pompéienne" (no. I-22) and supplied decorative bronzes for the imperial residences, including four Louis XVI-style girandoles in gilded bronze delivered in 1863 to Compiègne (Arch. nat. 0⁵ 1681). At the Union Centrale exhibition of 1863 Barbedienne showed a pair of Louis XVI candelabra designed "for the study of the Emperor" (Union Centrale 1863, no. 163). At the London International Exhibition of 1862 Barbedienne introduced "cloisonné" enamels in Byzantine styles (see no. II-34), the first examples of metalwork to reproduce Oriental models (The Builder, 1862, pp. 384–85) and to use "Eastern" or "Chinese" techniques, and won medals in three different classes: furniture, reproduction and casting in bronze, and fine works in silver. As jury reporter Barbedienne was hors concours at the Exposition Universelle of 1867, although his display, like that of 1862, featured cloisonné enamels. Barbedienne himself was named officer (1867) and commander (1878) of the Legion of Honor and was awarded the Jean Goujon Gold Medal by the Société d'Encouragement pour l'Industrie Nationale in 1886. At Barbedienne's*

*death, his nephew and former associate Gustave Leblanc-Barbedienne succeeded as proprietor of the firm.*

K.B.H.

Bibliography:
Arch. nat. 368 AP 1,2 [Barbedienne papers]; de Champeaux, 1886, pp. 59–68; Rossigneux, 1886; Champier, 1891–92, pp. 289–92; Barbedienne, 1893

Ferdinand Barbedienne

## III-1
## Incense Burner

1855

Bronze, silvered and oxidized
Incense burner height 51 cm, width 25.5 cm;
salver diameter 29 cm; stand height 5.1 cm

Provenance:
Purchased from the maker at the Exposition Universelle of 1855 for 48 pounds by the South Kensington Museum (now the Victoria and Albert Museum, London); transferred to the Bethnal Green Museum (inv. no. 2707-1856)

Exhibitions:
1855, Paris, Exposition Universelle; 1862, London

Bibliography:
*Inventory, London, Victoria and Albert Museum, 1852–67,* 1856, p. 30; Waring, 1863, vol. I, pl. 10; Aslin, 1973, no. 11 (repro.)

In his report on the state of design at the Paris Exposition Universelle of 1855, Richard Redgrave praised Barbedienne generally for designs "in the Greek style... of great merit and beautiful execution" (R. Redgrave, in *Reports 1855,* part 3, p. 389). When the incense burner, exhibited first in 1855, was shown again in London in 1862 it was its "Greek" aspect that Waring chose to emphasize: "The vase is intended for a *brule-parfum,* and is a good example of that peculiar development of the Greek style which has distinguished the ornamental designs of France for the last few years, called 'Néo-Grec.'" In 1855 the incense burner anticipated later extravagant and bizarre inventions which were often "Greek" in ornament only: here palmettes decorate a form that is essentially Islamic (although the curious and spiky handles add a Neo-Gothic note to the profile) with pierced openings and calligraphic strapwork that also suggest Near Eastern

sources. Superimposed on these exotic forms are naturalistic decorations — including the dragonfly applied prominently at the neck — which anticipate in style, if not in intent, Japanizing influences of the 1870s and 1880s. At the 1855 exposition Barbedienne also showed archaeologically correct Greek designs, including a tripod designed by Henri Cahieu (after a first-century A.D. candelabrum or lamp stand; Victoria and Albert Museum, London, 2704-1856) and two vases, described in *The Art Journal Catalogue* as "formed, and ornamented, on the best models of the ancient Greeks" *(Art Journal Catalogue 1855,* p. 41). Both aspects of Barbedienne's innovative Greek style were ap-

III-1

parent in the display by Sèvres (q.v.) at the 1862 exhibition, which included fantastic porcelains designed by Nicolle (q.v.) and Solon (q.v.) and historically imitative pieces by Forgeot (q.v.).

K.B.H.

Bethnal Green Museum, London

## Louis-Constant Sévin

### Versailles 1821–1888 Paris

*Son of an itinerant actor, Sévin was apprenticed at thirteen to the Parisian sculptor Marneuf. In 1839 he formed a partnership with the sculpteurs-modeleurs Phenix and Joyau to produce ornamental metalwork on consignment — Sévin as designer — for such firms as Denière (q. v.), François-Désiré Froment-Meurice (q.v.), and Morel and Duponchel. During the Revolution of 1848 Sévin joined Morel (q. v.) in London and as chef d'atelier designed a number of the pieces that Morel exhibited at the Crystal Palace exhibition of 1851, including two Renaissance-style hard-stone footed vases with gold and enamel decorations (Art Journal Catalogue 1851, repro. p. 113; Travaux 1851, vol. VI, p. 160), which anticipated Sévin's single most important work for Morel, the gold, jasper, and enamel vase executed for Henry Thomas Hope (no. III-33). In 1851 Sévin returned to France and Limoges, where he supplied designs for the porcelain firm of Jouhanneaud and Dubois. At the Paris Exposition Universelle of 1855 Jouhanneaud exhibited ceramics decorated with relief sculptures in seventeenth-century Italian and German styles after metalwork examples, which were designed by Sévin (Ravenez, 1855, pp. 74–76). Returning to Paris in 1855, Sévin accepted a position as sculpteur-ornemaniste with Barbedienne (q.v.), where he remained until the end of his life. From the late 1850s Sévin designed bronzes for the Hôtel de Païva (1855–66) and, after the death of Prince Albert in December 1861, gilded-bronze column bases, capitals, and four large pendant lamps for the Royal Mausoleum at Frogmore (Berkshire), which was dedicated in 1862. At the London exhibition of 1862 Sévin received a medal "for the high artistic excellence displayed in the furniture designed by him and exhibited by Barbedienne" (Medals 1862, p. 328). Sévin also won a second-class medal at the Union Centrale's exhibition of 1863 (Union Centrale 1863, p. 46, no. 60) for the design of the Emperor's gilded-bronze Louis XVI-style candelabra whose ornaments were described as "full of spirit and of delicacy" (Union Centrale 1863, p. 35). At the 1867 exposition, where Sévin was awarded a gold medal as coopérateur (Récompensés 1867, p. 44), Barbedienne remarked that*

posterity would remember Sévin's compositions, and praised the designer's knowledge of the history of ornament and his ability to work in a variety of styles in a manner consistently "sober and pure" (F. Barbedienne, in Rapports 1867, vol. III, pp. 309–10). On his use of historic styles, Sévin himself commented that "if I borrow from the styles of the past . . . I always interpret" (Champier, 1888–89, pp. 173–74). The most singular object Sévin designed for Barbedienne was a monumental gilded-bronze Renaissance-style clock, four meters high, which won the designer a gold medal and Barbedienne a Grand Medal at the Exposition Universelle of 1878 (Catalogue 1878, group III, class XXV, p. 122).

K.B.H.

Bibliography:
Champier, 1888–89; Vever, 1906–8, vol. I, pp. 267–68, 275

## Désiré Attarge

### Saint-Germain-en-Laye c. 1820–1878 Paris

*A metal chaser of great skill, Attarge worked for François-Désiré Froment-Meurice (q.v.), and for Morel and Duponchel during the 1840s. In 1848 Attarge followed Morel (q.v.) to London where he wrought a number of pieces of gold jewelry shown at the 1851 Universal Exhibition. By 1855 Attarge had returned to Paris and a position as ciseleur-ornemaniste with Barbedienne (q. v.). He remained with Barbedienne for the rest of his career, although at the 1867 Exposition Universelle Attarge is also reported to have chased gold and silver gun ornaments (a hunting relief with weasels pursuing birds) for the armorer Gastine-Renette (Darcel, 1867, "Galvanoplastie," p. 565). In 1862 and 1864 Attarge won the Concours Crozatier and 500 francs for chased objects "executed with the greatest perfection" (Lami, 1881–88, vol. III, p. 491). At the 1867 exposition, where Attarge was awarded a silver medal as coopérateur (Récompensés 1867, p. 44), Darcel complimented Attarge's technical ability to model smoothly and with great precision the broad surfaces and details of his reliefs : "It is impossible to handle the tool with more precision and more breadth, or to create a greater richness, despite the preciousness of the details. Thus treated, bronze becomes goldsmith's work" (Darcel, 1867, "Bronze," p. 425). Barbedienne, too, praised his craftsman's skill and intelligence "under which the metal becomes supple and takes on delicate forms" (F. Barbedienne, in Rapports 1867, vol. III, p. 310), and like Lami,*

who compared Attarge to Gouthières (Lami, 1881–88, vol. III, p. 491), considered Attarge the equal of any goldsmith of the past.

K.B.H.

Bibliography:
Lami, 1881–88, vol. I, p. 380; Vever, 1906–8, vol. I, p. 267

Ferdinand Barbedienne; designed by Louis-Constant Sévin and chased by Désiré Attarge

## III-2
## Covered Ewer, Ewer, and Goblet

1862
Mark : F. BARBEDIENNE
Silver, decorated with repoussé reliefs; parcel-gilt interiors
Covered ewer height 29 cm; ewer height 28 cm; goblet height 17 cm

Provenance:
Gift of Mme Leblanc-Barbedienne to the Musée National du Château, Compiègne, 1962 (inv. nos. C 63.020/1; C 63.020/2; C 63.020/3)

Exhibition:
1862, London

Bibliography:
Compiègne Archives C 63.020/9, C 63.020/10 [letters from Lemaître to Barbedienne, April 27, May 5, 1862], C 63.020/11 [letter from Sévin to Barbedienne, May 1, 1862]; Bouilhet, 1908–12, vol. III, pp. 159–60

Described in the firm's correspondence as the "garniture argenté" and valued at 18,000 francs, the silver table service which included these pieces was sent to the London International Exhibition in the spring of 1862 along with two Chinese incense burners, a Chinese enameled "boat," and two Louis XVI flower holders. The naturalistic floral ornaments raised and chased by Attarge derive in style from Late Hellenistic silver wares — such as the first-century B.C. cup decorated in relief with myrtle branches which was found at Alise-Sainte-Reine (ancient Alesia, Côte d'Or) in September 1862, reproduced by Barbedienne (Union Centrale 1863, "supplement," p. 97) and given by the Emperor in 1867 to the Musée des Antiquités Nationales at Saint-Germain-en-Laye (Nieuwerkerke, 1869, p. 133). During the 1860s and 1870s Sévin and Attarge produced a series of vessels with similar, but not identical, naturalistic ornaments. The 1862 service anticipates this series and differs from the later pieces in that the Classical ornaments (including the friezes of lotus and palmette and tongues) here decorate forms more Renaissance than Greco-Roman. However, by 1867 Barbedienne had adopted appropriate Classical

III-2

forms for this naturalistic style, exhibiting a silver kantharos with wild heather in relief *(Art Journal Catalogue 1867,* vol. VII, repro. p. 200), and in 1878, a kylix with mask and vine ornament (Bouilhet, 1908–12, vol. I, repro. p. 160). Barbedienne claimed that Greek art was the "basis" of Sévin's beliefs, his "first rule of study" (F. Barbedienne, in *Rapports 1867,* vol. III, p. 309). Here Sévin subscribes his Hellenism to the conception prevalent in both France and England from about 1850 — that the nature of ornament should suggest the purpose of the object it adorns. The covered ewer, serving as a wine jug, is decorated with a mask of Dionysius and naturalistic sprays of vine and vineyard creatures, including snails and lizards; the water jug is correspondingly decorated with a mask of Poseidon, seaweed, cockle and snail shells, and a frog at the base of the handle.

K.B.H.

Musée National du Château, Compiègne

## Charles Christofle
*Paris 1805–1863 Brunoy (Essonne)*

Charles Christofle came from a family in Lyons who owned a silk factory but became impoverished in 1814. Obliged to discontinue his studies, he entered the jewelry firm founded in 1812 in Paris by his brother-in-law Calmette, where he remained an apprentice for three years and a craftsman for one year before being taken on as a partner in 1825. As of 1831 he was sole director of the firm, which was established at 76, rue Montmartre. He registered his mark on August 1, 1832, and manufactured, especially for export, jewelry that won him a gold medal at the Exposition des Produits de l'Industrie in 1839. Christofle obtained in 1842 and 1843 for ten years the exclusive use of the patents taken out by Elkington (in 1840 and 1842) and Ruolz (in 1841 and 1842) for the galvanic process of gilding and silvering (Almanach du Commerce), and in the following years was embroiled in many lawsuits to preserve his

rights until the patents entered the public domain. The factory for silverwork was established on the rue de Bondy (now rue René Boulanger), at number 54 (Almanach du Commerce), then at 56 (Almanach du Commerce, 1851), and remained there until 1934. In 1844 Christofle exhibited for the first time, along with jewelry, silver- and gold-plated objects that earned him a gold medal, then the Legion of Honor. Christofle took his nephew and collaborator Léon Rouvenat as a partner in the jewelry firm, then ceded it to him in 1849. Christofle obtained a gold medal for his silver-plated work in 1849 and another medal also in 1851. On April 4, 1853, he registered a mark for silver. In 1854 he took his son-in-law Ernest de Ribes as his partner. In 1855 his factory employed more than 1,200 workers, and Christofle added a second factory in Karlsruhe in 1859. He received the Grand Medal of Honor in 1855 (fifteen of his collaborators also received awards) and a medal at the exposition of 1862, after which he was named officer of the Legion of Honor. He and Ernest de Ribes both died the same year, and the direction of the firm passed in 1863 to Christofle's son and nephew Paul Christofle and Henri Bouilhet. The work of Christofle under the Second Empire, both in silver and silver plate, fell into three categories: standard silversmith's work (table services, articles for the Levant, toilet articles, lights), luxury silverwork, and objets d'art.

D.A.

Bibliography:
Arch. de la Garantie, Insculpations 1820–41, fol. 23, 1841–54, fol. 25; Christofle, 1855; *Rapports 1855*, pp. 462, 912, 925–26, 1409–10; *Catalogue 1862*, p. 212, "Renseignements," pp. 167–68; *Christofle*, 1862; Dalloz, 1862; Darcel, 1862, pp. 316–21; Luchet, 1862, "Christofle"; Vever, 1906–8, vol. II, pp. 183–88; Bouilhet, 1908–12, vols. II, III, passim; Lefébure, 1977, pp. 9–19

---

## Henri Bouilhet

*1830–1910 Villerville (Calvados)*

## Paul Christofle

*Paris 1838–1907 Paris*

*Paul Christofle devoted himself particularly to administrative and commercial matters, and drew up the report on silversmith's work at the 1867 exposition (*Rapports 1867, *vol. III, pp. 257–73). Bouilhet, nephew of Charles Christofle and a chemical engineer from the Ecole Centrale des Arts et Manufactures in 1851, subsequently worked for his uncle (he received a silver medal in 1855 as* coopérateur*), and at his death took over the direction of manufacturing. In 1867 the Christofle firm employed 1,418 workers, including 400 women, in Paris and Karlsruhe; it was* hors concours *at the Exposition Universelle, but three of its collaborators received awards.*

*While Christofle's production was solely industrial at the beginning, its artistic merit actually increased thanks to Bouilhet, with the collaboration of Rossigneux and Reiber (q.v.) and of famous sculptors. Bouilhet was responsible, besides, for the technical progress made by the firm. He took an active part at the beginning of the Second Empire in the invention of "massive" (relief) and three-dimensional galvanoplasty (electroforming), a procedure consisting of casting a metal in the shell obtained by galvanoplasty in order to give it the appearance and properties of a casting. Massive galvanoplasty makes it possible to obtain objects or parts of objects of the type made by silversmiths (examples exhibited in 1855) and bas-reliefs employed in furniture and architectural decoration. Three-dimensional galvanoplasty produces large-size statues, two examples of which were exhibited as early as 1862. During the Second Empire the Christofle firm executed by these processes the gilded and silver-plated decoration for*

the railway car presented to the Pope by the Pio-Latina society (1859; Museo di Roma, Rome); the gilded Louis XVI "bronzes" for the Empress's apartments in the Tuileries, after Lefuel (q.v.); the statue of the Virgin (9 meters high) for the Church of Notre Dame de la Garde in Marseilles; the two groups by Gumery crowning the facade of the Opéra (5 meters high); the doors of the Church of Saint Augustin in Paris. Bouilhet continued his pursuits under the Third Republic. He created a second Christofle factory at Saint-Denis, and at the same time played an important role in the Union Centrale des Arts Décoratifs. As did his uncle, he left valuable publications for the history of nineteenth-century French silversmith's work.

D.A.

Bibliography:
*Récompensés 1867*, group III, pp. 38–39; Ducuing, 1868, vol. I, pp. 438–41, vol. II, pp. 227–29, 463, 478–79; Mesnard, 1867, vol. I, pp. 89–112, vol. II, pp. 90–99, 205–16; Luchet, 1868, pp. 340–50; Mantz, 1868, pp. 134–39; Champier, 1894–95, "Christofle"; Bouilhet, 1908–12, vol. III, passim

Charles Christofle

## III-3
## Central Ornament from the Centerpiece of the Empress's Regiment of Dragoons

c. 1857

Mark: maker, Christofle, silver plate
Signed: CHRISTOFLE; crown and imperial arms surmounting crowned monogram E in cartouche in middle of long sides; inscribed under

cartouches: A SON REGIMENT DE DRAGONS/L'IMPERATICE
Silver plate
Height 45 cm; length 109 cm; depth 53 cm

Provenance:
Presented by the Empress to the Regiment of Dragoons; Simon-Antoine-Eugène Sautereau-Dupart (1819–1888), major in Regiment of Guides of the Imperial Guard (June 3, 1854), colonel of Empress's Regiment of Dragoons (December 19, 1868), brigadier general (October 27, 1870); private coll.

In the middle of this piece, a little girl with a cornucopia is surrounded by four putti, each with an attribute: plowshare, anvil, ewer, caduceus (lost). Four eagles flank the base. On either side are groups of two putti, representing sculpture and architecture and possibly dream and action. Like similar objects by Christofle, the piece was cast and chased, some elements being obtained by "massive" galvanoplasty. It is an example of the many centerpieces furnished by Christofle after Napoleon III had commissioned from him a centerpiece and service in silver plate for the Tuileries (exhibited in part in 1855, burned in 1871). Christofle later delivered to the Empress a Louis XVI centerpiece and dessert service and, to the Emperor, a Louis XVI gilded bronze centerpiece exhibited in 1867; for the Hôtel de Ville he supplied a centerpiece (exhibited in part in 1862) and dessert service, also burned in 1871. In addition to these exceptional commissions, Christofle produced silver-plated centerpieces related to this one, especially for the ministries. A piece he exhibited in 1855, commissioned by the duc de Morny for the Palace of the President of the Corps Législatif, seems similar: "A silver-plated

III-3

central ornament, the groups of children in oxidized silver, represent the works of the Arts, Commerce, and Industry spreading abundance under the protection of the eagles that form part of the middle groups" (Christofle, 1855, p. 4).

This central ornament, belonging to the so-called Louis XVI Eagles centerpiece, was eventually furnished in other forms: longer, with more feet, and including, instead of the middle group, a basin, and in place of the side groups, putti with other attributes, or a faun and a bacchante. The central ornament of the so-called Louis XVI Dolphins centerpiece shows many points in common with this one: plan, pedestal, feet, cartouches; but dolphins take the place of the eagles, the composition of the groups and the dimensions being subject to the same variations as on the Eagles centerpiece (see Christofle Archives, "Modèles de l'Orfèvrerie Christofle," vol. XII, nos. 3121–35). Christofle exhibited in 1862 a large piece from a Louis XVI Dolphins centerpiece with fourteen feet (Waring, 1863, vol. II, pl. 192). Thus he shrewdly offered elements in series whose combination allowed his clients to choose their own ensembles. Besides the central ornament, the centerpieces included table end pieces and candelabra, and were accompanied by dessert pieces. The ornament exhibited is matched by two end pieces with putti (32 × 48 × 33 cm). Christofle employed the same groups of putti on other centerpieces, such as those of the type of Maximilian's centerpiece (see no. III-4). The central group was used alone as a centerpiece on different pedestals (Christofle Archives, "Modèles de l'Orfèvrerie Christofle," vol. VIII, no. 2864, vol. XIII, no. 3200); an example was executed in aluminum and presented to Napoleon III by Sainte-Claire-Deville (see no. III-23) in 1858 (Compiègne). The creation of centerpieces with putti likely dates from the beginning of the Second Empire, although it is not known who was responsible for the models.

The formation of the Regiment of Dragoons of the Imperial Guard, decreed by Napoleon III on December 20, 1855, was carried out on July 1, 1856. By decree of January 1, 1857, it took the name of the Dragoons of the Empress. The regiment distinguished itself on August 16, 1870, at Gravelotte, where its colonel, Dupart, was wounded (Vincennes, Archives de la Guerre, Historiques du 13e régiment de dragons, dossier GB, 2e série, 3847 [General Sautereau-Dupart]). It is most likely that the Empress presented this centerpiece at the time the regiment took her name.

D.A.

Private Collection

III-4

Charles Christofle

## III-4
## Jardiniere from the Centerpiece of the Emperor Maximilian

c. 1865
Signed: CHRISTOFLE A PARIS; monogram MI under imperial crown of Mexico, in cartouche in middle of long sides
Silver plate
Height 96 cm; length 144 cm; depth 76 cm

Provenance:
Part of the service purchased from Christofle, 1865, by Maximilian (1832–1867), Emperor of Mexico (1864–67); service dispersed on fall of Maximilian, except for certain pieces in the National Palace in Mexico City, assigned to the Museo Nacional de Historia, 1879, and deposited there at that time, or, as the jardinieres, in 1919

Bibliography:
Cozic, 1865, p. 110, repro. p. 109; Dussieux, 1876, p. 256; Catalogue, Mexico City, Museo Nacional de Historia, 1976, no. 146, repro. pp. 14, 31

As part of his effort to create a European court in Mexico by transforming the palace of Chapultepec and by importing furnishings, Maximilian decided to acquire, like Napoleon III, a Christofle service, one even more lavish than that of the Emperor of the French. L'Illustration specified when this service was shown in the Christofle exhibition galleries before its delivery: "The work numbers no less than 60 ornamental and dessert pieces, 3,159 separate pieces, such as dishes, casseroles, etc..., 1,703 pieces of small silverwork, and 16 candelabra, not counting the clusters of lights that surmount the main pieces; total 4,938 pieces" (Cozic, 1865). The catalogue of the work of Christofle preserved in the Museo Nacional in Mexico City now includes only 228 pieces and a few fragments in silver plate, in addition to three objects in silver. Among the pieces in silver plate, some, more restrained and bearing the monogram MC of Maximilian and Carlota, undoubtedly must belong to another service. But the main elements of the centerpiece enumerated in L'Illustration remain: the central ornament (271 cm long); four jardinieres, including this one, on which the basin could be replaced by a candelabrum; and four flower baskets. This ensemble was not created especially for Maximilian, but was composed of pieces whose date of manufacture ranged from 1858 to 1865, as is shown by the order numbers appearing on all these objects except the central ornament and the jardinieres. Christofle offered different models of Louis XV centerpieces: this one was entitled Louis XV Rinceaux. It was adorned, as seen here, with groups of putti, which appear also on other centerpieces (see no. III-3; Christofle Archives, "Modèles de l'Orfèvrerie Christofle," vol. VIII, nos. 2852–66), or with different animals (vol. VIII, nos. 2884–2902). The 1862 Christofle price list offered and reproduced a "modèle Louis XV riche" service that included as principal pieces a flower basket and a pair of candelabra of the same model as those of the Maximilian service (3,000 and 3,200 francs). A central ornament similar to that of Maximilian, but shorter in length (202 cm), belongs to the Mobilier National (Connaissance des Arts, 1957, repro. p. 153). Each piece of the centerpiece includes one, two, or three putti, engaging mainly in bucolic activities: they play, fish, hunt, eat, or drink amid animals and plants. On the large pieces mentioned above, as well as on some of the candelabra, the scene represented by the putti is placed within a large cartouche formed by two Louis XV branches, or "rinceaux." It is possible that this composition had been suggested by a pair of Louis XV chandeliers in gilded bronze, executed for Mme de Pompadour and now in the Bibliothèque Mazarine, on which the central part is likewise formed by a large cartouche created by three rocaille branches, separated at their lower part by three putti bearing different attributes. Although the two rocaille shells adorning the basin of the jardiniere constitute another Louis XV element, the decoration of the base derives rather from the style of Louis XVI.

D.A.

Museo Nacional de Historia, Castillo de Chapultepec, Mexico City

## Eugène Capy
### Paris 1829–1894

*This sculptor, a student of Drolling and Pradier, entered the Ecole des Beaux-Arts in 1849, exhibiting chiefly portrait busts at the Salon, from 1849 to 1853, after which he ceased to exhibit. It was probably at this time that he joined the firm of Christofle; he was permanently attached to it a few years later when he and Madroux (q.v.) conceived the first project for the centerpiece of the Hôtel de Ville. This project was redone by Baltard (q.v.), but Capy and Madroux still provided the model for the ornamental part of the final work, and Capy modeled the tritons on each end of the central ornament. He also collaborated in the execution of the figures for the gilded-bronze centerpiece of Napoleon III.*

D.A.

Bibliography:
Dalloz, 1862; Ducuing, 1868, vol. II, p. 228; Bouilhet, 1908–12, vol. III, pp. 40–41; Lami, 1914–21, vol. I, pp. 250–51

## Pierre-Louis Rouillard
### Paris 1820–1881 Paris

*Rouillard, son of a woodturner, entered the Ecole des Beaux-Arts in 1837, where he was a pupil of the sculptor Cortot. He was already a specialist in animal sculpture when he first exhibited at the Salon that same year, and he continued to exhibit at the Salons until his death. Under the Second Empire he contributed to the sculpted decoration of such Parisian monuments as the Louvre, the Muséum d'Histoire Naturelle, and the Opéra (see no. I-10). Like Barye (q.v.), he worked for goldsmiths from the beginning of his career, supplying models for François-Désiré Froment-Meurice (q.v.), notably, the model for one of the four bas-reliefs (horse pursued by tigers) ornamenting the silver shield designed as a racing trophy and displayed by the goldsmith in 1844. At Froment-Meurice's death Rouillard signed the petition drawn up by his collaborators.*

*Rouillard worked for Christofle and made, among others, the model for the oxen in the centerpiece of Napoleon III, the eagle guiding the ship in the central ornament of the centerpiece of the Hôtel de Ville and the groups of sea horses at each of its ends, as well as agricultural competition prizes.*

*Rouillard was awarded the Legion of Honor in 1866 and became professor at the Ecole des Arts Décoratifs. The Musée des Arts Décoratifs has in its collection a hunting-crop handle decorated with a horse race by Rouillard and chased by Honoré (q.v.).*

D.A.

Bibliography:
Dalloz, 1862; Burty, 1883, pp. 38–39, 65–66, 77; Bouilhet, 1908–12, vol. III, pp. 41–42; Lami, 1914–21, vol. IV, pp. 194–98

Christofle; from models by Eugène Capy (Ceres) and Pierre-Louis Rouillard (animals)

## III-5
## Prime d'Honneur of the Regional Agricultural Competitions

1866
Marks: standard, silver, Paris, after 1838; maker Christofle, silver, *barrette* CHRISTOFLE; guaranty, The Netherlands, since 1953
Signed, in engraving, on base: CH. CHRISTOFLE FᵀT 1866; order number: 548 204 [corresponding to 1866]; inscribed on pedestal of Ceres: DECERNEE A; around base of pedestal: CONCOURS REGIONAL AGRICOLE D'AUXERRE; around *coupe*: MINISTERE DE LAGRICULTURE DU COMMERCE ET DES

TRAVAUX PUBLICS. MDCCCLXVI; below bas-reliefs of *coupe*: PATURAGE; MOISSON; VENDANGE; LABOURAGE
Silver
Height 65.5 cm; diameter 49.5 cm

Provenance:
Presented by the Ministry of Agriculture to Charles Martenot, landowner at Maulne, commune of Cruzy-le-Châtel (Yonne) at the regional competition in Auxerre, 1866; acquired by the Musées de la Ville d'Auxerre, 1969 (inv. no. 69.3)

In 1866 there were two series of regional agricultural competitions, the first in six regional centers, among them Auxerre, where the award ceremony took place on May 5 and the *prime d'honneur* consisted of this *coupe* and a sum of 5,000 francs. The following day the Emperor and Empress made a triumphal visit to Auxerre (*Le Moniteur,* May 6, 8, 1866).

Thanks to two collections of old photographs of *objets d'art* by Christofle made in the nineteenth century for the Ministry of Agriculture (Christofle Archives), we know that the figure of Ceres was by Capy, and the animals, by Rouillard, who probably also designed the bas-reliefs. Rouillard exhibited at the Salon of 1861 (no. 3594) a "*coupe,* gold and silver" presented at the regional competitions of 1861, its sculpture done in collaboration with Capy and Madroux (q.v.). Could it have been the prototype of this *coupe*? In fact, in 1862 Christofle did exhibit in London a *coupe* of this type (Darcel, 1862, p. 318, repro. p. 321; Waring, 1863, vol. I, pl. 46). The outline and composition recall those of the four large *coupes* from the Emperor's silver-plated centerpiece (Bouilhet, 1908–12, vol. II, repro. pp. 295, 297). The figure of Ceres, still Neoclassical, contrasts with the rest of the decoration. In the four reliefs rural life is evoked realistically and set in an industrial environment by means of the reaper (identified by K. A. Citroen as an English Burgess and Key reaper, produced in 1854) and the factory chimney in the background of the relief entitled *Plowing.* In a variation of this *coupe,* the basketwork motif from the lower part continues upward (Christofle Archives, "Modèles de l'Orfèvrerie Christofle," vol. XXVI, no. 4256, pedestal also with imperial arms). Many of the elements that make up this object are found on other Christofle agricultural trophies. The figure of Ceres alone was used as a prize (Christofle Archives, "Modèles de l'Orfèvrerie Christofle," vol. XXVI, no. 4269, presented in 1868). In 1867 the prize for the agricultural schools was a different figure of Ceres, on a pedestal decorated with a square bas-relief incorporating the left half of *Grazing* (Mesnard, 1867, vol. II, pp. 91–96, repro.). On another prize, *Plowing* appears on the pedestal supporting the figure of a laborer (Christofle Archives, "Modèles de l'Orfèvrerie Christofle," vol. XXVI, no. 4274) while *Grape Picking* and *Plowing* decorate the bellies of two different vases (Christofle Archives, "Modèles de l'Orfèvrerie Christofle," vol. XXVI, no. 4282, presented in 1876; no. 4283). The cow on the pedestal was also used on the pedestal of another *coupe* (Christofle Archives, "Modèles de l'Orfèvrerie Christofle," vol. XXIX, no. 1938, presented in 1883).

The agricultural prizes under the Second Empire and at the beginning of the Third Republic were generally composed of suitable allegorical figures while animals, tools, and vegetation contributed a more domestic note. The originality of this *coupe* resides in the realism of its reliefs, foreshadowing the spirit of the competition launched among silversmiths by the Ministry of Agriculture in 1887, when naturalistic themes would prevail on this type of object (*see* Champier, 1887–88; Bouilhet, 1908–12, vol. III, pp. 177–91).

D.A.

Musées de la Ville d'Auxerre

III-5

---

## Mathurin Moreau

### Dijon 1821–1912 Paris

*Moreau, the son of the Dijon sculptor Joseph Moreau, was trained first with his father, as were his two younger brothers, also sculptors, and then, beginning in 1841, at the Ecole des Beaux-Arts in Paris. There he was the student of the sculptors Ramey and Dumont, and in 1842 won the second Grand Prix de Rome. He first showed his work at the Salon of 1848, and continued to exhibit at the Salons throughout his life. The most characteristic aspect of his work was his representation of female figures in the eighteenth-century manner. Among the sculptures he executed during the Second Empire were* Fairy with Flowers, *bronze, commissioned by the State (Salon of 1853; Musée des Beaux-Arts, Dijon);* The Spinner, *marble, commissioned by the State (Salon of 1861; deposited by the Louvre in Dijon);* Saint Jerome *and* Saint Gregory, *stone, 1863 (facade of the Church of La Trinité, Paris); and* Studiosa, *marble, commissioned by the State (Salon of 1866; Musée des Beaux-Arts, Marseilles). Frequently awarded prizes under the Second Empire (he took second prize for sculpture at the Exposition Universelle of 1867), he became chevalier of the Legion of Honor in 1865. Thereafter he pursued a brilliant official career, and was a member of the jury at the exposition of 1900.*

*Concurrent with his sculpture, Moreau supplied models for statuettes to bronze manufacturers, and worked for Christofle, for whom he made, notably, the models for certain figures in the centerpiece of the Hôtel de Ville and the gilded-bronze centerpiece of Napoleon III. When Christofle was put in charge of producing the objets d'art given to the prize winners in agriculture at the Exposition Universelle of 1867, Moreau created the prize for the winner of the gold medal (the "Renommée").*

*In 1869 a Louis XV-style service with figures by Moreau, made for the Oppenheims, bankers of Co-*

*logne, was exhibited at Christofle's. Their collaboration continued for a long time: for example, Christofle was indebted to Moreau for the two bronze figures on the jewel cabinet exhibited in Vienna in 1873 and for prizes for agricultural competitions in 1887.*

D.A.

Bibliography:
Rémy, 1867, "Les Prix," pp. 300–301; Dussieux, 1876, p. 224; Champier, 1887–88, pp. 86, 89; Bouilhet, 1908–12, vol. III, pp. 41, 84, 89, 120, 182, 188; Lami, 1914–21, vol. III, pp. 478–84; Ancet, 1974

## Auguste Madroux
### Died 1870

*Madroux was a skilled modeler of ornaments employed by the sculptor François Gilbert (1816–91), Christofle's collaborator from 1849, for the decorative work on the silver-plated service of Napoleon III. He left Gilbert in order to work for Christofle as an ornamentalist, and there he managed this area of work until his death. He executed, with Capy (q.v.), the first project, and then the ornamentation, for the centerpiece of the Hôtel de Ville, produced the models for the dessert service of the Hôtel de Ville, and the ornamentation for the gilded-bronze centerpiece of Napoleon III. At the Exposition Universelle of 1867 he received a silver medal as coopérateur. Christofle displayed in 1869 two services made for the Oppenheims, bankers of Cologne, for which Madroux did the ornamentation.*

D.A.

Bibliography:
*Récompensés 1867*, group III, p. 38; Mantz, 1868, p. 135; Dussieux, 1876, p. 224; Bouilhet, 1908–12, vol. III, pp. 40–42, 51, 53, 84

Christofle; from models by Mathurin Moreau (central relief) and Auguste Madroux (ornamentation)

## III-6
## "Education of Achilles" Vase

1867
Marks: standard, silver, Paris, after 1838; maker, Christofle, silver
Signed in engraving on base: PAUL CHRISTOFLE ET HENRI BOUILHET. ORF; arms of Napoleon III on back of belly
Silver
Height 75 cm; width 26.5 cm; depth 13 cm

Provenance:
Gift of Napoleon III to the Cercle des Patineurs as a prize in the international pigeon-shooting competition organized by the club in 1867; won by Frank Heathcote, secretary of the Hurlingham Club, London; The Citroen Collection

Exhibition:
1867, Paris, Exposition Universelle

Bibliography:
Mesnard, 1867, vol. I, p. 98; Rémy, 1867, "Orfèvrerie," p. 11, repro. p. 12; Ducuing, 1868, vol. II, pp. 228, 443–44, repros. pp. 229, 445; Bouilhet, 1908–12, vol. III, p. 69; Hansen, 1970, pp. 290–91, repro., p. 187; Mulder-Hijmans, 1971 (repro.)

Christofle's display at the Exposition Universelle of 1867 included the table (no. II-20)

III - 6

and three remarkable *objets d'art: Navigation*, after Carrier-Belleuse (q.v.); *Victory*, after Maillet (q.v.); and this vase. Moreau and Madroux worked together for Christofle, producing, in 1863, models for the decoration of the three doors of Saint Augustin in Paris from designs by Baltard (q.v.), Moreau providing the figures and Madroux the ornamentation—as they did here. It is not known, however, who created the form of the vase. The neck seems inspired by Far Eastern porcelains, while the foot is reminiscent of those of the cups of the dessert service made for the Empress by Christofle, which have similar profiles and attached consoles (Bouilhet, 1908–12, vol. II, repro. p. 307). These two elements, oval, and decorated in the same manner, are separated by the flat belly, ornamented in a completely diffent style.

Given the subject, the vase could have been conceived originally as a racing prize. The central bas-relief, created by Moreau, represents Chiron training Achilles in running. The same subject was painted by Jean-Baptiste Regnault in 1783 in his reception piece at the Académie des Beaux-Arts (Louvre), circulated in engravings, and by Delacroix (q. v.) in the library of the Palais Bourbon, whose decoration was completed in 1847.

Although the composition of these paintings is different from the relief's, Moreau could have borrowed certain elements from them. The theme of the centaur was favored in silverwork in 1867: for example, the centaurs forming the feet of the P.-H. Emile Froment-Meurice (q. v.) candelabra have an attitude similar to that of Chiron, while Klagmann's coffret, displayed by Christofle, was surmounted by a group representing the Rape of Dejanira, after Guido Reni (Bouilhet, 1908–12, vol. III, p. 76, repro. p. 88). The two genii forming the handles—probably also by Moreau—enrich the scene with a moral tone: with one holding spurs and the other a bit, they symbolize Emulation and Prudence. The conception of handles in the form of human figures and the style of these genii derive from sixteenth-century Mannerism. Their attitude is the same as on the two Goujon statues in the Salle des Caryatides in the Louvre (Hansen, 1970).

For the other elements of the vase, Madroux took inspiration from sixteenth-century French gold- and silverwork for the bunches of fruit—which he had already used in the centerpiece and dessert service of the Hôtel de Ville—and the masks and strapwork, and from seventeenth-century French examples for the gadrooned base. But the decoration is above all representative of a major current at Christofle, appearing in the silver-plated table service of Napoleon III. On Bouilhet's suggestion its decoration, created by Gilbert, with contributions by Madroux, was in the form of plant motifs arranged in an airy and disciplined manner, but handled naturalistically. This principle, found again in such later work as the centerpiece of the Hôtel de Ville or this vase, predated the similar decoration inspired in silverwork by the Hildesheim treasure (discovered in 1868), copied by Christofle in 1869, as well as *fin-de-siècle* plant ornamentation.

The activities of the Cerle des Patineurs at the Pelouse de Madrid in the Bois de Boulogne centered around skating and pigeon shooting. The club had close ties with the Hurlingham Club of London, which also specialized in pigeon shooting (*Annuaire des Cercles et du Sport*, Paris, 1883, pp. 523–30, 588).

D.A.

The Citroen Collection, Amsterdam

Christofle; from model by Pierre-Louis Rouillard

## III-7
## Trophy of a Regional Agricultural Competition

1868

Signed on base of group: Rouillard Sc., CHRISTOFLE & CIE; order number under gilded-bronze base: 657066; inscribed on cartouche in middle of marble base: MINISTERE DE L'AGRICULTURE/ET DU COMMERCE/1870
Silverplate; red marble and gilded-bronze base
Height 33 cm; width 41 cm; depth 28.5 cm

Provenance:
Presented to Alphonse Tiersonnier (1819–1895), gentleman farmer in Gimouille (Nièvre), by the Ministry of Agriculture, 1870; Comte Henri de Martimprey

III - 7

Alphonse Tiersonnier, an acquaintance of the chemist and agronomist Eugène Chevreul, created a model farm for the breeding of Charolais cattle on his Colombier estate in Gimouille, which earned him numerous prizes both during and after the Second Empire. This group, as ascertained from two collections of old photographs of *objets d'art* executed by Christofle for the Ministry of Agriculture in the nineteenth century, was the trophy for all breeding animals in the bovine class in the regional agricultural competitions until 1879. In the same vein Rouillard created two other groups in the round depicting pigs (two versions) and sheep, which constituted the same prize for the porcine and ovine classes.

The order number has led us to discover that this copy, although presented in 1870, was actually made in 1868. A bull pulling up branches near a fence, along with a cow and a calf, make up this peaceful scene. Rouillard especially liked to do cattle, as can be seen by his entries in the Salons (*Cow,* plaster, 1839; *Bull,* plaster, 1843; *Cow,* plaster, 1866; the same, bronze, 1869; *Bulls Fighting,* wax, 1870; the same, silver, 1874; *Bull,* bronze, belonging to Christofle, 1880).

This group is reminiscent of the four oxen pulling the Chariot of Peace in the central ornament of the silver-plated centerpiece of Napoleon III (Compiègne), "Rouillard's chef-d'œuvre, which for power and movement, is only comparable to the famous *Ploughing* by Rosa Bonheur [q.v.], which it recalls, but surpasses" (Magne, 1855). The group exhibited also recalls Troyon (q.v.) and Bonheur, whose brother Isidore worked with Rouillard in 1865 on the sculpted decoration of the Beylerbey Palace built by the sultan in Constantinople (Dussieux, 1876, pp. 388–89).

In 1877 Tiersonnier received as a prize the same group except that the bull's tail is erect (collection of Comte Henri de Martimprey).

D.A.

Collection Comte Henri de Martimprey, Gimouille (Nevers)

---

### Fannière Frères
*Paris, 1839–1900*

*François-Auguste (1818–1900) and François-Joseph-Louis (1820–1897) Fannière were unique among Second Empire silversmiths for their craftsmanlike practice of both designing and executing, through each separate stage of manufacture, the works produced by their firm. As Paul Christofle (q.v.) remarked, "The Fannière Frères alone today are at once designers, sculptors, chasers, and manufactors" (Rapports 1867, vol. III, p. 261). The Fannière Frères were trained in Paris during the 1830s by their uncle, Jacques-Henri Fauconnier (1776–1839), the first of the Restoration goldsmiths to introduce the Renaissance style. Auguste entered the atelier of the painter Michel-Martin Drolling and after 1838 studied sculpture at the Ecole des Beaux-Arts. In 1841 Auguste made his Salon debut, and continued to exhibit sculptures there until 1876. At the death of Fauconnier in 1839, the brothers opened*

*a small workshop with Auguste as sculpteur and Joseph as ciseleur. For the next two decades the firm produced works for the principal gold- and silversmiths of Paris, including Lebrun, Duponchel, Odiot, François-Désiré Froment-Meurice (q.v.), and Christofle (q.v.), and for the armorer Lepage-Moutier. As coopérateurs of "eminent merit," "Fagnières frères [sic]" were awarded two first-class medals at the Exposition Universelle of 1855 (Ledagre, in Rapports 1855, p. 924), at the close of which Auguste was named chevalier of the Legion of Honor. Much of the firm's work during the 1850s was executed for Froment-Meurice, including the chasing of ornaments for the cradle of the Prince Imperial (no. II-17).*

*It was not until 1862 that the Fannières exhibited works independently under their own names (Catalogue 1862, no. 3629). According to Darcel, they were "tired of always being at the mercy of others and of making the reputation as well as the fortune of manufacturers who exploited them" (Darcel, 1862, p. 322). At the exhibition, where Fossin declared the Fannières "at the head of our artists"(Rapports 1862, vol. VI, pp. 457–58), the firm was awarded a medal, and Joseph Fannière in turn was named chevalier of the Legion of Honor. At the Union Centrale exhibition of 1865, Fannière Frères won a gold medal and the patronage of the Emperor who purchased from their vitrine the silver beer jug. The firm was given a number of important official commissions, including in 1859 a gilded-silver lamp offered by the Empress to the Church of Notre Dame des Victoires, a racing cup commissioned by the Emperor* in 1867, and in 1869 the nef presented by the Empress to de Lesseps. At the Paris exposition of 1867 the firm won a gold medal for an "exceptional" display that included an embossed steel shield for the duc de Luynes (G.J. Cayley, in Reports 1867, vol. II, pp. 489–90).

At the death of Auguste Fannière in 1900, the passing of the brothers was mourned for the loss of craftsmanship which could be compared only to that of "artists of the Middle Ages" (Robert, 1900, p. 129).

K.B.H.

Bibliography:
Quépat, 1887, pp. 162–63; Bouilhet, 1908–12, vol. III, pp. 61–66; Vever, 1906–8, vol. II, pp. 198–208; Lami, 1914–21, vol. II, pp. 337–38

Fannière Frères; designed by François-Auguste Fannière and chased by François-Joseph-Louis Fannière

## III-8
## Beer Jug

1865
Mark: maker's mark in diamond-shaped lozenge: [Falcon head/clasped hands] FANNIERE/FRES [three pearls]
Inscribed on base and inside lid: FANNIERE FRES
Silver, with repoussé and chased decoration
Height 26.1 cm; diameter 13.5 cm

Provenance:
Purchased by William Walters; Walters Art Gallery (inv. no. 57.2025)

Bibliography:
P. Burty, in Rapports 1865, p. 402; Gersaint, 1865, p. 378, repro. p. 377; Burty, 1869, Chefs-d'œuvre, repro. p. 363; Lami, 1881–88, vol. III, fig. 306; Bouilhet, 1908–12, vol. I, p. 21 (repro. en suite), vol. III, p. 63, repro. p. 67

This is a slightly elongated version of the celebrated jug purchased by the Emperor from the Union Centrale exhibition of 1865. The body of the jug is cast in the form of a wooden barrel, banded with hooped staves and ornamented in low relief with a hop vine and insects. While the rustic style of the jug is not typical of the elaborate historicizing forms usually associated with the Fannière production, the refined chasing of the relief and textured wood decoration, as well as the modeling of the handle with thick vines of silver, demonstrate the technical skills for which the firm was famous. In reviewing Fannière's exhibit in 1865, Gersaint described the jug as "the most interesting piece in their display" (1865, p. 378) and

Burty remarked that it represented "a thoroughly modern sentiment" (Rapports 1865, p. 402). In point of fact, this type of decorative jug bearing naturalistic ornament was an English invention of the 1830s, produced in pottery in both France and England during the 1840s. Moreover, decorating a beer container with a hop vine subscribed to the mid-century notion that ornament should suggest the function of the object it adorned. Burty pointed out that hops "suggest [the] use" of the jug (Burty, 1869, Chefs-d'œuvre, p. 363) and praised a table service also exhibited by Fannière in 1865 as "varied by motifs appropriate to its purpose" (P. Burty, in Rapports 1865, p. 402). The somewhat retardataire English realism of the jug is, however, reshaped by "modern" ideas: the comparative austerity and formality in the design of the vine ornament, the scattering of insects over the surface in decorative patterns, and the crouching mouse forming the thumbpiece suggest the

new interest in Japanese arts which Burty himself championed and was to label as "Japonisme" in 1872.

K.B.H.

The Walters Art Gallery, Baltimore

Fannière Frères; designed by François-Auguste Fannière and chased by François-Joseph-Louis Fannière

## III-9
## Nef

1869
Inscribed on poop: a Mr Fd de Lesseps/L'Impératrice Eugénie/XVII Novbre M.D.C.C.L.XIX/Suez; on prow: Fannières frès 1869; on base:

III-8

Offert à Ferdinand de Lesseps par l'Impératrice Eugénie, Présidant à l'inauguration du Canal de Suez le 17 Novembre 1869/Don de M. Charles de Lesseps
Silver, cast and chased; green marble base
Height 72 cm; width 72 cm; depth 24 cm

Provenance:
Gift of the Empress to Ferdinand de Lesseps at the inauguration of the Suez Canal, November 17, 1869; Comte Charles de Lesseps; gift to the Musée des Arts Décoratifs, 1909 (inv. no. 15.688)

Exhibitions:
1871, London; 1874, Paris, Union Centrale; 1900, Paris, Exposition Universelle Centennal; 1963, Biarritz, no. 82; 1973, Brive-la-Garde, no. 134; 1973–74, Paris, Legion d'Honneur, no. 201

Bibliography:
A. Viollet-le-Duc, in *Rapports 1871*, p. 17; *Art Journal Catalogue 1871*, vol. X, repro. p. 87; Sandoz, 1875, p. 6; Bouilhet, 1908–12, vol. I, repro. p. 21, vol. III, pp. 65, 94, 95 (repro.); Jullian, n.d., p. 147, fig. 3; Catalogue, Paris, Musée des Arts Décoratifs, 1934, p. 205; Babelon, 1946, p. 101

On November 17, 1869, sixty-eight ships from various nations, led by the French *Aigle* with the Empress Eugénie on board, began the first passage from the Mediterranean to the Red Sea through the Suez Canal (*Le Moniteur*, November 29, 1869). In 1854 Ferdinand de Lesseps had obtained a concession from the Viceroy of Egypt to form the Compagnie Universelle du Canal Maritime de Suez for the purpose of constructing a ship channel through the Isthmus of Suez, which would shorten by more than half, the maritime route between Europe and the Orient. Work on the canal began at Port Said in 1859 and was subsidized in 1864 by the Emperor, who indemnified the company in the amount of 38,000,000 francs. To honor de Lesseps at the inauguration, the Empress presented him with this silver nef in the form of a Roman galley, decorated by Fannière Frères with mythological and allegorical figures that symbolize the purpose and construction of the canal: on the poop Mercury, the gods' swift messenger and patron of Commerce, is borne on a shield supported by winged allegorical figures of Science and Industry; from the prow, which is decorated with imperial robe, scepter, and crown (*see* no. III-24), emerges a trumpeting Fame with a palm of victory; on the sides of the galley are chased reliefs representing the construction and inauguration of the canal; the foot is formed by two nereids who support the galley, and a base with sea shells in high relief. The nef was shown by Fannière Frères at the London International Exhibition of 1871 where Adolphe Viollet-le-Duc described it as "a rare and precious piece of goldsmith's work, a chased silver vessel ornamented with charming figures which was presented to Mr. de Lesseps" (*Rapports 1871*, p. 17).

III-9

Ship forms or nefs were adopted in France from the thirteenth century in metalwork for secular table use and ornament, and for ecclesiastical use as incense boats and *ex-votos*. A gold nef complete with masts and rigging in a sixteenth-century style and, like Fannière's ship, supported by a nereid and base with marine reliefs, was presented in 1530 to Eléonore, second wife of Francis I, by the city of Bordeaux. A famous pair of ornamental nefs in silver gilt, from the coronation service of Napoleon I, made by Henry Auguste in 1804 (Musée National du Château, Malmaison), were used by Napoleon III at important diplomatic dinners during the Second Empire: like Fannière's nef, the coronation nefs are in the form of galleys, with reliefs on the side and a winged figure at the prow. Auguste Fannière has here enriched the Classical (and Neoclassical) galley form with a Romantic figurative and decorative vocabulary inherited from such Neo-Renaissance designers and silversmiths of the 1830s and 1840s as Fauconnier and Jean-Jacques Feuchère (see Carlier). The Fannières here multiply effects of movement in the figures of Fame, Mercury, the nereids, and even the galley's wedge-shaped beak, which seem at once to fly, point, and twist in space — enriched by delicate chasing and subtle differentiation of surface textures. Theatrical and exuberant, the nef is embellished by the Fannières for the festive occasion.

K.B.H.

Musée des Arts Décoratifs, Paris

---

## P.-H. Emile Froment-Meurice

*Paris 1837–1913 Paris*

*A third-generation silversmith and jeweler, P.-H. Emile Froment-Meurice succeeded to a firm founded by his grandfather, which became the most important in Paris under his father François-Désiré Froment-Meurice (q. v.). After his father's death in 1855, his mother took over direction of the firm. Emile learned the trade from his father's apprentices — the chefs orfèvres Babeur, Croville, Dumoulin, and Wièse (q.v.), and ciseleurs Poux, Mulleret, Alexandre, and Louis and Philibert Audouard. The firm completed works left unfinished at Froment-Meurice's death, including those for the Exposition Universelle of 1855, where it won a Medal of Honor for silverwork (Ledagre, in Rapports 1855, p. 911) and "M. Froment-Meurice fils" a mention pour mémoire for damascened jewelry (Fossin, in Rapports 1855, p. 915). The reputation and quality of production continued undiminished throughout the 1850s with major public commissions such as the cradle of the Prince Imperial (no. II-17) and private commissions for Isaac Pereire and the duke of Medinaceli. In 1859 Emile became director of the firm, which still employed such collaborators of his father as the Audouards (Mantz, 1863, "Orfèvrerie," p. 429). Froment-Meurice did not exhibit in London in 1862 and, as a member of the Conseil Manufacturier, was hors concours at the Union Centrale exhibition of 1865. Not until 1867 did the firm, under Emile's direction, enter international competition; that year it won a gold medal for an exceptional display that included two imperial commissions: a bust of the Emperor carved from an aquamarine for the Salon de l'Empereur at the Hôtel de Ville and the silver and rock crystal centerpiece (P. Christofle, in Rapports 1867, vol. III, pp. 263–64; Mantz, 1868, pp. 127–34). Burty commented that Froment-Meurice pursued "a very specialized taste"*

*in combining hard stones (and ivory) with metal (Burty, 1869, "Industries," p. 536) — a style initiated in F.-D. Froment-Meurice's chryselephantine Leda of 1851, but greatly developed by Emile in his 1867 exhibition pieces. Froment-Meurice continued to produce works of major importance for a rich clientele only partly inherited from his father. Froment-Meurice, like his father, surrounded himself with craftsmen of great ability, including Henry Cameré, who designed a ewer for the duc de Montpensier in 1867 and most of the orfèvrerie and jewelry exhibited by the firm at the Union Centrale in 1869, and Léopold Hubert, director of the factory and himself a bijoutier-orfèvre, who also exhibited jewelry for Froment-Meurice in 1869 (Mantz, 1868, p. 130; Sandoz, 1875, p. 6).*

K.B.H.

Bibliography:
Rossigneux, 1892, pp. 9–24; Vever, 1906–8, vol. II, pp. 278–85; Bouilhet, 1908–12, vol. III, pp. 32–40

---

## Emile-François Carlier

*Paris 1827–1879 Paris*

*A pupil of the great Romantic sculptor Jean-Jacques Feuchère, Carlier made his Salon debut in 1859 with plaster and bronze figure groups, The Wolf Hunter and Drunkenness. Like his master, who had provided a number of models for François-Désiré Froment-Meurice (q.v.), from about 1865 Carlier was similarly associated as sculpteur-ornemaniste with Emile Froment-Meurice. For the Paris Exposition Universelle of 1867 Carlier collaborated on the sculptural decoration of two important works which Froment-Meurice himself designed: a clock of hard stones decorated with Renaissance deities in ivory, described as "carved from ivory by an able sculptor, E. Carlier," and the Emperor's centerpiece ornamented with fauns, centaurs, and putti in chased silver (Mantz, 1868, p. 130). At the Union Centrale exhibition of 1869 Froment-Meurice exhibited a pair of candelabra "in the stately style of Bérain," which were modeled by Carlier and described by Burty as "elite works for an elite clientele" (Burty, 1869, "Industries," p. 538). During the 1870s Carlier supplied Froment-Meurice with sculptural models for works in the Louis XVI and Renaissance styles: in 1872 a Louis XVI tea service offered by Australia to the French consul-general; in 1874 a Louis XVI table service offered jointly by the English and American governments to the Italian minister to Washington; in 1878 a silver Renaissance-style racing trophy decorated with a centaur and Victory similar in style to the fauns and centaurs that ornament the imperial centerpiece. Carlier exhibited two*

*bronze groups for the last time in the Salon of 1879 and died later that same year.*

K.B.H.

Bibliography:
Dussieux, 1876, pp. 297, 615; Lami, 1914–21, vol. I, pp. 252–53

---

Designed by P.-H. Emile Froment-Meurice; modeled by Emile-François Carlier

## III-10
## Coupe

1867
Chased bronze, silver, and crystal glass
Height 59 cm; width 55 cm; depth 40 cm

Provenance:
Froment-Meurice sale, September 1907; purchased by the Musée des Arts Décoratifs (inv. no. 14.338)

Bibliography:
P. Christofle, in *Rapports 1867*, vol. III, p. 263; H. Friswell, in *Art Journal Catalogue 1867*, vol. VII, p. 262; Mantz, 1868, p. 130, repro. p. 129; O. Lacroix, in Ducuing, 1868, vol. II, pp. 21–22 (repro.); Bouilhet, 1908–12, vol. III, pp. 39–40, repro. p. 37; Vever, 1906–8, vol. II, p. 284; Catalogue, Paris, Musée des Arts Décoratifs, 1934, p. 207; Connaissance des Arts, 1957, p. 106, no. 3 (repro.); Grandjean, 1962, p. 84; Steingräber, 1966, p. 146, no. 69, repro. p. 145; Jullian, n.d., p. 142, fig. 3

This *coupe* and a pair of candelabra (Musée des Arts Décoratifs, 14.338 b,c) were Froment-Meurice's bronze- and silver-mounted models for the celebrated *surtout de table* commissioned by the Emperor. The imperial centerpiece, in silver, silver gilt, and rock crystal, was praised for its use of materials by Christofle (q.v.), who described it as "one of the most comprehensive works in his [Froment-Meurice's] exhibit" (*Rapports 1867*, vol. III, p. 263). Friswell declared that "there was nothing so beautiful in England, nor indeed of its kind in the Exposition [than]... the group of candelabra and a centrepiece in *cristal de roche* and silver... which stands alone" (H. Friswell, in *Art Journal Catalogue 1867*, vol. VII, p. 262). The clear crystal bowl of this model is banded by twining violet stems and ornamented with putti which, as Bouilhet pointed out, were designed to conceal the joins between the several pieces of rock crystal that compose the original *coupe*. From the top springs a bouquet of crown imperial flowers (Fritallaria imperialis), chosen undoubtedly in allusion to the patron. Froment-Meurice's use of such a rich and exotic material as rock crystal was inspired by Italian and German goldsmiths' work of the late sixteenth and

III-10

### Frédéric-Jules Rudolphi

*Active Paris after c. 1840*

*After having worked in Copenhagen, Rudolphi became, in Paris, the collaborator of the goldsmith and jeweler Charles Wagner. On December 14, 1842, living at 36, rue Montmartre, he registered his mark. Following Wagner's premature death, he exhibited under Wagner's name at the Exposition des Produits de l'Industrie in 1844 and took over his workshop with the same creative spirit. He, too, favored diverse materials and enjoyed the collaboration of artists such as Geoffroy-Dechaume and Steinheil. After having a shop at 3, rue Tronchet, and a workshop at 11, rue du Mail until 1853, he established himself at 23, boulevard des Capucines* (Almanach du Commerce, 1854). *His many faceted production included jewelry in chased silver, often decorated with figures;* objets d'art *(vases; coffrets; racing trophies; shields, such as the one ordered by the king of Denmark, exhibited in 1862), which sometimes attained large dimensions (a gueridon in cast silver decorated with figures, exhibited in 1851; an enameled prie-dieu and gueridon with enamel and lapis lazuli decoration, both exhibited in 1862); and finally, religious silverwork, his most famous piece being a large enameled reliquary exhibited in 1862. After the London Universal Exhibition of 1851, where he was awarded a medal, Rudolphi's success gained him the Legion of Honor. He received a silver medal at the Exposition Universelle of 1855—with honorable mention being bestowed on two chasers working for him—and another medal in 1862. In 1867 he had his son Frédéric-Aristide as his partner, and had a branch in Denmark; he was still established at 23, boulevard des Capucines, but was about to move to 1, place de Wagram and 87, boulevard de Neuilly (now avenue de Villiers). Although he received a silver medal in 1867 and his* chef ciseleur, *Léon Binder, won an honorable mention, his exhibit was judged by Paul Christofle (q.v.) as "slightly outmoded in style."*

D.A.

Bibliography:
Arch. de la Garantie, Insculpations 1841–54, fol. 107; Arch. nat. F[12] 3042 [Exposition Universelle of 1867]; *Rapports 1855*, pp. 912, 926; *Catalogue 1862*, p. 213; Darcel, 1862, pp. 324, 541–43; Waring, 1863, vol. I, pl. 1, vol. III, pls. 254, 275; *Récompensés 1867*, group III, pp. 36, 39; *Rapports 1867*, vol. III, pp. 264–65; Vever, 1906–8, vol. I, pp. 163–66, 190–92; Bouilhet, 1908–12, vol. II, p. 266, vol. III, p. 67

early seventeenth centuries, to which the lush, spiky profile of the crown imperials and violets overgrowing the crystal add a contemporary sense of undisciplined naturalism. The bowl is supported by a family of fauns, chased fully in the round and seated on a footed base draped with animal skins and trophies—sixteenth-century-style figures remembered partly by Carlier from Feuchère's Romantic Renaissance vocabulary of the 1830s and 1840s, although here at once more stylized and freely adapted as decorative supports. It was a style that Mantz described as "a new taste and charming invention" (1868, p. 130), which made its first important appearance in Froment-Meurice's 1867 exhibition pieces—a rich polychromatic style combining figurative and decorative elements in different and precious materials. Along with the centerpiece, Froment-Meurice exhibited in 1867 a gold-crowned bust of the Emperor carved from a green aquamarine, a clock of hard stones decorated with Renaissance-style figures in ivory by Carlier, and a rock-crystal ewer encrusted with blue and green enamels made for the duc de Montpensier.

K.B.H.

Musée des Arts Décoratifs, Paris

III-11

Frédéric-Jules Rudolphi

## III-11
## Tankard

c. 1855
Silver, ivory, turquoises, rubies
Height 23 cm; width 17.5 cm

Provenance:
Purchased from the Exposition Universelle of 1855 for the Museum of Ornamental Art, later the South Kensington Museum (1857), then the Victoria and Albert Museum (1899); deposited in the Bethnal Green Museum (inv. no. C. 2653-1856)

Exhibition:
1855, Paris, Exposition Universelle

Bibliography:
Redgrave, 1856, p. 395; Catalogue, London, South Kensington Museum, 1878, p. 271; Aslin, 1973, no. 14 (repro.)

The body of this tankard consists of a section of elephant tusk inlaid with turquoises and adorned in its central part with rubies; the mount is of engraved silver, and the pierced lid and the hinge are also embellished with rubies. The general form is of German Renaissance inspiration, but the openwork decoration of the double handle may derive from twelfth- and thirteenth-century ironwork—grilles, strap hinges—which had been the subject of several articles in the *Annales Archéologiques* in the pre-ceding years (*see,* for example, vol. XI, 1851, pp. 133–36, 238–39; vol. XII, 1852, pp. 51–53). Always looking to the past, Rudolphi took inspiration for his works from both periods, in an original way. The combination of materials in the form of inlay, a taste transmitted by Wagner to Rudolphi, is quite characteristic of their production, which makes use of niello, damascening, or, as here, inlaid stones. The Musée des Arts Décoratifs has a steel brooch by Wagner incrusted with malachites (Vever, 1906–8, vol. I, repro. p. 165). Like his master, Rudolphi had a taste for stones: he had been accused especially of overdoing lapis lazuli. Here the choice of materials and the arrangement of the motifs suggest an influence from the Muslim East, Persia, or India, while it also constituted a modest attempt at chryselephantine silverwork, which was being revived at the same time in spectacular pieces combining ivory figures and precious metals—the monumental statue of Minerva made by Duponchel for the duc de Luynes (1846–51; château of Dampierre), the bacchante and the *Toilette of Venus* by François-Désiré Froment-Meurice (1851), the figures of the Muses on the Pompeiian centerpiece of Prince Napoleon made by Christofle (q.v.; exhibited 1862)—although this type of work did not become prevalent until the end of the century. Rudolphi's curious works aroused certain reservations among French critics, but the silversmith, who in 1862 exported 35 percent of his production, was admired by the British. Various other works by Rudolphi, bought at the expositions for the Museum of Ornamental Art, are now reassembled in the Bethnal Green Museum: a silver vase exhibited in 1844 (Aslin, 1973, no. 3); two silver coffrets, one of them parcel gilt (Aslin, no. 6), both exhibited in 1851; a steel vase damascened in gold and silver (Aslin, no. 13), also acquired in 1855 and which, like this tankard, has openwork decoration and turquoise inlays.

D.A.

Bethnal Green Museum, London

# Silverwork (Ecclesiastical)

## Thomas-Joseph Armand-Calliat

*Abbrets (Isère) 1822–1901 Lyons*

Armand-Calliat was by the end of the Second Empire one of the two principal manufacturers of ecclesiastical metalwork in France, the chief competitor of Poussielgue-Rusand (q.v.). T.-J. Armand succeeded to the firm founded in Lyons in 1820 by his father-in-law, François Calliat, which he directed after 1853 under the name Armand-Calliat. In 1855 Armand-Calliat et Sœur participated in the Exposition Universelle in Paris (Catalogue 1855, p. 113). Armand-Calliat himself described his staff in 1867 as large, although the firm produced only church plate, and bronzes by special commission. In 1858 Armand-Calliat first became associated with the architect Pierre Bossan to whom he credited his first successes and the stylistic orientation of the firm's work. At the London International Exhibition of 1862, the firm won a medal for gold and silver devotional articles which included an "exceptional... Byzantine" monstrance designed by Bossan for the Church of the Immaculate Conception in Lyons (Fossin, in Rapports 1862, vol. VI, p. 461).

During the 1860s Armand-Calliat received a number of important commissions for church furnishings in the Romanesque and Byzantine styles which Bossan had made popular in 1862: a communion service for the "new catholic Church at Geneva"; various objects including a silver monstrance for Sir James Hope, at Galashiels; a monstrance for the cathedral of York; and a monstrance commissioned by Napoleon III for presentation to the bishop of Saint-Jean-de-Maurienne. By the exhibition of 1867 Armand-Calliat could boast that his works "penetrated all Catholic countries." Armand-Calliat won a gold medal at the 1867 exhibition and high praise from Paul Christofle (q.v.), who stated that Calliat's production was comparable in quality to that of Poussielgue (Rapports 1867, vol. III, p. 266).

Armand-Calliat took great pride in having re-created an important metalwork industry in Lyons, competitive with Paris, which he described in 1888 as "the first attempt at independence, the first effort to constitute a distinct art" in two hundred years. In 1867 he had noted that Lyons offered particular advantages to specialists in church furnishings: a "marvelously appropriate" milieu in "the most religious town in Catholic Europe"; an inspiring contemporary Christian artistic tradition, exemplified by the work of Flandrin (q.v.); and competition and encouragement among Lyons's related industries including textile firms which produced the major por-

tion of France's ecclesiastical vestments (see no. II-7). Armand-Calliat's firm continued to flourish in the decades following the Second Empire. In 1888 Armand-Calliat was received into the Académie des Sciences, Belles-Lettres et Arts of Lyons. At his father's death, Armand-Calliat's son Joseph succeeded as director of the firm.

K.B.H.

Bibliography:
Armand-Calliat, 1867, pp. 6–10; Dussieux, 1876, pp. 297, 611; Armand-Calliat, 1888, pp. 27, 34–37; Bouilhet, 1908–12, vol. III, pp. 26–27, 166-69; Audin and Vial, 1918–19, vol. I, pp. 21–23

## Pierre Bossan

*Lyons 1814–1888 La Ciotat*

Urged by his father, a stonecutter, Bossan studied architecture at the Ecole des Beaux-Arts in Lyons, then in the atelier of Labrouste (q.v.) in Paris. In 1844, having already built the church of the Demi-Lune (1842) in Lyons, he was entrusted with the construction of the Gothic-style church of Saint Georges. His stay in Italy (1847–52) and his conversion by the curé of Ars were crucial events in his life. Having decided to devote himself thenceforth to Christian art, he remained marked by his Italian and Sicilian memories. Bossan embarked on an intensive building program, constructing the church of Valfleury (Loire) in 1853 and the church of Couzon (Rhône) in 1854, which like the Monastery of the Visitation (Lyons), still betrayed archaeological tendencies. The turning point in his work came around 1856 with the Church of the Immaculate Conception in Lyons. The same year he erected the church of Régny (Loire); in 1861, the Jesuit chapel in Lyons and the Dominican chapel in Oullins (Rhône); in 1862, the churches at La Mulatière (Rhône) and Ars (Ain) and the Trappist monastery of Les Dombes; in 1864, the church of Echallon (Ain); in 1866, the Chapel of the Dames de Sainte Marthe in Valence; in 1869, the Dominican convent in Saint-Maximin (Var); in 1873, the churches of Aouste and La Bégude (Drôme); in 1874, those of Grane (Drôme) and Oullins, then of Pradelle and Saint-Genais (Drôme); in 1879, the Dominican convent in Marseilles. In 1887 he completed the Church of the Holy Sacrament in Lyons.

The basilicas of La Louvesc (Ardèche) and especially of Fourvière in Lyons are his most important works. The design for Notre Dame de Fourvière,

completed in 1866, was carried out after the war of 1870; it embodied Bossan's concern for the creation of an original Christian art freed from archaeology, his search for unity in plan and volumes, and for contrasts, established by an ornamental crescendo in the upper elements. The interiors of his buildings reveal his efforts to create an overall decoration in an appropriate style (altars, ciboria, pulpits, polychromy) and his interest in symbolism, seen also in his designs for religious silverwork.

J.-M.L.

Bibliography:
Sainte-Marie-Perrin, 1889; Thieme and Becker, 1907–50, vol. IV, pp. 398–99 (bibl.); Thiollier, 1891

Thomas-Joseph Armand-Calliat; designed by Pierre Bossan

## III-12
## Ciborium

1867

Marks: guaranty, silver, departments, after 1838; maker, Armand-Calliat
Inscribed in red enamel around lid: + VBI / CUM / QVE / FVE / RIT / COR / PVS / ILLVNC / CON / GRE / GA / BUN / TVR / ET / AQVILAE [Luke 17:37]
Gilded silver, enamel, amethysts
Height 37 cm; width 18 cm; diameter (bowl) 15.2 cm

Provenance:
Purchased from Armand-Calliat et Fils for 5,000 francs by the Musée des Arts Décoratifs, 1895 (inv. no. A.8190)

Exhibition:
1867, Paris, Exposition Universelle

Bibliography:
Armand-Calliat, 1867, pp. 25–29; Rapports 1867, vol. III, p. 266; Rapports des délégations 1867, vol. III, "Orfèvres," pp. 62–64, repro. p. 70; Thiollier, 1891, p. 19; Bouilhet, 1908–12, vol. III, p. 26, repro. p. 28

At the Exposition Universelle of 1867 Armand-Calliat exhibited, like his Paris colleagues, Gothic objects; however, his principal pieces were an ensemble created by Bossan, in a new Christian spirit, which did not display gratuitous archaeological decoration but was adorned with figures which alluded to their function. In commenting on them, Armand-Calliat mentioned first the monstrance exe-

III-12

cuted for Notre Dame de la Garde in Marseilles (Bouilhet, 1908–12, vol. III, repro. p. 27) as a "poem of the Eucharist." The other pieces constituted a bishop's altar service: chalice, crozier, ewer and basin, processional cross (Bouilhet, 1908–12, vol. III, repro. p. 29), and ciborium, to which Thiollier added a pectoral cross, cruets, and candle holder not mentioned by Armand-Calliat. Concerning the ciborium Armand-Calliat wrote: "At the base are four dragons, 'the enemies of the dove,' defeated and fleeing. On the knot, kneeling angels carrying the Eucharistic harvest and the golden sickle. On the bowl, doves with golden robes represent, in the scrolls rich with sheaves of wheat, the communion of the faithful. Among them stand eagles, whose presence is explained by an inscription on the lid.... At the top is the sacrificial lamb...." Although the form is reminiscent of such medieval pieces as the Royal Gold Cup probably made for Charles V (British Museum), the completely modern decoration

is surprising, especially its polychromy. The colors of the painted enamel do not refer to those of medieval enamels. Some of the ornamental motifs—the scrolls of the belly particularly—seem to have been inspired by bronzes of Louis XVI furniture. In addition to their religious purpose, the eagles and the inscription may have been included by Armand-Calliat to attract the Emperor's attention.

All the collaborators on this ensemble were from Lyons or had worked for Armand-Calliat for a long time: Charles Dufraine (1827–1900), a religious sculptor and Bossan's collaborator (Lami, 1914–21, vol. II, pp. 235–37), who modeled the figures with the help of Révérend, the sculptor, attached to Armand-Calliat for fifteen years, who also provided, along with Bador, models for the ornaments; several chasers, including Hervier-Méray, for the statuettes, and Adolphe Frémonteil; several silversmiths, including the foreman Jules Frémonteil, brother of Adolphe, and Charlin; the enameler A. Geffroy, a collaborator of Armand-Calliat for nine years. As coopérateurs, Bossan received a silver medal, Hervier-Méray, a bronze medal, and Charlin, an honorable mention (Récompensés 1867, group III, pp. 36, 38, 39; Rapports des délégués lyonnais 1867 [those for silverwork being Charlin and Révérend], pp. xi, 57, 180–81).

The subsequent fate of these pieces is confused. According to Thiollier, the crozier was offered to Monseigneur Callot, bishop of Oran from 1867 until his death in 1875, and the other pieces to Pius IX by the Fathers of the Vatican Council. Bouilhet confirms the presence of the cross in the Vatican, as does Dussieux (1876, p. 506), according to whom Armand-Calliat in 1869 "executed" a cross presented by an Englishman to Pius IX for the opening of the Council, and in 1870, an altar service commissioned by the Fathers for him. Why did the ciborium not follow the other pieces, or were there two identical ciboria, or even two identical altar services? The ciborium executed later by Armand-Calliat, after Bossan, for Notre Dame de Fourvière in Lyons, recalls this one (Thiollier, 1891, pls. 111–12).

Under the Second Empire, the originality of the decorative arts of Lyons, encouraged by the creation of courses of study and a museum of industrial arts (founded 1864), also appeared in other fields such as textiles and even furniture (for example, the secretary by Daubet and Dumarest, 1855, at Compiègne).

D.A.

Musée des Arts Décoratifs, Paris

## Alexandre Chertier
### Active Paris after c. 1850

A "very capable foreman at the House of Bachelet" in Paris, Chertier won a bronze medal as coopérateur at the Exposition Universelle of 1855. He founded in 1857 his own firm located at 48, rue Mazarine, and moved to 7, rue Férou in 1866. Chertier, a specialist like Bachelet in ecclesiastical silver- and bronze work in the style of the Middle Ages, showed chalices, ciboria, candlesticks, and reliquaries in London in 1862, but nothing in 1867. He executed many works based on diocesan architects' plans: for the Bordeaux cathedral, based on Danjoy (1806–1862), a statue of the Virgin in embossed and gilded copper (6.50 m high), also shown in 1862, made for the top of the Pey-Berland bell tower where it remains, as well as a silver altar intended for the Chapel of Saint Joseph (1863); the tomb of Saint Martin in Tours, in gilded and enameled bronze, based on a Verdier design (1867); five marble altars decorated with enameled bronze after a design by Chabrol for the Limoges cathedral (1868); then, after 1870, important works for the church of Mont-Saint-Michel, for the cathedrals of Saint-Omer, Reims, Moulins, Strasbourg, and for the churches of Saint Augustin and Saint Laurent in Paris. He made the altar service for the château of Roquetaillade (see no. II-1). Another Chertier, a jeweler, was established at 42, rue Neuve Saint Augustin during the Second Empire.

D.A.

Bibliography:
Almanach du Commerce; Rapports 1855, p. 925; Chertier, 1859; Catalogue 1862, pp. 211–12; Waring, 1863, vol. II, pl. 157; de Champeaux, 1886, pp. 283–84; Bouilhet, 1908–12, vol. III, pp. 25–26

Alexandre Chertier; designed by Eugène-Emmanuel Viollet-le-Duc

## III-13
## Missal of Notre Dame de Paris

1867–68
Mark: guaranty, silver, Paris, after 1838
Signed on each clasp: A. CHERTIER/Orfèvre/A PARIS; inscribed around busts on bottom cover: S^TA GE/NOVEF; S^S LU/DOVICV; S^TA CLO/TIL: CAROLU/MAGNU

Headband and inside edges gilded silver; partially gilded and enameled copper, partially gilded bronze, red morocco
Height 38.3 cm; width 26.8 cm; depth 8.5 cm

Provenance:
Executed for the chapter of Notre Dame de Paris; deposited by the chapter library in the Museum

It is well known how hard Viollet-le-Duc tried to complete his restorations of religious buildings by furnishing them with liturgical objects in precious metals or bronze in the style of the Middle Ages. Three goldsmiths executed his projects: Bachelet, who exhibited works designed by the architect in 1855, 1862, and 1867, Poussielgue-Rusand (q.v.), and Chertier. For Notre Dame in Paris, whose architectural restoration kept Viollet-le-Duc busy from 1844 to 1865, his numerous creations include celebrated pieces by Poussielgue-Rusand: the Reliquary of the Crown of Thorns exhibited in 1862 (Treasury of Notre Dame); the Reliquary of the Holy Nail and the True Cross (Treasury of Notre Dame); an altar service commissioned by the chapter, exhibited in 1867, including a monstrance (Treasury of Notre Dame), a tabernacle, two large candelabra, and a candlestick (*Etudes sur l'Exposition 1867*, p. 239, figs. 421, 422, 424). To the same period belongs the execution of three sacred books, whose designs, signed by the architect, are kept in the museum of Notre Dame.

The drawing for this missal (42 × 58 cm), bearing the legend "Missel en vermeil et émail pour Notre-Dame de Paris/28 mars 1867/E Viollet le Duc," shows for the top cover, the figure of the Virgin and the decoration of the left half; for the back cover, the figure of Saint Marcel, bishop of Paris from 417 to 436, the four busts, and the left half. This project was faithfully executed. The influence of thirteenth-century Limousin champlevé enamel bindings is obvious in the composition of both covers: a rectangular enameled plaque, with an applied figure in embossed copper and an enameled border. Limousin enamels also inspired other decorative elements: rosettes in the borders, scrolls in the central plaques, close, for example, to those on the tomb of Prince Jean, son of Saint Louis (Viollet-le-Duc, 1858–75, vol. II, pl. 43). The same enamels also suggested the choice of colors; but red, used only for details in Limoges, abounds here, covering the ground of the mandorla. The two figures were inspired by thirteenth-century statuary, Saint Marcel, his feet on a dragon, recalling in particular, *gisant* statues. The Virgin holds a scepter ending in a fleur-de-lis, like Jeanne d'Evreux's Virgin in the Louvre. More independent in iconography, Viollet-le-Duc placed the Virgin, patroness of the cathedral, inside a mandorla held by two angels, an arrangement reserved for Christ during the Middle Ages.

The missal was printed in 1868. The designs for the Evangelistary and the Epistolary, dated January 1867, show that the bindings of these two books, now lost, were decorated according to the same principle: the cover of the Evangelistary bore the embossed figure of Christ, the Epistolary, the figure of Saint Paul; the corner nails and clasps are the same as those on the missal. The Treasury of Notre Dame has two reliquary busts of Saint Denis and of Saint Louis, also executed by Chertier after Viollet-le-Duc's designs, as well as a large enameled cross and two *paces* by the same goldsmith (Auzas, n.d., pp. 10–11).

D.A.

Ministère de la Culture et de la Communication — Musée de Notre Dame de Paris

III-13

## François-Désiré Froment-Meurice

### Paris 1802–1855 Paris

*After the death of the silversmith François Froment, his widow married the silversmith Pierre Meurice. The family workshop took the name of Froment-Meurice, which Froment's son François-Désiré retained when he took over its direction in 1832. He received his training in this workshop, then with the chaser Lenglet, and also studied sculpture and drawing, and received advice from Charles Wagner. Established first at 2, rue de Lobau (Almanach du Commerce, 1848), later at 52, rue du Faubourg Saint Honoré (Almanach du Commerce, 1849), Froment-Meurice became known when he first exhibited at the exposition of 1839, receiving two silver medals, for gold- and silverwork. He became so successful that he was given the title of orfèvre-joaillier de la ville de Paris. He received gold medals in 1844 and 1849, and triumphed in London at the Universal Exhibition of 1851. This latter-day "Benvenuto Cellini" was celebrated by such friends and clients as Hugo (q.v.), Gautier, and Balzac. His production owed much to the art of the*

Renaissance, and still more to the artists who supplied him with designs: the sculptors Cavelier (q.v.), Feuchère, Geoffroy-Dechaume, Klagmann, Liénard, Préault (q.v.), Rouillard (q.v.), Schoenewerk (q.v.), the designer Rambert (q.v.). Their designs were executed by collaborators who would have brilliant careers: the chasers Vechte, whom Froment-Meurice employed as early as 1839, Honoré (q.v.), and Dalbergue (q.v.); the enamelers Lefournier, Sollier, and Grisée; the silversmiths Jules Fossin and Wièse; the jeweler Fossin (q.v.); and Fannière Frères (q.v.). Froment-Meurice died suddenly in 1855, before the Exposition Universelle, where his firm received a gold medal. An article by Gustave Planche, accusing Froment-Meurice of exploiting the work of his collaborators for his own profit, provoked a signed protest on their part in 1855.

Among his major works are the vase presented by the City of Paris to the baron de Feuchères (exposition of 1844; Musée des Arts Décoratifs); a silver racing trophy in the form of a shield with reliefs showing the history of the horse; the centerpiece of the duc de Luynes (expositions of 1849 and 1851); the dressing table of the duchess of Parma, designed by Duban (exposition of 1851). After having worked for the family of Louis Philippe, Froment-Meurice was approached by Napoleon III early in the reign: he furnished on January 28, 1853, a flask in jasper for the future Empress for 1,200 francs (Arch. nat. O⁵ 2301).

D.A.

Bibliography:
Rapports 1855, pp. 911, 915; Dussieux, 1876; Burty, 1883; Vever, 1906–8, vol. I, pp. 165–83; Bouilhet, 1908–12, vol. II, pp. 232–40, 252–60, 273–81, 306; Dumont, 1956

## Jules Wièse

### 1818–1890

During his lifetime Wièse was sometimes incorrectly referred to as Wiset. Trained by Hossauer, a well-known Berlin goldsmith, Wièse emigrated to Paris, where he worked for Jean-Valentin Morel (q.v.), and then, beginning in 1839, for François-Désiré Froment-Meurice, where he later became foreman. He set up his own workshop in 1844. On November 2, while living at 63, rue de la Tixanderie, he registered his maker's mark. He was established at 7, rue Jean Pain Mollet in the Marais, then 1, rue Saint Nicaise and 6, rue de Rivoli (Almanach du Commerce, 1853); 48, rue de l'Arbre Sec (Almanach du Commerce, 1854–63); and 90, rue de Richelieu (Almanach du Commerce, 1864). At first he worked only for Froment-Meurice, which brought him a medal as coopérateur at the Exposition des Produits de l'Industrie in 1849 and at the

Universal Exhibition in London in 1851. Later he also collaborated with Duponchel. At the Exposition Universelle of 1855, where he exhibited for the first time under his name, he showed Renaissance-style jewelry and enameled "pièces d'art," achieving wide recognition and receiving two silver medals for gold-and silverwork. One of his major works was the sword designed by Schoenewerk (q.v.) and presented in 1860 to Marshal MacMahon by his native city of Autun, on the occasion of the victory of Magenta. Wièse exhibited it at the International Exhibition in London in 1862, along with coupes of hard stones with mounts, and a clock and a pair of candelabra in the Greek style, these last designed by Rossigneux, and he won a medal for the group. In 1867, when he was criticized for showing works that were already known, he received a bronze medal. His son Louis succeeded him in 1880.

D.A.

Bibliography:
Arch. de la Garantie, Insculpations 1841–54, fol. 126; Catalogue 1855, p. 115; Rapports 1855, pp. 912, 917; Catalogue 1862, p. 214, "Renseignements," p. 172; Darcel, 1862, p. 322; Mantz, 1863, "Orfèvrerie," p. 540; Waring, 1863, vol. I, pl. 100; Récompensés 1867, group IV, p. 107; Rapports des délégations 1867, vol. I, "Bijoutiers," p. 16; Burty, 1883, pp. 45, 58, 77; Vever, 1906–8, vol. II, pp. 207–13

François-Désiré Froment-Meurice; made by Jules Wièse and chased by Honoré (Honoré-Séverin Bourdoncle)

## III-14
## Reliquary of the Talisman of Charlemagne

1855
Marks: guaranty, silver, Paris, after 1838; maker, J. Wièse
Signed on back of base: FROMENT-MEURICE 1855; inscribed on glass panes: LANGE DE N.S. JESUS-CHRIST; ROBE DE LA Sᵀᴱ VIERGE; TALISMAN DE CHARLEMAGNE; LINCEUL DE Sᵗ JEAN-BAPTISTE; OS DU BRAS DROIT DE CHARLEMAGNE
Parcel gilt, enamel, ivory, glass, precious stones, pearls
Height 63 cm; width 42 cm; depth 25.5 cm

Provenance:
Executed for Napoleon III; placed in the Louvre, 1871 (Louvre Archives Z 15A); returned to Empress, 1873; gift (with contents) of the Empress to Cardinal Luçon, archbishop of Reims, for the Treasury of the Cathedral, 1919 (see Paléologue, 1928, pp. 265–68); Association Diocésaine de Reims, since 1927

Exhibition:
1855, Paris, Exposition Universelle

Bibliography:
Moultat, 1858, p. 17; Honoré, 1859, p. 162; Rapports des délégations 1867, vol. III, "Orfèvres," pp. 32–33; Clouzot, 1925, p. 144; Taralon, 1966

This reliquary was made mainly to receive the object known in the nineteenth century as the "Talisman of Charlemagne," a Carolingian gold reliquary (height 6.5 cm; width 7.3 cm) that was supposedly found around Charlemagne's neck in the year 1000 or in 1165, when his body was exhumed at Aix-la-Chapelle (Aachen). In 1804 the chapter of Aix-la-Chapelle presented the Empress Josephine with several reliquaries belonging to the cathedral Treasury including the Talisman; these were divided among her children after her death. Queen Hortense's share, which passed to Napoleon III, included, according to his own statement around 1866, the Talisman, a bone of Charlemagne, pieces of Christ's swaddling clothes and of the robe of the Virgin. Superstitiously devoted to the Talisman, and attempting like Barbarossa and Napoleon I to link himself to Charlemagne, the Emperor kept these relics, as well as a relic from the shroud of Saint John the Baptist, in this reliquary, where they remain (except for the Talisman, which is shown separately in Reims).

It is difficult to find traces of the commission of the reliquary, which the Emperor probably paid for personally. The design may be by Viollet-le-Duc (q.v.), who was always responsive to the wishes of the sovereigns. Totally new, the composition does not recall any type of medieval reliquary; it is possible, however, that another work, also linked to Charlemagne, contributed to its conception: the Screen of Charlemagne from the Abbey of Saint Denis. This spectacular object, melted down during the Revolution and known only from an eighteenth-century engraving (Félibien, 1706, pl. 4), consisted of three superimposed rows of arcades resting on "a reliquary in the form of an elongated box, fitted with glass panes that allowed the bones of saints to be seen" (Viollet-le-Duc, 1858–75, vol. II, pp. 173–74). The overall appearance of the "box," gilded silver adorned with precious stones, is found again, along with arcades, on this reliquary. Froment-Meurice put the execution in the hands of his former collaborator Wièse (mark identified by François Macé de Lépinay). The chasing is by Honoré (q.v.): a reliquary for the Emperor was mentioned among his works exhibited in 1855 (Moultat, 1858). Honoré himself noted that the "Byzantine" reliquary commissioned by the Emperor to adorn the chapel of the palace of Saint-Cloud was widely admired in 1855. It does not, however, appear in Saint-Cloud inventories, and other sources indicate that this reliquary was actually in the Emperor's bedroom in the Tuileries, to the right of the bed.

The reliquary combines two aspects of medieval religious objects, enamelwork and

III-14

*Achille Legost*

*Active Paris*

*A bronze manufacturer and enameler of religious ornaments, domiciled at one time in the rue du Faubourg Saint Denis (Poitiers, Diocesan Archives), at another in the rue Saint Anastase (Louvre Archives M 21)—enamelers being generally established in the Marais—Legost contributed, at the instigation of Lassus (q.v.) and Viollet-le-Duc (q.v.), to the technical rediscovery of "Byzantine" enamels, executing for Monseigneur Sibour a clasp and a crozier in enamel, and restoring, under Viollet-le-Duc's direction, the plaques of the tombs of the children of Saint Louis in the Church of Saint Denis. He restored some works in the collection of Prince Soltykoff, to whom he had probably been introduced by Lassus. In 1855 he exhibited furniture decorated with enamels in accordance with the processes of the Middle Ages, receiving also a bronze medal as coopérateur for silverwork and a bronze medal for furniture, and later executed a tomb in enamel for a Russian prince. Although he did not exhibit in London in 1862, about that date he began "a colossal cross in enamel, modeled after the one that M. L. Steinheil has painted in such a deceptive manner to support the fine twelfth-century Christ in the Cluny museum" (Darcel, 1862, p. 539). In 1867, when he was established at 8, rue des Trois Pavillons (rue Elzévir) (Almanach du Commerce), he won a bronze medal for his enameled bronzes. Legost was considered a pioneer in the rediscovery of the techniques of medieval enamel, especially in the difficult pursuit of the color red.*

J.-M.L.

Bibliography:
Didron, 1854, pp. 58–62; *Rapports 1855*, pp. 925, 1126; Darcel, 1862, pp. 533–55; *Récompensés 1867*, group III, p. 43; Darcel, 1868, p. 76

ivory statuettes. They are found together on late-twelfth-century Rhenish reliquaries in the form of a church (one, then in the collection of Prince Soltykoff in Paris, is now in the Victoria and Albert Museum). The decoration is borrowed from various medieval periods: Romanesque arches, enamel columns inspired by Rhenish and Mosan reliquaries, and Gothic foliage. The Gothic angels recall the statuettes of angels, also holding the Instruments of the Passion, that surmounted an altar in the former cathedral of Arras, which appear in a drawing published by Lassus (*Annales Archéologiques*, vol. IX, 1849, pp. 1–9). To these motifs were added symbols giving the object a political meaning: arms of the Holy Roman Empire beneath the imperial Germanic crown, the so-

called crown of Charlemagne (Schatzkammer, Vienna; Willemin and Pottier, 1839, vol. I, pl. 19; described by Viollet-le-Duc, 1858–75, vol. III, pp. 307–8). The statuettes, inspired by Romanesque statuary, testify that ivory sculpture was not neglected by religious art. Exhibited the same year, at the Exposition Universelle of 1855, were an ivory tabernacle by Pierre Poisson (Church of La Trinité, Paris) and at the Salon, an altar by Moreau-Vauthier (q.v; Valabrègue, 1889–90, p. 383, repro. p. 387), both Gothic, while Armand-Calliat (q.v.) used ivory figures on objects exhibited in 1867.

D.A.

Association Diocésaine de Reims, on deposit in the Treasury of the Cathedral of Reims (Palais du Tau)

*Jean-Baptiste-Antoine Lassus*

*Paris 1807–1857 Vichy*

*Rejecting the Greco-Roman tradition, Lassus elaborated an artistic doctrine based on the study of medieval architecture, which by its qualities of logic and aesthetics was, in his view, adapted to climatic and functional conditions and suitable for regenerating contemporary architecture. His work was simultaneously that of archaeologist, restorer, and creator. As an archaeologist he frequented the circle of the* Annales Archéologiques *and the Comité des Arts et Monuments, and published the* Monographie de la Cathédrale de Chartres *and numerous articles. As a restorer and creator, he worked on the restoration, design, and construction of numerous ecclesiastical structures throughout*

France (see also *biography preceding no. I-15*). In these works he sought to recreate a Gothic "milieu" by conceiving also the objects, furniture, ornaments, silverwork, and stained glass.

In addition to his ecclesiastic architectural activities, he participated in the competition for the tomb of Napoleon I, completed with Préault (q.v.) and Pyanet the tomb of the Abbé de l'Epée in the Church of Saint Roch, built a block of flats in the rue Taitbout, the Hôtel Soltykoff (since destroyed) in Paris, and a private mansion in the style of Louis XIII in Maisons-Laffitte; he prepared restoration plans for the château of Saint-Parres-lès-Vaudes (Aube), for the comte de Maupas, Napoleon III's Prefect of Police. Finally, he executed, either alone or in collaboration, festival decorations for the Sainte Chapelle and Notre Dame (especially for the Emperor's marriage in 1853 and the baptism of the Prince Imperial in 1856), and participated in the special edition, adorned with illuminations reproduced by industrial processes, of *De Imitatione Christi*, exhibited in 1855.

A model of conscientiousness as a restorer, Lassus, though standing at the beginning of a renaissance in the decorative arts, remained too erudite perhaps to become a true inventor, but from his position as a pioneer he appeared as the most outstanding among the Neo-Gothic architects of the Second Empire.

J.-M.L.

Bibliography:
Leniaud, 1976

Achille Legost; designed by Jean-Baptiste-Antoine Lassus

## III-15
## Reliquary of Saint Radegunda

1852
Signed inside: + Hanc. capsam... benedixit, in eaqve sacra ossa reclvsit Lvdovicvs Edvardvs Pie, pictaviensis anno Domini MDCCCLII operis magister et delineator Johannes Lassvs celavit Achilles Legost
Enameled bronze
Height 75 cm; length 53 cm; depth 27 cm

Provenance:
Commissioned by Monseigneur Pie, bishop of Poitiers, 1851 (Poitiers, Diocesan Archives; Bib. nat., Mss. Nouv. acq. fr. 24002)
Bibliography:
Didron, 1854, pp. 58–62; Leniaud, 1976

The reliquary form underwent considerable development in the nineteenth century, no doubt due to the arrival of numerous relics in France during the first half of the century—such as those of Saint Philomena, Saint Flavia in Nevers, and Saint Theodosia in Amiens—to such an extent that the study of these objects could truly lead to a more tangible appreciation of the religious feeling of the period. In 1851 Monseigneur Pie, bishop of Poitiers, decided to have a reliquary made to hold the relics of Saint Radegunda; on the advice of Paul Durand, the scholar from Chartres, he turned to Lassus, after having considered choosing Fathers Cahier and Martin. In 1852 the design of the reliquary (exhibited at the Exposition Universelle in 1855) was ready, the architect having successively rejected the idea of a simple enameled reliquary, and then the idea of placing the bust of the saint behind a grill on one side of the reliquary. Legost executed the work in 1852, with the help of Steinheil, who carried out the designs for the enamels, and of Geoffroy Dechaume, Prinssay, and Pyanet for the sculptures. In 1854 the reliquary was exhibited at Didron's, and Lassus declared to Monseigneur Pie: "I have never done anything that interested me so much." It had cost 11,819 francs.

The reliquary has the structure of a Rhenish reliquary, a rectangular box supported by claw feet and topped by a double-sloped roof with a crest and balls above the gables; the whole was strongly influenced by the reliquary of Saint Julie in Jouarre and that of Saint Eleutherius of Tournai, published in the *Annales Archéologiques* (vol. VIII, 1848, p. 136; vol. XIII, 1853, p. 113). On the ends, a reliquary head and a reliquary arm add a stylistically heterogeneous note. Finally, the enamels themselves suggest Limousin enamels. Should one see this as an eclectic work, produced by the man who wrote: "Electicism is the scourge of art?" In Lassus's opinion, eclecticism did not consist in combining different medieval tendencies, but rather different historical styles, such as ancient art, the art of the Renaissance, and so on.

The iconography, worked out by Monseigneur Pie, demonstrates a good deal of research. On one side is a relief representing Saint Radegunda offering the Host to Pientius, bishop of Poitiers, with the commentary, "iste panis non est communis cum aliquo," flanked by Saint Agnes and Saint Disciole within trefoil niches; the two enamel medallions above show Saint Radegunda at the feet of Saint Medardus, who lays his hands upon her, and the saint, pursued by a warrior, taking refuge in the field of a peasant who is sowing. On the other side, in relief, the saint and Euphronius hold a reliquary containing pieces of the True Cross, with the commentary "Fulget crucis mysterium," flanked by Saints Fortunatus and Junianus; in one of the upper medallions Christ appears to the saint, while the other represents her burial. Finally, the arms of Poitiers and of Monseigneur Pie are placed beneath each gable. This iconography, so complex and learned, derived from miniatures and texts by Etienne de Fleury, and serving more for the delectation of clerics than as a Bible for the poor, is typical of the religious and medievalist pursuits that developed under the Second Empire. The reliquary itself was to remain a model, until the end of the century, for a whole line produced by the workshop of Poussielgue-Rusand (q.v.).

J.-M.L.

Abbaye Ste-Croix, Poitiers

## Placide Poussielgue-Rusand
### 1824–1889

Poussielgue-Rusand's parents, booksellers in Paris connected with Choiselat, a manufacturer of church bronzes (established at 8, rue de Pot de Fer Saint Sulpice, now rue Bonaparte), published works of archaeology written by Fathers Charles Cahier and Arthur Martin. Under these influences, Placide Poussielgue-Rusand, who studied design, became a manufacturer of sacred objects with the advice and designs of Father Martin and of the silversmith Cahier, Father Cahier's brother (who, obliged to close his own shop, worked for him). Poussielgue worked first in partnership with Choiselat at 36, rue Cassette (Almanach du Commerce, 1847–50), then alone at 34, rue Cassette (Almanach du Commerce, 1851–61), and later at 15, rue Cassette (Almanach du Commerce, 1862). The Dreux-Brézé altar service won Poussielgue a medal in 1851 and a success that his talents as a dealer advanced. He had the title of fabricant de N.S.P. le Pape (Almanach du Commerce, 1857). His enormous production included works in precious metals, copper, and bronze after designs by such architects and restorers as Viollet-le-Duc (q.v.), Corroyer, Duthoit (q.v.), Gay, and Sauvageot. He supplied furnishings for numerous churches in Paris, restored objects, and did a good deal of exporting. The high altar of the Church of Saint Martin d'Ainay in Lyons, executed in Romanesque style after Questel, architect of the palace of Versailles, won him a silver medal at the exposition of 1855. He obtained a medal in 1862 when he exhibited, among other things, the Reliquary of the Crown of Thorns and became chevalier of the Legion of Honor in 1863. In 1867, he executed the high altar of the cathedral of Quimper after Boeswilwald, and an altar for the cathedral of

*Amiens by Viollet-le-Duc, which despite some criticism for his lack of development, won him a gold medal. At the same time two of his collaborators received bronze medals as* coopérateurs. *An officer of the Legion of Honor, Poussielgue presided over the jury for silverwork at the exposition of 1889 but died shortly thereafter, leaving his firm to his son Maurice, his partner since 1885.*

D.A.

Bibliography:
*Rapports 1855*, pp. 912, 925–26, 1150–51; Waring, 1863, vol. I, pl. 83; *Catalogue 1867*, vol. III, p. 41; *Récompensés 1867*, group III, pp. 36, 38, 39; *Rapports 1867*, vol. III, p. 265; *Rapports des délégués lyonnais 1867*, pp. 179–80; *Rapports des délégations 1867*, vol. III, "Orfèvres," p. 66; Dussieux, 1876, passim; Champier, 1889–90; Bouilhet, 1908–12, vol. II, p. 134, vol. III, pp. 11–23, 165–67, 217–21, 354

Placide Poussielgue-Rusand; designed by Father Arthur Martin*

## III-16
## Chalice

c. 1865
Marks: standard silver, Paris, since 1838; maker, Pl. Poussielgue-Rusand
Inscribed on enamels on bowl; HOC EST/CORPUS MEUM; PRO VOBIS/EFŪNDETEUR; MORTEM D̄/AÑŪNCIA; DOMINUS MEUS/ET DEUS MEUS
Gilded silver, enamel, niello, garnets, pearls
Height 26.5 cm; diameter (top) 11.4 cm; diameter (foot) 16.2 cm

Provenance:
Part of the service presented by Napoleon III to canon de Place, titular canon of Notre Dame of Paris (*Almanach National*, 1850); *théologal* (*Almanach Impérial*, 1862), *théologal* and archpriest (*Almanach Impérial*, 1864), at close of Lent in 1865, which he had preached at the Tuileries; gift of the canon to the Trésor de Notre Dame de Paris
Bibliography:
Auzas, n.d., p. 15, repro. p. 9

The four large lobes of the base of the chalice are ornamented with enamel scenes: *Moses Striking the Rock, The Brazen Serpent, The Grapes of the Promised Land,* and *The Inscription of the Tau.* Four enameled medallions, with the Tetramorph, appear on the knot, and four more ornament the bowl: *The Last Supper, Christ on the Cross between the Church and the Synagogue,*

III-16

*The Entombment,* and *The Incredulity of Saint Thomas.* Besides this chalice, the altar service included a paten, two ciboria, two cruets with salver, and a hand bell (lost). This service was reproduced in several copies, and the chalice appears as number 1 in the Poussielgue-Rusand catalogue of 1893, offered in various materials for various prices.

The first example of this medieval-style service was produced in 1850 for Monseigneur de Dreux-Brézé, who on becoming bishop of Moulins, undertook to promote the Neo-Gothic style in religious art. One might see in the case of this young, forty-year-old prelate, an artistic manifestation of ultramontanism, the Gallican tradition remaining embodied by Neoclassicism. To build in the Neo-Gothic style

and create Neo-medieval objects was obviously a political-theological declaration preaching a return to the century of Saint Louis, considered the golden age of a union between the temporal and the spiritual. This service (the ciborium alone is extant; cathedral of Moulins), displayed in London in 1851, was designed by Father Martin, as can be seen from the Poussielgue-Rusand catalogue and two preparatory drawings (Centre de Recherches des Monuments Historiques). One shows a work more squat in shape, with a wider bowl, but with the same arrangement of enamels in circular medallions on a filigree background and the same knot; the other constitutes a sketch for the work with the same proportions, rows of pearls, garnets, and indications of iconography. However, the Tetramorph is replaced by simple crosses, the medallions of the foot and bowl have six lobes, the dragons are not yet present, and the placement of the enamels on the foot is different, and the design lacks both filigree work and scenes.

The work was hailed as a stylistic and technical rebirth of the silversmith's art, although Poussielgue did not reproduce medieval techniques: instead of champlevé enamels, the medallions were enameled on stamped grounds; the colors of the enamels are few; the checkerwork is stamped; and the filigrees of the base are fixed from behind with screws. Although the dragons suggest those of Limoges and the filigree recalls the work of Hugo d'Oignies, the arrangement of the decoration on the bowl, knot, and foot derives instead from fourteenth- and fifteenth-century models, giving the whole a heterogeneous appearance. Nevertheless— and herein lies its originality—everything was planned for industrial reproduction. The Gothic revival, in order to impose itself on the religious art market, utilized appropriate marketing methods, catalogues, different versions with different prices (another version of the chalice, in Notre Dame, shows the same scenes in mosaic), and reduction of handwork, with the result that this art, launched through special commissions, in fifty years conquered all the sacristies (*see* Bouilhet, 1908–12, vol. III, pp. 12–17).

J.-M.L.

Ministère de la Culture et de la Communication — Trésor de Notre Dame de Paris

# Goldwork

## Gustave Baugrand

*1826–1870 Paris*

Son of Victor Baugrand (1803–1872), a stone setter and jeweler, Baugrand was himself first established as a joaillier in 1852 in partnership with Paul Marret, whose family firm had enjoyed considerable success under Louis Philippe. Following Marret's death in 1853, Baugrand directed the firm with Marret's widow for over a decade, participating in the international exhibitions in Paris and London under the name Marret and Beaugrand [sic]. In 1855 the firm won a Medal of Honor for jewelry in the naturalistic floral styles popular since the late 1830s, including a "garland of cornflowers of very beautiful workmanship" (Fossin, in Rapports 1855, p. 916). In the same year, the firm set stones belonging to the imperial family (Arch. nat. 0⁵2319). Inspired by Classical jewelry in the Campana collection, in 1862 Marret and Baugrand showed an "Etruscan" diadem and won an exhibition medal for "excellence of design and workmanship" (Medals 1862, p. 359, no. 3205) and praise from Fossin for jewelry judged "rich without being tasteless... the form is nowhere sacrificed to the effect" (Rapports 1862, vol. VI, p. 446). On July 26, 1864, Baugrand registered his maker's mark at the Garantie: a row of small pearls and the monogram GB. By 1867 Baugrand was sole proprietor of a business of considerable importance: his designers included Fauré and Fossey, his jewelers and enamelers, Massin, Meyer (q.v.), and Tard (q.v.). At the Paris 1867 exposition, Baugrand was hors concours as a member of the jury, although his dazzling display of Neo-Egyptian pieces and prominent use of colored enamels were highly praised by one reviewer as "thoroughly modern" (Boutell, in Art Journal Catalogue 1867, vol. VII, p. 154). Among Baugrand's clients in 1867 was the queen of Portugal, for whom the firm executed a stomacher in rubies, pearls, and brilliants. In 1870, during the siege of Paris, Baugrand died, and his firm was subsequently sold to Ernest Vever.

K.B.H.

Bibliography:
Arch. de la Garantie, Insculpations, 1855–81, no. 7.634; Vever, 1906–8, vol. II, pp. 120, 300–303

Gustave Baugrand; designed by P. Fauré*; chased by Honoré (Honoré-Séverin Bourdoncle) and Fannière Frères; enamels painted by Théophile Soyer* and Solié Frères*; enameled by Gagneré*; rock crystal engraved by Ernest Hue*

## III-17
## Clock

1867
Signed and dated at bottom: PARIS/BAUGRAND/ANNO/1867: monogram C.I.F. ["Comme je fus," the Dudley motto] on base
Case silver, parcel-gilt, chased, engraved, and enameled with decorations in gold, painted enamel and lapis lazuli; side plates rock crystal with engraved decoration; base silver, parcel-gilt
Height 37.5 cm

Provenance:
Purchased by William, First Earl of Dudley (1817–1885) from the Exposition Universelle of 1867; acquired at an unknown date "from a sale, New York" by Henry Walters (1848–1931); The Walters Art Gallery (inv. no. 58.230)

Exhibition:
1867, Paris, Exposition Universelle

III-17

Bibliography:
Friswell, in *Art Journal Catalogue 1867*, vol. VII, p. 272, repro. p. 288; Mesnard, 1867, vol. I, pp. 140–42, repro. p. 141; Vever, 1906–8, vol. II, repro. p. 301

*See* Colorplate

Described in 1867 as "ornamented with enamel and many rare jewels, a production of surpassing elegance in design and execution… acquired by the Earl of Dudley" (*Art Journal Catalogue 1867*, vol. VII, p. 272), this table clock, recalling sixteenth- and seventeenth-century models, is in tower form with a large engraved rock crystal front for the dial and an enameled dome covering the bell. Renaissance in style, the architecture of the case is enriched with a wealth of jewel-like figurative and decorative elements, an intricately detailed fantasy sharing the technical conceit and preciosity, as well as the style, of its sixteenth-century sources. Allegorical figures ornament the clock, with chimeras driven by putti at the base; atlantes supporting the case; the Four Seasons, putti, and griffins at the base of the dome; and Urania, Muse of astronomy, as a finial. According to Mesnard, the clock, composed of 120 single pieces, required eighteen months for fabrication by distinguished craftsmen, all of whom were rewarded with medals as *coopérateurs* at the 1867 exposition.

The clock was one of the few Renaissance objects exhibited by Baugrand in 1867 among a display primarily Egyptian in style, and was praised by Mesnard as "completely French in character, and for the taste which was responsible for its creation," a work "which Ducerceau would not have disavowed" (Mesnard, 1867, vol. I, pp. 140, 142). If Renaissance revival designs had by 1867 been largely replaced in Baugrand's repertory by exotic styles, they were nonetheless suited to the conservative tastes of the "rich English and Americans" described as among Baugrand's patrons at the exhibition (H. Friswell, in *Art Journal Catalogue 1867*, vol. VII, pp. 272, 288).

K.B.H.

The Walters Art Gallery, Baltimore

---

## Charles-Martial Bernard

*1824–1896*

Charles-Martial Bernard's father, Jean-Benoît-Martial, a jeweler, established himself at 1, rue de la Paix in 1826 (*Almanach du Commerce, 1827*). A talented designer, he placed his son as an apprentice in the workshop of the jeweler Jules Chaise (1807–1870), who was known for his fine craftsmanship, and at the same time had him take

courses at the Ecole des Beaux-Arts. Charles-Martial was later in charge of design at his father's establishment, before succeeding him after his death in 1846. This firm's clients included the royal family at the end of the Restoration and under the July Monarchy. As fournisseur du Ministère des Affaires Etrangères, the firm executed snuffboxes and other objects bearing the initials of Louis Philippe and Marie Amélie which were offered as gifts by the sovereigns, and the firm kept this title under the Second Empire. Bernard did not take part in the international exhibitions until 1867, when, showing a jeweled frontlet and a brooch in topaz and gold of several colors representing The Fox and the Grapes, he received a bronze medal, while his foreman Baroux won an honorable mention.

Bernard led a very active public life particularly in matters affecting his profession's interests. He became a judge at the Tribunal de Commerce de la Seine (1869–73), then, after distinguishing himself during the siege of Paris, became municipal councilor (1871–80). At the exposition of 1889, he presided over the international jury for goldwork and jewelry. His son succeeded him.

D.A.

Bibliography:
Arch. nat. F¹² 3049 [Exposition of 1867]; *Récompensés 1867*, group IV, pp. 107, 111; *Rapports des délégations 1867*, vol. I, "Bijoutiers," pp. 4, 15; Vever, 1906–8, vol. I, pp. 208–17

Charles-Martial Bernard

## III-18
## Snuffbox

1853
Mark: guaranty, gold, Paris, after 1838
Signed inside: Martial Bernard rue de la Paix 1; number engraved inside: 307; inscribed on trophy on cover: 27 Mai 1853; around box: ON NE SAUVE PAS L'AVENIR D'UN PAYS PAR LES ABUS DE LA FORCE LA VIOLATION DES LOIS; monogram on bottom in gold of several colors: AE [?]
Gold of several colors, enamel
Height 2.2 cm; width 8 cm; depth 5.1 cm

Provenance:
Pierre-Antoine Berryer (1790–1868), lawyer, Legitimist deputy; purchased by Mrs. John Bowes (see no. II-30) in Paris from the dealer Lamer (30, rue Drouot; *Almanach du Commerce*, 1865, the last year he was listed) for 700 francs, March 19, 1869 (Bowes Museum Archives); gift of John Bowes to the Bowes Museum (inv. no. X 5465)

Bibliography:
*French Art*, n.d., frontispiece

Although the form of this snuffbox refers to the eighteenth century, it recalls more the toilet

boxes of that period than the snuffboxes, which had different contours and proportions. Coating the box with translucent green enamel on a guilloche background also stems from the eighteenth century. The ornamentation consists, on the one hand, of applied gold reliefs on the cover, and on the other, of reserves in gold and white enamel. The themes are also dual.

Motifs of Legitimist inspiration give the object a political meaning: on the center of the cover a trophy in eighteenth-century style, in yellow, green, and white gold, includes white flags with fleurs-de-lis, two scepters with fleurs-de-lis, a hand of Justice, and a sword, while the field is scattered with fleurs-de-lis and framed by four larger ones which are flanked by field lilies. Fleurs-de-lis reappear on the banderole which bears the inscription and which is edged with field lilies and ivy leaves. On the bottom, these last motifs encircle the monogram. But this emblematical ornamentation is updated by the white Moresque interlacings on the cover and the bottom. Vever reproduced a drawing by Jean-Benoît-Martial Bernard showing a snuffbox with the monogram of Louis Philippe and whose decoration includes similar interlacings. This type of object is characteristic of the work of Martial Bernard,

III-18

who in 1867 showed several snuffboxes "with applied reliefs of gold of several colors" (*Rapports des délégations 1867*, vol. I, "Bijoutiers," p. 15). Perhaps the box also reflects, at the beginning of the Empire, the political ideas of the jeweler who had been compromised under the preceding regime.

According to Lamer's bill, this was "a gold snuffbox from the Berryer sale, gift of the comte de Chambord, with an excerpt from one of his most beautiful speeches following the coup d'etat." The extent to which Berryer had defended the Legitimist cause is well known. He died in Augerville (Loiret) on November 29, 1868; as early as November 30, the comte de Chambord wrote from Frohsdorf: "France has lost, in the person of M. Berryer, one of her noblest sons, the cause of law, its most eloquent supporter, and I, one of my most faithful friends" (*Derniers adieux de M. Berryer à Mᵍʳ le comte de Chambord*, n.p., n.d., pp. 3–4). The sale catalogue of the Berryer estate (Paris, Hôtel Drouot, room 2, March 15, 1869) does not mention the box, but notes that various uncatalogued objects were to be sold under lot 125. Perhaps this box, bought four days later by Mrs. Bowes, was one of them.

D.A.

The Bowes Museum, Barnard Castle, England

---

## Ecole Municipale d'Horlogerie

*Besançon, established 1862*

*The creation of this school attests to the growing concern for professional training under the Second Empire. In 1840 the prefect Tourangin tried to establish a watchmaking school in Besançon, but failed owing to the hostility of professionals who feared competition. In 1862 following the "Exposition Internationale Universelle," organized in Besançon in 1860, where the importance of Besançon watchmaking was publicly demonstrated, the school was founded by the municipality, under the mayor César Clerc de Landresse, and established in the place Labourey. In 1867 it was said that the city spent 20,000 francs a year for the school. Its first director, Courvoisier, a master watchmaker of Swiss origin, wanted to train specialists, while his successor, Georges Sire, a doctor of sciences, preferred that his pupils be both theoreticians and practical watchmakers; he was opposed to division of labor, he explained in a speech delivered at the first distribution of prizes in 1865. The school, which proved to be a great success, had forty pupils in 1865, all with scholarships, thirty of whom came from outside Besançon. At the Paris Exposition Universelle of 1867, where its achievements gained recognition, the school was awarded a bronze medal, as were the three other great watchmaking schools of Europe—Cluses (Haute-Savoie), Geneva, and Le Locle.*

D.A.

Bibliography:
*Récompensés 1867*, group III, pp. 47–48; *Rapports 1867*, vol. III, p. 325; Luchet, 1868, pp. 22–23; Fohlen, 1964–65, vol. II, pp. 334, 355

Ecole Municipale d'Horlogerie; designed by Georges Sire* and chased by Denis-Auguste Krachpeltz*

## III-19
## Pocket Watch

c. 1866
Signed: KRACHPELTZ SCULP; monogram on cover: LN; inscribed under stem, on two sides: FRANCE; imperial arms on case
Gold of several colors
Height 6.7 cm; diameter 4.5 cm

Provenance:
Deposited in the Musée des Beaux-Arts by the city of Besançon, 1871

Exhibition:
1962, Besançon

Bibliography:
Catalogues, Musées de Besançon, 1886, no. 1092, 1955, no. 6558

According to the 1886 catalogue of the Besançon museum, this watch was executed by the Ecole Municipale d'Horlogerie after a design by its director Georges Sire. It was made for presentation to the Prince Imperial as a souvenir of a visit that the Emperor and Empress intended to pay to Besançon in 1866, but which was canceled. The monogram is the same as that of the Emperor. The watch is a stem-winder, a type that was slowly supplanting the key system, and the stem takes the form of the imperial crown. The cylinder movement, of a standard type, was constructed under the direction of three teachers by a group of thirteen students (four from Besançon, two from the Doubs, the others from the region of Paris or the East). The purely emblematic decoration was engraved free of charge by a Besançon watchmaker, Denis-Auguste Krachpeltz, who exhibited in the Exposition Universelle of 1867 (*Catalogue 1867*, vol. III, p. 55).

Watchmaking, brought to Besançon in 1793 by political refugees from Neuchâtel in Switzerland, had become the leading industry there, employing in 1867 close to 15,000 of the 50,000 inhabitants. The work, specializing in the finishing and decoration of watches made in Montbéliard and in Switzerland, was performed in small workshops. Besançon watch production, in part exported, kept growing: in 1847 the watchmakers presented to the Bureau de la Garantie of the city 61,024 watches, 9,667 of them in gold (the rest in silver); 211,811 in 1860, of which 76,146 were gold; and 305,435 in 1866, of which 101,309 were gold—that is, 98 percent of the total French production. Though the Second Empire represented for Besançon an era of great progress in trade, ur-

III-19

ban growth, hygiene, and standard of living, its citizens maintained a reticent attitude toward Napoleon III, who did not succeed in exploiting the marked local division between the Left and the Legitimist party. When on August 18, 1850, the Prince-President came to Besançon—whose votes he had received in the election—the reception was rather cold and assassination rumors circulated. The marquis de Conegliano, chamberlain of the Emperor, and the official candidate, was elected deputy in 1857 and 1863, but defeated in 1869. Besançon, which had become predominantly Republican, voted No in the referendum of May 1870, and the Republic was proclaimed on September 4 (*L'Horlogerie à Besançon*, 1867; *Rapports 1867*, vol. III, pp. 324–27; Fohlen, 1964–65, vol. II).

D.A.

Musée des Beaux-Arts, Besançon

---

## Alexis Falize

*Liège 1811–1898 Moret*

*At the death of his father, a bootmaker, Alexis Falize went to Paris to complete his studies in the school where he later became a professor and, notably, taught drawing. In 1833 he became a clerk with Mellerio Frères on the rue de la Paix. As a result of* this connection he began to design jewelry, first for Mellerio, then in 1835 for the jewelry firm of Janisset, fashionable under Louis Philippe, where he worked until 1838. That year he bought the firm of the jewelry maker Aristide Joureau-Robin, at Palais Royal, promising, as had his predecessor, to work only for the Janisset firm. From 1840 to 1871 he was at 6, rue Montesquieu. He registered his maker's mark on June 4, 1841. After the Janisset firm failed in 1848, his services were used by other great jewelers, such as Boucheron in 1867. Unknown by the public, never exhibiting under his own name, but very well thought of by other members of his profession, Falize became in 1864 the first president of the Syndicat de la Bijouterie. Always making his own designs, Falize helped revive the art of jewelry under the Second Empire, creating in particular works inspired by Greek and then Egyptian art. He retired in 1876. A number of jewelry designs in watercolor by Alexis Falize are preserved in the Cooper-Hewitt Museum in New York.

D.A.

Bibliography:
Arch. de la Garantie, Insculpations 1841–54, fol. 42; Vever, 1906–8, vol. II, pp. 60–88

## Lucien Falize

*1842–1897 Paris*

The son of Alexis Falize, Lucien began to work with his father in 1856. He studied carefully the works of the past in museums as well as through his contact with the erudite Alfred Darcel. In 1871 he became his father's partner. The firm of Falize, which moved to 55, avenue de l'Opéra (Almanach du Commerce, 1873), was directed by Lucien alone as of 1876 and exhibited for the first time in 1878. At the death of Alfred Bapst in 1879, his son Germain (1853–1921) became Lucien Falize's partner. They moved to 6, rue d'Antin but separated in 1892 because Bapst wanted to devote himself to study. Falize's three sons directed the establishment after his death.

Lucien Falize's role in jewelry and silverwork was very important at the beginning of the Third Republic as a result of his creations, his publications (scholarly studies; articles published under his name or that of "Monsieur Josse"), his lectures, and his activities within the Union Centrale des Arts Décoratifs. His taste for plant ornamentation made him a precursor of Art Nouveau.

D.A.

Bibliography:
*Revue des Arts Décoratifs,* vol. XII (1891–92), p. 401, vol. XVII (1897), pp. 320, 351–52; Vever, 1906–8, vol. III, pp. 484–522; Bouilhet, 1908–12, vol. III

## Antoine Tard

*Active Paris after c. 1860*

An unassuming enameler, Antoine Tard reinvented, without knowing the ancient precedents, the technique of cloisonné. His efforts elicited the interest of Paul Christofle (q.v.) and Henri Bouilhet (q.v.), who had Tard execute for the Exposition Universelle of 1867 objects of cloisonné enamel on copper with decoration of Persian or Indian inspiration. The Bethnal Green Museum in London has a plate which must have been the first piece of this type they produced, the bottom of which bears the enameled inscription: "EMAUX/à cloisons rapportées/CHRISTOFLE & CIE/PARIS/1867/TARD EMAILLEUR." The same museum owns a teapot, a coffeepot, and a sugar bowl of the same authorship from the exposition of 1867. At the exposition the goldsmith Emile Philippe also showed cloisonné objects by Tard. This novelty was greatly applauded. During the following years Tard executed for Christofle, after Japanizing designs of Emile Reiber (q.v.), more and more spectacular enameled objects of which a number are in the Musée Christofle in Saint-Denis. At the same time Tard enameled gold jewelry for Falize using the same technique. He was still working for Lucien Falize at the time of the exposition of 1878, where he won a bronze medal as a collaborateur. He was also employed by Baugrand (q.v.) and, notably for the exposition of 1889, by Boucheron.

D.A.

Bibliography:
*Rapports des délégations 1867,* vol. III, "Orfèvres," pp. 43–44; *Récompensés 1878,* p. 229; Falize, 1882–83, pp. 332–35; Vever, 1906–8, vol. II, p. 302, vol. III, pp. 456, 491–94, 496

Alexis Falize and Lucien Falize; enameled by Antoine Tard

## III-20
## Necklace and Earrings

c. 1870
Marks (on each earring): guaranty, gold, Paris, after 1838; maker, Alexis Falize (no mark on necklace)
Gold, cloisonné enamel
Necklace length 40 cm, largest pendant diame-

III-20

ter 3.5 cm; earrings length 5.4 cm, diameter 2.9 cm

Bibliography:
Oxford University, *Ashmolean Museum, Report of the Visitors,* 1964, p. 33; Gere, 1975, pp. 51, 67, 150, repro. p. 50

The necklace consists of ten convex plaques, separated by ten gold flowers of two alternating types; five pendants are attached to the necklace, including a pair the same size as the earrings. Every part of the set is enameled on both faces with opaque enamels in many colors. The decoration on the earrings is similar but reversed. Alexis Falize was always especially interested in enamel, using painted enamel on his jewelry in collaboration with

**III-20**

Meyer (q.v.), Lepec, and Popelin (q.v.) (Vever, 1906–8, vol. II, p. 80). The Tard pieces shown by Christofle (q.v.) in 1867 astonished both the elder and younger Falize, who, using the same enameler, wanted to adapt the cloisonné technique to gold jewelry. During this time Japanese objects were beginning to enter France, and Lucien Falize discovered Japanese prints, which the ceramic manufacturer François-Eugène Rousseau (q.v.) and the critic Burty lent him, or which he bought. Taking inspiration from Japanese decorative motifs, the Falizes tried to reproduce in enamel the colors of ancient Chinese cloisonnés, which were more highly colored than contemporary

Japanese cloisonnés. Their investigations were completed by 1868, when they executed their first jewelry of this type for Martz, a jeweler at 2, rue de la Paix, some of which was published by Burty the same year. After this date the Falizes made all sorts of jewelry in cloisonné enamel (several pieces are in the Musée des Arts Décoratifs).

The date of the pieces shown is problematic. According to the donors, they were acquired in 1867, which is unlikely since Lucien Falize himself said that his house had not executed any such objects until 1868. Burty published an illustration of a pair of earrings composed of a round medallion with a gold-beaded edge, like these. The set shown could, therefore, be contemporary, but Vever reproduced and ascribed to 1874 two round medallions with a similar beaded edge and a third decorated with birds like those on one of the faces of the earrings, and he also published related jewelry which he dated 1876. The decoration of the earring mount, inspired by ironwork, could be later than the Second Empire. How long did the Falize workshop execute this type of object? Lucien Falize spoke about it as a past endeavor in 1882–83. However, the donors of this set gave the Ashmolean Museum a bracelet of the same kind signed and dated by Bapst and Falize in 1883. Whatever its date, it is certain that the Falizes executed jewelry in the same style and technique by the end of the Second Empire. Afterward, Lucien Falize pursued different investigations in enameling using translucent enamels. (*See Rapports 1867,* vol. III, p. 277; Burty, 1868, *Emaux cloisonnés,* pp. 54–70; Darcel, 1868, pp. 75–76; Falize, 1882–83, pp. 332–37; Vever, 1906–8, vol. III, pp. 347–49, 491–94.)

D.A.

The Visitors of the Ashmolean Museum, Oxford

## Prosper-Eugène Fontenay

*Paris 1823–1887*

*The son and grandson of Parisian goldsmiths, Prosper-Eugène Fontenay was apprenticed to Edouard Marchand, then became a worker with Dutreih, two goldsmiths renowned for the quality of their workmanship, before establishing himself at 2, rue Favart in 1847, then 19, place du Marché Saint Honoré in 1858 (Almanach du Commerce). Erudite, an excellent technician, designing his pieces himself, Fontenay produced goldwork for the trade*

*and, on order, jewelry in a Classical style, or for export to the Orient. Under the Second Empire he executed for India, Turkey, the king of Siam, the shah of Persia, and the viceroy of Egypt, Said Pasha, many luxurious gold objects in the Oriental style, decorated with enamel and precious stones, sometimes enormous: weapons, tableware, pipes, fly whisks, lights, etc. He registered his maker's mark on July 24, 1863. He exhibited under his own name for the first time in 1867, and published on this occasion a collection of nine etchings, which he himself had made, picturing his most spectacular works: a diadem made for the Empress (1858) and pieces for the Orient (1858–67). Fontenay received a gold medal for his jewelry in 1867, while his collaborators, whose names he submitted to the jury, also received awards: Henri Smets, his foreman, a bronze medal, and Homassel, his pupil, an honorable mention. He exhibited in the Salon, notably landscapes, from 1867 to 1870. Having pursued actively the interests of his profession and been a member of the jury at the Expositions Universelles of 1873 and 1878, Fontenay retired in 1882, leaving his firm to Smets. He devoted himself to writing* Les Bijoux anciens et modernes, *which was published in the year of his death. He is best known for his "Néo-Grec" jewelry.*

D.A.

Bibliography:
Arch. de la Garantie, Insculpations 1855–81, fol. 47; Arch. nat. F¹² 3049 [Exposition of 1867]; *Récompensés 1867,* group IV, pp. 105, 110–11; Fontenay, 1867; Bellier and Auvray, 1882–87, vol. I, p. 563; Falize, 1886–87; Vever, 1906–8, vol. I, p. 226, vol. II, pp. 147–81, 275, 322, vol. III, pp. 375, 393, 449

## Félix Samper

*Active Paris until 1879*

*Félix Samper et Cie, jeweler-goldsmith, supplier to the royal house of Spain, was established at 16, rue de la Paix and 18, boulevard des Italiens in Paris and, at the same time, on the Calle del Carmen in Madrid (Almanach du Commerce, 1867). Although he called himself a manufacturer, he seems to have been accustomed to selling works done by colleagues. For the Exposition Universelle of 1867, for example, he had Oscar Massin execute almost his entire presentation but finally decided not to exhibit. Debut and Coulon, former employees of Boucheron, succeeded Samper in 1879.*

D.A.

Bibliography:
Vever, 1906–8, vol. II, pp. 232–33, vol. III, p. 592

Prosper-Eugène Fontenay; made for Félix Samper

## III-21
## Earrings

c. 1867
Marks: guaranty, gold, Paris, after 1838; maker (illegible)
Signed on one earring on reverse of upper snake: FONTENAY FAB; F. SAMPER & Cᵒ
Jade and gold
Height 5.4 cm; width 1.5 cm

Provenance:
Gift of Mme René Fouret to the Musée des Arts Décoratifs, 1919 (inv. no. 21 192)
Exhibition:
1867, Paris, Exposition Universelle
Bibliography:
Vever, 1906–8, vol. II, repro. p. 155

III-21

An etching by Fontenay showing some of the jewelry he exhibited in 1867 includes a pair of earrings identical to this one (*Rapports des délégations 1867,* vol. I, "Bijoutiers," repro. p. 4). Vever also pictured an identical earring. Both illustrations probably represent this pair which Fontenay executed for Samper, as signed. Perhaps they were originally intended for the display at the Exposition Universelle that Samper planned but canceled. Excited and inspired by the jewelry of the Musée Napoléon III, Fontenay was a champion of "Campana jewelry" for many years. He created works in many different forms, but the amphora appeared often in jade or in gold in his brooches or earrings (*see* Vever, 1906–8, vol. II, repro. pp. 155, 157, 177). Fontenay himself published antique jewelry—earrings, necklaces—composed of amphoras, notably a Hellenistic earring from the Campana collection (Clément, 1862, no. 119), whose two-handled amphora, decorated with granulation, though much smaller, could have inspired these (Fontenay, 1887, pp. 110-11). But he was not content, like his colleagues, to rely only on ancient forms and decorations. He endeavored, like Castellani, to rediscover certain techniques, as seen in the use of granulation, here on the necks and the bands around the bellies. Rather than making a pastiche of archaeological pieces, he introduced diverse materials into his jewelry: painted enamels representing Pompeian scenes by Richet, Couture's student; and pearls, coral, and hard stones. The Musée des Arts Décoratifs has a pair of "Néo-Grec" earrings by Fontenay, each decorated with the bust of a child in lapis (Vever, 1906–8, vol. II, repro. p. 152). The use

of jade, however, seems to have been an innovation, and Fontenay particularly called it to the attention of the jury in 1867: "I would point out several green jade jewels in my case. I believe it is the first time this stone has been worked in France or even in Europe. It seems to me a point of interest for the history of our industry to mention this fact to you" (Fontenay, 1867, p. 4). He later wrote: "For a relatively short time, green jade was used in making jewelry. This experiment, made possible by the introduction into France of a block of green jade from the Summer Palace, could not be followed up" (Fontenay, 1887, p. 374). Actually, jade had been worked in Europe during the Renaissance. Vever published other jade jewelry by Fontenay, in antique and other styles (Vever, 1906–8, vol. II, pp. 155, 158–59, 174).

D.A.

Musée des Arts Décoratifs, Paris

---

## Jules-Jean-Baptiste Fossin
*Paris 1808–1869 Vasouy (Calvados)*

*Nitot Fils,* joaillier de l'Empereur, 15, place Vendôme (Almanach du Commerce, *1815*) retired in 1815, leaving his firm to his chef d'atelier Jean-Baptiste Fossin (1786–1848), who established it at 78, rue de Richelieu (Almanach du Commerce, *1818–32*), then at 62, rue de Richelieu (Almanach du Commerce, *1833*). Fossin and his son Jules,

who became his partner (Almanach du Commerce, *1835*), received the title of joailliers du Roi under Louis Philippe, and for some years Jean-Valentin Morel (q.v.) worked as their chef d'atelier. Designers and modelers, they simultaneously produced jewelry and "pièces d'art," and collaborated with François-Désiré Froment-Meurice (q.v.). The elder Fossin retired in 1845. Jules Fossin, who had numbered the Empress among his customers, obtained on the occasion of her marriage several commissions, as did Lemonnier (q.v.): he made modifications to the Crown jewels; he furnished bracelets and bodice and shoulder brooches; in addition he made the setting for a parasol in green enamel, embellished with rose diamonds, which he delivered to Mme Fould on March 7, 1853, and billed on April 25 for 3,700 francs (Arch. nat. 0⁵ 2301).

But official patronage did not continue: having been joaillier du Roi, he is thought to have refused at the beginning of the Second Empire the title of joaillier-bijoutier de l'Impératrice, which went instead to his manager, F. Kramer. But Fossin was so respected in his profession that he became a judge in the Tribunal de Commerce de la Seine and was a member of the international juries and the reporter for goldwork and jewelry at the expositions of 1855, 1862, and 1867. Prosper Morel, son of Jean-Valentin Morel, Fossin's manager in 1854, replaced him in 1862; his son-in-law, J. Chaumet, succeeded him in 1889.

D.A.

Bibliography:
De Beauvoir, 1853; *Rapports 1855,* p. 909; *Rapports 1867,* vol. IV, pp. 409–38; Bellier and Auvray, 1882–87, vol. I, p. 570; Vever, 1906–8, vols. I, II

---

## Henri-Léon Curmer
*Paris 1801–1870 Paris*

Having founded in 1834 in Paris a publishing house specializing in luxury editions and bindings, Curmer published religious and secular works, illustrated notably by Tony Johannot, Français (q.v.), and Meissonier (q.v.), and reproductions of ancient manuscripts. He was also a specialist in "marriage books, illustrated prayer books, illustrated books of hours, euchologia, first communion books, mourning books" and "illuminated prayers in imitation of the finest manuscripts." In 1856 he was commissioned to print and bind an album devoted to the birth and baptism of the Prince Imperial (Arch. nat. 0⁵ 2303). He was awarded a bronze medal at the Exposition Universelle of 1855 and a silver medal at the Exposition Universelle of 1867.

D.A.

Bibliography:
*Rapports 1855,* p. 1252; *Catalogue 1862,* pp. 178–79, "Renseignements," pp. 145–46; *Récompensés 1867,* group III, p. 3; *Dictionnaire de biographie française,* vol. IX, Paris, 1961, col. 1408

Compiled by Henri-Léon Curmer; binding by Jules-Jean-Baptiste Fossin, illuminations by Eugène Lami and Charles Leblanc*

## III-22
## Marriage Book of the Empress

c. 1853
Full-page illuminated title: LIVRE DU MARIAGE... PARIS.— L. CURMER. 49, RUE RICHELIEU; full-page illumination signed, lower left: Eugène Lami 1840; three full-page illuminations signed, lower left: ch. leblanc; lower right: L. CURMER éd; monogram on back cover: E
Gold, silver, enamel, parchment, illuminations on vellum
Height 13.8 cm; width 10.8 cm; depth 3.3 cm

Provenance:
Used by the Empress Eugénie during her marriage ceremony in the Cathedral of Notre Dame, Paris, January 30, 1853; descended in imperial family

Exhibitions:
1962, Paris, Louvre, "Joaillerie," no. 132; 1973–74, Paris, Légion d'Honneur, no. 214

Bibliography:
De Beauvoir, 1853: *Relation générale,* 1853, pp. 59–60; Vever, 1906–8, vol. II, pp. 44, 47

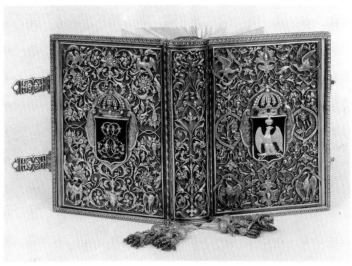

III-22

This missal was said to have been given to the Empress by Princess Mathilde, but this is not mentioned in texts of the period or in biographies of the princess. Rather, the book appears among the official purchases made for the Empress: "We have just admired most of the masterpieces created... on the occasion of this marriage.... The setting of the Empress's missal has been composed by Fossin. This book is covered in white velvet adorned with chased silver. On one side is the eagle on the field of gules surmounted by an imperial crown in diamonds; on the other are the initials of Her Majesty, likewise on a field of gules and surmounted like the eagle by an imperial crown in diamonds. The manuscript, though modern, is admirable" (de Beauvoir, 1853). During the marriage ceremony, the missal was held for the Empress by the Grande-Maîtresse (*see* no. III-25).

A printed missal of 364 pages (imprimatur of 1838), the marriage book includes illuminations in the body of the text; in addition, several fully illuminated title pages have been intercalated, as well as five illuminations, one

by Lami (q.v.) in the "Style Troubadour," and four by Leblanc (scenes from the Bible, one unsigned). Although sources mention that the binding was white velvet, it appears now in parchment. The missal is set in an armature of cast and chased silver with decorations recalling the works of French ornamentalists of the first half of the seventeenth century. In the center of each cover an Oriental-style cartouche inscribed with a shield of translucent red enamel: on the front cover are a crowned eagle of gold and a silver thunderbolt— whereas on the imperial arms the uncrowned eagle and the gold thunderbolt are on a field of azure—surmounted by a crown of enameled gold (not diamonds as described by de Beauvoir).

There was little time to complete this work: after the official announcement of the marriage on January 22, the date for the ceremonies was set for January 29 and 30. At first the intention must have been to order a missal made especially for the occasion, since on March 26, 1853, Curmer billed Mme Fould, wife of the Ministre d'Etat et de la Maison de l'Empereur, 50 francs for "preparations and beginning of the execution of a Marriage Book for H.M. the Empress" (Arch. nat. $0^5$ 2301). The invoice for the missal ultimately delivered no longer seems to be extant; Curmer must have had the missal and illustrations already in stock, as is shown by the date of Lami's illumination (1840) and the address appearing on the title page—49, rue de Richelieu (on the invoice to Mme Fould, Curmer is located at 47 [formerly 49], rue de Richelieu). Curmer added an illuminated page

showing the first name of the Empress as well as, in the text of the wedding mass, the illuminated first names of the spouses. It is possible that the binding by Fossin, Curmer's neighbor, also existed before, the jeweler having been content to add the two cartouches. The binding is typical of the taste launched under Louis Philippe by the bookbinder Gruel for precious bindings designed for books of piety and for albums. Traditional binding under the Second Empire lacked originality, but these works are innovative in the diversity of their materials. A binding executed by Gruel after Rossigneux in 1844 is composed of boxwood reliefs including scrolls similar to those of Fossin's binding (Devauchelle, 1959–61, vol. II, p. 202, pl. 71). The period's most celebrated binding by a goldsmith was that of the *Histoire de Jules César* by Napoleon III, adorned with "Néo-Grec" reliefs by A. Falize (q.v.) and exhibited by Boucheron in 1867 (*Délégation des ouvriers relieurs 1867,* vol. II, repro.).

D.A.

Collection S.A.I. Prince Napoléon Paris

---

*Honoré (Honoré-Séverin Bourdoncle)*
*Sedan 1823–1893 Le Raincy (Seine–Saint-Denis)*

*Born to parents who ran a military canteen, reared like an enfant de troupe, taught by a minor craftsman, Honoré became one of the best Parisian chasers. He lived successively at 10, rue des Beaux-*

Arts (Almanach du Commerce, 1853–64); 13, rue des Vieux Augustins (Almanach du Commerce, 1865–67); 3, rue de Laval Prolongée (now rue Condorcet) (Almanach du Commerce, 1868–69); and 39, rue Condorcet (Almanach du Commerce, 1870–79). Employed by the largest manufacturers, he received silver medals as coopérateur at the Expositions Universelles of 1855 and 1867. Among the works to which he contributed were the reliquary of the Talisman of Charlemagne (no. III-14); the silver-plated centerpiece of Napoleon III, exhibited by Christofle (q.v.) in 1855 and on which many other chasers worked; the silver figure of an hermaphrodite executed by Duponchel for the Prince Napoleon; the Wièse (q.v.) sword presented to MacMahon; the clock by Baugrand (no. III-17); and jewelry shown by Frédéric Boucheron in 1867. On March 3, 1859, Honoré gave a lecture in defense of French metal chasing to the Société du Progrès de l'Art Industriel, which was later published.

Under the Third Republic, he collaborated with Boucheron, Lucien Falize (q.v.), Alphonse Fouquet, and after the Exposition Universelle of 1878, where he won a gold medal as collaborateur, was named chevalier of the Legion of Honor. He was the teacher of Jules Brateau, a reviver of pewter work under the Third Republic. The Musée des Arts Décoratifs preserves jewelry chased by Honoré, as does the Musée de la Comédie Française (a silver lorgnon which belonged to Augustine Brohan).

D.A.

Bibliography:
Rapports 1855, p. 924; Moultat, 1858, pp. 16–17; Honoré, 1859; Récompensés 1867, group IV, p. 108; Mesnard, 1867, vol. I, pp. 140–42; Récompensés 1878, p. 228; Burty, 1883, p. 77; Vever, 1906–8, passim

## Charles Rambert

### Active Paris after c. 1848

A mystic caught up in social questions, Rambert published lithographs inspired by religion and philosophy between 1848 and 1863, including a series dedicated to his friend Piat (q.v.). To make a living he became "a most capable industrial designer, especially in furnishings." Also working in metal, he signed in 1855 the protest drafted by the collaborators of François-Désiré Froment-Meurice (q.v.). At the 1855 Exposition Universelle, recognized by Paillard (see no. II-5), he received a bronze medal as coopérateur. The Almanach du Commerce for 1867 lists him at 153, rue de Vaugirard.

D.A.

Bibliography:
Rapports 1855, p. 925; Burty, 1883, p. 77; Beraldi, 1885–92, vol. XI, pp. 167–69

III-23

Honoré (Honoré-Séverin Bourdoncle); designed by Charles Rambert

## III-23
## Rattle of the Prince Imperial

1856
Signed, on each medallion: B. honoré; monogram on breast of woman holding medallion of Emperor: N E
Gold, aluminum, coral, emeralds, and diamonds
Length 20.5 cm; width 4.7 cm

Provenance:
Commissioned by the Ministre d'Etat et de la Maison de l'Empereur for Eugène-Louis-Jean-Joseph Napoléon, Prince Imperial (1856–1879); the Empress Eugénie; Prince Napoléon

Bibliography:
Moultat, 1858; Sainte-Claire-Deville, 1859, p. 140; Vever, 1906–8, vol. II, pp. 285–86; Castelot, Decaux, and Koenig, 1969, pp. 128–29, 147 (repro.)

The Empress kept in a display case in her study at the Tuileries the Prince Imperial's rattles and his first toys (Carette, n.d., vol. I, p. 136). This rattle, whose lower part is shaped into a whistle, was famous in its time. Designed by Rambert and chased by Honoré, both collaborators of François-Désiré Froment-Meurice (q.v.), the rattle is decorated with figures reminiscent of those used in his jewelry. Other elements of decoration evoke the recipient of the object: the imperial crown, cushion embroidered with bees, engraved sign of Pisces (the Prince was born March 16), profiles of the sovereigns, which were undoubtedly inspired by medals. The Emperor's profile resembles those on a series of medals by Barre, Caqué, A. Dubois, and Longueil that appeared at the beginning of his reign. The Empress's profile recalls above all, as Michel Pastoureau suggested, a medal executed by Bovy after Peyre in 1853.

Coral, so popular in jewelry since the end of the Restoration, was worked notably in Marseilles (Vever, 1906–8, vol. I, pp. 346–47) and was used for superstitious reasons on this type of object. More unexpected, the two medallions and the four statuettes in aluminum constitute one of the earliest examples of the use of this material. Discovered in Germany in 1827, the metal was limited to laboratory use until the chemist Henri Sainte-Claire-Deville (1818–1881) succeeded, with financial aid from Napoleon III, in making it practical for industrial use in 1854–55. A factory in the Glacière quarter on the outskirts of Paris and then in Nanterre, since 1857, directed by Paul Morin, produced the metal whose initial selling price put it in a class with precious metals.

Consequently, it was used at first for "novelty objects," and Honoré and Christofle (q.v.) were among its earliest users. "The first art object made of aluminum was chased by M. Honoré; it was a rattle for the Prince Imperial," wrote Sainte-Claire-Deville, who predicted the widespread use of this metal. Honoré used it for several years in jewelry sometimes decorated with gold and for other objects mentioned by contemporaries: a bracelet which would have been exhibited in 1855 and would have been bought by Queen Victoria; a small cup decorated with medals of the sovereigns, perhaps of the same type used on the rattle; a cup in the Renaissance style (gilded by P. Mourey, the inventor of the technique for gilding aluminum) given in 1858 by the inhabitants of Saint-Germain-en-Laye to their mayor, M. de Breuvery. Other aluminum jewelry by Honoré is preserved today in the Musée des Arts Décoratifs (two bracelets) and in the Cooper-Hewitt Museum in New York. Another bracelet by Honoré was reproduced in *The Connoisseur* (vol. CLXXXIX, April–August 1975, p. 118). As the price of the metal dropped, it tempted other silversmiths and jewelers to specialize in jewelry, buttons, art objects, tableware, and ecclesiastical objects made out of aluminum or aluminum-bronze (*see* Lambert, 1858, pp. 60–61, 70–72; Moultat, 1858, pp. 16–17; Sainte-Claire-Deville, 1859; *Almanach du Commerce*).

D.A.

Collection S.A.I. Prince Napoléon, Paris

---

## Gabriel Lemonnier

*Died c. 1882 Paris*

*Formerly employed by Bury, a jeweler in the rue de Richelieu in Paris, Lemonnier attracted attention at the London Universal Exhibition of 1851, where he displayed among other things two sets of jewels executed for Isabel II of Spain and was awarded a medal. This gained him the appointment of joaillier du Prince-Président. Like Fossin (q.v.), he was asked by the Emperor at the time of his marriage to supply jewelry, and was charged with the execution of the necklace offered by the City of Paris, which the Empress refused. Named joaillier de la Couronne by decree of the Ministre d'Etat et de la Maison de l'Empereur on May 31, 1853 (Arch. nat. O⁵ 48), he was established at 25, place Vendôme. In 1855 he won a silver medal at the Exposition Universelle for "imperial crowns of simple taste, good design, and careful execution" with P.-J. Maheu "jeweler, manufacturer for M. Lemonnier" receiving a silver medal as* coopérateur. *Five brooches in pearls and diamonds executed by Lemonnier appeared in 1887 in the sale of the diamonds of the Crown (Bloche,*

*1888, pp. 76–77, 85, repro.), but after 1855 the settings of these seem to have been entrusted particularly to Bapst et Neveu (Charles and Alfred Bapst). Lemonnier was also jeweler to the queen of Spain and became a chevalier of the Legion of Honor. He knew how to use such able collaborators as Maheu, and Oscar Massin, who in 1864 executed for him a diadem adorned with sprays designed for the duchess of Medinaceli in Madrid, the first important piece of this type and which had great success. This was probably the piece whose loan was denied Lemonnier in 1867, which prevented him from exhibiting. His business began to fail after 1870, and the jeweler ended his career in the employ of a colleague. The Bowes Museum of Barnard Castle preserves a snuffbox in red enameled gold, bearing the monogram of Napoleon III in diamonds, which is signed Lemonnier.*

D.A.

Bibliography:
Arch. nat. F¹² 3049 [Exposition Universelle of 1867]; de Beauvoir, 1853; *Rapports 1855*, pp. 916, 925; Ducuing, 1868, vol. II, pp. 276–77; Vever, 1906–8, vol. II, pp. 14–20, 40–42, 220–23

III-24

III-24

Gabriel Lemonnier

## III-24
## Crown of the Empress

1855
Signed and inscribed on original red morocco case: Gouverneur, gaînier / Aux 4 fils Aymon / 37 quai de l'Horloge / Couronne de l'Impératrice
Gold, gilded silver, diamonds, and emeralds
Height 13 cm; diameter 15 cm

Provenance:
Executed for the Empress Eugénie (Arch. nat. 0⁵ 2319); descended in imperial family

Exhibition:
1962, Paris, Louvre, "Joaillerie," no. 127

Bibliography:
Twining, 1967, p. 63, pl. 25b

In the Winterhalter portraits of the Emperor and Empress exhibited at the Salon of 1855, an imperial crown appears beside each of the sovereigns. The composition of these crowns, which are close to each other, have elements in common with the crown shown here: above the frontlet are eight eagles (behind each rises a hoop) separated by eight fleurons. Eagles do not appear on crowns created during the first Empire. In 1855 a number of pieces executed partially with Crown diamonds and intended to be shown at the Exposition Universelle were commissioned from eight well-known jewelers, among them Lemonnier, who supplied a crown for the Emperor and one for the Empress. The invoices of the other jewelers generally date from June and July 1855. Lemonnier's invoices are not preserved with the others, but for each crown there is a detailed statement of the sums owed the jeweler (24,144.55 francs for the Emperor's crown and 33,622 francs for the Empress's), drawn up by the imperial administration and signed by Lemonnier on September 24.

Regarding the Empress's crown, it is thus known that on February 13, 1855, Lemonnier was supplied with 102 brilliants forming part of the Crown diamonds (32 carats 10/32). The stones he furnished consisted of 1,252 brilliants (107 carats 4/32; 18,079 francs), bringing their total to 1,354; 1,136 rose diamonds (1,620 francs) and 56 emeralds (26 carats 16/32; 1,696 francs). This accounting corresponds to the exhibited crown and its description in the inventory of the Crown jewels of 1875, published in 1962. It may have been designed by Adolphe Devin, a former craftsman with the Bapst firm, who, having directed the jewelry workshop of Hunt and Roskell in London (*L'Art au Dix-Neuvième Siècle,* vol. IV, 1859, p. 167), knew Louis Napoleon in England and became *inspecteur des diamants de la Couronne* (*see* Vever, 1906–8, vol. II, pp. 216–18; Bloche, 1888, p. 45). The form of the exhibited crown with widening hoops, recalling the crown of Charles X created by Bapst in 1825, displays sixteen branches, eight eagles alternating with eight palmettes prolonged by a palm. These last motifs seem rather a reminiscence of the first Empire than a reflection of the emerging "Néo-Grec" style. The crown is surmounted by the globe and cross, like that used for the coronation of the Empress Josephine and the ones in the Winterhalter portraits.

For the crown of Napoleon III, eight brilliants for the eight palmettes and ten others for the cross, belonging to the Crown, were delivered to Lemonnier on February 13. This is probably the crown visible in the Emperor's Cabanel portrait (Salon of 1865): closely resembling the exhibited crown, it is formed by eight eagles alternating with eight palmettes and hoops, these motifs being separated as they

are on the exhibited crown by sixteen emeralds; it is surmounted by the globe and cross. This crown was destroyed in 1886–87 (Twining, 1960, pp. 173–74). Vever (1906–8, vol. II, p. 41) recounts surprisingly: "The imperial crown was commissioned from Lemonnier, who entrusted its execution to Maheu. Unfortunately, this work... for which the Fannière Frères [q.v.] had modeled the eagles, was never finished.... Only the cross that surmounted it was set.... This cross was sold separately, at the time of the sale of the Crown jewels." In fact, a cross composed of ten brilliants, like that of the crown of 1855, was sold in 1887 (Bloche, 1888, p. 100). So the Fannières could be the authors of the similar eagles seen on this crown.

D.A.

Collection S.A.I. Princesse Marie-Clotilde Napoléon, Comtesse de Witt, Paris

## III-25
## Insignia of the Grande-Maîtresse

c. 1853–61
Enameled gold, diamonds
Height 9 cm, width 4.8 cm

III-25

Provenance:
Executed for the princesse d'Essling (née Anne Debelle, 1802–1887); private coll.

Exhibition:
1922, Paris, Musée des Arts Décoratifs, no. 739

Bibliography:
Dayot, 1900, repro. pp. 41, 182

## III-26
## Insignia of the Dame d'Honneur

c. 1853–61
Enameled gold and diamonds, miniatures on ivory
Jewel with monogram height 9 cm, width 4.8 cm; medallion with miniatures height 9 cm, width 4.3 cm

Provenance:
Executed for the duchesse de Bassano (née Pauline-Marie-Ghislaine van der Linden d'Hooghvorst, 1814–1867); son, Napoléon, duc de Bassano (1844–1906); daughter, comtesse de Viel-Castel (née Marie de Bassano); daughter comtesse Napoléon Lepic

Exhibition:
1973–74, Paris, Légion d'Honneur, no. 248

An imperial decree of January 25, 1853, four days before the marriage of Napoleon III and Eugénie, named the members of the Household of the Empress, including a female honor guard of a Grande-Maîtresse, a title borrowed from the German courts and not previously used in France; a Dame d'Honneur; and seven Dames du Palais, to which six more were added by the decree of January 29, 1855 (Arch. nat. O$^5$ 126). The Grande-Maîtresse and the Dame d'Honneur were in charge of presentations and audiences and appeared only on ceremonial occasions. The Grande-Maîtresse also organized the daily routines of the Dames du Palais.

The princesse d'Essling (the daughter-in-law of Masséna) was named Grande-Maîtresse and the duchesse de Bassano (Maret's daughter-in-law and the wife of the Grand Chamberlain), Dame d'Honneur. They flank the Empress in Winterhalter's painting (no. VI-110). Both performed their duties with kindness and dignity. After the duchesse de Bassano's much regretted death in 1867, she was replaced by the comtesse Walewska by the decree of November 8, 1868 (Arch. nat. O$^5$ 126). Later, the princesse d'Essling would be caught in the crowd trying in vain to join the Empress before she fled the Tuileries on September 4, 1870.

The insignias of the Grande-Maîtresse and the Dame d'Honneur are the same, consisting

III-26

blue for the arms, decorated with guilloches. The fragmentary archives of the Household of the Empress do not indicate from whom or on what date they were ordered. They were added to a portrait of the duchesse de Bassano, signed 1853 by the Belgian painter Gustav Wappers (collection of Comtesse Napoléon Lepic). On December 19, 1854, the baron de Pierres, equerry of the Empress, paid 80 francs "to Mr. Basset, for a drawing of the Empress's monogram, commissioned by the order of Her Majesty" (Arch. nat. 0⁵ 979). The duc de Conegliano, who mentioned the wearing of these insignia as an established prerogative, had been chamberlain in the Household of the Emperor since 1855. Vever wrote, however: "The principal jewelers had [in 1856] so many orders that there was a steep increase in the price of diamonds, which is perhaps what prevented the realization of the gracious thought in high places of giving the Empress's Dames d'Honneur an insignia created for them and consisting of a knotted blue ribbon, to be pinned to the shoulder by two entwined circles of diamonds" (Vever, 1906–8, vol. II, pp. 126–27). The insignias could therefore be later than 1856, but must be earlier than 1861, because the duchesse de Bassano wears them in a photograph taken that year (collection of Comtesse Napoléon Lepic). Mme Carette, named Dame du Palais in 1866, wears the insignia with monogram in her portrait by Cabanel (Dayot, 1900, repro. p. 186).

D.A.

Private Collection (no. III-25) and Collection Comtesse Napoléon Lepic, Paris (no. III-26)

of two pieces: "In the evening, the Dames [du Palais], like Her Majesty the Empress, wore low-cut but simple dresses with little jewelry. On the left side of their bodices they always wore their insignias of office, the Empress's monogram in diamonds on a blue enamel ground; the imperial crown in diamonds surmounted the monogram. This jewel was attached to the bodice with a blue ribbon bordered in white. The Dames rarely wore this jewel on a high-necked dress, and then only for important, ceremonial occasions.... The Grande-Maîtresse and the Dame d'Honneur in addition wore on their bodices, secured by the same type of ribbon, a two-sided jewel, bearing the Emperor's portrait on one side and the Empress's on the other, both surrounded by diamonds; the Gouvernante des Enfants de France wore the same type jewel" (Conegliano, 1897, pp. 348–49).

The piece with the monogram has a translucent enamel background, red for the crown,

# Arms

## Louis-Félix Delacour
### Active Paris until c. 1870s

A manufacturer of swords established in Paris at 20, rue aux Fers (rue Berger) (Almanach du Commerce, 1852), then at 7, rue des Trois Pavillons (rue Elzévir), (Almanach du Commerce, 1857), Delacour executed swords and sabers for ceremony and for war, and hunting knives, designing the models himself. He rediscovered the lost method for preparing sharkskin. Having created models for official swords—swords for deputies, for senators, for the Household of the Emperor, numerous others

for the army, the administration, the diplomatic corps—he received a certificate as fourbisseur de l'Empereur. After having received a bronze medal at the Expositions des Produits de l'Industrie in 1844 and in 1849, and two honorable mentions at the London Universal Exhibition in 1851, he was awarded a gold medal at the Exposition Universelle in 1855, and a medal and an honorable mention in 1862. In 1867 he was in partnership with Backes and received a silver medal, while honorable mentions were awarded to three of his workmen, Joseph Aimable, fitter, Blancheteau, modeler, and Rouget, chaser. Backes, succeeding Delacour, exhibited alone in 1878.
D.A.

Bibliography:
Arch. nat. F¹² 3049 [Exposition Universelle of 1867]; Rapports 1855, p. 709; Catalogue 1862, p. 105, "Renseignements," pp. 87–88; Récompensés 1867, group IV, pp. 114, 119; Récompensés 1878, p. 231; Jarlier, 1976, col. 78

## Charles Goutzwiller
### Altkirch (Haut-Rhin) 1810–1900 Coincy (Aisne)

An art historian and a designer, Goutzwiller first published an album of lithographs on Altkirch in 1841–42. First secretary in the Colmar town hall *under the Second Empire, he executed a small bas-relief for the base of the bronze statue of General Rapp by the sculptor Frédéric-Auguste Bartholdi, both natives of Colmar, which was dedicated on the Champs de Mars in Colmar on August 31, 1856. He was then asked for the models for the two swords presented to the victors of Sebastopol. He published the second catalogue of the Colmar museum in 1866 and other works about Alsace. Having fled to Paris after the annexation, he provided illustrations for books of art history and the* Gazette des Beaux-Arts.

D.A.

Bibliography:
Kaeppelin, 1889, p. 215; Thieme and Becker, 1907–50, vol. XIV, p. 450; *Catalogue général des imprimés de la Bibliothèque Nationale*, Paris, 1929, vol. LXII, cols. 1240–42

Louis-Félix Delacour; designed by Charles Goutzwiller

## III-27
## Dress Sword of Marshal Pélissier

1855–63
Marks: standard, silver, Paris, after 1838; maker (illegible, most likely L.-F. Delacour)
Signed in engraving on back of guard: Delacour. Fourbisseur de S. M. l'Empereur/à Paris; inscribed in relief on grip, front: SEBASTOPOL, back: 1855; inscribed in relief on guard above the coat of arms of Colmar: LA VILLE DE COLMAR AU MARECHAL PELISSIER; inscribed in relief and gilt letters on blade: 8. SEPTEMBRE 1855./

HOMMAGE DE LA VILLE DE COLMAR
Gilded silver hilt; chased steel blade, partially gilded; black leather scabbard mounted in gilded silver
Length 97 cm; width 13 cm

Provenance:
Presented by the city of Colmar to Amable-Jean-Jacques Pélissier (Maromme [Seine-Maritime] 1794–Algiers 1864), Marshal of France (September 12, 1855), duc de Malakoff (July 22, 1856), Governor General of Algeria (November 24, 1860); Musée Franchet d'Espérey, Algiers; placed in the Musée de l'Armée by decree of June 12, 1962 (inv. no. J 16376)

Exhibition:
1862, London

Bibliography:
Goutzwiller, 1856; Waring, 1863, vol. III, pl. 215; Burty, 1866, pp. 391–92; Kaeppelin, 1889, p. 215; Waltz, 1902, p. 377

Both French victors of Sebastopol were connected with Colmar. One was Pélissier, who became commander-in-chief of the Army of the Orient on May 16, 1855, and later Marshal of France after Sebastopol; his father had been *commissaire en chef des poudres et salpêtres* in Colmar under the Restoration. The second, Vice-Admiral Bruat, born in Colmar in 1796, was appointed commander-in-chief of the Navy of the East in 1854, becoming admiral on September 15, 1855 (*see* Foltz, 1887, pp. 339–40; Derrécagaix, 1911; Scherlen, 1931).

Proud of the victory of Sebastopol, the City Council of Colmar decided on September 21 to present each victor with a dress sword. A subscription brought in 3,023 francs, and the city made up the difference. Bruat died during his return from the Crimea, and the sword was accepted by his widow. The model for the two identical swords was made by Goutzwiller, who published it in *L'Illustration* on January 16, 1856. By that time, forging had already been assigned to Delacour who displayed both swords in London in 1862. Seemingly he executed the silverwork himself. On November 8, 1861, he registered his silversmith's mark, which was later canceled on May 31, 1878 (Arch. de la Garantie, Insculpations 1855–81, fol. 34).

The gift of dress swords to commemorate important events was practiced throughout the world in the nineteenth century. Their decoration was essentially symbolic. The sword offered by the City of Paris to the comte de Paris in 1841, by Klagmann and François-Désiré Froment-Meurice (q.v.; Vever, 1906–8, vol. I, pp. 254–58, repro.), which served as a model for those which followed, includes, like the one exhibited here, a serpent and imbricated discs on the knuckle bow. Froment-Meurice exhibited in 1849 two swords presented to Generals Changarnier and Cavaignac

III-27

(Burty, 1883, pp. 54–55, repro.). At the London Universal Exhibition of 1851, the sword offered to the Columbian general Mosquera, executed by Christofle (q.v.) and Rouvenat about 1848, with a lion, a serpent, and imbricated discs on the knuckle bow, and arms in the center of a trophy on the guard (Vever, 1906–8, vol. I, p. 187, repro.) was noted; as in 1862 was the MacMahon sword by Wièse (q.v.), the knuckle bow of which also bears a serpent and imbricated discs; the sword by Gueyton offered to Marshal Baragueys d'Hilliers (Vever, 1906–8, vol. II, p. 27); and the swords of Francis II, king of the Two Sicilies, and of Marshal Bosquet by Duponchel (Darcel, 1862, p. 322).

In addition to the inscriptions and arms of the city, many symbols appear on Pélissier's sword: the imperial eagle, Bellona, stars, laurel, and marshal's batons. The other motifs are taken from the past: Renaissance (cartouche with strapwork), eighteenth century (shells, palms linked by a ribbon).

Delacour also exhibited a sword in 1862, presented by the fishermen of Boulogne to d'Estremont de Maucroix (Waring, 1863, vol. III, pl. 215). The sword of the Argentinian general Mitre, manufactured by Delacour at the same period, has elements in common with Pélissier's, with Bellona decorating the knuckle bow, and the arms of Buenos Aires on the guard (*L'Illustration*, vol. XXXIX, January – June, 1862, repro. p. 304).

D.A.

Musée de l'Armée, Paris

---

*Louis-François Devisme*

*Born c. 1806*

*After modest beginnings Louis-François Devisme became one of the three great gunsmiths under the Second Empire, together with Gastinne-Renette, arquebusier de l'Empereur, and Lepage-Moutier. Entering the workshop of the gunsmith Deboubert in 1819, he was an apprentice there for four years, then a worker, and foreman in 1826. Devisme became director of the firm in 1834. He manufactured hunting and military firearms, sabers, hunting spears, hunting knives, and gun barrels. The creator of numerous refinements, Devisme invented among others, the salon pistol (1835), the steel-tipped bullet (1846), the Devisme revolver (patented in 1854), the explosive bullet for hunting big game (patented in 1857), the bullet mold for casting hollow and channeled bullets (patented in 1858). Established at the*

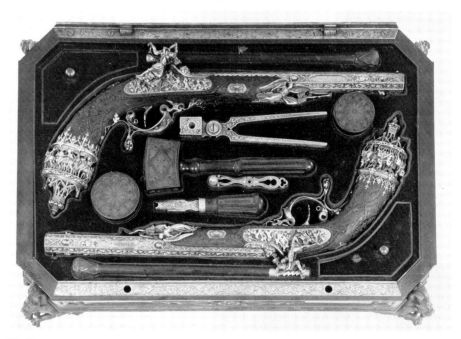

III-28

*corner of 36, boulevard des Italiens and 12, rue du Helder, he also had a workshop at 23, rue Moncey which employed 60 workers in 1862. His works received a number of awards, in particular a bronze medal at the Exposition des Produits de l'Industrie in 1844 (where he showed notably a gun presented by Louis Philippe to Prince Albert the same year; now at Kensington Palace, London); another bronze medal at the exposition of 1849; a medal in 1851; a silver medal in 1855; a medal at the exhibition of 1862, after which he was made a chevalier of the Legion of Honor, and finally a silver medal in 1867. He was a captain in the National Guard.*

D.A.

Bibliography:
Arch. nat. F¹² 3049 [Exposition Universelle of 1867]; Arch. nat. F¹² 5129 [Legion of Honor]; *Rapports 1855*, p. 710; Waring, 1863, vol. I, pl. 6, vol. III, pl. 215; *Récompensés 1867*, group IV, p. 114; Jarlier, 1976, col. 87

Louis-François Devisme

## III-28
## Case of Pistols

c. 1862–67
Marks on pistols: guaranty, silver, Paris, after 1838

Signed on upper part of barrels, in Gothic letters and in relief: Devisme à Paris; inscribed under barrels in gilt letters: EXPOSITION 1867; inscribed on thumb rests: NAPOLEON III/ au /GENERAL LE-BRUN/SOUVENIR; monogram, at center of case lid: LB; inscribed on lining inside lid in gilded letters: DEVISME/A PARIS
Ebonized wood, ebony, steel, silver
Box height 15 cm, width 52.5 cm, depth 35.5 cm; pistols height 19 cm, length 42.5 cm

Provenance:
Gift of Napoleon III to General Barthélemy-Louis-Joseph Lebrun (1809–1889); gift of widow of General Lebrun (née Joséphine Maurice) to the Musée de l'Armée, 1906 (inv. no. Cc533)

Exhibition:
1867, Paris, Exposition Universelle

This case, in ebonized wood, with a lid decorated with Gothic interlaces in relief around the monogram, rests on four winged dragons reminiscent of gargoyles. The engraved steel hinges are decorated with Islamic cartouches, Gothic foliage, and ivy leaves. The interior, lined in blue velvet, contains a pair of pistols and their accessories. The identical pistols have ebony handles carved in low relief in the Gothic style with fenestrages and ivy leaves, while the theme of the steel and silver decorative elements is borrowed from the Crusades. On the barrel, which has eight chased steel facets, a facet chased with Gothic scrollwork alternates with a facet decorated with applied silver reliefs which include European or Muslim trophies and six masks. The hammer is composed of a group in steel, the combat of a Crusader against a Turk. The rest of the fittings are in silver: the lockplate and nail plate, each with a different bas-relief showing a battle between Crusaders and Turks; the trigger guard, shaped like a dragon; the butt, showing the departure of six knights for the Crusades accompanied by foot soldiers. Under the barrel are three figures in silver, Fame and two Victories. The accessories in ebony and steel include a bullet mold, a bullet case, a powder box, a mallet, a screwdriver, a packing rod, and a cleaning rod. While the Gothic style remained important at the end of the Second Empire in religious metalwork or furniture, the inspiration of the "Style Troubadour" in the design of these objects would be surprising in 1867; however, this design is not new. At the Exposition Universelle of 1855, a work by Devisme was noted: "Valu-able pistols in a box (10,000 francs); the ornaments are in chased silver; the design is quite remarkable" (*Rapports 1855*, p. 710). Could it be this pair? Waring pictured a pistol exactly like these, which Devisme showed in London in 1862 (Waring, 1863, vol. I, pl. 6), but he did not specify whether or not there was only one such weapon. Was this group in existence already in 1862, or was it completed after 1862? Was another version made for the exposition of 1867? The delegation of the gunsmiths, after having mentioned the more utilitarian weapons shown by Devisme in 1867, noted " a lovely pair of pistols with chased silver fittings, Oriental style, completed M. Devisme's exhibit" (*Rapports des délégations 1867*, vol. I, "Arquebusiers," p. 7). This description seems to fit these weapons, which Napoleon III acquired at an unknown date and presented to Lebrun, "a good worker and a scholar, simple, modest, gentle, likeable, and kind" (Conegliano, 1897, p. 328). Lebrun was an *officier d'état-major*, a colonel in 1855, and took part in the Oriental campaign (1855–56). He became brigadier general in 1859, taking part in the Italian campaign, where he was much esteemed by Mac-Mahon. He became *chef d'état major-general* in the Imperial Guard on May 19, 1860, division general in 1866, aide-de-camp to the Emperor on October 23, 1869. In May–June 1870, he was entrusted by Napoleon with a mission to Franz Joseph of Austria to establish a Franco-Austro-Italian campaign plan in case of war with Prussia. Perhaps the presentation of these pistols was made on that occasion. Lebrun participated later in the campaign against Germany, during which he was imprisoned at Sedan and asked to be relieved of his command in 1879 (Archives de la Guerre, Vincennes, dossier Gd, 2e série, 1426).

D.A.

Musée de l'Armée, Paris

# Enamels

## Manufacture Impériale de Sèvres (Enamel Workshop)

*Sèvres, 1845–1872*

*Although there had been earlier attempts at enamel, and there are at Sèvres designs for painted enamels dating back to 1839, the enamel workshop at Sèvres (see history preceding no. IV-4) was not officially founded until October 31, 1845. Jacob Meyer-Heine (1805–1879), ornamental painter at the factory and enameler was put in charge of the workshop: on January 1, 1846, he was named peintre émailleur, and on June 1, 1848, émailleur chef. Ebelmen, then director of the manufactory, especially wanted to produce large-size plaques of enameled sheet metal for use in the exterior decoration of buildings. But research in this area eventually proved unprofitable. At the same time, thanks to the interest shown by Paul Delaroche, a member of the Conseil Supérieur de Perfectionnement des Manufactures Nationales created in 1848 under the Second Republic, Sèvres became involved in the production of painted enamel on copper. At Ebelmen's request, in order to help develop this technique, Delaroche supplied him with painters chosen from among his students: Picou and Hamon (who showed little interest in the work), then Gobert (q.v.). From that time on, for a period of about twenty years, the factory produced objects in enameled copper, some of them mounted in gilded bronze at Sèvres itself. At first, both form and decoration were frequently conceived by Jules Diéterle (q.v.), directeur des travaux d'art from 1848 to 1855, in the Indian or Renaissance styles. In 1855, when the factory, alone in the class of ceramics, received the Grand Medal of Honor, its "enamels on iron, on copper, on platinum, and on gold" were cited. It is to the investigations made in the field of enameling that we owe the invention of pâte-sur-pâte decoration on porcelain. The Sèvres enamel workshop, like that for faïence, was closed for reasons of economy in 1872.*

D.A.

Bibliography:
Sèvres Archives, Armoire F XIV; *Rapports 1855*, p. 948; Doat, 1891–92, pp. 45–46; Falize, 1893–94, vol. IX, pp. 427–32, vol. X, p. 486

## Emile Renard

*Paris 1825–1882*

*Renard was already working as a designer at the Sèvres factory in 1846, but it was not until March 1, 1856, that he permanently held this position, which he retained until his death. In addition to his designs for the "Indian" vase, seven other watercolor designs by Renard for enamels in the Indian or Renaissance styles, executed between 1860 and 1862, are in the Sèvres Archives. At the Salon of 1868 and 1869 Renard exhibited prints showing vases from the Musée de Céramique at Sèvres.*

D.A.

Bibliography:
Sèvres Archives Y 10, fol. 87r, Y 11, fol. 82v; Sèvres Archives, Armoire F XIV; Bellier and Auvray, 1882–87, vol. II, p. 356; de Chavagnac and de Grollier, 1906, p. 349

## Jean-Baptiste-César Philip

*Avignon 1815–1877*

*An expert enameler, Philip was working in Paris for the firm of Charlot, which specialized in enameled silverwork, when Ebelmen singled him out for technical work—preparation of plaques, firing — at the enamel workshop at Sèvres. Entering the factory as an assistant enameler on July 29, 1846, he was permanently registered as an employee on January 1, 1848. On February 1, 1857, he was promoted to enameler, and he kept this position until his death.*

D.A.

Bibliography:
Sèvres Archives Y 10, fol. 68r, Y 11, fol. 45v; Falize, 1893–94, vol. IX, pp. 422–30

Manufacture Impériale de Sèvres; designed by Jules-Pierre-Michel Diéterle and Emile Renard, enameled by Jean-Baptiste-César Philip

## III-29
## "Indian" Vase

1854–55
Handwritten label on base: 53.4/2000
Enameled metal
Height 84.5 cm; diameter 34 cm

Provenance:
Delivered by the factory as number 53.4 with the value of 2,000 francs in December 1876 (decree of December 30, 1876; Sèvres Archives Vaa³, fol. 94 v) to the Musée de Céramique (inv. no. 7680)

The taste for Indian decoration also appeared at Sèvres in porcelain, during the same period, when the "Delhi" vase (1851) and the "Indian" ewer with inlays (1852) were created (1975, Sèvres, nos. 199, 165). The designs seem to have come from the study of actual Indian objects: the factory archives (Armoire F XIV) contain a watercolor bearing the date June 6, 1848, which represents an Indian dagger in enameled copper, belonging to the collection of the painter Jollivet and decorated with polychrome flowers in polylobate frames, as well as three watercolor designs for enamel objects, inspired by this dagger and dating from June and July 1848. Two watercolors, also in the Sèvres Archives (Armoire F XIV), show full-size designs for the decoration that is repeated three times around this vase. One, made for the lid (a palmette), bears a notation written by V. Regnault, director of the factory, above his sig-

III-29

nature: "Jules Diéterle et Renard, 20 Juillet 1853." The second shows the designs for the vase itself: neck (a fleuron), molding, belly (a cartouche, but without the bird later inscribed inside), and base; it includes the following commentary: "Vase en Email Style indien J. Diéterle inv. Renard ex. 20 Sept. 1853." Renard was indeed devoting himself partially "to Indian designs" in June 1853, and he spent the following August on "a design for an Indian vase" (Sèvres Archives Vj' 59, "Travaux de peinture…," fol. 203 r, v), probably references to these watercolors, executed on Diéterle's instructions. The object faithfully follows the color scheme: dark blue, red, green, white, black, and—on the vase alone—pink and yellow for the seeds represented beneath the molding.

The dominant gilded background gives this vase an appearance of champlevé enamel. Actually, the form and relief champlevé were ob-

tained by galvanoplasty. The enameling was entrusted to Philip, who experimented with the process at the beginning of 1854: "enameling trials on galvanized metals" (February), "trial with galvanized copper tray" (March). Among other operations, he enameled between June and August a "lid, process galvanoplasty" and between September 1854 and February 1855 a "ball-shaped 'Indian' vase" (Sèvres Archives Vj' 60, fols. 102 r, 103 r, Vj' 61, fol. 126 r). These notices undoubtedly concern this vase, which seems to have been intended for exhibition in 1855. Indeed, Mme Tamara Préaud observed that among the nineteen enamels that were expected to be shown was "an Oriental-style vase: form and decoration by Mr J. Diéterle… champlevé enamel; made by M. Philip" (Sèvres Archives U.9, "Notice sur les Principales Pièces mises à l'Exposition Universelle de 1855"), very likely this one, which they must have given up the idea of exhibiting since this mention is crossed out.

The factory was to produce other "Indian" vases of various sizes, but similar in decoration. Fontainebleau has a smaller one (height 69 cm; diameter 25 cm), whose decoration with its champlevé appearance is identical with the vase exhibited, but rendered in different colors. Such vases were also executed in painted enamel, like the second "Indian" vase enameled by Philip, between October 1854 and August 1855, and which is described "with black background" (Sèvres Archives Vj'60, fols. 102 v, 103 r, Vj'61, fols. 126 r, v); this may be the one that entered the Sèvres museum along with the exhibited vase (MNC 7681; height 94 cm, diameter 34 cm), which combines the Indian influence and that of Venetian painted enamels; or another, also preserved at Fontainebleau (height 69 cm, diameter 33 cm). The factory likewise executed large round bowls in the same style.

D.A.

Musée National de Céramique, Sèvres

## Alfred-Thompson Gobert

*Paris 1822–1894 La Garenne-Colombes (Hauts-de-Seine)*

*The son of a miniaturist, and a student of Gleyre and Delaroche, Gobert exhibited paintings at the Salons from 1848 to 1850; later he devoted himself to enamel when, on the recommendations of Delaroche and Ingres (q.v.), he joined the Sèvres (q.v.) factory* on February 15, 1849, as a figure painter and was permanently employed there by January 1, 1852. Although he did some outside work (see no. II-38), he produced his most important works for Sèvres: plaques (see II-17), bowls, vases ("Pénicaud" vase, for example), ewers. The decoration, painted most often from his own compositions, is generally executed in grisaille or in blue monochrome on a dark background. He received a silver medal as coopérateur in 1855, and was named chevalier of the Legion of Honor in 1867. When the Sèvres factory gave up enamelwork, Gobert painted porcelain vases that display similar characteristics. He became directeur des travaux d'art at Sèvres on August 1, 1887, replacing Carrier-Belleuse (q.v.), and was retired on December 15, 1891. Although a certain number of his works in enamel had been presented as gifts by Napoleon III, some of them remain in the Sèvres and Fontainebleau museums.

D.A.

Bibliography:
Sèvres Archives Y 10, fol. 74 v, Y 11, fol. 56 v, Ob 6; Sèvres Archives, "Notes sur Gobert par son gendre, le docteur Keller"; Rapports 1855, p. 953; Doat, 1891–92, pp. 76–77, 79–80; Falize, 1893–94, vol. IX, pp. 429–32, vol. X, pp. 431, 436; L. A., 1894–95, pp. 177–79

Manufacture Impériale de Sèvres; enameled by Alfred-Thompson Gobert

## III-30
## "Chalice" Vase

1869
Signed in gold letters on medallion of Winter, lower right: Sèvres; on medallion of Spring, lower right: GOB-R.1869
Embossed and enameled copper
Height 86 cm; diameter 33.5 cm

Provenance:
Delivered by the factory with an estimated value of 6,850 francs in August 1875 (Sèvres Archives Vaa³, fol. 87 r) to the museum (inv. no. 7503)

The decoration of this vase is in grisaille on a black background, with a few highlights in gold. On each of the four convex oval medallions on the lid are two naked winged putti playing or hunting, accompanied successively by a lion, birds, a sea monster, and stars, symbolizing the Four Elements. Four other medallions of similar form are on the belly representing the Four Seasons, each personified by a woman and a cherub; between these cartouches, three winged putti hang a crown of

III-30

flowers on an arrow, this theme being differently interpreted each time. The reverse of the lid and the inside of the vase, except for the bottom, are enameled in black and decorated with white and gold rosettes; the back of the foot is enameled black.

Gobert conceived and painted the decoration for three vases of this shape, each for 3,200 francs, the first two in 1866–67 and 1867–68 (Sèvres Archives Vj' 72–74, "Travaux de peinture..."). On the third, the one shown here, prepared by Philip (q.v.) in 1868 (Sèvres Archives Va' 60, "Travaux des tourneurs...," fol. 203 r), the figures were painted by Gobert in 1869 (Sèvres Archives Vj' 75, fol. 8 r, v). The borrowings from sixteenth-century Limousin

enamels—masks, strapwork, female figures—were slight and much transformed, the decoration revealing mostly Gobert's taste for the representation of women and children. Of the two other vases, one, with turquoise blue and white decoration on a black ground, entered the Sèvres museum at the same time as this one; the other, decorated in grisaille and whose belly also displays four embossed oval medallions, each decorated with a female figure, is in Fontainebleau.

D.A.

Musée National de Céramique, Sèvres

---

## Bernard-Alfred Meyer
See no. II-38

---

## Claudius Popelin
Paris 1825–1892 Paris

The son of a businessman, Popelin acquired his training as a painter first in the atelier of Picot and then, after a visit to Italy (1846–48), in the atelier of Ary Scheffer. He exhibited for the first time at the Salon of 1852. As an enthusiast of the Renaissance, from which he derived the subjects for his paintings, he began to study the decorative arts of that period as a scholar, which lead him, about 1860, to execute some works in faïence imitating Italian majolica. Finally, he found his calling in enamelwork, a technique he learned in 1862–63 from Alfred Meyer (q.v.). In 1863 Popelin set up his own enameler's kiln at Yerres (Essonne) and exhibited his first enamels at the first Exposition de l'Union Centrale. Success came in the following years, during which the artist executed historical portraits, decorative panels, and bookbinding plaques, receiving commissions from the Princess Mathilde, Ludwig II of Bavaria, Count Guido Henckel von Donnersmarck, and the duc d'Aumale. Popelin became a chevalier of the Legion of Honor in 1869. After 1870 he devoted himself to portraits of contemporary celebrities, executed in gold on black in the manner of Fouquet's self-portrait. If Popelin was not exactly the reviver of painted enamel, he was its "ardent popularizer" (Falize, 1893–94), and exerted considerable influence through his work and writings: L'Email des peintres (1866), L'Art de l'émail, leçon faite à l'Union Centrale des Beaux-Arts, le 6 mars 1868 (1868), Les Vieux Arts du feu (1869). Popelin translated and published Li Tre Libri dell'Arte del Vasaio by Piccolpasso (1860), De Statua and

De Pictura *by Alberti (1868), and* Hyp-
nerotomachia Poliphili *(1883). He also published
collections of poems. The Musée des Arts Décoratifs in
Paris has several of his enamels.*

D.A.

Bibliography:
Burty, 1868, *L'Email;* Falize, 1893–94; de Bouchaud,
1894

Claudius Popelin

## III-31
## Napoleon III

1865
Signed in gold letters on central plaque and
large lower horizontal plaque: Claudius Popelin; on left vertical plaque: Cl. P.; at top of
frame, enameled shield with the arms of the
Fialin de Persigny family, under ducal crown
and surmounting motto: JE SERS; inscribed under central plaque: Napoleo tertius; on four
round plaques: CAROLUS MAG. FRANC. IMP.,
NAPOLEO MAG. FRANC. IMP., CLODOVICUS REX
CRINITUS, HUGO CAPET REX FRANC.; on upper horizontal plaque: AFRICA/ITALIA/COXINSINA/RUSSIA/
SYRIA/SINA/MEXICUM; on lower horizontal
plaque: MAGENTA/SOLFERINO/VITA J. CAESARIS./OP-
ERA VARIA./EX UTROQUE CAESAR; on four central
horizontal plaques: GENEROSITAS, FORTITUDO,
SAPIENTIA, JUSTITIA
Painted enamel on copper, blackened wood
95 × 74.3 cm

Provenance:
Executed for Jean-Gilbert-Victor Fialin, comte, later
duc (1863) de Persigny (1808–1872), Minister of the
Interior (1852–54), ambassador to England (1855–58,
1859–60), Minister of the Interior (1860–63); sold by
his heirs to the antiquary Sichel; purchased by the
comte de Camondo, owner of the object in 1893
(handwritten data on a copy of the 1893 exposition
catalogue in library of the Louvre); Frédéric Masson;
bequest, with his collection, to the library of the Institut de France, 1922 (inv. no. 2264)

Exhibitions:
1865, Paris, Salon, no. 2733; 1893, Paris, Palais de
l'Industrie, no. 3
Bibliography:
Falize, 1893–94, vol. IX, pp. 513–16

*See* Colorplate

At the Salon of 1864 Popelin exhibited a
large enamel panel representing Julius Caesar.
According to L. Falize, the subject had been
suggested to him by his friend Dardenne de La
Grangerie, a relative of Persigny (*see* V-31), for
the purpose of attracting official attention,
Popelin being at the time in need of money.

III-31

Indeed, Napoleon III was at this time preparing
his *Histoire de Jules César,* which was to appear in
three volumes in 1865–66. The enamel was
noticed, and gained for Popelin a commission
from Persigny for a portrait of the Emperor.
Persigny may have wanted in this way to demonstrate his continued loyalty: on June 23,
1863, after the elections, he had had to resign
his post as minister, bringing about the end of
his political career, the Emperor having broken
off with this too outspoken friend. The content
of the work, undoubtedly set by Persigny, systematically flatters the sovereign, whose image,
bordered by a garland of violets, is surrounded
by allusions to his virtues, his military and literary talents, and his dynastic designs. Falize
(1893–94, vol. IX, p. 513) published the drawing executed by Popelin for the bust of the
Emperor. The artist obtained a medal at the
Salon of 1865. In *L'Email des peintres,* written in

the style of earlier technical treatises, Popelin
described the successive operations of the
work: embossing the copper plaques to make
them convex; application and baking of a
counter-enamel on the concave reverse side of
the plaques and of a dark background on the
face; transfer of the subject; applications of
white enamel to obtain the modeling in
*grisaille,* which he left exposed on the flesh
tones and banderoles or which he covered with
translucent enamels; final decoration of gold
highlights executed in gold ground and mixed
with spirits and applied with a brush. Instead of
being applied over white enamel, the translucent enamels could also be applied directly on
silver foil, a procedure that had already been
revived by Alfred Meyer. Popelin, who unlike
Gobert (q.v.), valued this decoration, employed
it here for the crown of laurel and parts of the
Emperor's armor. From the Limousin enam-

elers of the sixteenth century, Popelin borrowed not only the technique, but also the style of the two female figures, the taste for inscriptions that he advocated in his treatise, and the practice of incorporating enamels of smaller dimensions within the frame of a portrait. Popelin's frames were most often of blackened wood. The distribution of smaller plaques elaborating the theme around a central plaque occurs frequently, in particular in two of his other principal works: *The Rebirth of Letters*, exhibited at the same Salon (Muzeul de Arte al

R.S. România, Bucharest), and *Truth*, a panel executed for Count Henckel and finished in 1867 (location unknown).

D.A.

Institut de France—Musée Frédéric Masson, Paris

---

*Antoine Tard*

*See* no. III-20

# Hard Stones

## Adolphe David

*Baugé (Maine-et-Loire) 1828–1895 Paris*

*A pupil of the sculptor Jouffroy and, beginning in 1854, at the Ecole des Beaux-Arts in Paris, David became a sculptor, but especially an engraver of semiprecious stones. He lived in Paris at 56, rue du Montparnasse (1857) and later at 12, rue Campagne Première (1860). Usually he executed rather large cameos. He exhibited for the first time at the Salon of 1857, where his cameo The Wreck of the Medusa after Géricault attracted notice. The maker of two cameos of the Prince Imperial that were owned by the Empress in 1860, David gained official encouragement in the following years, chiefly the commission for the cameo of The Apotheosis of Napoleon I. Modesty Resisting Love, a cameo after Jouffroy, exhibited at the Salon of 1863, was purchased on July 17 for 4,000 francs by the Ministre de la Maison de l'Empereur et des Beaux-Arts, exhibited in 1867, and then given by the Emperor in 1869 to the Bibliothèque Impériale (10 × 7.1 cm; Babelon, 1897, no. 485). In 1864 the same ministry, having acquired with David in mind a block of blue-gray sardonyx costing 1,500 francs, commissioned him on December 21 to execute busts of the Emperor and Empress for the sum of 5,000 francs, raised to 10,000 francs in 1866. This commission was cancelled in 1868 after the price of The Apotheosis of Napoleon had been raised, and the engraver was obliged to return the stone on which he had not begun to work. But on July 5, 1870, he was asked to create for the Emperor a three-layer cameo in carnelian representing the sovereigns (7 × 9 cm) for 4,000 francs, of which he received one quarter; it is not known if this cameo was ever executed. The Bibliothèque Nationale has another cameo of his, Amalthea (12.6 × 9.1 cm; Babelon, 1897, no. 443), exhibited in 1889.*

D.A.

Bibliography:
Arch. nat. F²¹ 131, dossiers 19–21; Louvre Archives 2 DD 20, p. 120, N 6; *Catalogue 1867*, vol. I, p. 58; Thieme and Becker, 1907–50, vol. VIII, pp. 448–49; *Dictionnaire de biographie française*, vol. X, Paris, 1962, pp. 338–39

Adolphe David; after Jean-Auguste-Dominique Ingres

### III-32
### The Apotheosis of Napoleon I

1861–74
Signed, lower left: INGRES. PINX., lower right: A. DAVID. SCULP.
Agate onyx
Height 23 cm; length 20.5 cm; depth 2.8 cm

Provenance:
Commissioned by decree of the Ministre d'Etat et de la Maison de l'Empereur, April 2, 1861 (Arch. nat. F²¹ 131, dossier 19); entered the Musée du Luxembourg, 1874; Louvre, 1886–95; Musée du Luxembourg; deposited in the Musée Fabre, 1933 (inv. no. D 33-1-1)

Exhibitions:
1874, Paris, Salon, no. 3212; 1878, Paris, Exposition Universelle

Bibliography:
Chabouillet, 1879 (repro.); Babelon, 1902, pp. 229–31, pl. 17; Ternois, 1971, p. 114

Napoleon III bears the responsibility for supporting the commission of the largest cameo of modern times and of known cameos, second only to the "Great Cameo" of France (Bibliothèque Nationale, 31 × 26.5 cm). *The Apotheosis of Napoleon I* by Ingres, destroyed by fire in 1871, is known today from various documents (*see* no. VI-69). At the same time that Oudiné (q.v.) made a bas-relief and a medal

after the *Apotheosis*, David executed a small cameo on shell (Salon of 1859). Eager to interpret the same theme in stone, and with the support of Ingres, who promised to help him, as did Jouffroy, David tried to obtain an official commission. He petitioned in a letter of January 27, 1860, to Achille Fould, Minister of State, but the minister replied that the administration did not commission cameos. However, Walewski, Fould's successor, decided to grant the commission in the amount of 12,000 francs. By a decree of March 27, the stone was acquired, a gray agate with white veins, from Auguste Lhérie of Chatou for 3,200 francs. In the plaster model prepared with Ingres's help, the figures at the bottom of the painting were replaced by the island of Saint Helena. The model, in Angers (Catalogue, Musée d'Angers, 1887, no. 870), twice the size of the cameo (46 × 42 cm), shows at right the temple and clouds, which ultimately were not reproduced.

By December 1862 the masses were completely indicated on the stone, and David worked on it until December 1864, when he fell victim of accidental poisoning and had to interrupt his work for three years. Impecunious, he turned to Nieuwerkerke: "I am, Monsieur le Comte, more enthusiastic than ever over my big stone. It is a monument such as one does in architecture for future centuries, but even more durable.... I think I can say without fear of being mistaken that the Apotheosis of Napoleon cannot be engraved in less than five years, and *without doing anything else.*" A decree of December 20, 1867, accordingly raised the fee to 18,000 francs. In December 1869, the cameo was two-thirds finished and on April 9, 1870, the *inspecteur des Beaux-Arts* Henry d'Escamps reported: "The main figures... are well along. The two Fames and two Horses in the background alone remain to be done. In a year,

III-32

or two, the cameo will be engraved and French glyptic art will have its rarest monument." On December 14, 1871, d'Escamps stated that David still needed another year, and a decree of February 20, 1873, raised the total price of the work to 25,000 francs. The cameo, almost finished in September 1873, was sent to a polisher, whose work took several months more. The delivery certificate, issued on May 22, 1874, granted David the balance of his commission — 2,000 francs. The cameo was exhibited at the Salon the same year, receiving but a lukewarm reception.

Did David succeed in rivaling the largest Classical cameos, a goal he and his contemporaries set? Although the stone did not allow him to obtain the polychrome effects of the ancient cameos, this courageous work illustrates the interest in reviving a decadent art in France, one which was to attain its most fruitful period at the end of the century.

D.A.

Musée Fabre, Montpellier

## Jean-Valentin Morel
*Paris 1794–1860 Passy (Paris)*

*Valentin Morel (1761–1833), a Parisian lapidary, provided his son Jean-Valentin with a thorough knowledge of this art. Jean-Valentin also studied under the goldsmith Adrien Vachette. He first worked on his own, producing gold snuffboxes and objects in* piqué *tortoise shell and hard stones. He registered his mark on August 2, 1827, and worked on the Ile de la Cité at 17, rue de la Calandre (Almanach du Commerce, 1827–28), then 5, rue de la Vieille Draperie at least from 1833 (Vever, 1906–8, vol. I, p. 254; Almanach du Commerce, 1840–42). From about 1834 he was employed by Fossin (q.v.) as* chef *d'atelier, working notably on the famous sword for the comte de Paris, the execution of which, partially entrusted to Fossin by François-Désiré Froment-Meurice (q.v.), was finished in 1841. Through Klagmann, designer of the sword, Morel was put in touch with Charles-Edmond Duponchel (1794–1868). A former student at the Ecole des Beaux-Arts, where he studied architecture,*

*Duponchel, co-director of the Opéra from 1835 to 1842 and again from 1847 to 1849, entered into partnership with Morel in 1842, providing him with capital and advising him on artistic matters. Their firm, established on the rue Neuve Saint Augustin at 39 (Almanach du Commerce, 1843–48), then at 47 (Almanach du Commerce, 1849), became famous, producing gold- and silverwork primarily inspired by the Renaissance. Some of their designs were furnished by Jules Peyre and Constant Sévin (q.v.). In 1844 Morel, who employed eighty workers including lapidaries and enamelers, won a gold medal at the Exposition des Produits de l'Industrie. But the dissolution of the partnership brought about a lawsuit that resulted in Morel's being prohibited thenceforth from maintaining an establishment in the Department of the Seine. Duponchel then directed the firm by himself (Almanach du Commerce, 1850), while Morel went to London in 1848. There he surrounded himself with distinguished collaborators: Sévin (q.v.), Attarge (q.v.), Henri Fourdinois (q.v.), Néville (later a designer for Fourdinois), the enameler Lefournier, and Willms (q.v.). Morel triumphed in 1851 at the London Universal Exhibition where the duc de Luynes and Laborde praised his work. New financial difficulties brought him back to France in 1852 and he settled at Sèvres. In 1855 his exhibit, including the Hope coupe, earned him the Grand Medal of Honor for goldwork and jewelry. In 1857 Morel became a chevalier of the Legion of Honor.*

D.A.

Bibliography:
Arch. de la Garantie, Insculpations 1820–41, fol. 94; *Rapports 1855*, pp. 916, 925; de Laborde, 1856, vol. I, pp. 209, 375; Wièse, 1860, pp. 43, 51–53; Mantz, 1863,"Orfèvrerie," pp. 534–37; Dussieux, 1876, pp. 301–7; Champier, 1888–89, pp. 168–71; Vever, 1906–8, vol. I, pp. 201, 220, 252–84, vol. II, p. 332; Bouilhet, 1908–12, vol. II, pp. 223–31, 260–61, 281

## Pierre-Alexandre Schoenewerk
*Paris 1820–1885 Paris*

*The "sculpture" of the Hope coupe, by which is undoubtedly meant the model for the enameled gold decoration, was by Schoenewerk (Dussieux) or by Schoenewerk and Willms (Deville). Coming from a family of German origin, Schoenewerk became naturalized as a French citizen. He studied sculpture with Triqueti and David d'Angers, making his debut at the Salon of 1841 and continuing to exhibit there throughout his life. Mythological themes appeared frequently in his work (for example,* Leda and the Swan, *marble, Salon of 1863; park of the château of Compiègne). Under the Second Empire he participated in the sculptural decoration of the Louvre, the*

Tuileries, and the Church of Saint Augustin in Paris. Interested in silverwork, he did work for various silversmiths. François-Désiré Froment-Meurice commissioned him to make, notably, the model for one of the four bas-reliefs (the race course at Chantilly) ornamenting the racing trophy in the form of a shield that he exhibited in 1844: "Schoenewerck [sic] pulled it off with a great deal of skill and imagination" (Théophile Gautier). He also provided the models for a number of figures on the centerpiece (1842–45) of Prince Léon Radziwill created by Sévin (q.v.), the most celebrated work by Morel and Duponchel. This depicted a thirteenth-century hunting scene in Lithuania, inspired by the history of the Radziwills. He later designed for Wièse (q.v.) the sword that was presented in 1860 to Marshal MacMahon.

In 1867 Schoenewerk resided at 22, rue de Fleurus and had his workshop at 27 (Almanach du Commerce). Suffering from mental illness since 1866 and disappointed by the reception given his work at the Salon of 1885, Schoenewerk committed suicide that year.

D.A.

Bibliography:
Waring, 1863, vol. I, pl. 100; Dussieux, 1876, p. 253; Burty, 1883, pp. 40, 65; Lami, 1914–21, vol. IV, pp. 242–47; Vever, 1906–8, vol. II, pp. 210–11

## Albert Willms

### Active Paris and London

An ornamental sculptor of Parisian origin, Willms worked with Diéterle (q.v.), Klagmann, and Sévin (q.v.) before emigrating to London in 1848. There he contributed some of the works exhibited by Jean-Valentin Morel in 1851. On his return to Paris he was employed by Christofle (q.v.) and François-Désiré Froment-Meurice (q.v.); recognized by Paillard (see no. II-5), he received a silver medal as coopérateur in 1855. In the following years he became "chief artist" for Elkington in Birmingham, where he was asked to make a table service for the duc de Brabant. At the 1862 London International Exhibition, Elkington's exhibit included works designed by Willms: a parcel-gilt ewer and basin, decorated with medallions showing the Elements and executed by the chaser Morel-Ladeuil, and a dessert service in parcel-gilt and enameled silver in the "Néo-Grec" style. In 1867 Elkington exhibited other celebrated objects composed by Willms, ornamented with bas-reliefs.

D.A.

Bibliography:
Rapports 1855, p. 925; L'Art au Dix-Neuvième Siècle, vol. V, 1860, p. 20; Darcel, 1862, pp. 330, 543; Waring, 1863, vol. II, pl. 102, vol. III, pl. 211; Luchet, 1868, pp. 354–55; Champier, 1888–89, p. 170

## Alexandre Dalbergue

### Active Paris until c. 1863

The name of this ciseleur, who was responsible for the chasing of the Hope coupe, is sometimes spelled Daubergue. After having worked in the workshop of Vechte, he became a chaser of some repute, employed both by bronze founders and by silversmiths, especially for major undertakings. At the Exposition des Produits de l'Industrie of 1849 his works were exhibited by several silversmiths: Rudolphi (q.v.); François-Désiré Froment-Meurice (q.v.; the centerpiece of the duc de Luynes, the chasing of which was done by Dalbergue and three other famous chasers, Mulleret, Poux, and J. Fannière, q.v.); Lebrun (Louis XV service of the grande duchesse Helen of Russia, chased by Dalbergue, Poux, and others). At the Universal Exhibition of 1851 Dalbergue won an honorable mention as Froment-Meurice's collaborator. The chasing of the silver-plated service for Napoleon III, executed by Christofle (q.v.), occupied all of the great chasers of the period, especially Honoré (q.v.), Fannière, Deurbergue, Poux, and Dalbergue. In 1855 he was awarded a silver medal as coopérateur of the bronze manufacturer Denière (q.v.) and honorable mention as coopérateur of Aucoc, maker of silver traveling cases. During Second Empire he lived at 11, rue de l'Oseille (now rue de Poitou), according to the Almanach du Commerce which mentioned him for the last time in 1863.

D.A.

Bibliography:
Rapports 1855, pp. 925, 1212; Dussieux, 1876, p. 571; Burty, 1883, pp. 45, 58; Vever, 1906–8, vol. I, p. 190; Bouilhet, 1908–12, vol. II, pp. 266, 300

## Richard (Family of Painters)

### Active Sèvres

Morel had intended to entrust the enameling of the mounts for the Hope coupe to his regular enameler Louis-Auguste-Hippolyte Lefournier (1802–1859). An outstanding enameler, he had followed Morel to London, then returned to Paris, where he was also working for François-Désiré Froment-Meurice (q.v.) and Wièse (q.v.). Because he did not have enough time, Lefournier did not want to undertake this work, which Morel, according to Dussieux, then had done by Richard, a painter at the manufactory at Sèvres (q.v.).

Six members of a family named Richard—two brothers and their two respective sons—worked at Sèvres in the nineteenth century. Among them, three painters can be identified. Pierre-Nicolas Richard, called Richard Aîné (the elder; Chantilly 1779–Sèvres 1855), worked at Sèvres as a gilder (doreur) from 1815, and was recorded as a permanent employee under this title from 1816 until his

retirement in 1848. His oldest son Nicolas-Joseph (born Paris 1805), employed at the manufactory as peintre d'ornements beginning in 1830 and recorded as a permanent employee in 1833, was named peintre-décorateur in 1856 and retired in 1872. The second son, Eugène (born Paris 1808), who was listed as a flower painter as of 1838, also retired in 1872. The brother of Pierre-Nicolas, Louis-Auguste-Victor Richard (born Chantilly 1786), was employed as a doreur beginning in 1818, recorded as a permanent employee in 1821, and left in 1848. François-Gervais (born Paris 1814), the oldest son of Louis-Auguste-Victor, was perhaps the most talented (see no. IV-4). Recorded as employed by April 1, 1833, working as a doreur sur porcelaine at the manufactory's dépôt in Paris (18, rue de Rivoli), he was recalled to Sèvres when the dépôt was closed on July 1, 1841, and was given the title of peintre-ornemaniste on January 1, 1843. Having won an honorable mention as a coopérateur at the Exposition Universelle of 1855, he was named peintre-décorateur as of March 1, 1856, and retired on January 1, 1875. His brother Paul-Eugène (born Paris 1820–died 1892) worked at the manufactory as painter of grounds of hard-paste porcelain from 1854 until 1880. Morel's collaborator could thus have been Nicolas-Joseph, Eugène, or François-Gervais.

D.A.

Bibliography:
Sèvres Archives Y 10, fols. 26v, 27r, 40v, 48r, 83r; Sèvres Archives Y 11, fols. 16r, v, 22v, 77r; Sèvres Archives Ob 10 [dossiers Richard]; Rapports 1855, p. 954

## Jean-Baptiste Salmson

### Stockholm 1799–1859 Paris

The creator of the jasper cameo representing a mask of Medusa, on the Hope coupe, said by Dussieux and the 1855 exposition reports (Reports 1855) to have been Morel (q.v.), was unequivocally shown by Deville (1856) to be Salmson.

A member of a family of Swedish artists and an engraver of medals and semiprecious stones, Salmson began working in Stockholm, where some of his production is preserved, then established himself in Paris in 1822, where he was a student of Bosio and became a naturalized French citizen. He won a third-class medal at the Exposition Universelle of 1855 for the engraving of semiprecious stones. He seems to have executed mainly portraits, and exhibited notably, at the Salon of 1855, two engraved gems representing the Emperor (cornelian) and Empress (onyx). At the Salon of 1859 he showed intaglios of the king and queen of Spain. He was the father of the sculptor Jean-Jules Salmson (q.v.).

D.A.

Bibliography:
*Rapports 1855*, p. 1378; Andréï, 1859, p. 284; Thieme and Becker, 1907–50, vol. XXIX, p. 352–53; Lami, 1914–21, vol. IV, pp. 228–30

Jean-Valentin Morel; designed by Louis-Constant Sévin, models of sculpture by Pierre-Alexandre Schoenewerk and Albert Willms; chased by Alexandre Dalbergue; enameled by Richard; cameo by Jean-Baptiste Salmson

## III-33
## Coupe with the Story of Perseus and Andromeda

1855
Mark: maker, Jean-Valentin Morel
Signed at base on jasper: MOREL/1855; inscribed on banderoles held by putti: AT SPES NON FRACTA
Jasper (bloodstone); base gilded silver, mounts repoussé and enameled gold; opaque and translucent enamel
Height 65.5 cm; width 50 cm; depth 22 cm

Provenance:
Executed for Henry Thomas Hope (1808–1862), son of the architect Thomas Hope (*Dictionary of National Biography*, s.v.; Baumgarten, 1958, pp. 231–32); Mrs. H.T. Hope, née Adèle Bichat; sale, London, Sotheby, December 5, 1960, no. 93; sale, New York, Parke-Bernet, October 6, 1971, no. 118 (repro.); Walter Godny

Exhibitions:
1855, Paris, Exposition Universelle; 1971, London, no. 134 (repro.)

Bibliography:
*Rapports 1855*, p. 916; Deville, 1856, pp. 80–81; Wièse, 1860, p. 53; Mantz, 1863, "Orfèvrerie," pp. 536–37; Dussieux, 1876, pp. 306–7; Champier, 1888–89, pp. 170–71; Vever, 1906–8, vol. I, p. 275

Morel's success in 1851 was due largely to a series of hard-stone vases, created for the most part by Sévin, the mountings of which represented foliage, figures, and so forth, in repoussé and enameled gold, and enameled by Lefournier. Certain of these vases anticipate the composition of the one exhibited here, such as a *coupe* in agate, the mounting of which comprises as the handle, a female figure riding a dolphin, and as the foot, a female figure supported by a triton reclining on marine plants (*The Art Journal*, n.s., vol. I, 1855, p. 151, repro. p. 150). This piece was subsequently acquired by the Museum of Ornamental Art, and almost all the others by English collectors, which probably led to the Hope commission. A watercolor showing a full-scale model for the *coupe* was signed "ne varietur" by Morel and Hope on November 29, 1854 (Chaumet coll., Paris). But by this time, the execution, at least of the stone, had been underway for some time;

III-33

it is possible, given the choice of collaborators and the length of the execution, that the work was begun in London. The watercolor could therefore precede the date shown. But the gold and silver base at least was not yet finished by the end of 1854, since its final appearance is different from that in the watercolor.

The *coupe* consists of four pieces of bloodstone; the shell rests on three superimposed blocks. Two putti hold the Hope device and their crest (in part consisting of a terrestrial globe), while Pegasus evokes the gold horse figuring on the Hope arms.

Morel "found or rather invented ways to carve the jasper and to give it, despite its hardness over which one can triumph only with the help of emery mixed with powdered diamonds, a suppleness of contours and of forms that can only be found in antique works" (*Rapports 1855*, p. 916). "The *coupe* is extracted from a block of jasper that weighed 80 pounds; it is the largest piece of jasper known; its cutting required three years of work and the invention of numerous procedures" (Dussieux, 1876). Actually, in the sixteenth and seventeenth centuries, larger jasper objects were carved. Morel was responsible for the cutting of the stone. Dussieux also attributed the repoussé work to him. The design was by Sévin, the probable author of the watercolor mentioned above.

The vase was inspired by the hard-stone vases of the sixteenth and seventeenth centuries, and particularly by those of Louis XIV, then exhibited at the Louvre. The general form recalls two shell-shaped vases in particular: one in jade (Catalogue, Paris, Louvre, 1914, no. 942), the other in sard, surmounted by a dragon in enameled gold (Catalogue, Paris, Louvre, 1914, no. 1107). The decoration of volutes and gadroons in very low relief, characteristic of works executed in Prague during the seventeenth century, appeared notably on a bloodstone vessel (Catalogue, Paris, Louvre, 1914, no. 975). The figures were inspired by those on a group of French seventeenth-century mounts: the male masks are close to a satyr's mask ornamenting a lapis lazuli nef (Catalogue, Paris, Louvre, 1914, no. 990, repro.); the dragon recalls that of the sard *coupe* noted above; these figures evoke above all a Louis-XIV sard ewer stolen from the Louvre in 1830, then in the possession of A.J.B. Beresford-Hope, brother of Henry Thomas (*see* Waagen, 1857, p. 191; since returned to the Louvre). The ewer includes, notably, a dragon that serves as a handle. The mounting borrows also from French art of the sixteenth century: the Moorish motifs and strapwork of the cameo mount and the female masks of the base.

The Hope *coupe* must have influenced certain vases exhibited in 1862: an agate *coupe* by Wièse (q.v.) supported by a siren; a *coupe* in rock crystal by Duponchel surmounted by a bird; and above all a vase with Perseus and Andromeda, in smoked crystal and enameled gold, designed by the French sculptor Chesneau for the London goldsmith Harry Emanuel (Waring, 1863, vol. I, pl. 100, vol. II, pl. 174, vol. I, pl. 94).

D.A.

Collection Walter Godny, London

# Ceramics and Glass

The Second Empire witnessed the beginning of a distinction between mass-produced, commercial factory wares, and studio wares, produced in limited quantities by individual artist-potters and glassmakers. This distinction was not without exception, however, as commercial manufacturers produced wares which expressed a craftsman's regard for his material, and studio artists adapted industrial techniques for their original designs. The large commercial manufactories entered in the production of art wares by creating unique and self-consciously novel designs for competition at the international exhibitions held in London in 1851 and 1862 and in Paris in 1855 and 1867, and at national exhibitions held in Paris and at various provincial centers. Such exhibition pieces, a number of which are included here, won medals and prestige for their designs and methods of manufacture, but seldom resulted in any commercial benefit[1]—leading certain critics to decry the sacrifice of usefulness to "art" by manufacturers "who return with no other reward than the astonished or distracted regards of the public."[2] Studio artists adopted mechanical processes from industry: commercial slip-casting (coulage) was applied by the studio-potter Tite-Henri-Clément Ristori in his award-winning 1855 exhibition pieces[3] and France's first artist-glassmaker, Philippe-Joseph Brocard (q.v.), adapted the commercial technique of muffle-firing a specific range of vitrified colors on glass during the 1860s in his enameled and gilded glasswares.

The state-subsidized imperial manufactory at Sèvres (q.v.) occupied a unique position between studio art and industry. By virtue of its role as a progressive "school" for industry, Sèvres had survived attempts to suppress the national manufactories during the Second Republic,[4] a purpose reiterated during the Second Empire by Prosper Mérimée, who considered it Sèvres's mission to "instruct" private industry by producing ceramics "whose quality, choice of models, and... decoration are superior to those which private industry can produce."[5] While the imperial manufactory was ostensibly not a commercial competitor, its inclusion in the 1851 exhibition occasioned complaints that it was "unjust" to admit Sèvres to competition with private industry,[6] although Léon Arnoux, art director at Minton, argued that Sèvres's sponsorship of "the highest regions of art" in ceramic manufacture would encourage commercial manufacturers to proper competition "based upon the improvement of... quality,

which is the true mode of establishing a good reputation."[7]

It was through international competition that the ceramics and glass industries learned and developed advanced industrial methods first successfully applied during the Second Empire—notably the conversion to coal from wood fuel and the use of the Siemens furnace. In the early nineteenth century wood was abundant and cheap in France. By the 1830s, however, rising costs of wood and inadequate supplies prompted experiments in coal-firing by the Limoges porcelain manufacturer Ruaud and at the great industrial glacerie of Saint-Gobain (Aisne). The first successful coal-firing of porcelain was produced by Vital-Roux at his manufactory at Noirlac (Cher) between 1846 and 1848, an achievement which won him a gold medal at the Paris industrial exposition of 1849. In 1848 Vital-Roux was appointed chef des fours à pâtes at Sèvres, where he remained until 1856, establishing the imperial manufactory's first coal-burning kilns, which were 75 percent cheaper to fire than wood ovens.[8] In 1849 Ebelmen warned that since England, too, possessed the raw materials necessary to coal-fire hard-paste porcelain, "our manufacturers... [must] immediately [modify] their processes by this experiment which has just been proved effective."[9] The problems of inaccessibility and high transportation costs of coal to the porcelain manufacturers of Limoges were relieved by the opening of railroads from Paris to Limoges in 1857, and from Limoges to Montluçon in 1865.

The proximity of the cristalleries to forests slowed the conversion of the glass industry to coal. In 1862 Pelouze chided glass manufacturers who continued to burn wood at four francs a cord instead of coal at twenty-five francs a ton when English and Belgian crystals were underselling French products,[10] and as late as 1867 furnaces at Baccarat (q.v.) were still burning wood. The regenerative furnace developed by Karl Wilhelm Siemens greatly increased the utilization and economy of coal as fuel for the glass industry. In 1861 Siemens first successfully applied his furnace at Henry Chance's glassworks in Smethwick, near Birmingham, England: by 1862 Baccarat had two Siemens furnaces in operation, and was followed soon after by Saint-Louis (q.v.), whose factory director Didierjean modified the system to permit the working of crystal in open vessels. By 1867 the faïence manufactory of Lebeuf-Milliet et Cie at Creil (q.v.) was also operating a

Siemens furnace, with two others under construction; Girard estimated this lowered the firing costs at Creil by 40 percent.[11] With such economic use of fuel, Péligot and Bontemps viewed the Siemens furnace as "the greatest progress made in our time."[12]

Inspired by English, German, and Venetian colored and decorated glasswares, the commercial glass manufacturers from the late 1830s through 1870 invented a number of decorative techniques which for the first time put French glass at the forefront of European colored and novelty wares. While most commercial glasswares were produced mechanically by pressing or blowing the glass into molds, many of the new techniques—particularly those reflecting the influence of historical Venetian glass—involved traditional hand processes, whereby the glass was manipulated at the furnace with pincers and tongs (see no. IV-21). In their handmade irregularity and varied color and texture, the Venetian glasses mark the beginning of a reaction against the over-brilliant, clear white commercial crystal, which during most of the nineteenth century remained one of the most valued products of the industrial revolution.

In 1839 the Société d'Encouragement pour l'Industrie Nationale awarded prizes to manufacturers for "Bohemian" glasswares: to François-Eugène Fontenay, director of the verrerie at Vallerysthal, for cased and flashed glass; to Georges Bontemps, director of the verrerie-cristallerie at Choisy-le-Roi, for colored glass;[13] and to Fontenay and Louis Robert (q.v.) for glass with muffle-fired painted decorations.[14] During the late 1830s and early 1840s came the first experiments by Bontemps in highly complicated Venetian color techniques such as filigrane (latticino) and millefiori glass after sixteenth- and seventeenth-century prototypes.[15] In 1855 Saint-Louis first exhibited imitations of semiprecious stones after Venetian calcedonio, and Joseph Maes, proprietor of the Cristallerie de Clichy, his black "obsidian" glass made with sulphur. By 1860 Hautefeuille was producing commercial quantities of spangled aventurine glass, which was improved by Pelouze in 1865 with a green glass "harder than the Venetian aventurines."[16] Following English examples, Maréchal (q.v.) in Metz and the cristalleries of Baccarat and Saint-Louis produced glasswares with acid-etched decorations after 1854, when Kessler first successfully applied this method of engraving with hydrofluoric acid (see no. IV-24). Although admitting in 1867 that clear crystal glass was better made in England than in France, Péligot and Bontemps considered French novelty, colored, painted, and engraved wares equal and superior to rival European products.[17]

Unlike in the glass industry, major technical innovations in ceramics were made during the Second Empire not by commercial manufacturers, but by the imperial manufactory at Sèvres in porcelain, and by independent artist-potters in earthenware. While Prosper Mérimée considered it Sèvres's "mission... to constantly perfect its processes of manufacture,"[18] Burty felt that Regnault's administration at Sèvres was "too much given to the system of working out theoretical experiments," sacrificing "art" to science to such an extent that by 1862 the "productions of the... English Ceramists, Minton and Copeland, were almost equal" in quality to those of the imperial manufactory at Sèvres.[19] In 1850 Ferdinand de Lasteyrie praised recent improvements at Sèvres in the process of slip-casting which permitted the manufacture of large-scale, thin-bodied porcelains, and new methods of decoration which included high-firing colors, and slip-reliefs (pâtes colorées) developed by Louis Robert, head of Sèvres's painting and gilding studio.[20] The application of Robert's process in porcelains decorated with successive layers of slip in reliefs known ás pâte-sur-pâte was Sèvres's most important innovation during the Second Empire.[21] It was not until the 1860s that the slip reliefs, introduced by Sèvres at the Paris exposition of 1850 and the international exhibitions of 1851 and 1855, were adopted by the commercial manufacturers of Limoges, including Henri Ardant in 1862 and Gibus et Cie (q.v.) in 1867.

Sèvres also contributed to technical progress in the ceramics industry by reviving or rediscovering materials and processes of manufacture long disused or forgotten, much as the glass manufacturers had reproduced historical Venetian techniques, and it was by these means also that individual artist-potters were able to advance the development of French earthenwares and stoneware. In the early 1850s Sèvres reestablished production of soft-paste porcelain, and examples in this celebrated eighteenth-century medium cast from Sèvres's earlier molds were first displayed at the Paris Exposition Universelle of 1855.[22] In 1852 Sèvres organized its first studio for the production of earthenwares where historical techniques were often combined within a single piece in a manner considered so "original" by Mérimée that it "would soon inspire private industry."[23]

However, the most advanced work in earthenware and stoneware was done by artist-potters working alone outside the commercial or state factories, on a relatively small scale—which Darcel described in 1863 as a "resurrection of the art of pottery in France."[24] From about 1840 to 1856, Jules-Claude Ziégler revived at Voisinlieu, near Beauvais, the production of brown salt-glazed stoneware after sixteenth- and seventeenth-century European models, its rough finish and mottled color the antithesis of flawlessly glazed and technically perfect factory products. Ziégler's wares mark the beginning of the art pottery or studio movement in French ceramics, guided self-consciously by the qualities of the material.[25] Ziégler's most influential designs were not his specific imitations of sixteenth-century prototypes, but a series of jugs decorated naturalistically with running plant patterns, described by Burty as "really modern" in style[26] which were reproduced by English manufacturers such as T.J. & J. Mayer and Ridgway and Abington during the later 1840s, and by the French firms of Gille and Mansard for the 1851 exhibition.[27]

During the 1840s while Ziégler was rediscovering stoneware as an artistic medium, Charles-Jean Avisseau (q.v.) revived in Tours the production of glazed earthenwares by recreating the techniques and styles of the sixteenth-century potter Bernard Palissy. Avisseau's technical achievements in recreating Palissy's rustic wares were highly praised by contemporaries, and imitated by a number of manufacturers including his brother-in-law and former associate, Joseph Landais of Tours, Lesme Frères of Limoges, Victor Barbizet of Paris, and Minton in England—all of whom were listed as exhibitors of Palissy wares at the Paris exposition of 1855. Avisseau led the general revival of interest in historical European earthenwares, and the rediscovery of these historical ceramic materials and techniques remained bound, as in Avisseau's own pottery, to the styles with which they were originally associated. Tin-glazed earthenwares were produced in Italian and French Renaissance and French seventeenth-century styles from 1847 by Joseph Devers—who was responsible for renovating the technique of painting colors over unfired glaze—and from 1854 by Ristori at Marzy (Nièvre); from 1859 by Auguste Jean in Paris; and from 1855 by Jean-Jude Ulysse (called Besnard) at Blois. France's greatest artist-potter of the nineteenth century, Théodore Deck (q.v.), also began his career by rediscovering medieval and Renaissance processes of ceramic manufacture and decoration. At the 1861 Exposition des Produits de l'Industrie in Paris, Deck exhibited Henri II-style earthenwares, inlaid with colored clays, and at the London International Exhibition of 1862, metallic luster glazes in Hispano-Moresque and Italian Renaissance styles.

Yet Deck's most important innovation during the Second Empire was his production in 1861 of Islamic earthenwares—the first art pottery to depart from European precedents both in medium and style of decoration (see nos. IV-14, IV-15)—which were described later by Deck himself as "the beginning of a new era" in faïence.[28] After prolonged experiments Deck succeeded in reproducing "Persian" colors which were highly praised by his contemporaries for their "fine quality" and "intensity of tones,"[29] and the Islamic technique of firing them in a single operation between a white ground below and clear glaze above. During the 1860s French potters and the glassmaker Brocard followed Deck in the production of Near Eastern wares, including Eugène-Victor Collinot (q.v.) and Auguste Jean, who were listed as exhibitors of these wares at the 1863 exhibition of the Union Centrale; Charles Longuet, at the Union Centrale exhibition of 1865; and Leon Parvillée at the Exposition Universelle of 1867.

Deck's discovery of non-Classical, non-Western traditions illustrates an important change in attitude toward medium which French studio-potters and glassmakers championed during the Second Empire and later nineteenth century—in which materials and techniques became in themselves a legitimate end for art wares. In 1862 Mérimée warned that certain manufacturers were "strangers to the practice of their industry... the part of their work which lasts. In that regard we cannot too highly recommend a complete study of ceramic means,"[30] and earlier, in 1850, Sèvres's illusionistic painted decorations were judged inappropriate because they denied the forms to which they were applied and masked the qualities of the ceramic material itself.[31] This new concern for material means was implicit in the rediscovery of historic European ceramic techniques, but it was often overlooked in criticism of the imitative forms associated with these techniques. While Avisseau himself was praised for his technical discoveries, the imitators of Palissy in general were dismissed for "servile reproductions" that would never equal their models.[32] Deck's earthenwares and Brocard's enameled glasswares in Islamic styles were often as imitative of specific prototypes as historicizing wares in European styles, but partly from lack of familiarity with their models, and partly because of their superb craftsmanship, they were consistently given important awards at the international exhibitions, heralded as original and novel,[33] and judged "as successful as their models."[34] The interest in Near Eastern and Far Eastern ceramics and glass which developed during the Second Empire was viewed by Burty as the "return of taste... [from which] we may date all serious discussion concerning the principles of decorative art."[35] It was a movement which manifested itself in freedom from Classical preconceptions,[36] and emulating the spirit of the Oriental models themselves, gave new impulse to materials and techniques as principal artistic concerns.

An attempt to imitate Chinese celadons decorated with white reliefs led about 1850 to the invention at Sèvres of the high-firing celadon glazes and slip reliefs in *pâte-sur-pâte*. In 1875 Sèvres's Commission de Perfectionnement recalled these earlier experiments in "Oriental" bodies and enamels and recommended that Sèvres produce new transparent colors and colored grounds after Chinese models.[37]

Félix Bracquemond (q.v.) introduced "Japanism" into French ceramics with his celebrated service of 1866 (*see* no. IV-18). Yet while this Japanese style remained during the Second Empire a superficial borrowing of motifs from Japanese print albums and illustrated books, the disappearance of borders, the asymmetry, and the undecorated surfaces learned from these prints by such artists as Camille Moreau (q.v.) and Escallier (q.v.) led eventually to a new, freer conception of painted decoration.

The revival of both European and Oriental techniques was strongly encouraged by the national collections at the Louvre and Cluny museums, and particularly at Sèvres's Musée Céramique, where both studio artists and commercial manufacturers were able to study in original works the historical processes of manufacture and decoration. In 1835 Alexandre Brongniart, Sèvres's *administrateur*, acquired Bohemian glasses for the museum which Montalivet claimed were the "first models... to inspire" the *cristalleries* to produce colored glasswares.[38] The Sèvres decorator Solon (q.v.) attributed the invention of *pâte-sur-pâte* decorations to Denis-Désiré Riocreux, curator of the Musée Céramique from 1823 to 1872, who so admired a Chinese vase in the museum decorated with a celadon ground and white floral reliefs "that he induced one of the modellers at the factory, Mr. Fishback [Charles Fischbag, *réparateur*, 1834–50], to undertake the necessary trials, in view of obtaining similar effects with... Sèvres porcelain."[39] Private collections of historical material were exhibited at the "Musée Rétrospectif" organized by the Union Centrale in 1863 and 1865, at the "Musée Oriental" organized by the Union Centrale in 1869, and at special exhibitions held at and in conjunction with the international exhibitions. In 1864 Reiber (q.v.) spoke of public taste "purified" by the arts of the past "whose remarkable specimens daily enrich our museums and private collections and direct the efforts of artists... especially in the most practical applications of art."[40] Certain printed sources were also of particular importance to ceramists and glassmakers in providing models for their designs. These included the *Description méthodique du musée céramique de la manufacture royale de porcelaine de Sèvres* by Brongniart and Riocreux (1845); *Etudes céramiques* by Ziégler (1850); *Recueil de dessins pour l'art et l'industrie*, published by Adalbert de Beaumont and Collinot in 1859; *L'Art pour Tous*, a periodical design book published from 1861 by Reiber; and *Les Merveilles de la céramique* published by Albert Jacquemart in 1868.

Studio artists and commercial manufacturers of ceramics and glass in the Second Empire were equally excited by the possibilities of progress. Made ambitious by international competition, they pursued advanced industrial methods and developed new processes of manufacture and decoration. In 1865 Horace de Viel-Castel observed with satisfaction "the truly marvelous progress" made by the ceramics and glass industries which would assure in the near future "an incontestable superiority over foreign products."[41] If during the Second Empire other industries complained of their own lack of progress, glassmakers could boast of their superiority in producing colored wares, and Adalbert de Beaumont declared the "supremacy" of French faïence over its European—and particularly English—rivals,[42] an idea echoed by Victor de Luynes when he declared France to have given "the first impulse" to art pottery in all countries, and in 1873 to be "still at the head" of the movement.[43]

K.B.H.

*Notes*

1. Grellier reports (1908, p. 263), for example, that at the 1867 exhibition, Limousin porcelain manufacturers won seven silver medals and a Medal of Honor, and complained of no appreciable commercial results.

2. Blanqui, in *Rapport 1849*, vol. III, p. 405.

3. Salvetat, in *Rapports 1855*, p. 944.

4. *Le Moniteur*, March 29, 1849, pp. 1142–43, July 3, 1850, pp. 2270–71.

5. *Rapports 1862*, vol. VI, p. 573.

6. *Travaux 1851*, vol. VI, XXV^e Jury, p. 21.

7. *Reports 1855*, part II, p. 366.

8. Ebelmen, in *Rapport 1849*, vol. II, p. 893.

9. Ebelmen, in *Rapport 1849*, vol. II, pp. 893–94.

10. Pelouze, in *Rapports 1862*, vol. VI, p. 541.

11. A. Girard, in *Rapports 1867*, vol. III, pp. 149–50.

12. E. Péligot and G. Bontemps, in *Rapports 1867*, vol. III, p. 64.

13. Which Bontemps produced as early as 1825 for use in stained window glass (Péligot, 1877, p. 197; Bontemps, 1868, p. 710).

14. Péligot, 1877, p. 421, a technique later adapted by Brocard (q.v.).

15. His experiments in 1838–39 were published before the Société d'Encouragement in 1845 (Bontemps, 1868, pp. 601–2).

16. Péligot, 1877, p. 459.

17. E. Péligot and G. Bontemps, in *Rapports 1867*, vol. III, pp. 67, 74–75.

18. *Rapports 1862*, vol. VI, p. 573.

19. Burty, 1869, *Chefs-d'œuvre*, pp. 163–64.

20. De Lasteyrie, 1850, pp. 138–39.

21. Duc, 1875, p. 22.

22. L. Arnoux, in *Reports 1855*, part 2, pp. 368–69.

23. P. Mérimée, in *Rapports 1862*, vol. VI, pp. 583–84.

24. Darcel, 1863, p. 72.

25. "I accept responsibility only for my works, for the enterprise, and the material which has not lost favor since [the time of] Palissy" (Ziégler, 1850, p. 5).

26. Burty, 1869, *Chefs-d'œuvre*, p. 127.

27. In 1849 Ziégler wrote "Most of the factories in Europe have copied my models, which have inspired them" (Ziégler, 1850, p. 5).

28. Deck, 1887, p. 245.

29. *Union Centrale 1865*, p. 46; especially a turquoise blue, much remarked at the 1862 exhibition: V. de Luynes, in *Rapports 1871*, vol. III, p. 120.

30. *Rapports 1862*, vol. VI, pp. 590–91.

31. De Lasteyrie, 1850, pp. 141–42.

32. A. Girard, in *Rapports 1867*, vol. III, p. 158.

33. A. Girard, in *Rapports 1867*, vol. III, p. 154.

34. De Beaumont, 1867, p. 157.

35. Burty, 1869, *Chefs-d'œuvre*, p. 5.

36. Burty, 1869, *Chefs-d'œuvre*, p. 5: It "disturb[ed] the souls of the disciples of the old classic school."

37. Duc, 1875, pp. 22–24.

38. De Montalivet, 1851, p. 133.

39. Solon, 1894, p. 120.

40. *L'Art pour Tous*, 4^th year, 1864, introduction.

41. *Union Centrale 1865*, p. 40.

42. "Everyone was struck by the important role which French faïence played at the exposition of 1867, and we do not hesitate to declare the supremacy it has achieved over that of other countries" (de Beaumont, 1867, p. 157).

43. *Rapport 1873*, vol. III, p. 23.

# Porcelain

## Gibus et Cie

*Limoges, 1853–1872*

*In 1853 a hard-paste porcelain factory located at 2, rue des Trois Chatains was taken over by Justin Gibus (1821–1897) in association with Martial Redon and Alpinien Margaine. Under the name Gibus et Cie the firm exhibited table services and decorated porcelain objects at the Paris Exposition Universelle of 1855 (Catalogue 1855, no. 5507). At the exposition Ravenez praised the "beautiful whiteness and fine firing" of Gibus's porcelain, which he felt guaranteed a promising future for the new firm (Ravenez, 1855, p. 80). During the 1850s and 1860s Gibus et Cie also produced white porcelains which were sold to and decorated at other factories, including that of Haviland (q.v.): in 1864 the firm earned income in the amount of 463,000 francs from the porcelains that it sold in Paris (288,000 francs) and Limoges (175,000 francs). At the 1867 Exposition Universelle, where the firm won a silver medal (Récompensés 1867, p. 18), Gibus was judged by Arnoux "very little behind Sèvres in the production of the pâte sur pâte" and the best of the Limoges manufacturers "for beauty of materials, good models neatly manufactured, and lightness united to elegance of form" (L. Arnoux, in* Reports 1867, *vol. II, p. 410). At the 1870 exhibition of the Société des Amis des Arts of Limoges, the porcelains of Gibus et Cie were thought superior to those of Sèvres: "These vases with varied grounds and designs... possibly surpass in distinction the most beautiful examples of Sèvres" (Burty, 1870, "Limoges," p. 229). In 1872 the factory was moved to 7, faubourg des Casseaux and the firm reorganized as Gibus et Redon. In 1881 Gibus retired from the firm, which until 1896 was known as Redon et Cie.*

K.B.H.

Bibliography:
Leroux, 1904, pp. 89, 155, 164; de Chavagnac and de Grollier, 1906, p. 771; Giacomotti and Verlet, 1965, pp. 71, 75, 78; d'Albis and Romanet, n.d.

## Alpinien Margaine

*Limoges 1825–1878 Limoges*

*Educated at the schools of drawing and modeling of the Société d'Agriculture of Limoges, Margaine was associated with the porcelain firm of Gibus et Cie from its establishment in 1853 until his retirement in 1871. Margaine served as artistic director of the firm,* and for the 1855 Exposition Universelle *"created numerous models" praised by Ravenez as "remarkable for the elegance of their execution" (Ravenez, 1855, p. 80). At his death in 1878 Margaine was remembered for his skill at fashioning porcelain shapes "whose beauty, elegance, purity of form, irreproachable taste characterize the production of this firm" and which were cited as evidence of "the greatest artistic progress that the fabrication of porcelain has made at Limoges." Margaine bequeathed sums of money to various relief funds for porcelain workers and to the city of Limoges for the creation of a professional ceramics school.*

K.B.H.

Bibliography:
"Margaine," 1879–80.

Gibus et Cie; designed by Alpinien Margaine, mounts manufactured by Christofle et Cie

## IV-1
## Ewer and Stand

c. 1870
Marked in green: G & C[IE]
Hard-paste porcelain, colored and glazed, with white *pâte-sur-pâte* decorations; silver handle and collar
Ewer height 38.9 cm, diameter 17.3 cm; stand height 4.7 cm, diameter 33.5 cm

Provenance:
Bequest of the designer to the Musée Adrien-Dubouché, 1879 (inv. no. 4604)

Exhibitions:
1878, Paris, Exposition Universelle; 1879, Limoges
Bibliography:
Ch. D., 1878; Dubouché, 1878; Leymarie, 1879; "Margaine," 1879–80; Giacomotti and Verlet, 1965, p. 75

Designed by Margaine and manufactured by Gibus prior to the reorganization of the firm in 1872, the ewer and stand were not publicly exhibited until the Paris Exposition Universelle of 1878, where the ewer was described by Adrien Dubouché as "high fired, with applied ornaments, executed with a precision worthy of the richest metals" and in *Le Courrier du Centre* as "adorned with sculpted ornaments in the taste of the sixteenth century, executed with a precision worthy of gold and silver...." The ewer and stand were exhibited again in 1879 in Limoges, where Camille Leymarie praised "the decoration of these two pieces, figures and arabesques, [which] are perfectly correct and astonishingly executed.... The form, the ornamentation belong to the realm of gold- and enamelwork." After the death of Margaine, "the porcelain ewer with mounts by Christofle" was listed among his works bequeathed to the Musée Adrien-Dubouché.

The ewer and stand are decorated with grotesque ornaments and medallions enclosing mythological figures that imitate in style the decoration of sixteenth-century Limoges enamels. These ornaments, painted in successive layers of white slip on a deeply colored ground by the process known as *pâte-sur-pâte*, also imitate the *grisaille* effect, if not the actual technique, of the black and white layering of sixteenth-century copper-ground enamels. However, the ornamental designs, the chocolate-brown color of the ground, and the form of the ewer, which recalls early nineteenth-century prototypes, are inventions of Margaine that carry the pieces beyond the level of imitation. Gibus et Cie was much praised at the 1867 exposition for having "perfectly succeeded" in producing *pâte-sur-pâte* decorations (F. Dommartin, in *Rapports 1867*, vol. III, p. 173) and for "new research in applying colored slips to *biscuit* grounds" (Hervé, 1867). The firm at this period had no means in Limoges of manufacturing the ewer's metal handle, which was consequently produced in Paris by Christofle (q.v.).

Versions of Limoges enamels in porcelain and earthenware were produced from the late 1850s through the 1880s by ceramic manufactories other than Gibus, including Sèvres (Musée National de Céramique, Sèvres, MNC 15726), Gien (Conservatoire des Arts et Métiers, Paris, 10.189), and Minton in England (1976, London, Victoria and Albert Museum nos. G1, G2, G3, G5). Historical interest in Renaissance enamels, developed in France in the 1830s, was reflected during the Second Empire in a number of important private collections, notably those of the Rothschilds (Alphonse, James, Gustave, and Baroness Salomon de Rothschild), which were exhibited at the South Kensington Museum, London, in 1862 at a special exhibition of "Works of art of the Medieval, Renaissance, and more recent periods"; at the "Musée Rétrospectif" of the Union Centrale exposition in 1865; and in the "Histoire du Travail" exhibition of the Paris Exposition Universelle of 1867. At the same time, scholarly catalogues (de Laborde, 1853; Darcel, 1867,

IV-1

*Emaux*) disseminated information about the French national collections of enamels. Capitalizing on this specific taste in a period of general enthusiasm for the Renaissance, Gibus's ewer and stand delighted critics as a metamorphosis in porcelain of sixteenth-century metalwork techniques.

K.B.H.

Musée National Adrien-Dubouché, Limoges

## Haviland & Co.
### Limoges, established 1842

Haviland & Co. was founded in Limoges in 1842 by an American, David Haviland (1814–1879), who from 1838 imported English tablewares in New York with his brother Daniel Griffin Haviland, under the name D. G. and D. Haviland. On the champ de Juillet in Limoges, David opened an atelier for the creation of models and the decoration of porcelain in shapes and patterns suitable for American tastes: these were imported, distributed, and sold by the New York firm under Daniel's direction. Not until 1865 did Haviland actually manufacture—as well as decorate—its own white ware at a factory on the avenue Garibaldi; until that time blanks were being furnished according to Haviland's designs by several firms, including Gibus (q.v.). At the 1855 Exposition Universelle, as a décorateur sur porcelaine, Haviland won a second-class medal, as well as praise from Regnault for employing large numbers of painters and workers ("a great service to the country") and for producing porcelains at modest prices (Rapports 1855, p. 952). Ravenez also praised Haviland for reaching a popular and widely based market, and declared the firm "the résumé and the crowning example of all the types of fabrication adopted at Limoges" (Ravenez, 1855, p. 34). In 1862 Haviland was still listed as a decorating firm (Catalogue 1862, p. 220, no. 3330); its first award for "white and decorated porcelain" was a silver medal at the Paris Exposition Universelle of 1867 (Récompensés 1867, p. 19). Dommartin reported that Haviland had revolutionized the American market in porcelains and set an example "to be followed by all French exporters" (Rapports 1867, vol. III, pp. 178–79). In 1850 Haviland's exports to the United States had been valued at about 100,000 dollars; by 1880 exports reached a total of 1,500,000 dollars.

In 1864 David Haviland made his two sons, Charles and Theodore, partners in the firm: they continued the business jointly after David Haviland's death in 1879, with Charles as director of the factory until 1892, when the partnership was dissolved. To supplement the traditional Rococo and floral patterns manufactured for export in Limoges, Haviland opened a studio at Auteuil in 1872, directed by Bracquemond (q.v.), where for the next decade innovative slip-decorated, or barbotine, earthenwares with Japanizing and Impressionist decorations were produced.

K.B.H.

Bibliography:
De Chavagnac and de Grollier, 1906, pp. 669–70; Wood, 1951, pp. 17–21; T. Haviland [June 19, 1952], in Schleiger, 1964, pp. 1–3

IV-2

Haviland & Co.; blank manufactured by Gibus et Cie, decorated by Saquet*

## IV-2
## Sugar Bowl

1867
Hard-paste porcelain, with colored enamel and gilded decoration and modeled figures in *biscuit*
Height 19 cm; diameter 24.5 cm

Provenance:
Made for exhibition and retained by Haviland & Co. (inv. no. 46)

Exhibition:
1867, Paris, Exposition Universelle

Bibliography:
Guillemot, 1867; de Lasteyrie, 1867

Although Haviland's new factory for white ware opened in 1865 under the direction of Charles Haviland, it was not until the 1870s that the factory produced porcelain in sufficient quantities to supply Haviland's export needs. During the late 1860s Haviland supplemented its own production with blanks furnished by a number of firms, including Gibus et Cie (q.v.), as documented by correspondence between 1865 and 1869 (Haviland S. A. Archives, letters of August 28, 1865, March 4, 1869). The com-

bination of *biscuit* figures with painted decorations, which appears in this covered bowl, was a specialty of Gibus much remarked at the 1867 Exposition Universelle (Hervé, 1867; L. Arnoux, in *Reports 1867*, vol. II, p. 410; *Art Journal Catalogue 1867*, vol. VII, p. 300). It was adopted by Haviland for this sugar bowl from the "Gothic" service, which was also shown at the 1867 exposition. The bowl is one of four pieces from the service—described by Lasteyrie as "forming at the same time a *surtout de table*"—still preserved in the firm's collections. Among the artists at Haviland whose names have been associated with the service are Berthauzé, *modeleur*; Hayon and Saquet, *peintres-décorateurs* (the latter having decorated this sugar bowl); and Dominique, *doreur*. This "blue service with gold banding and white reliefs" was praised by Guillemot as "elegant and original; the décor, although rich, is not gaudy; the tones are fine and distinguished.... the compotes supported by lovely figures in *biscuit* and a sugar bowl supported on each side by two kneeling female figures" (Guillemot, 1867).

K.B.H.

Haviland, Limoges

## Pouyat Frères
*Limoges, 1842–1883*

By 1780 François Pouyat (died 1811) owned kaolin quarries at Saint-Yrieix, near Limoges, which he increased in 1785 and 1786 through purchases of land. A wholesale merchant, Pouyat supplied clay and raw materials from his quarries to a number of Parisian porcelain factories, including, in 1797, the firm of Russinger at La Courtille in the rue Fontaine au Roy. By 1800 the principal creditor of Russinger, Pouyat took over their La Courtille factory, which he sold in 1810 to Jean Pouyat and his two other sons. In 1820 the Pouyat brothers acquired from their sometime partner, Le Bourgeois, a second factory at Fours (Nièvre), which remained in the family until 1865. The Pouyats sold the La Courtille factory in 1823, but continued to market porcelain in Paris (including their own products from Fours) at a shop on the rue du Temple. In 1842 Jean Pouyat established a factory in Limoges, on the place des Carmes, which achieved great renown in succeeding decades for the production of blancs—white porcelains bearing no painted decoration.

At Jean's death in 1849 the factory was taken over by his three sons, Emile, Léonard, and Charles-Louis, under the name Pouyat Frères; in the same year, the Pouyats opened a second factory at nearby Saint-Léonard. In 1843 the firm produced income in the amount of 278,000 francs; by 1855 the gross income of Pouyat Frères exceeded 700,000 francs (V. Regnault, in Rapports 1855, p. 949). Pouyat Frères won a first-class medal at the 1855 Paris Exposition Universelle (Rapports 1855, p. 949) and a medal at the 1862 International Exhibition in London (Commission Rapport 1862, p. 221). In 1855 Ravenez declared that the firm's exhibit rivaled that of Sèvres and earned "a genuine right to the recognition of the country"; in 1862 Darcel praised Pouyat's porcelain, next to Sèvres, as the leading porcelain, "of a body so thin and so white, and of a form so elegant..." (Darcel, 1863, p. 66). In 1883 A. Dubreuil and the baron de la Bastide succeeded Emile Pouyat in the management of the firm, which adopted the name La Céramique but retained the mark JP/L for Jean Pouyat, Limoges.

K.B.H.

Bibliography:
Ravenez, 1855, pp. 80–87; de Chavagnac and de Grollier, 1906, pp. 438–39, 472, 491–92, 580, 767–68; Gauthier, 1959, pp. 35–39; Hosotte-Reynaud, 1964, pp. 167–72; de Guillebon and Lasserre, 1966, pp. 103–7; de Guillebon, 1972, pp. 268–70, 272–73

## Paul Comoléra

*Paris 1818–1898 Paris*

*A student of François Rude, Comoléra made his Salon debut as an* animalier *in 1847 with a plaster study of* Female Golden Pheasant *(no. 2053), which he exhibited in bronze at the Salon of 1848 (no. 4675). Comoléra continued to exhibit animal sculptures and figure groups at Salons through 1891, in plaster and terra-cotta, or bronze, cast by such firms as Susse. Around 1855 Comoléra accepted a position as* sculpteur *in Limoges with the porcelain firm of Pouyat Frères, who according to Ravenez, sought through Comoléra to reproduce metalwork forms and details in their porcelains. Described by Ravenez as "one of the most distinguished ornamentalists of Paris," Comoléra designed a number of pieces exhibited by Pouyat at the 1855 Exposition Universelle, including the "Cérès Riche" and the "Etruscan" services (Musée Adrien-Dubouché, Limoges). The style of the large footed basin from the "Cérès Riche" service, decorated with palm trees and herons, recalls Comoléra's many bird groups, including* A Wounded Heron *exhibited at the Salon of 1853 (no. 1333).*

K.B.H.

Bibliography:
Ravenez, 1855, p. 83; Lami, 1914–21, vol. I, pp. 412–13; MacKay, 1973, pp. 58–59

Pouyat Frères; designed by Paul Comoléra

## IV-3
## Tureen with Cover and Platter

Designed 1855
Marked in green: JP/L; marked in red: POUYAT FRERES EXPOSITION UNIVERSELLE FRANCAISE 1855, MEDAILLE DE 1ᴱᴿ CLASSE
White hard-paste porcelain, with clear glaze and cast-relief decoration
Tureen height 30 cm, length 52 cm, width 28 cm; platter height 5.8 cm, length 51 cm, width 32.8 cm

Provenance:
Gift of the manufacturer to the Musée Adrien-Dubouché, 1867 (inv. no. 3535)

Exhibition:
1949, Limoges, no. 178

Bibliography:
Ravenez, 1855, p. 84; Tresca, 1855, p. 646; *Catalogue 1855,* no. 5525; V. Regnault, in *Rapports 1855,* p. 949; Gauthier, 1959, p. 39, fig. 1; Giacomotti and Verlet, 1965, p. 69, fig. 25

Part of the "Cérès Riche" service first exhibited by Pouyat at the Paris Exposition Univer-

selle of 1855, the tureen is decorated with molded wheat sheaves and a vegetable bouquet in *biscuit* relief and has handles and feet in the form of leafy stalks. Both the Rococo form of the tureen and its elaborate naturalistic relief decoration recall mid-eighteenth-century examples in metalwork and faïence, but the continuous, flaccid curves which shape its contours convert a Louis XV revival style into proto-Art Nouveau. For Ravenez the linear and elongated handles were "a completely new form." Other pieces bearing similar naturalistic ornament were designed by Comoléra for Pouyat in 1855: an extravagant footed basin in *biscuit* with palm trees and herons, the centerpiece of the "Cérès Riche" service, and a service with wheat stalks in relief commissioned by Alexander II of Russia. At the exposition of 1855 Pouyat Frères was listed as both wholesale supplier and porcelain manufacturer, and a first-class medal was awarded Pouyat in recognition of both aspects of the firm's trade—"for the quality of material and good production." The superior quality of Pouyat's white porcelain body, praised for its "whiteness and transparency," naturally lent itself to Comoléra's bold relief decoration, here left uncolored, or *blanc,* both in the *biscuit* state and under a clear glaze. Arnoux commented that among French manufacturers of porcelain it was Pouyat who showed the material to its greatest advantage "as regards execution as well as beauty of material" (*Reports 1855,* part 2 p. 365).

K.B.H.

Musée National Adrien-Dubouché, Limoges

## Manufacture Impériale de Sèvres

*Vincennes, established 1738; transferred to Sèvres 1756*

*With the coup d'etat of December 1852, subsidy of the national manufactory of Sèvres was returned to the civil list and household budget of the Emperor.*

*By 1869 Sèvres's annual operating budget had increased to 593,600 francs (Arch. nat. 0⁵ 17) from the 307,000 francs allotted by the Second Republic (de Montalivet, 1851, p. 313). Throughout the Second Empire, Victor Regnault was director of the manufactory; appointed in 1852, he remained* administrateur *until his retirement in 1871. Like his predecessor, Jacques-Joseph Ebelmen (1847–52), Regnault, a chemist, was chiefly concerned with technical developments of production, ceding artistic direction to the factory's* chefs des travaux d'art, *Diéterle (q.v., 1852–55) and then Nicolle (q.v., 1856–71).*

*As early as the Exposition Universelle of 1855, Regnault was credited with seeking "to realize improvements on all sides at once, and [for] the variety and excellence of his contributions" (L. Arnoux, in* Reports 1855, *part 2, p. 367). There Sèvres was awarded the Grand Medal of Honor for technical contributions (some of which had been initiated under Ebelmen's direction): a new range of colors, high-firing in both reducing and oxidizing atmospheres; their application in slip reliefs (pâte-sur-pâte) and tinted bodies; reestablishment of soft-paste porcelain production; production of faïence; and establishment of an ornamental metalwork studio (V. Regnault, in* Rapports 1855, *p. 948). These new materials and techniques dominated the reports*

IV-3

of the international exhibitions and were specifically encouraged through imperial commissions, such as the Empress's tea and coffee services in the new soft-paste porcelain (Sèvres Archives Vbb 12 fols. 4, 29 [March 1854, January 1860]) and the Emperor's centerpiece with pâte-sur-pâte ornaments (Sèvres Archives Vbb fol. 15 [June 1856]).

Sèvres also continued to produce porcelains with figurative and landscape decorations (often in eighteenth-century forms and styles, by such artists as François Richard, q.v., Joseph-Ferdinand Regnier, Abel Schilt, and Jules André)—favorite gifts of the Emperor to foreign heads of state (Dussieux, 1876, pp. 218, 240, 335, 355, 394, 402, 518, 603). While its technical and mechanical perfection was unrivaled during the Second Empire—Sèvres won a medal at the London exhibition of 1862 but was hors concours in 1867—a growing concern for the integrity of the ceramic medium, reflected in criticism leveled at Sèvres's traditional illusionistic decorations in the 1850 and 1875 reports of the Conseil and Commission de Perfectionnement, led to radical reforms there later in the century. (See also history preceding no. III-29.)

K.B.H.

Bibliography:
De Lasteyrie, 1850, pp. 137–49; P. Mérimée, in Rapports 1862, vol. VI, p. 255; Duc, 1875, p. 22, passim; Lechevallier-Chevignard, 1908, vol. I, pp. 156–64; 1975, Sèvres, pp. 23–36

Manufacture Impériale de Sèvres; designed by Jules-Pierre-Michel Diéterle, decorated by François Richard

## IV-4
## "Diéterle" Vase

Designed 1851, decorated 1855
Marked under glaze: S.54 [in oval]; marked on glaze: [crowned] N/55 [surrounded by] DECORE A SEVRES; incised: h 54-10
Hard-paste porcelain, with painted decoration
Height 110 cm; diameter (at neck) 38 cm

Provenance:
Entered sale room of Sèvres factory, July 31, 1858 (Sèvres Archives Pb 13, fol. 36); delivered to the Mobilier de la Couronne for the furnishing of the palace of Fontainebleau, by decree of September 15, 1860 (Sèvres Archives Vbb 12); entered Fontainebleau for general service, March 20, 1861; placed in the Salle des Colonnes under the Second Empire; transferred to the Galerie des Cerfs at end of nineteenth century (inv. no. F 236 C)

This type of vase was created in 1851 by Jules Diéterle (q.v.), artiste en chef from 1848 to 1852, then chef des travaux d'art at the Sèvres factory from 1852 to 1855 (Sèvres Archives

IV-4

Vr' l fol. 126 r, v). This particular vase is the work of the tourneur François-Julien Hutray (1824–1877), active in the factory from 1848 to 1875; he began to rough out the vase in August 1854 and worked at it on the wheel until the month of December (Sèvres Archives Va' 46 fol. 50 v). The decoration was painted by François Richard, doreur and peintre-décorateur at Sèvres from 1833 to 1875. Between April 1853 and October 1856 he decorated four such "Diéterle" vases with flowers, butterflies, and insects (three of these are preserved at Fontainebleau in the Musée National du Château). In May 1853 he was given the four lithographic designs that were to be used for their decoration (Sèvres Archives Vj' 59 fol. 40 r; Vq' 6 fol. 133 r). The vase exhibited here was painted between May and October 1855 (Sèvres Archives Vj' 61 fol. 36 r, v), and the artist received 1,300 francs for his work in December of the same year (Sèvres Archives Vq' 6 fol. 162 r).

The form and decoration of the vase are among the original Sèvres creations under the

Second Empire. The death of the director of Sèvres, Alexandre Brongniart, in 1847 and the fall of the July Monarchy signaled in fact a stylistic renewal at the Sèvres factory: the painted cartouches surrounded by palmettes or rosettes in gold and platinum disappeared to make room for purely decorative compositions, and flora and fauna now played a predominant role, literally invading the entire available surface.

B.C.

Musée National du Château, Fontainebleau

Manufacture Impériale de Sèvres; decorated by Guyonnet,* mounts manufactured by Christofle et Cie

## IV-5
## "Cordelier" Vase

Decorated 1857
Marked on glaze: [crowned] N/57 surrounded by DECORE A SEVRES; incised DZ PL11–DL25–11
Hard-paste porcelain, with painted and gilded decoration, and chased and gilded-bronze mounts
Height 69 cm; diameter (at neck) 37 cm

Provenance:
Entered sale room of Sèvres factory, May 31, 1858 (Sèvres Archives Pb 13 fol. 27); delivered to the Mobilier de la Couronne for the furnishing of the palace of Fontainebleau, by decree of September 15, 1860 (Sèvres Archives Vbb 12); entered Fontainebleau for general service, March 20, 1861; in bedroom of apartments of Marie Antoinette, 1894 (inv. no. F 660 C)

The shape of the "Cordelier" vase was created in 1800. The body of this example had been thrown in November 1812 by Louis Petion (1751–1822), tourneur at Sèvres between 1770 and 1817 (Sèvres Archives Va' 19 fol. 52 r, v) and the foot, in November 1825 by Louis Davignon (1785–1827), a Sèvres tourneur since 1803 (Sèvres Archives Va' 26 fol. 78 r). This shows that the different parts of the vases were mass-produced, kept in storage, and mounted when they were decorated.

The intertwined gold monograms of the Emperor and Empress formed from two garlands, one of laurel, the other of roses, are the work of the doreur Guyonnet, active at Sèvres from 1853 to 1857; he decorated this vase from July to October 1857 (Sèvres Archives Vj' 63); he had asked 60 francs for his work, a fee that was reduced to 50 francs (Sèvres Archives Vq' 6).

IV - 5

During the first half of the nineteenth century the handles of "Cordelier" vases generally took the form of a ram's head. However, in 1856, Tranchant, *sculpteur-modeleur* at the factory from 1852 to 1858, was asked to create a new form of handle for this form of vase; from January to May, 1856, he worked on a model in plaster (Sèvres Archives Va' 48 fol. 193; R 57), which he submitted to the management May 29, 1856 (Sèvres Archives, ''Registre d'entrée de modèle de toutes sortes de la Manufacture royale de Sèvres,'' 1847–90). The eleven pairs of bronze handles, made from the plaster model, were cast and gilded by Christofle (q.v.), which presented its bills to the Sèvres factory on June 18, 1856, and October 18, 1858 (Sèvres Archives R 58, R 61); the chasing and mounting were most certainly carried out as customary in the factory's workshops.

This vase seems to have been the first to receive the new type of handles. Their truly extraordinary form, which appears to foreshadow the motifs of Art Nouveau, in fact takes its inspiration from the typical floral repertoire of the period; the transposition of this foliage into three dimensions is surely what bestows its exceptional character.

B.C.

Musée National du Château, Fontainebleau

Manufacture Impériale de Sèvres; designed by Jules-Pierre-Michel Diéterle, gilded by Louis-Joseph Charpentier*

## IV-6
## "Rimini" Vase

Designed 1850; manufactured 1863; gilded 1864; decorated 1867
Mark printed in green under glaze: S.63 [in oval]; printed in red under glaze: [crowned] N/64 [surrounded by] DORE A SEVRES and [crowned] N/67 [surrounded by] DECORE A SEVRES: incised: B.5C.12
Hard-paste porcelain, celadon ground, with painted decoration in blue, and gilding
Height 45.5 cm; diameter 26.7 cm

Provenance:
Entered sale room of Sèvres factory, July 31, 1868 (Sèvres Archives Vr', 1re série, vol. II, fol. 106 v; Vbb 12, fol. 52 [November 1868]); gift of the State to the Musée Adrien-Dubouché, August 1868 (inv. no. 4208)

Exhibition:
1975, Sèvres, no. 552

Designed in 1850 by Jules-Pierre-Michel Diéterle (q.v.; Sèvres Archives Vr', 3e série, vol. I, fol. 85 [April 1850, appréciation en blanc]), then *artiste en chef* at Sèvres, the original version of this vase was praised in Lasteyrie's 1850 report of the Conseil de Perfectionnement (de Lasteyrie, 1850, pp. 139–40) as one of Diéterle's new shapes in the "Italian style." Lasteyrie described the vase, executed in white and blue, as particularly noteworthy for its twisted handles, skillfully cast by Pierre-Adrien-Jacques Derivière, *mouleur*, 1834–51, "in the form of snakes, whose execution in porcelain presented certain difficulties." The vase was reproduced frequently during the Second Empire—on the occasion of the baptism of the Prince Imperial, as an imperial gift (Sèvres Archives Vbb 12, fol. 17 [October 1856]), and in 1864 with painted decorations by Jules-Eugène Humbert.

This version of the vase was valued for sale in July 1868 and presented to the museum at Limoges shortly thereafter. Unlike earlier examples, this one is decorated simply with glaze in Chinese celadon, its ornament restricted to the "Italian-style" Chinese dragon handles modeled in relief, and decorative bands painted at foot, neck, and lid. The vase was gilded by Louis-Joseph Charpentier, a *doreur* at Sèvres in 1852 and from 1854 to 1879. Diéterle himself designed the first examples of colored celadons exhibited by Sèvres—a pair of vases and a cup of "Chinese design" which were shown in London in 1851 (*Crystal Palace 1851*, p. 171). "Bluish celadons," like the present

example, were listed by Regnault as among the new high-firing colors exhibited in 1855 (*Rapports 1855*, p. 948), although by the 1860s when this vase was produced, the range and subtlety of celadon colors—obtained by exposing chrome oxides in both reducing and oxidizing atmospheres—had considerably expanded. With the belly of this vase left otherwise unadorned, color is conceived as a principal means of decoration—a revolutionary Far Eastern-inspired idea introduced at Sèvres about 1850, but demonstrated in only a few examples during the Second Empire. It was, in fact, a recommendation of the 1875 Commission de Perfectionnement that Sèvres pursue its early experiments in Oriental decoration and specifically in the production of Chinese colored glazes (Duc, 1875, pp. 22–25).

K.B.H.

Musée National Adrien-Dubouché, Limoges

## Léopold-Jules-Joseph Gély
### *1820–1893*

*Gély decorated porcelains at Sèvres between 1851 and 1889, specializing in the method of decoration known as* pâte-sur-pâte, *which had been developed at the factory about 1850. Although not the originator of this process of decoration, Gély rapidly became its leading practitioner, and was awarded a second-class medal and a silver medal as* coopérateur *in* pâte-sur-pâte *sculpture at the Paris Expositions Universelles of 1855 and 1867 (V. Regnault, in Rapports 1855, p. 953; Récompensés 1867, p. 22). At the 1855 exposition, the South Kensington Museum (then at Marlborough House) purchased a tray and covered sugar bowl decorated by Gély in* pâte-sur-pâte *(Victoria and Albert Museum, London, 2684a, b-1856), which Richard Redgrave described as "a beautiful and exquisitely finished example of this material. It presents some novelties for the study of our manufacturers in the interchange of celadon green and murrey colour... modelled with gem-like beauty and completion" (Reports 1855, part 3, p. 380). At the exposition of 1867, Léon Arnoux remarked that "for the last 15 years the [Sèvres] manufactory has chiefly directed its exertions on its production [of pâte-sur-pâte], and, thanks to Mr. Gely, they have been crowned with perfect success" (Reports 1867, vol. II, p. 409).*

*Porcelains decorated by Gély in* pâte-sur-pâte *were purchased by the State for Compiègne, including a large basin decorated with birds and flowers (C 385 C), which entered Compiègne in 1863 for the*

IV-6

*Salon des Aides de Camp, and two vases with fables from La Fontaine (C450C), which entered in 1868 for the Salon des Huissiers. In 1868, in addition to acquiring porcelains for the imperial household, the Emperor made gifts of vases decorated by Gély in* pâte-sur-pâte *to the emperor of Austria and the king of Portugal (Dussieux, 1876, pp. 158, 540).*

K.B.H.

Bibliography:
De Chavagnac and de Grollier, 1906, p. 325; Lechevallier-Chevignard, 1908, vol. I, p. 157, vol. II, p. 132

Manufacture Impériale de Sèvres; decorated by Léopold-Jules-Joseph Gély

## IV-7
## "Bijou" Vase

1862
Signed: J. Gély; marked: [crowned] N/62 [surrounded by] DECORE A SEVRES
Hard-paste porcelain, gray ground, with polychrome decoration in *pâte-sur-pâte*
Height 18.5 cm

Provenance:
Registered in works of sculpture and relief studios at Sèvres factory, 1862 (Sèvres Archives Va' 54, fol. 117); entered the Musée National de Céramique, 1863 (inv. no. 5964²)

Exhibition:
1975, Sèvres, no. 169

Bibliography:
Lechevallier-Chevignard, 1908, vol. I, repro. p. 158

This "Bijou" vase, originally covered, was produced at Sèvres in 1862 along with a number of other "Néo-Grec" works by Nicolle (q.v.), Forgeot (q.v.), and Solon (q.v.); a version of the vase was also purchased by the State for Compiègne, and entered there in 1867 for the music room. The form of the vase and the precious quality of its decoration are reminiscent of Hellenistic painted vases from southern Italy, although the form was also adopted during the Renaissance in such examples as the rock crystal vase in the Galerie d'Apollon of the Louvre (MR 299), which entered the collection of Louis XIV between 1684 and 1701 and may well have been known to Gély. To this Classical form, Gély applied Classical ornament in imitation of Roman cameos, a style of decoration current at Sèvres during the late Empire and the Restoration. Here, however, the cameos are not cast in relief like the earlier examples, but painted in thin layers of transparent slip in the

IV-7

new pâte-sur-pâte technique. Gély's particular delicacy of style and handling, as well as his revival of cameos in pâte-sur-pâte, later inspired the Sèvres decorator Taxile Doat (active 1879–1905), who specialized in such pâte-sur-pâte cameo ornaments.

K.B.H.

Musée National de Céramique, Sèvres

## Marc-Louis-Emmanuel Solon

*Montauban 1835–1913 Stoke-on-Trent*

*The process of* pâte-sur-pâte *is most frequently associated with Solon's name—due largely to the enormous success, his* pâte-sur-pâte *decorations brought Minton after he emigrated to England in 1870. Solon received his earliest artistic training in the mid-1850s in the Parisian atelier of Lecoq de Boisbaudran, and pursued independently his interest in decorative and applied art at the Cluny museum and the Louvre, where he studied Greek vases and terra-cottas. Solon etched a series of original designs for decorative bronzes and sculptures, one of which was sold to the director of Sèvres, Victor Regnault. In 1857 Regnault hired Solon as*

décorateur *for Sèvres, where according to Solon, "the process of decoration in 'Pâte sur Pâte' was just on its trial, and M. Regnault thought that my small abilities might be turned in that direction. Nothing could have pleased me more than to be asked to execute some figure subjects in these delicate and transparent reliefs. All facilities were afforded to the artists for the execution of their work; we were never limited as to time or to cost, and I may say that it was only from that moment that I began in earnest my art studies, as applied to decoration"* (Solon, 1894, p. 118).

*In the early 1860s Solon was commissioned by Eugène Rousseau (q.v.) to produce, outside Sèvres, pâte-sur-pâte decorations, which were sold at Rousseau's shop under the acronym "Miles." Solon-Rousseau porcelains were exhibited at the Union Centrale exhibition in 1863* (Rapports 1863, p. 48), *and again in 1865, where "Miles" won a bronze medal for his "modeling with transparent paste on colored grounds... with a good style and with a facile and correct execution" (A. Jacquemart, in Rapports 1865, p. 408). At the Paris Exposition Universelle of 1867, Solon won a bronze medal as coopérateur (Récompensés 1867, p. 23) and Sèvres exhibited a vase decorated by Solon in pâte-sur-pâte described as among the manufactory's "best specimens... the fine vase of antique shape, painted by Mr. Solon, in which the effect of the different shades of white on the dark-greenish colour of the ground is exceedingly good" (L. Arnoux, in Reports 1867, vol. II, p. 410). In 1867 Solon also provided designs for Emile Froment-Meurice (q.v.; Mantz, 1868, p. 132; see also L. Falize, in Rapports 1889, p. 455). At the outbreak of the Franco-Prussian War, Solon left Sèvres for Stoke-on-Trent and Minton, where he designed and painted pâte-sur-pâte decorations until his retirement in 1904, and in a free-lance capacity until his death.*

K.B.H.

Bibliography:
Solon, 1894; 1976, London, Victoria and Albert Museum, pp. 13, 71

Manufacture Impériale de Sèvres; designed by Marc-Louis-Emmanuel Solon, gilded by François-Bernard-Louis Pine*

## IV-8
## Coffeepot

1862
Dated on base: 1862
Hard-paste porcelain, gray celadon ground; painted with white slip and gilded
Height 19.8 cm

Provenance:
Entered sale room of Sèvres factory, March 1862 (Sèvres Archives Vr', 3ᵉ série, vol. II, fol. 280, appréciation en blanc; Vr', 1ʳᵉ série, vol. I, fol. 147 [April 30, 1862], appréciation); purchased for 4 pounds 16 shillings by the South Kensington Museum (now Victoria and Albert Museum, London), 1862; transferred to the Bethnal Green Museum (inv. no. 8055-1862)

Exhibitions:
1862, London; 1962, London, Victoria and Albert Museum, no. 12 (repro.); 1975, London

Bibliography:
Solon, 1866, pl. 5; Aslin, 1973, no. 19 (repro.).

Hitherto unidentified as a design by Solon, the "cafetière éléphant" was first valued for sale at Sèvres in March 1862 and shown by the manufactory at the London International Exhibition soon thereafter. The design was also published as plate 5 in Solon's 1866 book, *Inventions décoratives, choix de compositions et de motifs d'ornementation,* along with a number of other three-dimensional models in the "Néo-Grec" style (pls. 14, 41). Solon did not regularly design ceramic shapes for Sèvres; he was employed as a decorator in *pâte-sur-pâte,* the technique he used for the white slip reliefs in Classical palmette patterns that ornament the body and lid of the coffeepot. In 1869 Burty described the *pâte-sur-pâte* technique as Solon's speciality: "One of the happiest efforts of decoration realized in our day consists in applying white pastes on céladon, toned grey, fresh green, coffee, or clear chocolate.... A young sculptor, M. Solon, has almost made it his own by the skill and taste with which he handles it" (Burty, 1869, *Chefs-d'œuvre,* p. 167). Although isolated examples were shown by Sèvres at the Paris exposition of national manufactories (1850, Paris, Palais National) and the international exhibitions of 1851 and 1855, and commissioned by the Emperor as early as 1856 (Sèvres Archives Vbb 12 fol. 15 [June 1856]), the manufactory's celebrated slip-decorated celadons made their first major appearance in 1862, with the coffeepot among six examples in this technique acquired from the exhibition by the South Kensington Museum. Solon's coffeepot, an original Oriental fantasy, with faint reminiscences of the "vase à éléphants" produced at Sèvres from the 1750s, and a "confiturier égyptien" created there for Napoleon I in 1806–7 (Sèvres Archives), represents one of the more exaggeratedly Romantic "Néo-Grec" designs produced under the direction of Nicolle (q.v.).

K.B.H.

Bethnal Green Museum, London

## Claude-Edouard Forgeot

*Moule (commune of Lays-sur-le-Doubs [Saône-et-Loire]) 1826; active Sèvres 1856–87*

*A student of François Rude, Forgeot made his Salon debut in 1853 with a plaster* Christ on the Cross, *which was commissioned by the* collège *at Gray (1853, Paris, Salon, no. 1348). He continued to exhibit at the Salon and is last mentioned there in 1891 as the winner of an honorable mention ("Récompensés," 1891, p. xv). In 1856 Forgeot accepted a position at Sèvres as* sculpteur-modeleur, *becoming the factory's chief specialist in figure sculptures. At Sèvres, Forgeot modeled figures in several styles, including a Venus after an eighteenth-century model by Pigalle (Musée National de Céramique, Sèvres, 5460) and a flambeau, purchased by the State in 1867 for Compiègne (C 768 C); and the large "Néo-Grec" centerpiece with figures produced between 1862 and 1867. At the Exposition Universelle of 1867, where the centerpiece was shown, Forgeot was awarded a silver medal as* coopérateur *(Récompensés 1867, p. 22). In 1875 the French government presented to the imam of Zanzibar, Forgeot's biscuit portrait bust of Marshal MacMahon, a version of which was also acquired by the Musée Baron Martin at Gray (Dussieux, 1876, p. 614; Catalogue, Gray, Musée Baron Martin, 1959, p. 78, no. 256).*

K.B.H.

Bibliography:
Lechevallier-Chevignard, 1908, vol. II, p. 147

Manufacture Impériale de Sèvres; modeled by Claude-Edouard Forgeot

## IV-9
## Figures from a Centerpiece

1862–67
Hard-paste porcelain, celadon ground, with painted polychrome enamels
Height 72 cm (each)

Provenance:
Entered sale room of Sèvres factory, April 1862 (Sèvres Archives Vr', 3e série, no. 2, fols. 286, 287, 288, appréciation en blanc) and June 14, 1867 (Sèvres Archives Vr', 3e série, no. 3, fol. 185, appréciation en blanc); deposited by the State in the Musée d'Art Décoratif, Troyes, 1896; Musées des Beaux-Arts, Troyes (inv. nos. D.896.3,4)

Bibliography:
L. Arnoux, in *Reports 1867*, vol. II, p. 410; *Art Journal Catalogue 1867,* vol.VI, repro. p. 53; Ducuing, 1868, vol. II, repro. p. 104; Catalogue, Troyes, Musée d'Art Décoratif, 1904, nos. 45, 46; 1975, Sèvres, no. 343

IV-8

IV-9

These two figures—a *porte-étagère* and a *porte-lumière*—were part of the same table centerpiece, the *surtout aux figures* designed by Forgeot between 1862 and 1867. Originally the *porte-étagère* held a gilt-bronze tray with putti and sweetmeat dishes (a sort of *marchande d'amours*) and the *porte-lumière*, a mount for candles. Of the five pieces included in the centerpiece, all modeled with classically draped female figures, the *porte-étagère* was the second produced (in April 1862), following by a month the *surtout's* central group, a *porte-bouquet*. The *surtout* was not completed until June 1867, when three more pieces were registered for sale: a jardiniere with four reclining Seasons, a candelabrum, and the *porte-lumière*. The *surtout* was shown by Sèvres at the 1867 Exposition Universelle in Paris, where the highly stylized polychromy of the jardiniere's celadon-colored figures shocked Arnoux: "The first impression is one of surprise; being so unlike what the eye has been used to, it is hard to determine whether to like it or not, and those greenish figures, with dresses of different shades of neutral tints, have certainly a strange look. Fortunately, there are some touches of gold here and there to relieve the whole. The composition is creditable to the modeller, Mr. Forgeot, who has also modelled the other pieces of the same set, but with less success, the pretension to quaintness being carried too far. We prefer his graceful *etagère*, in the form of a standing female figure, holding a ring of bronze gilt, in which are fitted four tazzas with cupids seated between" (*Reports 1867*, vol. II, p. 410). By 1867 Forgeot's archaeologically conceived version of the "Néo-Grec" style should have come as no surprise to Arnoux, despite its fanciful polychromy. Freely following the fashion set by the furnishings and decorations of the "Maison Pompéienne" (1856–60; no. I-22), including Christofle's *surtout* with accurately reproduced polychromed figures of Classical muses (Bouilhet, 1908–12, vol. II, repro. p. 289), Forgeot's classicizing figures are less radical than other "Néo-Grec" pieces produced at Sèvres during the 1860s (*see* no. IV-10). In their decorative and utilitarian function, their elaborate costumes (the *porte-lumière* wearing an aegis-like ornament with lion's head), and their slender proportions, the figures seem to reflect a Roman adaptation of Hellenistic models—a "Néo-Grec" invention by Forgeot in the decorative manner of Roman eclecticism.

K.B.H.

Musées des Beaux-Arts, Troyes

## Joseph Nicolle

*Santenay (Côte-d'Or) 1810–1887 Paris*

At his death in 1887 Nicolle was mourned as an architect who had never fulfilled his youthful promise: "There was certainly within the soul of Nicolle the [undeveloped] germ of the genius of architecture" ("Nicolle," 1887). As early as 1859 he was regarded as an artist of talent and originality who had not received the recognition or the commissions his talents merited (Daly, 1859, p. 70). One of the younger generation of Romantic Rationalist architects who practiced during the Second Empire, Nicolle studied architecture from 1826, first with Louis-Pierre Baltard, and then in 1832, with Duban (q.v.) at the Ecole des Beaux-Arts. He made his debut at the Salon of 1833 with a project for a public fountain. During the 1830s Nicolle traveled in Italy and Sicily. In 1842 he opened his own atelier in Paris and served first as sous-inspecteur under Théodore Ballu at the Church of Sainte Clotilde (1849–57) and later as architecte en second under François-Alexis Cendrier at the Gare de Lyon (1859–60). At the Salon of 1852 he was awarded a second-class medal, and in 1864, received the Legion of Honor.

In 1856 Nicolle replaced Diéterle (q.v.) at Sèvres as chef des travaux d'art and administrateur-adjoint to Regnault—and although he continued to practice architecture (including a project submitted in competition for the Paris Opéra), his activities were thereafter chiefly restricted to the manufactory. As chef des travaux d'art at Sèvres, Nicolle bore responsibility for the aesthetic quality of the production. César Daly defended what he termed the "happy influence" of his colleague against the "presumptuous incapacity" of Regnault. During the 1860s Nicolle seems to have inspired a "Néo-Grec" movement among designers at Sèvres (for example, Solon, Forgeot, Gély, q.q.v.), and Nicolle was himself an inventive designer of shapes to whom his successors at Sèvres, including Carrier-Belleuse (q.v.), were indebted. In 1871, following the Franco-Prussian War, Nicolle was retired from Sèvres with Regnault.

K.B.H.

Bibliography:
Daly, 1887, pp. 245–46; "Nicolle," 1887; Lechevallier-Chevignard, 1908, vol. I, p. 157, vol. II, p. 124

IV - 10

Manufacture Impériale de Sèvres; designed by Joseph Nicolle, ornamented by Adolphe-Théodore-Jean Briffaut* and Jean-Charles-Girard Derichsweiler*

## IV-10
## "Nicolle" Jug

Designed 1862, manufactured 1867
Mark printed in green under glaze: S.67 [in oval]; printed in red under glaze: [crowned] N/67
Hard-paste porcelain, celadon ground, with painted enamel decorations and gilding
Height 31 cm

Provenance:
Registered in works of sculpture and relief studios (Sèvres Archives Va', no. 59, fol. 45) and painting and gilding studios at Sèvres factory, 1867 (Sèvres Archives Vj', no. 73, fol. 54); Musée National de Céramique, 1869 (inv. no. 6747)

Exhibition:
1975, Sèvres, no. 179

Recalling sources in ancient metalwork, the form of Nicolle's jug is derived from an Etruscan beaked oinochoe with acrobat handle, transformed by way of the seventeenth century in its high, narrow proportions and sculptural preciosity. The ornament, applied by Adolphe-Théodore-Jean Briffaut (*sculpteur* at Sèvres, 1848–90) and by Jean-Charles-Girard Derichsweiler (*décorateur* at Sèvres, 1855–84), refers to Classical Greek precedents, with the belly of the jug decorated with palmettes and lotuses and the foot with grooved tongues. Like other Romantic Rationalist architects, Nicolle taught the "Néo-Grec" style in his atelier; he was remembered by a student for his understanding of antiquity and for numerous drawings after the Antique which he had made in Italy (Hardy, 1887). In this radical example of "Néo-Grec" design, the highly evocative silhouette, the sinuous interplay of human and abstract shapes, and the sense of continuous curvilinear movement anticipate essential elements of Art Nouveau.

K.B.H.

Musée National de Céramique, Sèvres

## Antoine-Léon Brunel-Rocque

*Paris 1822; active Sèvres 1852–55, 1859–83*

*A student of the Ingriste painter Amaury-Duval (q.v.), Brunel-Rocque made his Salon debut in 1844 and until 1880 regularly exhibited portraits and religious and genre subjects in classicizing styles. In 1852 Brunel-Rocque accepted a position as a figure painter at Sèvres, where he spent almost his whole career decorating vases with miniature subject paintings—a practice which had been criticized in the 1850 report of the Conseil de Perfectionnement but which continued to be favored by the imperial family. In 1856 the Emperor gave Prince Albert a large porcelain vase which Brunel-Rocque had decorated with an allegory of world powers bringing their national products to the Paris Exposition Universelle of 1855 (Dussieux, 1876, p. 295). At the Paris exposition of 1867, Brunel-Rocque was awarded a bronze medal as coopérateur (Récompensés 1867, p. 23). In addition to his work at Sèvres, in 1857 Brunel-Rocque was commissioned to paint the altarpiece for the chapel of Saint Cecilia in the Church of Saint Eustache—a Saint Cecilia and Tiburtius Crowned—for which the artist was paid 1,500 francs (Inventaire général, 1878–86, vol. I, p. 84). In 1874 Brunel-Rocque was listed as professor of painting on faïence and porcelain at the Ecole Nationale de Dessin pour les Jeunes Filles (Bulletin de l'Union Centrale, vol. 1, no. 6, January 1875, p. 153).*

K.B.H.

Bibliography:
Lechevallier-Chevignard, 1908, vol. II, p. 128

Manufacture Impériale de Sèvres; painted by Antoine-Léon Brunel-Rocque

## IV-11
## Vase Commemorating the Visit of the Empress Eugénie to Amiens during the Cholera Epidemic of 1866

1867
Signed and dated: Brunel 1867; inscribed: A
EUGENIE IMPERATRICE PARIS–AMIENS 1865–66 [en-

IV-11

circled by] SEMPER HONOS NOMEN QUE TUUM LAUDES QUE MANEBUNT
Hard-paste porcelain, with enamel decoration and gilding
Height 91 cm; diameter 41 cm

Provenance:
Registered in works of painting and gilding studios at Sèvres factory, 1867 (Sèvres Archives Vj', no. 73, fol. 12; Vv, no. 7, fol. 62); registered at Sèvres for delivery May 9, 1870 (Sèvres Archives Vbb, fol. 56; Vbb bis, no. 1, fol. 191v–192); gift of Napoleon III to the city of Amiens; Musée de Picardie

Bibliography:
Catalogue, Amiens, Musée de Picardie, 1876, p. 198, no. 2137

From the summer of 1865 to the winter of 1866 there were many outbreaks of cholera throughout France, the worst epidemic since 1832. On June 30, 1866, the Emperor sent the Minister of Agriculture and Commerce and the Inspector of Medical Services to Amiens, where the epidemic had been particularly severe, and contributed in his own name and that of the Prince Imperial 5,000 francs and 1,000 francs, respectively, for the relief of the victims (*Le Moniteur,* July 4, 1866). Four days later, on July 4, the Empress herself made a charitable visit to Amiens, inspecting hospitals and other institutions (*Le Moniteur,* July 5, 1866). Although the Empress's visit was unannounced, she was apparently greeted with much acclaim and gratitude by the citizens of Amiens: Prosper Mérimée described her visit as "not very reasonable, but noble" (Mérimée to Panizzi, July 5, 1866, in Mérimée, 1881, vol. II, p. 125). In December 1865 the Empress had visited the cholera-stricken at the Beaujon hospital in Paris, an event commemorated by the Municipal Council in 1866 with a bronze medal (*Inventaire général,* 1878–89, vol. II, p. 501). To record the Empress's visit to Amiens, this vase, decorated by Brunel-Rocque, was commissioned from Sèvres. Payments were made to Brunel-Rocque in 1866 and 1867 for a "vase... painting of figures, the Empress during the cholera [epidemic]," which included 500 francs for the original oil composition (signed "Brunel, 1866," now in the Musée National du Château de Compiègne, MMPO 208) and 1,500 francs for the execution of the vase. The vase was valued for sale at Sèvres in June 1867 in the amount of 6,200 francs, and delivered to Amiens's "Musée Napoléon in the name of S. M. the Emperor" by May 1870.

Within an oval cartouche on a classic amphora, the Empress Eugénie is shown triumphant over the dragon Cholera, which lies at her feet, framed by allegorical figures of Paris and Amiens. Noted as a painter of religious subjects, Brunel-Rocque deliberately referred to Christian iconography in his image of the Empress, who, cast in the attitude of a victorious saint, expunges the evil disease. Brunel-Rocque's conventional classicism, referring to Raphaelesque precedents in sixteenth- and seventeenth-century religious paintings, was a style particularly suited both to the ceremonial nature of the gift and to the conservative tastes of his patrons and audience.

K.B.H.

Musée de Picardie, Amiens

# Earthenware and Stoneware

## Charles-Jean Avisseau
*Tours 1796–1861 Tours*

In 1843 Avisseau established in Tours a small family-operated faïence manufactory specializing in works in the style of the sixteenth-century potter Bernard Palissy. Avisseau's rustic recreations of plants and animals colored with lead glazes combined Romantic antiquarian and naturalistic interests already prevalent in France during the 1840s, although he was first to discover them in Palissy. In recreating Palissy's ceramic techniques and processes, Avisseau led the revival of artistic faïence in France. Although certain critics complained that in regard to design his pottery was imitative and non-utilitarian (L. Arnoux, in Reports 1855, part 2, pp. 357–58), his technical achievements were consistently praised (Bougon, in Rapport 1849, vol. II, p. 852; Salvetat, in Rapports 1855, p. 944) and regarded posthumously as the way of progress in the industry (A. Girard, in Rapports 1867, vol. III, pp. 152–53; V. de Luynes, in Rapports 1871, p. 123).

Apprenticed at an early age in a faïence factory at Saint-Pierre-des-Corps, Avisseau in 1825 was appointed surveillant-contremaître in the baron de Bezeval's ceramic manufactory at Beaumont-les-Autels (Eure-et-Loire). There he first saw a dish by Palissy, but it was not until almost two decades later that Avisseau began independent and successful production of Palissy ware at his establishment in the rue Saint Maurice in Tours. In 1845 Brongniart purchased a dish for the Musée Céramique at Sèvres (q.v.), and this official recognition was followed by a number of important commissions, including an epergne for Princess Mathilde.

In 1849 Avisseau won an honorable mention in the Exposition des Produits de l'Industrie in Paris; in 1851 and 1855 he exhibited in the universal exhibitions in London and Paris, receiving in the latter a second-class medal. At the request of the Municipal Council of Tours, Avisseau made for the official visit of Louis Napoleon to Tours, October 15, 1852, a footed dish which decorated the Prince-President's apartment in the Prefecture (Journal d'Indre-et-Loire, October 19, 1852). During the 1850s Avisseau's production expanded through the collaboration of family members, including his son Edouard, daughter Caroline, and brother-in-law Joseph Landais, and his assistants Léon Brard and Auguste Chauvigne. After Avisseau's death, the Municipal Council purchased two objects from his studio for the museum (Le Monde Illustré, February 23, 1861, p. 122) and organized a public subscription for his funerary monument, dedicated to the "renovator of the art of Bernard Palissy."

K.B.H.

Bibliography:
*Journal d'Indre-et-Loire,* September 28, 1846; Dussieux, 1856, pp. 78, 152, 192, 246, 378; Morain de Sourdeval, 1859; Giraudet, 1885, pp. 9–10; Carré de Busserolle, 1966, vol. I, pp. 91–92; Maury, 1970; Heuser, 1974, pp. 58–67

IV-12

Charles-Jean Avisseau

### IV-12
### Dish

1854
Signed and dated: Avisseau à Tours 1854; marked: AV [monogram]
Earthenware, decorated with colored lead glazes
Height 19 cm; length 62 cm; width 50 cm

Provenance:
Maître Faucheux, Tours; purchased by the Musée des Beaux-Arts, Tours, 1922 (inv. no. 922-601-1)
Exhibitions:
1934, Tours, no. 225; 1974, Tours

Although Avisseau was criticized as a mere imitator of Palissy, his works, such as this dish, are not direct copies of actual sixteenth-century pieces, but rather free inventions in the style of Palissy's "figulines rustiques." In order to reproduce the natural colors of his models, Avisseau, like Palissy, experimented with low-temperature lead glazes colored with different metallic oxides: iron oxide for yellow glazes; manganese and cobalt oxides for violet; cobalt oxide for blue; copper oxide for green; iron and manganese oxides for yellow-brown (according to Deck, 1887, p. 243). These colored glazes were difficult to control as they fused at close but different temperatures, as Palissy himself had complained: "The green for the lizards was burned before the color for the snakes had melted, and the color for the snakes had fluxed before the white had acquired any beauty" (Palissy, 1961, p. 319). Avisseau's palette, however, is broader than that of Palissy, the enamels brighter and shinier; these drew particular praise from the exhibition reporter of 1849: "The variety of the colors, their freshness and the transparency of the glaze create a beautiful effect" (Bougon, in *Rapport 1849*, vol. II, p. 852). Moreover, while Palissy's plant and animal forms were cast from nature, Avisseau's were freely modeled "and never twice recopied" (Morain de Sourdeval, 1859, p. 2). Bougon praised the "originality and diversity" of Avisseau's subjects, "skillfully imitated in form and color," and Burty considered Avisseau's naturalistic models more "artistic" than Palissy's casts (Burty, 1869, *Chefs-d'œuvre*, pp. 93–94). In 1849 Bougon reported that Avisseau himself modeled, painted, fired, and sold all works that issued from his shop—an integrated potting process which Victor de Luynes viewed in the works of Edouard Avisseau as a mark of the craftsman's integrity and originality: "Heir to the processes of his father, Avisseau knows how to stamp his works with complete originality. All of his works are made by hand—he never uses a mold. At once a naturalist, modeler, painter, enameler, and firer, he finds the time to compose the subjects that he then executes himself" (*Rapports 1871*, p. 124).

Despite the collaboration of his family from the 1850s, Avisseau's production remained limited and costly. That Avisseau consciously strove to create works of art rather than wares for a commercial market is evidenced by his "obstinate" refusal to counterfeit Palissy for "the rich merchants of Paris and London who would have sold the works as authentic" (*Gazette des Beaux-Arts*, vol. IX, 3rd year, March 1861, p. 318); consequently, all pieces produced by Avisseau bear, as does this dish, his signature and/or monogram.

K.B.H.

Musée des Beaux-Arts, Tours

## Eugène-Victor Collinot

*Died 1882 Paris*

*In 1859 Collinot and Adalbert de Beaumont published the* Recueil de dessins pour l'art et l'industrie—*a design book of European and Near and Far Eastern architecture and objects seen by the authors in their travels. The* Recueil *created the earliest interest in Near Eastern ceramics and glass among French applied artists, and it was in this style that Collinot and de Beaumont specialized when they established a faïence manufactory in 1863. The factory's kiln and workshop—described by Burty as "one of the greatest curiosities of the new Bois de Boulogne... decorated with blue and white Islamic dishes"—was located on the boulevard d'Auteuil in the Parc des Princes (Boulogne-sur-Seine, now Boulogne-Billancourt).*

*Collinot first exhibited "Persian" faïence from his manufactory "with the artistic collaboration of M. Adalbert de Beaumont" in 1863 at the Union Centrale* (Union Centrale 1863, p. 106). *There, he and de Beaumont both won first-class medals, Collinot for the production of Persian wares, de Beaumont for "the promotion of the industry in France" and for "publications which furnished industries with models of Persian ornament" (Rapports 1863, p. 45). In 1865 the ceramics of Collinot and de Beaumont were praised for their "superiority... the ideal in utilitarian ceramics and luxury wares" (H. Trianon, in* Rapports 1865, *p. 155) and in the same year, Collinot was decorated by the shah of Persia for having "revived Persian ceramic art" (Catalogue 1869, p. 203). Collinot's manufactory reached the height of its success at the Paris Exposition Universelle of 1867, with a silver medal and extravagant praise from the exhibition reporter, who commented that "for the reproduction of Oriental faïence, M. Collinot is second to none..." (A. Girard, in* Rapports 1867, *vol. III, p. 155). Collinot was compared to Deck (q.v.) and found, if less original, more skillful and sure as a ceramist (A. Girard, in* Rapports 1867, *vol. III, p. 154). At the Union Centrale exhibition of 1869, Collinot both exhibited Persian wares from his manufactory (he was* hors concours) *and lent original Islamic material to the Union's "Musée Oriental" (1869, Paris, "Musée Oriental," pp. 37, 39). After de Beaumont's death in 1869, Collinot seems to have received artistic advice from Adrien Dubouché, director of the museum at Limoges, in the design of certain exhibition pieces (Burty, 1869, "Industries," p. 543). During the 1870s Collinot exhibited predominantly Islamizing works, and his collection in 1878 was judged "the most beautiful exhibit in Ceramics" (de Liesville, 1878, p. 680).*

K.B.H.

Bibliography:
Burty, 1869, *Chefs-d'œuvre*, pp. 116–17

Eugène-Victor Collinot

## IV-13
## Footed Bowl

1867
Signed on base: EC 60 B
Earthenware, with polychrome enamel decoration partly formed in relief and outlined
Height 13 cm; diameter 23.5 cm

Provenance:
Purchased from the maker for 3 pounds 4 shillings by the South Kensington Museum (now Victoria and Albert Museum, London), 1867; transferred to the Bethnal Green Museum (inv. no. 742-1869)

Exhibition:
1867, Paris, Exposition Universelle

Although at the 1867 Exposition Universelle, Collinot was listed as an exhibitor of "Persian" faïences (*Récompensés 1867*) and known as a specialist in Near Eastern styles and decorative techniques, this bowl (one of a pair), and other works by him exhibited in 1867, place Collinot, like Bracquemond (q.v.) and Escallier (q.v.), among the early enthusiasts for Japanese art. Japanese designs were prominent in Collinot's 1859 *Recueil de dessins pour l'art et l'industrie*, providing an early, if not immediately influential, source for French artists. The bird and flowering branch design that decorates the bowl was later published by Collinot in his 1883 *Ornements du Japon* (pl. 35). The design is colored with thickened enamel and outlined in black, giving it a slight relief and somewhat the appearance of wire fillets separating the colored fields of cloisonné enamels. This decorative technique was invented by Collinot and described in detail by Girard in his 1867 exhibition report: "Over the ground—sometimes white, sometimes colored—Collinot lightly sprinkles flowers to which he gives considerable relief by successive thicknesses of enamel. A special process allows him to terminate the contours with absolute precision; this process consists of outlining each flower, using a copper compound, with a line of color which when fired forms a metallic cell; this confines the enamel and prevents it from running onto the ground" (A. Girard, in *Rapports 1867*, vol. III, pp. 155–56).

Deck discounted Collinot's (and Girard's) claim that these outlines kept the colored enamels physically separate in the manner of cloisons, and complained that the process was improperly termed "cloisonné": "Collinot and Adalbert de Beaumont introduced what is improperly called 'cloisonné enamel,' the production of which consists of encircling the decorative motifs with a black line to which they

IV-13

ascribe the property of retaining the enamel" (Deck, 1887, p. 217). Deck also criticized Collinot's Persian wares as improperly and inauthentically decorated; this suggests that whatever early association may have existed between the artists (Burty, 1869, *Chefs-d'œuvre*, pp. 116–17), their competition in the Near Eastern fashion in ceramics had made them rivals. At the exposition of 1867, Deck and Collinot were compared by all observers (D. Wyatt, in *Reports 1867*, vol. II, p. 328; L. Arnoux, in *Reports 1867*, vol. II, p. 398; A. Girard, in *Rapports 1867*, vol. III, p. 155) and awarded equal prizes.

K.B.H.

Bethnal Green Museum, London

---

## Joseph-Théodore Deck

*Guebwiller (Alsace) 1823–1891 Sèvres*

*Théodore Deck was the most influential and technically progressive ceramist in France in the second half of the nineteenth century. At his faïence factory in Paris in the late 1850s and 1860s, Deck developed grounds inlaid with colored clays in the* style of Saint Porchaire earthenwares, "Persian" enamel colors, and luster glazes from Hispano-Moresque pottery, and in the 1870s produced "Chinese" transparent and cloisonné enamels and flambé glazes, and gold grounds inspired by Venetian mosaics. In his book La Faïence (1887), Deck provided formulas and technical instructions for the manufacture of his ceramics. Also in 1887 Deck was appointed administrateur at Sèvres, the first practicing potter to achieve that distinction.

*After coming to Paris from Strasbourg in 1851, Deck worked for the firm of Dumas, which produced glazed earthenware stoves with inlaid decorations. By about 1856 Deck was decorating and firing ceramics for himself, the earliest of which were sold to Victor Paillard, the bronze manufacturer, and to Eugène Rousseau (q.v.). By 1858 he had established his own kiln and atelier on the boulevard Saint Jacques, where such artists as Jean-Louis Hamon (q.v.), Victor Ranvier, Eugène Gluck, Bracquemond (q.v.), and Escallier (q.v.) decorated ceramics which Deck produced. At the Paris Exposition des Produits de l'Industrie in 1861, Deck first exhibited his innovative Islamic earthenwares, won a silver medal, and praise for faïence "whose dazzling hues seem like electric sparks" (Dalloz, 1861), although it was pointed out that the glazes tended to craze. At the London International Exhibition of 1862, Deck introduced his metallic luster glazes with a copy of the "Alhambra" vase, and won a medal, despite continued criticism for crazing and underfired bodies*

(Darcel, 1863, p. 71). Although his technical difficulties persisted through the 1860s, Deck was awarded a first-class medal and Prize of Honor at the Union Centrale exhibitions of 1863 and 1865 respectively (Ménard, 1876, p. 140; Rapports 1863, p. 46), and a silver medal at the Exposition Universelle of 1867 (A. Girard, in Rapports 1867, vol. III, pp. 154–55). By 1867 Deck was considered "in the first rank of French faïence makers" (L. Arnoux, in Reports 1867, vol. II, p. 398), and in 1871 the acknowledged "lead[er] in ceramic art... an artist of great, recognized, and appreciated ability" (Art Journal Catalogue 1871, vol. X, p. 59). In 1874 Deck joined Sèvres's Commission de Perfectionnement and later ceded direction of his atelier to his brother Xavier when he became administrateur at Sèvres.

K.B.H.

Bibliography:
Ménard, 1876; Gerspach, 1882–83; Deck, 1887; Gerspach, 1890–91; Lechevallier-Chevignard, 1908, vol. II, pp. 17–20; Heuser, 1974, pp. 68–82 (bibl.)

---

Joseph-Théodore Deck

## IV-14
## Dish

1867
Incised: TH. DECK
Earthenware, with polychrome enamel decoration on and under glaze
Height 7.2 cm; diameter 41.2 cm

Provenance:
Purchased by subscription from the Paris Exposition Universelle of 1867; Musée Adrien-Dubouché, November 1867 (inv. no. 6823)

Exhibition:
1867, Paris, Exposition Universelle

This dish is characteristic of Deck's "Persian" faïence, which he developed through much research in the later 1850s and first exhibited publicly in 1861 at the Exposition des Produits de l'Industrie in Paris. It was his ambition to study the fabrication of Near Eastern pottery and to create works which might be comparable to their prototypes "in the brilliance and seductiveness of the colors" (Deck, 1887, p. 245). About 1856 Deck acquired an Islamic tile, decorated, as he discovered (and as is typical of such wares), first with a white alkaline slip containing tin oxide and then with a transparent glaze applied over enamel colors. It was this primary technique of applying a white slip ground that Deck adopted from Islamic pottery.

His formula for "white or Persian slip" contains frit, tin enamel, and white earth (Deck, 1887, p. 250). When fired, the white ground provides a uniform, slightly translucent surface for decoration, and the enamel colors, set off and fused against it and the clear glaze above, appear pure, vibrant, and luminescent. Prominent in the decoration of this dish is Deck's most famous color, his Persian blue—a turquoise later known as "bleu de Deck"—which was described by a contemporary as "deep, limpid, pure in tone... transparent" (Gerspach, 1882–83, p. 292).

In regard to the style of his Islamic wares, Deck frequently copied floral decorations from specific Turkish (Isnik—at that time called Rhodian) sixteenth- and seventeenth-century pieces: a dish made by Deck in 1866 (Musée Adrien-Dubouché, Limoges, 6812) reproduces a design from an Isnik dish then in the museum at Sèvres, which Deck later illustrated as figure 10 in *La Faïence*. In other works—as in this dish—Deck assembled motifs from various Isnik prototypes; because of the originality and application of their colors, they were described as important "departures from the pure imitation" of Oriental wares (A. Jacquemart, in *Rapports 1865*, p. 406). Other versions of this dish are reproduced by Maury (1969, p. 38) and H. Ludwig (1972, Munich, pp. 28–30, no. 86).

K.B.H.

Musée National Adrien-Dubouché, Limoges

Joseph-Théodore Deck

## IV-15
## Vase

1867
Impressed on base: T-D
Cream earthenware, with impressed and incised decoration colored in red enamel
Height 36 cm; diameter 23.5 cm

Provenance:
Purchased from the maker for 6 pounds by the South Kensington Museum (now Victoria and Albert Museum, London), 1867; transferred to the Bethnal Green Museum (inv. no. 705a-1869)

Exhibitions:
1867, Paris, Exposition Universelle; 1972, Munich, no. 197, repro. p. 39

Bibliography:
Aslin, 1973, no. 25 (repro.)

It was Adalbert de Beaumont who, according to Burty, first led Théodore Deck to the study of Near Eastern ceramics and glass: "The Brothers Deck were first urged to imitate Oriental—and especially Persian—produce, by M. Adalbert de Beaumont.... It was he who directed all the first attempts of the Brothers Deck" (Burty, 1869, *Chefs-d'œuvre*, pp. 116–17). Despite Théodore Deck's later criticism of de Beaumont's (and Collinot's) ceramic wares (*see* no. IV-13), the form of this vase as well as the armorial device inscribed in cartouches around the neck derive from a fourteenth-century Islamic glass mosque lamp from the collection of Alphonse de Rothschild, reproduced by de Beaumont and Collinot in their 1859 *Recueil de dessins* (pls. 58, 73). Deck, however, transformed the Rothschild lamp from glass to earthenware and the Arabic inscriptions that cover its surface into a floral ground based on fourteenth-century Islamic decorations—a style adopted by Brocard (q.v.) in an Islamic-style glass lamp, which was also exhibited in 1867 (Österreichisches Museum für angewandte Kunst, Vienna, 7552/G1553). This was not Deck's first use of the mosque lamp form: in 1864, at the second exhibition of the Société du Progrès de l'Art Industriel (of which Deck was the only member among the exhibiting artists), he showed a similar vase decorated with inlaid enamels, which was described as an "Arabic vase in cloisonné enamels. The form is taken from the mosque lamps of Cairo" (1864, Paris, Société du Progrès, no. 5). From this exhibition the South Kensington Museum purchased four pieces by Deck, having previously purchased three of Deck's works at the London International Exhibition of 1862. This earthenware vase, one of a pair, was acquired by the museum from the 1867 Paris Exposition Universelle.

K.B.H.

Bethnal Green Museum, London

IV-14

---

*Marie-Caroline-Eléonore Légerot Escallier*

*Poligny (Jura) 1827–1888 Sèvres*

*A pupil of the history painter and potter Jules-Claude Ziégler, Eléonore Escallier made her Salon debut in 1857 with two flower paintings (nos. 900,*

IV-15

chives N 6 [June 26, 1869]). In 1874, when Deck
was made a member of Sèvres's Commission de Perfectionnement, Escallier entered the national manufactory as a flower and animal painter. She remained at Sèvres until her death and is recorded
there, along with Gély (q.v.), as a specialist in colored slip reliefs.

K.B.H.

Bibliography:
Lechevallier-Chevignard, 1908, vol. I, p. 157, vol. II,
p. 131; Heuser, 1974, p. 70

Produced by Joseph-Théodore Deck; designed
and painted by Marie-Caroline-Eléonore Légerot Escallier

## IV-16
## Dish

1867
Signed: E. Escallier; on reverse: T.H. DECK 1867
Earthenware, with decoration partly in relief
and painted on and under glaze
Diameter 60 cm

Provenance:
Peter Rose and Albert Gallichan

Bibliography:
A. Girard, in *Rapports 1867*, vol. III, pp. 154–55

Decorated with a pair of Central American
quetzals *(Pharomachrus mocino)*, laburnum
*(Laburnum vulgare)*, and plum *(Prunus)*
branches and a hellebore *(Helleborus)* plant, this
dish is identical to one shown by Escallier at the
Paris Exposition Universelle of 1867 and acquired by the Musée des Arts Décoratifs
(20475B). Another dish of nearly equal dimensions, decorated with a single male quetzal,
was also exhibited by Escallier in 1867 and
purchased from the exposition by the South
Kensington Museum (Victoria and Albert
Museum, London, 703-1869). These exotic
bird dishes, designed and painted by Escallier
and manufactured by Deck, received particular
praise for both their style and their technique
from the exhibition reporter: "These magnificent plates on which Mme Escallier has painted
such beautiful blue birds.... The effect produced in these principal pieces, where the subject, modeled by means of layers, stands out
vigorously against the white or colored ground,
is as picturesque as it is striking" (A. Girard, in
*Rapports 1867*, vol. III, p. 155). By the late 1860s
Deck had begun to develop a range of transparent colored enamels—particularly blue and

901). From 1857 to 1859 she worked both in Paris
and in Dijon—where Ziégler had briefly been director of the Ecole des Beaux-Arts. Like her master,
Escallier was both painter and ceramist, exhibiting
fruit and flower paintings at the Salons through
1880 and at the same time decorating and exhibiting
ceramics. Although her ceramic techniques owe
nothing to Ziégler's salt-glazed stonewares, the exotic
style of his Moorish vases may have led her, about
1860, to the studio of Théodore Deck (q.v.), who was
then experimenting with Islamic ceramic techniques
and decorations. Deck's first public exhibition of
ceramics in 1861 included pieces that were decorated
by various artists and sold, according to Deck's usual
arrangement, at profits divided equally between decorator and potter. Escallier was invariably listed
among Deck's earliest collaborators (Ménard, 1876,
p. 139; Gerspach, 1882–83, p. 296), although by

1863 she was listed as a "new exhibitor" under her
own name at the Union Centrale exhibition (Union
Centrale 1863, "Table du supplement," no. 81
bis).

In 1866, explaining that she raised her family
with the "remuneration of her talent," Escallier
petitioned the State to purchase her painting Flowers from the Salon exhibition (no. 672), and it was
acquired for the museum of Lons-le-Saunier for
1,500 francs (1974, Paris, Grand Palais, p. 68,
no. 76). By the late 1860s her fortunes had improved: at the Paris Exposition Universelle of 1867,
ceramics she decorated for Deck were purchased by
the South Kensington Museum for 20 pounds; in
1868 she was awarded a medal for her Salon paintings ("Recompenses," 1868, p. xxix); and in 1869 a
Salon painting, Chrysanthemums (no. 885) was
purchased by the State for 1,200 francs (Louvre Ar-

turquoise blue—which could, as in the almost iridescent crest and tail covert of the quetzals, be applied independently in layers or over modeled reliefs. Deck himself described this method: "The thicker the enamel, the more powerful the effect; the modeling can be achieved by means of accumulation, or with a white relief as the ground" (Deck, 1887, p. 265).

In style this naturalistic and Japanizing design of Escallier breaks with the predominantly Persian and genre subjects then popular among Deck and his collaborators, and with the traditional still lifes which Escallier herself continued to paint for the Salon exhibitions. Although the quetzal is indigenous to Central America and the flowering trees and plant to Europe and Asia, they were apparently known to Escallier from the Jardin des Plantes or from prints. Their asymmetrical arrangement on an otherwise unadorned and borderless ground surface suggests a new Japanizing influence. As innovative, if not perhaps as influential, as the Bracquemond-Rousseau service also first exhibited in 1867 (no. IV-18), Escallier's dish anticipates a more independent, interpretive, Japanizing style in French ceramics of the 1870s. In 1878 Escallier's were among the "very Japanese" works exhibited by Sèvres,

where de Liesville noted a tendency toward "large, simplified, and intensely colored decorations" created "under the influence of Asiatic models" (de Liesville, 1878, p. 682).

K.B.H.

Collection Peter Rose and Albert Gallichan

## Camille Nélaton Moreau
### Paris 1840–1897 Paris

*Daughter of a Parisian surgeon, Camille Nélaton first studied drawing in the studio of her uncle Jules Nélaton. There she met the watercolorist and engraver Adolphe F. Moreau, whom she married in 1858. After her marriage, Camille studied painting with the animalier Auguste Bonheur, brother of Rosa Bonheur (q.v.). Sharing her master's interest in animal painting and influenced particularly by the works of Troyon (q.v.), she made her debut in the Salon of 1865 (nos. 1537, 1538). In 1867, inspired by the Bracquemond-Rousseau service, Moreau first became interested in ceramics, painting a pre-glazed, undecorated family table service with Japanese-style designs of flowers, birds, and fish—after Brac-*

*quemond, Japanese prints, and directly from nature. In the same year she began to decorate ceramics that were fired in the kilns of Théodore Deck (q.v.), and although not among the artist-decorators who collaborated exclusively with Deck, her association with the potter lasted until about 1874. At the same time she continued to paint and exhibit paintings—as well as large decorative ceramics—in the Salons (see 1869, Paris, Salon, nos. 1743, 1744 [painting], nos. 2986, 2987 [faïence]). During the 1870s Moreau attempted to increase her technical knowledge of ceramic manufacture: in the summers of 1871 and 1872 she designed ceramic forms (executed for her by others), decorated those pieces herself with ceramic colors, and supervised their firing in the ovens of a tile factory at Jaulgonne. Encouraged by her success, Camille Moreau continued experiments between 1872 and 1874 in Paris, assisted by Laurent Bouvier, painter and ceramist, who provided her with the clays that he himself used and taught her to mix enamel colors. Bouvier also reinforced Moreau's interest in Japanese sources, which continuously inspired her ceramic decorations. Moreau's first and greatest public success as a ceramist occurred at the Paris Exposition Universelle of 1878, where she sold a number of works to the ceramic museums of Sèvres and Limoges. In 1882 Adolphe Moreau died, and shortly thereafter Camille fell victim to a long illness which interrupted her work entirely between 1889*

IV-16

IV-17

and 1891. From 1892 until her tragic death in the Bazar de la Charité fire, Camille Moreau continued to produce Japanizing ceramics.

K.B.H.

Bibliography:
Moreau-Nélaton, 1899; Heuser, 1974, pp. 90–91

Produced by Joseph-Théodore Deck; designed and painted by Camille Nélaton Moreau

## IV-17
## Footed Dish

1868
Signed and dated: c$^{lle}$ M. 68; incised: TH. DECK; marked in blue: MALNOVE
Tin-enameled earthenware, with polychrome enamel decoration
Height 3.5 cm; diameter 30 cm

Provenance:
Gift of the designer to the Musée Adrien-Dubouché, August 20, 1870 (inv. no. 6803)

Exhibitions:
1972, Limoges; 1973, Saint-Omer

Bibliography:
Weisberg, 1973, "Moreau and Dammouse," p. 125, fig. 2

This footed dish, painted with an iris, flowering branch, and insect, is similar in style to, and contemporary with, the large table service that marked Camille Moreau's debut as a ceramic decorator. Begun in 1867 and inspired by nature and the Bracquemond-Rousseau Japanese service produced the previous year (no. IV-18), the table service was executed for her own family in collaboration with her husband, in large part between 1867 and 1868, although it was completed only about 1876 (Moreau-Nélaton, 1899, vol. II, pl. 1).

Following Bracquemond, Camille Moreau borrowed designs from Japanese print albums and illustrated books including Hokusai's Manga, or "sketchbooks," and the "Fish Series" album of Hiroshige, although she also made studies directly from nature. Individual studies of flowers, birds, and insects were adapted in Japanizing fashion to the various forms of the service, placed asymmetrically on the predominantly white ground and freed from border patterns and contours. Here Moreau's iris, seemingly observed from nature although recalling those of the Manga and by Bracquemond, is encircled by the flowering branch—a composition denser and more complex than the sparse decorations after Bracquemond. This elaboration is characteristic of

contemporary works by Deck, and of those pieces designed by Camille Moreau in collaboration with him, including those exhibited in the Salon of 1869 (no. 2987; Moreau-Nélaton, 1899, vol. II, pl. 3). Moreover, while Camille Moreau's first table service was painted in low-temperature colors on tin-glazed faïence, this dish and others of her works produced by Deck were decorated in high-temperature colors on unfired tin enamel. Requiring more technical skill from the artist, this technique produced softer and richer colors due to the fusing of the enamels with the opaque tin glaze during firing (Deck, 1887, pp. 212–13).

K.B.H.

Musée National Adrien-Dubouché, Limoges

---

## François-Eugène Rousseau
### Paris 1827–1891 Paris

Merchant and artist, Rousseau was one of the most influential figures in the decorative arts of the later nineteenth century, both because of the innovative works he commissioned from leading designers and sold at his Paris shop and because of the highly original glass that he himself produced. Rousseau succeeded his father in 1855 as proprietor of a shop at 41, rue Coquillière, which had specialized for nearly a century in the sale of porcelain and faïence. In 1862 Rousseau's decorative ceramics won a medal and "universal admiration" at the London International Exhibition (Art Journal Catalogue 1862, vol. II, p. 235). A founding member of the Union Centrale des Arts Décoratifs, Rousseau introduced at its first exhibition in 1863 the slip reliefs ("pâtes rapportées") of the Sèvres decorator Solon (q.v.), for which he was awarded a first-class medal (Union Centrale 1863, p. 115, no. 225; Rapports 1863, pp. 47–48).

In 1866 Rousseau commissioned from Bracquemond the celebrated "Japanese" service for which Rousseau won a bronze medal at the Exposition Universelle of 1867. During the late 1860s Rousseau is reported to have owned a number of Japanese print albums (which were studied by such artists as Fâlize, q.v.; Josse, 1882–83, p. 333), and in 1874, he exhibited at the Union Centrale a "Japanese" service commissioned from the Sèvres painter Henri Lambert. At the 1869 Union Centrale exhibition (where as an organizing committee member he was hors concours, as he had been in 1865), Rousseau showed a service decorated by Lefèvre-Deumier in a sketchy, Impressionist style that attracted almost as much attention as had the Bracquemond service (Catalogue 1869, no. 224; Burty, 1869, "Industries," p. 544; Fourcaud, 1884–85, p. 259).

It was Rousseau's interest in Japanese art that seems to have led him, in the mid-1870s, to glass decoration. His first glasswares, which bore engraved Japanizing decorations after his own designs, were exhibited at the Exposition Universelle of 1878 (de Liesville, 1878, p. 696); by 1884 the variety and originality of his decorative methods had grown considerably, and included imitations of hard stones and coloristic and textural effects in cased glass. In 1887 Rousseau sold his firm and models to a friend and collaborator, Ernest Léveillé.

K.B.H.

Bibliography:
Fourcaud, 1884–85; Champier, 1890–91; Rapport 1900, p. 130; Brunhammer et al., 1976, pp. 488–89 (bibl.)

---

## Félix-Joseph-Auguste Bracquemond
### Paris 1833–1914 Paris

One of the most important graphic artists and engravers of the nineteenth century, Bracquemond began formal training with the Ingriste painter Joseph Guichard and, encouraged by Guichard, learned etching independently from Diderot's Encyclopedia and animalier prints of Boissieu. In 1852 Bracquemond made his Salon debut with a portrait of his grandmother and in the same year created his first important etching, The Top of a Half-Door, which was printed by Delâtre. It was at the shop of Delâtre that Bracquemond is said to have discovered a volume of Hokusai's Manga, thereby inaugurating the cult of Japanism which swept through French art during the last third of the nineteenth century. In 1862 Bracquemond founded the Société des Aquafortistes, exhibiting in the society's collection of that year the Japanizing etching The Unknown. Bracquemond participated in the Salon des Refusés in 1863, and in 1867 joined a small group of artists and critics in the Japanese Société du Jing-lar.

During the 1860s Bracquemond became interested in ceramic decoration, working first in the studio of Deck (q.v.) and then in 1866 independently for Eugène Rousseau, who commissioned from him the celebrated Japanese table service. Also in 1866 Bracquemond applied for appointment to the imperial manufactory of Sèvres (q.v.), but succeeded in being named head of the painting and gilding ateliers there only in 1870. Bracquemond remained at Sèvres for less than a year and in 1872 accepted the offer of Charles Haviland to be director of the new Auteuil studio of Haviland & Co. (q.v.), which under Bracquemond's direction specialized in the production of barbotine earthenwares, painted with colored slips and lead-glazed in loose Impressionist and

*Japanizing styles. In 1881 Bracquemond retired as director at Auteuil, devoting the remainder of his career principally to his graphic work, but serving as art critic and theoretician (Du dessin et de la couleur, 1885), director of various artistic societies, and sometime interior designer (notably a billiard room for Baron Vitta shown at the 1902 Société National des Beaux-Arts Salon).*

K.B.H.

Bibliography:
Burty, 1878; de Lostalot, 1884; Beraldi, 1885–92, vol. III, pp. 5–16, 143–54; Bénédite, 1905; 1972, Mortagne; 1974, Paris, Bibliothèque Nationale, Bracquemond; Heuser, 1974, p. 88; 1974–75, Paris, Bibliothèque Forney, nos. 10, 12, 19

## Lebeuf-Milliet et Cie

*Creil and Montereau, 1840–1875*

*In the late eighteenth century manufactories were founded separately at Creil and Montereau to produce earthenwares that would rival English products. Although during the first quarter of the nineteenth century this endeavor met with little success, by 1855 the factories were considered the equal of their foreign rivals and by 1867 were counted the second largest producers of fine earthenwares in France (next to Utzschneider, q.v.; A. Girard, in* Rapports 1867, *vol. III, p. 124). In 1840 the separate manufactories of Charles Saint-Cricq-Casaux at Creil and Louis Lebeuf at Montereau were united as the Fayenceries de Creil et Montereau under the name Lebeuf et Milliet for the production of "fine earthenware, opaque and transparent porcelain... stoneware and pottery." At the industrial exhibitions of 1844 and 1849, Creil-Montereau received gold medals, in the latter for the production of hard ironstone-like earthenware (pétrocérame), examples of which were purchased for the museum at Sèvres (MNC 3325). First-class and gold medals were also won by Lebeuf-Milliet at the Expositions Universelles of 1855 and 1867 respectively. In 1855 Salvetat praised the "perfection" of the firm's products (*Rapports 1855, *p. 945) and in 1867 the innovative use of Siemens furnaces at Creil was "of greatest interest to the entire ceramic industry" (A. Girard, in* Rapports 1867, *vol. III, pp. 149–50).*

*Printed decorations were applied at Creil before 1810. During the Second Empire, the manufactory produced commemorative plates printed with such contemporary subjects as the Voyage of Napoleon III in Brittany, the Syrian Campaign, and the Exposition of 1867, as well as the innovative Bracquemond-Rousseau service. In 1875 the name of the firm was changed to Lebeuf et Cie; a year later, when Lebeuf himself died, Henry-Félix-Anatole Barluet, director*

IV-18

*of the manufactory at Creil, became general director of the firm, which carried his name, Barluet et Cie, until his death in 1884. In 1895 the manufactory at Creil was closed, bringing to an end the combined productions of Creil and Montereau.*

K.B.H.

Bibliography:
*Rapport 1900,* pp. 149–52; Aries, 1974

Produced by François-Eugène Rousseau; designed by Félix-Joseph-Auguste Bracquemond; manufactured by Lebeuf-Milliet et Cie

## IV-18
## Dish

1866–67
Marked in black: CREIL L M & C^IE MONTEREAU MODELE E. ROUSSEAU A PARIS; incised: 2
Earthenware, with decoration printed and painted on glaze
Height 4.8 cm; length 42.8 cm; width 35.9 cm

Provenance:
Purchased by the Musée Adrien-Dubouché, May 1869 (inv. no. 4939)

Exhibition:
1867, Paris, Exposition Universelle

Bibliography:
A. Girard, in *Rapports 1867,* vol. III, p. 145; Champier, 1890–91, pp. 88–89; Valotaire, 1930, pl. 1; Connaissance des Arts, 1957, repro. p. 96; Weisberg, 1969,
pp. 278–79; 1972, Mortagne, nos. 11, 40, 41; Heuser, 1974, pp. 88–89; 1974–75, Paris, Bibliothèque Forney, no. 1; 1975–76, Cleveland, nos. 22, 194

A faïence dinner service of over two hundred pieces decorated with plants, birds, and fish was commissioned from Félix Bracquemond by Eugène Rousseau in 1866 (for 600 francs, according to Goncourt and Goncourt, 1956, vol. II, pp. 726–27). Bracquemond etched a large series of preparatory studies, which eventually served as transfers for the images printed on the service. The etchings copy motifs directly from a number of Japanese print albums and illustrated books, including Hokusai's *Manga* and *Picture Book of Flowers and Birds (Kwacho Gwafu),* Hiroshige's "Fish Series" album, Isai's *Minute Drawings of Flowers (Kwacho Sansui Zushiki),* and Hokusen's *Pictures of Flowers and Birds (Kwacho Gaden)* (1975–76, Cleveland, nos. 22, 194). The images of lobster and eggplants which appear on this dish from the service are borrowed from two separate colored woodcuts in the "Great Fish" series *(Uo Zukushi),* c. 1832, by Hiroshige. They are combined in reverse in Bracquemond's preparatory etching for the service (Beraldi, 1885–92, vol. III, no. 550), the artist substituting Hiroshige's lobster for the flatheads which originally appeared between eggplants.

The Bracquemond-Rousseau service represents the earliest example of Japanism in French ceramics (Chesneau, 1878, pp. 391–92;

Allemand, 1964, pp. 197–98; Weisberg, 1973, "Rousseau," pp. 210–11)—in which specific Japanese designs are freely and asymmetrically applied to European shapes in a fashion and medium as suggestive of Rococo japonaiserie as it is Japanese. The painted earthenware service, with its combed borders and molded relief ornament, derives from eighteenth-century French faïence, despite Bracquemond's Japanese motifs and their random disposition over the ground in Japanizing style. The service was first exhibited at the Paris Exposition Universelle of 1867; while Girard reported on Rousseau's "original service, where large fish... isolated and strewn at random, are spread over the white ground" (*Rapports 1867*, vol. III, p. 145), the manufactures of Lebeuf-Milliet received a gold medal and praise for the superiority of their "imitation of old faïence" (Aries, 1974, p. 108). The Bracquemond-Rousseau service attracted much subsequent attention: in 1869 Burty remarked that it was still creating a furor (Burty, 1869, "Industries," p. 544) and Rousseau exhibited the service again at the Paris exposition of 1878 (de Liesville, 1878, p. 687). The commercial success of the service is indicated by the fact that it was reissued in the early 1880s by Lebeuf-Milliet's successor Barluet and it was copied directly and indirectly by decorators such as Camille Moreau (q.v.); by Eugène Millet for J. Vieillard & Cie, Bordeaux; and by W. S. Coleman for Minton. During the 1870s Bracquemond designed for Haviland three other table services inspired by motifs from Japanese prints: the "Parisian" service (1876), the "Grand-Feu" service (1877), and the "Flowers and Ribbons—Barluet" service (1879) which, however, were more evocative and less specifically imitative of their sources than the Rousseau service.

K.B.H.

Musée National Adrien-Dubouché, Limoges

---

*Jean-Denis Larue*

*Born Paris–1884 Paris*

*A student of the Romantic sculptor Jean-Baptiste-Jules Klagmann, Larue made his Salon debut in 1845 with a plaster portrait bust (no. 2127). He continued to exhibit portrait busts and medallions at Salons until 1852 (no. 1436). In 1853 Larue accepted a position as* sculpteur-modeleur *at Sèvres, where he remained until 1882, confining his work exclusively to the manufactory.*

K.B.H.

Bibliography:
Bellier and Auvray, 1882–87, vol. I, p. 914; Lami, 1914–21, vol. III, p. 225; Lechevallier-Chevignard, 1908, vol. II, p. 148

Manufacture Impériale de Sèvres; designed by Jean-Denis Larue

## IV-19
## Flower Basket

Designed 1863, manufactured 1867
Inscribed: Sevres 1863 J Larue sculp.
Earthenware, with colored glazes
Height 51 cm; diameter 49.5 cm

Provenance:
Registered in works of sculpture and relief studios at Sèvres factory 1863 (Sèvres Archives Va'55, fol. 115); valued for sale at Sèvres May 1867 (Sèvres Archives Vv', no. 7, fol. 56 v, appréciation), June 1867 (Sèvres Archives, Vr', 3ᵉ série, no. 3, fols. 175, 176 [entry of June 14, 1867], appréciation en blanc; Vy' bis, no. 24, p. 65), and December 27, 1867 (Sèvres Archives Vy' bis, no. 24, p. 164); Musée National de Céramique, 1910 (inv. no. 15537)

Bibliography:
Connaissance des Arts, 1957, p. 57, fig. 5

In 1863 Larue was paid to provide sketches for this central group of a centerpiece described as "a group of three putti carrying a basket for flowers." Larue had already designed in 1862 as *pièces de côté* a "group of two putti carrying a flower or cornet" (Sèvres Archives Va' 54 [1862], fol. 118), which was apparently replaced from 1863 with groups of "two individual putti"—putti with swans bearing reticulated baskets. The groups were not produced immediately and are recorded in the sales inventory of the manufactory only in May 1867 as: "No. 83a; a central basket with three putti by Larue... 1,450 francs; No. 84: two side baskets with one putto by Larue, idem 750 francs." Several examples of each model must have been made in addition to those delivered to the Sèvres museum: in June 1867 a version of this centerpiece was sold to the

IV-19

duchesse de Chevreuse. Larue's boldly modeled basket, with putti representing the continents of Europe, Africa, and America, is decorated with brightly colored glazes after the fashion of Minton's majolica wares—first introduced at the 1851 London exhibition in imitation of Italian Renaissance wares and developed thereafter into the most popular earthenware in England. While the form of the basket and sculptural style of the putti refer to models of about 1850, such intensely colored glazes were commonly used at Sèvres only in the 1860s. Although earthenware was produced at Sèvres for only two decades (1852–72), the interest in color and in colored glazes associated with heavily modeled earthenwares such as this basket survived as one of the principal reforming ideas of the 1875 Commission de Perfectionnement.

K.B.H.

Musée National de Céramique, Sèvres

---

## Utzschneider et Cie

*Sarreguemines (Moselle), established 1778*

*Utzschneider was the largest producer of fine earthenwares in France during the nineteenth century and a major manufacturer of stonewares. In 1855 Utzschneider's factory at Sarreguemines employed 1,100 workers and grossed more than 1,500,000 francs; by 1867 the firm employed 2,000 workers in three factories and earned 4,000,000 francs.*

*A faïence factory was founded in 1778 in Sarreguemines by Nicolas-Henri Jacobi, Paul-Augustin Jacobi, and Joseph Fabry. After 1799 the Jacobi interests were ceded to François-Paul Utzschneider (1771–1844), who formed a new partnership with Fabry for the production of "English" earthenware and stoneware. Utzschneider's price lists of 1810 describe products "in the English taste" including queen's ware, black basaltes, and agate and marble wares. Known as the French Wedgwood, Utzschneider continued to specialize in such wares, winning gold medals for them at industrial exhibitions in Paris (1806, 1819, 1823, 1827, 1834). In 1836 Utzschneider turned over direction of the factory to his son-in-law Alexandre de Geiger (1808–1891), who remained in partnership with Fabry's heirs. At the Paris exposition of 1849, where the firm won a gold medal, Bougon praised de Geiger's development of new products, including a "demi-porcelaine" (ironstone) remarkable for its high quality and low price (Rapport 1849, vol. II, pp. 856–57).*

*At the Exposition Universelle of 1855, Utzschneider won a first-class medal and praise for the firm's continued progress (Salvetat, in Rapports 1855, p. 946). At the Paris exposition of 1867, where the firm won a gold medal, Utzschneider showed a new group of earthenwares with painted decorations, among which Girard described "magnificent luxury vases, painted by Langlois, of Sèvres, and by Sabaurin, with original decorations, landscapes monochromatic in the foreground, tinted in the background, for which the prices, despite the signature of an artist such as Langlois, are affordable even for those of modest means" (Rapports 1867, vol. III, p. 159). It was just such earthenwares with painted landscape decoration that the Emperor was reported to have purchased from Utzschneider at the exposition (Modern Industries, 1868, p. 13).*

*Paul de Geiger (1837–1915) became director of the firm in 1859 and continued his father's policy of expansion. New factories were built in 1858 and 1862, and construction of a third was interrupted in 1870 by the Franco-Prussian War. After Sarreguemines was annexed to Germany, de Geiger opened new factories at Digoin (1876) and Vitry-le-François (1900).*

K.B.H.

Bibliography:
Rapport 1900, pp. 156–58; Solon, 1903, pp. 146–47; Ernould-Gandouet, 1969, pp. 84–85, 88, 92; Brossard, 1975

IV-20

---

Utzschneider et Cie

## IV-20
## Tobacco Jar

c. 1869
Mark applied in relief: [Eagle]/N/[laurel branches]
Unglazed fine colored stoneware, cast, with relief and gilded decoration
Height 31 cm; diameter 22.5 cm

Provenance:
Gift of Baron Alexandre de Geiger to the Conservatoire National des Arts et Métiers, 1869 (inv. no. 8131)

Bibliography:
Ernould-Gandouet, 1969, repro. p. 91; Brossard, 1975, p. 34, repro. p. 26

In his exhibition report of 1867, Chandelon praised Utzschneider's stonewares as worthy of comparison with English products "with respect to the fineness of the paste, the variety of the colors, and the purity of the forms" (Rapports 1867, vol. III, p. 108). Fine stoneware bodies such as that of the tobacco jar were originated by Josiah Wedgwood in the late eighteenth century and developed by Utzschneider in imitation of, and in competition with, the English market. Classicizing jaspers and basaltes with the cameo-like white relief decoration usually associated with the Wedgwood firm formed a major portion of Utzschneider's luxury stonewares during the first half of the nineteenth century. However, from the 1840s and 1850s, Utzschneider also produced monochrome tan- and buff-colored stonewares like the tobacco jar, decorated with popular, naturalistic reliefs. In style and coloration, the tobacco jar is also faintly reminiscent of Wedgwood's canewares, commonly decorated with molded animal ornaments like the jar's boar finial, although here updated with a contemporary hunt subject and running plant pattern. The intertwining oak branches that adorn the base and lid of the jar suggest the influence of the artist-potter Jules-Claude Ziégler, who produced during the 1840s at Voisinlieu (near Beauvais) stoneware jugs decorated with such naturalistic plant motifs. In its expensive decorative details—the complicated sculptural reliefs that are exacting in molds, and the areas of gilding—the jar demonstrates the high quality which Utzschneider offered on a commercial scale to its widely based market.

K.B.H.

Musée National des Techniques—C.N.A.M., Paris

# Glass

## Cristalleries de Baccarat
*Baccarat (Lorraine), established 1764*

Throughout most of the nineteenth century, Baccarat was the largest producer of fine glasswares in France. By 1862 the firm was earning about 4,000,000 francs in gross income, as compared to some 2,400,000 francs for Saint-Louis (q.v.), 800,000 francs for Clichy, and 500,000 francs for Monot (q.v.; Pelouze, in Rapports 1862, vol. VI, p. 534). A glass factory under the name Verrerie Sainte Anne was founded at Baccarat in 1764. In 1816 Aimé-Gabriel d'Artigues, proprietor of a glassworks at Vonèche, Belgium, purchased the factory, and in 1819 constructed Baccarat's first furnace for the manufacture of English-type lead crystal. In 1822 d'Artigues sold the factory to Pierre-Antoine Godard-Desmarets, who in association with Colot and Lescuyer founded the Société Anonyme des Cristalleries de Vonèche-Baccarat, afterward known as the Compagnie des Verreries et Cristalleries de Baccarat. Jean-Baptiste Toussaint was appointed director (as he had been under d'Artigues) and, with François-Eugène Fontenay as sous-directeur from 1841, remained in that position until his death in 1858.

The firm did not exhibit at the London international exhibitions of 1851 and 1862, but won the Grand Medal of Honor at the Paris Expositions Universelles in both 1855 and 1867, against strong foreign competition. In 1855 the French reporter claimed that Baccarat's clear crystal glass "bears comparison with the most beautiful English crystal; it is quite superior to the most beautiful Bohemian glass, in which the tint is always a little yellow" (E. Péligot, in Rapports 1855, p. 935). In 1867 the French crystal was considered by Péligot and Bontemps superior even to English wares "with respect to the diversity of the products, to the variety and tastefulness of the forms" (Rapports 1867, vol. III, p. 67).

Toussaint was succeeded as director by Emile Godard, the son of Pierre-Antoine. Until his death in 1867 he endeavored to expand Baccarat's foreign markets (following the Anglo-French commercial treaty of 1860) and to increase the factory's means of production by converting the glass furnaces at Baccarat from solid to more economical gaseous fuels. In 1862, only a year after Siemens first successfully applied his invention in Birmingham, Baccarat built the first two Siemens furnaces in France, which uniquely derived their clean-burning gas from the distillation of wood rather than coal. By 1867, when Paul Michaut was named director, the annual gross income of the firm had risen to 5,000,000 francs ("Baccarat," 1869, p. 77).

K.B.H.

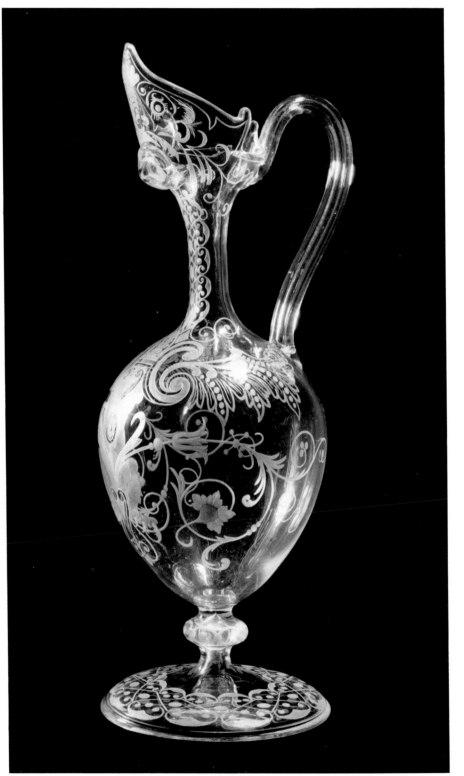

IV-21

Bibliography:
Turgan, 1863, vol. III, pp. 273–326; Lami, 1881–88, vol. I, pp. 418–19; Amic, 1952, pp. 65–66

Cristalleries de Baccarat

## IV-21
## Ewer

1855
Crystal glass, with furnace-formed handle and rim and wheel-engraved decoration
Height 36 cm; diameter 12 cm

Provenance:
Made for exhibition and retained by Baccarat; Musée de la Cristallerie de Baccarat

Exhibition:
1855, Paris, Exposition Universelle

This ewer is a forerunner of the crystal glassware decorated by engraving (*see* no. IV-22), which during the Second Empire and through the 1870s eclipsed the cut styles of decoration that had been fashionable in France since the first decades of the nineteenth century. In 1862 Pelouze reported that whereas formerly in France much elaborately patterned cut glass had been produced, "for a long time light objects have been preferred to heavy objects" (*Rapports 1862*, vol. VI, p. 542). As alternatives to these styles, which concentrated attention on the cut decoration rather than on the shape, glassmakers at Baccarat from the mid-1850s sought models for vessels in historic glass—Venetian sixteenth-century furnace-manipulated glass and Central European engraved glass of the seventeenth and eighteenth centuries—which would reflect the molten quality of glass formed by blowing, with decoration subordinate to shape.

The rim, spout, and handle of this ewer were cut and shaped at the furnace in a manner derived from Venice, and both its general form and the engraved decoration of naturalistically treated Renaissance arabesques were inspired by sixteenth-century designs. However, the ewer's thin, elongated neck and ovoid body are inventions, demonstrating the characteristic virtuosity of an exhibition piece. The ewer was not produced commercially by Baccarat, and its innovative shape remained untried even by P.-H. Emile Froment-Meurice (q.v.), who in 1867 exhibited an otherwise similar Renaissance ewer in rock crystal decorated with enamel arabesques (Darcel, 1868, repro. p. 83).

K.B.H.

Baccarat, Paris

IV-22

Cristalleries de Baccarat

## IV-22
## Table Service: Two Decanters, Covered Bowl, Goblet, and Tray

c. 1867
Clear crystal glass, with wheel-engraved and cut decoration
Decanter height 40 cm; decanter height 20.5 cm; bowl height 19.5 cm, diameter 11.5 cm; goblet height 16.5 cm, diameter 7.5 cm; tray diameter 31.5 cm

Provenance:
Musée de la Cristallerie de Baccarat

The light cutting on the necks of the decanters and stem of the goblet, supplementing the wheel-engraved ornament, was a feature of glass decoration reintroduced at the Exposition Universelle of 1867 both by Baccarat and by such British firms as Apsley Pellatt, Henry Greene, and W. T. Copeland & Sons. In 1869 Burty described the manufacture of a decanter at Baccarat, decorated both by cutting and engraving: "Lastly, these are conveyed to the carving and cutting-room (taillerie), where a finishing touch is given to them by means of grinding wheels, which are turned at a great speed.... The engraving of them, either by means of the hydrofluoric acid, or with the help of small wheels made of iron or copper wire, on which is sprinkled a certain quantity of emery, gives the concluding touch" (Burty, 1869, *Chefs-d'œuvre*, p. 198). The engraved arabesque ornament is partly polished in a sumptuous style also developed during the late 1860s, with the engraved lines left in their abraded state to contrast with the brighter, polished highlights. In style, the engraved decoration of foliage, scrolls, and strapwork derives from late-seventeenth- and early eighteenth-century ornamental designs, which greatly influenced Central European glass decoration of the eighteenth century, and in turn, glasswares of the 1860s, which sought to rival earlier Bohemian styles and techniques. This style was particularly suited to a reforming fashion of the 1860s, which emphasized the virtues of clear lead crystal. In 1867 George Wallis praised Baccarat's engraved tablewares as "elegant in design, and eminently artistic in the distribution of the lines of ornamental construction. The details are kept light and in tendrils, rather than given in masses, and thus the crystalline character of the material is never interfered with" (*Art Journal Catalogue 1867,* vol. VI, p. 101).

K.B.H.

Baccarat, Paris

Cristalleries de Baccarat

## IV-23
## Decanter

1867
Clear crystal glass, with cut decoration
Height 32 cm

Provenance:
Made for exhibition and retained by Baccarat; Musée de la Cristallerie de Baccarat

Exhibition:
1867, Paris, Exposition Universelle

This dignified and supremely functional design for a decanter was shown by the Baccarat firm at the 1867 Exposition Universelle and provides a striking contrast in style with the Baccarat engraved service (no. IV-22) also made in or about 1867. The latter shows every feature of the new international glass style which was developing in the 1860s—the Classical amphora shape, the thinly blown walls of the vessel, and the complex, wheel-engraved decoration—while the decanter typifies a conservative taste in its heaviness, both in shape and in actual weight. Its thick walls and deeply cut pattern of split hexagons, its low-bellied shape (echoed in the stopper), and its functional double neck ring make up a design more typical of glasswares of the 1850s.

Cut glass reached a peak of technical perfection and popularity in Europe during the first half of the nineteenth century, with the British factories, being the most advanced technically, setting the leading styles. However, by about 1860 a reaction against cut glass came about both in England and in France, and, although most factories continued production, heavy cut glass suffered a decline during the Second Empire. It was not until the 1880s that there was a renewal of interest in the technique of cutting, which resulted in new and very different designs. Like other French factories, Baccarat continued to produce cut-glass designs such as the "Juvisy" service, to which this decanter belongs, for conservative patrons during the 1860s, and George Wallis had high praise for Baccarat's display of tablewares at the 1867 exhibition: "The table glass, especially the cut specimens, are decidedly the best among the French. The forms are generally excellent, and

IV-23

in a pure style, while the arrangement of the ornamentation in facets approaches the perfection of geometric arrangement in proportionate quantities, the larger masses being well contrasted with the smaller details. This gives a variety of light and shadow, so to speak, rarely seen in cut glass" (*Art Journal Catalogue 1867,* vol. II, pp. 100–101).

B.E./K.B.H.

Baccarat, Paris

Cristalleries de Baccarat

## IV-24
## Covered Vase

1867
Amber glass layered over crystal, with etched decoration
Height 41 cm; diameter 15 cm

Provenance:
Made for exhibition and retained by Baccarat; Musée de la Cristallerie de Baccarat

Exhibition:
1867, Paris, Exposition Universelle

Bibliography:
*Art Journal Catalogue 1867,* vol. VII, probably repro. p. 308

This Egyptian-style vase demonstrates Baccarat's technical virtuosity in the new process of acid etching, used to produce its amber tones, varied surface textures, and linear decoration. The crystal body of the vase, covered with a layer of amber glass, was coated with an acid-resisting substance, and Egyptian designs were cut through the resist in the manner of an engraving. The vase was then dipped in hydrofluoric acid in stages, which etched the cutaway patterns, leaving the protected, top layer a glossy dark amber, and inner layers successively reduced in color and with the characteristic mat finish that results from the action of the acid. The inner layers include the dark outlines of the forms, the lighter amber figurative and decorative elements, and the white glass beneath, from which the amber layer was entirely etched away. At the 1867 Exposition Universelle, George Wallis described this technique as "the most novel method of decorating glass in the whole Exhibition" and praised a punch service decorated in this manner (*Art Journal Catalogue 1867,* vol. VI, p. 102).

Although acid etching had been known since the seventeenth century, its commercial application was entirely a development of the nineteenth century, practiced in England from

IV-24

## Jean-Baptiste Simon

*Active Baccarat 1840–70*

*Simon is said to have learned glass engraving in Germany, where during the 1820s and 1830s a number of able artists decorated Biedermeier glass with naturalistic subjects in a new pictorial style. In 1840 Simon was engaged by Baccarat as an engraver and, during the course of a thirty-year career with the firm, established an important engraving work-shop-studio. At Baccarat, Simon specialized in pictorial engraving with designs of naturalistically treated figures, flowers, birds, and foliage, frequently on flashed or stained glass in the German and Bohemian fashion. At the Paris Exposition Universelle of 1867, Simon was awarded an honorable mention as coopérateur (Récompensés 1867, p. 17).*

K.B.H.

Cristalleries de Baccarat; designed by Jean-Baptiste Simon

## IV-25
## Vase

1867
Signed and dated on rim of medallion: J Bᵗᵉ Simon. Gᵛʳ a Baccarat. 1867.
Ruby glass layered over crystal, with wheel-engraved and cut decoration; gilded bronze base
Height 72.5 cm; diameter 27 cm

Provenance:
Gift to Aldebert de Chambrun, 1867; bequest to the Musée de la Cristallerie de Baccarat, 1894

Exhibition:
1867, Paris, Exposition Universelle

Bibliography:
*Art Journal Catalogue 1867*, vol. VII, p. 308; H. Chance, in *Reports 1867*, vol. II, pp. 373–74; E. Péligot and G. Bontemps, in *Rapports 1867*, vol. III, p. 72

*(Shown in Paris only)*

This is one of a pair of richly colored vases that were exhibited with a matching tazza at the 1867 Exposition Universelle and described by Henry Chance as "two very large vases and a centre tazza of white and ruby glass (flashed), the cutting showing the clear glass. The ruby colour is very brilliant, the engraving is well designed and most carefully executed" (*Reports 1867*, vol. II, pp. 373–74). Following Central European styles and techniques of the 1820s and 1830s, Baccarat produced colored glasses on a commercial scale from 1839 (Amic, 1952, p. 69), including glasses formed, as here, of

---

the 1830s. It was not, however, until 1854, when L. Kessler patented a printing process for engraving with hydrofluoric acid, that etched decoration was produced in France by the major *cristalleries*; Baccarat did not begin producing such decoration until 1862 (Amic, 1952, p. 77). At the exposition of 1867 Baccarat and Saint-Louis (q.v.) showed etched glass for the first time. As exhibition reporters, Péligot and Bontemps described acid etching as a "new mode of decoration" and commented on its use to produce—as in this vase—mat surfaces in both clear and layered glass (*Rapports 1867*, vol. III, pp. 67–68).

Based generally on the form of Egyptian glass vessels, Baccarat's vase with conical lid resembles an inverse amphora with tall handles. Inspired by the Suez Canal project and Egyptian archaeological finds made during the 1850s and 1860s by Auguste Mariette which were displayed in the "Egyptian Temple" at the 1867 Exposition Universelle, other exhibitors such as Baugrand (q.v.) and P.-H. Emile Froment-Meurice (q.v.) also showed Egyptian-style objects at the 1867 exposition.

K.B.H.

Baccarat, Paris

contrasting layers, the outer layer being used to provide a colored ground for engraving. In its scale, its elaborate decoration, and its cost of manufacture, this vase is a consciously designed exhibition piece (Baccarat records that Simon's wheel engraving occupied a one-and-a-half-year period); in its massive form and deeply cut intaglio engraving the vase evokes late-seventeenth- and early eighteenth-century Central European glasswares, which were similarly covered with floral and mythological designs rendered in relief by the process of grinding on the wheel. The figurative and floral ornaments engraved on the vase are united by a marine theme, which centers on the medallion with Venus, riding a dolphin, and Cupid: the rinceaux disclose crayfish, snails, and toads; hippocampi appear among the lateral flower sprays; and fish trophies are displayed below the masks. In 1867 the vases were presented to Aldebert de Chambrun, an associate of Emile Godard and later a benefactor of the firm, who bequeathed the pieces to the *cristallerie*.

K.B.H.

Baccarat, Paris

Cristalleries de Baccarat

## IV-26
## Vase

c. 1870
Clear crystal glass, with cut decoration; chased and gilded bronze mounts
Height 116 cm; diameter 31 cm

Provenance:
Musée de la Cristallerie de Baccarat

Large-scale ornamental vases such as this were typically produced by Baccarat for the international exhibitions, where manufacturers of all countries tried to outdo one another in feats of scale and technique. At the Exposition Universelle of 1867, Baccarat showed a fountain 7.3 meters high, the largest object among a display of "large decorative pieces and... great vases mounted in bronze," which Péligot and Bontemps claimed could be put to use by architects (*Rapports 1867*, vol. III, p. 72). A glass vase of this size and form is virtually impossible to make in one piece, and therefore had to be produced in separate parts according to complex measurements and profiles worked out in plan and then fitted together. The gilded-bronze mounts at base, foot, and lid are both functional and decorative, serving to join together the separate parts of the vase as they form part of the design. The gilded bronze enhances by contrast the diamondlike brilliance of the crystal glass, in much the same way that jewelry of the Second Empire was often embellished with gold mounting.

The cut decoration of the vase anticipates in certain respects the widespread revival of cutting techniques in the 1870s and 1880s. The deceptively simple design of convex ribs is a difficult form to shape. This design is interrupted at the shoulder and neck of the vase by a band of intricate and reflective "rose cutting," a method of cutting much used and developed at the end of the century in table glass, to which it added a particularly ornate and brilliant appearance. In this case, however, reflective faceting has been kept to a minimum and the vase relies for effect mainly on its form—an attenuated version of the classical amphora shape, which was widely used (especially for ceramics) during the decade of the 1870s.

B.E.

Baccarat, Paris

---

## Philippe-Joseph Brocard
*Active Paris 1867–96*

*Brocard was France's first modern artist-glassmaker, and like Deck (q.v.), rediscovered in Near Eastern forms and decorative processes new possibilities of his medium. At first reproducing Islamic enameled and gilded glasses of the thirteenth and fourteenth centuries and later borrowing forms from Islamic inlaid bronze work, Brocard revived the craft of enameling on glass, known in France during the first half of the nineteenth century, but little practiced, and never before in Islamic styles. A collector and restorer of art objects, Brocard found inspi-*

IV-25

IV-26

ration for his glass in the Egyptian and the Syrian mosque lamps in the Cluny museum and those shown at the Union Centrale's "Musée Rétrospectif" of 1865. Self-taught, Brocard made his exhibition debut in 1867 with enameled glasses displaying the full vocabulary of Islamic forms and ornamentation that would characterize his work in the following two decades. His sources were specific pieces from museums and private collections, such as a reproduction of a fourteenth-century lamp with floral decorations from the Charles Davillier collection (now Louvre A.O. no. 3110 bis; Art Journal Catalogue 1871, vol. X, repro. p. 57) as well as designs published by de Beaumont and Collinot (1859). At the Union Centrale exhibition of 1869, Brocard, listed as émailleur sur verre at 216, rue du Faubourg Saint Honoré, showed enameled glasses (Catalogue 1869, p. 201, no. 186; Burty, 1869, "Industries," p. 543) while, simultaneously, historical Islamic pieces were again being exhibited in the Union's "Musée Oriental." By the London International Exhibition of 1871, Antonio Salviati of Venice was also exhibiting Islamic-style glasses (as would Lobmeyr in 1873), although "the originality and merit" (V. de Luynes, in Rapports 1871, pp. 124–25) of Brocard's productions, called "novelties in modern art" attracted "very general attention in the court allotted to France" (Art Journal Catalogue 1871, vol. X, p. 57).

Brocard received acclaim at the Paris exposition of 1878, where his enameling won "superiority" for France in glassmaking (de Liesville, 1878, p. 696) and first demonstrated its influence in the early enameled glasswares of Emile Gallé. During the 1880s Brocard, influenced by Gallé's floral naturalism, began using European forms and decorations. From 1884 Brocard was associated with his son Emile at 23, rue Bertrand; after his death in 1896, the firm continued under the name Verrerie Brocard.

K.B.H.

Bibliography:
"Rapport," 1874; 1972, Munich, nos. 193–204; Bloch-Dermant, 1974, pp. 22–27; Brunhammer et al., 1976, p. 467

Philippe-Joseph Brocard

## IV-27
## Footed Bowl

1870
Signed and dated: Brocard 1870
Glass, lightly tinted in green, painted with polychrome enamels and gilding
Height 17.7 cm; diameter 21 cm

IV-27

Provenance:
Musée Adrien-Dubouché (inv. no. V. 309)

Bibliography:
De Beaumont and Collinot, 1859, pls. 196–97; V. de Luynes, in Rapports 1871, p. 125; Art Journal Catalogue 1871, vol. X, repro. p. 57; Gerspach, 1885, pp. 102–3

Decorated with animal friezes, eagle medallions, and stylized Arabic poetic phrases in Mameluke Neskhi, Brocard's footed bowl is a reproduction of a thirteenth-century Syrian enameled glass coupe which belonged, in the nineteenth century, to the collector Charles Schefer. The coupe, probably exhibited among Schefer's Islamic glasswares at the Union Centrale in 1865 and 1869, was first published in de Beaumont and Collinot's Recueil de dessins (1859) as "found at a barber's in Damascus," and accompanied by a free but sound translation of the Islamic compliments. Schefer's coupe was also published in 1885 by Gerspach, who identified the arms as those of "Berdr-el-Din-ed-Dhahery (died 1277)."

At the London International Exhibition of 1871, where Brocard displayed a version of this footed bowl (identical, apparently, except for the interlaced ornament at foot and rim), Victor de Luynes remarked that the high price of Brocard's wares was due to the "long and delicate" process of production. Such a process,

declared by the 1871 Art Journal Catalogue to be "a secret of the inventor," was finally patented by Brocard in 1891 after it had long been practiced by such French glassmakers as Gallé, Ernie, Pfulb, and Imberton ("demande de brevet d'invention," August 20, 1891, in Bloch-Dermant, 1974, pp. 26–27): Brocard's designs were outlined with "cloisons" of gold or thick enamel or both (evident here in the red and gold lines which border the script and interlaced ornament), and painted in vitrifiable colors. The pieces were muffle-fired, during which the softened enamel colors adhered to the heated surface of the vessel. In his demande of 1891 Brocard declared that his enamel decorations could be applied to glasswares of all types and dimensions, and adapted to particular uses ("We can, according to the circumstances, vary the proportions of the various elements which we use"), and it was this ability to create ornament "in harmony" with the form of the vessel that de Luynes admired in 1871. In praising Brocard's glasses as blown, not molded, and painted by hand ("the glass is always blown and doesn't have that regularity of form that is found in molded pieces. All of the decoration must therefore be applied by hand"), de Luynes was also praising Brocard's new freedom from conventional ideas of crys-

tal-clear and mechanically perfect glass—a first
step toward the non-Classical directions art
glass was to take in the next decades.

K.B.H.

Musée National Adrien-Dubouché, Limoges

---

### Charles-Laurent Maréchal

*Metz 1801–1887 Bar-le-Duc*

*Leader of a group of artists known as the "School
of Metz," Maréchal became the most important glass
painter in France. He entered the Paris atelier of
Victor Regnault but in 1825 returned to Metz where
he specialized in pastel landscapes and peasant
scenes. In 1840 Maréchal made his Paris Salon debut
with pastels, for which he was awarded a third-class
medal; at subsequent Salons he won a second-class
medal (1841) and two third-class medals (1842 and
1855) and was named chevalier (1846) and officer
(1855) of the Legion of Honor. In 1841 Maréchal first
exhibited painted-glass windows for the cathedral of
Metz, which led immediately to other commissions
(Saint Vincent de Paul and Sainte Clotilde in Paris),
that increased when the glass-painting studio at
Sèvres closed in 1852.*

*At the London Universal Exhibition of 1851
Maréchal received a first-class medal but was criticized for his pictorial technique of painting opaque
colored enamels on sheets of white glass, which denied the transparency of the medium and was contrary to medieval methods—favored by Gothic re-
formers—of constructing mosaic windows with
small pieces of strongly colored glass. Such criticism
did not, however, affect the awarding of a commission to Maréchal to paint three windows of the Palais
de l'Industrie for the Exposition Universelle of 1855.
These windows won Maréchal a first-class medal at
the exposition, although criticism of his colors and
style "more appropriate to oil painting" persisted (de
Caumont, in* Rapports *1855, p. 954). At the London International Exhibition of 1862 Maréchal won
a medal for windows of "the highest artistic and
executive merit" as did his son, Charles-Raphael
Maréchal (*Medals *1862, p. 364). During the 1860s
Maréchal painted windows both for public buildings
(Saint Augustin) and for private ones—a chapel
in Luxembourg (Dussieux, 1876, pp. 401–2) and
Viollet-le-Duc's studio (exhibited at the Exposition
Universelle of 1867). By 1867 even Didron, himself a*
peintre-verrier, *who as editor of the* Annales Archéologiques *was a critic of Maréchal's pictorial
methods, conceded the "incontrovertible talent" of the
artist who had "planted the flag of the Renaissance
for painting on glass."*

K.B.H.

IV-28

Bibliography:
Ménard, 1876, pp. 448–53; Lami, 1881–88, vol. VI, p. 308; de la Fizelière, 1861; Didron, 1868, p. 8

Charles-Laurent Maréchal

## IV-28
## The Artist

1867
Signed, bottom left: L.-C. MARECHAL; inscribed and dated, bottom right: METZ. 1867; dated above, in roundel: 1867
White glass, painted and stained with colored enamels
430 × 175 cm

Provenance:
Purchased by the Emperor from the Exposition Universelle of 1867 for 5,000 francs; placed in the château of Fontainebleau, 1869, in "the central window opposite the corridor forming the antechamber to the Galerie des Fastes on the main floor" (Arch. nat. F²¹ 802, dossier 46-1868); dismantled, 1938

Exhibition:
1867, Paris, Exposition Universelle

Bibliography:
M. Chevalier, in *Rapports 1867*, vol. III, p. 91; T.-G. Parry, in *Reports 1867*, vol. II, p. 379; Didron, 1868, pp. 11–12; Ménard, 1876, p. 450

This leaded-glass window, *The Artist*, created for the Exposition Universelle of 1867, bears witness to the virtuosity Maréchal had attained with the help of Tessié du Motay, a glass technician. Various techniques freeing the artist from the traditional restrictions of stained glass (lead mullions, solid colors, and uniform gray flesh tones) are introduced here. Acid etching allowed the intensity of colors to be varied, for example, in the face or the portfolio made of red glass which was then lightened. Certain parts are of double thickness, also lightly etched, which further increased the possibilities for nuances. The large sizes of the pieces of glass, which avoid the necessity of breaking the unity of the design with lead, are themselves a tour de force, but what the critics admired most was the quality of the enamels applied to the white glass—especially the remarkable yellows and oranges of the carpet.

For the central part of the window—the artist himself—Maréchal obviously was inspired by Rubens, as is clearly indicated by the arms of Antwerp and Venice, the two great centers of painting, which are placed above. (Contrary to earlier opinions, this figure is not a self-portrait, but rather a tribute to all artists.)

"In my opinion, this figure is a perfect example of what happens when one starts off in the wrong direction," wrote Didron (1868,

p. 11), who preferred faithful reproductions of sixteenth-century stained glass; but the public was enthusiastic, and the Emperor bought the window. This gave great encouragement to Maréchal, who by unveiling this portrait of an artist at the same time as his *Reapers*, executed for the studio of Viollet-le-Duc, was promoting the use of stained-glass windows with secular subjects for private residences.

The window had to be modified and enlarged to fit into its new setting (Arch. nat. F²¹ 802, dossier 46-1868; Fontainebleau Archives); this cost 1,500 francs in addition to the 5,000-franc purchase price. These enlargements include the upper portion—the figures of Fame flanking the medallion, dating from 1867—and all the lower parts under the balcony, where cornucopias frame the Emperor's monogram surmounted by the imperial crown (the monogram L N which appears here was used concurrently with N alone or N III throughout the Second Empire).

Ménard (1876, p. 448) reproduces the central part of a stained-glass window of *The Artist* in a different version, and the Metz museum has a study for a head in the style of Rembrandt that is probably also related to the development of this work.

C.S.-V.

Palais de Fontainebleau, Direction de l'Architecture

---

Monot et Cie
(Cristallerie de La Villette,
later Cristallerie de Pantin)

*La Villette, established 1851; transferred to Pantin 1855*

*In 1851 E. S. Monot, a "modest worker" (E. Péligot and G. Bontemps, in Rapports 1867, vol. III, p. 73) from the Cristallerie de Lyon, founded the Cristallerie de La Villette, which was renamed the Cristallerie de Pantin after the factory moved to Pantin in 1855. Specializing in clear glass with cut decoration, the factory was still located at La Villette when Monot et Cie won an honorable mention at the Paris Exposition Universelle of 1855. Péligot described Monot's production as consisting chiefly of ordinary tablewares, although he praised "some rather large pieces, well executed" (Rapports 1855, p. 940). At the London International Exhibition of 1862, where Pantin and Clichy were the only French glasshouses to exhibit, Monot won a medal for table services "of all types... distinguished by their fine execution and by their quite moderate*

*price" (Pelouze, in Rapports 1862, vol. VI, p. 545) and for a varied production of molded, cut, engraved, and gilded-bronze mounted wares, of which one third were manufactured for export (Catalogue 1862, p. 218, no. 3308). During the 1860s Monot, following Baccarat (q.v.) and Saint-Louis (q.v.), introduced a variety of color techniques and effects in quasi-Venetian styles. At the Exposition Universelle of 1867, where the firm won a gold medal, Péligot and Bontemps praised Monot's colored glass and "imitations of Venetian glass" as well as the firm's clear crystal wares for "the elegance of their form... the whiteness and brilliance of the glass" (in Rapports 1867, vol. III, p. 73). By 1878 the firm— under the name Monot Père et Fils et Stumpf—was ranked with Clichy "just after Baccarat" (de Liesville, 1878, p. 698), and at the Paris Exposition Universelle of that year exhibited progressive wares in Chinese forms with "rock crystal" engravings, as well as opaline, Venetian-style, and enameled glasses. Before 1889 Monot retired from the firm, which was reorganized as Stumpf, Touvier, Viollet et Cie and continued production under Stumpf's direction until after 1900.*

K.B.H.

Bibliography:
Amic, 1952, pp. 117–18; Bloch-Dermant, 1974, p. 15; Brunhammer et al., 1976, p. 486

Monot et Cie (Cristallerie de La Villette)

## IV-29
## Vase

1855
Opaque-white opaline glass, with painted enamel decoration and gilding
Height 69.5 cm; diameter 30 cm

Provenance:
Gift of the maker's son to the Conservatoire National des Arts et Métiers, 1906 (inv. no. 14006²)

Exhibition:
1855, Paris, Exposition Universelle

Bibliography:
Catalogue, Paris, Conservatoire National des Arts et Métiers, 1908, p. 270, no. 14006; Amic, 1952, pp. 55, 118, pl. 40; Connaissance des Arts, 1957, no 8, repro. p. 145; Bloch-Dermant, 1974, p. 15

Impressive in its proportions and perfection of shape and finish, this vase (one of a pair) is undoubtedly one of the pieces Péligot had in mind when he praised "some rather large pieces, well executed" (in *Rapports 1855*, p. 940) among Monot's glasswares at the Exposition Universelle of 1855. Opalines such as this vase with painted polychrome decoration were made commercially by French firms from the

IV-29

late 1830s following technical innovations of Jean-François Robert and François-Eugène Fontenay in the muffle-firing of vitrified colors on glass. At the Paris exposition of 1839, Bontemps showed such painted opalines, a number of which he donated to the Musée Céramique at Sèvres (Bontemps, 1868, pp. 590–91). Robert and Fontenay were themselves inspired by painted Biedermeier glass of the 1820s and 1830s: Fontenay's *brevet d'importation* of 1836 describes a method for reproducing "the decorative effects of Bohemian glasswares" (Amic, 1952, p. 173). In 1843 Robert himself opened an independent glass-decorating studio at Sèvres, and the style and technique of the floral decorations which appear on this vase are similar to those he produced for such firms as Baccarat (q.v.), Saint-Louis (q.v.), and Choisy-le-Roi during the 1840s. The lush array of roses, anemones, narcissus, fuchsias, convolvulus, and delphiniums which overrun the neck and belly of the vase represents a free and natural-

istic style of flower decorations at its height—a style begun in the 1840s and used also in painted porcelains of the period. The bands of formalized gilded ornament separating the floral ornamentation already anticipate the more austere historicizing decorative styles of the 1860s, which Monot was to adopt in his exhibition pieces of 1867 and 1878.

K.B.H.

Musée National des Techniques–C.N.A.M., Paris

---

## Cristalleries de Saint-Louis

*Saint-Louis, established 1767*

*Founded 1767 by grant of Louis XV, the Verrerie Royale de Saint-Louis was reorganized in 1774 as François Lassalle et Cie. During Lassalle's ownership (1774–88), the factory, under the direction of de Beaufort, began the production of lead crystal, the first crystal of English type manufactured in France. In 1797 the company was reorganized as Seiler, Walter et Cie, which was known from 1829 as the Compagnie des Verreries et Cristalleries de Saint-Louis. From 1839 Saint-Louis specialized, like Baccarat (q.v.), in colored and opaline glasses after Central European models, which remained popular through the Second Empire. Saint-Louis seems to have led the other French cristalleries in creating new shapes for its glasswares, and its products were also distinguished by the brightness of their colors. Saint-Louis was Baccarat's major rival during the nineteenth century, although between 1832 and 1855 the firms sold their wares together in the Paris showroom of Launay, Hautin et Cie. By 1850 the gross incomes of the two companies were nearly identical, with Saint-Louis earning 1,800,000 francs and Baccarat 2,000,000 francs (Pelouze, in Rapports 1862, vol. VI, p. 533). Saint-Louis did not participate in the London international exhibitions of 1851 and 1862, but won a Medal of Honor in 1855 and a gold medal in 1867 at the Expositions Universelles in Paris. In 1855 Péligot praised Saint-Louis for a varied production of high quality and for "the spirit of invention that ceaselessly inspires its directors" (Rapports 1855, p. 936). Among objects first manufactured by Saint-Louis, Péligot listed "pieces imitating malachite, agate, marble" which were actually produced at Saint-Louis after Bohemian examples as early as 1844. The factory at Saint-Louis was directed successively during the mid-nineteenth century by F. A. Seiler (1817–57), Majorelle (1857–62), and Didierjean (1862–95). Didierjean was responsible for adopting Siemens furnaces at Saint-Louis, which from 1864 were coal-fired, with*

*the temperature regulated to permit the working of glass in open vessels. Didierjean's system was the most advanced in France, superior to the wood-burning process of Baccarat, and was highly praised by Péligot and Bontemps in 1867 (Rapports 1867, vol. III, pp. 62–63).*

K.B.H.

Bibliography:
Lami, 1881–88, vol. VIII, pp. 26–28; Amic, 1952, pp. 80–90

Cristalleries de Saint-Louis

## IV-30
## Ewer and Goblet

c. 1867
Clear crystal glass decorated with twisted opaque-white and pink threads; gilded bronze foot
Ewer height 39.5 cm; goblet height 21.5 cm

Provenance:
Compagnie des Cristalleries, Saint-Louis

Bibliography:
Schlumberger, 1977, repro. p. 30

The important sixteenth-century Venetian decorative technique of embedding threads of opaque-white (*latticino*) or colored glass within clear glass was revived in France in the late 1830s. Georges Bontemps produced filigree glass at Choisy-le-Roi in 1838 and 1839, and first described the technique in 1845 at a meeting of the Société d'Encouragement pour l'Industrie Nationale (Bontemps, 1868, pp. 601–2). By 1847 Saint-Louis was producing "filigranes rubannés," which Launay, Hautin et Cie complained sold at higher prices than those made at Clichy (Amic, 1952, p. 84). The method by which this ewer and goblet were decorated consisted of using a gather of clear glass to collect spirally twisted threads of white and pink glass from an open mold; by manipulating the gather, crossing and interlacing patterns were formed in the glass, which was subsequently blown in the usual way. The center of the ewer was pressed through, making a hole, after the fashion of certain late-sixteenth- and early seventeenth-century glass flasks. Glass with the more intricate patterns of these pieces is (and was during the nineteenth century) known as *vetro de trina*, or "lace glass."

Although such Venetian sixteenth-century decorative methods as the use of twisted threads and waved edges came into fashion in the 1840s and 1850s (*see Tarifs de la Compagnie des Cristalleries de Saint-Louis*, part 2, 1858), it was not until the 1860s that these techniques

IV-30

were applied, as in this ewer, to sixteenth-century forms in conscious, if not necessarily scrupulous, historicist fashion. In 1862 Clichy showed "glasses and large Venetian *coupes*" (Darcel, 1863, p. 75) in *latticino* (*Art Journal Catalogue 1862*, vol. II, repro. p. 213) and agate *calcedonio*. In 1867 Monot (q.v.) exhibited "imitations of Venetian filigrana vases and tazze" (H. Chance, in *Reports 1867*, vol. II, p. 374);

Baccarat exhibited a Venetian flask with a pressed-out circular hole, similar to that of the ewer; and Saint-Louis was praised by Péligot and Bontemps for its "Venetian filigree glass" (*Rapports 1867*, vol. III, p. 72).

K.B.H.

Compagnie des Cristalleries, Saint-Louis

# Sculpture

The state of French sculpture during the Second Empire was suggested by the critic Jules Claretie while commenting on Carpeaux's *Dance* (*see* no. V-8), unveiled in 1869 on the facade of the still uncompleted Paris Opéra: "It personified well the art of the Second Empire, that aphrodisiac art whose execution, this time superb, did not compensate for its vulgarity.... The truth is that it seemed to us of mediocre taste, and that the sculpture made a bawdy can-can out of the dance of the fairies."[1] In characterizing the period through this flamboyant group—perhaps the most important architectural decoration of the 1860s—Claretie revealed a conservative's despair at the erosion of the "grand style" in its most traditional and its most important mode: public sculpture.

The history of nineteenth-century sculpture can be viewed as the gradual downfall of the traditional "high" art of the Académie, but with no single acceptable alternative ready to take its place, regardless of how the critics cried for new, universal forms that would speak to the present. The legacy of the Romantic movement of the first half of the century, which sought almost any alternatives to academic principles, succeeded in further weakening an already enfeebled tradition. What artistic coherence remained was splintered, leaving both the practice and the criticism of sculpture without an established goal.

The Second Empire represents the critical point in the process of aesthetic fragmentation and institutional degeneration through which a new "modern" phase begins to emerge, marked by a more liberal official attitude and greater public acceptance of diversity. This transition is perhaps more dramatically evident in the history of sculpture than in that of any other art form since sculpture had more direct and traditional dependencies on classical forms.

Responding in part to a new diversity of attitudes, the primary state teaching instrument, the Ecole des Beaux-Arts, went through several changes during the period, and to a great degree it was able to maintain its prestige.[2] The Prix de Rome, its highest award, was still a coveted prize and a near guarantee of later commissions. Students selected masters largely on the basis of their success in producing Prix de Rome winners.[3] Other state-sponsored teaching institutions also existed, although not intended for practitioners of "high" art. The Muséum d'Histoire Naturelle had a program of instruction, attracting mostly *animalier* sculptors, such as Barye (q.v.), who taught there, but also many others, including Rodin (q.v.). The Ecole Gratuite de Dessin (commonly known as the Petite Ecole), established in the eighteenth century, became a state-sponsored school for ornamentalists during the July Monarchy and served as the initial, if not the only, source of education for many artists, including Carpeaux (q.v.), Carrier-Belleuse (q.v.), Frémiet (q.v.), and Rodin. Some sculptors did not enter any of these schools. Robert (q.v.), for example, studied only at the studios of David d'Angers and Pradier, although both also taught at the Ecole. Furthermore, one of the most influential teachers of the Second Empire, François Rude, was independent of the state-sponsored institutions, and many well-known sculptors studied with him.

The fact that a great diversity of sculptural style and opinions could survive and find an audience at the same time is a reflection of the general economic prosperity of France during the Second Empire and of the State's decision to encourage the production of sculpture as a tool to affirm the legitimacy of the Empire. Following Louis Philippe, who consecrated Versailles to the glories of France, Napoleon III capitalized on French nationalism and established himself as heir to the illustrious heroes of France by commissioning their effigies: monuments were erected to Vercingétorix by Petit (1858), Millet (1861), Claudet (1862), Delhomme (1867), Bartholdi (1870); to Charlemagne by Pascal (1859), Le Véel (1865), Rochet (1867); to Joan of Arc by Fabisch (1855), Clère (1863), Chapu (1870); to Francis I by Clésinger (1856), Etex (1864), Cavelier (1869); and to Henri IV by Bonnassieux (1856) and Ottin (1868). In turn the monuments of Napoleon I are nearly countless: those by Nieuwerkerke (1854; La Roche-sur-Yon); Rochet (1853; Versailles); Le Maire (1854; Lille); Le Véel (1857; Cherbourg); Jouffroy (1857; Auxonne); Cavelier (1861; formerly collection Prince Napoléon); Vital Dubray (1865; Rouen); Barye (1865; Ajaccio); Frémiet (1866–67; Grenoble); Pajol (1867; Montereau)—preceding the no less numerous monuments to Napoleon III himself.

Grand architectural statements, accompanied by elaborate and abundant decoration, promoted the image, suggested the wealth, and affirmed the might of imperial power.[4] During the eighteen years of the Second Empire, a provincial city such as Marseilles, for example, would receive the new Cathedral of Notre Dame de la Garde; the Palais du Pharo (Palais de l'Impératrice); the Palais de Longchamp, with its luxuriant *mise-en-scène* by Cavelier (q.v.); a superb city hall; the Palais de Justice; the Bourse; the Grand Hôtel, all noteworthy buildings with sculptural programs. The provincial capitals competed with one another, and the fever of construction (and speculation) went hand in hand with the fever of ornamentation. But it was Paris that received the greatest attention.

The Louvre and the Tuileries represented the most important complex in Paris, the image of the Empire itself. The variety of sculptors involved in the decoration of both the old and new sections bespeaks the liberal policy of imperial patronage, both stylistically and iconographically. The major commissions of the 1850s went to academicians, whose works maintained a sober dignity. The facade of the Pavillon de Rohan was executed by Diébolt; that of the Pavillon de Turgot by Cavelier, who, with Guillaume, also contributed its caryatids; that of the Pavillon Richelieu by Duret, with caryatids by Bosio, Pollet (q.v.), and Cavelier. The Pavillon Colbert and Pavillon Daru received their facade sculpture and caryatids from Vilain; the Pavillon Sully, caryatids by Simart (q.v.) and Duret; the Pavillon Denon, facade from Simart with caryatids by Brian, Jacquer, Ottin, and Robert; and the Pavillon Mollien, facade and caryatids by Jouffroy. However, Barye also contributed significantly to the Louvre during the Second Empire. The Pavillon de Flore, one of the last to be completed, includes the work of such artists as Mme Léon Bertaux (lunette figure of *Navigation*). The major commission went to Carpeaux (having received no commissions for the Cour Napoléon), who produced for it in 1866 *Imperial France Bringing Light into the World and Protecting Agriculture and Science* and the lively *Triumph of Flora*.[5]

The new Opéra (*see* no. I-10) was also conceived with lavish sculptural ornamentation.[6] With the exception of Carpeaux's *Dance*, most of the sculpture on the exterior of Garnier's opulent and flamboyant structure is markedly restrained. The sculptors employed included Jouffroy, Jean-Joseph Perraud, Guillaume, and Aimé Millet. On the interior, the sculpture is more animated, and more in the spirit of the lavish decoration. If the works of Chapu (q.v.), Paul Dubois (q.v.), and Pollet (q.v.) go only so far as to blend with the overall opulence of the Opéra, the dramatic Neo-Mannerist conception of the *Pythia* by Marcello (q.v.) stands out as a more fully charged element, as do Carrier-Belleuse's chimney caryatids and his torchères flanking the Grand Staircase.

A quite different set of sculptural problems was presented by the complete and radical restoration of the Cathedral of Notre Dame, a project initiated under Louis Philippe. Its style and its importance logically encouraged the use of artists conversant in the Gothic idiom like the ornamentalist Bièze and a sculptor such as Michel-Pascal. The supervisor of sculpture, Geoffroy-Dechaume, became primarily a Gothic specialist, contributing the Apostles on the roof near the new spire. Commissions for other churches were approached with less historical accuracy, and conventional decorum was sought primarily through assigning the major works to academicians. Pradier designed bas-reliefs for the new church of Sainte Clotilde, which were completed by his students Eugène Guillaume and Eugène-Louis Lequesne in the 1850s, who in turn received further commissions for the church. François Jouffroy in 1862 executed the pedimental sculpture for the principal facade of the Church of Saint Augustin. While not an academician, Carpeaux, in his first public commission in the 1860s (and his only religious commission in Paris) showed an unusual restraint in his figure of Temperance for the Church of La Trinité.

A still greater diversity in sculptural outlook appears in the public monuments commissioned by the Empire. The Vendôme column was one of a number of first Empire monuments restored to their former appearance: Augustin Dumont's antique figure of Napoleon I of 1863 approximates Denis-Antoine Chaudet's earlier version, and even includes the surviving Victory in his hand. Direct references to the Antique and their implied political allusions to the Neoclassicism of the first Empire are also found in Barye's equestrians: his relief of Napoleon III, commissioned in 1860 for the "guichets" of the Louvre (destroyed September 1870; *see* no. I-20) evokes the equestrian Marcus Aurelius on the Campidoglio in Rome as does his figure of Napoleon I for the most important of the many Second Empire tributes to the Bonaparte family, the monument in Ajaccio. Erected in the Bonaparte birthplace in 1865 and supervised by Viollet-le-Duc (q.v.), Barye's equestrian of Napoleon I as a Roman emperor reigns over the figures of the four brothers by Gabriel-Jules

Thomas, Aimé Millet, Louis Petit, and Jacques-Léonard Maillet (q.v.).

On a somewhat smaller scale, but no less abundant, were the portraits produced for the new court. Jean-Auguste Barre was probably the most active imperial portraitist of the 1850s and early 1860s. He produced at least twelve portraits of the Emperor in a severely Neoclassical style, and many of the Bonaparte family. The numerous imperial portraits of Lequien (q.v.) recall Houdon's crisply modeled bust *à l'antique* of Napoleon I. Yet, commissioned formal portraiture, like much of the public Bonapartist sculpture, does not bear a consistent kinship with the first Empire; rather, it frequently responds to a new realistic outlook. The full-length 1861 marble of the Emperor in uniform by Auguste Ottin (Compiègne) is a conspicuous example of a literal, if tedious, representation. More informal portraits, rather genre in character, were also undertaken, such as those by Chatrousse (q.v.) and Mme Lefèvre-Deumier (q.v.).

The imperial couple avoided designating an official court sculptor,[7] although Carpeaux seems to have served that function informally during the 1860s. Despite his very proper educational credentials, he gave little credence to academic goals and it was probably his personal style that initially brought him the public notoriety that also won the attention of the Empress and Emperor. The focus of his activity for the imperial family during the Second Empire was the artistic education and portrayal of the young Prince Imperial (*see* no. V-7). He also executed a bust of the Empress in 1866 and one of the former Emperor after 1871 (*see* no. V-9). The formal dignity and full-state regalia that characterize Princess Mathilde's portrait (no. V-6) are conspicuously lacking in the imperial portraits. This very low-key approach to "court" sculpture shows how blurred the division between the court and the people of France had become. The imperial portraits are as informal and expressive as those made of the bourgeoisie.

The absence of a clear official goal within court portraiture is reflected on a still more complex level within the most vital proving ground for the Second Empire artist: the Salon. Providing the indispensable link between artist and patron, the Salon was especially important to the sculptors, given the particularly public role of the medium. Exhibition alternatives, because of this, were largely overlooked. Few sculptors submitted to the rotating exhibitions on the boulevard des Italiens and when they did, it was usually informal portraits or works already familiar from the Salon that might be found there. Similarly,

works that received some note in the Salon were at time shown again in the provinces.[8] But the Salon des Refusés of 1863, featuring some of the most progressive painters in France, did not interest significant independent sculptors.[9]

The admissions policy for sculpture was remarkably liberal during the Second Empire. Unlike painting, few works considered important then or now were rejected and a number of them were duly recognized with awards, like Carpeaux's important entries of 1863, which won a first-class medal. The great "Romantics" of the 1830s and 1840s (absent from the July Monarchy Salons either out of choice, like Barye, or by force, like Préault and Rude and his students) had been guiltily welcomed during the Republic and were highly visible in the Salons of the Second Empire. They and all their minor *confrères* provided the initial variety in the galleries, echoed subsequently by younger artists encouraged by their example. Presumably in the name of artistic open-mindedness, the jury's indulgence permitted a wide range of quality as well.

The entries in the Salon and the criticism they precipitated reveal the aesthetic issues most frequently raised during the period. The "grand style" in sculpture was generally synonymous with Classicism. Its medium was marble, supreme in the traditional hierarchy of materials, its form, the idealized nude. Many, like Théophile Gautier, felt sculpture excluded other forms: "Nudity is the essential condition of sculpture... the representation of the human body, abstracted from all particularities and accidents, constitutes ideal beauty...."[10] "It [sculpture] seems to have received from antiquity its definitive form... without the gods and heroes of mythology who give him the plausible pretext of the nude and draped forms which he needs, the sculptor can do nothing...."[11] Sculpture with Classical subjects continued to dominate to the point that the critic Paul Mantz, conservative as he was, credited the prevalence of the traditional repertory as a sign of crisis in modern sculpture. While praising the aesthetic quality of many pieces in the Salon of 1865, he complained: "The monotony of subject matter handled by our sculptors reveals of them a persistent lethargy, a perfect sterility of imagination. Today, as yesterday, a young girl in conference with a dove, a child bitten by a snake, a gladiator falling in the arena, the soldier Marathon, etc.... shepherdesses, seasons, muses...."[12] For all his support, the vast quantities of sculpture produced in the Classical mode were mediocre, the exceptions being those works of antique theme extending beyond traditional forms and bringing to these subjects either a quality of archaeological domestic genre as in the work of Salmson (q.v.) or technical virtuosity and surface complexity as that of Maillet (q.v.).[13]

The search for impact within this idiom led many artists to emphasize the inherent erotic potential of the nude and the sensuality of highly finished marble surfaces. The *antiquité voluptueuse* of Pradier's supple nudes was carried far beyond his coy suggestiveness. Clésinger's *Woman Bitten by a Serpent* of 1847 initiated a more blatantly sexual type which had particular importance for the next generation; for example, Cavelier's *Truth* of 1853 (destroyed); Christophe's *Human Comedy* of 1859, celebrated by Baudelaire (Tuileries gardens); Arnaud's *Venus of the Golden Hair* (no. V-1) of 1862; Claude Vignon's *Daphne Transformed into a Laurel Tree* of 1866 (Marseilles museum); Clésinger's *Andromeda* of 1869 (Périgord museum); and Delaplanche's *Eve* (Saint-Quentin museum). A greater sensuality is also apparent in male subjects, in a virile figure such as Delhomme's *Wounded Gaul* of 1867 (Belfort), after a Hellenistic model, as well as in androgynous youths such as Dubois's *Narcissus* (Louvre), shown in 1867. The use of an adolescent boy, be it in a Saint John type by Moreau-Vauthier (q.v.) or a Neapolitan fisherboy by Carpeaux, seems to have a similar propensity.

Sterner aspects of Classicism continued to be seen; Pierre-Charles Simart (q.v.) was a particularly conspicuous practitioner of this style during the 1850s. His work had all the gravity and nobility of the grand style, evident especially in his earlier projects for the tomb of Napoleon at the Invalides, and he continued to be favored with official commissions. Eugène Guillaume, who dominated the Ecole des Beaux-Arts for decades, was elected director in 1864. He had attracted attention at the Salon of 1852 with his marble *Anacreon* (Louvre) and in the 1860s executed a series of marble portraits of Napoleon I for the "Maison Pompéienne" (the initial full-length figure of Napoleon I as a Roman emperor of 1859 [now at Arenenberg] is seen in Boulanger's painting, no. VI-12). Although best known for his "Roman" Classicism, Guillaume was remarkably adaptive and his subject matter largely determined his style. For example, his 1858 monument to Colbert at Reims is as lively and full of lace as his Augustan portrait of Napoleon I is solemn and heavy with Roman togas.

Despite the honor given to the Classical tradition, the Second Empire openly embraced Romanticism after its many years of struggle. Top awards at the Exposition Universelle of 1855 went to Romantic works of the 1830s and 1840s: Duret's *Grape Picker Playing Music* and *Neapolitan Fisherman*; Rude's *Fisherboy* and Barye's animal sculpture. This gesture represented tacit acceptance of the genre quality of the subjects as well as the "unclassical" principles of expression, movement, naturalism, and the particular.

By the 1850s, despite its long lineage, animal sculpture was recognized as a significantly anti-classical, therefore modern, genre. The Goncourts commented in 1852: "The historical school is dying, in the art which makes things palpable just as is happening in the art which makes things visible. Landscape replaces it in painting; animals replace it in sculpture. Nature succeeds man. That is the evolution of modern art."[14]

While the antique character of Barye's *Centaur and Lapith*, shown in 1850, continued to be praised by the conservatives, it was the familiar dramatic naturalism of his *Jaguar Devouring a Hare* (no. V-2), shown in 1850 and 1852, that proved so significant. Bronze was the Romantic medium and in the hands of Barye, a craftsman par excellence (he ran his own foundry for a short while), this ductile material perfectly suited his formal and expressive concerns. Barye's work was the primary model for succeeding *animaliers.* His discriminating naturalism became the basis for Landseer-like tableaux in bronze by Isidore Bonheur, Pierre-Jules Mêne, Jules Moigniez, and Frémiet. With the large-scale works of Cain (q.v.), however, the heroic tradition of Barye continued until the end of the century.

An informal figural art with a strongly documentary character, be it exotic or familiar, sprang up under the impetus of naturalism. Cordier's vigorous African portraits begun in the 1840s became particularly popular during the 1850s and 1860s (*see* no. V-16). Frémiet's statuettes of the French army for the Emperor are accurate in detail and lively in attitude; though minor, they were hailed in the Salons for their truth, much like his subsequent historical equestrians. Many anecdotal sculptural subjects were based on sentimental literature, perhaps best exemplified by Chatrousse's two groups of Heloise and Abelard, shown initially in plaster in 1857. Mathurin Moreau (q.v.) and J.-L.-D. Schroeder (*Falling Leaves*, 1858; Tours museum) displayed a tender Romantic feeling that English observers particularly appreciated and likened to their own Baily.

By the late 1850s the lessons of Rude's *Fisherboy* had taken hold, and Carpeaux's bronze *Fisherboy with Seashell* was no isolated incident in the Salon of 1859, where five other similar subjects were shown. Carpeaux's happened to be the version that caught the public's imagination. Endowed with exuberant animation, its relationship with the early Romantics was quickly noticed: "It deserves to be shown in the same gallery as the *Fisherboy* by Rude, the *Dancer* by Duret.... Without pursuing the dangerous foolishness of the ideal, he holds strictly to nature."[15]

The respect for nature, which would lead eventually to naturalism, appears in other works inspired by the Antique, such as *Discovery at Pompeii* by Moulin (Salon of 1864; Louvre): a shovel (an object to which Dalou, q.v., would bring honor) rests on the shoulder of a triumphantly dancing young excavator, recalling the popular Hellenistic figure, *The Dancing Faun* from Pompeii.

The Renaissance also became a fertile source. Falguière (q.v.) added another dimension to his work with his *Winner of the Cock Fight* (Louvre), shown in 1864. An allusion much appreciated by critics, this figure was a modernized version of the *Mercury* of Giambologna. Similarly praised at the Salon were "the simplicity and individual character" of Paul Dubois's "Michelangelesque" *Narcissus*, his "Raphaelesque" *St. John the Baptist* (Louvre), and the "Donatellesque mannerism" of his very popular *Florentine Singer* (no. V-17).[16]

Finally, the Neo-Rococo, already prevalent in the decorative arts, thanks partly to Carrier-Belleuse, was introduced in Salon sculpture in the 1850s. Few commented on the "Rococo" flavor of Louis Veray's *Sleeping Harvester* of 1853 (Musée Calvet) or Carrier-Belleuse's own *Love and Friendship* of about 1857, but its effect on portraiture was much discussed. In the early 1860s both Carpeaux and Carrier-Belleuse explored the eighteenth-century idiom in portraits, giving them a vivacious intimacy and plastic richness unlike the ponderous realism of contemporaries such as Oliva, Iselin, and Ottin. These portraits were both successful publicly and influential aesthetically, particularly upon a sculptor such as Rodin. Of the two it was Carpeaux whose impact on "serious" art still seems the most profound. For all his popularity, most of his Salon entries and public commissions raised lively critical controversy. His range of subjects and conceptual depth took him into areas into which Carrier-Belleuse would never venture.

Typical of the period, Carpeaux and Carrier-Belleuse made their work accessible to the public through the production of variants and reductions. Carrier-Belleuse's involvement with the art industry was particularly significant. The commercial arts had been given impetus in the nineteenth century with the rise of bourgeois patronage and the equating of material progress and social development. An important facet of the art industry was the revival of art bronzes. While other European countries were highly active in this area, France was their recognized leader, winning top awards at most international exhibitions during the period. Technical innovations introduced during the 1830s and 1840s—*fonte de fer*, galvanoplasty (*see* Christofle), and particularly Achille Collas's reduction process purchased by Barbedienne (q.v.)—allowed manufacturers to produce an incredible variety of objects, from inexpensive reductions in zinc to extremely fine luxury objects like the torchères designed by Carrier-Belleuse and executed by Charpentier (no. V-10).

The proliferation of sculpture as commercial art was a conspicuous facet of the vulgarization of art bemoaned by Claretie. Efforts to expand artistic focus to include a wider audience and to increase the options allowed by high art, together with the struggle of Classicists themselves to give their idiom significant form, provided the art world with a diversity that challenged the perspective of even the most catholic of critics. Yet within this diversity, geniuses did appear and were widely recognized, capable of articulating the truths of their time, yet contributing as well to future generations. Other artists also enjoyed the support of an increasingly involved public and that of a tolerant, if not incisive, government. The Second Empire thus emerges as one of the most vital periods in the history of sculpture since the seventeenth century.

S.G.L./A.P./J.R.

*Notes*

1. Claretie, 1873, p. 194.
2. *See* Boime, 1977.
3. Guiffrey's *Listes des Pensionnaires de l'Académie de France à Rome* reveals Francisque Duret (member of the Institut de France since 1843, professor at the Ecole since 1852) as the most frequently mentioned master of Prix de Rome winners and runners-up during the Republic and Second Empire, followed by François Jouffroy (Institut, 1857; Ecole, 1863) and Alexandre-Augustin Dumont (Institut, 1838; Ecole, 1852). Carpeaux defected from his admired François Rude to Duret's studio hoping to win the Prix de Rome, which he did.
4. The utilization of sculpture under the Second Empire on facades and in public places was massive compared with the percentage of work entering museums and imperial collections. The inventory of the "domaine privé" of Napoleon III for sculpture includes 196 contemporary works (159 numbers). Only 43 are reported on the inventory of the Louvre. Certain acquisitions by the Empress or the Emperor do not appear on the inventory of the "domaine privé." *Le Moniteur* of March 28, 1869, published the report of Marshal Vaillant to the Emperor (March 26) and to Nieuwerkerke (July 30), noting the considerable accomplishment of increasing the artistic collections in fifteen years by some 45,000 works. For sculpture, however, one finds only 67 listings at the Louvre (including sculpture from the Middle Ages to modern times), 200 at the Luxembourg (this representing sculpture and painting which are not distinguished), 400 at Versailles (same confusion of sculpture and paintings).
5. *Flora* was dubbed "Triumph" by the Emperor, who allowed the public to decide its fate upon protests about its unconventionality by the architect Lefuel (Riotor, 1927, pp. 61–62). Its survival represents not only a defeat of an established stylistic approach but also that of the control exercised by architects and governing committees.

6. *See* Garnier, 1878–81, vols. I, II.
7. Lami quotes a letter which may articulate just such a decision. A marginal note on a request from Mme Lefèvre-Deumier for the title of *Sculpteur de la Maison de l'Impératrice* reads: "Le titre, non, mais des commandes" (Lami, 1914–21, vol. III, p. 283).
8. Bronze casts of Carpeaux's *Fisherboy with Seashell* were exhibited in Nantes, Lyons, and Metz after the debut of the work in plaster at the Ecole in 1858 and appearance in bronze in the Salon of 1859, where it won a second-class medal.
9. Thirty-seven sculptors were listed in the catalogue, among them Jean-Baptiste Baujault, Albert Fautsas, and Charles Iguel, who entered two minor commissions for the Louvre (Wildenstein, 1965, p. 147). That achievement alone makes Iguel the most apparently successful of the lot, for the majority remained in obscurity.
10. Gautier, 1855–56, vol. I, p. 117.
11. Benoist, 1928, p. 35.
12. *Gazette des Beaux-Arts*, vol. XVIII, 1865, pp. 33–34.
13. There would seem to be an unconscious desire to respond against the technical perfections of certain works prompted both by the imitation of antique sculpture, known more often than not in a mutilated form, but also an involuntary demonstration of the frequent absence of spirituality during this time (despite the construction of numerous churches it is necessary in general to note the absence of a true religious or funerary sculpture); Gautier in *Le Moniteur*, September 1, 1863, noted apropos of *The Childhood of Bacchus* by Perraud: "Had it been broken... it would easily pass as a masterpiece"; Rambosson (1898, p. 5) observed that "what one says of a fragmented arm of a Greek statue, one could also say of the head or the hands of *The Martyr* by M. Falguière" (*see also* Girodie, 1901, p. 3; Baudelaire, 1965, p. 206; Goncourt and Goncourt, 1956, May 19, 1861).
14. 1852, Paris, Salon, p. 124.
15. Fidière, 1894, p. 26.
16. *The Art Journal*, n.s., vol. VI, 1867, p. 155.

## Charles-Auguste Arnaud

*La Rochelle 1825–1883*

*Arnaud attended the Ecole des Beaux-Arts in Angers before entering the studio of François Rude in Paris. He first exhibited at the Salon of 1846 and subsequently obtained a number of official commissions, the best known among them being the Hunter and the Artilleryman for the Pont de l'Alma, Paris. He apparently had financial difficulties and suffered mental disturbances, and he did not exhibit after 1865. He was confined in the Sainte Anne asylum, from which he was discharged in 1869; he does not seem to have produced any sculpture after this date.*

*In May 1852 he had urgently solicited a commission from the Ministry of Fine Arts, asserting that it had been promised him (Arch. nat. F²¹ 62). His biographer, Saché, explains this aberration on the grounds that he was "disappointed in his hope of obtaining the commission for the statue of Don Pedro, King of Portugal" and strongly affected by the lack of success of his* Venus of the Golden Hair *(1859). Indeed, in a series of letters in the Archives Nationales, we see that legal action was brought against him in 1859. He had been given the commissions for the two decorative statues for the Pont de l'Alma, and for a statue of Summer for the Louvre, commissions involving a total of 27,000 francs. But he failed to pay either his workers or restaurant owners who provided food for him and his assistants, and he incurred transportation expenses which exceeded the sum owed him. At this time Arnaud was in Portugal, trying for the commission for the statue of Don Pedro, on which he was desperately counting. (Carpeaux, q.v., also failed to obtain this commission, which in fact went to Elias Robert, q.v.)*

*After the lawsuit had been decided against him, all his possessions were confiscated and put up for sale. In a letter to the director of the Sainte Anne asylum, he wrote: "The small-scale model of the statue of Summer, ordered for the cour de Louvre, and the entire contents of my studio were sold while I was in Portugal. The fact that I could not return from Portugal and oppose this sale of all my worldly goods, effected under such sad circumstances, explains the illness that has driven me here to Sainte Anne to await the time when I will be able to take up my work again."*

O.S.

Bibliography:
Bellier and Auvray, 1882–87, vol. I, p. 22; Thieme and Becker, 1907–50, vol. II, pp. 123–24; Lami, 1914–21, vol. I, pp. 20–22.

V-1

## Charles-Auguste Arnaud

### V-1
### Venus of the Golden Hair

Completed 1862
Signed and dated, lower left: AVG. ARNAUD, SC. PARIS A. MDCCCLXII
Marble
210 × 56 × 56 cm

Provenance:
Purchased by the Emperor after the Salon of 1863 (?) for 20,000 francs (Louvre Archives 2 DD 20); placed in his private garden at Saint-Cloud (Louvre Archives 38 DD 7 no. 109); taken by the Germans to the Prefecture of Versailles; stored at Versailles, March 19, 1870 (Louvre Archives 8 DD 4); deposited at Compiègne, 1881 (Compiègne Archives 41 ter); exhibited in the Salle des Colonnes (Louvre Archives S 12 [July 27, 1887]); Musée National du Château (inv. no. 38 C 7)

Exhibitions:
1859, Paris, Salon, no. 3053; 1863, Paris, Salon, no. 2222

Bibliography:
Aubert, 1863; Auvray, 1863, p. 80; de Callias, 1863, *Salon*, pp. 5–6; Cantrel, 1863, p. 190; T. Gautier, *Le Monde Illustré*, vol. I, 1863, p. 298; Gautier, 1863, "Salon"; Merson, 1863; de Sault, 1863, pp. 238–39; Thoré-Bürger, 1863, p. 433; Yriarte, 1863, "Vénus"; Bellier and Auvray, 1882–87, vol. I, p. 22; Lami, 1914–21, vol. I, pp. 20–22; Saché, 1918, pp. 5, 19

Although this *Venus* bears no traces of Arnaud's psychological problems, the letters which he wrote about it in 1863 to the comte de Nieuwerkerke suggest the sculptor's agitated state of mind. "I neither can nor should send my statue until you yourself have decided upon the place it is to occupy; otherwise its transport is impossible. I would not press my position with such incomprehensible insistence and in such bad taste were it not justified by the exceptional nature of my work..." (Louvre Archives X [April 13, 1863]). Two days later he wrote again: "You will judge later whether a work of this importance, the result of five years of labor and considerable expense, does not fall outside the usual rules."

Is this *Venus*, the object of so much attention, the one exhibited at the Salon in 1859? It would seem so, and yet it is signed 1862. It is likely that after the 1859 exhibit, Arnaud retouched it, added color, and signed it for presentation at the Salon of 1863, where it enjoyed a certain success, especially if we remember that critics then took little interest in sculpture.

However, fault was found with the conception of the subject and the technique of its execution. Aubert and Mantz took to task its lack of moral elevation and accused it of "representing a purely fortuitous type instead of one in which we may find eternal beauty." This corresponded to a critical current that called for a pure and noble art with idealistic purpose and abominated sensuality and realism, which were both relegated to a low level. For like reasons there was criticism of the abundance of color. Thoré, who praised "the graceful softness of the flesh tones," said that the marble was "rather loosely worked."

Other critics extolled Arnaud for the very same characteristics. Auvray liked the "natural shapes, broadly modeled... but not imitative of the classics." De Sault excused the polychromy, considering it "a form of coquetry akin to the beauty marks of our grandmothers." Yriarte and Gautier recalled the fact that polychromy was used by the ancient Greeks. Finally, Cantrel remarked that Arnaud "is already a little Horace Vernet of sculpture."

Arnaud's *Venus* was also noted and appreciated by the Emperor. This should not surprise us, for its sensual and ungodlike character is in keeping with Second Empire taste. And the heavy, cascading curls remind us that hair was not only a sign of noble birth and distinction but also a fetish and an erotic symbol, celebrated by Baudelaire and Courbet and later by de Maupassant.

O.S.

Musée National du Château, Compiègne

---

*Antoine-Louis Barye*

*Paris 1796–1875 Paris*

*Barye was first apprenticed to the engraver Fourier; in 1816 he entered the studio of the sculptor François-Joseph Bosio, then that of the painter Antoine-Jean Gros, before being admitted, in 1818, to the Ecole des Beaux-Arts.*

*Despite an honorable mention for engraving (1819) and a second prize for sculpture (1820), he failed to win the Prix de Rome in 1824. The previous year he had begun to sculpt animals for Jacques-Henri Fauconnier, jeweler to the duchesse d'Angoulême. At the same time he took courses in anatomy and dissection at the Jardin des Plantes.*

*Barye exhibited for the first time at the Salon of 1827 and, during the reign of Louis Philippe, created his finest hunting scenes and animal combats:* Tiger Devouring a Gavial *(1831),* Lion and Snake *(1833–36), and numerous animal hunts for the duc d'Orléans. His more monumental works foreshadow the classical style of the* Walking Lion *on the July Column (1836).*

*His rejection by the 1837 Salon caused him to stop exhibiting until the Revolution of 1848 changed the Salon's method of selection. Commissions continued through the Second Republic and the Second Empire, including* Lapith and Centaur *(1849),* Jaguar Devouring a Hare *(1850), the frieze of the Pavillon de l'Horloge of the Louvre (1855), and* Napoleon III on Horseback *(1860) for the "Guichets" du Carrousel (see no. I-20). In the provinces he executed four fighting animals (1869) for the Palais de Longchamp, Marseilles, and the equestrian Napoleon I for Ajaccio.*

*Barye was appointed curator of plaster casts and director of casting at the Louvre (1848–50). When this post was eliminated he became professor of natural-history drawing at the Ecole Agronomique of Versailles and then professor of zoological drawing at the Muséum (1854–74). In 1855 he was made a member of the jury for the Salon, and in 1863, president of the advisory commission of the Union Centrale des Arts Appliqués à l'Industrie, of which he was a founder. He set up his own foundry (1849–52), which was ultimately a failure. He had many founders—not counting his numerous counterfeiters (see G. Benge, in 1975–76, Cambridge, pp. 79–88).*

*A chevalier (1833) and officer (1855) of the Legion of Honor, he won a gold medal at the Exposition Universelle of 1855 (Industry Section, a purposeful and significant choice on his part; see no. II-35) and another gold medal at the exposition of 1867 and was elected a member of the Institut de France in 1868.*

A.P.

Bibliography:
Alexandre, 1889; Ballu, 1890; Lami, 1914–21, vol. I, pp. 69–85 (bibl.); Benge, 1969; Pivar, 1974; G. Benge, in 1975–76, Cambridge, pp. 77–107 (bibl.)

Antoine-Louis Barye

## V-2
## Jaguar Devouring a Hare

1850
Signed on base behind jaguar's left rear paw: A.L. Barye
Bronze
$39.5 \times 38.6 \times 103.7$ cm

Provenance:
Commissioned by the Ministry of the Interior, October 8, 1851, after exhibition of plaster model in the 1850 Salon (Arch. nat. F$^{21}$63); assigned to the Direction des Musées Impériaux, January 24, 1853, and exhibited in the rotunda of bronzes in the Musée du Luxembourg (Louvre Archives S 16); reverted to the Louvre, May 3, 1874, but not transferred until 1886; considered lost after 1939 San Francisco exhibition; discovered by Jean-René Gaborit at the Palace of the Legion of Honor, 1973; returned to the Louvre (inv. no. RF 160)

Exhibitions:
1852, Paris, Salon, no. 1295; 1855, Paris, Exposition Universelle, no. 4245; 1934, Paris, Muséum d'Histoire Naturelle, no. 126; 1935, Brussels, no. 983; 1937, Paris, Palais National des Arts, no. 1080; 1939, San Francisco, no. 163; 1976–77, Paris, Muséum d'Histoire Naturelle, no. 251

Bibliography:
De la Fizelière, 1851, p. 97; Goncourt and Goncourt, 1852, pp. 123–25; Loudun, 1852, p. 21; Malitourne, 1852, p. 165; Planche, n.d., vol. II, p. 321; Vignon, 1852, p. 59; T. Gautier, Le Moniteur, December 8, 1855; Gebaüer, 1855, pp. 276–77; Loudun, 1855, p. 195; Planche, 1855, p. 1160; de la Rochenoire, 1855, p. 94; Vignon, 1855, p. 153; Catalogues, Paris, Luxembourg, 1858–86; Mantz, 1867, "Barye," pp. 121, 122; Genevay, 1875, p. 37; Goncourt, 1886, pp. 3–7; Bonnat, 1889, pp. 379–82; Ballu, 1890, pp. 104, 107–9; Migeon, 1903, p. 17; Focillon, 1913, pp. 168–69, repro. p. 171; Vitry, 1912, pp. 93–94; Isay, 1937, pp. 32–35; Benge, 1969, no. 128 (bibl.); 1975–76, Cambridge, p. 78

The subject may have been prompted by the delayed success of Barye's bronze *Tiger Devouring a Gavial*, shown in plaster in 1831, cast in 1832, and finally purchased by the State in 1848, thanks to Charles Blanc. It remained at the Ministère de l'Intérieur throughout the Second Empire.

Comparison of these two groups reveals a stylistic evolution toward greater realism and away from the ornamental. Surface treatment is less dependent on chasing. The jaguar is no longer merely poised on an oval base with scattered leaves; rather, the powerful tension of its body relates to the irregularity of the rock. Its composition emphasizes asymmetry to accentuate the vertical thrust of the jaguar's neck and hare's body, whereas the 1831 group makes an almost perfect arc.

Critics often reveal more about themselves than about the work under analysis. In 1852 Gustave Planche praised this group "which can be compared to the most beautiful monument of antique art" and yet concluded his discussion by condemning realism. That same year Edmond de Goncourt described it as "one of those imitations of living nature beyond which sculpture cannot go."

Critical acclaim was unanimous, from Ballu's view that it was the "synthesis of his art," the masterpiece of his life" to Bonnat's unforgettable exclamation: "It is as beautiful as Michelangelo's *Slave* at the Louvre."

The original plaster (RF 1563) and the bronze proof model (RF 1553) were gifts to the Louvre in 1912 from J. Zoubaloff. Numerous full-scale bronzes exist: aside from the three listed by Benge in American public collections, there are casts at the Newark Museum, the Minneapolis Institute of Arts (anonymous loan), and the Musée Bonnat, Bayonne.

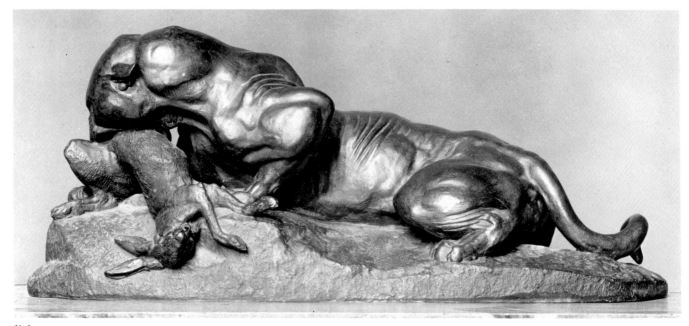

V-2

The bronze was distributed commercially after 1855; Barye's fourth catalogue lists it under number 65 (44 × 105 cm; 30 francs) and his fifth and final catalogue offers it at 35 francs under number 78. Edited by Barbedienne, it appears unnumbered in the 1877 catalogue (same dimensions; 1,800 francs) and the 1880 catalogue (same price). The reproduction studio of the Musées Nationaux distributed a plaster (42 × 85 cm), number C3964 in the 1955 catalogue. Zieseniss (1954) published six related watercolors (C 13–18).

A.P.

Musée du Louvre, Paris

Antoine-Louis Barye

## V-3
## War

1855
Patinated plaster (original model, at one-third scale)
105 × 62 × 90 cm

Provenance:
On January 17, 1855, proposals submitted for two groups, *Peace* and *War*, for the facade of the Pavillon Denon of the Louvre; contract drawn up and approved February 6, 1855, by Achille Fould; payment of 5,000 francs made for one-third-scale models, June 2, 1855; final acceptance of the works, January 13, 1856 (Arch. nat. 64 Aj 189); models in sculptor's studio until 1876; sale, Paris, Hôtel Drouot, February 7–12, 1876; F. Barbedienne; J. Zoubaloff, 1892; anonymous gifts to the Louvre, 1912 (inv. no. RF 1556)

Exhibitions:
1875, Paris, Ecole des Beaux-Arts, no. 3; 1889, Paris, Ecole des Beaux-Arts, no. 573; 1956–57, Paris, Louvre, no. 88, pl. 6

Bibliography:
Planche, 1855, p. 1160; Mantz, 1867, "Barye," pp. 107–23; Henriot, 1870, pp. 771–72; Genevay, 1875, pp. 39–40; Silvestre, 1878, pp. 194, 202, 208; Alexandre, 1889, p. 86; De Kay, 1889, p. 86; Ballu, 1890, pp. 109–13; Guillaume, 1900, pp. 520–22; Vitry, 1912, p. 95, pl. 29; Focillon, 1913, p. 161, repro. p. 165; Lami, 1914–21, vol. I, pp. 72, 77–78; Saunier, 1925, *Barye*, pp. 35, 40–42, pl. 15; Remington, 1940, pp. 34–36; Benge, 1969, vol. I, pp. 363–65, vol. II, pp. 539–41; Lewis, 1977, pp. 3–11

One of the most impressive projects of Napoleon III's reign, the construction of the New Louvre, was completed in five years (1852–57). Motivated by a social goal (the simultaneous employment of 335 sculptors, for example), as well as a political one, the New Louvre was an administrative feat demonstrating the regime's skill in managing grandiose projects while asserting itself as successor, thus rightful heir, to the work of the kings (*see* nos. I-19, I-20). In Mme Molimard's 1970 study of the series of Hector Lefuel's projects, she observes a progressive proliferation of ornamentation which grows proportionally like tropical vegetation; this was an unconscious manifestation of the vigorous growth of the national economy.

Contrary to the opinions of Ballu and Saunier, who felt that *War* and *Peace* were placed higher than originally intended, documents deposited at the Archives Nationales (by the Agence des Bâtiments), leave no doubt that their present locations are in fact as planned (confirming Lewis's hypothesis). Sometimes called *Victory* during its execution, the original title of this group, *War*, has survived. It is, however, less accurate, for the man is already crowned with laurel, has already sheathed his sword, and the fallen horse has endured a grueling battle. The iconographic program is unusual (it lacked the guidance of a Charles Le Brun). At the corners of the Pavillon Richelieu, at this same attic level, two allegorical reliefs were installed (since replaced by consoles), subjects which also occur on the Pavillon Denon: *Order* and *Work* by Maillet (q.v.).

The pyramidal composition of this group of three figures is less surprising than the wild-eyed appearance of the horse. Should *War*, as Benge suggests, be compared with Guillaume Boichot's *Force?* If so, their ancestors are the numerous antique figures of the reclining Hercules. On the other hand, Benge astutely observes the influence of the young man in Rude's *Departure of the Volunteers in 1792 (La Marseillaise)* on Barye's young trumpet player, even though it is La Marseillaise herself whose head is similarly turned away from the direction of the march. Two sides of Barye's personality after the age of fifty are at work here, that of the architect of Classical forms and, first revealed through his acute realism, that of the Romantic visionary.

Bronzes based on these models were edited by Barbedienne during Barye's lifetime in three different sizes (100 × 75 cm; 50 × 40 cm; 36 × 30 cm). William P. Walters gave the city of Baltimore a set of bronzes the size of the models which was installed in Mount Vernon Square. According to a letter from the sculptor (Gardet to Paul Vitry, December 3, 1912), only one other cast of each was made by Barbedienne. The *War* and *Peace* recently purchased by the Museum of Fine Arts in St. Petersburg, Florida, are undoubtedly those he described for they bear the stamp: "Collection F. Barbedienne."

Reductions from an unknown caster (measuring 50 cm) are at the Shepherd Gallery, New York, and the Metropolitan Museum of Art (40.23.1).

A.P.

Musée du Louvre, Paris

---

## Auguste-Nicolas Cain
*Paris 1821–1894 Paris?*

*Cain studied with the wood sculptor Alexandre Guionnet and with François Rude. During the 1840s he worked for the Fannière Frères (q.v.; Hargrove, 1977, p. 7) and supplied models for the jeweler Frédéric Rudolphi (q.v.; Vever, 1906–8, vol. I, p. 190). Cain was later associated with the animalier Pierre-Jules Mêne, marrying his daughter in 1852 and producing commercial editions in his studio, which Cain operated after Mêne's death in 1879.*

*His initial Salon entries were small-scale works but he later exhibited monumental pieces, attracting many state commissions. The first was a vulture group commissioned in 1849 and shown at the Salon of 1850 and at the Exposition Universelle of 1855. Four casts of this group were executed as supports for a table in the Louvre's Egyptian Museum. An important imperial commission was a series of four bas-reliefs of predators chasing their prey, which, in 1869, was installed as a decoration in one of the imperial kennels. Four bronze lionesses now flanking the Louvre entrances on the Cour du Carrousel date from the late 1860s.*

*Both his small-scale work and public commissions continued after 1871. The Tuileries gardens alone received three lion and tiger groups. An equestrian monument to Charles II of Brunswick was installed in Geneva in 1874. A prolific artist, Cain produced and exhibited until his death.*

*His small-scale work could be as delicate as Jules Moigniez's or as vigorous as Mêne's. Unlike his colleagues, Cain produced few animal portraits or groups that included human figures. Domestic animals occasionally appeared but he preferred wildlife. His large-scale sculpture is distinctive: though naturalistic, his forms have been articulated with strong aesthetic judgment. Théophile Gautier commented: "M. Cain is not content to represent lions, tigers, and crocodiles faithfully; he endows them with style and grandeur" (Gautier, 1920–21, p. 327).*

S.G.L.

Bibliography:
Lami, 1914–21, vol. I, pp. 233–38; Horswell, 1971, p. 249; MacKay, 1973, p. 58

Auguste-Nicolas Cain

## V-4
## Vulture and Sphinx

1864
Signed on socle at right: A CAIN; inscribed and dated on socle at left: F. BARBEDIENNE FONDEUR/ PARIS 1864
Bronze
165 × 80 × 90 cm

Provenance:
Exhibited at the Salon of 1863, the plaster model was purchased by the State, July 17, 1863; bronze commissioned by the Ministère de la Maison de l'Empereur et des Beaux-Arts, July 17, 1864; placed in the Jardin des Plantes after 1867; transferred to the Musée du Luxembourg, 1872; placed in the Dépôt des Marbres, 1926; erected in Thann, 1946

V-3

Exhibitions:
1865, Paris, Salon, no. 2890; 1867, Paris, Exposition Universelle, no. 640
Bibliography:
Catalogue Illustré, Paris, Luxembourg, 1892, p. xlix, no. 379; Catalogue, Paris, Luxembourg, 1896, p. 118, no. 439; Lami, 1914–21, vol. I, pp. 234–35; MacKay, 1973, pp. 58, 147

A sphinx head surmounted by a vulture has no known close parallels in art. The composition itself is rare in large sculpture; it was perhaps suggested by earlier decorative work or by Barye's (q.v.) small bronze *Stork Standing on a Tortoise.*

The iconography is puzzling, having something of the symbolic character of antique gems. The critic Louis Auvray found the group a particularly picturesque achievement: "M. Cain... has shown himself to be an artist this year; there is conceptual depth to his wild vulture, poised on that head of a sphinx, in the midst of the desert sand, stalking the caravans that pass and the corpses left behind" (1863, p. 101).

The strange imagery may simply reflect the revived interest in Egypt prevalent since the late eighteenth century. Current events may also have contributed: Auguste Mariette's important archaeological work begun in the 1850s was much publicized, as was another important French project, the Suez Canal. There were also specific Napoleonic associations with Egyptian iconography. The Egyptian military and scientific expeditions of Napoleon I expanded early Romantic interest in the exotic. The vulture briefly represented the Empire: it was the emblem of the Vautours de Bonaparte, a secret society of the Restoration intent on reestablishing the Empire (Larousse, 1866–90, vol. XV, p. 815).

Cain's sphinx may represent the Great Sphinx at Giza, which, though cleared of sand to its base numerous times, was most frequently visible only above the shoulders. The deliberately abraded nose of Cain's bronze may duplicate the Great Sphinx's, which, as one legend has it, was shot off by a French soldier (Herold, 1962, p. 160).

The regal dignity associated with the sphinx has even been noted in the vulture. The historian Jules Michelet admired this predator's imposing grandeur, calling the Algerian vultures of the Jardin des Plantes, "Turkish Pashas, adorned with superb cravats, draped with a noble cloak" (Larousse, 1866–90, vol. XV, p. 816). The critic Charles Yriarte similarly found grandeur in Cain's juxtaposed figures (1863, "Sculpture," p. 46). Certainly this is an arresting group, with its emphasis on verticality, pervasive diagonals, and sharp and simple profiles.

V-4

Another bronze version appeared in the 1900 Exposition Universelle, and a large ceramic version was recently with a Paris dealer. This group was also available in reduction through Cain's studio and later through Susse Frères.

S.G.L.

City of Thann

---

## Jean-Baptiste Carpeaux

*Valenciennes 1827–1875 Courbevoie*

*On October 20, 1844, presented by François Rude, Carpeaux entered the Ecole des Beaux-Arts in Paris. That same year (according to a letter he wrote to Dutouquet on January 15) he left the studio of Rude for that of Francisque-Joseph Duret, an advantage for the competition for the Grand Prix.*

*Ten years of hard work and patience followed. Finally, with his relief* The Emperor Receiving Abd-el-Kader at Saint-Cloud *(1853), he won the attention of Napoléon III. The Emperor gave Carpeaux his support, and the artist produced the finest visual representations of the festive occasions of the Second Empire.*

*He was runner-up for the Prix de Rome in 1852 and the following year won the top honor; however, the prize was not awarded. Finally he won the Grand Prix in 1854. After spending thirteen months finishing various official commissions, he went to the Villa Medici in Rome, where he stayed from 1856 to 1862, except for occasional trips to Naples, Florence, and France.*

*Carpeaux's Fisherboy with a Seashell, exhibited in Rome in 1857 and in Paris in 1858, was criticized by the Institut. His project for* Ugolino *brought him into conflict with Jean-Victor Schnetz, director of the Académie de France in Rome. However, the marquise de la Valette, the marquis de Piennes, and James Tissot, whose portrait busts he would execute, took an interest in him.*

*In Paris, Carpeaux had worked previously on the decoration of the Louvre's Pavillon de Rohan (1853–55); upon his return to France, Lefuel (q.v.) entrusted him with decorative friezes for the south facade of the Pavillon de Flore (1863–66). In 1865 he finished a figure of Temperance for the Church of La Trinité and received commissions for the statue of the Prince Imperial and for the group entitled* Dance *for the new Paris Opéra. This latter work, heavily criticized, provoked a scandal in 1869.*

*After the Second Empire, Carpeaux fell out of favor; he went in exile to London, but after a while returned to France, where he died in 1875.*

A.P.

V-5

Bibliography:
1975, Paris, Grand Palais; 1975, Valenciennes; A. Braunwald and A.M. Wagner, in 1975–76, Cambridge, pp. 109–43

Jean-Baptiste Carpeaux

## V-5
## Portrait of an Unknown Lady

c. 1860–70
Signed on left shoulder at rear (in script): J.B. Carpeaux; inscribed on socle at right:[..] VE TO [..] LOYΣ
Plaster
67.3 × 48.9 × 33.6 cm

Provenance:
Private coll., Paris; Heim Gallery, London; The Art Institute of Chicago (inv. no. 1972.1168)

Exhibition:
1977, Chicago, Antiquarian Society, no. 119

Bibliography:
The Art Institute of Chicago, *Annual Report*, 1972–73, p. 44, repro. p. 43

Generally associated with elegant, youthful female images, Carpeaux could also depict older women with tender honesty. This faculty is evident in his plaster bust of the marquise de la Valette (1861; Louvre) but is more apparent in his two-dimensional studies such as the 1869 crayon sketch of his mother-in-law, the vicomtesse de Montfort (Petit Palais, Paris), or the oil portrait at Valenciennes of an old woman, thought to be the dowager marquise de Piennes.

The Chicago plaster particularly resembles these portraits in the sympathetic rendering of an aging woman of character. The sitter has not been identified, but the strong psychological portrayal suggests she may have been well-known to Carpeaux. Like the subjects of his sketches, she may be the mother or wife of a close friend.

Identity notwithstanding, the portrait is compelling. Carpeaux here reveals himself a master of the richly modeled "living" portrait much as Houdon was. The loosely gathered drapery and absence of lavish accessories bespeak its informality. The heavily lidded eyes

V-6

Jean-Baptiste Carpeaux

## V-6
## Princess Mathilde

1862
Plaster
94 × 71 × 41 cm

Provenance:
Mme Carpeaux (?); Manzi coll.; sale, Paris, Manzi, Joyant & Cie, March 14, 1919, no. 227; Fabius Frères, Paris

Exhibitions:
1922, Paris, Musée des Arts Décoratifs, no. 455; 1957, Paris, Petit Palais, no. 300; 1959, Florence, no. 128; 1975, Paris, Grand Palais, no. 182

Commissioned in 1862 by Princess Mathilde and shown at the Salon the following year, the official marble portrait was enthusiastically received, helping to launch Carpeaux's career. The portrait's conscious historicism was quickly noticed by critics. Paul Mantz compared it to the work of Antoine Coysevox and Guillaume Coustou, saying that it had "something rich and princely" about it. He encouraged Carpeaux to continue these portraits "in the French manner" (1863, "Salon," p. 51).

Inspired by earlier French portraiture at its most stately, Carpeaux has created a grand and unapproachable image. Mathilde wears full regalia: ermine, a dress decorated with the Bonaparte bees, the imperial eagle diadem, and the pearl necklace given to her mother by Napoleon I (Kühn, 1935, p. 253). A previous court style has been consciously revived here, providing an opulent alternative to the first Empire Neoclassicism still respected in state portraiture. Carpeaux's later court portraits, even for the imperial family, would not repeat its majestic dignity.

The plaster exhibited displays not only Carpeaux's characteristically sensitive handling, but a vibrant energy that is absent in the marble. Its powerful volumes are crisply articulated, the texture of the modeling evident throughout. Although details are defined, the sense of scale and sweeping baroque movement prevent it from appearing overly fastidious.

The original plaster is now in the Ny Carlsberg Glyptotek in Copenhagen, and the marble is in the Louvre. Plasters are also at Lille and Valenciennes. Another plaster, identified as a cast made by the Louvre, was at the Hôtel Drouot on January 19, 1945, and on May 31, 1946, but apparently was not sold. A crayon study and two sketches are also in the Louvre.

An informal variant was commissioned

and sagging flesh are handled with great sensitivity and a warmth of expression is conveyed through the gentle smile, while the deeply incised, "dotted" eyes impart a sparkle to the face.

As with his other original plasters, the surface has been directly reworked after casting. The hair and face show particularly thoughtful tooling. Evidence of the casting process itself—airholes and shim lines—remains, giving further informality and energy to the surface. The nicks, chips, and repairs do not detract from the bust's vitality; together with the mottled patina, they reveal constant handling over the years.

No other versions are known, enticing one to believe it is unique, a private tribute by the artist to a friend. Because the sitter is unidentified, this bust must stand entirely on its formal merits, which are considerable. Its powerful modeling and lively surfaces are as appealing as the quiet radiance of its subject.

S.G.L.

The Art Institute of Chicago, Gift of the Antiquarian Society

immediately after the formal bust. The original plaster was sold in the Manzi sale (Paris, May 30, 1913, no. 60). A tinted plaster is at Valenciennes and Charles-Augustin Sainte-Beuve's plaster is in the Louvre. Alexander Dumas fils's purported bronze is apparently lost.

S.G.L.

MM. Fabius, Paris

Jean-Baptiste Carpeaux

# V-7
## The Prince Imperial and His Dog Nero

1865
Signed on plinth at right: JB$^{te}$ Carpeaux Tuileries 15 Août 1865; inscribed on dog's collar: AUX TUILERIES
Marble
140 × 65 × 61 cm

Provenance:
Commissioned late 1864; begun April 17, 1865 (plaster exhibited, Salon of 1866, no. 2668); Italian marble (block no. 1178) assigned by Dépôt des Marbres, November 4, 1865 (Arch. nat. F$^{21}$ 479); executed by Carpeaux's *praticien* Emile Bernaërts; payment of 15,000 francs from the Emperor's private purse made to Carpeaux, October 25, 1866; after Exposition Universelle of 1867, installed in the Galerie de Diane at the Tuileries (old photograph, Bibliothèque Nationale, Cabinet des Estampes, Va 219c. fol.); as private property, transported to Arenenberg (Switzerland), 1871, then to Farnborough (England), where it was placed in the funerary chapel, 1879; sale, Farnborough Hill, Farnborough, Hants, Hampton & Sons, July 18, 1927, no. 1317; Raymond Fabius; gift to the State by Mme Raba Deutsch de la Meurthe, July 27, 1930; exhibited at Compiègne, 1956–69; transferred to the Louvre, 1969 (inv. no. RF 2042)

Exhibitions:
1867, Paris, Exposition Universelle, no. 23; 1928, Malmaison, no. 73; 1955–56, Paris, Petit Palais, no. 97

Bibliography:
Gautier, 1866, p. 982; Jahyer, 1866, p. 251; *The Art Journal*, vol. VI, 1867, p. 156; T. Gautier, "Salon de 1868," *Le Moniteur*, July 19, 1868, p. 1076; Zola, 1868; Chesneau, 1880, pp. 92–97, 274; Delorme, 1889, p. 16; Vitry, 1912, *Carpeaux*, pp. 53–54, pl. 19; Mabille de Poncheville, 1925, pp. 79–80, pl. 11; Sarradin, 1927, p. 45; Huyghe, 1930, pp. 3–4 (repro.); Vitry, 1930, pp. 52–54 (repro.); Vitry, 1933, no. 1655; Clément-Carpeaux, 1934–35, vol. I, pp. 172–82

At the end of November 1864, Carpeaux wrote the marquis de Piennes: "I have, as you know, been assigned by the Emperor to do, not the bust of the Prince Imperial that I had expressed the desire to do, but a full-length statue to be cast in silver like the small Henry IV which is in the Louvre....Amazed at the Emperor's idea and his confidence in the outcome of the

V-7

work, I hastened to tell the Empress about it. Her reaction was not enthusiastic" (Clément-Carpeaux, 1934–35, vol. I, p. 172).

The Empress preferred a bust, the Emperor a full-length statue. Both were commissioned at the same time. Francis Monnier, the Prince Imperial's tutor, wrote Carpeaux on April 16, 1865: "Her Majesty the Empress has asked me to write and tell you that you can begin work on the bust of His Majesty the Prince Imperial. You can come tomorrow morning at eight-thirty and bring whatever you need" (Clément-Carpeaux, 1934–35, vol. I, p. 179). Sittings were held in a studio set up in the Orangerie of the Tuileries. An *enfant de troupe,* J. Turtoglia, posed for the costume. On May 6 Carpeaux told the marquis de Piennes about the visit of the Empress and her entourage and the "extraordinary bravos" that he received from them (Clément-Carpeaux, 1934–35, vol. I, pp. 179–80).

The plaster elicited fewer comments at the Salon of 1866 than Carpeaux's model for the sculpture crowning the Pavillon de Flore. As diffused as the boring official busts of the imperial couple by such artists as Nieuwerkerke, Henri-Frédéric Iselin, or Pollet (q.v.), Carpeaux's portrait group has in its favor the gracefulness of a "Florentine singer" in modern costume (*see* no. V-17), a direction followed by Jules Franceschi (*Young Boy,* 1868; Compiègne C 55 D 10) and Chapu (q.v.; *Young Robert Desmarres,* 1877; Louvre, RF 1451).

The original plaster is at Valenciennes; plasters are also at Compiègne and in Lille. Two silvered bronzes were produced: one exhibited at the Salon of 1868 and sent to the Hôtel de Ville (destroyed 1871); the second, commissioned by the Empress on the death of Napoleon III (purchased by the Ny Carlsberg Glyptotek, Copenhagen, 1907). In 1927 the Prince Napoleon gave a bronze to Malmaison for the Prince Imperial's mausoleum, where it remains. There are several preliminary drawings and modeled sketches (*see* 1975, Paris, Grand Palais, nos. 168–81).

Commercial edition of this work and the bust made Carpeaux's fortune. Reductions in all materials were produced after 1867 by his studio, Barbedienne (q.v.), and Christofle (q.v.). The archives at Sèvres (q.v.) indicate editions in *biscuit* in three different sizes after 1869. Immensely popular, this work continued to be produced after the fall of the Empire under the title *Boy with a Dog.*

A.P.

Musée du Louvre, Paris

V-8

Jean-Baptiste Carpeaux

## V-8
## Dance (Preliminary Study)

1866
Signed at top of base at right: J-B^te CARPEAUX
Plaster
54.5 × 34 × 29.8 cm

Provenance:
Carpeaux sale, Paris, 1894, no. 334 bis; acquired by the Louvre by decree of June 20, 1894 (inv. no. RF 983)

Exhibitions:
1955–56, Paris, Petit Palais, no. 107, pl. 23; 1964, Paris, Louvre, no. 102 (repro.); 1967, Paris, Académie des Beaux-Arts, no. 45 (repro.); 1975, Paris, Grand Palais, no. 306 (repro.)

Bibliography:
Gautier, 1869, p. 1047; C. Garnier, 1878–81, vol. I, pp. 431–59; Clément-Carpeaux, 1927, pp. 285–300; A. Braunwald and A.M. Wagner, in 1975–76, Cambridge, pp. 125–41 (bibl.)

Approached by Garnier to execute a statue for the vestibule of the Opéra (to replace Pierre-Jules Cavelier, who was detained by his work on the Palais de Longchamp, Marseilles), Carpeaux wrote to Louis Dutouquet: "I am overjoyed because I have just been chosen by Garnier to fill one of the most beautiful spaces of the Opéra. I am assigned to do one of the large bas-reliefs on the facade in the spirit of those on the Arc de Triomphe" (December 25, 1863).

However, the history of this project is difficult to trace from this point on. Garnier's correspondence with the artist (Bibliothèque de l'Opéra, RES. 880) was not dated by the architect and not always by Carpeaux in his replies. Garnier, who advised him to visit Jean-Baptiste-Eugène Guillaume, François Jouffroy, and Jean-Joseph Perraud, all sculptors of an earlier generation who had already begun their proposals for the project, wrote: "The two subjects between which we still must choose are the Bacchic dance and the dance of love (or any other dance) and Comedy and Tragedy [already chosen by Perraud, however]. Think ahead to the overall arrangement, for there must not be three figures lined up like sticks one next to the other." This advice was followed, even to the point that the architect would have difficulty in restraining this *ronde,* which he was so quick to claim to have inspired.

Putting aside the other themes explored by Carpeaux (namely two models for Drama and Comedy; Louvre), the progress of the idea of *Dance* is as follows. The marquis de Piennes's proposal for a minuet which would be "serious, with great style" was rejected in favor of "a nimble *ronde* encircling an inspiring genie" for which Garnier gave Carpeaux essential credit. "He took a pen, a scrap of paper, and in an instant sketched a few lines intersecting marvelously, a few beautifully composed movements, and in a brief five minutes his group was found! It was, with very few changes, the outline of the group that he later executed and that created such a sensation in the world" (C. Garnier, 1878–81, vol. I, p. 434). While Garnier's memory was not always accurate, the scene he described seems to be true considering the years Carpeaux spent studying movement, from the Classical female dancers to the group of the Laocoön, from the figure of Peace in the *Holy Alliance of the People* (1848) to the drawing of Flora at the Fogg. He was to add as many as one figure a day to his composition hereafter, Garnier noted in jest, but as both of them fought to defend this work, it was on a basis of reciprocal admiration.

This sketch of five dancers around a female genie (later replaced by a young man) is the only extant example of the proposal at this stage, sufficiently developed for Garnier to present to the ministry; therefore it can be dated 1866, after March 7, the date on which he wrote to Garnier, "my thought is not yet completely resolved" (ninth letter in the series).

This model and a similar one without a back were edited in plaster and terra-cotta during Carpeaux's lifetime, a milestone in being an early reflection of the later taste for the "unfinished."

Reflecting the great fame of *Dance,* finished variants in all materials exist in great quantities, executed initially by Carpeaux's studio. Susse Frères cast numerous editions after 1909 and A. A. Hébrard produced a limited lost-wax edition in 1927.

A.P.

Musée du Louvre, Paris

Jean-Baptiste Carpeaux

## V-9
### A. Napoleon III

1873
Signed and dated on left shoulder (in script):
Chiselhurst/13 Janvier 1873/JB^te Carpeaux;
inscribed on front: NAPOLEON III
Marble
52 × 36 × 27 cm

Provenance:
The Empress and Prince Victor Napoleon; sale, Farnborough Hill, Farnborough, Hants, Hampton & Sons, July 12–21, 1927, no. 1347; Raymond Fabius, Neuilly; The Metropolitan Museum of Art (inv. no. 1974.297)

Exhibitions:
1928, Malmaison, no. 72; 1935, Paris, Orangerie, no. 87; 1939, New York, no. 319; 1955–56, Paris, Petit Palais, no. 213; 1975, New York, p. 250

Bibliography:
Mantz, 1876, p. 624; Chesneau, 1880, pp. 141, 276; Carpeaux, 1899; Lami, 1914–21, vol. I, pp. 273–74; Clément-Carpeaux, 1934–35, vol. I, pp. 340, 348, 366–68, 373, vol. II, pp. 31, 49, 83, 110

*(Shown in Philadelphia and Detroit only)*

### B. Napoleon III

Signed and dated on left shoulder (in script):
Chiselhurst/13 Janvier 1873/JB^te Carpeaux;
inscribed on front: NAPOLEON III
Plaster
51.5 × 35.5 × 24 cm

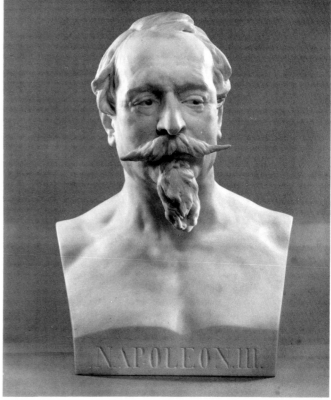

V-9

Provenance:
Mme Carpeaux; acquired by the Louvre, 1895; deposited at Compiègne, March 8, 1972 (inv. no. RF 1057)

Exhibitions:
1894, Paris, Ecole des Beaux-Arts, no. 402 (?); 1975, Paris, Grand Palais, no. 147

Bibliography:
Mantz, 1876, p. 624; Chesneau, 1880, pp. 141, 276; Carpeaux, 1899; Lami, 1914–21, vol. I, pp. 273–74; Clément-Carpeaux, 1934, vol. I, pp. 340, 348, 366–68, 373, vol. II, pp. 31, 49, 83, 110

*(Shown in Paris only; not illustrated)*

Although Carpeaux evidently planned to executed a full-length statue of the Emperor in 1864, no finished portrait by his hand exists from the Second Empire. Mme Clément-Carpeaux states that the Prince Imperial commissioned this bust in 1871 when Carpeaux visited the exiled imperial family at Chislehurst in England. Sittings began in 1872 but the desperately ill former sovereign could not continue them. Carpeaux was summoned from Paris to complete the portrait when Napoleon III died on January 9, 1873.

According to Mme Clément-Carpeaux, the Prince Imperial and the Empress watched Carpeaux finish the model, advising further emphasis on "the remoteness of the gaze, the bitterness about the lips" (1934–35, vol. I, p. 367). The plaster was completed on January 13, 1873; the definitive marble reached the Empress after May 1874. The bust was never exhibited during Carpeaux's lifetime: apparently it was intended only as a private family memento.

Carpeaux has achieved a powerful portrait with unusual economy of means: adopting a herm format and eschewing all accessories, he focused directly on the man, producing a compelling psychological characterization. Carpeaux's sensitive modeling of the sagging flesh, drawn brow, and brooding, deeply cut eyes conveys the troubled inwardness of a man whose goals were thwarted and who sensed his end drawing near.

The loose, lively treatment of the hair, moustache, and goatee complements the subtle volumes of the face. The carving of the beautiful marble has been achieved with great sensitivity and sureness of hand, giving the portrait its full expressive power and arresting physical presence. It ranks among the most masterly and beautiful portraits of the nineteenth century.

The Heim Gallery in London has an authorized reproduction executed shortly afterward for Paul Demidoff. An unfinished marble at Compiègne is described by Mme Clément-Carpeau as a studio replica for the Prince Imperial, abandoned at his death in 1879. A reduced marble, formerly belonging to the Emperor's equerry Firmin Rainbeaux, is with Fabius Frères, Paris, as is the terra-cotta from the Manzi sale (Paris, May 30, 1913), purchased subsequently by the prince de la Moskowa. The museum in Compiègne now owns the original plaster model for reductions (Manzi sale, Paris, December 8–9, 1913, no. 55). Two drawings of the Emperor in his coffin, both signed by Carpeaux and one dated January 13, 1873, are in the Louvre.

S.G.L.

The Metropolitan Museum of Art, New York, Purchase, 1974, Anne and George Blumenthal Fund; Munsey and Fletcher Funds; Funds from Various Donors; Agnes Shewan Rizzo Bequest and Mrs. Peter Oliver Gift (V-9A) and Musée National du Château, Compiègne (V-9 B)

V - 10

## Albert-Ernest Carrier-Belleuse

### Anizy-le-Château 1824–1887 Sèvres

*Carrier-Belleuse initially worked for a chaser know only as Bauchery, the goldsmith Jacques-Henri Fauconnier, and his nephews, the Fannière Frères (q.v.). He was enrolled briefly at the Ecole des Beaux-Arts but left to study at the Petite Ecole. He produced models in England for Minton for five years and returned to Paris in 1855.*

*Immensely prolific, he succeeded in almost every area of art production. He exhibited regularly at the Salon, beginning in 1857. His groups with strong erotic appeal, such as the 1863* Bacchante *(Tuileries gardens) and the 1869* Sleeping Hebe *(Louvre), were praised for their naturalism and were enormously successful. His quietly dramatic* Messiah, *shown in 1867 and purchased for the Church of Saint Vincent de Paul, won a Medal of Honor and the Legion of Honor cross.*

*His many portrait busts, drawn primarily from café or theater society and his intimate circle of friends, were inspired by informal eighteenth-century portraiture. Among his architectural projects were the 1865 relief of Abundance for the Pavillon de*

*Flore and stucco work in the Grand Gallery of the Louvre; sculpture for the facade of the new Vichy casino; and the famous caryatids for the Grand Foyer of the Paris Opéra (see no. I-10). Executed in the mid-1860s, his most complex program was for the Hôtel de Païva (now Travellers Club; see no. II-22), highlighted by his sinuous, Neo-Renaissance chimney nymphs in the marquise de Païva's bedroom.*

*A charter member of the Union Centrale des Arts Décoratifs, Carrier-Belleuse made enormous contributions to the improvement of the industrial arts.*

*He produced models continuously for manufacturers, and his own studio sold innumerable decorative objects. Later, as chef des travaux d'art at Sèvres (q.v.), he improved the quality of its designs and revived the use of biscuit. In 1885 he was made an officer of the Legion of Honor for his outstanding role in the decorative arts.*

*Carrier-Belleuse was endowed with an immense talent for modeling and design, and his inventive compositions used the human form for every conceivable aesthetic purpose. His work was naturalistic yet elegant and eclectic, enjoying widespread and long-lasting popularity.*

S.G.L.

Bibliography:
Lami, 1914–21, vol. I, pp. 276–85; Ségard, 1928; Hargrove, 1977

Albert-Ernest Carrier-Belleuse

## V-10
## Torchères

c. 1862
Left figure signed on socle at left: CARRIER; right figure signed on socle at right: A CARRIER; both inscribed at rear (in script): Charpentier/Bronzier/Paris
Silver-gilt, bronze; black onyx bases with red marble plaques
278.1 × 68.6 × 68.6 cm (each)

Provenance:
Private coll., Saint Paul; The Minneapolis Institute of Arts (inv. nos. 74.27.1,2)

Bibliography:
Hargrove, 1974, pp. 34–39, figs. 7, 8; Hargrove, 1977, pp. 207–8, fig. 174

*See* Colorplate

Anthropomorphic torchères were made as early as the seventeenth century. They reached the peak of their popularity during the Second Empire, thanks to technological advances and the increased demand for luxury items. Carrier-Belleuse produced many torchère models, his most famous being the flamboyant groups on the Grand Staircase of the Paris Opéra (*see* no. I-10).

This lovely pair of torchères was probably intended for domestic use. The quality of design, craftsmanship, and materials marks them as luxury objects of high caliber. The opulence of the combined materials has been tastefully controlled: the mellow gleam of the bronze figures is enlivened with bright gilt detail, and the onyx bases provide a handsome contrast. The figures have been expertly cast and sensitively chased, a credit to the fine reputation enjoyed by Charpentier. The design emphasizes delicacy, verticality, and even proportions. Unencumbered by the weight of the candelabra, the slender figures merely steady the stems and sway in interestingly varied *contrapposto* poses.

The torchères are unusually subdued in style. The effect is vaguely antique and many motifs are Classical— the jewelry and coiffures, and the foliated scrolls and palmettes on the girandoles. The graceful poses, clinging

drapery, and crisp handling are Neo-Renaissance, an effect heightened by the tight curls and the faces, which are reminiscent of the sixteenth-century *Diana of Anet* (Louvre).

Although lighter in scale and more fluid in form, the figures are similar to those on Carrier-Belleuse's *Tazza* (Victoria and Albert Museum, London), exhibited in the 1862 London International Exhibition, and suggest a date around the early 1860s. These torchères, if not other casts, may have been shown by Charpentier in the same exhibition: engravings of one of the torchères appeared in 1863 (*Art Journal Catalogue 1862,* supplement, p. 305) and in a German catalogue (Brockhaus, in Hargrove, 1974, p. 36). Carrier-Belleuse also exhibited them in the Union Centrale exhibition of 1863 (Hargrove, 1974, p. 42). Variants with white fluted bases were shown in the 1867 Exposition Universelle. Alfred Darcel's description pinpoints their distinctive elegance: "Carrier-Belleuse has modeled two charming figures of young girls, French by their features and easy grace, Greek by their stiff bearing and the near symmetry of the drapery and poses— Parisians trying their hand at Greek dignity" (Darcel, 1867, "Bronze," p. 425).

S.G.L.

The Minneapolis Institute of Arts, Gift of Mrs. Maud H. Schroll

Albert-Ernest Carrier-Belleuse

## V-11
## The Comtesse de Castiglione as Queen of Etruria

1864
Signed and dated on base at right: Carrier-Belleuse, 1864
Patinated plaster
72 × 30 × 32 cm

Provenance:
Comtesse de Castiglione; sale, 1901 (no. 357); Dr. Hugenschmidt; F. Bac; gift to the Musée National du Château, Compiègne, 1953 (inv. no. C53.C50)

Exhibitions:
1953, Compiègne, no. 46; 1953, Paris, Castiglione

Bibliography:
Loliée, 1928, p. 110; Ségard, 1928, p. 14; Terrier, 1959, no. 56; Hargrove, 1976, p. 412; Decaux, 1976, p. 256; Hargrove, 1977, pp. 124–25

The subject of this statue, Virginia Oldoini, became by her marriage the comtesse Verasis

de Castiglione. It is said that she was sent by her cousin the Italian statesman Cavour to persuade Napoleon III, by whatever means she chose, to intervene in Italy. Napoleon III was fascinated by her, and she herself claimed to be the most beautiful woman of the century. She had a genius for theatrics: setting the stage, placing herself upon it, creating her own myth.

All her life she tried unsuccessfully to play a behind-the-scenes role in European politics, and when she wanted her "memoirs" written, it was her intelligence rather than her beauty that she wished to emphasize. And yet she passionately cultivated all the testimonies of her beauty, an attitude perceptively recorded by Barrès: "She also had a morbid interest in attempting to arrest the passage of hours, to stem the flow of minutes, which drove her to save old finery, to preserve in alcohol all her small dead dogs, to keep countless photographs showing her in innumerable poses... to shed

V-11

bitter tears on the assaults of time.... She spent much of her time being photographed in the poses most calculated to immortalize the highlights of her life. To what avail? The efforts to idolize her body, to cheat death, to become a goddess."

Reports that the comtesse attended a ball at the Tuileries on February 9, 1863, in the guise of Salammbô, attired in a revealing costume— and subsequent art-historical opinions that she commissioned this statue to prove the decency of her costume—are contradicted by a letter written by the photographer Pierson (q.v.): "I swear she never wore such a costume. I saw... on the evening of the ball, the comtesse attired as Queen of Etruria in a high-neck gown that fully covered her and had a long train. In the photographs I took the following day, I had her uncover only one arm, so as to achieve a more artistic effect, as did my friend the sculptor Carrier-Belleuse for the statue he modeled in my presence...."

The judgment of J.E. Blanche, who thought that Carrier-Belleuse was not equal to rendering such a personality, seems severe. Carrier-Belleuse certainly showed the abundant hair, the fineness of her features, and the determination of the "divine countess" to inspire awe, but it must be admitted that he was more at ease modeling the pretty face of Marguerite Bellanger, another mistress of Napoleon III.

The comtesse distributed plasters of the statue to her friends, and surely would have sent one to her husband. The duc d'Aumale had one (Chantilly), as did the famous nerve specialist Dr. Blanche. Another was bought at the sculptor's studio sale on March 20, 1893 (no. 211). The provenance of the one in the Calais museum is unknown.

O.S.

Musée National du Château, Compiègne

---

## Pierre-Jules Cavelier
### Paris 1814–1894 Paris

*Cavelier was one of the important sculptors active during the reign of Napoleon III; given the great scale of his major work he is of necessity only poorly represented here. He won the Grand Prix de Rome in 1842, and upon his return to France was given commissions for many of the official decorative projects in Paris and Marseilles. He became famous for his figure of Penelope, which was reproduced countless times, especially by Barbedienne (q.v.). He also executed most of the decorative scheme for the Palais de Longchamp in Marseilles.*

*Cavelier was awarded a first-class medal and a Medal of Honor in 1849, was made an officer of the Legion of Honor in 1861, and after 1864 held an influential position as a professor at the Ecole des Beaux-Arts. He was elected a member of the Institut de France in 1865, replacing Francisque-Joseph Duret.*

A.P.

Bibliography:
Lami, 1914–21, vol. I, pp. 305–11

---

## André Vauthier-Galle
### Paris 1818–1899 Paris

*Vauthier-Galle was the grandson on his mother's side of the engraver André Galle and brother-in-law of Oudiné (q.v.), who had married his sister. In 1834 he entered the Ecole des Beaux-Arts, and in 1839 won first prize in metal engraving. A regular exhibitor in the Salon from 1845 until 1868, he was awarded a second-class medal in 1852 and another in 1866. He also sculpted in the round; however his poor eyesight forced him to stop working twenty years before his death.*

A.P.

Bibliography:
Forrer, 1904–30, vol. VI, pp. 210–12; Lami, 1914–21, vol. IV, pp. 349–50

Pierre-Jules Cavelier; engraved by André Vauthier-Galle

## V-12
## Medal: The City of Paris Presenting the Cradle of the Prince Imperial to the Emperor and Empress

1856
Mark: Paris, mint, 1841–80
Obverse signed at left: J. CAVELIER SCULPTEUR. at right: VAUTHIER GALLE GRAVEUR; inscribed: PACATVMQUE REGET PATRIIS VIRTVTIBVS ORBEM [text from Virgil's *Eclogues* 4.17; communication of J. R. Gaborit]; reverse inscribed: LA VILLE DE PARIS OFFRE A L'EMPEREUR ET A L'IMPERATRICE LE BERCEAU DU PRINCE IMPERIAL. on exergue: XVI MARS MDCCCLVI. on arms and device of Paris: FLUCTUAT NEC MERGITUR
Struck bronze
Diameter 7.7 cm

Provenance:
Musée du Luxembourg; transferred to the Louvre

Bibliography:
Forrer, 1904–30, vol. VI, p. 212, repro. p. 211 (as Vauthier-Galle)

On August 1, 1856, the Prefect of the Seine asked the Municipal Council of Paris for a credit of 20,000 francs to have a medal struck commemorating the birth of the Prince Imperial. This credit was given to him from funds for "emergency expenses." By an order of September 25, the Prefect commissioned Cavelier to make the models for the medal and Vauthier-Galle to reproduce it in engraving. Each was to receive 4,000 francs. The architect Baltard (q.v.) was to supervise the engraving and printing. The dies, which have not been found, belong to the City of Paris (Archives de la Seine V.R. 143).

Unlike Oudiné (q.v.), who both conceived and executed his medals, Cavelier turned to Vauthier-Galle to do the engraving for his first

V-12

commission from the City of Paris (Archives de la Seine 10 626/72/1 liasse 40). It is interesting to compare the obverse of this medal with the reverse of *The Accession of Napoleon III to the Empire* (no. V-25) by Oudiné. Both compositions are strictly conventional with a central figure framed by two female figures and supported by an eagle. However, the stylistic interpretations are quite different. In Cavelier's medal commemorating the gift of the Cradle of the Prince Imperial (no. II–17) to the Emperor and Empress, everything is in motion: the figures of Abundance and Victory, the draperies, even the eagle resting on the globe seems poised for flight. The relief is modeled with a pictorial softness. In Oudiné's medal the composition is monumental and severe. The eagle supports a shield that would prevent him from flying; the figures are fully clothed, their draperies hanging straight down at their sides. Even the ribbons of the crown, which fill some of the empty spaces, seem to be made of zinc. In contrast, the palm and olive branches on Cavelier's medal are awkwardly designed, while the signs of the zodiac serve to fill in the lower part of the composition, which otherwise would be top-heavy.

A.P.

Musée du Louvre, Paris

---

## Henri-Michel-Antoine Chapu
*Le Mée 1833–1891 Paris*

*Chapu was admitted to the Ecole des Beaux-Arts in 1849 after studying at the Petite Ecole. He was a student of Jean-Jacques Pradier until the latter's death in 1852; he then worked with Francisque-Joseph Duret and the painter Léon Cogniet. Chapu won the Prix de Rome for sculpture in 1855. The last of his envois from the Villa Medici,* Mercury Inventing the Caduceus, *was purchased by the State in 1862.*

*Upon his return to Paris in 1861, he was commissioned to execute decorative sculpture for several new houses. For public buildings he created the figure of Mechanical Art (1865) on the staircase of the Tribunal de Commerce and the figures of Saint John and Saint Louis of Gonzaga (1867) for the Church of Saint Etienne du Mont.*

*His Salon debut took place in 1863 with his marble* Mercury, *for which he won a third-class medal. Aside from his* Sower, *shown in 1865, and* Clytie, *shown the following year, most of his entries during the Second Empire were portrait medallions. Chapu's first great Salon success was his* Joan of Arc

at Domrémy, *exhibited in plaster in 1870, acquired by the State, and executed in marble for the Salon of 1872. That and his figure of Youth (1876), part of his monument to Henri Regnault (q.v.) at the Ecole des Beaux-Arts, made him famous. His most noteworthy later projects were commemorative monuments such as the tomb of Jean Reynaud at Père Lachaise, whose Genius of Immortality of 1880 was reproduced on his own monument at Le Mée. Chapu was made a chevalier of the Legion of Honor in 1867, promoted to officer in 1872, and elected to the Académie des Beaux-Arts in 1880.*

*Early in his career he declared his stylistic guides to be "the Antique and nature" (Fidière, 1894, p. 47). His large-scale figures are clearly handled with a naturalism tempered by Classical simplicity and grace. Rarely dramatic, his work has a gentle charm born of a disposition which early on earned him the affectionate nickname, Monsieur l'Abbé.*

S.G.L.

Bibliography:
Fidière 1894; Gonse, 1895, pp. 307–9; Lami, 1914–21, vol. I, pp. 328–42

---

Henri-Michel-Antoine Chapu

## V-13
## Caryatid

1867
Plaster model
134 × 32 × 13 cm

Provenance:
Commissioned for the Exposition Universelle of 1867; gift of the sculptor, along with two other smaller models which were actually chosen, to the Musée Chapu (inv. no. 22)

Bibliography:
Fidière, 1894, p. 68; Catalogue, Le Mée, Musée Chapu, 1977, pp. 12, 13

Ten years after his first *envoi* from Rome, *Christ with Angels* (which for technical reasons could not be exhibited here), Chapu executed this model for the last great international exhibition of the Second Empire. As early as December 9, 1866, Krautz, the *directeur des travaux d'art* for the Exposition Universelle, asked the comte de Nieuwerkerke, who had dealt with the sculptor before, for advance payment for Chapu even though a contract had not yet been concluded. On December 12 Nieuwerkerke replied that the price would be less than 8,000 francs; Chapu would thus have to invest more than 3,000 francs while receiving a payment of only 5,000 francs "for three months of constant labor carried out under arduous conditions."

V-13

A series of unsigned and undated notes in the Archives Nationales (F²¹ 522) provide interesting details about the project. Chapu's expenses were listed: workers, helpers, clay, armatures, firing. Each figure would be five meters high, not including the base and the capital. Sixty-four replicas would be made (it was common practice to use the same model of a caryatid several times over). Chapu would remain in the studio until February 1, and the casters would occupy it until April 1. On January 21, 1867, Chapu asked Nieuwerkerke to come and look at his "fully completed" project because he wanted to have his impressions and advice before proceeding with the finished work.

Chapu was made a chevalier of the Legion of Honor for the Exposition Universelle (Mercury, Louvre, RF165; The Sower). In addition—and probably for his caryatids—he received a certificate from Frédéric le Play, organizer of the exposition (January 5, 1868). "The Imperial Commission presents M. Chapus [sic], sculptor and contractor, with two medals in commemoration of the service he has rendered to the international undertaking" (Fidière, 1894, p. 222).

This decorative project, however ephemeral, did not allow free run of the sculptor's imagination. He appears here economical and prudent. Instead of this rigid, draped caryatid, in which the classic grace of Chapu's female figures is felt—apropos this, there is a significant note by the sculptor accompanying the address of a model written on a sketch preserved in the Bibliothèque Doucet (ms. 427 F°44), "Mlle Mauvis, elegant arms, 24, rue M. le Prince"—the standing models, with swaying hips and abundant jewelry more in harmony with the imperial display, would ultimately be selected for the exposition.

A.P.

Musée Municipal Henri Chapu, Le Mée

---

## Emile Chatrousse

*Paris 1829–1896 Paris*

*Chatrousse came from a modest background, and the beginning of his career was difficult. After being apprenticed to a cutter and engraver of jewels, he studied under the painter Abel de Pujol and first exhibited at the Salon of 1848. Taking the advice of Nieuwerkerke, who had saved him from conscription (Louvre Archives S 5 [May 27, 1859]), he entered the studio of François Rude (Louvre Archives S 5 [June 11, 1851]). In spite of his protection from above, Chatrousse battled financial difficulties all his life, but thanks to his official commissions he was able to survive. His work centered around the decoration of the public buildings of Paris. For the Louvre he did* Autumn *(1857) and* Christian Art *(Salon of 1859); for the Tuileries,* Ceres *(1866); for the Conseil d'Etat,* Portalis *(1867; now at the Palais*

*de Justice); for the Châtelet theater,* Comedy*; for the Hôtel de Ville,* Mme Roland *(1882); for the Church of Saint Eustache,* Angel with Incense Jar *(1873) and* Blessed Are They That Mourn...*; for Saint Sulpice,* Resignation *(Salon of 1859; now at Saint Eustache); for Saint Leu,* Saint Giles, Sixth-Century Hermit *(Salon of 1861); for Saint Ambroise,* Saint Joseph *(Salon of 1861); for La Trinité,* Saint Simon *(Salon of 1865). Like other sculptors of his time he received orders for portrait busts of government officials, civil servants (General Beuret; Versailles), and great personalities of the past (Marquise de Pompadour; Salon of 1866).*

*Chatrousse early demonstrated markedly nationalistic feelings that suited those of Napoleon III (see L'Artiste, 1862; Louvre Archives S 30 [April 20, 1869]). Only after 1870 did this source of inspiration appear in his work with his project for a monument to the martyrs of national independence;* Joan of Arc *and* Vercingétorix *Musée des Beaux-Arts, Clermont-Ferrand);* Joan of Arc, Liberator of France *(1887; boulevard Saint Marcel, Paris); and* War Crimes *(Salon of 1876; Musée des Beaux-Arts, Nancy). One of his last works,* Pity *(Salon of 1895), representing a French soldier giving a Prussian soldier something to drink, received much adverse criticism, understandable in the context of mounting French nationalism.*

*Chatrousse was an art critic for* L'Artiste, Le Pays, Le Bien Public, *and* Le National.

O.S.

Bibliography:
Thieme and Becker, 1907–50, vol. VI, p. 432; Lami, 1914–21, vol. I, pp. 358–64

---

Emile Chatrousse

## V-14
## Queen Hortense and Her Son Prince Louis Napoleon

1852
Signed and dated on base at left: Emile Chatrousse 1852
Marble
87 × 57 × 75 cm

Provenance:
Ordered in 1853 by the Ministère de la Maison de l'Empereur for the Emperor's private collection (Louvre Archives 22 DD 20 no. 13, "Livre d'inventaire des commandes et acquisitions, 1853–70") for 5,000 francs (Arch. nat. 0⁷ 1707, ordinance 4305; 0⁷ 1708, ordinance 2311; 0⁷ 1708, ordinance 2698); sent to Versailles museum, 1858 (Louvre Archives 2 DD 16 p. 9); deposited at Malmaison, 1912; transferred to the Musée National du Château, Compiègne, 1969 (inv. no. C 69 D 1)

Exhibition:
1855, Paris, Exposition Universelle, no. 4280

Bibliography:
De la Rochenoire, 1855, p. 93; Soulié, 1859, vol. I, p. 482; Lagrange, 1860, p. 268; Nieuwerkerke, 1868, p. 162; Vapereau, 1870, pp. 379–80; Jahyer, 1876, vol. II; Bellier and Auvray, 1882–87, vol. I, pp. 241–42; Nohlac and Pératé, 1896, p. 335; Times, December 30, 1896; L'Eclair, December 16, 1896; Thieme and Becker, 1907–50, vol. VI, p. 432; Lami, 1914–21, vol. I, pp. 359–60; Bénézit, 1948–54, vol. II, p. 461

The plaster model of this group was shown at the Salon of 1853 (no. 1268), bought by the State, and sent to the museum in Bagnères-de-Bigorre (Catalogues, Bagnères-de-Bigorre, 1857, p. 37, 1864, p. 14). The piece is now lost.

The genesis of the work can be followed through the correspondence between Chatrousse and the comte de Nieuwerkerke, his protector (Louvre Archives). In an undated letter (S 30) the artist requested that a mold be made of the death mask of Queen Hortense. Probably he had begun to model his likeness from the bust by François-Joseph Bosio. He also asked for a portrait of the Emperor as a child, declaring: "I am working day and night on my group, which has taken shape and is going well. Everyone speaks of it encouragingly. Rude, who saw it just recently, was very pleased." On March 14, 1853, Chatrousse announced that the group was finished (S 8) and offered a cast to Nieuwerkerke, who was "very satisfied with what he had done." On July 13 Chatrousse requested marble for his statue, which Nieuwerkerke refused (S 30). By August 12, 1853, however, Nieuwerkerke had obliged him with the marble (S 30) but Chatrousse realized that he would have to reduce its size by a quarter. Thanking Nieuwerkerke for the marble (S 8 [mismarked March 26, 1853]), he said he had ceded rights to a bronze edition to M. Paillard, and offered to give Nieuwerkerke a cast. On March 10, 1854, Chatrousse changed his offer, this time offering Nieuwerkerke a plaster. He apologized, saying: "I cheer myself up with the idea that, although the material is more frail, the artistic worth is greater, since bronze is further from the original than plaster" (S 8). Finally, on March 28, 1855, Chatrousse petitioned for a good place for his group, probably at the Exposition Universelle. "I shall be happy when it finds its place; in this way my maternal scene should have more of a chance to please Their Majesties" (S. 5).

The iconography of this work is set forth in the Salon catalogue: "Queen Hortense... instructs her son about the events leading to the Peace of Tilsit [Sovetsk], in which the Kingdom of Holland received recognition (1812)." Although the artist received an honorable mention, his work went unnoticed in the enormous exposition of 1855. Only the critic J. de la

V-14

George Sand *(1864)* for the Théâtre Français, or equestrians, *Napoleon I and Charlemagne for the Palais de l'Industrie (1864)*, and a bronze *Napoleon III (1866)*, later placed at Chislehurst.

Clésinger's career was interrupted by the fall of the Second Empire. He exhibited mostly busts from 1875 to 1880; his major project of four equestrians for the Ecole Militaire remained unfinished.

Clésinger's Salon pieces made him famous. His portraits could be grand, like the Neo-Baroque bust of Cardinal Antonelli (The Art Institute of Chicago), or romantic, like that of Thomas Couture (Los Angeles County Museum of Act). Clésinger produced variants of his successful Woman Bitten by a Serpent *and repeated its compelling voluptuousness in similar subjects. Where dramatic poses were not used, surface treatment was accentuated, sometimes with polychromy. His 1859* Sappho *and 1869* Cleopatra *(both lost) were tinted and bore jewelry by P.-H. Emile Froment-Meurice (q.v.).*

Much commented on by critics, his particular attributes were aptly described by Castagnary in 1864: "The fecundity of this rapid improviser is astonishing. He is as audacious with marble as Puget and Michelangelo... above all a man of temperament.... perfection is irreconcilable with the passion and energy of his natural instincts" (1892, vol. I, pp. 214–17).

S.G.L.

Bibliography:
Estignard, 1900; Lami, 1914–21, vol. I, pp. 398–405; Benoist, 1928, "Clésinger," pp. 283–96; Hargrove, 1974, pp. 28–34

---

Rochenoire noted "a charming group of Queen Hortense and Prince Louis Napoleon, by M. Chatrousse" (1855). The group was probably conceived by Nieuwerkerke for the purpose of attracting the attention of the Emperor and Empress. The appeal of its subject was inherent in the imperial mythology, which knowingly fostered the Napoleonic myth. Within the genre this group, executed when the artist was only twenty-three, does not, except for the quality of its execution, typify the artist. His subsequent production, no longer bound by the demands of official commissions, developed in the direction of a pathetic lyricism or, depending on the subject, a "1900" preciosity.

O.S.

Musée National du Château, Compiègne

## Jean-Baptiste Clésinger
*Besançon 1814–1883 Paris*

*Clésinger studied with his father, the sculptor Georges-Philippe Clésinger, and briefly with Bertel Thorvaldsen and David d'Angers. Settling in Paris in 1845, he achieved his first public success with the marble* Woman Bitten by a Serpent *(Louvre), shown in 1847. The sensual drama and palpitating realism of the work caused a sensation he was never able to repeat.*

*After his equestrian statue of Francis I was heavily criticized in 1856, Clésinger left for Italy, sending back submissions to the Salons of 1859 and 1861. Upon his return to Paris in 1864, he was made an officer of the Legion of Honor.*

*His public commissions were mostly full-length portraits such as* Rachel as Tragedy *(1852) and*

Jean-Baptiste Clésinger

## V-15
## Bacchante and Faun

1869
Signed and dated on base at right: J. CLESINGER 1869
Marble
87.5 × 67.3 × 34.3 cm

Provenance:
Shepherd Gallery, New York; The Minneapolis Institute of Arts (inv. no. 73.13ab)
Bibliography:
*Gazette des Beaux-Arts*, vol. LXXXII, February 1974, supplement, p. 138; Hargrove, 1974, pp. 28–34, figs. 2, 3

This group is based on lost pendants of a *Bacchante* and a *Seated Faun* sent to the 1863 Salon from Rome. Like them, it is less dramatic and emphatically modeled than most of

Clésinger's work. The erotic potential is nonetheless fully developed: the languid caress of the bacchante's left hand communicates willingness as the faun goes about his seduction. In its playful fashion, this mutual engagement resembles that of a sixteenth-century bronze by Andrea Riccio, *Satyr and Satyresse* (Victoria and Albert Museum, London); the satyr's hand on his companion's chin is similarly expressive. The protagonists' faces in Clésinger's group are unusually eloquent; as in most of his sculpture, poses typically tell all.

Evidence of Clésinger's study in Rome of Michelangelo and the Antique can be seen here. The new, restrained handling of the bacchante may be due to antique sculpture, while the influence of Michelangelo is evident in the muscular, dynamic forms of Clésinger's faun and in the contrasting surfaces—polished and smooth opposed to mat and rough.

The relaxed, undulating planes are, however, inspired by eighteenth-century examples, revealing Clésinger's familiarity with the popular Rococo idiom. The subject is a typical one; the light-hearted mood, restless outlines, careful details, and rippling patterns of the hair and drapery are Clodionesque. Yet Clésinger's figures, particularly the faun, are stockier than the slender, elongated Clodionesque types sometimes used by Carrier-Belleuse (q.v.). Clésinger's composition is more subdued than the often exuberant Neo-Rococo groups. Unlike Clodion or Carrier-Belleuse, whose genius lay in modeling, Clésinger preferred to work in marble. This group reveals his facility with stone, its handling alternating between lively description and restrained smoothness.

No other documented versions of this work are known. Despite certain inconsistencies, it might possibly relate to three versions of a *Faun and Faunesse* listed in Clésinger's auction catalogue (Paris, Hôtel Drouot, April 16, 1870). Although said to have been executed in Rome, the marble listed in this group (no. 10) has dimensions that are approximately the same (90 × 82 cm) as the Minneapolis piece. The marble in the sale may be identified with the one mentioned by Estignard, said to date from 1870 (1900, pp. 56, 165). Clésinger's auction catalogue further lists a bronze (no. 50) of similar size as the marble in the same sale, as well as a terra-cotta of unknown size (no. 36). The 1893 Barbedienne catalogue (p. 48) lists a *Bacchante* and *Satyr* available in four sizes; perhaps these are derived from the 1863 pendants of the *Seated Faun* and *Bacchante*.

S.G.L.

The Minneapolis Institute of Arts, Purchase, The John R. Van Derlip Fund

V-15

---

### Charles-Henri-Joseph Cordier
*Cambrai 1827–1905 Algiers*

Cordier studied drawing in Cambrai. Given a grant by the town, he entered the Ecole des Beaux-Arts in Paris in 1846, but he soon left to follow his "venerated master, M. Rude." An early success at the Salon may have determined his vocation, as he recalled in his memoirs: "A superb Sudanese turned up at the studio. Within a fortnight I did his bust and sent it to the Salon, feeling quite sure that it would be accepted. Just then the Revolution of 1848 burst out, and the jury was democratically elected. Trembling, I got up my nerve to send in the Sudanese bust anyway, and it was a revelation to the art world. Standing in front of it, Pradier said: 'Who did this? Here is a fellow who will be a sculptor!' My teacher, who was a member of the jury, stepped forward and said: 'My student, Charles Cordier.' Some people turned away, but this did not interfere with success. Indeed, I won an honorable mention. My genre had the freshness of something new, revolt against slavery, the budding science of anthropology.... I revitalized the value of sculpture and created the study of race, widening the circle of beauty by showing that it existed everywhere." This began a series of busts documenting "modern types to be compared with those of the Antique."

Cordier also worked on Parisian buildings: the Tour Saint Jacques, Sainte Clotilde (1851), Saint Augustin (1862), the Théâtre du Vaudeville (1867), the Opéra (1866–72), the château of Ferrières (1864; four admirable polychrome caryatids), and the cathedral of Monaco (1887–89). He was also commissioned to do major monuments abroad: Algeria (1857–58), Christopher Columbus (1872–74), Ibrahim Pasha, Viceroy of Egypt (shown at the Salon of 1872), and numerous busts of bishops, admirals, and marshals in France.

Although he faced financial worries in later years, he attracted famous buyers, including Queen Victoria, Princess Mathilde, Rosa Bonheur, the duc de Morny, and the Marquis of Hertfort. He won many awards at the Salon; a third-class medal (1851), a second-class medal (1853), a rappel (1857), as well as an honorable mention at the 1855 Exposition Universelle and the Legion of Honor in 1860.

A.P.

Bibliography:
Cordier, Memoirs, ms., priv. coll.; Gautier, 1865, p. 37; Lami, 1914–21, vol. I, pp. 417–23

Charles-Henri-Joseph Cordier

## V-16
## Negro in Algerian Costume

1856–57
Signed, lower right: C. CORDIER
Bronze and onyx
76 (extended at the bottom 4.5 cm) × 66 × 36 cm

Provenance:
Probably bought by the State after the Salon of 1857 (Arch. nat. $0^5$ 1698, decree of September 30, 1857, certificate of delivery of October 2); in storage at the Louvre, September 4, 1870; exhibited Musée du Luxembourg, after 1872; transferred to the Louvre (inv. no. RF 2997)

Exhibitions:
1857, Paris, Salon, no. 2818; 1889, Paris, Exposition Universelle Centennale, no. 59; 1931, Vincennes (not in catalogue); 1951, Paris, Atelier de Delacroix,

V-16

no. 79; 1952, Paris, Atelier de Delacroix (not in catalogue)

Bibliography:
Vignon, 1852, p. 42; T. Gautier, Le Moniteur, December 8, 1855; Vignon, 1855, pp. 161–62; L'Artiste, vol. LIX, 1857, p. 93; Auvray, 1857, p. 98; du Camp, 1857, p. 172; T. Gautier, L'Artiste, vol. LIX, 1857, p. 183; About, 1858, p. 241; Andréï, 1860, pp. 188–89; Cordier, 1860, nos. 14, 15; Trapadoux, 1860, no 8; Thoré-Bürger, 1861, p. 162; Courrier Artistique, March 1, 1862; Chatrousse, 1862, p. 125; Auvray, 1863, p. 97; Mantz, 1863, "Salon," p. 59; Thoré-Bürger, 1863, pp. 433–34; Waring, 1863, vol. II, pl. 145; de Sault, 1864, p. 246; Dax, 1865, p. 72; Jahyer, 1866, p. 97; Catalogues, Paris, Luxembourg, 1879–96; Bénédite, 1899, pp. 478–79; Lami, 1914–21, vol. I, p. 420 (confuses the busts of 1857 and 1860); Vitry, 1922, no. 1081; Benoist, 1928, p. 160; Rheims, 1972, repro. p. 408

See Colorplate

In his letter of January 28, 1854, to Achille Fould (Arch. nat. $F^{21}$ 72), Cordier asked to be sent on a six-month mission to Algeria "in order to reproduce there the various types that are at the point of merging into one and the same people." In 1856 he obtained 1,000 francs for work in Algeria studying "from the point of view of art the different types of the native human race" (Arch. nat. $F^{70}$ 201).

He returned with twelve busts for the Salon of 1857. One of them, Negro of the Sudan

(no. 2813), a bronze bust (Musée de l'Homme, Paris), is the face that served as the model for later examples in bronze and onyx, a type which the artist would do in several versions; hence the persistence of the general title Negro of the Sudan to refer to Cordier's busts. In addition, in Cordier's volume of photographs in the Bibliothèque Nationale (this use of photography is further proof of the sculptor's scientific spirit), number 14 is labeled: "Type Ethiopian, Race Sudanese."

It was to Cordier that the Second Empire owed its renewed interest in polychrome statuary that accompanied periods of luxury. From antiquity (at the Louvre he was able to see the fine examples from the Borghese, Albani, and Mazarin collections) to Venetian blackamoors, including the great decorations of the Renaissance and Baroque, polychromy continued to enchant, until it was rejected by the Neoclassicists.

But this revival of polychromy was not easily accepted. In 1899 Bénédite wrote: "It is a long time since the elder Cordier attracted attention by the use of polychrome materials. His two busts in the Luxembourg have remained completely isolated for years and years. One might say they have been in quarantine, since sculptures in colored material have been deliberately treated as commercial sculpture. Color discredited art."

"Isolated" is excessive. Simart's chryselephantine Pallas Athena created a sensation at the Exposition Universelle of 1855. Arnaud (q.v.) in 1863 and Clésinger (q.v.) in 1852 gilded their marbles. The latter exhibited a polychrome Cleopatra with jewels in 1869; Rochet, a polychrome Cassandra in 1870; and Carpeaux (q.v.) dreamed of patinas of color for his fountain at the Observatoire.

Nevertheless, polychromy remained the prerogative of architecture and decoration. The premature enthusiasm of Gautier, which was confirmed in each of his Salon reviews in Le Moniteur, the official newspaper of the French Empire, collided with the criticisms of Mme Vignon in 1855 ("Let us execrate polychrome sculpture") and of Sault, Auvray, and Mantz. Thoré-Bürger wavered. Favorably disposed in 1861, he was less so in 1863: "These luxurious attractions have the misfortune of allowing one to neglect somehow the face and physiognomy." Although this may be true for Cordier's Jewess of Algiers from the Salon of 1863, it does not apply to this figure, with its "look of a Roman emperor" (Trapadoux, 1860), all the more proud for his sumptuous costume.

A.P.

Musée du Louvre, Paris

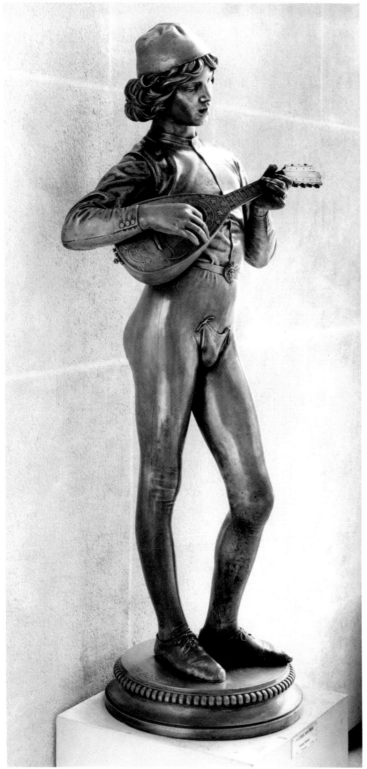

V - 17

## Paul Dubois

*Nogent-sur-Seine 1829–1905 Paris*

*Although Dubois was the son of a notary who wanted him to study law, he was able to pursue his inclination to become a sculptor. He studied with Armand Toussaint and made his debut at the Salon of 1857, under the name of Dubois-Pigalle (he was the great nephew of Jean-Baptiste Pigalle, the sculptor of the marquise de Pompadour). Dubois was admitted in 1858 to the Ecole des Beaux-Arts but left almost immediately and went to Italy, where he spent four years that were very important for his work and his connections. His submissions to the Salon of 1863 — plaster sculptures,* Saint John the Baptist *and* Narcissus *— won a second-class medal. This marked the beginning of an uninterrupted success: three Medals of Honor, in 1865, 1876, and 1878 (Exposition Universelle); election to the Institut de France in 1876; and grand cordon of the Legion of Honor in 1896.*

*He was made curator of the Musée du Luxembourg in 1873 and was director, from 1878 to 1905, of the Ecole des Beaux-Arts, which he had left some twenty years earlier. He made busts and painted portraits of his contemporaries and carried out important public commissions: a* Virgin *for the Church of La Trinité;* Song *for the Paris Opéra;* Monument to General Lamoricière *in the cathedral of Nantes;* The High Constable Anne de Montmorency *at Chantilly;* Joan of Arc *in front of the cathedral of Reims (repeated in front of the Church of Saint Augustin in Paris); and the funerary statue of the duc d'Aumale at Dreux.*

*His subtle and refined sculpture, strongly marked by Florentine influence, enjoyed great public success. Commercial reproduction by Barbedienne (q.v.) and the Manufacture de Sèvres (q.v.) further expanded his audience.*

A.P.

Bibliography:
Lami, 1914–21, vol. I, pp. 217–22; du Castel, 1964; Delahaye, 1973

Paul Dubois

## V-17
## The Fifteenth-Century
## Florentine Singer

1865
Signed and dated on top of base at left: P. DUBOIS.
1865; inscribed at right: F. BARBEDIENNE FONDEUR
Silvered bronze
155 × 58 × 50 cm

Provenance:
Commissioned by the State for 7,000 francs by decree of June 24, 1865 (Arch. nat. F²¹135); later, silvered at request of Nieuwerkerke, for an additional 945 francs; placed in the quarters of Nieuwerkerke (Louvre Archives S 4 [October 23, 1866]); entered Musée du Luxembourg, 1871 (LUX 41); transferred to the Louvre, 1920 (inv. no. RF 2998)

Exhibitions:
1867, Paris, Exposition Universelle, group I, class 3, no. 76; 1873, Vienna, no. 909; 1889, Paris, Exposition Universelle Centennale, no. 67; 1932, Paris, Grand Palais; 1957–58, Paris, Musée Rodin, no. 62; 1961, Vichy, no. 67; 1967–68, Nice, no. 4

Bibliography:
Arch. nat. AP 368 [Barbedienne papers]; Catalogue, Paris, Luxembourg, 1865, pp. 388–90; Claretie, 1865, pp. 228, 229; Jahyer, 1865, pp. 220–24; de Montifaud, 1865, p. 9; Privat, 1865, p. 199; Thoré-Bürger, 1865, p. 267; Gautier, 1866, p. 1002; The Art Journal, vol. VI, 1867, pp. 155–56; Mantz, 1867, "Exposition," p. 342; de Navery, 1868, pp. 83–84; Thoré-Bürger, 1868, pp. 539–40; "Galvanoplastie," Magasin Pittoresque, 1868, pp. 259–62, 287–88; Catalogues, Paris, Luxembourg, 1872–1914; Veron, 1875, pp. 147–48; Guillaume, 1879, pp. 923–24; Guillaume, 1900, p. 522; Riotor, 1906, p. 93; Lami, 1914–21, vol. II, p. 218; du Castel, 1964, p. 34; 1973, New York, Shepherd Gallery, no. 50; Delahaye, 1975, nos. 5–6, pp. 338–43 (bibl.)

Executed upon Dubois's return from Italy, the plaster version of *The Florentine Singer* was exhibited at the Salon of 1865 and won the Medal of Honor. On June 23, 1865, Dubois wrote to the founder Barbedienne: "Apart from the cast intended for the Minister, I believe I will make another cast of my *Florentine* so that I will be able to send it to exhibitions when needed and to have it at my home; but I will limit myself to that... fearing that the Administration might take exception to reproductions of my figure in its original size" (Arch. nat. 368 AP 3). And indeed, even before having received its piece, the Administration des Beaux-Arts in the person of Nieuwerkerke was surprised to read in Barbedienne's letter of invitation to visit its new collections in December 1865 that the most important work was "*The Florentine Singer* of M. Paul Dubois... of which several reductions are completed" (Arch. nat. F²¹135).

Because of its commission of the bronze, the Administration found itself the owner of the plaster. Therefore, did it not have exclusive rights to the work in the same size? On March 26, 1866 (Louvre Archives S 30), Dubois explained his chronology to Nieuwerkerke: Originally, three life-size casts were made. The first cast was defective; the second, commissioned for Princess Mathilde, was delivered to her as soon as it was finished; the third went to the State. After restoration, the first was used by Barbedienne, provoking by its premature exhibition the official resentment.

An edition contract signed with Barbedienne was limited to bronzes of a maximum of three-fourths of the original size. This contract was renewed repeatedly until finally the foundry broke the contract on December 17, 1953, stating: "For several years now this edition has not produced any results" (Arch. nat. 368 AP 3). Nevertheless, the edition had a remarkable longevity with six sizes obtained through the use of the Collas method. Examples also exist in wax, terra-cotta, and *biscuit* (Manufacture de Sèvres, three sizes). A marble was executed in 1869 by Fabbrucci under the direction of Dubois.

The immense popularity of this piece has two causes: it pleases and it reassures. While it is a new work, it is at the same time the product of an intellectual culture that Dubois studied in Tuscany. Though the poses found in the pages of his sketchbooks were taken from the frescoes of Benozzo Gozzoli or Pintoricchio, the details of costume and musical intruments have their equivalents in the works of Raphael (Gonse). Paul Mantz compared him to Masaccio, but pointed out the danger in "this extreme love of archaism." However, in the same article, he expressed great admiration for *The Florentine Singer*, the fruit of a "liberal education."

A.P.

Musée du Louvre, Paris

---

## Alexandre-Jean-Joseph Falguière
### Toulouse 1831–1900 Paris

*Falguière's work is so obviously a product of the Third Republic that one overlooks the fact that two of his youthful but best-known sculptures,* Winner of the Cock Fight *and* Tarcisius, Christian Martyr, *were acquired during the Second Empire. Indeed, one of Falguière's works,* Winner of the Race, *concluded the list of sculptures privately owned by Napoleon III (Louvre Archives 2 DD 20). Shown at the Salon of 1870, it was a marble version of a work he had sent back from Rome in 1864.*

*Falguière went to Paris with a grant from his native Toulouse and pursued a successful career. He entered the Ecole des Beaux-Arts in 1854 as a pupil of François Jouffroy, made his first appearance at the Salon in 1857, and won the Prix de Rome in 1859. He was awarded a third-class medal in 1864, a second-class in 1867, a first-class at the Exposition Universelle of 1867, a Medal of Honor in 1868, and a rappel ten years later. He succeeded Jouffroy as professor at the Ecole des Beaux-Arts and as a*

*member of the Institut de France in 1883. After his snow statue of the Resistance of 1870, he was made a chevalier of the Legion of Honor and in 1889 a commander.*

*As a teacher and head of the "Toulouse clan," he had many friends and admirers; he enlisted the aid of his pupils—Antonin Mercié, Laurent-Honoré, Victor Peter—in the execution of numerous commemorative monuments commissioned during the Third Republic, including his replacement for Rodin's Balzac (1899). He was an adroit and worldly portraitist, whose sketches were most highly valued. His southern temperament, in which Mantz detected "the breath of modern life," was often lost in the final execution.*

*He also tried his hand at painting and exhibited successfully at the Salon between 1873 and 1892. From 1894 to 1895 he frescoed the ceiling of the Salle des Illustres at the Capitole in Toulouse.*

*Falguière affords a convenient point of reference for art historians due to the abundance of his works and his sensitivity to the values of his time. His creativity was quickly exhausted but his lively, professional hand and his sensuality explain both his success and the temporary oblivion into which he has fallen.*

A.P.

Bibliography:
*La Plume*, June 1, 1898, no. 219; Bénédite, 1902; Lami, 1914–21, vol. II, pp. 324–35

---

Alexandre-Jean-Joseph Falguière

## V-18
## Tarcisius, Christian Martyr

1868
Signed and dated on top of base at right: A. FALGUIERE 1868; inscribed on front chamfer of plinth: TARCISIM. SANCTVM. CHRISTI. SACRAMENTA.GERENTEM.CVM. MALESANA. MANVS. PETERET. VULGARE. PROFANIS. IPSE. ANIMAM. POTIVS. VOLVIT. DIMITTERE. CAESVS. PRODERE. QVAM. CANIBVS. RABIDIS. COELESTIA. MEMBRA [after Pope Damese, cemetery of Callistus]; inscribed on back: A and UU; inscribed on Host: CORPVS DOMINI JESVS CHRISTI
Marble
64.5 × 140.7 × 59.9 cm

Provenance:
Plaster exhibited at Salon of 1867 (no. 2252), transferred to Exposition Universelle (no. 225) [acquired by State June 14, 1867]; marble commissioned by decree of December 16, 1867, for 4,500 francs (Arch. nat. F²¹138); entered the Musée du Luxembourg, August 12, 1871 (LUX 43); transferred to the Louvre, January 27, 1926 (inv. no. RF 174)

V-18

Exhibitions:
1868, Paris, Salon, no. 3578 (Tarcinus; Medal of Honor); 1878, Paris, Exposition Universelle Internationale, no. 1228; 1889, Paris, Exposition Universelle Centennale, no. 78; 1932, Paris, Grand Palais; 1937, Paris, Palais National des Arts, no. 1126

Bibliography:
Castagnary, 1868, p. 325; T. Gautier, "Salon de 1868," Le Moniteur, July 19, 1868, p. 1075; de Navery, 1868, pp. 92, 94; Thoré-Bürger, 1868, p. 540; Mantz, 1869, p. 20; Thoré-Bürger, 1869, p. 287; Catalogues, Paris, Luxembourg, 1872–1906; Veron, 1875, p. 71; Renaud, 1876, p. 160; Bergerat, 1878, pp. 100–103; Jouin, 1879, pp. 177–78; L. Ménard, 1879, repro. p. 237; Barbezieux, 1897; Javel, 1898, pp. 339, 340, 356, 360, 362; Rambosson, 1898, p. 5; Geffroy, 1900, "Falguière," pp. 397, 402, 406, repro. p. 397; Guillaume, 1900, p. 522; Girodie, 1901, "Falguière," repro. p. 3; Bénédite, 1902, pp. 70, 71, 77–79; 1902, Paris, Ecole des Beaux-Arts, pp. 1–24; Lami, 1914–21, vol. II, p. 325; Dimier, 1930, p. 17; Vitry, 1933, vol. III, no. 1806; Peyrefitte, 1973, pp. 58–59; Pingeot, 1977

In 1854 Cardinal Wiseman, archbishop of Westminster, published a novel entitled Fabiola, or, the Church of the Catacombs intended for the "Popular Catholic Library." It was to attain international success. Falguière saw a translated and reedited version when he was in Rome as a pensionnaire at the Villa Medici. The chapter called "The Viaticum," devoted to the story of Tarcisius, a child martyr, inspired one of Falguière's most famous works, which took the form of a tableau vivant.

In the archives of the Musée Rodin, there is a startling photograph of the model for this work (Bénédite, 1902, repro.). This ambiguous type of "small thin boy," denounced by the critic Thoré-Bürger, was used intentionally by Falguière. He admired the dying children in Carpeaux's Ugolino of 1864, especially the youngest one: "The lifelike quality of his pose, the suppleness of his little concave torso, the grace of his limbs, the anatomical precision of his joints, fill me with admiration. I found it extraordinarily audacious to have rendered with such truth those thin bodies, that poor and shrunken flesh through which the skeleton is visible; I understood how beautiful and new it was."

But the representation of recumbent adolescents occurs frequently in antiquity. It was revived in the Hyacinth of François-Joseph Bosio (1817), Bara by David d'Angers (1839), Dying Abel by Giovanni Dupré (1844), and Saint Benedict on a Bed of Thorns by Antoine Etex (1865), and it would have numerous descendants such as the Dead Abel by Vincent-Emile Feugère des Forts (1869), that of Lange Gug-lielmo (1877), Abel by Jean-Antonin Carlès (1881), Pro Patria by Emile Peynot (1886), Death of Hyacinth by Léon-Jean-Baptiste Grandin (1888), Ishmael by Just Becquet (1889), Eve Finding Abel's Body by Albert-Gaston Guilloux, and Saint Philomena by Louis-Noël (1897).

The history of the execution of this marble shows us a young Prix de Rome grappling with the Administration. On June 6, 1867, Falguière responded to Nieuwerkerke's request to buy the plaster: "I gratefully accept your proposal; however, there is one condition, and that is that I be granted permission to do it in marble." Nieuwerkerke agreed, and a block of marble was assigned to him by decree of July 11, followed by another for the plinth (decree of October 19). This block proved to be flawed but despite the artist's complaints it was not replaced, and faults remain, most evident on the thigh, the left elbow, the left eyebrow, and in the hair.

Several other full-scale versions in plaster, marble, and bronze exist, as do editions of just the head.

A.P.

Musée du Louvre, Paris

## Emmanuel Frémiet

*Paris 1824–1910 Paris*

Many aspects of Frémiet's art can be understood if one examines his artistic formation: "He took his first drawing lessons from his aunt, Sophie Frémiet, who had married the great sculptor Rude. Soon after he worked with Werner, a natural history painter to whom he was distantly related. Without any inheritance, he was forced to earn a living. He executed preparatory drawings for lithographs illustrating comparative osteology, restored anatomical models for the Orfila museum, and in a truly gruesome occupation, served for a short time as a morgue painter.... Subsequently, while studying at the Muséum and taking courses at the Petite Ecole, he modeled religious figures for commercial sale" (Lami, 1914–21, vol. II, pp. 405–6). He then entered Rude's studio while diligently continuing his visits to the Jardin des Plantes, where he drew animals from life. He thus acquired the detailed knowledge of anatomy which is evident in all of his work.

He began his career as an animalier. From the Salon of 1843 until 1855 he exhibited mostly dogs, cats, and herons. Then he was commissioned to do a series of statuettes representing different military types (1855). The Gallic Horseman (Salon of 1863) and the Roman Horseman (Salon of 1866), both half life size, were executed for Saint-Germain-en-Laye.

The equestrian statue of Napoleon I, ordered in 1866, and that of Louis d'Orléans for Pierrefonds, commissioned in 1869, mark the beginning of the period of his monumental groups. Until that time he had enjoyed only modest success; his greatest fame was achieved during the Third Republic. After he was commissioned to do the statue of Joan of Arc for the place des Pyramides (1874), other important commissions followed: Saint Michael (1879), Stefan al Mare (1882; Romania), Meisonnier (1894; Poissy), Rude (1907; Dijon), Bolivar (1910; Colombia).

In the meantime he had not forgotten his animals; this time, however, he tried to instill his compositions with philosophical meaning, an approach that was not always appreciated. His Gorilla Dragging the Body of a Woman, prepared for the Salon of 1859, was criticized for being in extremely bad taste, and as a result was refused. He nevertheless made a great effort to see that his art embodied a moral lesson. Frémiet returned to this moralizing theme several times, notably with his Gorilla Abducting a Negress, which was accepted for the Salon of 1887. (See also no. II-23.)

O.S.

Bibliography:
Bricon, 1898; de Biez, 1910; Lami, 1914–21, vol. II, pp. 405–19; Fauré-Frémiet, 1934

V-19

Emmanuel Frémiet

## V-19
## Ravageot and Ravageode, Basset Hounds

1853
Signed on base: E. Frémiet
Bronze
Height 60 cm; diameter 80 cm

Provenance:
Commissioned from the artist on June 10, 1852; following Salon of 1853 sent to Compiègne where it was placed in apartment A, by 1855 (Louvre Archives H2758 [December 3, 1855]); decorated the chimney of the Salle des Gardes by 1861; Musée National du Château (inv. no. C 69 C)

Exhibitions:
1853, Paris, Salon, no. 1355; 1855, Paris, Salon, no. 4392

Bibliography:
Malitourne, 1853, p. 23; Pétroz, 1855; Notice, 1867; Vapereau, 1870, p. 708; Saint-Ogan, 1887, p. 166; de Biez, 1896, p. 54; de Biez, 1910, p. 50; Lami, 1914–21, vol. II, pp. 406, 409; Fauré-Frémiet, 1934, p. 48; Horswell, 1971, repro. p. 188; Rheims, 1972, p. 297; Cooper, 1975, pp. 149, 156 (repro.)

Ravageot's companion has been given several different names (Ravageole, Ravageotte, etc.) but we prefer to use the one from the Salon catalogues of 1853 and 1855, Ravageode. The 1855 catalogue entry also reads: "In plaster, Salon of 1848." In 1848 Frémiet had exhibited "Ravaude and Mascareau, dogs from M. de V's kennel." Cooper (1975, p. 156) states that this group of two basset hounds was commissioned for the palace at Compiègne following its successful reception at the Salon of 1851. Unfortunately, in reality, the situation was far less pleasant for Frémiet. The documents concerning this commission in the Archives Nationales (F$^{21}$81) are extremely confusing because the ministry did not always specify the names and breeds of the dogs, mentioning only a commission for "a group of animals." However, one can try to reconstruct the chronology of events concerning this group.

On September 7, 1850, Frémiet solicited a commission for a group in bronze. His request was left unanswered. On June 5, 1851, he was apparently hard-pressed and begged the Director of Fine Arts to come to his aid. Two days later he formulated a specific request: "Please entrust me... with the execution of a bronze group of two life-size basset hounds, which were in the last exhibition.... I am heavily in debt.... The cost of the casting is one thousand francs for the bronze and six hundred francs for the zinc." Thus, it is clear that Frémiet exhibited a group of basset hounds in plaster at an earlier date without success, but following this letter the Minister of the Interior commissioned from him (October 8, 1851) "an animal group the model for which must be presented for the approval of the administration" for the sum of 2,000 francs. We know that this animal group is identical with *Ravageot and Ravageode* because on June 10, 1852, the artist was asked "to execute a bronze group representing bassets after the plaster model which was commissioned from him 8.8.^bre, 1851 for the sum of one thousand francs." On March 10, 1853, the work was completed and Frémiet received payment.

This minutely detailed piece was hardly noticed by his contemporaries even though an attempt at life-size animal sculpture was rather unusual. However Pétroz wrote: "M. Frémiet, in particular, seems to believe that one should disdain nothing in nature, and that all of its objects are of equal interest. This theory is certainly debatable, especially in the case of sculpture, but one must acknowledge that *Ravageot and Ravageode* are portraits that are perfect in the observation of detail and in execution. The poses of the two bassets, one with his head held high, the other sniffing at a snail that has his horns extended, are extremely convincing. The turned out paws, the modulations in their coats, the chain, the small bell that hangs under the throat could not be more accurately rendered."

Frémiet had smaller versions of his hounds done, and the Minister bought two of them in 1858 for 90 francs! The sculptor also made separate sculptures of the two dogs. They also exist in reductions as two separate figures (*see* Horswell, 1971, p. 189). A drawing by Frémiet of *Ravageot and Ravageode* is at Compiègne.

O.S.

Musée National du Château, Compiègne

---

*Marie-Louise Lefèvre-Deumier*

*Argentan 1816–1877 Paris*

*Since the eighteenth century a number of women painters had been active; women sculptors emerged in the nineteenth century. Among them were Princess Marie d'Orléans; Mlle de Fauveau; the duchesse de Castiglione-Colonna, who used the pseudonym Marcello (q.v.) to exhibit her work; F. Dubois d'Av-esnes; A. Grégoire; Mme Claude Vignon; and Mme Lefèvre-Deumier. It seems that many of these women practiced sculpture as a pastime rather than as a means of livelihood. However, Mme Lefèvre-Deumier showed her works quite regularly at the Salon, beginning in 1850, and she received frequent commissions from the government. Had she friends at court, as Lami seemed to think? Apparently the imperial couple had no artist friends, and Mme Lefèvre shared with many other artists the ministerial manna that was scattered yearly.*

*Critics often had kind words for this artist's entries in the Salon, especially the* Young Shepherd on the Island of Procida, *a marble commissioned in 1853 for the grand sum of 9,000 francs. It was exhibited again in the 1857 Salon, this time with the title* Virgil as a Child *(Louvre Archives S 30 [letter from Mme Lefèvre-Deumier asking that this work be sent to the Caen museum]). Also of interest is* The Morning Star, *a marble statue exhibited in the 1863 Salon (Rouen museum).*

*Mme Lefèvre had the honor, not shared by Carpeaux (q.v.), of doing a bust of the Prince-President (a mediocre bronze version is at Compiègne) and of the Empress, a marble which was shown in the 1859 Salon (Marseilles museum). She was commissioned, as were practically all sculptors of the Second Empire, to do the portrait of some official for Versailles, in her case General Sibuet (Salon of 1869), and she participated in the great campaign of Parisian works for the Cour de Louvre with her nymph* Glycera, *commissioned in 1858. After the fall of the Second Empire, Mme Lefèvre's production ceased. She exhibited only once more, in the 1873 Salon; just before her death, she completed the work that was to decorate the family tomb (Salon of 1877).*

O.S.

Bibliography:
Thieme and Becker, 1907–50, vol. XXII, p. 558; Lami, 1914–21, vol. III, pp. 283–85

---

Marie-Louise Lefèvre-Deumier

## V-20
## Souvenir of Notre Dame

1853
Signed and dated on base at left: Mme LEFÈVRE-DEUMIER, 1853; inscribed on base: SOUVENIR DE NOTRE-DAME
Plaster
Height 70 cm; depth 62 cm

Provenance:
Gift of Dr. Hugenschmitt to the museum at Malmaison; entered Musée National du Château, Compiègne, May 22, 1953 (inv. no. MMPO 1253)

Bibliography:
Vignon, 1855, p. 171; Besnard, 1856, p. 200; Bour-

V-20

guignon, n.d., p. 22; Lami, 1914–21, vol. III, p. 284; *Le Journal de la France*, 1970, repro. p. 1408

This plaster statuette represents the Empress Eugénie on her wedding day. It is probably one of several plasters made after the model for the marble statuette which was commissioned from Mme Lefèvre-Deumier by the Minister of State. The plaster statuette is dated 1853, and on March 14, 1854, Mme Lefèvre-Deumier wrote to the Minister: "From the day on which, as a result of your suggestions and kind support, Their Majesties were willing to accept my statuette of the Empress, the benevolent appreciation of it that they have expressed gave me the idea that they would perhaps like to consecrate this remembrance of one of the most beautiful days of their lives in a material more durable than plaster and more worthy of Their Majesties. If they should express to the Minister of State the desire to have me execute this work in marble for the palace at Versailles, I would be very happy.... I could have the sculpture ready for the exposition of 1855, and it would be easy for me to improve the likeness and to come even closer to the beauty of the model" (Arch. nat. F^21 93).

On June 8, 1854, the minister commissioned a marble statuette for the sum of 6,000 francs. We do not know what became of the marble, and none of the statuettes was exhibited at the Salon, Vignon (1855) regretting its absence.

This statuette defines exactly the limits of Mme Lefèvre-Deumier's talents. While it faithfully reproduces the costume of the Empress, it totally lacks life and sensitivity.

There are two other plaster versions of the *Souvenir of Notre Dame* at Compiègne. One is the same size but more mediocre in quality (38-429); the other is smaller (height 47 cm), with several "variations" which are simply the result of bad restorations. It is probably the same size as the original model since the commission for the marble stipulated that "this statuette should be of the same proportions as the plaster model," and Mme Lefèvre-Deumier used a white Italian marble block which measured 48.6 cubic centimeters.

This work was popularized through black-and-white and color lithographs by Pauquet. A drawing for the lithographs is in the Rouen museum.

O.S.

Musée National du Château, Compiègne

V-21

### Alexandre-Victor Lequien
*Paris 1822–1905*

*Little is known of this forgotten artist except that he was a pupil of François Devaulx. Essentially he sculpted portraits and seems to have lived on subsidies from the State, which continually commissioned effigies of officials of the Empire to fill Versailles and administrative offices. Besides the various portraits of Napoleon III, also notable is that of the marshal, Comte d'Ornano (Salon of 1863; formerly Ajaccio museum), as well as those of General de Laumière dating from 1863 (Versailles museum), Admiral de Genouilly in 1869 (Versailles), and Comte Colonna Walewski, which was exhibited in the 1870 Salon (Versailles). After the end of the Second Empire, Lequien continued his career as official portraitist.*

O.S.

Bibliography:
Thieme and Becker, 1907–50, vol. XXIII, p. 109; Lami, 1914–21, vol. III, pp. 327–30

Alexandre-Victor Lequien

## V-21
## Napoleon III

1869
Signed and dated: A/dre Lequien 1869
Bronze, heavily patinated
63 × 35 × 27.5 cm

Provenance:
Prince Napoléon
Bibliography:
Lami, 1914–21, vol. III, p. 328

Lequien executed at least three different busts of Napoleon III: one in marble in 1860, one in bronze in 1868, and another in marble for the Salon of 1869. Did the Emperor perhaps have a preference for Lequien? No more than for Gayrard, Iselin, Oliva, Pollet (q.v.), Ponscarme, Roux, Barre, Denécheau, Eude, Fontana, Carrier, Prosper d'Epinay, Chardigny, Devaulx, and Hébert, all of whom sculpted busts of Napoleon III (not to mention equestrian or full-length statues). It is remarkable that there are no famous names among Lequien's fellow sculptors. Even Carpeaux did not receive an official commission for the bust of Napoleon III while the Emperor was in power (*see* no. V-9). Napoleon III apparently did not prefer any particular artistic style or any one artist. There is nothing surprising about this; what it meant was that the Emperor, the

author of *L'Extinction du paupérisme,* gave a bit of work to everyone.

This bronze bust was ordered for the price of 700 francs with nine other casts at 450 francs by the Ministère de la Maison de l'Empereur in response to a request by Lequien (Arch. nat. F[21] 156). The Musée National du Château in Compiègne owns two of the less expensive casts; their patinas are not as beautiful as that of the original.

Although this bust is dated 1869 and is different from the other likenesses of the Emperor in marble, Lequien perhaps based it on an earlier model. It is known that the Emperor did not like to pose and so it is hardly likely that he would have agreed to new posing sessions for each portrait. Moreover, the heavy features of the Emperor are similar to those in photographs of the 1860s or in the portrait by Flandrin (*see* no. VI-55). Nevertheless, Lequien made it a point to give it an energy not found in the busts of Eude, Pollet, Iselin, or Barre—an energy that probably did not exist. The gloomy expression and vague look, which all the memorialists describe, would never have been suitable for a head crowned with laurel. Carpeaux also was to transform the Emperor's expression in his portrait of 1873, giving it the spirituality typical of all his works.

O.S.

Collection S.A.I. Prince Napoléon, Paris

### Jacques-Léonard Maillet
*Paris 1823–1895 Paris*

*Maillet, the son of a carpenter, won the second Prix de Rome as Jean-Jacques Feuchère's student, and then the first, as James Pradier's student in 1847. On his return from the Villa Medici, he was awarded a first-class medal for his envoi in the 1853 Salon. He received many honors during the Second Empire. As a "sculptor-poet, Greco-Roman throughout" (Veron, 1876, p. 208), he drew his inspiration from ancient or Biblical themes before he began making models for goldwork and doing genre subjects. "This regenerator of our great art" (Veron, 1876, p. 213) who received many official commissions in Paris—for the Louvre, the Opéra, the Hôtel de Ville, and the churches of Saint Séverin, Sainte Clotilde, Saint Leu, La Trinité, and Saint Joseph—is one of the sculptors most unjustly ignored today.*

A.P.

Bibliography:
Veron, 1876, pp. 208–13; Veron, 1877, pp. 337–39; Chevalier, 1878, pp. 92–97; Lami, 1914–21, vol. III, pp. 372–75

V-22

Jacques-Léonard Maillet

## V-22
## Agrippina Bearing the Ashes of Germanicus

1859
Signed on base at left: JACQUES MAILLET; inscribed on urn: GERMA/NICUS
Plaster
188 × 65 × 50 cm

Provenance:
Gift of the sculptor to the Musée des Beaux-Arts, Angers, 1883, by request of M.A. Giffard (Catalogue, Angers, Musée des Beaux-Arts, 1887, supplement, no. 861)

Exhibitions:
1859, Paris, Salon, no. 3369; 1900, Paris, Exposition Universelle, no. 1720

Bibliography:
Astruc, 1859, p. 341; Auvray, 1859, p. 82; Chesneau, 1859, p. 156; du Camp, 1859, p. 182; *Notices explicatives*, 1861, p. 79; *Magasin Pittoresque*, vol. XXIX, 1861, pp. 223–24; Aubert, 1861, p. 277; du Camp, 1861, p. 190; Gautier, 1861, p. 405; le Guillois, 1861, p. 63; Thoré-Bürger, 1861, p. 174; Veron, 1875, p. 156; Veron, 1876, pp. 209, 210; Chevalier, 1878, p. 92; Lami, 1914–21, vol. III, p. 374; Charageat, 1931, no. 25; Hargrove, 1977, p. 44

Neither the 1859 plaster cast nor the marble, which won him the Legion of Honor in 1861 when shown at the Salon (no. 3465) and a third-class medal in the Exposition Universelle of 1867 (RF 184; today exposed to the weather on the terrace of the fort of Mont Valérien), left the critics indifferent. They were divided into two camps. Some, carried away by the subject matter, quoted Tacitus or M.J. Chenier (*Magasin Pittoresque*, vol. XXIX, 1861, pp. 223–24; Veron, 1876), while others, the greater majority, were interested in the problem of veiled transparency in sculpture, which Maillet had explicitly investigated. His letter of February 18, 1860, requesting a block of marble of the first quality makes this clear (Arch. nat. F²¹ 159).

In 1859 du Camp wrote: "This is less art than it is difficulty overcome," while Aubert, in 1861, said: "This is an excellent piece, but I hope it is the last of its kind: the veiled woman is hackneyed." The same year Gautier commented: "A *tour de force* easier to do than the layman would think… many a Neapolitan sculptor made this apparent impossibility… his unique means of success. M. Maillet does not fall into this category; he has enough serious qualities to get beyond this bit of charlatanism"—or this virtuosity—which never ended in Italy (as in the work of Corradini, Sanmartino, Spinazzi, Monti).

In France, Jules Bonnaffé exhibited *Beautiful Night*, a woman draped in veils, at the Salon of 1857; Mathurin Moreau (q.v.), a work entitled *The Future*; Carrier-Belleuse (q.v.), a *Veiled Vestal Virgin* (Laon museum) at the Salon of 1859; and later François-Etienne Captier repeated this process for his two busts of *Woman of Bresse* in the museum in Mâcon.

The following description appeared in the entry for Maillet's work in the Salon catalogue of 1859: "Agrippina left Syria in order to carry the ashes of her husband to Rome. The Senate, the people—in fact everyone—filed before the urn with as much respect as would have been given the effigy of some god." Du Camp, in 1861, asked: "Why, in the catalogue, does M. Maillet tell us that the ashes were in an urn and then go ahead and put them in a kind of jewel box in Agrippina's hands?" This inspired le Guillois (1861) to write one of his light verses: "Maillet is the inventor of this square urn,/ Young Agrippina's sorrowful concern,/Are ducats behind all this fuss,/Or just the ashes of Germanicus?"

This figure is a testimony to the training received (a constraint sometimes more enriching than sterilizing) by the *pensionnaires* at the Villa Medici. What would have become of Maillet's talent without this discipline, which is even more perceptible in his earlier *Agrippina and Caligula* (RF 10) from the 1853 Salon?

Like Gabriel-Jules Thomas's contemporary *Virgil* (RF 2224), this noble work belongs to the most official, but no less interesting, statuary of the Second Empire.

A.P.

Musée des Beaux-Arts, Angers

---

## Marcello (Adèle d'Affry, Duchesse de Castiglione-Colonna)
*Givisiez (Switzerland) 1836–1879 Castellammare (Italy)*

*Widowed in 1856 after several months of marriage to Carlo Colonna, Adèle d'Affry turned to a career in art. As a woman, her access to professional training was limited. She had studied drawing in Nice with Joseph Fricero and had been a student of the sculptor Heinrich Maximilian Imhof in Rome in 1853. Later, in Paris, she obtained special permission to study anatomy at the Ecole Pratique de Médicine. Her interest in sixteenth-century Italian art, particularly Michelangelo, greatly influenced the character of her own work. In 1861 she met Carpeaux (q.v.) in Rome and their mutual passion for Michelangelo sparked a lifelong friendship. Each lent valuable help to the other over the years.*

*Aside from portraiture, her work consists mainly of images of women in history or mythology. Although most are small or bust-length, she produced numerous large-scale pieces as well:* Hecate and Cerberus, *purchased about 1867 for the Hôtel de Ville and destroyed in 1871; the marble portrait statue of Princess Czartoryska of 1869, now in Fribourg; and, best known of all, the dramatic bronze* Pythia, *shown in the Salon of 1870 and purchased for the Paris Opéra by Charles Garnier (q.v.).*

Marcello exhibited in the Paris Salons from 1863 to 1870. One of her initial entries, the marble bust of Bianca Capello, was purchased for the Luxembourg collections, as was her bust of an Abyssinian chief shown in 1870.

The marble bust of a Gorgon, now at Fontainebleau, was shown at the Salon of 1866; a bronze cast was also exhibited that year in London at the Royal Academy and purchased for the South Kensington Museum (now the Victoria and Albert Museum). One of the seven entries in the Exposition Universelle of 1867 was the bust of Diana, which was purchased by the Emperor.

Marcello bequeathed her collection to Fribourg. Her studies, numerous finished works, replicas, and paintings by friends such as Delacroix, Hébert, and Courbet (q.q.v.) can be seen there and at her studio at Givisiez.

S.G.L.

Bibliography:
D'Alcantara, 1961; Bessis, 1967; Avery, 1972; Bessis, 1975

Marcello (Adèle d'Affry, Duchesse de Castiglione-Colonna)

## V-23
## Bianca Capello

1863
Signed at right: A. Marcello; inscribed on pedestal: Bianca Capello
Marble
95 × 63 × 37 cm

Provenance:
Purchased ("domaine privé") by the Emperor for 4,000 francs by decree of August 8, 1864 (Louvre Archives 2 DD 26, n⁶ [1864]); sent to Fontainebleau, March 7, 1865 (Louvre Archives S 12 [1865]); transferred to the Musée des Beaux-Arts, Marseilles, April 17, 1894 (Louvre Archives S 12 [1894])

Exhibition:
1863, Paris, Salon, no. 2471

Bibliography:
Auvray, 1863, pp. 96–97; de Callias, 1863, p. 5; de Rialle, 1863, p. 135; du Pays, 1863, pp. 85, 235; de Sault, 1864, p. 245; Thoré-Bürger, 1870, p. 437; d'Alcantara, 1961, pp. 60–61, 63, 78

This colossal bust established Marcello's reputation at the very first showing of her work. The artist explained in her notes that she conceived it not as the portrait of a historical personality, but as a study of expression and character: "Having been invited to the marriage of an Italian couple, I...observed a lady with a proud bearing, a hawklike nose, and a look both domineering and alluring which she occasionally chose to direct toward some unknown victim of hers. I left, deeply preoccupied, having memorized the features of a woman about whom I knew nothing. I said to myself that here was a type of rare quality, and the means of reproducing that tragic head without altering its beauty came to me. What would have happened in the sixteenth century to that perverse, haughty, passionate woman? In the end the model became a mere pretext. But in order to create a type, one must look further. I had already done a great deal of work on the bust, and I was looking for a name which, for the public, would symbolize the perfidious charms of my heroine when the name of Bianca Capello struck me" (d'Alcantara, 1961, p. 60). "The superb and daring coiffure" she found in a drawing by Michelangelo in the Uffizi (Dussler, 1959, no. 491, p. 186), and she also took from the drawing the shape of the collar and the sleeves of the bodice.

In order to find out more about the character she had chosen, Marcello asked for background information from the former diplomat and author, the comte de Circourt. The explanatory note on the life of Bianca Capello that appeared in the Salon catalogue may have been written by him. "Bianca Capello, daughter of a great Venetian family, eloped when she was eighteen with a young Florentine, taking with her the family jewels. Having found refuge in Florence, she became the mistress of Francesco de' Medici, falsely claimed to be pregnant, got rid of her accomplices, and per-

V-23

suaded her lover to marry her. Having become Grand Duchess of Tuscany, Bianca Capello tried to poison her brother-in-law, Cardinal de' Medici, but when her husband mistakenly partook of the readied dish, she too swallowed some of it and died."

This work received many favorable notices. Théophile Gautier in *Le Moniteur* of September 1, 1865, wrote: "This bust could easily be taken for the work of one of the Renaissance masters. It has the slender pride, the haughty elegance of sculptures of that period. The head, with its bizarre coiffure, shows a cruel grace, an imperious beauty, a deadly charm...."

Another marble version of this bust was bought in 1872 by the Administration des Beaux-Arts at Adolphe Thiers's request (decree of July 19, 1872; Arch. nat. F²¹ 205) and entered the Luxembourg on March 29, 1873. It remained there until October 30, 1890; then, because it was thought to be the original, it was sent to Fontainebleau on April 17, 1894, as a replacement for the version exhibited here.

Between these two versions, Marcello seems to have executed another marble reproduction, shown in 1867 at the Exposition Universelle. This marble perhaps belonged to one of her friends, Princess Isabelle Czartoryska, the comtesse Dzialynska. A bronze version of Bianca Capello was exhibited in Lille in 1866 (no. 1034). This was probably the same cast that Marcello sent to the international exhibition in Vienna in 1873 (Ménard, 1873, p. 208) and which she exhibited at the Société des Beaux-Arts of Nice in 1877 (no. 16). A marble version is in the museum at Arras.

J.-P.S.

Musée des Beaux-Arts, Marseilles

---

## Moreau-Vauthier (Augustin-Jean Moreau)

*Paris 1831–1893 Paris*

*Moreau-Vauthier represents a new type of sculptor, one who brought to the profession the background of a craftsman and never abandoned his original means of expression. Following his father, he worked in ivory and bequeathed this métier to his sculptor son, Paul Moreau-Vauthier.*

*He entered the Ecole des Beaux-Arts as a student of Armand Toussaint in 1850 and exhibited at the Salon from 1857 to 1892 (including a posthumous submission in 1893). He added "Vauthier" to his*

name in 1865 so that he would not be confused with any of the numerous other late-nineteenth-century sculptors called Moreau.

*In the album of mementos (Bibliothèque Doucet Msc. 275) gathered by Roger-Marx, who delivered the eulogy at his funeral, is a list drawn up by the sculptor himself of the works he exhibited and the awards he won from 1850 on. It demonstrates the importance he attached to industrial art: in the category of industry at the Expositions Universelles, he won a first-class medal in 1855 and two medals in 1867, gold (class 90) and silver (class 26); honorable mentions in 1861 and 1863 at the Ecole des Beaux-Arts; at the Salons, a medal (1865), a second-class medal (1875), chevalier of the Legion of Honor (1877), and a third-class medal (1878); and a silver medal (not mentioned in Moreau-Vauthier's list) at the Exposition Universelle of 1889; finally, he was made an officer of the Académie des Beaux-Arts in 1885. He also won medals abroad: London (1872), Vienna (1873 and 1882), Philadelphia (1876), Amsterdam (1883), and Antwerp (1885).*

*From 1864 to his death the State purchased eleven of his works. In 1885 he was made a professor at the Ecole des Arts Décoratifs. He was frequently a member of the jury for the exhibitions of the Union Centrale and presented to it a figure of Fortune and three models for the Hôtel de Ville.*

A.P.

Bibliography:
Roger-Marx, 1893; Lami, 1914–21, vol. III, pp. 484–87

---

Moreau-Vauthier (Augustin-Jean Moreau)

## V-24
## The Little Drinker

1869
Signed and dated at rear, on top of base: A. MOREAU-VAUTHIER M DCCC LXIX
Marble
68 × 49 × 88 cm

Provenance:
Purchased privately by the Emperor from the Salon

V-24

of 1869 for 4,000 francs, June 26, 1869 (Louvre Archives 2 DD 20, 2 DD 25, S. 160, Inventaire du domaine privé, no. 152); installed in the English garden at Compiègne, August 22, 1872, replacing Spalla's *Hymen;* transferred to the Musée du Luxembourg, November 22, 1878 (LUX 78); deposited at the Sénat, January 12, 1917; returned to the Louvre, 1976 (inv. no. RF 152)

Exhibitions:
1869, Paris, Salon, no. 3607; 1878, Paris, Exposition Universelle Internationale, no. 1364; 1900, Paris, Exposition Universelle Centennale, no. 1750

Bibliography:
Jahyer, 1865, p. 232; Jahyer, 1866, p. 266; Auvray, 1869, p. 85; T. Gautier, *Le Moniteur,* May 24, 1869, p. 744; Thoré-Bürger, 1869, p. 290; *Le Moniteur,* April 22, 1871; Catalogues, Paris, Luxembourg, 1879–98; Lami, 1914–22, vol. III, pp. 484–85

Moreau-Vauthier first exhibited a *Little Drinker* in bronze in the Salon of 1865 (no. 3086; third-class medal) and the Exposition Universelle of 1867. It was purchased by the State on November 11, 1867, for 3,500 francs (Arch. nat. F²¹ 164) and is now in the museum in Carcassone. Four years later he exhibited the marble in the Salon of 1869 (no. 3607). Chennevières sent Nieuwerkerke a list of works which had attracted the attention of the Emperor and Empress at the Salon (Louvre Archives Z 21 [June 12, 1869]). Napoleon III selected two pieces of sculpture: the *Huntsman on Horseback,* a wax by Pierre-Jules Mêne, and the bronze *Young Italian Shepherd* by Moreau-Vauthier. However, this *zampognaro* already had a purchaser, so the Emperor chose *The Little Drinker* instead. The Administration des Beaux-Arts neglected to adjust the price and the 4,000 francs offered for the bronze were simply transferred to the marble. The sum was not sufficient but Moreau-Vauthier "did not request an increase..., that would have been out of keeping with his character and position" (Louvre Archives N 6 [June 26, 1869]). By contrast, he later became concerned about the condition of his sculpture, "badly placed" in the park at Compiègne, "on a base which is too high and too large. For my sake and for the preservation of the marble, which was not intended for the outdoors, it is urgent that it be moved" (Louvre Archives S 2 [February 14, 1878]).

In 1895 Moreau-Vauthier's children voiced the same concern. They offered his *Bacchante* (RF 2225) from the Salon of 1892 as a replacement for *The Little Drinker,* then at the Luxembourg, probably hoping that the latter would go to the Louvre (Louvre Archives S 8 [July 10, 1895]).

The subject of this work is representative of the adolescent figures which invaded the Salon (*see also* no. VI-2). Gautier's interest reflects the appeal of this marble: "We linger with pleasure before *The Little Drinker...* a boy who could teach even Diogenes about excess and inspire him to throw away his clay cup....The youth is ten or twelve years old and his youthful slenderness lends itself to subtle anatomical details. M. Moreau-Vauthier has treated this figure without dryness: his little body is as slender as a Saint John by Donatello."

The mention of Saint John is inevitable; the reference to Donatello is more doubtful. By his choice of subjects and his love of material, less delicate in his compositions than Delaplanche, Moreau-Vauthier is among the most typical artists of the Second Empire.

A.P.

Musée du Louvre, Paris

---

## Eugène-André Oudiné

*Paris 1810–1887 Paris*

*Oudiné's official career began with a Prix de Rome for medal engraving in 1831. He won second-class medals for engraving and sculpture in 1837, 1848, and 1855, first-class medals in 1839 and 1843, a rappel in 1857 and, in the same year, the Legion of Honor. He was continually in pursuit of commissions and, backed by numerous recommendations, usually obtained them. Quick to foresee a coming event, he prepared the sketch of a commemorative work in advance. One of his original ideas was to send out photographs of his compositions (Arch. nat. F²¹ 168).*

*Oudiné produced considerable sculpture but he was primarily a medalist. "No influence was comparable in importance to that which Oudiné exercised for a span of forty years," wrote Roger-Marx (quoted by Forrer, 1904–30). "He took up the efforts of his predecessors, explored them, synthesized them." Babelon discovered in him "a very modern feeling: he was the one who initiated the rejuvenation that turned a sterile, dead art into the one we know, timid and conventional at times, or too willfully realistic, but always alive." The Bibliothèque Nationale owns eighty of his medals and the Louvre eleven, but these form only a small part of his total production.*

A.P.

Bibliography:
Forrer, 1904–30, vol. IV, pp. 346–51; Lami, 1914–21, vol. IV, pp. 32–38; Babelon, 1927, pp. 205–6; 1967, Paris, Hôtel de la Monnaie, nos. 640–58; Darnis, 1975

V-25

Eugène-André Oudiné

## V-25
## Medal: The Accession of Napoleon III to the Empire

1852
Signed at bottom: E. A. OUDINE F.; inscribed: AVENEMENT DE NAPOLEON III A L'EMPIRE; inscribed on exergue: II. DECEM^BRE MDCCCLII; inscribed on ribbons of crown of oak leaves held above head of Napoleon III; 7824189 SUFFRAGES
Struck copper
Diameter 7.2 cm

Provenance:
Musée du Luxembourg; with nos. V-26 and V-27, possibly part of the "series of medals by Oudiné entering the museum in 1889," loaned to the Exposition Universelle of 1900, and returned December 11, 1900 (Louvre Archives 2 HH 24 [Catalogue of activities of the Luxembourg, p. 123]); transferred to the Louvre

Bibliography:
Malitourne, 1852, p. 166; Catalogue, Paris, Musée Monétaire, 1892, p. 476; Darnis, 1975, p. 206

The vicissitudes of French nineteenth-century history often forced artists to make sudden changes in iconography. Oudiné, who won a first prize in the medal competition with his *Establishment of the Republic in 1848,* exhibited at the Salon of 1851 the plaster for the *Commemorative Medal of December 2, 1851:* "Louis-Napoleon Bonaparte, Guided by Wisdom, Vanquishes the Hydra of Anarchy; A Grateful France Bestows on Him the Civic Crown" (description given in the Salon catalogue, no. 1507). He repeated the composition

V-26

This versatile obverse was used for at least three medals: *The Annexation of Savoy and the County of Nice*, June 12, 1860 (diameter 7.2 cm, reduction 4.1 cm); *The Suez Canal: Joining of Two Seas*, 1864; and *Photography: Homine Dirigente Sol Artifex*, 1866. The Paris Mint still issues the first and third of these medals with dies reconstructed after the originals it possesses (Darnis, 1975, p. 206).

In addition, this "laureate type" composition was used from 1861 until 1870 to strike award medals (with a crown on the reverse) in two sizes: 5 centimeters and 3.2 centimeters.

The "velvety" appearance of Oudiné's medals, praised by Dr. Weber (Forrer, 1904–30, vol. IV, p. 346), is less evident here than in the two profiles of the Emperor and the Prince Imperial on the medal of *The Plebiscite of 1870* (no. V-27), but is quite noticeable in his work executed directly on steel.

A.P.

Musée du Louvre, Paris

Eugène-André Oudiné

## V-27
## Medal: The Plebiscite of 1870

1870–72

Obverse: signed at left: OUDINE; inscribed: NA-POLEON. EUGENE.LOUIS.PRINCE.IMPERIAL/NAPOLEON III.EMPEREUR.DES.FRANCAIS; reverse: signed at right: OUDINE; inscribed: PLEBISCITE/MDCCCLXX; inscribed in banderole at top: 7,350,000, repeated on urn carried by figure at left; inscribed on tablet held by Napoleon III: CONSTI/TUTION; inscribed on exergue: VIII/MAI
Struck copper
Diameter 7.3 cm

Provenance:
*See* no. V-25
Bibliography:
Darnis, 1975, p. 206

This medal, commemorating an event that was held in vain, was commissioned from Oudiné by a decree of August 4, 1870, for the sum of 6,000 francs payable in 1871! It required that he furnish two dies and one stamp for each side of the medal, or six pieces in all. The fall of the Empire one month later did not disconcert the sculptor for long. On January 10, 1872, he sent plaster proofs of the medal to Charles Blanc, the new Director of Fine Arts, and re-

quested partial payment: the molds had been cast, and he had only to finish the inscriptions and engrave them. His request included the fact that his home had been sacked during the Commune. On January 24 he was paid 2,000 francs. On April 30, Oudiné asked Blanc to have his four medals struck by the Dépôt Légal. Blanc sent Abel de Pujol to reason with him. On May 17, de Pujol wrote a report in which he assured Blanc that Oudiné had withdrawn his request and intended to deposit his dies and stamps at the Mint, which in fact was done on May 22. In the margin the director noted: "It is appropriate that M. Oudiné be reimbursed with some new commissions." The final payment for the medal was made on June 18.

Two years later Oudiné took up the fight again. He wanted to have the medal struck in order to complete his personal collection and to

V-27

in 1852 but was obliged to change both the title, which became *The Accession of Napoleon III to the Empire,* and the spirit: "the annointment by universal suffrage" supported by the imperial eagle took the place of "Napoleon receiving the civic crown."

The obverse of the medal of 1852 was also changed to suit the new political climate. The Prince-President of the Republic was replaced by the Emperor. The signature (E. A. OUDINE. F.) and the absence of the crown of laurel leaves (which does not appear on award medals until after 1861) differentiate it from the single-faced proof exhibited here.

A.P.

Musée du Louvre, Paris

Eugène-André Oudiné

## V-26
## Medal: The Emperor Napoleon III (Single-Faced Proof)

1860–70

Signed at bottom: OUDINE; inscribed:
NAPOLEON III /EMPEREUR
Struck bronze
Diameter 7.3 cm

Provenance:
*See* no. V-25
Bibliography:
Catalogue, Paris, Musée Monétaire, 1892, pp. 478, 479; J. Jacquiot, in 1971, Paris, Hôtel de la Monnaie, pp. 392, 393, no. 87

submit it to the appropriate department of fine arts at the Institut de France in order to prepare his candidacy for membership. The Prefect of Police asked for the opinion of the Minister of Public Instruction, who, on January 22, 1875, granted permission for ten medals to be made, six for the artist and four for the Dépôt Légal. Nevertheless, the medal is not found in the Cabinet des Médailles at the Bibliothèque Nationale. The example from the Mint's collection was exhibited in 1967 (no. 644).

The reverse takes up again the composition of *The Accession of Napoleon III* (*see* no. V-25); however, the tired Emperor is seated. The back of the throne recalls the volutes on the tomb of Napoleon I (an unconscious recollection: in 1852 Oudiné had executed the medal of the *Inauguration of the Tomb* in the Hôtel des Invalides). The poses of the figures illustrate the mechanism of the right of hereditary succession based on universal suffrage. The 7,350,000 votes (474,189 fewer than in 1852) collected in the urn lead the figure of France to lean on the right shoulder of the Emperor who, in turn, leans on his son's shoulder. Could Carpeaux have inspired Oudiné five years later in his representation of the Prince Imperial in modern dress?

A.P.

Musée du Louvre, Paris

V-28

## Joseph-Michel-Ange Pollet
*Palermo 1814–1870 Paris?*

*Pollet was a student in Italy of Valerio Villareale, Bertel Thorvaldsen, and Pietro Tenerani. He settled in Paris after 1836, having looked for work in several cities.*

*He exhibited regularly at the Salon from 1846 to 1869. His best-known work is the allegorical figure* An Hour of Night. *Commissioned in 1848 and exhibited that year in plaster, the marble won a first-class medal at the Salon of 1850. Now at Compiègne, it was installed initially at Saint-Cloud. A bust of a Bacchante, shown in the 1853 Salon and at the Exposition Universelle of 1855, was acquired for the Tuileries.*

*Pollet produced numerous imperial portraits that were also placed at state residences. His marble bust of the Empress was acquired in 1856 for the Tuileries, with replicas at Saint-Cloud, Compiègne, and the apartments of the Minister of State. Replicas of his portrait of Napoleon III, shown in 1859, were installed in the same locations.*

*Among other projects, Pollet also executed commissions for several churches: a stone figure of Saint Radegunda for the porch of Sainte Clotilde (1851); two angels and decorative work for an organ case at Saint Eustache (1852); and a stone bas-relief of the Virgin of Mercy for the facade of Sainte Elizabeth.*

*Pollet was awarded numerous lesser medals for his Salon entries and received the Legion of Honor cross in 1856.*

S.G.L.

Bibliography:
Bellier and Auvray, 1882–87, vol. II, part 2, p. 292; Lami, 1914–21, vol. IV, pp. 93–96

Joseph-Michel-Ange Pollet

## V-28
## Eloa

1862
Signed and dated on front of cloud bank (in script): J. Pollet/1862; inscribed at right: F^{DU} PAR V^{OR} THIEBAUT
Bronze
152 × 102 × 71 cm

Provenance:
Group initially commissioned in stone by the Ministry

of State on March 23, 1861, but executed in marble following a decree of July 14, 1863 [marble installed after 1869 in the Luxembourg gardens; sent to the town hall of Oued-Zénati, Algeria, c. 1897 (F²¹173)]; the exhibited version, a half-size model, was acquired on June 6, 1864, by the Administration des Beaux-Arts; deposited at the Musée des Beaux-Arts, Rouen, 1868

Exhibition:
1863, Paris, Salon, no. 2526

Bibliography:
Bellier and Auvray, 1882–87, vol. II, part 2, p. 292; Catalogues, Rouen, Musée des Beaux-Arts, 1890, p. 110, no. 980, 1911, p. 161, no. 1298; Lami, 1914–21, vol. IV, pp. 95–96

This group was inspired by Alfred de Vigny's *Eloa, ou la Sœur des Anges*, written in 1823. It presents a sequel to the fall from Grace: bent on retribution, the beautiful rebel Lucifer attracts the attention of the angel of compassion, Eloa, who comes to console him in his pain, thus effecting its own downfall. Unlike Friedrich Klopstock's Eloa, Vigny's is a beautiful, female angel. The innocence of compassion is complicated by sexual desire, transforming Lucifer's revenge into sinister seduction.

The subject is quintessentially Romantic; it deals with *douleur* and the demonic, the dissociation of beauty and virtue, and the fallibility of even the most chaste. Although other Romantic artists also represented Satan and the fall from Grace, Pollet's *Eloa* is the latest and the only presently located example of three known to have been inspired by Vigny's poem. It departs from the text by presenting Eloa wingless and actually carried bodily. In the poem this is merely suggested in Lucifer's words as they descend to Hell: "I abduct my slave and I possess my victim" (Vigny, 1935, p. 35).

Critics regarded Pollet's *Eloa* as Romantic, both in content and in style. Théophile Gautier commented on the marble in 1869: "We find only that, because of the treatment of the hair, the character of the features, and that Byronic *sneer* that curls his lips, the demon's head has too modern and too Romantic a physiognomy" (Larousse, 1866–90, vol. VII, p. 377).

Despite its contemporaneity of style and subject, the composition is based on a sculptural prototype traditional to mythological abduction subjects. His group bears some resemblance to one formerly in the Tuileries gardens, *Boreas Carrying Off Orithyia*, by Gaspard Marsy and Anselme Flamen (Louvre). Even in this half-size version it is clear that Pollet was composing on a grand scale, with strong emphasis on sweeping diagonal forms.

It is not known if the full-scale, three-meter-high marble version still exists. A marble reduction of unknown size and date was lo-

cated several years ago in a private Libyan collection.

S.G.L.

Musée des Beaux-Arts, Rouen

---

## Antoine-Augustin Préault
*Paris 1809–1879 Paris*

*Préault was the object of great interest to the avant-garde of the Second Empire and has become of interest in our century. The convention dictating that sculpture be enduring rather than an occasion to experiment — the attitude at least of patrons — was upset by his vision. His medium was relief, a pretext for the pictorial in sculpture. He had a loud, assertive manner, not the least Romantic of his characteristics.*

*His principal three-dimensional works were all government commissions. Despite the great number of active sculptors' studios, the Second Empire neglected few, and Préault received his fair share: saints for the facades of three Parisian churches (Saint Gervais, Sainte Clotilde, and Saint Paul et Saint Louis); retrospective marble figures at Versailles (J. Hardouin Mansart, 1852–59; Le Nôtre); a stone statue in the Cour Napoléon of the Louvre (André Chenier, 1855); a bronze at Chartres (Marceau, 1851); decorative groups on the Pont d'Iéna (1849–53) and the canal of Fontainebleau (1867–70).*

*But his reliefs — The Massacre (1834), Silence (1842), Vitellius (1864), Mickiewicz (1868), Ophelia (1850–76) — are what distinguish him as an exceptional artist. He was not appreciated by each succeeding generation, but Brière wrote, on May 15, 1905: "I am sure that Préault's renown would almost certainly be revived by the sight of these fugitive but lively and expressive works [the forty medallions at Lille]. What he never brought off in his colossal works and his other abandoned, fantastic projects he successfully achieved in these hasty waxes.... Poor Préault! After admiring his medallions I went to Amiens and, in contrast to the grandiose and restful group by Puvis, I was shocked to see four monstrous busts that destroy the harmonious beauty of the stairway. 'Who is the jackass who placed them here?' I asked myself. Then I saw that the heads of Poussin, Puget, etc. were by Préault [this is inaccurate; Préault did only the Poussin, and there is no Puget].... The execution of large-scale works for the outdoors destroyed him. In spite of what the great Michelet says, he will endure because of his plaques."*

A.P.

Bibliography:
Malitourne, 1853, pp. 22–23; Pelletan, 1879, pp. 96–98; Lami, 1914–21, vol. IV, pp. 112–19

V-29

Antoine-Augustin Préault

## V-29
## Dante

1852
Signed and dated at bottom: Auguste Préault/ 1852; inscribed at left: DANTE/ALIGHIERI/NE.A/ FLORENCE/1265/MORT/1321; inscribed at right: LA/ VITA.NUOVA/./.LA/DIVINA/COMMEDIA/. ; inscribed at bottom: F^derie de Eck et Durand
Bronze
95 × 85 × 23 cm

Antoine-Augustin Préault

## V-30
## Virgil

1853
Signed and dated at bottom: PREAULT/STATUAIRE 1853; inscribed at left: F^DERIE DE ECK ET DURAND; inscribed at right: .P. VIRGILIUS.
Bronze
95 × 85 × 23 cm

Provenance:
Commissioned by decree of July 12, 1853, for the Service des Musées Impériaux and intended for Napoleon III; delivery dated July 20, 1853; only one of the medallions, probably mistakenly, listed in the inventory of the Emperor's private residence: "no. 7 Dante, medallion, Salon 1853, 2,600 francs, storage"; 1857 checklist (Louvre Archives 8 DD 5) indicates

V-30

they were stored in the former guard room in the Louvre (inv. nos. RF 4, 3)

Exhibition:
1853, Paris, Salon, no. 1481 (both)

Bibliography:
Malitourne, 1853, pp. 22–23; Eaton, 1913, p. 214; Locquin, 1920, p. 459; Barré, 1922, p. 26; Vitry, 1922, nos. 1460, 1461; Benoist, 1928, p. 133

Information concerning payment for these medallions is contradictory. According to a file entitled "Encouragement of the Arts" (Arch. nat. 0⁵ 1707), payment of 2,600 francs was made to Préault on July 29, 1853. The medallions were listed in the sculpture inventory of the Louvre. But, according to Préault's correspondence (Louvre Archives S 30), on June 14, 1853, he asked Nieuwerkerke for final payment for "Dante and Virgil commissioned by M.J. Lefèvre-Deumier for the Household of the Emperor." Préault reminded him that the price established for each bronze was 1,800 francs (3,600 for two) and that he had received payment of only 1,000 francs. This discrepancy has not been resolved.

In 1856 Silvestre described Préault's apartment (1878, p. 287): "He lives alone in a sixth-floor dormered room, the walls of which are covered from the tile floor to the ceiling with old engravings…(works by Goltzius at their most muscular, by Rubens at their most apoplectic, and by Dürer at their most pensive)." Among those that surrounded his bed were "the *Ugolino* by Reynolds, the *Dante and Virgil* by Delacroix, copied by Courbet." *The Divine Comedy*, then, occupied a choice spot. The illustration of this poem had been exceptionally

popular since its creation, but the Romantic period gave it a new vitality, and to it the nineteenth century owes a number of its masterpieces.

Delacroix's painting, done when he was twenty-four years old and acquired by the Louvre at the Salon of 1822, belongs to the sixth category of iconography for Dante, according to Marchisio's classifications (*see* Marchisio, 1956, pp. 131–58). In this category, the iconography is created purely by the artist's imagination with no relationship to any other work. This was not the case with Préault. He closely followed the vigorous modeling of the *Bust of Dante* (Museo Nazionale, Naples), tentatively dated as fifteenth century. He added a crown of laurel leaves and changed the treatment of the hair in the back so that it fell in a straight line. As in the Naples bust, large letters identify the subject depicted.

Virgil, who was portrayed as a bearded old man in early-fifteenth-century miniatures, was represented younger and crowned with laurel in the work of Luca Signorelli. Préault celebrates Virgil's beauty, which he contrasts to the angular face of Dante. In the hair he plays with parallel lines as he had done with the hair of the angels on the tomb of the Abbé Liautard (1849), or, as he would do later in the drapery of the group of *Jupiter and the Sphinx* in the park at Fontainebleau.

Before the Second Empire, Préault, whose style was sometimes called "Dantesque," had already sketched a striking composition of *Dante and Virgil in Hell* (Chartres museum), prefiguring Rodin. He again joined those who were inspired by *The Divine Comedy* when he created the medallions of *Dante* and *Virgil*. Among those who were to sculpt the same two figures were Henri-Joseph-François Triqueti, *Dante and Virgil* (Museum of Fine Arts, Boston); Gabriel-Jules Thomas, *Virgil* (marble, 1861 or 1865; Louvre RF 2224); Louis-Ernest Barrias, *Virgil*; and Jean-Paul Aubé, *Dante* (two full-length statues for the stairway in the Hôtel de Païva).

A.P.

Musée du Louvre, Paris

---

*Louis-Valentin-Elias Robert*
*Etampes 1821–1874 Paris*

*In the Salon catalogues Robert credited David d'Angers and Jean-Jacques Pradier as his teachers. His Salon debut took place in 1845 with two portrait*

busts. *When the imperial propaganda campaign intensified after 1851, Robert quickly found favor as a portraitist of distinguished Bonapartists. Among them were busts of outstanding army officers such as the comte Pajol and the comte de Bailly de Monthion, and Napoleon I's father, Charles-Marie Bonaparte. These works were commissioned in 1852 for Versailles. A marble figure of the zoologist Etienne-Geoffroy Saint-Hilaire, a member of the scientific expedition to Egypt, was erected in 1857 in Etampes, birthplace of both Robert and Saint-Hilaire.*

*Among his public projects were the major allegorical relief for the facade of the new Palais de l'Industrie, figures of Rabelais and Jacques Cœur for the former Cour Napoléon III at the Louvre, and caryatids and allegories for the facades of the Opéra and the Gare d'Austerlitz.*

*In 1865 he won the coveted Portuguese commission for the monument to Don Pedro, King of Portugal. Collaborating with the architect Gabriel Davioud, he completed it in 1868 and it was erected in Lisbon in 1870. The monument consists of a gilded-bronze figure of Pedro IV on a column, surrounded by allegorical reliefs and marble figures of Prudence, Force, Justice, and Temperance. The fall of the Second Empire eliminated Robert's major source of patronage. A few uncommissioned busts, a figure of Comedy, and a sketch for the top of the Arc de Triomphe (Etoile), all shown at the Salon, are his only documented later works.*

*Robert received the Legion of Honor cross in 1858, a fact probably more indicative of official support than of public acclaim, as he was rarely discussed by critics.*

S.G.L.

Bibliography:
Bellier and Auvray, 1882–87, vol. II, part 2, pp. 395–96; Lami, 1914–21, vol. IV, pp. 148–52; Michel, 1905–29, vol. VIII, part 2, pp. 838, 840; Thieme and Becker, 1907–50, vol. XXVIII, p. 419

Louis-Valentin-Elias Robert

## V-31
## Comte de Persigny, Minister of the Interior

1852
Marble
78 × 54 × 33 cm

Provenance:
Commissioned by the Ministry of State on August 10, 1852, for the city of Roanne; Musée Joseph Déchelette (inv. no. 147)

Exhibition:
1853, Paris, Salon, no. 1486

V-31

Bibliography:
Bellier and Auvray, 1882–87, vol. II, part 2, p. 395;
Lami, 1914–21, vol. IV, p. 149

Jean-Gilbert Fialin became an ardent Bonapartist in the 1830s, attaching himself to Louis Napoleon in 1835 and working for the reestablishment of a Bonapartist empire. Styling himself the comte de Persigny during the Republic, he became Minister of the Interior in 1852. The office was responsible for a vast number of public commissions, and Persigny's two-year initial tenure saw the beginning of the city's redevelopment under Baron Haussmann. He also increased the appropriation for the new civil list to 25,000,000 francs, the sum purportedly granted to Napoleon I in 1795 (d'Ambès, 1912, vol. I, p. 371). A controversial figure, he never stayed long in one position, serving later as Ambassador to London, a member of the Privy Council, and again as Minister of the Interior in 1860. Harsh with those he considered enemies of the regime, Persigny was asked to resign by the Emperor in 1863. He retired from public life with a ducal title as compensation.

This commission of 1852 documents Persigny at the height of his career: that year witnessed his first imperial appointment and his marriage to a granddaughter of Marshal Ney,

Albine-Marie-Napoléone-Eglé Ney de la Moskowa. Robert's portrait, in its emphasis upon likeness and fastidiously detailed formal period attire, is reminiscent of state portraits of the first Empire, in particular Houdon's well-known bust of Marshal Ney, which had been commissioned in 1804 for the Salle des Maréchaux at the Tuileries. Both Ney and Persigny are in full dress uniform, with unsmiling faces and lofty expressions emphasizing their mutual sense of purpose. Given the family connection, the similarity between the two portraits was perhaps no coincidence. Ney's memory was being especially honored during the time that Robert received the commission for the bust of Persigny. In fact, Persigny was personally responsible for the final version of the most important monument to Ney in Paris, that by François Rude, also commissioned in 1852.

Used by François-Joseph Bosio for subsequent portraiture as well, this type of formal portrait bust, with its crisply articulated surface, reflects a less severe aspect of French Neoclassicism. The descriptive handling of Robert's bust became characteristic of much of the portraiture produced after the late 1850s, especially by Auguste-Louis-Marie Ottin, Pierre-Bernard Prouha, and Henri-Frédéric Iselin (witness his 1860 portrait of Boileau). The contemporaneity and opulent surfaces of this type, in fact, made it popular in formal portraiture well into the twentieth century.

S.G.L.

Musée Joseph Déchelette, Roanne

## Auguste Rodin

*Paris 1840–1917 Meudon*

*Rodin studied at the Petite Ecole from 1854 to 1857. Refused admission to the Ecole des Beaux-Arts, he entered into a long association with decorative sculptors. Carrier-Belleuse (q.v.) employed him from 1864 to 1870 for commissions such as the Hôtel de Païva, but he produced mainly commercial models.*

*His earliest surviving sculptures, two portraits, resemble David d'Angers's work. The first, dated 1860, is of his father; the second, depicting Father Pierre-Julien Eymard and dated 1863, was executed during his brief novitiate in Eymard's religious order.*

*The* Man with the Broken Nose *was produced shortly thereafter. Rejected for the 1864 Salon, the mask was his only submission to the jury during the Second Empire. Rodin nonetheless prized the mask, later saying, "it determined all my future work" (Bartlett, 1965, p. 21).*

*His relationship with Rose Beuret began around 1864. She posed for the full-length* Bacchante *(later destroyed) and several busts, beginning with the* Mignon *of the late 1860s.*

*During the 1870s Rodin worked in Brussels, briefly with Carrier-Belleuse, then as an independent ornamentalist and as a collaborator with Antoine Van Rasbourg. He went to Italy in 1876 to study Michelangelo, a turning point in his career. Upon his return he completed* The Age of Bronze, *which caused a sensation in Brussels and Paris in 1877. Many criticized it as cast from life but artists convinced otherwise marveled at this "astounding piece of modeling" (Bartlett, 1965, p. 100). It marked the emergence of his mature style; thanks partly to Michelangelo, it possessed a new grandeur and expressive depth.*

*Rodin considered sculpture synonymous with modeling and learned important lessons from ornament makers. Constant Simon taught him to see form as emerging volumes. Carrier-Belleuse showed him how to create lively surfaces and acquainted him with several revival styles, including the Rococo. In addition, Rodin was a great admirer of Carpeaux (q.v.). The grandeur and realism of Carpeaux's figures, together with their expressive movement, appealed to Rodin, and he tried to develop these qualities in his own art.*

S.G.L.

Bibliography:
Gsell, 1911; Dujardin-Beaumetz, 1913; Cladel, 1936; Bartlett, 1965; Mirolli, 1966; Catalogue, Philadelphia, Rodin Museum, 1976

Auguste Rodin

## V-32
## Young Girl with Roses on Her Hat

c. 1865–70
Terra-cotta
69 × 33 × 30 cm (with pedestal)

Provenance:
Gift of the artist to the Musée Rodin, 1916 (inv. no. j10)
Exhibition:
1962–63, Paris, Louvre, no. 6
Bibliography:
Goldscheider, 1962, p. 15, repro. p. 51; Mirolli, 1966,

pp. 118–20, pl. 85; Jianou and Goldscheider, 1967, p. 83; Pitoëff, 1971, repro. p. 114; Rheims, 1972, repro. p. 251; Catalogue, Philadelphia, Rodin Museum, 1976, p. 576, fig. 105.2; Hargrove, 1977, p. 212, pl. 223

*See* Colorplate

A group of busts of young girls, dating probably in the late 1860s, demonstrates Rodin's facility with the Rococo type then being produced by Carrier-Belleuse. A few of these busts are of mythological subjects, like *Flora* (Musée Rodin, Paris; Rodin Museum, Philadelphia) or the *Bacchante* (Musée Rodin, Meudon; The Metropolitan Museum of Art, New York), but Rodin focused mainly on the youthful beauty of the sitters and the costume details, creating winsome, contemporary images.

*Young Girl with Roses on Her Hat* is one of the most masterly of this group. The stylish, flowered hat and the informality of the pose are clearly indebted to Neo-Rococo examples. Even the physical type of the model—wide-eyed, pert-nosed, with a bee-stung mouth and full cheeks—appears in Carrier-Belleuse's fantasy busts. The frequently mentioned "breathless" quality of Rodin's terra-cotta also reflects the animation of Carrier-Belleuse's work.

V-32

Nonetheless, at this early stage in his career, Rodin was beginning to develop his own personal style of handling, albeit influenced by Carpeaux and Carrier-Belleuse. Instead of following the crisp, descriptive treatment of the hair and clothing of Carrier-Belleuse's female busts, Rodin has rendered these forms as loose, powerfully modeled volumes similar to those in Carpeaux's *Portrait of an Unknown Lady* (no. V-5). Rodin has taken full advantage of the tactile quality of the terra-cotta, creating fluid surfaces, energetic contours, and a sharp chiaroscuro achieved by the varying degrees of depth of the modeling. Like Carrier-Belleuse's bust of Daumier (Versailles), Rodin's *Young Girl* has delicately tooled skin while the clothing has a lightly "hatched" texture. Rodin's portrait particularly emphasizes what Paul Audouy calls the "protected fragility" of Rodin's women: sweet and innocent, she charms with her vulnerability (Hargrove, 1977, p. 137).

Other examples of this group include: *Young Girl with Disheveled Hair* (Musée Rodin, Paris); *Mme Cruchet* (three terra-cottas extant); *Bust of a Young Girl (Mme Cruchet?)* (National Gallery of Art, Washington, D.C.); *Woman with Daisies in Her Hat* (Musée Rodin, Paris); and *Young Girl with Flowers in Her Hair* (plaster, Musée Rodin, Paris; bronzes in Musée Rodin, Paris, and National Museum of Western Art, Tokyo).

S.G.L.

Musée Rodin, Paris

---

*Jean-Jules Salmson*

*Paris 1823–1902 Coupvray*

*Salmson, the son of the medalist Jean-Baptiste Salmson (q.v.) was a pupil of Etienne-Jules Ramey, Armand Toussaint, and Augustin Dumont at the Ecole des Beaux-Arts. He exhibited at the Salon from 1859 to 1891. Under the Second Empire he was awarded a medal in 1865, two second-class medals, in 1863 and at the Exposition Universelle of 1867, and in the same year, the Legion of Honor.*

*In Paris he worked for the Church of Saint Bernard (1861), the Tribunal de Commerce (1864), the Théâtre du Vaudeville (1867), the Tuileries, and the Opéra (Handel, 1875–87). After the Franco-Prussian War he went to London and then, in 1877, to Geneva, where he was head of the Ecole des Arts Industriels. Salmson, who modeled statuettes of celebrated personalities for commercial edition (Lord Byron, Sir Walter Scott, Shakespeare, etc.), maintained a constant interest in the applied arts.*

*"For twenty years," he wrote to the Empress on October 22, 1865 (Arch. nat. F²¹ 252), "I have rendered innumerable services to the decorative arts." On April 15, 1866, a calling card announced the new addresses of his two decorator studios and his own personal studio (Arch. nat. F²¹ 179). In 1892 he published a book containing anecdotes about his contemporaries, Entre deux coups de ciseau: Souvenirs d'un sculpteur, which allows one to follow his dual career in the applied arts and sculpture.*

A.P.

Bibliography:
Louvre Archives S 30, 1862–67 [six letters to Nieuwerkerke]; Salmson, 1892; Lami, 1914–21, vol. IV, pp. 228–30

Jean-Jules Salmson

# V-33
# The Winder

1863
Signed and dated on plinth, at left: J. SALMSON F 1863
Bronze
121 × 68 × 94 cm

Provenance:
Aquired by the State at the Salon of 1863 for 6,500 francs (Arch. nat F²¹ 179); exhibited at the Musée du Luxembourg (LUX 94); transferred to the Direction des Musées Nationaux by decree of May 3, 1874; entered the Louvre, January 27, 1926

Exhibition:
1863, Paris, Salon, no. 2555

Bibliography:
Thoré-Bürger, 1863, p. 435; de Sault, 1864, p. 244; de Montifaud, 1865, p. 10; Privat, 1865, p. 221; Thoré-Bürger, 1865, p. 262; Mantz, 1867, "Exposition," p. 344; Catalogues, Paris, Luxembourg, 1867–96; Salmson, 1892, pp. 86, 240–43, 313, 315, 316; Jouin, 1908, p. 407; Lami, 1914–21, vol. IV, pp. 228–29

In searching among earlier styles for its identity, the new society of the Second Empire found a noble security in the "Antique," which the Campana collection had brought back into fashion.

This *Winder*, which followed *The Spinners* by Mathurin Moreau (q.v.; 1861, Louvre, RF 189; marble, 1890, RF 1089), gave Salmson a pretext for showing his erudition (note the chair and basket taken from Cavelier's *Penelope* of 1849) which Jean-Louis-Nicolas Jaley had not done in his *Remembrance of Pompeii* of 1852 (RF 1354; deposited in the Musée des Beaux-Arts, Troyes).

Salmson was touchingly overjoyed when

V-33

Following the examples of Moreau-Vauthier (q.v.) and Mathurin Moreau, who did the same work in bronze and then in marble, Salmson exhibited a marble version of *The Winder* at the 1865 Salon. The Empress stopped in front of it, expressed her admiration, and asked whether it had already been bought. Salmson hoped to sell this version but, in spite of a petition to the Empress, was not successful (Arch. nat. F²¹ 252), an episode not included in his memoirs. Instead, he published a letter from G.J. Thomas dated November 16, 1869(?), which told Salmson that after having seen his *Winder* at the Salon, Garnier (q.v.), who had commissioned from him two figures for the arcades of the Grand Foyer of the Opéra, decided to request of Salmson one of the four large statues of composers for the Vestibule (1892, p. 86).

After a decree of 1870 established automatic governmental acquisition of all Salon prize winners, Salmson asked for its retroactive application to his marble, which had been awarded prizes in 1865 and in 1867 at the Exposition Universelle. "I have rarely asked favors from the government," he wrote. "I believe in private initiative and have long been satisfied with what I have done on my own" (Arch. nat. F²¹ 252). The marble, which Salmson tried to sell to the State, is now in the Ny Carlsberg Glyptotek, Copenhagen.

A second *Winder* (plaster, RF 1359) was to enter the Louvre, inventoried on its return from the Palais de l'Elysée in 1903. Another is in the museum in Angers (Goffard bequest, 1894), possibly a copy from the workshop of the Musées Nationaux, which cast the work in 1881, sharing expenses with Salmson, who received a trial copy. An earlier cast owned by Richard Wallace was destroyed during the Franco-Prussian War (Salmson, 1892, p. 316).

Reductions in at least two different sizes were issued, according to an acknowledgment in Salmson's hand of January 12, 1876 (Bibliothèque Doucet, carton 41 sculpteur). And, for a clock ornament, Salmson again used his *Winder* bending toward a little cupid playing with a ball (sale, Paris, Hôtel Drouot, November 23, 1977).

A.P.

Musée du Louvre, Paris

he heard from Nieuwerkerke that his work had been acquired from the Salon of 1863. He was concerned, "above all, that his sculpture [recipient of a second-class medal] should be placed in the Luxembourg for he had no other work on permanent exhibition" (Louvre Archives S30 [July 29, 1863]). Obliged to earn his living by making industrial models, he had neglected the Salon and been passed over for commissions, but now began to solicit them (letter to Maréchal Vaillant, August 11, 1863, Arch. nat. F²¹ 179).

# Painting

It is by the tens of thousands that one must number the paintings produced under the Second Empire and shown, in the course of these years, to the curious and the amateurs who by the hundreds of thousands visited the Salons and the Expositions Universelles of 1855 and 1867. With a scale so vast as this, no selection for exhibition or publication could but indicate the diverse artistic directions of the time, the traditional, the official, and the innovative, while for obvious physical reasons, it is impossible to show in a satisfactory fashion the large paintings made to decorate public buildings, palaces, and churches. Moreover, an entire area of major decorative undertakings, exemplified here by Ingres's sketch for the destroyed ceiling of *The Apotheosis of Napoleon I* (no. VI-69), has disappeared, in part through the burning during 1870–71 of the Hôtel de Ville, the palace of Saint-Cloud, the Cour des Comptes, the Conseil d'Etat, and the Tuileries itself.

The paintings presented here have been chosen with a constant regard for historical revisionism, which during the past ten years has become evident through a number of monographic exhibitions, returning to a position of importance such figures as Tissot (q.v.),[1] Gérôme (q.v.),[2] Bouguereau (q.v.),[3] Jules Breton (q.v.) and his brother Emile,[4] and Léon Belly,[5] as well as Puvis de Chavannes (q.v.)[6] and Bazille (q.v.)[7] alongside of those exhibitions devoted to the incontestable masters of the period, Delacroix (q.v.)[8] and Ingres (q.v.),[9] and more recently Millet (q.v.)[10] and Courbet (q.v.).[11] General exhibitions have also fostered the rediscovery of work reflecting other aspects of nineteenth-century art[12] and the resurrection, from the obscurity into which they had fallen, of the official paintings chosen at the same time for the collection consecrated to the works of living artists at the Musée Impérial du Luxembourg in Paris (since dispersed).[13] To gain a fair understanding of the artistic reality of the times, it is valuable to consult some of the rare photographic documents which allow us to recapture the atmosphere of the Salons, those periodic manifestations to which all artists, practically without exception, attached such great importance. The best example is provided, just at the midpoint of the Second Empire, by the album showing the Salon of 1861 comprising forty-two photographs by Richebourg, which allows us after a fashion to

visit the Salon.[14] One sees the pictures stacked up frame against frame in the halls of the Palais de l'Industrie, hung in alphabetical order by the artists' names according to an arrangement devised by Philippe de Chennevières, *chargé du service des expositions,* in order to avoid any objections from the artists, and which resulted in a host of unexpected juxtapositions. In contrast with the Salon of 1853, where special galleries were set aside for still lifes and for flower paintings, here everything is intermixed, and only a certain regard for symmetry in the hanging provides for some sense of order. Underneath gigantic paintings illustrating episodes from contemporary history (the Crimean War, the Italian campaign, ceremonies in Paris) might be placed a group of small genre scenes or landscapes, while elsewhere were hung the "flood of portraits" which, as noted by Zola, "rose each year and threatened to overflow the Salon."[15]

Organized by the imperial administration, the Salon was controlled through almost the entire Second Empire (until 1869) by the comte de Nieuwerkerke. At first *directeur général des musées* in the Ministère de la Maison de l'Empereur, he became Superintendent of Fine Arts in June 1863, when the division of the Fine Arts, which depended until then on the Ministry of State, was integrated, under his authority, into the new Ministère de la Maison de l'Empereur et des Beaux-Arts. But paradoxically, there had never yet been a period when this venerable institution was so unstable in its organization, and indeed for the first time in its history, in serious danger of collapse.

The first blow to the prestige of the Salon was undoubtedly the changing of its location. Installed until 1848 in the very heart of the Louvre, specifically the Salon Carré and the adjoining galleries, the Salon had been transferred during the Second Republic first to the Tuileries and then to the Palais Royal. The provisionary buildings constructed for these Salons were then transported in 1853 for the first Salon of the Second Empire far from the center of the city to Menus Plaisirs, at the corner of the rue Richer and the rue du Faubourg Poissonnière. It must be noted that at each Salon a new "Salon Carré," or hall of honor, had been reconstituted, as was also done in the building constructed for the fine arts on the avenue Montaigne for the Exposition Universelle of 1855. In 1857 the Salon was held—as it would be for nearly half a century thereafter—in the Palais de l'Industrie, on the Champs Elysées, also built for the exposition. Henceforth, the painting exhibition was held on two levels of galleries surrounding the sculpture garden, which occupied more than half of the huge glass nave. There it alternated with agricultural and industrial exhibitions and no longer was associated with the prestigious presentation of the masterpieces of the Louvre. It was perhaps to regain a sense of dignity that, in 1864, the ceremony marking the presentation of awards, previously held at the Palais de l'Industrie, was moved back to the Salon Carré of the Louvre.

The organization of the Salon underwent a steady sequence of modifications. In 1853 Nieuwerkerke, in an attempt to encourage quality, instituted a two-year interval between exhibitions—so that artists would not have to rush to complete an important work every spring. This lasted until 1863, after which, for exactly the opposite reasons, the Salon was reestablished as an annual event. The desire to establish a standard rather than to encourage the commercial side of the Salon (so important for the artists) also caused the Administration at intervals to limit the number of works an artist could present within each section: three works were permitted in 1853 and again in 1863, the year of the crisis, although between these two dates there was no limit, perhaps because there was ample space in the new exhibition halls. With the renewal of restrictions in 1864, the figure was set at two submissions.

Given the fact that from the beginning of the Second Empire the painting section of the Salon always included a small proportion (12 to 15 per cent) of drawings and prints, the total number of entries grew from 1,208 works in 1853 to 1,915 in 1863 then 3,045 in 1859 and 3,146 in 1861; at the end of the period the equally impressive, but somewhat more manageable, entries numbered 2,587 in 1868 and 2,991 in 1870.

The variation in the number and nature of the works exhibited was primarily a result of the attitude of the admissions jury, which was largely determined by its composition, rather than by any regulations. In 1853, as the last vestige of the liberalism of 1848, one half of the painting jury was composed of elected members (seven, of whom five were painters: Delacroix, Paul Delaroche, François-Édouard Picot, H. Flandrin, Adrien Dauzats) while the second half was designated by the Administration. Those eligible to vote in the jury selection were the artists whose works had been admitted to any previous exhibition, except that of the unjuried Salon of 1848.

The prestigious selection jury for 1855 included the painters Jacques-Raymond Brascassat (the Paulus Potter of the nineteenth century, immensely respected in his old age), Abel de Pujol (a quite conservative member of the Institut), Couture (q.v.), Hippolyte Flandrin (q.v.), Heim (q.v.; winner of the first Grand Prix de Rome in 1807!), H. Lehmann, Léon Cogniet (an important teacher through the Ecole), Müller (q.v.), Horace Vernet (the revered Romantic painter of battles honored with a retrospective that same year), and Troyon (q.v.). To the awards jury, overlapping somewhat with the selection committee, were added the names of Delacroix, Ingres, and Winterhalter (q.v.), in all a rather broad representation of attitudes, even if Courbet was not among them.

The power of the Institut de France, which had slowly been waning, was reaffirmed in 1857, when Nieuwerkerke, who had just been elected to its membership, restored to his colleagues some of their previous privileges. A single jury, composed of the first four sections of the Académie des Beaux-Arts as well as its "free" members, was in charge of all Salon admissions, thereby creating a pattern in which the established figures of Romanticism (Vernet and Delacroix) were dominated by those of Classicism (Ingres, Heim, Abel de Pujol, Jean-Victor Schnetz, Cogniet, and H. Flandrin). This continued, with the interesting addition of Meissonier (q.v.) in 1863.

The excessive severity of certain members of these juries, Emile Signol, for example, rendered them increasingly unpopular. Protests abounded. In all likelihood it was one of those petitions in response to the harshness of the jury that gave rise to the celebrated Salon des Refusés of 1863. The Emperor had visited the Salon on April 22, 1863, while it was in preparation, in order, it was said, to examine the refused works. Two days later Le Moniteur announced the news "that the works that have been refused should be shown in another part of the Palais de l'Industrie." Without a doubt the Emperor was only putting into practice an idea that had been submitted to him two years before by Théodore Veron, whose picture After the Battle: The Emperor Visiting the Wounded had been refused. This artist and art critic had already suggested to the Administration on April 8, 1861, that "all works be shown in the Palais de l'Industrie," a vast space after all, and that they be clearly classified into six categories from "A, a treasure of art, to F, bad works [œuvres mauvaises]." On April 11, 1861, addressing himself directly to Napoleon III in the name of his fellow rejected painters and sculptors, he had suggested that "our works be placed in a hall which would be reserved for

this purpose at the Palais de l'Exposition."[16] This phrase, carefully underlined in red, was transmitted to the appropriate department and perhaps gave rise to the famous exhibition. The Salon des Refusés opened May 15, five days after the regular Salon, and despite numerous withdrawals (it was optional to exhibit there) 604 paintings were shown. One can find in the catalogue prepared by the exhibitors themselves the names of Adolphe Cals, Jean-Charles Cazin, Chintreuil (q.v.), Fantin-Latour (q.v.), Harpignies (q.v.), Jongkind (q.v.), Jean-Paul Laurens, Legros (q.v.), Manet (q.v.; with three pictures, including the Bath, or Luncheon on the Grass), Pissarro (q.v.), Vollon (q.v.), and Whistler.

In the great tide of administrative reforms of 1863, the Institut and the Ecole des Beaux-Arts saw their influence diminish considerably. It was only by their individual qualifications that members of the Institut could comprise part of the jury (and they often would be a part). The only chance given the Institut to regain some power as a body—the August 22, 1866, notice, which announced that one third of the jury in 1867 would be designated from members of the Académie—was modified in January 1867 by a new ruling, when it was decided that the jury would be composed of a majority of elected members. From 1864 to 1869, the electors consisted either of members of the Institut or of those decorated or those who had received medals (the list is printed at the beginning of each catalogue), which is to say, those who had already been exempt from the examination of the jury. Falsely liberal, this system did no more than perpetuate the same tendencies, and the young artists complained still more.

One of the four sections of the jury was devoted to painting. It was composed of twelve members in 1864 and 1865, twenty-four in 1866 (three fourths elected, one third nominated) then eighteen in 1868 and 1869 (two thirds elected, one third nominated). Finally, in 1870, shortly preceding the creation of the Ministry of Fine Arts, the electorate was expanded to include all those who had previously been admitted to a Salon (with the exception of that of 1848) with eighteen members of the jury elected, thereby arriving finally at a firmly liberal position. A listing of the 1870 jury gives some idea of the shift that open election brought about (although the passing of time had eliminated many of the entrenched defenders of academic principles): Daubigny, Corot, Bonnat (q.q.v.), Gérôme, Pierre-Charles Comte, Millet, Fromentin (q.v.), Gleyre (q.v.), Joseph Robert-Fleury, Cabanel (q.v.), Isidore Pils, Nicolas Cabat, Delaunay, Meissonier, Edouard-Louis Dubuffe, and Félix Ziem with

Chaplin (q.v.), Vollon, Baudry (q.v.), Bida (q.v.), Courbet, and Gustave Brion serving as supplements, having received in order the next greatest number of votes. With the possible exception of Cabanel and Baudry, no strong protagonist of history painting was included among this broad representation of genre and landscape painters.

Following the example of 1863, and perhaps the first suggestion of Théodore Veron, the regulations for the Salon of 1864 assigned to the jury a special task: "The jury will be required to judge those works too weak to participate in the competition for awards.... [and] those will be shown in special galleries, but this exhibition will be optional...."[17] It was therefore a year without any actual rejections, although there were a few hundred voluntary withdrawals; however, the new galleries of works not admitted into competition for awards (283 paintings) were barely noticed and not one remarkable painting seems to have been shown in this section.

A repetition of the Salon des Refusés would not again be attempted; however, the petitions did not cease. In 1866 a letter of petition from Cézanne was thus annotated by an official hand: "It is well known that the exposition of the Refusés was of little suitability for the dignity of art and it will not be reinstituted."[18] The same response was given by the Administration in a letter of 1867 to twenty-five artists, including Bazille, Pissarro, Monet (q.v.), and Renoir (q.v.), who had addressed a petition to obtain a "special exposition for rejected works," stating that "the refusal of an artistic production from the Salon is always a painful mortification for the artist but it can become a cause for further ruin and it is this hypothesis that seems serious enough to us to urge, if for this reason alone, a renewal of our request."[19]

Such a request emphasizes the economic importance of the Salon, which encouraged artists' relationships with private collectors and dealers, and established their reputation. It was also from the Salon that representatives of the Administration—the Administration of Fine Arts and the civil list—made their selections.[20] For the civil list, it happened that the Emperor, the Empress, or even the little Prince Imperial would designate works that pleased them and which they hoped to acquire if they were available.[21]

But the Salons and retrospective exhibitions organized within the context of the expositions of 1855 and 1867 were not the only means of exhibition available to the painters during the Second Empire. Works were sent to exhibitions in Marseilles, Lille, Rouen, and Nantes. For example, the museum of Nantes,

following the Exposition Nationale which opened there August 10, 1861, was enriched by the purchase (from a total fund of 35,000 francs) of four important pictures: *The Corn Sifter* by Courbet, already shown in Paris in 1855, for which they paid 3,000 francs (the artist asking 5,000); *Charlotte Corday* by Baudry, 12,000 francs; *The Prisoner* by Gérôme, 10,500 francs; and *The Conjuror* by Hamon (q.v.).[22] Many regional governments also contributed toward the financial support of young painters from their areas—marking a remarkable number of careers launched through the enlightened benevolence of provincial authorities.

A significant accounting of sales achieved by means other than the Salon is provided by the manuscript catalogue of the works of Ernest Hillemacher, compiled by the painter himself.[23] The destination and price of each work is carefully indicated; they traveled within France and abroad, to Brussels, Ghent, London, Manchester, Liverpool, Lyons, Toulouse, Bordeaux, Besançon, Dijon, Lille, Marseilles, and Strasbourg, and often the sales took place on the spot. His genre scenes, usually historical, found their way to a large number of collectors through individual dealers: Mme Jeanne Nordmann, Thomas, Gambart, A. Moreau, or the specialists in reproductive engravings and photographs, Goupil, Bulla, Jouy, and Dusacq et Cie.

One can also cite other dealers who served as correspondents for provincial artists as well as for painters working in Paris: Haro, Carpentier, Cadart, and Binant. Galleries such as Martinet's on the boulevard des Italiens, which received, for example in 1864, the Société Nationale des Beaux-Arts, provided an alternative exhibition space to artists and met with a ready market, while a whole entrepreneur system developed in Paris to satisfy a new appetite for pictures.

Certain dealers such as Gambart were specialists with foreign clients, with the New York offices of figures such as Goupil or Avery giving further evidence of this broad diffusion of French works, particularly in America, where the formation of large collections was beginning in earnest at this time.[24] The chapter in Zola's *L'Œuvre* in which the dealer discourages his pet artist from showing in the Salon because the *new* clients seem to prefer the illusion of discovering the works for themselves in a painter's luxurious and exotic studio, is undoubtedly a true if harsh depiction of an emerging pattern.[25] In turn, this new market had a strong effect on the nature of popular subjects. Landscape, genre, animal painting, and peasant pictures found a much more ready

audience at this level than traditional history subjects.

Stylistically, the Second Empire began with the inherited conflict of the Romanticists and the Classicists, although already considerably tempered. Delacroix and Ingres continued to be the dominant figures, certainly through their fame if not their direct stylistic influence, throughout the 1850s. Both were given awards and commissions by the State and honored as representing the highest achievement of French art with large retrospective exhibitions in adjoining galleries at the Exposition Universelle of 1855. Delacroix, however, shared his space with Decamps (q.v.) and Horace Vernet, while Ingres was given exclusive privilege to his. Delacroix was by far the more active in the art politics of his time. Ingres lived very privately and only emerged with force during this period to pronounce his famous statement about the purpose of art in opposition to the reforms at the Ecole des Beaux-Arts in 1863. However, Delacroix often complained in his journals about his sense of detachment from contemporary art activities—finding himself progressively more introverted—and Ingres, toward the end of his immensely long career, seems on the whole to have heeded contemporary events very little.

The influence of Ingres was the most immediately felt during the Second Empire, although his style was no less personal than that of Delacroix. Its exact import is difficult to appraise since he was so often viewed as embodying all forms of idealized Classicism. Amaury-Duval (q.v.), his student, represented one adaptation of an Ingresesque manner during the Second Empire: cool and purely colored, elegantly linear, but with a frankness of naturalism, which replaced idealized elegance with a certain modernity and chic. Hippolyte Flandrin was, perhaps, the most profound direct heir of the master—especially in his high seriousness and dependence on a somewhat flattened use of form. Louis-Charles Timbal and Pichon (q.v.; who successively carried an Ingresesque Classicism well into the 1880s) responded, in turn, to his scale of forms and pure areas of color, while the so-called "Néo-Grecs," first emerging in the late 1840s (with Gérôme's *Cock Fight*) adapted through a variety of means exercised by Hamon, the young Auguste Toulmouche, and, in part even Gleyre, one aspect of Ingres as best represented in such works as his *Antiochus and Stratonice.* The artist who would take up his inheritance most brilliantly was Degas (q.v.), who was completely devoted to Ingres throughout his life.

The influence of Delacroix is still more elusive; until his death in 1863 Delacroix continued to stand as the hero of the Romantic movement. With his own contemporaries—many of whom continued actively into this period—he pursued his essential premise of the primacy of color and a free handling of paint. The most important, all quite independent in their styles, would be Huet (q.v.) in landscape, Dedreux (q.v.; although somewhat more mundane than Delacroix), and also Boulanger (q.v.). To these can be added the figures of Eugène Isabey and Diaz de la Peña, who carried, although with a more Louis Philippe flavor, certain aspects of Romantic attitudes and styles into the Second Empire. Chassériau (q.v.) honored Delacroix while never completely forsaking his master Ingres, and it is perhaps, in figures who at first seem more distant from Delacroix, that one finds the most vital adaptation of his brilliant use of color and animated composition: for example, in Léon Riesener (whose pictures were purchased by Delacroix), Emile Lévy, Jules-Elie Delaunay, Fromentin, Gustave Moreau (q.v.), the young Puvis de Chavannes, and Fantin. However, if his influence seems pervasive yet indirect (as it would for Manet and the young Impressionists), there continued to be rather startingly direct homages to him, represented here by the splendidy dramatic *Joash* (no. VI-78) by Henri Lévy.

Courbet, whose rough genius would introduce quite a new force into painting in the 1850s, is as much defined by his choice of subjects as by his style and manner of painting. Realism—at its sharpest definition—had passed by 1852 although the word would continue to be a rallying cry as much for social concerns as for any easily understood style. Whereas his emphasis on painting on a dark ground with a palette primarily limited to somber colors would have an immediate effect on Bonvin (q.v.), and Carolus-Duran (q.v.), others who followed this approach—most notably Ribot and Vollon —were then responding as much to a revived interest in Spanish painting of the seventeenth century as to Courbet's style. While the young Monet and Renoir were struck by Courbet's egoism and ferocity of attack on established systems and attitudes, their painting was more affected by the grandeur of his forms and his determination to work directly from the model than by his convictions about color or technique (although Monet did, with disastrous effects, try one picture on a dark ground on Courbet's advice). It can be argued that Courbet's influence is more directly apparent in the paintings of artists working outside of France, particularly in Belgium and Germany.

Couture was the second major figure to introduce an essentially "dark manner" into painting, again originating from the late 1840s. His greatest importance in the period was as a teacher. His teaching methods were very precise; generally, his method of working with thick impasto—quite light in tone—on a deep brown ground introduced a dramatic and strongly modeled style to which his most famous pupil, Manet, owed a heavy debt, but no clearly defined school formed around his methods. Charles Müller continued to work in a somewhat similar manner, although with a greater emphasis on drawing and observed detail, but even here it is more a matter of parallel attitudes than direct influence.

The styles of all of these figures—Ingres, Delacroix, Courbet, and Couture—were clearly established, mature and formed, by the beginning of the Second Empire. The new sources of influence—the next generation of seminal forces—are more difficult to discern and it was not until Manet that a figure of equal stature, in terms of influence and art-historical significance, emerged, but the power of his originality (and its effect on yet another generation) was not clearly felt until well into the 1870s. Cabanel and Bouguereau, reflecting the continued vitality of the Ingresque tradition in their great purity and use of local color and their dependence on the elegance of drawing, seem more the continuation of a tradition than the realization of a new set of attitudes, although their refined execution and suave manner would continue to affect other painters until the end of the century. Gérôme, with his extremely detailed brushwork and ability to record observed detail and movement with great accuracy, would form the style of a broad range of students including the American Thomas Eakins. This style had a parallel in the work of Meissonier and his student Detaille (q.v.). However, none of these figures—with the advantage of art-historical hindsight—formed a stylistic "ism" and one of the major features of painting during the Second Empire was, in fact, the absence of a given stylistic categorization. Through a newly emerging tendency for the painter to specialize in specific genres, stylistically the Second Empire was not a time for easily defined movements and the rather useless terminology of "academic painting" or the "art of the Salon" has little substance when one confronts the actual pictures. This phenomenon has somewhat prompted later critics and historians to neglect so much of interest from the Second Empire, just because of the immense complexity—without clear stylistic coherence—of the state of painting at this time. Given this circumstance, it is therefore of more use to discuss painting of the Second Empire in terms of its subject matter than of its style.

With each speech given at the conclusion of the Salons throughout this period, the primacy of "high" art—a figurative art depicting historical subjects founded on the principles of the Académie, taught at the Ecole des Beaux-Arts and the Villa Medici in Rome—reiterated: "Turn your studies toward the grand form in art."[26] The continuity of this tradition, which dates from David and before him Le Brun, was assured at the beginning of the Second Empire through the presence of Delacroix and Ingres, who, even with the great independence of their interpretation of these subjects, continued with complete devotion to honor the importance of narrative figure painting above all other genres.

However, the history of painting during this period could be written simply in terms of the decline in dominance of historical subjects. Through the work of such figures as Henri Lévy, Gustave Moreau, Delaunay, Puvis de Chavannes, Paul Chenavard, and even the young Degas there was a progressive tendency to turn antique or historical subjects away from strictly narrative interpretations to a new emphasis on idealism or already to a form of Symbolism. While it was extremely difficult for contemporary critics to grasp the closeness of the relationship, the vast figurative compositions by Courbet are, in fact, a continuation of this attitude, which, since the seventeenth century, carried with it the tradition of a grand scale. Manet, perhaps even more so, continued the rebellion of honoring contemporary life with the same ceremony and heroic scale of traditional history painting. He himself was continually haunted by references to the past and from him—although with the narrative element diminished still more—stem the large early figural compositions of the young Monet, Bazille, and Renoir.

Yet another aspect of history painting, clearly established through the work of Delaroche and even Ingres, was a representation of narrative drawn not from antiquity but from more recent phases of history and it underwent a new revival of interest, be it with medieval subjects such as those of Penguilly-L'Haridon (q.v.) or those from the Renaissance and the seventeenth century, these especially through Gérôme and Meissonier. But, particularly with the latter, there was a tendency to eliminate the heroic element—and with it the moral implications—of the subjects and to reduce this tradition to a new form of genre in which an accuracy of historical detail was more praised than the importance of the event depicted.

Within the ever-broadening description of "history painting" there continued—sparked by state commissions—the tradition of battle pictures begun during the first Empire which attracted a broad group of specialists including Hippolyte Bellangé, Adolphe Yvon, Pils, Henri Philippoteaux, Meissonier, and John-Lewis Brown (q.v.). However, Manet's *Execution of the Emperor Maximilian* is perhaps, ironically, one of the most serious attempts to show contemporary military and political history.

This elevation to an important level of what was previously felt to be a lesser form of painting—genre—had a varied and complex history during the period. There continued in Rome—very much in the genre practice of the 1830s and 1840s—a form of peasant subject, usually peopled with young women from the countryside, well represented here by the work of Hébert (q.v.). In France this new attitude toward peasant subjects—prompted somewhat by the vigor of Courbet's Realism— would find its master in Millet, who brought to it all the high seriousness and dignity previously restricted to depictions of historical narrative. Breton, who added a somewhat more idealized feature to this genre, would bring it to a still more accessible level.

Animal painting, closely linked to depictions of rural life as presented by Millet and Breton, was nearly the exclusive interest of some of the most engaging artists of the period: Philippe Rousseau, Troyon, and Rosa Bonheur (q.q.v.). And their success—both critical and in terms of prices fetched—indicates still more the elevation of what were traditionally held to be lesser subjects and the erosion of the academically sponsored ranking of subject matter.

With the broadening diversification within figurative painting and the inevitable decline of the traditional hierarchy within genres of painting, other forms took on a new importance. Portraiture, as it developed to serve both the State through the very necessary production of public images as well as the bourgeoisie, began a growing specialization to the point that an artist such as Bonnat, who by training began as a history painter, would devote nearly all of his energies to its lucrative practice. In turn, still-life painting, especially prompted by a re-

vived interest in the works of this genre from the seventeenth and eighteenth centuries, underwent a new vitalization, attracting artists such as Vollon, Blaise Desgoffe, and Fantin, who practiced it with a sense of specialization not previously known in the nineteenth century.

Finally, one must mention another form of figurative painting very typical of the Second Empire, which is elusive by its very nature: these are the narrative pictures of a subjective and fantastic nature which increased in number and seem particularly in temper with this epoch. Originating perhaps with the more erotic work of Delacroix, such as his *Turkish Women Bathing* (no. VI-44), or Ingres's treatment of the same subject, there emerged a lyrical and poetic mood often drawn from obscure literary sources of privately defined allegories. Jalabert (q.v.) perhaps represents it best in this exhibition, but it is a form of fantasy-dream which would touch the works of Fantin, Hamon, Glaize (q.v.), and particularly Gustave Moreau, who would carry it to the more Symbolist lyrical works of the 1890s and the turn of the century.

The fascination with North Africa and the Near East, further prompted by the Crimean War and the Suez Canal activities, grew in importance with Decamps and with Delacroix, who continued well into the Second Empire to paint Oriental subjects of particular drama. However, the younger artists brought to their subjects a still more emphatic realism of observed detail, while at the same time eliminating some of the heroic romance of the older tradition, and with Belly and Gérôme an entirely new attitude toward information—objective and accurate—emerged within the genre.

Clearly established as a dignified, yet separate category since the founding of the Académie, with its own Prix de Rome (until 1863), landscape underwent tremendous change within these eighteen years. Figures such as Français (q.v.) and Bénouville (q.v.) continued firmly within the classical tradition, with works composed and lit in the Italian manner ultimately derived from Claude. To

this set of conventions Corot brought, particularly in the 1850s and 1860s, his own highly personalized dreams of haze and mist, elevating the form to a new level of lyrical idealization which would be as untranslatable, in terms of influence, as it would be popular. Courbet, working more massively and in a darker manner, paralleled the Barbizon landscapists— particularly Troyon and Théodore Rousseau (q.v.)—in an adaptation of closely observed motifs noted out of doors which would be arranged and modified in the studio, an attitude which created as much a subjectively heroic effect of expansive grandeur as a sense of place. Cibot (q.v.), not unlike Courbet, witnessed and arranged but to a gentler end, while Daubigny (q.v.), interested more in decorative painting, composed elegantly within a simplified palette. Figures outside the main Parisian activities— Guigou (q.v.) from the south and Jongkind and Boudin (q.v.) on the Channel coast—brought a character of a new literalism to landscape and while their insistence on painting out of doors at least in the preliminary stage of a work derived from Barbizon painting, they worked with a new intensity of color and freshness of observation which would have a great affect on the work of Sisley (q.v.), Pissarro, Renoir, and Monet. While this group would not clearly emerge as a movement until four years after the fall of the Second Empire with the first Impressionist exhibition, the newness of their vision, as well as its dependency on what went before, was evident by the late 1860s.

The Second Empire, in short, witnessed a radical transition within its history of painting, both in terms of the new diversity of works produced, perhaps unprecedented in their range of attitudes, and within those institutions, particularly the Salons, most closely related to painting as it was seen and criticized. Within this vast array, works of considerable quality were produced and artists of genius flourished, albeit within a context of institutional tensions which progressively encouraged the primacy of the individual. This was indeed a time of abundance; the pleasures to be found within it are vast.

G.L./J.R.

*Notes*

1. 1968, Providence, Toronto.

2. 1972–73, Dayton, Minneapolis, Baltimore.

3. 1974–75, New York.

4. 1976–77, Arras.

5. 1977, Saint Omer.

6. 1976–77, Paris, Grand Palais; 1977, Ottawa.

7. 1978, Chicago.

8. 1963, Paris, Louvre.

9. 1967–68, Paris, Petit Palais.

10. 1975–76, Paris, Grand Palais; 1976, London, Hayward Gallery.

11. 1977–78, Paris, Grand Palais; 1978, London.

12. 1973, Paris, Musée des Arts Décoratifs.

13. 1974, Paris, Grand Palais.

14. Paris, Bibliothèque Nationale, Cabinet des Estampes.

15. E. Zola, *Le Bon Combat*, Paris, 1974, p. 101.

16. Arch. nat., F$^{21}$ 528.

17. Paris, Salon, 1864, pp. xxv–xxvi.

18. P. Cézanne, *Correspondance*, Paris, 1937, p. 96.

19. Louvre Archives, X [Salon of 1867].

20. *See* Arch. nat., series F$^{21}$, as well as Louvre Archives.

21. Beginning in 1864 the purchases by the State—as many as 150 artists might benefit each year—were fortunately photographed at the end of the Salon by Michelez (Paris, Bibliothèque Nationale, Cabinet des Estampes). It is interesting to note that a large part of the funds for these purchases was gained through the accumulation of entrance fees, an innovation of the Second Empire. Another means of funding acquisitions was the lotteries which multiplied in Paris, particularly in 1859 and 1861.

22. Souverin, 1977, p. 2.

23. A copy of this document is preserved in the Service d'Étude et de Documentation du Département des Peintures, Musée du Louvre.

24. *See* M. Fidell-Beaufort's study (in preparation) on the archives of Samuel P. Avery.

25. E. Zola, *L'Œuvre*, chap. 6.

26. Vaillant, in Paris, Salon, 1863, p. xiii.

## Eugène-Emmanuel Amaury-Duval

*Montrouge 1808–1885 Paris*

*A student of Ingres (q.v.), Amaury-Duval exhibited at the Salon beginning in 1830. He was introduced to a contemporary audience in 1974 with an exhibition at the Hôtel de Ville in Montrouge, which presented about thirty paintings and drawings (see no. VII-1)—portraits and history paintings. The catalogue listed another forty works, portraits as well as decorative (for the château of Linières, begun in 1865) and religious subjects. He worked also for Parisian churches, decorating the Chapel of Saint Philomena (1840–44) in the Church of Saint Merry and the Chapel of the Virgin (1844–46) in the Church of Saint Germain l'Auxerrois, and, from 1849 on, for the church of Saint-Germain-en-Laye. He left many unpublished writings—accounts of trips to Italy, for example—and a number of books:* L'Atelier d'Ingres: Souvenirs *(1878) as well as* Souvenirs 1829–1830 *(1885).*

G.L.

Bibliography:
1974, Montrouge

VI-1

Eugène-Emmanuel Amaury-Duval

# VI-1
# Tragedy (Portrait of Rachel)

1854
Signed and dated, lower right: AMAURY-DUVAL 1854
Oil on canvas
167.5 × 115 cm

Provenance:
Rachel (?); Emile de Girardin; purchased by decree of April 15, 1880, by the Ministère de l'Instruction Publique et des Beaux-Arts for 5,000 francs for the Comédie Française; delivered June 8, 1880 (Arch. nat. F²¹ 191) (inv. no. CF 338)

Exhibitions:
1855, Paris, Exposition Universelle, no. 2421 (as *Tragedy*); 1934, Paris, Galerie Jacques Seligman, no. 47; 1962, Versailles, no. 324 (repro.); 1967, Montauban, no. 164; 1974, Montrouge, no. 14 (repro.); 1974–76, France, Musées de Province, no. 108 (repro.)

Bibliography:
About, 1855, p. 144; du Camp, 1855, p. 263; Gebauër, 1855, p. 186; de la Rochenoire, 1855, pp. 48–49; Vignon, 1855, p. 197; Gautier, 1855–56, vol. I, pp. 148–49; About, 1858, p. 59; Monval, 1897, p. 117, no. 338; Dacier, 1905, pp. 141, 189; Lacambre, 1969, p. 101, repro. p. 102

In 1852, unveiling his plans for the expansion of the museum of the Comédie Française to the Director of Fine Arts, Romieu, Arsène Houssaye, then administrator, wrote: " Eugène Delacroix will endeavor to paint Mlle Rachel as the Muse of tragedy " (Delorme, 1878, p. 26). Delacroix did not do so, but shortly afterward he sold to the State for 1,500 francs his *Portrait of Talma*, destined for the foyer of the Théâtre Français (Arch. nat. F²¹ 74).

On March 6, 1854, Amaury-Duval received the commission to produce *Tragedy* for 4,000 francs, Ingres having always maintained that he was not competent to paint such a portrait. This was abandoned by the government and while the reason is not known, the unfaithfulness of the celebrated actress Rachel to the Comédie Française may have had something to do with it. After returning in May 1854 from a triumphant tour of Russia, she considered resigning several times and prepared to leave for the United States. It is interesting to note that while in 1851 Clésinger (q.v.) sculpted *Rachel as Tragedy*, Duret's *Tragedy* of 1855 (Salon of 1857) was not modeled after her (Arch. nat. F²¹ 78); and it was only after her untimely death in 1858 that she became once more the incarnation of Tragedy (again by Duret, 1865; all three statues now at the Comédie Française).

The early history of Amaury-Duval's painting is not clear. A receipt for 5,000 francs (photocopy at the Comédie Française) indicates that Rachel did buy a portrait by Amaury-Duval, and this is not likely to have been the other, surely smaller version, now lost (1974, Montrouge, no. 54), nor the sketch showing slight variations that belonged to a friend of Amaury-Duval at Riom during the nineteenth century (private coll.). No painting resembling this has appeared in any of the sales of her effects (July 27–30, 1857; April 12, 1858) nor is it mentioned in descriptions of her various residences. However the first certain owner of *Tragedy*, Emile de Girardin, was very close to Rachel: it was he who in 1855 intervened to end the offensive silence of the press which was then acclaiming a new tragedienne, Adelaide Ristori.

The Classical background of this painting is of course part of the symbolism of Tragedy, but it also reflects Rachel's taste, for she had a dining room decorated in the Etruscan style in her house at 4, rue Trudon (see Houssaye, 1884, p. 312). This background should be compared with that of two paintings by Ingres: *Cherubini* (Louvre) and *Antiochus and Stratonice* (Musée Condé, Chantilly).

*Tragedy* was generally poorly received at the Exposition Universelle. The critic About talked of "dry drawing" and "disastrous color," and Vignon asked "What is this Rachel in painted plaster all about?" "Is it an epigram against tragedy?" questioned Théophile Gautier who, however, did admire "the nobility and purity of the drawing, modeling so delicate in its softened relief, the perfect taste of arrangement, the accuracy of the Classical details, indeed all the subtlety and discipline of the master."

G.L.

Collections de la Comédie Française, Paris

## Paul Baudry

*La Roche-sur-Yon (Vendée) 1828–1886 Paris*

*At first a student of Antoine Sartoris, Baudry was given a scholarship by the town of his birth to complete his studies in Paris. He entered the atelier of Michel-Martin Drolling and was admitted to the Ecole des Beaux-Arts in 1845. He was awarded a second prize in the 1847 competition, then the Grand Prix de Rome in 1850, at the same time as Bouguereau (q.v.). In January 1851 he left for Italy, where he studied the Italian Primitives, and especially the painters of the Renaissance, among whom he particularly admired Correggio, Raphael, and the Venetians. He was then painting antique and mythological subjects. Upon his return to France, the State acquired* Torture of a Vestal Virgin *(Lille museum) before it was exhibited in the Salon of 1857, the first in which any of his work appeared, and where he exhibited his other* envoi *from Rome,* Venus and Cupid *(Fortune and the Child; Musée du Luxembourg, later the Louvre), and* Saint John the Baptist *(Amiens museum), both purchased from the civil list. He was immediately awarded a first-class medal. His prices were already very high, and he soon acquired a reputation as a portrait painter. The State purchased* The Repentant Magdalene *at the Salon of 1859 (Nantes museum). In 1861 he received a* rappel *and was made chevalier of the Legion of Honor. In 1863 he exhibited his famous composition* The Pearl and the Wave *(Prado, Madrid).*

*An accomplished decorative painter, he was commissioned to do a great many private mansions and, in 1865, the Grand Foyer of the Opéra (see no. VII-4). This was to be his major undertaking. He worked eight years on it, having first prepared himself for the task by trips to Rome to study Michelangelo's Sistine ceiling and to London to copy Raphael's cartoons. His official advancement was swift and continued under the Third Republic. In 1870 he was elected to the Institut de France to fill the vacancy left by Jean-Victor Schnetz.*

G.L.

Bibliography:
About, 1876; Breton, 1886; Ephrussi, 1887; Goarin (in preparation)

Paul Baudry

## VI-2
## Portrait of the Son of the Comtesse Swieytowska as the Young Saint John

1860
Signed and dated, lower left: Paris. 1860 Paul Baudry
Oil on canvas
115 × 82 cm

Provenance:
Baron Gustave de Rothschild, Paris (probably after 1882); private coll.

Exhibitions:
1861, Paris, Salon, no. 158; 1882, Paris, Galerie Georges Petit, no. 25 (as *The Young Saint John,* without indication of ownership; probably the artist); 1886, Paris, Ecole des Beaux-Arts, no. 58 (Baron Gustave de Rothschild)

Bibliography:
Cantaloube, 1861, p. 77; du Camp, 1861, p. 32; Gautier, 1861, p. 42; Lagrange, 1861, pp. 332–33; Delaborde, 1866, pp. 178–79; Breton, 1886, p. 15; Lafenestre, 1886, p. 402; Ephrussi, 1887, p. 318; Breton, 1890, p. 233

VI-2

In the Salon of 1857 Baudry had exhibited a *Saint John the Baptist* as a child sitting with a lamb in his arms (oval canvas 85 × 95 cm). It was purchased by Napoleon III for 5,000 francs (Louvre Archives 2 DD 25, no. 201 on the civil list), a sum indicative of the instant success the artist had achieved. The painting remained in the domaine privé until 1879, when it was assigned to the national museums (exhibited, beginning in 1881, in the Musée du Luxembourg, then sent to Amiens).

In 1860 Baudry did a painting of young Jean Swieytowski, showing him with the attributes of his patron saint: a reed shepherd's crook in the shape of a cross and an emblem bearing the inscription "Agnus Dei." Despite an overabundance of picturesque details—cherries, a spider web—which a number of critics regretted, the picture delighted the public at the Salon. Du Camp considered it "the outstanding piece in M. Baudry's exhibit," which consisted of no less than eight works, among them *Charlotte Corday* (Nantes museum). "This type of historical portrait" appealed enormously to Théophile Gautier for it "allows the entry of a much greater amount of art into works that otherwise are too easily bourgeois." The poet concluded: "It would be difficult to imagine anything more divinely childlike and with a more delicate coloration than this little Polish

Saint John. The landscape is sketched in with a knowing ease, so characteristic of the painter, which sets off the figures to advantage. Were it to be given a coat of golden varnish, Leonardo would welcome this beautiful child into one of his holy families."

G.L.

Private Collection

Paul Baudry

## VI-3
## Portrait of Charles Garnier, Architect

1868
Signed, dated, and inscribed, upper left: P¹ BAU-
DRY A SON AMI Cˢ GARNIER 1868
Oil on canvas
103 × 81 cm

Provenance:
Charles Garnier; widow, Mme Charles Garnier; bequest to the Musées Nationaux for the Versailles museum, 1922 (inv. no. MV 5903)

Exhibitions:
1869, Paris, Salon, no. 145; 1866, Paris, Ecole des Beaux-Arts, no. 103; 1961, Vichy, no. 3

Bibliography:
About, 1869, p. 747; Lafenestre, 1886, pp. 408–10; Ephrussi, 1887, p. 318; Roujon, n.d., *Baudry*, pp. 58, 73

From the time of his stay at the Villa Medici to which he had gone in January 1851, Baudry had been a friend of Charles Garnier (q.v.), the latter having won the Prix de Rome in 1848. Appointed architect of the Opéra in 1861, Garnier put Baudry in charge of the decoration of the Grand Foyer, an enormous task to which Baudry devoted all his energies beginning in 1865. When Baudry painted this portrait, which was done in the tradition of eighteenth-century presentation portraits for inauguration into the Académie des Beaux-Arts, the facade of the Opéra had just been dedicated, bringing fame to its architect.

Another friend of Baudry's, Edmond About—they had met in Naples in 1853—gave an enthusiastic description of this work in the *Revue des Deux-Mondes*: "The *Charles Garnier* by M. Baudry is a letter addressed to posterity; it is not only alive now but it will go on living. It is a strong work, intimate, profound, doubly personal: it sprang, so to speak, from the collaboration of a model and an artist, men who have shared their lives and who have no secrets from one another. All portraits of outstanding men ought to be handled in this way, sittings being merely a recapitulation, a summing up of

VI-3

thousands of previously made observations.... M. Garnier's portrait provokes shouts of admiration from artists, but somewhat surprises the public at large. I have heard Sunday visitors saying to one another: 'Who is this? A savage? A man from ancient times? Surely he does not belong here.' No, good people, he belongs neither to our country nor to our times; he is a sixteenth-century Florentine, and his work states it as eloquently as does his face. The new Opéra, with its forms, colors, marbles, metals, and that profusion of strange, brilliant, extraordinary things, could certainly not be the product of a Parisian brain; it is the work of a unique man especially created to eradicate the vulgarity of your new Paris."

G.L.

Musée National du Château, Versailles

---

## Frédéric Bazille
*Montpellier 1841–1870 Beaune-la-Rolande*

*Born into a prosperous and cultivated Protestant family in Montpellier, Bazille had the good fortune during his youth to live opposite Alfred Bruyas (see no. VII-20), and so witnessed the formation of Bruyas's remarkable collection of contemporary painting. It is not surprising on that account that he soon wished to become an artist himself, and enrolled at the newly founded Ecole des Beaux-Arts in Montpellier. However, his parents wanted him to pursue a more serious profession, and it was only through a compromise reached in the fall of 1862, by which he studied painting half of the time and medicine the rest, that he was allowed to depart for Paris.*

*Bazille entered the studio of Gleyre (q.v.), then in its last months of existence, and soon established close friendships with Renoir, Monet, and slightly later, Sisley (q.q.v.). With them he traveled to the country to paint in the open air (he posed at Chailly in 1865 for Manet's* Luncheon on the Grass, *which he subsequently bought to help out the artist), and shared the friendships of Fantin-Latour, Gérôme, Manet, and Courbet (q.q.v.). Unlike his close contemporaries, he was prosperous and mixed broadly in society (as did Manet and Degas), forming many friendships in theatrical and musical circles.*

*Bazille's landscapes have a particular intensity of color that sets them apart from those of his colleagues, and reflects his visual sensibility as a southerner (see Guigou). Most of his surviving works are figure paintings, and while, like Monet's, these were often posed out of doors, Bazille's forms rarely succumb to the dissolving quality of light, which would mark the biggest single departure in the developing styles of the young Impressionists. The most successful of his figure compositions—*The Artist's Family *and* View of the Village—*were done during return visits to Montpellier.*

*It is perhaps because of the more finished quality of his painting that Bazille met with greater success at the Salon than many of his progressive contemporaries. He exhibited there in 1866, 1868, 1869, and 1870. In the last two years his works were well hung and received some critical comment.*

*With the Prussian invasion in August 1870, Bazille enlisted, serving with the prestigious Third Zouave, and was killed later the same year.*

J.R.

Bibliography:
Poulain, 1932; Rewald, 1946; 1950, New York, Wildenstein, "Bazille"; 1950, Paris, Galerie Wildenstein; Daulte, 1952; 1959, Montpellier; Daulte, 1970; 1978, Chicago

Frédéric Bazille

## VI-4
## Negress Arranging Peonies

1870
Signed and dated, lower left: F. Bazille 1870
Oil on canvas
60 × 75 cm

Provenance:
Artist's family; gift of Marc Bazille to the Musée Fabre, 1918 (inv. no. 18-1-3)

Exhibitions:
1927, Montpellier, no. 29; 1941, Montpellier, no. 34;
1973, Paris, Musée des Arts Décoratifs; 1978, Chicago,
no. 55

Bibliography:
Joubin, 1929, no. 365; Poulain, 1932, no. 39; Daulte,
1952, pp. 79, 129, 188, no. 51

Painted in the spring of 1870 in his studio on the rue des Batignolles in Paris, this hauntingly mute and beautiful picture recalls several works of Bazille's immediate circle, most immediately, Manet's *Olympia*, in which a black maid presents a bouquet to her mistress (this was a time when Bazille's relationship to Manet was particularly close and when he made frequent visits to Manet's studio). The actual idea of doing a flower piece may also have been prompted by Bazille's steady visits to Fantin-Latour (q.v.), where he was posing for his portrait in *A Studio in the Batignolles Quarter* (Jeu de Paume). However, neither reference explains all the elements in this particular picture. If it is a modest homage to the *Olympia*, it takes the form of a detail; and also the composition of a figure with a still life is quite unlike Fantin.

As early as the fall of 1864, Monet had advised Bazille on the pleasure of painting flowers (Rewald, 1946, pp. 111–12), and Bazille made several floral pieces beginning in 1866. They are like those of Monet and Renoir in their fresh abundance; however, the inclusion of the figure was a new departure. Its source most likely lies in several such works by Courbet (for example, Toledo Museum of Art; coll. Lucie

Germain, Paris), which combine the sensuality of a model with a full and rich arrangement of flowers. It is tempting also to speculate whether the young artist was aware of the use of this juxtaposition by his friend Degas in *Woman and Chrysanthemums* (1866–68; Metropolitan Museum of Art, New York). Yet, despite these possible associations, the picture is uniquely Bazille's in its studied, calm detachment—depicting a variety of colored substances (cloth, skin, the vase, the flowers) in an even, clear light.

Daulte commented on the general use of black models during the period, and referred to Bazille's loose reference to the assertive, Romantic works of the Orientalists, but exoticism is very mild here. It seems likely that Bazille was simply prompted to make still further use in his paintings of the handsome, black model he was employing. In a more pointed reference to Arabic themes, he was preparing *The Toilette* (Montpellier) that same spring for the Salon.

This subject seems to have particularly interested Bazille, since another version exists (a unique case in his known work) in the collection of Paul Mellon (Daulte, 1970, repro.), in which the same model arranges flowers in a basket, but looks directly out at the viewer, her right hand holding a blossom. Its relationship to the exhibited version is unclear; both pictures seem to have been painted simultaneously, and if the version shown here is perhaps a reference to Courbet, the Mellon picture with flowers completely filling the lower third of the

canvas is a nod to Delacroix, whom Bazille admired with almost pious devotion.

J.R.

Musée Fabre, Montpellier

---

## Léon Bénouville
*Paris 1821–1859 Paris*

*The brother of Jean-Achille Bénouville, six years his elder, Léon studied with him at the same time. As a student of François-Edouard Picot, he entered the Ecole des Beaux-Arts on March 27, 1837, and in 1845 he and his brother were both awarded the Prix de Rome: Léon for* Jesus before the Roman Court *(Ecole des Beaux-Arts, Paris) and Jean-Achille in the area of historical landscape.*

*Léon made his debut at the Salon of 1838 and continued to show his work successfully in the Salons until 1845. As a* pensionnaire *at the Villa Medici he did not send* envois *to Paris, and did not exhibit again until the Salon of 1852, when he showed several works, among them a large watercolor called* Martyrs Being Brought to Torture *(Musée du Luxembourg, then, in 1877, Cabinet des Dessins, Louvre). This composition, done during his stay in Rome, won him a second-class medal; in 1854 he received a commission for the large painting based on it, which was ready for the Exposition Universelle of 1855 (Louvre). His submission to the Salon of 1853,* The Dying Saint Francis, *awarded a first-class medal, made him famous. In 1855 he won a second-class medal at the Exposition Universelle and the Legion of Honor. He also painted portraits, historical genre scenes, and worked on large decorations, such as those in the church of Saint-Germain-en-Laye, with Amaury-Duval (q.v.), and the Hôtel de Ville in Paris. His early death in 1859 met with a general expression of grief.*

G.L.

Bibliography:
Blanc, 1863, vol. III, appendix, pp. 70–71

Léon Bénouville

## VI-5
## The Dying Saint Francis Carried to Santa Maria degli Angeli, Blessing the Town of Assisi

1853
Signed and dated, lower right: Léon-

VI-4

VI-5

Bénouville 1853
Oil on canvas
93 × 240 cm

Provenance:
Purchased at the Salon of 1853 by the Ministère de la
Maison de l'Empereur by decree of June 24, 1853, for
4,000 francs; destined for the Musée du Luxembourg
(Louvre Archives X [Salon of 1853]); entered the
Luxembourg, September 12, 1853; transferred to the
Louvre, November 13, 1874 (inv. nos. MI 9 and
RF 62)

Exhibitions:
1853, Paris, Salon, no. 79; 1855, Paris, Exposition
Universelle, no. 2525; 1967, Montauban, no. 170 (repro.)

Bibliography:
D'Auvigny, 1853, p. 19; Delaborde, 1853, pp.
1141–42; Henriet, 1853, p. 12; Horsin-Déon, 1853,
p. 15; Nadar, 1853, no. 179; Vignon, 1853, p. 60;
About, 1855, p. 148; du Camp, 1855, p. 211; Gautier,
1855, Le Moniteur, p. 934; Lavergne, 1855, p. 77;
Loudun, 1855, p. 136; Perrier, 1855, p. 102; Vignon,
1855, pp. 197–98; Catalogues, Paris, Luxembourg,
1855–74; Pelloquet, 1858, p. 18; Dumesnil, 1859, p.
85; Lépinois, 1859, p. 87; Viardot, 1859, p. 85; Delaborde, 1866, pp. 80, 125; Beulé, 1867, p. 345; Castagnary, 1892, vol. I, p. 45; Laurens, 1901, p. 306;
Brière, 1924, no. 17; Sterling and Adhémar, 1958–61,
vol. I, no. 58, pl. 14; Catalogue, Paris, Louvre, Paintings, 1972, vol. I, p. 30

In the catalogue of the artist's death sale
(Paris, May 3–4, 1859), there was a plan for the
decoration of a chapel of Saint Francis of Assisi
(no. 48) which included three subjects: Saint
Francis blessing the town of Assisi, corresponding to this painting; Saint Clare receiving
the body of Saint Francis at the convent of
Santa Maria degli Angeli (Salon of 1859;
Musée Condé, Chantilly), as well as an
apotheosis of Saint Francis, which was never
executed.

At the Salon of 1853, The Dying Saint Francis
Carried to Santa Maria degli Angeli, Blessing the
Town of Assisi was a huge success—which
explains its rather numerous reductions and
copies—and although it was classified as a historical painting, critics did not hesitate to emphasize the contrast between the subject and

the style, calling it "a graceful little picture"
(Boyeldieu d'Auvigny). "In a word it is great
painting in a small frame," summed up Horsin-
Déon. Others praised its feeling and poetry
(Vignon), seeing in it "a calm, an austerity
which is moving... an elevated style" (Horsin-
Déon) and "the serenity of the monks, the majesty of the scene, the grandeur of the landscape" which "imparts some of the mystical
elevation from the most beautiful pages of the
life of Saint Bruno" (Henriet, 1853, p. 12).

In 1855 Théophile Gautier wrote: "This is
Zurbaran tempered by Lesueur; for a lan-
guishing grace, a morbid sweetness, soften
these heads on whose faces may be read a nostalgia for heaven." Perrier noted that "the color
is as sober as M. Flandrin's." In 1858 Pelloquet,
in his incisive Dictionnaire de poche des artistes
contemporains, proved less satisfied: "As in all
works said to be by draftsmen, the drawing
lacked truth and study, and the coloring took
on a bottle-green harmony which many people
greatly admired."

In the end, in 1859, a few weeks after the
painter's death, emotion won out: Paul Mantz
noted that it was "the strongest and the tender-
est of his works," that it "marks in the short life
of Léon Bénouville a point of relative perfection which he never surpassed." This is the
work most often linked with the name of its
creator.

Perceived for the most part as a small-for-
mat historical painting, the picture was interpreted in a different way by Jules Castagnary,
who cited it in his Salon of 1857 as a genre
painting because "with genre, a new principle—action—was introduced." Thus this representation of the death of Saint Francis of Assisi would be one of the earliest examples of
historical genre painting, which played a dominant role during the Second Empire.

G.L.

Musée du Louvre, Paris

## Maria-Rosa Bonheur
Bordeaux 1822–1899 Le By (Seine-et-Marne)

Maria-Rosa Bonheur was the eldest of four children, all of whom followed the profession of their
artist father, Raymond Bonheur, a Saint-Simonian
socialist. One of the strong beliefs of that group was
equality for women, a belief so innate to their revolutionary movement that a female messiah was
sought and a female component of the Trinity postu-
lated. Bonheur's energetic and independent nature
thrived in this atmosphere, and as an adult she chose
to work in male clothing, an indiscretion for which
she had to obtain a waiver from the police in 1855.
She was a good friend of George Sand and is said to
have borrowed her idea for Plowing at Nivernais
(Fontainebleau) from a passage in Sand's novel La
Mare au Diable. Bonheur bought a château in the
village of Le By near the Forest of Fontainebleau;
there, in order to study animals from nature, she
kept—in addition to dogs, cats, cows, and sheep—a
yak, a gazelle, monkeys, an eagle, and a lion.

The artist won an international reputation with
her vast and highly praised Horse Fair, exhibited at
the Salon of 1853 and sold immediately to an English
dealer. (Cornelius Vanderbilt bought it in 1887 for
52,000 dollars, an enormous sum at that time for a
nineteenth-century painting, and gave it to the Metropolitan Museum of Art.) Bonheur had been
awarded two gold medals by 1853 and would receive
another in 1855. She was awarded the cross of the
Legion of Honor by the Empress Eugénie (who came
to Le By and presented the medal in her studio in
1865), and was the first woman to be made an officer
of the Legion of Honor, a title she received in 1894,
five years before her death.

Bonheur generally did not impose sentimen-
talized morality or human psychological states on her
animals; rather, she simply studied each in its
habitat or at animal fairs or slaughter houses, making drawings for use in later paintings. Nonetheless,
although she was preeminently a Realist, her passion
for animals shared in the Romantic tendencies of her
predecessors, Géricault and Delacroix (q.v.), for
whom certain animals evoked a kind of primitive
energy and grace.

N.D.

Bibliography:
Hamerton, 1895, pp. 98–103; Stranahan, 1902, pp.
294–97; Klumpke, 1909; Tufts, 1974; 1976–77, Los
Angeles, etc., pp. 223–25

VI-6

Maria-Rosa Bonheur

## VI-6
## Deer in Repose

1867
Signed and dated, lower left: Rosa Bonheur 1867
Oil on canvas:
104.1 × 84 cm

Provenance:
D.M. Ferry, Detroit; daughter, Queen Ferry Coonley; gift to the Detroit Institute of Arts, 1920 (inv. no. 20.93)
Exhibitions:
1924, Poughkeepsie; 1964, Detroit
Bibliography:
*Bulletin of the Detroit Institute of Arts,* vol. II, no. 4, January 1921, pp. 34–35, repro. p. 34

While depictions of animals, were the nearly exclusive concern of Rosa Bonheur's art, few subjects absorbed her more than the representation of deer, a subject that took on great importance after she established her studio at Le By, in 1860. Here in the Forest of Fontainebleau she had frequent opportunity to observe deer. Indeed, the catalogue of her studio sale (Paris, Galerie Georges Petit, May 30–June 2, 1900, nos. 320–415) lists ninety-five paintings of stags, roebucks, and hinds.

Stanton recounts an anecdote giving some idea of her working method: "One day, not fifty rods from the Carrefour de la Pointe d'Iray.... Rosa Bonheur was driving when she saw a stag couched under the foliage, with the sun playing on him through the leaves.... On returning home, she immediately made a study of this little scene, which was an exact reproduction of form and colour of what we had been gazing at a few moments before. Rosa Bonheur had acquired great skill in this art of photographing on her mind all she saw and then reproducing it faithfully with her brush as soon as she reached her studio" (Stanton [ed.], 1910, p. 299).

One has a sense that this process, perhaps supported with drawings made of animals in captivity, is what happened here, particularly because there is a distinct sense of place—with the light filtering through the oak onto the ferns. Bonheur's style, formulated almost entirely on that of her father and encouraged by her two artist brothers, is hermetic in its freedom from contemporary influences. She felt herself, both personally and artistically, detached from society. Apart from her own family, Troyon was the only painter whom she mentioned frequently with respect in letters. However, with this picture, one is tempted to question her knowledge of Courbet, who at the Salon the previous year, had shown *Covert of Roe-Deer by the Stream of Plaisir-Fontaine, Doubs* (Louvre) which Bonheur's great supporter, the Empress, had attempted to buy. Although Courbet's is much grander in scale, they share the same sharp sense of observation, as well as an effect of light gently filtered through trees, although Courbet's picture has a stronger element of anthropomorphic sentimentality which he recognized when he commented that his doe was "like a lady receiving company in her drawing room" (Courthion, 1948–50, vol. I, p. 222).

J.R.

The Detroit Institute of Arts, Gift of Mrs. Avery Coonley

---

## Léon Bonnat

*Bayonne 1833–1922 Mouchy-en-Brie (Oise)*

*In 1847 Bonnat's father took his family to Madrid, where the young artist's first masters were José Madrazo and his son, Federigo, at the Real Academia de Bellas Artes de San Fernando. But in his search for a strong chiaroscuro, and the interest in naturalism that marks even his earliest works, the paintings he saw at the Prado—and particularly his profound sympathy for Velázquez and Ribera—were the greater influences. In 1852 he returned to Paris, his abilities having been developed well enough for him to win a scholarship from his native city of Bayonne, which continued annually until 1860. He entered the studio of Léon Cogniet in 1854, and in 1857 joined the competition for the Prix de Rome, winning only a second place. Rather than wait another year, however, he used his pension to go immediately to study at the Villa Medici. There, under the instruction of Jean-Victor Schnetz and Chapu (q.v.), he studied, copied, and traveled, often joined by his fellow* pensionnaires, *most notably Lefebvre, Henner (q.v.), Delaunay (q.v.), and by Gustave Moreau (q.v.).*

*Bonnat returned to Paris in 1860 and through his Salon successes and his work as a portraitist, his reputation grew rapidly. He ran an independent atelier where, among others, Thomas Eakins and Toulouse-Lautrec came to study. He was elected to serve on the Salon juries sixteen times between 1868 and 1888. After 1870 his official honors multiplied, and in 1900, he was awarded the grand cross of the Legion of Honor. His international fame rests today on the portraits he painted of famous Frenchmen of his day (Thiers, Pasteur, Renan, Hugo, Dumas, and Taine, to list a few). He made a substantial fortune from these (receiving 15,000 francs a work by the 1880s) and had practically a monopoly on portraits of the barons of industry visiting from America.*

*Bonnat turned nearly all of his wealth over to the perceptive and avid buying of art, with a particular interest in Renaissance drawings. He left most of these, as well as many of his own works, to a museum named in his honor in Bayonne, the city that had with foresight supported him in his youth.*

N.D./J.R.

Bibliography:
Meynell, 1881, pp. 238–42; Claretie, 1882–84, vol. II, s.v.; Van Dyke, 1896; Stranahan, 1917; Bénédite, 1923; Cuzacq, 1940; Bean, 1960; Ackerman, 1969, pp. 235–56

Léon Bonnat

## VI-7
## Adam and Eve Finding the Dead Abel

1860–61
Signed: L. Bonnat
Oil on canvas
173 × 250 cm

Provenance:
Purchased by the State from the Salon of 1861 for the

Musée des Beaux-Arts, Lille (inv. no. 628)

Exhibition:
1861, Paris, Salon, no. 327

Bibliography:
Catalogue, Lille, Musée des Beaux-Arts, 1872, p. 19; Gonse, 1874, p. 344; Fouquier, 1879, pp. 61–65, 73–74; Claretie, 1882–84, vol. II; Bénédite, 1923, p. 10

*Adam and Eve Finding the Dead Abel* was the assigned competition subject for the Prix de Rome of 1858 (*see* Henner's winning version, Ecole des Beaux-Arts); while Bonnat's direct competition had ceased in 1857, it is not surprising that this subject would appeal to him, both as a demonstration of his ability to present the nude and as a continuation of the success of his earlier submission of a Biblical subject to the Salon of 1859, *The Good Samaritan* (no. 298), which had won him an honorable mention and been purchased by the State for the museum of Bayonne. However, his motivation must have been still stronger, since the subject allowed him to demonstrate his indebtedness to two masters: Michelangelo and Ribera. His devotion to Spanish painting, from his earliest training in Madrid, and to Velázquez and Ribera in particular (verbally honoring the former, but in practice drawing infinitely more from the latter) is well documented. The sprawling figure of the dead Abel here can be taken as a direct homage to the lean male nudes of similar poses (fallen, dead, or dying) that people the works of Ribera, especially the *Saint Sebastian* in the Prado, as well as, based on his more recent experience of a visit to Naples, the *Pietà* in the convent of San Martino. Claretie noted (p. 132), in addition, that he was particularly

haunted by Michelangelo (as was his friend in Rome, Gustave Moreau, q.v.) and he even dreamed of painting a large *Creation*, but this was thought, by his professors, to be too ambitious. Therefore, the relationship between Adam and the poses of two of the Athletes from the Sistine ceiling (particularly in the spread legs, one folded back) and between Eve whose hunched pose and crossed ankles echo Michelangelo's Eve in the ceiling (*The Fall*) is intentional, if somewhat audacious. The simplicity of the landscape and the intense orange and blue of the background might also reflect his interest in Michelangelo's frescoes. However, these figural sources are adjusted through a close observance of nature, the figures being drawn in the most refined, academic manner.

Bonnat sent two other pictures to the Salon the same year—an Italian peasant figure study, *Mariuccia*, as well as an unidentified portrait. This demonstrates the diversity of his interests (to which he would soon add Oriental subjects, drawn from his travels in the Near East with Gérôme, q.v.) and may also indicate that while he would continue to do large figurative paintings throughout the 1860s (his *Saint Vincent in Chains* at the Salon of 1866 was a particular success) he did not feel altogether at ease with this style—according to some critics, quite rightly. As Bénédite noted (1923, p. 10), while the young artist had high visions and noble ambitions, history painting was not his natural domain; his reality was too often confined to the reality of the body and not to the psychological or emotional truth. However, even in its staged and somewhat eclectic quality, this *Adam and Eve* represents, perhaps better

than any other selection in this exhibition, a young artist striving within the tradition of history painting and the grand style and, in turn, demonstrates—just in its scale and simplicity—the purity of that ambition.

J.R.

Musée des Beaux-Arts, Lille

---

## François Bonvin
*Vaugirard (Paris) 1817–1887 Paris*

*From a modest background, Bonvin practiced various trades and trained himself by studying above all at the Louvre or by cultivating collectors, such as Laperlier and La Caze. He was an admirer of Chardin, the seventeenth-century Dutch masters, and the Le Nain brothers, whom the Realist critic and novelist Champfleury had restored to a place of honor.*

*He painted still lifes, interior scenes—kitchens, taverns, classrooms, convents (see no. VII-7)—and a few rare landscapes. These works put him foremost among the Realists. He was in addition a friend of Courbet (q.v.), Théodule-Augustin Ribot (q.v.), and Whistler.*

*He exhibited regularly at the Salon from 1847 on; he won a number of awards under the Second Republic: a third-class medal in 1849 and a second-class medal in 1850–51. During the Second Empire he lived under rather wretched conditions, even though he regularly obtained aid from the State through modest acquisitions. He died blind and paralyzed.*

G.L.

Bibliography:
Moreau-Nélaton, 1927; Weisberg, 1974

François Bonvin

## VI-8
## Interior of a Tavern

1859
Signed and dated, lower left: F. Bonvin 1859
Oil on canvas
54.5 × 65 cm

Provenance:
Purchased by the Ministry of State on October 25, 1859, for 1,200 francs, paid in two installments: 500 francs on November 3, 1859, 700 francs on January 28, 1860 (Arch. nat. F$^{21}$ 65); deposited, after the Salon of 1861, at the Musée des Beaux-Arts, Arras, 1862

Exhibitions:
1859, Paris, Théâtre de l'Odéon; 1861, Paris, Salon, no. 336

VI-7

VI-8

Bibliography:
Cantaloube, 1861, p. 88; Catalogues, Arras, Musée des Beaux-Arts, 1864, no. 4, 1867, no. 4, 1880, no. 10; Lefort, 1888, pp. 140–41; Thoré-Bürger, 1893, pp. 39–40, 114–15; Catalogue, Arras, Musée des Beaux-Arts, 1907, no. 24; Moreau-Nélaton, 1927, pp. 54–55, 57–58, fig. 31; Vergnet-Ruiz and Laclotte, 1962, p. 227; Weisberg, 1970, p. 362, fig. 3; Pillement, 1974, p. 243, pl. 261; Weisberg, 1974, pp. 307, 311; Ten-Doesschate-Chu, 1974, p. 40, pl. 62

A note dated October 20, 1859 (Arch. nat. $F^{21}$ 65) outlines the circumstances of the acquisition of this work: "M. Bonvin is at present in a most precarious situation and he has only one way out: to sell to the Ministry the painting he brought me, which I have had taken to M. de Mercey's office." The previous commission, *Christian School* (Besançon museum) had been bought for 1,500 francs; this one—"the painting in question is at least as important"—fetched only 1,200 francs. The payment, not scheduled until January of 1860, was advanced—possibly at a renewed request from the painter—and the first installment of 500 francs was paid on November 3.

This episode clearly illustrates the difficulties encountered by a Realist artist who had been favorably received during the Second Republic, but whose works did not appeal to collectors of the Second Empire, avid for sentimental genre or historic subjects (compare, for example, the prices a Meissonier could command!).

In spite of his repeated efforts to exhibit in Paris and the provinces and to promote his works—on April 29, 1861, he asked the marquis de Chennevières, who was in charge of the exhibitions, for permission to "varnish and clean" his painting before it was shown in the Salon (Moreau-Nélaton)—Bonvin stated in a letter of June 3, 1861, to the Minister of State: "The little I have realized from my works in the past few years has not been enough to cover the expenses incurred for them" (Arch. nat. $F^{21}$ 120).

This painting, which may have been inspired, if one is to believe Moreau-Nélaton, by the family tavern at Vaugirard, did not go unnoticed in the Salon. Cantaloube, admiring, nevertheless threw light on the atmosphere prevailing at the time: " This painter is considered sad because he has a taste for the stark and finds beauty in hovels where frivolous people cannot see it." Thoré-Bürger, who ranked Bonvin with Courbet and Millet (q. q.v.), wrote: "He too is master in his modest genre." (Compare this painting with Courbet's *After Dinner at Ornans*, shown in the Salon of 1848, now in Lille, so different in spirit.) He added: "There is also in his work something reminiscent of the Le Nain brothers, Chardin, and the Dutch." While there is a temptation to compare the 1859 painting with Le Nains' *Peasants Eating*, which was acquired by the Louvre only in 1869 through the La Caze bequest, one must bear in mind that Bonvin had come to know this work—and other works of the Le Nains—

through his friend Champfleury, the champion of the Le Nains.

In this particular painting Bonvin was clearly influenced more by the tavern interiors of David Teniers the Younger, highly thought of at the time, than by Pieter de Hooch, of whom Thoré was reminded, or by Chardin, from whom Bonvin took the notion of reducing the size of the characters depicted. Was it not said, besides, that the atelier of Bonvin on the rue Saint Jacques, in which were exhibited in 1859 some rejected works by his friends Whistler, Ribot, and Fantin-Latour, was a "Flemish" atelier? This bears out his exclusion from official art and explains the comparison with Gérôme (q.v.)—flattering to Bonvin—made by Thoré in his description of the painting: "Workers are drinking, smoking, and *reading*. The main figures are about one foot high, but they are depicted as though they were of normal height. They could easily put into their shirt pockets all M. Gérôme's Areopagites, and the Phryne and the Aspasia ['Néo-Grec' entries by Gérôme in 1861] besides."

Weisberg mentions a small picture on a similar subject, *Three Men Seated at a Table* (45 × 37 cm), also dated 1869, in the Van Marle collection in Amsterdam.

G.L.

Musée des Beaux-Arts, Arras

---

## Eugène Boudin

### Honfleur 1824 — 1898 Deauville

*Boudin served as a cabin boy on a ship from Le Havre to the West Indies; later he became a stationer and framer in Le Havre. In his shop he exhibited works by artists living in the area, such as Troyon (q.v.) and Millet (q.v.), who encouraged him to paint. Thanks to a scholarship granted by the city council, he was able to go to Paris and work in 1850, but he would often return to Normandy in order to do studies of the sky, sea, and countryside (see no. VII-8). In 1858 he met young Claude Monet (q.v.), and persuaded him to paint outdoors, as he did; later he met Courbet (q.v.) and Baudelaire. Although he entered some local exhibitions, he did not exhibit in Paris until 1859; from 1864 on he regularly submitted landscapes of Normandy and Brittany to the Salon. In 1860 he settled in Honfleur and became acquainted with the group of landscape artists at the farm of Saint-Siméon, where he met Corot (q.v.). His art, despite the advice of Isabey and Troyon, was more influenced by the work of*

*Jongkind (q.v.). After 1871, as his reputation grew, each summer he made more frequent trips to Belgium, Holland, and Bordeaux; later he went to the Midi and even to Venice, but he never neglected the coast of Brittany and Normandy.*

*In 1874, continuing to exhibit at the Salon, he took part in the first exhibition by the Impressionists.*

G.L.

Bibliography:
Jean-Aubry, 1968; Schmit, 1973

Eugène Boudin

## VI-9
## "Pardon" of Sainte-Anne-la-Palud, Gulf of Douarnenez (Finistère)

1858
Signed and dated, lower right: Eugène Boudin 1858; on cart at left: E. BOUDIN—1858
Oil on canvas
78 × 155 cm

Provenance:
Purchased from the artist by the city of Le Havre, for 500 francs, around April 20, 1860 (*see* Jean-Aubry, 1968, pp. 24, 46), for the Musée des Beaux-Arts (inv. no. B.1)

Exhibitions:
1859, Paris, Salon, no. 330; 1964, Rennes, no. 4 (repro.); 1968–69, Paris, Petit Palais, no. 468 (repro.); 1977, Leningrad, no. 1; 1978, Peking, Shanghai, no. 4

VI-9

Bibliography:
Darcel, 1859, p. 9; Catalogue, Le Havre, Musée des Beaux-Arts, 1887, no. 117; Cahen, 1900, pp. 28–35; Jean-Aubry, 1922, p. 178; Roger-Marx, 1927, p. 34; Benjamin, 1937, p. 180; Arnould, 1954, p. 27; Jean-Aubry, 1968, pp. 23–27, repro. p. 26; Schmit, 1973, no. 185, repro. p. 59; Baudelaire, 1976, p. 665

Boudin traveled in Brittany during the summers of 1857 and 1858 and was attracted from the very first by the picturesque "beautiful costumes" that peasant women donned for marriages and pilgrimages, or "pardons," which were the occasions of picnics and outdoor festivities. The area of Douarnenez particularly appealed to him. He wrote to his brother on July 14, 1857: "I have just been to the famous pilgrimage of Sainte-Anne-la-Palud. I have discovered this area too late, for this is what I have been dreaming of; I shall return." One wonders if July 14 is indeed the date he actually wrote, for Boudin must have witnessed the "petit pardon" which, on the Sunday nearest the feast of Saint Anne (July 26) brings together local pilgrims—the coifs of Porzay, Quimper, and Pont-l'Abbé in evidence—rather than the "grand pardon" on the last Sunday in August, when Bretons from all regions come pouring in. Numerous tents and stalls were set up for the occasion near the Chapel of Sainte Anne la Palud, which is located five hundred meters from the shore in a bare, uninhabited spot; this was what Boudin chose to paint.

Using sketches made on the spot he composed a painting which he later sent to the Salon for his first exhibit there. However, this

project, in which the influence of his teacher Isabey was still evident, did not satisfy him completely, for he wrote in his notebook on January 25, 1859: "My picture (the Pardon) is full of shortcomings, I dream of doing better.... I must capture more purity, more glow, more finesse." Might he have felt hampered by his efforts to conform to the rules of official art, any infraction of which could mean being turned down by the jury?

The few critics who did notice the *"Pardon"* were already familiar with the works of the artist: Alfred Darcel, who wrote about Norman artists for the *Journal de Rouen,* thought that Boudin's contributions to the Le Havre exhibition the preceding year were more outstanding than this and in his lengthy description of the picture, he betrayed his disappointment and severity: "This cold Breton fair is nothing but a sketch in which blues and green are too prominent...." Baudelaire, who had visited Boudin's atelier in Honfleur and who was to be the first to speak enthusiastically about his talent, responded somewhat to this charge as he noted that the *"Pardon"* is a "good and careful picture" and suggested to landscapists that they use more imagination. "If they had been with me recently in the studio of M. Boudin... they would have seen several hundred pastel-studies, improvised in front of the sea and sky, and would then have understood what they do not yet seem to understand—the gulf which separates a study from a picture" (Baudelaire, 1965, p. 199). Baudelaire takes a quite justifiable stand apropos this somewhat unusual painting by Boudin on one of the major problems of the period: whether or not the artist—in this case Boudin and later the Impressionists—has the right to consider a work completed when it is neither smooth nor slick although the artist achieves, as he does here, a marvelous atmosphere.

G.L.

Musée des Beaux-Arts "André Malraux," Le Havre

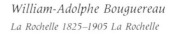

*William-Adolphe Bouguereau*
*La Rochelle 1825–1905 La Rochelle*

*Born in La Rochelle, a city to which he was fervently loyal throughout his life, Bouguereau showed at an early age an extraordinary ability to draw the figure. After having attended the Ecole des Beaux-Arts in Bordeaux for two years, he earned* enough money by painting portraits to send himself to Paris. There, he enrolled in the studio of François-Edouard Picot and, shortly thereafter, at the Ecole des Beaux-Arts. In 1848 he placed second (with Boulanger, q.v.) in competition for the Prix de Rome, as he did again in 1850. That fall he departed for Italy with Paul Baudry (q.v.), where he was particularly taken by the frescoes of the Renaissance. He copied all the Giottos at Assisi, and through a copy of Raphael's Galatea, which was sent back to Paris as his second year envoi, he began his permanent devotion to this artist.

The great success of the Triumph of the Martyr (Louvre) at the Salon of 1854 established Bouguereau's reputation. His work during the Second Empire was varied: secular decoration of private houses, murals in churches, and easel paintings, which brought continued success at the Salons (Théophile Gautier being a particularly strong admirer). His subject matter, however, remained almost entirely within a Classical mold. His one venture into contemporary history, Napoleon III Visiting the Flood Victims at Tarascon in 1856 (Hôtel de Ville, Tarascon), was not a success, and he never returned to this genre. His Scenes of the Life of Saint Louis and Saint Clotilde won for him the title of chevalier of the Legion of Honor in 1859; in 1865 he received the commission to decorate the newly completed concert hall in the Grand Théâtre in Bordeaux (see no. VII-9).

As Isaacson points out (1975), it was not until the 1870s that Bouguereau began to achieve his broad, international fame. And while he is often referred to as an artist of the Second Empire many of this best-known subjects—idealized peasant women and children—were not painted until the Third Republic. In 1876 he was made a member of the Institut de France, as well as an officer of the Legion of Honor. The previous year he began his long career as a teacher at the Ecole des Beaux-Arts, and he also taught at the Académie Julien.

J.R.

Bibliography:
Baschet (ed.), 1885; Vachon, 1900; 1974–75, New York, Cultural Center; Isaacson, 1975

William-Adolphe Bouguereau

## VI-10
## Spring

1858
Signed and dated, lower left: W. Bouguereau 1858
Oil on canvas
49.7 × 151.8 cm

VI-10

Provenance:
Hôtel Pereire, Paris, 1857; Shepherd Gallery, New York, 1975; Harry Glass, Old Westbury, New York, 1976

Exhibitions:
1857, Paris, Salon, no. 521 (?); 1974–75, New York, Cultural Center, no. 118

Bibliography:
Baschet (ed.), 1885; Vachon, 1900, p. 53

Shortly after his return from Rome in 1854, Bouguereau began a series of commissions for the decoration of private villas and hôtels, which were to establish his reputation in this genre, and stand as some of the most elegant and inventive work of his early career. The first was a set of Four Seasons, for the villa of his patroness, Mme Moulun, in the village of Angoulins, near La Rochelle. With his arrival in Paris, through the suggestion of his teacher, Picot, Bouguereau took up the more ambitious task of providing two ceilings and nine panels for the Hôtel Barthélemy on the rue de La Rochefoucauld, again using pastoral and allegorical subjects. The following year (1855) he began a second Barthélemy project, for the son, Etienne, on the rue de Verneuil, and in 1857, he was commissioned, along with Cabanel (q.v.), to decorate the Hôtel Pereire on the rue du Faubourg Saint Honoré.

At the Salon of 1857 Bouguereau showed five works simply noted as "decoration of a Salon," including Spring (no. 521), and it has been suggested that this may have been the picture shown here (1974–75, New York, Cultural Center, p. 118). However, the critic Saint-Victoire explicitly described these paintings as being in wax (which the present picture is not) and on a black background, thereby placing them more within the non-Pompeian mode

(see no. VI-12). Here, the frieze of figures is placed against a scored ground of gold leaf, a general reference to late-sixteenth- and early seventeenth-century French architectural decoration. However, Saint-Victoire's general praise does apply equally well here: "These groups at rest breathe the melancholy poetry exuded by Virgil's elegy. No modern nuance alters their faces, imbued, in grace as in sadness, with a silent solemnity... isolated from the outside world, wrapped in an atmosphere of the past, absorbed in the serene fixity of the symbol" (quoted by Vachon, 1900, p. 50).

Baschet (pls. 14–15) states that this work was done for the Hôtel Pereire, and the gold ground and general coloration do compare closely to other works with this same provenance: an oval Birth of Venus (collection of Lincoln Kirstein, New York) and two panels recently on the London market (Isaacson, 1975, p. 83, no. 2).

For the banker Emile Pereire, Bouguereau decorated two rooms, Cabanel doing a third, and the whole project was one of the most lavish private undertakings of the time. Gautier bluntly described the decoration as "the most sumptuous in the world" and continued in praise of Bouguereau's restraint and charm, "for no luxury can rival the luxury of intelligence, and one would not have the right to say to the celebrated banker, in going through his residence, 'You have made it lavish, being unable to make it beautiful'" (Vachon, 1900, p. 51).

J.R.

Collection Mr. and Mrs. Harry Glass, Old Westbury, New York

William-Adolphe Bouguereau

## VI-11
## All Souls' Day

1859
Signed and dated, lower right: W. BOVGVEREAV-
1859
Oil on canvas
147 × 120 cm

Provenance:
Purchased by the city of Bordeaux, 1860; Musée des
Beaux-Arts (inv. no. 6262)

Exhibitions:
1859, Paris, Salon, no. 335; 1860, Bordeaux;
1974–75, New York, Cultural Center, no. 4

Bibliography:
Baschet (ed.), 1885, p. 16; Vachon, 1900, pp. 95, 146

Bouguereau rarely took up a subject which had an implicit literary narrative, and among those that he did (for example, *The Thank Offering*, 1867; Philadelphia Museum of Art), some border on maudlin sentimentality. However, with this picture showing a mother and daughter placing a wreath on a grave (the husband/father?), he escapes the inherent pitfalls of the subject, and creates a picture which is gently restrained, seriously dignified, and remarkably beautiful, especially the rich purple-blue dresses against the silver light of the autumnal day.

When shown at the Salon of 1859, the work received high praise, particularly from Gautier and Emile Cantrel, who celebrated its effective

VI-11

treatment of emotion in a contemporary event. Yet it was Paul de Saint-Victor who realized best that the success of the work depended just on its idealized, uncontemporary quality: "Under our mourning clothes, the funeral scene remains as Athenian as an elegy of Bion.... In the harmony of its lines, expertness of its poses, the pathetic group would be worthy of weeping on the tomb of a young Greek killed at Marathon or Salamis" (quoted by Vachon, 1900, p. 95). This is excessive praise, perhaps from Saint-Victor's desire to intensify romantically the pathos of the scene, but it is insightful; and while a specific source for the two kneeling figures has yet to be discovered, one imagines that they may have their origins in a Roman Niobe sarcophagus, albeit seen through the filter of Raphael, such as the mourning woman on the right in his Borghese *Entombment*.

J.R.

Musée des Beaux-Arts, Bordeaux

---

### Gustave-Clarence-Rodolphe Boulanger
*Paris 1824–1888 Paris*

*Boulanger, of Creole ancestry, was orphaned at fourteen. He was brought up by his uncle A.M. Desbrosses, who supported his interest in art by sending him for instruction to the history painter Pierre-Jules Jollivet. Continuing to live with Jollivet, Boulanger moved after 1840 to the atelier of Paul Delaroche. There he met the group of young artists whose art in the 1840s and 1850s would be called "Néo-Grec," a style characterized by careful archaeological research, tight linear control, and a preference for antique genre rather than heroic subject matter. Gérôme's* Cock Fight, *shown at the Salon of 1847, is the model of this style, which Boulanger as well as the artists Hamon (q.v.) and Picou favored.*

*Boulanger made his first trip to Algeria in 1845 and his love for North Africa and the Near East was parallel to that of his good friend, Gérôme (q.v.). (The two visited this area together in 1872.) Boulanger entered the Ecole des Beaux-Arts in 1846 and won a Prix de Rome in 1849, and his ensuing studies in Italy (until 1856) concentrated on the ruins of Pompeii and the life, customs, and costumes of ancient Rome. His Salon entry of 1869,* The Via dei Sepolcri at Pompeii *and of 1874,* The Via Appia in the Time of Augustus, *are full of authentic detail. "Antiquity captured in daily life" wrote Jules Claretie (1876, p. 351), although it has been suggested recently that his figures also reveal some of the movements and mood of bourgeois Parisians of his own day (1975, New York, Shepherd Gallery, p. 248).*

*Boulanger received commissions for large-scale decorations for the ceiling of a Paris café, a Monte Carlo theater, and the* mairie *of the XIIIth arrondissement in Paris. He also painted for Labrouste in the Foyer of the Dance at the Paris Opéra (see no. I-10) four large panels representing the dances of warriors, mythological figures, lovers, and nymphs.*

N.D.

Bibliography:
Lavoix, 1886; Claretie, 1876, passim; *Chronique des Arts*, 1888, p. 248; Stranahan, 1902, pp. 320–21; Thieme and Becker, 1907–50, vol. IV, p. 446; 1975, New York, Shepherd Gallery, pp. 247–52

Gustave-Clarence-Rodolphe Boulanger

## VI-12
## Rehearsal of "The Flute Player" in the Atrium of the House of H.I.H. the Prince Napoleon

1861
Signed and dated, lower left: Gustave Boulanger MDCCCLXI
Oil on canvas
83 × 130 cm

Provenance:
Princess Mathilde; bequest to the Musée National du Château, Versailles, 1904 (inv. no. MV 5614)

Exhibitions:
1922, Paris, Musée des Arts Décoratifs, p. 27; 1973, Paris, Petit Palais, no. 350; 1973, Paris, Musée des Arts Décoratifs (repro.); 1976–77, Paris, Archives Nationales, p. 134, no. 636

Bibliography:
Gautier, 1861; Stranahan, 1902, pp. 320–21

*See* Colorplate

Boulanger's interest in Pompeian wall painting is put to good use in this illustration of the Pompeian atrium in Prince Napoleon's house, the "Maison Pompéienne" (no. I-22) on the avenue Montaigne in Paris. The composition is based on the delicate Pompeian "Second Style" decorations, in which panels of two-dimensional architectural fantasy are interspersed with panels of three-dimensional figures interacting in space. The subject, most appropriately, is a play called *The Flute Player*, an improvisation based on a painting in The House of the Tragic Poet in Pompeii. The roles were not played by models dressed in Classical attire, however, but by friends of the artist and the Prince: the critic Théophile Gautier, the dramatist Emile Augier, the Comédie Française

VI-12

actor Got, and the actresses Madeleine Brohan and Marie Favart. The Prince himself also takes part in the production. Boulanger is said to have happened on this scene when he visited the Prince, and it is said that he also reproduced a similar painting, *The Wife of Diomedes,* derived from the same Pompeian source. He afterward copied these two paintings directly onto the walls of the Prince's house.

The painting provides both an account of the manners of the aristocracy of the Second Empire, in which intellectuals, artists, and actors joined in the social life of the court, and an indication of the serious interest in the Classical world in the 1860s, which had not died with David and Neoclassicism. It serves also as a reminder that the theater, both professional and amateur, was an important aspect of the life of the period. "Elegant modern fantasy on an ancient theme. The composition is up to the level of the setting, that is to say, an ingenious, successful excursion into the realm of the past," wrote A. de la Fizelière in his criticism of the work at the Salon of 1861. He, like modern viewers and perhaps like the participants themselves, sensed the artificiality of this amalgam of past and present, real and unreal, as illustrated by the illusionistic art of painting.

N.D.

Musée National du Château, Versailles

---

## Jules Breton

*Courrières (Pas-de-Calais) 1827–1906 Paris*

*Jules Breton's first teacher was Félix de Vigne, whose daughter he was to marry. Subsequently he studied under Baron Wappers in Antwerp, then under Michel-Martin Drolling at the Ecole des Beaux-Arts in Paris, which he entered on October 6, 1847. He first exhibited at the Salon of 1849, and the works he submitted under the Second Republic (now destroyed) had elements of the realism one finds in the large paintings of Antigna or Courbet (q.v.).*

*The peasant subjects that were responsible for Breton's success appeared in 1853. In 1855 he won a third-class medal; in 1857 a second-class medal; in 1859 a first-class medal, in 1861 a rappel; and finally, a first-class medal at the Exposition Universelle in 1867. He was named chevalier of the Legion of Honor in 1861 and officer in 1867. These awards predicted the brilliant course of his career and his entrance into the Institut de France in 1886.*

*Breton emerged as the official painter of life in the fields and took care to give Classical nobility to his models; for example, one critic saw "beautiful rustic caryatids" in the* Return of the Gleaners *in the Salon of 1859. Although most of his themes were drawn from his native village of Courrières, in the Artois, and present an attitude which may seem similar to that of Courbet, Breton was not included in the Realist movement by his contemporaries; indeed, he was advised by the press of his time not to become part of the movement. By captivating the urban*

public of his day, he paved the way for an entire generation of naturalistic artists. Breton was the author of several works of art criticism and reminiscences, La Vie d'un artiste (1890), Un Peintre paysan (1896), Nos Peintres du siècle (1899), as well as the poems Les Champs et la mer (1875), of which a number are dedicated to Millet (q.v.).

G.L.

Bibliography:
Vachon, 1899; 1976–77, Arras

Jules Breton

## VI-13
## Monday

1858
Signed and dated, lower right: Jules Breton Courrières 1858
Oil on canvas
76 × 111.5 cm

Provenance:
Gambart coll., Courrières (Pas-de-Calais), 1859; John Hoey; sale, New York, American Art Galleries, 1893(?); Charles Parsons, Saint Louis, 1904; gift with life interest to Charles P. Pettus (died 1923), to Washington University, Saint Louis (inv. no. WU 2101)

Exhibitions:
1859, Paris, Salon, no. 411; 1914, Saint Louis, no. 10 (repro.) (coll. of Charles P. Pettus?); 1970, Saint Louis

Bibliography:
Astruc, 1859, pp. 229–30; Auvray, 1859, p. 41; du Camp, 1859, pp. 37–38; Dumesnil, 1859, pp. 33–34; Lépinois, 1859, pp. 149–50; Breton, 1890, p. 233; Breton, 1891, p. 241; Marcel, 1905, p. 217

Jules Breton was called "the Balzac of the commune of Courrières" (Lépinois). The four paintings (including the *Return of the Gleaners,* Arras museum) that he submitted to the Salon of 1859, which on the whole were well received after the artist's success in 1857, show various aspects of the life of this village of the Pas-de-Calais. *Monday,* however, aroused divided opinions, and was to remain—perhaps because of this reception—a most unusual type of composition in Breton's *oeuvre.* Auvray and du Camp greeted him as a new genre painter but warned him against the danger of Realism. "Let M. Breton look at M. Courbet in order to despise the realism to which he is coming closer than he thinks; let him remain with the real, that would be better" (du Camp). Dumesnil, who found a tavern interior "remarkable for its air of truth," also noted in almost identical terms that "Breton verges on vulgar realism." Paul Mantz was more severe: "M. Breton does not have the temperament of Brouwer and Ostade, and his rather superficial painting here shows us nothing but flat village caricatures."

VI-13

But those who could not accuse him of placing himself under the banner of the new school reproached him on the contrary for being too timid. Astruc deplored the fact that he took "M. Biard as his leader and model" rather than Courbet, and while putting all his hopes on the artist's talent, noted in his long commentary: "It is an interior scene... moral and amusing. It has the proper expression. But here the leanness of the paint is too obvious.... What was needed was an orgy of paint," as in Rubens *(The Flemish Kermesse)* or Rembrandt *(The Slaughtered Ox)*. It is interesting to conclude with another observation by Astruc, for whom Breton was "an active and studious personality, very fond of naturalism"—thus making this painting one of the first to be called by the name of the style that was to have such great importance at the end of the nineteenth century.

G.L.

Washington University Gallery of Art, Saint Louis

Jules Breton

## VI-14
## The Rest

1864
Signed and dated, lower right: Jules Breton

Courrières juillet 1864
Oil on canvas
74.5 × 60 cm

Provenance:
Acquired by the Musée des Beaux-Arts, Arras, 1864

Exhibitions:
1962, Le Touquet; 1976, Chartres; 1976–77, Arras, no. 20

VI-14

Bibliography:
Catalogues, Arras, Musée des Beaux-Arts, 1864, no. 8, 1867, no. 8, 1880, no. 16; *Bulletin de l'Union Artistique du Pas-de-Calais,* 1904 (repro.); Catalogue, Arras, Musée des Beaux-Arts, 1907, no. 35

This painting, an example of a rare excellence in Breton's work, was not presented at the Paris Salon, but instead immediately entered the museum of the capital of the Pas-de-Calais, the department in which Courrières is located—a good illustration of how a provincial city took interest in local painters who also had careers in Paris. This painting is a variation on the theme of peasant life in Courrières, and may be compared with the work entitled *Evening* (1860, Salon of 1861; acquired by the State for the Musée du Luxembourg, now in the *mairie* of Cuisery), in which the principal figure stands out against a background of fields where several figures appear. The costume—shirt with rolled-up sleeves, the wide skirt and apron—is the same and their feet are bare. This last detail can also be found in the *Return of the Gleaners* (Arras museum). This faithfulness to reality was opposed to the method of a Puvis de Chavannes (q.v.), who would represent in his Amiens murals figures wearing a costume of no specific period, in contemplative poses, but the format and the composition of this painting are similar to those of a number of Millet's paintings, such as *Woman Carding Wool,* from the Salon of 1863 (1975–76, Paris, Grand Palais, no. 162).

G.L.

Musée des Beaux-Arts, Arras

---

### John-Lewis Brown
*Bordeaux 1829–1890 Paris*

*A pupil of Camille Roqueplan and Belloc, Brown specialized in genre painting. He first exhibited at the non-juried Salon of 1848, and then, beginning with the Salon of 1859, he regularly showed paintings, watercolors, and etchings with animal subjects— dogs and hunting scenes—and military scenes. In 1862, in "L'Eau-forte est à la mode," Baudelaire hailed him as "a successor, more daring and refined, of Alfred Dedreux [q.v.], and perhaps a rival of Eugène Lami [q.v.]" (Baudelaire, 1976, p. 736). He won medals in 1865, 1866, and 1867, and in 1870 was awarded the Legion of Honor. From 1865 on, numerous purchases of his work were made by the civil list of Napoleon III and the Administration of Fine Arts, and at times both were in competition with each other for his work, as was the case in 1866. His* Episode from the Seven Years War *from the Salon of 1868 was sent to the museum of Bar-le-Duc,* and his submission to the Salon of 1869, to the museum of his native city, Bordeaux, which shows the usual attitude on the part of the Administration with regard to first purchases made from an artist and foreshadows his success with the Emperor as well as with a vast private clientele. Thus in 1869, in addition to the picture destined for the Bordeaux museum, he sent to Munich his Battle Horses of H. M. Napoleon III, owned by General Fleury.

G.L.

Bibliography:
Hédiard, 1899

John-Lewis Brown

## VI-15
## Battle of June 17, 1815, Seven O'Clock in the Evening

1869
Signed and dated, lower left: JOHN LEWIS BROWN 1869
Oil on canvas
124 × 158 cm

Provenance:
Purchased by the State (Administration of Fine Arts)

for 3,000 francs by decree of May 28, 1869 (Arch. nat. F$^{21}$ 122); deposited in the Musée des Beaux-Arts, Bordeaux, 1872 (inv. no. 6267; formerly 703)

Exhibitions:
1869, Paris, Salon, no. 342; 1869, Munich, no. 1297; 1953, Bordeaux, no. 20; 1971, Bordeaux, no. 172; 1971–72, Nagoya, etc., no. 40

Bibliography:
Guédy, n.d., p. 102, no. 397; Catalogues, Bordeaux, Musée des Beaux-Arts, 1875, no. 601, 1877, no. 601, 1879, no. 601, 1881, no. 398, 1894, no. 438; Galibert, 1906, pl. 44; Catalogue, Bordeaux, Musée des Beaux-Arts, 1910, no. 349, repro. p. 45; Saunier, 1925, p. 129; Manciet, 1931, p. 13, repro. p. 50; Catalogue, Bordeaux, Musée des Beaux-Arts, 1933, no. 204; Vergnet-Ruiz and Laclotte, 1962, p. 228

In the Salon catalogue an explanatory text taken from Adolphe Thiers's Waterloo described the subject: "Napoleon, conqueror of the Prussians at Ligny, afraid they would join ranks with the English above Brussels, deployed General Milhaud's cuirassiers in order to be sure of the English position at Mont-Saint-Jean. This movement exposed 50 pieces of artillery, and decided the next day's attack." Thus this is an episode preceding the decisive day of the defeat of Waterloo, on June 18, 1815. True to historical fact—and it is known what role bad weather played in the outcome of the battle—the artist showed his characters under a heavily clouded sky. It is tempting to see in such

a theme, done in 1869, a precursor of contemporary events and the imminent fall of the Second Empire. But it should be noted that already in 1864, Hippolyte Bellangé obtained a state purchase of the Battle of Waterloo for the Musée Napoléon in Amiens (Arch. nat. F$^{21}$ 117) and that during those same years he did additional pictures dealing with the defeat of Napoleon. In the Salon of 1865, Bellangé's Cuirassiers at Waterloo was mentioned by the critic Léon Lagrange for its dramatic interest as "the only battle picture in the Salon," with other painters depicting only "military episodes" (Lagrange, 1865, p. 165). In treating the episode of Waterloo in the twentieth volume of his Histoire du Consulat et de l'Empire published in 1862— reissued often since the Second Empire— Thiers removed the event beyond partisan quarrels and into the realm of history. Nevertheless, as if to guard against any unfavorable political interpretation of his painting, Brown was careful not to use the word Waterloo in his title and to begin the commentary with the words "Napoleon, conqueror...."

G.L.

Musée des Beaux-Arts, Bordeaux

VI-15

## Alexandre Cabanel
*Montpellier 1823–1889 Paris*

*Alexandre Cabanel received in his lifetime all the official honors of a favorite of the imperial court, a popular teacher, and an expert craftsman. Born in 1823 he entered the Ecole des Beaux-Arts in 1840 as a student of François-Edouard Picot, and received the Prix de Rome in 1845 for his Christ in the Praetorium. He was awarded the cross of the Legion of Honor in 1855, made an officer in 1864, and a commander in 1878. He was appointed a member of the Institut de France in 1863, filling the chair previously occupied by David, Lebarbier, and Horace Vernet, and that same year he was given a professorship at the reformed Ecole des Beaux-Arts along with Gérôme (q.v.) and Pils. In additon to many lesser medals, Cabanel was awarded the Grand Medal of Honor in 1865, 1867, and 1878. In 1886, 112 artists in the Salon listed him as their teacher. He served on the Salon jury seventeen times between 1868 and 1888.*

*Cabanel was more than an artist, he was an institution. In 1889 George Lafenestre wrote a memorial article on this artist who had died earlier that year. Cabanel's atelier, he wrote, "is not at all, however, a salon; it is rather a laboratory. Every-*

thing there seems prepared for regular, peaceful, pleasant labor. The painter, in a costume of black velvet, well-proportioned and sturdy in his bulk, standing with his head straight, his posture erect, brushes the canvas with his white hand with a confident tranquillity that fits in perfectly with the calm order of the surroundings" (Lafenestre, 1889, pp. 265–66). (See also no. VII-10.)

N.D./J.R.

Bibliography:
Blanc, 1876, pp. 427–28; Meynell, 1886, pp. 271–76; Stranahan, 1888, pp. 398–401; Lafenestre, 1889, pp. 265–80; 1975, Montpellier

Alexandre Cabanel

## VI-16
## Nymph Abducted by a Faun

1860
Signed, lower right: ALEX. CABANEL 1860
Oil on canvas
245 × 142 cm

Provenance:
Purchased by Napoleon III; assigned to the Musée du Luxembourg by decree, 1879; transferred to the Musée des Beaux-Arts, Lille, 1886 (inv. no. 525)

Exhibitions:
1861, Paris, Salon, no. 495; 1867, Exposition Universelle, no. 120

Bibliography:
Delaborde, 1861, p. 879; Blanc, 1876, p. 428; Bellier and Auvray, 1882–87, vol. I, p. 184; Lafenestre, 1889, p. 275

*Nymph Abducted by a Faun* was exhibited at the Salon of 1861 along with *Mary Magdalene, A Florentine Poet,* and three portraits. It was purchased by the Emperor, who later bought for his collection Cabanel's famous *Birth of Venus,* the *cause célèbre* in the Salon of 1863. Imperial tastes, often more circumspect, strayed willingly in the case of these two luscious and suggestive paintings, and Napoleon III reexhibited his *Nymph Abducted by a Faun* at the Exposition Universelle of 1867.

Charles Blanc, often critical of Cabanel's art, wrote of this painting: "If David saw the *Nymph Abducted by a Faun,* he would no doubt say: 'There's still one of them who is French.' These mythological beings, whose forms moreover are choice and whose colors are delicate, have not been brought up in the woods of fable; they come from the city, they are Parisian. In the manner of drawing they belong to the French school of the last century; in her blond and pink coloring, pale and faint, the nymph has some affinity with those of Natoire" (Blanc, 1876, p. 427). To Blanc's comparisons with

VI-16

eighteenth-century painting can also be added Cabanel's probable awareness of the sculptural treatments of this theme. While the subject originated in antiquity (frequently found on Bacchantic sarcophagi), Cabanel's figures relate most directly to Clodion's playfully sensuous nymphs of the late eighteenth century, a genre of sculpture which was undergoing a revival just at this time both through new casts after Clodion's *Nymphs and Satyrs* and through free adaptations of these by Carrier-Belleuse (q.v.) and Clésinger (*see* no. V-15). Within Cabanel's erotic subjects there is consistently a reflection of eighteenth-century works; however, even at his most directly literal (such as the clear reference to Boucher in the *Birth of Venus*), the freer handling of paint of the Rococo period never dissuaded him from his firm and disciplined linearism, as loaded as his brush might have been.

N.D./J.R.

Musée des Beaux-Arts, Lille

Alexandre Cabanel

# VI-17
# Napoleon III

1865
Signed, lower left: Alex Cabanel; lower right: Ale Cabanel
Oil on panel
42 × 32 cm

Provenance:
W.T. Walters, by 1893; Walters Art Gallery (inv. no. 37.146)

Bibliography:
*Walters Collection*, 1893, no. 161

VI-17

This small and highly finished likeness is a replica of Cabanel's large portrait of Napoleon III, painted in 1865 for the apartments of the Empress in the Tuileries. Charles Blanc wrote: "In the portrait of the Emperor, the head is little developed, softly outlined. The subject seems to have put on his Sunday best, that look produced by cosmetics, the finish of cold cream. Edges are obliterated, the relief smoothed, blemishes hidden and removed so that the candor of nature is effaced by the flattery of painting" (Blanc, 1876, p. 431). Blanc's strong criticism of the lackluster, characterless quality of the portrait was not shared by the imperial family, for whom the likeness was infinitely preferable to the first commission for the Empress's apartments, given to Hippolyte Flandrin (no. VI-55). Claretie reported that the

Princess Mathilde said of that work: "Sire, you appear to be plotting the death of your son" (Claretie, 1876, pp. 235–36), a comment that precipitated the removal of Flandrin's painting from its original location to the Musée du Luxembourg, and thence to the Tribunal de Commerce, and the placement of Cabanel's portrait in the Tuileries. The gentle, noncommittal character of the Emperor, which Claretie said served to "*make him aristocratic* to the point of anemia" (Claretie, 1876, p. 35), his nonmilitary attire, his domination of the space without theatrical pose and gesture were qualities of the Cabanel portrait that pleased the imperial taste. Meynell explained: "In this system of the Second Empire, the expression of

a portrait was an important matter; to look happy was a point of some moment. To M. Cabanel thereupon was entrusted the production of a portrait which should be more expressive of the stability, suavity, and prosperity of the Empire" (Meynell, 1886, p. 274).

The original destination of this small replica is not known, but its existence is not surprising considering the importance the court placed on Cabanel's portrait for the Empress. It is interesting to see this smaller Baltimore version (lacking the large version whose location is presently unknown) opposed, as it was in the Second Empire, to its rival by Flandrin.

N.D./J.R.

The Walters Art Gallery, Baltimore

Alexandre Cabanel

# VI-18
# The Governess

c. 1865–70
Signed, lower left: A. Cabanel
Oil on canvas
114.3 × 99 cm

Provenance:
Frank S. Schwarz and Son, Philadelphia; purchased by the Philadelphia Museum of Art, 1977 (inv. no. 1977-80-1)

Bibliography:
*Philadelphia Museum of Art Bulletin*, vol. LXXIII, no. 319, December 1977, repro. p. 11

This picture, shown here for the first time, is not recorded in Cabanel's *œuvre*. The attribution to Cabanel is supported by stylistic comparison: the sturdily constructed women and the small, soulful boy rest easily within his style. The criticism of Cabanel's strong sensitive female portraits may aptly be applied here. Both women are "at once proud and charming," both have "that shape of a provocative majesty" that Claretie praised in the portrait of Mme la comtesse de M. A. in the Salon of 1873 (Claretie, 1876, p. 114). The tentative date is based primarily on costume, since Cabanel's mature work has a consistency that makes precise dating on the basis of style difficult.

The present title, which comes from the English label on the frame, must be accepted until documentation on the painting is uncovered because the woman is dressed in a costume often worn by governesses, although it was also worn by women in mourning. There is a record of a painting by Cabanel called *The Widow of the Choirmaster* (Bellier and Auvray, 1882–87, vol. II, p. 184) and another by Hébert (q.v.) simply called *A Widow* which suggest that the subject of bereaved women, silent, competent, brave in their grief, was a topic of some interest to the Second Empire, a period in which concern for women was a recognizable theme in art and literature, as it was in England at that time.

The composition of this painting is not inconsistent with other interiors of the 1860s. Figures are brought up close to the picture plane, which necessitated the cropping of furniture and a picture on the wall. The viewer shares the intimacy by his own position in space, contrived by the artist to be close to the scene depicted. One finds similar experimentation within the works of Tissot (q.v.), Whistler, and Carolus-Duran (q.v.). Degas, in his famous portrait of his Italian relations, the Bellelli family, moved in the same direction as did Cabanel

in *The Governess*, albeit with far more daring. Cabanel's work stands structurally between academic formalism and modern developments in composition, yet, spiritually, it belongs to the Second Empire.

N.D./J.R.

Philadelphia Museum of Art, Purchased, The Edward and Althea Budd Fund

---

## Carolus-Duran (Charles Durand)
*Lille 1837–1917 Paris*

*Durand, the son of an innkeeper of modest means, first attended the Ecole Municipale de Dessin in Lille. As soon as he had arrived in Paris in 1855, he adopted the pseudonym Carolus-Duran. Through the art critic Zacharie Astruc, whom he had known in Lille, he made the acquaintance of Courbet (q.v.), Manet (q.v.), and other artists of the Realist circle. He perfected his technique by copying at the Louvre and enrolling at the Académie Suisse. He began exhibiting at the Salon in 1859, was awarded the* Prix Wicar in Lille in 1861, and spent four years in Italy at the expense of his native city.

*In Rome he made friends with Jean-Jacques Henner (q.v.) and Falguière (q.v.), pensionnaires at the Villa Medici. He was awarded a medal for his large painting* The Assassination, *which he had brought back from Italy for the Salon of 1866 (he received two additional medals in 1869 and 1870); the painting was purchased by the State for the Lille museum. He then traveled in Spain, where his admiration for Velázquez was confirmed. (His copy of a dwarf by Velázquez is now in the Ministère des Finances in Paris.) He soon achieved fame as a portraitist and exhibited in the Salon of 1869 a portrait of his wife entitled* Lady with a Glove *(Louvre).*

*During the Third Republic his brilliant career as a portraitist, decorative artist, and teacher continued. In 1890 he became one of the founders of the Société Nationale des Beaux-Arts, and in 1899 its president. He was elected to the Académie des Beaux-Arts in 1904 and from that year until 1913 he was director of the Académie de France à Rome.*

G.L.

Bibliography:
Alexandre, 1903; le Gal, 1974

VI-18

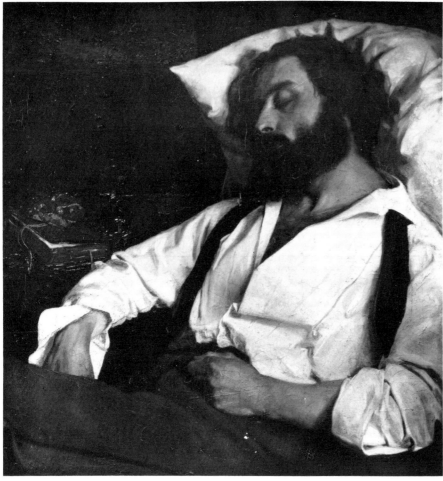

VI-19

of the painter, whom he had met through his friendship with Zacharie Astruc.

Carolus-Duran developed the theme of the sleeping man in a painting entitled *The Convalescent*, more precisely known as *The Wounded Man*, which was hung in the Luxembourg in 1919 (Catalogue, Paris, Luxembourg, 1924, repro. p. 5) and in 1933 transferred to Grenoble.

G.L.

Musée des Beaux-Arts, Lille

Jean-Baptiste Carpeaux

## VI-20
## A Ball at the Tuileries

1867
Signed and dated, lower right: B<sup>te</sup> Carp...
X 1867
Oil on canvas
65.2 × 54.5 cm

Provenance:
Carpeaux sale, 1906, no. 88; purchased by the Louvre (inv. no. RF 1599)

Exhibitions:
1894, Paris, Ecole des Beaux-Arts, no. 9; 1896, Brussels, no. 2; 1922, Paris, Musée des Arts Décoratifs, no. 35; 1927, Valenciennes, no. 552; 1928, Compiègne, no. 61; 1928, Copenhagen, Stockholm, Oslo, no. 3; 1935, Paris, Orangerie, no. 142; 1955–56, Paris, Petit Palais, no. 142; 1969, Paris, Bibliothèque Nationale, no. 299; 1973, Brive, no. 68; 1974, Paris, Grand Palais, no. 10; 1975, Paris, Grand Palais, no. 192

Bibliography:
Carpeaux, 1899, p. 5; Riotor, 1906, p. 100; Jamot, 1908, pp. 191–92; Leprieur, 1909, p. 260; Vitry, 1912, *Carpeaux*, pp. 59–60; Margueritte, 1914, pp. xii, 70–71; Henriot, 1922, p. 100; Brière, 1924, no. 873; Regamey, 1925, p. 35; L. Clément-Carpeaux, in 1927, Valenciennes, pp. 80–81; Lecomte, 1928, p. 171; *Le Figaro Artistique*, April 25, 1929; Jamot, 1929, vol. III, p. 128; Clément-Carpeaux, 1934–35, vol. I, pp. 206–7; Clément-Carpeaux, 1937, p. 2, no. 219; Besson, 1934, vol. II, p. 43; Cartier, 1956, p. 149; Sterling and Adhémar, 1958–61, vol. I, no. 172; Catalogue, Paris, Louvre, Paintings, 1972, vol. I, p. 52

Carolus-Duran (Charles Durand)

## VI-19
## Sleeping Man

1861
Signed and dated, lower right: Carolus Duran 1861
Oil on canvas
87 × 85 cm

Provenance:
Gift of the artist to the Musée des Beaux Arts, Lille, 1862 (inv. no. 584)

Exhibitions:
1861, Paris, Salon, no. 972; 1900, Paris, Exposition Universelle Centennale, no. 78

Bibliography:
Lagrange, 1861, p. 52; Riat, 1906, p. 197; de Forges, 1973, pp. 16–17, no. 17

The *Sleeping Man* was considered a large study and received little critical notice in the Salon of 1861. Léon Lagrange rightly ranked it among those realistic works which, he said, "are noteworthy almost entirely because of the energetic way in which they were executed." As Riat suggested in 1906, this particular painting is probably an echo of Courbet's *Wounded Man* (Louvre), which Carolus-Duran may have seen either at the time of his arrival in Paris in 1855 at Courbet's private showing, in the "Pavilion of Realism," or later in the atelier

According to tradition, *A Ball at the Tuileries* represents the Empress Eugénie making her entrance on the arm of Czar Alexander in 1867. But the charm of Carpeaux's painting has little to do with the identity of the subjects; rather it stems from his ability to recreate the atmosphere of the fete "imperial": bright silhouettes, shimmering and undulating colors. The painting seems a snapshot from his memory. Carpeaux painted it for his own pleasure, for he had been overwhelmed by these unique moments. Paul Jamot accurately described his technique: "He loves texture and handles it beautifully, using his intuition; he throws the paint onto the canvas as he would pieces of clay onto a sculpture; he speckles, splashes, and works with wide brushstrokes."

O.S.

Musée du Louvre, Paris

## Charles Chaplin
*Les Andelys 1825–1891 Paris*

*To the degree that Chaplin is remembered in this century (in* Claudine, *Colette puts a picture by him in her heroine's wonderfully old-fashioned house), it is for his vaporously erotic, thinly veiled women (usually half length), very much in the style of Greuze and very much to the taste of the Third Republic and the Edwardian period. However, while paintings of this style certainly are in the majority in his œuvre, his work has considerable variety and, particularly from the period of the Second Empire, a charmingly modest distinction.*

*Born of an English father and French mother (he would not become a naturalized French citizen until 1886), he had a temperament that seems to have followed his father's: "Chaplin was tall and blond, of a cool and phlegmatic manner which had a certain allure and immediately recalled his English origin" (quoted in Bénézit, 1911–24, vol. II, p. 432). In 1841 he entered the Ecole des Beaux-Arts and studied also at the studio of Michel-Martin Drolling. Entering the Salon in 1845, he continued to exhibit there regularly throughout his life, winning a third-class medal in 1851, a second-class in 1852, as well as a Medal of Distinction (unclassified after 1863) in 1865. That same year he was made a chevalier of the Legion of Honor and became an officer in 1881. His first exhibited works were portraits and landscapes (often watercolors); he also showed religious subjects,* The Vision of Ezekiel *of 1869 having been particularly praised. In 1861 he was in considerable demand as a decorative painter, and was given commissions to execute the ceiling and overdoors of the Salon des Fleurs in the Tuileries and a section of the Salon de l'Hemicycle in the Elysée palace. He also provided eight panels and four over-doors painted on glass for the Empress's dressing room in the Tuileries (1864). However, beginning in the 1850s, his reputation became firmly established through his genre subjects, usually of children or young women, in an eighteenth-century manner. In these he refers —both in the subjects and the manner of painting—to Chardin and Lepecie or, depending on the age of the girls, Boucher and Greuze. Silvery and blond, rose and peach often with diffused lightly brushed-in backgrounds, these paintings also recall Gainsborough. He was also adept at pastels and his prints (landscapes and genre) were widely collected.*

J.R.

Bibliography:
Delaborde, 1861, vol. XXXII, p. 882; Claretie, 1876; Montrosier, 1881–84; vol. I, pp. 9–11; H.C., *Revue Encyclopedique,* vol. I, 1891, pp. 342–3; Stranahan, 1902, p. 406; Bénézit, 1911-24, vol. II, pp. 432–3

VI-20

Charles Chaplin

## VI-21
## The Dream

1857
Signed, center right: Ch. Chaplin
Oil on canvas
106 × 92 cm

Provenance:
Acquired from the artist by the Musée des Beaux-Arts, Marseilles, 1860 (inv. no. B.A. 137)

Bibliography:
Catalogues, Marseilles, Musée des Beaux-Arts, 1876, no. 29, 1900, no. 75, repro. p. 45

In 1859, the year before this picture was acquired, Chaplin caused a sensation at the Salon; the jury rejected a nude *Aurora* on the stated grounds that it was too erotic. Nothing could be farther from this painting of a sleeping girl, which, while gently sensuous in the slumbering pose of the figure, has the lovely innocence and propriety of quite another aspect of Chaplin's temperament. While not drawn from any known source, the work recalls certain eighteenth-century variations on this subject, especially those of Pietro Rotari. The costume and the sense of intimacy might also derive from Chardin, although without the intentional sense of direct reference, as in such works as *Girls Playing Lotto* (Salon of 1865; Rouen) and *Soap Bubbles* (Salon of 1864; Louvre). The oval format, so frequent in Boucher, adds to the rather wistful nostalgia for

VI-21

Church of Saint Philippe du Roule (see no. VII-11) in place of the plan rejected by the Minister of Public Works, to decorate the Salle de Diana in the Louvre. He finished this vast project in 1855, having obtained the commission from the City of Paris the previous year to decorate the walls of the baptismal chapel of the Church of Saint Roch. To the Exposition Universelle of 1855, where he received a second-class medal, Chassériau submitted important paintings, including Defense of the Gauls by Vercingétorix and Susanna and the Elders. A few weeks after the

November 18, 1856 (Arch. nat. F²¹ 70): "It would be a real consolation for the family also to see admitted to the Louvre two great paintings that even in my brother's lifetime were esteemed by the most enlightened judges and by the public as well." The Defense of the Gauls was acquired the following year for the museum in Clermont-Ferrand, but it was only in 1881 that the Susanna finally entered the Louvre, thanks to the generosity of Alice Ozy, whith whom Chassériau had had a liaison as early as 1849. Numerous works—some not completed— that had been left in the artist's studio were given to French museums beginning in 1933 by Baron Arthur Chassériau. (See also no. VII-12.)

G.L.

Bibliography:
Sandoz, 1974

---

the eighteenth century, which Chaplin so often evoked. However, in choosing a model of the highest elegance and dressing her so finely, Chaplin was clearly painting a contemporary subject in, moreover, a contemporary setting.

It is perhaps this combination of elements—echoes of the ancient regime blended with very up-to-date elegance—that attracted the Empress to this artist. The Goncourts (1956, vol. I, p. 1298 [July 15, 1863]), in discussing paintings depicting contemporary women of the world, relate Gautier's anecdote of a visit to the Empress at Compiègne where she showed the critic her pictures by Chaplin, which hung in her bedroom, with the comment, "Je me mets dans mes meubles," taken to mean "I discover myself among my furnishings."

J.R.

Musée des Beaux-Arts, Marseilles

---

### Théodore Chassériau

*Santa Bárbara de Samaná (Santo Domingo)*
*1819–1856 Paris*

*Chassériau's family returned to France in 1822, and by 1831, Théodore, a very precocious artist, was in Ingres's studio. He exhibited for the first time at the Salon of 1836, obtaining a third-class medal. In 1837 he visited Lille, Belgium, and Holland; in 1840, Italy, where he met up with Ingres (whom he had begun to reproach for not being receptive to modern ideas and to change); then in 1846, Algeria. He was a portraitist and a painter of mythological creatures and Biblical and Oriental scenes. Very early in his career he obtained many commissions for churches and public buildings; the decoration for the staircase of the Cour des Comptes was completed in 1848 (destroyed in 1871; fragments are in the Louvre). Though he received a second-class medal in 1844, a number of his works were rejected by the Salon, particularly in 1840, 1845, and 1847. He became a chevalier of the Legion of Honor in 1849.*

*In 1852 Chassériau obtained from the Ministry of the Interior the commission to decorate the apse of the*

---

Théodore Chassériau

## VI-22
## Tepidarium: The Hall Where the Women of Pompeii Came to Rest and Dry Themselves on Emerging from the Bath

1853
Signed and dated, lower right: 1853 Théodore Chassériau
Oil on canvas
171 × 258 cm

Provenance:
Acquired by the State on May 30, 1853 (under the title "A Bath Hall at Pompeii") for 7,000 francs, paid in two installments: 4,000 francs on January 3, 1885, 3,000 francs on March 6, 1855 (Arch. nat. F²¹ 70); placed in the Musée du Luxembourg, March 1, 1856; transferred to the Louvre, November 12, 1874 (inv. no. RF 71)

Exhibitions:
1853, Paris, Salon, no. 228; 1855, Paris, Exposition Universelle, no. 2689; 1933, Paris, Orangerie, "Chassériau," no. 66

Bibliography:
De Calonne, 1853, p. 147; Delaborde, 1853, pp. 1147–49; Vignon, 1853, p. 75; About, 1855, pp. 187–89; Gautier, 1855–56, vol. I, pp. 249, 255–57; Perrier, 1855, "Beaux-Arts," p. 115; de la Rochenoire, 1855, p. 33; Vignon, 1855, p. 206; Catalogues, Paris, Luxembourg, 1863–74; Delaborde, 1866, pp. 91–92; Gautier, 1874, p. 369; Chevillard, 1893, p. 174, no. 79; Brière, 1924, no. 120; Bénédite, 1932, vol. II, pp. 419–32, pl. 43; Sterling and Adhémar, 1958–61, no. 322, pl. 84; Rosenblum, 1968, pp. 48, 172, fig. 67; Angrand, 1968, p. 321; Sandoz, 1970, p. 50; Catalogue, Paris, Louvre, Paintings, 1972, vol. I, p. 72; Sandoz, 1974, pp. 354–56, no. 218, pl. 174 (bibl.)

The inspiration for this painting came from one of the rooms of a Pompeian public bath that was unearthed in 1826 near the Porta di Stabia, cleared in 1828, and immediately published by Mazois in the third volume of *Les Ruines de Pompei* (begun in 1827). It shows the general arrangement of the decorated vault and some benches as well as the central brazier that served to heat the tepidarium (*see* Mazois, 1824–38, vol. III, pp. 75–76, pls. 47, 49). An overall study, preserved in the Cabinet des Dessins of the Louvre (RF 25858), which is closer to Mazois's plates than this final composition, shows clearly the source of the artist's documentation.

Théophile Gautier, who was immediately enthusiastic about the *Tepidarium*, called it "an ancient fresco stolen from the walls of Pompeii." He was followed by Claude Vignon, who considered the painting an "event": not only does one "rediscover a moment in the milieu of Pompeii... with such powerful realism," but the artist "seems for a moment to reconcile the two rival schools of drawing and color. Here indeed is a consummate colorist, a perfect colorist, simultaneously a realist and a harmonist, with whose drawing no critic can find fault." Everyone did not share this opinion, however. H. Delaborde declared: "Try as he may, M. Chassériau does not belong to the school of colorists," and he found him mistaken in looking to Delacroix as his model. He scolded him for his "customary disdain for perspective" and the disproportion of the figures. Alphonse de Calonne was cruelly ironic: "The scene takes place in an oven. In the center a green billiard table holds burning coals that, without fail, ought to consume the figures surrounding it, unless they are made of clay and have been placed there through the efforts of a terra-cotta maker."

The disagreements subsided somewhat in 1855. Charles Perrier noted with regard to the *Tepidarium* that "there the sun of Delacroix already produces a fatal effect," while Claude Vignon saluted "Chassériau's excellent work," and Gautier and Edmond About confirmed his

VI-22

success, admiring in Chassériau an art that consists in restoring life to a deserted but well-preserved ancient site: "This crowd is real; this variety of colors, poses, and costumes does not only satisfy the eyes, it leads one to think, and the mind profits thereby" (About). Well displayed in the French Gallery of the Exposition Universelle and then in the Luxembourg museum, the painting harkened back to compositions of Neoclassical inspiration while introducing figures whose languor evoked the exoticism of Delacroix's harem scenes and perhaps foreshadowed Ingres's *Turkish Bath*.

G.L.

Musée du Louvre, Paris

---

## Antoine Chintreuil

*Pont-de-Vaux (Ain) 1814–1873 Septeuil (Seine-et-Oise)*

*Chintreuil was counseled by Corot (q.v.), whose pupil he claimed to be; he also mentioned as his teachers Delaroche in 1845 and Bertin in 1847. A romantic dreamer, he must have had a hard time making a living from his painting.*

*He was repeatedly turned down by the Salon during the reign of Louis Philippe; none of his works were exhibited in 1843, 1844, 1845, or 1846, and it was only with the intervention of Béranger, who never stopped helping and encouraging him, that one of his pictures was finally shown in the Salon of 1847.*

*Beginning in 1843 the Administration of Fine Arts and that of museums commissioned five copies of religious paintings for village churches; the most interesting, done in 1845, was of the Luxembourg Adulteress by Signol (Arch. nat. F²¹ 21), which he modified by adding in the background a vast landscape (church of La Gacilly, Morbihan).*

*At this period he definitively turned to naturalistic landscapes. The abolishing of the Salon jury by the Second Republic, in 1848, gave him a chance to become known. Between 1848 and 1852 four paintings were acquired by the State, for modest sums (notably, museums of Niort, Montpellier), and then purchases were made in 1854 and 1856 (Salon of 1857) for the Bourg museum, in 1858 (Salon of 1859), for that of Mende. In 1863 he participated in the Salon des Refusés. Beginning in 1864 he sold one work each year to the Administration, for the museums in Mâcon, Saint-Malo, Rodez (the last two destroyed), Rochefort, Troyes, Amiens, and for the Musée du Luxembourg. He received a medal at the Salon of 1867 and the Legion of Honor in 1870.*

*His fame was chiefly posthumous; the fresh tonality of his landscapes of the region around Paris (valley of the Bièvre, then Septeuil, where he spent the last sixteen years of his life), which surprised his contemporaries by their luminosity, must have been*

VI-23

welcome at a time when the boldness of the Impressionists was found to be upsetting.

G.L.

Bibliography:
De la Fizelière, Champfleury, and Henriet, 1874; 1973, Bourg-en-Bresse

Antoine Chintreuil

# VI-23
# Expanse

1869
Signed, lower right: Chintreuil
Oil on canvas
102 × 202 cm

Provenance:
Acquired by the State on June 15, 1869 for 2,500 francs (Arch. nat. F²¹ 127); deposited at the Musée du Luxembourg after being shown in Munich, 1869 or 1870; transferred to the Louvre, December 18, 1883 (inv. no. RF 381)

Exhibitions:
1869, Paris, Salon, no. 483; 1869, Munich, no. 1575 (as *Plain*); 1873, Vienna, no. 133; 1878, Paris, Exposition Universelle Internationale, group I, class 1, no. 168; 1958, Munich, no. 15; 1973, Bourg-en-Bresse, no. 42, repro. p. 40; 1974, Paris, Grand Palais, no. 50 (repro.)

Bibliography:
Mantz, 1869, p. 508; Catalogues, Paris, Luxembourg, 1872–82; de la Fizelière, Champfleury, and Henriet, 1874, no. 362; de Montaiglon, 1875, p. 25; Montrosier, 1881, p. 194; Chennevières, 1883–89, vol. II, p. 35; Saunier, 1911, vol. I, repro. p. 109; Brière, 1924, no. 362; Focillon, 1928, p. 102; Catalogue, Paris, Jeu de Paume, 1947, no. 6; Sterling and Adhémar, 1958–61, vol. I, no. 336, pl. 90; Zola, 1959, pp. 119, 222; Decour, 1963, pp. 29, 35; Catalogue, Paris, Louvre, Paintings, 1972, vol. I, p. 78; Miquel, 1975, vol. III, p. 659

The announcement of the awarding of a medal to Chintreuil for his *Expanse* at the Vienna exhibition in 1873 was made only after the artist's death. His friends saw in this more of the bad luck that had dogged the artist throughout his life. The painting had been well reviewed in the Salon of 1869 and its purchase by the State for the Luxembourg was looked upon as putting the seal on his reputation. He was credited with a "keen sensitivity to light." Paul Mantz, however, thought the sky too serene to withstand a comparison with Rembrandt or a "Koning" who "liked those panoramas that enable one to take in at a single glance several acres of land." On the other hand, this new view of nature, precisely because it did not follow the accepted norm, filled another critic with enthusiasm: "The perspective is immense; it unfolds in full light, without a distracting foreground, in the glorious joy of the morning" (quoted by Miquel, 1975). It was only at a later date that the artist's originality was appreciated. Zola, in 1878, judging him to have "considerable" talent, wrote about this work: "One senses an artist who is striving to go beyond the leaders of the Naturalist school of landscape painting and who, although faithfully copying nature, attempted to catch her at a special moment difficult to transcribe."

The area depicted is in the neighborhood of La Tournelle-Septeuil, in the environs of Paris.

G.L.

Musée du Louvre, Paris

---

*Edouard Cibot*

*Paris 1799–1877 Paris*

*A student of Guérin and Picot, Cibot exhibited at the Salon from 1827 on. At first his paintings were primarily genre scenes and history paintings, several* of which were done for the historical museum founded by Louis Philippe at Versailles. His work The Loves of the Angels during the Floods *(Salon of 1834; Brest museum)* shows a poetic inspiration quite close to that of Ary Scheffer. After a trip to Italy in 1838–39, he concentrated more on religious subjects, working from 1844 to 1866 on decorations for the Church of Saint Leu in Paris. After 1850 he painted several landscapes of the outskirts of Paris. The Pit near Seine-Port (Seine-et-Marne), *purchased in 1864 for the Luxembourg, is now in the museum of Rochefort-sur-Mer.*

Cibot was awarded a second-class medal for history painting in 1836 and a first-class medal in 1843. During the Second Empire, he received rappels *in 1857 and 1863 as a landscape painter, and he was awarded the Legion of Honor in 1863.*

G.L.

Edouard Cibot

my landscapes purchased together, as a consolation at least, or even one of them should my request for both seem too outrageous?" In the end, the *View at Neauphle-le-Château (Seine-et-Oise)* did not become part of the state collections, and the modest fate of the *View at Bellevue,* purchased for a small sum and sent to Lisieux, indicates that this was very much a solicited purchase made only to help the artist. That same year a request from Jongkind (q.v.), sponsored by Eugène Isabey, was answered by a purchase, for the modest sum of 700 francs, of his large *View of Paris* sent to the museum in Angers.

It is said that Cibot became a landscape artist on the advice of Dauzats, and that he was successful at it during the Second Empire. He proved to be a sensitive observer, aware of the light and dark effects in the underbrush, at the same time wild and civilized, of this old park on the outskirts of Paris, which had become a place for leisurely walks. Even in his first works in the genre, he chose an altogether naturalistic approach, possibly with a view toward the aesthetic of 1848.

G.L.

Musée du Louvre, Paris

## VI-24
## View at Bellevue, near Meudon

1852
Signed and dated, lower right: E. Cibot 1852
Oil on canvas
64 × 88 cm

Provenance:
Purchased by the Direction Générale des Musées Impériaux for 800 francs, paid out of "a sum calculated on the total amount of admission fees plus the checking of walking sticks and umbrellas during the exhibition of 1853" by decree of September 22, 1853; registered in the inventory of the Louvre and sent immediately to the museum in Lisieux; returned to the Louvre, May 1970 (inv. no. MI. 38)

Exhibitions:
1853, Paris, Salon, no. 258; 1971, Vannes, Brest, no. 10 (repro.); 1973, Besançon, Bourg-en-Bresse, Aix-les-Bains, no. 29 (repro.)

Bibliography:
Horsin-Déon, 1853, p. 27; Henriet, 1853, p. 19; Catalogue, Lisieux, museum, 1925, no. 15

Cibot had sent three paintings to the Salon of 1853: *Caritas* and two landscapes. He was hoping to receive some encouragement from the government in his search for "ideal beauty" with the government's purchase of *Caritas.* Receiving no response, he wrote again to the Directeur Général des Musées Impériaux on July 29, 1853, and rephrased his request in a more subtle way: "Or rather could I hope to see both

## Jean-Baptiste-Camille Corot
*Paris 1796–1875 Ville d'Avray*

*Corot's career, like that of other progressive artists, was profoundly affected by the Revolution of 1848. After a late start as a painter and a slow climb toward recognition during the 1830s, Corot saw his public career go into partial eclipse in the early 1840s with the rejection of a number of his paintings by the reactionary Salon juries of the period. By the latter half of the decade the critics had become more friendly, and the artist had even been decorated with the Legion of Honor. Nevertheless, though now over fifty and well known, Corot still found few buyers for his works.*

*With the Revolution, Corot was made a member of the hanging committee of the Salon, and received a first-class medal in 1848. The following year he was placed on the jury; from this time on Corot was to use his growing influence generously on behalf of younger artists, including his friends among the Barbizon painters. More significantly, by the beginning of the Second Empire he had finally begun to receive more commissions from collectors. In the 1860s this demand became a torrent which was met by the artist through the extensive use of studio assistance.*

VI-24

Throughout the period Corot continued his established practice of traveling widely through the provinces in search of subjects in the spring and summer months, while working in his Paris studio during the winter. His powers in no way declined with advancing age, and in fact he developed several major new genres during his late period. He continued to produce works of striking clarity painted from nature, such as the great Port of La Rochelle of 1852 (Yale University Art Gallery, New Haven). At the same time he inaugurated a new manner of "poetic" landscape, characterized by a hazy, damp atmosphere, a lyrical, elegiac mood, and silvery colors sometimes heightened by the use of numerous flecks of white. Corot at this period also developed a renewed interest in painting the single figure, particularly in small yet monumental canvases of women, often in exotic costume; though much admired by some of his artist friends, these works aroused little enthusiasm in the public during Corot's lifetime. (See also nos. VII-14, VII-15.)

D.R.

Bibliography:
Moreau-Nélaton and Robaut, 1905; 1975, Paris, Orangerie

Jean-Baptiste-Camille Corot

## VI-25
## Nymph Playing with a Cupid

1857
Signed, lower left: COROT
Oil on canvas
78.5 × 57 cm

Provenance:
Acquired from the artist by M. Quatrain; presented to Dr. Charcot, by 1878; Alfred Chauchard; bequest to the Louvre, 1909 (inv. no. RF 1782)

Exhibitions:
1857, Paris, Salon, no. 594; 1857, Marseilles, no. 93; 1962, Paris, Louvre, no. 50 (repro.); 1975, Paris, Orangerie, no. 76 (repro.); 1975–76, Rome, no. 53 (repro.)

Bibliography:
Beslay and Paisant, 1857, p. 17; Chaumelin, 1857, p. 266; Roger-Milès, 1891, p. 150; Moreau-Nélaton and Robaut, 1905, vol. I, pp. 168–69, 179, 181, vol. II, no. 1100 (repro.), vol. IV, p. 174; Catalogue, Paris, Louvre, 1910, Chauchard coll., no. 7 (repro.); Bénédite, 1911, p. 106; Moreau-Nélaton, 1924, vol. I, pp. 108, 110, 113, fig. 142; Brière, 1924, no. CH 7; Jamot, 1929, p. 32, pl. 38; Tabarant, 1942, p. 283; Sterling and Adhémar, 1958–61, vol. I, no. 415, pl. 119; Catalogue, Paris, Louvre, Paintings, 1972, vol. I, p. 93; Bazin, 1973, p. 269

When he wrote to his friend Brandon on March 31, 1857, Corot anticipated sending five pictures to the Salon. This one, of which he provided a sketch with the notation "the figure against a clear sky," was then entitled Venus and Cupid. He finally sent seven paintings, since the Salon did not open that year until June 15. Thus, though nearly all the critics mentioned Corot's name in their reviews of the Salon, he being considered by Gustave Planche the "happiest representative of the poetic landscape" (1857, p. 399), few of them lingered specifically over the Nymph Playing with a Cupid. It is this picture that Castagnary evoked when he wrote: "Do not disturb these nymphs and cupids who wander over these primitive regions, pure as Eden and as moist and overgrown" (1892, vol. I, p. 25). Théophile Gautier remarked that Corot's landscapes are all alike, but "one loves this Elysian verdure.... A mysterious life animates these confused forms, and the breast of ancient Cybele throbs under this indistinct terrain. So it is not necessary to describe the Nymph Playing with a Cupid. We know how Corot treats these subjects: it is like La Fontaine translating Anacreon with good-natured nonchalance, and yet it is closer to ancient meaning than to the laborious research of the scholars."

The year 1857 saw the height of Corot's lyrical period, and the theme of this painting recalls Morning: Dance of the Nymphs of the Salon of 1850–51, which by then had been hanging on the walls of the Luxembourg museum. Beslay and Paisant, in their Causeries à deux sur le

VI-25

Salon de 1857, called Corot a "spoiled and unruly child of the naturalist school" and reproached him for this "heavy, luminous, transparent fog that... spreads over nature like a veil of fine batiste.... His canvases are most carefully bathed in this colorless tint that is initially attractive, for a moment charming, and very soon tiresome to the point of distastefulness." Despite repeated observations, he did not mend his ways, "a nymph with a cupid" proving "that M. Corot has resolved to die impenitent."

G.L./M.N.

Musée du Louvre, Paris

Jean-Baptiste-Camille Corot

## VI-26
## Recollection of Mortefontaine

1864
Signed, lower right: Corot
Oil on canvas
65 × 89 cm

Provenance:
One of eight pictures purchased by the Emperor from the Salon of 1864 (Louvre Archives N 6) for 3,000 francs, paid by decree of July 5, 1864, and noted in the inventory of the civil list, no. 509 (Louvre Archives 2 DD 25, 2 DD 26); hung in Fontainebleau (Louvre Archives 2 DD 20; cited July 18, 1872 [Fontainebleau Archives, "L'État des tableaux du Domaine privé]); assigned, February 12, 1879, to the Musées Nationaux by decree of the Tribunal Civil de la Seine on August 2 (recorded August 4), 1880 (Louvre Archives Z 15 [May 29, 1880]); hung, in 1888, in the Galerie des Cerfs at Fontainebleau (Fontainebleau Archives); sent to the Louvre, March 16, 1889; entered the Louvre inventory, 1889 (MI 692 bis)

Exhibitions:
1864, Paris, Salon, no. 442; 1932, London, no. 305 (repro.); 1936, Paris, Orangerie, no. 75; 1936, Lyons, no. 80; 1955, Paris, Bibliothèque Nationale, no. 282; 1959, London, no. 78; 1962–63, San Francisco, etc., no. 16 (repro.); 1975, Paris, Orangerie, no. 78 (repro.; bibl.)

Bibliography:
Lagrange, 1864, p. 110; Barral, 1864, p. 17; du Camp, 1867, p. 87; Chennevières, 1883–89, vol. II, p. 4; Castagnary, 1892, vol. II, p. 206; Moreau-Nélaton and Robaut, 1905, vol. I, p. 221, vol. III, no. 1625, repro. p. 137; Michel, 1906, pl. 27; Moreau-Nélaton, 1924, vol. II, p. 16, fig. 185; Brière, 1924, no. 141; Jamot, 1929, p. 34, pl. 44; Sterling and Adhémar, 1958–61, vol. I, no. 427, pl. 124; Leymarie, 1966, repro. p. 89; Durbé and Damigella, 1969, pl. 25; Catalogue, Paris, Louvre, Paintings, 1972, vol. I, p. 86; Bazin, 1973, pp. 48, 49, 57, repro. p. 225; Miquel, 1975, vol. II, p. 45

A photograph of the room in which Corot died shows a reproduction of Recollection of Mortefontaine above his bed (Moreau-Nélaton

VI-26

and Robaut, 1905, vol. I, pp. 324–25). Undoubtedly the artist attached special importance to this painting, which was acquired by Napoleon III and hung at Fontainebleau, where the court gathered during the summer. (An earlier purchase from Corot also appears in the civil list.)

When the comte de Nieuwerkerke announced the purchase of this entry from the Salon of 1864, the painter responded simply: "It gives me great pleasure on this Thursday, May 19, 1864, to acknowledge the receipt of your letter announcing that H. M. the Emperor has acquired my painting number 442; this makes me very happy" (Louvre Archives P 30 [Corot]). The painting had received mixed

notices, but the Emperor's choice had perhaps been guided by the name of the place represented: was it not the beautiful English-style park near Senlis that had been embellished a number of times at the beginning of the century by Joseph Bonaparte? One can hardly suspect Corot of having done his painting with this in mind, but other artists, for example, Daubigny (q.v.) in 1865, and J.-A. Bénouville in 1870, were not above such flattery to attract the attention of the Administration or the Emperor.

Among the Salon reviewers, Barral wrote: "M. Corot is always the first among the first," and Maxime du Camp was touched by this "small canvas filled with brightness, which

contains and diffuses an essential, native kind of light." Chateaubriand had said that "our best poetry consists in memories," and Corot's contemporaries were aware of his lyricism, his sentimental, poetic Romanticism, but they felt uneasy about what appeared clumsy to them. The vaporous technique, possibly influenced by the blur of photographic landscapes—Corot had a large collection of photographs (*see* Scharf, 1968)—and the balance of values achieved by the minuscule colored spots of small-scale figures make this work one of the most representative of the painter's late style.

G.L.

Musée du Louvre, Paris

## Gustave Courbet

*Ornans 1819–1877 La Tour-de-Peilz (Switzerland)*

*Honored in 1977–78 by an important exhibition in Paris and then in London, Courbet, one of the greatest painters of his time, offers insights into the artistic policies of the Second Empire. He arrived in Paris in the autumn of 1839 and remained outside academic training, studied for a time in Steuben's atelier, later listened to Hesse's advice, but devoted much time to visiting museums, often in the company of his friend Bonvin (q.v.). His entries in the Salons, beginning in 1841, were rejected with three exceptions— 1844, 1845, and 1846. The elimination of the jury in 1848 by the Second Republic made it possible for him to become known through ten of his works. His friend Champfleury predicted that "he will be a great painter." In 1849 he was awarded a medal (which in most years freed him from the verdicts of the jury), and he became famous. His works, especially the* Burial at Ornans *(Salon of 1850–51; Louvre), were the object of lively controversy.*

*During the Second Empire, Courbet's relations with official circles, whose political ideas he did not share (his* Bathers *in the Salon of 1855 shocked the Emperor and the Empress), were punctuated with numerous distinguished achievements. In 1855, near the Exposition Universelle, he opened the "Pavilion of Realism," which made him the undisputed leader of this new aesthetic. He repeated the experiment in 1867 and thus was the first to jar the official institution of the Salon. Despite his enormous*

VI-27

public success, which began in 1861 with his hunting scenes, landscapes, and portraits, his Stag Fight *(Louvre) was turned down by the Luxembourg museum and Napoleon III refused to award him the Legion of Honor. In 1866 there was a new controversy with the comte de Nieuwerkerke about the* Woman with a Parrot.

*Courbet, who was active during the Commune, served a prison sentence of several months' duration as the result of charges brought against him for aiding in the overturning of the Vendôme Column. He subsequently returned to Franche-Comté and then went into voluntary exile in Switzerland, near Vevey.*

G.L.

Bibliography:
Riat, 1906; Nochlin, 1976; 1977–78, Paris, Grand Palais

Gustave Courbet

## VI-27
## A Spanish Woman

1854–55
Signed and dated, lower right: G. Courbet 55
Oil on canvas
81 × 65 cm

Provenance:
Consigned by the artist to the Galerie Durand-Ruel, 1873; Juliette Courbet; Courbet sale, Paris, 1881, no. 9; Galerie Durand-Ruel; Jules Paton; sale, Paris, Hôtel Drouot, 1883, no. 31; John G. Johnson, Philadelphia, between 1914 and 1917; John G. Johnson Collection, Philadelphia (inv. no. 2265)

Exhibitions:
1855, Paris, Exposition Universelle, no. 2808; 1867, Paris, Rond-Point de l'Alma, no. 84; 1882, Paris, Ecole des Beaux-Arts, no. 21; 1939–40, San Francisco; 1948–49, New York, no. 9; 1949, Fort Worth; 1951, Birmingham; 1956, New York, no. 5; 1956-57, Providence; 1959–60, Philadelphia, Boston, no. 21; 1977–78, Paris, Grand Palais, no. 41; 1978, London, no. 39

Bibliography:
Catalogue, Philadelphia, John G. Johnson Collection, 1941, p. 59, inv. 2265

Eleven of the pictures submitted by Courbet to the combined Salon and art section of the Exposition Universelle of 1855 were accepted, while two were rejected, presumably because of limited space. This has often been seen as a major concession on the part of the organizing committee, but it must be noted that several others (aside from Decamps, Delacroix, Ingres, q.q.v., and Vernet, who were given full retrospectives) were represented in similar number: Antigna with thirteen; Cibot (q.v.), ten; Jean-Paul Flandrin, thirteen; Gudin,

twenty-two; Hamon, eight; Charles Lehmann, twenty-one; Theodore, who served on the jury, thirteen. Yet even within this vast exhibition, which had some 1,800 works in the French painting section alone, hung to disadvantage in a long lateral gallery, and lit from the side, Courbet's paintings received a full share of criticism, nearly all of it negative. Of the seven pictures shown for the first time (*The Stone Breakers* of the Salon of 1850–51 still taking the greatest abuse), *A Spanish Woman* sparked the harshest observations, both from the visitors (she was caricatured as being done in Russian leather) and from the critics, who found in her a level of offense and corruption of female beauty new even for Courbet.

The model for this painting has always been thought to be the young woman, probably of Spanish origin, who nursed Courbet briefly in Lyons, where he fell ill at the end of the summer of 1854 on his return from visiting Alfred Bruyas (*see* no. VII-21) in Montpellier (Borel, 1955, p. 24; 1977–78, Paris, Grand Palais, no. 41). However, that she could have been painted on the spot in Lyons seems unlikely, although a letter written by Courbet implied it, since x-rays of *A Spanish Woman* reveal a completely finished portrait of a different woman underneath. One can hardly suppose that the artist would have traveled to and from Montpellier with a finished picture that he would have so readily painted out. Many scholars have tried to connect this woman with the dark and exotic beauty who appears in both *Sleep* (1866) and *The Awakening* (1866), even though the difference in dates and the definite youth of the model would seem to make this an impossibility. More likely, the strange and immediate sensuality of this Spanish woman was to establish a certain canon of beauty for Courbet, who would search well into the 1860s for these qualities in other models.

This type of portrait study of a model would haunt Courbet throughout the later 1850s and early 1860s. The rich spill of hair and the hand entangled in it and the languorous pose reappear in such later works as the *Portrait of Mme Gabrielle Borreau* (1862), the versions of his portrait of *Jo Heffernan* (1865?), and *The Reflection* (1864), the last bearing in the blue dress with pink ribbons a particularly close relationship to *A Spanish Woman*.

Paul Burty, in his introduction to the 1883 sales catalogue of Courbet's work, wrote what is probably the most evocative description of this remarkable work: "... cascading hair, smoldering eyebrows and eyelashes, ardent eyes, dark and flushed tones, thin arms and a throat of great refinement, the languorousness of a cat, such is the description of this person, an

VI-28

etching of whom could well serve as an illustration to the *Fleurs du mal*" (Burty, 1883, p. 20).

J.R.

John G. Johnson Collection, Philadelphia

Gustave Courbet

## VI-28
## Landscape: The Hidden Brook

1865
Signed and dated, lower right: 65 G. Courbet
Oil on canvas
94 × 135 cm

Provenance:
Selected in Courbet's studio by the comte de Nieuwerkerke; delivered August 1865 (letter from Courbet to Nieuwerkerke, August 17, 1865; Louvre Archives P 30 [Courbet]); purchased for 2,000 francs for Napoleon III by decree of September 23, 1865 (Louvre Archives 2 DD25, 2 DD26; "Inventaire des peintures de la liste civile," no. 555); sent to Saint-Cloud and later the Elysée palace; transferred by Chennevières to the Musée du Luxembourg, September 29, 1870 (Louvre Archives 2 DD20; "Livre des mouvements de peintures"); exhibited at the Luxembourg until 1873; transferred to the Louvre during settlement of the Emperor's estate; retained by the State in 1880 pursuant to a decision by the Tribunal Civil de la Seine, February 12, 1879; registered in the inventory of paintings in the Louvre; sent to the Luxembourg, January 19 (or 21), 1881; transferred to the Louvre, January 8, 1903 (inv. no. RF 275)

Exhibitions:
1867, Paris, Exposition Universelle, no. 174 (as *Landscape*, Ministère de la Maison de l'Empereur et des Beaux-Arts); 1882, Paris, Ecole des Beaux-Arts, no. 55 (as *Hidden Brook*); 1928, Cairo, no. 27; 1954, Lyons, no. 30; 1954, Venice, no. 26; 1955, Paris, Petit Palais, no. 62; 1967, Montreal; 1977–78, Paris, Grand Palais, no. 91 (repro.); 1978, London, no. 88 (repro.)

Bibliography:
De Montifaud, 1867, p. 247; Catalogues, Paris, Luxembourg, 1872 ff., 1882–1900 (as *Brook in the Puits-Noir*), 1887, no. 57, repro. p. 102; Catalogue, Paris, Louvre, 1903, no. 146A; Riat, 1906, p. 252; Castagnary, 1912, p. 21 (reprinted in Courthion, 1948, p. 210); Brière, 1924, no. 146A; Léger, 1948, pp. 106, 113; Bazin, 1957, repro. p. 270; Sterling and Adhémar, 1958–61, vol. I, no. 477, pl. 145; Leymarie, 1962, p. 144, repro. p. 145; Chamson-Mazauric, 1968, pp. 27–28, 32, 35, repro. p. 34; Catalogue, Paris, Louvre, Paintings, 1972, vol. I, p. 101; Lacambre, 1974, p. 4 (repro.)

A document published by Chamson-Mazauric suggests that this painting had been exhibited at the Salon of 1865, under the title *Entrance of the Valley of the Puits-Noir (Doubs): Dusk*. This should be reconsidered, for the annotation in the document is a much later addition. Two other paintings bought under the same decree (the third one is a copy) were hastily confused with other works exhibited that same year at the Salon, for example, *Deer and Fox Fighting* by Viardot was confused with *Hounds Quenching Their Thirst after the Hunt* (no. 2163 in the Salon), a quite different subject.

If this painting had been the one exhibited at the Salon, Courbet and the organizers would have kept its title, but it continued to be called *Landscape* until 1881, except when Courbet referred to it as the *Hidden Brook* in the catalogue of his private exhibition in 1867 (under no. 10, *Woman with a Parrot*; see no. VI-30). This title should be retained, rather than that of *Brook in the Puits-Noir*, used in the catalogue of the Luxembourg, even though it refers to the same location.

This locale, near Ornans, repeatedly served as an inspiration to Courbet: it had already appeared in the title of a landscape in the Exposition Universelle of 1855 (no. 2810). But Courbet more likely executed this beautiful version of it (repeated often) during his stay in Franche-Comté in 1864 and at the beginning of 1865. In addition to the painting in the Salon of 1865, distinct from that chosen by Nieuwerkerke, Courbet sent another painting entitled the *Brook in the Puits-Noir (Franche-Comté)* to the Exposition des Beaux-Arts in Lille (1866, no. 385).

Among the compositions showing the same view, except for slight variations, that in the Kunsthistorisches Museum in Vienna has similar dimensions, those in Toulouse—also at dusk—and in Besançon are smaller, and that in Chicago is dated 1868. *Solitude,* from the Bruyas collection (Musée Fabre, Montpellier), should also be mentioned.

These landscapes became extremely popular. Castagnary said that one cannot look at them without "feeling a breath of fresh air." The review in *L'Artiste* by Marc de Montifaud, at the Exposition Universelle, noted that "M. Courbet has given us one of his most notable works. It is a landscape of a sunken stream, flanked by broken boulders, moist and deliciously covered by moss...."

In choosing this painting, the Superintendent of Fine Arts, whom we know had a stormy relationship with the painter, was following the vogue for Courbet's work. One wonders how much attention the Emperor paid to this landscape: it did not go to the Tuileries, but to Saint-Cloud and later to the Elysée palace, which at the time was used as a residence for visiting dignitaries.

G.L.

Musée du Louvre, Paris

Gustave Courbet

## VI-29
## Mme Proudhon

1865
Oil on canvas
73 × 59 cm

Provenance:
Gift to Mme Proudhon from the artist on August 19, 1868; remained in her home until her death in 1900; daughter, Mrs. Felix Henneguy (Catherine Proudhon), until 1947; granddaughters, Mme Emmanuel Fauré-Frémiet and Mlle Suzanne Henneguy; gift to the Louvre, subject to life interest, 1958; at the Louvre since 1970 (inv. no. RF 1958-15)

Exhibitions:
1867, Paris, Rond-Point de l'Alma, no. 68; 1952–53, Paris, Musée Carnavalet, no. 20 (repro.); 1953, London, no. 23, pl. 7; 1955, Paris, Petit Palais, no. 58 (repro.); 1967–68, Paris, Orangerie, no. 350 (repro.); 1969–70, Rome, Milan, no. 26 (repro.; bibl.); 1977–78, Paris, Grand Palais, no. 84 (repro.); 1978, London, no. 81 (repro.)

Bibliography:
Riat, 1906, pp. 108, 223, 236, 253; Léger, 1947, pp. 7,9,10; Léger, 1948, pp. 104–5, 110–11; Catalogue, Paris, Louvre, Paintings, 1972, vol. I, p. 102; Bowness, 1978, "Proudhon," p. 128, fig. 4

The history of this painting closely relates to the large *Portrait of Pierre-Joseph Proudhon in 1853* (Petit Palais, Paris), the group portrait that Courbet executed as a token of gratitude for his friend and supporter, who had died in Paris on January 19, 1865. He finished the work within thirty-six days in Ornans and sent it to the Salon on March 18, 1865. He had painted the philosopher from documents; from memory he had done a "temporary figure" in place of Proudhon's wife. According to a letter addressed to the dealer Luquet, he was planning, before the opening of the Salon on May 1, to do "on a piece of canvas and from life, a portrait of Mme Proudhon, upon my arrival in Paris" and later to transfer it to his large painting. But he was forbidden by the organizers to execute this change at the Salon. Therefore, we cannot be sure that he began this portrait of Louise-Euphrasie Proudhon, née Piégard (1822–1900) as early as April, although it is known from a newspaper clipping that it was completed by August 11.

The large painting was severely criticized at the Salon, especially Mme Proudhon's figure—"the woman has been squeezed, so to speak, into a corner of the painting," said Thoré-Bürger. Her pose is "grotesque," thought L. de Laincel, who called the ensemble "frightful caricatures" (1865, pp. 2–3). These remarks deeply angered Proudhon's widow.

According to family tradition, she granted

VI-29

Courbet only three sittings, probably at her home at 10, Grande Rue in Passy. These probably gave the artist the opportunity to achieve in this portrait the charming spontaneity and the soft expression that characterized this woman of "simple and noble" qualities. He may also have worked from a photograph taken by his friend H. Carjat (preserved in the Louvre), which shows Mme Proudhon wearing the identical dress, a widow's garment.

On April 6, 1866, Courbet wrote to Cuénot when he was working again on the *Portrait of Proudhon and His Family*: "I am going to use the Mme Proudhon that I have at home, already completed." He was referring to the portrait in question. But he eventually decided against this, and the family portrait appeared at his private exhibition in 1867 in its final form: Mme Proudhon had been painted out and replaced—as a reminder of her daily chores—by a sewing basket placed on a garden chair.

G.L.

Musée du Louvre, Paris

Gustave Courbet

## VI-30
## Woman with a Parrot

1865–66
Signed, lower left: 66 Gustave Courbet
Oil on canvas
129.5 × 195.5 cm

Provenance:
Purchased from the artist by Jules Bordet, Dijon, 1870–89; H.O. Havemeyer, 1919; bequest of Mrs. H.O. Havemeyer to the Metropolitan Museum of Art, 1929 (inv. no. 29.100.57)

Exhibitions:
1866, Paris, Salon, no. 463; 1867, Paris, Rond-Point de l'Alma, no. 10; 1869, Munich; 1870, Dijon; 1882, Paris, Ecole des Beaux-Arts, no. 13; 1889, Paris, Exposition Universelle Centennale, no. 210; 1919, New York, no. 24; 1930, New York, no. 21; 1932, London, no. 436; 1956, Cleveland, no. 8; 1959–60, Philadelphia, Boston, no. 60; 1977–78, Paris, Grand Palais, no. 96; 1978, London, no. 1

Bibliography:
Catalogue, New York, Metropolitan Museum of Art, French Paintings, 1966, vol. II, pp. 124–27 (bibl.); Chamson-Mazauric, 1968, pp. 27–36, no. 1

Optimistic and self-assured as ever, Courbet wrote to his father in 1860 that popular acclaim and official recognition were about to be his: "All Paris expects me to be decorated and my pictures bought for the Luxembourg" (*Les Amis*, 1957, p. 20, no. 20). But such a triumph eluded him yet again that year, and it was not until the *Woman with a Parrot* that he achieved a substantial success with the public and came closer than he ever would during the Second Empire to entering the Luxembourg. Comte Nieuwerkerke saw this picture in Courbet's studio in November 1865, at the same time that he negotiated the purchase of *The Hidden Brook* (no. VI-28), and seems to have implied firmly that the State might acquire the picture, even though it was still unfinished. However, as recorded in a series of very heated letters (Chamson-Mazauric, 1968, pp. 27–36, no. 1), Nieuwerkerke was either unable or unwilling to act on his promise, and the picture eventually was sold privately.

It is not surprising that by 1865 the Administration would consider purchasing a major work by this artist who only a few years before had been considered so controversial. Courbet's reputation was by then firmly established and even his strongest enemies had to admit the power of his work. He was selling well, at relatively good prices, and perhaps most important, from the point of view of Nieuwerkerke, the assertive crudeness, both of subject matter and handling, of his early work had waned considerably. This is nowhere more apparent than in *Woman with a Parrot*. This painting is well within the grand tradition of the nude, which, as Toussaint points out, had met with continued official success throughout the Second Empire (1977–78, Paris, Grand Palais). Its high degree of finish (with very little use of the palette knife) and emphasis on drawing are representative of a new departure for Courbet in the mid-1860s, and this, with the immediate sensuous appeal of the figure, made the work a considerable popular success at the

VI-30

Salon. Critical opinion was more varied, ranging from About's comment that "Courbet after a long eclipse reappears with more vitality and brilliance than ever" (1867, p. 47) to those, particularly critics who had defended Courbet earlier, who found it a compromise with popular taste.

The Goncourts, sensing a concession to the bourgeoisie, were the most brutal; on a visit to Courbet's exhibition at the place d'Alma in 1867 they noted this picture and his work in general: "Ugliness, always ugliness! An ugliness without great character; an ugliness even without the beauty of ugliness" (1956, vol. II, p. 376).

The subject of this work was first introduced in the bust length *Woman with a Parrot* dated 1861 (coll. Alfred Daber, Paris). The figure is adapted from the Psyche of *The Awakening*,

1864 (in several variants, one of which, perhaps postdating the Metropolitan picture, includes a parrot) and also includes a twisted bedpost. Thoré-Bürger noted that a suggestion from him may have been the inspiration for this composition (1870, pp. 277, 283ff.). In this context, it is tempting to speculate that some aspect of this subject may have derived from Dutch seventeenth-century painting, where women with parrots abound, often with the same erotic overtones, and more especially from Rembrandt's *Danaë*, which employs the same raised arm and particularly the heavily ornamented bed drape.

J.R.

The Metropolitan Museum of Art, New York, Bequest of Mrs. H.O. Havemeyer, 1929, The H.O. Havemeyer Collection

## Thomas Couture

### Senlis 1815–1879 Villiers-le-Bel

*In response to a request for a biography, Couture wrote: "I am a student of Gros [later of Delaroche]. I first won a second Grand Prix in 1836. Having no aptitude for academic painting, I dropped out of the competition to paint the way I wanted. I made my debut in the Salon in 1840 with* A Young Venetian after an Orgy. *This canvas attracted some attention, was purchased, and I soon had the rare pleasure of selling all my paintings for high prices. I completed in succession* The Prodigal Son, Troubadour, Love of Gold, *and a great many portraits and imaginative paintings. In 1847 I exhibited my* Decadence of the Romans.

*"I thought I might as well take advantage of the public's infatuation by painting the many portraits I*

had been commissioned to do. In 1850 I exhibited a number of them thinking to prove to my dear colleagues that it was possible to please both the public and the art lovers by painting portraits in an artistic fashion. I obviously mistook the situation; both artists and critics alike were severe in their judgment of me. In 1854 I finished the great work for the Chapel of the Virgin in Saint Eustache. . . .

"In 1855, at the time of the Exposition Universelle, I showed Decadence of the Romans and The Falconer. The award I received was of a secondary level and I was excluded from the great fete given for French painters. It was a cruel and bitter pill to swallow and, as a result, I lost my interest in exhibiting. I finally understood that since I had the bad luck of being too popular, I must retire altogether" (Bertauts-Couture, 1932, pp. 74–75: probably written after his "retirement" to Villiers in 1868).

It seems remarkable that Couture omitted mention of The Enrollment of the Volunteers, commissioned in 1848, as well as other commissions he received but never completed during the Second Empire: The Baptism of the Prince Imperial, Return of the Troops from the Crimea, and the decoration of the Pavillon Denon.

When Couture retired to the country he continued to produce genre paintings, purchased for the most part by American collectors. However, still another disaster befell him: in 1870 many canvases and drawings were taken by the Prussians.

O.S.

VI-31

Thomas Couture

## VI-31
## The Empress Eugénie (Study for "The Baptism of the Prince Imperial")

c. 1856–62
Signed, bottom right: T.C.
Oil on canvas
53 × 64.5 cm

Provenance:
Artist's family; gift of M. and Mme Bertauts-Couture to the Musée National du Château, Compiègne, 1964 (inv. no. C 64.030)

Exhibitions:
1880, Paris, Palais de l'Industrie, no. 86; 1936, Paris, Petit Palais, no. 186

Bibliography:
Dimier, 1914, p. 196; Colombier, 1931; Doria, 1931, p. 4; Kunstler, 1931; de Maricourt, 1931; Bertauts-Couture, 1932, pp. 33, 43; Bertauts-Couture, 1955–56, p. 196; Le Journal de France, 1970, repro. p. 1511

Bibliography:
Couture, 1867; 1880, Paris, Palais de l'Industrie; Bertauts-Couture, 1932; Boime, 1969; 1970, College Park; Vaisse, 1977, "Couture"; Vaisse, 1977, "Second Empire"; Boime (in preparation)

Thomas Couture

## VI-32
## Napoleon III (Study for "The Baptism of the Prince Imperial")

c. 1856–62
Oil on canvas
81 × 65 cm

Provenance:
Artist's family; gift of M. Bertauts-Couture to the Musée National du Château, Compiègne, 1950 (inv. no. C 50.064)

Exhibitions:
1880, Paris, Palais de l'Industrie, no. 305; 1953, Compiègne, no. 67

Bibliography:
Bertauts-Couture, 1955–56, p. 196; Le Journal de France, 1970 (repro.)

Thomas Couture

## VI-33
## The Grande Duchesse Stéphanie de Bade (Study for "The Baptism of the Prince Imperial")

c. 1856–62
Oil on canvas
55 × 46 cm

Provenance:
Artist's family; gift of M. Bertauts-Couture to the Musée National du Château, Compiègne, 1950 (inv. no. C 50.069)

Exhibitions:
1880, Paris, Palais de l'Industrie, no. 83 (as Head of Woman); 1953, Compiègne, no. 69 (as Portrait of Admiral Brust's Wife)

Bibliography:
Bertauts-Couture, 1955–56, p. 196 (as Mme de Sancy); Terrier, 1959, no. 43 (as Mme de Sancy-Parabère)

Thomas Couture

## VI-34
## The Grande Duchesse Stéphanie de Bade (Full-Length Figure) (Study for "The Baptism of the Prince Imperial")

c. 1856–62
Oil on canvas
65 × 81 cm

VI-32

VI-33

June 1862 (Vaisse, 1977, "Second Empire," p. 49). The work was never completed (although the only major blank is the head of Napoleon III).

The *Baptism*—with Couture's other unfinished official commissions—stands as one of the great enigmas of his career. Its fate is closely linked with *The Enrollment of the Volunteers* as well as the projected program for the Pavillon

Provenance:
Artist's family; gift of M. Bertauts-Couture to the Musée National du Château, Compiègne, 1950 (inv. no. C 50.065)

Exhibitions:
1880, Paris, Palais de l'Industrie, no. 85; 1953, Compiègne, no. 68 (as *Admiral Brust's Wife*)

Bibliography:
Bertauts-Couture, 1955–56, p. 196; Chevalier, 1957, p. 703

Thomas Couture

## VI-35
## Choirboy (Study for "The Baptism of the Prince Imperial")

c. 1856–62
Signed at right: T.C.
Oil on canvas
55 × 46 cm

Provenance:
Artist's family; gift of M. Bertauts-Couture to the Musée National du Château, Compiègne, 1950 (inv. no. C 50.068)

Exhibition:
1953, Compiègne, no. 72

Bibliography:
Bertauts-Couture, 1955–56, p. 196

Couture's huge painting, *The Baptism of the Prince Imperial* (gift of Couture's granddaughter, Mme Moatti, to the Musée National du Château, Compiègne) represents the court as well as the clergy gathered in Notre Dame for the baptismal ceremony, while Napoleon I, with the imperial eagle, appears on a cloud above the crowd witnessing the celebration of the continuity of his dynasty.

Although the official decree of commission is dated May 29, 1861, the decision to confer this work to Couture seems to have been made even before the actual event on June 14, 1856. The artist received a first payment on July 2, 1856, and three others thereafter, the last in

Denon of the Louvre. Couture never complained, nor publicly explained the real reason why these canvases were not finished. This silence has prompted art historians to conclude that he was incapable of completing large compositions.

In an important article Vaisse gives a logical explanation for the incompletion of these works based upon evidence confirmed by the papers in the Couture donation to Compiègne. The matter of the *Volunteers* is simple, notes Vaisse, and Couture himself alluded to it in a letter to Nieuwerkerke, the Superintendent of Fine Arts: "M. de Persigny [Minister of the Interior] told me that I could keep the advances as indemnity but that he did not want a painting of demagogues. Those were his very words. I regretfully withdrew and stopped painting those demagogues of 1792, who had saved their country."

The problems surrounding the *Baptism* and the Pavillon Denon reflect similar difficulties with the Administration. They were both

VI-34

rules over everything. The army, in its turn, will protect him simply and with devotion. But the most imposing of forces—memory—surfaces: Napoleon I descends to earth to bless his descendant and touches his eagles with his fearful sword.

"The Prince is presented to the Legate. The women carrying him lift him up to the throne, and the drapery surrounding them forms a cradle which makes him look like a little Moses on the waters [*see* no. VII-16].... His mother, his poor mother...forgive me for a moment, the Empress, prays for her child. Everything pales before this maternal love.... Small vanities disappear and bathe this mother in a religious glow.... As for the Emperor, he will let the Empress play the lead, and his modesty will make him seem all the the greater.... In this way, I will tell of the great human forces, and I will make them loved by painting their fragility poetically" (Couture, 1867, pp. 280–82).

Couture himself has chosen the pose of the Empress (no. VI-31), which allowed him to emphasize her profile, which he especially liked. To do this he had been granted several posing sessions, but it was probably to avoid tiring the Empress that she was photographed in the dress worn at the baptism (*see* no. VIII-16), and the photographs were given to Couture, together with the Empress's train, to facilitate the artist's studies. These objects are preserved today at Compiègne. This dazzling sketch of the Empress testifies to the passion of Couture's brushstroke. Couture always prepared his pic-

VI-35

commissioned, orally, by Achille Fould, Minister of State. Vaisse gives the following reconstruction of the case: "Fould transmitted orally the commission for the decoration of the Salle d'Etat, then asked for a painting in return. Since Couture did not understand that the painting was to be a bribe, Fould did not follow through with the commission." But there must have been something more than a bribe involved since Couture later wrote Nieuwerkerke: "This misunderstanding had been straightened out in a relaxed sort of way by his Majesty the Emperor who decided that the work [the decoration of the Pavillon Denon] was too large a job for only one artist, and divided it up, leaving me to choose my half. Relying on the imperial word, I continued my work on the composition for the Pavillon Denon.... [Also] it was you, Superintendent, who interfered with the work [the *Baptism*], which was in quite an advanced state, when you said: '...nothing has been done and you will not be awarded this commission; I have disposed of it in some other way....' You forced me into a false position, that of a tactless person obtaining work by devious means.... It was you who made me appear unreliable and deprived me of the opportunity of working for the Administration.... And if, having disrupted my career as an artist, you succeed in ruining me...."

A close look at the note confirming the commission of the *Baptism*, which was not signed until 1861 (Arch. nat. F²⁴ 129), reveals that it came from the Ministère de la Maison de l'Empereur to which Nieuwerkerke was at-

tached, even though the painting was destined for the historical museum at Versailles. Thus, this all fell within Nieuwerkerke's realm. The negotiations had been possible because Fould headed both ministries, but Nieuwerkerke must have found it difficult to admit that orders for the decoration of the Louvre and paintings for Versailles could be commissioned without his involvement. It seems that Nieuwerkerke did not care for Fould, and thus Couture was victim both of the rivalry between Fould and Nieuwerkerke and of his own pride. As Vaisse noted, Couture subsequently changed his mind and made several requests for an atelier sufficiently large to enable him to finish his *Baptism*, but his requests were never granted.

In the painting of *The Baptism of the Prince Imperial* the figure of the Empress occupies a privileged place between the group of presiding clergymen and the group of spectators, but not just for aesthetic reasons. Couture, an artist in the tradition of great history painting, conceived his picture as a page of didactic morality. "This ceremony, by which the Church receives the child into its fold, if shown realistically, would depict only aspects relevant to Christian unity. But you will note that this instance involves a Prince who must continue a national dynasty, a national hope.... The nation sees a direct heir to the dynasty which she acclaims. She sees in this child guarantees of order buttressed by memories of greatness—in the last analysis, the present consolidated in the future.... This child will be received into the fold of the Church, that great spiritual force which

tures by means of many sketches such as these until he "knew the piece by heart."

The sketch of the Emperor (no. VI-32) is especially interesting for in the final painting his head is unfinished. By drawing the Emperor with a modestly bowed head, Couture emphasized the Empress. At the same time, he astutely resolved the difficult problem of the Emperor's vague and inexpressive gaze which stumped so many artists. One of the preparatory sketches for the painting at Compiègne, a drawing with a study of Napoleon's head (C 52.011/6), seems to have been taken from life. It may have been executed during the baptism, or perhaps during Couture's stay in Compiègne in 1856, at exactly the same time the commission was given.

The woman holding the Prince Imperial first was thought to be the wife of Admiral Brust, but then was called Mme de Sancy-Parabère, a Dame du Palais. The identification as Mme de Sancy is unlikely, for she was not even mentioned in the accounts of the ceremony. According to Le Moniteur, the Prince Imperial was taken to Notre Dame by the Gouvernante des Enfants de France, therefore Admiral Brust's wife, assisted by Mesdames Brancion and Bizot, and it was the Admiral's wife who handed the Prince Imperial to Napoleon III to hold up to the crowd.

But the moment in the ceremony that Couture chose to represent was the most important one from the point of view of Catholic ritual, that is, the Benediction, since the infant had been privately baptized at the Tuileries prior to the ceremony at Notre Dame. It is logical that at the most important moment it would be the godmother who would hold the infant. Thus, this sketch for the figure of the woman holding the child (no. VI-33) would be of the grande duchesse Stéphanie de Bade, who represented the Prince's godmother, the queen of Sweden, who could not attend the ceremony.

In support of this is a letter to Couture from Lazay-Marnesia, the Empress's chamberlain (in the Couture donation at Compiègne): "The grande duchesse is afraid that she cannot give you enough time tomorrow for you to take the trouble to come to Saint-Cloud. But she *expressly* asked me to tell you that she would be very pleased to see you in Germany." It is highly unlikely that Couture asked for posing sessions only to portray the back of the grande duchesse and, the figure depicted from behind must instead be the wife of Admiral Brust.

This study of Stéphanie de Bade, which retains so much impromptu charm, illustrates well Couture's technique at that time, washing a brown glaze on the background, painting in the dark parts lightly, and using a heavy im-

pasto in the light areas. The rapid sketch of the full-length figure study of Stéphanie de Bade (no. VI-34) also gives an idea of the ease with which Couture painted. Although he quickly put the outline and highlights down on canvas, he had studied each character with obvious care, for he made precise drawings not only of the bodice (Compiègne C 34 D 2) and train (Compiègne C 34 D 1) but also of the front of the dress, which would not even show in the finished picture.

Couture painted this study on a canvas on which can be seen a sketch of a nude male model, which is attributed to Edouard Manet (q.v.) because of the inscription on the back. Manet was Couture's student for six years and Couture's influence on Manet is no longer disputed today.

The freshness and luminosity of the rapidly painted figure of the choirboy (no. VI-35) make it apparent why even his most vicious detractors could not fault Couture's studies for the *Baptism*.

In addition to the exhibited works, another eight painted sketches (C 53.025, 64.024, 32.042, 48.056, 50.066, 50.067, C 67 D2, C 64.024) and forty drawings (C 50.071, C 53.020, 21, C 64.020, C 34 D1, D2, D3, D4, C 71.183–C 71.206, C 520/1–7) are at Compiègne. Other painted portraits are known also: Monseigneur Patrizzi, Don Petro Nardi, and portraits of women (exhibited 1880, Paris, Palais de l'Industrie); studies for the footman, the zouave, the clergymen (private colls.); the canon of Notre Dame (Chalons museum), as well as the sketches of Monseigneur Sibour (wrongly identified as Monseigneur Eglée; Worcester Museum of Art, Mass.); and Monseigneur Patrizzi (private coll., U.S.A.). A study for a figure of a bishop was exhibited in London in 1975, one of a clergyman, at the Shepherd Gallery in New York in 1971 (no. 30), while another sketch shown there (no. 29) was listed erroneously as a preparatory sketch for Monseigneur Sibour's hand, but it is actually a sketch for the hand of Monseigneur Patrizzi sold in Paris in 1972 (Prouté, no. 65). Recently, a study for the Emperor's sword was sold twice in Paris, in 1970 and in 1977.

O.S.

Musée National du Château, Compiègne

Thomas Couture

## VI-36
## Damocles

1866
Signed on cushion, at left: T.C. 1866
Oil on canvas
285 × 155 cm

Provenance:
Purchased from the artist by Charles Noël through Barbedienne (q.v.) for 12,000 francs, 1866; Noël sale, 1891; Barbedienne sale, 1892, no. 17; Noël Barbé; gift to the Musée des Beaux-Arts, Caen, 1901 (inv. no. 39)

Exhibitions:
1872, Paris, Salon, no. 407; 1880, Paris, Palais de l'Industrie, no. 141

Bibliography:
Clément, 1872; Fabius, 1872; Pelletan, 1872; Duranty, 1872; Wolff, 1872; Castagnary, 1872; Bonnin, 1872; de Vaudrey, 1872; Stella, 1872; Mantz, 1872; Cherbulliez, 1872; G. Lafenestre, Le Moniteur, June 12, 1872; Saint-Victor, 1872, pp. 253–54; de Montifaud, 1872, p. 240; Bertall, 1872, p. 19; Ballu, 1880, "Couture"; 1880, Paris, Palais de l'Industrie, p. xxiv; Drumont, 1880; Duranty, 1880; Trianon, 1880; Claretie, 1882–84, vol. I, pp. 344, 346–47; Spoll, 1882; Fournel, 1885; Mireur, 1901–12, vol. II, p. 298; Catalogues, Caen, Musée des Beaux-Arts, 1913, no. 213, 1928, no. 207; Bertauts-Couture, 1932, pp. 41, 153, repro. p. 136; Bertauts-Couture, 1955–56; Lacambre, 1972, p. 71 (repro.); Vaisse, 1977, "Second Empire," pp. 43–49 (repro.)

"The most remarkable puzzle at the Salon is undeniably the Damocles of M. Couture," declared G. Lafenestre, and with him, all the critics at the Salon. Poor Couture, once again misunderstood! He had to wait until 1977 when Pierre Vaisse deciphered the riddle whose key Couture had carefully given in the inscription at the top of his canvas: POTIOR MIHI PERICULOSA LIBERTAS QUAM SECURA ET AUREA SERVITUS ("I prefer the storms of liberty to the golden security of servitude"). The poet Damocles, who preferred prison and solitude when threatened with censure (i.e., the scissors), is Couture under the Second Empire: "A profession of faith and a spiritual self-portrait, Damocles does not simply illustrate the situation of the artist or official poet. It is the work of circumstance, the denunciation of a specific regime, the Second Empire" (Vaisse). Not only was this work misunderstood but its technique was also rather violently denounced: "Damocles is not the victim of M. Couture's false generosity. He is too fine an observer not to see that the fruits put within his grasp are made out of felt and cardboard, the silver and gold coins out of paper. Out of despair, he has just swallowed the sword that made him so famous. He will have a hard time recovering from it…. Couture too" (Bertall, 1872, p. 19). Stella defended Couture, calling

VI-36

his painting "the most imposing work at the Salon," while Lafenestre praised its "open and fresh, rich and luminous execution" and noted that "this proud way of painting is no longer stylish."

Today we are no longer bothered by incised contours or by the violent, heavy impasto used in the light tones, which were characteristic of Couture's technique at that time. Therein lies the ambiguity of Couture's work: his didactic mission and art of composition were rooted in the grand tradition while his technique was innovative.

This work was probably conceived in the 1860s; a sketch was finished in 1863, and in 1865 in the accounts on Couture with Barbedienne, a sketch of Damocles given to Barbedienne is mentioned as well as a painting of the same subject which was to be delivered (Compiègne Archives, fonds Couture). It must have been nearing completion in 1866, since Couture received the balance of the sum agreed upon at that time. Couture's papers at Compiègne make it clear indeed that a replica and a "small-scale sketch" of *Damocles* were finished around 1863. Carpeaux (q.v.) praised "the severity of the drawing, the high distinction of its characters, and the exalted poetry of the whole." Several other versions and replicas exist, among them preparatory drawings at Compiègne (C 71.208; C 51.811/208). Couture himself kept his own "memento" of this work, a fine small sketch of the whole composition, almost identical to the painting in Caen (given to Compiègne by Mme Moatti, née Grodet-Thomas Couture, the painter's granddaughter; C 71.207).

O.S.

Musée des Beaux-Arts, Caen

---

## Paul-Alfred de Curzon

*Le Moulinet (near Poitiers) 1820–1895 Paris*

*A student of Drolling, Curzon entered the Ecole des Beaux-Arts in Paris in 1840. Having had little interest in the figure, in 1841 he decided to study landscape painting with Cabat. He visited Italy for the first time in 1846–47 with his friend Louis-Georges Brillouin, but he was more attracted to the countryside than to the museums. Although he placed second in 1849 in the competition for the Prix de Rome for his historical landscape* (The Death of Milo of Croton), *he petitioned the Académie and was granted a* pension *for four years at the Villa Medici. During that time he traveled in Italy, and, in 1852, visited Greece.*

*Curzon began to exhibit at the Salon in 1843, and in 1857 was awarded a second-class medal, followed by several* rappels. *In 1865 he was named chevalier of the Legion of Honor and in 1867 received a third-class medal at the Exposition Universelle. During the Second Empire three of his works entered the Musée du Luxembourg:* Psyche *(Salon of 1859; now in the Mairie, Sermaize-les-Bains),* Dominicans Decorating Their Chapel with Paintings *(Salon of 1867, deposited in Poitiers, 1896; the museum houses a number of drawings by the artist), and* View at Ostia during the Flood of the Tiber *(Salon of 1868; location unknown). All this is indicative of a rather successful career.*

*Although he worked in every area, he was especially celebrated for his landscapes of Greece and Italy, as well as his Italian genre scenes, and he was an outstanding draftsman (see no. VII-17).*

*In 1916 his son Henri de Curzon published the artist's biography along with his correspondence and a catalogue of his works.*

G.L.

Bibliography:
De Curzon, 1916

---

VI-37

Paul-Alfred de Curzon

## VI-37
## A Dream in the Ruins of Pompeii (The Spirits of Its Ancient Inhabitants Return to Visit Their Homes)

1866
Signed and dated, lower right: A. de CURZON 1866
Oil on canvas
71 × 104 cm

Provenance:
Charles Paravay; Saint-Albin coll. (*see* de Curzon, 1916, vol. II, p. 249); Mme Duruy; gift in memory of her mother, Mme Achille Jubinal, to the Musée Municipal, Bagnères-de-Bigorre, 1877 (inv. no. 146)

Exhibition:
1866, Paris, Salon, no. 477

Bibliography:
Jahyer, 1866, p. 89; de Montifaud, 1867, May 1, p. 176; T. Gautier, "Salon de 1866," *Le Moniteur,* June 12, 1866; About, 1867, pp. 256–57; de Curzon, 1916, vol. I, p. 186, vol. II, pp. 25–26, 249, no. 59

During his *pension* at the Villa Medici in Rome, Curzon traveled through Campania in 1851. He left Rome in March with his friend Bouchaud and reached Naples on May 23. With Bouguereau (q.v.), whom he met there, he continued his travels, visiting the ruins of Pompeii in the company of Bouguereau in August. It was possibly at this time that he made the drawing of the House of the Faun (de Curzon, 1916, vol. II, p. 249, no. 1479), which became the genesis of this painting destined for the Salon of 1866.

By situating this scene—a poet draped in a flowing cloak, seated on the edge of an impluvium, envisioning the ancient figures he dreams about (note, in particular, the old man at the right, dressed in white, who seems to talk of the smoking Mount Vesuvius)—in a rather faithful representation of the ruins of Pompeii, Curzon departed from the Neoclassical tradition of recreating antiquity and its décor, and even more from the "Néo-Grec" school of his time which was reinventing Greek and Roman genre scenes following Gérôme (q.v.) and Hamon (q.v.). According to F. Jahyer, Curzon "gives a much better idea of this unique city than M. Hamon." Edmond About, who had traveled with Curzon to Greece, recorded his "sophisticated and refined taste," his unique talent, "austere but sensitive." "M. Alfred de Curzon seems to have resolutely moved away from landscape painting. His *Resurrection of Pompeii* is a history painting, except for its size." Marc de Montifaud, enthusiastic about it, entitled the work "A Summer Night's Dream among the Ruins of Pompeii," showing himself sensitive to the mystery and poetry that emanate from the work. He noted its nocturnal light, its starlit sky and the moonlight, as well as the sphinx in the center, with wings fully extended, formulating his "question...amid tranquillity and silence." As for the peacocks, are they not symbols of immortality rather than Juno's pets and signs of her vanity?

There is no doubt that this Roman city, buried under the ashes of Vesuvius and exhumed toward the end of the eighteenth century, evoked a very particular nostalgia. It inspired painters, such as P. H. de Valenciennes (Salon of 1814; Musée des Augustins, Toulouse) and the Russian Brulliov (Salon of 1833; Leningrad) as well as writers, such as Théophile Gautier, who understood Curzon's purpose and wrote: "When one walks through the city...even the most rational minds naturally indulge in this type of evocation. Even we have written a story, *Areia Marcella*, based on that same retrospective phantasmagoria.... M. de Curzon draws the monuments like an architect and colors them like a painter. He also does the figures very well and his dream has an aspect at the same time fantastic and real; fantastic, because the figures are only shadows; real, because its architecture has the solidity of the real thing."

Lacking the poetic ambiguity of Curzon, Pompeian subjects were numerous during the Second Empire, for instance, *The Last Day of Happiness in Pompeii*, by Pierre-Olivier Coomans (Salon of 1863; bought from

Napoleon III's civil list) or *A Walk along the Via dei Sepulcri in Pompeii*, by Boulanger (q.v., Salon of 1869).

G.L.

Musée Municipal, Bagnères-de-Bigorre

---

## Charles-François Daubigny
### Paris 1817–1878 Paris

*Daubigny's father, a painter of Classical landscapes, was his first teacher. He visited Italy when he was seventeen years old, and later worked for a time in the restoration studio of the Louvre. In 1838 he entered the atelier of Paul Delaroche and made his debut at the Salon, where he continued to exhibit paintings, along with some etchings (the State purchased a series of twenty prints from him in 1856; Arch. nat. F²¹ 73). The mountainous landscape in the* Saint Jerome *(Salon of 1840; Amiens museum) shows his early interest in the region of the Dauphiné, where a group of landscape artists had formed around Crémieu and Optevoz, a local version of the Barbizon School, which influenced him after 1840. His reputation as a landscape painter was established after 1844 and he received numerous awards: a second-class medal in 1848, a first-class medal in 1853, with* rappels *in 1857 and 1859, the Legion of Honor in 1857, a third-class medal at the Exposition Universelle in 1855 and a first-class medal in 1867.*

*Daubigny had a brilliant official career during the Second Empire, a rather unusual distinction for a landscape painter at the time. The Musée du Luxembourg exhibited two of his works:* Lock in the Optevoz Valley *(Exposition Universelle of 1855; Rouen museum) and* Spring *(Salon of 1857; Louvre); the Emperor purchased privately* The Pond of Gylieu *(Salon of 1853; Cincinnati Art Museum) and also the* Great Valley of Optevoz *(Salon of 1857; Louvre).*

*Daubigny became interested early in studying the effects of water and sky and set up a studio on a boat, the* Botin, *which floated up and down the Seine, Marne, and Oise rivers; he was one of the first artists who lived in Auvers-sur-Oise (1860), where Corot (q.v.)—whom he had known since 1848—and Daumier (q.v.) came to visit him. In 1870–71 he traveled in Holland and to London, where he became acquainted with Claude Monet (q.v.). Thus was established a link with the future Impressionists. (See also no. VII-18.)*

G.L.

Bibliography:
Henriet, 1875; Moreau-Nélaton, 1925; Fidell-Beaufort and Bailly-Herzberg, 1975

Charles-François Daubigny

## VI-38
## The Park of Saint-Cloud

1862–65
Signed and dated, lower left: Daubigny 1865
Oil on canvas
124 × 201 cm

Provenance:
Commission by the State of a "landscape, a preliminary sketch of which must be submitted first" by decree of August 9, 1862, for 3,000 francs; referred to as a "view of Saint-Cloud" in certificate of payment of the first installment (1,000 francs) on December 24, 1862; for second payment (1,000 francs), on July 22, 1863, the *inspecteur* Dubois reported on July 17: "The painting is well under way and looks quite good"; completed work delivered to the Superintendent of Fine Arts before payment of the balance of 1,000 francs, September 10, 1864; placed in the Dépôt des Marbres and temporarily sent on January 11, 1867, to "M. Doucet, Superintendent of Theaters" (Arch. nat. F²¹ 130); deposited in the Museum in Châlons-sur-Marne, about 1871 (inv. no. D 871.1.1)

Exhibitions:
1865, Paris, Salon, no. 570 (Ministère de la Maison de l'Empereur et des Beaux-Arts); 1922, Paris, Musée des Arts Décoratifs, no. 54; 1937, Sceaux, no. 13; 1961, Vichy, no. 50

Bibliography:
Jahyer, 1865, pp. 185–86; de Laincel, 1865, p. 94; Privat, 1865, p. 113–15; *Magasin Pittoresque*, August 1866, repro. p. 261 (engraved by Sargent); Henriet, 1875, pp. 77, 235, no. 570; Laran, 1913, p. 85; Moreau-Nélaton, 1925, pp. 85–86, 88, 91–92, fig. 68; Tabarant, 1942, p. 418; Vergnet-Ruiz and Laclotte, 1962, p. 232; Miquel, 1975, vol. III, p. 690; Fidell-Beaufort and Bailly-Herzberg, 1975, p. 55; Hellebranth, 1976, repro. p. 8, no. 13

In a letter dated March 21 addressed to the Minister of State, certainly from 1862, Daubigny applied for a new commission. He mentioned the two views of the Tuileries on the grand staircase in the Ministère d'Etat (today the Ministère des Finances), which he had painted in 1860: "I would be delighted to obtain a commission for a series of paintings representing the imperial parks and châteaux. Joseph Vernet has left a reminder, both historical and picturesque, of the ports of France. I feel that the imperial parks and châteaux, treated the same way, would also be of great interest..." (Arch. nat. F²¹ 130). Only the view of the Park of Saint-Cloud was done. It represents, as one would have seen them from the banks of the Seine, the Great Fountain, forty-two meters high; the Great Cascade by Lepautre and Mansard; as well as the château, one of Napoleon III's favorite summer residences (which was to be destroyed by fire on October 12, 1870). Although Daubigny gave the sketch now in the Musée Condé in Chantilly the date 1865 (repro. by mistake as the

VI-38

painting of the Salon by Fidell-Beaufort and Bailly-Herzberg, 1975, p. 56), he actually executed it as well as the large painting as early as 1862. Thus he chose to indicate the date of the Salon, following a common procedure: the painting, "well under way" in 1863 was continued in May and June, 1864, in Auvers, and completed in Paris during the second half of July, according to a letter to Henriet dated July 16, 1864 (published by Moreau-Nélaton). At the Salon of 1865 the critics admired the other work Daubigny had submitted, *Moonlight,* but a number remained cold toward *The Park of Saint-Cloud,* which they felt was too conventional a locale, a "sad subject in painting" (Jahyer); de Laincel wrote that the painting "looks like a beautiful colored lithograph," while, on the contrary, Jahyer noted that "M. Daubigny achieved a tour de force by being able to hide the stiffness of the quincuncial shapes and by avoiding any possible resemblance to a colored lithograph.... He was able to infuse a great deal of air and light throughout the foliage." On contemplating it, Gonzagne Privat imagined a romance among the thick bushes near the fountain.

Daubigny was to be inspired several times by Saint-Cloud. The view of Saint-Cloud reproduced by Arthur Mangin in *Les Jardins* (Tours, 1867) together with the preliminary drawing (Cabinet des Dessins, Louvre) were taken from another viewpoint.

G.L.

Musées de Châlons-sur-Marne

## Alexandre-Gabriel Decamps
*Paris 1803–1860 Fontainebleau*

*There was little in Decamps's humble origins to suggest that he would become a well-known artist or that his brother Maurice-Alexandre would become an art critic and essayist. When he was about fourteen Decamps began to study with the painter Etienne Bouhot; late in 1818 he entered the studio of Abel du Pujol, where he met the animal painter Godefroy Jadin, who remained his lifelong friend. Leaving the studio around 1819–20, he embarked on a career as a professional painter, draftsman, and printmaker.*

*After a period of some economic success during the early 1820s, Decamps made his debut at the Salon of 1827–28 and exhibited consistently until 1855. His first great success came at the Salon of 1834 with his most famous painting,* The Defeat of the Cimbrians *(Louvre). Decamps received all the major awards and recognitions bestowed on contemporary artists (see Mosby, 1977, vol. I, pp. 366–67). The crowning point of his career was the Exposition Universelle of 1855, where he was given a retrospective exhibition, as were Ingres (q.v.) and Delacroix (q.v.), all three of whom won the Grand Medal of Honor.*

*Decamps is best known for having created a vogue for Oriental themes, although he rendered all types of subjects throughout his career. He was masterful at depicting effects of light, and achieved an inimitable, golden, brittle texture, his "cuisine." Decamps believed that art was primarily a visual*

*experience, stating: "for me a painting achieving its effect is a finished painting." He placed great importance on originality; however, he admired, and put to work for his own ends, the art of such diverse masters as Raphael, Titian, Giovanni da Bologna, Rembrandt, Poussin, Léopold Robert, and Géricault.*

*Decamps worked tirelessly for the rights of artists and for a reorganization of the Salon. His friends urged him to apply for the seat in the Académie des Beaux-Arts left vacant by the death of Delaroche in 1856, but he refused because of his poor health. His significance was recognized by Napoleon III, who along with the Empress, paid him an impromptu visit on June 18, 1858. Among his friends were Barye (q.v.), Comairas, Corot (q.v.), and Huet (q.v.).*

D.F.M.

Bibliography:
Chaumelin, 1861; Moreau, 1869; Mosby, 1977

Alexandre-Gabriel Decamps

## VI-39
## Job and His Friends

c. 1853
Oil on canvas
119.4 × 85.7 cm

Provenance:
Commissioned by the State for the Musée du Luxembourg, 1849 (Arch. nat. F²¹ 24, 5ᵉ série, dossier no. 23 [June 16, 1849]); but never delivered (*see* Louvre Archives P 4 [March 21, 1862]); in studio after death; sale, Paris, Hôtel Drouot, April 29–30, 1861, no. 2; Broët coll., Paris; van den Eynde coll., 1889; Durand-Ruel et Cie, Paris, 1892; P. A. B. Widener, Philadelphia and Paris; Durand-Ruel et Cie, Paris, 1913; James J. Hill, Minneapolis; Mrs. Erasmus C. Lindley, Minneapolis; gift to the Minneapolis Institute of Arts, 1939 (inv. no. 39.48)

Exhibition:
1866, Paris, Palais des Champs-Elysées, no. 246 (?)

Bibliography:
Chaumelin, 1861, p. 19; Moreau, 1869, pp. 124 (no. 123), 289; Widener, 1900, no. 33; Davis, 1950, repro. cover; Catalogue, Minneapolis, Institute of Arts, 1971, no. 118 (repro.); Mosby, 1977, vol. I, pp. 228–29, vol. II, no. 185, pl. 100-B

Well over a year before the coup d'etat of December 1851, the State had begun to encourage the arts by commissioning five sculptures and twenty paintings from several artists (Louvre Archives Z 4 [August 14, 1851]); Decamps alone was permitted to execute a subject of his own choice. Why Decamps chose to paint this subject from the Book of Job (II: 9–11) is

VI-39

The artist did not generally turn to the earlier masters for visual sources at this time. However, he could have borrowed from Ribera's *Martyrdom of Saint Bartholomew* (Grenoble) for the figure of Job. Indeed, he owned a copy after Ribera's painting by François Bisson (sale, Paris, Hôtel Drouot, April 21–23, 1853, no. 42).

Decamps's approach to *Job,* especially in his use of light, may be seen as one of the early attacks on the traditional method of modeling with light and dark. This tentative step would be developed fully in the art of Manet (q.v.).

Decamps did not exhibit *Job and His Friends,* but we do have an important contemporary view of the work. Delacroix saw it in his atelier and remarked in his *Journal* (Delacroix, 1951, p. 178 [April 29, 1853]) : "Returned to the Salon with E. Lami to make some inquiries, then on to see Decamps, whose studio was in utter confusion. He showed me some admirable things, including the enlarged version of his *Job,* intended for the Ministry ; it is quite as fine as the small one and I think that he has carried it further."

Decamps painted a smaller oil version of this subject in 1853 (81 × 65 cm), which is lost, and the larger work was reproduced as a lithograph by Jules Laurens. There are no known preparatory drawings for the painting, as is frequently the case with Decamps's works.

D.F.M.

The Minneapolis Institute of Arts, Gift of Mrs. Erasmus C. Lindley

---

unknown ; however, he was interested in Biblical themes during the early part of the Second Empire. Although he is best known as a genre painter, as early as the mid-1830s he had aspired toward the grand manner. Here Decamps selected the moment when, as a challenge from Satan to God, the wealthy and virtuous Job is stripped of his riches ; he is shown lying in a dung heap ; he is tormented by his wife who stands on the balcony, and is ridiculed by his friends. In spite of his calamitous experience, Job retains his moral excellence, raising his arm to ask blessings for his adversaries.

Decamps placed the scene in an architectural setting of the ancient world, in this instance, Idumaea in Palestine. In addition to imbuing the Biblical scene with an appropriate appearance (an invention of Decamps during the 1830s), the architecture is the key to the composition. The buildings permit logical juxtapositions of shapes, and a complex system of perspective, which leads the eye to the background but carries it back to the foreground. This directional movement is emphasized by the sharp contrasts of light and dark. For example, the highlighted background advances toward the lighter values of the foreground but is kept in place by the penetrating angles of the architecture. The bright sky too seems to advance but it is held visually in place by the tree which is blown toward the right, returning the eye to the highlights of the foreground. Color plays a minor role in the composition, as does Decamps's "cuisine." The figures, or the true subject, have little impact as conveyors of cerebral actions, which is evidence that Decamps's primary concern was "art for art's sake."

## Alfred Dedreux

*Paris 1810–1860 Paris*

*The son of an architect, Dedreux was raised in an artistic ambience ; during his youth he was frequently taken by his uncle, the painter Pierre-Joseph Dedreux-Dorcy, to the atelier of Géricault, whose work had a lasting influence on him. Although he studied with Léon Cogniet, he had little interest in his master's history painting ; rather, Dedreux admired the works of Stubbs, Morland, Constable, and Landseer, and after the fall of the July Monarchy, he joined his friends Lami (q.v.) and Gavarni in England, where he studied the English masters. He returned to Paris in 1849, and soon deliberately aligned himself with the Second Empire (Doin, 1921, p. 247).*

*Dedreux exhibited first at the Salon in 1831 and showed regularly for three decades ; he received several medals (Bellier and Auvray, 1882–87, vol. I, p. 374) and was awarded the Legion of Honor in 1857. The facile manner and elegance of his works were quickly appreciated by the nobility; he painted a portrait of the duc d'Orléans (1843; Bordeaux) and worked for the duc d'Aumale and Queen Victoria (Doin, 1921, p. 249). During the Second Empire, Dedreux was commissioned by many notables, including the comte d'Orsay, the actress Mme Doche, and the Emperor himself (two equestrian portraits: Salon of 1853, no. 338; 1858, Musée de l'Armée, Paris).*

*By 1838 Dedreux had achieved the imaginative, brooding light of the Romantics and the compositional balance seen in his most famous work* Two Lovers in the Country *(1840, Paris, Salon, no. 378). His mature period, beginning around 1848, is characterized by luminous color, crisp light, and massive horses (*Woman on Horseback, *Detroit Institute of Arts, 75.61); by the late 1850s his brushwork became broader, as in* Men and Women on Horseback beside the Lake at Pierrefonds *(c. 1859, Louvre, RF 2609).*

*Dedreux was extremely prolific, and numerous lithographs, were made after his works. Yet he is little known today, possibly because his paintings are generally privately held and because sporting subjects were long out of favor. However, his mature works compare favorably with those of his compatriots: his compositions are clearer and simpler than Lami's, and his drawing less spotty than Guy's (q.v.). Dedreux's horses are a link between the fiery steeds of Géricault and the calculated, racetrack animals of Degas.*

D.F.M.

Bibliography:
Doin, 1921; 1928, Paris, Musées Nationaux; de Fouquières, n.d.; Renauld et al., 1976

Alfred Dedreux

## VI-40
## Imperial Guard: The Colonel Commanding the Guides

c. 1853–55
Oil on canvas
120 × 80 cm

Provenance:
Comte Emile-Félix Fleury coll. (probably by 1855); descended in family; private coll.

Exhibition:
1855, Paris, Exposition Universelle, no. 2900

The subject of this painting is Emile-Félix Fleury (1815–1884), who like Dedreux, had a brilliant career during the July Monarchy and became a resolute follower of Louis Napoleon.

Fleury participated in the coup d'etat and was named colonel of the Regiment of Guides and head of the imperial stables soon after the proclamation of the Second Empire (Larousse, 1866–90, vol. VIII, p. 481). In March 1856, Fleury was made brigadier general and soon after had an apartment at the Louvre. He received numerous awards and decorations, and was raised to the peerage. Fleury's passionate interest in the stables of the Emperor, one of the finest ever assembled by any sovereign, and Dedreux's love for horses would suggest that there was a natural affinity between the two men. However, the absence of Fleury's name from the exhibition title of the painting hints that he may not have commissioned it, for another work shown at the same time does include the name of the sitter: *Equestrian Portrait of M. le Comte Klein* (1855, Paris, Exposition Universelle, no. 2901). It was not at all unusual for French artists to paint similar military subjects because, traditionally, they were a guarantee of success (*see* Mosby, 1969).

Dedreux depicts Fleury mounted on Adonis, one of the Emperor's horses given exclusively to the service of the colonel, followed by two members of the imperial guard. Through position and clarity of execution, Dedreux made Fleury and Adonis the focal point of the painting although the character of the sitter is not delineated. The composition is animated through the contrast of the erect position of the well-disciplined soldiers and the nervous actions of the animals. Dust, which flies brusquely about, adds to the life of the composition, and joins with the sky to create a sense of infinite space. The entire scene is bathed in a crisp, natural light so characteristic of Second Empire paintings.

The composition of this painting is closely

VI-40

related to Dedreux's 1853 equestrian portrait of Napoleon III, and both works echo the idea of the equestrian portrait of the duc d'Orléans. The ultimate source for all three paintings is Géricault's work, and the portrait of Fleury is particularly indebted to the *Mounted Trumpeter of the Chasseurs* (coll. Stavros S. Niarchos, Paris).

This work can be dated between 1853 and 1855 because of its stylistic similarity to the 1853 portrait of Napoleon III, its appearance at the Exposition Universelle of 1855, and the stages of Fleury's military career. In April 1855,

VI-41

it was reported that the rich, dark-brown stallion Adonis, which Fleury rides, "was recently purchased from Mr. Mason, of London, for a very large stake" ("The Emperor's Stud," *Illustrated London News*, p. 375).

A drawing by Dedreux in the Uffizi (M.887) relates to the mounted figure of Fleury, and an exact copy of the painting is in the Musée de l'Armée, Paris (EA 327¹.01107). Dedreux also painted a larger version of the subject (1860[?], private coll., Paris).

D.F.M.

Private Collection

## Edgar-Hilaire-Germain Degas
*Paris 1834–1917 Paris*

*Until his death forty-seven years after the fall of the Second Empire, Degas continued to make innovations in the techniques of sculpture, pastel, and monotypes of which the artists and teachers of his youth could not have dreamed. Yet in his devotion to the figure as the essential subject of art, and drawing as its primary means of expression, he continued many of the principles first learned in the 1850s and he can be placed, with Renoir (q.v.), as one of the artists who carried the classical tradition into our century.*

*Trained at the Lycée de Louis le Grand (1845–53), he quickly turned away from the study of law encouraged by his banker father and, in 1853, studied briefly with Félix-Joseph Barrias, moving later that year to the studio of Louis Lemothe, a student of Ingres (q.v.) and Flandrin (q.v.). After a brief period at the Ecole des Beaux-Arts (1855–56) he departed in 1856 for Italy, where he worked in Rome at the Villa Medici and became particularly close friends with Gustave Moreau (q.v.). He returned to Paris in 1859 and began a history painting,* The Spartan Girls *(London and Chicago). The notebooks of this time (Reff [ed.], 1976) are full of ideas for illustrations of Biblical, Classical, and Renaissance literature. In 1861 he began visiting the Café Guerbois, where he came to know Pissaro, Sisley, Fantin, Stevens, and Manet (q.q.v.) as well as Zola and the Realist critic and novelist Duranty. During the 1860s his work expanded from a purely Ingres classicism to a greater sense of Delacroix (encouraged through van Dyck and the Venetians),* The Daughter of Jephthah *being the clearest point of transition. It was perhaps through Manet that he began to depict subjects of modern life (*The Wounded Jockey, *1866), however this interest was already present in many of his portraits (most of his œuvre during the later 1860s) with their profound quality of psychological narrative. He first submitted to the Salon in 1865 and exhibited there in 1868, 1869, and 1870. In 1874 he helped organize the first Impressionist exhibition in the studio of Nadar (q.v.); however, while placing himself firmly in their ranks, he would never work in a purely Impressionist technique or share their desire simply to depict, rather than interpret, the subject before them.*

N.D./J.R.

Bibliography:
Lafond, 1918–19; Jamot, 1924; Guérin and Halevy (eds.), 1931; Rewald, 1944; Rouart, 1945; Lemoisne, 1947–49; Fevre, 1949; Boggs, 1958; Reff, 1976, *Degas*; Reff (ed.), 1976

Edgar-Hilaire-Germain Degas

## VI-41
## The Daughter of Jephthah

c. 1861–64
Signed, lower left: Degas
Oil on canvas
195.5 × 224.5 cm

Provenance:
Degas studio sale, Paris, Galerie Georges Petit, May 6–8, 1918, no. 6a; Carlos Baca-Flor; Jacques Seligman, New York; sale, New York, American Art Association, January 27, 1921, no. 71; Wildenstein; purchased by the Smith College Museum of Art, 1933 (inv. no. 1933:9)

Exhibitions:
1933, Northampton, no. 5; 1935, Kansas City, pl. 5; 1935, Rochester, no. 7; 1936, Philadelphia, no. 7; 1956, Brooklyn, no. 25; 1960, New York, no. 7; 1961, Cambridge, Mass., no. 17; 1969, Minneapolis

Bibliography:
Lafond, 1918–19, vol. II, p. 2; Jamot, 1924, p. 31; *The Art Digest*, vol. VIII, December 1, 1933, p. 38; Abbot, 1934, pp. 2–12; Mitchell, 1937, pp. 175–89; Tietze-Conrat, 1944, p. 420; Lemoisne, 1947–49, vol. I, pp. 48–49; Huttinger, 1960, pp. 29–31, repro. facing p. 11; Pool, 1964, pp. 310–11

VI-42

This canvas, the largest of Degas's works and the most complex of his early history paintings, illustrates the Biblical story of Jephthah (Judges 11), the "mighty warrior," who, in return for his defeat of the Ammonites, had vowed to sacrifice the first person who came out of his tent on his arrival home. The tragic outcome of his victory was that his daughter, playing on the timbrels with her handmaidens, ran out first to meet her father. Jephthah kept his vow and sacrificed the girl. Degas's painting depicts in the foreground the despairing general and his startled troops, while, beyond, the handmaidens console the distraught daughter.

The dating of this painting by scholars has varied from Jamot's of 1856–60 to Guerin's of 1865–70. This discrepancy is due to Degas's custom of endlessly reworking his canvases. This one, still in his studio at his death in 1917, along with thirty-five studies for it, was probably retouched often by the artist, which makes precise dating by brushstroke and color scheme impossible. The date of c. 1861–64 given here, which refers only to the original conception of the subject, concurs with the known dates of his other history paintings, the last of which, *The Misfortunes of the City of Orléans*, was shown at the Salon of 1865, and also with his return from Italy in 1861.

At this time his mind was still full of the copies of old masters he had been making for the last eight years, both at the Bibliothèque Nationale (first registered 1853) and throughout Italy. *The Daughter of Jephthah* contains quotations from many of his copies. From a work by Girolamo Genga in Siena he borrowed two men, the semi-nude prisoner with arms tied, cropped by the right edge of the canvas, and the soldier with his back turned in the right foreground. The helmeted head of this same soldier is after a head in an *Adoration of the Magi* by Cesare da Sesto that Degas had copied in the Museo Nazionale in Naples. The horse's head comes from his copy of a cast of one of the horses of the Parthenon pediment. The soldier carrying a banner at left is a copy of Degas's drawing after Mantegna's *Triumph of Caesar* and the handmaidens and daughter of Jephthah repeat the positions of the Marys in the predella panel of the Crucifixion from Mantegna's Saint Zeno altarpiece in the Louvre. Poussin's *Rape of the Sabines*, of which Degas made a copy in 1863, is similar in its concentrated action and intense interrelationship of figures. Finally, the equestrian warriors from Delacroix (q.v.) suggested to him the appearance of Jephthah on his horse. Delacroix's color was important for him, also, for an undated notation in a sketchbook in the Louvre states: "For the red of

Jephthah's robe, remember the orange-red tones of the old man in the... of Delacroix" (Lemoisne, 1921, p. 222 n. 3).

Such multiple borrowings are an indication of Degas's traditionalism, but the composition itself, with its complex juxtaposition of figures, turned away from the viewer, cropped by the frame, and radically disparate in scale to suggest a deep space, are indications that Degas would become the most radical formal innovator of the Impressionist circle, a radicalism that is particularly startling because of the artist's deep roots in the past.

N.D./J.R.

Smith College Museum of Art, Northampton, Massachusetts, Purchased, 1933

Edgar-Hilaire-Germain Degas

## VI-42
## Edmondo and Thérèse Morbilli

1867
Oil on canvas
115 × 89.5 cm

Provenance:
Degas studio sale, Paris, Galerie Georges Petit, May 6–8, 1918; René de Gas, Paris; sale, Paris, November 10, 1927, no. 71 (repro.); Wildenstein & Co., New York; Robert Treat Paine, 2nd, Brookline, Mass.; gift to the Museum of Fine Arts, Boston, 1931 (inv. no. 31.33)

Exhibitions:
1933, Northampton, no. 33; 1936, Philadelphia, no. 10 (repro.); 1941, Boston, no. 144; 1973, Boston, no. 1

Bibliography:
Lemoisne, 1927, p. 314; Hendy, 1932, pp. 43–45; Lemoisne, 1947–49, vol. II, pp. 66, 80; Boggs, 1962, pp. 18, 24, pl. 39; Boggs, 1963, pp. 274–76; Peters, 1974, pp. 124–25

The figures in this portrait are Degas's sister Thérèse and their first cousin Edmondo, whom she married in Naples in 1863. Degas's grandfather had fled to Naples during the French Revolution and had established a bank there. His son Auguste returned to Paris and married Mlle Musson from New Orleans; their children Edgar, Achille, Marguerite, Thérèse, and René kept close ties with their families in the native cities of their parents, René marrying his maternal aunt's daughter in New Orleans and Thérèse, with special dispensation from the Pope because of their close blood relationship, her paternal aunt's son in Naples.

In another portrait of this newly married couple, in the National Gallery of Art, Wash-

ington, D. C., both are seated, Thérèse on a long sofa, and Edmondo behind her on the back rest. The work was never finished. In the Boston painting, done shortly afterward, Edmondo dominates the composition by occupying more than three-quarters of the pictorial space and by the detailed manner in which he is painted. Thérèse, behind him (almost a twin in features to her brother), hesitantly touches her husband's shoulder, searching for the reassurance that her pale, worried expression seems to indicate she seeks. Her face is overshadowed by the bulk of her husband's frame, and her clothing blurred in relation to his. "Within his formal vocabulary," wrote Jean Boggs, Degas has "painted a convincing and tender portrait of this young couple in the complexities of their defenses with each other and the outside world" (1962, p. 18).

Boggs saw in the portrait an example of the influence of the daguerreotype, a process that Degas had already been studying by this time. She cites the neutral background found in a studio instead of a domestic interior, the conventional poses typical of contemporary photography, and Degas's way of handling the values (Boggs, 1962, p. 16). Peters noted how Degas, in this composition held so close to the picture plane, still emphasized certain elements by painting them in careful detail and subordinated others by painting them broadly, as if he were trying to replicate the concept of peripheral vision of both the eye and the camera lens with the medium of paint (Peters, 1974, p. 125).

Degas did not sell any of his many family portraits, but kept them in his studio. In 1918 René de Gas removed this portrait from the posthumous sale of his brother's atelier, and it did not leave the family until René died in 1927.

N.D.

Museum of Fine Arts, Boston, Gift of Robert Treat Paine, 2nd

Edgar-Hilaire-Germain Degas

## VI-43
## Mlle Fiocre in the Ballet "La Source"

c. 1866–68
Oil on canvas
130 × 145.1 cm

Provenance:
Degas studio sale, Galerie Georges Petit, Paris, May 6–8, 1918, no. 8; Jacques Seligman, Paris; sale, New York, American Art Association, January 27, 1921, no. 68; purchased through Durand-Ruel and presented to the Brooklyn Museum by James H. Post, John T. Underwood, and A.A. Healy (inv. no. 21.111)

Exhibitions:
1868, Paris, Salon, no. 686; 1949, New York, no. 14; 1953, New Orleans, no. 73; 1960, New York, no. 13; 1960, Paris, Galerie Durand-Ruel, no. 4; 1971, New York, Philadelphia, no. 63

Bibliography:
Jamot, 1924, pp. 25, 57, 58, 97, 135–36; Mongan, 1938, pp. 290–302; Lemoisne, 1947–49, vol. I, pp. 60, 62, 63, vol. II, p. 74; Browse, 1949, p. 51; Wegener, 1954, pp. 8–10; Rewald, 1961, pp. 158, 175, 186; Reff, 1964, pp. 250–59; Reff, 1976, *Degas,* pp. 29, 30, 214, 232, 298, 306, 327

From the age of twenty Degas held a season ticket to the Opéra, and throughout his life his interest in theater, opera, and particularly ballet was the sustaining inspiration for much of his art.

*La Source* was the second stage subject he chose for a submission to the Salon; the first, *Semiramis Founding a City* (Salon of 1861; Louvre), had been based on a recent production at the Opéra. This subject was taken from the ballet *La Source* (book by Muitter and Saint-Leon, music by Minkus and Delibes), first performed on November 12, 1866. A Persian fantasy, staged primarily as a mime spectacle (the horse and pond were actually on the stage), the dancing was nonetheless much praised, particularly that of Mlle Eugénie Fiocre in the character of Nouredda. At the peak of her career and fame (Carpeaux, q.v., did her bust in 1869) Fiocre gave a performance that was for Paul de Saint-Victor "nearly an exact reproduction of the paintings one sees in Persian miniatures" (*La Presse,* July 15, 1866, quoted by Browse, 1949, p. 51). To Théophile Gautier she appeared as "the prettiest houri to have worn the bonnet and corset of pearls in the Mohammedan Paradise" (quoted by Guest, 1974, p. 219).

Reff noted the very convincing relationship to Whistler's *Symphony in White, No. 3* (Barber Institute of Fine Arts, Birmingham, England), which Degas knew and noted in a drawing (Reff, 1976, *Degas,* pp. 29–31). However, in his fascination with the reflection of water, the rich costumes, and the complexity of color, Degas seems some distance from his American friend, echoing Delacroix (q.v.) or Chassériau (q.v.) to a greater degree. The static quality of the scene may also derive from the lyrical stillness of Whistler, but this could equally relate to the plot of the ballet, since the moment in the first act that Degas has chosen is one of considerable drama, a pause between great activity and

VI-43

spectacle. Nouredda, having just finished dancing the famous *pas de la Guzla* (the prettiest moment in the ballet, according to Gautier), kicks off her shoes, dips her feet in the pond, and sinks into the deep thoughts that lead to the abandonment of her suitor to certain death and her grand departure (with caravan) to marry the prince. When this painting was shown at the Salon (where it seems to have received little attention) the work was simply entitled *Portrait of Mlle E.F. . . . Apropos the Ballet La Source.* It was the portrait of a dancer in a narrative context rather than in movement that Degas chose to emphasize.

According to Ernest Rouart, upon the return of the painting to the studio, "the artist, dissatisfied with the surface, began to remove the varnish and, in the process, seems to have damaged the surface somewhat and put the picture aside. About 1894 he had a professional restorer complete the removal of the varnish and, at that time, retouched the picture, although to what degree is uncertain" (quoted by Lemoisne). Two preparatory oil sketches survive, one (Buffalo; Lemoisne, 1947–49, no. 149) showing the two seated figures nude, which reflects Degas's continued devotion to the working methods of Ingres and the Ecole des Beaux-Arts.

J.R.

The Brooklyn Museum, New York

## Eugène Delacroix
*Charenton-Saint-Maurice 1798–1863 Paris*

By the early 1850s Delacroix had solidified the position he had held somewhat reluctantly since the 1820s as the leader of the Romantic movement, and was regarded as an important painter by all but the most conservative critics. An aura of his early reputation as a Romantic rebel contributed to his being denied membership in the Académie des Beaux-Arts until 1857, when he was near the end of his career. On the other hand, since the 1830s Delacroix had been favored with an exceptional number of important state commissions. Early in Napoleon III's reign, he was at work on the mural decorations for the Salon de la Paix of the Hôtel de Ville (completed 1854; now destroyed). Delacroix's greatest public commission, however, was for the murals of the Chapel of the Holy Angels in the Church of Saint Sulpice; work on the preparation and execution of this project took up much of his time from 1854 to 1861 (see no. VII-22).

Delacroix in his later years led a highly disciplined existence centered around his work. Withdrawing to a great extent from the worldly pastimes of his youth, the artist through his reserved and somber manner discouraged approaches by all but a few close friends. In addition to directing his large decorative projects and producing many smaller works, Delacroix during this period wrote the bulk of his celebrated Journal and continued to publish art criticism. The retrospective exhibition of Delacroix's work at the Exposition Universelle of 1855 added to his prestige; however, as late as 1859 his Salon works could still evoke such hostile reactions as that of Maxime du Camp, who suggested that the painter might more profitably devote himself to literary studies and music (du Camp, 1859, p. 34).

Delacroix was probably the last great artist to think of himself primarily as a "history" painter. To the avant-garde of the 1850s he was a respected older independent artist, but one whose goals were no longer those that seemed most pressing. Among his loyal admirers, on the contrary, he had become an institution almost beyond reproach. Delacroix perhaps had these attitudes in mind in 1859 when he wrote to his defender Charles Baudelaire, who had praised him highly, "You treat me as one treats only the great dead. You make me blush even as you give me great pleasure" (1936–38, vol. IV, p. 111 [June 27, 1859]). (See also nos. VII-20, VII-21.)

D.R.

Bibliography:
Robaut and Chesneau, 1855; Delacroix, 1932; Delacroix, 1936–38; Trapp, 1971

Eugène Delacroix

# VI-44
## Turkish Women Bathing

1854
Signed and dated, lower left: Eug. Delacroix 1854
Oil on canvas
92 × 78 cm

Provenance:
Possibly commissioned by J.J. Berger, Prefect of the Seine; Goupil coll., 1864; sale, Paris, March 4, 1868; John Saulnier, Bordeaux, 1868–86; sale, Paris, June 5, 1886, no. 39 (repro.); Jagoux coll.; Ferdinand Blumenthal; Cecil Pecci-Blunt; Comtesse Pecci-Blunt, Paris, 1933; Mr. and Mrs. R. L.; Paul Rosenberg, New York, 1952; purchased by the Wadsworth Atheneum, 1952 (inv. no. 1952.300)

Exhibitions:
1864, Paris, Société Nationale des Beaux-Arts; 1885, Paris, Ecole des Beaux-Arts, no. 197; 1933, Paris, Orangerie, "Delacroix," no. 195; 1963, Paris, Louvre. no. 451; 1975, Providence, no. 87

Bibliography:
Robaut and Chesneau, 1885, no. 1240; Moreau-Nélaton, 1916, vol. II, p. 137, fig. p. 361; Escholier, 1926–29, vol. III, p. 192 (repro.); Delacroix, 1932, vol. II, pp. 163, 167, 175–76, 204, 232; Cunningham, 1952, p. 1 (repro.); Sérullaz, 1963, no. 457 (repro.); Huyghe, 1963, pp. 302–3, 418, 471, pl. 219; Trapp, 1971, pp. 141, 193, fig. 71; Bortolatto, 1972, no. 693

Delacroix was at work on this painting by April 13, 1854, and finished it on June 22 of that year (Delacroix, 1932, vol. II, pp. 163, 204). The traditional title seems to be a misnomer, since Delacroix refers to the painting in the Journal only as his Bathers or his Women at the Fountain. The change of locale by later critics to Turkey (a country never visited by Delacroix) may be the result of the popularity of the image of women in the Turkish bath, a theme treated by major European artists from Hogarth (Saint Clair, 1973, no. 44) to Ingres (q.v.; Turkish Bath, 1852–63).

The subject may have been suggested to Delacroix by his viewing of the Bathers by Courbet (q.v.) in 1853 (Bortolatto, 1972, no. 693). Although the two paintings seem to have little in common other than their theme, Courbet's picture had made a strong impression on Delacroix; he praised the vigor of the execution, though he was greatly annoyed by the figures' "meaningless" gestures. He also complained that the figures in Courbet's painting had been put into the landscape afterward, without connection with their surroundings, and he continued: "This brings up the question of harmony between the accessories and the principal object, a thing lacking in the majority of great painters" (Delacroix, 1932, vol. II, p. 19 [April 15, 1853]). While painting his own Bathers Delacroix wrote at length about the technical problems involved in painting the trees which, he said, should be modeled with colored reflections, as in the painting of flesh (Delacroix, 1932, vol. II, p. 175). Implicit in this discussion is the desire for the unified treatment of figures and landscape which Delacroix found lacking in Courbet, Poussin, and other gifted artists.

Delacroix later wrote that he had painted the picture under conditions that did not please him (1932, vol. II, p. 232). Although Trapp (1971, p. 141) suggested the artist was referring to an unpleasant incident that took place during this trip to Morocco in 1832, Delacroix probably was speaking about the actual execution of the picture in 1854. The source of the motif is not to be found in Delacroix's Moroccan recollections but in the charming bathing scenes of the Rococo; the landscape, with the statue turned away from us, recalls those in such works as Watteau's Mezzetin (Metropolitan Museum of Art, New York). This subject was taken up again during the "Rococo revival" of the Romantic period; Delacroix's friend, the Orientalist painter Jules-Robert Auguste, had already treated the theme as early as the 1820s in a pastel Bathing Girl with a Mirror (Musée des Beaux-Arts, Orléans). In choosing to paint this traditional subject, using only the most generalized references to the Orient, Delacroix was adopting for his coloristic experiments a vehicle later to be used for the most ambitious formal statements of Renoir (q.v.), Cézanne, and Matisse.

D.R.

Wadsworth Atheneum, Hartford, The Ella Gallup Sumner and Mary Catlin Sumner Collection

Eugène Delacroix

# VI-45
## Rebecca Abducted by the Knight Templar during the Sack of the Castle of Front-de-Boeuf

1858
Signed and dated, lower center: Eug. Delacroix 1858
Oil on canvas
105 × 81 cm

Provenance:
Hartmann coll., Mulhouse; sale, Paris, Hôtel Drouot, May 11, 1876; Kramer coll., 1878; Arnold & Tripp, April 21, 1882; purchased same day by E. Secrétan; Thomy Thiéry coll., 1889; bequest to the Louvre, 1902 (inv. no. RF 1392)

Exhibitions:
1859, Paris, Salon, no. 824; 1878, Paris, Galerie Durand-Ruel, no. 148; 1930, Paris, Louvre, no. 175; 1936, London, no. 8; 1951–52, Paris, Bibliothèque Nationale, no. 509; 1963, Paris, Louvre, no. 498; 1964, Edinburgh, no. 68; 1969, Kyoto, Tokyo, no. H. 39 (repro.)

Bibliography:
Astruc, 1859, pp. 265–66; Mantz, 1859, pp. 137–38; Auvray, 1859, p. 19; Robaut and Chesneau, 1885, no. 1383, repro. p. 372; Brière, 1924, no. T. 2850; Joubin, 1950, vol. II, pp. 449, 460; Sterling and Adhémar, 1958–61, vol. II, no. 706, pl. 251; Sérullaz, 1963, no. 501 (repro.; bibl.); Bessis, 1969, p. 222, no. 440; Calvet-Sérullaz, 1971, p. 128, no. 7; Catalogue, Paris, Louvre, Paintings, 1972, vol. I, p. 129; Kemp, 1973, pp. 226–27; Georgel and Rossi-Bortolato, 1975, no. 748 (repro.)

The subject of this painting was taken from Sir Walter Scott's novel Ivanhoe (1819), the first French translation of which dates from 1820; it was to become a frequent source of inspiration for Delacroix. He listed twenty-four possible themes from this book in his Journal (December 23–29, 1860). This particular episode takes place in chapter XXXI, which had already been illustrated in the 1846 Salon painting, The Abduction of Rebecca (Metropolitan Museum of Art, New York). Delacroix took a few liberties with the text for, actually, Rebecca, kidnapped by the Knight Templar Bois-Guilbert from a

VI-45

Eugène Delacroix

## VI-46
## Horses at the Fountain

1862
Signed and dated, lower left: Eug. Delacroix 1862
Oil on canvas
76 × 91 cm

Provenance:
G. coll.; sale, Paris, April 23, 1866; Khalil Bey; sale, Paris, January 16, 1868, no. 21; Constant Say, 1868; Comtesse de Tredern (née Say); Prince de Wagram; Baillehache coll., 1916; Marcel Kapferer; Etienne Bignou, 1930; Chester Beatty, London; Paul Rosenberg & Co., New York, 1950; Philadelphia Museum of Art (inv. no. W'50-1-2)

Exhibitions:
1930, Paris, Louvre, no. 197A; 1932, London, no. 374

Bibliography:
Moreau, 1873, p. 273; Robaut and Chesneau, 1885, no. 1442; Moreau-Nélaton, 1916, vol. II, pp. 168, 203, 261, fig. 388; Escholier, 1926, p. 256; *Philadelphia Museum of Art Bulletin*, vol. XLVI, no. 229, 1951, p. 43, repro. p. 50; Huyghe, 1963, pp. 295, 304, fig. 233; Bortolatto, 1972, no. 798

Near the end of his life Delacroix often returned to themes inspired by his Moroccan impressions of thirty years earlier: *Arabian Horses Fighting in a Stable* (1860, Louvre); *Lion Hunt* (1861; Art Institute of Chicago); *Visit of a Caid in Morocco* (1862; de Noailles coll., Paris); *The Sultan of Morocco and His Court* (1862; Bührle coll., Zurich); and *Arabs Skirmishing in the Mountains* (1863; National Gallery of Art, Washington, D.C.). The scene depicted here does not seem to correspond to any experience recorded in the Moroccan sketchbooks of 1832, but clearly represents an idealized recollection of that memorable journey.

The setting has been constructed somewhat arbitrarily: a preparatory pencil sketch for this composition (Robaut and Chesneau, 1885, no. 1443, repro.) shows that Delacroix made numerous changes in the final version. In the sketch the man at the right is shown mounted on his horse, and the men approaching the well on horseback in the background do not appear. A more important alteration is the addition of the final version of the architecture at the left, changing the locale from countryside to town. These buildings must have been adapted from those Delacroix saw during his journey. The tower at the far left in particular recalls the large, severe minarets of western medieval Islamic architecture; a famous example in altered form that was certainly known to Delacroix is the Giralda, now the bell tower of the cathedral of Seville.

The subdued air of the composition, the

high chamber in the castle where Ivanhoe was also prisoner, leaves the flaming castle, not in the arms of the knight, like a Sabine woman, but on a horse led by the slaves of the Saracen Templar, who is waiting for her in the foreground.

In his *Journal* entry for May 26, 1856, Delacroix noted that he had sketched on a previously used canvas the *Knight Templar Abducting Rebecca*. The next day he left Champrosay and did not return to it until the following month, writing on June 29, "I was not satisfied yesterday, when I returned, with what I had left behind...the Bois-Guilbert abducting Rebecca." Finished in 1858, the painting was exhibited in the Salon of 1859, the last in which Delacroix was represented. Traditional critics, surprised by the passion shown in the composition, evinced scorn for what appeared to them to be only a sketch. However, Zacharie Astruc

was enthusiastic: "It is impossible to be more clear-eyed, lucid, dramatic, to achieve greater accuracy, to render a more riveting vision of light and color. It is impossible to create that Gothic Orient more effectively...What fire! What vibrancy! One is transported by the movement, the picturesque quality, the dauntless vigor, the curious romantic presence. Walter Scott is there, totally, but enhanced by the painter's fiery genius." Paul Mantz thought that there was "much in it that is truly admirable...There is a strange charm, a touching, virile grace in the bent figure of the young captive who is fighting off her abductor and who, delightfully clad in blue, orange, and white, shines out in the midst of this scene of carnage like a flower in a field devastated by a storm."

G.L.

Musée du Louvre, Paris

VI-46

Jules-Elie Delaunay

VI-47
**The Death of Nessus**

1869–70
Oil on canvas
95 × 125 cm

Provenance:
Purchased by the State, by decree of June 25, 1870, for 6,000 francs (Arch. nat. F²¹ 132); entered the Musée du Luxembourg, January 10, 1874; transferred to the Louvre, October 19, 1885; inscribed in the painting inventory (inv. no. RF 542); deposited in the Musée des Beaux-Arts, Nantes, December 12, 1885, after a request of June 9, 1872 (Arch. nat. F²¹ 132) (inv. no. 916)

Exhibitions:
1870, Paris, Salon, no. 778; 1878, Paris, Exposition Universelle Internationale, group I, class 1, no. 245; 1889, Paris, Exposition Universelle Centennale, no. 278; 1974, Paris, Grand Palais, no. 67 (repro.)

Bibliography:
Chaumelin, 1870, p. 390; Ménard, 1870, p. 512; Catalogues, Paris, Luxembourg, 1875–85; Ménard, 1878, pp. 491–92; Montrosier, 1881–84, p. 194; Catalogues Illustrés, Paris, Luxembourg, 1884, 1887, repro. p. 101; Gonse, 1900, p. 251; Catalogues, Nantes, museum, 1903, no. 849, 1913, p. 349, no. 916, 1953, p. 85

Delaunay painted *The Death of Nessus* after the success of his *Plague in Rome* (now in the Louvre) in the Salon of 1869. Indeed, in addition to the twelve drawings—studies of details and of the whole—in the Nantes museum, there is a painted sketch, dated 1869 (24 × 32 cm) in a private collection in Paris. The subject was drawn from Book IX of Ovid's *Metamorphoses*: the centaur Nessus, after the rape of Dejaneira, is pursued by Hercules who, from the other side of the river Evenus, shoots him with a poisoned arrow. As in his earlier compositions, Delaunay imbues the dramatic gesture of the arms with an eloquent and theatrical character. The influence of his Italian sojourn is still visible, especially in his predilection for Classical landscapes as well as, perhaps, the influence of Domenichino. His contemporaries did not always like the importance given to the landscape, which, in the eyes of René Ménard, for instance, diminished "the dramatic impact of the subject" and obliged the artist "to limit his scope; it is a pity in the case of the principal group which was grandiosely conceived; it could have made a beautiful page; instead, it is a pretty picture." This type of comment bears out the importance ascribed to large formats for history paintings at the end of the Second Empire as well as at the beginning (see Benouville). Nonetheless, Ménard admitted, in 1878, that "there is expression, passion, and style in this small picture."

classicism of the poses (as in the woman at the left), and the warm accord of dark red, green, and brown are all in keeping with Delacroix's vision of men living in complete harmony with their environment in the Moroccan countryside. "They are closer to nature in a thousand ways," he had written in 1832 (1932, vol. I, p. 152 [April 28, 1832]). At the same time, the almost dejected attitude of several of the figures suggests a weariness of mood that occasionally overtook the aging artist.

D.R.

Philadelphia Museum of Art, Purchased for the W. P. Wilstach Collection

*Jules-Elie Delaunay*

Nantes 1828–1891 Paris

*Delaunay, a pupil of Lamothe and Hippolyte Flandrin (q.v.), two disciples of Ingres, entered the Ecole des Beaux-Arts on April 7, 1848. He was awarded a second prize at the Prix de Rome competition in 1853 and in the same year made his debut in the Salon. In 1856 his Return of Young Tobias (Ecole des Beaux-Arts, Paris) won him the Grand Prix de Rome. He was awarded a third-class medal for his work in the Salon of 1859, then, after his return from Rome in 1861, exhibited quite regularly: in 1863 he won a second-class medal, repeated in 1865, and then at the Exposition Universelle in 1867. The Administration of Fine Arts bought a number of his works: The Death of Lucretia in 1862 for the Tours museum, the Communion of the Apostles (done in Rome before his return to France) in 1864 for the Musée du Luxembourg (now at the Hôpital Saint Jacques in Nantes) and The Death of Nessus in 1870. The civil list supported the acquisition of The Plague in Rome from the Salon of 1869, which hung also in the Luxembourg, where Delaunay, during the last years of the Second Empire, became one of the best represented young artists. He also devoted much of his time to the decoration of churches in Nantes and in Paris and several rooms in the Conseil d'Etat. He kept up his brilliant official career during the Third Republic, was elected to the Institut de France in 1879, and became a professor at the Ecole des Beaux-Arts in 1889.*

G.L.

VI-47

This painting should be compared with drawings and paintings on the same subject by Gustave Moreau (q.v.).

G.L.

Musée des Beaux-Arts, Nantes

## Jean-Baptiste-Edouard Detaille
*Paris 1848–1912 Paris*

*Edouard Detaille displayed from a very early age the two features that were to create his fame and govern his life: a remarkable skill for drawing in minute detail and a strong curiosity about, and appetite for, all things related to the army. His parents, who encouraged him in this, recognized his ability early, and in 1865 sent him to the studio of Meissonier (q.v.), the well-established painter of military subjects as well as of portraits and historical genre. His training with the master was intense and severe, following the routine of the Ecole des Beaux-Arts. He first declared his independence at the Salon of 1869, where he met with great success, and from that date his career grew and expanded with all the honors and acclaim of an established master. During the Franco-Prussian War he joined the army and traveled in the environs of Paris, making drawings and watercolors of the troops, which are some of the most touching and evocative records of the war.*

*In the 1870s and 1880s, with his friends Alphonse de Neuville and Berne-Bellecour (with whom he traveled to Algiers in the spring of 1870), he continued as a specialist in military subjects, receiving very high prices, particularly from Americans. Unlike Meissonier, he rarely attempted historical subjects, even of the Napoleonic campaigns: The Skirmish between Cossacks and the Imperial Bodyguard, 1814 (Salon of 1870; Metropolitan Museum of Art, New York) was not a complete success, as would have been expected from his reception the previous year, and it was only through collaboration with de Neuville on the large-scale commissioned works of 1882 and 1883 that he undertook historical subjects. At the end of his life, he received commissions to decorate two panels for the Hôtel de Ville (1902) and one for the Panthéon (1905), an act of patronage that would seem ironic for an artist whose reputation, from the Second Empire, had rested on his remarkable ability to paint on a small scale. This indicates, however, the immensity of his reputation at the time.*

J.R.

Bibliography:
Duplessis, 1874; Masson, 1895; Vachon, 1898; Masson, 1913; Forbes and Kelly, 1977

Jean-Baptiste-Edouard Detaille

## VI-48
## Rest During Maneuvers, Camp of Saint-Maur, 1868

1869
Signed and dated, lower right: Edouard Detaille 1869
Oil on canvas
60.3 × 90.8 cm

Provenance:
William L. Elkins; Philadelphia Museum of Art, by 1896 (inv. no. E'24-3-82)

Exhibition:
1869, Paris, Salon, no. 743

Bibliography:
Duplessis, 1874, pp. 424–28; Vachon, 1898; Masson, 1895; *Elkins Collection*, 1900, vol. I, no. 15

While having shown in two previous Salons (*A Corner of the Studio of M. Meissonier* in 1865 and *The Halt of the Tambour* in 1868), Detaille first achieved his reputation in 1869 with the exhibition of this picture at the Salon. Its reception was, especially for the work of so young a man, remarkably enthusiastic. It was outspokenly praised by nearly all the powerful critics, and, as Duplessis mentions (1874, p. 428), was one of the popular favorites of the Salon. This immediately created commercial success for the artist, who was besieged by dealers, demanding anything from his hand. Much later, in 1896, the artist recalled the picture in a letter to William Elkins (known only from an English translation in the Philadelphia Museum of Art Archives):

"I learned with great pleasure that you had bought my painting entitled, 'Grenadiers at the Camp of St. Maur.' This painting certainly recalls to my mind the pleasantest souvenirs of my youth. I was then 20 years old, and when I painted it, it naturally produced (with my first medal at the Salon) every little self-satisfaction which accompanies a happy beginning.

"At the opening of the Salon, and on the part of Emperor Napoleon III, it was asked for the Imperial Prince, but was already sold.

"It was painted at Poissy, where I resided at the time, working in the studio of my master, Meissonier. Before executing this painting I made numerous studies for each figure on small wood panels, which remained in the studio at Poissy, and when the war of 1870 broke out, the Prussians took away these panels no doubt thinking they had studies from Meissonier, who, however, had carefully emptied his studio only leaving the 'Grenadiers' in a conspicuous place.

"The subject of the painting is derived from the last years of the Empire, when the troops of the Imperial Guard in turn went to camp at St. Maur, near Paris, to exercise. It is the moment of repose, music is played before the Staff Officers, in the background appears the donjon of Vincennes at the horizon of the field for drilling: the soldiers are in undress uniform, the same as the Cuirassiers of the Guard who serve as Escort to the General.

"I must confess that it is not without curious emotion that I would see this canvas again, to which are attached so many souvenirs, and if my signature has been remarked at the time, I have always tried to do honor to it...."

Meissonier did not show in the Salon that year, and it may have been through the absence of the immediate comparison to his master that Detaille's work received such high acclaim. Much of the praise of the picture—its minute veracity of detail, its clarity in observing movement and gesture, and, above all, its implicit scale "seen large, executed small"—are very much the features that had earlier brought Meissonier such fame. However, the one element that set Detaille apart from his master, and would mark his work throughout his long career, is his predilection for showing military figures at a casual, non-glorious moment. This he did with a candor more akin to photography than painting. As such, he left us with a curiously vivid and intimate record of military life shortly before the collapse of the imperial army.

J.R.

Philadelphia Museum of Art, William L. Elkins Collection

VI-48

## Gustave-Paul Doré
*Strasbourg 1832–1883 Paris*

*Gustave Doré, the son of a civil engineer and a mother with whom he lived happily until her death in 1881, made use in his lifetime of "all the modes of expression that art has pressed into the service of the idea, drawing, engraving, etching, aquarelle, painting, sculpture" (Stranahan, 1902, p. 420). Stranahan wrote that he had completed 50,000 designs by the age of thirty-two, and he kept up this level of production until he died in January 1883.*

*Doré first visited Paris in 1847, after five years spent at a lycée in the city of Bourg, where his family had moved in 1842. In Paris he succeeded in signing a three-year contract to do illustrations for the Journal pour Rire, then under the direction of the liberal editor and friend of Daumier, Philipon. Although pressed by family and friends to enter an art school, Doré continued his successful career as an illustrator in the 1850s with his well-known publications of Rabelais, Balzac, and Pierre Dupont. These led him into his later illustrations for the works of most of the great European authors: Shakespeare, Tennyson, Dante, Cervantes, Chateaubriand, and La Fontaine, among others.*

*Doré first entered the Salon in 1851 with a landscape called* Wild Pines, *but in 1853, a more significant entry included two works in which his carefully observed realism was imbued with moral overtones. Many of Doré's later paintings have religious subjects, one of which,* Tobit and the Angel *(Salon of 1865), was bought for the Musée du Luxembourg.*

*Doré was a popular guest at Compiègne during the Second Empire, and was even asked to accompany the imperial party on the trip to Suez. His first visit to London, in 1868, led to the opening of the Doré Gallery at 35 New Bond Street and to a friendship with the Prince of Wales. Although he was a friend of the critics About, Gautier, and Balloz, his art was little honored in France. Jules Comte expressed the popular estimation in 1885 when he wrote: "Gustave Doré, in spite of his extraordinary knowledge as an illustrator, has never produced anything in which one senses that intensity of thought, or that search for character, or that passion for nature that are the mark of the masters" (1885, p. 374). (See also nos. VII-24, VIII-32.)*

J.R.

Bibliography:
Comte, 1885, pp. 367–74; Roosevelt, 1885; Blanchard, 1891; Rosenberg, 1894, vol. I, pp. 271–74; Stranahan, 1902, pp. 414–26; Leblanc, 1931; Rose, 1946; Gosling, 1974

Gustave-Paul Doré

## VI-49
## Summer

c. 1860–70
Signed, lower left: G. Doré
Oil on canvas
268 × 202 cm

Provenance:
De Vries, Paris; Richard Baker; gift to the Museum of Fine Arts, Boston, 1873 (inv. no. 73.8)

Exhibitions:
1871, Boston, no. 138; 1871–72, Boston, no. 214; 1872, Boston, no. 68; 1873, Boston, no. 60; 1963, Philadelphia, repro. p. 137; 1964, Houston

Bibliography:
Downes, 1888, p. 507

William Downes's commentary on the paintings in the then new Museum of Fine Arts in Boston included a paragraph on Gustave Doré's *Summer*. He called it "a huge upright painting of wild flowers and weeds in rank profusion; a scythe of the sort that Father Time uses lies idle among the green growths; mountains close in the distance; and the colors are all out of time. This is a strangely insignificant work, considering the author's genius in graphic expression" (Downes, 1888, p. 507).

Following the lead of Downes, and in recognition of the sobriquet "Painter-Preacher" given to Doré by his English admirers, it is probable that this undated work is an allegory. Its subject seems to be the eternal rejuvenation

VI-49

of nature, as contrasted to the transience of the labors of man. The scythe, here a figurative symbol of the "Grim Reaper," lies rusted in the foreground. Hollyhocks, symbols of fecundity, press against the picket fence to join the encroaching tangle of weeds, morning glories, dandelions, daisies, and thistles outside the garden. Butterflies and dragonflies alight on the trumpetweed to feed and to begin again the life of the flowers by scattering pollen. The luxuriance of nature is omnipresent, while in the background, one of Doré's familiar ruined buildings both recalls his memories of a youth spent in the Bavarian Alps and, like his scythe, illustrates the theme of impermanence.

In Leblanc's catalogue of Doré's work published in 1931, twenty-one landscapes are listed, seven of Scottish scenery, nine of mountains and castles evoking his youthful *wanderjahre* in eastern France. None seems to share the careful botanical observation and the seemingly moral intent of the still enigmatic and highly individualistic *Summer*.

N.D.

Museum of Fine Arts, Boston, Gift of Richard Baker

---

*Henri Fantin-Latour*

*Grenoble 1836–1904 Buré (Orne)*

*Fantin-Latour was the son of a painter of portraits and religious subjects in Grenoble. When he was six, the family moved to Paris, where he received an early and rigorous instruction in drawing from his father. In 1850 he entered the Ecole de Dessin of* Lecoq de Boisbaudran, where he was trained in the master's method of rapid observation and rendering from memory (see Luard [ed.], 1914). An attempt to enter the Ecole des Beaux-Arts in 1854 failed. However, even earlier, he had begun the practice of copying, central to the academic method of instruction, and from 1853 until the early 1870s produced large-scale copies of paintings at the Louvre and Versailles. His artist friends were the more restless and independent painters, and perhaps his greatest influence was Whistler, who introduced him to England, where he was to find early and sustained patronage. Among the older generation, he was most closely drawn to Delacroix (whose works he frequently copied), Courbet, and Manet (q.q.v.).

He enjoyed his first success at the Salon of 1864 and during the 1860s his reputation as a portraitist and painter of flower pieces grew, providing him with a steady, if modest, income. In 1862 he joined the Société des Aquafortistes, and his continuing interest in printmaking allowed him to experiment and pursue his taste for other themes while—especially in later years—he increasingly confined his paintings to portraits and still lifes. Throughout his life he exhibited at the Salons, having refused, with Manet, an invitation to join the Impressionists in 1874.

Even in his earliest work during the Second Empire, influences on his style are extremely difficult to discern, and the most distinctive elements of his mature style derived from an assimilation of older masters and a sharp observation of nature—the "truth" (to which he makes frequent reference). As he explained in 1866 to his friend and patron Edwin Edwards: "I even believe that the time of schools and artistic movements is past. After the Romantic movement, born of classicizing exaggeration, after the Realist movement, product of the follies of Romanticism, it may be seen that there is great foolishness in all these ideas. We are going to achieve a personal manner of feeling" (Jullien, 1909, p. 23). (See also no. VII-25.)

J.R.

Bibliography:
Jullien, 1909; Fantin-Latour, 1911; Luard (ed.), 1914; Lucie-Smith, 1977

Henri Fantin-Latour

## VI-50
## Tannhäuser on the Venusberg

1864
Signed and dated, lower left: Fantin 1864
Oil on canvas
97.4 × 130.1 cm

Provenance:
Alexander Ionides, London; Rosenberg coll.; F. Gerard; Montagu Napier; Mrs. R.A. Workman, Lon-

don; Paul E. Cremetti, London; Cyril Davis, London; Mr. and Mrs. Charles Boyer; gift to the Los Angeles County Museum of Art, 1959 (inv. no. 59.62)

Exhibitions:
1864, Paris, Salon, no. 678; 1906, Paris, Ecole des Beaux-Arts, no. 151; 1920, Glasgow; 1942, London, no. 6

Bibliography:
Bénédite, 1906, pp. 27, 29, pl. 34; Jullien, 1906, pp. 36–37; Jullien, 1909, pp. 25, 49, 50, 93, 94, 196; Fantin-Latour, 1911, no. 233; Gibson, 1927, p. 29; Rewald, 1946, p. 101; Curry, 1964; Lucie-Smith, 1977, p. 152, no. 90

Two pictures by Fantin were accepted at the Salon of 1864, the work shown here and the well known *Homage to Delacroix* (Jeu de Paume, Paris), both tributes to a contemporary.

Fantin's deep devotion to the music of Wagner lasted throughout his life. In this painting he chose the moment in Tannhäuser (act I, scene I) when the hero, having lived on the Venusberg for 101 days, has realized that he must abandon this paradise and return to the mortal world of his beloved Elisabeth. (This, even while Venus slumbers on his chest and her nymphs continue their bacchantic dance.) *Tannhäuser on the Venusberg* was his first presentation in painting of a Wagnerian subject; however, his interest in poetic and fantastic subjects had been declared the previous year when he exhibited at the Salon des Refusés the *Display of Enchantments* (Museum of Fine Arts, Montreal).

In style, the work—as with many of Fantin's narrative subjects—depends as much on old masters as on artists of his own period. The figure of Tannhäuser is drawn directly from Giorgione, and a notation on one of the preparatory drawings for the painting specifically mentions the influence of Rubens, perhaps most evident here in the dazzling light of the landscape. Among his contemporary sources, the intensity and variety of the colors derive from Delacroix, although the very density of the glazes also indicates a knowledge of English painting, particularly George Frederic Watts. However, none of these sources fully explains the languorous sensuosity of the work, which in its ponderous brooding and dreamlike fantasy finds closer parallels, in the context of this exhibition, with Ingres, Gleyre, and Jalabert (q.q.v.).

The subject first appeared in Fantin's work in a lithograph of 1862, although it was considerably altered and enriched by 1864. Four preparatory drawings survive; three in the Louvre (all dated 1863) and one in Grenoble (dated 1864).

J.R.

Los Angeles County Museum of Art, Gift of Mr. and Mrs. Charles Boyer

VI-50

Henri Fantin-Latour

## VI-51
## Fruit and Flowers

1865
Signed and dated, lower right: Fantin 1865
Oil on canvas
59.7 × 73 cm

Provenance:
C. de Hele, Brussels; Julien Tempeleare, Paris; A. Reid, Glasgow; Cargill coll., Scotland, Reid & Lefevre Gallery, London; John T. Spaulding; bequest to the Museum of Fine Arts, Boston (inv. no. 48.540)

Exhibitions:
1932, New York, no. 25; 1934, London, no. 9; 1940, New York, no. 13

Still-life and flower painting underwent a notable revival during the Second Empire in both the variety and the quantity of works executed. They range from the delicate flower pictures of Simon Saint-Jean (which carried on a tradition of purism from the 1830s and 1840s) to the exotic masses of precious objects by Blaise-Alexandre Desgoffe; from the gentle and modest Chardin-inspired kitchen pieces of Bonvin, Vollon, and Philippe Rousseau (q.q.v.) to the monumental works in this genre by Manet (McCoubrey, 1964, pp. 39–53). By 1863 this production reached such a point that Castagnary noted with approval that still lifes were proliferating like rodents at the Salon and threatened to gnaw away at the higher foun-

dations of that institution (Castagnary, 1892, vol. II, p. 161). And while much of this popularity can be attributed to the growing prosperity of the bourgeois collector, traditionally the market for still lifes (as well as genre painting), there was, especially by the later 1860s, a discernible and growing acceptance on a critical level.

Fantin-Latour was to find financial success in this revived interest, since by far the majority of his output was devoted to still lifes and flower pieces. While it has often been noted that these were for him a tedious means of subsistence, taking him away from his preferred subject paintings, there is no doubt, especially with a work of the quality exhibited here, that they can stand comparison in their formal complexity and textural and coloristic sophistication with his more "serious" paintings.

Although *Fruits and Flowers* is not listed in Mme Fantin's inventory of works for 1865, another painting of nearly the same dimension incorporating many of the same elements, dahlias, pears, grapes in a basket, a knife, is listed (no. 276 bis). It was not at all unusual for Fantin to re-use a set of elements within a formal arrangement, almost as a series. In the following year, when he first submitted a still life to the Salon (National Gallery of Art, Washington, D.C.), there were at least three close variations of this work (*see* Chiego, 1974, pp. 30–31). Certain elements such as the knife blade projecting beyond the table recall similar *trompe l'œil* devices in Dutch seventeenth-cen-

VI-51

Bibliography:
Poncet, 1864; Delaborde, 1865; Flandrin, 1902; Cambas-Lanvin, 1967

Hippolyte-Jean Flandrin

## VI-52
## The Passage of the Red Sea (Study for the Nave of Saint Germain des Prés)

1858
Dated, lower right: 1858
Oil on cardboard
48.5 × 57 cm

Provenance:
Flandrin studio sale, Paris, May 15–17, 1865, no. 5; M. le comte de XXX (Lambertye) sale, Paris, December 17, 1868, no. 23; Shepherd Gallery, New York

Exhibitions:
1865, Paris, Ecole des Beaux-Arts, no. 86; 1976, New York, no. 65; 1977, London, p. 36

Bibliography:
T. Gautier, in Lambertye sale, Paris, December 17, 1868, p. vii; Mireur, 1901–1912, vol. III, p. 171

tury painting (for example, Pieter Claesz); however, in the coolly witnessed elements and particularly the recess of space under the tabletop, Fantin demonstrates yet again his great independence. The essential chasteness and restraint, even within such a variety of good things, also suggest the fundamentally reclusive and watchful aspect of his nature.

J.R.

Museum of Fine Arts, Boston, Bequest of John T. Spaulding

---

## Hippolyte-Jean Flandrin
*Lyons 1809–1864 Rome*

*Flandrin began his art studies in Lyons, but in 1829 went to Paris, where he entered the atelier of Ingres (q.v.; see no. VII-40). "He retained until the end of his life that deferential and charming attitude toward him... in which an expression of filial love was mingled with a sort of religious veneration" (Fournel, 1884). Indeed, Ingres and Catholicism were the two dominant influences giving direction to Flandrin's painting.*

*After receiving the Grand Prix de Rome in 1832, awarded for his* Theseus Recognized by His Father *(Ecole des Beaux-Arts), he went to study at the Villa Medici. His envois from Rome attracted*

*attention at the Salons:* Saint Clare Healing the Blind *(cathedral of Nantes) earned him a gold medal in 1837, and his* Jesus and the Little Children *(Lisieux museum) enjoyed a certain success. Upon his return to Paris he was entrusted with the decoration of the Chapel of Saint John in the Church of Saint Séverin. Between 1842 and 1846 he worked on the transept of the Church of Saint Germain des Prés, where his two large compositions,* The Entry of Jesus into Jerusalem *and* Christ on the Road to Calvary *were acclaimed by Christian contemporaries who saw in Flandrin the first great French religious painter since Lesueur, Flandrin having succeeded in giving form to their concept of religion. Flandrin worked in the Church of Saint Paul in Nimes, in 1849 he did his famous "Christian Panathenaea" for Saint Vincent de Paul, in Paris, and in 1856 began the decoration of the nave of Saint Germain des Prés.*

*Although almost all his critics recognized Flandrin's talent, they differed in characterizing it. Charles Blanc could see only the religious painter, considering him incapable as a portraitist of infusing life into his subjects; others, among them Chesneau, thought Flandrin's religious work lifeless and weak, and saw strength only in his portraits. Some were enraptured by his skill in painting women, "good women" (Théophile Gautier) like the girl with a carnation (Salon of 1859); others looked upon the portrait of Napoleon III as his best work. Although he achieved a notoriety rather than a real popularity, he may be seen today as one of the truly great religious painters of the nineteenth century.*

O.S.

In 1856 Flandrin began the decoration of the nave of the Church of Saint Germain des Prés, which he was unable to complete. For his conception, he returned to the idea, dear to the Middle Ages, according to which the Old Testament announces the New Testament, and thus each scene from the Gospel was juxtaposed with a scene from the Old Testament "prophesying" this event. As his biographer, Louis Flandrin, so justly observed, this preconceived notion had certain disadvantages: "The unity of these compositions is apparent to the mind, but not to the eye; each forms a separate picture, enclosed within its own frame and with no visible link to the neighboring ones." It was for this reason that the public was disappointed by them. Delaborde saw in the nave of Saint Germain des Prés the logical development of Flandrin's style, but Galimard complained of its monotony, its confusion, and quibbled about iconography. In defense of the artist it must be said that the task was not an easy one, for a system of arcades does not lend itself to the harmonious unfolding of great compositions, and the light was insufficient.

In the fourth bay of the nave, *The Passage of the Red Sea* is paired with *The Baptism of Christ* because "the waters of baptism establish between the Christian and the pagan an insurmountable barrier, just as the waters of the Red Sea forever separated the people of God from the Egyptians who pursued them. The artist chose the moment when the Israelites, on reaching the opposite side, watch the destruction of their enemy" (Flandrin, 1909, p. 302). Flandrin followed almost literally the text of the Bible where the Hebrews rejoice at the destruction of their enemy (Exodus 14-15). This composition was widely praised, especially the figure of Moses, who "looms up grandiose and fierce," and even a lukewarm admirer such as Mantz (1864, p. 85) esteemed this work in which "by their eloquent gestures and their proud forms these figures are linked to the School of Raphael." The strength of the composition is even more sensitively rendered in the sketch than in the final composition.

In the Flandrin studio sale, grouped under number 29, were five preliminary drawings, purchased by the dealer Haro, that reappeared in the Lambertye sale (no. 48), accompanied by a tracing for the Moses. Two preliminary studies for the whole composition are now in a Parisian collection, as are the drawings for Moses, while the study for the group of the woman and child in the foreground is in the Musée des Beaux-Arts in Lyons.

O.S.

Shepherd Gallery, Associates, New York

VI-52

Hippolyte-Jean Flandrin

## VI-53
## The Mission of the Apostles to Unite the Nations in a Single Faith (Study for the Nave of Saint Germain des Prés)

1861
Signed and dated, lower right: Hte Flandrin 1861
Oil on cardboard
43.5 × 55.5 cm

Provenance:
Flandrin studio sale, Paris, May 15–17, 1865, no. 14; acquired by the Musée des Beaux-Arts, Poitiers, 1974 (inv. no. 974-17-2)

Bibliography:
Mireur, 1901–12, vol. III, p. 171; Cambas-Lanvin, 1967; "Acquisitions," 1976, p. 393

The title of this painting is the one used in the catalogue of the exhibition sale of 1865 and by all the critics when the paintings for Saint Germain des Prés were unveiled. As required by the iconographic program for the nave, this

VI-53

scene is juxtaposed, in the ninth bay, with an episode from the Old Testament, *The Scattering of the Nations at the Base of the Tower of Babel.* Critics and art historians have generally misunderstood the relationship between these two compositions, which they interpreted as being antithetical: "It would be difficult to find fault with this ingenious arrangement although sometimes the meaning of the texts had to be stretched in order to obtain the desired paral-

lelism. In one or two cases even, Flandrin had to substitute antithesis for analogy, hence the scattering of the nations after the destruction of Babel as a pendant for the uniting of the nations at the behest of Christ" (Mantz, 1864, p. 84). Yet it is plain that after giving the keys to Saint Peter, Jesus asked the Apostles to go forth and teach the nations; in order to do this surely it was necessary for them to disperse.

This painting was clearly inspired by that of

Flandrin's master, Ingres (Musée Ingres, Montauban), who had himself borrowed it from Raphael (Victoria and Albert Museum, London). In addition, Paul Flandrin had made a reduced copy of the *Christ Giving the Keys to Saint Peter*. Flandrin, in his arrangement of the Apostles around Jesus Christ, gave the scene an almost boring symmetry, which Ingres and Raphael had succeeded in avoiding. Modern critics have generally had little appreciation for this scene. In fact, although there are some superb portions, such as the heads of the Apostles in the foreground, it is easy to see how those artists who were inspired by this painting withdrew all spirituality from it, and their work consequently sank into the "plaster saint" kind of art.

In the 1865 Flandrin studio sale, there were two lots of drawings. Number 113 was made up of five drawings, among which was the figure of Christ (no. VII-27); while number 114 had seven sheets of studies, among them two faces of Christ, two faces of Saint Peter, and the face of Saint John. The Musée Fabre in Montpellier has a drawing for the Apostle shown in right profile (no. VII-26), erroneously catalogued by Claparède as a "study probably for the decoration of the nave of Saint Vincent de Paul." A drawing for the face of Jesus Christ, another for the group of Apostles on the right, and two for the face of Saint Peter are now in private collections in Paris.

O.S.

Musée des Beaux-Arts, Poitiers

Hippolyte-Jean Flandrin

## VI-54
## The Prophet Habakkuk
## (Study for the Nave
## of Saint Germain des Prés)

c. 1856–61
Signed, at left: H. Flandrin
Paper laid to canvas
32 × 13 cm

Provenance:
Flandrin studio sale, Paris, May 15–17, 1865, no. 37; M. le comte de XXX (Lambertye) sale, Paris, December 17, 1868, no. 25 (mentioned by Hunolstein); sale, Paris, Hôtel Drouot, December 4, 1973; Musée des Beaux-Arts, Poitiers, 1974 (inv. no. 974-17-1)

Exhibition:
1865, Paris, Ecole des Beaux-Arts, no. 87

VI-54

Bibliography:
Mireur, 1901–12, vol. III, p. 171; "Acquisitions," 1976, p. 393, no. 18 (repro.)

Above the twenty large compositions in the nave of Saint Germain des Prés are "solemnly lined up an assembly of patriarchs, prophets, holy figures—forty-two of them can be counted—who in one way or another foretold or symbolized the coming of Jesus Christ" (Flandrin, 1902, p. 232). Among them is Habakkuk, in the second arcade, represented as he was "being seized by the hair and borne off by the Angel of the Lord to Babylon in order to provide food for Daniel in the lion's den: he holds in his hand a basket of fruit." This study makes it possible to appreciate the figures that are otherwise difficult to discern in the nave given the great height at which they are placed.

O.S.

Musée des Beaux-Arts, Poitiers

Hippolyte-Jean Flandrin

## VI-55
## Napoleon III
## (Full-Length Portrait)

c. 1860–61
Oil on canvas
212 × 147 cm

Provenance:
Officially ordered for 20,000 francs by decree of June 12, 1862, while the picture was on exhibit in London; after the Salon of 1863 remained for several months in the Dépôt des Marbres for the first copies to be made (Arch. nat. F$^{21}$ 120); sent to the Musée du Luxembourg (Louvre Archives L 2, and "Livre rapport de... Nieuwerkerke," 1868); gift of Napoleon III to the Tribunal de Commerce of the Seine, 1866 (Louvre Archives P 10 [April 14, 1868]); reclaimed for the Musées Nationaux and sent to Versailles (Louvre Archives P 4 [May 3, June 25, 1884]) (inv. no. MV 6556)

Exhibitions:
1862, London, class 38, no. 177; 1863, Paris, Salon, no. 704; 1865, Paris, Ecole des Beaux-Arts, no. 5; 1867, Paris, Exposition Universelle, no. 255; 1937, Lyons, no. 119; 1959, Milan, p. 9, pl. XV

Bibliography:
Astruc, 1863; Auvray, 1863, p. 24; de Callias, 1863, *Salon*, p. 214; Cantrel, 1863, p. 195; Chesneau, 1863; T. Gautier, *Le Monde Illustré*, vol. I, 1863, p. 298; T. Gautier, *Le Moniteur*, May 23, 1863; Lagarde, 1863; Merson, 1863; de Rialle, 1863, pp. 18–21; de Sault, 1863, pp. 4, 5, 8, 9–15; Viollet-le-Duc, 1863; Yriarte, 1863, "Exposition," p. 409; Beulé, 1864, p. 19; Delaborde, 1864, p. 851; Galimard, 1864, p. 43; Lagrange, n.d., p. 753; Mantz, 1864, p. 80; Saglio, 1864, p. 249; *L'Artiste*, 1864, p. 158; Claretie, 1865, p. 225; Delaborde, 1865, pp. 77, 101, 422, 430, 439; Merson, 1865; de Montifaud, 1865, p. 27; Nathaniel, 1865, p. 416; Jannet, 1866, p. 43; de Montrond, 1866, p. 30; Stevens, 1866, pp. 12–13; Duret, 1867, pp. 160–61; Saint-Pulgent, 1869, p. 531; Blanc, 1876, p. 271; de Montrosier, 1882, pp. 71–72; Fournel, 1884, pp. 255, 270, 276; Castagnary, 1892, pp. 109, 111–12; Thoré-Bürger, 1893, pp. 193, 372; Masson, 1900, p. 27; Flandrin, 1902, pp. 123, 259–62; Geffroy, 1904, repro. p. 95; Thieme and Becker, 1907–50, vol. II, p. 13; Flandrin, 1909, pp. 256–59; Schommer, 1927, p. 458; Mauricheau-Beaupré, 1949, p. 119; Cambas-Lanvin, 1967; Rosenblum, 1967, repro. p. 37; Angrand, 1968, p. 316; Lacambre, 1969, p. 110 (repro.); Lanvin, 1975, pp. 66, 68–71

In 1853 Nieuwerkerke submitted to the minister a plan for the use of 20,000 francs set aside for the encouragement of the fine arts, proposing Flandrin as "the artist most capable of executing a large historical portrait of the Emperor." An official order was passed in 1853 (Louvre Archives Z 6 [April 1, 1853]), then cancelled (Louvre Archives Z 6 [April 26, 1853]). A hint of this commission can be found in Flandrin's diary, which notes: "Visit of the Princess Mathilde—she is extremely pleasant, but talks to me about the portrait of the Emperor [May 24, 1853]." Like his master Ingres, Flandrin did not much like being distracted from his major works to do portraits, yet it was the Emperor himself who did not follow up on the project, probably because he preferred the services of Winterhalter (q.v.). Flandrin, however, did execute the portrait around 1860–61, but the order was only regularized on June 12, 1862 (Arch. nat. F$^{21}$ 80).

The portrait had enormous popular success in London (Callias), then in Paris at the Salon of 1863, where it was badly lit (Louvre Archives X [May 13, 1863]) and hung on an unflattering background (Louvre Archives X [June 2, 1863]) but found favor with the public (Merson). The critics were divided. Only Astruc railed violently against this "radically defective painting." Chesneau, Cantrel, de Sault, and Thoré-Bürger found many good qualities in this work, but were shocked by the Emperor's cloudy gaze. However, according to eye-witnesses from the court, "his pupils were dulled by the continual, silent tone of melancholy; they lay heavy under his eyelids which sink beneath the weight and seem as if infiltrated with fog." And Théophile Gautier, who knew the Emperor well, declared that "it is assuredly the first 'true' portrait we have seen of His Majesty." It is enough to compare photographs of Napoleon III with this picture in order to observe that he was right.

This is an intimate, psychological portrait despite the costume and accessories designed to fix the Emperor's official image, surrounded by symbols of Napoleonic ideology. And we can say with Gustave Geffroy: "Everything serves to make this work a profound, tragic portrait (and a very real one, without useless artifice or magical lighting) of a second-rate adventurer, a contemplative sociologist, an emperor of the coup d'etat and the political ambush." There is no doubt that it displeased because the portrait was a bit too true to life. The Emperor preferred to convey the spirited image Winterhalter and Cabanel (no. VI-17) had given him, and as soon as Flandrin was dead, he gave the portrait to the Tribunal de Commerce, where copies were habitually hung.

O.S.

Musée National du Château, Versailles

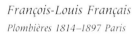

VI-55

## François-Louis Français
*Plombières 1814–1897 Paris*

*Français came to Paris in 1829 and worked for several years as an illustrator. By 1834 he was studying in the studio of Jean Gigoux, and he soon* became friendly with Corot (q.v.), whose work had a profound influence on him. The well-to-do Corot helped Français undertake a lengthy visit to Italy (1845–1849), and the younger man frequently reproduced the works of the leading Barbizon painters in his lithographs.

Exhibiting at the Salon as early as 1837, Français began receiving medals in 1841, and by 1853 had been made a chevalier of the Legion of Honor. He was almost exclusively a landscapist, though he occasionally painted mythological scenes with prominent landscape backgrounds. His most frequent subjects include the Roman countryside, the provinces of France, and the region around Paris.

Although Français is sometimes regarded as a belated follower of the classicizing landscape tradition developed by Valenciennes and Bidault around the turn of the nineteenth century, his work is strongly related to the realism of Corot in both subjects and composition. The hybrid character of this style, combining direct observation of nature with careful premeditation, was recognized by Charles Baudelaire, who praised Français's merit: "A merit somewhat like that of Corot, and one that we should be inclined to characterize as 'love of nature'; but it is already less naïve, more artful—it smacks much more of its painter—and it is also easier to understand" (Baudelaire, 1956, p. 30).

D.R.

Bibliography:
Girodie, 1901; Gros, 1902

VI-56

François-Louis Français

## VI-56
## Idyllic Landscape

1864
Signed and dated, on rock, lower right: FRANÇAIS 1864
Oil on canvas
109 × 134 cm

Provenance:
Purchased by the State; deposited in the Musée des Beaux-Arts, Lille, 1865 (inv. no. 437)

Exhibitions:
1864, Paris, Salon, no. 742 (as *Sacred Wood*); 1867, Paris, Exposition Universelle, no. 264 (as *Sacred Wood*); 1898, Paris, Ecole des Beaux-Arts, no. 50; 1918, Valenciennes, no. 325; 1956, Hazebrouck, no. 34

Bibliography:
Merson, 1867, p. 251; Catalogues, Lille, Musée des Beaux-Arts, 1872, no. 163, 1893, no. 313; Gros, 1902, pp. 180–81; Benoit, 1909, vol. III, p. 394

Français painted a number of large pictures of wooded glades inhabited by diminutive mythological figures. The forest growth is usually dense and, in the foreground areas, highly detailed; the artist often used a high horizon line that shuts out the sky almost completely. The similarity of the positions of the figures in this painting to those in the larger work *Daphnis and Chloe* (1872; Musée des Beaux-Arts, Stras-

bourg) suggests that the mythological staffage of Français's pictures was to a certain extent interchangeable. In this case, however, the figural group is taken directly from a Classical prototype, the well-known Hellenistic sculptural group of a satyr teaching a shepherd boy to play the panpipes (versions in the Museo Nazionale, Rome; Uffizi, Florence). Français's reading of Virgil's *Eclogues*, some of which are related in content, may also have influenced his choice of subject (Gros, 1902, pp. 180–81). The psychological realism of the lecherous satyr and the shy youth in the sculpture has here been distanced and transformed. The picture is an unusual amalgam of generalization and detail, of the ideal and the naturalistic.

D.R.

Musée des Beaux-Arts, Lille

---

*Eugène Fromentin*

*La Rochelle 1820–1876 Saint-Maurice (near La Rochelle)*

Fromentin first studied law, and did not begin to paint until 1843, when he entered the atelier of the academic landscape painter Rémond, which he soon left for that of Cabat. He pursued simultaneously a career as a writer and art critic as well as that of a painter.

In 1846 a six-week trip to Algeria at the invitation of one of his friends, the watercolorist Charles Labbé, was the event that determined the course of his life. He returned to Algeria twice, in 1847–48 and 1852–53.

Algeria and the Sahara were almost the only sources of his inspiration, from the Salon of 1847, the first in which he exhibited, until the end of the Second Empire. His work was notably absent, however, from the Exposition Universelle of 1855. He won a second-class medal in 1847, a rappel in 1857, a first-class medal and the Legion of Honor in 1859. He was a member of the jury of the Exposition Universelle of 1867 and became an officer of the Legion of Honor in 1869. From then on he led a very social life. Among his best-known friends were George Sand, Gustave Moreau (q.v.), and the landscape painter Charles Busson, at whose home in Montoire he stayed on several occasions.

Among his literary works are Un Eté dans le Sahara and Une Année dans le Sahel, published as books in 1857 and 1859, both drawing from the same inspiration as his paintings. He was also the author of the famous novel Dominique, published in 1863. In 1869 he was invited to the opening of the

Suez Canal and visited Egypt, and in 1870 he went to Venice; after a trip to Belgium and Holland in 1875, he wrote his study of Dutch and Flemish painting Maîtres d'autrefois.

G.L.

Bibliography:
1970, La Rochelle

Eugène Fromentin

## VI-57
## Falconry in Algeria: The Quarry

1863
Signed, lower right: Eug. Fromentin
Oil on canvas
162 × 118 cm

Provenance:
Purchased by the State by decree of June 22, 1863, for 7,000 francs (Arch. nat. F$^{21}$ 141); entered the Musée du Luxembourg, 1863; transferred to the Louvre, August 10, 1886; loaned, then deposited, in the Musée des Colonies, Paris, 1947; re-entered the Louvre, December 16, 1968 (inv. no. RF 87)

Exhibitions:
1863, Paris, Salon, no. 736; 1928, Cairo, no. 51; 1929, Paris, Hôtel Charpentier, no. 369; 1947, Paris, Musée des Colonies; 1970, La Rochelle, no. 21 (bibl.); 1974, Paris, Grand Palais, no. 90 (repro.; bibl.)

Bibliography:
Mantz, 1863, "Salon," pp. 496–97; Catalogues, Paris, Luxembourg, 1863–86; Chesneau, 1864, p. 219; de Sault, 1864, pp. 169, 170; du Camp, 1867, pp. 19–20; Thoré-Bürger, 1870, p. 385; Gonse, 1881, p. 79, repro. facing p. 81; Catalogues Illustrés, Paris, Luxembourg, 1884, 1887, 1893, p. 13; Chennevières, 1883–89, vol. II, p. 35; Blanchon, 1912, pp. 159, 179–82; Brière, 1924, no. 305; Dorbec, 1926, pp. 72, 80, 86, repro. p. 109; Jamot, 1929, p. 114, repro. p. 125; Catalogue, Paris, Louvre, Paintings, 1972, vol. I, p. 168

This large composition, which is the most famous of Fromentin's works, appeared as an illustration of his writings on Algeria. It was praised for the feeling of celebration that emanates from it, for its brilliant color and the almost Ingres-like perfection of its draftsmanship (see also no. VII-28). Du Camp, however, criticized the "dryness of execution" in "certain sections, and generally in the accurately copied details of the clothing" and did not find the artist's usual qualities in the work. Noting that Fromentin was seeking to "render nature such as it is," du Camp found it useless to bring up the "danger" of Realism: "He will never be a Realist—what is likeable in his paintings is not nature itself, but his way of interpreting it"

G.L.

Musée du Louvre, Paris

## Auguste Gendron
*Paris 1817–1881*

Gendron became a pupil of Paul Delaroche at the Ecole des Beaux-Arts, which he entered in 1837. Traveling in Italy from 1844 to 1847, he became interested in the art of antiquity and the Middle Ages. He exhibited at the Salon beginning in 1840, and was awarded a third-class medal in 1847 and a second-class medal in 1849.

Under the Second Empire he was given a great number of commissions for decorative painting: the Salle des Pas Perdus in the Palais d'Orsay (1852–59, destroyed in 1871); a room in the palace at Saint-Cloud (1856, destroyed in 1871); the ceiling of the Salle des Fêtes in the Ministère d'Etat (1861, now the Ministère des Finances); the Chapel of Sainte Catherine in the Church of Saint Gervais (1861–66); and private mansions, for example, the Hôtel Pereire (1859). At the 1855 Exposition Universelle he was awarded a third-class medal and the Legion of Honor for A Sunday: Fifteenth-Century Scene in Florence, which was sent to the Musée du Luxembourg (now at Fontainebleau). It is a vast, historical genre scene—he also liked Venetian subjects—which his contemporaries preferred to the huge canvases evoking the world of legends and poetic mythology. Nonetheless, this type of work, such as The Voice of the Torrent and the Nymphs at the Tomb of Adonis (Salon of 1864; Musée des Augustins, Toulouse) were bought on a regular basis by the State.

G.L.

VI-57

VI-58

to say that on this occasion he was "even more immaterial...." fading "into the vague phantasmagories of dream." In this fantastic painting of a kind that was occasionally produced in this era — *The Mourning Oceanides* of Lehmann (q.v.) for example (Salon of 1851, Exposition Universelle of 1855, then in the Luxembourg; now in the museum in Gap) — Gendron, whose tastes were eclectic and who was passionately drawn to the tradition of grand decorative painting, embraced some of the themes that had already been exploited in vast canvases with which he was undoubtedly familiar; first, Rubens's *Education of Marie de Médicis,* which at that time hung in the Grand Gallery of the Louvre (cascade and musicians motif, in the foreground) and perhaps also Ingres's *Dream of Ossian* which Reveil had engraved for the *Oeuvres de J.A. Ingres,* published by Magimel in 1851. This musical vision — still in the Romantic tradition — in which a multitude of female figures spring from the cascading water in the background and gradually take shape in the ray of light coming from the right, although remaining faithful to academic technique, heralds the subjects dear to Fantin-Latour (q.v.) and the Symbolist lore collected by Léon Frédéric at the end of the century (*The Stream,* in Brussels, was inspired by Beethoven). The whirling movement of the figures is accentuated by the placement of the faces; only one woman, in the center, is looking straight at the viewer.

G.L.

Musée des Beaux-Arts "André Malraux," Le Havre

---

Auguste Gendron

## VI-58
## The Voice of the Torrent

1857
Signed, lower left: A. Gendron
Oil on canvas
197 × 112 cm

Provenance:
Acquired by the Administration of Fine Arts of the Ministry of State for 3,000 francs by decree of November 19, 1857 (Arch. nat. F²¹ 83); deposited at the Musée des Beaux-Arts, Le Havre (inv. no. D.159)

Exhibition:
1857, Paris, Salon, no. 1148

Bibliography:
T. Gautier, "Salon de 1857–XIV," *L'Artiste,* September 13, 1857, p. 19; About, 1858, p. 348

The Salon catalogue explained the title of this painting with the following lines: "The abyss was aglow with an immortal light/Alive with spectral forms/tall, slender, ghostly women/Uttering wails and sighs that reached the very heavens." These lines could only confirm Pelloquet's general criticism of the artist (1858, p. 113): "I can see how one might have a penchant for spirits and fairies of lakes and torrents and for all sorts of phantasms, though far too transparent, of songs and ballads, but such devices should be used sparingly; it is a mistake to indulge too freely; and that is M. Gendron's error." Edmond About briefly praised the elegance of the composition, while Gautier meditated at length on the painting: "M. Gendron is a poet, perhaps even too much of a poet... it looks as if he has assumed the position of official painter to Titania." Gautier went on

## Jean-Léon Gérôme

*Vesoul 1824–1904 Paris*

*Jean-Léon Gérôme, the son of a wealthy goldsmith in Vesoul in eastern France, received his baccalaureate in Vesoul at sixteen and went to study with Paul Delaroche in Paris in 1841. He traveled with his master in Italy in 1844 and then returned to study in the atelier of Charles Gleyre (q.v.). His first success at the Salon was* The Cock Fight, *which competed for praise with Couture's* Romans of the Decadence *in 1847. The large, solid figures and the Antique genre subject represented the epitome of the style of Gérôme's early maturity, often called "Néo-Grec" or Pompeian. In 1848 Gérôme entered the competition for the ideal figure of the Republic proposed by the short-lived Second Republic.*

*Gérôme's real success and the travels in the Near East (see nos. VII-29, VII-30) and Africa that in-*

VI-59

spired so many of his paintings began during the
Second Empire. By the mid-1850s he was an accepted
figure at Compiègne, and a frequent visitor to the
salon of Princess Mathilde in Paris. He embarked on
African safaris and hunted with the Rothschilds. In
1855 he exhibited at the Salon a massive compilation
of ancient history, The Age of Augustus. After this
time his serious subjects from early Christian and
imperial Rome commingled with subjects from mos-
ques and harems of the Orient and scenes from the
court of Louis XIV.

Gérôme received the Grand Medal of Honor three
times, in 1867, 1874, and 1878. In 1863 he became
a member of the Institut de France after four rejections, and was a professor at the Ecole des Beaux-
Arts. His name has been vilified by those who felt he
thwarted the attempts of the Impressionists to
legitimize their art in official circles. His friends included Degas, Monet, and Bazille (q.q.v.), and his
own experiments in composition and, later on, in
sculpture, deny the rigid conservatism of which he
has been accused.

N.D.

Bibliography:
Arago, n.d.; Gautier, 1847; Chesneau, 1868;
Galichon, 1868; Claretie, 1882–84, vol. I; Hering,
1892; Stranahan, 1902, pp. 308–19, 329ff.; Spiel-
man, 1904, pp. 200–208; Moreau-Vauthier, 1906;
Zola, 1959, pp. 111–13; Ackerman, 1967, "Gérôme";
Ackerman, 1967, "Vassar"; Ackerman, 1967,
"Realist"; Boime, 1971, "Contest"; Boime, 1971,
"Gérôme"; Boime, 1972; 1972–73, Dayton, Min-
neapolis, Baltimore; Ackerman, 1973; Meyer, 1973

Jean-Léon Gérôme

## VI-59
## Reception of the Siamese Ambassadors by Napoleon III and the Empress Eugénie at Fontainebleau, June 27, 1861

1861–64
Signed and dated, lower left: J.L. GEROME.
MDCCCLXIV
Oil on canvas
120 × 260 cm

Provenance:
Commissioned by the Minister of Fine Arts for the
museum of Versailles, 1861 (inv. no. MV5004)

Exhibitions:
1865, Paris, Salon, no. 889; 1960, Nice, no. 135;
1969, Minneapolis

Bibliography:
T. Gautier, Le Moniteur, June 13, 1865; Hering, 1892,
pp. 111–12; Merimée, 1941–61, vol. IV, pp. 311–13;
1972–73, Dayton, Minneapolis, Baltimore, pp. 54–55

Gérôme was commissioned by the Minister
of Fine Arts to illustrate the visit of the ambassadors from Chai-Pha-Mongkout, the Emperor
of Siam, to Napoleon and the Empress, who
received them in the Salon d'Hercule at the
château of Fontainebleau in 1861. Their meeting commemorated a treaty Siam had made
with France, one of several signed in the 1850s,
which gave England, France, and the United
States trading access to the formerly closed
country. The gifts offered by the ambassadors
and painted here by Gérôme are today in the
museum at Fontainebleau, part of a collection
of Orientalia made by the Empress.

The artist was given an invitation to the
reception, and painted his self-portrait as well
as the portraits of the painters Jadin and Meissonier (q.v.), the three in light-colored civilian
dress in front of the large window to the left. He
also painted over eighty other portraits (identified in Strahan, 1881, vol. II, pl. 52) from
careful drawings as well as from photographs
by his friend Nadar (q.v.), all made after the
event. This mammoth undertaking took him

three years to complete, and was a task, as Ackerman notes, in which the realist was nearly "overruled by the demands of reality" (1972–73, Dayton, Minneapolis, Baltimore, p. 55). In order to include the entire scene, he drew back, diminishing the figures to a relatively small scale, allowing the grand hall with its frescoes, stuccoes, and rugs to dominate. Although Merimée, in a first-hand report, commented on the actual tedium of the event (1941–61, vol. IV, pp. 311–13), Gérôme has presented an august and splendid moment in the Second Empire, a meeting of East and West, in a setting equal to the grandeur of both nations.

Commissions to commemorate the great events of the Empire were liberally spread among the respected artists of Paris. *The Baptism of the Prince Imperial* by Couture is another important example of this custom (*see* nos. VI-31 – VI-35). Gérôme's fascination with Oriental subjects, even in countries far to the west of Siam, made him an excellent choice for this project. While both works look back to David's *Coronation,* they each, in quite different ways, attempt to record the event with an even more intense emphasis on literal accuracy.

N.D.

Musée National du Château, Versailles

Jean-Léon Gérôme

## VI-60
## The Death of Caesar

1860–67
Signed and dated, lower left: J. L. Gerome
MDCCCLX
Oil on canvas
85.5 × 145.5 cm

Provenance:
John Taylor Johnson, New York; sale, New York, 1876, no. 188; John Jacob Astor; Boussod Valadon et Cie, Paris; James B. Haggin; sale, New York, April 5, 1917, no. 148; Walters Art Gallery (inv. no. 37.884).

Exhibitions:
1867, Paris, Exposition Universelle; 1872, New Haven, no. 12; 1972–73, Dayton, Minneapolis, Baltimore, no. 20

Bibliography:
Gautier, 1858, "Les Ateliers"; Hering, 1892, p. 116; Ackerman, 1967, "Gérôme"; Drost, 1971, pp. 256–85; Boime, 1972, pp. 51–54

"*The Death of Caesar* rivals *The Christian Martyrs,* in this writer's eyes, as Gérôme's masterpiece," wrote Gerald Ackerman in 1972 (1972–73, Dayton, Minneapolis, Baltimore, p. 63), and Ackerman's discussion should certainly be consulted for his views about this extraordinary painting. Gérôme placed the dead Caesar at the foot of the statue of Pompey, whence he struggled as his enemies attacked him, according to Plutarch and Suetonius. This

VI-60

same juxtaposition of marble Republican and defeated Emperor can be seen in what Ackerman maintained a probable source for the painting: Vincenzo Camuccino's *The Death of Caesar* of 1798, seen by Gérôme in the royal museum in Naples. Another possible source of inspiration was Kaulbach's pencil drawing of the assassination, published in a set of photographs of his drawings in 1857.

Gautier described a painting of this subject, either a study or the unfinished version, in 1858 in *L'Artiste*: "Never did a scene of history appear more real. If photography had existed in Caesar's day, one could believe that the picture was painted from a photograph taken on the spot at the very moment of the catastrophe" (May 16, 1858, p. 17). Such adulation illustrates the broadly held belief in the accuracy of Gérôme's realism which the artist had created by his precise technique. However Gérôme's apparent archaeological accuracy is deceiving. His recreation of ancient buildings was as often motivated by dramatic needs as by historical accuracy. Franklin Sayre pointed out, for instance, that the grand circular sweep of the Colosseum was not erected when the Emperor Vitellius, who ruled for only one year, A.D. 69, received the salute of the dying gladiators in Gérôme's 1850 *Ave, Caesar, Moritorii Te Salutant* (Yale University Art Gallery), but Gérôme needed that space to dramatize his composition. He made use of a similar grand and imaginary stage set for *The Death of Caesar.*

The popularity of this work can be indicated by the use of the foreshortened Caesar by Manet (q.v.) for his *Dead Toreador* (National Gallery of Art, Washington, D.C.), although perhaps drawn more directly from Gérôme's large *Dead Caesar* (218.4 × 317.5 cm), shown at the Salon of 1857 (formerly Corcoran Gallery, Washington, D.C.; now lost). Its fame also spread across the ocean where it was used by Thomas Nast in a satire about Andrew Johnson's termination of office (Boime, 1972). Nast called his wood engraving *The Political Death of the Bogus Caesar.*

Gérôme's surface is the result of his clear, true colors and many layers of glazing, his almost precisionist effects, the fruit of his careful analysis of each object in light. Gérôme's friendship with Degas can be understood through this painting, in which control of the composition is absolute, not in the academic sense of bilateral symmetry, but by an asymmetrical balance of forms and light.

N.D./J.R.

The Walters Art Gallery, Baltimore

---

## Auguste-Barthélemy Glaize
*Montpellier 1807–1893 Paris*

*A pupil of Eugène and Achille Devéria, Glaize began exhibiting in 1836 at the Salon with history and genre paintings, as well as portraits. He received a third-class medal in 1842, second-class in 1844, first-class in 1845, second-class in 1848 and 1855, the year he was also decorated with the Legion of Honor. Under the Second Empire, despite official recognition, he led a difficult life; his composition entitled* The Distribution of the Eagles on the Champ de Mars on May 10, 1852, *commissioned in 1856 for the Versailles museum and exhibited in 1859, struck everyone, both critics and administration officials, as a failure. In spite of his repeated solicitations, he had to wait until 1864 before the State bought another of his pictures,* The Reefs, *for the Luxembourg museum (now in the Musée de Picardie, Amiens), where since 1844 his* Saint Elizabeth of Hungary *had been displayed (trans-*

*ferred in 1872 to the Valenciennes museum). His works, academic in style but giving proof of a highly personal philosophical and allegorical inspiration, did not easily find buyers, as the painter himself pointed out in a letter to the Administration of Fine Arts dated May 8, 1865: "My kind of painting and the nature of my interests making it impossible for me to place my pictures with the public, I cannot live without the encouragement of the State"* (Arch. nat. F²¹ 143).

G.L.

---

Auguste-Barthélemy Glaize

## VI-61
## Misery the Procuress

1860
Signed and dated, bottom center: A. Glaize 1860
Oil on canvas
155 × 260 cm

Provenance:
Prévost-Hommet coll.; gift to the Musée des Beaux-Arts, Rouen, 1874 (inv. no. 874-6)

Exhibitions:
1861, Paris, Salon, no. 1315; 1862, Rouen, no. 416

Bibliography:
De Callias, 1861, p. 268; du Camp, 1861, pp. 45, 135–38; Cantaloube, 1861, p. 79; Gautier, 1861, pp. 190–91; Claretie, 1882–84, p. 201; Catalogue, Rouen, Musée des Beaux-Arts, 1890, no. 224; Lafond, n.d., p. 61; Catalogue, Rouen, Musée des Beaux-Arts, 1920, p. 16; Vergnet-Ruiz and Laclotte, 1962, p. 237

VI-61

A number of critics at the time of the Salon took pleasure in writing lengthy descriptions of this painting, which captivated them by its singularity and its fantastic appearance. The subject is treated in the form of allegory, which Théophile Gautier found reassuring, since "given its modernity, it could have led to realism in bad taste." Maxime du Camp found it "a rather lugubrious composition extremely agitated and remarkable... absolutely fantastic and nevertheless fantastically real, comprehensible to all." Everything is organized in order to bring out the contrast between the foolish virgins and the wise virgins, between the "young women adorned for pleasure and sensuality" (Cantaloube) riding in a carriage toward a brightly lit city—Babylon or Sodom, Hell or the labyrinth where the Minotaur lurks—which the old woman, who personifies Misery, points to with her crooked finger, and the young women still working humbly by the light of a flickering candle. For they too are subject to temptation, as the artist explains in the Salon catalogue: "How many young women, giving up work, throw themselves into all the vices brought on by debauchery in order to escape this specter that seems always to pursue them?"

H. de Callias saw it as a moral allegory: "Misery, do not confuse it with poverty, holy poverty... misery is the mother of despair and infamy, of prostitution of all kinds"; Maxime du Camp offered social observations on "girls of ill repute who are today a new element in our society in transition," on prostitutes and the leveling aspect of the mixing of social classes as it results from the "mission" of these beautiful girls born from the "lower classes of our society," a mission that would "seem to be to ruin and cretinize the upper bourgeoisie and the remnants of the nobility."

G.L.

Musée des Beaux-Arts, Rouen

---

## Marc-Gabriel-Charles Gleyre
*Chevilly (Switzerland) 1808–1874 Paris*

*For the critic Hippolyte Taine, who more than any of his contemporaries stressed the union between art and the historical present, Gleyre achieved near perfection: "In the creation of style, and a grand style, he had few superiors; by his taste, science, and ideas, through perpetual research and nearly constant devotion to pure beauty and perfection, physical and moral, Christian and pagan, he is of the first order" (Taine, 1903, pp. 237ff). Yet even with such praise, Gleyre stands out as one of the most enigmatic figures of his time.*

*Born in the Swiss canton of Vaud (and fervently loyal throughout his life to his native land), he was taken as an orphan at the age of eight to Lyons, where he worked in the silk factories, perhaps establishing there his interest in the applied arts (1974–75, Winterthur, etc., p. 106). In 1825 he went to Paris and entered the studio of Hersent and*

VI-62

then took a long, arduous voyage to Italy and the Near East. Reestablishing himself in Paris in 1838, he emerged during the next five years as an artist of considerable importance, his most significant commission being from the duc de Luynes for the staircase of the château at Dampierre (destroyed). In the Salon of 1843 he gained an immense success with Evening (Louvre). However, after the Salon of 1849, he refused to show publicly in Paris, retreating into his studio on the rue du Bac (which he had inherited from Delaroche in 1843). There, in his free and open classes, he became one of the most significant and influential teachers of the period (1974–75, Winterthur, etc.), and is perhaps best known today as the master of many of the Impressionists, including Renoir, Bazille, Monet, and Sisley (q.q.v.).

Reclusive and melancholy, often plagued by his inability to complete satisfactorily his complex compositions, he was, nonetheless, a friend of many leading liberal intellectuals of the Second Empire. Politically, he was an outspoken Republican (partially explaining his refusal to exhibit after the Second Republic); this is best reflected in the two works commissioned by his native canton: Major Daval (Lausanne) and Romans Passing under the Yoke (Lausanne). While refusing the Legion of Honor, he did allow himself to be elected to the Salon jury, to which he was named every year from 1864 to 1870.

J.R.

Bibliography:
Mantz, 1875, "Gleyre"; Clément, 1878; Taine, 1903, pp. 237ff.; 1974–75, Winterthur, etc.

Marc-Gabriel-Charles Gleyre

## VI-62
## The Bath

1868
Dated, lower left: 1868
Oil on canvas
89 × 63.5 cm

Provenance:
Goupil et Cie, Paris (?); John Taillor, New York, until 1876; Charles S. Smith, New York; anonymous sale, New York, 1935; John H. McKay, New York, until 1969; Walter B. Chrysler, New York; gift to the Chrysler Museum at Norfolk (inv. no. 71.2069)
Exhibition:
1974, Hemstead, p. 52
Bibliography:
Mantz, 1875, "Gleyre," p. 411; Clément, 1878, nos. 109–11, nos. 407–12; 1974–75, Winterthur, etc., pp. 46, 102, 161, 186, 187

Speaking of the later development of Gleyre's art, Paul Mantz noted (p. 406):

"Gleyre settled into a style of grace. He returned to the smiling subjects which pleased his fantasies and only rarely made excursions into religious history; the last years of his career were consecrated to a commentary on the poem which is woman." The Bath is one of the most effective of these late works—calm, lovely, radiant—the full quality of which was for Mantz "a savoring of the tenderness of flesh and the flowering of life."

Earlier in his life, through his personal, formalized romanticism, Gleyre had turned to "Néo-Grec" subjects, a style of Classical genre that had particular influence on Hamon (q.v.) and Gérôme (q.v.); in returning to this form in the 1860s, he brought to it a new refinement of literal Antique detail and idealized beauty. Yet, for all the calm abstraction of this work, his strength of observation is quite apparent, and it is not surprising to note that Clément listed some six finished preparatory drawings for the subject, as well as two smaller oil versions (Clément, 1878, nos. 407–12). For all his fantastic poetry, this is still the artist famous for correcting a student's rigid figure drawing by commenting, "Have you never seen a woman playing with a child?" (1974–75, Winterthur, etc., p. 102).

Since the painting seems to have come almost immediately to America, it was known to contemporary critics only by photographs and a study of the head in the collection of Clément (and was listed as missing as recently as the 1974–75 Gleyre exhibition). However, even on this limited basis, it received from Paul Mantz the highest praise: "It is a picture of a penetrating suavity, which, in its clarity of tone, makes one realize that, while observing nature, the artist was also recollecting Leonardo da Vinci" (Mantz, 1875, "Gleyre," pp. 411–12).

J.R.

Chrysler Museum at Norfolk, Virginia, Gift of Walter P. Chrysler, Jr.

---

### Eva Gonzalès
*Paris 1849–1883 Paris*

*The daughter of Emmanuel Gonzalès, a journalist and celebrated author of serialized novels, Gonzalès studied at first with Chaplin (q.v.). Later, on meeting Manet (q.v.), who asked her to pose for a portrait, she left her professor and in 1869 entered Manet's studio on the rue Guyot, where Berthe Morisot considered her a rival. She showed in Lon-* don in 1869, then irregularly in Paris at the Salon starting in 1870. A painter and pastelist, she followed Manet's example and did not take part in the Impressionist exhibitions. In 1879 she married the engraver Henri Guérard and died in 1883 a few weeks after Manet.

G.L.

Bibliography:
Roger-Marx, 1950; 1959, Paris, Galerie Daber

Eva Gonzalès

## VI-63
## The Little Soldier

1870
Signed, bottom right: Eva Gonzalès
Oil on canvas
130 × 98 cm

Provenance:
Purchased by the State on July 18, 1870, for 2,000 francs (Arch. nat. F²¹ 144), paid in two installments (1,000 francs on July 27, 1870; 1,000 francs on July 28, 1871); deposited at the Mairie, Villeneuve-sur-Lot for the museum, 1874; transferred to the Musée Rapin, 1970 (inv. no. PG 1)

Exhibitions:
1870, Paris, Salon, no. 1219; 1959, Paris, Galerie Daber; 1976–77, Los Angeles, etc., no. 97 (repro.)
Bibliography:
Bertrand, 1870, p. 319; Castagnary, 1892, pp. 428–29; Roger-Marx, 1950; Bazin, 1972, p. 82 (repro.); 1974, Paris, Grand Palais, p. 11; Lacambre, 1974, p. 4 (repro.)

This painting was shown at the Salon of 1870 beside Manet's portrait of Eva Gonzalès seated, painting at an easel (Tate Gallery, London). The Little Soldier (Enfant de Troupe) put Eva Gonzalès forever in Manet's entourage and not, as the Salon catalogue indicated, as "M. Chaplin's pupil."

A tribute to Manet's Fifer (Jeu de Paume, Paris), which was refused by the Salon of 1866, and to Gonzalès's contemporaries, the painting appeared as a stroke of brilliance coming from a twenty-year-old girl. Karl Bertrand claimed: "There, I tell you, is a real artist, one who will leave her style and her mark. Already her brush is accustomed to drawing, and her palette is resourceful." However, he was disturbed by Manet's unhealthy influence, "a man of spirit who has spoiled her," and he agreed with Jules Castagnary who wrote, after having judged the painting "important" despite some imperfections: "What is most urgent for Mlle Eva Gonzalès is for her to leave M. Manet to his faults. Her work is a bit too black, with an inclination

VI-63

draw from nature, perhaps under the instruction of the young poet Frédéric Mistral (Daulte, 1960, p. 71). In 1854 he moved to join his parents in Marseilles, where he sought the advice of Emile Loubon, director of the Ecole des Beaux-Arts. Through the kind support of this painter, who had brought a new artistic vitality to the city, Guigou pursued his painting with greater energy and in 1854 began to exhibit in the annual exhibition of the Société Artistique des Bouches-du-Rhône. The importance of these shows, partially organized by Loubon, is often overlooked. In 1855 he made a brief visit to Paris, but it was not until 1862 that he gained his parents' approval for a career as an artist, and he moved to Paris, where he took a studio in Montmartre.

By the time he was twenty-eight his style was firmly established, as was his almost exclusive taste for landscape, and while he painted various locales in the Ile-de-France (Moret, Triel, Villars), doing rapid and brilliant studies at the site, which he would enlarge and finish in his studio, his primary source continued to be Provence, where he returned each summer, often working in the valley of the Durance with his good friend Monticelli. He first exhibited in the Salon of 1863 and was accepted each year thereafter, although he gained little recognition, either in the critical press or in the awarding of prizes. It was not until Roger-Marx included him in the 1900 Exposition Universelle Centennale that his reputation became broadly established.

J.R.

Bibliography:
Gouirand, 1901; Duret, 1912; Rey, 1927, pp. 556–59; 1959, Marseilles (bibl.); Daulte, 1960; 1970, Paris, Galerie Daber

to leave out halftones as that artist does. There we have a dangerous path which leads not to the practice of art, but to mannerism." He went on to advise her to paint outdoors.

Although the painting was bought by the State, this came about only because of the recommendation of Emmanuel Gonzalès, then delegate and honorary president of the Société des Gens de Lettres. A note dated June 28, 1870, and addressed to the Minister (Arch. nat.) sets forth the recommendation. Since the choice was to a certain extent imposed on the Administration, the work waited a few years before being given its modest home, in a provincial museum, which at the time of acquisition did not exist.

G.L.

Musée Gaston Rapin, Villeneuve-sur-Lot

## Paul-Camille Guigou
*Villars (Vaucluse) 1834–1871 Paris*

*Guigou is often presented in modern literature as a precursor of the Impressionists, and while he certainly knew Monet, Pissarro, and Sisley (q.q.v.) at the Café Guerbois by the mid-1860s (and they would later take up several of his favorite sites along the Loing and the Marne), he is an artist of distinctly separate attitude and style. The foremost painter of the hard landscape and dry light of the South, he represents a vital and considerably independent tradition of painting that emerged in Provence during the Second Empire.*

*Born into a family of prosperous landowners, he was apprenticed to a notary in 1851, and followed this career with lessening interest, having begun to*

Paul-Camille Guigou

## VI-64
## The Hills of Allauch

1862
Signed and dated, lower right: 62 Guigou
Oil on canvas
108 × 199 cm

Provenance:
Acquired from the family of the artist by the Musée des Beaux-Arts, Marseilles, 1881 (inv. no. BA 505)

Exhibitions:
1863, Paris, Salon, no. 854; 1927, Marseilles, Galerie Detaille, no. 17; 1927, Paris, Luxembourg, no. 14; 1959, Marseilles, no. 3 (bibl.); 1969, Minneapolis, p. 13; 1970–71, Leningrad, Moscow, p. 13

Bibliography:
Daulte, 1960, repro. p. 75

VI-64

This broad panorama of the hills behind Marseilles was one of three works accepted by the jury in 1863, and marked Guigou's first showing at the Salon in Paris. Importantly, all three are Provençal subjects, even though Guigou had been living in Paris since the spring of 1862. Like his exhibition in later Salons, his preference was always to be shown as a painter of that region.

While Courbet (q.v.), whom he first admired on a visit to Paris for the Salon of 1859, may be partially credited for the density of the paint surface, the breadth of the subject and the complete understanding of the bleaching light of Provence derive directly from his own intense experience of his native landscape, and his training under Loubon. François Daulte characterized Guigou's landscapes as having a "well-ordered grandeur" and, as such, Guigou sustained an attitude toward subjects that would be found again in Cézanne.

The paint itself has a lean and gritty quality, and even the inclusion of figures and the rutted road only slightly tempers the vast, sharply defined emptiness of the space. Speaking of these qualities, Duret noted: "His works have a dusty aspect, the plants bleached by the sun, the atmosphere limpid, the sky covered with a thin spread of clouds" (Duret, 1912, p. 99).

J.R.

Musée des Beaux-Arts, Marseilles

## Jean-Louis Hamon
*Plouha (Côtes-du-Nord) 1821–1874 Saint Raphaël*

*Hamon was one of the most esteemed representatives of the "Néo-Grec" school that derived from the art of Ingres (q.v.). He was considered one of the masters of this Pompeian style, which he interpreted in a wholly personal way, using a thin, transparent pigment at a time when Courbet (q.v.) was making strenuous efforts to impose on the Salon a technique in which the paint was rich, solid, and alive.*

*Born into a very poor family, this "Pompeian" was self-educated until his arrival in Paris in 1841, where he entered Delaroche's atelier and completed his training in the studio of Gleyre (q.v.), who helped him enter the Sèvres (q.v.) manufactory in 1848, where he remained as a decorator and potter until 1852. "This period at Sèvres had the most fortunate influence on his talent; there his palette was to be surprisingly lightened, his colors took on that simplicity, limpidness, and transparency, if I may say so, that was to astonish Théophile Gautier so much, but which was also the original stamp of his very personal artistic production" (Hoffmann, 1903, p. 63).*

*Hamon exhibited* The Human Comedy *at the Salon of 1852, but his first real success came in 1853 with a small "idyll,"* My Sister Is Not There, *bought by the Empress to decorate her apartments at Saint-Cloud. (Hoffmann claimed that this work was burned in the Tuileries fire, but it seems nevertheless*

to have turned up in the Rainbeaux sale of 1936, no. 32). The great Pompeian vogue of the mid-1850s was his moment of glory. But the fashion soon ended, and in 1859 Clément de Ris was already noting in L'Artiste the silence of the public with regard to Hamon's works.

The fact is that Hamon's style underwent almost no development. In 1860 he exhibited The Conjuror (Nantes), a pendant to The Human Comedy, but with no success. Discouraged, he left Paris for Rome in 1862. He sent Dawn to the Salon of 1864, and it too was bought by the Empress. He moved to Capri in 1865. His stay there inspired his large painting, The Muses Weeping over Pompeii, which was in a more noble and severe style than had been his custom. It did not bring him further recognition and, as of 1867, he stopped exhibiting but continued to paint for foreign collectors. He sent his last painting, Sad Shore, to the Salon of 1873.

O.S.

Jean-Louis Hamon

## VI-65
## The Human Comedy

1852
Signed, lower left: J.L. HAMON
Oil on canvas
137 × 316 cm

Provenance:
Purchased by the Ministry of the Interior for 3,000 francs in 1852 (Arch. nat. F²¹ 86); sent to the Musée du Luxembourg, 1878; transferred to the Louvre, by 1885; transferred to Compiègne, June 25, 1953 (inv. no. C 53 D 25)

Exhibitions:
1852, Paris, Salon, no. 607; 1855, Paris, Salon, no. 3270; 1939, Paris, Musée Galliéra, no. 762

Bibliography:
Esnault, 1852, pp. 70–77; Goncourt and Goncourt, 1852, pp. 43–44; Grün, 1852, pp. 15–20; de Ris, 1852, p. 116; Vignon, 1852, pp. 121–25; About, 1855, pp. 158–59; de Belloy, 1855; Delécluze, *Journal des Débats*, November 24, 1855; T. Gautier, *Le Moniteur*, October 11, 1855; Gebauër, 1855, pp. 117–18; Pétroz, 1855; Planche, 1855, pp. 1154–55; Vignon, 1855, pp. 231–37; de Belloy, 1859, pp. 3–4; Gautier, 1861, p. 196; Lafenestre, 1875, p. 396; Fol, 1875, pp. 122–26 (repro.); Bergerat, 1877, n.p.; Adams, 1881, pp. 200, 201, 205; Claretie, 1881, pp. 52–65; Bellier and Auvray, 1882–87, vol. I, p. 740; Dumas, 1884, no. 80 (repro.); Fournel, 1884, pp. 399–406; Rosenberg, 1884–85, p. 281; Hoffmann, 1903, pp. 70–79, 89, 92; *Chronique des Arts*, 1904, p. 123; le Braz, 1906, p. 28; Thieme and Becker, 1907–50, vol. XV, p. 571; Brière, 1924, p. 127; Focillon, 1928, p. 91

Hamon himself explained the subject of this picture, the inspiration for it having come to him while reading Dante. The mind of the spectator is transported to the Elysian Fields,

VI-65

realm of the Blessed, and along with all the great men of the past, he contemplates the spectacle in which "Love is hanged, Bacchus is thrashed, and Minerva, who eternally settles everyone's accounts, provides plenty of amusement for the curious and the strollers in the ideal abode where I place my spectators... [for] the old man has acquired wisdom when he has settled his account with Love, which overpowered his body in his youth. Bacchus, too, the drunkenness of life at a more advanced age, ambition, in a word all the passions, even the most sublime, must be muzzled by wisdom. That is the moral of my picture." Although the critics at the Salon of 1852 had deciphered the subject, they complained of its obscurity because they were disconcerted. The content of the idea was scarcely different from that of numerous history paintings in the Classical tradition, but the form that Hamon had given it was completely disorienting. People were not accustomed to seeing the great men of this world at a puppet theater. Vignon guffawed: "M. Hamon smokes opium, that's for sure," and he mocked the painting's "maid's-room sensibility." In general, the freshness of the children sitting with Socrates was applauded.

It was actually in compositions of this kind that Hamon subsequently struck his happiest notes. On the other hand, reservations were expressed about the execution. Hamon was

often reproached for the lack of correct drawing, the anatomical faults, the too gray and insipid colors. The Goncourts delivered the harshest blows: "This cosmopolitan and 'chronopolitan' nightmare, which seems modeled on those pieces of verse known as galimatias... is illuminated as in a daytime eclipse. Only two colors, sickly yellow and purple, share M. Hamon's palette. The drawing is flaccid, feeble, wavering.... One's view of each object is offended by incredible anatomical inaccuracies.... M. Hamon's characters have no eyes." Indeed, although there was a good deal of talk and many onlookers around this picture, the critics hastened to inform Hamon that this was only because of its oddity.

In 1855, when the canvas was reexhibited at the Exposition Universelle, reactions were much more laudatory, with, however, some reservations; the "Néo-Grec" fashion was in full swing and people had become accustomed to the originality of the subject.

Pétroz, like Théophile Gautier, let himself be seduced by this picture, which "is such that it makes you dream," and even though Gautier quite wrongly begged Hamon "to try when he paints to put a little color on the end of his brush," he went into raptures with E. About over the delightful "babies."

The Hermitage has a painted sketch in which each character has his name inscribed

above his head. *The Human Comedy* was lithographed by Aubert.

O.S

Musée National du Château, Compiègne

---

## Ernest Hébert

*Grenoble 1817–1908 La Tronche (Isère)*

*After a precocious start in Grenoble as a student of Rolland, Hébert simultaneously pursued studies at law school and at the Ecole des Beaux-Arts in Paris, which he entered March 1839, having first worked in the ateliers of Monvoisin, David d'Angers, and Delaroche. In his first competition, the Prix de Rome in 1839, he placed tenth, the last competitor considered, but he emerged with a first. The same year he submitted to the Salon* Expilly Visiting Tasso in Prison, *a rare example for him of a painting with a historic subject, which he gave in 1840 to the Grenoble museum.*

*During his stay in Rome, under the directorship first of Ingres, then of Schnetz, Hébert tried to find his own artistic individuality and began to take an interest in sketching Italian peasant girls. His works reappeared in the Salon only in 1848 and he first attained success in the Salon of 1850–51 with his*

Malaria *(Louvre), for which he was awarded a first-class medal. Already clearly defined in this work was his particular technique, in which he combined a play of light on figures with a certain sfumato, and which he was to use throughout his life. He enjoyed a brilliant career during the Second Empire: he was a society portrait painter (see no. VII-35) and a friend of Princess Mathilda. He continued to be interested in Italy, revisiting the Roman States and the Kingdom of Naples from 1853 to 1856. In December 1866 he was made a director of the Villa Medici. He became a chevalier of the Legion of Honor in 1853, then officer in 1867. His works were well represented in the Musée du Luxembourg, where his* Malaria, Kiss of Judas *(1853) and* Girls of Cervara *(1859) could be seen.*

*His success was reaffirmed during the Third Republic; upon his return from Rome in 1874 he was elected a member of the Institut de France and in 1882 became professor at the Ecole des Beaux-Arts. From 1886 to 1891 he was again director of the Villa Medici. An important gift to the Musées Nationaux in 1977 endowed Paris with the Musée Hébert, which complements the one established in the painter's family house in La Tronche.*

G.L.

Bibliography:
Péladan, 1910

Ernest Hébert

## VI-66
## Girls of Alvito: Kingdom of Naples

1855
Oil on canvas
220 × 152 cm

Provenance:
Marquise de Broc, in 1910; sale, Paris, Hôtel Drouot, December 6–7, 1926, no. 104 (repro.); Mme Hébert, widow of the painter, 1926; Musée Hébert, La Tronche; gift of M. d'Uckermann to the Musées Nationaux for the Musée Hébert, Paris, 1977

Exhibitions:
1855, Paris, Exposition Universelle, no. 3280; 1977, Paris, Musée Hébert, no. 68 (repro.)

Bibliography:
About, 1855, p. 162; du Camp, 1855, p. 213; Gebauër, 1855, pp. 95–96; Loudun, 1855, pp. 136–37; Vignon, 1855, p. 224; Castagnary, 1858, p. 81; Lépinois, 1859, pp. 123–24; Péladan, 1910, pp. 132, 137, 270, repro. p. 133; Roujon, n.d., *Hébert,* p. 51

*(Shown in Paris only)*

"M. Hébert is the most vigorous painter to have emerged for some time from the Villa Medici," Maxime du Camp wrote in 1855, finding that the *Girls of Alvito* "is certainly one of

the best [paintings] presented to us at this great exhibition of modern painting." The critics were unanimous in their praise and the artist was awarded for his submissions—he had also entered *Crescenza in the Prison of San Germano: Kingdom of Naples,* executed from November 1853 to January 1854—a first-class medal at the Exposition Universelle.

Alluding to a general criticism—Hébert's models were consumptive—Edmond About wrote: "The Alvito girls are feeling better; they are starting their convalescence. But they are so beautiful, so simple, so majestic, so queenly, and so peasant-like that I haven't the gall to quibble about the state of their health. One can criticize the painting of M. Hébert—but one likes it." Théophile Gautier thought they had the "anguished mask of Antigone or Iphigenia" and looked as though they were ready to enter Mycenae through the Lion Gate for libations at mysterious sacrifices. Hébert knew how to link an Italian genre scene with a history painting. He probably painted the picture in Italy, under circumstances similar to those for the *Crescenza,* known from the unpublished diary his friend Imer had kept at the beginning of their sojourn together in Italy in 1853–54 (Musée Hébert). The artist would conceive an idea for a picture, then have young girls from the village where he was staying pose for him, making them

VI-66

come back to sit again and again over a period of several weeks. Two drawings (Musée Hébert; 1977, Paris, Musée Hébert, nos. 69,70) show, on the same scale as the picture, the heads of the two models and bear on the reverse the date 1855. Thus it was only a few months before the Exposition Universelle that the artist painted the picture.

G.L.

Musée Hébert, Paris

---

## Jean-Jacques Henner
*Bernwiller (Haut-Rhin) 1829–1905 Paris*

*Henner began studying drawing very early at Altkirk, then in Strasbourg, and at the end of 1846 came to work in the atelier of Michel-Martin Drolling. In 1847 he was accepted at the Ecole des Beaux-Arts, where he studied under François-Edouard Picot. In 1858 he won the first Grand Prix de Rome and spent six years studying in Italy. There he perfected his painting of the nude from live models, did many landscape studies, and copied the old masters, especially Titian, Giorgione, and Correggio, who later inspired his vaporous technique. Back in Paris in 1864, he moved into a house at 43, rue de Villiers, which, after his death, became the Musée Henner. He made his debut at the Salon of 1863 where he won a third-class medal. At that Salon the State purchased his* Young Bather Sleeping *for the Colmar museum. In 1865 and 1866 he won medals and under the Third Republic he continued to receive honors.*

*Gradually a particular technique, characterized by a strong chiaroscuro and blurred outlines, began to become evident in his portraits, his female nudes especially, as well as in religious compositions, which were often a pretext for a nude study, which sometimes shocked his contemporaries.*

G.L.

Bibliography:
1973, Strasbourg

Jean-Jacques Henner

## VI-67
## Chaste Susanna
## (Susanna Bathing)

1864
Signed, lower right: J.-J. Henner
Oil on canvas
185 × 130 cm

Provenance:
Following a request of the artist (letter of October 25, 1864), the picture was purchased for 6,000 francs by the Direction des Beaux-Arts by a decree of January 17, 1865; taken on January 23, 1865, by the artist from the Ecole des Beaux-Arts, where the *envois* from Rome were shown, and delivered to the Dépôt des Marbres, February 4, 1865 (Arch. nat. F²¹ 147); entered the Musée du Luxembourg, 1867; assigned to the Musées Nationaux by decree of May 3, 1874; transferred to the Louvre, January 30, 1929 (inv. no. RF 94)

Exhibitions:
1864, Paris, Ecole des Beaux-Arts; 1865, Paris, Salon, no. 1027; 1867, Paris, Exposition Universelle, no. 347; 1873, Vienna, no. 331; 1958, Munich, no. 58; 1974, Paris, Grand Palais, no. 121 (repro.)

Bibliography:
Mantz, 1865, pp. 496, 498, repro. p. 497; Boetzel, 1865 (repro.); Gallet, 1865, p. 27; de Laincel, 1865, p. 59; Privat, 1865, pp. 88–89; Catalogues, Paris, Luxembourg, 1868–1927; Claretie, 1882–84, p. 81; Chennevières, 1883–89, vol. II, p. 35; Catalogue Illustré, Paris, Luxembourg, 1887, no. 139, no. 16 (repro.); Muther, 1893–94, vol. I, repro. p. 360; Focillon, 1928, p. 98, repro. p. 95; Sterling and Adhémar, 1958–61, vol. III, no. 1071, pl. 385; Crespelle, 1966, p. 106, no. 158 (repro.); Catalogue, Paris, Louvre, Paintings, 1972, vol. I, p. 210; Beyer, 1973

This painting, about which Henner wrote in his letter of October 25, 1864, saying that it was "a summation of my long period of study," was his final year's *envoi* as *pensionnaire* at the Villa Medici. In fact, the idea came to him in Rome, both from studying Guercino's *Susanna at the Bath* (Galleria Colonna), which he copied in one of his notebooks, most likely around 1862, and from Titian's *Sacred and Profane Love*. The critics were often harsh. Paul Mantz remarked that it was really more a study—in the sense of a nude academic exercise—than a painting and noted that it looked better among the exercises sent from Rome exhibited in the galleries on the quai Malaquais at the Ecole des Beaux-Arts than at the Salon where the standard was higher. He found the head "lacking something," and F. Jahyer pointed out that in it there was a mistake in idealization: "The head of Susanna should be more noble. Looking at it, it seems to me, one gets the feeling in spite of oneself, that it was copied directly from a model who was not very distinctive." The legs and feet were declared "a little heavy" by L. Gallet, and Jahyer criticized another detail, the reflection in the water: "It is no doubt true to life but it is not graceful."

G. Privat's censure was more serious: "Why, M. Henner, this contempt for the subject? Why not simply call a bather a bather. And what could possibly have made you think that putting an old man in the background would be enough to turn it into a *Chaste Susanna*?" He suggested that with a simple change in décor it could just as easily become a Bathsheba.

But as conscientious teachers, they admitted he had great ability, a "practiced hand," and put all their hopes on Henner's submission to the next Salon. Despite these mixed reviews, the work had a brilliant official career, being shown at universal expositions and hung in the Luxembourg. It was often reproduced as an engraving (Boetzel in 1865; C. Waltner at the Salon of 1875; and E. Gaujean in 1877, for example), as a lithograph (Pirodon), and on porcelain (Mme F. Fleury, Salon of 1869).

G.L.

Musée du Louvre, Paris

VI-67

## Paul Huet

*Paris 1803–1869 Paris*

Huet began his artistic studies with drawing courses under Deltil in 1816, then entered the studio of Guérin in 1818 and that of Baron Gros in 1819. From the outset he was in revolt against the preceding generation of Neoclassical landscape artists. Around 1820 he formed a friendship with Richard Bonington and in 1822 with Delacroix (q.v.). He first participated in the Salon of 1827 with a View of the Environs of La Fère *and was to become one of the promoters of Romantic landscape.*

He was named professor to the duchesse d'Orléans in 1837 and gradually won a number of honorary titles, receiving the Legion of Honor at the Salon of 1841. This eternal traveler, enamored of dark forests and rocks battered by the sea, was forced to settle in the south of France due to delicate health. Returning to Paris in 1848, Huet won a gold medal at the Salon. After the coup d'etat, according to his biographers, he was "blacklisted by the Emperor" (Miquel, 1962, p. 13) and his sincere Republican opinions cast a shadow over his career. However, the State, through the intermediary of different administrations, did buy or commission paintings rather regularly, including in 1852 Morning Calm (Louvre); 1855, The Flood at Saint-Cloud (Louvre); 1861, Under the Trees (Alençon museum); 1866, Pierrefonds Restored (formerly collection of the Empress), and The Forest at the Hague (Orléans museum); 1868, Pierrefonds in Ruins (Compiègne).

During the Second Empire the paintings that Huet presented at the Salon were a little old-fashioned in their conception, and he never won popular acclaim. His ravishing studies made from nature, which seduce all who appreciate Impressionist painting, were seen only by his intimates during his lifetime. The works which could have exercised an influence are those that were presented at the Salon, and they almost always display a Romantic conception and a more finished execution. His true worth was defined by Sainte-Beuve (Miquel, 1962, p. 239): "You are one of the fathers of the rebirth of natural landscape; no one conceived as broadly as you did its spirit, poetry, and life: others were able to succeed and to excel in parts and corners of landscape, but 'the soul' of nature, who has grasped and understood it as you have?"

O.S.

Paul Huet

# VI-68
# Pierrefonds in Ruins

c. 1868
Signed, lower left: Paul Huet
Oil on canvas
107 × 160 cm

Provenance:
Purchased at the Salon of 1868 for 3,000 francs (Louvre Archives 2 DD 25); turned over to the Empress on May 29, 1880 (Louvre Archives Z 15); sale, Farnborough, 1927; Mlle Marie Dechaux; gift to the Musées Nationaux, 1928; deposited at Compiègne (inv. no. C 28.093)

Exhibitions:
1868, Paris, Salon, no. 1279; 1949–50, London, no. 199

Bibliography:
Chesneau, 1868, Le Constitutionnel; Auvray, 1868, p. 40; G. Lafenestre, Le Salon de 1868, 1868, p. 41; Thoré-Bürger, 1893, p. 495; Burty, 1869, p. 104; Bellier and Auvray, 1882–87, vol. I, p. 789; Huet, 1911, pp. 411, 462–65, 524; Terrier, 1959, no. 27; Miquel, 1962, p. 224; Miquel, 1975, p. 245

VI-68

This painting showing the ruins of the château of Pierrefonds was exhibited at the Salon of 1868, although the restoration work on the château, carried out under the direction of Viollet-le-Duc, had begun a decade earlier in 1857 (see no. I-29). In 1866 Huet had already exhibited another painting representing Pierrefonds restored. In October 1864 he was at Compiègne awaiting "a little work that [he] hoped to have . . . the two views of the Château of Pierrefonds" (Miquel, 1962, p. 224). In 1865 Viollet-le-Duc asked him: "And your Pierrefonds, what are you doing with it?" (Huet, 1911, p. 397), indicating that it was still a question of only one painting, Pierrefonds Restored, on which Huet was to work in 1865. In September he wrote to Legrain: "I have worked a great deal this summer and progressed, at least I believe so without being certain about it, on a painting that was commissioned from me and that I want to put in a forthcoming exhibition: The restored Château of Pierrefonds. I want to combine it with its pendant, the ruins, of which I have had the studies for at least thirty-five years!" It is clear from this letter that only Pierrefonds Restored was commissioned, while the pendant, Pierrefonds in Ruins, was purchased only at the Salon of 1868 (contrary to the assertions of Miquel). This is confirmed by Burty (1869) and Bellier and Auvray. Huet's idea to do a pendant was a good one since he knew that the Empress was infatuated with Pierrefonds. However, the price paid to Huet seems rather modest.

The reviewers said very little about this painting. Auvray criticized him for aiming at effect and preferred the Château of Pierrefonds by Justin Ouvrié; Only Thoré-Bürger found it to have "great expanse" and Lafenestre saluted Huet, who, "faithful in his old age to the aspirations he had when he was twenty years old, continues to sound the great fanfare of 1830." In 1868 Huet's painting was a little out of fashion, as he wrote to his wife, "Alas, my work will not cause a revolution" (Huet, 1911, p. 407).

In the very subject of the painting: a medieval château, ruins, a storm, can be found all of the components of a Romantic landscape, a landscape that reveals the moods of the artist's soul. Huet was, moreover, a friend of Lamartine and a fervent admirer of his poetry as well as that of Victor Hugo.

Two small painted sketches of Pierrefonds in Ruins are known (Musée de l'Ile-de-France, Sceaux; Compiègne, with variations). A drawing, very close to these sketches, was exhibited in 1969 at the Heim Gallery in London (no. 21). In the final version Huet eliminated the cow lying in the foreground which created an inappropriate element of serenity in a stormy atmosphere, while he added two slender trees unfortunately bent by a wind from a direction contrary to the wind blowing the woman's scarf.

O.S.

Musée National du Château, Compiègne

## Jean-Auguste-Dominique Ingres

*Montauban 1780–1867 Paris*

*Ingres's artistic production during the Second Empire consisted exclusively of his completing works he had conceived earlier, for example, the portraits of Mme Moitessier (done between 1844 and 1856) and Mme Gonse (from 1845 to 1852), and such famous paintings as the* Virgin with the Host, The Source, Antiochus and Stratonice, Jesus among the Doctors, *and* The Turkish Bath *(see no. VII-42). Such variations on themes, repeated time and again (see no. VII-41), symbolize not only the somewhat earlier period when they first appeared but also epitomize the Second Empire, with the contrast between its academic concerns and its aesthetic modernity. Nor should one forget the influence Ingres exerted through his style and subject matter on a great many artists, not all of whom had actually been his pupils.*

*His fame was tremendous, even after he had decided to stop exhibiting his works in the Salon and to keep them for selected admirers. Nonetheless, in December 1853, he was appointed, along with Delacroix (q.v.) to the imperial commission presided over by Prince Napoleon to direct and supervise the 1855 Exposition Universelle. At that time an entire gallery was given over to a vast retrospective of his works. After his death in 1867, a large show was mounted at the Ecole des Beaux-Arts, while the museum of the city of Montauban, his birthplace, was enriched by the bequest of his collections and works from his atelier. This city thus has become, through exhibitions and publications, one of the privileged sources for the study of Ingres and his works. (See also no. VII-40.)*

G.L.

Bibliography:
Wildenstein, 1954; Rosenblum, 1967; Rosenblum, 1968; Ternois and Camesasca, 1971

Jean-Auguste-Dominique Ingres

## VI-69
## The Apotheosis of Napoleon I (Study for the Hôtel de Ville)

1853
Oil on canvas
48 × 48 cm

Provenance:
E. Gatteaux (?); purchased from M. David by the city

VI-69

of Paris, 1899; entered the Musée Carnavalet, 1903 (inv. no. P 443)

Exhibition:
1967, Montauban, no. 134

Bibliography:
Lapauze, 1911, p. 473; Wildenstein, 1954, no. 271, pl. 100; González-Palacios, 1967, p. 78, pl. 52; Rosenblum, 1968, pp. 41–43, repro. no. 55; Ternois and Camesasca, 1971, no. 152b (repro.)

This study, which shows the transition from a rectangular to the definitively adopted circular format, was done for the ceiling of the Salon de l'Empereur in the Paris Hôtel de Ville, which was destroyed in the fire of 1871 as was the Salon de la Paix, the ceiling of which Delacroix (q.v.) had painted at about the same time.

The painting was done in 1853 in Gatteaux's atelier on the rue de Lille, where the Emperor and the court came to admire it on February 1854, and was shown at the Exposition Universelle of 1855, a pendant to *The Apotheosis of Homer,* in the center of one of the walls of the Ingres gallery (*see* photographs of the installation in Trapp, 1965, p. 304).

The catalogue of the 1855 exposition described the subject (no. 3343): Napoleon I "is being taken in a chariot to the temple of Glory and Immortality; Fame crowns him and Victory leads the horses; France mourns him; Nemesis, the Goddess of Vengeance, crushes Anarchy." The iconography derives from Flaxman's *Iliad* and from Greek vases from the Hamilton collection engraved by Tischbein.

Théophile Gautier observed that "M. Ingres conceived and executed this dazzling and difficult subject as an artist of the age of Pericles or of Augustus would have done it. The ceiling designed for the Hôtel de Ville could easily have come from the picture gallery of the Propylaea."

Ingres made numerous preparatory sketches of details (Musée Ingres, Montauban; Fogg Art Museum, Cambridge, Mass.; *see also* no. VII-39) and the full work (Musée Bonnat, Bayonne; Cabinet des Dessins, Louvre). In 1874 Bastien-Lepage made copies from the engravings, one of which was bequeathed to the Louvre by Gatteaux and is on deposit in Montauban. Adolphe David remained faithful to the aesthetic of Ingres in his reproduction of the composition as a cameo (no. III-32).

G.L.

Musée Carnavalet, Paris

Jean-Auguste-Dominique Ingres

## VI-70
## Joan of Arc

1854

Signed and dated, lower left: I. INGRES P$^{IT}$. 1854;
inscribed on cartouche, lower left: "et son
bûcher se change en trône dans les cieux. Em.
Deschamps"
Oil on canvas
240 × 178 cm

Provenance:
State commission of October 8, 1851, of 20,000 francs
for a "painting whose subject and sketch you should
submit for the Minister's approval" (letter to Ingres,
October 16, 1851) refused by Ingres in a note of
November 8, 1851; commission changed to the acquisition of works in the course of execution, including "a Joan of Arc at the Coronation of Charles VII in
the Cathedral of Reims, standing, whose composition
is already engraved and forms part of Le Plutarque
français," which is "on the easel," for 10,000 francs;
regularized by decree of November 8, 1851; 4,000
francs paid on August 12, 1852; by decision of January 12, 1855, Ingres having added several figures,
the allotted sum raised to 15,000 francs; balance of
11,000 francs paid on February 12, 1855 (Arch. nat.
F$^{21}$ 88); sent to the Musée du Luxembourg, as coming
from the Ministry of State in early March 1856
(Louvre Archives Z 4); returned to the Louvre, December 26, 1862; sent to Versailles, January 28,
1863; inscribed in the Louvre inventory in August
1863 as a gift of the Ministry of State for the Versailles
museum; reentered the Louvre; sent to the Corps
Législatif, December 1865; reentered the Louvre,
April 1867; again sent to the Luxembourg after the
Ingres exhibition of 1867; reentered the Louvre,
November 1874 (inv. no. MI 667)

Exhibitions:
1854, Orléans; 1854, Paris, Atelier Ingres; 1855, Paris,
Exposition Universelle, no. 3356; 1867, Paris, Ecole
des Beaux-Arts, no. 59; 1968–69, Paris, Petit Palais,
no. 264

Bibliography:
Vinet, 1854, pp. 615–18; About, 1855, p. 129; du
Camp, 1855, pp. 54, 72–73; T. Gautier, Le Moniteur,
October 11, 1855, pp. 155–56; Gebauër, 1855, p. 28;
de la Rochenoire, 1855, pp. 38, 40–41; Vignon, 1855,
pp. 191–92; Catalogues, Paris, Luxembourg, 1858,
1862, no. 82, 1868, no. 123, 1870–74, no. 136; Catalogue, Paris, Galerie du Corps Législatif, 1866,
no. 21; Larousse, 1866–90, vol. VI, p. 114; Nieuwerkerke, 1869, p. 123; Chennevières, 1883–89, vol. II,
p. 35; Momméja, 1898, p. 42; Flandrin, 1902, p. 151;
Lapauze, 1911, pp. 465, 473–74; Brière, 1924, no.
420; Wildenstein, 1954, no. 273, pl. 111; Schlenoff,
1956, pp. 271, 275–77; Sterling and Adhémar,
1958–61, no. 1117, pl. 408; Houyoux and Sulzberger,
1964, p. 184; Trapp, 1965, p. 304; Rosenblum, 1967,
pp. 160–63, pl. 45; Angrand, 1968, pp. 318–46;
Gaudibert, 1970, p. 9, pl. 68; Ternois and Camesasca,
1971, no. 153 (repro.); Catalogue, Paris, Louvre,
Paintings, 1972, vol. I, p. 210; Naef, 1973, pp. 23–24;
Baudelaire, 1976, vol. II, p. 589

See Colorplate

The history of the commission of Joan of Arc
demonstrates the modifications introduced by

VI-70

the artist during the execution of the painting.
As M. de Mercey, chef de la section des Beaux-Arts,
explained in 1855 in a note proposing to raise
the price even though the picture was finished:
"M. Ingres, in executing the Joan of Arc, abandoned himself to his inspiration and instead of
limiting himself to reproducing the figure of the
heroine alone, which was all he had promised
to do, has composed a picture showing her
surrounded by her pages and followers witnessing the coronation of King Charles VII in
the church of Reims" (Arch. nat. F$^{21}$ 88). The
catalogue of the Exposition Universelle
specified the identity of these figures: "She is
accompanied by her squire Doloy, her chaplain
Jean Paquerel, an Augustinian monk, and her
pages." Ingres gave his own features to Doloy,
shown standing at left.

Although the painting was judged "quite
beautiful" by Hippolyte Flandrin (q.v.), who
saw it as early as July 6, 1854, and Théophile
Gautier was enthusiastic—"Thanks to M. Ingres, Joan of Arc at last possesses an image
worthy of herself"—most of the critics were
perturbed. Baudelaire, who of course was prej-
udiced, wrote: "As for his Joan of Arc, a picture
whose most obvious distinction is an inordinate
technical pedantry—I do not trust myself to
speak of it.... I prefer to believe that the loftiest
talent always reserves certain rights to make
mistakes" (Baudelaire, 1965, p. 135). Edmond
About declared: "The Joan of Arc is a bad painting in which steel and copper play the principal

role." It was Joan's armor in particular that
provoked the most insulting remarks: J. de la
Rochenoire found that it "kills the picture";
E. Gebauër quipped: "Joan of Arc, color of
tin"; and later, in 1877, Fernand Khnopff,
whose taste for smooth painting is well known,
wrote to his friend L. Houyoux that she is
"dressed in an armor which, like painted
cardboard, is of an admirable finish." It was
only with Robert Rosenblum's brilliant analysis
that this much discredited painting was at last
restored to its proper place. He rightly insists on
the "visual fascination" of the work, its extraordinary density, the contrasts of color and
the subtle play of counterpoint of the materials—fabrics and metals—and shows how such
a picture falls perfectly within the aesthetic of
the 1850s, if one compares it with the decorations of Neo-Gothic churches in Paris such
as Saint Eugène and Sainte Clotilde.

The city of Orléans wished to obtain a copy
of Joan of Arc, and Ingres had one executed
under his own direction by his pupil Pichon
(q.v.). In this version, Joan's costume—a coat
of mail and armor—corresponds faithfully to
the illustration Ingres had supplied in 1846 for
Le Plutarque français.

G.L.

Musée du Louvre, Paris

Jean-Auguste-Dominique Ingres

## VI-71
## The Source

1820–56
Signed and dated, lower left: J. Ingres 1856
Oil on canvas
163 × 80 cm

Provenance:
Purchased by the comte Charles-Marie Tanneguy-
Duchâtel (1803–1867), Minister of the Interior under
Louis Philippe, for 25,000 francs in 1857; comtesse
Duchâtel; bequest to the Louvre, 1878 (inv. no.
RF 219)

Exhibitions:
1856, Paris, Atelier Ingres; 1861, Paris, Galerie Martinet; 1862, London, no. 76; 1867, Paris, Ecole des
Beaux-Arts, no. 31; 1868, Bordeaux, no. 363; 1932,
London, no. 440; 1945, Paris, Louvre, no. 26; 1955,
Rome, Florence, no. 62, pl. 28; 1956, Warsaw, Moscow, Leningrad, no. 56, pl. 23; 1964–65, Munich,
no. 149 (repro.); 1965, Lisbon, no. 70 (repro.); 1967,
Montauban, no. 137, pl. 15; 1967–68, Paris, Petit
Palais, no. 252 (repro.; bibl.); 1973–74, Paris, Louvre,
no. 1

Bibliography:
Gautier, 1857, "La Source," pp. 113–14; Blanc, 1859,

VI-71

p. 18; de Banville, 1861, p. 359; Turner Palgrave, 1862, p. 122; Taylor, 1862, p. 117; Delaborde, 1862, pp. 14–18, repro. facing p. 14; Blanc, 1863, pp. 13–14, 22; Auvray, 1863, pp. 70, 104; Lecomte, 1863, pp. 245–47; Delaborde, 1870, no. 29; Gigoux, 1885, pp. 92, 93; Thoré-Bürger, 1893, pp. 192, 288, 321–22; Lapauze, 1911, pp. 196–98, 489, 495–96 (re-pro.); Brière, 1924, no. 422; *Commemorative Catalogue 1932*, no. 416, pl. 91; Wildenstein, 1954, no. 279 (re-pro.); Schlenoff, 1956, pp. 292–94; Goncourt and Goncourt, 1956, vol. I, p. 1035; Sterling and Adhémar, 1958–61, vol. III, no. 1119, pl. 410; Mesuret, 1964, p. 4; Rosenblum, 1967, p. 43, fig. 58; Gaudibert, 1970, pp. 24, 27, pl. 70; Sandoz, 1970, p. 45; Ternois and Camesasca, 1971, no. 155, pls. 53, 54; Catalogue, Paris, Louvre, Paintings, 1972, vol. I, p. 211; Guizot, 1972, p. 31; Georgel, 1975, p. 71, re-pro. p. 16; Haskell, 1975, pp. 65, 76; Méras, 1976, p. 7; Foucart, 1976, pp. 20–21

In his 1881 guide to Paris, Baedeker men-tioned *The Source*, hung in the Salle Duchâtel in the Louvre, as "perhaps the most perfect specimen of the treatment of the nude among modern paintings." The painting was be-gun, according to Amaury-Duval (q.v.), at the beginning of Ingres's stay in Florence in 1820; for a long time it remained merely a study from nature, the model wearing red stockings half-way above her knees, and although Ingres oc-casionally went back to it, it was not completed until 1856—at that point within a fortnight, it was said—with the help of two students, Paul Balze (pitcher and reflections in the water) and Alexandre Desgoffe (background). Amaury-Duval, who regretted the alterations, reported that "only the torso remained intact"; the posi-tion of the arms was changed, while the legs were made "heavier," as Ingres "possibly wanted to avoid making them too realistic."

*The Source*, whose pose was inspired by a bas-relief in the courtyard of the Hôtel Sully in Paris (as noted by Edmond de Goncourt in his *Journal* (1957 [June 11, 1892]), is somewhat akin to the *Venus Anadyomene*, completed in 1848 (Musée Condé, Chantilly).

The painting was tremendously successful when it was exhibited privately in Ingres's atelier and was immediately snapped up for 25,000 francs by the comte Duchâtel, who out-bid five other collectors. Guizot, in a letter dated May 7, 1857, wrote that the count had hung the painting in a room of its own, "surrounded by large aquatic plants and flowers, to make the nymph of *The Source* appear even more real." She was a source for inspiration for the writers Théophile Gautier (1857, "La Source") and Théodore de Banville (1861), who charac-terized her as a "silvery naiad." She was often copied by artists, in engravings (Flameng, etc.), in enamel (Balze, 1863; L.-M. Berthon, 1876; E.-C. Chanson, 1872), on porcelain (Mme D. de Cool; Mlle M. Leclerc, 1868; Mlle Bergeron, 1873), in cameo (H.-L. François, 1870); she appears placed in the cella of the nymphaeum in Nîmes in a drawing by Simil (Bibliothèque de l'Architecture, Paris). Later, Seurat and Derain copied her in drawings; she was a direct source of inspiration for Hippolyte Petitjean and Magritte (*Halcyon Days of M. Ingres*, 1943); others, like Jules Lefebvre in his *Truth* (Amiens museum), would paraphrase her image. A smaller version, without doubt a studio piece, but signed and dated by Ingres in 1859, was bequeathed to the Musées Impériaux in 1867 by Marcotte-Genlis and exhibited, beginning in 1868, in the Luxembourg (now, Louvre).

Gautier looked upon her as "pure Paros marble, rosy with life," while to Blanc she was a vision: "I felt transported, as in a dream, to that remote time, incalculably long ago, when the human form suddenly freed itself from the forces of a life-giving, beneficent nature, when a youthful Eve awoke under the palm trees of Asia in the light of the dawn." But the Goncourts were severe, writing on March 11, 1862, in their *Journal*: "It is a restoration of the body of a young girl of antiquity, a painfully wrought restoration, polished, ingeniously stupid," and Gustave Moreau observed in a notebook (Musée Gustave Moreau, Paris, cahier IV, pp. 95–100) that the painting is "academic (old style), in short, executed by an outstanding scholar...."

G.L.

Musée du Louvre, Paris

Jean-Auguste-Dominique Ingres

## VI-72
## Louis XIV and Molière

1857
Signed and dated, lower left: J. Ingres 1857
Oil on canvas
50.5 × 71 cm

Provenance:
Gift of the artist, in appreciation for the lifetime pass he had been granted, to the Comédie Française on January 1, 1858

Exhibitions:
1967, Montauban, no. 139; 1974–76, France, Musées de Province, no. 7

Bibliography:
Gautier, 1858, pp. 21–23; Blanc, 1859, pp. 16–18 (repro. Flameng engraving); Delaborde, 1870, no. 69; Delorme, 1878, pp. 26–28, 184, no. 7; Monval, 1897, no. 217; Lapauze, 1911, pp. 366, 502–4; Joubin, 1936, p. 91; Wildenstein, 1954, no. 281, fig. 185; Schlenoff, 1956, p. 287; Ternois and Camesasca, 1971, no. 159a (repro.)

VI-72

In a long letter dated September 1852 to Romieu, Director of Fine Arts, Arsène Houssaye, who was at the time administrator of the Comédie Française, announced his plans for the enlargement of the museum: "M. Ingres, who does not know how to thank me for his pass, and especially for that of Mme Ingres, asks only to paint the portrait of an actor." However, it was Houssaye's successor, M. Empis, who received from Ingres, after much hesitation, this picture of Molière dining with Louis XIV at Versailles. The subject, as referred to by Ingres's notebook (carnet X), was taken from an anecdote recounted in Mme de Campan's *Mémoires* (1822): in order to make his courtiers respect the actor, Louis XIV invited Molière to his table one morning at the time of his "petit lever" and summoned his courtiers. "You find me," the King said, "attending to Molière's meal; my footmen do not consider him good enough company for themselves." In a letter dated July 3, 1857, to Magimel, Ingres wrote: "I have prepared... this picture of Molière, on which I have cleaned up what was done and finished sketching." This sentence leads one to believe that the painting was begun as a studio piece. On August 25, 1857, he wrote to Marcotte (letter published by Schlenoff): "I have very nearly finished the large sketch of Molière which I want to give to the Théâtre Français."

Théophile Gautier and Charles Blanc admired the painting's bright, intense colors, but Blanc expressed some surprise that Ingres took up such an anecdotal subject, reminiscent of some of his larger canvases dating from the

Restoration. Soon after, Ingres undertook a new version of the same subject on which he worked during the summer of 1859 and which was sold for the substantial sum of 25,000 francs on January 25, 1861, according to the civil list of Napoleon III (Louvre Archives 2 DD 25, "Inventaire de la liste civile", no. 410). Remitted under the terms of the 1879 decree as part of the "domaine privé," it entered the collection of the Empress on January 17, 1881 (Louvre Archives Z 15 A), and is now part of the Wildenstein collection in New York. Other artists took up the same theme: Gérôme (q.v.; Public Library, Malden, Mass.) and Jacques-Edmond Leman (*The Petit Lever of the King*; Arras museum) in the Salon of 1863 and Jean-Hégésippe Vetter in the Salon of 1864 (now in the Sénat, Paris).

G.L.

Collections de la Comédie Française, Paris

---

*Charles-François Jalabert*
*Nîmes 1819–1901 Paris*

*Jalabert's art and life belong, in spirit if not completely in date, to the courtly and elegant side of the Second Empire. "His talent," wrote Théophile Gautier, "... has something tender, delicate, and feminine about it that charms and prevents you from wishing for more force. It is not that he cannot raise*

VI-73

Bibliography:
Lagrange, 1861, p. 335; Lagrange, 1866, p. 399;
Mantz, 1872, p. 38; Blanc, 1876, p. 474; Claretie,
1876, p. 115

Charles-François Jalabert

## VI-73
## Orpheus

1853
Signed and dated, lower left: ch. Jalabert 1853
Oil on canvas
111.8 × 91.8 cm

Provenance:
Goupil et Cie, Paris; unknown coll., Liège; Alexander
White, Chicago; Samuel P. Avery; W.T. Walters, by
1878; Walters Art Gallery (inv. no. 37.37)

Exhibition:
1853, Paris, Salon, no. 646

Bibliography:
Strahan, 1878–80, vol. I, repro. facing p. 93; Bellier
and Auvray, 1882–87, vol. I, p. 818; Walters Collection,
1884, no. 108; Champlin and Perkins, 1886–87,
vol. III, p. 330

The full name of this work, entitled *Orpheus*
in the Walters catalogue, is *Nymphs Listening to
the Songs of Orpheus*. It was exhibited at the
Salon of 1853 with an *Annunciation*, which was
bought by the State, and the portrait of an
unidentified woman. This variety in his Salon
entries indicates Jalabert's versatility. He received the cross of the Legion of Honor for
*Christ on the Mount of Olives* in 1855; his portraits
of the Duchess of Alba, the Countess Montijo,
and the duchesse d'Aumale, among others, exhibited "a character of delicacy, sensitivity, and
sweetness, the presence of spirit," according to
Charles Blanc (1876, p. 474). The beauty of his
mythological genre canvases brought him two
private commissions for ceilings and panels in
Paris, *Night Unfolding Her Wings* in the Hôtel
Pereire and *Homage to the Dawn* at the Hôtel Say.

The subject of Orpheus charming the wood
nymphs by his song does not illustrate a specific
text, but is simply a romantic notion that allowed the artist to subjugate the sights and
sounds of nature to his will. Jalabert's predecessors were Titian, Rubens, and Boucher,
but like his contemporaries Corot (q.v.) and
Diaz, he did not impose his figures upon the
landscape; rather, he incorporated them into it,
like flowers or wild animals. They appear
among the foliage as if in the dream of the
viewer, and seem capable of dissolving back
into it at will.

Jalabert's most powerful tool was his color.
"One must applaud the charming fashion in

*himself to vigorousness when he wants, but his real
nature is gracefulness" (1855–56, vol. I, p. 8). His
obituary in* Chronique des Arts *in 1901 concluded:
"The fall of the Empire put an end to Jalabert's
previously uninterrupted success... the wind having
changed, little by little the taste of the public abandoned the delicate and slightly mannered painting of
the earlier period for a more solid kind of painting."*

*Jalabert was born in Nîmes, where he studied
with Alexandre Colin at the Ecole de Dessin. He
entered the Ecole des Beaux-Arts in Paris in 1839
and was a pupil of Paul Delaroche, whom he followed to Rome in 1843. He returned to Paris in 1846
and submitted to the Salon of 1847* Virgil, Horace,
*and Varius at the House of Maecenas, which was
highly acclaimed. He regularly exhibited genre,
Classical, and Biblical subjects in the Salons from
this time until 1882. For these and his gallery of
royal portraits he was made chevalier of the Legion of
Honor in 1855 and officer in 1867.*

*Jalabert sold his work through the dealer Goupil
(whose daughter would marry Gérôme, q.v.). The
increasing power of dealers, and their close relationships with artists, is illustrated by Goupil's
providing a house for Jalabert in 1858.*

N.D./J.R.

which M. Jalabert has translated his caprice onto the canvas," wrote Claretie. "His pinks, his blues, his pleasing tones are of an intimate sweetness. It is the adorable in the false, it is seduction in the impossible. It's a bouquet of fresh flowers, a creamy... bedizened image" (Claretie, 1876, p. 116).

The photogravure illustration by Goupil et Cie in Strahan shows the picture with an arched frame, since removed. H. Mireur noted a painting of the same title (40 × 90 cm) sold at the 1863 Gilkinet sale for 8,900 francs (1901–12, vol. IV, p. 35).

N.D.

The Walters Art Gallery, Baltimore

---

## Johan-Barthold Jongkind
*Latrop (Holland) 1819–1891 La Côte-Saint-André (Isère)*

*While Jongkind showed frequently at the Salons during the Second Empire and achieved some official recognition early in his career (third-class medal, Salon of 1851; works purchased by the State, 1851 and 1853), during this period he rarely attracted the attention of any but the most progressive critics (i.e., Champfleury), and his influence, so important for later landscape painting, was limited to a small circle of painters, namely his friends of the Barbizon School, Boudin (q.v.) and Monet (q.v.).*

*Born in a small town near the Dutch-German border, he began his official training at the age of eighteen with Andreas Schelfhout in The Hague. In 1845, through the indirect assistance of Nieuwerkerke, who was visiting The Hague to unveil his statue of William of Orange, it was arranged that Jongkind would go to Paris on a stipend from the Prince of Holland to study with Eugène Isabey. There he met Théodore Rousseau (q.v.), Couture (q.v.), and Boudin, and on the advice of Troyon (q.v.), studied briefly with François-Edouard Picot. In 1847 he visited Normandy and Brittany for the first time, and returned with Isabey in 1850 and 1851. During the early 1850s he began to find an audience for his pictures, especially with the help of the dealer Pierre-Firmin Martin. However, in 1855 he was rejected by the Salon and this, along with the death of his mother the same year, caused a depression that sent him into retreat in Holland. It was only through the proceeds of a sale held to sponsor him in 1860 that he was able to resettle in Paris, where he established a liaison with the remarkable Mme Joséphine Fesser-Borrhée. He resumed his work, alternating between Paris and the Channel coast, and his output during the rest of his life was immense.*

*A man of rustic manners and considerable charm, Jongkind was firmly rooted in the traditions of seventeenth-century Dutch marine painting and cityscapes. With Boudin and the young painters around Le Havre, he established an informal school which would, on many levels (see 1976–77, Northampton, Williamstown), have considerable influence until the end of the century.*

J.R.

Bibliography:
Hefting, 1969; Hefting, 1975; 1976–77, Northampton, Williamstown

Johan-Barthold Jongkind

## VI-74
## Shipyard (Port in Normandy)

1852
Signed, lower right: Jongkind, 52
Oil on canvas
43 × 60.7 cm

Provenance:
Boussod Valadon and Co., New York; John G. Johnson, Philadelphia, October 1889; John G. Johnson Collection, Philadelphia (inv. no. cat. 1013).

Exhibitions:
1958, Baltimore; 1976–77, Northampton, Williamstown, p. 35, no. 4

Bibliography:
*Johnson Collection*, 1892, p. 44, no. 131; *Johnson Collection*, 1914, vol. III, p. 122, no. 1013; Catalogue, Philadelphia, John G. Johnson Collection, 1941, p. 62, no. 1013; Hefting, 1975, p. 90, no. 109

An old pencil inscription on the stretcher of this painting notes: "Fecamp." Several elements do bear a certain similarity to a view of this small fishing village between Le Havre and Dieppe of the same date, now in Hartford (Hefting, 1975, no. 110). Jongkind visited this area with Isabey in 1850, and perhaps again in 1851. However, it should be noted that for all the freshness of his watercolors and drawings done outdoors, his finished oils, especially of this early period, often are studio composites of arranged elements (so clear here in the perspective of the two small boats in the foreground on the right) from earlier notations, with the primary sense of place depending on a remembrance of light and atmosphere. It was this quality which would so influence the young Impressionists. As with Corot and Théodore Rousseau, the pervading "Jongkind light"—silvery and radiant—should not be taken as a rejection of *plein air* painting; however, in the relationship of on-the-spot studies to finished work, Jongkind has more in common with Constable than with the following generation.

J.R.

John G. Johnson Collection, Philadelphia

---

## Alphonse Legros
*Dijon 1837–1911 Watford*

*Legros first studied drawing at the Ecole des Beaux-Arts in Dijon and then went to Paris, where he enrolled in the course given by Horace Lecoq de*

VI-74

*Boisbaudran at the Ecole de Médecine. Like other artists he completed his training by studying at the Louvre. His first painting exhibited at the Salon, in 1857, was a portrait of his father (Tours museum), which reflects the influence of Holbein. Champfleury remarked on this work, and in 1859 Baudelaire was to sing the praises of* The Angelus *(private coll.). In 1861 he was labeled a Naturalist or Realist because of his* Ex-Voto *(Dijon museum), which was to have its fervent admirers as well as its detractors. This same canvas, exhibited in London in 1864, firmly established the artist's reputation in England.*

*In 1863, victim of numerous material difficulties, he went to England on the invitation of Whistler. Subsequently he established himself in that country while continuing to send paintings to the Paris Salon, among them* Making Amends, *which was purchased for the modest sum of 3,000 francs at the Salon of 1868. Beginning in 1876 he taught drawing for eighteen years, then took up his art again, working intensely.*

*Legros did not limit himself to painting, but experimented with many areas of artistic expression: drawing, engraving, medals, semiprecious stones, and decoration. In 1863 (Le Salon, May 14) Astruc described his talent: "Among everything, I recognize in him a well-defined character: —the accent; —he distinguishes himself by a tighter style, by a profoundly studied construction. He works in the grand manner—he already has within him all the authority of an audacious and knowing artist, ample and precise." To these qualities should be added that of the originality of the subjects treated by Legros. In a contemplative mood he often depicted subjects taken from contemporary life or religious scenes.*

O.S.

Bibliography:
Soulier (ed.), 1904; 1957, Dijon

Alphonse Legros

## VI-75
## The Vocation of Saint Francis

1861
Signed and dated, lower left: A. Legros. 61
Oil on canvas
140 × 195 cm

Provenance:
Gift of the artist to the Musées d'Alençon, 1862 (inv. no. 862.1.1)

Exhibitions:
1861, Paris, Galerie Martinet; 1957, Dijon, no. 5; 1968–69, Paris, Petit Palais, no. 529

Bibliography:
Astruc, 1863; Poulet-Malassis, 1875, p. 12

VI-75

This youthful work by Legros shows his knowledge of the Spanish painters. Baudelaire emphasized this: "M. Legros, always enamored of the harsh sensualities of religion, produced two magnificent paintings, one of which could be admired at the last exhibition held on the Champs Elysées *(Women Kneeling before Dense, Luminous Landscape);* the other a more recent creation, representing monks of different ages prostrate before a holy book from which they humbly endeavor to interpret certain passages. These two paintings, the second of which makes one think of the most solid Spanish compositions, are hung close to a famous canvas by Delacroix, and in spite of it, in this dangerous location, they have a life of their own." This Spanish influence can be found again in *Making Amends* (Tribunal de Commerce, Niort) which is very clearly inspired by Zurbaran (*see* 1974, Paris, Grand Palais, no. 154). The originality of Legros's inspiration should also be emphasized since religious painters were rare during the Second Empire.

O.S.

Musées d'Alençon

---

### Karl-Ernest-Rodolphe-Heinrich Lehmann

*Kiel (Holstein) 1814–1882 Paris*

*After his arrival in Paris in 1831, Lehmann became one of the most distinguished and dedicated students of Ingres (q.v.). His initial training under his father, the portraitist Leo Lehmann, followed by study under the German academicians G. Hardorff the Elder and S.D. Bendixen in Hamburg, laid the ground for his peculiarly intensified Ingresque portraits of such well-known figures as Baron Haussmann, Stendhal, Lamartine, Thorvaldsen, Meyerbeer, Chopin, and Liszt. His most famous female portrait, exhibited in 1844, was of the Princess Belgiojoso, a spirited and socially minded belle. The artist's accentuation of her large eyes became a trademark of his portraits of women and it is this singular intensity that ultimately separates Lehmann's work from Ingres's purer Neoclassicism. Although he became a French citizen in 1847 and studied extensively in Rome, his Germanic background continued to influence his work.*

*In Paris, Lehmann won a second-class medal in 1835 with* Tobias and the Angel *and first-class medals in 1840, 1848, and 1855. In 1855 he exhibited, with the diversity typical of his production, five works:* The Infant Jesus and the Magi, Jeremiah, The Adoration, Venus Anadyomene, *and* Ondine. *Such a combination of religious and quasi-erotic subjects, along with his successful portrait business, can be compared to the multi-faceted art of his master, Ingres.*

*Lehmann was elected to head the Ecole des Beaux-Arts in 1861 and became a member of the Institut de France in 1864. In 1875 he replaced Isidore Pils as professor at the Ecole des Beaux-Arts, where he struggled to preserve the academic disciplines of his youth. According to Stranahan, at his death in March of 1882, "he left in the terms of his bequest for a prize, a perpetual expression of his contempt for 'the degradation which the unclassic doctrines of the day favor'" (Stranahan, 1902, p. 290).*

N.D.

Bibliography:
Fournel, 1884, pp. 311–20; *Chronique des Arts*, 1882, p. 107; Thieme and Becker, 1907–50, vol. XXII, p. 581; Stranahan, 1902, pp. 289–90; 1975, New York, Shepherd Gallery, pp. 167–72

Karl-Ernest-Rodolphe-Heinrich Lehmann

## VI-76
## Decorative Panel

1862
Signed and dated, lower middle: Hr. LEHMANN MDCCCLXII
Oil on panel, with borders in gold and *grisaille*
51.6 × 72.7 cm

Provenance:
Private coll., New York

Exhibitions:
1975, New York, Shepherd Gallery, p. 171, no. 71, repro. p. 172; 1978, Chapel Hill, no. 46

Lehmann completed a number of decorative projects for religious, state, and private buildings. Beginning in 1842 with an altarpiece for the Church of Saint Nicolas in Boulogne-sur-Mer, followed by a chapel in the Church of Sainte Marie in Paris (1844) and by chapels in the Institut pour les Aveugles Jeunes in Paris (1845–48), he went on to state commissions, and completed fifty-six compositions for the Galerie des Fêtes at the old Hôtel de Ville, two hemicycles for the new throne room at the Sénat, and work for the Palais de Justice.

Lehmann's official work for church and state was supplemented by such private commissions as this panel (*see* 1975, New York, Shepherd Gallery, p. 121). We see in it the influence of his sojourns in Rome. The decorative border panels with their delicate arabesques and corner sphinxes are reminiscent of the imagery of the Domus Aurea, a richly decorated imperial Roman building of great importance to artists since the Renaissance. The influence of the amorous subject matter of this panel, and Lehmann's knowledge of Guido Reni's *Aurora* is seen in the light-filled background and the stability of the figures floating through space.

The putti in roundels seem to illustrate the power love has to tame the savage instincts, as does Cupid in his chariot standing on a reclining lion. The embracing couple are bound together to the chariot, and it seems that Venus triumphant over Mars is not yet free from "the problematic dilemmas of love" (1978, Chapel Hill, p. 95). French society of the Second Empire, with its penchant for courtesans and romantic liaisons, is reflected in the sensuous overtones in this work, which is simultaneously rich in allusions to the Antique in a tradition that Lehmann tried to sustain.

N.D.

Private Collection, New York

---

### Hector Leroux
*Verdun 1829–1900 Angers*

Leroux took a public drawing class at the collège of Verdun and in 1848 received a scholarship of 600 francs from the General Council of the Department of the Meuse to pursue the study of art for three years. He became a student of Picot and was admitted to the Ecole des Beaux-Arts on April 5, 1849. In order to survive he later executed copies and illustrations. He won only a second place for the Prix de Rome in 1857, and again in 1859, when he reached the maximum age for entering the competition; however, through the recommendations of Picot, Cogniet, Robert Fleury and Hippolyte Flandrin (q.v.), and aided by the intervention of Halévy from the Institut (who believed a trip to Rome would allow him to complete his studies), he was commissioned by the State on April 16, 1860, to copy in Rome, Titian's Sacred and Profane Love (Arch. nat. F²¹ 94).

In Rome he established for himself the genre that he practiced thereafter: scenes of Roman life, "the intimate aspect of pagan mores" (Ménard). Thus he appeared for the first time at the Salon of 1863 with the New Vestal (Verdun museum), commissioned by the State, January 15, 1862; the Administration helped him again the following year, when he executed a copy of Guido Reni's Aurora, life size, to be used as a cartoon at the Gobelins manufactory.

At the Salon of 1864, the Funeral in the Columbarium of the House of the Caesars was admitted to the Musée du Luxembourg (now in Saint-Dizier museum) confirming his success as a painter; a smaller version of it, dated 1869, was in the collection of his friend Henner (q.v.; Musée Henner, Paris).

In 1867 the State bought Serenade for the museum in Saint-Germain-en-Laye, and his work was known and purchased by collectors in France and America (for example, Sleeping Vestal, from the Salon of 1880, now in the Walters Art Gallery, Baltimore).

His works, of a delicate finish, are often small in size. However, his Herculaneum (Salon of 1881), which was also sent to the Luxembourg (now in Dijon), is a vast composition, exaltingly dramatic.

G.L.

VI-76

Hector Leroux

## VI-77
## The Believers (Prayer to the Goddess Hygeia)

1862
Signed and dated, lower left: H^or Leroux Rome 1862
Oil on canvas
94 × 67 cm

Provenance:
Private coll., Germany; acquired by the city of Verdun, 1974 (inv. no. 74.2.345)

Exhibition:
1863, Paris, Salon, no. 1199

Bibliography:
De Sault, 1864, p. 71; Ménard, 1876, p. 441, repro. p. 442; "Acquisitions." 1976, p. 394, fig. 28

"Among the Néo-Grecs the palm this year goes to M. Leroux for his small painting entitled

VI-77

*The Believers*, a poetic work, touching and full of delicacy," wrote the critic de Sault in his review of the Salon of 1863. In his enthusiasm he added a very detailed description of the work, which thus corroborates that it was indeed the composition later known as *The Offering to Hygeia.*

It had been composed at the same time as the *New Vestal*, commissioned by the Direction des Beaux-Arts, January 15, 1862, and executed in Rome with the same meticulous attention to archaeological detail. This picture shortly thereafter was sent to the museum in Verdun, Leroux's birthplace. For both works he received a third-class medal. In quick order, he had made for himself "..a special place among the lovers of antiquity"(Ménard).

*The Believers* is one of the most successfully rendered scenes in the Neo-Antique genre of the Second Empire. The subject is like a Roman transcription of a vow to the Madonna, a subject frequently treated by artists traveling in

Italy and illustrated repeatedly by Schnetz, who was at that time director of the Villa Medici, and responsible, therefore, for the supervision of the proper execution of the works commissioned from Leroux (Arch. nat. F^21 157). Hygeia, goddess of health, is represented, as is Aesculapius, with whom she is often linked, with a serpent for an emblem. The artist rendered the nostalgic feeling befitting the scene with tremendous subtlety in the choice of tones—an understated harmony of grays and browns relieved only by the blue of the dress of one of the votive figures. To quote de Sault again: "The landscape still shows the harshness of winter, but a breath of spring murmurs a word of hope." And to follow him still further, there are subtle analogies between the broken urn, the ruined columns, the almost bare branches, the figure crouching at the right—winter, old age—and the weakness of the sick woman. Leroux had a very Ingresque taste for finish—perhaps halfway between Ingres and Meissonier—and the work, the draped figures especially, evokes at the same time the Nazarenes and Feuerbach, or the English contemporary Neoclassicists Alma-Tadema and Leighton.

A reduced version (on panel, 64 × 44 cm) passed through sales twice at Chickering Hall, New York: February 17, 1893 (no. 25) and then January 27, 1899 (no. 25), under the title *Suppliants to Hygeia.* It was part of the collection of Walter Richmond of Providence, Rhode Island. It would not seem to correspond to the example acquired by the Yale University Art Gallery (1972-51) which, while also on panel, is much smaller (36 × 24 cm).

G.L.

Musée de la Princerie, Verdun

---

## Henri-Léopold Lévy
### Nancy 1840–1904 Paris

*A student of Picot and Cabanel (q.v.) at the Ecole des Beaux-Arts in Paris, which he entered on April 3, 1856, Lévy also studied with Fromentin (q.v.). Beginning in 1862 he made several unsuccessful attempts to win the Prix de Rome, but gave up after failing, in 1865, the test for admission to the final competition. He exhibited the same year for the first time at the Salon, earning a medal for* Hecuba Discovering the Body of Her Son Polydorus on the Shore, *which was not purchased by the State, in spite of his request, but which soon entered the*

*Roubaix museum. During this period Lévy was apparently leading a rather impoverished life, which compelled him to formulate numerous requests to the administrations, since his paintings, on account of their size and historical subjects were fit only for museums. He earned medals for his submissions to the Salons of 1867 and 1869, and in 1867 the State purchased* Joash *for the Arras museum and in 1869,* A Captive Hebrew Crying over the Ruins of Jerusalem, *which, after having been sent to the Munich exhibition of 1869, was listed in the Nancy museum (since destroyed). It was during the Third Republic that Lévy achieved full success: in 1872* Herodias *(sketch in the Nancy museum) brought him the Legion of Honor. He participated in numerous programs for the decoration of buildings, notably, the Panthéon, the Hôtel de Ville in Paris, and the Conseil d'Etat.*

G.L.

Henri-Léopold Lévy

## VI-78
## Joash Saved from the Massacre of Athaliah's Grandsons

1867
Signed and dated, lower right: Henri Lévy 1867
Oil on canvas
312.5 × 237.5 cm

Provenance:
Purchased by the State by decree of June 14, 1867, for 3,000 francs (Arch. nat. F[21] 157); deposited in the Musée des Beaux-Arts, Arras, 1867

Exhibitions:
1867, Paris, Salon, no. 970; 1867, Paris, Exposition Universelle, no. 659

Bibliography:
Mantz, 1867, "Salon," p. 519; de Montifaud, 1867, June 1, pp. 450–51; Ménard, 1876, p. 444; Catalogues, Arras, Musée des Beaux-Arts, 1880, no. 119, 1907, no. 234

VI-78

Lévy did not draw his inspiration, as did Paul Delaroche in 1822, from Racine's tragedy, *Athalie* (*Joash Saved from the Dead by Jehosheba, His Aunt*; Musée du Luxembourg, transferred to Troyes, 1872) but from the Bible (2 Kings 11). He aimed, as he had already stated in a request to the Administration in May 1865 (Arch. nat. F[21] 157), which proved fruitless, to paint history and to return to the sources. Only the State could encourage this genre. Thus, in 1867, he took the precaution of being recommended by Claire Benoit Champy, who was received at the receptions of the comte de Nieuwerkerke, and who was thus fulfilling "the promise made to a poor young man even more shy than myself" (letter registered May 8,

1867). The request was inscribed, and, a few weeks later, the artist responded affirmatively to an offer of purchase of May 31. In addition he himself had written as early as April 15: "On account of its size, I could not entertain any hopes to have this painting purchased by a private individual," but had received only a noncommital letter in reply.

At the Salon, M. de Montifaud, with many reservations, however, noted the "accent of savage and robust beauty" of the canvas, placed in the Salon d'Honneur, while Paul Mantz remarked: "The particular characteristic of M. Lévy, and probably what is appealing to us in his talent, is the fact that he shows his debt to Delacroix, quite a feat indeed on the part of a student of M. Picot.... The main figure of his

painting, that of Jehosheba saving young Joash from the slaughter, bears a strong resemblance to the glorious *Medea* of the immortal master. The twisted draperies, the purple tones, are definitely taken from him. One may even find that the reminiscence is too close. But M. Lévy, who is not yet out of his period of trial and error, has taken a great stride on the path that he intends to follow. He possesses a true feeling for color: his *Joash Saved* is a great animated and lavish work, in which everything is in motion, and where everything is arranged with a sense of display and brilliance. M. Lévy truly appears to love his craft; for him, painting is a joy."

G.L.

Musée des Beaux-Arts, Arras

## Edouard Manet

*Paris 1832–1883 Paris*

*Manet, regarded as one of the greatest French painters of the nineteenth century, remains one of its most enigmatic. Recent research, especially into the sources and content of his paintings, has—if anything—added still more to the perplexing dilemma. For his contemporaries, the bold and seemingly innovative subjects were best understood purely on a stylistic level, yet most of his major works, especially during the Second Empire, were the creation of a remarkably complex network of progressive and traditional impulses, drawing their style and form from references to both past and contemporary art (see Gérôme). Son of a high-ranking and prosperous government official, the well-educated artist retained throughout his life the personal elegance and urbane manners of a well-born Parisian, and his persistence in attempting to gain prominence through the Salons and official channels, even when, with the Impressionist exhibition of 1874 an alternative means of showing existed, indicates his conservatism.*

*In 1850 he entered the studio of Couture (q.v.), where, despite several sharp disagreements, he remained for six years (see no. VI-34). The early 1850s were marked by frequent travel (Venice, perhaps Florence in 1853; Belgium, Holland, Germany, Austria, and Italy in 1856), and his first attempt to show at the Salon—*The Absinthe Drinker *(Copenhagen)—was rejected in 1859. However, two pictures were accepted in 1861 (Portrait of M. and Mme Manet and* The Spanish Singer*) and the young artist was awarded an honorable mention. The rejection of three works in 1863, including* Luncheon on the Grass, *and their subsequent display at the Salon des Refusés, established his power to provoke public scandal and critical abuse, while the acceptance in 1865 of* Christ Mocked *and* Olympia *and the ensuing criticism made the artist a* cause célèbre *and established the rebellious image he was to retain throughout his life. The following year two works were refused, perhaps prompting his absence in 1867. Two works were accepted in 1868 (Portrait of Zola and* Woman with a Parrot*), although badly hung, as were those in 1869 and 1870. During the early Third Republic, with the exception of 1873 when* The Bon Bock *(Philadelphia Museum of Art) achieved popular success, Manet's official reception was as varied and it was not until the early 1880s that he met with any general success. (See also no. VII-45.)*

J.R.

Bibliography:
Rouart and Wildenstein, 1975, vol. I (bibl.); Hanson, 1977 (bibl.).

VI-79

Edouard Manet

## VI-79
## Young Woman Reclining in Spanish Costume

1862
Signed, lower right: A mon ami Nadar, Manet
Oil on canvas
93 × 113 cm

Provenance:
Gift of the artist to Nadar (q.v.), Paris; sale, Paris, November 11–12, 1895, no. 60; Edouard Arnhold, Berlin; Stephen Carlton Clark, New York; bequest to the Yale University Art Gallery, 1961 (inv. no. 1961.18.33).

Exhibitions:
1863, Paris, Galerie Martinet, no. 130; 1867, Paris, Avenue de l'Alma, no. 35; 1884, Paris, Ecole des Beaux-Arts, no. 20; 1912, Dresden; 1926, Berlin, no. 19; 1954, New York, no. 6; 1966–67, Philadelphia, Chicago, no. 52; 1972, New York, no. 37

Bibliography:
Bazire, 1884, p. 54; Meier-Graefe, 1899, p. 64 (repro.); Duret, 1902, pp. 30–31, no. 46; Meier-Graefe, 1907, p. 83; Duret, 1910, pp. 26, 217, no. 46; Meier-Graefe, 1912, pp. 57 (repro.), 65–66; Proust, 1913, pp. 53, 164; Dormoy, 1926, pp. 242–43; Moreau-Nélaton, 1926, vol. I, pp. 44–47, 51, 86, no. 47, fig. 45; Jamot, 1927, "Manet," p. 32; Jamot and Wildenstein, 1932, no. 63; Rich, 1932, p. 4; Lambert, 1933, p. 377 (repro.); Jedlicka, 1941, pp. 82–83 (repro.); Tabarant, 1942, pp. 367, 462, 488; Tabarant, 1947, pp. 55, 137, 492, no. 57 (repro.); Gardner, 1954, p. 36 (repro.); Comstock, 1954, p. 289 (repro.); Sandblad, 1954, p. 96; *Art Quarterly*, no. 24, 1961, p. 400 (repro.);

*Chronique des Arts*, no. 146, February 1962, p. 40; Bowness, 1967, p. 186 (repro.); Hahn, 1968, pp. 15–17, pl. 12; Farwell, 1969, pp. 204, 205 (repro.), 206; Rouart and Orienti, 1970, no. 52; Rouart and Wildenstein, 1975, vol. I, no. 59; Hanson, 1977, pp. 88–89; Reff, 1977, *Manet*, pp. 63–66

*(Shown in Philadelphia and Detroit only)*

It has often been felt that, given the relationship between Goya's *Maja Nude* and *Maja Clothed*, this picture may have served as a pendant for Manet's *Olympia*, which caused a sensation at the Salon of 1865. Although their sizes are quite different and no documentation has been found to prove that this was in Manet's mind, the *Young Woman Reclining in Spanish Costume* can, as Reff notes (1977, *Manet*, p. 65), be taken as a precedent for the *Olympia*, if it is not actually a source.

The sensual inertia—felt all the more in contrast to the animated kitten—and the staring gaze do strongly recall Goya. Nadar (q.v.) to whom Manet gave the picture (and whose mistress it perhaps represents) may have owned copies after both *Majas*, purchased on the advice of Baudelaire. However, the general mood, exotic and languorous, may also have derived in part from the odalisques of Delacroix (q.v.; *see* Hanson, 1977, p. 88 no. 154).

Things Spanish held a particular appeal for Manet in the early 1860s (anticipating his trip of 1865) and the costume here may have been from his collection, since it appears again in the *Mlle Victorine in the Costume of an Espada* (Metropolitan Museum of Art, New York) done the same year. Spanish art—in Manet's case, specifically Velázquez and Goya—would have a strong influence during the Second Empire, replacing for some (*see* Ribot and Vollon) the role that Raphael and the High Renaissance held for Ingres and the Académie des Beaux-Arts. On a broader level still, contemporary Spanish costume, dance, and music enjoyed great fashionability in France (*see* no. VII-12), encouraged by the Empress's taste for her native country.

As Richardson points out (1967, pp. 109, 116, 211, 216) women dressed as men—as here—were given particular play at the time in the world of the demimonde. This observation adds still further to the already disconcerting quality of this picture in its aspect as a costume portrait, placing it closer to his friend Guys (q.v.) than nearly any other work, although as always with Manet, it is permeated with historical references and private associations.

J.R.

Yale University Art Gallery, New Haven, Bequest of Stephen Carlton Clark, B.A. 1903

Edouard Manet

## VI-80
## The Battle of the Kearsage and the Alabama

1864
Signed, lower left: Manet
Oil on canvas
134 × 127 cm

Provenance:
M. de L. sale, Paris, Hôtel Drouot, March 23, 1878, no. 32; Georges Charpentier, Paris; Durand-Ruel, Paris, 1884; T. Duret, Paris, 1887–88; Durand-Ruel, Paris and New York; John G. Johnson, Philadelphia, 1888; John G. Johnson Collection (inv. no. cat. 1027)

Exhibitions:
1867, Paris, Avenue de l'Alma, no. 22; 1872, Paris, Salon, no. 1059; 1872, Brussels, no. 489; 1884, Paris, Ecole des Beaux-Arts, no. 35; 1886, New York, no. 178; 1933, Philadelphia; 1937, New York, no. 9; 1939, San Francisco, no. 149; 1945, Boston, no. 13; 1945, New York, no. 34; 1946–47, New York, no. 14; 1954, Fort Worth, no. 59; 1965, Paris, Petit Palais, no. 21; 1966–67, Philadelphia, Chicago, no. 62

Bibliography:
Claretie, 1872; Guillemet, 1872; Meier-Graefe, 1912, pp. 158, 160, 312; *Johnson Collection*, 1914, vol. III, p. 128, no. 1027; Jamot, 1914, p. 445; Moreau-Nélaton, 1926, vol. I, pp. 60–61, 137–38, fig. 63; Moreau-Nélaton, n.d., no. 54; Jamot and Wildenstein, 1932, no. 87; Rewald, 1946, p. 93, repro. p. 94; Hanson, 1962, pp. 322–36 (repro.); Rouart

and Orienti, 1970, no. 66; Rouart and Wildenstein, 1975, vol. I, no. 76; Hanson, 1977, pp. 121–25
*See* Colorplate

From 10:57 a.m. to 12:24 p.m. on Sunday, June 19, 1864, the most significant naval battle of the American Civil War took place in Cherbourg harbor, the engagement of the Confederate frigate *Alabama* with the Union *Kearsage*. The event, visible from the roads outside Cherbourg, as well as within sight of the city, was much publicized in advance since the captain of the *Alabama*, Raphael Semmes, forced by the French authorities to leave the neutrality of the harbor, had some five days earlier announced his intention to fight. Large crowds gathered to witness the encounter, the allure even further increased by the wide reputation of Semmes and his English crew, who during the previous two years had captured and sunk fifty-seven Union ships. That such an advance warning of the event was given is of particular importance, since there is considerable disagreement as to whether Manet (who was in Boulogne later that summer) actually witnessed the battle (*see* Hanson, 1977, pp. 121–22 for summation of the arguments). Whether he was an eyewitness or not, Manet must have taken up the subject with considerable excitement and energy since only a month later the picture was shown in the dealer Cadart's shop window on the rue de Richelieu and was noted by Philippe Burty in *La Presse*, July 18, 1864.

Manet's immediate response to a dramatic contemporary event was to be repeated, although on a more complex and elaborately plotted scale, in his reaction to the assassination

VI-80

of the Emperor of Mexico, Maximilian, the same day in June, three years later. It provided Manet with the perfect response to the frequently heard critical and official pleas for artistic depictions of contemporary history. However, despite its contemporaneity, Manet chose not to submit *The Battle of the Kearsage and the Alabama* to the Salon of 1865 and it was not seen, after its brief view at Cadart's, until it went relatively unnoticed in Manet's privately funded exhibition in 1867 at the place de l'Alma and did not receive full recognition until it was shown at the Salon of 1872, where it was received positively by the majority of critics.

Although the originality of the composition and its possible origins in Japanese prints—especially the high horizon and the rushing perspective up the picture plane—have been frequently noted, the subject itself is not unusual and depictions of contemporary naval battles were often seen at the Salon. No other treatment of the subject was shown in the Salon of 1865, as Burty had predicted, but there were several ship paintings shown, perhaps the most noteworthy being one submitted by the most established painter in the genre, Théodore Gudin. Manet's dependence on popular illustrations of the event has been a point of speculation, but no convincing evidence of borrowing has been established.

J.R.

John G. Johnson Collection, Philadelphia

Edouard Manet

## VI-81
## Still Life with Fruit and a Melon on a Buffet

c. 1866–67
Signed, lower right: Manet
Oil on canvas
69 × 92.2 cm

Provenance:
Léopold Baugnée, Brussels; sale, Brussels, Galerie Ghémar, March 22, 1875, no. 44; Durand-Ruel, Paris; Mr. and Mrs. Eugene Meyer, Washington, D. C.; gift to the National Gallery of Art, 1960 (inv. no. 1549)

Exhibitions:
1867, Paris, Avenue de l'Alma, no. 36; 1913, New York, Durand-Ruel Galleries, no. 17; 1920, New York, no. 9; 1921, New York, no. 63; 1966–67, Philadelphia, Chicago, no. 99

Bibliography:
Meier-Graefe, 1912, pl. 82; Proust, 1913, p. 140; Moreau-Nélaton, 1926, vol. I, p. 89, fig. 92; Moreau-Nélaton, n.d., no. 94; Jamot and Wildenstein, 1932, no. 131; Tabarant, 1947, pp. 130–31, no. 127; Hamilton, 1954; Catalogue, Washington, D. C., National Gallery of Art, 1968, no. 1549; Rouart and Orienti,

1970, no. 110; Rouart and Wildenstein, 1975, vol. I, no. 121; Hanson, 1977, p. 70, pl. 29

Still-life and flower painting, as independent subjects or as elements of larger figural compositions (for example, the picnic items and cloths in *Luncheon on the Grass* or the bottles in the *Bar at the Folies Bergère),* interested Manet throughout his life. However, he practiced this genre with particular concentration during two periods: 1864–69 and 1880–83. It has been noted that with this first group the artist made a rapid progression from domestic arrangements echoing Chardin to more opulently laid out compositions of rich stuffs, which, it may be argued, drew more from seventeenth-century Dutch works. Hanson, speaking specifically of *Still Life with Fruit and a Melon on a Buffet,* notes: "The coarse tables and rustic kitchen equipment are now replaced by sparkling glassware, fine damask and silver, and even a casually abandoned flower. There is, as well, a remarkably strong sense of the people who have left the table in such casual disarray, disdainful of the abundance spread out before them.... These pictures speak of 'la vie moderne' as persuasively as some of the portraits or street scenes which record other forms of affluence and pleasure" (Hanson, 1977, pp. 69–70).

This work is not dated, but it has consistently been placed in the mid-1860s (Wildenstein dates it c. 1866; Hanson, 1867) and it is frequently compared to the *Luncheon in the Studio* (1868; Bayerische Staatsgemäldesammlungen, Munich), which includes a very similar cloth. The buffet, with its brass keyhole, appears also in *The Salmon* (c. 1866–69, Shelburne Museum, Shelburne, Vt.). If at this point Manet had a motivation for doing still lifes other than his obvious pleasure in witnessing the abundance of his household, it is not known. He included several still lifes, including this picture, in his large private exhibition at the place de l'Alma in 1867. However, the argument set forth that these pictures were done to reach a more ready audience is somewhat weakened by the absence of recognition they received in 1867 and further, by the price list recorded by Moreau-Nélaton (1926, vol. I, pp. 132–34) in Manet's first set of sales to Durand-Ruel in 1871 where, at 2,000 francs, this work fetched the same as figure subjects of a similar scale (for example, *The Guitar Player* and *The Smoker*). It should be noted in turn that certain larger and more controversial works went for even less, *The Fifer* being sold at 1,500 francs!

J.R.

National Gallery of Art, Washington, D. C., Gift of Eugene and Agnes Meyer, 1960

VI-81

Edouard Manet

## VI-82
## View of the Exposition Universelle in Paris

1867
Dated, lower right: Juin 1867; signed, lower right, by Mme Manet: Ed. Manet
Oil on canvas
108 × 196.5 cm

Provenance:
Manet inventory, 1883, no. 16; Manet sale, Paris, Hôtel Drouot, February 4–5, 1884, no. 67; Mme Besnard, Paris; Auguste Pellerin, Paris (1902, 1909); Bernheim Jeune, Paris, 1907; Mme Angelot, Paris, 1919; Tryggve Sagen, Oslo; Klaveness Bank, Oslo; gift of the Friends of the Nasjonalgalleriet, 1923 (inv. no. 1293)

Exhibitions:
1884, Paris, Ecole des Beaux-Arts, no. 41; 1922, Stockholm, Copenhagen, Oslo, no. 6; 1928, Berlin, Galerie Matthiesen, no. 20; 1928, Paris, Galerie Bernheim-Jeune, no. 80; 1932, London, no. 414; 1932, Paris, Orangerie, no. 25

Bibliography:
Duret, 1902, no. 92; Meier-Graefe, 1912, pl. 85;

VI-82

Moreau-Nélaton, 1926, vol. I, p. 92, fig. 107; Moreau-Nélaton, n.d., no. 100; Jamot, 1927, "Manet," p. 30; Meier-Graefe, 1928, pp. 86, 88 (repro.); Jamot, 1929, "Norvège," pp. 80 (repro.), 85; Jamot and Wildenstein, 1932, no. 137; Meier-Graefe, 1932, p. 253; Lambert, 1933, p. 381 (repro.); J.L., 1945, p. 1; Tabarant, 1947, p. 140, no. 131; Florisoone, 1947, pp. xx, xxviii, 43 (repro.); Sandblad, 1954, p. 30, no. 20; Richardson, 1958, pl. 29; Lambert, 1960, pp. 121, 122; Bowness, 1961, pp. 276–77; Rewald, 1961, pp. 172–73 (repro.); Bodelsen, 1968, p. 344, no. 67; Rouart and Orienti, 1970, no. 114; Bazin, 1972, pp. 42, 77 (repro.); Catalogue, Oslo, Nasjonalgalleriet, 1973, no. 537; Rouart and Wildenstein, 1975, vol. I, no. 123; Hanson, 1977, pp. 201–2, pl. 125

*(Shown in Paris only)*

Prompted perhaps by his young friends Renoir (q.v.) and Monet (q.v.), who took up views of Paris in 1866, or by Berthe Morisot, whose 1866 *View of the Seine below the Pont d'Iéna* was shown at the Salon the following year, Manet turned to this subject in 1867 (one of his few attempts), showing a panoramic view of the Exposition Universelle from the top of the park of the Trocadéro. The exposition was inaugurated in May 1867 by a series of grand ceremonies, and on May 24, Manet opened his own exhibition in a temporary structure at the place de l'Alma. Having decided not to submit to the Salon that year (and not having received an invitation from the selection committee to show in the art section of the exposition) and prompted by Courbet (q.v.), who staged a similar private retrospective nearby, Manet exhibited over fifty pictures, dating as early as 1859, including *Luncheon on the Grass* and *Olympia*. The exhibition was neither a critical nor a popular success, receiving very little notice in the press, and attracting only small crowds, who were on the whole more curious than interested.

However, if this brought him great disappointment, he did not show it here in one of his freest and most loosely handled pictures of the 1860s. Manet's dependence on secondary visual sources, prints or photographs, is well documented, and he may have derived this composition from one of the numerous engraved views of the exhibition site, with its oval hall by Frédéric le Play surrounded by towered pavilions on the grounds of the Champ-de-Mars. In fact, the particularly casual viewpoint, as well as the distortion of the perspective and topography (the Seine should be somewhat between the hill and the first row of buildings), suggests more likely that he freely remembered the panorama from a spring visit to the site.

Cited sometimes as one of Manet's failures (Richardson, 1958, p. 13), this randomly composed work does fall beyond any conventional canon of observation or landscape arrange-

ment. However, it is one of Manet's most adventurous and bold pictures, in a category of independent oil paintings without more finished pictures intended, which the artist did in response to a particularly pleasing view. Its closest comparisons all document a summer day full of gay animation, for example, *Beach at Boulogne* (1869; Le Havre museum) and *Departure of the Folkstone Boat* (1869; Philadelphia Museum of Art). The personal pleasure that this picture must have held for Manet is further witnessed by the inclusion in the lower right of his natural son, Léon Leehof, leading a dog, and the balloon of his good friend Nadar (q.v.), bobbing over the fairgrounds.

J.R.

Nasjonalgalleriet, Oslo

Edouard Manet

## VI-83
## Portrait of Emile Zola

1867–68
Oil on canvas
146 × 114 cm

Provenance:
Gift of the artist to Emile Zola; gift of Mme Zola, reserving life interest, to the Louvre, 1918; entered the Louvre, 1925 (inv. no. RF 2205)

VI-83

Exhibitions:
1868, Paris, Salon, no. 1660; 1883, Paris, Ecole des Beaux-Arts, no. 304; 1884, Paris, Ecole des Beaux-Arts, no. 42; 1903, Paris, Galerie Bernheim-Jeune, no. 33; 1905, Paris, Salon d'Automne, no. 7; 1928, Berlin, Galerie Matthiesen, no. 22; 1928, Paris, Galerie Bernheim-Jeune, no. 6; 1932, Paris, Orangerie, no. 30; 1937, Warsaw, Prague, no. 15 (repro.); 1938, Lyons, no. 42; 1939, Belgrade, no. 71; 1941, Montpellier; 1952, Paris, Orangerie; 1952, Paris, Bibliothèque Nationale, no. 87; 1970–71, Leningrad, Moscow, no. 50; 1971, Madrid, no. 40; 1974, Paris, Grand Palais, "Impressionnisme," no. 20

Bibliography:
T. Gautier, *Le Moniteur*, May 11, 1868; Thoré-Bürger, 1870, vol. II, p. 532; Jamot and Wildenstein, 1932, pp. 83, 135, no. 146, fig. 149; Faison, 1949, pp. 163–68; Adhémar, 1960, pp. 286–87; Sterling and Adhémar, 1958–61, pl. 444; Catalogue, Paris, Louvre, Paintings, 1972, vol. I, p. 250; Catalogue, Paris, Jeu de Paume, 1973, p. 149, repro. p. 54; Zola, 1974, pp. 104–6; Rouart and Wildenstein, 1975, vol. I, pp. 15, 122, no. 128, repro. p. 123 (bibl.); Reff, 1975, pp. 35–44; Reff, 1977, *Manet*, fig. 24

*(Shown in Paris only)*

It was at the Café Guerbois in 1866 that Zola made the acquaintance of Manet, whom he was to defend the following year when the artist held his own exhibition on the perimeter of the Exposition Universelle. His essay on the painter, published in the *Revue du XXᵉ Siècle* of January 1, 1867, was shortly—in June of the same year—issued by Dentu in a slender pamphlet seen here on Zola's desk, in the portrait executed by Manet in gratitude for the writer's support. It was probably in November 1867 that Manet set to work on it, and in February 1868 Zola wrote to Théodore Duret: "Manet is doing my portrait for the Salon." The setting is the apartment occupied at that time by the writer in the rue Moncey, at the corner of the rue de Clichy, close to the Café Guerbois (the inkstand, for example, was still preserved by his descendants in 1960; *see* Adhémar, 1960). The composition of the painting can be compared to that of Degas's *Print Collector* (1866; Metropolitan Museum of Art, New York), especially the frame in the upper right enclosing a number of prints. They were obviously chosen as an expression of interests shared by the painter and his critic: we see a reproduction—photograph or engraving?—of the *Olympia* of the Salon of 1865 in front of a partially visible engraving after Velázquez's *Triumph of Bacchus*, probably executed by Nanteuil, which symbolizes their common attraction for Spanish realism. Finally, several elements attest to Zola's interest in the art of Japan: the partly visible screen on the left and a print by Utagawa Kuniaki II, *The Wrestler Onaruto Nadaemon from the Province of Awa*, one of those late *ukiyo-e* works in lively colors that were to inspire artists in their search for simplified color. (A copy of this print is in Boston.)

Though badly hung at the Salon, Manet's painting did not go unnoticed and provoked considerable controversy. Zola defended it at length: "Would that I had ten newspaper columns to repeat aloud what I was thinking to myself during the sittings, while watching Edouard Manet struggle with nature inch by inch.... I remember the long posing sessions.... I thought for whole hours of that fate of individual artists that makes them live apart in the solitude of their talent." For him, Manet was first of all a "naturalist. His eye sees and renders objects with elegant simplicity.... This portrait is an ensemble of difficulties overcome.... everything is held within a knowing, clear, and dazzling range, so real that the eye overlooks the accumulation of objects and sees simply a harmonious whole."

G.L.

Musée du Louvre, Galerie du Jeu de Paume, Paris

---

## Jean-Louis-Ernest Meissonier

*Lyons 1815–1891 Paris*

*Meissonier's academic training was brief—he spent a short time in the atelier of Jules Potier and then in that of Léon Cogniet.* A Visit to the Burgomaster, *his first submission to the Salon, in 1834, was a pastiche of Dutch seventeenth-century painting, and Meissonier was to exploit this vein of contemporary taste all his life (see no. VII-46). He painted countless readers, smokers, and other good, simple people. At the same time, he supplied illustrations for books, notably,* Paul et Virginie *and* La Chaumière indienne *(1838).*

*Under the Second Empire his fame grew, and along with Courbet (q.v.), he was an easy target for caricaturists because of the small scale of his works: "Great Scott! The devil of a fly that alighted on the Meissonier is covering up the whole painting!" (Cham, 1857). The Maison de l'Empereur purchased* The Brawl *for the considerable sum of 25,000 francs; one of the most expensive paintings acquired by the Ministry, it was presented to Prince Albert and Queen Victoria on their visit to France (Arch. nat. 0⁵ 1709).*

*The Italian campaign, in which Meissonier was assigned to the staff of Napoleon III in order to depict the various events, marked a turning point in his career. Military scenes became his second area of interest, and he developed a personal devotion to Napoleon I and dreamed of immortalizing him in five paintings that would celebrate the important dates in his life: 1796, 1807, 1810, 1814, and 1815. But it was under the Third Republic that Meis-*

*sonier's glory attained its apogee. Then, after a long "purgatory," when he was condemned like so many other artists who were shelved under the label of* pompiers, *he aroused renewed interest.*

*The minutely detailed art of Meissonier, although often repetitive in character, has interesting and unexpected aspects. One can regret his concept that the role of painting was to recreate history, for this led him to an excessively documentary approach. On the other hand, when he allowed his personal sensitivity to react directly to nature or political events, he was able to create compositions that were among the most moving of his artistic production.* The Barricade *(1848),* The Tuileries *(1870), and* The Siege of Paris *make us regret that Meissonier did not allow himself to be guided by his emotions more often in order to create these "syntheses for which his soul thirsted" (Meissonier, in Gréard, 1897, p. 228).*

O.S.

Bibliography:
Roujon, n.d., *Meissonier*

Jean-Louis-Ernest Meissonier

## VI-84
## Antibes: The Artist and His Son on Horseback

1868
Signed and dated, lower left: E. MEISSONIER 1868
Antibes
Oil on canvas
46 × 76 cm

Provenance:
Fop. Smit, Rotterdam; Chauchard coll.; bequest to the Louvre, 1906 (inv. no. RF 1858)

Exhibitions:
1878, Paris, Exposition Universelle Internationale,

no. 627; 1893, Paris, Ecole des Beaux-Arts, no. 56; 1936, Antibes, no. 41; 1958, Munich, no. 83; 1960, Nice, no. 176

Bibliography:
Chaumelin, 1887, no. 221; Gréard, 1897, pp. 90, 402; Bénédite, 1910, p. 111; *Chauchard Collection,* 1911, p. 83; Cabanne, 1957; Sterling and Adhémar, 1958–61, vol. III, no. 1244; Crespelle, 1966, p. 54; Catalogue, Paris, Louvre, Paintings, 1972, vol. I, p. 258

In 1868 Meissonier made a trip to Antibes from which he returned with numerous studies. This site on the Salice road seems to have been particularly attractive to him since it served as the setting for several compositions having a more or less similar viewpoint. Besides this work, one can include in this group another horseman on the road to Antibes (1893, Paris, Galerie Georges Petit, no. 82), *The Salice Road* (1893, Paris, Galerie Georges Petit, no. 1062), *Playing Bowls, Antibes* (Elmira, New York), and *A General and His Aide-de-Camp* (Metropolitan Museum of Art, New York). This procedure was typical of Meissonier, who frequently explored a theme in an almost obsessive way; indeed, he stated that leaving well enough alone was a proverb of the lazy.

Meissonier not only explored a theme in multiple variations, but he also captured each detail through innumerable documentary studies. Thus the known studies for the landscape on the Salice road are numerous (*see* 1893, Paris, Galerie Georges Petit). One should add to them the study for the horse his son rides (1893, Paris, Galerie Georges Petit, no. 334) and a study for his son's arm (Louvre RF 1859 verso). It should be mentioned that the horse ridden by the artist is none other than "that poor bachelor" whose portrait he painted (1893, Paris, Galerie Georges Petit, no. 89) and whom he occasionally loaned to Napoleon I in some of his compositions. This patient prepara-

VI-84

tion later permitted him to paint directly on his canvas without a sketch, as he was to affirm in his *Entretiens* (*see* Gréard, 1897, p. 204).

In 1869, after finishing this canvas, Meissonier executed a watercolor based on the painting, which was engraved by Manchon. This work, bathed in warm southern light, reveals Meissonier's talent as a landscape artist. It is regrettable that he did not exercise his gifts of observation as often in his formal compositions as he did in his small genre paintings.

O.S.

Musée du Louvre, Paris

Jean-Louis-Ernest Meissonier

## VI-85
## The Siege of Paris

1870
Signed and dated, lower right: 70. E. MEISSONIER
Oil on canvas
53.5 × 70.5 cm

Provenance:
Bequest of Mme Meissonier, widow of the artist, to the Louvre, 1898 (inv. no. RF 1249)

Exhibitions:
1884, Paris, Galerie Georges Petit, no. 146; 1893, Paris, Galerie Georges Petit, no. 110; 1893, Paris, Ecole des Beaux-Arts, no. 9; 1967, Paris, Hôtel Meurice; 1968, Berlin, no. 118; 1969, Minneapolis, no. 56; 1974, Castres, no. 145; 1977, Saint-Tropez

Bibliography:
Bénédite, 1910, pp. 36–37; Dayot, 1901, repro. p. 5; Roujon, n.d., *Meissonier,* p. 68; Chaumelin, 1887, pp. 33–36, no. 336; Delaborde, 1892, pp. 363–64; Gréard, 1897, pp. 65, 106, 227, 242–44, 250; Brière, 1924, no. 2969; Cabanne, 1957, p. 35; Sterling and Adhémar, 1958–61, vol. III, no. 1249; Rosenblum, 1969, p. 31; *Immortali,* 1970, p. 28; Catalogue, Paris, Louvre, Paintings, 1972, vol. I, p. 256; Vaisse, 1977, "Second Empire," fig. 13

Meissonier, in his *Entretiens,* told about the circumstances surrounding the creation of this sketch. In 1870 the artist, who had enlisted in the army, had suffered greatly from its defeats. He returned to Paris and participated in her defense. For Meissonier the siege saved the honor of the country. Following it he returned to his house at Poissy (*see* Detaille), and "it was while my house was invaded by the enemy that I imprisoned myself in my studio, where I painted the sketch of *Paris.* It was my revenge!" He intended to give a general meaning to this work: "As for 1870, even though it is the Siege, it is not any specific part of the Siege." The 1884 catalogue identifies the figures: in the foreground colonel de Dampierre, a young naval

VI-85

officer, still holds a sword in his right hand; behind him, leaning against a stele is Captain Després; close to the figure of the City of Paris is the painter Regnault (q.v.); in the foreground is Neverley, his leg crushed under a horse; to the left, the figure of a hospital orderly is that of Father Anthelme, while in the sky the spectre of Famine is accompanied by the Prussian eagle.

Meissonier took at least two months to paint this sketch for which he did numerous preparatory drawings (*see* Guiffrey and Marcel, 1907–38, vol. X, nos. 9697, 9632, 9633, 9634, 9636, 9627, 9629), a painted sketch of a dying soldier (1893, Paris, Ecole des Beaux-Arts, no. 13), and a wax model of the dying horse.

All his life he wanted to do a large version of this painting, the modifications of which he contemplated in relation to the sketch. He also wanted to engrave the work himself, but both of these wishes were to remain unfulfilled. Delaborde confirmed these facts at the time of the painter's death: "The noble composition imagined by Meissonier remained at the sketch stage even though until the end of his life the master had thought of converting this sketch into a painting."

Curiously, the point of view of Chaumelin, who would have hoped to eliminate from the composition "the giant woman with a lion's skin on her head and wearing a yellowish dress" (1887), coincides with that of Robert Rosenblum, who was not able to believe in patriotic rhetoric of this figure of France (its subject is actually the City of Paris and not France). However, without this ferocious giant, Meissonier would not have made anything but a butchery in the genre executed by those artists who did military paintings lauding the imperial victories. And if it is true that the artist rendered with exactitude the military uniform that he knew so well from his having worn and collected it, the conventional comment of the type "there isn't a gaiter button missing" (Cabanne, 1957) seems to us singularly out of place here. As for the dissonances of color of which Meissonier was aware, since he stated "that it needs to be given a little harmony, a little pulling together," they are no longer shocking today.

O.S.

Musée du Louvre, Paris

## Hugues Merle
*Saint-Martin 1823–1881 Paris*

*Hugues Merle was a student of Léon Cogniet and exhibited regularly in the Salon between 1847 and 1880. He received his first medal (second-class) only in 1861, won this honor again in 1863, and was named chevalier of the Legion of Honor in 1866. Merle was known for his "life-size pictures of subjects taken from the life of the poor, carefully drawn, but cold in color and often theatrical in treatment"(Champlin and Perkins, 1886–87, vol. III, p. 248). Stranahan wrote that he was a formidable rival of Bouguereau (q.v.) in this genre, although his works expressed with greater sensitivity the everyday life of the poor than did Bouguereau's idealized angel-orphans (Stranahan, 1902, p. 398). Such subjects as* A Beggar Woman *(Wallace Collection, London),* The Bible Reading *(Stedelijk Museum, Amsterdam), and* Mother Love *(Metropolitan Museum of Art, New York) are typical examples of this dimension of his work. A painting of his called* The Springtime of Life *had been owned by the Empress Eugénie.*

*Merle was particularly popular with American collectors, as was the work of his son, Georges Hugues Merle (with whom he is sometimes confused), who continued his father's manner but brought to it a greater degree of sentimentality typical of the Third Republic.*

N.D./J.R.

Bibliography:
Claretie, 1876, pp.152–53; *Chronique des Arts*, 1881, p. 103; *American Art Review*, vol. II, 1881, p. 261; Stranahan, 1902, p. 398

Hugues Merle

## VI-86
## The Scarlet Letter

1861
Oil on canvas
99.9 × 81.1 cm

Provenance:
Purchased from the artist's studio by W.T. Walters, through George Lucas for 2,000 francs, November 1861; Walters Art Gallery (inv. no. 37.172)

Bibliography:
*Walters Collection*, 1887, no. 59

This painting is an illustration of Nathaniel Hawthorne's novel of the same name, written in 1850. The American novel was translated under the title *La Lettre Rouge* as early as 1853 by

VI-86

a man calling himself "Old Nick." Merle must have made use of this edition because the next translation, by E.D. Forgues, was not until 1865, five years after his painting. This edition was republished four times before 1873, indicating the popularity of the work in France. Merle's composition leaves no ambiguity about the meaning he intended. The adultress with the "A" embroidered on her bodice and holding her child lives in lonely isolation from the Pilgrim fathers in the background.

One wonders if the agitation for new freedom for women, which aroused liberal circles in the Second Empire, was influential in Merle's choice of subject. This can not be judged, however, since the work was never exhibited in France. W.T. Walters, as a young man in Paris, bought *The Scarlet Letter* from the artist's studio; it was the beginning of his great collection.

Moralizing paintings were coveted by American patrons of French art in the second half of the nineteenth century, and the combination in *The Scarlet Letter* of an American source and a poignant lesson about tolerance was sufficient reason to attract Walters to the work. At a later date he also bought a drawing entitled *The Good Sister* from Merle's studio.

The *American Art Review*, an important document of American taste published in Boston between 1879 and 1881, gave space for an obituary of Merle. In it he was called "the well-known French figure painter," suggesting a reputation in America which is difficult to recreate today. "His paintings, somewhat waxy in treatment of flesh and cold in color, but refined and academically correct, enjoyed great popularity in the United States, and specimens of his work are to be found in most American collections" (*American Art Review*, vol. II, 1881, p. 261).

N.D.

The Walters Art Gallery, Baltimore

## Jean-François Millet

*Gruchy 1814–1875 Barbizon*

*Millet, one of the best-known painters of his time, was born into a peasant family in the village of Gruchy, near Cherbourg, on October 4, 1814. His parents encouraged his interest in art, and he began his training at Cherbourg with the local portrait painter Mouchel and then the Davidian Langlois (see 1976, London, Hayward Gallery, p. 21). Through a fellowship awarded by the city of Cherbourg, he entered the Parisian atelier of Paul Delaroche. The impact of these masters' styles on the mature Millet's choice of subjects and manner of execution was slight. Although extremely cultured and well versed in Classical literature, Millet embraced wholeheartedly the rural environment of his youth. This attitude accounts in part for his being a central figure in the Barbizon group and for his association with Diaz, Théodore Rousseau (q.v.), Jacque, Daumier (q.v.), Barye (q.v.), Dupré, and Troyon (q.v.). During the early phase of the Second Empire, he became friends with the Boston painter William Morris Hunt, which led to his acquiring many important American patrons.*

*Millet's career before the Second Empire was marked by struggles. He first achieved notoriety at the Salon of 1850–51, where he exhibited* The Sower. *Millet's works asserted the moral superiority of hard labor, and they were well suited to the policies of Napoleon III, which were at once authoritarian and benevolent, caring to improve the material lot of the workers (see Romier, 1960, p. 408). Millet received a state commission in 1852, Salon medals in 1853 and 1864, and the cross of the Legion of Honor in 1868. These recognitions do not mean that Millet was universally accepted by the apparatus of the government (see 1976, London, Hayward Gallery, passim).*

*Although Millet is frequently seen as a precursor of many later trends in modern art, his art was very personal. Even in landscape painting, for which he held a growing attraction after 1865, both the inner meaning as well as the social purpose were as important as in his earlier figure paintings. Robert Herbert explained best the position of the artist: "Millet's world was one of labour and well-earned repose that permitted the urban bourgeoisie to release itself into the realm of the seemingly untouched past, with its connotations of permanence, health, open air and simplicity of life" (1976, London, Hayward Gallery, p. 14). (See also no. VII-47.)*

D.F.M.

Bibliography:
1976, London, Hayward Gallery

Jean-François Millet

## VI-87
## Shepherdess and Her Flock

1863–64
Signed, lower right: J.-F. Millet
Oil on canvas
81 × 101 cm

Provenance:
Commissioned by Paul Tesse, Paris, 1863; accepted 1864; Van Praet coll., Brussels, 1864, in exchange for *The Angelus* (Louvre RF 1593); Alfred Chauchard, 1892; bequest to the Louvre, 1909 (inv. no. RF 1879)

Exhibitions:
1864, Paris, Salon, no. 1362; 1867, Paris, Exposition Universelle, no. 475; 1887, Paris, Ecole des Beaux-Arts, no. 30; 1913, Sao Paulo, no. 711 (repro.); 1937, Geneva, no. 58; 1939–41, Buenos Aires, etc., no. 93; 1954–55, Tokyo, no. 18 (repro.); 1956, Musées de France, no. 16; 1957, Fontainebleau, no. 77; 1958, Munich, no. 85 (repro.); 1964–65, Tokyo, Fukuoka, Kyoto, no. 37; 1970, Tokyo, Kyoto, Fukuoka, no. 19 (repro.); 1972, Seoul, no. 2 (repro.); 1973, Paris, Musée des Arts Décoratifs (repro.); 1975, Barbizon, no. 239 (repro.); 1975, Cherbourg, no. 12; 1975–76, Paris, Grand Palais, no. 163; 1976, London, Hayward Gallery, no. 87

Bibliography:
See 1976, London, Hayward Gallery, pp. 142–43

*The Shepherdess and Her Flock* was Millet's first universal success at a public exhibition. Its popular reception owed a great deal to the peaceful nature of the scene. Herbert (1976, London, Hayward Gallery, p. 142) noted that "the shepherdess is young and almost beautiful," and as a result did not raise bitter social questions as did *The Newborn Calf* (Art Institute of Chicago), which was shown at the same Salon (*see* 1976, London, Hayward Gallery, p. 145, no. 88).

The composition of *The Shepherdess and Her Flock* is characteristic of Millet's figure paintings during the 1860s. A panoramic landscape under a colorful sky is set off by a grouping in the middle ground—here the flock—with a figure (or figures) acting as vertical accent in the foreground. The key to the painting does not lie simply in skillful arrangements of figure and stuffs, brushwork or color, but in the emotional impact that they produce. One is compelled to speculate on the thoughts of the young woman standing alone in the tranquillity of nature. It is perhaps this factor that separates Millet from the Romantic painters, although his manner of execution is closely related to theirs.

Scenes of shepherds and shepherdesses with their flocks appear frequently in Barbizon School paintings. Probably the first work of the subject to receive notoriety was the 1843 *Return of the Shepherd* by Decamps (q.v.: Stedelijk Museum, Amsterdam; Mosby, 1977, vol. I, p. 180). Decamps's painting seems to have been the pictorial source for Millet's *Return of the Flock* (1857–60; formerly Pennsylvania Academy of the Fine Arts, Philadelphia, now Japanese art market), in which a solitary shepherd leads his flock across a plain in late winter. In turn, the latter painting must have

VI-87

provided the idea for this *Shepherdess and Her Flock*. In fact, disregarding the sizes, the works could be pendants. The serene shepherdess with dandelions in bloom around her feet, indicating late spring, stands in direct contrast to the Pennsylvania Academy painting in which the shivering shepherd braces the winter evening. One must wonder whether these works, taken as a pair, provided the initial impetus for the numerous depictions of the four seasons that Millet undertook during the following decade.

It should be mentioned that Millet's contemporaries did not group the paintings (*see* 1976, London, Hayward Gallery, nos. 79, 87). In fact, *Shepherdess and Her Flock* was viewed as different from Millet's other production, and his friend, patron, and biographer, A. Sensier, urged the artist to produce more works in this direction. He thought they were more marketable because they appealed to patrons who wished to be reminded more of rural idylls than of rural poverty. Robert Herbert relates several pastels, drawings, prints, and oils to the present painting.

D.F.M.

Musée du Louvre, Paris

---

## Oscar-Claude Monet
*Paris 1840–1926 Giverny (Eure)*

*In his choice of subjects and his fervent ambition to gain distinction at the Salons, Monet followed a tradition long established. Yet, in his manner of painting and his plainly witnessed rendering of subjects seen in outdoor light, he rapidly surpassed all others, and presented critics with an innovative manner which, with a few exceptions, transcended their standards of judgment. With the collapse of the Second Empire, Monet, with a small group of friends, abandoned any quest for official success, and in 1874, with the first showing of the Impressionists, launched a new vision of painting, and changed the role of the artist as well.*

*Born in Paris in 1840, Monet moved with his family to Le Havre (1845) where he was enrolled in the local schools, and showed an early, flamboyant talent for caricature drawing. At the age of sixteen he was introduced to Boudin (q.v.), who took the young artist with him on landscape-painting outings and essentially became his master. In 1859 Monet visited Paris for two months, studying with Charles Jacque and working at the Académie Suisse, where he met Pissarro (q.v.). From 1860 to 1862, he spent two years in Algeria in the army; but by December 1862, he was again in Paris, enrolled in Gleyre's large and*

*informal studio, where he met Bazille, Sisley, and Renoir (q.q.v.). With them, he made excursions into the country, painting in the open air. With the close of Gleyre's studio at the end of 1863, Monet's formal training, such as it was, ceased, and the next six years were marked by peripatetic life. He was often pursued by creditors, between Paris, where he shared a studio with Bazille (and, briefly, with Renoir), and Honfleur and the Norman coast; at Chailly (Forest of Fontainebleau); and in several villages along the Seine. In 1865 two seascapes were accepted at the Salon, and that same summer he took up his vast, but ill-fated project,* Luncheon on the Grass, *on which Courbet advised him. At the salon of 1866 he achieved his greatest early success with* Camille. *Following this brief triumph, which did not substantially increase his sales or his public reputation, and with his rejection at the Salon of 1867, there began a period of critical obscurity — often marked by severe misery—which scarcely lifted until the early 1880s. With the outbreak of the Franco-Prussian War, he fled to London (see Richardson, 1957).*

J.R.

Bibliography:
Geffroy, 1924; Richardson, 1957; Seitz, 1960; Wildenstein, 1971; Rewald, 1973; Wildenstein 1974

---

Oscar-Claude Monet

# VI-88
# Spring Flowers

1864
Signed and dated, upper right: Claude Monet 64
Oil on canvas
116.5 × 91 cm

Provenance:
Léon Monet, Rouen; Cleveland Museum of Art, 1953 (inv. no. 53.155)

Exhibitions:
1954, Detroit, no. 43, repro. p. 36; 1957, Saint Louis, Minneapolis, no. 1 (repro.); 1963, Philadelphia, p. 143; 1975, Chicago, no. 3

Bibliography:
Francis, 1954; Rewald, 1961, repro. p. 111; Wildenstein, 1971, p. 75; Wildenstein, 1974, no. 20

*See* Colorplate

In the autumn of 1864 Monet wrote to Bazille (q.v.): "There are a lot of us at the moment in Honfleur... Boudin [q.v.] and Jongkind [q.v.] are here; we are getting on marvelously. I regret very much that you aren't here, because in such company there's a lot to

VI-88

be learned and nature begins to grow beautiful; things are turning yellow, grow more varied; altogether, it's wonderful.... I'm sending a flower picture to the exhibition in Rouen; there are very beautiful flowers at present.... Now do such a picture, because I believe it's an excellent thing to paint" (Rewald, 1961, pp. 111–12).

Although Bazille seems not to have taken the advice until two years later (Rewald, 1946, p. 113), the exuberance of the twenty-year-old Monet projects with great vitality, and this flower piece is one of his most successful early pictures. Its sources are numerous, and whereas we cannot be sure if Monet knew the formal and balanced bouquets of Fantin-Latour (q.v.) at this date, it is almost certain that the reference here is to Courbet (q.v.), whom he had met in Paris in the spring of 1864. However, in close comparison with Courbet, for example, the *Trellis* of 1863 (Toledo Museum of Art), Monet's independence is clearly evident. Whereas he painted here on a dark ground (a warm brick red) probably on the direct advice of Courbet, the contrasts from shadow to highlight are not as abrupt as Courbet's, and the actual drawing is more concise, with no use of the palette knife, which was frequently employed by Courbet in his flower pictures. Rewald notes that this vigorous rendering shows the influence of Jongkind and Boudin; however, compared to Boudin's *Hollyhocks*, one of the few works surviving by either of them in this genre (Rewald, 1946, p. 113), Monet's composition is still more firmly drawn and arranged in space. In the variation of color and the freshness of the light, he had already established his central concerns, quite independent of any influences.

J.R.

The Cleveland Museum of Art, Gift of Hanna Fund

Oscar-Claude Monet

## VI-89
## Camille

1866
Signed and dated, lower right: Claude Monet 1866
Oil on canvas
231 × 151 cm

Provenance:
Purchased by Arsène Houssaye, editor of *L'Artiste* and Inspector of Fine Arts, for 8,000 francs, October 1868; sale, Paris, Hôtel Drouot, May 22–23, 1896, no. 158; Henri Houssaye, Paris; Galerie Durand-Ruel, 1898; Galerie Cassirer, Berlin, 1902; acquired by the Kunsthalle, Bremen, 1906 (inv. no. 298.1906/1)

Exhibitions:
1866, Paris, Salon, no. 1386; 1868, Le Havre, no. 856; 1899, Paris, Galerie Georges Petit, no. 60; 1901, Berlin, no. 181; 1902, Brussels, no. 122; 1906, Bremen, no. 241; 1951, Paris, Orangerie, no. 60

Bibliography:
D'Hervilly, 1866, p. 207; About, 1867, pp. 102, 124; Thoré-Bürger, 1870, vol. II, pp. 285, 286, 325; Catalogue, Bremen, Kunsthalle, 1925, no. 298; Rewald, 1955, pp. 103, 108, 113, 122, 132; Catalogue, Bremen, Kunsthalle, 1973, p. 67, fig. 578; Zola, 1974, pp. 66, 114, repro. p. 199; Wildenstein, 1974, pp. 29, 31, 32, 145, no. 65 (repro.; bibl.)

*(Shown in Paris only)*

In 1866 Monet made his second appearance at the Salon, gaining tremendous success with *Camille*, his first large figure. E. d'Hervilly published a poem about the picture in *L'Artiste*: "Parisian woman, O queen...." Thoré-Bürger was enthusiastic: "Henceforth Camille is immortal and she is called the Woman in the Green Dress," while Zola noted admiringly: "I confess that the canvas that made me pause the longest is M. Monet's *Camille*.... Oh yes, here is a temperament, here is a man in this crowd of eunuchs. Look at the canvases nearby and see what a pitiful showing they make alongside this window open onto nature. Here there is more than a realist, here is a strong and sensitive interpreter who has been able to render each detail without falling into dryness." On the same occasion, in referring to Monet and a few others, Castagnary used the word "naturalist"

for the first time. In addition, when the Salon closed, the firm of Cadart et Luquet ordered from the artist a smaller repetition of his painting (panel, 81 × 55 cm, Bucharest museum), and in 1868, at the exhibition in Le Havre, this picture was one of the two that gained Monet a silver medal.

Recalling perhaps the figure on the right in *The Painter's Studio* (Louvre) by Courbet (q.v.), *Camille* appeared to its contemporaries to resemble the work of Manet (q.v.), and satirical critics did not fail to play on the close similarity between the names of the two painters. As early as 1865 Manet had been quite irritated by "this scoundrel who so shamelessly imitates" his painting, and the tension reached its peak in 1866; thanks to Zacharie Astruc, the two men finally met after the Salon was over.

Monet had originally hoped to send his huge composition of *Women in the Garden* to the Salon, but he gave up the idea and very rapidly painted—in four days, according to Thoré-Bürger—this figure set against a neutral background. Being winter, he painted it in the studio. The model was a young woman from Lyons, the nineteen-year-old Camille-Léonie Doncieux (1847–1879), whom Monet was soon to marry and whom he later often represented in intimist portraits. In a letter of May 1, 1906, he confirmed this to the director of the Bremen museum: "It is indeed Mme Monet,

VI-89

my first wife, who served me as model, and though it was not necessarily my intention to do a portrait of her, but merely a Parisian figure of that time, the likeness to her is complete."

G.L.

Kunsthalle, Bremen

Oscar-Claude Monet

## VI-90
## The Garden of the Princess

c. 1867
Signed, lower right: Claude Monet
Oil on canvas
91.8 × 61.9 cm

Provenance:
Latouche, Paris, 1867; Frederic Bonner, New York; sale, January 24, 1912, no. 36; Galerie Durand-Ruel, New York; Horace Havemeyer, New York, by 1931; M. Knoedler and Co., New York; Allen Memorial Art Museum (inv. no. 48.296)

Exhibitions:
1952, Zurich, Paris, The Hague, no. 9, pl. V (Zurich), no. 5 (Paris), no. 6 (The Hague, repro.); 1954, New York, Oberlin, no. 59 (repro.); 1954, Detroit, no. 44 (repro.); 1957, St. Louis, Minneapolis, no. 3; 1958, Palm Beach, no. 1; 1962, London, no. 28 (repro); 1966, Minneapolis; 1968, Baltimore, no. 77; 1970, New York, no. 6; 1975, Chicago, no. 12

Bibliography:
Geffroy, 1924, p. 25; Rewald, 1946, p. 131, repro. p. 133; Stechow, 1948, p. 41, repro. p. 41; Salinger, 1957, pl. 18; *Allen Memorial Art Museum Bulletin*, vol. XVI, no. 2, 1959, pp. 72–73; Seitz, 1960, p. 68, repro. p. 69; Isaacson, 1966, pp. 4–22; Catalogue, Oberlin, Allen Memorial Art Museum, 1967, pp. 112–13, fig. 95; Wildenstein, 1971, p. 17; Wildenstein, 1974, no. 86

As he would do in London at the end of the century, Monet in 1867 and 1868 executed a series of pictures of Paris, all from essentially the same locale, which stand among his best early landscapes. There are three in all, each done from a lofty vantage point which must be either a window or the balcony on the Perrault facade of the Louvre. The first, showing the newly restored church of Saint Germain l'Auxerrois across the street is dated 1866 (Berlin); the other two (The Hague and Oberlin) both look southeast across the Seine at the Ile de la Cité, and beyond at the dome of the Panthéon. It has been reasonably argued that these date from the spring of 1867 (by Isaacson, 1966; he speculates that the Berlin picture may also be from this date, but was later misdated) and, therefore, are probably the pictures mentioned

VI-90

in a letter to Bazille in May of that year, noting that he and Renoir were at work on their views of Paris.

To establish stylistic precedents is difficult. Boudin (q.v.) and, to a degree, Jongkind (q.v.) are present in the understanding of the diffusing quality of light and in the limpid atmosphere, but as Richardson points out, early Corot (q.v.)—especially the views of Rome—is the closest source. However, unlike any of the others, Monet animated his panorama with anecdotes taken from daily life and, by this means, recorded a moment on a spring day in the heart of Paris, which is as vivid and acute as a passage from Zola.

J.R.

Allen Memorial Art Museum, Oberlin College, Ohio

Oscar-Claude Monet

## VI-91
## Portrait of Mme Gaudibert

1868
Signed and dated, lower right: Claude Monet 1868
Oil on canvas
217 × 138.5 cm

Provenance:
M. and Mme Louis Gaudibert, Le Havre, 1868; Mme Gaudibert's sister, Mme Edgar Lamotte, Le Havre; Maurice Lamotte, Sainte-Adresse; the Louvre, 1951 (inv. no. RF 1951 20)

Exhibitions:
1925, Paris, Musée des Arts Décoratifs, no. 46; 1928, Berlin, no. 9; 1931, Paris, Orangerie, no. 11; 1932, London, no. 958; 1952, Zurich, Paris, The Hague, no. 14 (Zurich), no. 11 (Paris), no. 11 (The Hague); 1957, Paris, Musée Jacquemart André, no. 208; 1957, Saint Louis, Minneapolis, no. 6; 1967, Paris, Orangerie, no. 420; 1973, Paris, Musée des Arts Décoratifs; 1975, Chicago, no. 16

Bibliography:
Mellerio, 1900, p. 19; Bulletin de la Vie Artistique, 1921, p. 496 (repro.); Jean-Aubry, 1922, pp. 72–74; Régamey, 1927, pp. 70, 78, 82; Poulain, 1932, pp. 120, 129, 130, 148, 149; Malingue, 1943, p. 23; Adhémar and Dreyfus-Bruhl, 1958, no. 229; Seitz, 1960, pp. 14, 18, 19, 25 (repro.); Sterling and Adhémar, 1958–61, vol. III, p. 26, no. 1352, pl. 503; Rewald, 1961, p. 184; Wildenstein, 1974, p. 121; Adhémar and Dayez-Distel, 1977, pp. 65, 156

By the spring of 1868 Monet's career had seriously faltered. After being accepted at the Salons of 1865 and 1866, he encountered a severe blow in the rejection of his *Women in the Garden* in 1867, which prompted his aunt, who also disapproved of his mistress, to withdraw her financial support. His participation at Le Havre in the International Maritime Exposition that spring, where he won a silver medal, might have heartened him somewhat; however, as noted in a letter from Boudin (q.v.) to the dealer P.-F. Martin (Jean-Aubry, 1922, p. 74), he sold nothing from the show, and after it closed his works were seized by his creditors, going for as little as 80 francs at auction. The buyer of some marines from this sale was a wealthy shipowner from Le Havre, Louis Gaudibert, whose support and patronage during this difficult time saved the young artist.

In a despairing letter to Bazille dated June 29, 1868, Monet noted: "I'm leaving Paris this evening to see about doing something for my amateur in Le Havre" (Poulain, 1932, p. 120). By December of that year he was able to write his friend: "Thanks to this gentleman from Le Havre who has come to my aid, I am enjoying perfect tranquillity" (Poulain, 1932, p. 130).

Gaudibert's support included purchase of new works, as well as the seascapes (Wildenstein, 1974, nos. 77, 109, 123), and some form of stipend, which continued at least as late as June 1869, after Monet and his family had left the coast and settled in Bougival (Rewald, 1946, p. 225). Perhaps the most important act of patronage was his commission of three portraits: two of Gaudibert himself (Wildenstein, 1974, nos. 120, 122; both lost) and one of his wife.

The work is well documented: September 3, 1868; "I've received by telegram from my amateur from Le Havre a commission to begin a portrait of his wife next Monday" (Poulain, 1932, p. 129); a notation from late October that he was working on the portrait at

Etretat (Poulain, 1932, p. 148), probably at the Château Ardennes-Saint-Louis, which belonged to Mme Gaudibert's father; and finally Boudin's letter to Martin of January 18, 1869, mentioning that he had seen the finished work (Jean-Aubry, 1922, p. 72).

A commissioned full-length portrait on this scale was new for Monet, even though in both the *Luncheon on the Grass* (1865–66) and the *Women in the Garden* (1866–67) he had shown elaborately dressed women in different poses, some with lost-profiles, as here. The more immediate comparison is to his success of the Salon of 1866, *Camille.* Here, however, he abandoned the simplicity of that work and included a much greater variety of elements, also giving the paint surface a greater complexity throughout.

This portrait falls clearly within a Second Empire tradition of fashionable portraiture, for example, Stevens, Carolus-Duran, and Winterhalter (q.q.v.). The use of the floral rug may also recall Whistler's *White Girl.*

The success of this picture as a portrait has frequently been debated and it must be admitted that we learn little more of Marguerite Gaudibert (1844–1877) than that she was a woman of limited beauty, but with a sense of fashion, at ease in a richly ornamented household. As the shrewd dealer Martin noted: "It is simply a painting, not a portrait" (Wildenstein, 1974, p. 445, document no. 22), a most portentious observation for the future development of Monet.

J.R.

Musée de Louvre, Galerie du Jeu de Paume, Paris

VI-91

---

## Gustave Moreau

*Paris 1826–1898 Paris*

*In 1846 Moreau entered the studio of François-Edouard Picot at the Ecole des Beaux-Arts, but left in 1849 after failing to win the Prix de Rome. His work between 1850 and 1855 very clearly reflected the influence of Delacroix (q.v.) and then of Chassériau (q.v.), and his admiration for these masters can be felt in the paintings he exhibited at the Salon: The Descent from the Cross (1852); The Song of Songs (1853; Dijon); and Darius Fleeing after the Battle of Arbela (1853; Musée Gustave Moreau, Paris). At the same time he undertook vast compositions on which he worked all his life without completion: The Pretenders and Hercules and the Daughers of Thespius.*

*In order to complete his artistic training in 1857, Moreau went to Italy where he spent two years (see no. VII-49). He did not exhibit again at the Salon until 1864, when his Oedipus and the Sphinx caused a sensation. He was a regular participant in the annual exhibitions until 1869, showing, among his major works, The Young Man and Death (Fogg Art Museum) at the Salon of 1865 and Diomedes Devoured by His Horses (Salon of 1866; Musée des Beaux-Arts, Rouen), and the Young Thracian Girl Carrying the Head of Or-*

*pheus (Louvre). After having exhibited Prometheus and Jupiter and Europa (Musée Gustave Moreau, Paris) in the Salon of 1869, not having to depend on the sale of his works for survival, he retired from public life.*

*At this time his style began to evolve, with the human figure diminishing in importance, giving way to fantastic architecture or imaginary landscapes. From then on he was surrounded by a group of faithful admirers who had become excited by his submissions to the Salon of 1876.*

*Moreau became a professor of the Ecole des Beaux-Arts in 1892, and his teaching seems to have been appreciated by a group of artists who were later known as the Fauves. His work was quickly discovered by the Symbolists and then rediscovered by a small group of Surrealists. It was only in the second half of his mature period, after 1870, that Moreau found a style which allowed him to exercise his fantasies in works that were sometimes precious but always exploding with colors of a violent beauty.*

O.S.

Bibliography:
1961, Paris, Louvre; Von Holten, 1965; 1974, Los Angeles; Mathieu, 1976

Gustave Moreau

## VI-92
## The Athenians Delivered to the Minotaur in the Labyrinth

1855
Oil on canvas
106 × 200 cm

Provenance:
Commissioned by the Minister of State for 4,000 francs on September 23, 1854; sent to the Musée de l'Ain, Bourg-en-Bresse, 1856 (inv. no. 856 1 E)

Exhibitions:
1855, Paris, Exposition Universelle, no. 3703; 1954, Bourg-en-Bresse, no. 122; 1969, Ambérieu-en-Bugey; 1973, Paris, Musée des Arts Décoratifs; 1974, Los Angeles, no. 12

Bibliography:
Du Camp, 1864, p. 705; Leprieur, 1889, p. 10; Renan, 1900, p. 132; Laran and Deshairs, 1913, p. 19; Roujon, 1914, p. 28; Focillon, 1928, p. 88; Vergnet-Ruiz and Laclotte, 1962, p. 246; Cadars, 1965, p. 44; Paladilhe and Pierre, 1971, p. 12; Wright and Moisy, 1972, p. 25; Dorra, 1973, pp. 129–40 (repro.); Frongia, 1973, fig. 1; Marquis, 1976; Mathieu, 1976, pp. 40, 44–45, 299, no. 29 (repro.)

The fact that Gustave Moreau, who in 1854 was just at the beginning of his career, obtained a commission for a painting was not unusual. However, the considerable sum of 4,000 francs might have been the result of influence, since his father had many connections. Who chose the subject is not known. It may have been the artist himself, since the commission had been given to him after he had submitted a preliminary sketch on the same theme (Arch. nat. F²¹ 99 [September 21, 1854]). That sketch may have been the small painting that Gustave Moreau gave to his cousin Jules Moreau, counselor at the court of Rouen, which Mathieu (1976) classifies as a variant of the painting in Bourg-en-Bresse. The variants of this canvas are of little importance since the essential elements of composition were already determined. The drawing in sanguine and watercolor listed by Mathieu (no. 31) represents an earlier stage, slightly more dramatic in conception, particularly for the central character. During the course of the execution of this painting, Moreau consciously made his composition calmer and more heroic, probably in order to try to throw off the influence of Delacroix, too evident in his previous submissions to the Salon. To counterbalance this influence, still apparent in the group on the left, he borrowed elements from other masters. The group in the center has often been compared with the *Oath of the Horatii* of David, and the kneeling man with Poussin's *Shepherds of Arcadia*. Although the canvas is very well composed, it lacks originality, for Moreau had not yet assimilated the lessons of the past, and indeed, this work did not receive critical attention when it was shown at the 1855 Exposition Universelle.

O.S.

Musée de l'Ain, Bourg-en-Bresse

Gustave Moreau

## VI-93
## Oedipus and the Sphinx

1864
Signed and dated, lower left: Gustave Moreau 64
Oil on canvas
206 × 104 cm

Provenance:
Purchased by Prince Napoleon for 8,000 francs, 1864; William H. Herriman, New York; bequest to the Metropolitan Museum of Art, 1921 (inv. no. 21.134.1)

Exhibitions:
1864, Paris, Salon, no. 1388; 1961, New York, no. 175; 1961, Paris, Louvre, no. 10 (repro.); 1974, Los Angeles, no. 28

Bibliography:
About, 1864, p. 73ff.; Auvray, 1864, pp. 54–57; de Callias, 1864, p. 219; Cantaloube, 1864; Clément, 1864; Drion, 1864; T. Gautier, *Le Moniteur*, May 27, 1864; Lagrange, 1864, pp. 506–8; Merson, 1864; Nettement, 1864, pp. 587–88; Parent, 1864; Paul, 1864; Rousseau, 1864; Saint-Victor, 1864; de Sault, 1864; de Thémines, 1864; Gallet, 1865, p. 24; T. Gautier, *Le Moniteur*, July 9, 1865; du Camp, 1867, pp. 109–19, 144, 147, 151, 209, 210, 341; Scribe, 1867, pp. 390–91; Chesneau, 1868, pp. 181–90; T. Gautier, *L'Illustration*, May–June 1869; de Savarus, 1879, p. 87; Phillipps, 1885, p. 230; Fourcaud, 1888; Lorrain, 1888; Leprieur, 1889, pp. 12–14, 31–43, 48–49; Castagnary, 1892, pp. 196–202; Larroumet, 1896, pp. 270–71; Thévenin, 1897, p. 14; p. 5; Breton, 1899, p. 178; Flat, 1899, p. 17; Geffroy, 1900, "Moreau," p. 3; Renan, 1900, pp. 27, 45, 50, 52, 181; Larroumet, 1904, p. 242; Schuré, 1904, pp. 369–70; R. de Montesquiou, in 1906, Paris, Galerie Georges Petit, p. 30; Loisel, 1912, pp. 15, 28; Deshairs and Laran, 1913, pp. 25–29; Desvallières, 1913, pl. 8; Roujon, 1914, pp. 35–38; Boisse, 1917, p. 424; Léger, 1920, p. 54; Coquiot, 1924, pp. 107–9; Bouyer, 1926; Desvallières, 1926; Rouault, 1926, "Moreau," p. 141; Praz, 1933, pp. 295–96; Tabarant, 1942, p. 391; Chassé, 1947, p. 34; Sloane, 1951, pp. 171–75; Bacou, 1956, vol. I, p. 254; Polak, 1958, p. 38; Von Holten, 1957, pp. 35–50; Von Holten, 1960, pp. 2–15; Von Holten, 1965, pp. 22, 30, 197; Crespelle, 1966,

VI-92

p. 164; Salinger and Sterling, 1967, pp. 1–5; Mathieu, 1971, pp. 277–78; Paladilhe and Pierre, 1971, pp. 25, 26, 75, 76, 80, 99, 137, 157; Wright and Moisy, 1972, p. 13; Dorra, 1973, pp. 130–40; Frongia, 1973, fig. 1; Mathieu, 1976, pp. 18, 28, 70, 81–85, 110, 241, 305, no. 64; Lacambre, 1977

Gustave Moreau worked for a long time on the theme of Oedipus. Before beginning this composition he had drawn a Sphinx on a high, steep peak to which were still attached the corpses of her victims, as well as an Oedipus rejecting a temptress-Sphinx; an Oedipus turning his back to the Sphinx; and an Oedipus seated opposite the Sphinx (*see* Mathieu, 1976). It was in a cameo that he finally found his composition, a Sphinx clutching onto the body of Oedipus (Musée Gustave Moreau, Paris, 2483), which he reversed. Two drawings at the Musée Gustave Moreau bear the inscription "first idea"; the one dated 1861 (517) is closer to the final composition; the other (2425) may have been done earlier. However the small column supporting a vase, but placed on the left, appears in the latter. The details of the composition demanded a great deal of work. Thus the column moved from left to right (2419, 2457, 2415, 2420) after appearing once in the middle (2509). Two drawings in the museum (2448, 2457) seem to show the definitive composition. Moreau, of course, was familiar with Ingres's painting of the subject, a sketch of which he had hastily executed, and it was very difficult for him to free himself of this model.

He studied at length the anatomy of his model (notably drawings 2476, 2478, 2484, 2496, 2497, 2501) and yet the weaknesses in the anatomy of the hero, especially his right leg, are noticeable. There are also numerous studies for the Sphinx. Moreau had in his studio the wing of a bird which he studied in great detail before attaching it to his figure. It is also interesting to examine the various mutations the monster's head underwent. In 1864 a number of critics commented unfavorably on the doll-like head. Yet Moreau had undoubtedly studied a living model (2454) to whom he had fused various influences, among them Leonardo's Isabella d'Este (2431) and the Thetis of Ingres (2441), an artist whom he detested. It is plain, from the number of sketches he made (2500, 2424, 2465, 2436, 2464, among others) that he attached great importance to the head of his Sphinx. For him it was endowed with special significance: "It is a terrestrial chimera, as vile as earthly matter and equally bewitching, represented by that charming head of a woman, with a winged body... promises of the ideal, but with the body of a monster, of the carnivore who tears prey to shreds" (Musée Gustave Moreau, cahier IV, p. 21).

VI-93

One sees here all of Moreau's fantasies—interpreting woman as a perverse temptress; his own fear of the flesh, of matter. Ragnar Von Holten justly observed that it is not the ancient Oedipus myth that is pictured here but the war of the sexes. Critics at the Salon of 1864 were particularly struck by the differences between this painting, which for them made reference to fifteenth-century Italy, especially Mantegna, and that of Ingres's reinterpretation of Greek art. Despite some detractors, votaries of Realism, the critics, on the whole, were pleasantly surprised by its innovation. Its purchase by one of the highest members of the court is proof of Moreau's success.

O.S.

Metropolitan Museum of Art, New York, Bequest of William H. Herriman, 1921

---

*Octave Penguilly-L'Haridon*

*Paris 1811–1870 Paris*

*A graduate of the Ecole Polytechnique, Penguilly L'Haridon also studied with the painter Nicolas Charlet. He began to exhibit drawings in the Salon in 1835 and from 1846 on he showed on a regular basis. At the Salon of 1846 Baudelaire noticed his* Parade: Pierrot Introducing His Friends Harlequin and Punchinello to the Audience *(Poitiers museum). He was awarded a third-class medal in 1847 and a second-class medal and the Legion of Honor in 1851. His success during the Second Empire was immense, especially with Napoleon III who bought a number of pictures. Some, like* The Little Seagulls *(Salon of 1859; Rennes museum), were sent to provincial museums; others were shown at the Musée du Luxembourg, several of which were returned in 1879 to the heirs of Napoleon III (*The Riding Lesson, *Salon of 1863;* Proteus and His Seals, *Salon of 1866). His landscapes, which were broadly worked and well composed according to Baudelaire, often bordered on the fantastic. His historic scenes, of great precison, were at first destined for Versailles (*Battle of the Thirty) *of for the château of Saint-Germain (*Roman Villa Built at the Foot of the Dauphiné Alps Some Time after the Conquest of the Gauls, *Salon of 1870; now Louvre). He did not overlook exhibitions in the provinces, sending two paintings to Lille in 1866, for example, and he gave his* Death of Judas *(Salon of 1861) to the museum in Nantes, a region through which he traveled often, as his landscapes show.*

*A genre painter as well as a painter of historic scenes and landscapes, he nonetheless continued his military career. In 1854 he became the curator of the Musée de l'Artillerie and in 1868, inspecteur des études at the Ecole Polytechnique.*

G.L.

Octave Penguilly-L'Haridon

## VI-94
## Battle of the Thirty (1350)

1857
Signed and dated, lower right: O. Penguilly 1857
Oil on canvas
140 × 260 cm

Provenance:
Purchased at the Salon of 1857 from the civil list of Napoleon III for 6,000 francs by decree of September 30, 1857, "Inventaire de la liste civiles," no. 281; sent to the Musée Historique, Versailles (Louvre Archives, 2DD 20, 2DD 25) and exhibited in a provisionary presentation; transferred to the Louvre, April 5, 1881; sent to the Elysée palace, April 27, 1881; returned to the Louvre, September 12, 1882, and entered in the inventory of paintings (RF 348);

VI-94

deposited at the Musée Municipal des Beaux-Arts, Quimper, April 28, 1894 (inv. no. D.894.1.1.)

Exhibition:
1857, Paris, Salon, no. 2102

Bibliography:
Gautier, 1857, "Salon," p. 377–78; Auvray, 1857, p. 42; du Camp, 1857, pp. 75–76; About, 1858, pp. 196–97; Catalogue, Versailles, Musée Historique, 1860, vol. II, no. 1933; Calvet-Sérullaz, 1971, p. 132, no. 8 (repro.); Catalogue, Quimper, Musée Municipal des Beaux-Arts, 1976, n.p.; Baudelaire, 1976, pp. 643, 1592

In a long commentary the 1857 Salon catalogue explained the historical event represented here, beginning with these lines: "On March 27, 1350, thirty Bretons on the side of Ch. de Blois having as their leader Beaumanoir, and thirty Englishmen on the side of Montfort, commanded by Bembrough, made their way on a plain between Josselin and Ploermel, to an oak tree midway in order to fight in a kind of enclosed camp. After a desperate battle, twice resumed, victory fell to the Bretons..." The critics were generally disappointed: for Edmond About, "this charming painter misguided his talent for the first time"; for Maxime du Camp, he "is not successful this year... his *Combat of the Thirty* is more a work of archaeology than of art." Yet Baudelaire, finding contemporary military painting monotonous, understood that "artists during their warlike hours, look more to the past, as did M. Penguilly in the *Combat of the Thirty,* for a plausible pretext for developing a fine variety of weapons and of costumes," and Théophile Gautier lingered a long time over this composition: "In order to represent this event so strongly imbued with the spirit of the Middle Ages this artist employed medieval methods. It could be said that his painting is the reduced copy of some mural painting or of some old contemporaneous tapestry found in Brittany in the manor house of a descendant of the heroes who participated in the battle. On the frame are inscribed the names of the Thirty accompanied, as is appropriate, by their arms. ..." And, based on the absolute accuracy of the arms that the artist was able to study in his Musée de l'Artillerie, Gautier concluded: "This terrible battle is rendered with all the action that it required and in the way that, in fact, it must have actually occurred."

G.L.

Musée Municipal des Beaux-Arts, Quimper

VI-95

## Pierre-Auguste Pichon
*Sorèze (Tarn) 1805–1900 Paris*

*A student of Ingres (q.v.), for whom he worked on several projects (for instance, the decorating of the château of Dampierre), Pichon exhibited at the Salon from 1835 on and successively won a third-, second-, and first-class medal in 1843, 1844, and 1846. These honors were reconfirmed during the Second Empire with rappels in 1857 and 1861 and the decoration of the Legion of Honor in 1861.*

*Pichon executed an impressive number of portraits and religious and historical paintings, some of which had been commissioned or bought by the State to be sent to the provinces: for instance,* The Last Supper *(1846) for the cathedral of Amiens; the* Holy Women at the Tomb *(1848) for the church of Freigné;* Saint Sulpice *(1852)—its composition similar to that of Ingres's* Joan of Arc—*for the church of Guilly; the* Rest on the Flight *(1876), with some lingering Nazarene accents, for the church of Tracy-sur-Loire. He decorated several chapels in Parisian churches, notably Saint Eustache (chapel of Saint Genevieve), Saint Sulpice (chapel of Saint Charles Borromeo), and Saint Roch.*

G.L.

Bibliography:
Lacambre and Lacambre, 1970, pp. 23–29

Pierre-Auguste Pichon

## VI-95
## The Annunciation

1859
Signed and dated, lower right: A. PICHON 1859
Oil on canvas
250 × 200 cm

Provenance:
Commissioned by the Ministry of State, March 19, 1857, for 1,500 francs, with a first installment of 800 francs paid on June 7, 1859, the balance of 700 francs on December 30, 1859; consigned to the

church of Cléry (Loiret) (Arch. nat. F²¹ 103); classified by the Monuments Historiques, December 8, 1975

Exhibition:
1859, Paris, Salon, no. 2439

Bibliography:
Aubert, 1859, p. 94; Jourdan, 1859, p. 111; Angrand, 1968, p. 311; Lacambre and Lacambre, 1970, p. 27, repro. p. 28

On February 6, 1857, Pichon, whose last commission (*Saint Sulpice* for the church of Guilly [Cher]) dated back to 1851, complained to the Administration: "...I have been completely forgotten."

His request, duly accompanied by a recommendation, was soon followed by the commission for *The Annunciation*. Shortly thereafter, on June 27, through the powerful intercession of Ingres, he received another commission, this time for 3,000 francs: he was to copy, under the direction of the master, his *Joan of Arc* for the museum of Orléans (today at the Hôtel de Ville). Pichon, who promptly delivered a beautiful copy (with some slight variations in the costume) in April 1858, seems to have ignored the commission for *The Annunciation* and solicited more work. The Administration of Fine Arts of the Ministry of State became somewhat confused and made mention of the delivery of the *Holy Women at the Tomb,* of which the purchase for the Musée du Luxembourg planned in 1848 had been put aside (this picture was actually acquired only in 1873 and sent to the church of Freigné [Maine-et-Loire]) and confirmed that the sum of 1,500 francs had been appropriated for *The Annunciation.*

This painting, shown in the Salon of 1859, was appraised by Alfred Arago, *inspecteur des Beaux-Arts,* as being "painted with talent." The critics scarcely noticed it, remarking instead on the *Saint Clement* done for the Church of Saint Séverin in Paris, which was shown at the same time. However, Jourdan did refer to it, noting: "M. Pichon's talent is sure, sober, and correct. No one is better at grouping masses and harmonizing tones; no one draws with a surer hand. However... something is missing in this painting... who knows, perhaps it is too pure... M. Pichon's talent will probably take another turn when he begins painting something other than chapels and church pictures." It is true that the artist, faithful to traditional iconography, pushed to its extreme the delicate classicism in a Nazarene, even "plaster-saint," spirit, perhaps, because certain dealers in religious art were reproducing vast quantities of work after the models set by the Düsseldorf School. As a faithful pupil of Ingres, Pichon doubtlessly sought inspiration even further back, from examples of Fra Angelico in Florence or Raphael (predella of *The Coronation of the Virgin* in the Pinacoteca Vaticana), but he retained more sobriety than Amaury-Duval (q.v.), whose 1860 *Annunciation* (Mâcon museum) is placed in front of an arbor. Even the Administration was less austere than he for it commissioned countless copies of Vasari's Manneristic *Salutation of the Angels* (Louvre) for provincial churches.

Finally, it should be noted that, on December 30, 1869, an *Annunciation* was acquired from Pichon for Napoleon III for 1,200 francs ("Inventaire de la liste civile," no. 690, returned to the heirs of Napoleon III in 1880; *see* Louvre Archives DD 25, Z 15-29 [May 1880]).

G.L.

Basilica of Notre Dame, Cléry

---

## Camille Pissarro

Saint Thomas (Danish West Indies) 1830–1903 Paris

*Pissarro is often cited as the "dean" of the Impressionists (Rewald, 1963, p. 9). Their senior in age (he was two years older than Manet), he was also the sustaining force of the movement in the 1870s and 1880s; in his own work he was remarkably open to new ideas and flexible in his attitudes.*

*Like all of the artists who first showed together at the studio of Nadar (q.v.) in May 1874, Pissarro had wanted to gain recognition during the Second Empire through the established channels—the Salons and the State. While his work during this period is sometimes appreciated only for its anticipation of Impressionism, he was by the mid-1860s a painter of considerable stature and independence, creating work of a scale and an assurance equal to that of his later painting.*

*Born in Saint Thomas in the Danish West Indies, son of a French emigré shopkeeper and his Creole wife—Pissarro was sent to France for his early education (1842–47). Despite his strong artistic leaning (encouraged by his teacher, Savary), he returned to work for his father in Saint Thomas for five years, until 1853, when he rebelled and went to Caracas with the Danish landscapist Fritz Melbye. He remained there for two years, drawing and doing watercolors (see 1965, New York).*

*In 1855 he returned to France, where he studied at the Ecole des Beaux-Arts and worked at the Académie Suisse. He also studied with Anton Melbye (1818–75), Fritz's brother, an established marine and landscape painter. He also visited Corot (q.v.), who encouraged him. After painting a series of tropical landscapes, reminiscent of Saint Thomas, he began the subject that would dominate his career: the landscapes and rural inhabitants of the environs of Paris.*

*In 1859 Pissarro was accepted at the Salon, but was rejected in 1861 and 1863, when he showed three works at the Salon des Refusés. In 1864 he was again accepted at the Salon, and continued to show in every Salon of the Second Empire with the exception of 1867.*

*Like Monet (q.v.), Pissarro spent the years of the Franco-Prussian War in England, while his house at Louveciennes was ransacked and many works destroyed, which explains the relative scarcity of his pictures from the 1860s.*

J.R.

Bibliography:
Tabarant, 1924; Pissarro and Venturi, 1939, vol. II; Rewald, 1946, passim; Rewald, 1963; 1965, New York

VI-96

Camille Pissarro

## VI-96
## On the Banks of the Marne in Winter

1866
Signed and dated, lower right: C. Pissarro 1866
Oil on canvas
91.8 × 150.2 cm

Provenance:
Camille Pissarro; sale, Paris, Galerie Georges Petit, December 3, 1928, no. 27 (repro.); S. G. Archibald, 1930; Reid & Lefevre Galleries, London, 1952; purchased by the Art Institute of Chicago (inv. no. 1957.306)

Exhibitions:
1866, Paris, Salon, no. 1564; 1930, Paris, Orangerie, no. 3; 1965, New York, no. 2

Bibliography:
Rousseau, 1866; Zola, 1866; Pissarro and Venturi, 1939, pp. 18–84, no. 47

Shown at the Salon of 1866, accepted through the influence of Daubigny (q.v.), who served on the newly reformed jury for the first time, this was the first painting by Pissarro to receive critical notice. Of it Jean Rousseau wrote: "One can say that M. Pissaro is not banal because he is not capable of being merely picturesque. On the contrary, he uses a robust and exuberant talent to accentuate the vulgarities of the contemporary world, in the same way as a satirical poet is so much the more eloquent for being brutally and spontaneously truthful" (1866). Without being certain of the critic's comparative references—perhaps the late landscapes of Corot—we do know that this was the first year that Pissarro dropped Corot (q.v.) as his acknowledged master in the Salon catalogue. Rewald (1963, p. 16) notes that the two had had a falling out that year, probably because of Pissarro's evolution toward a greater realism.

Pissarro first saw the work of both Corot and Courbet (q.v.) in 1855, but it was the former who would guide his early development. By the mid-1860s, however, in response to Courbet, his work took on a greater boldness and scale and, especially through the use of the palette knife, a gradual departure from the poetry of Corot. In addition, the intensity of the greens and the long rectangular format, with a high horizon, may in turn have partially derived from the work of his friend and supporter, Daubigny. However, at the age of thirty-six, Pissarro achieved his full independent maturity, with this picture perhaps more than any other of this period.

Zola, too, noted the picture in the Salon, and gave, like Rousseau, a clear sense of its

jarringly innovative effect: "Look, you choose a winter scene, you have a plain bit of avenue, then a slope in the background, and some empty fields [stretching] to the horizon. Not the least entertainment for the eyes. A grave, austere painting, an extreme care for truth and accuracy, a strong, severe will. You are a great blunderer, sir—you are an artist I love" (1866, p. 74).

In the 1928 Pissarro sale catalogue (Paris, Galerie Georges Petit, December 3, 1928, no. 27), the picture was entitled: Landscape of La Varenne-Saint-Hilaire, the village on the Marne where the artist had lived since 1863.

J.R.

The Art Institute of Chicago,
Mr. and Mrs. Lewis L. Coburn Fund

---

## Pierre Puvis de Chavannes
*Lyons 1824–1898 Paris*

*The Second Empire marked the beginning of Puvis's career as an artist, though it was not until the end of the period that he began to receive the great public acclaim that characterized his later years. The son of a well-to-do mining engineer in Lyons, Puvis studied law for a time in the late 1840s and made two lengthy trips to Italy. He also irregularly attended the studios of Scheffer, Delacroix (q.v.), and Couture (q.v.); of these, Scheffer was the only master for whom Puvis had any praise in later years.*

*After withdrawing from Couture's studio, Puvis worked independently for several years, making his debut at the Salon of 1850 with a* Dead Christ *(location unknown). From 1852 to 1859 all of Puvis's submissions were rejected, so that he was taken by some critics to be a "new" artist when his works were again accepted in 1861. Puvis worked in the 1850s primarily as an easel painter, producing portraits, religious subjects, and Oriental genre scenes. In 1854–55, however, he was given the opportunity to decorate the dining room of his brother's home in Brouchy. Although these decorative paintings never became known to the public, Puvis later wrote, "Through them I found my own road to Damascus" (1977, Ottawa, p. 456).*

*The purchase of* Concordia *by the State after the Salon of 1861 and its subsequent installation at the Musée de Picardie, Amiens, helped decide Puvis's vocation as a specialist in decorative projects. Beginning in 1865 he provided additional paintings for Amiens, and in 1867–69 he completed two large decorations for the Palais de Longchamp in Marseilles. In 1867 Puvis was named a chevalier of the Legion of Honor.*

*The exhibition of Puvis's large decorations at the Salons drew mixed reactions from the critics. By the end of the period, however, many had come to admire his decorative use of color and his mastery of composition. Despite his individualism, Puvis was in many ways in step with the ideals of his time. The idea that art must be elevated in subject and removed from everyday realities, long defended by Ingres and still widely held, created a critical atmosphere predisposed toward Puvis's aesthetic. This factor, and the immense undecorated wall surfaces made available by the economic and cultural expansion of the Second Empire, seemed to guarantee Puvis's eventual triumph as the most successful decorative painter of the late nineteenth century. (See also no. VII-51.)*

D.R.

Bibliography:
1975, Toronto; 1976–77, Paris, Grand Palais; 1977, Ottawa

---

Pierre Puvis de Chavannes

## VI-97
## Peace

1867
Signed, lower left: P. Puvis de Chavannes; inscribed, bottom center, on border: LA PAIX
Oil on canvas
108 × 148 cm

Provenance:
Purchased from the artist by Paul Durand-Ruel, Paris, c. 1872; Hiltbrunner coll., 1887; Galerie Durand-Ruel, 1888; John G. Johnson, 1888; John G. Johnson Collection, Philadelphia (inv. no. cat. 1062)

Exhibitions:
1867, Paris, Exposition Universelle, no. 526; 1868, Bordeaux, no. 504; 1881, Paris, Musée des Arts Décoratifs; 1887, New York, no. 56; 1887, Paris, Galerie Durand-Ruel, no. 22; 1894, New York, no. 16; 1904, Saint Louis, no. 49; 1975, New York, Shepherd Gallery, no. 110; 1975, Toronto, no. 7; 1976–77, Paris, Grand Palais, no. 36; 1977, Ottawa, no. 36

Bibliography:
Burty, 1868, "Bordeaux," pp. 496–500; Baignères, 1881, p. 421; *Johnson Collection*, 1914, vol. III, nos. 1062, 1063; Bell, 1920, p. 10; Brinton, 1922, p. 11; Durand-Ruel, 1939, vol. II, pp. 193, 219

---

Pierre Puvis de Chavannes

## VI-98
## War

1867
Signed, lower left: P. Puvis de Chavannes; in-

VI-97

VI-98

scribed, bottom center, on border: LA GUERRE
Oil on canvas
108 × 148 cm

Provenance:
*See* no. VI-97; John G. Johnson Collection, Philadelphia (inv. no. cat. 1063)

Exhibitions:
1867, Paris, Exposition Universelle, no. 526; 1868, Bordeaux, no. 505; 1881, Paris, Musée des Arts Décoratifs; 1887, New York, no. 55; 1887, Paris, Galerie Durand-Ruel, no. 21; 1894, New York, no. 17; 1904, Saint Louis, no. 53; 1975, Toronto, no. 6; 1976–77, Paris, Grand Palais, no. 37; 1977, Ottawa, no. 37

Bibliography:
*See* no. VI-97

In 1861 Puvis had shown at the Salon two large paintings entitled *Concordia* and *Bellum;* two years later he exhibited a matching pair, *Repose* and *Work.* All four paintings found their way by purchase or donation to the Musée de Picardie, Amiens. On the occasion of the Exposition Universelle of 1867, Puvis painted reduced versions of these works, exhibiting them as a unit and eliminating the Latin titles of the first pair. Although Puvis hoped that the four reductions would remain together, *Peace* and *War* are now in the John G. Johnson Collection in Philadelphia, and *Repose* and *Work* are in the National Gallery of Art, Washington, D.C.

The subject of the pendants is not new, allegorical representations of Peace and War having been fairly common since the Baroque period; nor were the large paintings of 1861 Puvis's first interpretation of the theme. Included in the decorative scheme of Puvis's Brouchy murals of 1854–55 is a pair of long, narrow overdoor canvases representing Peace and War by their attributes, a basket of fruits and vegetables and a still life of arms and armor (Ségard, 1914, pp. 10, 12); some of these elements reappear in the borders of the 1867 paintings. The Brouchy dining room also contains a second pair of overdoors depicting attributes of the Arts and Sciences; the subjects of the two pairs seem to have little to do with each other, as is true of the later pairing with *Repose* and *Work,* though in that case Puvis insisted the four compositions formed an "indivisible" group.

Photographs taken in Puvis's studio (1974, Los Angeles, Riverside, fig. 19) show that the artist intended *Peace* to be hung on the left, its pendant *War* on the right; the same arrangement had been followed in the overdoor still-life compositions at Brouchy, which are similar in their compositional lines to the later figural paintings.

Although *Peace* and *War* are early works, they already display many of the characteristics of the mature decorative style for which Puvis was to become famous. Of these the most striking to the critics of the time was the use of pale, fresco-like colors. In his subsequent work Puvis continued to use Arcadian settings, far removed from everyday life, but gradually reduced the complexity and depth of the figural groupings seen here. In Puvis's mature work there is a general avoidance of scenes of action or drama; in this sense *Peace* is more advanced stylistically than its pendant. Although the paintings are differentiated in coloring (*War* being the more somber of the two), they are united by the matching borders of devices, which had been painted over in the original large versions installed at Amiens.

*Peace* and *War* contain many echoes of Classical and Italian Renaissance art, and of the ordered compositions of Poussin; citing a more immediate antecedent, d'Argencourt (1977, Ottawa, nos. 36, 37) compares *War* to Delacroix's *Massacre of Chios* of 1824. Precedents for Puvis's style may also be found in the mural paintings of Delacroix, an artist whose temperament is usually thought to have been quite different from that of Puvis. When the 1867 reductions were exhibited in Bordeaux, Philippe Burty wrote: "I have not seen anyone, since the death of Delacroix, who has had more noble and refined ideas and who has expressed them with greater candor and fewer concessions to vulgarity" (Burty, 1868, "Bordeaux," p. 498). Despite Puvis's attempts to deny that he had been attracted in his youth by Delacroix's style, the subdued monumentality and simplified colors later characteristic of his works may be seen in the older painter's *Virgil Presenting Dante to Homer* of 1845–47 (cupola, Senate library, Luxembourg palace; Trapp, 1971, p. 278). In particular Delacroix's *Orpheus Civilizing the Greeks* (library, Palais Bourbon) anticipates the composition of *Peace* in its carefully balanced semicircular group of figures in the center, with subordinate groups performing everyday activities in the background to the left and right. The Palais Bourbon commission had been completed in December 1847, only a few months before Puvis entered Delacroix's studio. The adaptation by Puvis of the flying figures from the *Orpheus* in much later works, such as *The Dream* (1883; Louvre) and *The Sacred Grove, Beloved of the Arts and of the Muses* (1884; Musée des Beaux-Arts, Lyons), reemphasizes the depth of Delacroix's influence on his rebellious student.

D.R.

John G. Johnson Collection, Philadelphia

## Alexandre-Georges-Henri Regnault
*Paris 1843–1871 Buzenval*

*The death of Regnault, who fell in defense of Paris on October 31, 1871, was taken as the single greatest loss French painting suffered from the Franco-Prussian War. The memorial in his honor by Chapu (q.v.), financed through a subscription of artists and placed in the Cour du Mûrier of the Ecole des Beaux-Arts, stands as a moving testimony to the fame and admiration that this young painter had achieved.*

*The son of the famous chemist Victor Regnault (director of the manufactory at Sèvres, q.v.) he began his brilliant career at the Ecole at the age of seventeen, first studying drawing with Louis Lamothe and then entering the atelier of Cabanel (q.v.). Viewed by his teachers and fellow students as an artist of great precocity, he won the Prix de Rome in 1866. In Rome he fell under the spell of the flamboyant and extraordinary Spanish painter Mariano Fortuny, and his first great success,* Automedon with the Horse of Achilles *(Museum of Fine Arts, Boston), reflects the influence of Cabanel's classicism and of Fortuny's boldness of execution. In 1868 he visited Madrid, then in the throes of revolution, where he admired Velázquez (he copied* The Surrender of Breda *in the Prado as his fourth-year envoi) and Goya. He then moved to Morocco, where like Fortuny, his style took on a still more flamboyant and exotic quality, with his subjects straining toward sensationalism (for example,* Execution without Judgment under the Moorish Kings of Granada, *1870; Louvre).*

*He sent works to each Salon from 1864 to 1870, his* General Prim, *which received a gold medal in 1869, becoming a veritable sensation. The following year the award was repeated for* Salome with the Head of Saint John the Baptist *(Metropolitan Museum of Art, New York). Even though he was exempt from service, being a winner of a Prix de Rome, Regnault returned from Tangiers to defend his country.*

*Regnault's preference for dramatic subject matter led many critics to compare him to Delacroix (q.v.), but Charles Blanc made an important distinction between their work: "What occurs in Regnault is on the surface, his comprehension is completely external; his soul is constantly outside. In Delacroix, on the contrary, the painter's work accomplishes itself internally, in the intimacy of his being" (Blanc, 1876, p. 351).*

J.R.

VI-99

Bibliography:
Bailliere, 1872; Blanc, 1876, pp. 347–64; Claretie, 1882–84, vol. I, pp. 1–24; Marx, 1886; *Kunstchronik*, no. 22, 1887, pp. 164–65; Burty, 1886, pp. 47–52; 1973, Paris, Musée des Arts Décoratifs; 1974, Paris, Grand Palais, p. 152, under no. 197; 1975, New York, Shepherd Gallery, pp. 356–59

Alexandre-Georges-Henri Regnault

## VI-99
## Portrait of General Juan Prim

c. 1868–69
Oil on canvas
80.5 × 64.2 cm

Provenance:
Marie Sterner Galleries, New York; purchased by the Art Institute of Chicago, 1947 (inv. no. 1947.510)

Exhibitions:
1954, Santa Barbara, San Francisco, Kansas City, no. 35; 1970, Baltimore

Bibliography:
Blanc, 1876, p. 356

This small version of the large portrait of *General Juan Prim, Marqués de los Castillejos* (315 × 258 cm; Louvre) captures both the grandeur and the weakness of this Spanish soldier-statesman-adventurer, who commissioned the work from Regnault when the young artist arrived in Madrid in 1868. The Republican Prim with his friend Francisco Serrano led the successful revolt against Queen Isabella in 1868. The following year Prim was elected president of the council and his friend Serrano, regent, remaining in that position until a new king could be found for Spain. However, in December 1870, before Prince Amedeo of Savoy could be crowned, Prim was assassinated.

The image of Prim is a late evocation of the Roman imperial portrait type, revived in the Renaissance to glorify the military adventurers of the Italian city-states and transposed through Titian and Velázquez to honor the crowned heads of Baroque Europe. Prim is shown astride his horse on a rise; behind and below, as in many paintings by Goya, are the citizens of Madrid, painted with a mixture of caricature and realism. Prim rejected the portrait as too ugly, but it was purchased by the State for the Musée du Luxembourg in 1872, and respected as one of the treasures from the palette of the young martyr of the Franco-Prussian War, Henri Regnault.

Charles Blanc's description of the finished paintings helps to illuminate for viewers of this small portrait the startling effects of this work:

"Juan Prim, a little man with a pale face, with reddish eyes, is represented bareheaded, mounted on a large—too large—black horse, which he reins strongly by the bridle, throwing himself backward in order to enjoy the triumph accorded to him by the inhabitants of Madrid, flocking to see his passage. The face of the marshal, injected with bile, yellowed by ambition, has something epic in its pallor and, as if in order to make more triumphant the form of its master, Prim's horse, a horse with flowing mane and tail, rather similar to the heroically realistic horses of Velázquez, stops brusquely and lowers its head, twisting its neck. At some distance the silk of the waving flags and the crowd, mottled with bright colors, acclaiming its hero, form a brilliant entourage for the conqueror, whose uniform, soiled by dust, and black steed stand out forcefully against the brightness of the background" (Blanc, 1876, p. 356).

N.D.

The Art Institute of Chicago, The Wentworth Greene Field Fund

---

## Pierre-Auguste Renoir

*Limoges 1841–1919 Cagnes*

*At the age of thirteen Renoir was apprenticed to the Parisian porcelain decorators Lévy Frères, where he excelled in painting and decorating wares in the eighteenth-century manner. Four years later he worked for a supplier of religious pictures to missionaries, and there continued his art education, having already begun to copy in the Louvre (where he met Fantin-Latour, q.v.). He applied to the Ecole des Beaux-Arts in 1862 and that same year entered the studio of Gleyre (q.v.), where he met Bazille, Sisley, and Monet (q.q.v.). In the summers, with his friends from Gleyre's studio, he painted in the Forest of Fontainebleau. In 1864 he exhibited a painting at the Salon, and he would continue to show there during the Second Empire in 1865, 1868, 1869, and 1870 (being rejected in 1866 and 1867). In 1865 he met Courbet (q.v.), who would have a strong influence on him during the remainder of the decade, although Renoir's style comes from a rich variety of influences, both contemporary and from the art of the past, especially the eighteenth century.*

*The first indication of his public success was a picture of his mistress, Lise Trehot, painted out of doors (1867; Essen), shown at the Salon of 1868 and praised by several critics, most notably Thoré-Bürger. That same year he painted Lise nude as Diana (National Gallery of Art, Washington, D. C.), which strongly reflects his indebtedness to Gleyre. His early landscapes too (Pont des Arts;*

*Norton Simon Collection, Los Angeles) reflect a variety of influences (Diaz, Corot, Courbet) and a high degree of experimentation, and he also turned to still lifes and flower painting as well as to the informal genre of portrait groups, which would be one of the major contributions of Impressionism.*

*Renoir stands markedly apart from his fellow Impressionists. Throughout his long career, his major subject was the figure; yet, unlike Degas (q.v.) who shared this interest, his was a devotion that grew from an unpretentious taste for decorative painting (in 1868 he executed two ceilings for the hôtel of the prince George Bibesco: one in the style of Boucher, the other, Fragonard) and a firm allegiance to the French tradition of idealized figure painting. In this sense, he admirably carried this tradition from the Second Empire well into our century.*

J.R.

Bibliography:
Daulte, 1971, vol. I, pp. 61–74; Rewald, 1973, pp. 647–51

Pierre-Auguste Renoir

## VI-100
## Mlle Romaine Lacaux

1864
Signed and dated, right center: A. RENOIR. 1864
Oil on canvas
81 × 65 cm

Provenance:
M. Lacaux, Paris; M. Decap, Paris; M. and Mme Maurice Barret-Decap, Biarritz; sale, Paris, Hôtel Drouot, December 12, 1929, no. 12; Roger Bernheim, Paris; Jacques Seligman, New York; purchased by the Cleveland Museum of Art, 1942 (inv. no. CMA 42.1065)

Exhibitions:
1928, Paris, Galerie Charpentier, no. 100; 1932, London, no. 479 (exhibition no. 454); 1933, Paris, Orangerie, "Renoir," no. 1; 1941, New York, no. 1; 1948, New York, no. 4; 1950, New York, Wildenstein, "Renoir," no. 1; 1963, Cleveland, no. 88; 1963, Oberlin, no. 24; 1973, Chicago, no. 2

Bibliography:
*Le Bulletin de l'Art Ancien et Moderne*, 1928; Imbourg, 1929, repro. facing p. 18; Barnes and de Mazia, 1935, pp. 49–50, 374, repro. p. 225; Francis, 1943, pp. 92–98 (repro.); Pach, 1950, repro. p. 32; Towndrow, 1952; Venturi, 1953; Drucker, 1955; Daulte, 1971, vol. I, no. 12

The year 1864 marked the emergence of Renoir as an independent artist. Gleyre's studio had closed that spring, and in April he seems to have presented himself for the last time for examination at the Ecole. His *Esmeralda* (after Victor Hugo) was accepted at the Salon (no. 1618); the youthful intensity of his self-

VI-100

Gallery of Art, Washington, D. C.), which Renoir would have seen at the Salon des Refusés in 1863. Certainly the flat background, especially the flower panel (a window?, or wallpaper?), and the fixed stare of the figure echo that controversial work. Finally, its directness and simplicity remind one of Renoir's friendship with Fantin-Latour (q.v.).

Yet, through these comparisons, one becomes all the more aware of the essential independence of Renoir's picture. The complexity of the background and the full relief of the figure (both the head and the sweep of the *mousseline de soie* dress) already have the strength of his later work. The flatly decorative scallops of the dress (which occur with equal boldness in Monet's *Women in the Garden*) and the use of gradated reds (the flower in the hand, the earrings, the pink flowers beyond) give the work a masterly assurance and place it among the most effective of Renoir's early paintings. Throughout his long career he would continue to record the unsentimentalized innocence and alert intelligence of children, an aspect of his career that was well launched here.

J.R.

The Cleveland Museum of Art, Gift of Hanna Fund

---

## Théodule-Augustin Ribot
*Saint-Nicolas-d'Attez (Eure) 1823–1891 Colombes*

*Ribot went to Paris in 1844 or 1845 and studied in the atelier of Glaize (q.v.). Being penniless he was obliged to do odd jobs, notably, copying Watteaus for export. His own work was rejected several times by the Salon. As a consequence, in 1859 he exhibited some of his works in the atelier of his friend Bonvin (q.v.) along with those of others who had been turned down: Alphonse Legros (q.v.), Fantin-Latour (q.v.), and Whistler. Ribot came to the attention of Courbet (q.v.), and soon the dealer Cadart took over his etchings and paintings.*

*It was not until 1861 that he made his debut at the Salon with kitchen scenes, which attracted immediate attention and subsequently became his specialty. He went on to paint interiors, still lifes, portraits, as well as religious subjects, for which he was awarded medals in 1864 and 1865. At the Salon of 1865, the State bought his* Saint Sebastian *for which he had set the rather high price of 6,000 francs. The painting, which was sent to the Musée du Luxembourg and hailed as a masterpiece, is a felicitous example of Ribera's influence. The State, in 1868, also acquired* The Oyster and the

criticism is indicated by its destruction shortly after it was returned to him. During that spring he also took up portraiture (probably encouraged by commissions, although most are of friends) of which some six survive, dating from 1864 to 1866. One of these, the portrait of Sisley's father he liked well enough to send to the Salon in 1865 (no. 1802, the catalogue still listing Renoir as a student of Gleyre; Louvre); however, by far the most beautiful of the group is the seated, half-length portrait of the daughter of bourgeois friends of his parents: *Mlle Romaine Lacaux* (later Mme Lestrade).

Although the idea of placing a lovely face so near a panel of flowers derives from Courbet (q.v.), whose influence would be so strongly felt the following year, Courbet's handling and palette seem to have had little influence here. Douglas Cooper notes that already the admiration for Corot (q.v.) is apparent (Cooper, 1959, p. 163), and the three-quarter-length composition and the silvery gray-blue tones do relate to certain of the figure subjects that Corot was just beginning in the early 1860s. However, Champa (1973, p. 35) makes the more pointed comparison to Whistler's *Girl in White* (National

Litigants *for the Caen museum; in 1869, the* Philosophers; *in 1871, the* Good Samaritan, *which had been shown in the Salon of 1870 (Musée du Luxembourg, lost in Warsaw);* Christ among the Doctors *from the Salon of 1866, which was then sent to the Musée du Luxembourg and is now in the Arras museum; and a* Saint Vincent *from the 1867 Exposition Universelle (Lille museum). His official success did not deter critics from finding faults with his somber and harsh palette. Classified as a second-generation Realist, he achieved genuine success only in 1878, well after the end of the Second Empire.*

G.L.

Bibliography:
Fourcaud, 1885; Ribot sale, Paris, Hôtel Drouot, May 30, 1896

Théodule-Augustin Ribot

## VI-101
## The Torture by Wedges
## (The Torment of Alonso Cano)

1867
Signed, lower right: T. Ribot
Oil on canvas
150 × 209 cm

VI-101

Provenance:
Purchased from the artist by the city of Rouen for 4,000 francs, for the Musée des Beaux-Arts, 1869 (inv. no. 869-4)

Exhibitions:
1867, Paris, Salon, no. 1281 *(The Torture by Wedges);* 1869, Rouen, no. 319 *(The Torment of Alonso Cano);* 1880, Paris, Galeries de l'Art

Bibliography:
Du Camp, 1867, pp. 264–65; Mantz, 1867, "Salon," pp. 515–16; de Montifaud, 1867, pp. 454–55; Larousse, 1866–90, vol. XIV, p. 1259; Fourcaud, 1885, p. 10; Dolent, 1888, pp. 21–22; Lafond, n.d. pp. 75, 91; Vergnet-Ruiz and Laclotte, 1962, p. 249; Catalogue, Rouen, Musée de Peinture et de Sculpture, 1967, p. 106

Oddly enough, when *The Torture by Wedges* was exhibited in the Salon no one realized that its real subject was the torture of the painter Alonso Cano. Ribot indicated this only two years later at the time of the presentation of the work to the city of Rouen. This same illusive process occurred with *The Enameler,* now at the Narodowe museum in Warsaw (189 688), which, according to its description in the Ribot sale catalogue (Paris, Hôtel Drouot, May 30, 1896, no. 1), illustrates an episode in the life of another artist, Bernard Palissy.

The composition here is similar to that of the *Saint Sebastian* (Salon of 1865; Louvre), a work strongly reflecting Ribera, or at such least paintings attributed to him as *The Good Samaritan,* acquired in 1839 by the Rouen museum, which Ribot, a native of the area, could have

known. (It is now attributed to Luca Giordano.) Du Camp went so far as to speak of a painting that has a quality of a servile copy of a canvas by "Lo Spagnoletto" and made fun of the black patina which, in his opinion, the painter overdid. However, Mantz was of the opinion that with *The Torture by Wedges* Ribot "begins to come out of his cave." And indeed, black painting, linked to Realism, was often the target of critics. Nonetheless, except for this reservation, they all praised the strength and vigor of this work and, like Jean Dolent in 1880, speaking about this very painting, they could say "Ribot was a born painter...." Each of the critics expressed surprise that in this torture scene in which an executioner "with strong blows of a mallet drives a wedge into a wooden vice bound between the victim's legs," the victim's expression "betrays no sign of sorrow." The face is relatively impassive; it is believed that he is being forced to confess a crime to the inquisitors. This episode in the life of the famous seventeenth-century painter Alonso Cano, which appears in histories of Spanish painting and even in contemporary dictionaries and encyclopedias, explains the attitude of the tortured hero. There are several versions of the story, which are perhaps legendary: probably in 1664, after the murder of Alonso Cano's wife by a copyist who had been working in his atelier and then had disappeared, the painter, who had been away when the crime was committed but who had a reputation for a hot temper, nonetheless was charged with it. Immediately, or perhaps after a stay of several years in Valencia where he had fled, he was arrested and "withstood torture with indomitable strength, denying to the very end that he had committed the murder" (Blanc). He was acquitted in the end, perhaps through influence and because of his greatly admired talent. The picture was etched by Palémont and lithographed by Philippe Astruc.

G.L.

Musée des Beaux-Arts, Rouen

---

*Philippe Rousseau*

*Paris 1816–1867 Acquigny (Eure)*

*Although most biographers of Rousseau have followed the unknown source that said his teachers were Gros and Bertin, he was largely self taught. His first works were landscapes of Normandy, one of which he exhibited at the Salon of 1834, beginning a continuous succession of entries in the exhibitions that lasted until 1877. His earliest prize at the Salon* was a third-class medal in 1845 for one of his most popular works, City Rat and Country Rat. *By 1845 Rousseau had found the subjects for which he would be known, still lifes and domestic animals, or combinations of the two, often with witty anthropomorphic twists. Such a painting is* The Intruder *of 1850 (Louvre), in which a dog is startled on coming upon a mother cat with her kittens, or* The Rat Who Has Retired from the World *(Lyons), exhibited in 1852, the year Rousseau was made chevalier of the Legion of Honor.*

*Although to twentieth-century eyes Rousseau has merely "a place among the little masters of the School of 1830" (Bénézit, 1976, vol. IX, p. 136), he was a highly successful, well-patronized artist during the Second Empire. His decorative skills were sought for dining-room murals and panels by Baron J. de Rothschild, Mme Grandin, M. Closemann in Bordeaux, and Princess Mathilde, who also bought two of his canvases,* The Monkey Photographers *and a flower piece. He received a first-class medal in 1848 and another as late as 1878. Of the painting* Peaches *bought by W.P. Wilstach in Philadelphia in 1869, the new owner said in a letter : "Wylie [the artist R. Wylie] is delighted at my buying the Rousseau ; he writes me that he thinks I have probably one of the finest, if not the finest, still-life pictures of the modern French school" (Catalogue, Philadelphia, Museum of Art, Wilstach Collection, 1900, no. 117).*

*Rousseau was praised by Gautier (1861, pp. 321–24) for his realism and his color. He was a close follower of the Dutch seventeenth-century still-life painters, Pieter Claesz, Jan de Heem, and Wilhelm Kalf, and an admirer of Chardin, to whom he paid tribute in a painting of 1867,* Chardin and His Models. *Like his contemporary Bonvin (q.v.), he belonged not to the Romantic school of still life of Géricault and Delacroix but to the Dutch school in which an interest in shapes, textures, and reflected light was the motive for extraordinarily varied compositions of carefully observed objects.*

N.D.

Bibliography :
P. Rousseau sale, Paris, Hôtel Drouot, February 21, 1881 ; Bellier and Auvray, 1882–87, vol. II, pp. 430–31

Philippe Rousseau

## VI-102
## Still Life: Game and Guinea Pig

1857
Signed and dated, lower left : Ph. Rousseau '57
Oil on canvas
48.9 × 60 cm

VI-102

Provenance :
John G. Johnson Collection, Philadelphia (inv. no. cat. 1077)

Bibliography :
*Johnson Collection,* 1914, vol. III, p. 157, no. 1077

The history of Rousseau's still life cannot be specifically documented at this time. The painting illustrates, however, many of the peculiar characteristics of Rousseau's style and subject matter. The red claws and the bars of crimson on the bird's wings and the subtle confluence of grays and browns in the feathers and the background evidence his fine sense of color, which Lefort praised as "his exquisite coloristic tact, which makes his tones vibrate and sing by adroit contrasts or by harmonious juxtapositions" (Lefort, 1888, p. 133). The subject is typical also. The depiction of a live animal observing dead game was popular in the seventeenth century with such artists as Frans Snyders (Rousseau's interest in Baroque still lifes is well known). Often the live animal was a working dog who may have helped in the hunt, but cats and rats were also popular, as observers or as diabolical symbols, a kind of *memento mori* of the animal kingdom.

Here Rousseau depicted a guinea pig sitting on his haunches looking at dead birds. This animal was not commonly painted, but in one eighteenth-century still life by C.F. Desportes (1695–1774) called *Still Life with Guinea Pigs* (Manufacture National de Sèvres) a barnyard contains a cascade of melons, grapes, peaches, and around it are two rabbits, two guinea pigs, and an inquiring spaniel. Guinea pigs, native to Peru, Bolivia, and Paraguay, had been domesticated in France in small numbers for food since the mid-sixteenth-century. The still life by Desportes indicates that they lived on farms along with rabbits, both being vegetarian rodents and needing to be caged in small pens. Thus Rousseau's guinea pig does not represent an exotic beast nor one with evil intentions, but merely a gentle noncarnivorous observer, whose omnipresent cousin, the rat, Rousseau often used in his genre works. Nor is it surprising that from the great numbers in the animal world, he chose this quiet little creature, for his vocabulary was limited to small domestic animals or those who lived close to man.

Claretie praised Rousseau's roses, "marvels of freshness and seduction" and we await the discovery of the words, hidden in nineteenth-century criticism, in praise of his charming guinea pig.

N.D.

John G. Johnson Collection, Philadelphia

---

## Pierre-Etienne-Théodore Rousseau
*Paris 1812–1867 Barbizon*

*Although Théodore Rousseau was the most famous landscape painter of the Romantic school of 1830, he had been systematically excluded from the Salon from 1836 to 1849, giving rise to his sobriquet*

VI-103

Bibliography:
Sensier, 1872, p. 270 n.1; 1967–68, Paris, Louvre, p. 83

Even during Théodore Rousseau's lifetime, questions sometimes arose about the subjects of his works, to which the artist often gave only general titles. Though now exhibited as *A Clearing in the Forest of Fontainebleau*, the scene is nearly identical with that of a smaller canvas (43 × 64 cm) engraved in 1873 by A. Brunet-Debaines (Durand-Ruel, 1873, vol. I, pl. 18) under the title of *The Carrefour de la Reine Blanche*, a site in the forest near Barbizon. The differences between the two scenes are no greater than may be explained by the slightly differing viewpoints adopted by the artist.

Rousseau evidently was attracted to this view, which he painted on at least four occasions. The panel in the Louvre (28 × 53 cm; 1967–68, Paris, Louvre, no. 55), which appears to date from about 1862, differs from the two canvas versions in that it includes a cart and driver on the road at the center. In a second panel (14 × 23 cm; formerly Paris, Galerie Georges Petit, photograph no. 7992), known as *The Cattle Pond*, the section of the road in the foreground is replaced by a small pond. Nearby several cows rest on the road, watched by a peasant woman dressed in red, a tiny figure echoed in the distance in the canvas shown here. The freedom of technique in this panel contrasts with the high degree of finish in the canvas.

Alfred Sensier, Rousseau's biographer, reported that around 1862 the artist, whose popularity was then temporarily in eclipse, did a series of splendid paintings from nature at Barbizon. None of these was seen until the sale after Rousseau's death; one was a *Carrefour de la Reine Blanche* (Sensier, 1872, p. 270). The painting that appeared under that title in the 1868 atelier sale is described as "Springtime. Painting almost finished, 1860," and the work seems to have been bought in (4,000 francs) by the sale's organizers (Philadelphia, John G. Johnson Collection library, annotated studio sale catalogue). The dimensions of that painting (81 × 145 cm) indicate that almost certainly it is the work in the Chrysler Museum.

The Norfolk painting, far from being unfinished, appears to twentieth-century viewers quite detailed in its realism. Not only the location, but even the season and the time of day (late afternoon or early morning) seems specified by the clear light, emerging from behind some dark clouds. The balanced composition recalls forest scenes by Meindert Hobbema, while the isolation of the site conveys a hint of the Romantic drama of Rousseau's

---

*"le grand refusé." Rousseau's position, like that of Corot (q.v.), was drastically altered by the advent of the Second Republic: in 1848 he was placed on the organizing committee of the Salon. By the 1850s he began to find even more buyers. Unlike the older artist, however, Rousseau continued to experience fluctuations in his reputation and patronage, lapsing into poverty again for a time in the early 1860s.*

*During the years of the Second Empire, Rousseau traveled less frequently than before in the provinces of France, spending winters in Paris and summers at Barbizon in the Forest of Fontainebleau. There he was host to a growing circle of artist friends including Diaz, Barye (q.v.), Daumier (q.v.), and his closest associate, Millet (q.v.). Working steadily, Rousseau produced dozens of new compositions, depicting mainly the area around Barbizon. By 1850 he had largely abandoned the free brushwork and dramatic subjects of his youthful paintings for a more sober, considered style, strongly influenced by seventeenth-century Dutch painting. He now portrayed more subdued aspects of nature, adopting a darker palette and a higher degree of finish. During this period he also retouched many of his unsold pictures of earlier years, causing some of his admirers to complain that his works had become overfinished.*

*In 1862–63 Rousseau became one of the first major European painters to come strongly under the influence of Japanese prints, then only recently introduced into France. He repainted several landscapes in bright tonalities, accentuated contours, and flat modeling of the Oriental prints; the lasting effect of this interlude was a lightening of his palette. The sale of a large group of sketches to the dealers Durand-Ruel and Brame in 1866 finally freed Rousseau from his financial difficulties, and he was*

*granted exceptional honors at the Exposition Universelle of 1867. The satisfaction Rousseau derived from this recognition was brief, for he died within the year. Always jealously guarding his independence and integrity, Rousseau remained, with Corot, the most admired and influential landscape painter of mid-nineteenth century France.*

D.R.

Bibliography:
Sensier, 1872; Dorbec, 1910; 1962–63, San Francisco, etc.; 1967–68, Paris, Louvre

Pierre-Etienne-Théodore Rousseau

## VI-103
## A Clearing in the Forest of Fontainebleau (The Carrefour de la Reine Blanche)

c. 1860–62
Signed, lower left: P T ROUSSEAU
Oil on canvas
82.5 × 145.5 cm

Provenance:
Rousseau studio sale, Paris, Hôtel Drouot, April 27–May 2, 1868, no. 38; Arthur Stevens; Ernest Brugeman, Brussels; E. Le Roy, Paris; Arthur Tooth, London; Frank G. Logan, Chicago; Walter P. Chrysler, Jr., New York; gift to the Chrysler Museum at Norfolk, 1971 (inv. no. 71.2054)

Exhibitions:
1859, Paris, Salon, no. 2641?; 1960, Dayton, no. 30; 1965–66, New York, no. 20

youth. Nevertheless, the treatment is wholly in the tradition of nineteenth-century *plein air* naturalism, from the cloud studies of John Constable to the later, momentary visions of the Impressionists.

D.R.

Chrysler Museum at Norfolk, Virginia, Gift of Walter P. Chrysler, Jr.

---

### Alfred Sisley
*Paris 1839–1899 Moret-sur-Loing (Seine-et-Marne)*

*Although Sisley's English ancestry is often stressed, he was born in Paris and spent almost his entire life in France. His father, a well-to-do merchant, sent Sisley to London from 1857 to 1861 to obtain a commercial education, but, on his return to Paris he received his parents' permission to study painting, and in October 1862 entered the studio of the history painter Charles Gleyre (q.v.). There he met Renoir, Monet, and Bazille (q.q.v.), with whom he was to form the nucleus of the Impressionist group. Sisley was unhappy with Gleyre's lack of interest in landscape painting; he gained little from his stay in the studio, which Gleyre closed because of ill health in March 1863.*

*That spring Sisley joined his three friends at Chailly-en-Bière, near Barbizon, in the Forest of Fontainebleau. Sisley established a studio in Paris in 1864, remaining in the city until 1870 but frequently visiting the Fontainebleau region during the spring and summer months. His earliest surviving dated painting is from 1865, and relatively few works from the late 1860s are known, probably because the artist was financially independent and thus not obliged to produce paintings for sale. However, he did exhibit at the Salons, showing two street scenes of Marlotte in 1866 and two views of the canal Saint Martin in Paris in 1870, the only pictures by Sisley ever accepted at the Salon.*

*The Franco-Prussian War ruined the elder Sisley's business, perhaps contributing to his death soon thereafter. Deprived of his independent income, Sisley was forced to struggle for a living as an artist for the rest of his life. On the other hand, the support of the dealer Paul Durand-Ruel, who began buying Sisley's work in 1872, encouraged the artist for the first time to develop a truly personal style.*

D.R.

Bibliography:
Daulte, 1959; 1971, Nottingham

Alfred Sisley

## VI-104
## Avenue of Chestnut Trees near La Celle-Saint-Cloud

1867
Signed and dated, lower left: A. Sisley. 1867
Oil on canvas
89 × 116 cm

VI-104

Provenance:
Henri Haro, Paris; sale, Paris, Hôtel Drouot, December 12–13, 1911, no. 225; Durand-Ruel, Paris; Mme de la Chapelle, 1936; A.D. Mouradian; purchased through the Chipperfield bequest by the Southampton Art Gallery, 1936 (inv. no. 524)

Exhibitions:
1868, Paris, Salon, no. 2312; 1948, London, Arts Council of Great Britain, no. 26; 1953, Peterborough; 1955, Exeter, no. 34; 1962, London, Royal Academy, no. 229; 1970, London, no. 27; 1971, Nottingham, no. 1; 1974, London, no. 105

Bibliography:
Huyghe, 1931, repro. facing p. 154; Rewald, 1946, p. 161 (repro.); Daulte, 1959, no. 9 (repro.); Champa, 1973, p. 93, fig. 134; Rewald, 1973, p. 187

This early work shows Sisley working under the influence of the Barbizon School painters and Courbet (q.v.); he had not yet attained a recognizably "Impressionist" style. The hazy treatment of the leaves, the flowing branches, and subdued colors are closely related to the late style of Corot (q.v.); while strong areas of green and the presence of the deer crossing the clearing recall the forest scenes of Courbet (*see* R. Pickvance, in 1971, Nottingham, no. 1). Though lacking the bright colors of his later work, the painting already shows Sisley's characteristic interest in light, shade, and tonal values.

D.R.

Southampton Art Gallery

---

### Alfred-Emile-Léopold Stevens
*Brussels 1823–1906 Paris*

*William Rothenstein, remembering his student days in Paris, recalled Stevens as "one of the great figures of the Second Empire" (Rothenstein, 1931, vol. I, p. 59), and even though his career extended long after Sedan, Stevens and his pictures have always been closely associated with this period. He was the master recorder of a certain aspect of life in the 1850s and 1860s: the opulent interiors, the ease of long afternoons, the beauty of the women and the splendor and modishness of their dress. Stevens moved comfortably among the rich and fashionable Parisians; he was a standard fixture at the salons of the great hostesses, including the Princess Mathilde (see no. II-4), the vicomtesse de Pourtalès, and the Princess Metternich (all of whom lent him dresses for his models). He received the direct favor of the court (although a commissioned group portrait of 1868 seems never to have been finished) and, in turn, was granted many official honors: the purchase of a work by the State in 1853, three gold medals, and the highest compliment of having eighteen works shown at the 1867 Exposition Universelle.*

*His friendships among artists were wide and varied, and it seems to have struck no one as inconsistent that this most official artist would have had his portrait painted by Courbet (q.v.; Brussels), invited Delacroix (q.v.) to his marriage in 1858, maintained a long alliance with Manet (q.v.) and Berthe Morisot, and asked Degas (q.v.) to be the godfather of his first child.*

*Stevens trained in Brussels with F.J. Navez, but at twenty-one went to Paris where, except for the years 1849–52, he spent the rest of his life. His early style shows the marked influence of Courbet and, to a degree, Couture (q.v.), whom he met in the early 1850s. In such works as* Is This What Is Called Vagrancy? *(Salon of 1855; Compiègne) he also reflected somewhat the knowledge of his countryman, Baron Leys. However, by the late 1850s, he had arrived at the type of picture that was to establish his reputation and fortune: modest in scale, domestic in subject, and painted with a remarkable ability to show rich materials in an even and gentle light. These works won the special praise of Thoré-Bürger, who was quick to note that they related immediately back to the "petits maîtres" of the seventeenth century, particularly Metsu and Terborch.*

J.R.

Bibliography:
Lemonnier, 1878, pp. 160–74, 335–42; Lambotte, 1907; Boucher, 1930; Mitchell, 1973; Grenez, 1975; 1977–78, Ann Arbor, Baltimore, Montreal

VI-105

Alfred-Emile-Léopold Stevens

# VI-105
# Will You Go Out with Me, Fido? (Departing for the Promenade)

1859
Signed and dated, lower right: Alfred Stevens 1859
Oil on panel
61.5 × 49 cm

Provenance:
W.P. Wilstach, Philadelphia, by 1870; Anna H. Wilstach, until 1893; bequest to the Philadelphia Museum of Art (inv. no. W93-1-106)

Exhibitions:
1966, South Hadley; 1977–78, Ann Arbor, Baltimore, Montreal, no. 4

Bibliography:
Strahan, 1878–80, vol. III, p. 34; Catalogues, Philadelphia, Museum of Art, Wilstach Collection, 1910, no. 395, 1913, no. 410, 1922, no. 302, repro. facing p. 119

William Coles, in the recent Stevens exhibition catalogue (1977–78, Ann Arbor, Baltimore, Montreal), thoroughly reviews the relationship of this picture to Stevens's work, particularly noting the elegant interior (probably the artist's own house, into which he moved following his marriage in 1858) and the continued fascination that the cashmere shawl would have for him. To this we can only add that the coy title seems to be an American invention, since it first appears in the handwritten inventory from 1870 of the collection of Mrs. Wilstach (Philadelphia Museum of Art Archives).

In his concentration on the single figure, generally standing and simply posed, Stevens addressed a new attitude of assertively non-narrative art, with an emphasis on formal beauty, such as would be more aggressively employed in the next decade, particularly by Whistler and Manet (q.v.). In the figure, reminiscent of fashion illustration, one may find a relationship with the work of the young Monet (*see,* for example, nos. VI-89, VI-91). However, although one may make such comparisons with the more avant-garde artists of his day, Stevens rarely broke away from his immediately modish world. Within these limitations— the limitations of complete contemporaneity, after all—he achieved great mastery, as in this picture, where one is reminded of Camille Lemonnier's comment that a good picture by Stevens is like "a rare perfume concentrated

within a scent bottle" (Lemonnier, 1878, p. 170).

J.R.

Philadelphia Museum of Art, W.P. Wilstach Collection

---

## James-Jacques-Joseph Tissot
*Nantes 1836–1902 Buillon (Doubs)*

*Tissot, a pupil of both Louis Lamothe and Flandrin (q.v.), entered the Ecole des Beaux-Arts in Paris on April 9, 1857, and exhibited for the first time in the Salon of 1859. His friends included Whistler and Degas (q.v.). He traveled to Antwerp, where he visited the painter Henri Leys, adopting his archaizing, meticulous manner reminiscent of fifteenth- and sixteenth-century Flemish and German painters for his paintings inspired chiefly by Goethe, such as* The Meeting of Faust and Marguerite *(Salon of 1861; acquired by the State for the Musée du Luxembourg, now in the Mairie of Le Chambon-Feugerolles). As a portraitist and a painter of contemporary life, he was able, in 1867, to afford a fashionable atelier on the avenue de l'Impératrice (now avenue Foch), where he became one of the first adherents of Japanism. His famous portrait by Degas dates from this period (Metropolitan Museum of Art, New York).*

*Having taken part in the siege of Paris, then in the Commune, he went to London in May 1871, remaining there several years and becoming a popular painter of society. He refused to participate in the first exhibition of the Impressionists, despite Degas's urging, and reappeared in the Salon only in 1876, with two etchings. His work as a painter and engraver was restored to its position of importance in a show organized by H. Zerner in Providence and Toronto in 1968.*

G.L.

Bibliography:
1968, Providence, Toronto

James-Jacques-Joseph Tissot

# VI-106
# Attempted Abduction

1865
Signed, lower right: J.J.J. Tissot
Oil on canvas
57 × 93 cm

Provenance:
Acquired by the Musée des Beaux-Arts, Nantes, 1974 (inv. no. 974.13.I.P.)

Exhibitions:
1865, Paris, Salon, no. 2075; 1974, Nantes, no. 53 (repro.); 1976, Nantes, no. 1

Bibliography:
Gallet, 1865, p. 27; Jahyer, 1865, pp. 136–37; Mantz, 1865, p. 11; "Acquisitions," 1976, p. 396, no. 33 (repro.)

This work, particularly unusual with its meticulous technique and its figures stuck onto a landscape "quite false" (Gallet) in its perspective, is one of the last scenes from the past that Tissot painted before devoting himself to contemporary subjects. Its literary source, if there was one, was not specified, but in it Paul Mantz saw the evocation of a "sixteenth-century novel." Although he admired the "finely detailed execution" he encouraged the artist to renounce "the curiosity shop of archaism" where he had, for a long time, been enclosed. The critics reflected this same opinion, even though they noted "great originality... a very sure hand" (Jahyer), a "singular attraction" (Gallet). The taste for paintings of pre-Raphaelite inspiration or those in the manner of the Antwerp painter Henri Leys, had passed. Claude Souviron justly observed that in that same Salon of 1865, Degas, a friend of Tissot, also exhibited his last history painting, an indeterminate subject, *War Scene during the Middle Ages* (Jeu de Paume), which is in fact an allegory of the misfortunes of New Orleans.

G.L.

Musée des Beaux-Arts, Nantes

---

## Constant Troyon

*Sèvres 1810–1865 Paris*

*In 1855 Maxime du Camp wrote: "We speak first of M. Troyon, who is perhaps, in his manner of understanding nature, the strongest artist we have in France today. We have already been following M. Troyon for a long time; each year we have seen his manner widen, grow, and elevate itself to arrive now at that beauty which Plato defined, the splendor of the truth. I do not know anything in this genre that is not inferior to the animals of M. Troyon" (du Camp, 1855, pp. 243–44).*

*Constant Troyon was the son of a porcelain worker at Sèvres (q.v.). He had no formal training in Paris, only the friendly advice and criticism of Camille Roqueplan and Théodore Rousseau (q.v.), but he always acknowledged as his teacher D.D. Riocreux, a porcelain painter at Sèvres, who would become the founder and keeper of the ceramic museum there.*

*Troyon first entered the Salon in 1833 with three landscapes painted that same year in the vicinity of Sèvres. These were the first of many studies he made in the regions of France, for although he is closely linked to the Barbizon painters, working in the Forest of Fontainebleau, he studied and painted nature in Normandy, Brittany, the Touraine, and Limousin as well.*

*In 1847 Troyon traveled to Holland. This was the critical journey of his life, for he saw in Amsterdam*

VI-106

*the works of the seventeenth-century Dutch animaliers, Albert Cuyp and Paul Potter, and he studied the palette and brushstroke of Rembrandt. When he returned to Paris, Troyon began incorporating animals into his landscapes and was highly praised for the way he integrated his cows, sheep, and dogs into their settings through a skillful use of light. "His incomparable talent," wrote Charles Blanc, "rests in his expression of the presence of atmosphere, in plunging his figures in a bath of light" (Blanc, 1876, p. 322). In 1849 Troyon received a first-class medal from the hand of Napoleon, President of the Republic, and this honor brought the artist the financial success that was to sustain him the remainder of his life.*

N.D./J.R.

Bibliography:
Du Camp, 1855, pp. 242–44; Mantz, 1865, vol. XVII, pp. 393–407; Blanc, 1876, pp. 313–23; Hustin, 1889, vol. XXXXVI, pp. 77–90, vol. XXXXVII, pp. 85–96; Stranahan, 1902, pp. 258–61; Thieme and Becker, 1907–50, vol. XXXIII, pp. 443–44

Constant Troyon

## VI-107
## Pointer

1860
Signed and dated, lower left: C. TROYON 1860
Oil on canvas
163 × 131 cm

Provenance:
A. Dreyfus, 1885; E. Secrétan, 1889; Prosper Crabbe; Galerie Durand-Ruel; F.L. Ames; Mrs. Louis A. Frothingham; gift to the Museum of Fine Arts, Boston, 1924 (inv. no. 24.345)

Exhibitions:
1908, Boston, no. 68; 1962–63, San Francisco, etc., no. 106, p. 195

Bibliography:
*Boston Museum of Fine Arts Bulletin,* vol. XXII, 1924, p. 36

The majority of Troyon's earlier animal paintings are of cows and sheep, following the tradition of the Dutch *animaliers* who had first inspired him. He began subjects such as this one of hunting dogs in 1854, when he made his first of eight successive summer visits to his friend M. Loizel who kept a kennel in the Touraine.

Earlier in the century J.R. Brascassat (1804–1867) had revived animal painting in France. His subjects were often angry bulls and wolves, although he also occasionally painted sheep. Troyon did not intend to evoke the Romantic expression of primitive bestial energy as had Brascassat; rather, he sought a gentle, poetic depiction of light as it fell on the animals and vegetation, here focusing on the light on the white of the dog's coat and the trunks of the trees beyond. Neither landscape nor animal is at rest. The dog sniffs the air, with his tail outstretched and legs spread apart; the distant, threatening clouds excite the animal's tenseness and sense of expectation. Mantz wrote of Troyon's work in 1865, the year of his death: "He had kept a little black at the tip of

VI-107

the brush.... There is nearly always a menace in the setting suns of Troyon... a little night almost always remains in his dawns" (Mantz, 1865, p. 401). Likewise in this painting, we are simultaneously aware of bright sunlight and an approaching storm; the tension of the animal and the transience of the light.

N.D.

Museum of Fine Arts, Boston, Gift of Mrs. Louis A. Frothingham

---

*Antoine Vollon*

*Lyons 1833–1900 Paris*

*Vollon first worked in Lyons for an enameling shop, then as apprentice to the metal engraver Chrasse, who enrolled him, in 1851, at the Ecole des Beaux-Arts in Lyons, where he studied engraving with Victor-Joseph Vibert and took lessons in paint-ing. He was awarded a first prize in Lyons in 1853 and exhibited in the local Salon beginning in 1858. At about this time he went to Paris to study the great masters, as he pointed out in a letter requesting work sent to the Administration of Fine Arts, registered July 4, 1860, and accompanied by recommendations from Daubigny (q.v.) and Flandrin (q.v.; Arch. nat. F²¹ 189). Gradually he obtained small commis-sions; a copy of Ribera's Adoration of the Shep-herds, in 1862, sent to the church of Saint-Jean-le-Blanc (Loiret), as well as a commission for the por-trait of the Emperor in 1864.*

*In 1864 he began to exhibit his works in the Paris Salon. Each subsequent year one of his entries was purchased by the Administration (for example, in 1865, Kitchen Interior for the Nantes museum; in 1866, Monkey Playing the Accordion for the Lyons museum; in 1868, Curiosities; in 1870, Fish of the Sea for the Musée du Luxembourg, now at the Louvre). Only in 1869 was there no purchase, but he was awarded a medal for the third time (the others dated from 1865 and 1868), and in 1870 he was made chevalier of the Legion of Honor. His still lifes—he had a predilection for representing ar-*

mor—and his genre paintings all contributed to his great success both with private collectors and in offi-cial circles.

G.L.

Bibliography:
Audin and Vial, 1918–19, vol. II, pp. 307–8

Antoine Vollon

## VI-108
## Curiosities

1868
Signed, lower right: A. Vollon
Oil on canvas
264 × 192 cm

Provenance:
Commissioned by the State, January 2, 1868, for 8,000 francs; 3,000 francs paid on January 29, 1868, 5,000 francs on April 16, 1868 (Arch. nat. F²¹ 189); sent to the Musée du Luxembourg, c. 1871; consigned to the Musées Nationaux by decree of May 3, 1874, and entered in the inventory of paintings of the Louvre; transferred from the Luxembourg to the Dépôt des Oeuvres d'Art de l'Etat, February 1, 1926; sent to the Nancy museum, January 31, 1927; trans-ferred to the Musée Municipal, Lunéville, 1929 (inv. no. RF 117 LUX 260)

Exhibitions:
1868, Paris, Salon, no. 2531; 1878, Paris, Exposition Universelle Internationale, France, group I, class 1, no. 839; 1974, Paris, Grand Palais, no. 233 (repro.)

Bibliography:
De Navery, 1868, p. 15; Catalogues, Paris, Luxem-bourg, 1872–1924; Catalogues Illustrés, Paris, Luxembourg, 1884, 1887, 1891, repro. p. 138; Chen-nevières, 1883–89, vol. II, p. 35; Castagnary, 1892, vol. I, p. 301; Ladoué, 1936, p. 188

This ambitious canvas, rather than *Kitchen Interior* (200 × 130 cm) from the Salon of 1865 (Nantes museum), is undoubtedly the one to which the artist referred in his letter of May 10, 1864, to the Administration (Arch. nat. F²¹ 189): "I have a very large canvas on my easel for the next Salon, but in order that I may complete it properly it will require expenses beyond my means." He did not obtain a com-mission for it until the beginning of 1868, but he then finished it in a few months. For him it was one of those "serious pieces of work quite different from those one is obliged to undertake in order to live," which are the dream of every artist.

Vollon was not the only artist who was tempted to show precious objects in a work of considerable size—almost comparable to that of history paintings. One critic, Raoul de Na-very, gauged it accurately: "It is a large canvas, very decorative, certain portions of which are marvelously successful. Breadth and art reign in this disorder; it is a Desgoffe painted with broader brushstrokes, and with a warmer effect." This was an allusion to the painter Blaise-Alexandre Desgoffe, who had specialized in a meticulous representation of the most precious objects in the Galerie d'Apollon of the Louvre. But this was not to the taste of that defender of naturalism, Castagnary: "Ah, archaism! Ah, Middle Ages! Ah, the taste for knickknacks so deplorably propagated by Romanticism! Will these never cease? And now we come upon a man who has fearlessly inscribed on an immense canvas the poetry of this odious bric-a-brac.... All the residue of past centuries, all the rejects that fill the rooms of rich collectors, are gathered in M. Antoine Vollon's canvas entitled *Curiosities.* Even if the artist had contrived a more felicitous composition, thrown more ideas on his canvas, tightened and focused his

effect, I should still just as vigorously have risen up in protest against this ill-conceived work." However, one can be sure that here Vollon remained faithful to the taste of the Second Empire and that the depiction of objects in carefully studied disarray was very much in the spirit of the times.

G.L.

Musée Municipal, Lunéville

---

### Franz-Xaver Winterhalter
*Menzenschwand 1805?–1873 Frankfurt*

*Winterhalter's work has remained eminently popular. His portraits of various European sovereigns are well known but as for the man, his early life remains a mystery. His biographers are not in* *agreement on the date of his birth, 1805 or 1806, and his birthplace in Baden is variously spelled. The chronology of his youth is uncertain; it is generally agreed that in 1818 he entered the Herdersche Kunstinstitut in Fribourg where he learned engraving, but he is also said to have trained as a miniaturist under Stieler (Dayot, 1928, "Winterhalter"). In 1824 he obtained a scholarship that allowed him to study in Munich. He traveled in Italy in the 1830s (Pecht, 1873) or 1833–34 (Thieme and Becker, 1907–50). There he painted Italian peasant children in the style of Léopold Robert. His portraits of the ducal family of Baden are generally ascribed to the period after his return from Italy. Arriving in Paris in 1834 he made his debut at the Salon of 1835. In 1837 his* Decameron *made him famous, and his success at the court of Louis Philippe was thenceforth assured. Several times he painted portraits of the royal family.*

*Winterhalter went to England during the unrest of 1848 and gained the same success as in France, to which he returned in 1853. He was immediately commissioned to paint portraits of the Emperor and Empress. It was in this period that he was asked to do the Compiègne series, painting the Empress at least nine times, as well as all the ladies of the court. He again left France in 1870, returning to Germany, where he died.*

*Although he was esteemed by high society, contemporary critics were less indulgent. The critic of* L'Artiste *stated: "As for M. Winterhalter, the best thing I can do for him is to say no more." Those who dared to say something attacked his works as "the most gaudy, the most slipshod, the most vulgar" (Vignon, 1855, p. 242), while sparing the portrait of the Empress. But in 1858 Pelloquet went so far as to say: "It is a dry painting, very adroitly executed, clothed in colored paper that imitates fabrics."*

*Today, Winterhalter's works have acquired the charm of all that conjures up a past period; one cannot deny the extraordinary virtuosity of this artist.*

O.S.

Bibliography:
Bellier and Auvray, 1882–87, vol. II, p. 724; Wild, 1894

Franz-Xaver Winterhalter

## VI-109
## The Empress Eugénie in Eighteenth-Century Costume

1854
Signed and dated, lower right: Winterhalter 1854
Oil on canvas
92.7 × 73.7 cm

VI-108

Provenance:
The Empress Eugénie; Farnborough Hill sale, London, Christie, Manson & Wood, June 7, 1927; Seligman et Cie, Paris; Germain Seligman, New York

Exhibitions:
1928, Paris, Hôtel de Sagan; 1933, London; 1936, London "Winterhalter"; 1938, Toronto; 1940, New York, World's Fair, no. 289; 1942, San Francisco; 1943, New York, no. 83; 1952, Minneapolis, no. 38

Bibliography:
Dayot, 1928, "Winterhalter," p. 41

*(Shown in Philadelphia only)*

VI-109

While the early history of this charming painting is not known (it may be one of the portraits of the Empress "en pied" shown at the Salon of 1855, no. 4206 or 4207), it seems to have been the property of the Empress throughout her life, sold only after her death in 1920. Of Winterhalter's many portraits of Eugénie, it stands unique, since here, on a relatively intimate scale, he showed her not in a contemporary dress, but rather in a Second Empire adaptation of a Louis XVI gown, perhaps a direct depiction of a costume worn by the Empress at one of the early masked balls at the Tuileries. (The Princess Metternich gave an elaborate description of one such eighteenth-century fancy-dress costume of the Empress, albeit of a slightly later date, in her memoirs; de Metternich, 1922, pp. vii–ix.)

The Empress's strong interest in the late eighteenth century and her fascination particularly for Marie Antoinette is well documented *see* no. II-2). Viel-Castel mentioned that the Empress specifically requested him on May 19, 1854, to search for memorabilia and objects related to Marie Antoinette, noting: "The Empress attaches great importance to all things that belonged to that unhappy monarch and especially any souvenir of the Queen" (Viel-Castel, 1883–84, vol. III, pp. 27–28). Some described her ironic passion for Marie Antoinette as a mania, and in one of the sharper pages in the Goncourts' journals, Princess Mathilde is quoted as exploding with rage on this particular point: "And this cult for Marie Antoinette! It is absolutely mad, ridiculous, and indecent! Do you know what she keeps in her private room?... The bust in Sèvres of Marie Antoinette [*see*, for example, deliveries of two busts in *biscuit*, Sèvres Archives Vbb fol. 5 (June 1854), Vbb 12, fol. 27 (October 1859)], a portrait of the Dauphin and, on the table, a volume of *L'Histoire de Marie Antoinette*, which we never read, since she never reads anything, occupying herself with nothing" (Goncourt and Goncourt, 1956, vol. II, p. 536).

However, whatever direction this absorbing taste would take by the end of the Empire, Winterhalter's depiction of the Empress shortly after her marriage, her hair powdered, wearing yellow taffeta with blue ribbons, standing in a garden of lilacs, is innocent of any obsessive reference, and one is free to speculate whether Winterhalter (on the suggestion of the Empress?) was evoking only a general recollection of earlier portraits—the closest parallel being that of *Marie Antoinette in the Park at Versailles* by Adolf-Ulrich Wertmüller.

In comparison to the large group portrait of the Empress and her ladies (no. VI-110), this work allows a more delicate reading of Winterhalter's abilities to handle color and to charm, and if he did not completely escape his almost forgivable difficulty of confusing the priorities of faces and fabrics in official portraits, this work does succeed, above almost all others, in bringing us closer to the curiously illusive beauty of this woman—a beauty which, while noted by almost all who saw her, seems to have defeated nearly all of her portraitists. It is a beauty perhaps best expressed in this context of fantasy "dress up." One is reminded here of the Goncourts' begrudgingly positive description of the Empress when they first met her: "The woman is charming, after all. She has eyes which seem only to smile, grace and prettiness of gesture, and indescribable loveliness in the way she passes before you. Neither a queen nor a princess,—an empress of others, not the French, perhaps of some fairy place such as Baden. If you wish, Marie Antoinette at the Mabille" (1956, vol. I, p. 1219).

J.R.

Estate of Germain Seligman, New York

Franz-Xaver Winterhalter

# VI-110
# The Empress Eugénie Surrounded by Her Ladies-in-Waiting

1855
Signed and dated, at left: Fr. Winterhalter 1855
Oil on canvas
300 × 420 cm

Provenance:
The Empress Eugénie; displayed at Fontainebleau during the Second Empire; returned to the Empress (Louvre Archives Z15 [February 28, 1881]); Farnborough Hill sale, London, July 1, 1927, no. 98; acquired by the baronne d'Alexandry d'Orengiani, with the aid of the vicomte de Noailles, the baron de Beauverger, and the comte de Cambacérès, to be presented to the museum in Malmaison; entered the Musée National du Château, Compiègne, December 19, 1952 (inv. no. MMPO 941)

Exhibitions:
1855, Paris, Salon, no. 4209; 1928, Paris, Hôtel de Sagan, p. 6; 1953, Compiègne, no. 257

Bibliography:
C. Delécluze, *Journal des Débats*, November 24, 1855; C. Delécluze, *Journal des Débats*, November 30, 1855; du Camp, 1855, p. 261; du Pays, 1855, p. 286; Loudun, 1855, pp. 149–50; *L'Illustration*, vol. I, 1856, p. 412; Vapereau, 1870, p. 1863; Pecht, 1873; Dayot, 1900, p. 23; Wild, 1894, pp. 24, 46; Loliée, 1905, p. 396; *Comoedia*, August 11, 1926; *Le Temps*, July 4, 1927; Monda, 1927, "Les Meubles"; Monda, 1927, "Portrait"; Sanvoisin, 1927; *Le Figaro*, July 23, 1927; *Gazette de Lausanne*, August 21, 1927; Schommer, 1927, pp. 457–59; Dayot, 1928, p. 253; Bolles, 1943, vol. I, p. 300; Thieme and Becker, 1907–50, vol. XXXVI, p. 88; Mérimée, 1941–61, vol. I, pp. 480–81; Francastel, 1955, vol. II, p. 100; Terrier, 1959, no. 10; Genaille, 1964, p. 32; Richardson, 1971, p. 44; Graham, 1973, p. 29

*See* Colorplate

No trace of the payment for this painting has been found: It does not appear in the commissions given by the Ministry of State or those by the Ministère de la Maison de l'Empereur. It is thus likely that it was paid for out of the private funds of the Empress. In any case, the picture was considered as her property since it was returned to her in 1881, and it hung in the main entrance of her English residence of Farnborough Hill.

The Empress, who holds in her hand a bunch of violets, is surrounded by her ladies-in-waiting; to the left, the princesse d'Essling, Grande Maîtresse; the baronne de Pierres and the vicomtesse de Lezay-Marnésia, Dames du Palais; to the right, the duchesse de Bassano, Dame d'Honneur; the comtesse de Montebello, the baronne de Malaret, the marquise de las Marismas, and the marquise de la Tour-Maubourg, Dames du Palais. The idea for this composition, arranging a group of women in a park, echoes that of an earlier work *Florinda* (Salon of 1853), where exactly the same trees can be seen in the background. But in the tableau of *The Empress Eugénie Surrounded by Her Ladies-in-Waiting,* the crinolines are effusive, while the nymphs who accompany Florinda are more in dishabille. Beyond this immediate reference, one must go back to the eighteenth century and its mythological portraits in the style of Nattier.

When this painting was presented at the Salon of 1855—it could not be missed, given its size and the place of honor it occupied—the critics had little to say; in 1855 censorship was still harsh, and one feared that comments on the painting would be interpreted as an attack on the imperial model. Mérimée confirmed this: "The portrait of the Empress by Winterhalter is detestable in my opinion, but nothing must be said about it to the court. It is a troop of tarts in a garden, all dolled up, with little affected looks. It could be used as a dance hall signboard for the Bal Mabille." A few critics did, however, whisper some reproaches. Delécluze attacked the crinolines. Loudun scolded Winterhalter for being more interested in ribbons and lace than in his models. Maxime du Camp, who shared this viewpoint, criticized "its dry and jarring treatment, its loud and harsh colors." Although little was said about the painting in 1855 in the newspapers, it was at this time that the sharpest criticism was leveled against Winterhalter.

A painted sketch showing slight variations is in the collection of the prince de Fürstenberg. Another sketch, very slight but much closer to the final painting, was sold on the Paris art market (location unknown). Winterhalter's picture was popularized through a lithograph by Lemoine and Léon Noël, but the success of this work goes beyond the sphere of engraving. It has been used for *tableaux vivants,* it has influenced the cinema, and though it was never used as a dance hall sign, it is often to be seen on boxes of chocolates. This work has had a surprising destiny, that of being loved at the same time by crowned heads and the masses but rejected by the critics of art.

O.S.

Musée National du Château, Compiègne

VI-110

# Drawing

A considered analysis of French drawing during the reign of Napoleon III points up the extreme diversity of styles that appeared during this relatively short period. It was at this time, in fact, that the artist came to free himself in a large part from the constraints that had bound him and to liberate the language of forms. It is interesting to note that in the nineteenth century, so often equated with Realism, drawing demanded an independence of its own instead of serving merely for the representation of appearances. And in this period of social movements it is also revealing that artistic individuality, as is so frequently the case, forced the draftsman to emphasize a manner that did not merely conform to the style he adopted but extended as far as possible into the realm of personal expression. The idea that one forms of art is close to the idea that one has of being. In this respect the distinction established by Baudelaire a few years earlier in the "Salon of 1846" proved to be prophetic: "There are several kinds of drawings, as there are of colour: the exact or silly, the physiognomic and the imaginative. The first is negative, incorrect by sheer force of reality, natural but absurd; the second is a naturalistic, but idealized draughtsmanship—the draughtsmanship of a genius who knows how to choose, arrange, correct, rebuke, and guess at nature; lastly the third, which is the noblest and strangest, and can afford to neglect nature—it realizes *another* nature, analogous to the mind and the temperament of the artist."[1]

With its pretext being a sort of "graphic journal," in which everyday reality came to life again through its individuality, drawing in the course of the nineteenth century became a passionate craze, as much among artists as among amateurs and collectors. Subjects were no longer limited to religious, mythological, allegorical, or historical scenes, nor to copies after antiquity or the old masters, but extended to all aspects of life. "Everything is a subject," declared Delacroix, in the sense that the artist could henceforth express himself with full freedom and not according to established norms; even when artists elaborated theories, these theories died quickly. On the other hand, the "metier" did remain, with all the possibilities it offered, from the unique and stylized drawn contour to shaded masses of light and shadow, from schematic lines to a suggestive density of strokes, from the precise rigor of the working drawing to a complete graphic exuberance, from the straight line to the single curve to their most complex variations. Techniques themselves became extremely varied: pencil, black crayon, sanguine, or a combination of these, charcoal with or without stump, colored crayons, pen, wash, watercolor, pastel, and so forth.

Such a diversity, however, did not exclude a certain form of fundamental unity in French drawing, beyond school groupings and beyond the tendencies which one is generally willing to ascribe to the mid-nineteenth century. The drawing of Ingres is not necessarily the drawing of a Classicist, no more than that of Delacroix is the drawing of a Romantic, or that of Millet purely realistic. Many contradictions do appear, particularly within the work of a number of the great masters, while certain affinities among the draftsmen of the beginning, middle, and end of the century are quite obvious.

No one has raised the "drawing of style" higher than Jean-Auguste-Dominique Ingres, he who had written, "style, it is nature." Heir to David's Neoclassicism and himself considered the leader of the Classical school in France, Ingres nevertheless departed from Davidian theories when he drew. David and his disciples sought their inspiration from Roman sculpture or bas-reliefs, while Ingres preferred the arabesque to volume and looked to Greek ceramics and to Raphael for his sources. Refashioning the human body to the measure of his own ideal by a series of "distortions," he combined the graphic purity of Greek vase painting with the exacerbated sensibility of forms of the Florentine Mannerists and of the School of Parma. A Classicist to be sure, but an exceptional innovator in the realm of form, Ingres foreshadowed the great modern masters, for example, Matisse and Modigliani. In his studies of female nudes (see no. VII-41), line itself becomes supple, voluptuous, sinuous, ever curving. In his portraits, on the other hand, the Antique is deliberately abandoned; binding himself to the most objective exactitude, Ingres insisted on placing his models in their milieu, rigorously drawing faces in their actual physical appearance, and lingering with relish over details of costume, always revealing himself to be an exceptional psychologist (see no. VII-40).

Ingres's "drawing of style" can still, for the period we are dealing with, be set against the drawing of Delacroix, with its multiple aspects. His is a "drawing of expression," of intimate testimony as well as of appeal to the great sensibilities of mankind—a dazzling lyricism, seeking suggestion in the intermingling of lines and shadows, of hatching and curves. But it is also subtle, attempting by a slow play of experiments to establish a perfectly balanced and rhythmical composition. "How could one conceive that the mind does not guide the artist's hand?" wrote Eugène Delacroix in effect, thereby declaring that lucid intelligence must control a feverish imagination. Contrary to the opinions generally expressed by critics of the time, Delacroix was without a doubt the nineteenth-century artist who best perceived the unlimited resources of drawing, using nature as his "dictionary." Endowed, to borrow Baudelaire's expression, with the "queen of faculties," that is to say, with a prodigious imagination, Delacroix unceasingly varied his drawing, not only during his development through the different stages of his life, but also stylistically in relation to the subject treated. Hence his drawing is "intelligent," on the level of the mind as well as in the realm of form: now in ovals or spirals (see no. VII-22), now by intertwining strokes (see no. VII-21).

To achieve a synthesis of the graphic obsession of Ingres and the passionate dynamism of Delacroix—such was the challenge accepted by Théodore Chassériau. His portrait drawings in pencil clearly reveal the influence of his teacher Ingres, but the rhythm of his style, all in curves, is closely related to that of Delacroix (see no. VII-11). Delacroix's example likewise left its mark on certain "Orientalists," from Eugène Fromentin (see no. VII-28) to Gustave Guillaumet (see no. VII-31), not to mention Alexandre Bida (see no. VII-5), even if each of these artists retained his own characteristics. Finally, with Barye we come back once more to Delacroix, with whom he frequently went to study at the Muséum d'Histoire Naturelle. His admirable studies of wild beasts executed in watercolor (see no. VII-3) go well beyond simple morphological studies, and the broad landscapes inhabited by his animals beckon the viewer like a call of the wild.

Assuredly Realists, Honoré Daumier and Jean-François Millet gave proof in their drawings of a creative strength going well beyond the strict representation of a figure or an event from contemporary life. Influenced both by the techniques of lithography and sculpture, which he practiced with equal skill, Daumier's handling plays with contrasted shadows and lights, or elaborates a wash of multiple overlapping strokes, stressing the musculature, the general forms, emphasizing the faces with incisive and schematic lines in order to convey more precisely their expressions (see no. VII-19). Likewise, the pseudo-realism of Millet, misunderstood by his contemporaries, is sublimated by style and a very great feeling for the nobility of man, most often expressed in the humble gestures of the peasant. A traditionalist in his conceptions of subjects, Millet did not hesitate to pursue with an innovative audacity plastic realization. The density of his "blacks," the quality of his "values" and of his sure and expressive strokes, make him one of the great forerunners not only of Pissarro, but of Seurat and Van Gogh (see no. VII-47).

Landscape, one of the fundamental aspects of French art, continued its evolution in the middle of the nineteenth century, starting with an objective and detailed representation of nature, then developing more toward the expression of atmosphere. Thus Camille Corot, from around 1850 until his death, drew in an increasingly free and spare manner, with a preference for charcoal or black crayon—with stump and highlights of white—on brown paper. Inspired by reality, his landscapes were transformed by the effect of a poetic and deeply lyrical reverie pervaded by a feeling of melancholy. Corot, beginning in 1860, was haunted by the problem of reflections, the fleeting and evanescent appearance of things (see no. VII-15). This late style of Corot's had an influence on the young Henri Harpignies, a charming petit maître with a delicate style, before he chose to devote himself almost exclusively to watercolor heightened by gouache, by which he rendered with equal success the sunlight of Mediterranean lands and the most subtle nuances of the Ile-de-France or the Morvan (see no. VII-34).

The refined sensibility of Adolphe Hervier already forecasted the landscape art of the Nabis (see no. VII-37). On the other hand, Auguste Ravier, from Lyons, remained resolutely apart from all schools, making his mark with a very individual style. His brilliant watercolors (see no. VII-52), flooded with an intense light that enshrouds nature in a bold harmony of reds, oranges, and yellows, calls to mind the work of Turner. Ravier's art, though imbued with a very personal poetry, remains nonetheless one of the milestones—quite different and yet necessary—toward the Impressionist evocation that Eugène Boudin (q.v.) directly preceded. One cannot fail to recall in this connection the surprise and enthusiasm of Baudelaire, discovering for the first time in 1859, in Honfleur, the views of beach, sea, and sky executed by Boudin in pastel and in watercolor, where the light, fluid touches "sweep" the paper in order to suggest the most fleeting reflections.

True "meteorological beauties," these views often bear added notations as to date, time, and wind; they unquestionably mark the emergence of the plein-air landscape that was to revolutionize the later nineteenth century.

It was also in the second half of the century that the broad tendencies in French drawing noted above became more pronounced and that the gap between "physiognomic drawing" and the "drawing of creation," as defined by Baudelaire, became much wider. Though many artists continued to exploit the traditions of the past and put their pencil or pen at the service of official "propaganda," there were many who henceforth responded to Baudelaire's call and devoted themselves to "modernity," that is, to "the transitory, the fleeting, the contingent, half of art, whose other half is the eternal and the immutable."[2] The contrast is to be seen, for example, between Eugène Lami (q.v.) or Henri Monnier (q.v.)— who never tired of depicting the piquant anecdote, capturing picturesque scenes of the Second Empire, simultaneously Napoleonic and bourgeois—and Constantin Guys (q.v.). For the latter went beyond his time by the instantaneity of his vision and by his ability to distinguish the essential, employing pen, brush, ink, and watercolor with an impressive freedom of expression. Though it may seem excessive praise to award Guys with the Baudelairean title of "the painter of modern life," a title that could as easily be justly claimed by Manet (q.v.), it would nevertheless be unfair not to recognize the innovative, "modern" character of his drawn chronicle of the historical events and diverse happenings of the Second Empire.

In their turn two draftsmen—Victor Hugo and Gustave Doré—although with rather different artistic conceptions, offered to later generations a new artistic language, an expression of the hitherto little explored realm of the unconscious. Poet of the night, uncontested leader of literary Romanticism, Hugo "inked" paper with his inspired dreams and conceived violently contrasted compositions of light and shadow from which emerged a terrible and visionary universe (see no. VII-38). Gustave Doré, for his part, though he likewise imagined the unreal in relation to the real, took his inspiration from literature or from contemporary life (see no. VII-24), whose picturesque or historical interest he transformed by a truly remarkable sense of the fantastic.

Is it therefore presumptuous to suggest that modern art began under the Second Empire? Could it have begun at a time when art was still under the thumb of academicism, faithfully championed in their various ways by Thomas Couture, Ernest Hébert, Paul Baudry,

Alexandre Cabanel, William Bouguereau, Jean-Léon Gérôme (q.q.v.), and others, at a time when bourgeois patronage considered anarchical all those who wished to transgress order and tradition and to escape from the codified discipline of contour drawing? If this idea seems too audacious, let us at least call attention to the multiple contradictions of the period, contradictions that could be expressed by Second Empire drawing itself. Let us not forget, in fact, that during the entire Second Empire, correct, strict, careful, and expert drawing was elevated to the height of an institution and extended its domain over all the other arts at the level of artistic formation: "Instruction," as the Superintendent of Fine Arts Nieuwerkerke was to observe in a report to the Emperor suggesting a reform of the Ecole des Beaux-Arts, "does not consist for painters, sculptors, and engravers in much more than a course in drawing.... Is it not extraordinary that in a school where painters are in the majority, there is no painting teacher?"[3] Oddly enough, however, drawing was scarcely shown at the Salon, where being included with paintings, no special attention was reserved for it. In order to satisfy their passion, the growing number of connoisseurs and collectors of drawings turned mostly to exhibitions, those organized while artists were still alive or right after their deaths by the Ecole des Beaux-Arts (Ingres in 1865, for example), or those undertaken privately and displayed in galleries (Galerie Martinet) or private houses (thus the Salon des Arts Unis, where an important group of drawings by Ingres, "taken from the collections of connoisseurs," including among others the portrait of Hippolyte Flandrin, no. VII-40, opened to the public in 1861).

The Second Empire certainly did not achieve the complete liberation of drawing, but it witnessed in this area the birth of profound changes. While the public progressively felt the need to meet artists outside a strictly official setting, artists for their part began to seek their way outside the academies, and we perceive after all that drawing would have been at the time the advanced element in the "modern" revolution, continuing to take reality in charge but also questioning the visible and departing further and further from the exact image and from imitation.

A.S

Notes

1. Baudelaire, 1965, p. 59 (see Baudelaire, 1976, p. 434).

2. See Baudelaire, 1976, p. 695.

3. Nieuwerkerke, 1863, pp. 564–65.

VII-1

Eugène-Emmanuel Amaury-Duval

## VII-1
## Young Girl Watching Doves

c. 1860
Signed, lower right: Amaury-Duval
Charcoal, heightened with white, on tinted paper
125 × 83 cm

Provenance:
Gift of the artist to the Musée des Beaux-Arts, Lille, 1867 (inv. no. 1345)

Exhibition:
1974, Montrouge, no. 24 (repro.)

Bibliography:
Gonse, 1877, p. 393

This drawing should be compared with the *Antique Bather* in the Musée des Beaux-Arts in Rouen (1974, Montrouge, no. 28, repro.), in which the cool, pure classicism corresponds to the artist's style around 1860–70. The general conception of the work clearly reflects the veneration Amaury-Duval felt for his teacher Ingres. But the charm of the slightly languid attitude of the woman and the rather dreamy sweetness of her face are entirely characteristic of Amaury-Duval, who was to develop this form of expression in his decorations for the château of Linières in the Vendée, begun around 1865. In the *Game of Shuttlecock,* one of the frescoes that adorned the billiard room (the château was demolished in 1912), one finds a young woman seated in a pose similar to that of the *Bather* (1974, Montrouge, no. 69, repro.).

A.S.

Musée des Beaux-Arts, Lille

---

## Henri Baron
*Besançon 1816–1885 Geneva*

*A pupil of Jean Gigoux, Baron made his debut at the Salon of 1837. He had returned from a trip to Italy with genre scenes which were very much in fashion at this time, and began to specialize in "costume and in historical anecdote, inspired by the Italian Renaissance and the eighteenth-century painters of* fêtes gallants.*" His reputation was already well established at the beginning of the Second Empire. At the Salon of 1852 in which he showed* The Skaters *(Lille museum), Grün (1852, p. 79) remarked: "M. Baron no longer has to identify himself: he is the one who perpetually recreates his elegant cavaliers, his lovely sixteenth-century ladies." The Goncourts (1852, pp. 86–87) found in the delicacy of Baron's likable talent reason for describing "silk and velvet, brocade in sunlight and mirroring waters, colonnades and pleasure gardens, canals overgrown with roses reflecting only flower-garlanded cupids, breezes laden with music and words of love—what a lovely domain! All is rose perfumes, scented oils, angel's water. All is perfumed mustachios, wavy hair adorned with jewels, Basque cloaks of silk, crimson velvet slippers slashed into shrimp whiskers, shimmering taffetas, golden cannetilles, Moorish stuffs with golden threads, plumes with glints of gold!"*

*In 1855 his* Grape Harvest in Romagna *(Niort museum) also received a favorable mention. His greatest success seems to have been the* Entrance to a Venetian Cabaret, *which was shown at the Salon of 1859 and gained for him the Legion of Honor. This picture was bought by the Empress and later appeared in the Rainbeaux sale (Paris, Hôtel Drouot, October 21–23, 1936, no. 9).*

*More often than not the critics continued to have a kind word for Baron at each Salon. C. Vignon (1855, p. 225) defined perfectly the reasons for this artist's success in Second Empire society: "M. Baron is always the stylish artist whom we know, with his adroit, well-arranged compositions and elegant, facile painting, all curls and speckles and ribbons, just made for the illustration of boudoirs and keepsakes."*

O.S.

Bibliography:
Montrosier, 1883, p. 289–304; Estignard, 1896

Henri Baron

## VII-2
## An Official Fete at the Palais des Tuileries during the Exposition Universelle of 1867

1867
Signed and dated at bottom, on banister:
H. Baron 1867
Watercolor
55 × 95 cm

Provenance:
Commissioned by the Ministère de la Maison de l'Empereur et des Beaux-Arts at the request of the Empress for 4,000 francs (Louvre Archives N6 [June 22, 1868]); placed in the apartments of the president of the Sénat; tranferred to the Musée du Luxembourg (Louvre Archives 2DD20); transferred to the Louvre (RF 137); deposited at Compiègne (inv. no. 38-2599)

Exhibitions:
1868, Paris, Salon, no. 2630; 1949, Arenenberg; 1953, Compiègne, no. 6; 1968, Dijon, no. 87

Bibliography:
De Navery, 1868, p. 69; Dayot, 1900, p. 3; Bellier and Auvray, 1882–87, p. 44; Chennevières, 1883–89, vol. I, pp. 5–6; Thieme and Becker, 1907–50, vol. II, p. 515; Fleury and Sonolet, n.d., repro.; Aubry, 1932, pl. 26; Guiffrey and Marcel, 1907–38, vol. I, no. 196; Terrier, 1959, no. 30; Le Journal de la France, no. 55, 1970, pp. 1514–15; Richardson, 1971, pp. 249–50

According to Chennevières, the Empress had wished to commemorate the imperial ceremonies "which were one of the institutions of the reign conceived to activate industries in Paris and Lyons," and Baron's watercolor was one of these commissions. Baron received a good price and de Navery gave it a favorable description in his criticism of the Salon of 1868: "M. Baron has painted the entire court with an extraordinary good temper. One never suspects that modern clothing is not the least bit gracious when one looks at this handsome page. Tulles, gauzes, ribbons, flowers mingle in the costumes of the women with an adorable grace; many portraits may be counted in this page of history, tasteful likenesses, tasteful successes. A great talent is required to come up with honors under such difficult circumstances." Actually Baron's brush evokes this supper with a precious, if somewhat superficial, grace. E. Cantrel in 1863 defined this painting (p. 196) as "false, lively, alert, gay, and showy; a picturesque, flexible drawing."

O.S.

Musée National du Château, Compiègne

Antoine-Louis Barye

## VII-3
## Tiger Rolling on Its Back

Signed, lower right: BARYE
Watercolor
23.3 × 29.5 cm

VII-2

VII-3

Provenance:
Probably Dr. Lereboullet coll.; unknown coll. (collector's mark, lower right, not in Lugt); private coll.

Exhibition:
1886, Paris, Ecole des Beaux-Arts, probably no. 273

Provenance:
Binder coll.; Henry O. Havemeyer; bequest of Mrs. H.O. Havemeyer to the Metropolitan Museum of Art, 1929 (inv. no. 29.100.586)

Exhibition:
1860, Paris, "Caisse de Secours des Artistes," no. 8

Bibliography:
*Havemeyer*, 1930, no. 134; Zieseniss, 1954, p. 65, no. B.19, pl. 12

Barye's watercolors have come to be as appreciated in our day as, in his lifetime, were the sculptures that officially established his reputation in a somewhat limited field—as an *animalier*. Barye studied animals throughout his life, from his first courses with Cuvier and with Geoffroy Saint-Hilaire until the time that he taught zoological drawing at the Muséum. His numerous drawings and watercolors, perhaps even more than his bronzes, permit one to follow the progress of his pursuits, which fell somewhere between Romanticism—Barye adopted its basic principles while rejecting its excesses—and the Barbizon School.

Of all the wild animals that Barye portrayed, he seems to have been particularly attracted to the tiger. Having had the chance to see one as early as 1828 at the Saint-Cloud menagerie, he used the tiger as the subject of a number of the watercolors he exhibited in the Salon of 1831. Yet it was especially from 1847–50 that he analyzed the animal in detail—whether it be lying in wait, lying down,

or, as here, rolling over on its back. Tigers were not easily acclimated to France, and they were shown at the Jardin des Plantes only from 1847 on, where Barye could study them at his leisure throughout the Second Empire. Even though this watercolor is not dated (which is true of all his watercolors), it can be situated in this time period—which the affixed signature in printed capital letters at the lower right confirms (*see* Zieseniss, 1954, p. 33).

A.S.

The Metropolitan Museum of Art, New York, Bequest of Mrs. H.O. Havemeyer, 1929, H.O. Havemeyer Collection

Paul Baudry

## VII-4
## Melpomene

c. 1868
Signed, lower right: Baudry; inscribed, bottom left: Melpomène; lower right: opéra
Charcoal, heightened with white, on brown paper
44.3 × 21 cm

This is an early idea, with variations, for one of the eight colossal figures of the Muses (310 × 150 cm) placed between the arches of the Grand Foyer of the Paris Opéra (no. I-10), the decoration of which was entrusted to Baudry in 1868. The pose of this figure of Tragedy is much closer to that finally adopted for the Muse Euterpe, the artist having in the end represented Melpomene with a mask raised off her face and clasping a sword against her knees.

Camille Renard, in describing the decorations for the Grand Foyer of the Opéra—which Baudry considered, according to Ephrussi (1887), "the most accurate, the most complete, the most deeply imbued with the very feeling of the artist"—stressed this with regard to the Muses: "Here is one aspect of the work that the artist, in my opinion, has stamped with his most powerful originality.

"Eight panels were offered for the master's interpretation. On them he inscribed what one might justly call the 'portraits' of the Muses. In choosing these great figures that antiquity so often celebrated in painting and sculpture, Baudry was fully aware of the difficulties he would encounter. Two serious obstacles had to be avoided: to follow tradition and produce only a repetition, or to indulge in fantasy but come up with nothing more than a fleeting expression of modernity. The artist rose above the two extremes. The Muses that his brush caressed were born in nature. They have not let themselves be dominated by the memory of the past; they owe nothing to the idealizations of Phidias, Raphael, or Veronese. Their forms are marked with a character that has become humanized by contact with our modern society; and such was the judicious spirit of their author that each of them seems to whisper in our ears the remembrance and the lamented name of some great celebrity of Song, Drama, and Dance" (Renard, 1874, in Ephrussi, 1887, pp. 228, 230).

The 1886 exhibition at the Ecole des Beaux-Arts included a series of drawings for the Foyer of the Opéra, in charcoal, pencil, or sanguine, frequently heightened with white (nos. 204–17, 219–29, 232–60, 261–89, 291–98). These include a number of drawings for the Muses (nos. 272–89), three of which relate to Melpomene: one dedicated to Mme Carpentier; the second, probably the drawing exhibited,

VII-4

belonged to Dr. Lereboullet; and the third, to Charles Garnier (q.v.).

A.S.

Private Collection

---

*Alexandre Bida*

*Toulouse 1823–1895 Bühl*

*A student of Delacroix (q.v.) for two years, Bida maintained a profound admiration for his master, retaining above all from his teaching a love of drawing. In fact, few paintings by this artist are known,* and all of his state commissions, as well as his submissions to the Salon, were drawings. "It is quite different with M. Bida," observed Baudelaire, "he... seems to have stoically repudiated colour and all its pomps in order to give more value and light to the human characters which his pencil undertakes to express. And he expresses them with a remarkable intensity and depth" ("Salon of 1859,"Baudelaire, 1965, p. 183). Having experienced the East during a trip to Constantinople and to Syria (1843), Bida devoted himself largely to Oriental subjects in which reality was very often blended with a kind of pathetic Romanticism.

*Bida made his debut at the Salon of 1847. From the beginning, the critics were favorable, and as a supreme honor, as early as 1849 the State bought* The Slave Market, *then* The Café in Constantinople *and* The Armenian Barber. *In 1850 Bida traveled to Egypt, bringing back a great number of drawings in black chalk and in sanguine. The trip he made in 1855 to Greece, Turkey, and the Crimea unquestionably inspired his most beautiful and celebrated compositions, including* Preaching in Lebanon, Jews Crying at the Wall of Solomon *(Salon of 1857),* Evening Call to Prayer in the Crimea *Salon of 1857; Louvre, Cabinet des Dessins, RF 138),* The Massacre of the Mamelukes *(Salon of 1861; Louvre, Cabinet des Dessins, RF 140). By this time Bida enjoyed great fame, and the critics continued to praise the works he presented at the Salon. After a fourth trip to Egypt and Palestine, to do illustrations for a Bible published by Hachette (Bibliothèque Nationale, Paris), Bida worked primarily on book illustrations ; shortly before his death, he completed his work for* Jeanne d'Arc *by Jules Michelet. An artist who was greatly appreciated during his lifetime and whose drawings were eagerly sought by collectors, Bida left a large body of works characterized by an attention to detail that was sometimes pushed to the extreme.*

A.S.

Bibliography:
G. Paris, 1895

Alexandre Bida

## VII-5
## The Ceremony of the Dosseh

1855
Signed, lower left: Bida
Black crayon, heightened with white
60 × 89.4 cm

Provenance:
Duc de Morny; Walters Art Gallery (inv. no. 37.901)
Exhibition:
1855, Paris, Salon, no. 2564

"In former times Sheik Sâad-Ed-Din, in order to prove the power of Mohammed, whom he served with love, rode on horseback over a road strewn with bottles without breaking any of them. Today, the chief of the order of the Dervishes, founded by Sâad-Ed-Din, carries out the same journey. Only, instead of bottles and glasses, men are placed under the hooves of his horse.... This is the Dosseh (trampling)" (described by Maxime du Camp in *Le Nil: Egypte et Nubie,* 1854).

A souvenir of Bida's second trip to the East, during which the artist executed important drawings in black crayon and sanguine, *The Ceremony of the Dosseh* attracted the attention of the critics when it was exhibited at the Salon of 1855. Théophile Gautier commented on it: "The artist has expressed with admirable depth the fatalist quietude of Islam and the ardent faith of these wretched people who pave the road of the impassive dervish with their bodies; the only one who feels any emotion among this multitude of fanatics is the horse; he lowers his head, sniffs, and lifts his hooves delicately in order not to injure anyone."

The very elaborate working of the drawing is absolutely typical of Bida's drawing style. As André Michel emphasized in the introduction to the catalogue of the sale held after the artist's death (Paris, Hôtel Drouot, April 26–30, 1895), this is one of those "persuasive" drawings in which one feels "the certainty and joy of the craftsman in full possession of his talents, in intimate rapport with nature and with life; the vision is penetrating, the execution alert and decisive, the individual character strongly underlined; the drawing, sober and at the same time supple and vigorous, abounds with success" (pp. 8–9).

In the 1855 Salon catalogue the drawing is mentioned as belonging to the duc de Morny. Could this same drawing have been acquired by the State on March 6, 1854, for the sum of 3,000 francs (Arch. nat. F $^{21}$–64; *see* Angrand, 1968, "L'Etat," p. 334) and paid for in three installments until January 23, 1855? In the catalogue of the Bida sale, there is a second drawing entitled *The Dosseh* (no. 42), but the drawing is smaller (48 × 72 cm) than that exhibited here. It would seem, therefore, that Bida executed two versions of this subject, just as he did two drawings representing *The Massacre of the Mamelukes* (one, in the Louvre, RF 140, was exhibited in the Salon of 1861; the other is in Mulhouse).

A.S.

The Walters Art Gallery, Baltimore

VII-5

Alexandre Bida

## VII-6
## Dalila (The Song of Calvary)

1857
Signed, lower right: Bida
Black crayon, gray wash, white highlights partially removed with an eraser, on gray paper
38.3 × 45 cm

Provenance:
Acquired from the Salon of 1857 by the city of Toulouse for the Musée des Augustins, 1858; later deposited at the Musée Paul Dupuy (inv. no. 7)

Exhibitions:
1857, Paris, Salon, no. 222; 1858, Toulouse

Bibliography:
Cicéron, 1858, pp. 93–94; Roschach, 1858, p. 299

Bida, who is associated primarily with works inspired by the Orient, was also very active as an illustrator. This drawing illustrates the following passage from Octave Feuillet's novel *Dalila* (1857): "All of a sudden I heard rise up from the depths of an orchard adjoining the cottage, the solemn and velvety sounds of a cello.... I recognized the bow... I recognized the hand!... I slipped unnoticed behind the trees, and I could see a group of three people who were protected from the rays of the setting sun by the foliage.... One of them was unknown to me, but I understood that he was a doctor.... As for the other two, I knew them. Only the old man appeared changed to me. The features of the young woman seemed hardly altered, and yet her pose, the armchair lined with pillows where she was half reclining, the unusual brilliance of her gaze, all told me that the doctor had come for her. Just as I arrived her father laid down his bow and asked her how she felt. 'Better,' she said smiling, 'better and better; but only Germany will cure me completely.' Then she closed her eyes and murmured some indistinct words. 'My child,' the old man said, 'confide in me. This secret that you keep so obstinately doubles your pain. Tell me everything, I beg of you; I promise not to denounce him. He deceived you, did he not?' She reopened her eyes: 'No, no,' she responded, 'I deceived myself; I love him still....' [The girl said] 'play *The Song of Calvary.*' 'No, no,' said the good man in a voice filled with poignant cheerfulness, 'your wedding day, my little girl.' The daughter smiled looking straight at him; he lowered his eyes without responding. With a suffering gesture… he took up his bow… I then heard *The Song of Calvary,* yes *The Song of Calvary!*… While he played, I saw large teardrops fall one by one on his poor emaciated and trembling hands…. He cried! The wood and the strings cried!… Only the daughter did not cry; she had no more tears. I left. I waited for the doctor at the door. I asked him if he held out any hope. He gestured toward heaven…."

The passage was quoted in an article in the *Magazin Pittoresque* (Cicéron, 1858, pp. 93–94), which continued: "This scene… lives again, for the eyes, under the knowing and energetic pencil of M. Bida, in such a way as to double the pleasure that the imagination derives from the book."

A.S.

Musée Paul Dupuy, Toulouse

François Bonvin

## VII-7
## Extern Sister Cutting Bread

1860
Signed and dated in pen, lower right: 1860 F. Bonvin
Watercolor and gouache on gray paper
33 × 22.5 cm

Provenance:
Grobet-Labadié coll.; gift to the city of Marseilles, 1919; Musée des Beaux-Arts (inv. no. G. 868)
Bibliography:
Pillement, 1974, "Bonvin" (repro.)

Bonvin repeated the composition of this watercolor, modifying it slightly, in *The Servant,* a painting somewhat larger in size (41 × 27.5 cm) and also dated 1860 (private coll.; Pillement, 1974, "Bonvin", fig. 258).

More than any other artist of a group that might be called "intimist Realists," Bonvin was in the habit of preparing his paintings by means of elaborate drawings or watercolors. As Gabriel Weisberg has kindly pointed out (monograph on Bonvin in preparation), this is a characteristic example of the artist's stylistic development around 1860.

His theme, revealing his admiration for the seventeenth-century Dutch "petits maîtres" and for Chardin, appears in a series of domestic scenes: cooks preparing meals, women doing laundry, ironing, and so on. In this period Bonvin was particularly fond of studying seated figures, placed off center and often in profile. Such a preference, as well as his division of the back wall into two unequal areas, is not with-

VII-6

out similarities, as Weisberg notes, to the composition of certain portraits painted by Whistler, in particular that of his mother (Louvre). The two artists were friends, and in 1859 Whistler exhibited in Bonvin's studio, along with Antoine Vollon, Auguste-Théodule Ribot, and Henri Fantin-Latour (q.q.v), all of whom had been rejected by the Salon.

A.S.

Musée des Beaux-Arts, Marseilles

Eugène Boudin

## VII-8
## On the Beach

1866
Dated in pencil, lower right: 66
Watercolor over pencil
20 × 32.5 cm

Provenance:
Part of a bequest of 5,742 drawings by the artist's heirs to the Musée du Luxembourg, 1899; transferred to the Louvre, 1930 (inv. no. RF 18.179)
Exhibitions:
1965, Paris, Louvre, no. 122; 1972, Darmstadt, no. 7 (repro.)

In 1862 Boudin, on the advice of the painter Eugène Isabey, began painting beach scenes,

VII-7

VII-8

William-Adolphe Bouguereau

## VII-9
## Study of Standing Female Nude Looking Left

c. 1865
Signed, lower left: W$^m$ Bouguereau
Pencil, heightened with white, on buff paper
46.3 × 30.3 cm

Provenance:
Marquise Landolfo Carcano; sale, Paris, May 30–June 1, 1912, no. 99; M. de Villeroy; sale, Paris, Georges Petit, April 28, 1922, no. 2; Knoedler, Paris; Robert Sterling Clark, 1922; Sterling and Francine Clark Art Institute, 1955 (inv. no. 1578)

chiefly in Normandy, where the seaside resorts of Trouville and Deauville, recently made fashionable by the imperial court, were frequented by "all the exotic, beautiful people that high society gathers into our watering places during the summer" (*see* Castagnary, 1892, vol. I, p. 374). Eager to "utilize nature as far as possible" in this new genre of seascape, the artist did a great number of drawings and watercolors, most of which are in the Louvre. They are not, strictly speaking, studies executed with a specific purpose, but rather notations taken from life, in which poetic feeling prevails over purely analytical precision. A tireless observer of the atmospheric changes of a varying and constantly renewed natural setting, Boudin, through his efforts to execute variations on a single theme, paved the way for the Impressionists.

This watercolor—in which the figures seem to merge with the surrounding landscape—clearly illustrates the intentions of Boudin, who "did not seek to individualize faces: his description remains a collective one. But if the figures keep their anonymity, what finesse he shows in establishing even the slightest silhouette" (Roger-Marx, 1957, p. 618). One should also note the subtlety of the color harmonies, grays and ochers predominating, warmed by three red spots: the coat of the woman standing to the left, the costume in the center, and the cape of the woman seated to the right under an umbrella.

A.S.

Cabinet des Dessins, Musée du Louvre, Paris

VII-9

Exhibitions:
1968, Bloomington, no. 6 (repro.); 1974, Binghamton, New York, Williamstown, no. 11 (repro.); 1976, Norton, no. 49
Bibliography:
Catalogue, Williamstown, Clark Art Institute, 1964, vol. I, no. 84, vol. II, pl. 118

This drawing is a study for the figure of Venus in the painting *Apollo and the Muses*, commissioned from Bouguereau in 1865 for the ceiling of the concert hall of the Grand Théâtre of Bordeaux and exhibited at the Salon of 1869 (no. 291). This decoration by Bouguereau, wrote Marius Vachon (1900, p. 82), "the first on a mythological theme that he executed after that for the Hôtel Pereire, reveals a decided development in composition and color. He abandons the flowing draperies of yellow, blue, and purple as a too facile means of expressing, against a strong background, the marmoreal delicacy of flesh; he seeks a general harmony of color, softer and more direct, and he boldly arrives at nudes that triumph in the glowing beauty of their forms."

A.S.

Sterling and Francine Clark Art Institute, Williamstown, Massachusetts

Alexandre Cabanel

## VII-10
## The Triumph of Flora

1869
Signed in pen and ink, bottom left: Alex. Cabanel
Pen and brown ink, watercolor, and gouache
46.5 × 27 cm

Provenance:
Gift of the artist to the architect Hector Lefuel (manuscript annotation on back of frame); Mme Lefuel; sale, Paris, March 30, 1973; purchased by the Louvre (inv. no. RF 35.727)
Exhibition:
1922, Paris, Musée des Arts Décoratifs, no. 221
Bibliography:
Chantelou, Le Monde, June 8, 1973, p. 21

*See* Colorplate

This delicate watercolor is a study for the ceiling of a grand staircase in the Louvre, commissioned in 1869 (now decorating the Cabinet des Dessins). Cabanel designed the ceiling as part of the renovations to the Pavillon de Flore, where Napoleon III wanted to establish an apartment for visiting royalty. The plan of Lefuel (q.v.) called for an apartment on the

VII-10

ground floor with an entrance that led to the monumental staircase of the "sovereigns," which was begun in 1867 and was to have been surmounted by Cabanel's ceiling. The Franco-Prussian War interrupted the project and the fire that ravaged the Tuileries in 1871 severely damaged Cabanel's ceiling, still in the process of execution (Aulanier, 1971, p. 91).

Three years later the artist undertook the necessary restorations. When the ceiling was exhibited in 1873 it delighted a number of the commentators, although on the whole they were rather reserved about it: "Cabanel's beautiful picture, unveiled this week at the Ecole des Beaux-Arts, will immediately be sent to the Exposition in Vienna. We are pleased that French painting will be able to be represented by a monumental work with a truly decorative character" (*Chronique des Arts et de la Curiosité,* March 29, 1873, pp. 120–21). Dominating the nuptial celebration set in great banks of clouds is the god of Hymen crowned with roses and armed with the symbolic torch. Zephyr leans toward Flora seated in a flower-laden chariot with a retinue of divinities in flight behind, strewing armfuls of flowers and playing instruments. Delaborde (1889, p. 14) cited a letter of Cabanel to his brother (*see* Nougaret, 1962), where the artist declared: "As

far as I'm concerned [the ceiling] is the best thing I've done to date. I took great pains, often making myself disliked, but nothing equals the satisfaction at finally seeing a finished work all one's own, a work which is the marrow of your bones, the essence of your heart, in a word, a true creation."

According to Fouquier (1889, p. 20): "The decoration of the Pavillon de Flore... demanded several years of work. Cabanel put into practice, more than any other artist, Ingres's phrase that draftsmanship is the conscience of the painter. He never began a composition without a series of studies, painted or drawn, always done with thoroughness. Confirming this remark, Cabanel's studio sale included three small paintings (Paris, Galerie Georges Petit, May 22–25, 1889, nos. 3, 41, 42) and thirty-one preparatory drawings (nos. 436–66) related to the ceiling.

A.S.

Cabinet des Dessins, Musée du Louvre, Paris

Théodore Chassériau

## VII-11
## Descent from the Cross
## (Study for the Church of Saint Philippe du Roule)

1852–55
Pencil on two unequally cut and juxtaposed sheets
29.1 × 44.5 cm

Provenance:
Chassériau studio sale, Paris, March 16–17, 1857 (collector's mark, lower right, Lugt 443); artist's nephew, Baron Arthur Chassériau; gift to the Louvre, 1935 (inv. no. RF 24.664)
Bibliography:
Sandoz, 1957, p. 34; Sandoz, 1974, p. 390, under no. 244

The ceiling—or, more precisely, the half dome—of the choir of the Church of Saint Philippe du Roule in Paris, built by Chalgrin between 1769 and 1784, and enlarged by Golde and Baltard in 1853 and 1854, was the last large decorative composition executed by Chassériau. He had been notified of the commission by a letter of February 28, 1852, from the Minister of the Interior. Three years later, the artist wrote to de Mercey: "My task is finally finished and you will no longer be worried over the hemicycle of Saint Philippe du Roule. I have accomplished my mission with devotion,

VII-11

The success of the Spanish ballet, brought to Paris around 1844, and the Hispanicizing fashion evident in French literature and painting in the mid-nineteenth century, undoubtedly spurred Chassériau, like other artists, to interest himself in this novelty. Petra Camara made her appearance on the stage of the Théâtre du Gymnase in 1851; a dancer so "sinister and beautiful as to drive one mad," she inspired a poem by Théophile Gautier in *Emaux et camées* (1852), "Inès de las Sierras, to Petra Camara": "Was it a wraith or woman seen,/A thing of dreams, or blood and flesh,/The flame that burst from out the sheen/Of beauty's undulating mesh?/I saw this phantom at the Gymnase,/All Paris drawn to this aura,/When in her shroud of thinnest gauze,/Appeared La Petra Camara./Closing her eyes with languor rare,/Impassive, passionate of art,/And, like the murdered Inès fair,/Dancing, a dagger in her heart!'

Chassériau made a number of sketches of the dancer, studies of movements and dance steps, executed at the theater itself (Bénédite, 1932, vol. II, repro. p. 505); facial expressions; and details of costume (Bénédite, 1932, vol. II, repro. p. 502). In the Szépművészeti Múzeum in Budapest there is a small painting on wood signed and dated 1852, showing Petra Camara in a more provocative pose than the one seen here. The Louvre drawing cannot fail to call to

preoccupied above all with what I will *leave* behind after this short life" (Bénédite, 1932, vol. II, p. 463).

Sandoz (1957, p. 32) cites a few sketches in the Louvre that seem to be related to an early idea, later abandoned, for a Calvary with three crosses (RF 24.651, RF 24.653, RF 24.712). Other studies, most of them in the Louvre, but some also in a private collection and in the Poitiers museum (Sandoz, 1957, pp. 33–34; Sandoz, 1974, pp. 390, 392), relate to the subject finally chosen: "Christ being taken down from the Cross," with the soldiers casting lots for his clothing on one side and a group of Jews watching the scene on the other. This fine drawing, which emphasizes the group of holy women to the left of the body of Christ, is certainly one of the most moving of the studies.

Overshadowed by his pursuits at the Church of Saint Roch (1854), the *Calvary* of Saint Philippe du Roule did not gain the attention of the critics, except for Théophile Gautier (*Le Moniteur*, October 13, 1856) and Paul de Saint-Victor. "The Descent from the Cross in Saint Philippe du Roule," he wrote, "elevates M. Chassériau, it attests to the sustained progress that he is making toward the heights of style and thought. With each new trial, his monumental painting reveals him to be more the master of his imaginings, more sure of his means, more advanced in that fusion of drawing and color that he pursues as a noble dream. No one in the Ecole has as much feeling and will

for great art as he, and he has shown himself to be a master in the vast composition that we have just described. It is one of those in the career of an artist that denotes, and in some way ushers in, his virility" (Saint-Victor, 1855).

A.S.

Cabinet des Dessins, Musée du Louvre, Paris

Théodore Chassériau

## VII-12
## The Dancer Petra Camara

1854
Signed and dated in pencil, lower right: Th^re Chassériau 1854
Pencil, heightened with watercolor
21.2 × 15.2 cm

Provenance:
Possibly Chassériau studio sale, Paris, March 16–17, 1857, no. 25 (wrongly classified among the paintings; *see* Sandoz, 1974, no. 179); artist's nephew, Baron Arthur Chassériau; gift to the Louvre, 1935 (inv. no. RF 24.430)

Exhibition:
1957, Paris, Louvre, no. 78, pl. 16

Bibliography:
Bénédite, 1932, vol. II, pl. 36; Sandoz, 1974, p. 322, under no. 179

VII-12

VII-13

mind two other portraits of Spanish dancers: Courbet's *Señora Adela Guerrero*, painted in Brussels in 1851 (Musées Royaux des Beaux-Arts, Brussels), and Manet's *Lola de Valence*, executed in 1862 (Jeu de Paume).

A.S.

Cabinet des Dessins, Musée du Louvre, Paris

## François-Nicolas Chifflart
*Saint-Omer 1825–1901 Paris*

*The son of a locksmith, Chifflart studied in Saint-Omer and later in Paris, winning the Grand Prix de Rome in 1851* (Pericles at the Deathbed of His Son). *He remained in Italy from 1851 to 1856 and made his debut at the Salon in 1859, showing two large charcoal sketches,* Faust in Combat *and* Faust at the Witches' Sabbath, *both acquired by the City of Paris in 1883 (now lost). Critics raved about these sketches: "Their style is truly fine and imposing," wrote Charles Baudelaire. "What a*

*dream of chaos!... I count it to M. Chifflart's greatest credit that he has treated these poetic subjects heroically and dramatically, and that he has thrust far from him all the accepted trappings of melancholy" (Baudelaire, 1965, p. 184). Nevertheless, the brilliant career that the artist could rightly expect after such high praise was soon to fall through his hands. Although Chifflart exhibited regularly at the Salon (1863, 1865, 1866, 1868, 1873, 1874, 1896 to 1900), he received few official commissions and led a more and more retired life. He devoted himself mainly to engraving and belonged to the Société des Aquafortistes from its formation in 1862. His masterpiece in this medium was* Improvisations, *published about 1865. In 1869 Hetzel published* Les

Travailleurs de la mer *by Victor Hugo (q.v.), with seventy illustrations by Chifflart, which won the poet's unreserved praise: "Chifflart superbly captured* Les Travailleurs de la mer, *especially its brutal side" (letter to Auguste Vacquerie, February 9, 1868). During the Franco-Prussian War, Chifflart worked for* Le Monde Illustré *and drew* The Charge of the Reichshoffen Cavalry, *whose masterful execution contrasts sharply with the heavy style of his allegorical works such as* The City of Paris Raising Up Her Children *(Salon of 1896). "Classical by education but... Romantic by temperament," was the comment of a critic at the Salon of 1865, who clearly identified the split personality that characterizes all of Chifflart's work. A draftsman and engraver of prodigious imagination, the artist deserves finally to emerge from the oblivion into which he slipped after his death.*

A.S.

Bibliography:
1972, Saint-Omer

François-Nicolas Chifflart

## VII-13
## Remorse

1864
Signed and inscribed in margin, lower right: A M^r F^x Le Sergeant de Monnecove. F. Chifflart reconnaissant
Charcoal on blue paper
93 × 126 cm

Provenance:
Félix Le Sergeant de Monnecove, mayor of Saint-Omer; gift to the town of Saint-Omer, 1897; Musée de l'Hôtel Sandelin

Exhibitions:
1900, Exposition Universelle, no. 813; 1972, Saint-Omer, p. 19, no. 21

Bibliography:
Noel, 1902, pp. 123–24, 151–52; Revillion, 1904, pp. 51–52, 60, no. 160

In January 1898 Chifflart stated in a letter to Félix de Monnecove: "Monsieur and dear compatriot, I have entitled the drawing in question *Remorse*.... An exaggerated sentiment perhaps, but my conception... perhaps also the influence of some literary work or other that affected me without my knowledge? I take this opportunity to thank you, my dear compatriot, for your present good wishes and also for the many efforts you have made on my behalf in the past" (Revillion, 1904, pp. 51–52). Thus we are not dealing here with a work of literary inspiration, such as the two charcoal drawings of *Faust in Combat* and *Faust at the Witches' Sabbath* after Goethe, much admired by Baudelaire at the Salon of 1859, or the drawings for Victor

Hugo's *Les Travailleurs de la mer* (1869), whose "brutal side" was so appreciated by the poet. Born of Chifflart's feverish imagination, this hallucinatory composition is another spectacular example of his tormented art, attracted as it is to the fantastic. One must admire, also, the skill displayed by the artist in using charcoal to render nocturnal illumination as it throws violent flashes of light on this almost infernal cavalcade.

A.S.

Musée de l'Hôtel Sandelin, Saint-Omer

Jean-Baptiste-Camille Corot

## VII-14
## Traveler Passing under Trees

1859
Signed, lower left: Corot
Charcoal on tracing paper
47.5 × 29.5 cm

Provenance:
Alfred Robaut; Georges Aubry; sale, Paris, February 22, 1937, no. 20 (repro.); Claude Roger-Marx;

VII-14

gift "in memory of his father, his brother, and his son, who died for France," to the Louvre, 1974 (inv. no. RF 35.834)

Bibliography:
Robaut, 1905, vol. IV, no. 2921 (repro.); Bacou, 1974, pp. 308–9, fig. 12

Alfred Robaut, the first great biographer of Corot and one of his friends, states in his 1905 catalogue that this beautiful drawing, which he owned, was executed in Douai in December 1859. The artist, already well known and sought after by the public, had exhibited six paintings that year in the Salon. The most innovative of them, *Landscape with Figures,* also entitled *The Toilette* (1859, Paris, Salon, no. 691), is related in its conception to the drawing shown here with its same deliberately vertical composition broken by the sweeps of stately tree trunks.

From 1848 on, Corot used charcoal more and more. This medium, which until then had been reserved for academic studies, allowed him to play with intense blacks in order to suggest a poetic and melancholy atmosphere, which characterized his work from this period on.

A.S.

Cabinet des Dessins, Musée du Louvre, Paris

Jean-Baptiste-Camille Corot

## VII-15
## Young Woman Seated in a Mournful Pose

c. 1870
Pencil, pen, and ink
42 × 30.5 cm

Provenance:
Corot sale, Paris, May 31–June 2, 1875 (stamp omitted; *see* Robaut, 1905, vol. IV, no. 3026); Alfred Robaut; P. Jamot; bequest to the Louvre, 1941 (inv. no. RF 29.288)

Exhibitions:
1962, Paris, Louvre, Cabinet des Dessins, no. 88; 1975, Paris, Orangerie, no. 166 (repro.)

Bibliography:
Robaut and Moreau-Nélaton, 1905, vol. IV, no. 3026 (repro.); Benoist, 1926, p. 171

Although Corot clearly favored the use of soft, smudged charcoal lines late in his career (*see* no. VII-14), he did not abandon the sharp outlines of pen and pencil. Around 1870—and even later—there appear many drawings similar to this one in which the execution is loose and there is attention to detail. The artist placed his figures against a landscape transplanted

VII-15

from Italy: the melancholy young woman here may be an evocation of music, poetry, or the theater.

A.S.

Cabinet des Dessins, Musée du Louvre, Paris

Thomas Couture

## VII-16
## Study for "The Baptism of the Prince Imperial"

c. 1856
Black crayon on blue-gray paper
31.5 × 41.5 cm

Provenance:
Shepherd Gallery, New York; The *Forbes* Magazine Collection (inv. no. P 74010-D)

According to his customary method, Couture conceived his vast composition of *The Baptism of the Prince Imperial* (see nos. VI-31–VI-35) with the help of numerous sketches and studies. "The amount of effort that went into the preparation of each idea for a work is really extraordinary," noted Roger Ballu in the foreword to the catalogue of the 1880 Couture exhibition (1880, Paris, Palais de l'Industrie, pp. x–xi). "He surrounded himself with every conceivable document that nature could sup-

ply: studies of arms and hands, studies of feet and legs, studies of details or the entire composition—one right after the other. On the whole these are superb studies, with powerful linearity and striking solidity. Through the intensity of their composition and execution some of them are finished pictures in their own right."

The principal participants in *The Baptism of the Prince Imperial* were painstakingly studied, first in pencil heightened with white, and then as oil sketches. But first of all, Couture made schematic drawings of groups or poses, as seen in this drawing, which is a quick sketch for the right side of the composition. One can see in the foreground the outlines of three kneeling women of the court holding the baby Prince Imperial, and of Monseigneur Sibour, surrounded by a number of prelates and choirboys. The reverse of this sketch shows a very schematic sketch of the officiating clergy.

A.S.

The *Forbes* Magazine Collection, New York

Paul-Alfred de Curzon

## VII-17
## The Woods of Castel Fusano

1869
Signed, lower right, with monogram
Charcoal
38.5 × 52.4 cm

Provenance:
Paravey coll., M. Raynaud; acquired by the Musée Tavet-Delacour, 1972 (inv. no. D. 72.1.7)

Exhibitions:
1869, Paris, Salon, no. 2645; 1976, Pontoise, no. 16, pl. 6

Bibliography:
De Curzon, 1916, vol. II, no. 560

When Curzon executed this melancholy landscape, he undoubtedly used sketches made during the three years he spent in Italy as a *pensionnaire* at the Académie de France (1850–53). Indeed, in the book that Curzon's son devoted to him, one finds mention of drawings done at Castel Fusano, a "vast villa in the middle of a stand of immense umbrella pines and green oaks" (de Curzon, 1916, vol. I, p. 96). These are either notations sketched on the pages of a notebook or more elaborate drawings (de Curzon, 1916, vol. II, pp. 298, 310, nos. 2317–21).

Along with watercolor, charcoal was one of Curzon's favorite techniques: "He used it in two ways; first, as a rough sketch, more or less developed, making a record, which would later prompt his imagination or memory, for the possible development (or rejection) of scenery, figures, or landscapes. Second, he used it for finished works, in the manner of those Romantic-looking black crayon drawings that caught one's attention in his first exhibitions. But unless he was using these drawings specifically to prepare a painting, he soon abandoned figures and tended more and more toward landscapes. These landscapes were very rarely

VII-16

VII-17

'invented'—ordinarily they were borrowed from some drawing, sketch, or painted study, with new proportions and with more vivid effects of light and sky, more suggestive of impressions. They were works which belonged to a separate genre. Despite their modest proportions, their highly finished execution made them just as capable of evoking a vast horizon or an imposing site as of capturing the intimacy of undergrowth or of an arbor" (de Curzon, 1916, vol. II, p. 264).

Even though in 1869 Curzon was principally working on four cartoons for the Opéra, which were the basis for a mosaic on the ceiling of the outer Foyer (the canvases are in the museum in Poitiers), he nonetheless did not abandon his landscapes. In the Salon, Curzon exhibited a *View of the Sorrento Coast (Bay of Naples)* (no. 592) and *The Banks of the Clain at Poitiers* (no. 593). These were favorably received—the critics appreciated the firmness of line, solidity of colors, and the grandeur of their style.

A.S.

Musée Tavet-Delacour, Pontoise

Charles-François Daubigny

## VII-18
## A Gathering under the Trees

c. 1865–67
Black crayon
25.7 × 40.9 cm

Provenance:
Daubigny studio sale, May 6–11, 1878 (collector's mark, lower right, Lugt 518); E. Calando (collector's mark, lower left, Lugt 837); acquired by the Louvre, 1970 (inv. no. RF 34.536)

Exhibition:
1972, Darmstadt, no. 21 (repro.)

There are great similarities between this drawing and the 1867 painting that Bazille (q.v.) exhibited in the Salon of 1868 under the title *The Family X (Family Gathering on the Terrace of the Château de Méric; Jeu de Paume)*. All the work for this painting was done out of doors. During the same period Monet (q.v.), on his part, was painting his large canvas *Women in the Garden* (1867; Jeu de Paume). A contemporary and friend of the artists of the Barbizon School, Daubigny was as adept as they were in working out of doors. He was thus a link between the Realism of Courbet or Daumier and pre-Impressionism. To suggest his figures here,

Daubigny used a "loose" stroke which enabled him to define the forms without imprisoning them, reminding one of Daumier's hand. In contrast, the rapid and elliptical treatment of trees as well as the suggestion of water are quite characteristic of Daubigny's drawing style.

A.S.

Cabinet des Dessins, Musée du Louvre, Paris

---

## Honoré Daumier

*Marseilles 1808–1879 Valmondois*

*Daumier's father, Jean-Baptiste-Louis, a glazier and picture-frame maker, also a poet and playwright, had settled in Paris in 1815; five years later he secured for his son a position as an errand-boy in a bailiff's office and later as a clerk to a bookseller. But young Honoré much preferred to study drawing. In 1822 he became a student of Alexandre Lenoir, a painter and former director of the Musée des Monuments Français, who loved sculpture. He then worked at the Académie Suisse and served his apprenticeship in lithography with Zéphirin-Felix Belliard.*

*Daumier's first lithographs were published in* La Silhouette *and* La Caricature *after the Revolution of 1830. He served a six-month sentence in jail for his caricature of Louis Philippe entitled* Gargantua (La Caricature, *December 15, 1831). Upon his release the artist became more and more involved in lithography. Because of censorship he gradually moved from political caricature* (The Legislative Body, *1834;* Rue Transnonain, *published April 15, 1834) to caricature of social manners* (Robert Macaire, *1836;* Marital Customs, *1840;* Old Story, *1844;* Lawyers and Justice, *1845–48, etc.).*

*Daumier did not start painting until 1848; that year he entered a competition for sketches for a painting celebrating the Republic (Louvre); the repression during the days of insurrection in June inspired his moving theme,* The Emigrants. *From then on Daumier executed paintings and prints. He became acquainted with such Barbizon painters as Corot, Millet, and Théodore Rousseau (q.q.v.), and during a three-year period when his collaboration with* Le Charivari *was interrupted (1860–63), he completed some of his masterpieces in oil (themes of actors, travelers in railway cars, and card players). His last years were unhappy: in dire poverty, he was losing his eyesight; hence the poignant and pathetic mood of his late works, in particular, the "Don Quixote" series. In 1865 he retired near Auvers-sur-Oise, at Valmondois, where Corot had bought him a house. He died there on February 11, 1879, and left*

VII-18

at the same time. K.E. Maison (1968, vol. II, nos. 47, 48, 50) catalogues three other sketches relating to this lithograph in which Carrier-Belleuse is portrayed full face.

Though still sketchy, this head is nonetheless interpreted with an expressive strength characteristic of Daumier's elliptical style at the end of his life. As Claude Roger-Marx observed in his preface to the catalogue of the Daumier exhibition in Paris in 1934: "A square but a few centimeters on a side often encloses a sketch so complete, so definitive, that it contains the substance of a great work, in the same way that the figurines that Rodin held in the hollow of his hands were to become statues."

A.S.

Cabinet des Dessins, Musée du Louvre, Paris

Eugène Delacroix

behind a considerable œuvre: *thousands of lithographs and wood engravings, many drawings, some two hundred paintings, and sculptures.*

A.S.

Bibliography:
Adhémar, 1954; Maison, 1968

Honoré Daumier

## VII-19
## Portrait of Albert-Ernest Carrier-Belleuse

1863
Signed, lower right: h.D.
Charcoal
29.7 × 21.5 cm

Provenance:
Heirs of Carrier-Belleuse; Claude Roger-Marx; gift "in memory of his father, his brother, and his son, who died for France" to the Louvre, 1974 (inv. no. RF 35.836)

Exhibitions:
1878, Paris, Galerie Durand-Ruel, no. 215; 1927, Paris, Galerie Dru, no. 15; 1934, Paris, Orangerie, no. 149; 1937, Philadelphia, no. 52; 1958, Paris, Bibliothèque Nationale, no. 194

Bibliography:
Fuchs, 1927, no. 177 (repro.); Adhémar, 1954, pl. 29; Maison, 1968, vol. II, no. 49, pl. 9; Bacou, 1974, pp. 307–9, fig. 11

This is one of the studies for the caricatured lithographic portrait of the sculptor Carrier-

Belleuse (q.v.) which Daumier published in *Boulevard* on May 24, 1863. Carrier-Belleuse had just been successful at the Salon with his *Bacchante* (no. 2275), acquired by the Emperor and placed in the Tuileries gardens. Daumier's lithograph showed him working on two busts

VII-19

## VII-20
## Portrait of Alfred Bruyas

1853
Signed, lower left: Eug. Delacroix
Pencil
27.5 × 11.5 cm

Provenance:
Gift of the artist to Bruyas upon completion of the painted portrait; bequest to the Musée Fabre, 1876 (inv. no. 876-3-103)

Exhibition:
1939, Paris, Orangerie, no. 143

Bibliography:
Bruyas, 1854, p. 49; Bruyas, 1876, pp. 346, 352, no. 71; Lafenestre and Michel, 1878, p. 282, no. 140; Robaut and Chesneau, 1885, no. 1208; Joubin, 1929, p. 12, repro. p. 53; Escholier, 1926–29, vol. III, repro. facing p. 170; Delacroix, 1936–38, vol. III, p. 144; Claparède, 1961, repro. p. 42; Claparède, 1962, no. 58 (repro.)

Alfred Bruyas (1821–1876), a native of Montpellier," was a curious art lover. He lived in Paris in the middle of the last century among the Romantic painters and the first Realists. He went from Delacroix to Courbet, and walked through their studios, displaying the elegance of a rich and consumptive man, his thin frame laden down with plaids and overcoats, his melancholy and his highly refined tastes. He requested his portrait of all those whom he admired" (see 1939, Paris, Orangerie, p. 10). Courbet painted four portraits of Bruyas, the most famous of which is the 1854 painting entitled *The Encounter,* or *Bonjour, Monsieur Courbet* (Musée Fabre, Montpellier).

This moving drawing is a study for Delacroix's 1853 portrait, also in the Musée Fabre. It was difficult at first for Bruyas to convince

VII-20

as a flame, sudden as a vision. Despite the instructive weaknesses and the systematic excesses of this drawing, especially risky in a portrait, never was Delacroix so harmonious in his lines as here..." (Bruyas, 1876, p. 340).

A.S.

Musée Fabre, Montpellier

Eugène Delacroix

## VII-21
## Study for "The Ascent to Calvary"

1859
Pencil
45 × 38 cm

Provenance:
Delacroix studio sale, Paris, February 22–27, 1864 (collector's mark, lower right, Lugt 838); Count

Doria; Claude Roger-Marx; gift "in memory of his father, his brother, and his son, who died for France," to the Louvre, 1974 (inv. no. RF 35.830)

Bibliography:
Robaut and Chesneau, 1885, no. 1378; Sérullaz, 1974, p. 303, fig. 3

Along with the pen drawing on glazed brown tracing paper, also in the Louvre (RF 1712), this is the only known study for the painting exhibited in the Salon of 1859 under the title *The Ascent to Calvary: Christ Faltering beneath the Cross* (no. 819). In addition, the Salon's catalogue indicates that "this composition was to have been carried out on a large scale at Saint Sulpice, in the baptismal chapel, whose purpose has now been changed" (*see* no. VII-22).

Through the intermediary of a painter and art lover from Metz, Charles-Laurent Maréchal (q.v.), with whom Delacroix maintained a friendship, the painting was acquired in 1861 by the city of Metz for the sum of 3,000 francs (Bellard, 1950, pp. 261–63). Baudelaire, once again, showed an almost unconditional admi-

VII-21

Delacroix to do his portrait, because, as Théophile Silvestre related, Delacroix "knew that while he had been blessed with the talents of an inventor, he had been denied the mental serenity and manual precision required of a portrait painter" (Bruyas, 1876, p. 342). After the two men met again unexpectedly on January 18, 1853, the artist suddenly made up his mind: "Come see me tomorrow; I will do your portrait."

Although the portrait was probably begun at the end of January, it was not completed until May. On March 9, Delacroix wrote to Bruyas: "Monsieur, would you agree to come tomorrow morning, Thursday, so that we can get back to work on your portrait? Excuse the interruption forced upon me by the necessity of working on my paintings for the Salon. Still, thanks to the drawing I made of you, you will find that I have made much progress on your portrait, and I hope that I will need only a few more sittings to finish it...' (Delacroix, 1936–38, vol. III, p. 144).

Indeed, there are only slight variations between the drawing and the painting—the model's melancholy and sickly expression is depicted here with great acuity. This "first scrawl" wrote Silvestre (Bruyas, 1876, p. 352), "this is the drawing of Delacroix, that is, it is the rapid flourish of a genius who is as naïve as he is refined, but who is always feverish and breathless. For him the most settled form in the calmest face is still as restless as a wave, glowing

ration for the religious works that Delacroix submitted to the Salon (*The Ascent to Calvary, The Entombment,* and *Saint Sebastian*): "The imagination of Delacroix! Never has it flinched before the arduous peaks of religion! The heavens belong to it, no less than hell, war, Olympus and love! In him you have the model of the painter-poet. He is indeed one of the rare elect, and the scope of his mind embraces religion in its domain" (Baudelaire, 1965, p. 166).

Other critics, however, were less enthusiastic: "Has death... struck M. Eugène Delacroix? I mean that premature death which paralyzes the hand, closes the eyes, deprives the mind of the notion of the just and the true. What are these ghostly paintings that are being exhibited under his name?" exclaimed Maxime du Camp (1859, p. 32). The main objection was the too "sketchy" character of the works.

Emile Perrin, in the *Revue Européenne* (June 15, 1854), wrote: "*The Ascent to Calvary* is the sketch for a composition which was to have been executed on a large scale, in a chapel of Saint Sulpice. It is regrettable that this project was never carried out—the figure of Christ succumbing under the weight of the Cross is admirable."

Such praise may well be applied to the drawing (which is only roughly sketched out in the background at the left and toward the upper right), where the attention focuses on the central group with Christ faltering on the ground. Although the essential lines of the painting are found here, the somewhat tighter composition of the drawing allows for a greater concentration on the action, thus increasing its emotional impact.

A.S.

Cabinet des Dessins, Musée du Louvre, Paris

Eugène Delacroix

## VII-22
## Heliodorus Expelled from the Temple (Study for the Church of Saint Sulpice)

c. 1861
Inscribed in artist's hand, at bottom: voir Jean Duvet pour les anges
Pencil
58.2 × 39.5 cm

Provenance:
Delacroix studio sale, Paris, February 22–27, 1864, part of no. 298 (collector's mark, lower right, Lugt 838); Dauzats coll.; Georges Aubry; Maurice Gobin; Philip Hofer; gift to the Fogg Art Museum, 1934 (inv. no. 1934.4)

VII-22

Exhibitions:
1925, Paris, Galerie Dru, no. 121; 1930, Paris, Louvre, no. 501; 1955, Cambridge, no. 31; 1963, Paris, Louvre, no. 513

Bibliography:
Robaut and Chesneau, 1885, no. 1333; Martine and Marotte, 1928, pl. 29; Escholier, 1926–29, vol. III, repro. p. 93; Graber, 1929, pl. 57b; Mongan and Sachs, 1940, vol. I, p. 307, no. 685, vol. III, fig. 359; Sérullaz, 1963, no. 512 (repro.)

From October 1849 until July 1861, while Delacroix was working on the ceiling of the Galerie d'Apollon in the Louvre (1850) and on the decoration of the Salon de la Paix in the Hôtel de Ville (1852), he began to concentrate his efforts on a commission by the Ministry of the Interior for the decoration of a chapel in the Church of Saint Sulpice. Originally this chapel, the first on the right, was to have contained the baptismal font, but it was later dedicated to the Holy Angels, which determined Delacroix's choice of subjects. On the ceiling he portrayed *Saint Michael Overthrowing the Demon*, an attached oval canvas, and on the side walls *Heliodorus Expelled from the Temple* and *Jacob Wrestling with the Angel*, painted in oil and wax. Here again he was assisted by his pupil and collaborator, Pierre Andrieu, as well as by Louis Boulangé, who worked on the ornamentation. Delacroix, already ill, put all his effort into this project, and through his correspondence one can follow the progression of the work. A significant number of preparatory drawings, from the most rapid first sketches to detailed analyses of ornamental motifs, are in the Louvre, but the two studies showing the principal scenes in total belong to the Fogg Art Museum.

This decoration, completed in 1861, was Delacroix's last undertaking. He died two years later. The reception given the work was mixed: in most of the accounts, there is a combination of praise and criticism. Paul de Saint-Victor's evaluation in *La Presse*, February 4, 1862, summarizes it well: "The master gives of himself completely in his last work, with its superior beauties and its excessive faults, its great imagination and its structural disorder. He looks for bearing and character as much as he scorns correctness and propriety, covering crude forms with magnificent color. In short, he is like a great barbaric poet."

A.S.

Fogg Art Museum, Harvard University, Cambridge, Massachusetts, Gift of Philip Hofer

Jules-Elie Delaunay

## VII-23
## Study of a Female Nude

c. 1860s
Black crayon, heightened with white, on tracing paper, backed
21.4 × 43.2 cm

Provenance:
Part of a bequest of 72 drawings by the artist to the Musées Nationaux, 1893 (Delaunay mark, lower right, Lugt 665); Musée du Luxembourg (Luxembourg mark, Lugt 1899); transferred to the Louvre (inv. no. RF 1794)

This drawing, with its sharp, clean lines, is a study for an unfinished picture representing *The Death of the Nymph Hesperia* (Delaunay studio sale, Paris, 1891, no. 7). The composition returns to a theme that Delaunay had painted in Rome in 1859, *The Nymph Hesperia Fleeing the Pursuit of Aesacus, Son of Priam*, for which the Nantes museum has a series of preliminary drawings.

Delaunay's stay in Italy reinforced his predilection for mythological themes: the nymph Hesperia is one of those that especially inspired him. As Georges Lafenestre indicated in the introduction to the catalogue of the Delaunay studio sale: "This graceful elegy is one of the four or five subjects which never ceased to haunt his restless, constant imagination; he made countless variations without ever reaching the point at which he considered one of them definitive" (1891, pp. 11–12).

A.S.

Cabinet des Dessins, Musée du Louvre, Paris

Gustave-Paul Doré

## VII-24
## Gathering the Flocks in the Bois de Boulogne

1870
Signed and dated, lower left: G. Doré 1870
Brown wash and white gouache on brown paper
64.5 × 97.5 cm

Provenance:
Sale of drawings and watercolors by Gustave Doré, Paris, May 22, 1875, no. 14; Doré studio sale, Paris, April 10–15, 1885, no. 71 (collector's mark, lower right, Lugt 681a); Mme Henri-Boisnard, great-niece of the artist; private coll., Paris; acquired by the Louvre, 1973 (inv. no. RF 35.722)

Exhibition:
1932, Paris, Petit Palais, no. 311

Bibliography:
Leblanc, 1931, p. 503; A. Sérullaz, 1973, pp. 117–18 (repro.)

Exceptional as much for its dimensions as for its subject matter and the distinction of its style; this drawing belongs to a series of compositions of equal importance which Doré executed between 1870 and 1871, inspired by different events of the siege of Paris and by the Commune (*see* catalogue of Doré studio sale, Paris, April 10–15, 1885, nos. 72–76, 78, 79, 81–83). Of all the subjects he treated, this one is probably the most anecdotal. However, the artist conceived a fantastic work in which his visionary spirit expressed itself completely.

VII-23

VII-24

One cannot fail to be struck by the hallucinatory quality of this "sea" of cattle and sheep crowding and jostling each other on all sides, whereas the silhouettes of soldiers on horseback, visible in the background against the light, accentuate the almost unreal appearance of the scene. Thus the illustrator of Rabelais, Balzac, Coleridge, Cervantes, and Shakespeare, among others, found in the more immediate and dramatic contemporary events a new pretext for letting his extraordinary imagination roam. Strangely, the visions of Doré and the Goncourts are parallel here (although the Goncourts were fierce critics of Doré's art), for their *Journal* describes the same scene: "Sunday, August 28, 1870. In the Bois de Boulogne, in a place where there had never been anything but silk among the green of the trees, I see a large bit of blue smock: the back of a shepherd near a little column of bluish smoke; and all around sheep are grazing, for lack of grass, on the foliage of forgotten fagots. In the lanes are open carriages. The large oxen, confused and disoriented, stray in herds.

"Sheep are everywhere. Here, at the edge of a path, lying on his side, is a dead ram. His head, with its curved horns, is flattened and oozes a bit of watery blood, enlarging a red spot in the sand—poor head, scenting, as if to kiss each passing ewe.

"In a moment, panic strikes. Through all the openings in the wood, through all the leafy gaps, one glimpses a herd of one hundred thousand bewildered beasts stampeding toward a gateway, toward an exit, like the avalanche of a Castiglione drawing. And in the sunlit dust, on the slope of the fortifications, the crowding lines of innumerable sheep seem to be small superimposed walls, which a blur of the eye would run together.

"And the Auteuil pond is half tainted by the ewes who drink, kneeling in its reeds" (Goncourt and Goncourt, 1959, vol. II, p. 586).

A.S.

Cabinet des Dessins, Musée du Louvre, Paris

VII-25

Henri Fantin-Latour

## VII-25
## The Embroiderers

c. 1860s
Charcoal on gray paper
22.7 × 29 cm

Provenance:
Musée du Luxembourg; transferred to the Louvre, 1930 (inv. no. RF 12.773)
Exhibition:
1972, Darmstadt, no. 37 (repro.)
Bibliography:
Fantin-Latour, 1911, no. 201

Fantin-Latour's first submission to the Salon, in 1859, was a painting showing two women in an interior, one reading and the other embroidering (Jullien, 1909, repro. facing p. 20). The work was refused. Subsequently, and up until 1881, Fantin returned several times to this theme of readers and embroiderers. In addition to this drawing, the Louvre owns another charcoal and a glazed watercolor (RF 12.774, RF 12.775) in which the artist also used his two sisters, Nathalie and Marie, as his models. The use of charcoal lends itself particularly well to the translation of the silent and contemplative atmosphere of the scene. Here there is a sense of Fantin's attachment to daily life, which constitutes one of the aspects of his complex temperament.

A.S.

Cabinet des Dessins, Musée du Louvre, Paris

VII-26

Hippolyte-Jean Flandrin

## VII-26
## Apostle (Study for "The Mission of the Apostles" for Saint Germain des Prés)

1852
Dated, lower left: X^{bre} 1852
Pencil
30 × 13 cm

Provenance:
Flandrin studio sale, May 15–17, 1865 (collector's mark, upper right, Lugt 933); gift of the artist's widow to the Galerie Bruyas; Alfred Bruyas; bequest to the Musée Fabre, 1876 (inv. no. 876-3-111)
Bibliography:
Bruyas, 1876, p. 496, no. 91; Claparède, 1962, no. 4

Because of its date, this drawing has been associated with the studies for the Church of Saint Vincent de Paul. Although Flandrin does not seem to have begun work on the nave of Saint Germain des Prés until 1856, there is no doubt that this figure appears, although reversed and with some variations, in *The Mission of the Apostles (see* no. VI-53). It is not unlikely that Flandrin reused an earlier study and integrated it in his picture. This work is very characteristic of the drawings of Flandrin, some-

VII-27

what bloodless and, in fact, sometimes laborious; yet one can see in this study how he was able to acquire considerable strength through the determination of his style.

O.S.

Musée Fabre, Montpellier

Hippolyte-Jean Flandrin

## VII-27
## Christ (Study for "The Mission of the Apostles" for Saint Germain des Prés)

1856–61
Pencil on blue paper
30.5 × 23.2 cm

Provenance:
Flandrin studio sale, May 15–17, 1865, part of no. 113 (collector's mark, lower right, Lugt 933); Haro coll.; private coll., purchased, 1977 (collector's mark, lower right, not in Lugt)

This drawing is a preparatory study for the decoration of the ninth bay in the Church of Saint Germain des Prés: *The Mission of the Apostles (see* no. VI-53). This is an early conception since Flandrin ultimately modified Christ's gesture—Christ raises up the key instead of holding it out to Saint Peter. The earlier gesture resembled the one Ingres had used in his treatment of the same subject (Musée Ingres, Montauban), yet gives less prominence to the key.

The four other drawings belonging to lot 113 of the Flandrin studio sale, which are in private collections in Paris, all relate to the same composition. One is a study of the overall composition, one for the figure of Saint Peter, another of the group of apostles on the right, and the last of Saint Peter's head.

L.-A.P.

Private Collection

Eugène Fromentin

## VII-28
## Study for "Falconry in Algeria: The Quarry"

1863
Pencil
60 × 38.5 cm

VII-28

Provenance:
Fromentin studio sale, Paris, January 30–February 3, 1877 (collector's mark, lower right, Lugt 957); private coll. (collector's mark, lower right, not in Lugt)

Bibliography:
Jullian, 1977, repro. p. 52

This is a study, with some variations, for the falconer on horseback at the far right of the painting exhibited in the Salon of 1863 under the title *Falconry in Algeria: The Quarry* (no. VI-57).

A.S.

Private Collection

Jean-Léon Gérôme

## VII-29
## Two Turkish Soldiers Playing Checkers

1856
Signed and dated, at left: J.L. Gérôme 1856
Black and red crayon, heightened with white, over traces of pencil, on buff paper
19.6 × 27.5 cm

Provenance:
Scott and Fowles, New York; Robert S. Clark, 1929; Sterling and Francine Clark Art Institute, 1955 (inv. no. 1656)

Exhibition:
1968, Bloomington, no. 59 (repro.)

Bibliography:
Catalogue, Williamstown, Clark Art Institute, 1964, vol. I, no. 203, vol. II, pl. 93

In 1856, thanks to 20,000 francs that came to him from the state's purchase of *The Age of Augustus* (Musée de Picardie, Amiens), Gérôme spent eight months in Egypt in the company of Frédéric Masson, Emile Augier, and the sculptor Frédéric-Auguste Bartholdi. He brought back various compositions inspired by picturesque street scenes. Four of them, exhibited at the Salon of 1857, were very well received by the critics. *L'Artiste* of July 5, 1875, printed a highly favorable commentary by Théophile Gautier: "Gérôme was the first to see the Orient as a history painter; he looked for style where others, for whom we do not lack admiration, sought only color". Indeed, Gautier gave Gérôme credit for a variety of talents: "An eye which perceives rapidly and accurately, a hand which executes knowingly and with assurance, etching every detail with a clarity as imperturbable as that of a daguerreotype and, above all, with a meaning which we may call, for want of a better designation, exotic. This enables him to discover immediately the characteristic differences between one race and another" (pp. 246–47).

The subject of this drawing, which was engraved by Henry Valentin, reappears in a painting by Gérôme signed and dated 1859, *Arnauts Playing Checkers* (location unknown; Catalogue, Williamstown, Clark Art Institute, 1964, vol. I, fig. 82). Because of its elaborate style, the drawing does not seem to be a preparatory study for the painting.

A.S.

Sterling and Francine Clark Art Institute, Williamstown, Massachusetts

Jean-Léon Gérôme

## VII-30
## The Old Arab

1855–70
Signed, at left: J.L. GEROME
Watercolor
29.9 × 23.5 cm

Provenance:
Geraldine Rockefeller Dodge; sale, New York, Sotheby Parke Bernet, October 7, 1975, no. 345 (repro.); purchased by the Yale University Art Gallery, 1975 (inv. no. 1975. 90)

This portrait of an old Arab is a remarkable example of the virtuosity with which Gérôme handled the medium of watercolor. It captures our attention as much by the manner in which he has rendered the smallest details of the man's costume and the decorative background as by the sensitive interpretation of the facial expression. The artist does not seem to have executed this watercolor toward a particular end (no painting of the subject exists). Although we cannot date it precisely, it seems reasonable, on stylistic grounds, to place it between the years 1855 and 1870.

A.S.

Yale University Art Gallery, New Haven, Everett V. Meeks, B.A. 1901, Fund

VII-29

VII-30

VII-31

## Gustave Guillaumet

*Puteaux 1840–1887 Paris*

*In 1857 Guillaumet entered the Ecole des Beaux-Arts, where he was the pupil of Picot, Abel de Pujol, and Barrias. He first showed at the Salon in 1861; the following year he took second place in the Prix de Rome. But instead of going to Italy as planned, he changed his itinerary at the last minute and sailed from Marseilles for North Africa, where he would return eleven times in twenty years. Guillaumet was fascinated by the desert, to which he devoted two books,* Lettres d'un voyageur *and* Tableaux algériens *(appearing in 1888, a year after his death), and it was the essential inspiration of his work, although he can be compared to Fromentin (q.v.) only from a literary point of view. True, he was an Orientalist, but actually he was more interested in depicting the life of simple people in the douars than the nobler, more adventurous life of the nomadic horseman. Numerous drawings done in the course of his various trips to Algeria — a representative selection of which is in the Louvre — make it possible for*

*us to follow Guillaumet's work on a motif even before he started the minute preparation for his paintings.*

*During the first half of the twentieth century, Guillaumet unjustly fell into oblivion, although during his lifetime he had attained considerable fame. He is among those painters whom present-day criticism must try to restore to a worthier position.*
A.S.

Bibliography:
Renan, 1887

Gustave Guillaumet

## VII-31
## Study for "Famine in Algeria"

1869
Signed, lower left: G. Guillaumet
Charcoal and sanguine, heightened with white chalk, on gray-green paper, squared for transfer
116 × 80 cm

Provenance:
Private coll., purchased, 1977

This powerful, pathos-ridden drawing is a study for the large painting (309 × 244 cm) that was exhibited in the Salon of 1869 under the title *Famine* (no. 1127); it was donated by the artist's widow to the museum in Oran in 1888 (since 1930 it has been in the Musée National des Beaux-Arts, Algiers). The two figures shown here can be found on the right side of the picture: an Arab, leaning against a house and holding up the arm of a nude adolescent who is half-collapsed on the ground. The profoundly dramatic composition of *Famine in Algeria,* reminiscent of Baron Gros's *Pest House at Jaffa* (Louvre), Théodore Géricault's *Raft of the Medusa* (Louvre), and works by Delacroix, evokes the terrible scenes Guillaumet must have witnessed on his fifth trip to Algeria (1868) when the country was ravaged by drought and the starving population wandered about the countryside and the towns in search of sustenance as described in *Tableaux algériens* (Guillaumet, 1888, pp. 233–36).

The Louvre has two drawings related to this painting, done in the same technique as this. The first, signed and dated 1868, relates to the three figures holding out their arms toward a loaf of bread being passed out of a dormer window (RF 12.297); the second, also signed, but undated, shows the dead woman and child in the left foreground (RF 12.390).

A.S.

Private Collection

---

## Constantin Guys

*Vlissingen (The Netherlands) 1802–1892 Paris*

*The name of Guys immediately evokes the Second Empire, of which he was the abundant and lively chronicler. Likewise, it is almost impossible to dissociate his name from that of Baudelaire, for the writer's important study, published under the title "Peintre de la vie moderne" (Baudelaire, 1863) contributed greatly to the artist's renown. There is no doubt that Guys was gifted, yet he remained a "minor master."*

*Compared to the length of his lifetime, the knowledge we have of Guys is limited. According to the photographer Nadar (q.v.), who was one of his few friends, Guys joined Lord Byron in his support of the Greek War of Independence against Turkey (1823). Then, about the 1840s, he was working in London as a correspondent for* The Illustrated London News. *In this capacity he followed the events of 1848 in France, and later filed on-the-spot reports of the major events of the Crimean War (1853–55). After having traveled throughout Europe and in the Orient, he returned to France for good around 1862. He continued to draw throughout his life, and led a quiet life in Paris, carefully avoiding all publicity.*

*In his preface to the* Fleurs du Mal *(1868), Théophile Gautier related how Baudelaire had been taken with this "mysterious personnage.... Guys was not what one would usually call an artist, but he had the particular gift for capturing the essence of things in a few minutes. In one glance, with unequaled clairvoyance, he discerned in everything its characteristic aspect—and that one alone—and placed it prominently, neglecting, either instinctively or on purpose, its subordinate features.... A talent of this nature could not fail to charm Baudelaire, who did, in fact, make much of Guys."*

A.S.

Bibliography:
Konody, 1930; Jamar-Rolin, 1956

VII-32

Constantin Guys

## VII-32
## The Box of the Emperor

c. 1855-60
Watercolor, with slight touches of pen and ink
21.6 × 34 cm

Provenance:
G. Lévy; purchased by the Louvre, 1942 (inv. no. RF 29.337); deposited at Compiègne, 1965

Exhibitions:
1937, Paris, Musée des Arts Décoratifs, no. 7; 1968–69, Paris, Petit Palais, no. 560 (repro.)

Bibliography:
Konody, 1930, pp. 113–14

This is one of the watercolors that inspired Baudelaire's lyrical description of the artist's work in chapter 7, "Pomp and Circumstance," of his study, "Peintre de la vie moderne": "In M. G.'s collections one frequently meets with the Emperor of the French, whose countenance he has reduced, without prejudicing the likeness, to an infallible formula, which he executes with the sureness of a flourish of his pen.... One these water-colours in particular has dazzled me by its magnetic character. In the front of a box of heavy and princely richness, the Empress appears in a quiet and restful attitude; the Emperor leans forward slightly as though he wanted to get a better view of the theatre; below, two guardsmen, standing in

military and almost hieratic immobility, receive on their brilliant uniforms the splashes of the footlights. Behind the streak of fire, in the ideal atmosphere of the stage, the actors sing, recite and gesticulate harmoniously; on the other side yawns an abyss of vague light, a circular space filled with human figures, tier upon tier: brilliancy and the public" (Konody, 1930, pp. 113–14; *see* Baudelaire, 1976, vol. II, p. 706). At right, the silhouette of the painter Delacroix (q.v.) can be discerned.

A.S.

Cabinet des Dessins, Musée du Louvre, Paris

Constantin Guys

## VII-33
## Woman in Blue Crinoline on a Yellow Background

c. 1860
Watercolor, heightened with gouache
31 × 22 cm

Provenance:
Musée Carnavalet; deposited in the Musée du Petit Palais, 1934 (inv. no. PPD 1525[5])

Exhibitions:
1937, Paris, Musée des Arts Décoratifs, no. 110; 1959, Paris, Musée Jacquemart-André, no. 59; 1968–69, Paris, Petit Palais, no. 570

Bibliography:
Geffroy, 1920, repro. p. 65; Konody, 1930, repro. p. 65; Sérullaz, 1966, no. 58 (repro.)

This is one of the most successful of Guys's watercolors. Baudelaire noted that Guys "attaches immense importance to the backgrounds which, whether they be strong or light, always have a quality and character to suit the figures" (Konody, 1930, p. 89). For Guys, "woman is, no doubt, a light, a glance, an invitation to happiness, a word sometimes; but she is above all a general harmony, not only in her deportment and in the movement of her limbs, but also in the muslins, the gauzes, the vast and iridescent clouds of stuffs in which she enwraps herself, which are like the attributes and the pedestal of her divinity.... What poet would dare, in painting the pleasure caused by the apparition of a beauty, to separate woman from her costume? Where is the man who, in the street, in the theatre, or in the park has not enjoyed, in the most disinterested manner, a cleverly composed *toilette*, and carried away

with the impression of it an inseparable picture of the beauty of her to whom it belonged, making thus of the two—of the woman and her dress—an indivisible whole?" (Konody, 1930, p. 143; *see* Baudelaire, 1976).

A.S.

Musée du Petit Palais, Paris

---

## Henri-Joseph Harpignies

*Valenciennes 1819–1916 Saint Privé (Yonne)*

*The son of the proprietor of a "fast transport" company, Harpignies decided in 1846 to devote himself to painting, and entered the Parisian atelier of the landscape painter Jean-Alexis Achard. From May to June, 1850, he made a short trip to Germany, and at the end of the year he went to Italy, where he stayed until 1852. Later, from 1863 to 1865, he made a second visit to Italy. His debut at the Salon was in 1853, where he exhibited three paintings:*

View of the Island of Capri, Bay of Naples; Sunken Road: Morning; *and* Near Valenciennes. *That same year he probably met Corot (q.v.), whom he idolized for some time. Having taken up painting late in life, Harpignies discovered watercolor even later, but it was a technique in which he soon excelled and continued to perfect until the end of his life. His watercolors show that he paid careful attention to values and nuances without neglecting form, which remained his chief concern.*

*Harpignies lived almost a hundred years and submitted to the Salons from 1853 until 1912, but he remained untouched by the major pictorial movements of the nineteenth century. Although a contemporary and admirer of Courbet (q.v.) and of the Barbizon School, he was not influenced by them, and while strongly attracted to Corot, he still remained independent. His pursuits in the field of landscape painting preceded those of the Impressionists. However, never espousing their new vision, he remained a staunch partisan of the primacy of form over color.*

A.S.

Bibliography:
1970, Valenciennes

VII-33

Henri-Joseph Harpignies

## VII-34
## Morvan, Autumn Landscape

1868
Signed and dated, lower left: H. Harpignies, 1868; inscribed, lower right: Morvan
Watercolor
30.4 × 22 cm

Provenance:
Dr. Vincent Paulet; bequest to the Musée Fabre, 1906 (inv. no. 06-5-17)
Bibliography:
Claparède, 1962, no. 108 (repro.)

This landscape dates fom Harpignies's visit to the Morvan in the summer of 1868. Several other works, two of which appeared in the Salon of 1869—*Rocky Path in the Morvan* (no. 1153) and *The River, Morvan* (no. 1154) — bear witness to the artist's interest in this region of France. His deep and sincere love of nature permeates this landscape, from which all picturesque elements have been eliminated and in which the subtle play of coloristic values in no way detracts from the structure of the composition.

The years 1868–69 marked a stage in Harpignies's artistic development: little by little he freed himself from the ascendancy of Corot and developed his own style, and it was specifically

VII-34

Ernest Hébert

## VII-35
## Portrait of Clotilde de Savoie, Princess Napoleon

1860
Signed, lower right: E. Hébert
Black crayon, heightened with white chalk, on beige paper
32 × 24.1 cm

Provenance:
Gift of Mme Ernest Hébert to the Louvre, 1924 (inv. no. RF 6320)

His numerous portraits, more than his history paintings or his Italian subjects, are what established Hébert's fame. Under the Second Empire especially, the artist occupied a privileged position in Parisian society with his much appreciated portraits of women. This unfinished drawing is a study for the portrait hung in the 1861 Salon (no. 1464) and housed in the museum at Versailles since 1868. It represents Clotilde de Savoie, the wife of Joseph-Charles-Raoul Napoleon — whose father, Jérôme, was king of Westphalia — and the sister-in-law of Princess Mathilde. According to the gossip of the day, this young woman did not share the broad taste in art of Princess Mathilde. It is said that Clotilde was against her husband's having Ingres's *Turkish Bath* (Louvre) in his collection because of its display of nudity!

On the back of this drawing is a quick sketch for the *Portrait of Emperor Napoleon III,* painted by Hébert.

A.S.

Cabinet des Dessins, Musée du Louvre, Paris

---

*François-Joseph Heim*
*Belfort 1787–1865 Paris*

*Heim, the son of a drawing teacher at the collège of Belfort, won a first prize for drawing when he was only eleven years old. In 1803 he entered the studio of Vincent and four years later he won the Prix de Rome with* Theseus and the Minotaur *(Ecole des Beaux-Arts, Paris). After his return from Italy he exhibited at the Salon from 1812 until 1859.*

*The peak of his career was reached during the Restoration, when he received important official commissions for paintings in churches in Paris and its surroundings and, notably, in the Louvre and at*

in watercolor, which he had been practicing since 1851, that he found his most personal means of expression. It was through his watercolors and not his paintings that he would later gain the admiration of a number of English and American collectors.

A.S.

Musée Fabre, Montpellier

VII-35

Le Cᵗᵉ de Nieuwerkerke

Institut : Académie des beaux arts.

VII-36

*Versailles. The painting which he exhibited at the
Salon of 1824,* Charles X Distributing Awards at
the End of the Exposition of 1824 *(Versailles),
was an enormous success such as he was not to know
again until the Exposition Universelle of 1855,
where a retrospective of his work included seven
paintings (among them* The Sack of Jerusalem,
The Martyrdom of Saint Hippolytus, *and* The
Distribution of Awards) *and sixteen portrait
drawings.*

*Almost entirely forgotten at his death, Heim left
behind a considerable number of Biblical, mythological, and historical works. He was a highly
esteemed painter of official portraits, and his pencil
studies (most of them now in the Louvre or the Musée
Bonnat in Bayonne), have an undeniable documentary interest. They are striking examples of the
artist's power of observation and acumen. Present
day critics have begun to appreciate Heim, drawing
on the tribute paid in 1867 by Philippe de Chennevières (under the pseudonym M. de Saint-Santin)
in the* Gazette des Beaux-Arts *to "the memory of
an artist of our century who upheld the honor of and
respect for great historical painting. . . . one of the
boldest in undertaking vast compositions which go
straight to the public's heart, a proud representative
of that dwindling race which, judging from the annual Salons, threatens soon to disappear; I refer to
those who paint the noble human face."*

A.S.

Bibliography:
Lafond, 1896–97

François-Joseph Heim

## VII-36
## Portrait of the Comte de Nieuwerkerke, Member of the Académie des Beaux-Arts

1859
Signed and dated, lower right: Heim 1859
Charcoal, heightened with white, on bluish
paper
38 × 25 cm

Provenance:
Gift of the artist's widow to the Louvre, 1866 (inv.
no. MI 999)

Exhibitions:
1859, Paris, Salon, under no. 1448; 1874, Paris,
Luxembourg, no. 270; 1959, Florence, no. 237;
1968–69, Paris, Petit Palais, no. 490

Bibliography:
De Tauzia, 1879, no. 1823; Guiffrey and Marcel,
1907–38, vol. VI, no. 4776 (repro.)

From a family of Dutch origin, Alfred-
Emilien, comte de Nieuwerkerke (1811–1892),
is less known for his sculpture (notably an
equestrian statue of Napoleon I, unveiled on
August 20, 1854, at La Roche-sur-Yon) than
for his official position at the court of Napoleon III. Superintendent of Fine Arts from 1863
to 1870, Nieuwerkerke left this post when a
Ministry of Fine Arts was created, but he retained his post as director of the museums of
the Louvre, conferred upon him in 1849. With
the fall of the Second Empire, he moved to
Italy, living near Lucca at the château de Gat-
tajola.

Nieuwerkerke was a handsome man of "a
noble, free, and easy bearing" (Chennevières,
1883–89, vol. II, p. 83). Frédéric Henriet

(1893, pp. 14–15) said, somewhat maliciously, that "he could not bear to be portrayed other than buttoned up tight in official garb, his hair curled and his chest studded with medals and ribbons. He was highly offended when a famous artist, Gavarni, brought him the sketch for a portrait showing him in a dressing gown and bedroom slippers, with his hair flowing in the breeze!"

This drawing belongs to a series of sixty-four portraits, dating from 1856 to 1859, of the principal members of the Institut de France, seated and in their academicians' uniforms. The series, preserved for the most part in the Louvre (Guiffrey and Marcel, 1907–38, vol. VI, nos. 4738–4807), was exhibited at the Salon of 1859 (nos. 1434–49, four per sheet and therefore under the same number). This was a continuation of the series of drawings executed by Heim between 1827 and 1829 as antecedents of three paintings (never carried out) commissioned by the vicomte de la Rochefoucauld to represent the various branches of the Institut (Guiffrey and Marcel, 1907–38, vol. VI, nos. 4701–37). "Among those artists who are content with the natural picturesqueness of the original," Baudelaire wrote, "the most outstanding are M. Bonvin [q.v.]... and M. Heim, at whom some superficial critics have mocked in the past, and who, this year again, as in 1855, has revealed to us a marvellous understanding of the human *grimace* in a whole cavalcade of sketches. I presume that you will not take this word in a disagreeable sense. I am alluding to the natural and professional grimace which belongs to each one of us" (Baudelaire, 1965, p. 192).

A.S.

Cabinet des Dessins, Musée du Louvre, Paris

VII-37

---

## Louis-Adolphe Hervier

*Paris 1818–1879 Paris*

*Son of the miniature painter Marie-Antoine Hervier, Louis-Adolphe Hervier was trained in the studios of Léon Cogniet, Decamps (q.v.), and Eugène Isabey. The events of his forty-year-long career are still largely unknown, except for his frequent travels throughout France, especially in Normandy. In spite of his talent and the support of such critics as Théophile Gautier, Champfleury, and Philippe Burty, Hervier had no official standing, and submitted only irregularly to the Salon, beginning in 1838.*

*With the freshness of the tones of his watercolors deriving from his master Isabey, Hervier constitutes a stage in the development of nineteenth-century* French landscape painting that should not be discounted. As Gautier recognized in 1856: "M. Hervier is an original talent, persevering and serious, who should be taken as in no way inferior to Théodore Rousseau [q.v.].... He has a deep feeling for Nature, which he observes, studies, and takes by surprise when she least expects it. He does not fear criticism and allows himself the amusement of bizarre effects."

A.S.

Bibliography:
Bouyer, 1896

Louis-Adolphe Hervier

## VII-37
## A Street in Saint-Germain (Seine-et-Oise)

1866
Signed and dated in ink, lower right: Hervier–1866–; inscribed in ink, upper right: St Germain Seine et Oise 7 mai 1866
Pen and ink over traces of pencil
23.9 × 19 cm

Provenance:
Perhaps Hervier sale, Paris, February 3, 1873, no. 7;
A. Pontremoli; sale, Paris, June 11, 1924; purchased
by the Société des Amis du Louvre; gift to the Louvre
(inv. no. RF 6162)
Bibliography:
Bauduin, 1972, no. 151

Signed, dated, and located, like most of
Hervier's watercolors and drawings, this work
is characteristic of what might be called the
artist's second style. In the 1850s he gave up the
muted tones, to which he had heretofore been
attached, in favor of more intense colors. Here,
the blues, greens, and browns are brightened
by the yellows and reds of the woman and child
climbing up the steep street. A. Baudin compares this watercolor to the one preserved in
the Cabinet des Estampes of the Bibliothèque
Nationale (Rés. legs, E.B. 96), *Steep Street at
Saint-Germain*. In addition, a watercolor from
the Granville collection, *The Hay Wagon*, now
in the museum of Dijon (1976, Dijon, no. 138,
repro.), seems to portray the same street from a
different angle.

A.S.

Cabinet des Dessins, Musée du Louvre, Paris

---

## Victor Hugo

*Besançon 1802–1885 Paris*

*After a childhood during which he moved fre-
quently because of the vicissitudes of the Empire,
Hugo spent a studious adolescence in Paris, where his
vocation as a writer was rapidly confirmed. Hugo,
who in 1822 had married his childhood sweetheart,
Adèle Foucher, worked unceasingly. Launching
himself in the theater, he wrote* Cromwell *(1827),
then* Hernani *(1830) and* Marion de Lorme
*(1831), while at the same time publishing* Odes et
ballades *(1828),* Les Orientales *(1829), and* Notre
Dame de Paris *(1831). During the following years,
Hugo, increasingly preoccupied with philosophical,
religious, and political questions, moved from the
Legitimism of his youth to Bonapartism and then to
a kind of social liberalism. Though he gained many
enemies, his prestige as a writer was nevertheless
maintained in the theater and poetry. In addition,
two trips to the Rhineland inspired a travel narrative,* Le Rhin *(1842). From 1843, the year of the
accidental death of his daughter Léopoldine, until
1851, Hugo wrote much but published nothing. He
let himself be drawn into active politics, and his
Republican sympathies were to force him, after the
coup d'etat of December 2, 1851, to leave France.
The poet's period of exile was to last until 1870, for he
refused the amnesty granted on August 15, 1859, by
the Emperor to banished foes of the regime. The Hugo*

*family lived for three years on Jersey (1852–55), and
then on Guernsey (1855–70), eighteen years in
which Hugo wrote* Châtiments *(1853),* Les Contemplations *(1856),* La Légende des siècles
*(1859), and completed* Les Miserables *(1862). At
the end of 1862 the* Bibliographie de la France
*announced the publication of* Les Dessins de Victor
Hugo, *engraved by Paul Chenay, and with a preface
by Théophile Gautier. After the fall of the Empire
and the proclamation of the Republic in September
1870, Hugo returned to Paris for good in 1873,
continuing to write and draw until about 1876–78.
When he died in 1885 after a brief illness, his national funeral was like that of Romanticism itself.
But his considerable œuvre has continued to grow
through a series of posthumous publications still going on. Though the figure of the writer—both admired and reviled—is well known, that of the artist,
creator of thousands of drawings whose originality
struck all of Hugo's contemporaries, has not yet been
completely described.*

A.S.

Bibliography:
1974, London, Victoria and Albert Museum

VII-38

Victor Hugo

## VII-38
## Marine Terrace

1855
Signed and dated, lower left: MARINE TERRACE
Victor Hugo 21 mai 1855
Pen and brown ink and brown wash, with
touches of gouache and rubbed charcoal
41 × 33 cm

Provenance:
Juliette Drouet (?); Paul Meurice; Mme Clemenceau-
Meurice; Mme R. Langlois-Berthelot; Mme Philippe
Devinat

Exhibitions:
1952, Paris, Bibliothèque Nationale, "Hugo," no.
368; 1955, Guernsey, no. 32; 1971–72, Villequier,
Paris, no. 68 (repro.); 1974, London, Victoria and Albert Museum, no. 33 (repro.)

Bibliography:
Picon, 1963, p. 103; Georgel, 1971, pp. 281–82

The giant initials of Victor Hugo and his mistress Juliette Drouet appear intertwined in the sky, seeming about to crush the isolated house—Marine Terrace, on Jersey, where the poet's family lived from 1852 to 1855. In representing it, Hugo used a photograph taken two years earlier by his son Charles (*see* Georgel, 1971). But it is the only realistic detail in this impressive composition, which is above all a new and striking affirmation of Hugo's ego. Georgel, in the catalogue of the exhibition "Dessins de Victor Hugo" (1971–72, Villequier, Paris, no. 68), interpreted the meaning of this fantastic and terrifying vision, seeing in Juliette's initials the image of the serpent, which is generally associated by psychoanalysis with that of woman. The drawing, apparently the largest of the Jersey period, is the proud and sublime illustration of an act of faith by Victor Hugo toward himself, on the eve of the poem "The Seers," completed on April 24, 1855, and published in *Les Contemplations*: "Is it not ineffable/To feel oneself to be immensity,/To illuminate what was thought to be fable/With what is found to be truth/To see to the bottom of the great crater/To feel entering into oneself/All the obscure trembling of the mystery/To go, a spark, to the stars/And say to oneself: I am the wing!/And say to oneself: I have the sky!/Go, priest! Go, genii!/Go seek the human note/In the supreme symphonies/Of the great starry abysses!/While awaiting the golden hour,/The ecstasy of sacred death,/Far from us, anxious herds,/Far from the laws we established,/Go and taste, sublime creatures,/The swooning of the heavens!"

A.S.

Collection Devinat, Paris

Jean-Auguste-Dominique Ingres

## VII-39
## Anarchy (Study for "The Apotheosis of Napoleon I" in the Hôtel de Ville)

1853
Black crayon, squared for transfer
26.5 × 34 cm

Provenance:
Gift of the artist to the city of Lille, 1866; Musée des Beaux-Arts, Lille (inv. no. 1482)

Exhibition:
1974–75, London, etc., no. 58, pl. 70

Bibliography:
Gonse, 1877, pp. 94–95, repro. p. 94; Pluchart, 1889, no. 1482

VII-39

Reviewing the Lille museum's recent acquisitions of contemporary works, L. Gonse (1877, pp. 94–95) commented on this drawing as follows: "It is... the Musée Wicar's good fortune to have been able to add to its Raphaels, its Andrea del Sartos, and its Davids, four superb drawings by Ingres... [one depicts] two nude male figures, in pencil, for the large ceiling of the Hôtel de Ville, *the Apotheosis of Napoleon I,* a controversial work in which there were some very fine parts, such as the figure of *Anarchy.* One of these two drawings is indeed the sketch for it from the model. It would be hard to imagine anything bolder and more virile. The drawing is doubly valuable since the painting itself perished in the fire of the Hôtel de Ville...."

In March 1853 Ingres received the commission to decorate the Salon de l'Empereur in the Hôtel de Ville and chose to represent *The Apotheosis of Napoleon I* on the ceiling. Although the burning of the Hôtel de Ville in 1871 during the Commune completely destroyed the composition, it is known through a photograph, an oil sketch (no. VI-69), two drawings of the complete composition (Bayonne; Louvre, RF 3608), and several drawings of particular details (Bayonne; Montauban; Musée Bourdelle, Paris).

Greeted with admiration by the critics, despite some reservations voiced by Delacroix, *The Apotheosis of Napoleon I* was especially acclaimed by Théophile Gautier in *L'Artiste* of February 15, 1854: "The ceiling of Homer now has its pendant, and the Hôtel de Ville will henceforth have no reason to envy the Louvre: Homer, Napoleon, the greatest poet of antiquity, the most famous modern warrior, transfigured, deified, elevated among the glories of apotheosis, in the heaven of the immortals! Perhaps only M. Ingres, at both extremes of his career, was capable of accomplishing this marvel of genius, art, and science.... *The Apotheosis of Napoleon I* is the artist's masterpiece and will bring honor to our century for posterity" (p. 17).

Gautier described the ceiling, including the lower section, to which this drawing relates: "A shrouded and empty throne stands on a dais against which leans a faithful eagle, fierce and severe.... From behind this throne, in a motion of blazing violence, a robust and formidable figure springs forth, her visage tragically contorted; there would have been no need to write her name in Greek letters on the red border of her white tunic for all to recognize it immediately as Nemesis. Her foreshortened arm is superb; it is worthy of Michelangelo for its knowledge of drawing and the strength of its musculature. This sudden apparition, by its very gesture, vanquishes a group of rebellious and furious figures [among them Anarchy] hideous phantoms into a black fog where the serpent of Anarchy lies hissing" (p. 18).

A.S.

Musée des Beaux-Arts, Lille

Jean-Auguste-Dominique Ingres

## VII-40
## Hippolyte Flandrin

1855
Signed, dated, and inscribed, bottom right: Ingres a Son ami et grand artiste hyppolite flandrin 1855
Pencil
32.2 × 25.3 cm

Provenance:
Gift of the artist to Hippolyte Flandrin; Mme Hippolyte Flandrin; artist's son, Paul-Hippolyte Flandrin; Mme Paul-Hippolyte Flandrin; bequest to the Musée des Beaux-Arts, Lyons, 1928 (inv. no. B-1553)

Exhibitions:
1861, Paris, Salon des Arts Unis, no. 52; 1866, Lille, no. 841; 1867, Paris, Ecole des Beaux-Arts, no. 333; 1884, Paris, Ecole des Beaux-Arts, Dessins, no. 407; 1905, Paris, Salon d'Automne, no. 39; 1921, Paris, Chambre Syndicale, no. 168; 1967–68, Paris, Petit Palais, no. 250 (repro.)

Bibliography:
Blanc, 1861, p. 191; Galichon, 1861, p. 358; Merson and Bellier, 1867, p. 121; Blanc, 1870, p. 236 (incorrect date); Delaborde, 1870, p. 296, no. 294 (incorrect date); Gatteaux, 1875, pl. 12 (detail); Flandrin, 1902, p. 148; Lapauze, 1903, no. 18 (repro.); Lapauze, 1911, repro. p. 479; Hourticq, 1928, pl. 106; Alazard, 1950, p. 107; Schlenoff, 1956, pl. 32; Ternois, 1962, fig. 2; Naef, 1962, pp. 1–25

VII-40

The dedication at the bottom of this portrait bears witness to the deep friendship that bound Ingres to his favorite pupil, Hippolyte Flandrin (q.v.). Ingres continually took a personal interest in Flandrin's career, while Flandrin, throughout his life, felt great admiration and respectful gratitude toward his master (see Flandrin, 1902, pp. 138–55).

This expressive portrait, in which the meditative and restless character of Flandrin is admirably rendered by sharp pencil strokes, was shown to the public for the first time in 1861 at the Salon des Arts Unis: "Until now Salons, almost always annuals, were the exclusive business of the government and imposed an obligation which, due to its annual nature, lost its importance, and even its worthiness, degenerating into a bother. Today we are beginning to understand that part of these cares should be given over to institutions such as ours. While the State should still organize, at greater intervals, solemn celebrations in which the nation would give itself a show of its progress—or a warning of its decadence—the private societies could undertake those more modest, everyday exhibitions which inspire daily production and untiring curiosity...."

The inauguration of this Salon took place on January 25, 1861. As Charles Blanc commented (1861, pp. 189–90): "It is charming to have at one's disposal, right in the center of Paris and as one would say, right at one's fingertips, a less solemn exhibition, but continuous, one which is destined to be constantly renewed by new works. Moreover, while the Salon des Arts Unis shows us paintings and sculptures by most of the artists we find in the Palais de l'Etat... it also offers us pieces which we would never have the occasion of seeing again, unique things which have never before been enjoyed and will no longer be available for enjoyment in a short while. As one might think, we are speaking precisely of this marvelous collection of a hundred drawings by M. Ingres. Here is something that has not been seen and will not be seen in the most magnificent government exhibitions."

The museum of Lyons also preserves the portrait of Mme Flandrin, made five years earlier, in 1850, and which was shown beside her husband's at the Salon des Arts Unis.

A.S.

Musée des Beaux-Arts, Lyons

VII-41

The drawing shown here was engraved by W. Haussoullier (Blanc, 1867, repro. facing p. 18).

A.S.

Cabinet des Dessins, Musée du Louvre, Paris

Jean-Auguste-Dominique Ingres

## VII-42
## Female Nude (Study for "The Turkish Bath")

1860–62
Pencil
23 × 12.8 cm

Provenance:
Bequest of the artist to the city of Montauban, 1867; Musée Ingres (inv. no. 867.1205)

Exhibitions:
1957, London, no. 70; 1967–68, Paris, Petit Palais, no. 264 (repro.)

Bibliography:
Lapauze, 1901, vol. IV, pl. 196; Momméja, 1905, no. 2021

VII-42

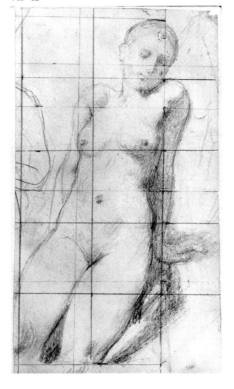

Jean-Auguste-Dominique Ingres

## VII-41
## Odalisque with Slave

1858
Signed and dated in pencil, lower left: J. Ingres 1858
Pencil and gray wash, heightened with white, on cream paper
34.5 × 47.5 cm

Provenance:
Emile Galichon; Roger Galichon; bequest to the Louvre, 1918 (inv. no. RF 4622)

Exhibitions:
1860, Paris, "Caisse de Secours des Peintres," no. 55; 1867, Paris, Ecole des Beaux-Arts, no. 150; 1967, Montauban, no. 140; 1967–68, Paris, Petit Palais, no. 255 (repro.)

Bibliography:
Blanc, 1867, p. 17; Blanc, 1870, pp. 106, 242; Delaborde, 1870, p. 284, no. 228; Brière, 1920, vol. II, pl. 52; Alazard, 1942, no. 14, pl. 14

Except for a few details (the locations of the perfume burner and the balustrade), Ingres here faithfully reproduced for his friend Emile Galichon the painting he had executed in 1839 for Marcotte (Fogg Art Museum, Cambridge;

Wildenstein, 1954, no. 228, fig. 149). In 1842 the artist executed a repetition—with variations—of the same painting; this canvas is in the Walters Art Gallery in Baltimore (1967–68, Paris, Petit Palais, no. 198, repro.). Although the subject of the composition (and especially its setting) expresses the Orientalist mode introduced by Romanticism around 1830, the point of departure for the odalisque's pose may be the *Sleeper of Naples,* painted for Caroline Murat around 1808 (lost in 1815). In a letter to Gatteaux of December 7, 1840, Ingres indicated that he had painted the *Odalisque with Slave* slowly and laboriously "from drawings, in the absence of a living model."

The fact that Ingres executed three versions of the same theme should come as no surprise, for this was his usual procedure. He painted three versions of *Antiochus and Stratonice*—in 1840 (Chantilly), a second in 1860 (private coll., Philadelphia; 1967–68, Paris, Petit Palais, no. 257, repro.), and the last in 1866 (Montpellier). And there are no fewer than five compositions of *Raphael and La Fornarina,* painted between 1813 and 1860 (*see* 1967–68, Paris, Petit Palais, no. 190, repro.). In addition, the Louvre has a late drawing of *Romulus, Conqueror of Acron* (RF 4623) and another of the *Dream of Ossian* (RF 1446).

This drawing is a study for the woman seated on the edge of the pool, on the left, in *The Turkish Bath* (1862; Louvre). It is well known that this figure was added by Ingres between 1860 and 1862 when he changed his painting, which at that time was square, into a circular format imitating the Italian *tondi* of the Renaissance. It illustrates a theme that obsessed the artist all his life (*see* folios 34, 37 v, 47 v, of notebook IX, where Ingres copied important passages from the *Turkish Letters* of Lady Mary Wortley Montagu).

*The Turkish Bath* is, in a way, the summation and the synthesis of all the drawings and paintings Ingres executed since 1807 (Toussaint, 1971). The Musée Ingres in Montauban preserves some fifty preparatory drawings, while the Louvre has a large sheet of charcoal studies on tracing paper (RF 12.199) and an ink sketch (RF 34.502).

A.S.

Musée Ingres, Montauban

VII-43

## Eugène Lami

Paris 1800–1890 Paris

In 1815 Lami entered the studio of Horace Vernet, where he met Bonington, who taught him the art of watercolor; with the aid of these two artists, his tremendously successful career was launched. A printmaker, watercolorist, painter, and architect, Lami was one of the primary chroniclers of high society of his day, on both sides of the channel. Baudelaire called him "the poet of official dandyism" ("Salon of 1846," in Baudelaire, 1965, p. 118).

Lami was from 1832 the official artist to Louis Philippe, and followed the king and his family into exile in England in 1848; however, on his return to Paris in 1852, he seems to have had no difficulty in adjusting to the politics of the new court, and the brilliant social activity of the Second Empire provided him with some of his best subjects. Lemoisne (1912, p. 134) recorded his famous statement, "Sovereigns may change, but the shoulders of the women remain."

Whereas he enjoyed the personal favor of the Emperor, whose costume he designed for the coronation (Lemoisne, 1912, pp. 149, 153), and executed watercolors for most of the court, his single most important patron during this period was the baron James de Rothschild, for whom he designed the Château Boulogne (1856) and took charge of the design of the immense country house at Ferrière. There he planned all the interiors and, with Joseph Paxton, had a hand in the exterior and the grounds

(Praz, 1964, pp. 358–62). While his lithography projects ceased in 1835, he continued to provide drawings for literary illustration (most notably the works of Alfred de Musset) as well as wood engravings for newspapers. He exhibited steadily at the Salon from 1828 until his death: prints, watercolors, and paintings (mostly military subjects). In 1862 he was named officer of the Legion of Honor.

His value and charm, and his attachment to the society he served so aptly, are perhaps nowhere more clearly stated than by Henri Beraldi (1885–92, vol. IX, p. 30): "One well recognizes in him an artist in love with modernity and the elegant portrayal of modern life, who knew how to see... a nineteenth century which is aristocratic, even glittering, a nineteenth century of elegant society, sport, the hunt, balls, fetes, revues, galas."

J.R.

Bibliography:
Beraldi, 1885–92, vol. IX, pp. 31–40; Lemoisne, 1912; Lemoisne, 1914; Lethieve and Gardey, 1963, vol. XXII, pp. 343–57; Praz, 1964, pp. 358–62

Eugène Lami

## VII-43
## Supper Given by the Emperor Napoleon III for Queen Victoria of England in the Theater of Versailles, August 25, 1855

1855
Signed and dated, lower right: E. Lami 1854
Watercolor
42 × 64 cm

Provenance:
Commissioned by the Emperor by decree of May 15, 1856 (Arch. nat. F² 190) as a replica of the watercolor presented to Queen Victoria, now preserved at Windsor Castle (Blunt, 1945, no. 475); deposited in the Musée du Luxembourg, about 1860; on permanent exhibit from 1863 to 1900; transferred to the Louvre, 1909 (inv. no. RF 141); deposited in the Versailles museum, 1937 (inv. no. MV 7307)

Exhibitions:
1857, Paris, Salon, no. 1542; 1953, Compiègne, no. 180

Bibliography:
Laran, 1912, p. 334, repro. p. 335; Lemoisne, 1912, pp. 136–39, repro. facing p. 160; Lemoisne, 1914, p. 123, no. 518

*See* Colorplate

There is no doubt that Lami was distracted when he dated this watercolor since this fete took place on August 25, 1855, and was part of the events organized in honor of the English sovereigns visiting Paris for the Exposition Universelle. Queen Victoria's diary reveals the splendors of the Versailles festivity: "The sight was truly magnificent. The whole stage was covered in, and four hundred people sat down to supper at forty small tables of ten each, each presided over by a lady and nicely selected—all by the Empress's own desire and arrangement.... We sat at a small table in the centre box, only with the Emperor and Empress, the two children, Prince Napoleon, Princesse Mathilde, and Prince Albert. It was quite one of the finest and most magnificent sights we have ever witnessed.... The supper over, we returned to the Salle des Glaces, where there was one more valse..." (*Journal*, 1961, pp. 126–27). Philippe de Chennevières echoed the wonder-struck memories of the Queen (1883–85, vol.

II, pp. 5–6): "This party was of artistic interest from various points of view: first there were Questel's ingenious and very tasteful inventions and the brilliant decorations he summoned from his imagination, he being at that time palace architect; then also because of the thought the Empress had in offering the Queen an album of the various facets of this memorable evening; each page was drawn in watercolor by our most able and elegant artists. Among others, I remember that Eugène Lami's talents were used for the supper in the theater, V. Chavet's for the Grand Gallery, Bonhomme's for the fireworks, with Questel furnishing each one with the architectural documents necessary for his subject matter.... Unfortunately, as often happens in these cases of ephemeral ceremony, the enthusiasm for this idea did not last; and all that was left finally was the charming watercolor by Eugène Lami,

representing, as I said, the supper in the theater, and which I saved for the public several years later by having it put in the drawing galleries of the Musée du Luxembourg."

While the essential interest of this work is historical, this large watercolor is not just an historic document, but demonstrates well the ability of the artist to bring together on one sheet of paper so many characters and to evoke the brilliant atmosphere of the festivity.

A.S.

Musée National du Château, Versailles

---

## Jean-Raymond-Hippolyte Lazerges
*Narbonne 1817–1887 Mustapha (Algeria)*

*A painter, and also a composer of melodies and songs, Lazerges was a pupil in Paris of the sculptor David d'Angers and the painter F. Bouchot. An unlucky artist, riddled with debts, he lived mostly off the proceeds of sales to the State. His career may be followed from 1841 to 1880 through the Salons, where he exhibited portraits and genre scenes (Albani in His Studio, 1856; Musée Fabre, Montpellier) and, above all, paintings of religious inspiration, mainly scenes from the life of Christ and the Virgin Mary. (His Descent from the Cross, painted in 1855, was purchased by the State, but destroyed during the Second World War.) After 1860 Lazerges journeyed frequently to Algeria, and his submissions to the Salon included many Oriental subjects (Kabyles Harvesting in the Plain of Mitidja, 1861, Tarbes; The Dance of the Aïssaouas, Perpignan). His son, Jean-Baptiste-Paul Lazerges (1845–1902), whose debut at the Salon dates from 1867, also dedicated himself to painting Oriental themes.*

A.S.

Jean-Raymond-Hippolyte Lazerges

## VII-44
## Head of Christ

1867
Signed and dated, in pencil, lower left: Hip^te Lazerges 1867; inscribed, lower right: Je leur ai donné mon amour, Ils m'ont donné leur haine....
Black and colored crayons on gray paper
63 × 48 cm

VII-44

Provenance:
Private coll., purchased, 1976 (collector's mark, lower left, not listed in Lugt)

The numerous figures of Christ and the Virgin Mary painted by Lazerges have been popularized by engravings (an important collection is in the Cabinet des Estampes of the Bibliothèque Nationale, AA3) and his various "holy cards."

This drawing is a perfect example of the artist's conception of Christ, with its characteristic forked beard. The Cabinet des Dessins of the Louvre has, among Lazerges's drawings, a head of Christ in pencil, dated 1859 (RF 6135), which is very similar to this one, although the influence of Couture (q.v.) is modified by an obvious concern for idealization.

A.S.

Private Collection

VII-45

Edouard Manet

## VII-45
## Study of a Female Nude

c. 1862–63
Signed, lower right: E. M.
Sanguine
24.5 × 45.7 cm

Provenance:
Henri Rouart; second sale, Paris, December 17, 1912, no. 207; Jacques Doucet; sale, Paris, December 19, 1917, no. 238; sale, Paris, March 30, 1935, no. 42, pl. 4; purchased by the Louvre (inv. no. RF 24.335)
Exhibitions:
1972, Darmstadt, no. 64 (repro.); 1976–77, Vienna, no. 46 (repro.)
Bibliography:
Jamot and Wildenstein, 1932, vol. I, p. 125; Tabarant, 1947, p. 76; de Leiris, 1969, pp. 61, 62, no. 195, fig. 225

Firmly committed to Realism and, it should be acknowledged, more of an independent than an Impressionist, Manet left relatively few drawings, but their extremely varied style constitutes a source of valuable information on the personality of the artist. This nude, whose form is defined by a continuous outline, a recollection of the tradition of Ingres, should be compared to *Olympia*, the celebrated painting accepted by the Salon of 1865 (Jeu de Paume). Victorine Meurend had posed for this painting for which several preparatory studies in watercolor and sanguine remain; one of them, pre-

served in the Bibliothèque Nationale (de Leiris, 1969, no. 194) is quite close to this drawing in technique as well as style.

A.S.

Cabinet des Dessins, Musée du Louvre, Paris

Jean-Louis-Ernest Meissonnier

## VII-46
## Cavalier in Louis XIII Costume

1866
Signed and dated, at right: Meissonnier 1866
Watercolor on brown paper
16 × 9 cm

Provenance:
Sale, New York, Parke-Bernet, September 17, 1969, no. 562 (repro.); Dr. and Mrs. Lambi Adams

This lovely watercolor painted with such great care is a characteristic example of the interest Meissonier maintained throughout his career in the seventeenth century, making him the true heir of the Dutch and Flemish "petits maîtres" so sought after in France from the middle of the eighteenth century.

Although it does not relate directly to any one known painting, this cavalier is probably one of the innumerable figure studies, both painted and drawn, that Meissonnier produced to satisfy the growing demand of collectors and dealers. The concern for the "authentic" document and the taste for the "finished" are fun-

VII-46

damental for the work of Meissonnier, who never undertook a painting without previously doing thorough and detailed research into the historical and social context of the subject chosen.

A.S.

Collection Dr. and Mrs. Lambi Adams, Worcester

Jean-François Millet

## VII-47
## Lobster Fishermen Throwing Their Traps: Night

1857–60
Signed, lower right: J. F. Millet
Black crayon
32.8 × 49.2 cm

Provenance:
Théodore Rousseau; sale, Paris, Hôtel Drouot, April 27–May 2, 1868, no. 561; Théophile Silvestre; Emile Gavet; sale, Paris, Hôtel Drouot, June 11–12, 1875, no. 35; Isaac de Camondo; gift to the Louvre, 1911 (inv. no. RF 4104)

Exhibitions:
1960, Paris, Louvre, Cabinet des Dessins, no. 21; 1964, Cherbourg, no. 87 (repro.); 1975–76, Paris, Grand Palais, no. 93 (repro.); 1976, London, Hayward Gallery, no. 75

Bibliography:
Soullié, 1900, p. 206; Guiffrey and Marcel, 1907–38, vol. X, no. 10.467; Lepoittevin, 1964, p. 10 (repro.); Bacou, 1975, p. 16, no. 46, pl. 46

The exact provenance and title of this sheet were specified for the first time in the catalogue of the Millet exhibition organized in Paris in 1975. According to Robert L. Herbert, who dates the drawing around 1857–60, Millet has here set down from memory an earlier impression from his stay in the Cotentin Peninsula in 1854. This kind of drawing is characteristic of the artist's style at that time, when he showed a certain preference for black crayon. He employed all of the conventions of the medium with the utmost subtlety. Without the slightest heightening with white, but by freely utilizing the white of the paper itself, Millet was able to suggest by drawing his lines closer together or farther apart, the partially illuminated horizon and the reflections of the moon in the water. The mysterious atmosphere emanating from this nocturnal seascape shows the extent to which Millet directly preceded Seurat as a draftsman in black and white. On the reverse of another Millet drawing, also in the Louvre (RF 5797; Guiffrey and Marcel, 1907–38,

VII-47

vol. X, no. 10.471), are two sketches for the boat and the fishermen throwing their traps; these should be dated slightly earlier, around 1854–55.

A.S.

Cabinet des Dessins, Musée du Louvre, Paris

---

## Henry Monnier
*Paris 1805–1877 Paris*

*A student first of Girodet and then Baron Gros, Monnier began to do caricatures in the 1820s after visiting London with Lami (q.v.). He gained recognition in 1830 following the publication of* Scènes populaires *in which he presented a character who would quickly achieve great popularity: Joseph Prudhomme. Endowed with a rich imagination and working steadily until his death, the artist produced illustrations for numerous books and contributed to such diverse newspapers and magazines as* Le Constitutionnel, Le Siècle, Le Figaro, La Vie Parisienne, Le Charivari, *and* La Caricature. *In addition to his work as a satirist, he was also a writer and an actor. Besides several novels (*Les Bourgeois de Paris, *1854;* Mémoires de M. Prudhomme, *1857), he also wrote plays which were performed at the Odéon, the Variétés, and the Palais Royal (including* Grandeur et décadence de

M. Prudhomme, *1852;* Le Roman de la Portière, Peintres et Bourgeois, *1855;* Les Métamorphoses de Chamoiseau, *1856), sometimes playing one of the roles himself. He was severely criticized by Baudelaire, but Balzac—who took Monnier as his inspiration for the character Bixiou in* Les Employés—*and Champfleury—who had met him in 1837 and gave the eulogy at his funeral—both admired his talent. Then as now, Monnier is remembered as the "father" of Joseph Prudhomme, a fictional character who enabled him to ridicule, indirectly, but with a biting wit, the self-satisfied bourgeoisie.*

A.S.

Bibliography:
Champfleury, 1879; Marie, 1931; Melcher, 1950

Henry Monnier

## VII-48
## Henry Monnier as M. Prudhomme

1860
Signed, dated, and inscribed in pen, lower right: Henry Monnier avril 1860. à mon ami Darrouy.
Varnished watercolor, heightened with gouache, over traces of pencil
14.9 × 25 cm

VII-48

VII-49

Provenance:
Darrouy coll.; Roger Galichon; bequest to the Louvre, 1918 (inv. no. RF 4630)

Joseph Prudhomme appeared for the first time in *Scènes populaires dessinées à la plume par Henry Monnier* (1830), and the artist continually improved on his character. When he himself was playing Prudhomme on stage at the Odéon theater, in a play he had written (*Grandeur et décadence de M. Prudhomme*), he came to fix definitively the physical characteristics that would be found thereafter in numerous exquisitely detailed watercolors, similar to this one. M. Prudhomme is a man of average height, pot-bellied, whose almost bald head contrasts with his mutton chops and whose face is squeezed into a high starched collar. The incarnation of the narrow-minded and incredibly self-satisfied bourgeois, he started in life as a writing master and eventually achieved financial independence and attained the rank of captain in the National Guard. According

to Champfleury, Monnier created in M. Prudhomme the greatest fictional character of the nineteenth century: "In the past the people used to be referred to as *Jacques Bonhomme*; today, the bourgeoisie is called *Monsieur Prudhomme.* This is unfortunate for the French nation, but it is so" (Champfleury, 1846). This sarcastic comment was echoed by the definition that Monnier himself presented through his intermediary, M. Prudhomme, writing in his *Mémoires*: "They said that I was a typical bourgeois; I do not deny this designation, very much to the contrary; who else in this day and age but the bourgeois has a right to talk about the bourgeois himself? For no matter what you do or say, everything has become bourgeois these days. The aristocracy does not exist any more, democracy has not come yet, all that is left is the bourgeoisie. You have only ideas, opinions, manners, literature, the arts—aptitudes for transition: salute Joseph Prudhomme, a man of transition, a man of the

bourgeoisie!... Son of Monsieur Prudhomme's son, that is who you are, not the son of Voltaire" (Schnerb, 1902, p. 496).

A.S.

Cabinet des Dessins, Musée du Louvre, Paris

Gustave Moreau

## VII-49
## Hesiod and the Muse

1858
Signed and dated in pen, lower left: GM [monogram]; Gustave Moreau. Rome. 1858
Pen and brown ink and chalk, heightened with white ink on beige paper
36 × 28 cm

Provenance:
Brame coll.; A. Marmontel; sale, Paris, January 25–26, 1883, no. 210 (as *The Spirit of Music Inspiring the*

*Shepherd*); sale, Paris, Hôtel Drouot, March 28–29, 1898, no. 173; Stephen Higgons; purchased by the National Gallery of Canada, 1966 (inv. no. 15213)

Exhibitions:
1866, Paris, Salon, no. 2430; 1969–70, London, Florence, Paris, no. 60, fig. 28

Bibliography:
Laran and Deshairs, 1913, pp. 37–38; Osler, 1968, (repro.); Mathieu, 1976, pp. 62, 301, no. 42 (repro.)

The subject of *Hesiod and the Muse*—which Delacroix had depicted on one of the ceiling pendentives in the library of the Palais Bourbon (1838–47)—seems to have particularly interested Gustave Moreau when he was in Italy (1857–59, again in 1867, and lastly around 1880). Of all of the versions, painted or drawn, the beautiful and poetic drawing in Ottawa is one of the most lyrical interpretations of the theme. Ernest Chesneau rightly analyzed its stylistic quality: "Hesiod receiving the chaste kiss of the Muse. The young and handsome herdsman, whose long, flowing locks escape from under his Phrygian cap. With eyes closed contemplatively, he listens to the inspired words which the Muse breathes into him. Descended from Olympus on her broad wings, she is all airy and suspended like a weightless cloud, her fingers and her perfumed breath brushing against the poet's forehead. The drawing is executed in bister with white highlights and is modeled by a delicate and loose pattern of shading along contours and muscles. The tone of the paper, tinted skillfully, presents contrasts in values and in tone, which give this little page all the charm and importance of a painting."

By its style and its reference to antiquity, this composition marks Gustave Moreau's momentary return to the Neoclassicism of his teacher Picot. As Pierre-Louis Mathieu pointed out (1976, p. 62): "The modeling of the figures, rendered by a network of hatchings, and the graceful features of Hesiod are reminiscent of certain drawings by Prud'hon, and by way of the French painter they hark back to Correggio, whom Moreau admired for the mellow smoothness of his forms."

A.S.

The National Gallery of Canada, Ottawa

---

## Charles-Lucien-Louis Müller

*Paris 1815–1892 Paris*

*Müller entered the Ecole des Beaux-Arts in October 1831 and was a student, with Couture (q.v.), of Baron Gros. When Gros died in 1835, Müller studied under Léon Cogniet. He entered the Salon*

VII-50

*first in 1834, and exhibited there regularly throughout his life. Of his work Bénézit wrote: "Charles Müller's cold, correct talent was immediately accepted by the public; he offended no tradition, loyally following the path traced by his teachers" (Bénézit, 1976, vol. VII, p. 589). Such slight praise for a man who had received first-class medals in 1848 and 1855, become a chevalier and an officer of the Legion of Honor, a member of the Institut de France in 1864, and then the director of the Gobelins tapestry works, may best be understood in the context of the career of Müller's friend Couture, who did not "toe the line" but angrily attacked the Académie and the imperial government. Couture and Müller had been the informal leaders of a group exhibiting with the art dealer Desforges. Their confidence in themselves was*

*unbounded in the 1840s. In 1847 Delacroix wrote of Müller: "The self-assurance of this cockerel is remarkable" (Delacroix, 1893–95, vol. I, pp. 254–55). After Couture's success at the 1847 Salon with* The Romans of the Decadence, *he wrote to Müller: "This year I am lending France to you; you can give it back to me next year."*

*Müller's first notable painting was* The Triumph of Heliogabalus *in 1841, a work whose moral position on the depravity of the late Roman Empire may have influenced Couture's* Romans of the Decadence *in 1847. In turn, Müller's* Victims of the Last Reign of Terror, *exhibited in 1850, has compositional similarities to Couture's triumph. In 1855 he was commissioned to illustrate the* Meeting of Queen Victoria and the Emperor and Empress at Saint-Cloud, *a painting which burned in the fire at that palace in 1870. He completed in 1860 an immense semicircular* Glorification of the Emperor *for the Louvre, linking the triumphs of Rome to the Second Empire in France.*

*Müller's historical subjects alternated at the Salon with works such as* The Snow Fairy *and* The May Dance, *whose frivolous themes contrast with his official rhetoric.*

N.D.

Bibliography:
Du Camp, 1855, pp. 199–201; Dimier, 1914, p. 195; Rosenthal, 1914, pp. 249–52; Giate, 1959, p. 162

Charles-Lucien-Louis Müller

## VII-50
## Two Women

1859
Signed, dated, and inscribed, lower left: A Monsieur Reynart tout petit souvenir affectueux de C.L. Müller. 1859
Black crayon, heightened with white chalk, on gray paper
52 × 46 cm

Provenance:
Gift of the artist to the Musée des Beaux-Arts, Lille, c. 1859–60 (inv. no. Pl. 1584)

Bibliography:
Pluchart, 1889, no. 1584

Creator of large compositions in a somewhat theatrical style popular with the bourgeoisie of the time, Müller seems also to have done numerous drawings, but this aspect of his work has hardly been studied. The drawings known at present (the majority in private collections) are mostly portraits or studies for paintings.

This drawing is a rather characteristic example of the artist's effortless, but somewhat soft, graphic style. It is dedicated to Edouard Reynart, who at the time was the curator of the museum of Lille and who ardently devoted himself to the development and study of the collections under his care from 1840 until 1878. He was responsible for the first "scientific" catalogue of the works in the museum. Most likely, Reynart suggested to Müller that he leave one his drawings in the museum, and the artist, as was frequently the custom in the nineteenth century, in turn dedicated it to him (information kindly provided by M. Oursel).

A.S.

Musée des Beaux-Arts, Lille

Pierre Puvis de Chavannes

## VII-51
## Study of a Male Nude Brandishing a Sword

c. 1869
Black crayon on blue-gray paper
27 × 20 cm

Provenance:
Gift of the artist's heirs to the city of Paris, 1898, for the Musée des Beaux-Arts (then in preparation); deposited in the Musée Galliéra, 1899; listed in the inventory of the Musée du Petit Palais at its inception, 1901 (inv. no. PPD 254[1])

Exhibitions:
1899–1900, Paris, Musée Galliéra, no. 3; 1963, Nancy, no. 91

Bibliography:
Lapauze, 1904, no. 369; Lapauze, 1906, no. 622; Gronkowski, 1927, no. 740; Davies and Gould, 1970, p. 116 (under no. 3266); Boucher, 1974, no. 48

This is a study for the executioner on the left of the *Beheading of Saint John the Baptist*, a composition existing in two versions, one signed and dated 1869 (Barber Institute of Fine Arts, Birmingham; 1977, Paris, Grand Palais, no. 77, repro.), the other, unfinished and probably earlier (National Gallery, London). We know of other studies executed in the same spirit for each of the figures (Lille, Lyons, Dijon, Toulouse, Marseilles, Amiens; Louvre and Petit Palais, Paris) but it is difficult to connect them precisely with one or the other of the paintings.

VII-51

This drawing seems to be closer to the London painting, since the man seems to be holding a sword and not a curved saber, as in the Birmingham work. The *Beheading of Saint John the Baptist* was done after the two murals that Puvis de Chavannes conceived between 1867 and 1869 for the new Marseilles museum, *Massilia, Greek Colony* and *Marseilles, Gateway to the East*, and which he exhibited at the Salon of 1869. The artist reached at this time the height of his stylistic maturity; through his slow and dogged effort toward formal purification, he henceforth expressed himself, in painting as well as in drawing, with an extraordinary economy of means, in his search above all for an expressive and synthesizing form of art. In this respect, this powerful drawing, with its deliberately simplified forms, is characteristic of Puvis's experiments in reaching that impersonal grandeur that is one of the fundamental aspects of his aesthetic.

A.S.

Musée du Petit Palais, Paris

---

*Auguste Ravier*

*Lyons 1814–1895 Morestel (Isère)*

*Ravier's father, a confectioner, wanted his son to study law and become a notary, but as a young man he was attracted by painting and chose to follow a different career. After a brief period at the Ecole des Beaux-Arts in Paris in the ateliers of Jules Cogniet and Caruelle d'Aligny, he went to Italy, where he stayed until 1845, although he made periodic trips back to Lyons and Paris. In Italy he met with Corot (q.v.), whom he had known earlier at Royat, and became friendly with Français (q.v.), Baron (q.v.), Anastasi, and Daubigny (q.v.). Returning to the region around Lyons, he lived at Crémieu (1852–68) and ended his days at Morestel, whose melancholy marshes and heavy vegetation inspired his paintings, drawings, and watercolors. Ravier led a secluded life, removed from contemporary art movements, pursuing in landscape his enduring interest in the relationship between light and color: "If we go in for too much color we risk becoming heavy and somber, and if we indulge in too much light our coloring is apt to be false or feeble." He was encouraged in his efforts by Félix Thiollier, an industrialist from Saint-Etienne, who tirelessly devoted himself to making the works of his friend known. Through what he wrote about Ravier, we are better able to understand the intriguing character of the "hermit of Morestel."*

A.S.

Bibliography:
Jamot, 1921; 1964, Reims

VII-52

Auguste Ravier

## VII-52
## The Plain: Sunset

c. 1868
Signed in black ink, lower right; F. Ate Ravier
Watercolor and gouache
26 × 36 cm

Provenance:
Gift of the artist's widow, through the mediation of
Félix Thiollier (along with four other watercolors and
four drawings) to the Louvre, 1907 (inv. no. RF 3445)

Without being able to date this landscape
exactly, we may place it around 1868, when
Ravier went to live at Morestel, an old hill town
on the border between the regions of Lyons and
the Dauphiné, midway between the plains and
the mountains. His works of this period are
characterized by their intense coloring and a
very personal use of watercolor and gouache.
On a coarsely grained paper Ravier superimposed large areas of color in as many as two or
three layers. The highlights of gouache enabled
him to obtain daring effects of brilliant light,
similar to those of Turner, a painter whom he
always sought to surpass.

"Considerable paper and canvas have been
wasted on reds, yellows, and violets in the attempt to imitate Ravier," Chenavard tells us.
"But what has not been successfully imitated is
his impression of grandeur, which he attained
by painting on a small scale, and his daring
color harmony, which I have never seen except
in his work and in Delacroix's."

A.S.

Cabinet des Dessins, Musée du Louvre, Paris

# Photography

Its glory was lavish abundance: "Photography today covers the whole world with its products," observed Philippe Burty in 1859.[1] Through the extent of its practice, photography fairly surpassed the opulence and vitality of all other forms of artistic expression during the Second Empire. In 1839 Louis Daguerre and the French government had generously bestowed the invention upon the population without patent restrictions. During the next thirty years, the curious, armed with cameras, invented a way of seeing which transformed epistemology. Photography engaged science, economics, history, politics, education, literature, architecture, painting, pageantry, taste, and gossip—sometimes all of them together. Photography has never been a pure art, separate and apart. It appears to have made the philosophy of materialism a closed case, but more important for the aesthetic concerns of modern times, it demanded a redefinition of the relationship between art and knowledge.

By 1854 there were already twenty-seven available variant processes from which to choose. Photographic technique was like medieval science, a discontinuity of unrepeatable recipes ever-increasing in number and variety in the search for standardization. Each of the processes, consisting of paper or glass negatives to support the infinitude of possible chemical combinations, offered a distinctive material structure which left its identifying mark on the reality portrayed in the paper print. Photographic materials thus reconstituted visual reality in their own images. Such a changeable complexion distinguishes photography during this period. But the number of technical alternatives also expressed the vast range of individual needs in the spectrum of personalities who worked to define photographic content.

The existence of eight or nine photographic reviews, simultaneously reporting events and issues or digesting the contents of the others, illustrates the politics of technique in Paris after 1850. Each review represented a different faction or emphasis. Several short-lived publications were sustained only long enough to express a single idea or to act as a partisan or mediator between battling forces.

For despite efforts to show that science and art were equally served by photography, mutual suspicion was forced into the open as well. For example, scientists reviewing in *Cosmos* attacked artists' trial-and-error methods of experimentation: they ridiculed the imprecision of language in their treatises; deplored the continued adherence to chemical formulas and equipment which defied progressive improvements; and belittled artistic issues involving questions of chance, predilection, or appropriateness. Confidently, amateurs, painters, and critics from *La Lumière*, with the perspective of history and the humanities to insulate them, retaliated in defense of artistic judgment; but above all, the humanists wrote with a knowledge of art's history and evolution and a clear recognition of its established conventions of picture-making, particularly the existent visual vocabulary of forms from other arts which specifically reflected the act of seeing.

International exhibitions, showplaces of the great universalization of progress, included photographic pavilions. While these were first set up in industrial palaces, by 1859 photographs hung in salons adjoining painting exhibitions. Societies encouraging art and industry featured photographic exhibitions and instituted prizes for photographic accomplishment—understood at the time to include all aspects of photographic activity, both artistic and technical. Special heliographic societies grew up in the big cities and in the provinces. Even the community of political exiles on the Channel Islands, namely Victor Hugo, his sons, and friends, photographed one another.

Artists, painters, and novelists such as Delacroix and Champfleury joined the societies in Paris. Critics like Francis Wey, Ernest Lacan, and Philippe Burty, the scientist Henri de la Blanchère, and the scientific popularizer Louis Figuier turned their attention toward inventing a language to explain and describe the appearance of the new pictures. The writers compared and connected photographs with other mimetic graphic structures of the visual arts, and they began to isolate photography's aesthetic uniqueness. "Photography always betrays her mechanical influence,"[2] reflected Burty in 1859. The same year, Delacroix wrote: "The most striking photographs are those in which certain gaps are left, owing to the failure of the process itself to give a complete rendering. Such gaps bring relief to the eyes, which are thereby concentrated on only a limited number of objects. Photography would be unbearable if our eyes were as accurate as a magnifying glass.... The confirmed realist corrects this inflexible perspective which, because of its very accuracy, falsifies our view of objects."[3] Baudelaire also contributed to early formulations of photographic aesthetic theory, but used photography as an excuse to condemn society's espousal of industry in general.[4] Baudelaire's conclusions about photography took the direction of social criticism. Nevertheless, they indicate that the poet was speaking from a knowledgeable and deeply felt position.

Photographic interest was multifaceted and contradictory: it was both popular and aristocratic, useful and indulgent, commercial and the ultimate in snob appeal. It was a mania which encouraged other manias, for example, that of glamour, and its accompanying relativism and amorality, all qualities the photographic medium was ideally suited to express. By 1866 a dismayed Englishman reporting from Paris had noticed the mania in photographic portrait collecting: "The photograph of Booth, the assassin of Lincoln, is, I am sorry to say, obtaining a very large sale, especially among the fair sex, who think him a very fine-looking man ('un très joli garçon'). The *carte-de-visite* of a strangler is also a very great success."[5]

With photography's popularity, the social world was classified anew according to photographic alliances linking Bohemian artists, socialists, members of the Institut de France, directors of railroad lines, sons of glovemakers, local archivists, Spanish bankers' sons, members of the Jockey Club, ichthyologists, writers on electricity, composers of light comedy, lithographers, architectural conservationists, builders, sculpture restorers, porcelain painters, and balloonists. The Emperor and Empress and their court quickly fell under this democratizing influence and understood its political usefulness. They learned the art of being photographed. The best photographers of the day presented Napoleon III and Eugénie with images symbolizing the beneficence of the Second Empire in splendidly bound albums showing new railway itineraries (no. VIII-2), a favorite military camp, or a newly constructed asylum (no. VIII-38).

Photography proclaimed a panorama of useful application.[6] Portraiture, big business from the beginning, was especially improved by hand coloring; portraits were pasted to mounts of visiting-card format. Eugène Disdéri, who is credited with this intriguing refinement of a well-established mode of etiquette, was rewarded with an official appointment to the court. Photography also allowed one to collect souvenirs of what one had never seen. It replaced travel with illusory stereoscopic vistas as remote and exotic as the Valley of the Kings or Broadway. Photography invented a new concept of the museum with grandiose reproductions of works of art. Among the first to enter the parlor and collector's cabinet alike were the engravings of Marcantonio Raimondi and the etchings of Rembrandt in two rival deluxe publications of 1853. Photography recorded under the microscope. It set down patterns of the stars and eclipses of the sun. It impressed pictures on enamel, fabricated niello on jewelry, and offered a chemistry which approximated the world in natural colors. It eventually superseded all informational and illustrational engraving accompanying the printed word. The photographic revolution also dramatically improved everything connected with its production. The demand for glass, paper, and chemicals increased markedly; with so much albumen used for prints, so did the egg business.

Materialism was celebrated by photography, not simply by recording the textures of objects in meticulous detail. It was actually because of photography's inexactitude, its confusion in capturing subject matter, that new versions of the visible world were established, and through this, new metaphors for expressing the structure of concreteness. Photography affirmed the universality of matter and its interconnectedness without necessitating an inventory of particulars. The camera, which was supposed to contain the technical secret for the pure apprehension of natural fact and material conservation, was quickly discovered by artists to be an instrument for tentatively suggesting possibilities. We are apt to forget how many times things went wrong in a nineteenth-century darkroom. Artists using the camera continually proved that a mistake might lead to discovery, which in turn could lead to new expressive forms. Nadar's famous little essay, "What They Don't Teach You in Photography,"[7] rings with the ironic twist of an experimentalist's confidence gained through error.

The indomitable presence of the machine allowed photography to be viewed as a great art of representation and inevitably of transformation. The pictures presented here demonstrate the beauty of a world constructed through photography's peculiar formal code. The existence of such abstract structuring of visual experience was as unequivocal in the nineteenth century as it is today. Walter Benjamin's observation that "it is a different nature which speaks to the camera than speaks to the eye"[8] is not really a twentieth-century insight. The pictures of LeSecq, Nadar, Marville, Robert, Nègre, LeGray, and the others shown here are based entirely on this fundamental understanding. The great masters of photography during the Second Empire proved that the "new photographic vision,"[9] a notion identified with purely modern photographic seeing, is as old as photography itself.

"Every period with a distinctive style of painting... has had an imitative photographic manner derived from the painterly trend of the moment."[10] This idea has been used to dismiss nineteenth-century pictures out of hand as being like painting. Gradually, the passage of time has enabled our modern gaze to appraise nineteenth-century photographs with an increased awareness of their photographic formality. Pictures once regarded as supreme renditions of fact, today, perhaps more than ever before, are revealed in their mysterious cloak of convention. We no longer see seamless extensions of natural appearance, but appreciate its rearrangement into radically formal hierarchies. The nudes of Vallou de Villeneuve (nos. VIII-41, VIII-42) are neither realistic nor strictly dependent upon forms derived from other arts, even though Vallou, a painter and one of the more prolific lithographers of the generation of 1830, had such repertoires of design to fall back on.

Leo Steinberg, writing about the art of representation, cited the example of old photographs to argue that there is no such thing as an absolute record of anything, that "technical capacity in the imitation of nature simply does not exist." He noted: "The encroaching archaism of old photographs is only the latest instance of an endless succession in which every new mode of nature-representation eventually resigns its claim to co-identity with natural appearance. And if appearances are thus unstable in the human eye, their representation in art is not a matter of mechanical reproduction but of progressive revelation."[11] The pictures exhibited here force a confrontation with this "encroaching archaism."

The lesson of photography is that the desire for artlessness is not self-fulfilling. As illusion, it too has to be invented. Realism in the arts is an attitude with a set of expressive conventions. Documenting is a form of rhetoric, as conventional as any historically commemorative painted "machine." In the mid-nineteenth century, the camera proposed a language of expressive discontinuity, interchangeable material surfaces, and framed arrangements offering a fragment for the whole. These attributes of photographic pictures do not automatically confer the status of art. As with all formal vocabularies, their use, combination, and reinvention by artists impose new meanings which transcend the original circumstances of their making.

During the Second Empire everything photographic took longer to do. In the search for the proper place to stand, the proper distance between camera and subject, the establishment of the frame, a photographer was not only making a photographic picture, he was literally collaborating with his instrument to invent a new language. Photography was a practice of recording visible matter which necessarily became an art of entering in, of meditative dreaming and gazing. Many Second Empire photographs bear witness to this passage of time in their making, and since their making, time has continued to idealize them. They are more unfamiliar than ever, more complete unto themselves. Without claims to knowledge, without answers, they recede from association with fact into the mysterious realm of the imagined, using the whole world as a metaphorical palette.

E.P.J.

*Notes*

1. Burty, 1859, p. 212.
2. Burty, 1859, p. 211.
3. Delacroix, 1951, p. 387. This notation is dated Strasbourg, September 1, 1859.
4. Baudelaire, 1965, pp. 149–55.
5. Peat, 1903, p. 178.
6. "Photographie," in Larousse, 1866–90, vol. XII, pp. 887–93.
7. Nadar, 1858.
8. Benjamin, 1977, p. 47.
9. Moholy-Nagy, 1967, passim.
10. Moholy-Nagy, 1967, p. 27.
11. Steinberg, 1972, p. 293.

## Edouard-Denis Baldus

*Westphalia 1820–1882 Paris?*

*After exhibiting paintings at four Salons in Paris between 1842 and 1850, Baldus gave up painting and took up photography, and by January 1851 was a founding member of the Société Héliographique. In the same year he was one of five photographers selected by the Commission des Monuments Historiques to document the endangered architectural treasures of France. Baldus's list of monuments took him to the Midi. In 1852 he received other assignments from the Ministry of the Interior and eventually achieved priority status as a photographer of Provence. During this time he invented a method of coating his prints with a gelatin solution rather than albumen and published a paper on the process.*

*In 1854 he traveled to Auvergne with Fortuné Petiot-Groffier, one of his students; the following year Baldus was photographing Paris. He also began to produce photographs for celebratory railroad albums, which were made on the occasion of the inauguration of new lines. Queen Victoria received one of Baldus's railroad albums as a souvenir of her journey to Paris for the Exposition Universelle of 1855.*

*Much of Baldus's work was shown at the exposition. His grandiose panoramas caused a sensation, and Baldus won a first-class medal. From 1854 through the period of the Second Empire, he exhibited in every important international photography exhibition and in nearly every exhibition of the Société Française de Photographie, of which he became a member in 1857.*

*Baldus's production was enormous. The most systematic survey of his work may be found in the publications of heliogravure prints made from his negatives, a process he helped reestablish. These publications include* Scènes d'inondations prises sur les bords du Rhône *(1859) and* Les Monuments principaux de France *(1875).*

*Baldus worked equally successfully with paper and glass negatives. He was an experimental printer, especially during the 1850s, concentrating in the next two decades on problems of print permanence and wide distribution, which heliogravure made possible. Baldus's prints from the 1850s show a radical taste for richness and a propensity for retouching, qualities which offended some of his contemporaries. His photographic style was perfectly suited to attract imperial patronage, and even today the powerful abstractions in his designs suit modern taste.*

E.P.J.

Bibliography:
Baldus, 1852; Gaudin, 1861

Edouard-Denis Baldus

## VIII-1
## Group in a Park

c. 1853
Salt print from waxed-paper negative
29 × 40.9 cm

Provenance:
Gérard Lévy, Paris; Musée Kodak-Pathé (inv. no. 2362)

To understand better how a nineteenth-century photographer actually saw his subject, it is useful to turn the photograph upside down, for such was the appearance of the image upon the ground glass of the camera. Right side up, this scene is a pleasant natural setting designed for picturesque effect. Inverted, its radical beauty more profoundly evokes its subject as it becomes perceived as an abstract arrangement. Moreover, the picture offers a lesson in photographic composing while it demonstrates some formal conventions of Impressionism evolved by the photographers of the 1850s.

Baldus carefully framed his image to balance the dark conifers on the left with the poplars on the right. The figures are placed so as to create a horizontal arrangement in keeping with the shape of the photograph. The sense of nature under the control of the landscape gardener is made explicit by the photographer's having synthesized the motif, thus more fully expressing the refined charm of the locale.

As he calculated the arrangement, Baldus must have counted on the houses in the distance to sustain interest against the superb reflections in the stream. The weakness of this photograph is not artistic but chemical. Too long exposure of the negative bleached out the sky.

Upside down, the photograph becomes a startling patchwork of verisimilitude in varying degrees of resemblance, literal description, and abstract effect. It is as silhouettes that the figures dominate the landscape. What a surprise it must have been for a photographer to discover through these reflections how little it took to identify and communicate the human form!

This photograph demonstrates a language of generalization which had been regarded as the exclusive province of Impressionist painting. When Michel Butor (1963) formulated Monet's radical "world upside down," he was probably not thinking of the spiritual communion with nature that the process of photographic picture-making had rendered necessary for every nineteenth-century photographer. He attributed this achievement to the eye of the painter alone. However, the reorganization of the natural world, the duality between figure and reflection, was made absolutely clear by photographic practice, since all photographers were forced to look reflections straight in the face in a manner that painters were not. In the work of Monet, Butor states, the upper portion of a painting corresponds to visual reality, the reflection below, to the activity of the painter. For the photographers of the 1850s this recognition was commonplace.

A variant of this photograph is in the Philadelphia Museum of Art (70-243-3).

E.P.J.

Musée Kodak-Pathé, Vincennes

VIII-1

Edouard-Denis Baldus

## VIII-2
## Album of the Chemins de Fer de Paris à Lyon et à la Méditerranée

c. 1855–56
Seventy albumen or gelatin prints from
waxed-paper and wet collodion on glass negatives pasted to album leaves
47 × 63 cm

Provenance:
André Jammes, Paris

Photograph exhibited:
**Pont de la Mulatière**
Signature stamp, lower right, below print: Baldus
Albumen or gelatin print from wet collodion on
glass negative
28.4 × 43.8 cm

VIII-2

By mid-century the English had become the
outstanding designers of fast locomotives. The
great English engineer T.R. Crampton built a
type of locomotive whose name came to stand
for speed. *The Crampton,* patented in 1843, was
long, low and sleek, and had attained a speed of
144 kilometers per hour. Three hundred of
these locomotives were constructed between
1849 and 1864, notably by Derosue & Cail, for
the Strasbourg and Lyons railroads and for several German lines.

It was with engines of this type that
Napoleon III was able to establish a record in
France that would not be broken for the next
eighty years. In 1855 he returned from Marseilles to Paris on a train pulled by *The Crampton*
at a commercial speed of 100 kilometers per
hour. This presentation album was made to
celebrate his journey as well as the inauguration of the new railroad line in Provence. Four
other railroad albums are known (two from the
1850s by Baldus, two from the 1860s by Col-
lard), all in the collection of André Jammes.

The pages of this album reveal Baldus's
photographic vision at its most regal and
majestic. On page after page, the bold vistas,
unbelievably simple in design, are perfect
abstract expressions of the Second Empire awe
of railroad technology. Funneling perspectives,
the pride of newly laid stretches of track, newly
engineered bridges, tunnels, and viaducts reflect spatial configurations complementary to
those envisioned by Baron Haussmann when
he transformed a Paris of medieval passage-

ways into a metropolis of thoroughfares. For
Baldus as well, the power of composition derived from a vision of spatial grandeur and
amplitude. But such spaces were inconceivable
without inhabitants. Always definitively
placed, singly or in groups, Baldus's figures
provide definable units within the larger
scheme. Their disposition may determine the
entire mood of a photograph, for they specifically intone Baldus's style as a language of
space.

Some of the negatives were made as early as
1851, when Baldus first photographed in the
Midi for the Commission des Monuments Historiques. In this album he mixed images from
glass and paper negatives, and since he could
produce pictures from both with equal clarity
and richness, even the most experienced eye
may not be able to distinguish between them.

Part of the excitement of this album comes
from the bold variety of means Baldus used to
create a picture, from almost hallucinatory
perspectives in the framing, long exposures
(the trailing forms of moving ships in the Marseilles harbor), or radical darkroom work and
printing. No other contemporary photographer
achieved such consistency between technique
and engineered design to produce images of
force and streamlined elegance similar to the
locomotive, to whose redesigning of the French
countryside this greatest of railway albums
pays tribute.

E.P.J.

Collection André Jammes, Paris

Attributed to Edouard-Denis Baldus

## VIII-3
## Private House, Paris

c. 1855
Albumen or gelatin print from wet collodion on
glass negative
41.7 × 32.9 cm

Provenance:
André Jammes, Paris

VIII-3

Attributed to Edouard-Denis Baldus

## VIII-4
## Private House, Paris: Windows and Doorway

c. 1855
Albumen or gelatin print from wet collodion on glass negative
43.8 × 33.2 cm

Provenance:
André Jammes, Paris

These photographs present what appears to be a new house: the trees in front are young, the masonry of the ground floor, the balconies, and the carved ornamentation have a clean-cut, unweathered look. At first glance the pictures could be mistaken for straightforward documentation. However, in the view of the full facade, the photographer did not place the camera directly in front; rather, a slight three-quarter vantage point was chosen, which strengthens the sculptural relief and causes the whole building to appear to tip backward, thereby breaking a cardinal rule of architectural photography.

There are other aberrations. A decidedly eerie light around the building seems to come from the movement of the trees, which are blurred because they are in front of the focal plane and because a breeze shakes their branches, causing vague shadows to dapple the facade. Something else pervades the scene and interferes with the structure of mimetic black and white: a flowed pattern, similar to that of marbling on endpapers of old books, has permeated this picture, while in the close up, curious dim veils of shadow descend diagonally across the architecture with increasing darkness.

That the emulsion on the photographic negative should have almost willfully insisted on its own presence as well is most peculiar; it is as if the emulsion were a phantom haunting the house. This thin, viscous film stirs with the foliage and, consorting with the painterly gust of wind, disembodies the trees. On the left, a tree literally seems to go up in smoke. The emulsion obliterates the door of the porte-cochere and spirits through its crevices. A tree trunk in front of the entrance disappears. Thus, an ordinary view of a house stirs the imagination and allows it to impose, in Poe's words, a certain "moral physique" on the place.

The windows add to this curious feeling of an unknown presence. In the time that elapsed between the taking of the full view and that of the detail, someone had come to lower the

VIII-4

blinds on the left. These windows are not the "vacant eyes" in Poe's "mansion of glory," but rather the telling "luminous squares" through which, Baudelaire wrote, "life lives, life dreams, life suffers."

These prints were discovered in an impressive album of photographs by a variety of photographers of Parisian buildings. They should be compared to a Paris album of thirty-two pictures from collodion on glass negatives (c. 1855–56) by Baldus in the International Museum of Photography in Rochester, New York (74.058), for their resemblance to certain examples in the album has led to the Baldus attribution.

E.P.J.

Collection André Jammes, Paris

---

### Bisson Frères

*Paris, established 1840 or 1841–1860s*

*At the time of the invention of photography, Louis-Auguste Bisson (born 1814) was employed as an architect for the City of Paris; his younger brother, Auguste-Rosalie (born 1826), worked with their father, a painter specializing in heraldry. Louis-Auguste could have been introduced to photography by Daguerre himself; based on* La Lumière *(no. 4, March 2, 1851, p. 14), it seems certain that the Bisson firm was established in 1840 or 1841 by the father and one or both sons (Bisson Père et Fils). At this time the Bissons were exclusively daguerreotypists, and until the early 1850s they were repeatedly recipients of prizes in the great expositions as portrait daguerreotypists. They worked as much together as independently, and the younger brother was also associated with several other photographers.*

*About 1852–53 they took up photographic reproduction of the work of the great engravers Rembrandt and Dürer. They then turned to scientific photography with Achille Devéria and the naturalist Louis Rousseau and were very active in the great movement of architectural photography, presenting outstanding prints from collodion on glass negatives of very large proportions to the Académie des Sciences in 1854. Their monumental work,* Reproductions photographiques des plus beaux types d'architecture, *appeared in installments from 1853 to 1862.*

*In 1853–54 the Bisson brothers had a prestigious studio at 35, boulevard des Capucines, an address frequented by the literary and artistic avant-garde of the period. In 1855 the Bissons participated in the vogue for photographs of colossal size along with Braun (q.v.) and Baldus (q.v.), whose work theirs rivaled. They were founding members of the Société Française de Photographie, where they exhibited their first photographs of the glaciers of the Alps.*

*In 1860, on the occasion of the reuniting of Savoy to France, they published a celebrated album of mountain photography, the first of its kind. In 1861 the younger Bisson made the first photograph on the summit of Mont Blanc, but by this time the public had diverted its attention from heroic photography and had become captivated by portraiture. As Le-Gray and Baldus had done before them, the Bisson brothers disappeared from the scene. They surrendered their studio in the Hôtel de Sourdéac at 8, rue Garancière to the photographer and photoengraver E. Placet; the elder Bisson brother stayed on as its director, while his brother went to work for Léon et Lévy, and later, in 1869, photographed in the Nile Valley on the occasion of the opening of the Suez Canal.*

E.P.J.

Bibliography:
Moigno, 1855

VIII-5

Bisson Frères

## VIII-5
## Mont Blanc Seen from the Garden

1860
Albumen print from wet collodion on glass
negative
29.4 × 43.5 cm

Provenance:
Gabriel Cromer; International Museum of Photography (inv. no. 175-429:21)
Bibliography:
Gernsheim and Gernsheim, 1969, p. 290, pl. 174; Pollack, 1969, pp. 110–12, 120–21

Members of the Société Française de Photographie, the Bissons had exhibited views of the Alps that were described by Moigno at the first exhibition of the society in 1855. They commemorated the tour that the Emperor and Empress had made in Savoy, which had been reunited with France in 1860, with the publication of a deluxe album, *Haute Savoie: Le Mont Blanc et ses glaciers; souvenirs du voyage de LL. MM. l'Empereur et l'Impératrice,* from which this view of Mont Blanc comes (plate 21). The Gernsheims supposed that this particular photograph was made by Auguste Bisson on his second ascent of Mont Blanc in the summer of 1861, during which he was accompanied by twenty-five porters and assistants. However, since the album that first contained the photograph is dated 1860, the Gernsheims seem to

have been mistaken. A similar confusion exists in Pollack.

E.P.J.

International Museum of Photography at George Eastman House, Rochester, New York

Bisson Frères

## VIII-6
## The Portal of Saint Ursinus at Bourges

1863
Stamp, lower right: Ancienne Maison Bisson Frères; blind stamp, lower left: E.P. [Placet]; blind stamp on mount: Placet successeur; stamp of distributor on mount: E. Quetier et Cie
Albumen print from wet collodion on glass negative
45.2 × 43.4 cm

Provenance:
Gérard Lévy, Paris

This splendid example of architectural detail is made even more remarkable by its size. The Bissons' preference for large scale vied only with the mammoth tableaux negatives of Baldus (q.v.). This study seems more like a care-

fully rendered architectural drawing than a portrayal of plan, mass, or ensemble. The selective placement of the focal plane in a narrow relief space calls attention to the way the raking light beckons intricately embroidered decorative surfaces from the massive architecture.

The tourist with his peculiar combination of hooded coat and silk top hat acts as a guide. He provides a scale of reference for the architecture, but he is also a mysterious extension of the hard-edged shadow at the left. By gazing at the sculptural detail, he draws attention to the central interest of the print. Without him, the photograph would be a handsome but much less memorable document.

The combination of a lone figure with a medieval architectural detail became a classic type of tourist picture in the 1850s, the most astonishing being Charles Nègre's portrait of Henri LeSecq with a gargoyle on the tower of Notre Dame (1853).

The Bissons probably made this negative around 1855, the time of Moigno's inventory of their work. It belongs to the collection *Reproductions photographiques des plus beaux types d'architecture,* a project that spanned several years (1853–62). E. Placet took over the Bissons' atelier after 1862 and printed their negatives (as Braun, q.v., had done for the firm of Mayer & Pierson, q.v.).

E.P.J.

Collection Gérard-Lévy, Paris

VIII-6

VIII-7

## Adolphe Braun

### Besançon 1812–1877 Dornach

*Braun, a fabric designer in Mulhouse, first experimented with daguerreotype, and then turned to collodion on glass negatives for photographing flowers. In 1848 he founded a photography publishing company in Dornach, and soon published six albums of flowers in their natural size to serve artists and decorators. His photographs were highly acclaimed at the Exposition Universelle of 1855: "Arranged by an artist, chosen by a botanist with exquisite taste, these bouquets breathe of spring. The slightest transparencies and reflections have been captured" (Ziègler, 1855, p. 33). Today Braun ranks with Roger Fenton and LeSecq (q.v.) as one of the greatest nineteenth-century still-life photographers, but he is better known for his documentation of Second Empire life, especially his stereoscopic views of the movement of the crowds on Paris boulevards (c. 1860).*

*By 1862 Braun's company had gained an international reputation for the reproduction of works of art. In order to develop the most appropriate and durable process for reproducing the subtleties of old master drawings, he adopted carbon printing, which gave a permanency to photographic prints and lent reproductions of drawings a coloration reminiscent of their originals.*

*Naomi Rosenblum (manuscript in preparation) clarifies Braun's role in the development of carbon processes by showing that his first carbon prints were labeled "Procès Poitevin et Swan, photog. Ad. Braun." Poitevin's carbon process had been patented in 1855. After 1866 Braun purchased exclusive French rights for the process Sir Joseph Wilson Swan had patented in 1864. Swan had perfected a ready-made carbon tissue paper, available in three contrast grades for negatives and in three colors.*

*In the 1860s Braun joined the fashionable rush to Switzerland and Savoy to capitalize on the commercial opportunities of alpine views. Braun's sublime mountain scenery and meticulous technique found a responsive audience among American photographers.* The Philadelphia Photographer *noted: "The detail is peculiarly wonderful. There are huge banks of lofty fleecy clouds, caught by some photographic prestidigitation which we cannot explain; magnificent snow-clad mountain peaks, miles away in perfect detail; huge rocks frozen and snow-covered, and mighty glaciers in close proximity to lovely valleys, and ripe harvest fields, so true to nature that one is forced to exclaim, Can photography be so real?" ("Carbon Photographs," 1867).*

E.P.J.

Bibliography:
"Braun," 1867; "Carbon Photographs," 1867; Lécuyer, 1945, pp. 110–11, 115–18; 1965, Paris, Musée des Arts Décoratifs, "Photographie," nos. 477–512; Scharf, 1968, pp. 101–2, 109, 276 n. 49

Adolphe Braun

## VIII-7
## Still Life with Hare and Ducks

c. 1865
Carbon print on tissue paper from wet collodion on glass negative, mounted
77.2 × 54.6 cm

Provenance:
Purchased by the Metropolitan Museum of Art, 1947 (inv. no. 47.149.52)

Adolphe Braun

## VIII-8
## Still Life with Deer and Wild Fowl

c. 1865
Carbon print on tissue paper from wet collodion on glass negative, mounted
77.2 × 59 cm

Provenance:
Purchased by the Metropolitan Museum of Art, 1947 (inv. no. 47.149.54)

Bibliography:
Lécuyer, 1945, repro. p. 118

The morbid splendor of these colossal compositions of dead game forces the viewer to perceive the material world through texture alone. These tableaux, for all their indebtedness to an age-old tradition of still-life painting, appear in photographic translation marvelous yet, oddly enough, naïve. It is this quality of naïveté that the camera's way of translating the world has exaggerated to a great degree. For a grandeur of conception is made to combine with a certain ghoulishness, suggesting a characteristic aspect of late-nineteenth-century taste that Braun clearly shared with his contemporaries. These pictures are practically larger than life: not enlargements, the photographs have been contact printed from gigantic negatives.

Daylight entering on the left, in the second photograph, takes inventory of two pheasants, a mallard, and a buck, plus two hunting horns, a powder horn, a game bag, a rifle, and a spray of evergreen, all tacked to a wall of planed pine. The chemistry and the light are unyieldingly descriptive. This description turns to classification: types of feathers are compared, as are types of horns. Following this formula, the mallard, hunting horn, powder horn, and rifle reappear against the same background in the other photograph, a hare replacing the deer. Light passes under and around the animals, who have surrendered in graceful conformity to a planned design. Yet in spite of the mystery of sacrifice surrounding them, the animals seem obscene; the abundance of texture is excessive and unmitigatedly registered. In this primeval rite of trophy-taking, it is not difficult to imagine the dangling hooves mounted on plaques in rows or severed and presented to the ladies of the hunting party, later to be trimmed in silver to form pillboxes, to hold snuff or tobacco, or to support a hassock or a pincushion. These photographs express such an intense curiosity about matter that viewing the hunt's glorious spoils becomes an experience more like identifying a corpse.

It is not surprising that besides photographers, certain late-nineteenth-century American painters were attracted to this type of work by Braun, especially the *trompe l'œil* painters for whom picture-making involved creating an experience that piqued curiosity. William Harnett may have depended on photographic compositions such as these for his renowned still life *After the Hunt*, 1885 (Fine Arts

Museums of San Francisco). Alfred Frankenstein, who indicated this connection (1953,
p. 66, figs. 58, 59), suggested that Harnett's
many imitators, who were anxious for "after
the hunt" subjects, may not have imitated Harnett at all, but may have actually been indebted
to Braun.

E.P.J.

The Metropolitan Museum of Art, New York,
McAlpin Fund, 1947

## Edouard Delessert

*Paris 1828–1898 Paris*

*Son of a Prefect of Police under Louis Philippe,
Delessert was the founder of L'Atheneum Française, a review of art and literature, as well as a critic
and a writer of travel books.* Vingt-et-un Jours à
la Mer Morte *(1851) and* Voyage aux villes
maudites *(1853) were souvenirs of two trips to
Palestine. In* Une Nuit dans la cité de Londres
*(1854) he described the appalling misery of the lower
classes in the old quarters of London. Other lighter
travel fantasies were* Le Chemin de Rome, s'il
vous plaît *(1860) and* Toujours tout droit *(1862).
As a member of a banking family, Delessert was
involved in financial affairs as well. He was a
member of the administrative council for the Chemin
de Fer du Nord de l'Espagne and the Chemin de Fer
de l'Ouest.*

*His cousin Benjamin had reproduced the prints
of Marcantonio Raimondi, using waxed-paper
negatives in a pioneering publication of 1853.
Edouard probably studied photography with LeGray
(q.v.), learning the dry waxed-paper process from
him after this date. He worked mainly with collodion
on glass negatives, reserving waxed paper for travel
(a standard practice for photographers in the first
half of the 1850s). As early as 1854 Ernest Lacan, the
editor of* La Lumière, *the most important photography periodical of the time, announced that Delessert and Count Aguado had invented the concept of
the* carte-de-visite *photograph which replaced the
name of a person with a "delicious little portrait."*

*Thus the two photographers were among several
others who preempted the revolutionary notion from
its historically acknowledged inventor, Eugène Disdéri.*

*Delessert, a member of the Société Française de
Photographie, invented other photographic improvements such as the* porte-lumière, *an apparatus for enlarging negatives, devised with Bian-
chi, which enabled him to produce life-size prints*

VIII-8

(see *Mayer & Pierson). The Goncourts were amused
in 1860 by Delessert's accounts of photographing the
local peasantry in Brittany and reported that he had
invented a conveyance of the type used by itinerant
dentists to carry his photographic equipment.*

E.P.J.

Bibliography:
Lacan, 1854; Lauzac, 1861; Goncourt and Goncourt,
1956, vol. I, p. 780

Edouard Delessert

## VIII-9
## Olive Trees near Sassari, Sardinia

1854
Signed, lower right : ED ; dated and inscribed on mount : Mai 1854 Oliviers près Sassari
Albumen print from waxed-paper negative, mounted
17.5 × 23.7 cm

Provenance :
Gérard Lévy, Paris
Exhibition :
1855, Paris, Exposition Universelle
Bibliography :
Delessert, 1855, pp. 16–17, 19, 55 ; Lacan, 1856, p. 26

This study of olive trees may be among the first of Delessert's travel photographs. It is fairly certain that he had not taken photographs on his trip in 1850 to the Dead Sea with Louis-Félicien de Saulcy, for he mentions only sketching the monuments and the terrain (*Vingt-et-un Jours à la Mer Morte*). However, *Six Semaines dans l'île de Sardaigne* mentions his photographic activities several times. It is clear in this account that Delessert is something of a novice, taking advantage of the least break in the clouds to make views. Of the olive trees that he found near Sassari he observed : "I have seen olive trees that were as beautiful in the Garden of Gethsemane at the gate of Jerusalem ; but in

Jerusalem, these veterans of other epoques, witnesses to such great events, seem to have lost consciousness of their own personal beauty, like certain people who, having reached a certain age, no longer feel required to care for themselves. Near Sassari, on the contrary, the olive tree appears to be full of self-love, puffed up with vanity by its rich branches and beautiful fruits" (1855, pp. 16–17).

The view exhibited here appears to be the sole survivor from what must have been a collection of souvenirs of Delessert's feelings on the trip as well as a record of his peregrinations in Sardinia. One edition of the book, however, was illustrated with two-toned lithographs, and it is possible that the photographs eventually served as models for the lithographic illustrator. Such collaborations were not at all uncommon ; some of the finest early photographers had been lithographers themselves.

E.P.J.

Collection Gérard-Lévy, Paris

---

## Delmaet et Durandelle

*Active Paris 1860s*

*This team of photographers has come to be associated with city planning and the documentation of demolitions, constructions, and reconstructions during the Second Empire, especially the construc-*

*tion of the new Opéra and the opening up of the avenue de l'Opéra. Other projects recording changes on the Ile de la Cité, the reconstruction of the Hôtel de Ville, and the construction of Sacré Cœur, which have been related to their collaboration, may have been done by Durandelle alone. For example, a year after the inauguration of the Opéra, Durandelle himself published forty-five photographs of the sculptural decoration in* Le Nouvel Opéra de Paris : Sculpture ornementale *(Paris, 1876). Communications by Durandelle to the* Bulletin *of the Société Française de Photographie in 1880 and in 1881 indicate that he also documented the Théâtre de Monte Carlo, the Abbey of Mont Saint Michel, and the entrance of the place du Carrousel. Neither Delmaet nor Durandelle was a member of the Société Française de Photographie.*

E.P.J.

Delmaet et Durandelle

## VIII-10
## Men on the Roof of the Paris Opéra Construction

c. 1864
Blind stamp on mount : Photographie de Delmaet et Durandelle 22, Bd. des Filles du Calvaire Portraits et Reproductions ; numbered, lower left : 186
Albumen print from wet collodion on glass negative, mounted
27 × 38.3 cm

Provenance :
Gabriel Cromer ; International Museum of Photography (inv. no. 175–318)
Exhibitions :
1971, Rochester ; 1977, Santa Barbara

In their view of the construction site of the Paris Opéra (*see* no. I-10), the photographers have eliminated all but a man-made landscape, a drawing board perspective with its own horizon. Against this dramatic vista, more prophetic somehow because of the upward tilt of the plane, human figures randomly populate the space, creating an effect of excitement only approached in views by contemporaries such as Félix Bonfils, Zangaki, or Francis Frith showing tourists in Egypt clambering over the pyramids. The design speaks not only for the aspirations of all urban planners and builders from the second half of the nineteenth century to modern times but for the vision of grandeur, applied to monuments that will endure, of all great civilizations.

VIII-9

VIII-10

Another example of this remarkable view is in the Bibliothèque de l'Opéra in a collection of photographs by Delmaet et Durandelle, A. Liébert & Cie, and Marville (q.v.). These document all stages of the planning and construction of the Opéra; the groups of artisans, sculptors, and engineers; and the sculptural ornamentation (in detailed views). Forty-three prints by Delmaet et Durandelle, all of the Opéra under construction, including five related prints attributed to the team, are in the International Museum of Photography in Rochester.

A variant of the view exhibited here, also in the Bibliothèque de l'Opéra, numbered 186 but bearing the stamp "A," may be regarded as a pendant. The frame is the same, but the central figure has moved toward the photographer and the other figures have rearranged themselves. Thus the pair of pictures gives a tantalizing impression of instantaneity, and the second version, by comparison, makes the delicately balanced pose of the central figure in the first seem even more precarious and attractive. Of the series devoted to the Opéra, numbers 186 and 186 A have an irresistible modernity. While thoroughness and professionalism were central to Delmaet et Durandelle's documentary pho-

tography, these examples transcend documentation at its very best.

E.P.J.

International Museum of Photography at George Eastman House, Rochester, New York

---

*Louis-Jean Delton*

*Active Paris 1860–80s*

*Delton's activities between 1835 and 1860 are shrouded in mystery. It is not known how he came to photography but he may have begun by photographing circus or vaudeville performers. In 1835 he became a member of the Jockey Club (founded in 1833), which was dedicated to the promotion of horse breeding and racing in France, favoring the thoroughbred English horse over the Arabian as a regenerating breed. Delton's photographic activity became more apparent with the establishment of the great racing prizes, and from 1860 on he used photography to record the forms and movements of prize winners, producing a pictorial equivalent of the Stud*

*Book. He was a photographer for the Société Hippique de France.*

*The Jockey Club, founded with a serious mission, grew into an organization associated with social self-importance and frivolity, and it became chic for popular writers, ambassadors, and the nobility to be portrayed on horseback by Delton. For this new genre of portraiture, Delton created an extraordinary garden promenade atelier where "sitters" could move about on their mounts or in carriages with attendants in full livery. The studio, located at 83, avenue de l'Impératrice, was pictured in a wood engraving showing riders passing before an enormous camera with a lens supported by its own tripod; the whole apparatus all but dwarfed its operator (Lécuyer, 1945, repro. p. 108).*

*A complete list of Delton's publications has not yet been established. Apart from the* Album hippique *(1866–67) and six miniature* Albums Delton *(1870) reproducing and identifying the repertoire of the studio, in all, 200 negatives, there were other publications with photogravures. Those in the International Museum of Photography, Rochester, include the* Album Delton *(1870) and* Le Tour de bois *(1884 and 1885), while the Bibliothèque Nationale lists* La Photographie hippique *(1889–94).*

*The preface to Delton's* Album hippique *reads: "Let us suppose that photography had existed during the period when racing had first been established in France. Today it would be possible to study the precise forms of the celebrated prize winners and compare them to the prize winners of today. Wouldn't such a study be enormously profitable? Today drawing and painting are influenced by personal taste, but photography is mercilessly* true. *It neither flatters nor makes ugly." With this unshakable belief in photography's absolute recording power, Delton became the most authoritative photographer of horses during the Second Empire and well afterward.*

E.P.J.

Bibliography:
Paton, 1884

Louis-Jean Delton

## VIII-11
## Thoroughbred English Stallion Belonging to Count Aguado

c. 1867

Inscribed on mount: 11 Etalon de pur sang anglais au Cte Aguado
Albumen print from wet collodion on glass negative, mounted
18.7 × 25.9 cm

VIII-11

Provenance:
Marguerite Milhau, Paris; André Jammes, Paris; Samuel Wagstaff, Jr., New York

"The head of the English horse approximates that of the Arabian. Its neck is slender and very fine at the attachment; its immense shoulder of a striking obliquity; its chest deeper and larger than that of the Arabian horse; the hindquarters... of a superior development; its flat legs, rather short from the knee to the hoof, not always ample enough, this is one of its drawbacks; the pastern is less oblique than that of the Arabian, but sufficiently long and of a perfect elasticity. The solid frame... [is] capable of enduring all strain; there is almost no belly so as not to overburden the legs with unnecessary weight. In a word, a perfect machine to attain the purpose in view: strength and speed.... A machine! Am I justified in speaking thus of the high spirit, courage, indomitable energy, the passion to excel that drives the thoroughbred to the very last heartbeat? We might add, as less important but characteristic details, that the thoroughbred is nearly always bay, bay-brown, or chestnut colored; there are a few blacks, very few of gray or white and even so they are not the best ones. No white horse has ever achieved olympic glory at our race courses" (M. L. Enault, *Revue Française*, quoted in "Courses," in Larousse, 1886–90, vol. V, p. 379).

Enault's views are borne out in Delton's *Album hippique*, where the only pure white horse shown is a prize-winning omnibus horse. The splendid English stallion in plate 11, shown

here, so mysteriously defined against a painted backdrop, must have belonged either to Count Olympe Clemente Aguado de las Marismas or to his brother, Count Onésipe Gonsalve, members of a Spanish banking family. Count Olympe Aguado was an early amateur photographer, a founding member of the Société Héliographique and the Société Française de Photographie. In his house at 18, place Vendôme he had an elaborate darkroom attended by servants. He specialized in studies of trees and animals and experimented with enlargements at an early stage, but is also known to have photographically printed counterfeit money, 20,000 francs of which a friend of his spent for a night with La Païva! (Goncourt and Goncourt, 1956, vol. I, p. 1278).

E.P.J.

Collection Samuel Wagstaff, Jr., New York

---

## Gustave LeGray

*Villiers-sur-Bel 1820–1882 Egypt*

*None of the outstanding photographers of the Second Empire studied the different photographic methods or employed them with a more profound understanding than LeGray. He evolved and refined much of photography's early subject matter, and through his writings suggested photography's primary aesthetic theory. By 1855 he had influenced, if* not taught, every important photographer in France. One student confessed he could not remember what he had specifically learned from LeGray other than to "love photography."

LeGray had been a painter of portraits and landscapes, having studied in the atelier of Paul Delaroche and exhibited in a few Salons, but during the 1840s he learned of the work of Alphonse-Louis Poitevin and was led into photographic chemistry. By 1850 LeGray had published his first treatise on paper-negative photography; his process was slow, but it almost guaranteed success. LeGray was convinced that the photographer's future lay with the use of paper. He had also experimented with glass negatives and was, in fact, the first to publish a formula for collodion on glass.

LeGray was a founding member of the Société Héliographique and the Société Française de Photographie and participated in every important international photography exhibition during the 1850s and 1860s. In 1851 he was sent by the Commission des Monuments Historiques to photograph in the Aquitaine and the Midi with his student, Mestral.

During the early 1850s he photographed in the Forest of Fontainebleau. The arrangement of light and shade that he achieved with paper negatives was not unlike that of the Barbizon painters. Landscape painters found what they were looking for as much in the abstract simplifications of light in such photographs as from nature directly.

In 1857 LeGray was asked to document the camp of Châlons, a military training ground of which Napoleon III was extremely proud. A rare collection of portraits of officers, all blind stamped "Gustave LeGray, photographe de l'Empereur," is at Compiègne (C 58.051).

Probably after the Exposition Universelle of 1855, LeGray moved into a studio at 35, boulevard des Capucines, which was furnished in great splendor. But LeGray's days as a fashionable photographer were limited and around 1859 he left Paris. He was photographing Palermo in 1860, and by 1865 he was in Egypt, teaching drawing. He submitted photographs to the London exhibition of 1861 and views of Egypt to the 1867 Exposition Universelle in Paris.

E.P.J.

Bibliography:
Nadar, 1900, pp. 194–207; Lécuyer, 1945, p. 59; 1965, Paris, Musée des Arts Décoratifs, "Photographie," nos. 371–72, 581–97; Scharf, 1968, pp. 102–3, 271 n. 37; 1969, Philadelphia, nos. 23, 63–69, 98–101; 1976, Paris, Bibliothèque Nationale, nos. 40, 103–5, 197

Gustave LeGray

## VIII-12
## Album of the Salon of 1852

1852
Ten salt prints from waxed-paper negatives pasted to album leaves
60.5 × 47.5 cm

Provenance:
André Jammes, Paris

Photograph exhibited:
**First Floor Gallery**
Blind stamp on print, at bottom: Gustave Le-Gray
24.2 × 38 cm

The precedent for documenting exhibition installations had been established at the time of the Great Exhibition in London in 1851. Nikolaas Henneman had produced 155 photographs to illustrate the reports of the juries in 115 presentation copies for Queen Victoria and Prince Albert. In contrast, this album by LeGray may be unique. It is not known who commissioned this modest attempt at reportage, and there is no information in the album to indicate imperial or state patronage or, for that matter, LeGray's status as a photographer in relation to the court.

The album selectively inventories an installation of pictures in a temporary wooden

structure erected in the *cour d'honneur* of the Palais Royal for the Salon exhibitions of 1850–51 and 1852. The photographs reveal paintings massed together in selected clusters. The effect is similar to that of a stamp collection. Its enchantment derives from this transformation through change of scale and lack of clearly established scale relationships. Even the portieres dividing the rooms, parted to allow further access to the pictures beyond, make the whole ensemble look like the model for an exhibition, rather than the installation itself. Because there are neither gallery visitors nor other intrusions, the impression is one of complete silence, with the animated figures in the paintings providing the only life.

Paper-negative photography is largely responsible for the suggestions of "aura," to use Walter Benjamin's apt characterization of the special atmosphere that locks nineteenth-century photographs into an impenetrable past. Here LeGray made an important aesthetic decision: he chose paper instead of glass for documentation, believing it would provide a truer approximation of a painting exhibition. It is important to realize that reportage was clearly understood by LeGray and many of his contemporaries to be a form of interpretation.

The photograph shown here, recording a long gallery on the first floor entirely illuminated by a skylight, is dominated by a vista of floor and ceiling. The larger pictures tip forward, almost forming an arcade. In this oblique inventory, one recognizes Courbet's large ver-

sion of the *Young Women from the Village* (1851) on the left. The halation contributed substantially to the effect of subtle circulation of air around the works of art. The light, ordered in this way, was a means of expression that an artist of LeGray's inclinations was quick to use to advantage. Contemporaries of LeGray such as Marville (*see* no. VIII-22) and Robert (*see* no. VIII-40), who recorded works of art, also understood the way light might be controlled to evoke the poetic spirit of an object rather than its literal photographic description.

E.P.J.

Collection André Jammes, Paris

Gustave LeGray

## VIII-13
## The Return of the Prince-President (Place de la Concorde)

1852
Blind stamp on print, lower right: Gustave LeGray
Salt print from wet collodion on glass negative, mounted
12.9 × 18.9 cm

Provenance:
Gérard Lévy, Paris; Lunn Gallery, Washington, D.C.
Exhibition:
1976, London, Colnaghi, no. 91 (repro.)
Bibliography:
Lacan, 1852; Nibelle, 1854, "Photographie"; Lacan, 1854, "Photographie"

At first glance nothing seems to be happening in this photograph. Pale configurations intimate time and place. Little specks, strewn then massed, suggest a collective intelligence below, maybe even an event. It is a scene, somehow like the past, but for memory's imperfect recollection, sadly out of reach. The vignetting lens intensifies this feeling. It frames the picture by asking us to peer down into it, as if into a well.

In the eyes of Ernest Lacan, this photograph was a miraculous achievement. In 1852 he devoted nearly an entire article in *La Lumière* to describing it: "M. LeGray, standing on the roof of the Admiralty, was able to capture a large section of the place de la Concorde. On the left, the trees in the Tuileries have been abstracted into a mass above the rostrums festooned with streamers. In the background the towers of the Church of Sainte Clotilde are still under con-

VIII-12

VIII-13

Exhibition:
1977, Zurich, p. 396

Bibliography:
Périer, 1855, part 4, p. 228; Scharf, 1968, pp. 275–76
n. 49

Paul Nibelle's article in *La Lumière* (1854) on the history of the château and the forest at Fontainebleau reflected the already well-established interest in this area among painters and expressed the more recent expansion of this interest among photographers. He interpreted the forest as a "museum," stocked with an infinite supply of pictures for the taking; this perfectly picturesque characterization allowed his readers to see how well photographic sketching might be fitted into such a search.

LeGray had photographed at Fontainebleau in 1851 using waxed-paper negatives. This process was considered an artist's medium, not simply because it could be manipulated to suggest visual characteristics found in charcoal, lithography, or even painting, but because in the right hands, paper might be used to suggest selectively the idea of a place.

The paper negative produced a light of its own, which had very little to do with the truthful appearance of natural sunshine. Rather, the effect was of a murky palpable atmosphere circulating around objects. The paper fibers, choked up with chemicals, prevented the image, so brightly registered on the ground glass, from recording the subject as clearly as might have been expected before the exposure.

A photographer soon discovered that he had to know what he wanted beforehand in order to attain it. He learned from trial and error to anticipate what details would be lost or overemphasized and how to plan ahead in the exposure or framing to compensate for the changes. All of this quickly led him away from simple copying. Nature was the subject matter of the photographer; but it was also his palette. Wind and weather, cloud movements and their shadows, offered the element of play that photographers learned to control and, in an important sense, to "paint" with.

LeGray and Flaubert shared similar interpretations of realism, both viewing it as an "eternal fusion of illusion and reality," to use Flaubert's expression. With the camera LeGray had discovered exactly what Flaubert would later write to Huysmans: "Art is not reality. Whatever one may do, one is obliged to choose amongst the elements which it provides" (quoted in Starkie, 1971, p. 380).

This print of the Futaie de Bas-Bréau must be dated later than 1851, when the negative was made, because the signature stamp on the mount was used only in the mid-1850s. The coloration marks a dramatic change in LeGray's

struction and the dome of the Invalides, slightly paler, rises in a far distant space, giving a feeling of greater depth above and beyond the quais, where quite a large crowd mills about. The triumphal arch, erected by workmen from the Louvre, is in the center with flags, beaklike columns, and banners. The setting sun illuminates the whole tableau obliquely. On the side of the pavement, delineated by the row formed by the National Guard, the crowd is more concentrated, the heads more dense; but in the foreground, on the asphalt, near the parapets where the trenches used to be, groups separate, spectators become isolated. There the figures, their costumes and postures, stand out very sharply in little animated shapes. These little figures, no larger than half a centimeter high, have expression, character, self-possession" (Lacan, 1852).

Lacan believed that LeGray's photograph was the best example of reportage he had ever seen. He envisioned a great future for photography in documenting historical events, especially public holidays, for he felt that during such times one discovered the truth about the present. For Lacan the photographer had the power to offer the palpitating heart of Second Empire citizenry to the future, in symbols of national pride gleaned from the shape of the crowd.

Lacan and the critic Francis Wey urged photographers to join with history painters and engravers for the popular press. *Le Monde Illustré* and *L'Illustration* are filled with wood engravings for which photographers have been given credit. LeGray's name appears in these periodicals on numerous occasions.

E.P.J.

Lunn Gallery/Graphics International Ltd., Washington, D.C.

Gustave LeGray

## VIII-14
## Undergrowth at Bas-Bréau (Forest of Fontainebleau)

c. 1855
Signature stamp, lower right: Gustave LeGray; blind stamp on mat: Gustave LeGray et Cie
Albumen print from waxed-paper negative
25.9 × 36.8 cm

Provenance:
Gérard Lévy, Paris

taste as a printer. The 1851 salt prints in the Fontainebleau album of André Jammes are opaque bronze-black, the result of gold chloride toning over particularly dark prints. By 1855, however, LeGray was printing with another idea in mind. Here, the print is a richer, sweeter translucent brown, given further luster by the albumen surface.

E.P.J.

Collection Gérard-Lévy, Paris

VIII-14

Gustave LeGray

# VIII-15
# The Imperial Yacht,
# "La Reine Hortense,"
# in the Port of Le Havre

1856
Signature stamp, lower right : Gustave LeGray
Albumen print from wet collodion on glass negative
32.3 × 40.1 cm

Provenance :
Gérard Lévy, Paris

Named after Hortense de Beauharnais, mother of the Emperor, this steamship made several voyages which were recorded in Le Monde Illustré and L'Illustration. On June 16, 1856, La Reine Hortense left Le Havre carrying the Prince Napoleon on an expedition to

Greenland and Spitsbergen, commanded by the baron de la Roncière le Noury, and accompanied by the ships Le Cocyte and L'Artemise. The party returned two months later, at the end of August.

The next year the yacht brought the Emperor and the Empress to England on one of the many friendly visits that followed the Crimean War and the Exposition Universelle of 1855. Departing from Le Havre on August 5, the yacht returned to the port on August 11.

LeGray, who was employed by the Emperor, was photographing at the camp of Châlons at the end of August and into September of 1857, and it hardly seems possible that he could have made this photograph at the time of the second trip. A date of 1856, the year LeGray made the first collection of seascapes along the Normandy coast, at Sainte-Adresse and Le Havre, is more likely for this view.

In this portrayal of the beautifully rigged light steamship, the smiling man who towers above all the other crew members might be the Prince himself. LeGray seems to have called to everyone on board to prepare for his picture-taking since the figures near the stern appear to be looking into the lens. The picture must have been taken from one of the attendant ships. The commercial ship in the background does not belong to the expedition.

In 1860 L'Aigle, made of sheathed iron, replaced La Reine Hortense as the imperial yacht. This "floating fortress" became the pride of France. Built in 1859, she was the first iron-clad battleship in the world. In 1860, on a voyage made by the Emperor from Toulon to Corsica and Algeria, three ships again made up the party : the Emperor sailed on the L'Aigle; La Gloire was an attendant frigate; and La Reine Hortense carried the entourage. The Victoria and Albert Museum possesses two views of the imperial yacht in its collection of photographs by LeGray.

E.P.J.

Collection Gérard-Lévy, Paris

VIII-15

Gustave LeGray

## VIII-16
## The Empress Eugénie Praying
## (Saint-Cloud)

1856
Signature stamp, lower right: Gustave LeGray;
blind stamp in margin: Photographie Gustave
LeGray et Cie, Paris
Albumen print from wet collodion on glass
negative, mounted
23 × 30.6 cm

Provenance:
Gérard Lévy, Paris
Bibliography:
Clouzot, 1925, p. 152; Dayot, 1900, repro. p. 115

Several variants of this photograph are
known. All appear to have been made in the
salon of the Empress at the château of Saint-
Cloud; a contemporary watercolor by Fortuné
de Fournier (q.v.) identifying the interior records the same writing desk and chairs, console
tables, sconces, and paneling (Terrier, 1959, pl.
23).

It would seem that the Empress's sitting for
LeGray occurred shortly after the baptism of
the Prince Imperial. The pictures were probably
made to provide Thomas Couture with photographic sketches for his painting honoring the
event, which took place in Notre Dame on
June 14, 1856 (see nos. VI-31–VI-35).

Neither Couture's oil sketches nor his
drawings for the painting indicate the painter's
direct use of LeGray's photographs. Nonetheless the pose in this photograph certainly reflects Couture's idea, and it is likely that LeGray
was directed or instructed by him. Many official
paintings for the court were produced in collaborations between the best official painters
and outstanding photographers. Another
example is Gérôme's probable use of Nadar's
portraits of the ambassadors visiting from Siam
(Collection Gérard-Lévy, Paris) for his painting
*Reception of the Siamese Ambassadors* (no. VI-59).

Of all the variants of the photographed
portrait of Eugénie, the example exhibited here
is the most abstract. The figure is formally and
spiritually detached from its setting. The Empress moved her head, thus flattening her face
into a mask; the focal emphasis thus shifts to
the outer flounce of the gown, the hands, and
the prie-dieu.

The Empress's expression is one that she
could not have considered flattering. Because
of this, the picture provides an unusual glimpse
of royalty backstage. For despite the overt piety
and the voluminous trappings, a sense of
fatigue has entered the scene. By contrast, two
photographs at Compiègne of the head and
bodice of the Empress and another—the gift to
the Compiègne museum from Couture's descendants—that shows her in the same gown
and posture but with a dark velvet cape do

justice to her beauty and are probably related to
this sitting.

It is tragic that virtually all of Eugénie's
photographic collection, a splendid panorama
of Second Empire tastes and conceits, rivaled
only by the collections of Nadar, Lacan, and
Queen Victoria, was lost in the destruction of
the Tuileries and Saint-Cloud in 1870 and
1871, making those pictures that have survived
all the more precious.

E.P.J.

Collection Gérard-Lévy, Paris

Gustave LeGray

## VIII-17
## The Great Wave

1857
Signature stamp, lower right: Gustave LeGray;
blind stamp on mount: Gustave LeGray et Cie,
Paris
Albumen print from two wet collodion on glass
negatives
34.4 × 41.1 cm

Provenance:
Gérard Lévy, Paris
Exhibitions:
1973, Turin (repro.); 1977, Zurich (not in catalogue)

In December 1856, LeGray exhibited a collection of seascapes at the Photographic Society
in London, views that suggest the Atlantic
coastline. It is believed that these pictures were
taken at Le Havre (see no. VIII-15) or Sainte-
Adresse. LeGray also photographed the
Mediterranean, notably from the port of Sète,
west of Montpellier. We can place him at the
port in 1857, when he traveled south to photograph the opening of the new railroad line from
Toulouse to Sète. *Le Monde Illustré* reproduced a
wood-engraved view of the port made from a
photograph by LeGray (May 9, 1857, pp. 8–9).

Some writers gather all the seascapes into
one undifferentiated group and date them
1856, presumably basing the date on the London exhibition. The two series are really separate efforts, however, and subtle differences
between them can be discerned. LeGray himself is responsible for mixing them up: he
exhibited them together; he may have added to
their number, although it seems unlikely. The
pictures were exhibited in Paris in 1857 and
1858, and by 1859 were very well known.

VIII-16

VIII-17

*The Great Wave* was made at Sète. Some of the brilliance of sea and sky results from Le-Gray's combination printing from two separate negatives: the sky of this scene may also be found in another seascape. The example here clearly shows retouching in the negative as well. The photograph has become a classic among seascapes. Yet, the wave is not very grand, no larger than the jetty in the distance. It is not threatening; neither does it evoke the sublimely Romantic notions of natural forces as metaphors for states of mind and human destiny. LeGray's wave does not impinge upon anyone; there is nothing of human scale against which to measure it.

Its grandeur may be associated with principles of Realism in France at mid-century. *The Great Wave* is great because it is durable. It seems to have very little to do with the overwhelming size and scope of the ocean. Instead, its texture makes it seem physically manageable. Aaron Scharf (1968, p. 102) has demonstrated that Courbet (q.v.) knew LeGray's seascapes and used at least one as the idea for a painting. It is not surprising that Courbet found what he was looking for in the photographer's work. The locale was perfect, but even more than this, the sea in LeGray's lens refuses to be ephemeral. The use of words such as "prairie" to describe the surface of the sea in LeGray's views or "tombstone" to suggest the sea as an impervious slab covering the dead below indicates one

London reviewer's response to an impression of permanence and opacity (*Journal of the Photographic Society*, February 21, 1857, p. 214). In this way LeGray's views of the sea corresponded perfectly to the world as Courbet understood it, and *The Great Wave* is their quintessence.

E.P.J.

Collection Gérard-Lévy, Paris

---

*Henri LeSecq*

*Paris 1818–1882 Paris*

*In the 1830s LeSecq entered the Ecole des Beaux-Arts as a student of Pradier, then worked with Granger, and finally Paul Delaroche. He became a painter of mediocre genre scenes, making his debut at the Salon of 1842 and winning a third-class medal in 1845. In spite of the triviality of his work, he exhibited at the Salon regularly until his death.*

*He learned photography after the Revolution of 1848. With Nègre (q.v.) he experimented with the available processes, especially the dry waxed-paper negative process of LeGray (q.v.). While other photographers quickly progressed to negatives on glass,*

*LeSecq restricted his photographic activity to paper. Initially using photography to make quick sketches of genre subjects for paintings, LeSecq then turned to architecture. Based on a series of early work documenting Amiens (1850–51), he was selected by the Commission des Monuments Historiques as one of five architectural photographers to photograph ancient and medieval monuments endangered by vandalism and neglect. LeSecq was assigned the provinces of Champagne, Alsace, and Lorraine; later he extensively documented the cathedrals of Strasbourg, Amiens, Reims, and Chartres.*

*For the seven or eight years he spent photographing, LeSecq made the most of the murky effects of the waxed-paper negative and its reticence in the rendering of detail. In 1852 he began making landscapes, probably in the woods around Montmirail, near Epernay. These studies, noted at the time for their resemblance to the painted works of Corot (q.v.), Théodore Rousseau (q.v.), Dupré, and Diaz, vary in size from colossal prints to others as small as postcards. They are among the most imposing landscape sketches of the mid-nineteenth century in France.*

*LeSecq rarely delved into portraiture. From 1849 to 1853 he documented the great architectural changes that were being made throughout Paris. He exhibited in every important photography exhibition in Europe and the British Isles. It was at the Exposition Universelle in 1855 that his accomplishments were summed up. Shortly after, he made a group of still lifes in his own studio which were his crowning achievement. Probably around 1856 LeSecq gave up photography.*

E.P.J.

Bibliography:
Lacretelle, 1853; Périer, 1855, part 3, p. 196; Lacan, 1856, pp. 87–88; Cromer, 1930; 1965, Paris, Musée des Arts Décoratifs, "Photographie," nos. 373–419; 1965–66, Essen, nos. 121–33; 1969, Philadelphia, nos. 19–22, 90, 213–19; 1973, Turin; Janis, 1976

Henri LeSecq

## VIII-18
## Album

1849–53

Inscribed on first page: Photographies relatives aux travaux de la ville de Paris 1849–1853 A. Berger; inscribed on second page: Legs de M. Amédée Berger, président de la cour de Comptes, fils de M.J. Berger, ancien préfet de la Seine, décède le 27 janvier 1881
Twenty-two salt prints from waxed-paper negatives pasted to album leaves
43 × 60 cm

VIII - 18

Provenance:
Jean-Jacques Berger; Amédée Berger; bequest to the Bibliothèque Historique de la Ville de Paris, 1881 (inv. no. F^mM^m17.643 Res. 68)
Bibliography:
Janis, 1976, pp. 21, 24 n. 9, 25 n. 40

Photograph exhibited:
**Demolition of the Place de l'Hôtel de Ville**
1852
Signed and dated, lower right: h. LeSecq. Paris 1852
23.5 × 33.5 cm

Born in Paris, LeSecq spent much of his life on the Ile Saint-Louis, first on the quai de Bourbon and then later, after a new street eliminated his family's dwelling, in a grander house on the quai de Béthune. As a connoisseur of his city and a self-appointed guardian of its medieval architectural treasures, he combed the center of Paris to conserve photographically the corners being destroyed by both prefects of the Seine, Berger and Haussmann. He was especially interested in the area being razed by the extension of the rue de Rivoli, for it was literally his old neighborhood. He was also interested in documenting the great monuments directly in view each day, such as Notre Dame, the largest form visible outside his window. As all Parisians had done, he had watched its reconstruction since the mid-1840s. After 1851 he regularly made photographic notes, some-

times in the company of Nègre (q.v.), to document the sculptural changes that were taking place on the pile. He conserved a memory of the old Pont Neuf, the Hôtel Dieu, public baths, and all the changes around the Hôtel de Ville, and he assembled these pictures in albums. In this way LeSecq "made his monument," to use the cliché of the period.

It is not known how this beautiful album came to be made. It is quite possible that Jean-Jacques Berger commissioned the photographs from LeSecq, but there is no evidence for this. It would seem that Berger bound them into the album himself. Berger was named Prefect of the Seine after the election of December 10, 1849. It was under his administration that the immense work of redesigning the city of Paris began, but he was not retained by Napoleon III because he was reluctant to spend the vast sums necessary to fulfill the Emperor's dream to beautify the city. After the coup d'état he was put on an advisory commission, and was succeeded by Baron Haussmann in 1853.

Several photographs in the album relate directly to etched views by Charles Meryon made during the same years: his views on page 5 should be compared to *Le Petit Pont*, 1850 (Delteil, 1869–1927 [Meryon] no. 24); page 16 to *L'Arche du Pont Notre Dame*, 1853 (Delteil no. 25); pages 17 and 18 to *La Pompe*

*Notre Dame*, 1852 (Delteil no. 31); and page 20 to *Le Pont Neuf*, 1853 (Delteil no. 33).

E.P.J.

Bibliothèque Historique de la Ville de Paris

Henri LeSecq

## VIII-19
## Rustic Scene (Corner of a Farm near the Quarries of Saint-Leu)

c. 1851
Salt print from waxed-paper negative
22 × 32.4 cm

Provenance:
Bibliothèque des Arts Décoratifs (inv. no. 27)

This photograph looks at first like an empty stage set for *Giselle* or *Faust*. In fact, it is a landscape which seems to be related to studies made in 1851 at Saint-Leu-d'Esserent. Situated directly north of Paris on the Oise River, Saint-Leu was the site of numerous quarries from which the famous Saint-Leu stone was excavated. One of the quarry studies is signed,

VIII - 19

dated, and identified in the collection of André Jammes (1969, Philadelphia, no. 90, repro.). There are several related landscapes in the Musée des Arts Décoratifs, Paris. In the Jammes example, abrupt contrasts of light and dark are crisp and detail is more apparent. Here, the subject is much more fragmentary, and the mystery lies in the recognizable peripheral detail framing the fathomless void. Another impression, cropped on top and sides and printed in Prussian blue as a cyanotype from ammoniocitrate of iron and potassium ferricyanide, may be found at the International Museum of Photography in Rochester, New York.

From 1851 on, LeSecq was severely criticized for the unattractive ruddy coloration of his prints. And it became clear to him after a few years that his prints were fading. This sad situation exists in nearly all the architectural prints that LeSecq presented to the Bibliothèque Nationale in 1854, which have faded to a disappointing reddish-yellow tint. Around the 1860s or 1870s, LeSecq re-pulled some of his negatives, perhaps with the hope of greater permanence, using the process of A. Marion (1872) or of Testud de Beauregard and made a series of blueprints of a number of sculptural details from his architectural works, landscapes, and still lifes.

E.P.J.

Bibliothèque des Arts Décoratifs, Paris

Henri LeSecq

## VIII-20
## Public Bath or Swimming School

c. 1852–53
Salt print from waxed-paper negative
12.5 × 17.4 cm

Provenance:
Bibliothèque des Arts Décoratifs (inv. no. 481)

"At present, the baths in Paris are numerous and afford every kind of accommodation at very low cost. Ecoles de Natation and baths of every kind are to be found each summer in floating establishments on the Seine, covered with canvas and fitted up with galleries, bathing rooms, plunging bridges, etc. Net or woodwork is placed at the bottom, which can be raised to the surface on occasion. Men are always in attendance to give instruction in swimming, and ropes and poles are in readiness either to aid pupils or prevent accidents. Their

price is generally twelve sous, but there are some [for] the lower order of people as low as four sous" (Galignani, 1852).

This bathing scene, possibly an as yet unidentified swimming school, appears to be unique in the history of early photography. (Two paper negatives related in subject are also in the Bibliothèque des Arts Décoratifs). Paris teemed with bathing establishments during the Second Empire and chances of identifying the one pictured here seem slim indeed. Guidebooks list several important ones, such as the Ecole Nationale de Natation at the Pont de la Concorde and the Ecole de Natation Henri IV, recorded in Charles Meryon's etching of the *Pont au Change*, 1854 (Delteil, 1869–1927 [Meryon], no. 34). Meryon's etching of another bathing place, the Bain-Froid Chevrier, beside the Pont Neuf, 1864 (Delteil no. 44), was a work commissioned from the artist by LeSecq himself.

In LeSecq's controlled structure, shots of bright light alternate with unfathomable shadows. Bathers stare into dark spaces as if into the inevitable void, each compartmentalized by the barrier bars of light between them. This effect has been enhanced greatly by

the obvious drawbacks in LeSecq's photographic technology and the fact that with the particular waxed-paper process he was using, exposures were several minutes long. Nevertheless, the limitations of calotype helped create the ground rules for its art. This meditative scene should be compared with the chaotic crowded compositions of Daumier's lithographs of the Bains Deligny (Delteil, 1869–1927 [Daumier], nos. 2863, 2864, 2866–75, 2877).

The figures, rare occurences in LeSecq's work, should be compared to those of Delmaet et Durandelle (q.v.) and to the master composer of figures in large-scale views, Baldus, in the railroad album (no. VIII-2), in order to observe several distinct manners invented by photographers to station human forms in space. More than simply providing a scale of reference, the figures are landmarks establishing intricate relationships within the surveyed spaces which become altered through the disorienting lens and ground glass.

E.P.J.

Bibliothèque des Arts Décoratifs, Paris

VIII-20

## Charles Marville
*Died c. 1879 Paris*

*Considering Marville's close relationship to the center of photographic activity before and during the Second Empire, it is surprising that the full story of his career is so difficult to establish. He is hardly mentioned in contemporary sources, and it is still not known where he was born or precisely how he came to photography.*

*Marville was a painter-engraver, from the 1830s worked as an illustrator, and was associated with a number of socialist publications. During the same period the name Marville is listed as collaborator on a number of light comedies written by Nadar's friend Auguste Lefranc. During the Second Empire, Marville had numerous civic commissions. In 1856, with Mayer & Pierson (q.v.) and Victor Plumier, he produced ninety-nine glass negatives of the baptismal ceremony of the Prince Imperial with special views of the crowds outside Notre Dame. He made reproductions of works of art as photographer to the Louvre, and he documented new constructions for the Administration des Bâtiments Civils. For the Musées Nationaux, he recorded renovations of older edifices and documented the new Opéra, and produced an album devoted to Bagatelle, the villa of the Marquess of Hertford.*

*Today, Marville's reputation as a photographer is based almost entirely on the magnificent compendium of pictures from glass-plate negatives documenting old Paris (Musée Carnavalet and Bibliothèque Historique de la Ville de Paris). This collection resulted from a methodical survey during the 1860s in which he ferreted out hidden medieval passageways and ancient structures which would soon be lost in the demolitions ordered by Haussmann.*

*They were the most important precedent for the equally impressive documentary projects of Eugène Atget forty years later.*

*Another body of pictures were done by Marville with paper negatives and produced in association with the printer and publisher Louis-Désiré Blanquart-Evrard of Lille. The origins of Marville's relationship with Blanquart-Evrard are unknown. In an exhaustive study of the career of the publisher, however, Isabelle Jammes in Paris has established that of the twenty-four different folio-collections produced by the printing establishment at Lille, ten contain work by Marville. Over one hundred of his calotype works may be found in Blanquart-Evrard's portfolios, including* L'Album photographique de l'artiste et l'amateur *(1851).* Mélanges photographiques *(1851), and* Etudes photographiques *(1853).*

E.P.J.

Bibliography:
Nadar, 1900, p. 202; Chéronnet, 1951, passim; 1965–66, Essen, p. 17, nos. 61, 65 (repro.); 1969, Philadelphia, nos. 35, 47–49; 1976, Paris, Bibliothèque Historique; 1976, Paris, Bibliothèque Nationale, nos. 108–9

VIII-21

Charles Marville

## VIII-21
## Man Reclining under a Horse Chestnut Tree

1853
Signed and dated on negative, lower left: Ch. Marville 1853; printed on mount: Blanquart-Evrard, éditeur Etudes photographiques série no. 1
Salt print from waxed-paper negative, mounted
21 × 16 cm

Provenance:
André Jammes, Paris

Exhibition:
1978, Chalon-sur-Saône

Bibliography:
Jammes, n.d., pl. 13; Christ, 1965, pl. 65

The intensity of Marville's interest in trees and his pleasure in sylvan "interiors" relate his work to the investigations of the Barbizon painters and to other photographers working in the Forest of Fontainebleau, all of whom knew one another. A photograph by Marville in the Bibliothèque Nationale shows Corot and Diaz seated on boulders in the forest.

Marville discovered that leafy trees provided the perfect conditions for exploring the endlessly varied relationships between figure and ground. This view of an old chestnut tree makes such a discovery its subject. Out-of-scale leaves, flattened by the light into large white cutouts, jump from the ensemble and establish their own surface in front of the focal plane. The languid young man in the white suit, his hat posed against his shadow, retires into a reverie. The details of his form are not as clear as the crisper wavy lines of the bark, which draw out twisting patterns to further vary and refine the piebald beauty of the light on the foliage. This picture illustrates perfectly Ruskin's observations on the difficulty of drawing leaves (*Elements of Drawing*, section 83–84).

Deep black spaces, obliterating all organic form and detail, mingle so subtly with the exquisite variety of highlights that the whole natural tapestry is abstractly reorganized into a completely new spatial environment. This photograph is one of many that might be cited as precursing by over a decade the mercurial lighting effects of Monet's picnic scenes set under the trees.

*Man Reclining under a Horse Chestnut Tree* is a plate from Blanquart-Evrard's *Etudes photographiques*, a series notable for its large number of studies of trees and the effects of snow and ice by other early pictorial photographers such as Edouard Loydreau, E. Benecke, and Victor Regnault. Although Blanquart-Evrard did not credit the photographers, their names appear on their negatives. This series must have contained more than eighty-seven prints, but only some sixty are known. Many of the photographs were intended for artists; others assisted in the general education of an artistically enlightened list of subscribers.

When the work of Marville and his contemporaries is properly assembled and understood, it will be necessary to review the history of the formative years of French Impressionism and properly integrate the activity of the photographers. For it is pictures such as this that make it undeniable that the conventions of vision established by the camera lens and by paper-negative chemistry during the 1850s played a paramount role in formulating the principles of the so-called "natural vision" of the avant-garde painters of the 1860s and 1870s.

E.P.J.

Collection André Jammes, Paris

Charles Marville

## VIII-22
## The Treasury of Reims Cathedral

1854
Signed, dated, and inscribed on negative, lower left: Reims. 332 ch. Marville 1854
Albumen print from waxed-paper negative
25.3 × 34.5 cm

VIII-22

Provenance:
André Jammes, Paris
Exhibition:
1969, Philadelphia, no. 10 (repro.)

"The concept of the diminutive in building exercises a most powerful fascination.... how deep is the appeal of 'the little house.'" In *Heavenly Mansions* (1963, p. 2), John Summerson speculated on the origins of ceremonial architecture from primal needs and fancies expressed in childhood games. This astonishing still life of reliquaries from Reims brings Summerson to mind. In some inexplicable manner the photograph has transformed great treasures of jewels, crystal, and finely wrought gold and silver into a conglomeration of mysterious little houses that seem almost like toys. These little temples, shrines whose functions from ancient times were symbolic and ceremonial, are here oddly quaint, and seem as strangely archetypal as the child's first extemporized "little shelter."

How unfamiliar and remote medieval religious symbolism and ceremony seem on viewing this collection! Yet the photograph inspires a certain awe as well. Marville could have avoided including the modern graffiti, but against its irreverent scrawl, the meticulous tracery on the objects touched by the harsh light seems all the more esoteric, wonderful,

and uncanny. What aspirations directed the hands responsible for these enchanted objects? Marville might have asked himself, for we are led to ask the same question faced with these ghostly "aediculae."

E.P.J.

Collection André Jammes, Paris

## Mayer & Pierson

*Active Paris 1850s–60s*

*Although sometimes referred to as Mayer Frères & Pierson, this association seems to have consisted of Héribert Mayer and Louis Pierson (1822–1913). Professional portrait photographers to the rich, noble, and notorious during the 1850s and 1860s, they worked separately as well as together. Each had his favorite portrait subjects: Pierson photographed the actresses Rachel and Ristori and some of the earliest and more erotic studies of Virginia, the comtesse de Castiglione (see no. V-11), who eventually became the Emperor's mistress. A compendium of self-idolatry in photographs, the album of portraits and costume studies (Metropolitan Museum of Art, New York) produced for her by the team admirably re-*

*cords her ingenious personal taste while it also reveals the nature of a sustained collaboration between a celebrity and her ever-present photographic celebrants.*

*Nadar (q.v.), who considered Mayer & Pierson inferior as portraitists, emphasized their obsession with profit, their slipshod technique, and their relinquishing of all artistic standards: "They restricted themselves, very profitably, to one style and even one size of picture.... Without a thought for composing the picture in a manner favorable to the sitter, nor for the expression on his face, nor for the way in which the light happened to be falling, they placed the client in a fixed position and made one rough and ready negative...." (in Braive, 1966, p. 93). The Castiglione album bears Nadar out, but in it are refreshing examples of Mayer & Pierson's work that contradict the usual assessment of their reputation, including remarkable studies of her feet, knees, elbows, and back, and certain costume studies (Roy, 1958, repro. pp. 16–17).*

*Mayer & Pierson were attracted to everything chic about photography, specifically, novel technical improvements which could become instant moneymakers and crowd-pleasers. According to Gernsheim and Gernsheim (1969, p. 294), Mayer & Pierson was the only firm of repute making ambrotypes in 1855. They competed with Delessert (q.v.) to make mammoth-size portrait enlargements, and were the first in France to have a special camera built to take eight separate portraits on one negative for speedier and more economical* carte-de-visite *portraits in 1860 (Gernsheim and Gernsheim, 1969, p. 302). In 1862 Mayer & Pierson published* La Photographie considérée comme art et industrie, *an apt expression of their equivocal reputation.*

E.P.J.

Bibliography:
Mayer & Pierson, 1862; Nadar, 1900, pp. 197–98; Aragon et al., 1942, repro. pp. 29, 43; Roy, 1958; Scharf, 1968, pp. 113–17; Gernsheim and Gernsheim, 1969, pp. 267, 294, 302, 315; Richardson, 1971, repro. p. 74; Coppens, 1974, pp. 34–39

Mayer & Pierson

## VIII-23
## The Prince Imperial on His Pony Being Photographed

c. 1859
Albumen print from wet collodion on glass negative
17 × 17 cm

Provenance:
Gérard Lévy, Paris

Bibliography:
Roy, 1958, repro. p. 6; Braive, 1966, repro. pp. 80–81

VIII-23

It is not known whether this engaging portrayal of the little Prince Imperial at about two or three years of age, precautiously bound to the saddle of his pony, Bouton d'or, was intended to be published and sold commercially by Mayer & Pierson. Indeed, examples exist in cards of cabinet-size format with all auxiliary elements cropped, leaving only the oddly swaddled prince, a tiny rigid figure staring ahead, backed by an expedient piece of studio drapery with the full length of the pony filling the frame.

Although the original negative was made by Mayer & Pierson, the photograph in the cabinet version was sold by the company of Adolphe Braun (q.v.), 18, rue Louis le Grand, avenue de l'Opéra, Paris, and Dornach. This has caused some confusion as to the authorship of the photograph, even though Braun was careful to state on the back of the mount that he was printing portraits by Mayer & Pierson from negatives of their former establishment "carefully conserved."

The uncropped version has been preserved intact in several examples. It has long been admired for qualities other than those associated with official portrayals of members of the imperial family. More than a portrait in this

state, it is a photograph which comments on the act of photographic portraiture.

The original idea behind the Prince sitting on a real pony was to produce a portrait which alluded to leisure and play, but by placing the child in a pose that seems to suggest his elevation on a throne, the image became hieratic as well. More likely than not, the photographers included the Emperor on the right of the picture without his knowledge. By doing so, they placed him in a position comparable to that of Bachon, the equerry; thus the Emperor becomes another accessory, a stroller who might have wandered in casually, a notion reinforced by the dog nearby. (According to Jean-Marie Moulin, the dog is too light in color to be the prince's pet, Nero.)

The Emperor and the attendant stand like supernumeraries in the wings. This gentle irony of reversals and changes in scale and emphasis bring to mind a grander, but not entirely unsimilar, elaboration of the same idea in Velázquez's *Las Meninas*. In Mayer & Pierson's modest photograph, casualness is set against unmitigated frontality. Hierarchical portraiture has become a pretext for a portrayal of another kind, which ultimately seeks to establish more clearly, if obliquely, a sense of the resonating relationships between those present, whether they are ostensibly being "portrayed" or not.

Finally the photographic "scene" is sufficiently incomplete so that the viewer comes away with the illusion that he has grasped the truth of its character by himself.

E.P.J.

Collection Gérard-Lévy, Paris

---

## F.-J. Moulin

*Active Paris 1850s*

*Moulin's work is first mentioned in 1852. With Nègre (q.v.), he was considered one of the creators of genre photography, but he became better known during the 1850s among photographers such as d'Olivier, Braquehais, Vallou de Villeneuve (q.v.), Malacrida, Eugène Durieu, and later Marconi and Achille Quinet, working in "fine arts photography." This was actually a rather formidable industry, specializing in "academic" nudes for artists.*

*Because it was unsigned, much of Moulin's work*

VIII - 24

*was grouped with that of others into a large and undifferentiated mass of stereoscopic daguerreotypes and prints on paper, which today are being assigned to their original ateliers. Many of these pictures, distinguished by great strength of design and erotic delicacy, transcend the limitations of a commercial market. Many betray characteristic styles that may be connected to individuals, but it is extremely difficult to make definitive attributions based exclusively on style.*

*The category of "erotic theater" had a particularly powerful allure in still photography during the 1850s and 1860s. Nudes, isolated or in contrived settings, were exploited by photography at every level of artistic interpretation. Quantities were universally available. The mode of presentation was not invented by photography; it followed conventions for erotic subjects found in popular lithography from the preceding generation, in the work of Achille Devéria, Vallou de Villeneuve (both of whom were photographing by the 1850s), Tassaert, Numas, Maurin, and others working on* Imagerie galante *and other collections of erotic pictures from the 1820s and 1830s. These lithographs were, of course, reconstitutions of standard erotic modes from the eighteenth century and earlier. Photographic staging brought something even more concrete to these fantasies,*

*especially in the detailed micro-universe of daguerreotype and the three-dimensional illusion through binocular vision in stereoscope.*

*The studio of Moulin, a family business, was extremely active during the 1850s. Besides nudes—Moulin's wife and daughter were among his models—and genre scenes in stereoscopic daguerreotype formats and works on paper, some also for stereoscopes, the atelier also produced "reportages," genre scenes with slightly more ethnographic character, in groups from Algeria and Tunisia (1856).*

E.P.J.

Bibliography:
"Moulin," 1853; "Epreuves stéréoscopiques," 1854

---

F.-J. Moulin

## VIII-24
## Seated Nude

c. 1855
Albumen print from wet collodion on glass negative
19.5 × 14.2 cm

Provenance:
Gérard Lévy, Paris
Exhibition:
1977, Zurich, no. 533 (as Braquehais)

Comparisons of atelier décors in signed prints by Moulin and others have made it possible for Gérard Lévy and François LePage to reattribute this study of a model, formerly ascribed to Braquehais, to Moulin. The nude, posed as a cameo in a still-life vignette of carefully arranged garments alternating with sensuous flesh, is further defined by earrings, necklaces, and other ornaments. This was a type of abstract erotic composition that Ingres (q.v.) had perfected in the first decades of the nineteenth century. Fleshly terrains, tastefully and seductively balanced with selections of accouterments of different scales and textures, were metaphors of sensuality in painting, which the camera was singularly equipped to explore to the fullest. Moulin's demure nude, with a sustained linear profile, also offers a collage of many smaller erotic features within the arrangement of the figure and garments. Many of Courbet's nudes display a similar mode to present the female body as a series of voyeur's keepsakes.

E.P.J.

Collection Gérard-Lévy, Paris

## Nadar (Gaspard-Félix Tournachon)

### Paris 1820–1910 Paris

*Journalist, caricaturist, aeronaut, and portrait photographer in Paris from 1854 to 1887 and a member of the Société Française de Photographie, Nadar had a colorful career and his ingenuous personality attracted numerous chroniclers. He was well established in his own time as the most important photographer of the Second Empire, and his reputation continues to grow even today. For a photographer, albeit a nineteenth-century notable, the literature devoted to Nadar is quite voluminous.*

*None of the publications about him has surveyed the scope of his activities as sucessfully as that of Jean Prinet and Antoinette Dilasser. Their study presents a thorough and lucid account of the important literary, artistic, technological, and legal issues involved in Nadar's career. It recounts his early collaboration with his brother Adrien in a studio at 11, boulevard des Capucines, the establishment of his own studio at 113, rue Saint Lazare in 1853 or 1854, and his eventual lawsuit against his brother, which resulted in Adrien's having to relinquish the use of the pseudonym Nadar, which Félix had established for himself.*

*The photography of Nadar speaks for itself as the works of few nineteenth-century photographers seem to do. Publishers have capitalized on the fact, and picture books on Nadar abound from all parts of the world. Certain of these books at least serve the pur-*

*pose of publicizing Nadar in a manner, one should add, that he might well have chosen for himself. It is hoped that aside from their obvious entertainment value, they will attract critics and writers who will eventually work to break the stereotype of Nadar that the books' very repetitions perpetuate.*

*As with all phases of nineteenth-century photography, a reformation in the critical study of Nadar will occur more quickly as previously unseen images are uncovered. Many of Nadar's pictures were part of his private collection and reflect his special tastes. Kept by his family, these photographs have until recently been accessible to only a few collectors. They are pictures which suggest other unrecognized dimensions of Nadar's sensibility. By exhibiting here a small selection of such exceptional images in the context of more familiar masterpieces, critical comparison might begin again, making possible a fuller interpretation of Nadar's supreme achievement.*

E.P.J.

Bibliography:
Nadar, 1900; Prinet and Dilasser, 1966; Vitali et al., 1973; Barret, 1975; Gosling, 1976; Kozloff, 1976; 1976, Düsseldorf

VIII-26

Nadar (Gaspard-Félix Tournachon)

## VIII-25
## Théophile Gautier

1854
Signed and inscribed: Nadar. 113 St. Lazare
Salt print from wet collodion on glass negative
24.4 × 19.5 cm

Provenance:
Descended in photographer's family; Gérard Lévy, Paris
Exhibition:
1977, Zurich, no. 474 (repro.)

According to Prinet and Dilasser (1966, p. 120), this portrait of the poet, critic, and novelist Théophile Gautier (1811–1872) in a big shaggy overcoat and a damask skullcap is one of the first from Nadar's Saint Lazare studio. This particular print was among the originals kept by Nadar in his personal collection. It remained in the family after the donations to the Cabinet des Estampes and the Départment des Manuscrits of the Bibliothèque Nationale. Another print, with a red signature stamp, is in the Bibliothèque Nationale.

E.P.J.

Collection Gérard-Lévy, Paris

Nadar (Gaspard-Félix Tournachon and Adrien Tournachon*)

## VIII-26
## Pierrot with a Basket of Fruit

1854–55
Blind stamp on print, lower left: Nadare jne; stamp on mount: Nadare jne
Print on gelatined paper (vernis-cuir) from wet collodion on glass negative
28 × 20.4 cm

Provenance:
Gérard Lévy, Paris
Exhibition:
1855, Paris, Exposition Universelle

The professional association between Félix and his brother Adrien at Adrien's studio on the boulevard des Capucines, which resumed for a second time in 1854, ended on January 16, 1855. In that year Adrien accepted a gold medal under the name of "Nadar jeune" for a series of studies of the actor Charles Deburau ("Têtes d'expression de Pierrot"). The next year his brother initiated a lawsuit against him which ended in Adrien's having to relinquish the use of the name of Nadar, which became exclusively Félix's pseudonym.

Prinet and Dilasser state that the brilliant *vernis-cuir* surface of the print was used exclu-

VIII-25

sively by Adrien but that certain pictures with that surface, such as the portrait of Gérard de Nerval and those of Deburau, were the result of a collaboration between the two brothers (Prinet and Dilasser, 1966, p. 124). After Félix's departure and his reestablishment in the Saint Lazare studio, where he supposedly began the celebrated series of portraits, Adrien did not hesitate to print the negatives of Deburau in his special manner and to stamp the photographs with his own stamp.

Charles Deburau (1829–1873), a mime, was the son of the most famous mime of the nineteenth century, Jean-Baptiste-Gaspard Deburau, who restored the character of Pierrot to the French theater. By 1854 the younger Deburau's popularity in Paris was declining, and in 1855 he left Paris to work in the provinces. This series of photographs was made during his last year at the Théâtre Funambules. Nigel Gosling (1976, p. 38) illustrates a print of Pierrot with a basket of fruit which bears the stamp "Adrien Tournachon, Jeune, 17, Boulevard des Italiens." Such a stamp seems to indicate that Adrien, after the gold medal and the trial, still considered the series his own.

E.P.J.

Collection Gérard-Lévy, Paris

Nadar (Gaspard-Félix Tournachon and Adrien Tournachon* )

## VIII-27
## Emmanuel Frémiet

c. 1854–55
Stamp, lower left: Nadar jeune; inscribed in Félix Nadar's hand on front: fremiet; inscribed in Félix Nadar's hand on back: Fremiet
Print on gelatined paper from wet collodion on glass negative
24.6 × 17.4 cm

Provenance:
Gérard Lévy, Paris
Exhibition:
1965, Paris, Bibliothèque Nationale, no. 222

This type of printing, with a highly glossed surface, is associated with Adrien Tournachon's studio at 11, boulevard des Capucines, as is the "Nadar jeune" stamp used from September 21, 1854. However, the two identifications in Félix's hand suggest his involvement as well. The print may have been made by Adrien but

VIII-27

the composition seems to be the work of Félix, who did not add the Saint Lazare address here, perhaps so that he could distinguish work made by him from that made in association with his brother.

This splendid portrait appears only once in the Nadar literature. In the Bibliothèque

VIII-28

Nationale exhibition catalogue, the sitter is described as having been photographed under an artificial light, although there is no evidence that he utilized artificial light before 1858. The particularly striking illumination, corresponding to the very earliest experiments of Félix Nadar, is in fact natural light. The magnificent sweep of drapery in the background also would seem to earmark this composition as the work of Félix.

In 1856, in the lawsuit against his brother, Nadar formulated his ideas about photographic portraiture. "What isn't taught about photography is the feeling for light, the artistic appraisal of effects of different kinds of light and their combinations. What isn't taught is that light may be studied and used depending on the artist's own temperament. What one is apprised of even less is the moral grasp of the subject, the instantaneous communication with the model which allows us to form an opinion about him, to determine his habits, to grasp ideas about him related to his character that permit us to produce not a banal, haphazard, and indifferent reproduction like that of any low level laboratory scientist but the most propitious kind of portrait and intimate likeness. What isn't taught is the psychological side of photography.... What isn't taught is the integrity of hard work : this is an aspect as delicate as the portrait itself, the enthusiasm, the tireless search, and the eager, even dogged, pursuit of something better" (Nadar, 1858).

Frémiet (q.v.), a nephew and pupil of François Rude, was a highly successful animal sculptor. His work was bought by the State, and he received numerous commissions from the Emperor. This portrait seems to date from the time of his early official success, during the mid-1850s.

E.P.J.

Collection Gérard-Lévy, Paris

Nadar (Gaspard-Félix Tournachon)

## VIII-28
## Théophile Gautier

1855–57
Signed and inscribed, lower right: Nadar. 113, St. Lazare; blind stamp on mount: Nadar et Cie Société de Photographie artistique. 113 rue St. Lazare
Albumen print from wet collodion on glass negative
23.8 × 18.6 cm

Provenance:
André Jammes, Paris
Bibliography:
Vitali et al., 1973, pp. 234–35; Barret, 1975, pp. 66–67; Gosling, 1976, pp. 112–13

This portrait was probably photographed in 1854 during the same sitting as that for Gautier wearing an overcoat (no. VIII-25). Gosling (1976, p. 10) mentions that the Société de Photographie Artistique was a short-lived organization formed by Nadar in 1855–56 after the final break with Adrien. It had a long list of shareholders. Thus, based on the stamp on the mount, the print itself must be ascribed to a later date.

E.P.J.

Collection André Jammes, Paris

VIII-29

Nadar (Gaspard-Félix Tournachon)

## VIII-29
## Study of a Seated Draped Female Nude

1856
Signed and inscribed, lower right: Nadar 113 St Lazare
Salt print from wet collodion on glass negative
11.1 × 10.4 cm

Provenance:
Gérard Lévy, Paris
Exhibition:
1977, Zurich (not in catalogue)
Bibliography:
Barret, 1975, pp. 126–27

This eloquent figure study is the only known print from a now-lost negative. One other photograph of a nude by Nadar is known from a late printing by Nadar's son Paul. The literature concerning that work is provided by Gernsheim (1962, pp. 98–101) where the author dates the photograph 1856, the same year as *The Source* by Ingres, (no. VI-71), and reports, although without citing his documentation, that Ingres "was in the habit of sending his sitters to Nadar's studio for preliminary photographs." Gernsheim identifies the sitter as Christine Roux, the original Musette of Henri Murger's *Scènes de la vie de Bohème*. While it is unknown whether Ingres sent any portrait "sitter" or "model" for nude studies to Nadar, the Roux sisters were indeed well known to Nadar and to Murger at the time of his *La Bohème* and *Buveurs d'eau* (1841–44) (*see* Prinet and Dilasser, 1966, pp. 18–19), and a daguerreotype of the two Roux sisters ("Le Nudisme," *Jazz*, 1930, repro. p. 36) belonged to Félix Nadar.

It is possible that the same model posed for both of Nadar's nudes. Nadar may have produced nude studies at the request of, or in collaboration with, certain artists, as Eugène Durieu had done with Delacroix. This pose may refer to a painting whose existence remains to be established or it may simply have been an idea for a figure study, never carried beyond an early photographic stage. Both nudes are delicate, shy, and reticent. This print has a special appeal for it seems as though the model, who stares directly into the lens, wished to guarantee that the study would also be a portrait.

E.P.J.

Collection Gérard-Lévy, Paris

Nadar (Gaspard-Félix Tournachon)

## VIII-30
## Gioacchino Rossini

1856
Inscribed in reverse, upper right: 443; inscribed in reverse, lower left: 146
Salt print from wet collodion on glass negative
24.5 × 18 cm

Provenance:
André Jammes, Paris
Bibliography:
Vitali et al., 1973, pp. 302–3; Barret, 1975, pp. 100–101; Gosling, 1976, pp. 110–11

This portrait of Rossini (1792–1868) wearing a wig is related to a number of variants from

VIII - 30

VIII - 31

VIII - 32

the same sitting; another is illustrated in Prinet and Dilasser (1966, p. 122). Probably the work dates from 1856, which, according to Vitali, was the year of the arrival of the Italian operatic composer in Paris. Prinet and Dilasser's dates of 1857–58 for this group are perhaps too late.

E.P.J.

Collection André Jammes, Paris

Nadar (Gaspard-Félix Tournachon)

## VIII-31
## Charles Philipon

c. 1857
Salt print from wet collodion on glass negative
21.5 × 16.2 cm

Provenance:
André Jammes, Paris

Bibliography:
Vitali et al., 1973, pp. 296–99; Barret, 1975, pp. 94–95; Gosling, 1976, pp. 58–59; Kozloff, 1976, p. 34

Vitali illustrates an example of this portrait from the collection of the Société Française de Photographie which has the Saint Lazare address in Nadar's hand, thus assuring its place in the great decade of the 1850s. This characterization of the journalist Charles Philipon (1800–1862) in the studio should be compared to his earlier effort of 1854 showing Philipon with a cigar, facing right, which was probably taken on the roof in full daylight (see Vitali et al., 1973, p. 297). The two examples of Philipon make it possible to begin to compare Nadar's earliest conceptions of portrait photography in the collaborations with his brother in 1853 and 1854 with later efforts showing his gradual control of the photographer's palette of light. "Light paints and draws but it does not think. Don't forget it," wrote Disdéri in his advice to photographers. "To make portraits the photographer must completely empathize with the sitter, feel the true palpitation of his life, spontaneously understand his character, his private life, his habits. More than photography, the photographer must produce a biography" (Disdéri, 1856).

E.P.J.

Collection André Jammes, Paris

Nadar (Gaspard-Félix Tournachon)

## VIII-32
## Gustave Doré

1857–58
Inscribed on print, at top: G. Doré
Salt print from wet collodion on glass negative
24.8 × 17.2 cm

Provenance:
André Jammes, Paris

This photograph is related to the better-known portrait of the painter and illustrator Gustave Doré (q.v.) seated and wearing the same checked trousers and dark frock coat, but with a short, checked wool scarf. The two poses seem to be from the same sitting (Vitali et al., 1973, pp. 222–23; Gosling, 1976, pp. 94–95). Here Nadar has wrapped a mass of checked fabric over Doré as if mocking the voluminous drapery of eighteenth-century portrait busts. Even the sitter, with his arch seriousness, seems to be stifling a good laugh. The Bibliothèque Nationale has an example of this print in a life-size enlargement of the head. Both portraits of Doré have been dated either 1854 or

1855 by Vitali and Gosling respectively. We are accepting a later date suggested by Prinet and Dilasser (1966, p. 120).

E.P.J.

Collection André Jammes, Paris

Nadar (Gaspard-Félix Tournachon)

## VIII-33
## Motherhood (Nadar's Son Paul in the Arms of Mme Auguste Lefranc)

c. 1858
Signed and inscribed, at right: Nadar. 113. St. Lazare; inscribed on back: Mme Auguste Lefranc; Michel Braive
Salt print from wet collodion on glass negative, mounted
Diameter 19 cm

Provenance:
Photographer's family; Michel Braive, Paris; Gérard Lévy, Paris

VIII-33

This composition, showing Nadar's son Paul (born 1856) asleep in the arms of Mme Auguste Lefranc, has an atmosphere of tenderness and emotional delicacy, particularly enhanced by the tondo format of the print. It is an altogether exceptional aspect of the work of Nadar and dates from the great period of the Saint Lazare studio. Although it is signed and inscribed, it was never exhibited or published, and remained in the collection of the Nadar family. The print appears to be unique and the location of the negative is unknown.

That Mme Lefranc is shown in a maternal pose with Nadar's son suggests the feelings of closeness that must have existed between the Tournachon and Lefranc families. Nadar's friendship with Pierre-Charles-Auguste Lefranc (1814–1878) probably dates from the late 1830s. Born in Bussières, near Mâcon, Lefranc completed his studies in the law in Paris and then devoted himself to literature. A poet, essayist, journalist—socialist and Republican—he mixed freely in the activities of the Parisian press, contributing to such publications as *La Vogue, Chérubin, Revue de France, Journal de Paris, L'Epoque, Revue des Théâtres,* and *Galerie des Artistes.* He worked for the smaller publications as well and managed two feuilletons, *Les Papillotes* (1841–42) and *L'Audience* (1839–45).

Soon after his arrival in Paris from Lyons in 1838, Nadar found himself in Lefranc's world, and it is likely that their friendship began at that time. Nadar also wrote for *La Vogue* and *L'Audience* during Lefranc's directorship. At the same time Lefranc created the religious journal *La Chaire Catholique,* he was collaborating on a seemingly endless string of light comedies, plays, and musicals with Eugène-Marin Labiche, also a former law student, and others.

Nadar introduced the Goncourts to Lefranc at the Moulin Rouge in 1857. They were unimpressed and used the occasion as an excuse to comment on the changing times: "Times are strange: you're introduced to a businessman, and he turns out to be a comedy writer. What an incredible mixture of circumstances, a real confusion of professions (Goncourt and Goncourt, 1956, vol. I, p. 353).

E.P.J.

Collection Gérard-Lévy, Paris

Nadar (Gaspard-Félix Tournachon)

## VIII-34
## Mother Jeanne Jugon

c. 1860
Albumen print from wet collodion on glass negative, mounted
23.3 × 18.5 cm

Provenance:
Paul Nadar; Gérard Lévy, Paris
Exhibition:
1977, Zurich, no. 477 (repro.)

Founded in 1842 at Saint-Servan by Abbot Le Pailleur and Mother Jeanne Jugon, the Order of the Little Sisters of the Poor was approved by Pius IX in 1854 and recognized by the State in 1856. Dedicated to the poor and aged, its members collected leftovers, which they served to their pensioners. An order of total humility, it was very popular and active during the Second Empire. In 1859 the Goncourts noted that their servant told them she had seen a "sister of charity" with a little cart passing in front of the Maison d'Or after a fancy dress ball to collect the remains of the supper (1956, vol. I, p. 588; cited by Richardson, 1971, p. 126).

This particular print was among a group of original proofs personally kept by Nadar. It was

VIII-34

VIII-35

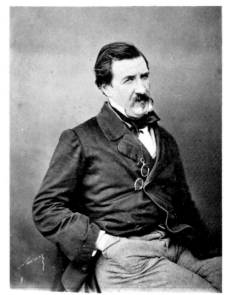

VIII-36

still in the collection of his son Paul after the donations of the Nadar prints and negatives to the Cabinet des Estampes and to the Département des Manuscrits in the Bibliothèque Nationale.

E.P.J.

Collection Gérard-Lévy, Paris

Nadar (Gaspard-Félix Tournachon)

## VIII-35
## Jean-François Millet

1860s
Signed and inscribed, lower right: Nadar. 113 St. Lazare. Millet
Albumen print from wet collodion on glass negative
24.5 × 18 cm

Provenance:
André Jammes, Paris

Bibliography:
Vitali et al., 1973, pp. 276–77 (as 1861); Barret, 1975, pp. 122–23; Gosling, 1976, pp. 120–21; Kozloff, 1976, repro. p. 35

This portrait of the painter Millet (q.v.) originally dates from the days of Nadar's Saint Lazare studio, about 1857, but it must have

been printed again in the 1860s or perhaps enlarged or cropped, leading us to assign it a date in the 1860s. Kozloff illustrates this portrait in a print where the signature and studio address have been unsuccessfully effaced, suggesting that Nadar continued to distribute the portrait after his Saint Lazare days.

E.P.J.

Collection André Jammes, Paris

Nadar (Gaspard-Félix Tournachon)

## VIII-36
## Champfleury (Jules Fleury-Husson)

c. 1865
Signature stamp, lower left: Nadar
Albumen print from wet collodion on glass negative
24.2 × 19.1 cm

Provenance:
André Jammes, Paris

Bibliography:
Vitali et al., 1973, pp. 194–95; Gosling, 1976, pp. 184–85; Kozloff, 1976, pp. 30–31

Kozloff (1976, p. 31) writes that in Nadar's

work — this portrait of the novelist Champfleury (1821–1889) for example — the sitters seem on the verge of addressing us. They suggest that the barrier between the activity of posing and normal intercourse had been relaxed or somewhat blurred in the interest of sociability or reportage.

E.P.J.

Collection André Jammes, Paris

---

### Charles Nègre
*Grasse 1820–1880 Grasse*

*Nègre studied painting with Paul Delaroche and Michel Drolling in Paris before turning his attention to photography around 1844. A consummate technical experimentalist, who eventually gave himself over almost entirely to photogravure, Nègre approached photography from the point of view of painting.*

*Even while he continued to exhibit paintings in the Salon during the late 1840s and early 1850s, when he won two gold medals, he developed formulas to shorten the exposure time of his daguerreotypes and experimented with the published treatises of LeGray (q.v.) to master paper-negative processes.*

*Nègre sold paintings to Napoleon III in the same year that he exhibited photographs at the Société Héliographique and designed a special lens to make near-instantaneous exposures.*

*Nègre was also interested in how architectural photographers might serve conservationists, architects, and artists as well as the manner in which photographs might educate the public about art. He created and financed his own photographic mission to the Midi. His* Midi de la France, *a collection of some two hundred photographs, remains one of the most important and beautiful bodies of paper-negative photography in the nineteenth century, establishing Nègre as one of the great early photographers. In these photographs Nègre searched for picturesque and romantic atmospheres, imbuing many of his pictures with a spirit of place. They reveal the characteristic photographic style of Nègre: his love of geometric arrangements and his use of light to divide and define edges, to draw out a perspectival space or a graphic surface.*

*In 1854 Nègre experimented with photogravure and reported his process to the Académie des Sciences. He was convinced that photogravure was the ultimate goal of photography for it assured permanence and cheap mass reproduction. With his own patented process he received numerous commissions for documentary architectural work.*

*He established a good relationship with the State, having obtained a commission to record the opening of the Imperial Asylum at Vincennes in 1859. By 1861 he had moved from Paris to Nice, where he worked as a commercial photographer and taught drawing.*

E.P.J.

Bibliography:
Jammes, 1963; 1963, Grasse; 1966, Munich; 1969, Philadelphia, nos. 24–34, 53–59, 107–10, 112–13, 185–86, 189; Borcoman, 1976

Charles Nègre

## VIII-37
## The Organ Grinder

Before March 1853
Salt print from waxed-paper negative
20.6 × 15.6 cm

Provenance:
André Jammes, Paris

Exhibitions:
1976, Ottawa, no. 101; 1977, Chicago, no. 121

Bibliography:
Jammes, 1963, pp. 17, 38; Borcoman, 1976, pp. 29–30, 53, pl. 101

The organ grinder was among many Paris street types—chimney sweeps, rag pickers, stonemasons, apple sellers—who interested Nègre during the first half of the 1850s. He made three compositions of this subject: a vignette of the old man alone at Nègre's door; the example exhibited here; and its variant, with the little girl accompanied by LeSecq (q.v.), giving alms to the musician.

Usually Nègre depicted the street people in their natural habitats. Choosing to convey a sense of naturalness, however calculated it might have been, was revolutionary. To accomplish this meant hunting through Paris armed with a heavy view camera, tripod, and plates of glass or papers. Nègre's pictures are successful not only because he knew how to instruct his sitters but also because of the manner in which he arranged the surrounding space.

In spite of the well-established tradition of such subjects in popular imagery even before photography adopted them, Nègre's figures seem fresh and innocent, with a charm that outweighs sentimentality. The critic Francis Wey described one of Nègre's compositions as "remarkable proof of the flexibility and the diversity of photography" (Wey, 1851; quoted in Borcoman, 1976, p. 17). They were "solid and airy" with the lightness and spontaneity of a painted sketch. Nègre may have regarded these studies, as he did most of his photographs of genre subjects, as preparatory sketches for his own paintings. A painted replica of *The Organ Grinder* hung in the July 1853 Salon.

It is easy to understand why Nègre's critics admired these little genre scenes. Ernest Lacan, who knew them well, wrote this detailed narrative about *The Organ Grinder* in 1853: "The play of light and shade on the wall against which the old man is leaning, and the dark vault which recedes behind him, remind us of

VIII-37

Decamps' [q.v.] most vigorous drawings, while
the finely drawn lines of the intelligent head,
thoughtful and sad, the minute details of his
yellowed velvet suit, creased and dirty, relate to
the most careful studies by Meissonier [q.v.].
Two children,… mouths open, arms hanging,
are listening to the sounds … of this popular
instrument. There is a strange contrast between
the attentive pose, the amazed faces of the children who have as yet seen so little, and the
expression of weariness and discouragement of
the old street musician who has seen so
much…. It is not us who says all that; it is
Nègre's print. It is not simply a cold reproduction of three figures posed by chance: it is a
planned picture, with its purpose and its lesson"
(Lacan, 1853, p. 147; quoted in Borcoman,
1976, p. 29).

E.P.J.

Collection André Jammes, Paris

Charles Nègre

VIII-38

## VIII-38
## Imperial Asylum, Vincennes:
## The Refectory

1859
Albumen print from wet collodion on glass
negative
32.5 × 42 cm

Provenance:
André Jammes, Paris; Musée Kodak-Pathé (inv. no.
1718)

Exhibition:
1969, Philadelphia, no. 55 (repro.)

Bibliography:
Jammes, 1963, pp. 35, 40; Borcoman, 1976, p. 231,
pl. 177

In May of 1859, Nègre received a government commission to produce a photographic
"monograph" of the Imperial Asylum in the
Bois de Vincennes, a charitable institution
founded by the Empress for disabled workmen
of the artisan class. Nègre was there to document the institution's opening in August. A
selection of twenty photographs, trimmed to
circular and oval formats, was mounted and
bound into the album *L'Asile impérial de Vincennes* (1861: *see* Jammes, 1963, p. 40). Nègre also
made enlargements of certain negatives from
this project.
Nègre's response to the assignment reveals
his knowledge of composition and a recognition of the ways in which the relationship between photographic form and direct representation might be clearly established to convey

the specifically desired impression of order, efficiency, and well-being. Nègre's task was to
describe a hospital; individually and collec-
tively his pictures do more. Room by room, the
photographer has documented the various
spaces incorporating the services offered by the
asylum. Nègre created an illusion with light. As
it enters the rooms, it illuminates the virtues of
the institution by touching upon the absorbed
and specialized activity of its servants. In the
kitchen, cooks arrange platters. In the dispen-
sary, a pharmacist grinds chemicals while his
associate returns a container to the shelf. Nuns
move noiselessly, folding and filing linen. Pa-
tients convalesce in smocks, straw hats, and soft
espadrilles. They are seen working the extensive gardens around the pavilions or gathering
at tables in large halls, everywhere joined by
attendants. A scene of a doctor's visit shows a
patient with a top-hatted physician, flanked by
seven male nurses and attendants.
Through the spatial vista all elements appear in harmonious relationship. In this view of
the refectory, light pours into a long hall divided by two rows of delicate cast-iron columns
alternating with gaslight chandeliers. Many
figures moved during the exposure, causing
images that blur with the light in startling confusion. Evidently this version of the refectory
was not the one favored by Nègre or his patrons, for the plates from the documentary album (Collection Gérard-Lévy, Paris) show a
variant of it. In the variant, seen from the same
vantage point, light is ordered in a strict pattern
of horizontals exactly matching the beams in

the ceiling and reinforcing the progression of
columns. The positions of the attendants
further clarify the space, and a circular format
formalizes Nègre's classic design to a greater
degree. But, the work here is not expressively
incompatible with Negre's intentions, though
formally it may appear so, for it is the light,
bathing the figures, that masses them into a
radiant community.

E.P.J.

Musée Kodak-Pathé, Vincennes

Charles Nègre

## VIII-39
## Lord Brougham with Family
## and Friends at Cannes

c. 1862
Albumen print from wet collodion on glass
negative
26 × 34 cm

Provenance:
André Jammes, Paris

Exhibition:
1976, Ottawa, no. 185

Bibliography:
Borcoman, 1976, p. 238, pl. 185

Nègre's fragile health forced him to retire to
the Midi in 1861. He taught drawing at the
Lycée Impérial and opened a professional

VIII-39

photographic studio in Nice. By 1863 he had settled there permanently. According to James Borcoman (1976, p. 47), Nègre made conservative studio portraits and views of the Riviera for the tourist trade during this time and, on commission, also photographed the English winter residents of Cannes and, for some clients, assembled the pictures into albums. In 1862 he delivered photographs made for Prince Leopold of Belgium, which included pictures of the Prince and Lord Brougham, who had a château in Cannes.

Henry Peter, Baron Brougham and Vaux of Brougham, born in Edinburgh in 1778, was, from 1834 to 1860, probably the most active member of the House of Lords. Notorious as a loquacious "reforming lawyer," he had distinguished himself by promoting public services, public education, and the abolition of slavery. However, *The Complete Peerage* (London, 1912, vol. II, p. 341) noted: "His mind ranged over so wide an area that he never acquired a *thorough* knowledge of any particular division of learning. It has been said of him that 'Science was his forte, and omniscience his foible'; and 'What Lord Brougham lacked in *learning* he was desirous to make up for in *haste.*'" In 1848 he expressed the wish of becoming a deputy in the French National Assembly but quickly realized that if he became a French citizen, he would have to give up his English rank and salary, and wisely withdrew his request. *Punch* featured a cartoon of him as "citizen of the world." It has been ironically noted that whereas Lord Brougham's name was given to a closed four-

wheeled carriage with an open driver's seat, a greater statesman, Gladstone, was "only god-father to a bag."

In a composition of rushing perspective, a characteristic vantage point preferred by Nègre, the photographer here has portrayed Lord Brougham seated on the terrace of his château surrounded by young people dressed for sport. Nègre stationed himself to allow the forms of the architecture to carve out a boxlike space and the shadows of the balustrade and figures to mark a stately recession of horizontals backed by a mass of trees in the distance. Thus, he enclosed a family in the secure geometry of its own universe.

E.P.J.

Collection André Jammes, Paris

---

## Louis-Rémy Robert

*1811–1882*

*Robert's primary occupation between 1848 and 1871 was chief of the workshop at the imperial manufactory at Sèvres (q.v.), which he entered in 1843; he was also a chemist and photographer. Robert must have found the atmosphere at Sèvres favorable to the development of his pastime, for between 1852 and 1871 the director of the manufactory was Victor Regnault. He too was a dedicated photographic experimentalist, working exclusively with paper nega-*

*tives during the first half of the 1850s. In fact, a small colony of photographers appears to have been at Sèvres with Robert and Regnault. Also at the manufactory were E. Béranger, possibly Jean-Baptiste-Emile Béranger, son of the figure painter Antoine Béranger; Jules Diéterle (q.v.), a decorator attached to the manufactory who formed an important collection of photography; and very likely others.*

*An enchanting series of views from paper negatives showing the gardens and fountains of Versailles and Saint-Cloud, printed and published by Louis-Désiré Blanquart-Evrard* (Souvenirs de Versailles) *around 1854, amply demonstrates Robert's taste and artistic affinity for the richly encrusted surfaces of eighteenth-century decorative forms. In his compositions of parks, Robert displayed his discovery of that fine veil of transparent light revealed as a luminous haze as it passed through the mists of playing fountains. In fact, everything Robert saw through the ground glass has a sad, dreamy opalescence. Objects seem magically alive, animated by decoration and piquant arabesques.*

*Robert became a member of the Société Française de Photographie in 1855. He succeeded Regnault as director of the manufactory of Sèvres from 1871 to 1879. After the Franco-Prussian War the factory was moved to Saint-Cloud and continued to operate there until 1876. Many photographs made in connection with porcelain works at Sèvres must have been lost in the bombings by the Germans in 1871, when Regnault's laboratory was completely destroyed. An extraordinary group of pictures from the Watelin and Diéterle collections, some by Robert depicting his family and friends, which included the painter Troyon (q.v.), and informal scenes showing Robert with Count Aguado and others, are illustrated in Lécuyer (1945), but have since apparently disappeared.*

E.P.J.

Bibliography:
Lécuyer, 1945, pp. 29–30, 69–70, 255, repro. pp. 80–83, 89; 1965–66, Essen, pp. 21–22

Louis-Rémy Robert

## VIII-40
## Vases from the Manufactory at Sèvres

1855
Signed on negative, lower left: L. Robert Photo^ie Sèvres; inscribed and dated on negative, lower right: Exposition de Sèvres 1855; inscribed on mount: à M. Laulerie L. Robert
Salt print from albumen on glass negative, mounted
32 × 25.5 cm

Provenance:
Presented by the photographer to Martin Laulerie, acting secretary of the Société Française de Photographie (inv. no. 360/6)

Exhibitions:
1856, Brussels; 1857, Paris, Société Française de Photographie; 1976, Paris, Bibliothèque Nationale, no. 133 (repro.)

Bibliography:
*La Lumière*, November 15, 1856, p. 181; *Bulletin de la Société Française de Photographie*, 1857, p. 289

In 1855 Robert was working with albumen on glass negatives. He exhibited a haunting series of still lifes of Sèvres porcelain vases; this example may be among the few survivors. They were advertisements for the modern achievements at Sèvres (q.v.) under imperial patronage, and Robert's choice of a more polished, brighter negative surface is significant in this respect. In 1860 the Goncourts, self-appointed champions of eighteenth-century taste, recorded their outrage after a visit to Sèvres: "As for the modern work from Sèvres, what a disgrace! This is the bourgeois ideal of what porcelain should be. This stupid school of plates covered with landscapes, of porcelain treated in the manner of paintings is going to defame French taste once and for all. There is nothing spontaneous here, no feeling of paint having been applied by a paintbrush as in those scattered bouquets on Dresden or Chinese export. No more raised gilding. A great art has gone to ruin. This degraded manufactory should throw everything away and begin again" (Goncourt and Goncourt, 1956, vol. I, p. 780).

With characteristic subtlety, Robert, making records of the pieces in this composition, has actually created an illusory effect. Light steals into the scene, producing no discernible shadows except those required to draw out delicately the most vital movements in the sumptuous relief surfaces and metallic appointments. The light is so soft that it fairly caresses the objects with a cosmetic veil, ameliorating the brittle new pastes and the strident polychromy and gilding favored by the court. The large pieces in the arrangement have been placed so that the ovoid silhouette of each is shown to best advantage. Hardly any of the pieces overlap, and Robert seems to be demonstrating a graduated scale of a single vase type. The overall impression is one of sensual exotic mystery, remote grandeur, and, above all, high technical achievement. Robert makes us believe that we are confronting splendid decorative animation of the highest order, and it becomes clear in such an image that the photographer's belief in the products of modern Sèvres and in his own role in the manufacture of these products was steadfast. From the photograph, it is difficult not to agree with him.

A delightful detail, easily overlooked, demonstrates Robert's light touch. The little measuring stick set up between the two pieces of porcelain on the right is intended to establish scale. Robert has placed it so that it seems to repeat the volute on the candelabrum and thus, like a chameleon, blends into its habitat.

E.P.J.

Société Française de Photographie, Paris

VIII-40

---

## Julien Vallou de Villeneuve
*Boissy-Saint-Léger 1795–1866 Paris*

*Vallou de Villeneuve made his debut as a painter in the Salon of 1814. During the 1820s and 1830s he achieved an international reputation as a lithographer of scenes of daily life, regional costume, and fashion in publications such as* Costumes des provinces septentrionales des Pays-Bas *(1826);* Souvenirs d'un artiste *(1829); and* Les Jeunes Femmes, groupes de têtes *(1839). His work was copied by numerous lithographers of the period. He also contributed to publications of erotica such as* Imagerie galante *(1830), along with Achille Devéria and others. Many of his lithographs are in the Bibliothèque Nationale.*

*According to Aaron Scharf, Vallou turned to photography around 1842, presumably in order to produce his popular subject matter more easily than with lithography. It is not known which photographic process he used then. Most likely he worked with daguerreotype and joined the ranks of photographers of erotic subjects who made daguerreotypes for stereoscopic views, but this is a speculation, for no daguerreotypes by him have been identified. It is certain that by 1853 Vallou was thoroughly grounded in paper-negative photography and had created a large repertoire of nudes and draped models for a collection called* Etudes d'après nature, *intended for artists' studios as well as for the general public. He also produced portraits of actors and actresses. He was a member of the Société Héliographique and the Société Française de Photographie. He was fond of retouching his negatives, a practice strenuously objected to by Eugène Durieu, who, with*

*Delacroix's help, also photographed nudes for artists. About sixty prints by Vallou, all from paper negatives, are in the Bibliothèque Nationale.*

E.P.J.

Bibliography:
Durieu, 1855, p. 67; Scharf, 1968, pp. 98–100, figs. 84, 88

VIII-41                          VIII-42

Julien Vallou de Villeneuve

## VIII-41
## Nude Viewed from the Back

1852 or 1853
Signed on negative, lower left: J.V.V.; inscribed, lower left: 1851
Salt paper print from waxed-paper negative, mounted
16 × 12.3 cm

Provenance:
Gérard Lévy, Paris

Julien Vallou de Villeneuve

## VIII-42
## The Shy Model

1852 or 1853
Salt paper print from waxed-paper negative, mounted
16.5 × 12.3 cm

Provenance:
Gérard Lévy, Paris

Both these studies may depict the same model. The unsigned example not only betrays the distinctive compositional style of Vallou, but includes the same piece of striped cloth. Vallou's work, always quite small in scale and meant for albums and intimate viewing, shows a hearty breadth of form. Figures are unencumbered by ornament or decorative trappings. The nude is arranged in carefully controlled light with accessories necessary to produce a clearly defined graphic idea. A crescent of white from a cap, a line of parted hair, a strong diagonal obscuring the face, light cutting off the line of a shoulder, a mass of gathered cloth from a shift, the curves of a hip and a thigh, all these develop into a sequence of distinct forms and directions, set against a supporting arm and hand. Chiaroscuro is used to synthesize the simplest of compositions without any suggestion of the flaccid prurience that characterizes some of Vallou's lithographs.

The model, placed beneath a skylight, must have moved until the forms desired by the photographer fell into place. Even in their small scale, these figures impose a strong physical presence, not by the intrusion of any single part but by the consistent relationship of all parts to a coherent whole. Working in this category of "academics," or studies for artists, a photographer such as Vallou did not simply offer models in poses that conformed to the existing repertoire of subjects in painting; he invented new conceptions of the nude. These studies were ideally suited to artists who wished to liberate the nude from the stock classical rhetoric and the theatrics of literary Romantic narrative and situation, to make them forcibly visual and tangibly concrete.

Similarly, the figure whose back is parallel to the picture plane and outlined sharply against the dark background is so impersonal and abstract that she may be read only as a composition. No delectable erotic vignette is depicted here—but a sensuality of a different order—providing inspiration for Courbet's "columns of flesh" in the notorious *Bather* of 1853, for example. Vallou's nudes are some of the most solidly constructed figure compositions from the early 1850s. One feature that distinguishes them from the work of Malacrida,

d'Olivier, Durieu, and others, besides the utter simplicity of the light and shade and chaste mood due to the abstraction, is Vallou's distinctive sense of proportion in relating the nude to the edges of the frame. The figure is always given adequate room. Spaces around it are felt spaces with their own scale and shape conforming comfortably to the design of the illuminated subject. The modesty and complete lack of coquetry seem to derive from a Northern tradition rather than a Latin one.

In 1852 *La Lumière* carried the following publicity: "Vallou de Villeneuve, models and other subjects achieved on paper with superior skill." Scharf (1968, p. 99) states that Courbet (q.v.) learned of the existence of these pictures through Alfred Bruyas in 1854. Since he compares one of Vallou's nudes to the *Bather* of 1853, Courbet's discovery must have occurred somewhat earlier. Considering the quantity of photographic studies of nudes available to Courbet in Paris by 1852, it is worth reflecting upon his particular attraction to Vallou. Vallou's nudes offered Courbet a conception of the female form that corresponded exactly to his own, being free of all historical and literary associations and having the allure of ingenuous modesty and the delectable corpulence of a Dutch hausfrau.

E.P.J.

Collection Gérard-Lévy, Paris

# Chronology of the Second Empire

## 1851

December 2. Coup d'etat: Louis-Napoleon Bonaparte (elected president of the Republic for 4 years on December 10, 1848) dissolves the Assembly and reestablishes universal suffrage
December 21–22. Plebiscite approves coup d'etat: 7,439,216 votes for; 647,737 against; 1,500,000 abstentions

## 1852

January 1. *Te Deum* at Notre Dame; Prince-President installed at the Tuileries
January 9. Seventy deputies deported (18 others "temporarily exiled"); Victor Hugo, in Belgium since December 11, 1851, officially exiled
January 14. Enactment of constitution; Louis-Napoleon becomes president of the Republic for 10 years with possibility of reelection
January 24. Titles of nobility reestablished
February 17. Decree places controls on the Press
March 18. Crédit Foncier instituted
March 25. Decree restricts right of public assembly
June 2. Bois de Boulogne annexed to Paris
July 17. Inauguration of railway to Strasbourg
September–October. Provincial tour of Prince-President
November 7. *Senatus consultum* proposes modification of constitution and reestablishment of Empire
November 17. Foundation of Crédit Mobilier
November 21–22. Plebiscite reestablishes Empire: 7,824,129 for; 253,149 against
December 1. Proclamation of Empire at Saint-Cloud
December 2. Solemn entry of Emperor into Paris

## 1853

January 29–30. Marriage of Napoleon III and Eugénie de Montijo, Countess of Teba
June 22. Baron Haussmann appointed Prefect of the Seine
September. Occupation of New Caledonia
October. Outbreak of cholera in Paris; episodes continue through 1855 (143,478 deaths)
Compagnie des Chemins de Fer du Midi established

## 1854

March 27. France and England in support of Turkey declare war against Russia
April 2. First issue of daily newspaper *Le Figaro*
September 14. French and English troops land in the Crimea

September. Visit of kings of Belgium and Portugal to France
September 20. Victory of Anglo-French forces against Russians at Alma River
September 30. Siege of Sebastopol
Compagnie des Chemins de Fer de l'Est established

## 1855

April 16–21. Visit of Emperor and Empress to London
April 28. Assassination attempt by Pianori, an Italian nationalist
May 2. Decree authorizing creation of Compagnie Générale Maritime
May 15. Opening of Exposition Universelle (closed November 15); 5,162,330 visitors, 24,000 exhibitors
August 17–28. Visit of Queen Victoria and Prince Albert to Paris
September 10. Anglo-French forces enter Sebastopol after evacuation by Russians
Compagnie des Chemins de Fer de l'Ouest established
Inauguration of the Paris-Lyon-Méditerranée railway

## 1856

March 16. Birth of Prince Imperial
March 30. Treaty of Paris, between Allies (France and England) and defeated Russians
June 1–5. Baptism of Prince Imperial
Autumn. First "series" at Compiègne for guests of Emperor and Empress
Bank of France given renewed privilege of issuing currency

## 1857

January 1. Law provides subsidies for three transatlantic maritime services: Le Havre (North America); Saint-Nazaire (Antilles); Bordeaux (South America)
May–July. Conquest of Kabyles of Algeria
June 14. Trade agreement with Russia
June 23. Law establishing trademark and industrial patent protection
August 6–10. Visit of Emperor and Empress to England

## 1858

January. Expedition to China; Canton taken by Anglo-French expeditionary force
January 14. Assassination attempt by Orsini, an Italian nationalist, in front of Opéra
February 1. Privy Council instituted
February 19. Law of *sûreté générale*, permitting

imprisonment or deportation without trial
June 27. Treaty of Tientsin
July 21–22. Verbal accord at Plombières between Napoleon III and Cavour, prime minister of Piedmont
October 9. Treaty of friendship and commerce with Japan
December 26. Compagnie Universelle du Canal Maritime de Suez formed by de Lesseps

## 1859

January 26. Treaty of Turin ratifying Plombières agreement: military alliance against Austria and creation of a North Italian kingdom, in exchange for cession of Nice and Savoy to France
January 30. Marriage of Prince Napoleon (Jérôme Napoleon), cousin of Emperor, and Princess Clotilde, daughter of Victor Emmanuel, king of Piedmont-Sardinia
May 3. France declares war on Austria after Austria invades Piedmontese territory; Emperor at battlefront, Empress named regent
May 20. Victory at Montebello
June 4. Victory at Magenta
June 24. Victory at Solferino
July 11. Armistice of Villa Franca, ending Italian campaign
August 4–5. Meeting of Emperor and Queen Victoria at Cherbourg
November 10. Peace of Zurich confirms agreement of Villa Franca

## 1860

January 23. Treaty of commerce with England reforms tariff and abolishes prohibitions and protective duties
March 12. Treaty with Piedmont confirms cession of Nice and Savoy (made public March 24)
April. Annexation of Nice and Savoy confirmed by ballot (Nice: 25,743 for, 160 against; Savoy: 130,533 for, 235 against)
May. Anglo-French expeditionary force lands in China
August 1. Law authorizing government loan to industry of 40,000,000 francs to assist manufacturers in meeting foreign competition occasioned by treaty of commerce
August–September. Emperor and Empress travel to Savoy, Nice, Corsica, Algeria
October. Capture of Peking; sacking and burning of Summer Palace by Anglo-French troops; second treaty of Tientsin
November 24. Decree permitting certain rights of assembly begins liberalization of Empire

1861
March 9. Trade treaty with Peru
April 6. Opening of Strasbourg-Kehl railway and bridge across Rhine
April 29. Trade treaty with Turkey
May 1. Trade treaty with Belgium
June 11. Declaration of French neutrality in United States Civil War
June 15. Siamese embassy arrives in Paris
August 6. Visit of king of Sweden to France
October. Visits of kings of Prussia and Holland to France
October 31. France, England, and Spain plan military intervention in Mexico
Foundation of *Le Temps*

1862
January 9. Landing of French troops in Mexico
March 27. Trade treaty with Prussia
April 8. Japanese embassy received in Paris
April. England and Spain withdraw troops from Mexico; France resumes hostilities
June 3. Treaty of Saigon between France and Annam; 3 provinces ceded to France
June. Emperor receives Bismarck and proposes alliance with Prussia

1863
January 17. Trade treaty with Italy
February 1. First issue of *Petit Journal*
June. Annexation of Cochin-China begins
June 10. French troops in Mexico City
June 23. Victor Duruy becomes Minister of Public Instruction; educational reforms begun
July 6. Crédit Lyonnais established
July 10. Archduke Maximilian of Austria offered crown as Emperor of Mexico, with support of France
August 11. Cambodia made French protectorate

1864
April 10. Maximilian accepts crown of Mexico
May 25. Law permitting trade associations virtually grants right to strike
June 28. Trade treaty with Bolivia
June 30. Trade treaty with Switzerland
July 19. Visit of king of Belgium to France
August 16. Visit of king of Spain to France
September. Bismarck visits Emperor at Biarritz
September 15. Franco-Italian meeting regarding evacuation of Rome by French
Société Générale established
Pope Pius IX issues Syllabus of Errors, containing attack on French policies

1865
March 4. Trade treaty with Sweden and Norway
May 5–June 8. Emperor travels to Algeria

May 23. Law authorizes payments by banker's check
July 7. Trade treaty with Low Countries
July. Paris branch of the International (established by Marx and Engels in London, 1864)
October 4. Bismarck received at Biarritz; obtains assurance of French non-intervention in conflict between Prussia and Austria
Cholera epidemics

1866
January 11. Trade treaty with Portugal
September. Evacuation of French troops from Mexico begins
October. Trade treaty with Austria
November 4. Opening of port of Dakar
December 11. Evacuation of French forces from Rome

1867
January 31. Decree gives right to raise questions in parliament
April 1. Opening of Exposition Universelle (closed November 3); more than 11,000,000 visitors, 50,000 exhibitors
June 6. Assassination attempt on czar of Russia, while visiting Paris, by a Pole, Berezowski
June 19. Execution of Emperor Maximilian at Querétaro
July 24. Law authorizing establishment of joint stock companies
July. Visit of Emperor to Germany
August 16–23. Meeting between Napoleon III and Austrian Emperor at Salzburg
October 28. French troops dispatched in defence of Papal States; defeat of Garibaldi at Mentana (November 3)

1868
January 14. Law reorganizing army
May 11. Law restoring greater freedom of Press
June 6. Law permitting limited right of public assembly

1869
May 24. Opposition makes gains in legislative elections
September 6. Act increasing powers of Sénat and Corps Législatif
November 17. Opening of Suez Canal in presence of Empress Eugénie, Prince of Wales, Crown Prince of Prussia, and Viceroy of Egypt
December 27. Napoleon III appoints Emile Ollivier chief minister and charges him to form new cabinet

1870
January 2. First meeting of Ollivier ministry
January. Resignation of Baron Haussmann as Prefect of the Seine

April 20. *Senatus consultum* proposing revised constitution
May 8. Plebiscite approves new constitution (7,358,000 for; 1,572,000 against; 2,000,000 abstentions)
July 3. Candidacy of Prince Leopold of Hohenzollern-Sigmaringen, a relative of the king of Prussia, for crown of Spain made public in Paris
July 12. Prince Leopold's candidacy withdrawn after hostile public reaction; France demands guarantees against further expansion of German influence in Europe; communication from king of Prussia to his chancellor condensed by Bismarck into Ems dispatch, published by German Press on July 14; taken as virtual provocation of war
July 19. France declares war on Prussia
July 23. Empress appointed regent while Emperor assumes command of army at Metz
August 4. French army under MacMahon defeated at Wissembourg
August 6. French armies defeated at Froeschwiller and Forbach
August 9. New French government formed under Cousin-Montauban, comte de Palikao, to prepare for defense of Paris
August 18. General Bazaine's army beseiged at Metz (surrendered October 27)
September 1. MacMahon's army and Emperor surrounded at Sedan
September 2. Emperor surrenders at Sedan (exiled to England, March 1871; dies January 9, 1873)
September 3. Princess Mathilde flees to Belgium (returns to Paris, June 1871)
September 4. Proclamation of the Republic at the Hôtel de Ville, Paris; the Empress and comte de Palikao leave Paris for Belgium; Eugénie later joins Emperor at Chislehurst in England

# Bibliography

## Books and Periodicals

*Names with the prefixes de and le are alphabetized under the second element*

Abbot, 1934
J. Abbot. "La Fille de Jephte." *Bulletin of Smith College Museum of Art,* no. 15 (June 1934), pp. 2-12.

About, 1855
E. About. *Voyage à travers l'exposition des Beaux-Arts.* Paris, 1855.

About, 1858
———. *Nos Artistes au Salon de 1857.* Paris, 1858.

About, 1864
———. *Salon de 1864.* Paris, 1864.

About, 1867
———. *Salon de 1866.* Paris, 1867.

About, 1869
———. "Le Salon de 1869." *Revue des Deux-Mondes,* June 1, 1869.

About, 1876
———. *Peintures décoratives du grand foyer de l'Opéra par Paul Baudry; notice biographique et description.* Paris, 1876.

"Accessions," 1961
Anon. "Accessions of American and Canadian Museums." *The Art Quarterly,* vol. XXIV, no. 4 (winter 1961), pp. 395–412.

Ackerman, 1967, "Gérôme"
G.M. Ackerman. "Gérôme and Manet." *Gazette des Beaux-Arts,* 109th year, vol. LXX (September 1967), pp. 163–76.

Ackerman, 1967, "Realist"
———. "Gérôme, the Academic Realist." *Art News Annual,* vol. XXXIII (1967), pp. 100–107.

Ackerman, 1967, "Vassar"
———. "A Gérôme Exhibition at Vassar." *The Burlington Magazine,* vol. CIX, no. 771 (June 1967), pp. 375–76.

Ackerman, 1969
———. "Thomas Eakins and His Parisian Masters Gérôme and Bonnat." *Gazette des Beaux-Arts,* 111th year, vol. LXXIII (April 1969), pp. 235–56.

Ackerman, 1973
———. "Gérôme: Reassessing a Scorned Painter." *Art News,* vol. LXXII, no. 1 (January 1973), pp. 32–35.

"Acquisitions," 1976
Anon. "Principales Acquisitions des musées de province 1973-1976." *La Revue du Louvre et des Musées de France,* nos. 5–6 (1976).

Adams, 1881
C. Adams. "Jean-Louis Hamon." *The American Art Review,* vol. II (1881), pp. 199–205.

Adhémar, 1954
J. Adhémar. *Honoré Daumier.* Paris, 1954.

Adhémar, 1960
———. "Le Cabinet de travail de Zola." *Gazette des Beaux-Arts,* 102nd year, vol. LVI (November 1960), pp. 285–98.

Adhémar and Dayez-Distel, 1977
H. Adhémar and A. Dayez-Distel. *Musée du Louvre, Musée de l'Impressionnisme, Jeu de Paume.* 3rd rev. ed. Paris, 1977.

Adhémar and Dreyfus-Bruhl, 1958
Paris, Musée du Louvre. *Catalogue des peintures, impressionnistes.* 3rd ed. By H. Adhémar, M. Dreyfus-Bruhl et al. Paris, 1958.

Alazard, 1942
J. Alazard. *Ingres, quatorze dessins.* (Collection de reproduction des dessins, Musée du Louvre, vol. XVII). Paris, 1942.

Alazard, 1950
———. *Ingres et l'Ingrisme.* Paris, 1950.

d'Albis and Romanet, n.d.
J. d'Albis and C. Romanet. *Histoire de la Porcelaine de Limoges* (in preparation).

d'Alcantara, 1961
O. d'Alcantara. *Marcello: Adèle d'Affry, duchesse Castiglione Colonna 1836–1879.* Geneva, 1961.

Alexandre, 1889
A. Alexandre. *Antoine-Louis Barye.* Paris, 1889.

Alexandre, 1903
———. *Carolus-Duran.* Paris, 1903.

*L'Algérie,* 1863
*Gouvernement général de l'Algérie: L'Algérie à l'Exposition Universelle à Londres, 1862.* 2 vols. Algiers, 1863.

Allemand, 1964
G.L. Allemand. "Le Rôle du Japon dans l'évolution de l'habitation et de son décor en France dans la seconde moitié du XIXᵉ siècle et au début du XXᵉ siècle." Thesis, Ecole du Louvre, 1964.

Amaury-Duval, 1878

E.-E. Amaury-Duval. *L'Atelier d'Ingres, souvenirs.* Paris, 1878.

d'Ambès, 1912
Baron d'Ambès [pseud.]. *Intimate Memoirs of Napoleon III. Personal Reminiscences of the Man and the Emperor.* 2 vols. Edited and translated by A.R. Allinson. Boston, 1912.

Amic, 1952
Y. Amic. *L'Opaline française au XIXᵉ siècle.* Paris, 1952.

Ancet, 1974
J.-C. Ancet. "Une Famille de sculpteurs bourguignons, Les 'Moreau.'" Thesis, Université de Dijon, 1974.

Andréi, 1859
A. Andréi. "Chronique." *L'Art au Dix-Neuvième Siècle,* vol. IV (1859), pp. 283–84.

Andréi, 1860
———. "Galerie anthropologique et ethnographique de M. Cordier." *L'Art au Dix-Neuvième Siècle,* vol. V (1860), pp. 188–89.

Angrand, 1968
P. Angrand. *Monsieur Ingres et son époque.* Lausanne and Paris, 1968.

Angrand, 1968, "L'Etat"
———. "L'Etat mécène—Période autoritaire du Second Empire (1851–1860)." *Gazette des Beaux-Arts,* 110th year, vol. LXXI (May–June 1968), pp. 303–48.

Appert and Henrivaux, 1894
L. Appert and J. Henrivaux. *Verre et verrerie.* Paris, 1894.

Arago, n.d.
A. Arago. *Œuvres choisis de J.-L. Gérôme.* Paris, n.d.

Aragon et al., 1942
Aragon, E. Sougez, G. Besson, and F. Tuefferd. "La Photographie ancienne." *Le Point, Revue Artistique et Littéraire,* vol. XXIII (1942).

Aries, 1974
M. Aries. *La Manufacture de Creil.* Paris, 1974.

Armand-Calliat, 1867
T.-J. Armand-Calliat. *L'Orfèvrerie religieuse lyonnaise à l'Exposition de 1867: Exposition de M. Armand-Calliat.* Lyons, 1867.

Armand-Calliat, 1888
———. *L'Orfèvrerie, discours de réception à l'Académie des Sciences, Belles-Lettres et Arts de Lyon, prononcé en séance publique le 19 juin 1888.* Lyons, 1888.

Arnould, 1954
R. Arnould. *L'Œuvre d'Eugène Boudin, 1824–1898, au Musée des Beaux-Arts du Havre.* Le Havre, 1954.

Art Journal Catalogue 1851
London, International Exhibition of 1851. *The Art Journal Illustrated Catalogue. The Industry of All Nations, 1851.* London, 1851.

*Art Journal Catalogue 1855*
Paris, Exposition Universelle of 1855. *The Exhibition of Art-Industry in Paris, 1855.* [supplementary to] *The Art Journal,* n.s., vol. I (1855).

*Art Journal Catalogue 1862*
London, International Exhibition of 1862. *The Art Journal Illustrated Catalogue of the International Exhibition.* [supplementary to] *The Art Journal,* n.s., vol. I (1862), pp. 1–199, n.s., vol. II (1863), pp. 200–324.

*Art Journal Catalogue 1867*
Paris, Exposition Universelle of 1867. *The Art Journal Illustrated Catalogue of the Universal Exhibition.* [supplementary to] *The Art Journal,* n.s., vol. VI (1867), pp. 1–122, n.s., vol. VII (1868), pp. 153–331.

*Art Journal Catalogue 1871*
London, International Exhibition of 1871. *The Art Journal Catalogue to the International Exhibition, 1871–72.* [supplementary to] *The Art Journal,* n.s., vol. X (1871), pp. 1–88, n.s., vol. XI (1872), pp. 1–64.

Aslin, 1973
London, Victoria and Albert Museum. *French Exhibition Pieces, 1844–78.* By E. Aslin. London, 1973.

Astruc, 1859
Z. Astruc. *Les 14 Stations du Salon, 1859.* Paris, 1859.

Astruc, 1863
———. *Le Salon,* May 14, 1863.

Aubert, 1859
M. Aubert. *Souvenirs du Salon de 1859.* Paris, 1859.

Aubert, 1861
F. Aubert. "Salon de 1861: Sculpture." *L'Artiste,* 1861, pp. 272–77.

Aubert, 1863
———. "Compte-rendu du Salon." *Le Pays,* June 24, 1863.

Aubry, 1932
O. Aubry. *Napoléon III.* Paris, 1932.

Audin and Vial, 1918–19
M. Audin and E. Vial. *Dictionnaire des artistes et ouvriers d'art du lyonnais.* 2 vols. Paris, 1918–19.

Aulanier, 1953
C. Aulanier. *Histoire du Palais et du Musée du Louvre.* Vol. IV: *Le Nouveau Louvre de Napoléon III.* Paris, 1953.

Aulanier, 1971
———. *Histoire du Palais et du Musée du Louvre: Le Pavillon de Flore.* Paris, 1971.

d'Auvigny, 1853
L. Boyeldieu d'Auvigny. *Salon de 1853 (Guide aux Menus-Plaisirs).* Paris, 1853.

Auvray, 1857
L. Auvray. *Exposition des Beaux-Arts, Salon de 1857.* Paris, 1857.

Auvray, 1859
———. *Exposition des Beaux-Arts, Salon de 1859.* Paris, 1859.

Auvray, 1861
———. *Exposition des Beaux-Arts, Salon de 1861.* Paris, 1861.

Auvray, 1863
———. *Exposition des Beaux-Arts, Salon de 1863.* Paris, 1863.

Auvray, 1864
———. *Le Salon de 1864.* Paris, 1864.

Auvray, 1868
———. *Le Salon de 1868.* Paris, 1868.

Auvray, 1869
———. *Le Salon de 1869.* Paris, 1869.

Auzas, n.d.
P.-M. Auzas. *Notre-Dame de Paris: Le Trésor.* Paris, n.d.

Avery, 1972
C. Avery. "From David d'Angers to Rodin—Britain's National Collection of French Nineteenth-Century Sculpture." *The Connoisseur,* vol. CLXXIX (April 1972), pp. 230–39.

"Avisseau," 1861
Anon. "Mouvement des arts et de la curiosité: Nécrologie: Charles Avisseau, de Tours." *Gazette des Beaux-Arts,* 3rd year, vol. IX (March 1, 1861), p. 318.

Babelon, 1897
E. Babelon. *Catalogue des camées antiques et modernes de la Bibliothèque Nationale.* 2 vols. Paris, 1897.

Babelon, 1902
———. *Histoire de la gravure sur gemmes en France.* Paris, 1902.

Babelon, 1927
J. Babelon. *La Médaille et les médailleurs.* Paris, 1927.

Babelon, 1946
———. *L'Orfèvrerie française.* Paris, 1946.

"Baccarat," 1869
Anon. "Cristallerie de Baccarat." *Moniteur de la Céramique, de la Verrerie, et des Industries qui s'y Rattachent,* vol. I, no. 3 (March 31, 1869), pp. 75–77.

Baccheschi, 1966
E. Baccheschi. *Gli ebanisti del XIX secolo.* Milan, 1966.

Bacou, 1956
R. Bacou. *Odilon Redon.* 2 vols. Geneva, 1956.

Bacou, 1974
———. "Donation Claude Roger-Marx." *La Revue du Louvre et des Musées de France,* nos. 4–5 (1974), pp. 307–12.

Bacou, 1975
———. *Millet, dessins.* Fribourg, 1975.

Baignères, 1881
A. Baignères. "La Peinture décorative au XIXᵉ siècle: M. Puvis de Chavannes." *Gazette des Beaux-Arts,* 23rd year, vol. XXIII (May 1, 1881), pp. 416–26.

Bailliere, 1872
H. Balliere. *Henri Regnault.* Paris, 1872.

Bailly, 1876
A.-N. Bailly. *Notice sur M. Henri Labrouste.* Paris, 1876.

Baldus, 1852
E. Baldus. *Concours de photographie. . . .* Paris, 1852.

Balfour, 1925
G. Balfour. *Catalogue of the Ceramic Library, Central School of Science and Technology, Stoke-on-Trent. . . .* Hanley, 1925.

Ballu, 1873
T. Ballu. *Notice sur M. Léon Vaudoyer.* Paris, 1873.

Ballu, 1880, "Couture"
R. Ballu. "Beaux-Arts, l'exposition des œuvres de Thomas Couture." Le Globe, September 17, 1880.
Ballu, 1890
———. L'Œuvre de Barye. Introduction by E. Guillaume. Paris, 1890.
Baltard, 1872
V. Baltard. "Exposition d'une collection de dessins de Félix Duban." Revue Générale de l'Architecture, vol. XXIX (1872), cols. 22–29.
Baltard and Callet, 1863
V. Baltard and F.-E. Callet. Monographie des Halles Centrales. . . . Paris, 1863.
de Banville, 1861
T. de Banville. "La Source d'Ingres." Revue Fantaisiste, vol. I (1861).
Bapst, 1889
G. Bapst. Histoire des joyaux de la Couronne de France. Paris, 1889.
Barbedienne, 1862
F. Barbedienne. Catalogue des bronzes d'art. Paris, 1862.
Barbedienne, 1875
———. Catalogue des bronzes d'art. Paris, 1875.
Barbedienne, 1877
———. Bronzes d'art : Œuvres de A.-L. Barye. Paris, 1877.
Barbedienne, 1880
———. Catalogue des bronzes d'art. Paris, 1880.
Barbedienne, 1880, Barye
———. Bronzes d'art : Œuvres de A.-L. Barye. Paris, 1880.
Barbedienne, 1884
———. Catalogue des bronzes d'art. Paris, 1884.
Barbedienne, 1893
———. Catalogue des bronzes d'art. Paris, 1893.
Barbedienne, 1900
———. Catalogue des bronzes d'art. Paris, 1900.
Barbet de Jouy, 1867
J.-H. Barbet de Jouy. Galerie d'Apollon : Notice des gemmes et joyaux. Paris, 1867.
Barbey d'Aurevilly, 1887
J. Barbey d'Aurevilly. Les Œuvres et les hommes : Sensations d'art. Paris, 1887.
Barbezieux, 1897
G. Barbezieux. "L'Art au Panthéon." La Paix, August 20, 1897.
"Barbizon," 1950
Anon. "Barbizon School Paintings from the Lindley Bequest." The Minneapolis Institute of Arts Bulletin, vol. XXXIX, no. 22 (June 3, 1950), pp. 106–12.
Barnes and de Mazia, 1935
A.C. Barnes and V. de Mazia. The Art of Renoir. New York, 1935.
Barral, 1864
G. Barral. Salon de 1864 — Vingt-Sept Pages d'arrêt!!! Paris, 1864.
Barrault and Bridel, 1857
A. Barrault and G. Bridel. Le Palais de l'Industrie et ses annexes. Paris and Liège, 1857.
Barré, 1922
L.-N. Barré. "Le Sculpteur Antoine-Augustin Preault." Bulletin Trimestriel de la Société Historique et Archéologique des IV et III Arrondissements de Paris, no. 81 (January 1922), pp. 15–32.
Barret, 1975
A. Barret. Nadar, 50 photographies de ses illustrés contemporains. Paris, 1975.
Bartlett, 1965
T.H. Bartlett. "Auguste Rodin, Sculptor." In A.E. Elsen, ed. Auguste Rodin : Readings on His Life and Work. Englewood Cliffs, N.J., 1965.
"Barye," 1888–89
Anon. "Les Oeuvres décoratives de Barye." Revue des Arts Décoratifs, vol. IX (1888–89), pp. 369–71.
Baschet (ed.), 1885
L. Baschet, ed. Artiste moderne : Catalogue des œuvres du W. Bouguereau. Paris, 1885.
Baudelaire, 1845
C. Baudelaire. Salon de 1845. Paris, 1845.
Baudelaire, 1863
———. "Un Peintre de la vie moderne." Le Figaro, November 26, 28, December 3, 1863.
Baudelaire, 1956
C. Baudelaire. "The Salon of 1845." In The Mirror of Art. Translated by J. Mayne. Garden City, N.Y., 1956.
———. Art in Paris 1845–1862 : Reviews of Salons and Other Exhibitions. Translated and edited by J. Mayne. London, 1965.
Baudelaire, 1970
———. "Windows." In Paris Spleen. Translated by L. Varèse. New York, 1970.
Baudelaire, 1976

———. Œuvres complètes. Vol. II compiled and annotated by C. Pichois. Paris, 1976.
Bauduin, 1972
A. Bauduin. Recherches sur la vie et l'œuvre du peintre François Adolphe Hervier (1819–1879).... Lille, 1972.
Baumgarten, 1958
S. Baumgarten. Le Crépuscule néo-classique : Thomas Hope. Paris, 1958.
Bazin, 1942
G. Bazin. Corot. Paris, 1942.
Bazin, 1957
———. Trésors de la peinture au Louvre. Paris, 1957.
Bazin, 1972
———. Manet. Milan, 1972.
Bazin, 1973
———. Corot. Paris, 1973.
Bazire, 1884
E. Bazire. Manet. Paris, 1884.
Bean, 1960
J. Bean. Les Dessins italiens de la collection Bonnat. Paris, 1960.
Beaulieu, 1975
M. Beaulieu. "Deux Bronzes romantiques d'inspiration classique." La Revue du Louvre et des Musées de France, no. 4 (1975), pp. 269–74.
de Beaumont, 1863
A. de Beaumont. "Les Arts industriels en France et l'exposition de 1863." Revue des Deux-Mondes, vol. XLVII (October 15, 1863), pp. 986–1001.
de Beaumont, 1867
———. "Les Arts décoratifs en Orient et en France : Une Visite à l'Orient à l'Exposition Universelle." Revue des Deux-Mondes, vol. LXXII (November 1867), pp. 138–60.
de Beaumont and Collinot, 1859
A. de Beaumont and E.-V. Collinot. Recueil de dessins pour l'art et l'industrie. Paris, 1859.
de Beauvoir, 1853
A.-R. de Beauvoir. "Toilettes de l'Impératrice." Le Constitutionnel, January 29, 1853, pp. 1–2.
Bell, 1920
H. Bell. "Temporary Exhibition from the Johnson Collection." Pennsylvania Museum Bulletin, vol. XVII, no. 66 (October 1920), pp. 4–10.
de Bellaigue, 1974
G. de Bellaigue. The James A. de Rothschild Collection at Waddesdon Manor : Furniture, Clocks and Gilt Bronzes. 2 vols. Fribourg and London, 1974.
de Bellaigue, 1975
———. "Queen Victoria Buys French in 1855." The Antique Collector, vol. XLVI, no. 4 (April 1975), pp. 37–41.
Bellard, 1950
A. Bellard. "Musées de Province : Metz et Delacroix." Musées de France, no. 10 (December 1950), pp. 261–63.
Bellier and Auvray, 1882–87
E. Bellier de la Chavignerie and L. Auvray. Dictionnaire général des artistes de l'école française depuis l'origine des arts du dessin jusqu'à nos jours. 3 vols. Paris, 1882–87.
Bellier and Auvray, 1934
———. Dictionnaire général des artistes de l'école française. Paris, 1934.
de Belloy, 1855
A. de Belloy. Assemblée Nationale, September 20, 1855.
de Belloy, 1859
M. de Belloy. "Salon de 1859." L'Artiste, vol. II (1859), pp. 3–6.
Bénédite, 1899
L. Bénédite. "Les Salons de 1899 : La Sculpture." La Revue de l'Art Ancien et Moderne, vol. V (1899), pp. 410–18, 473–84.
Bénédite, 1902
———. "Artistes contemporains : Alexandre Falguière." La Revue de l'Art Ancien et Moderne, vol. XI (1902), pp. 65–86.
Bénédite, 1903
———. "John Lewis-Brown." La Revue de l'Art Ancien et Moderne, vol. XII (1903), pp. 81–94.
Bénédite, 1905
———. "Félix Bracquemond, l'animalier." Art et Décoration, vol. XVII (February 1905), pp. 36–47.
Bénédite, 1906
———. L'Œuvre de Fantin-Latour. Paris, 1906.
Bénédite, 1908
———. "Artistes contemporains : J.-J. Henner." Gazette des Beaux-Arts, 50th year, vol. XXXIX (March 1, 1908), pp. 237–64, vol. XL (August 1, 1908), pp. 137–66.
Bénédite, 1910
———. Meissonier. Paris, 1910.
Bénédite, 1911
———. "La Collection Chauchard au Musée du Louvre." Gazette des Beaux-Arts, 53rd year, vol. V (February 1911), pp. 89–112.
Bénédite, 1923
———. "Léon Bonnat (1833–1922)." Gazette des Beaux-Arts,

65th year, vol. VII (January 1923), pp. 1–15.
Bénédite, 1932
———. Théodore Chassériau : Sa Vie et son œuvre. 2 vols. Paris, 1932.
Bénézit, 1911–24
E. Bénézit. Dictionnaire critique et documentaire des peintres, sculpteurs, dessinateurs et graveurs. 3 vols. Paris, 1911–24.
Bénézit, 1948–54
———. Dictionnaire critique et documentaire des peintres, sculpteurs, dessinateurs et graveurs. 8 vols. Paris, 1948–54.
Bénézit, 1976
———. Dictionnaire critique et documentaire des peintres, sculpteurs, dessinateurs et graveurs. 10 vols. Paris, 1976.
Benge, 1969
G.F. Benge. "The Sculptures of Antoine-Louis Barye in the American Collections, with a Catalogue Raisonné." 2 vols. Ph.D. dissertation, University of Iowa, Iowa City, 1969.
Benjamin, 1937
L.R. Benjamin. Eugène Boudin. New York, 1937.
Benjamin, 1977
W. Benjamin. "Short History of Photography." Translated by P. Patton. Artforum, vol. XV, no. 6 (February 1977), p. 47.
Benoist, 1926
L. Benoist. "Corot." L'Amateur d'Art, 1926.
Benoist, 1928
———. La Sculpture romantique. Paris, 1928.
Benoist, 1928, "Clésinger"
———. "Le Sculpteur Clésinger (1814–1883)." Gazette des Beaux-Arts, 70th year, vol. XVIII (November 1928), pp. 283–96.
Benoit, 1909
F. Benoit. La Peinture au Musée de Lille. 3 vols. Paris, 1909.
Beraldi, 1885–92
H. Beraldi. Les Graveurs du XIXe siècle. 12 vols. Paris, 1885–92.
Bergerat, 1877
E. Bergerat. "Hamon." Galerie Contemporaine, July–December 1877, n.p.
Bergerat, 1878
———. "A.-J. Falguière." In L'Art contemporain. Paris, 1878, pp. 100–103.
Bertall, 1872
Bertall. "Le Salon de 1872 de peint et dessiné par Bertall." Le Grelot au Salon, 3rd livraison, 1872.
Bertall, 1880
———. Paris-Journal, September 18, 1880.
Bertauts-Couture, 1932
G. Bertauts-Couture. Thomas Couture (1815–1879) sa vie — son œuvre — son caractère — ses idées — sa méthode, par lui-même et par son petit-fils. Paris, 1932.
Bertauts-Couture, 1955–56
———. "Thomas Couture, sa technique et son influence sur la peinture française du xive siècle." Etudes d'Art, nos. 11–12 (1955–56).
Bertrand, 1870
K. Bertrand. "Salon de 1870—Peinture." L'Artiste, 9th s., June 1, 1870.
Beslay and Paisant, 1857
F. Beslay and A. Paisant. La Peinture au Salon de 1857 : Causeries à deux sur le Salon de 1857. Paris, 1857.
Besnard, 1856
G. Besnard. "Madame L. Lefèvre-Deumier." Bulletin de la Société des Beaux-Arts de Caen, vol. I (1856), pp. 199–204.
Bessis, 1967
H. Bessis. "Marcello ou la duchesse Colonna." Bulletin de la Société de l'Histoire de l'Art Français, 1967 (published 1968), pp. 153–59.
Bessis, 1967, "Delacroix"
———. "Delacroix et la duchesse Colonna." L'Oeil, no. 14 (March 1967), pp. 22–29.
Bessis, 1969
———. "L'Inventaire après décès d'Eugène Delacroix." Bulletin de la Société de l'Histoire de l'Art Français, 1969 (published 1971).
Bessis, 1972
———. "Adolphe Thiers et la duchesse Colonna." Thesis, Paris, 1972.
Bessis, 1975
———. "Duo avec Carpeaux." Connaissance des Arts, vol. CCLXXVII (March 1975), pp. 84–91.
Besson, 1934
G. Besson. La Peinture française au XIXe siècle. Paris, 1934.
Beulé, 1864
M. Beulé. Notice sur la vie et les œuvrages de M. Hippolyte Flandrin. Paris, 1864.
Beulé, 1867
———. Causeries sur l'art. Paris, 1867.
Beulé, 1872
C.-E. Beulé. Eloge de Duban. Paris, 1872.
Beutler, n.d.
C. Beutler. "St. Eugène und die Bibliothèque Nationale." In

*Miscellanea pro Arte : Festschrift für Hermann Schnitzler.* Düsseldorf, n.d.

Beyer, 1973
  *See* 1973, Strasbourg.

Bezombes, 1953
  R. Bezombes. *L'Exotisme dans l'art et la pensée.* Paris and New York, 1953.

"Bibliographie," 1860
  Anon. "Bibliographie des ouvrages publiés en France sur les Beaux-Arts pendant le second semestre de l'année 1860: Photographies." *Gazette des Beaux-Arts,* 2nd year, vol. VIII (December 15, 1860), p. 386.

de Biez, 1896
  J. de Biez. *Un Maître imagier : E. Frémiet.* Paris, 1896.

de Biez, 1910
  ———. *E. Frémiet.* Paris, 1910.

Blanc, 1859
  C. Blanc. "Louis XIV et Molière: Tableau inédit de M. Ingres." *Gazette des Beaux-Arts,* 1st year, vol. I (January 1, 1859), pp. 16–18.

Blanc, 1861
  ———. "Le Salon des Arts Unis." *Gazette des Beaux-Arts,* 3rd year, vol. IX (February 1, 1861), pp. 189–92.

Blanc, 1863
  ———. "Du Style et de M. Ingres." *Gazette des Beaux-Arts,* 5th year, vol. XIV (January 1, 1863), pp. 5–23.

Blanc, 1866
  ———. "Salon de 1866." *Gazette des Beaux-Arts,* 8th year, vol. XXI (July 1, 1866), pp. 28–71.

Blanc, 1867
  ———. "Ingres, sa vie et ses ouvrages." *Gazette des Beaux-Arts,* 9th year, vol. XXIII (July 1, September 1, November 1, 1867), pp. 54–71, 193–208, 442–57.

Blanc, 1870
  ———. *Ingres, sa vie et ses ouvrages.* Paris, 1870.

Blanc, 1876
  ———. *Les Artistes de mon temps.* Paris, 1876.

Blanchard, 1891
  J. Blanchard. *The Life of Gustave Doré.* London, 1891.

Blanchon, 1912
  P. Blanchon. *Eugène Fromentin : Correspondance et fragments inédits.* 3rd ed. Paris, 1912.

Bloch-Dermant, 1974
  J. Bloch-Dermant. *L'Art du verre en France, 1860-1914.* Lausanne, 1974.

Bloche, 1888
  A. Bloche. *La Vente des diamants de la Couronne.* Paris, 1888.

Blouet, 1838
  A. Blouet. Foreword to *Expédition scientifique de Morée...* Vol. III. Paris, 1838.

Blunt, 1945
  A. Blunt. *The French Drawings in the Collection of His Majesty the King at Windsor Castle.* Oxford, 1945.

Bodelsen, 1968
  M. Bodelsen. "Early Impressionist Sales 1874–94 in the Light of Some Unpublished 'procès-verbaux.'" *The Burlington Magazine,* vol. CX, no. 783 (June 1968), pp. 331–49.

Boetzel, 1865
  M. Boetzel. *Année 1865. Le Salon.* Paris, 1865.

Boggs, 1958
  J.S. Boggs. "Degas Notebooks at the Bibliothèque Nationale." *The Burlington Magazine,* vol. C, nos. 662–64 (May–June 1958), pp. 163–71, 196–205, 240–46.

Boggs, 1962
  ———. *Portraits by Degas.* Berkeley, 1962.

Boggs, 1963
  ———. "Edgar Degas and Naples." *The Burlington Magazine,* vol. CV, no. 723 (June 1963), pp. 273–76.

Boime, 1969
  A. Boime. "Thomas Couture and the Evolution of Painting in Nineteenth-Century France." *The Art Bulletin,* vol. LI, no. 1 (March 1969), pp. 48–56.

Boime, 1969, "Salon des Refusés"
  ———. "The Salon des Refusés and the Evolution of Modern Art." *The Art Quarterly,* vol. XXXII (1969), pp. 411–23.

Boime, 1971, Academy
  ———. *The Academy and French Painting in the Nineteenth Century.* London, 1971.

Boime, 1971, "Contest"
  ———. "The Second Republic's Contest for the Figure of the Republic." *The Art Bulletin,* vol. LIII, no. 1 (March 1971), pp. 68–83.

Boime, 1971, "Gérôme"
  ———. "Jean-Léon Gérôme, Henri Rousseau's 'Sleeping Gypsy' and the Academic Legacy." *The Art Quarterly,* vol. XXXIV, no. 1 (spring 1971), pp. 3–29.

Boime, 1972
  ———. "Thomas Nast and French Art." *The American Art Journal,* vol. IV, no. 1 (spring 1972), pp. 43–65.

Boime, 1977
  ———. "The Teaching Reforms of 1863 and the Origins of Modernism in France." *The Art Quarterly,* n.s., vol. I, no. 1 (autumn 1977), pp. 1–39.

Boime (in preparation)
  ———. *Couture and the Eclectic Vision.* New Haven (in preparation).

Boisse, 1917
  L. Boisse. "Le Paysage et la nature dans l'œuvre de Gustave Moreau." *Mercure de France,* February 1, 1917, pp. 417–28.

Bolles, 1943
  M.P. Bolles. "A Second-Empire Flounce and Border." *The Metropolitan Museum of Art Bulletin,* vol. I, no. 10 (June 1943), pp. 300–302.

Bonnat, 1889
  L. Bonnat. "Barye." *Gazette des Beaux-Arts,* 31st year, vol. I (May 1, 1889), pp. 374–82.

Bonnin, 1872
  A. Bonnin. "Salon de 1872." *La Presse,* May 22, 1872.

Bontemps, 1868
  G. Bontemps. *Guide du verrier : Traité historique et pratique de la fabrication des verres, cristaux, vitraux.* Paris, 1868.

Borcoman, 1976
  Ottawa, National Gallery of Canada. *Charles Nègre 1820–1880.* By James Borcoman. Ottawa, 1976.

Borel, 1955
  P. Borel. "Ce que révèle une correspondance inédite, portraits et modèles d'Eugène Delacroix." *Tribune de Genève,* August 1955.

Bortolatto, 1972
  L.R. Bortolatto. *L'Opera pittorica completa di Delacroix.* Milan, 1972.

de Bouchaud, 1894
  P. de Bouchaud. *Claudius Popelin, peintre, émailleur et poète.* Paris, 1894.

Boucher, 1930
  F. Boucher. *Alfred Stevens.* Paris, 1930.

Boucher, 1974
  M.C. Boucher. "Catalogue de l'œuvre dessiné et peint de Puvis de Chavannes au Musée du Petit-Palais." Thesis, Ecole du Louvre, 1974.

Boudon et al., 1977
  F. Boudon, A. Chastel, H. Couzy, and F. Hamon. *Système de l'architecture urbaine ; le quartier des halles à Paris.* 2 vols. Paris, 1977.

Bouilhet, 1908–12
  H. Bouilhet. *L'Orfèvrerie française aux XVIII^e et XIX^e siècles.* 3 vols. Paris, 1908–12.

Bourguignon, n.d.
  J. Bourguignon. *Malmaison. Les Souvenirs du Second Empire.* Paris, n.d.

Bouyer, 1896
  R. Bouyer. "Petits Maîtres oubliés : Adolphe Hervier." *Gazette des Beaux-Arts,* 38th year, vol. XVI (July 1, 1896), pp. 61–72.

Bouyer, 1926
  ———. "Gustave Moreau 1826–1898 : A l'occasion du centenaire de sa naissance." *Le Figaro Artistique,* April 8, 1926.

Bowness, 1961
  A. Bowness. "A Note on 'Manet's Compositional Difficulties.'" *The Burlington Magazine,* vol. CIII, no. 699 (June 1961), pp. 276–77.

Bowness, 1967
  ———. "Manet at Philadelphia." *The Burlington Magazine,* vol. CIX, no. 768 (March 1967), pp. 188–89.

Bowness, 1978, "Proudhon"
  ———. "Courbet's Proudhon." *The Burlington Magazine,* vol. CXX, no. 900 (March 1978), pp. 123–30.

Boyer d'Agen, 1909
  Boyer d'Agen [A.-J. Boyé]. *Ernest Hébert, souvenirs d'atelier.* Paris, 1909.

Braive, 1966
  M. Braive. *The Photograph : A Social History.* Translated by D. Britt. New York and Toronto, 1966.

"Braun," 1867
  Anon. "Adolphe Braun." *The Philadelphia Photographer,* vol. IV, no. 48 (December 1867), p. 399.

le Braz, 1906
  A. le Braz. "Une Lettre de Hamon." *Chronique des Arts,* 1906, pp. 28–29.

Breton, 1886
  J.-A. Breton. *Notice sur M. Paul Baudry.* Paris, 1886.

Breton, 1890
  ———. *La Vie d'un artiste.* Paris, 1890.

Breton, 1891
  ———. *The Life of an Artist ; Art and Nature.* London and New York, 1891.

Breton, 1899
  ———. *Nos Peintres du siècle.* Paris, 1899.

Bricon, 1898
  E. Bricon. "Frémiet." *Gazette des Beaux-Arts,* 30th year,

vol. XIX (June 1, 1898), pp. 494–507, vol. XX (July 1, 1898), pp. 17–31.

Brière, 1920
  Paris, Musée du Louvre. *Le Musée du Louvre depuis 1914.* (Les Accroissements des musées nationaux français.) 3 vols. (1919–21). By G. Brière. Paris, 1920.

Brière, 1924
  Paris, Musée National du Louvre. *Musée National du Louvre. Catalogue des peintures.* Vol. I: *Ecole française.* By G. Brière. Paris, 1924.

Brinton, 1922
  C. Brinton. "The Johnson 'Modern Group.'" *International Studio,* vol. LXXVI, no. 305 (October 1922), pp. 7–13.

Brongniart and Riocreux, 1845
  A. Brongniart and D. Riocreux. *Description méthodique du Musée Céramique de la Manufacture Royale de Porcelaine de Sèvres.* Paris, 1845.

Brossard, 1975
  Y. Brossard. "Sarreguemines." *abc décor,* July–August 1975, pp. 23–28.

Browse, 1949
  L. Browse. *Degas Dancers.* London, 1949.

Brun, 1917
  K. Brun. *Schweizerisches Kunstler-Lexikon....* Vol. IV. Frauenfeld, 1917.

Brunet, 1953
  M. Brunet. *Les Marques de Sèvres.* Paris, 1953.

Brunhammer et al., 1976
  Y. Brunhammer et al. *Art Nouveau : Belgium, France.* Houston, 1976.

Bruyas, 1854
  A. Bruyas. *Explication des ouvrages de peinture du cabinet de M. Alfred Bruyas.* Paris, 1854.

Bruyas, 1876
  ———. *La Galerie Bruyas.* Translated by T. Silvestre. Paris, 1876.

Burty, 1859
  P. Burty. "Exposition de la Société Française de Photographie." *Gazette des Beaux-Arts,* 1st year, vol. II (May 15, 1859), pp. 209–21.

Burty, 1866, Chefs-d'œuvre
  ———. *Chefs-d'œuvre des arts industriels ; céramique, verrerie et vitraux, émaux, métaux, orfèvrerie et bijouterie, tapisserie.* Paris, 1866.

Burty, 1866, "Lille"
  ———. "L'Exposition des Beaux-Arts à Lille." *Gazette des Beaux-Arts,* 8th year, vol. XXI (October 1, 1866), pp. 379–90.

Burty, 1868, "Bordeaux"
  ———. "Exposition de la Société des Amis des Arts de Bordeaux." *Gazette des Beaux-Arts,* 10th year, vol. XXIV (May 1, 1868), pp. 496–500.

Burty, 1868, "L'Email"
  ———. "L'Email des peintres par L.M. Claudius Popelin." *Gazette des Beaux-Arts,* 10th year, vol. XXIV (June 1, 1868), pp. 587–97.

Burty, 1868, Emaux cloisonnés
  ———. *Les Emaux cloisonnés anciens et modernes.* Paris, 1868.

Burty, 1868, "Le Mobilier moderne"
  ———. "Le Mobilier moderne." *Gazette des Beaux-Arts,* 10th year, vol. XXIV (January 1, 1868), pp. 26–45.

Burty, 1869
  ———. *Paul Huet.* Paris, 1869.

Burty, 1869, Chefs-d'œuvre
  ———. *Chefs-d'œuvre of the Industrial Arts ; Pottery and Porcelain, Glass, Enamel, Metal....* London and New York, 1869.

Burty, 1869, "Industries"
  ———. "Les Industries de luxe à l'Exposition de l'Union Centrale." *Gazette des Beaux-Arts,* 11th year, vol. II (December 1, 1869), pp. 529–46.

Burty, 1870, "Bordeaux"
  ———. "L'Exposition de Bordeaux." *Gazette des Beaux-Arts,* 12th year, vol. III (June 1, 1870), pp. 552–60.

Burty, 1870, "Ecoles"
  ———. "Les Ecoles gratuites et le Musée céramique de Limoges." *Gazette des Beaux-Arts,* 12th year, vol. III (January 1, 1870), pp. 66–78.

Burty, 1870, "Limoges"
  ———. "L'Exposition de Limoges." *Gazette des Beaux-Arts,* 12th year, vol. IV (September 1, 1870), pp. 218–30.

Burty, 1875
  ———. *Union Centrale des Beaux-Arts appliqués à l'industrie. Exposition de 1874. Rapport présenté par le jury de la VI^e section.* Paris, 1875.

Burty, 1878
  ———. "Silhouettes d'artistes contemporains: Félix Bracquemond." *L'Art,* vol. XII (1878), pp. 289–98.

Burty, 1883
  ———. *F.-D. Froment-Meurice, argentier de la ville 1802–1855.* Paris, 1883.

Burty, 1883, "Courbet"

P. Burty. Introduction to Courbet sale catalogue, Paris, Hôtel Drouot, 1883.

Burty, 1886
————. "Henri Regnault : Quelques Lettres inédites." *L'Art*, 12th year, vol. XLI (1886), pp. 46–52.

Butor, 1963
M. Butor. "Claude Monet ou le monde renversé." *Art de France*, vol. I, no. 3 (1963), pp. 277–301.

Bye, 1921
A.E. Bye. *Pots and Pans ; or, Studies in Still-Life Painting.* Princeton, 1921.

Ch. D., 1878
Ch. D. "Compte rendu sur l'Exposition Universelle, Paris, 1878." *Le Courrier du Centre*, June 8, 1878.

Cabanne, 1957
P. Cabanne. "Quand le petit Meissonier." *Lecture pour Tous*, 1957.

Cadars, 1965
P. Cadars. "Les Débuts de Gustave Moreau." Thesis, Université de Toulouse, 1965.

Cahen, 1900
G. Cahen. *Eugène Boudin, sa vie et son œuvre.* Paris, 1900.

Caillaux, 1935
H. Caillaux. *Aimé-Jules Dalou.* Paris, 1935.

Cain, 1908
G. Cain. *La Place Vendôme.* Paris, 1908.

de Callias, 1861
H. de Callias. "Le Salon de 1861." *L'Artiste*, 7th s., vol. XI (1861), pp. 217ff., vol. XII, pp. 1ff.

de Callias, 1863
————. "Salon de 1863 : La Sculpture." *L'Artiste*, 8th s., vol. II (1863).

de Callias, 1863, *Salon*
————. *Salon de 1863.* Paris, 1863.

de Callias, 1864
————. "Salon de 1864." *L'Artiste*, 8th s., vol. I (1864), pp. 217–21, vol. V (1864), pp. 195ff.

Calmettes, 1912
F. Calmettes. "Deux Tentures au Palais de l'Elysée par Baudry et Galland." *Revue de l'Art Ancien et Moderne*, vol. XXXI (March 1912), pp. 205–18.

de Calonne, 1853
A. de Calonne. "Salon de 1853." *Revue Contemporaine*, vol. VIII (1853).

Calvet-Sérullaz, 1971
A. Calvet-Sérullaz. "A propos de l'exposition Baudelaire : L'Exposition de bazar Bonne-Nouvelle de 1846 et le Salon de 1859." *Bulletin de la Société de l'Histoire de l'Art Français*, 1969 (published 1971), pp. 123–34.

Cambas-Lanvin, 1967
Cambas-Lanvin. "Hippolyte Flandrin." Thesis, Ecole du Louvre, 1967.

Cantaloube, 1861
A. Cantaloube. *Lettre sur les expositions et le Salon de 1861.* Paris, 1861.

Cantaloube, 1864
E. Cantaloube. *Nouvelle Revue de Paris*, June 15, 1864, pp. 602–7.

Cantrel, 1859
E. Cantrel. "Le Salon de 1859." *L'Artiste*, vol. II (1859), pp. 130–32.

Cantrel, 1863
————. "Les Artistes contemporains : Salon de 1863." *L'Artiste*, vol. I (1863), pp. 190–204.

"Carbon Photographs," 1867
Anon. "Braun's Carbon Photographs." *The Philadelphia Photographer*, vol. IV, no. 48 (December 1867), pp. 401–2.

Carette, n.d.
Mme Carette. *Souvenirs intimes de la Cour des Tuileries.* 3 vols. Paris, n.d.

Carpeaux, 1899
C. Carpeaux. *La Galerie Carpeaux.* Paris, 1899.

Carré de Busserolle, 1966
J.-X. Carré de Busserolle. *Dictionnaire géographique, historique et biographique d'Indre-et-Loire et de l'ancienne province de Touraine.* 6 vols. 1878–84. Reprint. Mayenne, 1966.

Cartier, 1956
J.-A. Cartier. "J.-B. Carpeaux, sculpteur, peintre et dessinateur." *Galerie Jardin des Arts*, no. 15 (1956), pp. 146–49.

Castagnary, 1858
J.-A. Castagnary. *Philosophie du Salon de 1857.* Paris, 1858.

Castagnary, 1859
————. *Salon de 1859.* In Castagnary, 1892, pp. 181–82.

Castagnary, 1864
————. *Salon de 1864.* In Castagnary, 1892, pp. 214–20.

Castagnary, 1868
————. *Salon de 1868.* In Castagnary, 1892, pp. 320–26.

Castagnary, 1869
————. *Salon de 1869.* In Castagnary, 1892, pp. 384–89.

Castagnary, 1870
————. *Salon de 1870.* In Castagnary, 1892, pp. 431–36.

Castagnary, 1872
————. *Le Siècle*, May 18, 1872.

Castagnary, 1912
————. "Fragments d'un livre sur Courbet." *Gazette des Beaux-Arts*, 53rd year, vol. V (January 1911) pp. 5–20, vol. VI (December 1911), pp. 488–97, 54th year, vol. VII (January 1912), pp. 19–30.

Castelot, Decaux, and Koenig, 1969
A. Castelot, A. Decaux, and General Koenig. *Le Livre de la famille impériale.* Paris, 1969.

*Catalogue 1851*
*Great Exhibition of the Works of Industry of All Nations, 1851 : Official Descriptive and Illustrated Catalogue.* 3 vols. London, 1851.

*Catalogue 1855*
*Exposition des Produits de l'Industrie de Toutes les Nations, 1855 : Catalogue officiel publié par ordre de la Commission impériale.* Paris, 1855.

*Catalogue 1862*
*Exposition Universelle de 1862 à Londres. Section française : Catalogue officiel publié par ordre de la Commission impériale.* Paris, 1862.

*Catalogue 1867*
*Exposition Universelle de 1867 à Paris : Catalogue général publié par la Commission impériale.* 3 vols. Paris, 1867.

*Catalogue 1869*
*Palais de l'Industrie (Champs-Elysées). Union Centrale des Beaux-Arts Appliqués à l'Industrie. Exposition de 1869. Catalogue des œuvres et des produits modernes.* Paris, 1869.

*Catalogue 1878*
*Ministère de l'Agriculture et du Commerce. Exposition Universelle Internationale de 1878, à Paris. Catalogue officiel. Liste des récompensés.* Paris, 1878.

Celebonovic, 1974
A. Celebonovic. *Some Call It Kitsch.* New York, 1974.

*Chabal-Dussurgey*, 1903
Anon. *Biographie abrégée du peintre Chabal-Dussurgey.* Paris, 1903.

Chabouillet, 1879
A. Chabouillet. *Le Camée représentant l'Apothéose de Napoléon 1er gravé par M. Ad. David d'après le plafond d'Ingres.* Paris, 1879.

Cham, 1857
Cham [A. de Noé]. *Salon de 1857.* Paris, 1857.

Cham, 1863
————. *Au Salon de 1863.* Paris, 1863.

Champa, 1973
K.S. Champa. *Studies in Early Impressionism.* New Haven and London, 1973.

de Champeaux, 1886
A. de Champeaux. *Dictionnaire des fondeurs, ciseleurs, modeleurs en bronze et doreurs depuis le Moyen Age jusqu'à l'époque actuelle* [A–C]. Paris and London, 1886.

de Champeaux, n.d.
————. *Dictionnaire des fondeurs, ciseleurs, modeleurs en bronze et doreurs depuis le Moyen Age jusqu'à l'époque actuelle* [D–Z]. Ms. n.d. Paris, Bibliothèque des Arts Décoratifs.

Champfleury, 1846
J. Champfleury. "Tableaux de mœurs : M. Prudhomme au Salon." *La Silhouette*, March 22, 1846, pp. 848–51.

Champfleury, 1879
————. *Henry Monnier, sa vie, son œuvre, avec un catalogue complet de l'œuvre.* Paris, 1879.

Champier, 1882–83
V. Champier. "La Maison modèle...." *Revue des Arts Décoratifs*, vol. III (1882–83), p. 180.

Champier, 1887–88
————. "Le Concours d'orfèvrerie du Ministère de l'Agriculture." *Revue des Arts Décoratifs*, vol. VIII (1887–88), pp. 84–90.

Champier, 1888–89
————. "Les Artistes de l'industrie : I. Constant Sévin." *Revue des Arts Décoratifs*, vol. IX (1888–89), pp. 161–76.

Champier, 1889–90
————. "Nécrologie : Poussielgue-Rusand." *Revue des Arts Décoratifs*, vol. X (1889–90), pp. 260–62.

Champier, 1890–91
————. "Nécrologie : Eugène Rousseau, céramiste et verrier." *Revue des Arts Décoratifs*, vol. XI (1890–91), pp. 86–93.

Champier, 1891–92
————. "Ferdinand Barbedienne (1810–1892)." *Revue des Arts Décoratifs*, vol. XII (1891–92), pp. 289–90.

Champier, 1894–95, "Christofle"
————. "Le Cinquantenaire de la maison Christofle." *Revue des Arts Décoratifs*, vol. XV (1894–95), pp. 525–31.

Champier, 1894–95, "Piat"
————. "Le Musée F.-Eugène Piat à Troyes." *Revue des Arts Décoratifs*, vol. XV (1894–95), pp. 25–29.

Champier, 1896
————. "Les Artistes décorateurs. F. Thesmar." *Revue des Arts Décoratifs*, vol. XVI (1896), pp. 373–81.

Champier, 1901
————. "Une Visite à l'Hôtel Païva, la décoration sous le Second Empire." *Revue des Arts Décoratifs*, vol. XXI (1901), pp. 241–58.

Champier, 1902
————. *L'Hôtel Païva.* Bordeaux, 1902.

Champlin and Perkins, 1886–87
J.D. Champlin, Jr. and C.C. Perkins. *Cyclopedia of Painters and Painting.* 4 vols. New York, 1886–87.

Chamson-Mazauric, 1968
L. Chamson-Mazauric. "Comment on perd un tableau." *La Revue du Louvre et des Musées de France*, no. 1 (1968), pp. 27–36.

Charageat, 1931
M. Charageat. *Catalogues des sculptures des jardins du Louvre, du Carrousel et des Tuileries.* Paris, 1931.

Chassé, 1947
C. Chassé. *Le Mouvement symboliste dans l'art du XIXe siècle.* Paris, 1947.

Chatrousse, 1862
Chatrousse. "Les Statuaires français à l'Exposition Universelle de Londres." *L'Artiste*, 8th s., vol. LXXII (1862), pp. 121–26.

*Chauchard Collection*, 1911
H. F.-A. Chauchard. *Les Peintures de ... [sa] collection.* Paris, 1911.

Chaumelin, 1857
M. Chaumelin. "Société Artistique des Bouches-du-Rhône, Exposition de 1857 — 2e partie." *Tribune Artistique et Littéraire du Midi.* Marseilles, 1857.

Chaumelin, 1861
————. *Decamps, sa vie, son œuvre, ses imitateurs.* Marseilles, 1861.

Chaumelin, 1870
————. "Salon de 1870." *L'Art Contemporain*, 1870.

Chaumelin, 1887
————. *Portraits d'artistes ; E. Meissonier, J. Breton.* Paris, 1887.

de Chavagnac and de Grollier, 1906
X. de Chavagnac and G.A. de Grollier. *Histoire des manufactures françaises de porcelaine.* Paris, 1906.

Chavance, 1926
R. Chavance. "Claude Monet." *Le Figaro Illustré*, December 16, 1926.

Chennevières, 1883–89
P. de Chennevières. *Souvenirs d'un directeur des Beaux-Arts....* 5 vols. Paris, 1883–89.

Cherbulliez, 1872
V. Cherbulliez. "Lettres sur le Salon." *Le Temps*, June 6, 1872.

Chéronnet, 1951
L. Chéronnet. *Paris tel qu'il fut, 100 photographies anciennes.* Paris, 1951.

Chertier, 1859
A. Chertier. "L'Archéologie et ses rapports avec l'orfèvrerie religieuse." *L'Art au Dix-Neuvième Siècle*, vol. IV (1859), pp. 113–16.

Chesneau, 1859
E. Chesneau. *Libre Etude sur l'art contemporain : Salon de 1859.* Paris, 1859.

Chesneau, 1863
————. *Le Constitutionnel*, May 3, 1863.

Chesneau, 1864
————. *L'Art et les artistes modernes en France et en Angleterre.* Paris, 1864.

Chesneau, 1868
————. *Les Nations rivales dans l'art.* Paris, 1868.

Chesneau, 1868, *Le Constitutionnel*
————. *Le Constitutionnel*, July 1, 1868.

Chesneau, 1878
————. "Exposition Universelle : Le Japon à Paris." *Gazette des Beaux-Arts*, 20th year, vol. XVIII (September 1, November 1, 1878), pp. 385–97, 841–56.

Chesneau, 1880
————. *Le Statuaire J. B. Carpeaux, sa vie et son œuvre.* Paris, 1880.

Chevalier, 1878
F. Chevalier. "Jacques Maillet." *L'Artiste*, 9th s., vol. II (1878), pp. 92–97.

Chevalier, 1957
D. Chevalier. "Une Exposition reconstitue la vie sous le Second Empire." *Galerie Jardin des Arts*, September 1957,

pp. 702–4.

Chevillard, 1893
V. Chevillard. *Un Peintre romantique: Théodore Chassériau.* Paris, 1893.

Chiego, 1974
W.J. Chiego. "Two Paintings by Fantin-Latour." *Museum News: The Toledo Museum of Art,* n.s., vol. XVII, no. 2 (1974), pp. 27–39.

Christ, 1949
Y. Christ. *Le Louvre et les Tuileries.* Paris, 1949.

Christ, 1965
———. *L'Age d'or de la photographie.* Paris, 1965.

Christofle, 1855
C. Christofle. *Notice rédigée par Ch. Christofle pour MM. les membres du jury de l'Exposition Universelle.* Paris, 1855.

Christofle, 1862
Christofle et Cie, Paris. *Orfèvrerie Christofle: Tarif.* Paris, 1862.

Cicéron, 1858
Cicéron [pseud.]. "Le Chant du Calvaire." *Magasin Pittoresque,* 1858, pp. 93–94.

Cladel, 1936
J. Cladel. *Rodin: Sa Vie glorieuse, sa vie inconnue.* Paris, 1936.

Claparède, 1947
J. Claparède. *Les Peintres du Languedoc méditerranéen de 1610 à 1870 dans Languedoc méditerranéen et Roussillon d'hier et d'aujourd'hui.* Nice, 1947.

Claparède, 1961
———. "La Collection du Musée Fabre à Montpellier." *L'Œil,* no. 82 (October 1961), pp. 40–45.

Claparède, 1962
———. *Montpellier, Musée Fabre. Dessins de la collection Alfred Bruyas et autres dessins des XIXᵉ et XXᵉ siècles. (Inventaire des collections publiques françaises,* vol. VI). Paris, 1962.

Claretie, 1865
J. Claretie. "Deux Heures au Salon." *L'Artiste,* 8th s., vol. LXXVII (1865), pp. 224–29.

Claretie, 1872
———. "Salon de 1872." *Le Soir,* May 25, 1872.

Claretie, 1873
———. *Peintres et sculpteurs contemporains.* Paris, 1873.

Claretie, 1876
———. *L'Art et les artistes français contemporains.* Paris, 1876.

Claretie, 1881
———. *J.-L. Hamon.* Paris, 1881.

Claretie, 1882–84
———. *Peintres et sculpteurs contemporains.* 2 vols. Paris, 1882–84.

Clark, 1973
T. J. Clark. *The Absolute Bourgeois, Art and Politics in France, 1848–51.* Greenwich, 1973.

Clément, 1862
C. Clément. *Catalogue des bijoux du Musée Napoléon III.* Paris, 1862.

Clément, 1864
———. *Journal des Débats,* May 12, 1864.

Clément, 1872
———. "Salon de 1872." *Journal des Débats,* May 7, 1872.

Clément, 1878
———. *Gleyre, étude biographique et critique.* Paris, 1878.

Clement and Hutton, 1879
C.E. Clement and L. Hutton. *Artists of the Nineteenth Century.* 2 vols. Boston, 1879.

Clément-Carpeaux, 1927
L. Clément-Carpeaux. "Pour le Centenaire de Carpeaux: La Genèse du groupe de 'La Danse' (1863–1869)." *Revue de l'Art,* vol. LI (January–March 1927), pp. 285–300.

Clément-Carpeaux, 1934–35
———. *La Vérité sur l'œuvre et la vie de J.-B. Carpeaux (1827–1875).* 2 vols. Paris, 1934–35.

Clément-Carpeaux, 1937
———. "Carpeaux peintre." *Beaux-Arts,* no. 219 (1937), pp. 1–2.

Clouzot, 1925
H. Clouzot. *Des Tuileries à Saint-Cloud: L'Art décoratif du Second Empire.* Paris, 1925.

Clouzot, 1939
———. *Le Style Louis-Philippe* – Napoléon III. Paris, 1939.

Clouzot and Follot, 1935
H. Clouzot and C. Follot. *Histoire du papier peint en France.* Paris, 1935.

Clozier, 1940
R. Clozier. "La Gare du Nord." Université de Paris, 1940.

Collinot and de Beaumont, 1883, *Japon*
E. Collinot and A. de Beaumont. *Encyclopédie des arts décoratifs de l'Orient.* Series 4: *Ornements du Japon.* Paris, 1883.

Collinot and de Beaumont, 1883, *Perse*
———. *Encyclopédie des arts décoratifs de l'Orient.* Series 1: *Ornements de la Perse.* Paris, 1883.

Colombier, 1931
P. de Colombier. "Thomas Couture à Senlis." *Candide,* Au-

gust 6, 1931.

Commemorative Catalogue 1932
London, Royal Academy of Arts. *Commemorative Catalogue of the Exhibition of French Art, 1200–1900.* London, 1933.

Commission Rapport 1862
*Rapport de l'administration de la commission impériale sur la section française de l'exposition de 1862 suivi des documents statistiques et officiels et de la liste des exposants récompensés.* Paris, 1864.

Comstock, 1954
H. Comstock. "The Connoisseur in America." *The Connoisseur,* vol. CXXXIII (May 1954), pp. 289–94.

Comte, 1885
J. Comte. "Exposition de dessins, aquarelles et estampes de Gustave Doré." *Gazette des Beaux-Arts,* 27th year, vol. XXXI (April 1, 1885), pp. 367–74.

Conegliano, 1897
Duc de Conegliano. *Le Second Empire. La Maison de l'Empereur.* Paris, 1897.

Connaissance des Arts, 1957
Connaissance des Arts. *Le Dix-Neuvième Siècle français.* Paris, 1957.

Cook, 1888
C. Cook. *Art and Artists of Our Time.* 3 vols. New York, 1888.

Cooper, 1959
D. Cooper. "Renoir, Lise, and the Le Cœur Family: A Study of Renoir's Early Development." *The Burlington Magazine,* vol. CI, no. 674 (May 1959), p. 163.

Cooper, 1975
J. Cooper. *Nineteenth-Century Romantic Bronzes: French, English and American Bronzes, 1830–1915.* London, 1975.

Coppens, 1974
J. Coppens. "Pierson's portretten van 'La Castiglione.'" *Foto Universeel Tijdschrift,* December 1974, pp. 36–39.

Coquiot, 1924
G. Coquiot. *Des Gloires déboulonnées.* Paris, 1924.

Cordier, 1860
C. Cordier. *Sculpture ethnographique.* Paris, 1860.

Courthion, 1948–50
P. Courthion. *Courbet raconté par lui-même et par ses amis.* 2 vols. Geneva, 1948–50.

Courthion, 1964
———. *Autour de l'Impressionnisme.* Paris, 1964.

Couture, 1867
T. Couture. *Méthode et entretiens d'atelier.* Paris, 1867.

Cox, 1902
R. Cox. *Le Musée historique des tissus de la Chambre de Commerce de Lyon.* Lyons, 1902.

Cox, 1914
———. *Les Industries de la soie à l'Exposition Internationale de Lyon en 1914.* Lyons, 1914.

Cozic, 1865
H. Cozic. "Le Service de table de S.M. L'Empereur du Mexique." *L'Illustration,* vol. XLV (January–June 1865), pp. 109–10.

Crespelle, 1962
J.-P. Crespelle. *Les Fauves.* Neuchâtel, 1962.

Crespelle, 1966
———. *Les Maîtres de la Belle Epoque.* Paris, 1966.

Cromer, 1930
G. Cromer. "Un Photographe-Artiste dès milieu de XIXᵉ siècle, le peintre Henri LeSecq." *Bulletin de la Société Française de Photographie,* no. 10 (October 1930), pp. 287–95.

Crystal Palace 1851
*The Crystal Palace and Its Contents, Being an Illustrated Cyclopaedia of the Great Exhibition of the Industry of All Nations 1851....* [Published in weekly installments October 4, 1851–March 27, 1852, then bound with index, London, 1852].

Cunningham, 1952
C.C. Cunningham. "Eugène Delacroix (1798–1863) 'Turkish Women Bathing.'" *Wadsworth Atheneum Bulletin,* 2nd s., no. 35 (November 1952), p. 1.

Curry, 1964
L. Curry. "Henri Fantin-Latour's Tannhäuser on Venusberg." *Los Angeles County Museum of Art Bulletin,* vol. XVI, no. 1 (1964), pp. 3–19.

de Curzon, 1916
H. de Curzon. *Alfred de Curzon, peintre (1820–1895): Sa Vie et son œuvre d'après ses souvenirs, ses lettres, ses contemporains.* 2 vols. Paris, 1916.

Cuzacq, 1940
R. Cuzacq. *Bonnat, l'homme et l'artiste.* Mont-de-Marsan, 1940.

Dacier, 1905
E. Dacier. *Le Musée de la Comédie Française.* Paris, 1905.

Dalligny, 1901
*Catalogue des tableaux et étude peintes par Antoine Vollon.* Paris,

Hôtel Drouot, May 20–23, 1901. By A. Dalligny.

Dalloz, 1861
P. Dalloz. "Exposition des Arts Industriels." *Le Moniteur,* December 7, 1861.

Dalloz, 1862
———. "Exposition de Londres." *Le Moniteur,* May 25, 1862.

Dalloz, 1867
———. "Comptes rendus de l'Exposition Universelle de l'art et l'industrie, Galerie du Mobilier." *Le Moniteur,* May 26, July 29, August 11, October 5, 1867.

Daly, 1859
C. Daly. "Une Laiterie à Marly-le-Roi par M. Nicolle, arch." *Revue de l'Architecture et des Travaux Publics,* 1859, pp. 68–70.

Daly, 1887
———. "Nécrologie: Joseph Nicolle." *Revue de l'Architecture et des Travaux Publics,* vol. XLIV (1887), pp. 245–46.

Darcel, 1859
A. Darcel. *Les Artistes normands au Salon de 1859.* Rouen, 1859.

Darcel, 1862
———. "Les Arts industriels à l'Exposition de Londres." *Gazette des Beaux-Arts,* 4th year, vol. XIII (October 1, November 1, December 1, 1862), pp. 313–31, 437–45, 538–55.

Darcel, 1863
———. "Les Arts industriels à l'Exposition de Londres: La Céramique, la cristallerie, les meubles, tapisserie-étoffes." *Gazette des Beaux-Arts,* 5th year, vol. XIV (January 1, 1863), pp. 64–86.

Darcel, 1867, "Bronze"
———. "Exposition Universelle: Bronze et fonte modernes." *Gazette des Beaux-Arts,* 9th year, vol. XXIII (November 1, 1867), pp. 419–41.

Darcel, 1867, *Emaux*
———. "Maison de l'Empereur. Musée Impérial du Louvre. Musée du Moyen Age et de la Renaissance. Série D." In *Notice des émaux et de l'orfèvrerie.* Paris, 1867.

Darcel, 1867, "Galvanoplastie"
———. "Exposition Universelle: Galvanoplastie, ferronnerie, et damasquine." *Gazette des Beaux-Arts,* 9th year, vol. XXIII (December 1, 1867), pp. 559–71.

Darcel, 1868
———. "L'Emaillerie moderne." *Gazette des Beaux-Arts,* 10th year, vol. XXIV (January 1, 1868), pp. 75–84.

Darnis, 1975
J.-M. Darnis. "Eugène Oudine (1810–1887)." *Le Club Français de la Médaille Bulletin,* no. 49 (1975), pp. 200–207.

Dassy, 1887
L. Dassy. "Bulletin nécrologique de Ruprich-Robert." *Forum Artistique,* 2nd year, no. 7 (July 1887), pp. 97–102.

Daulte, 1950
F. Daulte. "Le Peintre de portraits." *Arts,* n.s., no. 266 (June 9, 1950).

Daulte, 1952
———. *Frédéric Bazille et son temps.* Geneva, 1952.

Daulte, 1959
———. *Alfred Sisley.* Lausanne, 1959.

Daulte, 1960
———. "Un Provençal pur: Paul Guigou." *Connaissance des Arts,* no. 98 (April 1960), pp. 70–77.

Daulte, 1970
———. "Bazille: Son Oeuvre s'achève en 1870." *Connaissance des Arts,* no. 226 (December 1970), pp. 86–91.

Daulte, 1971
———. *Auguste Renoir, catalogue raisonné de l'œuvre peint.* Vol. 1: *Figures.* Lausanne, 1971.

Davies and Gould, 1970
London, National Gallery. *French School, Early 19th Century, Impressionists, Post Impressionists....* By M. Davies, with revisions by C. Gould. London, 1970.

Davioud, 1873
G. Davioud. *Notice sur la vie et les œuvres de Léon Vaudoyer.* Paris, 1873.

Davis, 1950
R.S. Davis. "Barbizon School Paintings from the Lindley Bequest." *The Minneapolis Institute of Arts Bulletin,* vol. XXXIX (June 3, 1950), pp. 105–12.

Dax, 1865
P. Dax. "Chronique." *L'Artiste,* 8th s., vol. LXXVII (1865), p. 72.

Dayot, 1900
A. Dayot. *Le Second Empire (2 Décembre 1851–4 Septembre 1870).* Paris, 1900.

Dayot, 1901
———. *L'Invasion, le siège, la commune, 1870–1871, d'après des peintures, gravures, photographies, sculptures, médailles, autographes, objets du temps.* Paris, 1901.

Dayot, 1927
———. "Paul Guigou." *L'Art et les Artistes,* May 1927.

Dayot, 1928
See 1928, Paris, Hôtel de Sagan.

Dayot, 1928, "Winterhalter"
———. "Winterhalter — Painter to the Second Empire." *International Studio*, vol. XCI, no. 377 (October 1928), pp. 39–44.

Decaux, 1964
A. Decaux. *La Castiglione; dames de cœur de l'Europe, d'après sa correspondance et son journal intimes inédits.* Paris, 1964.

Deck, 1887
T. Deck. *La Faïence.* Paris, 1887.

Decour, 1963
A. Decour. *Le Mantois,* no. 14 (1963).

Degas, 1949
E. Degas. *Album des Dessins.* Preface by D. Halevy. Paris, 1949.

Dejean de la Bâtie, 1976
M.-C. Dejean de la Bâtie. "La Maison Pompéienne du Prince Napoléon, avenue Montaigne." *Gazette des Beaux-Arts,* 118th year, vol. LXXXVII (April 1976), pp. 127–34.

DeKay, 1889
C. DeKay. *Barye.* New York, 1889.

Delaborde, 1853
H. Delaborde. "Salon de 1853." *Revue des Deux-Mondes,* June 15, 1853.

Delaborde, 1861
———. "Salon of 1861." *Revue de Deux-Mondes,* vol. XXXII (1861), p. 882, vol. XXXIII (1861), p. 879.

Delaborde, 1862
———. "Les Cabinets d'amateurs: La Collection de tableaux de M. le comte Duchâtel. I. Ecole italienne, école française." *Gazette des Beaux-Arts,* 4th year, vol. XII (January 1, 1862), pp. 5–19.

Delaborde, 1864
———. "Hippolyte Flandrin." *Revue des Deux-Mondes,* 1864, pp. 862–92.

Delaborde, 1865
———. *Lettres et pensées d'Hippolyte Flandrin.* Paris, 1865.

Delaborde, 1865, "Amaury-Duval"
———. "Des Oeuvres et de la manière de M. Amaury-Duval." *Gazette des Beaux-Arts,* 7th year, vol. XVIII (May 1, 1865), pp. 419–28.

Delaborde, 1866
———. *Mélanges sur l'art contemporain.* Paris, 1866.

Delaborde, 1870
———. *Ingres, sa vie, ses travaux, sa doctrine, d'après les notes manuscrites et les lettres du maître.* Paris, 1870.

Delaborde, 1874
———. "Architectes contemporains: Victor Baltard." *Revue des Deux-Mondes,* 3rd s., vol. II (April 15, 1874), pp. 788–811.

Delaborde, 1878
———. *Notice sur la vie et les ouvrages de M. Henri Labrouste.* Paris, 1878.

Delaborde, 1882
———. *Notice sur la vie et les ouvrages de M. Lefuel.* Paris, 1882.

Delaborde, 1889
Paris, Institut de France, Académie des Beaux-Arts. "Notice sur la vie et les ouvrages de M. Cabanel." By H. Delaborde. In *La Séance Publique Annuelle du 19 octobre 1889, Paris.*

Delaborde, 1892
H. Delaborde. "Notice lue par M. le conseiller Henri Delaborde." In *La Séance Publique Annuelle de l'Académie des Beaux-Arts, 29 Octobre 1892.* In Gréard, 1897.

Delacroix, 1893–95
E. Delacroix. *Journal de Eugène Delacroix.* Paris, 1893–95.

Delacroix, 1923
———. *Oeuvres littéraires.* Paris, 1923.

Delacroix, 1932
———. *Journal de Eugène Delacroix. . . .* 3 vols. Paris, 1932.

Delacroix, 1936–38
———. *Correspondance générale. . . .* 5 vols. Paris, 1936–38.

Delacroix, 1951
———. *The Journal of Eugène Delacroix.* Edited with an introduction by H. Wellington. Translated by L. Norton. London, 1951.

Delacroix, 1960
———. *Journal. . . .* 2 vols. Paris, 1960.

Delahaye, 1973
J.-M. Delahaye. "Paul Dubois 1829–1905." Thesis, Ecole du Louvre, 1973.

Delahaye, 1975
———. Le 'Chanteur florentin' de Paul Dubois." *La Revue du Louvre et des Musées de France,* nos. 5–6 (1975), pp. 338–43.

Délégation des ouvrières relieurs 1867
Anon. *Exposition du 1867. Délégation des ouvrières relieurs.* Paris, 1869–75.

Delessert, 1855
E. Delessert. *Six Semaines dans l'île de Sardaigne.* Paris, 1855.

Delorme, 1878
L.-R. Delorme. *Le Musée de la Comédie Française.* Paris, 1878.

Delorme, 1889
———. "Carpeaux." *Galerie Contemporaine Littéraire et Artistique,* no. 56 (January 28, 1889).

Delteil, 1906–30
L. Delteil. *Le Peintre-graveur illustré.* 31 vols. Paris, 1906–30.

Demoriane, 1961
H. Demoriane. "Le Louis XVI qu'aimait Eugénie." *Connaissance des Arts,* no. 116 (October 1961), pp. 76–85.

Derrécagaix, 1911
General Derrécagaix. *Le Maréchal Pélissier, duc de Malakoff.* Paris, 1911.

Desfossé, 1855
J. Desfossé. *Note pour MM. les Présidents et Membres du Jury International.* Paris, 1855.

Deshairs and Laran, 1913
L. Deshairs and J. Laran. *Gustave Moreau.* Paris, 1913.

Desnoyers, 1863
F. Desnoyers. *Salon des refusés: La Peinture en 1863.* Paris, 1863.

Desvallières, 1913
G. Desvallières. *L'Oeuvre de Gustave Moreau.* Paris, 1913.

Desvallières, 1926
———. "L'Evolution de la pensée chrétienne dans l'œuvre de Gustave Moreau." *La Vie Artistique,* April 3, 1926.

Devauchelle, 1959–61
R. Devauchelle. *La Reliure en France, de ses origines jusqu'à nos jours.* 3 vols. Paris, 1959–61.

Deville, 1856
J. Deville. "Orfèvrerie, joaillerie, bijouterie, bronzes d'art et d'ameublement." *L'Art au Dix-Neuvième Siècle,* vol. I (1856), pp. 54–57, 79–81.

Deville, 1878–80
———. *Dictionnaire du tapissier, critique et historique de l'ameublement français depuis les temps anciens jusqu'à nos jours.* 2 vols. Paris, 1878–80.

Didron, 1854
A. Didron. "La Châsse de Sainte Radegonde." *Annales Archéologiques,* vol. XIV (1854), pp. 58–62.

Didron, 1868
E. Didron. *Les Vitraux à l'Exposition Universelle de 1867.* Paris, 1868.

Dimier, 1914
L. Dimier. *Histoire de la peinture française au XIXᵉ siècle.* 1914.

Dimier, 1930
———. "Tableaux qui passent." *Beaux-Arts,* no. 6 (June 20, 1930), p. 17.

Disdéri, 1856
E. Disdéri. "Renseignements photographiques." *Le Spectateur, Organe de la Photographie,* no. 1 (July 1856), n.p.

Doat, 1891–92
T. Doat. "Causerie d'un émailleur: Le Rôle actuel de l'émail." *Revue des Arts Décoratifs,* vol. XII (1891–92), pp. 39–46, 76–80.

Dognée, 1869
E.M.O. Dognée. *Les Arts industriels à l'Exposition Universelle de 1867.* Paris, 1869.

Doin, 1921
J. Doin. "Alfred de Dreux (1810–1860)." *Gazette des Beaux-Arts,* 63rd year, vol. IV (October 1921), pp. 237–51.

Doin, 1925
———. "Charles Séchan et son atelier de décoration théâtrale pendant le romantisme." *Gazette des Beaux-Arts,* 67th year, vol. XI (June 1925), pp. 344–60.

Dolent, 1888
J. Dolent. *Amoureux d'art.* Paris, 1888.

Dorbec, 1910
P. Dorbec. *Théodore Rousseau.* Paris, 1910.

Dorbec, 1926
———. *Eugène Fromentin.* Paris, 1926.

Doria, 1931
Comte A. Doria. "Thomas Couture à Senlis." *La Chronique des Arts et de la Curiosité,* 9th year, no. 8 (August 25, 1931), p. 4.

Dormoy, 1926
M. Dormoy. "La Collection Arnhold." *L'Amour de l'Art,* vol. VII (1926), pp. 242–43.

Dorra, 1973
H. Dorra. "The Guesser Guessed: Gustave Moreau's Œdipus." *Gazette des Beaux-Arts,* 115th year, vol. LXXXI (March 1973), pp. 129–40.

Downes, 1888
W. Downes. "Boston Painters and Paintings." *Atlantic Monthly,* October 1888, p. 507.

"Drawings," 1953
Anon. "Two Drawings by Delacroix." *The Baltimore Museum of Art News,* vol. XVII, no. 1 (October 1953).

Drexler (ed.), 1977
A. Drexler, R. Chafee, N. Levine, and D. Van Zanten. *The Architecture of the Ecole des Beaux-Arts.* Edited by A. Drexler. New York and London, 1977.

Dreyfous, 1903
M. Dreyfous. *Dalou, sa vie et son œuvre.* Paris, 1903.

Drion, 1864
Drion. *Journal du Soir,* June 8, 1864.

Drost, 1971
W. Drost. "Kriteria der Kunstkritik Baudelaires." In *Beitrage zur Theorie der Kunste im 19. Jahrhundert.* Frankfurt, 1971, vol. I, pp. 256–85.

Drucker, 1955
M. Drucker. *Renoir.* Paris, 1955.

Drumont, 1880
E. Drumont. "L'Exposition de Couture." *La Liberté,* September 4, 1880.

Dubouché, 1878
A. Dubouché. "Compte rendu sur l'Exposition Universelle Paris 1878." *Le Courrier du Centre,* October 31, 1878.

Duc, 1874
J.-L. Duc. *Rapport sur le concours de l'église du Sacré-Cœur.* Paris, 1874.

Duc, 1875
———. *Manufactures nationales; rapport adressé à M. le ministre . . . au nom de la commission de perfectionnement de la manufacture nationale de Sèvres.* Paris, 1875.

du Camp, 1854
M. du Camp. *Le Nil: Egypte et Nubie.* Paris, 1854.

du Camp, 1855
———. *Les Beaux-Arts à l'Exposition Universelle de 1855 — Peinture —Sculpture.* Paris, 1855.

du Camp, 1857
———. *Le Salon de 1857.* Paris, 1857.

du Camp, 1859
———. *Le Salon de 1859.* Paris, 1859.

du Camp, 1861
———. *Le Salon de 1861.* Paris, 1861.

du Camp, 1864
———. "Le Salon de 1864." *Revue des Deux-Mondes,* 1864, pp. 678–712.

du Camp, 1867
———. *Les Beaux-Arts à l'Exposition Universelle et aux Salons de 1863, 1864, 1865, 1866 et 1867.* Paris, 1867.

du Castel, 1964
F.-P.-D. du Castel. *Paul DuBois, peintre et sculpteur (1829–1905).* Paris, 1964.

Ducuing, 1868
F. Ducuing. *L'Exposition Universelle de 1867 illustrée.* 2 vols. Paris, 1868.

Duguet, 1897
R. Duguet. "Pierre Charles Simart, 1806–1857." *Les Contemporains,* no. 266 (November 14, 1897).

Dujardin-Beaumetz, 1913
H.-C.-E. Dujardin-Beaumetz. *Entretiens avec Rodin.* Paris, 1913.

Dumas, 1884
Paris, Musée du Luxembourg. *Livret illustré.* Compiled by F.G. Dumas. Paris, 1884.

Dumesnil, 1859
M. H. Dumesnil. *Le Salon de 1859.* Paris, 1859.

Dumont, 1956
F. Dumont. "Froment-Meurice, le Victor Hugo de l'orfèvrerie." *Connaissance des Arts,* no. 57 (November 1956), pp. 42–45.

Dumonthier, 1923
E. Dumonthier. *Mobilier national de France, le meuble-toilette.* Paris, 1923.

du Pasquier, 1975
J. du Pasquier. *Céramiques bordelaises du XIXᵉ siècle. Collection Douméezy.* Bordeaux, 1975.

du Pays, 1855
A.-J. du Pays. "Exposition Universelle des Beaux-Arts." *L'Illustration,* vol. II (1855), p. 286.

du Pays, 1863
———. "Salon de 1863." *L'Illustration,* vol. II (1863).

Duplessis, 1874
G. Duplessis. "M. Edouard Detaille." *Gazette des Beaux-Arts,* 16th year, vol. IX (May 1, 1874), pp. 419–33.

Durand, 1901
G. Durand. "La Cathédrale d'Amiens." In *Inventaire général des richesses d'art de la France.* Vol. III: *Monuments religieux.* Paris, 1901, pp. 59–140.

Durand, 1901–3
———. *Monographie de l'église Notre-Dame, cathédrale d'Amiens.* 2 vols. in 3. Paris, 1901–3.

Durand-Ruel, 1873
Galerie Durand-Ruel. *Recueil d'estampes gravées à l'eau-forte.* Introduction by T. Silvestre. 6 vols. Paris, 1873.

Durand-Ruel, 1939
P. Durand-Ruel. *Mémoires de Paul Durand-Ruel.* In L. Venturi. *Les Archives de l'impressionnisme.* Paris and New York, 1939.

Durant, 1860, "L'Algérie"
A. Durant. "A propos de l'Exposition d'Agriculture: L'Exposition des Produits de l'Algérie au Palais de l'Industrie. II." *L'Art au Dix-Neuvième Siècle,* vol. V (1860), pp. 166–67.

Durant, 1860, "Mouvement artistique"
———. "Mouvement artistique des ateliers." *L'Art au Dix-Neuvième Siècle*, vol. V (1860), pp. 227–29.
Duranty, 1872
P. Duranty. "Le Salon de 1872." *Paris—Journal*, May 13, 1872.
Duranty, 1880
———. "Thomas Couture." *La Chronique des Arts et de la Curiosité*, September 4, 1880, p. 232.
Durbé and Damigella, 1969
D. Durbé and A. M. Damigella. *La Scuola di Barbizon*. Milan, 1969.
Duret, 1867
T. Duret. *Les Peintres français en 1867*. Paris, 1867.
Duret, 1880
———. *Le Peintre Claude Monet : Notice sur son œuvre suivie du catalogue de ses tableaux exposés dans la galerie du journal illustré "La Vie Moderne."* Paris, 1880.
Duret, 1902
———. *Histoire d'Édouard Manet et de son œuvre*. Paris, 1902.
Duret, 1910
———. *Manet and the French Impressionists*. Translated by J.E. Crawford Flitch. London and Philadelphia, 1910.
Duret, 1912
———. "Un Grand Peintre de la Provence : Paul Guigou." *L'Art et les Artistes*, no. 87 (June 1912).
Durieu, 1855
E. Durieu. "Rapport présenté au nom de la Commission chargée de l'examen de l'exposition ouverte dans les salons de la Société Française de Photographie, du 1er août au 15 novembre 1855." *Bulletin de la Société Française de Photographie*, 1855, part 1, pp. 37–72, part 2, pp. 99–100.
Dussieux, 1856
L. Dussieux. *Les Artistes français à l'étranger....* Paris, 1856.
Dussieux, 1876
———. *Les Artistes français à l'étranger...* 3rd ed. Paris, 1876.
Dussler, 1959
L. Dussler. *Die Zeichnungen des Michelangelo*. Berlin, 1959.

Eaton, 1913
D. Cady Eaton. *A Handbook of Modern French Sculpture*. New York, 1913.
Ebénistes, 1963
*Les Ebénistes du XVIIIe siècle français*. Préface by P. Verlet. Paris, 1963.
Edgell, 1949
Boston, Museum of Fine Arts. *French Painters in the Museum of Fine Arts : Corot to Utrillo*. By G.H. Edgell. Boston, 1949.
Elkins Collection, 1900
*Catalogue of Paintings in the Private Collection of W.L. Elkins....* 2 vols. n.l., 1900.
Encyclopédie nouvelle, 1836–39
*Encyclopédie nouvelle*. 8 vols. Edited by P. Leroux and J. Reynaud. Paris, 1836–39.
Ephrussi, 1887
C. Ephrussi. *Paul Baudry, sa vie et œuvre*. Paris, 1887.
"Epreuves stéréoscopiques," 1854
Anon. "Epreuves stéréoscopiques : MM. Moulin, Gouin, Braquehais, Marlé, Bailly, Moonem." *Le Propagateur*, May 18, 1854, n.p.
Ernould-Gandouet, 1969
M. Ernould-Gandouet. *La Céramique en France au XIXe siècle*. Paris, 1969.
Escholier, 1926–29
R. Escholier. *Delacroix : Peintre, graveur, écrivain*. 3 vols. Paris, 1926–29.
Esnault, 1852
L. Esnault. *Le Salon de 1852*. Paris, 1852.
d'Espezel, 1939
P. d'Espezel. "Le Mouvement artistique." *La Revue de Paris*, April 15, 1939.
d'Espouy, 1900
H. d'Espouy. *Fragments d'architecture antique*. 2 vols. Paris, 1900.
Estignard, 1896
A. Estignard. *Henri Baron, sa vie, ses œuvres*. Paris, 1896.
Estignard, 1900
———. *Clésinger, sa vie, ses œuvres*. Paris, 1900.
Etoffes merveilleuses, 1976
Anon. *Etoffes merveilleuses du Musée historique des tissus de Lyon*. 2 vols. Tokyo and Gakken, 1976.
Etudes sur l'Exposition, 1867
Anon. *Gazette des Architectes et du Bâtiment. Etudes sur l'Exposition Universelle de 1867 à Paris*. Paris, n.d.

Fabius, 1872
Fabius. "Salon de 1872." *Le Français*, May 10–11, 1872.
Faison, 1949
S. L. Faison, Jr. "Manet's Portrait of Zola." *Magazine of Art*, vol. XLII, no. 5 (May 1949), pp. 162–68.
Falize, 1878
L. Falize (fils). "Exposition Universelle : Les Industries d'art au Champ de Mars. 1 : Orfèvrerie et bijouterie." *Gazette des Beaux-Arts*, 20th year, vol. XVIII (September 1, 1878), pp. 217–55.
Falize, 1882–83
L. Falize [M. Josse]. "L'Art japonais : A propos de l'exposition organisée par M. Gonse." *Revue des Arts Décoratifs*, vol. III (1882–83), pp. 329–38, 353–63.
Falize, 1886–87
———. "Nécrologie : M. Eugène Fontenay." *Revue des Arts Décoratifs*, vol. VII (1886–87), pp. 319–20.
Falize, 1893–94
———. "Claudius Popelin et la renaissance des émaux peints." *Gazette des Beaux-Arts*, 35th year, vol. IX (May 1, June 1, 1893), pp. 418–35, 502–18, vol. X (July 1, November 1, December 1, 1893), pp. 60–76, 426–37, 478–89, 36th year, vol. XI (February 1, 1894), pp. 130–48.
Fantin-Latour, 1911
V. Fantin-Latour. *Catalogue de l'œuvre complet (1849–1904) de Fantin-Latour*. Paris, 1911.
de Farcy, 1890
L. de Farcy. *La Broderie du XIe siècle jusqu'à nos jours d'après des spécimens authentiques et les anciens inventaires*. Angers, 1890.
Faré, 1962
M. Faré. *La Nature morte en France : Son Histoire et son évolution du XVIIe au XXe siècle*. 2 vols. Geneva, 1962.
Farwell, 1969
B. Farwell. "Manet's 'Espada' and Marcantonio." *Metropolitan Museum Journal*, vol. II (1969), pp. 197–207.
Fauré-Frémiet, 1934
P. Fauré-Frémiet. *Frémiet*. Paris, 1934.
Félibien, 1706
M. Félibien. *Histoire de l'abbaye royale de Saint-Denys en France....* Paris, 1706.
Fenaille, 1903–23
M. Fenaille. *Etat général des tapisseries de la manufacture des Gobelins, depuis son origine jusqu'à nos jours 1600–1900*. 6 vols. Paris, 1903–23.
Féraud, 1872
J.-B.-P.-H. Féraud. "Constant-Dufeux." *Revue Générale de l'Architecture*, vol. XXIX (1872), cols. 81–91, 132–37, 251–55.
Fêtes et cérémonies, 1860
Anon. Hôtel de Ville, Paris. *Fêtes et cérémonies à l'occasion de la naissance et du baptême de S.A. le Prince Impérial*. Paris, 1860.
Fèvre, 1949
J. Fèvre. *Mon Oncle Degas*. Geneva, 1949.
Fidell-Beaufort and Bailly-Herzberg, 1975
M. Fidell-Beaufort and J. Bailly-Herzberg. *Daubigny*. Paris, 1975.
Fidière, 1894
O. Fidière. *Chapu : Sa Vie et son œuvre*. Paris, 1894.
Filon, 1912
A. Filon. *Le Prince Impérial, souvenirs et documents*. Paris, 1912.
Fischel, 1921
O. Fischel. *Dante und die Künstler*. Berlin, 1921.
de la Fizelière, 1851
A. de la Fizelière. *Exposition nationale—Salon de 1850–1851*. Paris, 1851.
de la Fizelière, 1861
———. "Mouvement des arts et de la curiosité : Coup d'œil sur la prochaine exposition de Metz." *Gazette des Beaux-Arts*, 3rd year, vol. X (June 1, 1861), pp. 318–19.
de la Fizelière, 1861, Le Salon
———. *A-Z ou le Salon en miniature*. Paris, 1961.
de la Fizelière, Champfleury, and Henriet, 1874
A. de la Fizelière, J. Champfleury, and F. Henriet. *La Vie et l'œuvre de Chintreuil*. Paris, 1874.
Flandrin, 1902
L. Flandrin. *Hippolyte Flandrin, sa vie et son œuvre*. Paris, 1902.
Flandrin, 1909
———. *Un Peintre chrétien au XIXe siècle*. Paris, 1909.
Flat, 1899
P. Flat. *Le Musée Gustave Moreau : L'Artiste, son œuvre, son influence*. Paris, 1899.
Flaubert, 1964
G. Flaubert. *Sentimental Education*. 1874. Translated by R. Baldick. London, 1964.
Fleury and Sonolet, n.d.
J. Fleury and L. Sonolet. *La Société du Second Empire*. n.l., n.d.
Florisoone, 1947
M. Florisoone. *Manet*. Monaco, 1947.
Focillon, 1913
H. Focillon. "Artistes contemporains : Barye." *Revue de l'Art Ancien et Moderne*, vol. XXXIII (1913), pp. 161–73.

Focillon, 1928
———. *La Peinture aux XIXe et XXe siècles. Du Réalisme à nos jours*. Paris, 1928.
Fohlen, 1964–65
C. Fohlen. *Histoire de Besançon*. 2 vols. Paris, 1964–65.
Fol, 1875
W. Fol. "Jean-Louis Hamon." *Gazette des Beaux-Arts*, 17th year, vol. XI (February 1, 1875), pp. 119–34.
Foltz, 1887
C. Foltz. *Souvenirs historiques du vieux Colmar*. Colmar, 1887.
Fontenay, 1867
E. Fontenay. *Fontenay, Exposition Universelle de 1867 : Classe 36e pièces de joaillerie exécutées et gravées à l'eau-forte : A Messieurs les jurés*. Paris, 1867.
Fontenay, 1887
———. *Les Bijoux anciens et modernes*. Paris, 1887.
Forbes and Kelly, 1975
C. Forbes and M. Kelly. *War à la Mode : Military Pictures by Meissonier, Detaille, de Neuville, and Berne-Bellecour from the Forbes Magazine Collection*. New York, 1975.
de Forges, 1973
Paris, Musée National du Louvre. *Autoportraits de Courbet*. By M.-T. de Forges (Les Dossiers du département des peintures, no. 6). Paris, 1973.
Forrer, 1904–30
L. Forrer. *Biographical Dictionary of Medallists, Coin-, Gem-, and Seal-Engravers....* 8 vols. London, 1904–30.
Foucart, 1976
J. Foucart. "L'Ingrisme dans le monde." *Bulletin du Musée Ingres*, July 1976.
Fouquier, 1864
H. Fouquier. *Le Peuple*, May 11, 1864.
Fouquier, 1879
A. Fouquier. *L. Bonnat, première partie de sa vie et de ses œuvres*. Paris, 1879.
Fouquier, 1889
H. Fouquier. Preface to Cabanel studio sale catalogue, Paris, Galerie Georges Petit, May 22–25, 1889.
de Fouquières, n.d.
A. de Fouquières. *Alfred deDreux (peintre de chevaux) causerie*. Maisons-Lafitte, n.d.
Fourcaud, 1884–85
L. de Fourcaud. "La 8e Exposition de l'Union Centrale des Arts Décoratifs. Rapport général." *Revue des Arts Décoratifs*, vol. V (1884–85), pp. 231–66.
Fourcaud, 1885
———. *Théodule Ribot, sa vie et ses œuvres*. Paris, 1885.
Fourcaud, 1888
———. "M. Gustave Moreau." *Le Gaulois*, November 25, 1888.
Fournel, 1884
V. Fournel. *Les Artistes français contemporains*. Tours, 1884.
Fournel, 1885
———. *Les Artistes français contemporains. Peintres-sculpteurs*. 2nd ed. Tours, 1885.
Francastel, 1955
P. Francastel. *Histoire de la peinture française*. 2 vols. Paris and New York, 1955.
Francis, 1943
H.S. Francis. "'Mlle Romaine Lacaux' by Renoir." *The Bulletin of the Cleveland Museum of Art*, no. 6 (June 1943), pp. 92–98.
Francis, 1954
———. "'Spring Flowers' by Claude Monet." *The Bulletin of the Cleveland Museum of Art*, no. 2, part 1 (February 1954), pp. 23–24.
Frankenstein, 1953
A. Frankenstein. "After the Hunt," *William Harnett and Other American Still Life Painters 1870–1900*. Berkeley and Los Angeles, 1953.
French Art, n.d.
The Bowes Museum, Barnard Castle. *French Art*. n.l., n.d.
Frongia, 1973
M.-L. Frongia. "Il mito di Orfeo nella pittura simbolista francese." *Annali della Facoltà di Lettere, Filosofia et Magistero*, vol. XXXVI (1973; published 1974), pp. 352–94.
Fuchs, 1927
E. Fuchs. *Der Maler Daumier*. Munich, 1927.

de Gaigneron, 1977
A. de Gaigneron. "Le Salon de la princesse Mathilde, rendez-vous du Tout-Paris des arts sous le Second Empire." *Connaissance des Arts*, no. 310 (December 1977), pp. 94–99.
le Gal, 1974
M. le Gal. "Carolus Duran." Thesis, Ecole du Louvre, 1974.
Galibert, 1906
P. Galibert. *Chefs-d'œuvre du musée de Bordeaux*. Bordeaux, 1906.

Galichon, 1861
E. Galichon. "Description des dessins de M. Ingres exposés au Salon des Arts Unis." Gazette des Beaux-Arts, 3rd year, vol. IX (March 15, 1861), pp. 343–62.

Galichon, 1868
———. "M. Gérôme, peintre ethnographe." Gazette des Beaux-Arts, 10th year, vol. XXIV (February 1, 1868), pp. 147–51.

Galignani, 1852
A. & W. Galignani & Co. Galignani's New Paris Guide. Paris, 1852.

Galimard, 1864
A. Galimard. Les Peintures murales de Saint-Germain-des-Près. Paris, 1864.

Gallet, 1865
L. Gallet. Salon de 1865. Paris, 1865.

Gardner, 1954
A. TenEyck Gardner. "Metropolitan People and Pictures." Art News, vol. LII, no. 9 (January 1954), pp. 32–35.

C. Garnier, 1871
J.-L. C. Garnier. Le Théâtre. Paris, 1871.

C. Garnier, 1874
———. Notice sur Victor Baltard. Paris, 1874.

C. Garnier, 1878–81
———. Le Nouvel Opéra de Paris. 2 vols. and 1 atlas. Paris, 1878–81.

E. Garnier, 1882
E. Garnier. Histoire de la céramique, poteries, faïences et porcelaines chez tous les peuples depuis les temps anciens jusqu'à nos jours. Tours, 1882.

E. Garnier, 1886
———. Histoire de la verrerie et de l'émaillerie. Tours, 1886.

E. Garnier, 1893
———. Guide du collectionneur ; dictionnaire de la céramique, faïence, grès, porcelaine.... Paris, 1893.

L. Garnier, 1925
L. Garnier. "Charles Garnier, par Mme Garnier." L'Architecture, vol. XXXVIII, no. 21 (1925), pp. 377–90.

de Gary, 1978
M.-N. de Gary. "La Maison pompéienne du Prince Napoléon, Exposition de dix ans de donation au Musée des Arts Décoratifs." Cahiers de l'Union Centrale des Arts Décoratifs, no. 1 (February 1978).

Gasnault and E. Garnier, 1884
P. Gasnault and E. Garnier. French Pottery. Translated by M.P. Villars. London, 1884.

Gatteaux, 1875
E. Gatteaux. Collection de 120 dessins, croquis et peintures de M. Ingres.... 2 vols. Paris, 1875.

Gaudibert, 1970
P. Gaudibert. Ingres. Paris, 1970.

Gaudin, 1861
C. Gaudin. [Baldus.] La Lumière, June 15, 1861, p. 41.

Gaudin, 1877
P. Gaudin. Essai sur Eugène Fromentin. La Rochelle, 1877.

Gauthier, 1959
S. Gauthier. "Les Pouyat et leurs 'Blancs.'" Cahiers de la Céramique, no. 13 (1959), pp. 35–39.

Gautier, 1847
T. Gautier. Salon de 1847. Paris, 1847.

Gautier, 1853
———. "De l'Art moderne." L'Artiste, 5th s., vol. X (1853).

Gautier, 1854
———. "L'Apothéose de Napoléon (plafond de M. Ingres)." L'Artiste, 5th s., February 15, 1854.

Gautier, 1855, "L'Exposition"
———. "L'Exposition Universelle." Le Moniteur, October 11, 1855.

Gautier, 1855, Le Moniteur
———. "L'Exposition Universelle de 1855." Le Moniteur, August 25, 1855.

Gautier, 1855, Salon
———. Salon de 1855. Paris, 1855.

Gautier, 1855–56
———. Les Beaux-Arts en Europe—1855. 2 vols. Paris, 1855–56.

Gautier, 1856
———. [Chassériau]. Le Moniteur, October 13, 1856.

Gautier, 1857, "Salon"
———. "Salon de 1857." L'Artiste, 7th s., vol. I (1857), pp. 189ff., vol. II, pp. 1ff.

Gautier, 1857, "Simart"
———. "Nécrologie : Simart." L'Artiste, vol. LIX (1857), pp. 169–71.

Gautier, 1857, "La Source"
———. "La Source." L'Artiste, February 1, 1857.

Gautier, 1858
———. "Louis XIV et Molière, tableau de M. Ingres." L'Artiste, 7th s., January 10, 1858.

Gautier, 1858, "Les Ateliers"

———. "A Travers les ateliers." L'Artiste, 7th s., vol. XIV (May 16, 1858), p. 177.

Gautier, 1861
Gautier. Abécédaire du Salon de 1861. Paris, 1861.

Gautier, 1863, "Salon"
———. "Salon de 1863." Le Moniteur, September 1, 1863.

Gautier, 1864
———. Le Moniteur, May 27, 1864.

Gautier, 1865
———. "Œuvres des M. Cordier: Statues, bustes, statuettes et médaillons." Le Moniteur, January 13, 1865, p. 37.

Gautier, 1866
———. "Salon de 1866." Le Moniteur, August 3, 1866, pp. 981–82, August 10, 1866, pp. 1002–3.

Gautier, 1869
———. "Revue des théâtres : Le Nouvel Opéra—Variétés." Le Moniteur, August 2, 1869, p. 1047.

Gautier, 1870
———. "Salon de 1870." Le Moniteur, August 8, 1870, pp. 1384–85.

Gautier, 1874
———. Portraits contemporains. 3rd ed. Paris, 1874.

Gautier, 1920–21
———. "Salon de 1869." L'Illustration, May–June, 1869. In Tableaux à la plume. Paris, 1920–21.

Gautier, 1927
———. Histoire du romantisme. Paris, 1927.

Gautier, Houssaye, and Coligny, 1866
T. Gautier, A. Houssaye, and C. Coligny. Le Palais pompéien.... Paris, 1866.

Gebauër, 1855
E. Gebauër. Les Beaux-Arts à l'Exposition Universelle de 1855. Paris, 1855.

Geffroy, 1880
G. Geffroy. "Exposition des œuvres de Thomas Couture." La Justice, June 10, 1880.

Geffroy, 1900, "Falguière"
———. "Alexandre Falguière." Gazette des Beaux-Arts, 42nd year, vol. XXIII (May 1, 1900), pp. 397–406.

Geffroy, 1900, "Moreau"
———. "L'Œuvre de Gustave Moreau." L'Œuvre d'Art, July 5, 1900, pp. 1–33.

Geffroy, 1904
———. Versailles. Paris, 1904.

Geffroy, 1920
———. Constantin Guys, l'historien du Second Empire. Paris, 1920.

Geffroy, 1924
———. Claude Monet, sa vie, son œuvre. 2 vols. Paris, 1924.

Genaille, 1964
J. Genaille. "Portraits inédits du collectionneur Aguado, de Madame Aguado et de leurs enfants." Gazette des Beaux-Arts, 106th year, vol. LXIII (January 1964), pp. 23–36.

Genevay, 1875
See 1875, Paris, Ecole des Beaux-Arts.

Georgel, 1971
P. Georgel. "'Les Sources' des quelques dessins de Victor Hugo." Bulletin de la Société de l'Histoire de l'Art Français, 1971 (published 1973), pp. 281–95.

Georgel, 1975
———. "Les Transformations de la peinture vers 1848, 1855, 1863." Revue de l'Art, no. 27 (1975), pp. 62–77.

Georgel and Rossi-Bortolato, 1975
P. Georgel and L. Rossi-Bortolato. Tout l'œuvre peint de Delacroix. Paris, 1975.

Gere, 1975
C. Gere. American & European Jewelry, 1830–1914. New York, 1975.

Gernsheim, 1962
H. Gernsheim. Creative Photography, Aesthetic Trends, 1839–1960. New York, 1962.

Gernsheim and Gernsheim, 1969
H. Gernsheim and A. Gernsheim. The History of Photography from the Camera Obscura to the Beginning of the Modern Era. New York, 1969.

Gersaint, 1865
Gersaint. "Union Centrale des Beaux-Arts appliqués à l'industrie. Exposition des œuvres contemporaines." Gazette des Beaux-Arts, 7th year, vol. XIX (October 1, 1865), pp. 369–79.

Gerspach, 1882–83
E. Gerspach. "Théodore Deck." Revue des Arts Décoratifs, vol. III (1882–83), pp. 289–98.

Gerspach, 1885
———. L'Art de la verrerie. Paris, 1885.

Gerspach, 1887–88
———. "Etude sur la manufacture nationale des Gobelins." Revue des Arts Décoratifs, vol. VIII (1887–88), pp. 357–64.

Gerspach, 1890–91
———. "Théodore Deck ; son influence sur la céramique moderne." Revue des Arts Décoratifs, vol. XI (1890–91),

pp. 353–58.

Gerspach, 1893
———. Répertoire détaillé des tapisseries des Gobelins exécutées de 1662 à 1892. Paris, 1893.

Giacomotti and Verlet, 1965
J. Giacomotti and P. Verlet. Le Musée National Adrien-Dubouché a Limoges. Paris, 1965.

Giate, 1959
P. Giate. Deux Critiques d'art de l'époque romantique : G. Planche et T. Thoré. Stockholm, 1959.

Gibson, 1927
F. Gibson. The Art of Henri Fantin-Latour : His Life and Work. New York, 1927.

Gigoux, 1885
J. Gigoux. Causeries sur les artistes de mon temps. Paris, 1885.

Ginain, 1882
L. Ginain. Notice sur Lefuel. Paris, 1882.

de Girardin, 1855
Mme de Girardin. Le Chapeau d'un horloger. Paris, 1855.

Giraudet, 1885
E. Giraudet. Les Artistes tourangeaux.... Tours, 1885.

Girodie, 1901
A. Girodie. François-Louis Français. Moutiers, 1901.

Girodie, 1901, "Falguière"
———. "Alexandre Falguière, sculpteur de l'Institut. 1831–1900." Les Contemporains, no. 440 (1901), pp. 138–39.

Goarin (in preparation)
V. Goarin. "Baudry Catalogue." Université de Paris (in preparation).

Goldberg, 1976
M. Goldberg. "William Rimmer's Flight and Pursuit : An Allegory of Assassination." The Art Bulletin, vol. LVIII, no. 2 (June 1976), pp. 234–40.

Goldscheider, 1962
C. Goldscheider. Rodin : Sa vie, son œuvre, son héritage. Paris, 1962.

Goncourt, 1886
E. de Goncourt. Preface to Sichel sale catalogue, Paris, Hôtel Drouot, February 27, 1886.

Goncourt and Goncourt, 1852
J. de Goncourt and E. de Goncourt. Salon de 1852. Paris, 1852.

Goncourt and Goncourt, 1956
———. Journal, mémoires de la vie littéraire. 4 vols. Paris, 1956.

Goncourt and Goncourt, 1957
———. Journal, mémoires de la vie littéraire. Monaco, 1957.

Goncourt and Goncourt, 1959
———. Journal, mémoires de la vie littéraire. 2 vols. Paris, 1959.

Gonse, 1874
L. Gonse. "Musée de Lille : Le Musée de peinture." Gazette des Beaux-Arts, 16th year, vol. IX (April 1, 1874), pp. 341–51.

Gonse, 1877
———. "Musée de Lille : Le Musée Wicar." Gazette des Beaux-Arts, 19th year, vol. XV (January 1, April 1, 1877), pp. 80–95, 386–401, vol. XVI (November 1, 1877), pp. 393–409.

Gonse, 1878
———. "Musée de Lille : Le Musée Wicar." Gazette des Beaux-Arts, 20th year, vol. XVII (January 1, 1878), pp. 44–70.

Gonse, 1881
———. Eugène Fromentin, peintre et écrivain. Paris, 1881.

Gonse, 1895
———. La Sculpture française depuis le XIVe siècle. Paris, 1895.

Gonse, 1900
———. Les Chefs d'œuvre des musées de France. La Peinture. Paris, 1900.

González-Palacios, 1967
A. González-Palacios. David e la pittura napoleonica. Milan, 1967.

González-Palacios, 1969
———. Il mobile nei secoli. Vol. III : Francia. Milan, 1969.

Gosling, 1976
N. Gosling. Nadar. New York, 1976.

Gouirand, 1901
A. Gouirand. Les Peintres provençaux. Paris, 1901.

Goujon, 1870
J. Goujon. Salon de 1870 : Propos en l'air. Paris, 1870.

Gout, 1880
P. Gout. L'Oeuvre de Viollet-Le-Duc. Paris, 1880.

Goutzwiller, 1856
C. Goutzwiller. "Epées offertes à l'amiral Bruat et au maréchal Pélissier par la ville de Colmar." L'Illustration, vol. XXVII (January–June 1856), p. 16.

Graber, 1929
H. Graber. E. Delacroix, Zeichnungen, Aquarelle und Pastelle. Basel, 1929.

Grad, 1887
C. Grad. Jean-Jacques Henner. Nancy, 1887.

Grandgedor, 1869
J. Grandgedor. "Exposition de l'Union Centrale des Beaux-

Arts appliqués à l'industrie : Les Ecoles de dessin." *Gazette des Beaux-Arts*, 11th year, vol. XXVII (November 1, 1869), pp. 426–40.
Grandjean, 1962
S. Grandjean. *L'Orfèvrerie du XIXᵉ siècle en Europe.* Paris, 1962.
Gréard, 1897
O. Gréard. *Jean-Louis Ernest Meissonier, ses souvenirs, ses entretiens, précédés d'une étude sur sa vie et son œuvre.* Paris, 1897.
Grellier, 1908
C. Grellier. *L'Industrie de la porcelaine en Limousin : Ses Origines—son évolution.* Paris, 1908.
Grenez, 1975
*See* 1975, Charleroi.
Grodecki, 1965
L. Grodecki. "La Restauration du château de Pierrefonds, 1857–1879." *Des Monuments Historiques de la France,* nos. 1–2 (1965).
Gronkowski, 1927
C. Gronkowski. *Catalogue sommaire des collections municipales.* Paris, 1927.
Gros, 1902
A. Gros. *François-Louis Français : Causeries et souvenirs par un de ses élèves.* Paris, 1902.
Grün, 1852
A. Grün. *Salon de 1852.* Paris, 1852.
Gsell, 1911
P. Gsell. *L'Art (Entretiens réunis par Paul Gsell).* Paris, 1911.
Guadet, 1899
J. Guadet. *Charles Garnier, notice historique.* Paris, 1899.
Guédy, n.d.
T. Guédy. *Musées de France et collections particulières.* Paris, n.d.
Guérin and Halevy (eds.), 1931
M. Guérin and D. Halevy, eds. *Lettres de Degas.* Paris, 1931.
Guérinet, 1900
A. Guérinet. *Les Grands Prix de Rome d'architecture, 1850–1900.* Paris, 1900.
Guest, 1974
I. Guest. *The Ballet of the Second Empire.* London, 1974.
Guiffrey, 1886
J. Guiffrey. *Histoire de la tapisserie depuis le Moyen-Age jusqu'à nos jours.* Paris, 1886.
Guiffrey, 1908
———. *Liste des pensionnaires de l'Académie de France à Rome.* Paris, 1908.
Guiffrey, n.d.
———. *Les Modèles et le Musée des Gobelins.* Paris, n.d.
Guiffrey and Marcel, 1907–38
J. Guiffrey and P. Marcel. *Inventaire générale des dessins du Musée du Louvre et du Musée de Versailles. Ecole française.* 11 vols. Paris, 1907–38.
Guillaume, 1879
E. Guillaume. "Le Salon de 1879." *Revue des Deux-Mondes,* June 15, 1879, pp. 897–931.
Guillaume, 1900
———. "Les Arts à l'Exposition Universelle de 1900 : La Sculpture au XIXᵉ siècle." *Gazette des Beaux-Arts,* 42nd year, vol. XXIV (December 1, 1900), pp. 505–27.
Guillaumet, 1888
G. Guillaumet. *Tableaux algériens.* Paris, 1888.
de Guillebon, 1972
R. de Plinval de Guillebon. *Porcelain of Paris, 1770–1850.* New York, 1972.
de Guillebon and Lasserre, 1966
R. de Guillebon and C. Lasserre. "La Production de la manufacture de la Courtille XVIIIᵉ et XIXᵉ siècle." *Cahiers de la Céramique du Verre et des Arts du Feu,* no. 38 (1966), pp. 103–7.
Guillemet, 1872
J. Guillemet. "Le Salon de 1872." *Le Journal de Paris,* June 18, 1872.
Guillemot, 1867
R. Guillemot. "Compte rendu de l'Exposition Universelle Paris 1867." *Le Courrier du Centre,* April 6, 1867.
le Guillois, 1861
Le Guillois. *Diogène au Salon : Revue en quatrains.* Paris, 1861.
Guizot, 1972
Guizot. "La Source d'Ingres. Un Texte peu connu." *Bulletin du Musée Ingres,* July 1972.

Hahn, 1968
New Haven, Conn., Yale University Art Gallery. *French and School of Paris Paintings in the Yale University Art Gallery.* By F. Forster Hahn. New Haven and London, 1968.
Hamerton, 1895
P. Hamerton. *Contemporary French Painters.* Boston, 1895.
Hamilton, 1949
G.H. Hamilton. "Delacroix, Byron and the English Illustrators." *Gazette des Beaux-Arts,* 91st year, vol. XXXVI (July–December 1944), pp. 261–78.

Hamilton, 1954
———. *Manet and His Critics.* New Haven, 1954.
Hammer, 1968
K. Hammer. *Jakob Ignaz Hittorff : Ein Pariser Baumeister, 1792–1867.* Stuttgart, 1968.
Hansen, 1970
H. J. Hansen. *Das pompöse Zeitalter zwischen Biedermeier und Jugendstil. Kunst, Architektur, und Kunsthandwerk in der zweiten Hälfte des 19te Jahrhunderts.* Oldenburg, 1970.
Hanson, 1962
A.C. Hanson. "A Group of Marine Paintings by Manet." *The Art Bulletin,* vol. XLIV, no. 4 (December 1962), pp. 332–36.
Hanson, 1977
———. *Manet and the Modern Tradition.* New Haven and London, 1977.
Hardy, 1887
A. Hardy. "Nécrologie : Joseph Nicolle." *Revue de l'Architecture et des Travaux Publics,* 1887, pp. 243–44.
Hardy, 1970
C. E. Hardy. *John Bowes and the Bowes Museum.* Newcastle, 1970.
Hargrove, 1974
J. Hargrove. "Carrier-Belleuse, Clésinger and Dalou : French Nineteenth Century Sculptors." *The Minneapolis Institute of Arts Bulletin,* vol. LXI (1974), pp. 28–43.
Hargrove, 1976
———. "Sculptures et dessins d'Albert Carrier-Belleuse au Musée des Beaux-Arts de Calais." *La Revue du Louvre et des Musées de France,* nos. 5–6 (1976), pp. 411–24.
Hargrove, 1977
———. *The Life and Work of Albert Carrier-Belleuse.* [Ph.D. dissertation, New York University, 1975]. New York, 1977.
Harmand, 1959
J. Harmand. "Le Plus Ancien Château de Pierrefonds et ses problèmes." *Bulletin Monumentale,* vol. CXVII (1959).
Haskell, 1975
F. Haskell. "Un Monument et ses mystères. L'Art français et l'opinion anglaise dans la première moitié du XIXᵉ siècle." *Revue de l'Art,* no. 30 (1975), pp. 61–76.
Haussmann, 1890–93
G. Haussmann. *Mémoires du baron Haussmann...* 3 vols. Paris, 1890–93.
Hautecœur, 1928
L. Hautecœur. *Histoire du Louvre....* Paris, 1928.
Hautecœur, 1955
———. *Histoire de l'architecture classique en France.* Vol. VI : *La Restauration et le gouvernement de juillet, 1815–1848.* Paris, 1955.
Hautecœur, 1957
———. *Histoire de l'architecture classique en France.* Vol. VII : *La Fin de l'architecture classique, 1848–1900.* Paris, 1957.
Havard, 1879
H. Havard. "La Porcelaine française." In *L'Art et l'industrie de tous les peuples à l'Exposition Universelle de 1878.* Paris, 1879.
Havard, 1887–90
———. *Dictionnaire de l'ameublement et de la décoration depuis le XIIIᵉ siècle jusqu'à nos jours.* 4 vols. Paris, 1887–90.
Havemeyer, 1930
*The H.O. Havemeyer Collection.* Metropolitan Museum of Art. New York, 1930.
Hayward, 1964
J.F. Hayward. "A Present from the Paris Exhibition of 1855 : Mr. George Farrow's Gift to the Victoria and Albert Museum." *The Connoisseur,* vol. CLVII, no. 634 (December 1964), pp. 226–29.
Hédiard, 1899
G. Hédiard. *Les Maîtres de la lithographie : John Lewis-Brown.* Châteaudun, 1899.
Hefting, 1969
V. Hefting. *Jongkind d'après sa correspondance.* Utrecht, 1969.
Hefting, 1975
———. *Jongkind, sa vie, son œuvre, son époque.* Paris, 1975.
Hellebranth, 1976
R. Hellebranth. *Charles-François Daubigny, 1817–1878.* Morges, 1976.
Hendy, 1932
P. Hendy. "Degas and the de Gas." *Bulletin of the Museum of Fine Arts* [Boston], vol. XXX, no. 179 (June 1932), pp. 43–45.
d'Hennezel, 1930
H. d'Hennezel. *Pour comprendre les tissus d'art.* Paris, 1930.
Hennique, 1881
L. Hennique. "Art contemporain, Henri Lévy." In *Les Chefs-d'œuvre d'art au Luxembourg.* Paris, 1881.
Henriet, 1853
F. Henriet. *Coup d'œil sur le Salon de 1853.* Paris, 1853.
Henriet, 1875
———. *C. Daubigny et son œuvre gravé.* Paris, 1875.
Henriet, 1893
———. "Le comte de Nieuwerkerke." *Journal des Arts,* January 21, 25, 1893.

Henriot, 1870
C. de Henriot. "L'Art contemporain." *Revue des Deux-Mondes,* February 1, 1870, pp. 771–72.
Henriot, 1922
E. Henriot. "Le Décor de la vie sous le Second Empire." *Gazette des Beaux-Arts,* 64th year, vol. VI (July–August 1922), pp. 97–110.
Herbert, 1962
R.L. Herbert. "Millet Revisited." *The Burlington Magazine,* vol. CIV, no. 712 (July 1962), pp. 294–305, vol. CIV, no. 714 (September 1962), pp. 377–85.
Herbert, 1966
———. "Millet Reconsidered." *Museum Studies,* vol. I (1966), pp. 28–65.
Herbert, 1970
———. "City vs. Country : The Rural Image in French Painting from Millet to Gauguin." *Artforum,* vol. VIII, no. 6 (February 1970), pp. 44–55.
Hering, 1892
F.F. Hering. *The Life and Works of Jean-Léon Gérôme.* New York, 1892.
Herold, 1962
J.C. Herold. *Bonaparte in Egypt.* New York, 1962.
Héron de Villefosse, 1959
R. Héron de Villefosse. "L'Extravagant Hôtel de la Païva." *Connaissance des Arts,* no. 92 (October 1959), pp. 108–13.
Hervé, 1867
E. Hervé. "Compte rendu sur l'Exposition Universelle, Paris, 1867." *Le Courrier du Centre,* April 15, 1867.
d'Hervilly, 1866
E. d'Hervilly. "Les Poèmes du Salon : Camille." *L'Artiste,* 8th s., June 15, 1866.
Heuser, 1974
H.-J. Heuser. *Französische Keramik zwischen 1850 und 1910.* Munich, 1974.
Heuser, 1977
———. *Miscellanea 8.* Marxen am Berge, 1977.
Hoffmann, 1903
E. Hoffmann. *Jean-Louis Hamon, peintre.* Paris, 1903.
Honoré, 1859
Honoré. "La Ciselure : Causerie historique pour répondre au mémoire de Monsieur Richard Redgrave." *L'Art au Dix-Neuvième Siècle,* vol. IV (1859), pp. 76, 87–89, 99–100, 124–25, 149–50, 162–63.
Horeau, 1845
H. Horeau. *Examen critique du projet d'agrandissement et de construction des Halles Centrales....* Paris, 1845.
*L'Horlogerie à Besançon,* 1867
*Exposition Universelle de 1867 à Paris : Notice sur la fabrication de l'horlogerie à Besançon et dans le département du Doubs présentée à l'appui de son exposition collective.* Besançon, 1867.
Horsin-Déon, 1853
M. Horsin-Déon. *Rapport sur le Salon de 1853.* Paris, 1853.
Horswell, 1971
J. Horswell. *Bronze Sculpture of "Les Animaliers."* Woodbridge, Suffolk, 1971.
Hosotte-Reynaud, 1964
M. Hosotte-Reynaud. "Aperçus inédits sur une manufacture de porcelaine de Paris. La Courtille : De Locré à Pouyat." *Cahiers de la Céramique du Verre et des Arts du Feu,* no. 35 (1964), pp. 167–72.
Hourticq, 1928
L. Hourticq. *Ingres, l'œuvre du maître.* Paris, 1928.
Houssaye, 1884
A. Houssaye. *La Comédienne.* Paris, 1884.
Houssaye, 1896
———. *Un Hôtel célèbre sous le Second Empire : L'Hôtel Païva....* Paris, 1896.
Houyoux and Sulzberger, 1964
R. Houyoux and S. Sulzberger. "Fernand Khnopff et Eugène Delacroix." *Gazette des Beaux-Arts,* 106th year, vol. LXIV (September 1964), pp. 183–85.
Huet, 1911
R.-P. Huet. *Paul Huet.* Paris, 1911.
Hunisak, 1977
J.M. Hunisak. *The Sculptor Jules Dalou : Studies in His Style and Imagery.* [Ph.D. dissertation, New York University, 1975]. New York, 1977.
Hustin, 1889
A. Hustin. "Troyon." *L'Art,* 15th year, vol. XLVI (1889), pp. 77–90, vol. XLVII (1889), pp. 85–96.
Huttinger, 1960
E. Huttinger. *Degas.* Milan, 1960.
Huyghe, 1930
R. Huyghe. "Dans les musées nationaux." *Beaux-Arts,* April 1930, pp. 3–5.
Huyghe, 1931
———. "Lettres inédites de Sisley." *Formes,* no. 19 (November 1931), pp. 151–54.
Huyghe (ed.), 1957–61

R. Huyghe, ed. *L'Art et l'homme.* 3 vols. Paris, 1957–61.
Huyghe, 1963
R. Huyghe. *Delacroix.* New York and London, 1963.

Imbourg, 1929
P. Imbourg. "The B... and D... Collection." *Formes,* no. 1 (December 1929), p. 20.
*Immortali,* 1970
Anon. *Immortali.* Verona, 1970.
*L'Industrie de Mulhouse,* 1902
Anon. *Histoire documentaire de l'industrie de Mulhouse.* Mulhouse, 1902.
*Inventaire général,* 1878–86
Paris, Préfecture au Département de la Seine. *Inventaire général des œuvres d'art appartenant à la ville de Paris dressé par le service des Beaux-Arts.* Vols. I–IV: *Edifices religieux.* Paris, 1878–86.
*Inventaire général,* 1878–89
Paris, Préfecture au Département de la Seine. *Inventaire général des œuvres d'art appartenant à la ville de Paris dressé par le service des Beaux-Arts.* Vols. V, VI: *Edifices civils.* Paris, 1878–89.
*Inventory, London, Victoria and Albert Museum, 1852–67*
*Inventory of the Objects in the Art Division of Museum at South Kensington, Arranged According to the Dates of Their Acquisition.* Vol. I: *1852–67.* London, 1868.
Isaacson, 1966
J. Isaacson. "Monet's Views of Paris." *Allen Memorial Art Museum Bulletin,* vol. XXIV, no. 1 (fall 1966), pp. 4–22.
Isaacson, 1975
R. Isaacson. "The Evolution of Bouguereau's Grand Manner." *The Minneapolis Institute of Arts Bulletin,* vol. LXII (1975), pp. 74–83.
Isay, 1937
R. Isay. *Panorama des Expositions Universelles.* Paris, 1937.

J.L., 1945
J.L. "Documents inédits. Lettres d'Edouard Manet sur son voyage en Espagne." *Arts,* March 16, 1945, p. 1.
Jacquemart, 1859
A. Jacquemart. "Nécrologie." *Gazette des Beaux-Arts,* 1st year, vol. III (July 1, 1859), pp. 59–62.
Jahyer, 1865
F. Jahyer. *Etude sur les Beaux-Arts — Salon de 1865.* Paris, 1865.
Jahyer, 1866
———. *Deuxième Etude sur les Beaux-Arts. Salon de 1866.* Paris, 1866.
Jahyer, 1876
———. *Galerie contemporaine.* Paris, 1876.
Jamar-Rolin, 1956
L. Jamar-Rolin. "La Vie de Guys et la chronologie de son œuvre : Faits et propositions." *Gazette des Beaux-Arts,* 98th year, vol. XLVIII (July–August 1956), pp. 69–112.
Jammes, 1963
A. Jammes. *Charles Nègre, Photographe, 1820–1880.* Paris, 1963.
Jammes, n.d.
———. *Pour un musée idéal de la photographie.* Paris, n.d.
Jamot, 1908
P. Jamot. "Carpeaux : Peintre et graveur." *Gazette des Beaux-Arts,* 50th year, vol. XL (September 1, 1908), pp. 177–97.
Jamot, 1914
———. "La Collection Camondo au Musée du Louvre: Les Peintures et les dessins." *Gazette des Beaux-Arts,* 56th year, vol. XI (June 1914), pp. 441–60.
Jamot, 1921
———. *Auguste Ravier, étude critique suivie de la correspondance de l'artiste....* Lyons, 1921.
Jamot, 1924
———. *Degas.* Paris, 1924.
Jamot, 1927
———. "Etudes sur Manet." *Gazette des Beaux-Arts,* 69th year, vol. XV (January 1927), pp. 27–50.
Jamot, 1927, "Manet"
———. "Manet and the Olympia." *The Burlington Magazine,* vol. I, no. 286 (January 1927), pp. 27–35.
Jamot, 1929
Paris, Musée du Louvre. *La Peinture au Musée du Louvre. Ecole française. XIXᵉ siècle.* By P. Jamot. Paris, 1929.
Jamot, 1929, "Norvège"
P. Jamot. "L'Art français en Norvège." *La Renaissance de l'Art Français,* February 1929.
Jamot and Wildenstein, 1932
P. Jamot and G. Wildenstein. *Manet.* 2 vols. Paris, 1932.
Jamot, Wildenstein, and Bataille, 1932

P. Jamot, G. Wildenstein, and M.L. Bataille. *Manet.* Paris, 1932.
Janis, 1976
E.P. Janis. "The Man on the Tower of Notre Dame : New Light on Henri LeSecq." *Image,* vol. XIX, no. 4 (December 1976), pp. 13–25.
Jannet, 1866
C. Jannet. *Hippolyte Flandrin, sa vie et son œuvre.* Marseilles, 1866.
Jardel, 1962
M. Jardel. "Tassinari et Chatel, 1762–1962: Les Traditions de la soierie lyonnaise à travers l'histoire d'une grande maison." *La Revue Française,* no. 137 (February 1962).
Jarlier, 1976
P. Jarlier. *Répertoire d'arquebusiers et de fourbisseurs français.* Saint-Julien-du-Sault, 1976.
Javel, 1898
F. Javel. *La Plume,* no. 219 (June 1, 1898), pp. 323–411.
Jean, 1911
R. Jean. *Les Arts de la terre, céramique, verrerie, émaillerie, mosaïque, vitrail.* Paris, 1911.
Jean-Aubry, 1922
G. Jean-Aubry. *Eugène Boudin d'après des documents inédits.* Paris, 1922.
Jean-Aubry, 1968
———. *Eugène Boudin, la vie et l'œuvre d'après les lettres et les documents inédits.* Neuchâtel, 1968.
Jedlicka, 1941
G. Jedlicka. *Edouard Manet.* Zurich, 1941.
Jervis, 1974
S. Jervis. *Printed Furniture Designs before 1650.* London, 1974.
Jianou and Goldscheider, 1967
I. Jianou and C. Goldscheider. *Rodin.* Paris, 1967.
*Johnson Collection,* 1892
*Catalogue of a Collection of Paintings Belonging to John G. Johnson.* Philadelphia, 1892.
*Johnson Collection,* 1914
W.R. Valentiner. *Catalogue of a Collection of Paintings and Some Art Objects....* Vol. III : *Modern Paintings.* Philadelphia, 1914.
Josse, 1882–83
Josse. "L'Art japonais. A propos de l'exposition organisée par M. Gonse. Lettres de M. Josse à M. Louis Gonse, directeur de la *Gazette des Beaux-Arts.*" *Revue des Arts Décoratifs,* vol. III (1882–83), pp. 329–38.
Joubin, 1929
Montpellier. *Le Musée de Montpellier. Musée Fabre (Dessins).* By A. Joubin. Paris, 1929.
Joubin, 1936
A. Joubin. "M. Haro entre Ingres et Delacroix." *L'Amour de l'Art,* vol. XVII, no. 3 (March 1936), pp. 85–93.
Joubin, 1950
———. *Journal de Eugène Delacroix.* 3 vols. Paris, 1950.
Jouin, 1879
H. Jouin. *La Sculpture en Europe en 1878.* Paris, 1879.
Jouin, 1908
Angers, Musées d'Angers. *L'Inventaire général des richesses d'art de la France.* Vol. VIII by H. Jouin. Paris, 1908.
Jourdan, 1859
L. Jourdan. *Les Peintres français, Salon de 1859.* Paris, 1859.
*Journal,* 1961
*Queen Victoria : Leaves from a Journal. A Record of the Visit of the Emperor and Empress of the French to the Queen and of the Visit of the Queen and H.R.H., the Prince Consort, to the Emperor of the French, 1855.* New York and London, 1961.
Judex, 1897
Judex. "Chronique du mois." *Revue des Arts Décoratifs,* vol. XVII (1897), pp. 26–28.
Jullian, 1971
P. Jullian. "Les Conquêtes de Roquetaillade." *Connaissance des Arts,* no. 231 (May 1977), pp. 84–95.
Jullian, 1977
———. *The Orientalists.* Oxford, 1977.
Jullian, n.d.
———. *Le Style Second Empire.* Paris, n.d.
Jullien, 1906
A. Jullien. "Une Peinture mélomane — Fantin-Latour et la musique d'après des lettres inédites." *Revues des Deux-Mondes,* vol. XXXV (1906), pp. 36ff.
Jullien, 1909
———. *Fantin-Latour, sa vie et ses amitiés : Lettres inédites et souvenirs personnels.* Paris, 1909.

Kaeppelin, 1889
R. Kaeppelin. *Colmar de 1814 à 1871 : Récits d'un vieux Colmarien.* Paris, 1889.
Keim, 1930
A. Keim. *La Décoration et le mobilier à l'époque romantique et sous le Second Empire.* 7 vols. in 1. Paris, 1930.

Keller, 1966
L. Keller. *Piranèse et les romantiques français, le mythe des escaliers en spirale.* Paris, 1966.
Kemp, 1973
M. Kemp. "Scott and Delacroix with Some Assistance from Hugo and Bonington." In *Scott Bicentenary Essays.* Edinburgh, 1973.
Kjellberg, 1963
P. Kjellberg. "Le Palmarès 1850–1900 de la céramique française." *Connaissance des Arts,* no. 135 (May 1963), pp. 112–21.
Kjellberg, 1974
———. "Sur la piste des paysagistes provençaux." *Connaissance des Arts,* no. 269 (July 1974), pp. 70–77.
Klumpke, 1909
A.E. Klumpke. *Rosa Bonheur : Sa Vie, son œuvre.* Paris, 1909.
Konody, 1930
P.G. Konody. *The Painter of Victorian Life... with a Translation of Baudelaire's "Peintre de la vie moderne."* Edited by C.G. Holme. London, 1930.
Kozloff, 1976
M. Kozloff. "Nadar and the Republic of Mind." *Artforum,* vol. XV, no. 1 (September 1976), pp. 28–39.
Kühn, 1935
J. Kühn. *La Princesse Mathilde.* Paris, 1935.
Kunstler, 1931
C. Kunstler. "Thomas Couture à Senlis." *L'Art Vivant,* October 1931, pp. 549–50.

L. A., 1894–95
L. A. "Un Rénovateur de l'émaillerie française : A.-T. Gobert." *Revue des Arts Décoratifs,* vol. XV (1894–95), pp. 177–79.
de Laborde, 1853
Paris, Musée du Louvre. *Notice des émaux, bijoux et objets divers exposés dans les galeries du Louvre.* 2 vols. By L. de Laborde. Paris, 1853.
de Laborde, 1856
L. de Laborde. *De l'Union des arts et de l'industrie.* 2 vols. Paris, 1856.
Laboulaye, 1856
C. Laboulaye. *Essai sur l'art industriel... à l'Exposition Universelle de Londres en 1851 et à l'Exposition de Paris en 1855.* Paris, 1856.
Labourieu, 1857
T. Labourieu. "L'Orfèvrerie, les bronzes et le zinc d'art." *L'Art du Dix-Neuvième Siècle,* vol. II (1857), pp. 53–57.
Labrouste, 1885
L. Labrouste. *La Bibliothèque Nationale : Ses Bâtiments et ses constructions.* Paris, 1885.
Lacambre, 1969
J. Lacambre. "Les Elèves d'Ingres et la critique du temps." In *Colloque Ingres (1967).* Montauban, 1969, pp. 93–112.
Lacambre, 1972
———. "Les Expositions à l'occasion du centenaire de la Commune." *Revue de l'Art,* vol. XVIII (1972), pp. 68–71.
Lacambre, 1974
G. Lacambre. *Le Musée du Luxembourg en 1874.* (Le Petit Journal des Grandes Expositions). Paris, 1974.
Lacambre, 1977
See 1977, Le Mans.
Lacambre and Lacambre, 1970
G. Lacambre and J. Lacambre. "Pierre-Auguste Pichon élève d'Ingres." *Bulletin du Musée Ingres,* no. 28 (December 1970), pp. 23–29.
Lacan, 1852
E. Lacan. "Le Retour du Prince Président." *La Lumière,* October 30, 1852, p. 179.
Lacan, 1853
———. "Revue photographique." *La Lumière,* vol. III (September 10, 1853), p. 147.
Lacan, 1854
———. [Delessert.] *La Lumière,* October 28, 1854, pp. 170–71.
Lacan, 1854, "Photographie"
———. "La Photographie et les fêtes publiques." *La Lumière,* September 23, 1854, p. 149.
Lacan, 1856
———. *Esquisses photographiques... à propos de l'Exposition Universelle et de la Guerre d'Orient.* Paris, 1856.
Lacretelle, 1853
H. de Lacretelle. "Albums Photographiques. No. 2 — M. LeSecq." *La Lumière,* February 19, 1853, pp. 30–31.
Ladoué, 1936
P. Ladoué. "Le Musée du Luxembourg. Le 'Nouveau Musée' de 1886." *Bulletin des Musées de France,* December 1936.
Lafenestre, 1875
G. Lafenestre. "Jean-Louis Hamon." *L'Art,* 1st year, vol. I

(1875), pp. 394–99.

Lafenestre, 1886
————. "Paul Baudry et son exposition posthume." *Gazette des Beaux-Arts*, 28th year, vol. XXXIII (May 1, 1886), pp. 395–412.

Lafenestre, 1889
————. "Alexandre Cabanel." *Gazette des Beaux-Arts*, 31st year, vol. I (April 1, 1889), pp. 265–80.

Lafenestre, 1891
G. Lafenestre. Preface to Delaunay studio sale catalogue, Paris, 1891.

Lafenestre, 1897
————. *La Tradition dans la peinture française*. Paris, 1897.

Lafenestre and Michel, 1878
Montpellier, Musée de Montpellier. *Inventaire général des richesses d'art de la France, Province, Monuments civils*. Vol. I by G. Lafenestre and E. Michel. Paris, 1878.

Lafond, 1896–97
P. Lafond. "François-Joseph Heim." *Gazette des Beaux-Arts*, 38th year, vol. XVI (December 1, 1896), pp. 441–55, 39th year, vol. XVII (January 1, 1897), pp. 27–36.

Lafond, 1918–19
————. *Degas*. 2 vols. Paris, 1918–19.

Lafond, n.d.
Rouen, Musée des Beaux-Arts. *Le Musée de Rouen*. By P. Lafond. Paris, n.d.

Lagarde, 1863
L. Lagarde. *Le Pays*, May 2, 1863.

Lagrange, 1860
L. Lagrange. "Expositions de Province—Exposition de la Société des Amis des Arts de Lyon." *Gazette des Beaux-Arts*, 2nd year, vol. V (March 1, 1860), pp. 257–74.

Lagrange, 1861
————. "Salon de 1861." *Gazette des Beaux-Arts*, 3rd year, vol. X (May 15, June 1, 15, 1861), pp. 193–211, 257–82, 321–47, vol. XI (July 1, 1861), pp. 49–73.

Lagrange, 1864
————. "Le Salon de 1864." *Gazette des Beaux-Arts*, 6th year, vol. XVI (June 1, 1864), pp. 501–36, vol. XVII (July 1, 1864), pp. 5–44.

Lagrange, 1865
————. "Le Salon de 1865." *Le Correspondant*, May 25, 1865.

Lagrange, 1866
————. "Bulletin mensuel, Mars 1866: Exposition du cercle de l'Union Artistique." *Gazette des Beaux-Arts*, 8th year, vol. XX (April 1, 1866), pp. 398–400.

Lagrange, n.d.
————. *Hippolyte Flandrin*. n.l., n.d.

A. Lagrange, 1952
A. Lagrange. *L'Art de Fromentin*. Paris, 1952.

de Laincel, 1865
L. de Laincel. *Promenade aux Champs-Elysées*. Paris, 1865.

Laloux, 1916
V. Laloux. *Notice sur la vie et les œuvres de M. Alfred Normand*. Paris, 1916.

Lambert, 1858
E. Lambert. "L'Aluminium et ses applications artistiques et industrielles." *L'Art au Dix-Neuvième Siècle*, vol. III (1858), pp. 60–61, 70–72.

Lambert, 1933
E. Lambert. "Manet et l'Espagne." *Gazette des Beaux-Arts*, 75th year, vol. IX (June 1933), pp. 369–82.

Lambert, 1960
————. "Velàsquez et Manet." In *Actes du colloque tenu a la Casa Velàsquez*. 1960.

Lambotte, 1907
See 1907, Antwerp, Brussels.

Lami, 1881–88
E.-O. Lami. *Dictionnaire encyclopédique et biographique de l'industrie et des arts industriels*. 8 vols. Paris, 1881–88.

Lami, 1914–21
S. Lami. *Dictionnaire des sculpteurs de l'école française au dix-neuvième siècle*. 4 vols. Paris, 1914–21.

Lance, 1872
A. Lance. *Dictionnaire des architectes français*. Paris, 1872.

Langlois, 1958
R.-M. Langlois. *L'Opéra de Versailles*. Paris, 1958.

Lanoue, 1874
J. Lanoue. "Exposition de l'Union Centrale: L'Industrie moderne—Les Métaux." *Gazette des Beaux-Arts*, 16th year, vol. X (December 1, 1874), pp. 511–25.

Lanvin, 1975
C. Lanvin. "Les Frères Flandrin, Hippolyte et Paul, élèves d'Ingres." In *Actes du colloque international Ingres et le néo-classicisme*. Montauban, 1975, pp. 53–71.

Lapauze, 1901
H. Lapauze. *Les Dessins de J.-A.-D. Ingres du Musée de Montauban*. 5 vols. Paris, 1901.

Lapauze, 1903
————. *Les Portraits dessinés de J.-A.-D. Ingres*. Paris, 1903.

Lapauze, 1904
Paris, Palais des Beaux-Arts de la Ville de Paris. *Catalogue sommaire des collections municipales*. By H. Lapauze. Paris, 1904.

Lapauze, 1906
Paris, Palais des Beaux-Arts de la Ville de Paris. *Catalogue sommaire des collections municipales*. By H. Lapauze. Paris, 1906.

Lapauze, 1911
H. Lapauze. *Ingres, sa vie, son œuvre*. Paris, 1911.

Laran, 1912
J. Laran. "Eugène Lami." *Gazette des Beaux-Arts*, 54th year, vol. VII (April 1912), pp. 327–36.

Laran, 1913
————. *Daubigny*. Paris, 1913.

Laran and Deshairs, 1913
J. Laran and L. Deshairs. *Gustave Moreau*. Paris, 1913.

Larousse, 1866–90
P. Larousse. *Grand Dictionnaire universel du XIX* siècle français....* 17 vols. Paris, 1866–90.

Larroumet, 1896
B.-G.-P. Larroumet. "M. Gustave Moreau et le Symbolisme dans la peinture." In *Etudes de littérature et d'art*. Paris, 1896, pp. 253–98.

Larroumet, 1901
————. *Notice historique sur la vie et les œuvres de M. Gustave Moreau, membre de l'Académie*. Paris, 1901.

Larroumet, 1904
————. *Notice historique sur la vie et les travaux de M. Charles Garnier*. Paris, 1904.

Larroumet, 1904, *Portraits*
————. *Derniers Portraits*. Paris, 1904, pp. 209–54.

Lassus, 1845
J.-B.-A. Lassus. "De l'Art et de l'archéologie." *Annales Archéologiques*, vol. II (1845), pp. 69–78, 197–204, 329–35.

de Lasteyrie, 1850
F. de Lasteyrie. "Rapport présenté à M. le Ministre du commerce de l'agriculture...." *Bulletin du Comité Historique des Arts et Monuments*, vol. II (1850), pp. 136–52.

de Lasteyrie, 1867
————. "L'Exposition Universelle de 1867." *Le Courrier du Centre*, May 28, 1867.

Laurens, 1901
J. Laurens. *La Légende des ateliers*. Paris, 1901.

Lauzac, 1861
H. Lauzac. *E. Delessert*, n.l., 1861.

Lavergne, 1855
C. Lavergne. *L'Exposition Universelle de 1855*. Paris, 1855.

Lavoix, 1886
H. Lavoix. *G. Boulanger*. Paris, 1886.

Leblanc, 1931
H. Leblanc. *Catalogue de l'œuvre de Gustave Doré: Illustrations, peintures, dessins, sculptures, eaux-fortes, lithographies*. Paris, 1931.

Lechevallier-Chevignard, 1908
G. Lechevallier-Chevignard. *La Manufacture de porcelaine de Sèvres*. 2 vols. Vol. I: *Histoire de la manufacture 1738-1876*. vol. II: *Organisation actuelle et fabrication*. Paris, 1908.

Lecomte, 1928
G. Lecomte. *La Vie héroïque et glorieuse de Carpeaux*. Paris, 1928.

Lecomte, 1863
J. Lecomte. *Le Perron de Tortoni, indiscrétions biographiques*. Paris, 1863.

Lécuyer, 1935
R. Lécuyer. "Regard sur les musées de Provence." *L'Illustration*, November 9, 1935.

Lécuyer, 1945
————. *Histoire de la photographie*. Paris, 1945.

Ledoux-Lebard, 1965
D. Ledoux-Lebard. *Les Ebénistes parisiens du XIXᵉ siècle (1795–1870): Leurs Œuvres et leurs marques*. Paris, 1965.

Lefébure, 1977
A. Lefébure. "L'Orfèvrerie civile au Musée Condé (II)." *Le Musée Condé*, no. 13 (November 1977), pp. 5–23.

Lefort, 1883
P. Lefort. "La Collection de M.B. Narischkine." *Gazette des Beaux-Arts*, 25th year, vol. XXVII (March 1, 1883), pp. 219–25.

Lefort, 1888
————. "Les Artistes contemporains: Philippe Rousseau et François Bonvin." *Gazette des Beaux-Arts*, 30th year, vol. XXXVII (February 1, 1888), pp. 132–45.

Léger, 1920
C. Léger. *Courbet selon les caricatures et les images*. Paris, 1920.

Léger, 1947
————. "Proudhon et Courbet, histoire des portraits de Proudhon." *Bulletin des Amis de Gustave Courbet*, no. 2 (1947).

Léger, 1948
————. *Courbet et son temps (lettres et documents inédits)*. Paris,

1948.

de Leiris, 1969
A. de Leiris. *The Drawings of Edouard Manet*. Berkeley and Los Angeles, 1969.

Lemoisne, 1912
P.A. Lemoisne. *Eugène Lami, 1800–1890*. Paris, 1912.

Lemoisne, 1914
————. *L'Œuvre d'Eugène Lami (1800–1890): Lithographies, dessins, aquarelles, peintures, essai d'un catalogue raisonné*. Paris, 1914.

Lemoisne, 1921
————. "Les Carnets de Degas au Cabinet des Estampes." *Gazette des Beaux-Arts*, 63rd year, vol. III (April 1921), pp. 219–31.

Lemoisne, 1927
————. "Musée du Luxembourg: Le Portrait de Degas par lui-même." *Beaux-Arts*, no. 20 (December 1, 1927), pp. 313–14.

Lemoisne, 1947–49
————. *Degas et son œuvre*. 4 vols. Paris, 1946.

Lemonnier, 1870
C. Lemonnier. *Salon de Paris 1870*. Paris, 1870.

Lemonnier, 1878
————. "Les Artistes contemporains: Alfred Stevens." *Gazette des Beaux-Arts*, 20th year, vol. XVI (February 1, April 1, 1878), pp. 160–74, 335–42.

Leniaud, 1976
J.-M. Leniaud. "Recherches sur Jean-Baptiste Lassus, 1807-1857, archéologue et architecte." Thesis, Ecole des Chartes, Paris, 1976.

Lépinois, 1859
E. B. de Lépinois. *L'Art dans la rue et l'art au Salon*. Paris, 1859.

Lepoittevin, 1964
L. Lepoittevin. "Millet, peintre et combattant." *Arts*, November 19, 1964.

Leprieur, 1889
P. Leprieur. "Gustave Moreau et son œuvre." *L'Artiste*, March 1889, pp. 161–80, May 1889, pp. 338–59, June 1889, pp. 443–55.

Leprieur, 1909
————. "Les Récentes Acquisitions du département des peintures au Musée du Louvre (1907–1908)." *Gazette des Beaux-Arts*, 51st year, vol.I (March 1909), pp. 245–68.

Leroux, 1904
A. Leroux. *Histoire de la porcelaine de Limoges*. Vol. I: *Bibliographie, chronologie, statistique*. Limoges, 1904.

*Les Amis*, 1957
Anon. *Les Amis de Gustave Courbet*, no. 20 (1957), p. 20.

Lethieve and Gardey, 1963
J. Lethieve and F. Gardey. *Inventaire du fond français après 1800*. Vol. XII. Paris, 1963.

Levine, 1975
N. Levine. "Architectural Reasoning in the Age of Positivism: The *Néo-Grec* Idea of Henri Labrouste's Bibliothèque Sainte-Geneviève." Ph.D. dissertation, Yale University, 1975.

Lewis, 1977
D. Lewis, "The St. Petersburg Bronzes of Barye's *War* and *Peace*." *Pharos '77*, vol. XIV, no. 1 (1977), pp. 3–11.

Leymarie, 1879
C. Leymarie. *La Céramique à l'exposition des Beaux-Arts*. Limoges, 1879.

Leymarie, 1962
J. Leymarie. *La Peinture française: Le Dix-Neuvième Siècle*. Geneva, 1962.

Leymarie, 1966
————. *Corot*. Geneva, 1966.

Lienard, 1866
M. Lienard. *Livre d'ornements*. 3 vols. in 1. Paris, 1866.

de Liesville, 1878
A.R. de Liesville. "Exposition Universelle: Les Industries d'art au Champ de Mars. III: La Céramique moderne." *Gazette des Beaux-Arts*, 20th year, vol. XVIII (November 1, 1878), pp. 674–701.

Lionnard de Lens, 1956
E. Lionnard de Lens. "Le Décor intérieur à Fontainebleau sous Napoléon III." Unpublished ms., Ecole du Louvre, 1956.

Locquin, 1920
J. Locquin. "Un Grand Statuaire romantique: Auguste Préault, 1809–1879." *La Renaissance de l'Art Français*, no. 11 (November 1920), pp. 454–63.

Locroy, 1863
E. Locroy. *Le Courrier Artistique*, May 16, 1863.

Loisel, 1912
A. Loisel. *L'Inspiration chrétienne du peintre Gustave Moreau*. Paris, 1912.

Loliée, 1905
F. Loliée. *La Vie d'une impératrice: Eugénie de Montijo*. Paris, 1905.

Loliée, 1928
———. *Le Roman d'une favorite la comtesse de Castiglione d'après sa correspondance intime et les "Lettres des Princes."* Paris, 1928.
Lorrain, 1888
J. Lorrain. "Un Maître socier." *L'Événement*, November 29, 1888.
de Lostalot, 1884
A. de Lostalot. "M. Félix Bracquemond, peintre-graveur." *Gazette des Beaux-Arts*, 26th year, vol. XXX (1884), pp. 155–61.
Loudun, 1852
E. Loudun. *Le Salon de 1852.* Paris, 1852.
Loudun, 1855
———. *Exposition Universelle des Beaux-Arts. Le Salon de 1855.* Paris, 1855.
Lowry, 1963
B. Lowry. *Muse and Ego.* Claremont, 1963.
Luard (ed.), 1914
L.D. Luard, ed. *Horace Lecoq de Boisbaudran, l'éducation de la mémoire pittoresque et la formation de l'artiste.* Paris, 1914.
Luchet, 1862, "Barbedienne"
A. Luchet. "Courrier de l'Exposition Internationale : M. Barbedienne." *Le Monde Illustré*, vol. XI (July–December 1862), pp. 92–94.
Luchet, 1862, "Christofle"
———. "Courrier de l'Exposition Internationale : M. Christofle." *Le Monde Illustré*, vol. XI (July–December 1962), pp. 75–77.
Luchet, 1862, "Marchand"
———. "Courrier de l'Exposition Internationale : Bronzes d'art. M. Marchand." *Le Monde Illustré*, vol. XI (July–December 1862), pp. 219, 221.
Luchet, 1868
———. *L'Art industrielle à l'Exposition Universelle de 1867 : Mobilier, vêtement, aliments.* Paris, 1868.
Lucie-Smith, 1977
E. Lucie-Smith. *Fantin-Latour.* Oxford, 1977.
Lugt, 1938–64
F. Lugt. *Répertoire des catalogues de ventes publiques.* 3 vols. The Hague, 1938–64.

McClelland, 1924
N. McClelland. *Historic Wall-Papers, from Their Inception to the Introduction of Machinery.* Philadelphia, 1924.
McCoubrey, 1964
J.W. McCoubrey. "The Revival of Chardin in French Still-Life Painting, 1850-1870." *The Art Bulletin*, vol. XLVI (1964), pp. 39–53.
MacKay, 1973
J. MacKay. *The Animaliers: A Collector's Guide to the Animal Sculptors of the 19th & 20th Centuries.* New York, 1973.
Mabille de Poncheville, 1921
A. Mabille de Poncheville. *Carpeaux inconnu, ou la tradition recueillie.* Brussels and Paris, 1921.
Mabille de Poncheville, 1925
———. *Carpeaux.* Paris, 1925.
Magne, 1855
C.-P. Magne. "Exposition Universelle de 1855 : Le Service de l'Empereur, l'argenture et la galvanoplastie (Exposition de la maison Christofle)." *L'Illustration*, vol. XXVI (July–December 1855), pp. 331–32.
Magne, 1856
———. "Le Berceau offert au Prince Impérial de la Ville de Paris." *L'Illustration*, March 29, 1856, pp. 199–200.
Magne, 1913
L. Magne. *Décor du verre : gobeleterie, mosaïque, vitrail.* Paris, 1913.
Magonigle, 1922
H.V.B. Magonigle. *Architectural Rendering in Wash.* New York, 1922.
Maison, 1968
K.E. Maison. *H. Daumier: Catalogue raisonné.* 2 vols. Vol. I: *The Paintings.* Vol. II: *The Watercolours and Drawings.* London, 1968.
Malingue, 1943
M. Malingue. *Ingres.* Monaco, 1943.
Malitourne, 1852
P. Malitourne. "Salon de 1852." *L'Artiste*, 5th s., 1852, pp. 161–67.
Malitourne, 1853
———. "La Sculpture en 1853." *L'Artiste*, 5th s., vol. II (1853), pp. 20–24.
Malitourne, 1855
———. "Exposition Universelle des Beaux-Arts : La Sculpture. I. Sculpture française." *L'Artiste*, 5th s., vol. XVI (October 21, 1855), pp. 99–104.
Manciet, 1931

C. Manciet. *Le Musée de Bordeaux.* Paris, 1931.
Mandet, 1855
F. Mandet. *Notice nécrologique sur Charles Crozatier.* Paris, 1855.
Mangin, 1867
A. Mangin. *Les Jardins, histoire et description.* Tours, 1867.
Mantz, 1857
P. Mantz. "Ecole des Beaux-Arts : Les Concours—Les Envois de Rome." *L'Artiste*, 7th s., vol. II (1857), pp. 75–78.
Mantz, 1859
———. "Salon de 1859." *Gazette des Beaux-Arts*, 1st year, vol. II (May 1, 15, June 1, 1859), pp. 129–41, 193–208, 271–99.
Mantz, 1863, "Orfèvrerie"
———. "Recherches sur l'histoire de l'orfèvrerie française : V. Période moderne." *Gazette des Beaux-Arts*, 5th year, vol. XIV (May 1, June 1, 1863), pp. 410–29, 534–50.
Mantz, 1863, "Salon"
———. "Le Salon de 1863." *Gazette des Beaux-Arts*, 5th year, vol. XIV (June 1, 1863), pp. 481–506, vol. XV (July 1, 1863), pp. 32–64.
Mantz, 1864
———. "Artistes contemporains : Hippolyte Flandrin." *Revue Française*, n.s., nos. 1–8 (1864), pp. 71–86.
Mantz, 1865
———. "Salon de 1865." *Gazette des Beaux-Arts*, 7th year, vol. XVIII (June 1, 1865), pp. 489–523, vol. XIX (July 1, 1865), pp. 5–42.
Mantz, 1865, "Troyon"
———. "Artistes contemporains : Troyon." *Gazette des Beaux-Arts*, 7th year, vol. XVIII (May 1, 1865), pp. 393–407.
Mantz, 1867, "Barye"
———. "Artistes contemporains : M. Barye." *Gazette des Beaux-Arts*, 9th year, vol. XXII (February 1, 1867), pp. 107–26.
Mantz, 1867, "Exposition"
———. "Les Beaux-Arts à l'Exposition Universelle." *Gazette des Beaux-Arts*, 9th year, vol. XXIII (October 1, 1867), pp. 319–45.
Mantz, 1867, "Salon"
———. "Le Salon de 1867." *Gazette des Beaux-Arts*, 9th year, vol. XXII (June 1, 1867), pp. 513–48.
Mantz, 1868
———. "L'Orfèvrerie française en 1867." *Gazette des Beaux-Arts*, 10th year, vol. XXIV (February 1, 1868), pp. 126–46.
Mantz, 1869
———. "Salon de 1869." *Gazette des Beaux-Arts*, 11th year, vol. I (June 1, 1869), pp. 489–511, vol. II (July 1, 1869), pp. 5–23.
Mantz, 1872
———. "Salon de 1872." *Gazette des Beaux-Arts*, 14th year, vol. V (June 1, 1872), pp. 449–78, vol. VI (July 1, 1872), pp. 38–66.
Mantz, 1875, "Gleyre"
———. "Charles Gleyre." *Gazette des Beaux-Arts*, 17th year, vol. XI (March 1, May 1, 1875), pp. 233–44, 404–14.
Mantz, 1876
———. "Carpeaux." *Gazette des Beaux-Arts*, 18th year, vol. XIII (May 1, 1876), pp. 593–631.
Mantz, 1879
———. "Salon de 1879." *Le Temps*, June 8, 1879.
Marcel, 1905
H. Marcel. *La Peinture française au XIXᵉ siècle.* Paris, 1905.
G. Marchisio, 1956
G. Marchisio. *Il monumento pittorico a Dante in S. Maria del Fiore.* Rome, 1956.
"Margaine," 1879–80
Anon. "[Nécrologie] Margaine, Alpinien." *Almanach Limousin*, 1879, 1880.
Margueritte, 1913
V. Margueritte. Preface to Carpeaux studio sale catalogue, Paris, Galerie Manzi, December 8–9, 1913.
Margueritte, 1914
———. *J.B. Carpeaux 1827–1875.* Paris, 1914.
de Maricourt, 1931
A. de Maricourt. "Une Magnifique Expérience de décentralisation artistique : Thomas Couture à Senlis." *Le Courrier de l'Oise*, July 1931.
Marie, 1931
A. Marie. *L'Art et la vie romantique ; Henry Monnier.* Paris, 1931.
Marie, 1966
———. *Saint-Cloud, cité historique.* n.l., 1966.
Marion, 1872
A. Marion. *Procédés de photographie au charbon aux encres d'impression et aux sels d'argent.* Paris, 1872.
Marquis, 1976
J.-M. Marquis. "A Brou retour d'un chef-d'œuvre prodigue." *Le Progrès*, December 30, 1976.
Martine and Marotte, 1928
C. Martine and L. Marotte. *Eugène Delacroix, soixante-dix aqua-

relles, dessins. . . .* Paris, 1928.
Marx, 1886
R. Marx. *Les Artistes célèbres, Henri Regnault, 1843-1871.* Paris, 1886.
Masson, 1895
F. Masson. *Edouard Detaille and His Work.* London, 1895.
Masson, 1900
———. *Hippolyte Flandrin.* Lyons, 1900.
Masson, 1905
———. "Eugène Guillaume 1822–1905." *Les Arts*, no. 41 (May 1905), pp. 2–5.
Masson, 1913
———. "Edouard Detaille." *Les Arts*, vol. XII (February 1913).
Mathieu, 1966
P.-L. Mathieu. *Gustave Moreau, sa vie, son œuvre, catalogue raisonné de l'œuvre achevé.* Paris, 1966.
Mathieu, 1971
———. "Documents inédits sur la jeunesse de Gustave Moreau (1826–1857)." *Bulletin de la Société d'Histoire de l'Art Français*, 1971, pp. 259–79.
Mathieu, 1976
———. *Gustave Moreau with a Catalogue of the Finished Paintings, Watercolors and Drawings.* Boston, 1976.
Mauricheau-Beaupré, 1949
C. Mauricheau-Beaupré. *Versailles.* Paris, 1949.
Maury, 1969
R. Maury. "Théodore Deck." *abc décor*, no. 61 (November 1969), pp. 35–59.
Maury, 1970
———. "Faïences en relief : Les Figulines rustiques." *abc décor*, no. 66 (April 1970), pp. 56–82.
Mayer & Pierson, 1862
Mayer & Pierson. *La Photographie considérée comme art et industrie.* Paris, 1862.
Mazois, 1824–38
C.-F. Mazois. *Les Ruines de Pompeii.* 4 vols. Paris, 1824–38.
*Medals 1862*
*International Exhibition, 1862. Medals and Honourable Mentions Awarded by the International Juries with a List of Jurors and the Report of the Council of Chairmen.* London, 1862.
Meier-Graefe, 1899
J. Meier-Graefe. "Die Stellung Eduard Manet's." *Die Kunst*, no. 1 (October 1899), pp. 58–67.
Meier-Graefe, 1907
———. *Impressionisten.* Munich, 1907.
Meier-Graefe, 1912
———. *Edouard Manet.* Munich, 1912.
Meier-Graefe, 1928
———. "Ed. Manet, Zur Ausstellung in der Galerie Matthiesen." *Der Cicerone*, vol. XX, no. 3 (February 1928), pp. 85–94.
Meier-Graefe, 1932
———. "The Manet Centenary (1832–1883)." *Formes*, no. 24 (April 1932), pp. 251–53.
Melcher, 1950
E. Melcher. *The Life and Times of Henry Monnier: 1799–1877.* Cambridge, Mass., 1950.
Mellerio, 1900
A. Mellerio. *L'Exposition de 1900 et l'impressionnisme.* Paris, 1900.
Ménard, 1870
R. Ménard. "Salon de 1870." *Gazette des Beaux-Arts*, 12th year, vol. III (June 1, 1870), pp. 489–514.
Ménard, 1873
———. "Exposition de Vienne." *Gazette des Beaux-Arts*, 15th year, vol. VIII (September 1, 1873), pp. 185–214.
Ménard, 1876
———. *L'Art en Alsace-Lorraine.* Paris, 1876.
Ménard, 1878
———. *Les Curiosités artistiques de Paris—Guide du promeneur dans les musées, les collections et les édifices.* Paris, 1878.
Ménard, 1894
———. "Paul Baudry (et la décoration du foyer de l'Opéra de Paris)." *Gazette des Beaux-Arts*, 36th year, vol. XII (October 1, 1894).
L. Ménard, 1879
L. Ménard. "La Sculpture à l'Exposition Universelle de 1878 : La Section française." *L'Art*, vol. XVI (1879), pp. 233–37.
Méras, 1967
M. Méras. "Ingres et Prosper Mérimée." *Bulletin du Musée Ingres*, July 1976.
Mérimée, 1881
P. Mérimée. *Lettres à M. Panizzi, 1850–1870.* 2nd ed. 2 vols. Paris, 1881.
Mérimée, 1941–61
———. *Correspondance générale.* 17 vols. Annotated by M. Parturier. Paris and Toulouse, 1941–61.
Merson, 1863
O. Merson. "Compte-rendu du Salon." *L'Opinion Nationale*,

May 16, July 18, 1863.

Merson, 1864
———. *L'Opinion Nationale*, June 13, 1864.

Merson, 1865
———. "Hippolyte Flandrin." *L'Opinion Nationale*, May 8, 1865.

Merson, 1867
———. "Beaux-Arts." In Ducuing, 1867, pp. 249–51.

Merson and Bellier, 1867
O. Merson and E. Bellier. *Ingres; sa vie et ses œuvres.* Paris, 1867.

Mesnard, 1867
J. Mesnard. *Les Merveilles de l'Exposition Universelle de 1867.* 2 vols. Paris, 1867.

Mesuret, 1964
R. Mesuret. *Les Artistes toulousains à la Société des Amis des Arts de Bordeaux.* Toulouse, 1964.

de Metternich, 1922
P. de Metternich. *Souvenirs de la princesse Pauline de Metternich (1859–1871).* 20th ed. Preface by M. Dunan. Paris, 1922.

Meunier, 1927
P.-A. Meunier. *La Vie et l'art de Jean-Jacques Henner.* Paris, 1927.

Meyer, 1973
R.K. Meyer. "J.L. Gérôme: The Role of Subject Matter and the Importance of Formalized Composition." *Arts Magazine,* vol. XLVII, no. 4 (February 1973), pp. 31–34.

Meynell, 1881
A. Meynell. "Our Living Artists, Leon Bonnat." *The Magazine of Art,* vol. IV (1881), pp. 238–42.

Meynell, 1886
———. "Alexandre Cabanel." *The Magazine of Art,* vol. IX (May 1886), pp. 271–76.

Mezin, 1870
B. de Mezin. *Promenades en long et en large au Salon de 1870.* Paris, 1870.

Michel, 1905–29
A. Michel. "L'Art en Portugal." In *Histoire de l'art depuis les premiers temps chrétiens jusqu'à nos jours,* 8 vols. in 17. Paris, 1905–29.

Michel, 1906
E. Michel. *Les Maîtres du paysage.* Paris, 1906.

Migeon, 1903
G. Migeon. "Les Bronzes de Barye et le mobilier." *Les Arts,* no. 14 (February 1903), pp. 15–18.

Millet, 1882
E. Millet. *Henri Labrouste,... sa vie, ses œuvres (1801-1875): Notice biographique.* Paris, 1882.

Miquel, 1962
P. Miquel. *Paul Huet.* Sceaux, 1962.

Miquel, 1975
———. *Le Paysage français au XIXᵉ siècle, 1824–1874. L'Ecole de la nature.* 3 vols. Maurs-la-Jolie, 1975.

Mireur, 1901–12
H. Mireur. *Dictionnaire des ventes d'art.* 7 vols. Paris, 1901–12.

de Mirimonde, 1969
A.-P. de Mirimonde. "Un Prédécesseur de Gauguin à Tahiti: Charles Giraud." *Bulletin de la Société de l'Histoire de l'Art Français,* 1969 (published 1971), pp. 135–51.

Mirolli, 1966
R.B. Mirolli. "The Early Work of Rodin and Its Background." Ph. D. dissertation, New York University, 1966.

Mitchell, 1937
E. Mitchell. "La Fille de Jephté par Degas: Genèse et évolution." *Gazette des Beaux-Arts,* 79th year, vol. XVIII (October 1937), pp. 175–89.

Mitchell, 1973
P. Mitchell. *Alfred Emile Léopold Stevens, 1823–1906.* London, 1973.

*Modern Industries, 1868*
*Modern Industries: A Series of Reports on Industry and Manufactures as Represented in the Paris Exposition in 1867.* By Twelve British Workman, Visiting Paris under the Auspices of the Paris Excursion Committee. London, 1868.

le Moël, 1970
M. le Moël. "Les Hôtels Le Hon and Morny au rond-point des Champs-Elysées." In *Ville de Paris. Commission du Vieux-Paris. Procès-verbaux....* Paris, 1970, pp. 24–33.

Moholy-Nagy, 1967
L. Moholy-Nagy. *Painting Photography Film.* Translated by J. Seligman. Cambridge, Mass., 1967.

Moigno, 1855
F. Moigno. "MM. Bisson Frères." *Revue Photographique,* November 5, 1855, pp. 13–14.

Momméja, 1898
J. Momméja. "Les Collections et l'atelier de Jean-Auguste-Dominique Ingres." *Revue Populaire des Beaux-Arts,* 1898.

Momméja, 1905
Montauban, Musée de Montauban. *Inventaire général des richesses d'art de la France, Province, Monuments civils, Collection*

*Ingres au Musée de Montauban.* Vol. VII by J. Momméja. Paris, 1905.

Monda, 1927, "Les Meubles"
M. Monda. "Les Meubles et la tapisserie de l'Impératrice Eugénie vendus 2 576 000 fr." *Le Figaro,* July 10, 1927.

Monda, 1927, "Portrait"
———. "Le Portrait de l'Impératrice Eugénie au Louvre." *Le Figaro,* August 11, 1927.

Mongan, 1938
A. Mongan. "Degas as Seen in American Collections." *The Burlington Magazine,* vol. LXXII, no. 423 (June 1938), pp. 290–302.

Mongan and Sachs, 1940
Cambridge, Mass., Harvard University, William Hayes Fogg Art Museum. *Drawings in the Fogg Museum of Art.* 3 vols. By A. Mongan and P. J. Sachs. Cambridge, Mass., 1940.

de Montaiglon, 1875
A. de Montaiglon. "Le Salon de 1875." *Gazette des Beaux-Arts,* 17th year, vol. XII (July 1, 1875), pp. 5–43.

de Montalivet, 1851
M.-C. de Montalivet. *Le Roi Louis-Philippe: Liste civile,* new ed. Paris, 1851.

de Montifaud, 1865
M. de Montifaud. "Salon de 1865." *L'Artiste,* 8th s., vol. LXXVII (1865), pp. 217–24, vol. LXXVIII (1865), pp. 9–12.

de Montifaud, 1867, May 1
———. "Salon de 1867—Exposition Universelle—Salon de 1867—Exposition des portraits historiques au palais pompéien." *L'Artiste,* May 1, 1867.

de Montifaud, 1867, June 1
———. "Le Salon de 1867." *L'Artiste,* June 1, 1867.

de Montifaud, 1872
———. "Salon de 1872." *L'Artiste,* 9th s., June 1872, pp. 238–46.

de Montifaud, 1886
———. [M.-A. Chartroule]. "Salon de 1886." *L'Artiste,* May 15, 1886.

de Montrond, 1866
M. de Montrond. *Hippolyte Flandrin: Etude biographique et historique.* Lille, 1866.

Montrosier, 1881
E. Montrosier. "Le Musée du Luxembourg." *Les-Chefs-d'œuvres d'art au Luxembourg.* Paris, 1881.

Montrosier, 1881–84
———. *Les Artistes modernes.* 4 vols. Paris, 1881–84.

Montrosier, 1882
———. *Peintres modernes: Ingres, H. Flandrin, Robert-Fleury.* Paris, 1882.

Montrosier, 1883
———. "Henri Baron." In *Société d'Aquarellistes français.* 2 vols. Paris, 1883, vol. II, pp. 289–304.

Monval, 1897
G. Monval. *Les Collections de la Comédie française.* Paris, 1897.

Morain de Sourdeval, 1859
C. Morain de Sourdeval. *Une Nouvelle Poterie d'Avisseau.* Tours, 1859.

Moreau, 1869
A. Moreau. *Decamps et son œuvre.* Paris, 1869.

Moreau (ed.), 1893
G. Moreau, ed. *Revue Encyclopédique,* 1893.

Moreau-Nélaton, 1899
E. Moreau-Nélaton, ed. *Camille Moreau, peintre et céramiste, 1840–1897.* 2 vols. in 3. Paris, 1899.

Moreau-Nélaton, 1906
E. Moreau-Nélaton. *Manet, graveur et lithographe.* Paris, 1906.

Moreau-Nélaton, 1913
———. *Corot.* Paris, 1913.

Moreau-Nélaton, 1916
———. *Delacroix, raconté par lui-même.* Paris, 1916.

Moreau-Nélaton, 1924
———. *Corot raconté par lui-même.* Paris, 1924.

Moreau-Nélaton, 1925
———. *Daubigny raconté par lui-même.* Paris, 1925.

Moreau-Nélaton, 1926
———. *Manet raconté par lui-même.* 2 vols. Paris, 1926.

Moreau-Nélaton, 1927
———. *Bonvin raconté par lui-même.* Paris, 1927.

Moreau-Nélaton, n.d.
———. Catalogue of Manet's œuvre. Ms., Bibliothèque Nationale, Paris, n.d.

Moreau-Nélaton and Robaut, 1905
E. Moreau-Nélaton and A. Robaut. *L'Oeuvre de Corot: Catalogue raisonné.* 5 vols. Paris, 1905.

Moreau-Vauthier, 1906
C. Moreau-Vauthier. *Gérôme: Peintre et sculpteur, l'homme et l'artiste....* Paris, 1906.

Morin, 1894
L. Morin. "Quelques Artistes de ce temps: VI. Joseph Chéret." *L'Artiste,* n.s., September 1894, pp. 195–204.

Mosby, 1969
D.F. Mosby. "Military Painting in France 1830–1848." Thesis, University of California at Los Angeles, 1969.

Mosby, 1977
———. *Alexandre-Gabriel Decamps, 1803-1860.* [Ph.D. dissertation, Harvard University.] 2 vols. New York, 1977.

"Moulin," 1853
Anon. "Intérieurs d'ateliers: M. Moulin." *Le Propagateur,* December 4, 1853, n.p.

Moultat, 1858
L.-M. Moultat. "Chronique." *L'Art du Dix-Neuvième Siècle,* vol. III (1858), pp. 16–17.

Mulder-Hijmans, 1971
E.J. Mulder-Hijmans. "De Vaas met de Opvoeding van Achilleus door Chiron uit het Maison Christofle, ten tijde van Napoléon III." Thesis, University of Leyden, 1971.

Muther, 1893–94
R. Muther. *Geschichte der Malerei im XIX Jahrhundert.* 3 vols. Munich, 1893–94.

Muther, 1896
———. *The History of Modern Painting.* New York, 1896.

Muther, 1907
———. *The History of Modern Painting.* Rev. ed. New York, 1907.

Nadar, 1853
Nadar [pseud.]. *Nadar, jury au Salon de 1853.* Paris, 1853.

Nadar, 1858
———. "Ce qui ne s'apprend pas en photographie." *Le Photographe,* February 25, 1858, pp. 3–4.

Nadar, 1900
———. *Quand j'étais photographe.* Paris, 1900.

Naef, 1962
H. Naef. "La Famille Flandrin." Ms., 1962. (Typescript, Louvre Archives, Cabinet des Dessins).

Naef, 1973
———. "Une Exposition oubliée chez Ingres." *Bulletin du Musée Ingres.* December 1973.

"Napoléon III," 1954
Anon. "Le Décor de la vie sous Napoléon III." *Connaissance des Arts,* no. 32 (October 15, 1954), pp. 36–39.

Nathaniel, 1865
Nathaniel. "Chronique." *La Semaine des Familles,* March 25, 1865, pp. 415–16.

de Navery, 1868
R. de Navery [pseud.]. *Le Salon de 1868.* Paris, 1868.

Nénot, 1896
H.-P. Nénot. *Notice sur M. Gabriel-Auguste Ancelet.* Paris, 1896.

Nettement, 1864
A. Nettement. "Salon de 1864." *La Semaine des Familles,* 1864, pp. 584–88.

Nibelle, 1854, "Fontainebleau"
P. Nibelle. "Fontainebleau." *La Lumière,* April 15, 1854, pp. 59–60.

Nibelle, 1854, "Photographie"
———. "Photographie et les fêtes publiques." *La Lumière,* August 27, 1854, p. 135.

Nicolle, 1920
M. Nicolle. *Le Musée de Rouen, peintures.* Paris, 1920.

"Nicolle," 1887
Anon. "Nécrologie [Nicolle]." *La Semaine des Constructeurs,* December 17, 1887.

Nieuwerkerke, 1863
A.E. de Nieuwerkerke. "Ecole impériale et spéciale des Beaux-Arts: Rapport à l'Empereur." *Gazette des Beaux-Arts,* 5th year, vol. XV (December 1, 1863), pp. 562–72.

Nieuwerkerke, 1868
———. *Rapport... sur la situation des musées impériaux pendant le règne de S.M. Napoléon III (1853–1868).* Paris, 1868.

Nieuwerkerke, 1869
———. *Rapport... sur la situation des musées impériaux pendant le règne de S.M. Napoléon III (1853–1869).* Paris, 1869.

Nochlin, 1971
L. Nochlin. *Realism.* Baltimore, 1971.

Noël, 1902
L. Noël. *François Chifflart: Peintre et graveur français 1825–1901. Sa vie œuvre.* Lille, 1902.

Nohlac and Pératé, 1896
P. de Nohlac and A. Pératé. *Le Musée national de Versailles.* Paris, 1896.

*Notice, 1867*
Anon. *Notice sur les peintures et sculptures du palais de Compiègne.* Paris, 1867.

*Notice explicatives*
Anon. *Notices explicatives, historiques, biographiques sur les principaux ouvrages de peinture et de sculpture exposés.* Paris, 1861.

*Notre-Dame-de-la-Treille, 1856*
Anon. *Œuvre de Notre-Dame-de-la-Treille et de St.-Pierre:*

*Compte-rendu du concours.* Lille, 1856.

Nougaret, 1962
J. Nougaret. "Alexandre Cabanel, sa vie, son œuvre. Essai de catalogue." Thesis, Université de Montpellier, 1962.

Olander, 1974
W. Olander. "A Console Table by Dalou." *Toledo Museum of Art Museum News,* n.s., vol. XVII, no. 2 (1974), pp. 40–46.
Olligs (ed.), 1969–70
H. Olligs, ed. *Tapeten: Ihre Geschichte bis zur Gegenwart.* 3 vols. Brunswick, 1969–70.
Ollivier, 1903
A. Ollivier. *Eugène Fromentin, peintre et écrivain (1820–1876).* La Rochelle, 1903.
Osler, 1968
P.G. Osler. "Gustave Moreau: Some Drawings from the Italian Sojourn." *The National Gallery of Canada Bulletin,* vol. VI, no. 1 (1968), pp. 20–28.

Pach, 1950
W. Pach. *Pierre-Auguste Renoir.* New York, 1950.
Paladilhe and Pierre, 1971
J. Paladilhe and J. Pierrre. *Gustave Moreau.* Paris, 1971.
*Palais de Compiègne,* n.d.
Anon. *Monographie du Palais de Compiègne.* 2 vols. Paris, n.d.
Paléologue, 1928
M. Paléologue. *Les Entretiens de l'Impératrice Eugénie.* Paris, 1928.
Palgrave, 1862
F.T. Palgrave. *Handbook to the Fine Art Collections in the International Exhibition.* 2nd ed. 8 vols. London, 1862.
Palissy, 1961
B. Palissy. *Oeuvres complètes de Bernard Palissy. . . .* Paris, 1961.
Parent, 1864
P.C. Parent. *Le Courrier Artistique,* May 15, 1864.
G. Paris, 1895
G. Paris. "Souvenirs sur Alexandre Bida." *Gazette des Beaux-Arts,* 37th year, vol. XIII (April 1, 1895), pp. 332–45.
Pascal, 1881
J.-L. Pascal. "Notice sur Lefuel." *Revue Générale de l'Architecture,* vol. XXXVIII (1881), cols. 259–65.
Paton, 1884
J. Paton. Preface to *Le Tour de Bois, Photogravures, J. Delton; Photographie hippique du Bois de Boulogne et Boulevard Saint Germain, 1884.* Paris, 1884.
Paul, 1864
A. Paul. *Le Siège,* June 8, 1864.
Peat, 1903
A.B.N. Peat. *Gossip from Paris during the Second Empire, Correspondence 1864–1869.* New York, 1903.
Pecht, 1873
Pecht. *Allgemeine Zeitung,* July 8, 1873.
Peisse, 1841
L. Peisse. "Ecole des Beaux-Arts." *Revue des Deux-Mondes,* 1841, pp. 232–45.
Péladan, 1910
J. Péladan. *Ernest Hébert: Son Oeuvre et son temps.* Paris, 1910.
Péligot, 1877
E.M. Péligot. *Le Verre: Son Histoire, sa fabrication.* Paris, 1877.
Pelletan, 1872
C. Pelletan. "Le Salon." *Le Rappel,* May 11, 1872.
Pelletan, 1881
————. "Sculpteurs romantiques: Auguste Preault." *L'Artiste,* 9th s., vol. CIX (1879), pp. 96–98.
Pelloquet, 1858
T. Pelloquet [pseud.]. *Dictionnaire de poche des artistes contemporains.* Paris, 1858.
Périer, 1855
P. Périer. "Compte rendu de l'Exposition Universelle." *Bulletin de la Société Française de Photographie,* 1855, part 1, pp. 146–48, part 2, pp. 167–76, part 3, pp. 187–200, part 4, pp. 213–28, part 5, pp. 257–74, part 6, pp. 314–32.
Perrier, 1855, "Beaux-Arts"
C. Perrier. "Exposition Universelle des Beaux-Arts—La peinture française—Histoire." *L'Artiste,* 5th s., June 24, July 1, 1855.
Perrier, 1855, "L'Art"
————. "L'Art à l'Exposition Universelle." *L'Artiste,* 5th s., vol. XV (October 28, 1855), p. 15ff.
Peters, 1974
S.W. Peters. "Edgar Degas at the Boston Museum of Fine Arts." *Art in America,* vol. LXII, no. 6 (November–December 1974), pp. 124–25.
Pétroz, 1855
P. Pétroz. *La Presse,* July 31, September 10, 1855.
Peyrefitte, 1973

R. Peyrefitte. *Les Amitiés particulières: Roman.* Reprint. Paris, 1973.
Pfnor, 1853
R. Pfnor. *Vue perspective de la réunion de palais du Louvre et des Tuileries.* Paris, 1853.
Phillipps, 1885
C. Phillipps. "Gustave Moreau." *The Magazine of Art,* vol. VIII (1885), pp. 228–33.
Picon, 1963
G. Picon. *Victor Hugo dessinateur.* Paris, 1963.
Pillement, 1974
G. Pillement. *Les Pré-Impressionnistes.* Zug, 1974.
Pillement, 1974, "Bonvin"
————. "Bonvin, l'héritier des maîtres hollandais." *Galerie Jardin des Arts,* no. 134 (February 1974), pp. 52–56.
Pingeot, 1977
A. Pingeot. "Le Fonds d'atelier Falguière au Musée du Louvre." *Bulletin de la Société d'Histoire de l'Art Français,* 1977.
Pinkney, 1958
D. H. Pinkney. *Napoleon III and the Rebuilding of Paris.* Princeton, 1958.
Pissarro and Venturi, 1939
L.R. Pissarro and L. Venturi. *Camille Pissarro: Son art—son œuvre.* 2 vols. Paris, 1939.
Pitoëff, 1971
A. Pitoëff. "Sculpture, 19ᵉ siècle." *Connaissance des Arts.* November 1971, pp. 113–15.
Pivar, 1974
S. Pivar. *The Barye Bronzes.* Woodbridge, Suffolk, 1974.
Planche, 1855
G. Planche. "Exposition des Beaux-Arts—L'Ecole française." *Revue des Deux-Mondes,* September 15, 1855, pp. 1137–65.
Planche, 1857
————. "Le Salon de 1857." *La Revue des Deux-Mondes,* July 15, 1857.
Planche, n.d.
————. "Salon de 1852." *Etudes sur l'école française, 1831–1852.* Paris, n.d., vol. II, pp. 287–330.
de Plinval de Guillebon, 1972
R. de Plinval de Guillebon. *Porcelaine de Paris, 1770–1850.* Paris and Fribourg, 1972.
Pluchart, 1889
Lille, Musée des Beaux-Arts, Musée Wicar. *Notice des dessins, cartons, pastels, miniatures et grisailles exposés.* Introduction by H. Pluchart. Lille, 1889.
*La Plume,* 1898
*Alexandre Falguière, sculpteur et peintre.* Text by A. Silvestre et al. *La Plume* (special issue), nos. 21–22 (June–July 1898).
Polak, 1958
B. Polak. *Het Fin-de-siècle in de Nederlandse Schilderkunst.* Amsterdam, 1958.
Polak, 1962
A. Polak. *Modern Glass.* London, 1962.
Pollack, 1969
P. Pollack. *The Picture History of Photography, from the Earliest Beginnings to the Present Day.* Rev. and enl. New York, 1969.
Pollen, 1878
J.H. Pollen. *Ancient and Modern Gold and Silversmiths' Work in the South Kensington Museum.* London, 1878.
Pool, 1964
P. Pool. "The History Pictures of Edgar Degas and Their Background." *Apollo,* n.s., vol. LXXX, no. 32 (October 1964), pp. 306–11.
Popelin, 1866
C. Popelin. *L'Email des peintres.* Paris, 1866.
Poulain, 1932
G. Poulain. *Bazille et ses amis.* Paris, 1932.
Poulet-Malassis, 1875
A. Poulet-Malassis. *Monsieur Alphonse Legros au Salon de 1875: Note critique et biographique.* Paris and London, 1875.
*Poussielgue-Rusand,* 1893
*Catalogue Poussielgue-Rusand.* Paris, 1893.
Praz, 1933
M. Praz. *The Romantic Agony.* London, 1933.
Praz, 1956
————. *The Romantic Agony.* 3rd ed. Cleveland and New York, 1956.
Praz, 1964
————. *An Illustrated History of Furnishing, from the Renaissance to the 20th Century.* Translated by W. Weaver. New York, 1964.
Praz, 1964, *L'Ameublement*
————. *L'Ameublement, psychologie et évolution de la décoration intérieure.* Translated by M.-P. and C. Boulay and A.R. Salem. Milan and Paris, 1964.
Prinet and Dilasser, 1966
J. Prinet and A. Dilasser. *Nadar.* Paris, 1966.
Privat, 1865
G. Privat. *Place aux jeunes: Causeries critiques sur le Salon de*

*1865. Peinture, sculpture, gravure, architecture.* Paris, 1865.
Proust, 1913
A. Proust. *Edouard Manet. Souvenirs.* Paris, 1913.

Quépat, 1887
N. Quépat [R. Paquet]. *Dictionnaire biographique de l'ancien département de la Moselle.* Paris, 1887.
Questel, 1872
C. Questel. *Notice sur M. Duban.* Paris, 1872.
Questel, 1881
————. *Funérailles de M. Lefuel.* Paris, 1881.

Raimondi, 1958
R. Raimondi. *Degas, la sua famiglia in Napoli, 1893-1917.* Naples, 1958
Rambosson, 1898
See 1898, Paris, Nouveau Cirque.
*Rapport 1849*
*Rapport du jury central sur l'exposition des produits de l'agriculture et de l'industrie exposés en 1849.* 3 vols. Paris, 1850.
"Rapport," 1874
"Rapport général du jury des industries d'Art—Jury de la sixième section (art appliqué à la céramique et à la verrerie)." *Bulletin de l'Union Centrale,* vol. I, no. 4 (November 1874), pp. 108–9.
*Rapport 1900*
*Rapport du Comité d'Installation. Musée Centennal de la Classe 72, Céramique à l'Exposition Universelle Internationale de 1900 à Paris. Section française.* Paris, 1900.
*Rapports 1855*
*Exposition Universelle de 1855: Rapports de Jury mixte international, publiés sous la direction de S.A.I. le Prince Napoléon. . . .* Paris, 1856.
*Rapports 1862*
*Exposition Universelle de Londres de 1862. Rapports des membres de la section française du jury international sur l'ensemble de l'exposition sous la direction de M. Chevalier.* 7 vols. Paris, 1862–64.
*Rapports 1863*
*Rapports du jury de l'exposition des Beaux-Arts appliqués à l'industrie au Palais de Champs-Elysées en 1863.* Paris, 1865.
*Rapports 1865*
*Le Beau dans l'Utile. Histoire sommaire de l'Union Centrale des Beaux-Arts appliqués à l'Industrie suivie des rapports du jury de l'Exposition de 1865. . . .* Paris, 1866.
*Rapports 1867*
*Exposition Universelle de 1867 à Paris: Rapports du jury international. . . .* 13 vols. Paris, 1868.
*Rapports 1871*
*Exposition Internationale. Londres 1871. France. Commission supérieure. Rapports.* Paris, 1872.
*Rapports 1873*
*Exposition Universelle de Vienne, 1873—France. Commission supérieure. Rapports.* 5 vols. Paris, 1875.
*Rapports 1889*
*Exposition Universelle Internationale de 1889 à Paris. Rapports du jury international publiés sous la direction de M. Alfred Picard.* Paris, 1891.
*Rapports des délégations 1867*
*Exposition Universelle de 1867 à Paris: Rapports des délégations ouvrières. . . .* 3 vols. Paris, 1869.
*Rapports des délégués lyonnais 1867*
*Exposition Universelle de 1867: Rapports des délégués lyonnais publiés par la délégation avec le concours de la Commission ouvrière.* Lyons, 1869.
Ratouis de Limay, 1937
P. Ratouis de Limay. "Un Décorateur français en Turquie au XIXᵉ siècle: Charles Séchan." *Bulletin de la Société de l'Histoire de l'Art Français,* 1937, pp. 157–79.
Ravenez, 1855
L.-W. Ravenez. *Aperçu statistique de l'exposition de Limoges, en 1855.* Limoges, 1855.
*Récompenses 1867*
*Exposition Universelle de 1867 à Paris: Catalogue officiel des exposants récompensés par le jury international.* Paris, 1868.
"Récompenses," 1868
"Distribution des récompensés aux artistes exposants du Salon de 1868." In catalogue, Paris, Salon de 1869.
*Récompenses 1878*
*Ministère de l'Agriculture et du Commerce Exposition Universelle Internationale de 1878 à Paris: Catalogue officiel. Liste des récompensés.* Paris, 1878.
"Récompensés," 1891
"Distribution des récompensés aux artistes exposants du Salon de 1891." In catalogue, Paris, Salon de 1892.
*Recueil de documents 1862*
*Exposition Universelle de 1862 à Londres. Section française. Recueil*

de documents officiels. Publiés par ordre de la Commission Impériale. Paris, 1863.

Redgrave, 1856
R. Redgrave. Design as Applied to Manufacturers. London, 1856.

Reff, 1964
R. Reff. "New Light on Degas's Copies." The Burlington Magazine, vol. CVI, no. 735 (June 1964), pp. 250–59.

Reff, 1975
———. "Manet's Portrait of Zola." The Burlington Magazine, vol. CXVII (January 1975), pp. 34–44.

Reff (ed.), 1976
T. Reff, ed., The Notebooks of Edgar Degas. Oxford, 1976.

Reff, 1976, Degas
T. Reff. Degas: The Artist's Mind. New York, 1976.

Reff, 1977
———. "Degas: A Master among Masters." The Metropolitan Museum of Art Bulletin, vol. XXXIV, no. 4 (spring 1977).

Reff, 1977, Manet
———. Manet: Olympia. New York, 1977.

Régamey, 1925
R. Régamey. "Carpeaux." Art Vivant, vol. XIX (1925), pp. 33–35.

Régamey, 1927
———. "La Formation de Claude Monet." Gazette des Beaux-Arts, 69th year, vol. XV (February 1927), pp. 65–84.

Reinaud, 1903
E.-A. Reinaud. Charles Jalabert, l'homme, l'artiste, d'après sa correspondance. Paris, 1903.

Relation générale, 1853
Relation générale des cérémonies relatives au mariage de Sa Majesté l'Empereur Napoléon III.... Paris, 1853.

Remington, 1940
P. Remington. "Sculptures by Barye: Recent Acquisitions." The Metropolitan Museum of Art Bulletin, vol. XXXV, no. 2 (February 1940), pp. 34–36.

Rémy, 1867, "Orfèvrerie"
P.-A. Rémy. "La Galerie du mobilier: V. Orfèvrerie française et étrangère, joaillerie, bijouterie, etc." L'Illustration, vol. L (July–December 1867), pp. 11–13.

Rémy, 1867, "Les Prix"
———. "Exposition Universelle: Les Prix de l'Exposition Agricole." L'Illustration, vol. L (July–December 1867), pp. 300–301.

Renan, 1887
A. Renan. "Gustave Guillaumet." Gazette des Beaux-Arts, 29th year, vol. XXXV (May 1, 1887), pp. 404–22.

Renan, 1900
———. Gustave Moreau (1826–1898). Paris, 1900.

Renard, 1874
C. Renard. Etude sur les peintures de Paul Baudry au foyer du nouvel Opéra de Paris. Paris, 1874.

Renaud, 1876
V. Renaud. "Salon de 1876: Sculpture, II, Sculpture monumentale." L'Art, vol. V (1876), pp. 159–61.

Renauld et al., 1976
C. Renauld et al. "Un Cavalier du temps passé, Alfred Dedreux." Art et Curiosité, May–June 1976, pp. 27–33.

Reports 1851
Exhibition of the Works of Industry of All Nations, 1851. Reports by the Juries on the Subjects in the Thirty Classes into Which the Exhibition Was Divided. London, 1852.

Reports 1855
Reports on the Paris Universal Exhibition, 1855. 3 parts. London, 1856.

Reports 1867
Great Britain, Royal Commission for the Paris Exhibition, 1867. Reports on the Paris Universal Exhibition, 1867. Vol. II: Containing Reports on Oil and Other Paintings. Sculpture, Architecture....London, 1868.

Revillion, 1904
C. Revillion. Recherches sur les peintres de la ville de Saint-Omer. Saint-Omer, 1904.

Rewald, 1944
J. Rewald. Degas: Works in Sculpture. New York, 1944.

Rewald, 1946
———. The History of Impressionism. New York, 1946.

Rewald, 1947
———. Edouard Manet: Pastels. Oxford, 1947.

Rewald, 1961
———. The History of Impressionism. Rev. and enl. New York, 1961.

Rewald, 1963
———. Camille Pissarro. New York and London, 1963.

Rewald, 1973
———. The History of Impressionism. 4th rev. ed. New York, 1973.

Rey, 1927
R. Rey. "Paul Guigou." L'Art Vivant, no. 62 (July 15, 1927), pp. 556–59.

Reybaud, 1867
L. Reybaud. "L'Exposition de vêtement et de l'ameublement des industries de luxe." Revue des Deux-Mondes, August 15, 1867, pp. 929–63.

Rheims, 1972
M. Rheims. La Sculpture au XIXe siècle. Paris, 1972.

de Rialle, 1863
J. Girard de Rialle. A Travers le Salon de 1863. Paris, 1863.

Riat, 1906
G. Riat. ... Gustave Courbet, peintre. Paris, 1906.

Rich, 1932
D. C. Rich. "The Spanish Background for Manet's Early Work." Parnassus, vol. IV, no. 11 (February 1932), pp. 1–5.

Richardson, 1957
J. Richardson. Claude Monet. Edinburgh, 1957.

Richardson, 1958
———. Edouard Manet: Paintings and Drawings. London and New York, 1958.

Richardson, 1967
———. The Courtesans. Cleveland, 1967.

Richardson, 1971
———. La Vie parisienne, 1852–1870. London, 1971.

Riotor, 1906
L. Riotor. Carpeaux, biographie critique. Paris, 1906.

Riotor, 1927
———. Carpeaux. Paris, 1927.

de Ris, 1852
C. de Ris. "Le Salon." L'Artiste, 5th s., vol. VIII (1852), pp. 113–17.

Robaut and Chesneau, 1885
A. Robaut and E. Chesneau. L'Oeuvre complet de Eugène Delacroix. Paris, 1885.

Robaut and Moreau-Nélaton, 1905
See Moreau-Nélaton and Robaut, 1905.

Robert, 1900
A. Robert. "Auguste et Joseph Fannière: Orfèvres et sculpteurs." Revue de la Bijouterie, Joaillerie, Orfèvrerie, no. 8 (December 1900), pp.129–35.

de la Rochenoire, 1855
J. de la Rochenoire. Exposition Universelle des Beaux-Arts—Le Salon de 1855 apprécié à sa juste valeur pour un franc. Paris, 1855.

Roger-Marx, 1893
C. Roger-Marx. "Discours aux obsèques d'Augustin Jean Moreau-Vauthier." Le Journal des Arts, January 21, 1893.

Roger-Marx, 1927
———. E. Boudin. Paris, 1927.

Roger-Marx, 1950
———. Eva Gonzalès. Saint-Germain-en-Laye, 1950.

Roger-Marx, 1955
———. "Le Roi des ciels: Boudin." Connaissance des Arts, no. 40 (June 15, 1955), pp. 32–37.

Roger-Marx, 1957
———. "Boudin et la ville et la rivière." Galerie Jardin des Arts, no. 34 (August 7, 1957), pp. 615–20.

Roger-Milès, 1891
L. Roger-Milès. Corot. Paris, 1891.

Romier, 1960
L. Romier. A History of France. Translated by A.L. Rowse. London, 1960.

Roosevelt, 1885
B. Roosevelt [pseud.]. Life and Reminiscences of Gustave Doré. New York, 1885.

Roschach, 1858
Roschach. Revue de Toulouse, vol. VII (1858), p. 299.

Rose, 1946
M. Rose. Gustave Doré. London, 1946.

Rosenberg, 1884–89
A. Rosenberg. Geschichte der Modernen Kunst. 3 vols. Leipzig, 1884–89.

Rosenberg, 1894
———. Geschichte der Modernen Kunst. 3 vols. Leipzig, 1894.

Rosenblum, 1967
R. Rosenblum. Ingres. New York, 1967.

Rosenblum, 1968
———. Ingres. Paris, 1968.

Rosenblum, 1969
———. "The 19th-Century Franc Revalued." Art News, vol. LXVIII, no. 4 (summer 1969), pp. 26–31, 58–61.

Rosenthal, 1914
L. Rosenthal. Le Romantisme au réalisme. Paris, 1914.

Rossigneux, 1886
C. Rossigneux. Rapport fait à la Société d'Encouragement pour l'Industrie Nationale.... sur les titres de Ferdinand Barbedienne... la grande médaille d'or, dite de Jean Goujon. Paris, 1886.

Rossigneux, 1892
———. Rapport fait à la Société d'Encouragement pour l'Industrie Nationale...sur les titres de Emile Froment-Meurice...à la grande médaille d'or, dite de Jean Goujon. Paris, 1892.

Rothenstein, 1931
W. Rothenstein. Men and Memoirs. New York, 1931.

Rouart, 1945
D. Rouart. Degas à la recherche de sa technique. Paris, 1945.

Rouart and Orienti, 1970
D. Rouart and S. Orienti. Tout l'Œuvre peint d'Edouard Manet. Paris, 1970.

Rouart and Wildenstein, 1975
D. Rouart and G. Wildenstein. Edouard Manet: Catalogue raisonné. 2 vols. Vol. I: Peintures. Vol. II: Pastels, aquarelles et dessins. Lausanne and Paris, 1975.

Rouault, 1926, "Centenaire"
G. Rouault. "Gustave Moreau: A propos de son centenaire." Le Correspondant, April 10, 1926, pp. 141–43.

Rouault, 1926, "Moreau"
———. "Gustave Moreau." L'Art et les Artistes, April 1926, pp. 217–48.

Roujon, 1914
H. Roujon. Gustave Moreau. Paris, 1914.

Roujon, n. d., Baudry
———. Paul Baudry. Paris, n. d.

Roujon, n.d., Hébert
———. Hébert. Paris, n.d.

Roujon, n.d., Meissonier
———. Meissonier. Paris, n.d.

Rousseau,1864
J. Rousseau. L'Univers Illustré, May 28, 1864.

Rousseau, 1866
———. "Le Salon." L'Univers Illustré, July 1866.

Roux and Barré, 1870–75
H. Roux and L. Barré. Herculanum et Pompéi. 6 vols. Paris, 1870–75.

Rouyer, 1867
E. Rouyer. Les Apartements privés de S.M. l'Impératrice au Palais des Tuileries.... Paris, 1867.

Roy, 1958
C. Roy. "Le Second Empire vous regarde." Le Point, Revue Artistique et Littéraire, vols. LIII, LIV (January 1958).

Ruchel, 1895
A. Ruchel. Preface to Bida studio sale catalogue, Paris, Hôtel Drouot, April 25–30,1895.

Sache, 1918
M. Sache. "Notes sur le sculpteur Arnaud." In Mémoires de la Société Nationale d'Agriculture, Sciences et Arts d'Angers. Angers, 1918, pp. 3–23.

Saglio, 1864
E. Saglio. "Hippolyte Flandrin." Gazette des Beaux-Arts, 6th year, vol. XVII (August 1, 1864), pp. 243–52.

Saint Clair, 1973
A. Saint Clair. The Image of the Turk in Europe. New York, 1973.

Saint-Cyr de Rayssac, 1873
Saint-Cyr de Rayssac. "Le Plafond de M. Cabanel.." Gazette des Beaux-Arts, 15th year, vol. VII (May 1, 1873), pp. 424–27.

Saint-Ogan, 1887
L. Saint-Ogan. Compiègne. Paris, 1887.

Saint-Pulgent, 1869
Abbé Saint-Pulgent. "Hippolyte Flandrin et ses œuvres." Revue du Lyonnais, 1869, pp. 516–37.

de Saint-Santin, 1867
M. de Saint-Santin [P. de Chennevières]. "M. Heim." Gazette des Beaux-Arts, 9th year, vol. XXII (January 1, 1867), pp. 40–62.

Saint-Victor, 1855
P. de Saint-Victor. "Beaux-Arts, une descente de croix, par Théodore Chassériau." L'Artiste, December 16, 1855, pp. 211–14.

Saint-Victor, 1864
———. La Presse, May 7, 1864.

Saint-Victor, 1866
———. La Presse, July 15, 1866.

Saint-Victor, 1872
———. "Les Tableaux de style au Salon." L'Artiste, 9th s., June 1872, pp. 244–52.

Sainte-Claire-Deville, 1859
H. Sainte-Claire-Deville. De l'Aluminium: Ses Propriétés, sa fabrication et ses applications. Paris, 1859.

Sainte-Marie, 1975
J.-P. Sainte-Marie. "Un Ornemaniste français du XIXe siècle: Frédéric-Eugène Piat (Montfey, 1827—Paris, 1903)." Les Cahiers des Musées de Troyes, no. 2 (1975).

Sainte-Marie-Perrin, 1889
L.-J. Sainte-Marie-Perrin. Pierre Bossan, architecte. Lyons, 1889.

Salinger, 1957
M. Salinger. Claude Monet. New York, 1957.

Salinger and Sterling, 1967

New York, Metropolitan Museum of Art. *French Paintings: A Catalogue of the Metropolitan Museum of Art (XIX–XX Centuries).* By M.M. Salinger and C. Sterling. New York, 1967.

Salmson, 1892
J. Salmson. *Souvenirs d'un sculpteur.* Geneva, 1892.

Samoyault-Verlet, 1969
C. Samoyault-Verlet. "La Génération du Second Empire. Les Arts décoratifs." In "Histoire de l'Art," *Encyclopédie de la Pléiade,* vol. IV (1969), pp. 232–42.

Samoyault-Verlet, 1975
———. *Le Grand Livre de l'objet d'art.* 2 vols. Geneva, 1975.

Sandblad, 1954
N.G. Sandblad. *Manet: Three Studies in Artistic Conception.* Lund, 1954.

Sandoz, 1875
G. Sandoz. *Union Centrale des Beaux-Arts appliqués à l'industrie. Exposition de 1874. Rapport présenté par le jury de la Vᵉ section.* Paris, 1875.

Sandoz, 1957
M. Sandoz. "Esquisses et dessins inédits ou peu connus de Théodore Chassériau (1819–1856)...." *Bulletin de la Société d'Histoire de l'Art Français,* 1957, pp. 15–36.

Sandoz, 1970
———. "Les Peintures de la Renaissance à Fontainebleau et le maniérisme italien. Sources possibles de Théodore Chassériau et des premiers romantiques français." *Gazette des Beaux-Arts,* 112th year, vol. LXXV (January 1970), pp. 43–62.

Sandoz, 1974
———. *Théodore Chassériau, 1819–1856: Catalogue raisonné des peintures et estampes.* Paris, 1974.

Sanvoisin, 1927
G. Sanvoisin. "L'Impératrice Eugénie au Louvre." *Le Gaulois,* July 19, 1927.

Sarradin, 1927
E. Sarradin. *Carpeaux.* Paris, 1927.

de Sault, 1861
C. de Sault. "Expositions des Grands Prix de Rome à l'Ecole des Beaux-Arts." In *Essais de critique d'art.* Paris, 1864.

de Sault, 1863
*See* de Sault, 1864.

de Sault, 1864
———. *Essais de critique d'art: Salon de 1863: Peintures de Saint-Germain-des-Près....* Paris, 1864.

Saunier, 1911
C. Saunier. *Anthologie d'art français, la peinture, XIXᵉ siècle.* 2 vols. Paris, 1911.

Saunier, 1925
———. *Bordeaux.* 1909. 2nd ed. Paris, 1925.

Saunier, 1925, *Barye*
———. *Barye.* Paris, 1925.

Sauvageot, 1880
C. Sauvageot. *Viollet-Le-Duc et son œuvre dessiné.* Paris, 1880.

de Savarus, 1879
P. de Savarus. *Dix Années d'art.* Paris, 1879.

Scharf, 1968
A. Scharf. *Art and Photography.* London, 1968.

Scherlen, 1931
A. Scherlen. *Colmar, village et ville.* Colmar, 1931.

Schleiger, 1964
A. Schleiger. *Two Hundred Patterns of Haviland China. Book II.* 2nd rev. ed. Omaha, Neb., 1964.

Schlenoff, 1956
N. Schlenoff. *Ingres, ses sources littéraires.* Paris, 1956.

Schlumberger, 1977
E. Schlumberger. "Art et artifice des opalines." *Connaissance des Arts,* no. 306 (August 1977), pp. 26–33.

Schmit, 1973
R. Schmit. *Eugène Boudin 1824–1898.* Paris, 1973.

Schneider, 1977
D. Schneider. *The Work and Doctrine of Jacques-Ignace Hittorff (1792-1867): Structural Innovation and Formal Expression in French Architecture, 1810-1867.* [Ph.D. dissertation, Princeton University, 1970]. New York, 1977.

Schnerb, 1902
J.-F. Schnerb. "Henry Monnier et Joseph Prudhomme." *Gazette des Beaux-Arts,* 44th year, vol. XXVII (June 1, 1902), pp. 489–99.

Schommer, 1927
P. Schommer. "Le 'Decameron' de Winterhalter." *Renaissance,* 1927, pp. 457–59.

Schommer, 1930
———. "John Lewis-Brown." *Gazette des Beaux-Arts,* 72nd year, vol. III (March 1930), pp. 194–202.

Schuré, 1904
E. Schuré. *Précurseurs et révoltes.* Paris, 1904.

Schwartz and de Micheaux, 1964
P.-R. Schwartz and R. de Micheaux. *A Century of French Fabrics, 1850–1950.* Leigh, 1964.

Scribe, 1867

Scribe, 1867
L. Scribe. "Gustave Moreau [Exposition Universelle de 1867]." In Ducuing, 1968, pp. 390–91.

Sédille, 1874
P. Sédille. "Victor Baltard: Architecte." *Gazette des Beaux-Arts,* 16th year, vol. IX (May 1, 1874), pp. 485–96.

Ségard, 1914
A. Ségard. "Fresques inédits de Puvis de Chavannes." *Les Arts,* vol. XIII, no. 147 (1914), pp. 4–16, no. 150, p. 14.

Ségard, 1928
———. *Albert Carrier-Belleuse: 1824–1887.* Paris, 1928.

Seitz, 1960
W.C. Seitz. *Claude Monet: Seasons and Moments.* New York, 1960.

le Senne, 1910
E. le Senne. *Madame de Païva: Etude de psychologie et d'histoire.* Paris, 1910.

Sensier, 1872
A. Sensier. *Souvenirs sur Th. Rousseau.* Paris, 1872.

Sensier and Mantz, 1881
A. Sensier and P. Mantz. *La Vie et l'œuvre de J.-F. Millet.* Paris, 1881.

"Serre-Bijoux," 1957
Anon. "Les Serre-Bijoux de la Couronne." *Connaissance des Arts,* no. 63 (May 1957), pp. 82–87.

Sérullaz, 1939
M. Sérullaz. "Etudes." *Chronique des Arts,* April 20, 1939, p. 245.

Sérullaz, 1963
———. *Mémorial de l'exposition Eugène Delacroix organisée au Musée du Louvre à l'occasion du centenaire de la mort de l'artiste.* Paris, 1963.

Sérullaz, 1966
———. *Dessins français de Prud'hon à Daumier.* Fribourg, 1966.

Sérullaz, 1974
———. "Donation Claude Roger-Marx." *La Revue du Louvre et des Musées de France,* nos. 4–5 (1974), pp. 301–6.

A. Sérullaz, 1973
A. Sérullaz. "Cabinet des Dessins: Un Dessin de Gustave Doré." *La Revue du Louvre et des Musées de France,* no. 2 (1973), pp. 117–18.

Silvestre, 1876
*See* Bruyas, 1876.

Silvestre, 1878
T. Silvestre. *Histoire des artistes vivantes, français et étrangers, études d'après nature.* 1856. Reprint. Paris, 1878.

Sloane, 1951
J.C. Sloane. *French Painting between the Past and the Present: Artists, Critics, and Traditions from 1848 to 1870.* Princeton, 1951.

Sloane, 1962
———. *Paul Marc Joseph Chenavard, Artist of 1848.* Chapel Hill, N.C., 1962.

Société du Progrès, 1864
Anon. *Société du Progrès de l'art industriel Deuxième Exposition de l'art industriel au Palais de l'Industrie.* Paris, 1864.

Solon, 1866
L.-M. Solon. *Inventions décoratives, choix de compositions et de motifs d'ornementation.* Paris, 1866.

Solon, 1894
———. "Pâte sur pâte." *The Studio.* [London], vol. II, no. 10 (January 1894), pp. 117–22.

Solon, 1903
———. *A History and Description of the Old French Faience.* London, 1903.

Soubies, 1905
A. Soubies. *J.-J. Henner, 1829–1905; notes biographiques.* Paris, 1905.

Soulié, 1859
E. Soulié. *Notice du Musée Impérial de Versailles.* Paris, 1859.

Soulier (ed.), 1904
G. Soulier, ed. *L'Œuvre gravé et lithographié de A. Legros.* Paris, 1904.

Soullié, 1900
L. Soullié. *Peintures, aquarelles, pastels, dessins de Jean-François Millet, relevées dans les catalogues de ventes de 1849 à 1900....* Paris, 1900.

Souverin, 1977
C. Souverin. "Le Musée des Beaux-Arts et la peinture contemporaine—politique d'acquisition 1830–1914." *Art de l'Ouest,* 1977.

*Souvenirs de Labrouste,* 1928
Anon. *Souvenirs d'Henri Labrouste, architecte, membre de l'Institut: Notes recueillies et classées par ses parents.* Fontainebleau, 1928.

Spielman, 1904
M.H. Spielman. "Jean Léon Gérôme, 1824–1902: Recollections." *The Magazine of Art,* vol. II (1904), pp. 200–208.

Spoll, 1882
E.A. Spoll. "Thomas Couture et son œuvre." *La Vérité,* September 7, 1882.

Stanton (ed.), 1910
T. Stanton, ed. *Reminiscences of Rosa Bonheur.* New York, 1910.

Starkie, 1971
E. Starkie. *Flaubert: The Making of the Master.* London, 1971.

Stechow, 1948
W. Stechow. "Selected Acquisitions of European Art 1947–1948." *Allen Memorial Art Museum Bulletin,* vol. V, no. 2 (December 1948), pp. 24–45.

Steinberg, 1972
L. Steinberg. "The Eye Is a Part of the Mind." In *Other Criteria: Confrontations with Twentieth-Century Art.* London, 1972.

Steingräber, 1966
E. Steingräber. *Oreficeria dal Rinascimento al Liberty.* Milan, 1966.

Steinhauser, 1969
M. Steinhauser. *Die Architektur der Pariser Oper....* Munich, 1969.

Stella, 1872
C. Stella. "Salon de 1872." *L'Opinion Nationale,* May 29, 1872.

Sterling and Adhémar, 1958–61
Paris, Musée Nationale du Louvre. *Peintures, Ecole française, XIXᵉ siècle....* 4 vols. By C. Sterling and H. Adhémar. Paris, 1958–61.

Stevens, 1866
A. Stevens. *Le Salon de 1863.* Paris, 1866.

Strahan, 1878–80
E. Strahan [E. Shinn]. *The Art Treasures of America.* 3 vols. Philadelphia, 1878–80.

Strahan, 1881–83
———. *Gérome; A Collection of the Works of J.-L. Gérome in 100 Photogravures.* 2 vols. New York, 1881–83.

Stranahan, 1888
C.H. Stranahan. *A History of French Painting from Its Earliest to Its Latest Practice.* New York, 1888.

Stranahan, 1893
———. *A History of French Painting from Its Earliest to Its Latest Practice.* New York, 1893.

Stranahan, 1902
———. *A History of French Painting from Its Earliest to Its Latest Practice.* New York, 1902.

Stranahan, 1917
———. *A History of French Painting from Its Earliest to Its Latest Practice.* New York, 1917

Strong, 1966
D.E. Strong. *Greek and Roman Gold and Silver Plate.* London, 1966.

Tabarant, 1924
A. Tabarant. *Pissarro.* Paris, 1924.

Tabarant, 1942
———. *La Vie artistique au temps de Baudelaire.* 4th ed. Paris, 1942.

Tabarant, 1947
———. *Manet et ses œuvres.* 4th ed. Paris, 1947.

Taine, 1903
H. Taine. *Dernier Essai de critique et d'histoire.* Paris, 1903.

Taralon, 1966
J. Taralon. "Note technique sur le 'Talisman de Charlemagne.'" *Les Monuments Historiques de la France,* n.s., vol. XII (1966), pp. 24–43.

de Tauzia, 1879
Both de Tauzia. *Notice supplémentaire des dessins... de divers écoles exposées depuis 1869 dans la salle du premier étage au Musée National du Louvre.* Paris, 1879.

Taylor, 1862
T. Taylor. *Handbook of the Pictures of the International Exhibition of 1862.* London, 1862.

Ten-Doesschate-Chu, 1974
P. Ten-Doesschate-Chu. *French Realism and the Dutch Masters.* Utrecht, 1974.

Ternois, 1962
D. Ternois. "Lettres inédites d'Ingres à Hippolyte Flandrin." *Bulletin du Musée Ingres,* no. 11 (July 1962), pp. 5–26.

Ternois and Camesasca, 1971
D. Ternois and E. Camesasca. *Tout l'Œuvre peint d'Ingres.* Paris, 1971.

Terrier, 1959
Compiègne, Musée National de Compiègne. *Le Second Empire.* Preface by M. Terrier. Paris, 1959.

de Thémines, 1864
M. de Thémines. *La Patrie,* June 24, 1864.

Thévenin, 1897
L. Thévenin. *L'Esthétique du Gustave Moreau.* Paris, 1897.

Thieme and Becker, 1907–50
U. Thieme and F. Becker. *Allgemeines Lexikon der Bildenden Künstler von der Antike bis zur Gegenwart.* 37 vols. Leipzig, 1907–50.

Thiéry, 1787
Thiéry. *Guide des amateurs et des étrangers voyageurs à Paris.* 2 vols. Paris, 1787.

Thiollier, 1891
F. Thiollier. *L'Œuvre de Pierre Bossan, architecte.* Montbrison, 1891.

Thoré, 1847
E.-J.-T. Thoré [W. Bürger]. "Salon de 1847." In Thoré-Bürger, 1870.

Thoré-Bürger, 1861
———. "Salon de 1861." In Thoré-Bürger, 1870.

Thoré-Bürger, 1863
———. "Salon de 1863." In Thoré-Bürger, 1870.

Thoré-Bürger, 1864
———. "Salon de 1864." In Thoré-Bürger, 1870.

Thoré-Bürger, 1865
———. "Salon de 1865." In Thoré-Bürger, 1870.

Thoré-Bürger, 1868
———. "Salon de 1868." In Thoré-Bürger, 1870.

Thoré-Bürger, 1869
———. "Salon de 1869." *La Presse*, 1893.

Thoré-Bürger, 1870
———. *Salons de W. Bürger de 1861 à 1868.* 2 vols. Paris, 1870.

Thoré-Bürger, 1893
———. *Les Salons—Etudes de critique et d'esthétique.* Paris, 1893.

Tietze-Conrat, 1944
E. Tietze-Conrat. "What Degas Learned from Mantegna." *Gazette des Beaux-Arts*, 86th year, vol. XXVI (July–December 1944), pp. 412–20.

Toussaint, 1971
H. Toussaint. *Le Bain turc d'Ingres.* (Les Dossiers du département des peintures, no. 1). Paris, 1971.

Towndrow, 1952
K.R. Towndrow. "French Painters: I—Renoir." *Apollo*, vol. LV, no. 324 (February 1952), pp. 43–48.

Trapadoux, 1860
M. Trapadoux. *L'Œuvre de M. Cordier. Galerie anthropologique et ethnographique pour servir à l'histoire des races.* Paris, 1860.

Trapp, 1965
F. A. Trapp. "The Universal Exhibition of 1855." *The Burlington Magazine*, vol. CVII, no. 747 (June 1965), pp. 300–305.

Trapp, 1971
———. *The Attainment of Delacroix.* Baltimore, 1971.

Travaux 1851
*Exposition Universelle de 1851. Travaux de la Commission Française sur l'Industrie des Nations.* Paris, 1854.

Tresca, 1855
H. Tresca. *Visite à l'Exposition Universelle de Paris en 1855.* Paris, 1855.

Trianon, 1880
H. Trianon. *Le Constitutionnel*, October 30, 1880.

Troche, 1857
N. M. Troche. *L'Architecte Lassus.* Paris, 1857.

Tufts, 1974
E. Tufts. *Our Hidden Heritage, Five Centuries of Women Artists.* London and New York, 1974.

Turgan, 1863–75
J.-F. Turgan. *Les Grandes Usines: Etudes industrielles en France et à l'étranger.* 5 vols. Paris, 1863–75.

Twining, 1960
Lord Twining. *A History of the Crown Jewels of Europe.* London, 1960.

Twining, 1967
———. *European Regalia.* London, 1967.


Union Centrale 1863
*Palais de l'Industrie (Champs-Elysées). Exposition des Beaux-Arts appliqués à l'industrie.* Paris, 1863.

Union Centrale 1865
*Union Centrale des Beaux-Arts appliqués à l'industrie. Exposition de 1865 au Palais de l'Industrie.* Paris, 1866.


Vachon, 1898
M. Vachon. *Detaille.* Paris, 1898.

Vachon, 1899
———. *Jules Breton.* Paris, 1899.

Vachon, 1900
———. *W. Bouguereau.* Paris, 1900.

Vacquier, 1913
J. Vacquier. *Les Vieux Hôtels de Paris. La Place Vendôme.* Paris, 1913.

Vaisse, 1974
P. Vaisse. "Le Conseil supérieur de perfectionnement des manufactures nationales sous la Deuxième République."

*Bulletin de la Société de l'Histoire de l'Art Français*, 1974, pp. 153–71.

Vaisse, 1977, "Couture"
———. "Thomas Couture, ou le bourgeois malgré lui." *Romantisme: Revue du XIX\* Siècle*, vols. XVII–XVIII (1977), pp. 103–22.

Vaisse, 1977, "Second Empire"
———. "Couture et le Second Empire." *Revue de l'Art*, no. 37 (1977), pp. 43–68.

Valabrègue, 1889–90
A. Valabrègue. "L'Ivoire à l'Exposition Universelle de 1889." *Revue des Arts Décoratifs*, vol. X (1889–90), pp. 379–88.

Valotaire, 1930
M. Valotaire. *La Céramique française moderne.* Paris, 1930.

Van Brunt, 1861
H. Van Brunt. "Greek Lines." *The Atlantic Monthly*, vol. VII, no. 44 (June 1861), pp. 654–67, vol. VIII, no. 45 (July 1861), pp. 76–88.

Van Dyke, 1896
J.C. Van Dyke. *Modern French Masters.* New York, 1896.

Van Zanten, 1977
D. Van Zanten. *The Architectural Polychromy of the 1830's.* [Ph.D. dissertation, Harvard University, 1970]. New York, 1977.

Vapereau, 1858
G. Vapereau. *Dictionnaire universel des contemporains....* Paris, 1858.

Vapereau, 1870
———. *Dictionnaire universel des contemporains....* 4th ed. Paris, 1870.

Vapereau, 1893
———. *Dictionnaire universel des contemporains....* 6th ed. Paris, 1893.

de Vasselot, 1914
J.-J. Marguet de Vasselot. *Musée National du Louvre: Catalogue sommaire de l'orfèvrerie, de l'émaillerie et des gemmes du Moyen-Age au XVII\* siècle.* Paris, 1914.

Vaudoyer, 1847
L. Vaudoyer. "Histoire d'architecture en France." In *Patria.* 2 vols. Edited by J. Aicard. Paris, 1847, cols. 2113–98.

Vaudoyer, 1871
———. *Discours... prononcé aux funérailles de M. Duban.* Paris, 1871.

de Vaudrey, 1872
L. de Vaudrey. "Salon de 1872." *La Gazette de France*, May 26, 1872.

Venturi, 1953
L. Venturi. *De Manet à Lautrec.* Translated by J. Bertrand. Paris, 1953.

Vergnet-Ruiz and Laclotte, 1962
J. Vergnet-Ruiz and M. Laclotte. *Petits et grands musées de France—Ecole française.* Paris, 1962.

Verlet, 1913
R.-C. Verlet. *Institut de France, Académie des Beaux-Arts. Notice sur la vie et les œuvres de M. Emmanuel Frémiet....* Paris, 1913.

Verlet, 1972
P. Verlet. *Styles, meubles, décors.* 2 vols. Paris, 1972.

Veron, 1875
T. Veron. *De l'art et des artistes de mon temps.* Paris, 1875.

Veron, 1876
———. *Memorial de l'art et des artistes de mon temps.* Paris, 1876.

Veron, 1877
———. *Memorial de l'art et des artistes de mon temps.* Paris, 1877.

Véron, n.d.
E. Véron. *Union Centrale des Beaux-Arts appliqués à l'industrie. Histoire de l'Union Centrale: son origine, son présent, son avenir.* Paris, n.d.

Vever, 1906–8
H. Vever. *La Bijouterie française au XIX\* siècle.* 3 vols. Paris, 1906–8.

Viardot, 1859
L. Viardot. "Léon Benouville." *Gazette des Beaux-Arts*, 1st year, vol. I (March 1, 1859), pp. 309–11.

Viel-Castel, 1883–84
H. de Viel-Castel. *Mémoires du Comte Horace de Viel-Castel sur le règne de Napoléon III (1851–1864).* 6 vols. Paris, 1883–84.

Viel-Castel, 1942
———. *Mémoires du Comte Horace de Viel-Castel sur le règne de Napoléon III (1851–1864).* 2 vols. Paris, 1942.

Vignon, 1852
C. Vignon. *Salon de 1852.* Paris, 1852.

Vignon, 1853
———. *Salon de 1853.* Paris, 1853.

Vignon, 1855
———. *Le Salon de 1855—Exposition Universelle de 1855. Beaux-Arts.* Paris, 1855.

Vigny, 1935
A. de Vigny. *Les Poèmes.* Paris, 1935.

Vincent, 1956

M. Vincent. *La Peinture des XIX\* et XX\* siècles.* Lyons, 1956.

Vinet, 1854
E. Vinet. "La Jeanne d'Arc de M. Ingres." *Revue des Deux-Mondes*, August 1, 1854.

Viollet-le-Duc, 1854–68
E.-E. Viollet-le-Duc. *Dictionnaire raisonné de l'architecture française du XI\* au XVI\* siècle.* 10 vols. Paris, 1854–68.

Viollet-le-Duc, 1857
———. *Description du Château de Pierrefonds.* Paris, 1857.

Viollet-le-Duc, 1858
———. *La Cité de Carcassonne.* Paris, 1858.

Viollet-le-Duc, 1858–75
———. *Dictionnaire raisonné du mobilier français de l'époque carolingienne à la Renaissance.* 6 vols. Paris, 1858–75.

Viollet-le-Duc, 1862
———. "L'Enseignement des arts." *Gazette des Beaux-Arts*, 4th year, vol. XII (May 1, June 1, 1862), pp. 393–402, 525–34, vol. XIII (July 1, September 1, 1862), pp. 71–82, 249–55.

Viollet-le-Duc, 1863
———. *Journal des Débats*, May 12, 1863.

Viollet-le-Duc, 1863–72
———. *Entretiens sur l'architecture.* 3 vols. Paris, 1863–72.

Viollet-le-Duc, 1884
———. *Compositions et dessins de Viollet-le-Duc.* Paris, 1884.

Viollet-le-Duc, 1971
———. *Eugène-Emmanuel Viollet-le-Duc: Lettres d'Italie, 1836–1837.* Edited by G. Viollet Le Duc. Paris, 1971.

Visconti, 1853
L.-T.-J. Visconti. *Description du modèle... représentant l'achèvement du Louvre.* Paris, 1853.

Vitali et al., 1973
L. Vitali, J. Prinet, and A. Dilasser. *Nadar, Testi di Nadar, con 100 fotografie di Nadar e altri documenti.* Turin, 1973.

Vitet, 1866
L. Vitet. "Le Louvre et le nouveau Louvre." *Revue des Deux-Mondes*, July 1, 1866, pp. 57–93.

Vitry, 1898
P. Vitry. "L'Œuvre décorative de M. Frémiet." *Art et Décoration*, vol. IV (July–December 1898), pp. 65–77.

Vitry, 1912
———. "La Salle Barye au Musée du Louvre." *Bulletin des Musées de France*, 1912, pp. 93–96.

Vitry, 1912, Carpeaux
———. *Carpeaux.* Paris, 1912.

Vitry, 1922
———. *Musée National du Louvre. Catalogue des sculptures du Moyen Age, de Renaissance et des temps modernes.* Vol. II: *Temps modernes.* Paris, 1922.

Vitry, 1928
———. "La Sculpture romantique." In *Le Romantisme dans l'art.* Paris, 1928.

Vitry, 1930
———. "Sculptures modernes: La Statue du Prince Impérial, de Carpeaux." *Bulletin des Musées de France*, no. 3 (March 1930), pp. 52–54.

Vitry, 1933
———. *Musée National du Louvre, Catalogue des sculptures du Moyen Age, de la Renaissance et des temps modernes.* Vol. III: Supplement. Paris, 1933.

Von Holten, 1957
R. Von Holten. "Oedipe et le Sphinx, Gustave Moreau...." *Symbolister 3, Tidskrift för Konstvetenskap*, vol. XXIII (1957), pp. 36–50.

Von Holten, 1960
———. *L'Art fantastique de Gustave Moreau.* Preface by A. Breton. Paris, 1960.

Von Holten, 1965
———. *Gustave Moreau, Symbolist.* Stockholm, 1965.


Waagen, 1857
Dr. Waagen. *Galleries and Cabinets of Art in Great Britain.* London, 1857.

Wakefield, 1962
H. Wakefield. *Victorian Pottery.* London, 1962.

Walter, 1864
J. Walter. "Salon de 1864: Sculpture." *L'Artiste*, 1864, pp. 265–67.

Walters Collection, 1878
*Collection of W.T. Walters.* Baltimore, 1878.

Walters Collection, 1884
*Collection of W.T. Walters.* Baltimore, 1884.

Walters Collection, 1887
*Collection of W.T. Walters.* Baltimore, 1887.

Walters Collection, 1893
*Collection of W.T. Walters.* Baltimore, 1893.

Waltz, 1902
A. Waltz. *Bibliographie de la ville de Colmar.* Colmar, 1902.

Waring, 1863
J.B. Waring. *Masterpieces of Industrial Art & Sculpture at the International Exhibition, 1862.* 3 vols. London, 1863.

Watson, 1963
F. Watson. "Taste in Second Empire Furnishings." *Apollo,* n.s., vol. LXXVII, no. 16 (June 1963), pp. 467–71.

Wegener, 1954
H. Wegener. "French Impressionist and Postimpressionist Paintings in the Brooklyn Museum." *The Brooklyn Museum Bulletin,* vol. XVI, no. 1 (fall 1954), pp. 1–25.

Wehrle, 1911
L. Wehrle. "Lettres de Puvis de Chavannes (1888–1898)." *La Revue de Paris,* February 1, 1911, pp. 449–77.

Weisberg, 1969
G. P. Weisberg. "Félix Bracquemond and Japanese Influence in Ceramic Decoration." *The Art Bulletin,* vol. LI, no. 3 (September 1969), pp. 277–80.

Weisberg, 1970
———. "François Bonvin and an Interest in Several Painters of the Seventeenth and Eighteenth Centuries." *Gazette des Beaux-Arts,* 112th year, vol. LXXVI (December 1970), pp. 359–66.

Weisberg, 1973, "Moreau and Dammouse"
———. "Japonisme in French Ceramic Decoration; Part II: The Pieces by Camille Moreau and Albert Dammouse." *The Connoisseur,* vol. CLXXXIV, no. 740 (October 1973), pp. 125–31.

Weisberg, 1973, "Rousseau"
———. "Japonisme in French Ceramic Decoration; Part I: The Pieces for E. Rousseau, Paris." *The Connoisseur,* vol. CLXXXIII, no. 737 (July 1973), pp. 210–13.

Weisberg, 1974
———. "François Bonvin and the Critics of His Art." *Apollo,* n.s. vol. C (October 1974), pp. 306–11.

Wey, 1851
F. Wey. "Album de la Société Héliographique. Premier article." *La Lumière,* vol. I (May 18, 1851), p. 58.

Widener, 1900
P.A.B. Widener. *Catalogue of Paintings Forming the Private Collection of P.A.B. Widener, Ashbourne—near Philadelphia. Part 1: Modern Paintings.* Paris, 1900.

Wièse, 1860
J. Wièse. "Notice sur Lefournier, célèbre émailleur du dix-neuvième siècle." *L'Art au Dix-Neuvième Siècle,* vol. V (1860), pp. 41–43, 51–53.

Wild, 1894
F. Wild. *Nekrologe und Verzeichnisse der Gemälde von Franz und Hermann Winterhalter.* Zurich, 1894.

Wildenstein, 1954
G. Wildenstein. *Ingres.* London, 1954.

Wildenstein, 1965
"Le Salon des Refusés de 1863: Catalogue of documents. (Etudes et documents publiés sous la direction de Daniel Wildenstein)." *Gazette des Beaux-Arts,* 107th year, vol. LXVI (September 1965), pp. 125–52.

Wildenstein, 1971
D. Wildenstein. *Gli impressionisti: Claude Monet.* Milan, 1971.

Wildenstein, 1974
———. *Claude Monet: Biographie et catalogue raisonné.* Vol. I:*1840–1881—Peintures.* Lausanne and Paris, 1974.

Wilenski, 1940
R. H. Wilenski. *Modern French Painters.* New York, 1940.

Wilhelm, 1956
J. Wilhelm. "Les Salles du Second Empire et de la IIIᵉ République." *Bulletin du Musée Carnavalet,* June 1956.

Willemin and Pottier, 1839
N.-X. Willemin and A. Pottier. *Monuments français inédits pour servir à l'histoire des arts depuis le VIᵉ siècle jusqu'au commencement du XVIIᵉ.* 2 vols. Paris, 1839.

Williamson, 1883–85
E. Williamson. *Les Meubles d'art du Mobilier national.* 2 vols. Paris, 1883–85.

Wolff, 1872
A. Wolff. "Salon de 1872—Thomas Couture." *Le Figaro,* May 15, 1872.

Wolff, 1886
———. *La Capitale de l'art.* Paris, 1886.

Wood, 1951
S. Wood [G. LaVerne Freeman]. *Haviland—Limoges (China Classics II).* Watkins Glen, N.Y., 1951.

Wright and Moisy, 1972
B. Wright and P. Moisy. *Gustave Moreau et Eugène Fromentin: Documents inédits.* La Rochelle, 1972.

Young, 1960
D.W. Young. *The Life and Letters of J. Alden Weir.* New Haven, 1960.

Yriarte, 1863, "Exposition"
C. Yriarte. "Exposition des Beaux-Arts." *Le Monde Illustré,* vol. I (1863), pp. 408–9.

Yriarte, 1863, "Sculpture"
———. "Sculpture." *Le Monde Illustré,* vol. II (1863), pp. 45ff.

Yriarte, 1863, "Vénus"
———. "Exposition des Beaux-Arts—Vénus aux cheveux d'or." *Le Monde Illustré,* vol. II (1863), p. 96.

Yvon, 1911
M.-A. Yvon. "Notice sur la vie et les œuvres d'Alfred Normand." *L'Architecture,* vol. XXV (1911), pp. 89–92, 101–4.

Zauber, 1975
P. Zauber, "Grabreliefs römischer Freigelassener." *Jahrbuch des Deutschen Archäologischen Instituts,* 1975, pp. 265–315.

Ziégler, 1850
J. Ziégler. *Etudes céramiques: Recherche des principes du beau dans l'architecture, l'art céramique et la forme en général.* Paris, 1850.

Ziégler, 1855
———. *Compte rendu de la photographie à l'Exposition Universelle de 1855.* Dijon, 1855.

Zieseniss, 1954
C.O. Zieseniss. *Les Aquarelles de Barye: Etude critique et catalogue raisonné.* Paris, 1954.

Zola, 1866
E. Zola. "Mon Salon." *Le Figaro,* 1866.

Zola, 1868
———. "Causerie." *La Tribune,* August 30, 1868.

Zola, 1959
———. *Salons.* Edited by Hemmings and Niess. Paris, 1959.

Zola, 1974
———. *Le Bon Combat. De Courbet aux Impressionnistes.* Preface by G. Pichon. Paris, 1974.

# Exhibitions

1850, Paris, Palais National
Paris, Palais National. *Exposition des produits des manufactures nationales.* April-May 1850.

1852, Paris, Salon
Paris, Palais-Royal. *Salon de 1852.* April 1–June 30, 1852.

1853, Paris, Salon
Paris, Menus-Plaisirs. *Salon de 1853.* May 15–July 15, 1853.

1854, Orléans
Orléans. Fête de Jeanne d'Arc. December 1854.

1854, Paris, Atelier Ingres
Paris, Atelier Ingres. Private exhibition. 1854.

1855, Paris, Exposition Universelle
Paris, Champs-Elysées. *Exposition Universelle de 1855 à Paris.* May 15–November 15, 1855.*See also* 1855, Paris, Salon.

1855, Paris, Salon
Paris, Palais des Beaux-Arts. *Exposition Universelle des Beaux-Arts [Salon de 1855].* May 15–October 31, 1855.

1856, Brussels
Brussels, Association pour l'Encouragement et le Développement des Arts Industriels en Belgique. 1856. No catalogue.

1856, Paris, Atelier Ingres
Paris, Atelier Ingres. Private exhibition. 1856.

1857, Marseilles
Marseilles, Société Artistique des Bouches-du-Rhône. *Exposition annuelle,* 1857.

1857, Paris, Salon
Paris, Palais des Champs-Elysées. *Salon de 1857.* June 15–August 15, 1857.

1857, Paris, Société Française de Photographie
Paris, Société Française de Photographie, Studio of LeGray. 1857.

1858, Toulouse
Toulouse. *Exposition de l'Union Artistique de Toulouse.* 1858.

1859, Paris, Salon
Paris, Palais des Champs-Elysées. *Salon de 1859.* April 15–June 15, 1859.

1859, Paris, Théâtre de l'Odéon
Paris, Théâtre de l'Odéon. *Exposition des Peintures,* 1859.

1860, Bordeaux
Bordeaux. *Exposition de la Société des Amis des Arts.* 1860.

1861, Paris, Galerie Martinet
Paris, Galerie Martinet, boulevard des Italiens. *Ingres.* 1861.

1861, Paris, Salon
Paris, Palais des Champs-Elysées. *Salon de 1861.* May 1–July 1, 1861.

1862, London
London, South Kensington. *International Exhibition of 1862.* May 1–November 1, 1862.

1862, Rouen
Rouen. *Exposition municipale.* 1862.

1863, Paris, Galerie Martinet
Paris, Galerie Martinet. *Manet.* March 1863.

1863, Paris, Salon
Paris, Palais des Champs-Elysées. *Salon de 1863.* May 1–July 1, 1863.

1864, Oporto
Oporto. International exhibition of industrial arts, 1864.

1864, Paris, Ecole des Beaux-Arts
Paris, Ecole Impériale des Beaux-Arts. *Envois de Rome.* 1864.

1864, Paris, Salon
Paris, Palais des Champs-Elysées. *Salon de 1864.* May 1–June 15, 1864.

1864, Paris, Société du Progrès
Paris, Palais de l'Industrie. *Société du Progrès de l'Art Industriel. Deuxième Exposition de l'art industriel.* 1864.

1864, Paris, Société Nationale des Beaux-Arts
Paris, Société Nationale des Beaux-Arts, 26, boulevard des Italiens. *Exposition des œuvres d'Eugène Delacroix.* 1864.

1865, Paris, Ecole des Beaux-Arts
Paris, Ecole Impériale des Beaux-Arts. *Expositions des œuvres d'Hippolyte Flandrin.* 1865.

1865, Paris, Galerie Martinet
Paris, Galerie Martinet. *Manet.* From February 1865.

1865, Paris, Salon
Paris, Palais des Champs-Elysées. *Salon de 1865.* May 1–June 20, 1865.

1866, Lille
Lille. *Exposition des Beaux-Arts.* July 22–August 21, 1866.

1866, Paris, Ecole des Beaux-Arts
Paris, Ecole Impériale des Beaux-Arts. *Exposition de Paul Baudry.* 1866.

1866, Paris, Palais des Champs-Elysées
Paris, Palais des Champs-Elysées. *Exposition rétrospective, tableaux empruntés aux galeries particulières.* 1866.

1866, Paris, Salon
Paris, Palais des Champs-Elysées. *Salon de 1866.* May 1–June 20, 1866.

1867, Paris, Avenue de l'Alma
Paris, Avenue de l'Alma. *Edouard Manet.* 1867.

1867, Paris, Ecole des Beaux-Arts
Paris, Ecole Impériale des Beaux-Arts. *Exposition des tableaux, études peintes, dessins et croquis de J.-A.-D. Ingres.* 1867.

1867, Paris, Exposition Universelle
Paris, Champ de Mars, etc. *Exposition Universelle de 1867 à Paris.* April 1–November 3, 1867.

1867, Paris, Rond-Point de l'Alma
Paris, Rond-Point de l'Alma, Champs-Elysées. *Exposition des œuvres de M.G. Courbet.* 1867.

1867, Paris, Salon
Paris, Palais des Champs-Elysées. *Salon de 1867.* April 15–June 5, 1867.

1868, Bordeaux
Bordeaux, Société des Amis des Arts. *Exposition des peintures et des sculptures.* 1868.
1868, Le Havre
Le Havre. *Exposition maritime internationale du Havre.* 1868.
1868, Paris, Salon
Paris, Palais des Champs-Elysées. *Salon de 1868.* May 1–June 20, 1868.
1869, Munich
Munich, Glaspalast. *International Kunst Austellung.* 1869.
1869, Paris, "Musée Oriental"
Paris, Union Centrale des Beaux-Arts appliqués à l'industrie. "Musée Oriental." 1869.
1869, Paris, Salon
Paris, Palais des Champs-Elysées. *Salon de 1869.* May 1–June 20, 1869.
1869, Rouen
Rouen. *Exposition municipale.* 1869.
1870, Dijon
Dijon. *Exposition au profit des femmes des condamnés du Creusot.* 1870.
1870, Paris, Salon
Paris, Palais des Champs-Elysées. *Salon de 1870.* May 1–June 20, 1870.
1871, Boston
Boston, The Boston Athenaeum. *The 47th Annual Exhibition.* 1871.
1871, London, International Exhibition
London, South Kensington. *International Exhibition.* 1871.
1871–72, Boston
Boston, The Boston Athenaeum. *The 48th Annual Exhibition.* 1871–72.
1872, Boston
Boston, The Boston Athenaeum. *The 49th Annual Exhibition.* 1872.
1872, Brussels
Brussels. *Exposition générale des Beaux-Arts.* 1872.
1872, New Haven
New Haven, Yale University. *Fifth Annual Exhibition of the Yale School of Fine Arts.* 1872.
1872, Paris, Salon
Paris, Palais des Champs-Elysées. *Salon de 1872.* May 1–June 20, 1872.
1873, Boston
Boston, The Boston Athenaeum. *The 50th Annual Exhibition.* 1873.
1873, Vienna
Vienna, Prater. *Welt Ausstellung.* 1873.
1874, Paris, Ecole des Beaux-Arts
Paris, Ecole Nationale des Beaux-Arts. *Tableau, études et dessins de Chintreuil.* April 25–May 15, 1874.
1874, Paris, Union Centrale
Paris, Union Centrale des Beaux-Arts, Appliqués à l'Industrie. *Exposition de 1874.* 1874.
1875, Paris, Ecole des Beaux-Arts
Paris, Ecole Nationale des Beaux-Arts. *Œuvres de Antoine-Louis Barye.* 1875. Preface by A. Genevay.
1877, Nice
Nice, Société des Beaux-Arts. *Exposition de peinture et de sculpture.* 1877.
1878, Paris, Exposition Universelle Internationale
Paris, Champ de Mars, etc. *Exposition Universelle Internationale de 1878.* 1878.
1878, Paris, Galerie Durand-Ruel
Paris, Galerie Durand-Ruel. *Exposition rétrospective de tableaux et dessins de maîtres modernes.* 1878.
1878, Paris, Galerie Durand-Ruel, "Daumier"
Paris, Galerie Durand-Ruel. *Daumier.* 1878.
1879, Limoges
Limoges. *Exposition des Beaux-Arts.* 1879.
1880, Paris, Cluny
Paris, Musée de Cluny. *Viollet-le-Duc.* 1880.
1880, Paris, Galeries de l'Art
Paris, Galeries de l'Art. *Théodule Ribot, exposition générale de ses oeuvres.* 1880.
1880, Paris, Palais de l'Industrie
Paris, Palais de l'Industrie. *Thomas Couture.* 1880. Foreword and essay by R. Ballu.
1881, Paris, Musée des Arts Décoratifs
Paris, Musée des Arts Décoratifs. *Exposition de peinture et sculpture moderne de décoration et d'ornement.* 1881.
1882, Paris, Ecole des Beaux-Arts
Paris, Ecole Nationale des Beaux-Arts. *Exposition des œuvres de Courbet.* 1882.
1882, Paris, Galerie Georges Petit
Paris, Galerie Georges Petit. *Exposition internationale de peinture organisée par un groupe d'artistes—première année.* 1882.
1883, Paris, Ecole des Beaux-Arts
Paris, Ecole Nationale des Beaux-Arts. *Portraits du siècle.* 1883.
1883, Paris, Galerie Georges Petit

Paris, Galerie Georges Petit. *Cent Chefs-d'œuvre des collections parisiennes.* From June 12, 1883.
1884, Paris, Ecole des Beaux-Arts
Paris, Ecole Nationale des Beaux-Arts. *Exposition des Œuvres d'Edouard Manet.* June 5–28, 1884. Preface by E. Zola.
1884, Paris, Ecole des Beaux-Arts, "Dessins"
Paris, Ecole Nationale des Beaux-Arts. *Dessins de l'école moderne.* 1884.
1884, Paris, Galerie Georges Petit
Paris, Galerie Georges Petit. *Exposition Meissonier, au profit de l'hospitalité de nuit.* May 24–July 24, 1884.
1885, Paris, Ecole des Beaux-Arts
Paris, Ecole Nationale des Beaux-Arts. *Exposition Eugène Delacroix au profit de la souscription destinée à élever à Paris un monument à sa mémoire.* March 6–April 15, 1885.
1886, New York
New York, National Academy of Design. *Special Exhibition: Works in Oil and Pastel by the Impressionists of Paris.* 1886. Exhibition under the management of the American Art Association.
1886, Paris, Ecole des Beaux-Arts
Paris, Ecole Nationale des Beaux-Arts. *Paul Baudry, exposition au profit de l'association des artistes, peintres, sculpteurs, etc., et du monument à élever à la mémoire de Paul Baudry.* Essay by E. Guillaume. 1886.
1887, New York, National Academy of Design
New York, National Academy of Design. *Celebrated Paintings by Great French Masters.* 1887.
1887, Paris, Ecole des Beaux-Arts
Paris, Ecole Nationale des Beaux-Arts. *J.-F. Millet.* 1887.
1887, Paris, Galerie Durand-Ruel
Paris, Galerie Durand-Ruel. *Exposition de tableaux, pastels, dessins par M. Puvis de Chavannes.* November 20–December 20, 1887.
1889, Paris, Ecole des Beaux-Arts
Paris, Ecole Nationale des Beaux-Arts. *Les Œuvres de Barye.* April 1889. Catalogue by E. Guillaume.
1889, Paris, Exposition Universelle Centennale
Paris, Champ de Mars, etc. *Exposition Internationale. Beaux-Arts. Exposition centennale de l'art français (1789–1889).* 1889.
1893, Paris, Ecole des Beaux-Arts
Paris, Ecole Nationale des Beaux-Arts. *Exposition des œuvres de Meissonier organisée par sa veuve.* May 1893.
1893, Paris, Galerie Georges Petit
Paris, Galerie Georges Petit. *Exposition posthume de l'œuvre de Meissonier.* March 1893. Preface by A. Dumas.
1893, Paris, Palais de l'Industrie
Paris, Union Centrale des Arts Décoratifs, Palais de l'Industrie. *Exposition des œuvres de Claudius Popelin.* 1893.
1894, New York
New York, Durand-Ruel Galleries. *Paintings, Pastels, Decorations by Puvis de Chavannes.* 1894.
1894, Paris, Ecole des Beaux-Arts
Paris, Ecole des Beaux-Arts. *Exposition des œuvres originales et inédits de J.-B. Carpeaux.* May 20–28, 1894.
1896, Brussels
Brussels. "A la Toison d'or," Maison D'Art. *Exposition des œuvres originales et inédits de J.-B. Carpeaux.* June 1896.
1898, Paris, Ecole des Beaux-Arts
Paris, Ecole Nationale des Beaux-Arts. *Exposition des œuvres de Louis Français.* 1898.
1898, Paris, Nouveau Cirque
Paris, Nouveau Cirque, 251, rue Saint-Honoré. *A. Falguière.* 1898. Preface by Y. Rambossan.
1899, Paris, Galerie Georges Petit
Paris, Galerie Georges Petit. *Tableaux par Besnard, Cazin, etc.* 1899.
1899–1900, Galliéra
Paris, Musée Galliéra. *Les Dessins de Puvis de Chavannes.* 1899–1900.
1900, Paris, Exposition Universelle Centennale
Paris, Champ de Mars, etc. *Exposition Internationale Universelle de 1900 à Paris. Exposition centennale de l'art français de 1800 à 1889.* 1900.
1901, Berlin
Berlin. *Dritte Kunstausstellung der Berliner Secession.* 1901.
1901, Paris, Petit Palais
Paris, Petit Palais. *Exposition de l'enfance.* 1901.
1902, Brussels
Brussels. *Salon (9e Exposition de la Société des Beaux-Arts).* 1902.
1902, Paris, Ecole des Beaux-Arts
Paris, Ecole Nationale des Beaux-Arts. *Alexandre Falguière.* February 8–March 8, 1902. Catalogue by L. Bénédite; preface by G. Larroumet.
1903, Paris, Galerie Bernheim-Jeune
Paris, Galerie Bernheim-Jeune. *Œuvres de l'Ecole impressionniste.* 1903.
1904, Saint Louis
Saint Louis, Forest Park. *Louisiana Purchase Exposition.* 1904.

1904, Weimar
Weimar. *Monet, Manet, Renoir und Cézanne.* 1904.
1905, Paris, Grand Palais
Paris, Grand Palais. *Salon d'Automne, rétrospective Ingres.* 1905.
1905, Paris, Salon d'Automne
Paris, Grand Palais. *Salon d'Automne.* October 18–November 25, 1905. Introduction by E. Faure.
1906, Bremen
Bremen. *Internationale Kunstausstellung.* 1906.
1906, Paris, Ecole des Beaux-Arts
Paris, Ecole Nationale des Beaux-Arts. *Exposition de l'œuvre de Fantin-Latour.* May–June 1906.
1906, Paris, Galerie Georges Petit
Paris, Galerie Georges Petit. *Un Peintre lapidaire: Gustave Moreau.* 1906. Preface by R. de Montesquiou.
1907, Antwerp, Brussels
Brussels, Musée Moderne, Société Royale des Beaux-Arts et l'Art Contemporain. *L'Œuvre de Alfred Stevens.* April–May 1907. Also shown at Antwerp, Musée des Beaux-Arts. May–June, 1907. Catalogue by P. Lambotte.
1908, Boston
Boston, Copley Society. *The French School of 1830; Loan Collection.* March 1908.
1912, Dresden
Dresden. *Grosse Kunstausstellung.* From May 1, 1912.
1913, New York, Durand-Ruel Galleries
New York, Durand-Ruel Galleries. *Loan Exhibition: Paintings by Edouard Manet.* November 29–December 13, 1913.
1913, São Paulo
São Paulo, Comité Franco-Amérique. *Exposition d'art français de São Paulo.* 1913.
1914, Paris, Galerie Bernheim-Jeune
Paris, Galerie Bernheim-Jeune. *Eva Gonzales.* 1914.
1914, Saint Louis
Saint Louis, City Art Museum. *An Exhibition of Paintings Owned in Saint Louis.* 1914.
1918, Valenciennes
Valenciennes, Musée des Beaux-Arts. *Kunstwerke aus dem besetzten Nordfrankreich ausgestellt im Museum zu Valenciennes.* 1918. Catalogue by Dr. T. Demmier, Dr. A. Feulner, and Dr. H. Burgo.
1919, New York
New York, The Metropolitain Museum of Art. *Works of Gustave Courbet.* 1919.
1920, Glasgow
Glasgow, Royal Glasgow Institute of the Fine Arts. *Annual Exhibition.* 1920.
1920, New York
New York, The Metropolitan Museum of Art. *Fiftieth Anniversary Exhibition.* May 8–September 30, 1920.
1921, New York
New York, The Metropolitan Museum of Art. *Impressionist and Post-Impressionist Paintings.* May 3–September 15, 1921.
1921, Paris, Chambre Syndicale de la Curiosité et des Beaux-Arts
Paris, Chambre Syndicale de la Curiosité et des Beaux-Arts, associations franco-américaine d'expositions de peintures et de sculptures. *Ingres.* May 8–June 5, 1921. Preface by H. Lapauze.
1922, Paris, Musée des Arts Décoratifs
Paris, Musée des Arts Décoratifs, Pavillon du Marsan. *Décor de la vie sous le Second Empire.* May 27–July 10, 1922.
1922, Stockholm, Copenhagen, Oslo
Stockholm. *Föreningen Fransk Konst. . . Edouard Manet.* 1922. Also shown at Copenhagen and Oslo.
1924, Poughkeepsie
Poughkeepsie, Vassar College Art Gallery. *Vassar Alumnae Collections.* 1924. No catalogue.
1925, Paris, Galerie Dru
Paris, Galerie Dru. *Delacroix [Watercolors and Drawings].* April–May 1925.
1925, Paris, Musée des Arts Décoratifs
Paris, Musée des Arts Décoratifs. *Cinquante Ans de la peinture française 1875–1925.* May 28–July 12, 1925.
1926, Berlin
Berlin, Preussische Akademie der Künste. *Frühjahrsausstellung.* May–June 1926.
1927, Marseilles, Galerie Detaille
Marseilles, Galerie Detaille. *Guigou.* 1927.
1927, Montpellier
Montpellier. *Exposition internationale de Montpellier: Rétrospective Bazille.* 1927.
1927, Paris, Galerie Dru
Paris, Galerie Dru. *Aquarelles et dessins de Daumier.* 1927.
1927, Paris, Grand Palais
Paris, Grand Palais. *Salon des artistes français: Exposition rétrospective Carpeaux.* From April 30, 1927.
1927, Paris, Luxembourg
Paris, Musée du Luxembourg. *Paul Guigou 1834–1871.* 1927.
1927, Valenciennes

Valenciennes, Palais des Beaux-Arts. *Centenaire de la naissance de Carpeaux, exposition rétrospective.* June 12–July 31, 1927.
1928, Berlin
  Berlin, Galerien Thannhauser. *Claude Monet, 1840–1926.* February–March 1928.
1928, Berlin, Galerie Matthiesen
  Berlin, Galerie Matthiesen. *Ausstellung Edouard Manet: 1832–1883, Gemälde, Pastelle, Aquarelle, Zeichnungen.* February 6–March 18, 1928. Forewords by E. Waldmann, M. Friedlaender, and M. Liebermann.
1928, Cairo
  Cairo. *Exposition d'art français.* 1928.
1928, Compiègne
  Compiègne, Musée National de Compiègne. *Louis-Philippe et Napoléon III.* 1928.
1928, Copenhagen, Stockholm, Oslo
  Copenhagen, Ny Carlsberg Glyptotek. *Udstillungen af Fransk Malerkunst fra den forste halvdel af det 19. aarhundrede.* 1928. Also shown in Stockholm and Oslo.
1928, Malmaison
  Malmaison, Musée National de Malmaison. *Exposition 1928 de Napoléon Iᵉʳ à Napoléon III; souvenirs de la famille impériale, conservés par l'Impératrice Eugénie dans sa résidence de Farnborough et provenant de sa succession.* 1928.
1928, Paris, Galerie Bernheim-Jeune
  Paris, Galerie Bernheim-Jeune. *Exposition d'œuvres de Manet, au profit des ''Amis du Luxembourg.''* April 14–May 4, 1928. Preface by R. Rey.
1928, Paris, Galerie Charpentier
  Paris, Galerie Charpentier. *La Jeunesse et les peintres.* June 1–30, 1928.
1928, Paris, Galerie Georges Petit
  Paris, Galerie Georges Petit. *Camille Pissarro.* 1928.
1928, Paris, Hôtel de Sagan
  Paris, Hôtel de Sagan, Jacques Seligmann et fils. *L'Exposition Winterhalter: Portraits de dames du Second Empire.* May 1928. Preface by A. Dayot.
1928, Paris, Musées Nationaux
  Paris, Musées Nationaux. *Exposition rétrospective au château de Maisons-Laffitte: Alfred Dedreux peintre de chevaux.* May 25–July 1, 1928. Catalogue by M. Reitlinger; preface by R. Régamey.
1929, Paris, Hôtel Charpentier
  Paris, Hôtel Charpentier. *Cent Ans de vie française.* 1929.
1930, Paris, Louvre
  Paris, Musée du Louvre. *Centenaire du Romantisme. Exposition E. Delacroix, peintures, aquarelles, pastels, dessins, gravures documents.* June–July 1930.
1930, Paris, Orangerie
  Paris, Orangerie. *Centenaire de la naissance de Camille Pissarro.* February–March 1930.
1931, Paris, Orangerie
  Paris, Orangerie. *Monet,* 1931.
1931, Vincennes
  Vincennes. *Exposition coloniale internationale.* 1931.
1932, London
  London. Royal Academy of Arts, Burlington House. *Exhibition of French Art: 1200–1900.* January 4–March 12, 1932. *See also Commemorative Catalogue 1932.*
1932, New York
  New York, Museum of French Art. *Fantin-Latour: Loan Exhibition.* January–February 1932.
1932, Paris, Galerie Marcel Bernheim
  Paris, Galerie Marcel Bernheim. *Eva Gonzalès, exposition rétrospective.* Catalogue by P. Bayle.
1932, Paris, Grand Palais
  Paris, Grand Palais. *Cinquantenaire de la fondation du Salon des artistes français, 1882–1932.* 1932. Catalogue unnumbered.
1932, Paris, Orangerie
  Paris, Orangerie. *Manet: 1832–1883.* June 16–October 9, 1932. Catalogue by C. Sterling; preface by P. Valéry; introduction by P. Jamot.
1932, Paris, Petit Palais
  Paris, Petit Palais. *Exposition rétrospective Gustave Doré (1832–1883).* 1932. Preface by C. Gronkowski.
1933, Northampton
  Northampton, Mass., Smith College Museum. *Edgar Degas.* 1933.
1933, Paris, Orangerie, ''Chassériau''
  Paris, Orangerie. *Exposition Chassériau, 1819–1856.* 1933. Catalogue by C. Sterling; preface by J.-L. Vaudoyer.
1933, Paris, Orangerie, ''Delacroix''
  Paris, Orangerie. *Voyage de Delacroix au Maroc, 1832, et exposition rétrospective du peintre orientaliste M. Auguste.* 1933.
1933, Paris, Orangerie, ''Renoir''
  Paris, Orangerie. *Exposition Renoir, 1841–1919.* 1933. Preface by P. Jamot. 2 vols.
1933, Philadelphia
  Philadelphia, Pennsylvania Museum of Art. *Manet and Renoir.* November 29, 1933–January 1, 1934. Catalogue in

*Pennsylvania [Philadelphia] Museum of Art Bulletin,* vol. XXIX (December 1933), pp. 17–20. Catalogue unnumbered.
1934, London
  London, Reid & Lefevre Galleries. *Fantin-Latour.* November 1934.
1934, Paris, Galerie Jacques Seligmann
  Paris, Fondation de la Maison de Santé du gardien de la paix, Galerie Jacques Seligmann. *Portraits par Ingres et ses élèves.* 1934. Catalogue by C. Sterling; preface by P. Jamot.
1934, Paris, Muséum d'Histoire Naturelle
  Paris, Muséum d'Histoire Naturelle. *Art animalier ancien.* 1934.
1934, Paris, Orangerie
  Paris, Orangerie. *Daumier: Peintures, aquarelles, dessins.* 1934. Catalogue by C. Sterling; preface by A. de Monzie; introduction by G. Roger-Marx.
1934, Paris, Salomon de Rothschild
  Paris, Fondation Salomon de Rothschild. *Un Siècle de l'art lyonnais de la soierie. Centenaire de Jacquard 1834–1934.* June 13–30, 1934.
1934, Tours
  Tours, Hôtel de Ville. *La Céramique tourangelle du XVIIIᵉ au XXᵉ siècle.* May 5–13, 1934.
1935, Brussels
  Brussels, Exposition Universelle et Internationale. *Cinq Siècles d'art.* May 24–October 13, 1935.
1935, Kansas City
  Kansas City, Mo., The William Rockhill Nelson Gallery of Art. *One Hundred Years of French Painting.* 1935.
1935, Paris, Orangerie
  Paris, Orangerie. *Souvenirs du Prince Impérial.* 1935.
1935, Rochester
  Rochester, N.Y., University of Rochester. *French Exhibition.* March 1935.
1936, Antibes
  Antibes, Musée Grimaldi. *Le Portrait d'Antibes.* 1936.
1936, London
  London, Anglo-French Art and Travel Society, New Burlington Galleries. *Exhibition of Masters of French Nineteenth-Century Painting.* October 1–31, 1936.
1936, London, ''Winterhalter''
  London, War Service Legion. *Winterhalter.* 1936.
1936, Lyons
  Lyons, Palais Saint Pierre. *Corot.* 1936.
1936, Paris, Musée des Arts Décoratifs
  Paris, Musée des Arts Décoratifs. *Exposition internationale de la photographie contemporain, et section rétrospective, 1839–1900.* 1936.
1936, Paris, Orangerie
  Paris, Orangerie. *Corot.* 1936.
1936, Paris, Petit Palais
  Paris, Petit Palais. *Gros, ses amis, ses élèves.* 1936.
1936, Philadelphia
  Philadelphia, The Pennsylvania Museum of Art. *Degas, 1834–1917.* November 7–December 7, 1936. Prefatory note by P.J. Sachs; introduction by A. Mongan.
1937, Geneva
  Geneva, Musée d'Art et d'Histoire. *Le Paysage français avant les impressionnistes.* 1937.
1937, Lyons
  Lyons, Musée de Lyon. *Puvis de Chavannes et de la peinture lyonnaise du XIXᵉ siècle.* 1937.
1937, New York
  New York, Wildenstein & Co. *Edouard Manet 1832–1883.* March 19–April 17, 1937. Preface by P. Jamot.
1937, Paris, Musée des Arts Décoratifs
  Paris, Musée des Arts Décoratifs. *Un Peintre de la vie au XIXᵉ siècle, Constantin Guys (1802–1892).* January–February 1937.
1937, Paris, Palais National des Arts
  Paris, Palais National des Arts. *Les Chefs-d'œuvre de l'art français.* June–October 1937.
1937, Philadelphia
  Philadelphia, Pennsylvania Museum of Art. *Daumier 1808–1879.* November–December 12, 1937. Introduction by C. Roger-Marx; technical notes by H. Marceau and D. Rosen; catalogue by E. Van Hook.
1937, Sceaux
  Sceaux, Musées de l'Ile de France. *Les Environs de Paris Autrefois.* 1937.
1937, Warsaw, Prague
  Warsaw, Muzeum Narodowe. *Exposition de la peinture française de Manet à nos jours.* 1937. Also shown in Prague.
1938, Lyons
  Lyons. *Salon du Sud-Est, d'Ingres à Cézanne.* 1938.
1938, Toronto
  Toronto, Art Gallery of Toronto. *Paintings of Woman from the Fifteenth to Twentieth Century.* October 14–November 14, 1938.
1939, Belgrade
  Belgrade, Musée du Prince Paul. *La Peinture française au XIXᵉ*

*siècle.* 1939.
1939, New York
  New York, New York World's Fair, French Pavilion. *Five Centuries of History Mirrored in Five Centuries of French Art.* 1939.
1939, Paris, Musée Galliéra
  Paris, Musée Galliéra. *La Marionnette en France et à l'étranger.* June–October 1939.
1939, Paris, Orangerie
  Paris, Orangerie. *Les Chefs-d'œuvre du Musée de Montpellier.* March–April 1939. Also shown at Bern, Kunsthalle. Catalogue by M.A. Faré; preface by P. Valéry.
1939, San Francisco
  San Francisco, Golden Gate International Exposition. *Masterworks of Five Centuries.* 1939. Foreword by W. Heil.
1939–40, San Francisco
  San Francisco, California Palace of the Legion of Honor and M.H. de Young Memorial Museum. *Seven Centuries of Painting; A Loan Exhibition of Old and Modern Masters.* December 29, 1939–January 28, 1940.
1939–41, Buenos Aires, etc.
  Buenos Aires, Museo Nacional de Bellas Artes. *Exhibition of French Painting from David to the Present.* 1939–41. Also shown at Montevideo; Rio de Janeiro; San Francisco, The M.H. De Young Museum; Chicago, Art Institute of Chicago; New York, The Metropolitan Museum of Art.
1940, New York
  New York, Bignou Gallery. *French Painters of the Romantic Period.* November 1940.
1940, New York, World's Fair
  Nex York, World's Fair. *Masterpieces of Art.* 1940.
1941, Boston
  Boston, Museum of Fine Arts. *Portraits through Forty-Five Centuries.* February 19–April 6, 1941.
1941, Montpellier
  Montpellier, Musée Fabre. *Centenaire de la naissance de F. Bazille.* 1941.
1941, New York
  New York, Duveen Galleries. *Renoir, 1841–1941, Centennial Loan Exhibition for the Benefit of the Free French Relief Committee.* November 8–December 6, 1941. Foreword by A.M. Frankfurter; essay by H.B. Wehle.
1942, London
  London, National Gallery. *Nineteenth-Century French Paintings.* 1942.
1942, San Francisco
  San Francisco, California Palace of the Legion of Honor. *Vanity Fair: An Exhibition of Styles in Women's Headdress and Adornment through the Ages.* June 16–July 16, 1942.
1943, New York
  New York, Wildenstein & Co. Inc. *A Loan Exhibition of Fashion in Headdress, 1450-1943, for the Benefit of the New York Infirmary for Women and Children.* April 27–May 27, 1943.
1945, Boston
  Boston, Museum of Fine Arts. *A Thousand Years of Landscape East and West.* October 24–December 9, 1945.
1945, New York
  New York, Knoedler Gallery. *United States Naval Academy Centennial Exhibition.* September 24–October 13, 1945.
1945, Paris, Louvre
  Paris, Musée National du Louvre. *Exposition des chefs-d'œuvre de la région.* 1945.
1946–47, New York
  New York, Paul Rosenberg and Co. *Loan Exhibition: Masterpieces by Manet, for the Benefit of American Aid to France, Inc.* December 26, 1946–January 11, 1947.
1947, Paris, Musée des Colonies
  Paris, Musée des Colonies. *Histoire de l'Exotisme.* 1947.
1948, London, Arts Council of Great Britain
  London, Arts Council of Great Britain. *The Artist and the Countryside.* 1948.
1948, New York
  New York, Paul Rosenberg & Co. *Loan Exhibition of 21 Masterpieces by 7 Great Masters for the Benefit of the Public Education Association.* November 15–December 18, 1948.
1948, New York, ''Manet''
  New York, Wildenstein & Co., Inc. *Loan Exhibition of Manet for the Benefit of the New York Infirmary.* February 26–April 3, 1948. By G. Wildenstein.
1948–49, New York
  New York, Wildenstein & Co., Inc. *A Loan Exhibition of Gustave Courbet.* December 1948–January 1949.
1949, Arenenberg
  Arenenberg. *Napoléon III.* 1949.
1949, Fort Worth
  Fort Worth, Fort Worth Art Association. *Centennial Art Exhibition.* 1949.
1949, Limoges
  Limoges, Musée Municipal de Limoges. *Porcelaine de Limoges.* 1949.
1949, New York

New York, Wildenstein & Co., Inc. *A Loan Exhibition of Degas for the Benefit of the New York Infirmary.* April 7–May 14, 1949.

1949–50, London
London, The Royal Academy of Arts. *Landscape in French Art.* 1949–50.

1950, New York, Wildenstein, "Bazille"
New York, Wildenstein & Co., Inc. *Bazille.* 1950. Catalogue by J. Claparède and G. Sarraute.

1950, New York, Wildenstein, "Renoir"
New York, Wildenstein & Co. *A Loan Exhibition of Renoir for the Benefit of the New York Infirmary.* March 23–April 29, 1950. Catalogue by D. Wildenstein.

1950, Paris, Galerie Wildenstein
Paris, Galerie Wildenstein. *Bazille, Benefit Organized for the Montpellier Museum.* June–July 1950. Introduction by D. Wildenstein; essays by J. Claparède and G. Sarraute.

1950, Vienna
Vienna, Graphische Sammlung Albertina. *Meisterwerke aus Frankreichs Museen. Zeichnungen französischer Künstler vom ausgang des mittelalters bis Cezanne.* 1950.

1951, Birmingham
Birmingham, Al., Birmingham Museum of Art. *Catalogue of the Opening Exhibition.* April 8–June 3, 1951. Introduction by R. Foster; catalogue by H.B. Howard.

1951, Paris, Atelier de Delacroix
Paris, Atelier d'Eugène Delacroix, Atelier de Delacroix. *Delacroix et l'orientalisme de son temps.* From May 11, 1951.

1951, Paris, Orangerie
Paris, Orangerie. *Impressionnistes et romantiques français dans les musées allemands.* 1951. Catalogue by D. Roskamp; introduction by C.G. Heise.

1951–52, Paris, Bibliothèque Nationale
Paris, Bibliothèque Nationale. *Exposition du livre français.* 1951–52.

1952, Minneapolis
Minneapolis, The Minneapolis Institute of Arts. *Great Portraits by Famous Painters.* November 13–December 21, 1952.

1952, Paris, Atelier de Delacroix
Paris, Atelier de Delacroix. *Delacroix et les maîtres de la couleur.* From May 17, 1952.

1952, Paris, Bibliothèque Nationale
Paris, Bibliothèque Nationale. *Emile Zola.* 1952.

1952, Paris, Bibliothèque Nationale, "Hugo"
Paris, Bibliothèque Nationale. *Victor Hugo: Exposition organisée pour commémorer le cent-cinquantième anniversaire de sa naissance.* 1952. Introduction and catalogue by J. Prinet; preface by J. Cain.

1952, Paris, Orangerie
Paris, Orangerie. *Hommage à Manet.* 1952. No catalogue.

1952, Zurich, Paris, The Hague
Zurich, Kunsthaus. *Claude Monet.* May 10–June 15, 1952. Also shown at Paris, Galerie des Beaux-Arts, June 19–July 17, 1952; The Hague, Gemeente-museum, July 24–September 22, 1952. Separate catalogues: Zurich, foreword by G. Besson and R. Wehrli; Paris, foreword by D. Wildenstein; The Hague, foreword by G. Besson.

1952–53, Paris, Musée Carnavalet
Paris, Musée Carnavalet. *Chefs-d'œuvre des collections parisiennes.* 1952–53.

1953, Bordeaux
Bordeaux, Galerie des Beaux-Arts. *John-Lewis Brown.* 1953.

1953, Compiègne
Compiègne, Musée National de Compiègne. *Le Temps des crinolines.* July–September 1953. Catalogue by M. Terrier.

1953, London
London, Marlborough Fine Art Limited. *Gustave Courbet 1819–1877.* May–June 1953.

1953, New Orleans
New Orleans, Isaac Delgado Museum of Art. *Masterpieces of French Painting through Five Centuries, 1400–1900.* 1953.

1953, Paris, Castiglione
Paris, 10, rue de Castiglione. *La Chambre de Castiglione reconstituée.* 1953.

1953, Peterborough
Peterborough, Arts Council of Great Britain. *Exhibition of French Paintings.* 1953.

1953–54, Paris, Bibliothèque Nationale
Paris, Bibliothèque Nationale. *Prosper Mérimée.* 1953–54.

1954, Bourg-en-Bresse
Bourg-en-Bresse, Musée de l'Ain. *Le Centenaire du Musée.* 1954.

1954, Detroit
Detroit, The Detroit Institute of Arts. *Two Sides of the Medal: French Painting from Gérôme to Gauguin.* September 28–November 6, 1954. Foreword by E.P. Richardson; introduction by P.L. Grigaut.

1954, Fort Worth
Fort Worth, Fort Worth Art Center. *Inaugural Exhibition.* October 8–31, 1954.

1954, Lyons
Lyons, Palais Saint-Pierre. *Courbet.* 1954.

1954, New York
New York, Knoedler & Co. *A Collector's Taste.* January 12–30, 1954.

1954, New York, Oberlin
New York, Knoedler & Co. *Forty Paintings and Drawings from the Oberlin College Collection (Paintings and Drawings from Five Centuries).* February 2–21, 1954.

1954, Santa Barbara, San Francisco, Kansas City
Santa Barbara, The Santa Barbara Museum of Art. *The Horse in Art: Painting 17th to 20th Century.* July–August 1954. Also shown at San Francisco, California Palace of the Legion of Honor, August–September 1954; Kansas City, William Rockhill Nelson Gallery of Art, October–November 1954. Introduction by A. Story.

1954, Venice
Venice, XXVII Biennale. *Courbet.* 1954.

1954–55, Tokyo
Tokyo. *Exhibition of French Painting.* 1954–55.

1955, Cambridge, Mass.
Cambridge, Mass., Harvard University, Fogg Art Museum. *Delacroix in the New England Collections.* 1955.

1955, Exeter
Exeter, University Art Gallery. *Contemporary Paintings from Southampton.* 1955.

1955, Guernsey
Guernsey, Hauteville House. *Victor Hugo en exil.* 1955. Catalogue by J. Sergent.

1955, Paris, Bibliothèque Nationale
Paris, Bibliothèque Nationale. *Gérard de Nerval.* 1955.

1955, Paris, Petit Palais
Paris, Petit Palais. *G. Courbet.* 1955. Catalogue by S. Kahn, M. Ecalle, and L. Chamson; preface by A. Chamson.

1955, Rome, Florence
Rome, Palazzo delle Esposizioni. *Capolavori dell'Ottocento francese.* 1955. Also shown in Florence.

1955–56, Paris, Petit Palais
Paris, Petit Palais. *J.-B. Carpeaux, 1827–1875.* 1955–56. Preface by A. Chamson.

1956, Brooklyn
Brooklyn, Museum of Art. *Religious Painting. 15th–19th Century.* October 2–November 13, 1956.

1956, Cleveland
Cleveland, Cleveland Museum of Art. *The Venetian Tradition.* 1964.

1956, Hazebrouck
Hazebrouck. *Peintures françaises du 19ᵉ siècle.* 1956.

1956, Musées de France
Musées de France. *Le Paysage français de Poussin aux Impressionnistes.* 1956.

1956, New Haven
New Haven, Yale University Art Gallery. *Pictures Collected by Yale Alumni.* May 8–June 18, 1956.

1956, New York
New York, Rosenberg & Co. *Loan Exhibition of Paintings by Gustave Courbet (1819–1877).* January 16–February 11, 1956.

1956, Warsaw, Moscow, Leningrad
Warsaw, Muzeum Narodowe. *Peinture française de David à Cézanne.* 1956. Also shown in Moscow and Leningrad.

1956–57, Paris, Louvre
Paris, Musée du Louvre. *Barye, sculptures, peintures, aquarelles des collections publiques françaises.* October 1956–February 1957. Essays by G. Hubert, M. Sérullaz, and J. Bouchot-Saupique.

1956–57, Providence
Providence, Rhode Island School of Design. *Courbet.* 1956–57.

1957, Dijon
Dijon, Musée des Beaux-Arts, Palais des Etats de Bourgogne. *Alphonse Legros, peintre et graveur, 1837–1911.* 1957. Introduction by M. Geiger.

1957, Fontainebleau
Fontainebleau. *100 Ans de paysage français de Fragonard à Courbet.* 1957.

1957, London
London, Arts Council of Great Britain. *Ingres: Drawings from the Musée Ingres.* 1957. Also shown at Montauban, Manchester, and Leeds.

1957, Paris, Louvre
Paris, Musée du Louvre, Cabinet des Dessins. *Théodore Chassériau, 1819–1856, dessins.* Catalogue by M. Sérullaz and R. Bacou; preface by J. Bouchat-Saupique.

1957, Paris, Musée Jacquemart-André
Paris, Musée Jacquemart-André. *Le Second Empire.* 1957.

1957, Paris, Petit Palais
Paris, Petit Palais. *Un Siècle d'art français, 1850–1950.* 1957.

1957, Saint Louis, Minneapolis
Saint Louis, City Art Museum of Saint Louis. *Claude Monet, Loan Exhibition.* September 25–October 22, 1957. Also shown at Minneapolis, The Minneapolis Institute of Arts, November 1–December 1, 1957. Foreword by C. Nagel, W.N. Eisendrath, Jr., and R.C. Davis; catalogue by W.C. Seitz.

1957–58, Paris, Musée Rodin
Paris, Musée Rodin. *Rodin, ses collaborateurs et ses amis.* 1957–58. Preface by J. Cladel; catalogue by C. Goldscheider.

1958, Baltimore
Baltimore, The Walters Art Gallery. *Seven Steps to Impressionism.* January 25–March 2, 1958.

1958, Munich
Munich, Haus der Kunst. *München, 1869–1958. Aufbruch zur modernen Kunst.* June 21–October 5, 1958. Introduction by K. Martin; catalogue by S. Wichmann.

1958, Palm Beach
Palm Beach, Fla., Society of the Four Arts. *Paintings by Claude Monet.* January 3–February 2, 1958.

1958, Paris, Bibliothèque Nationale
Paris, Bibliothèque Nationale. *Daumier.* 1958.

1959, Florence
Florence, Palazzo Strozzi. *La Princesse Mathilde et son temps.* From April 27, 1959.

1959, London
London, Tate Gallery and the Arts Gallery. *The Romantic Movement: Fifth Exhibition to Celebrate the 10th Anniversary of the Council of Europe.* July 10–September 27, 1959.

1959, Marseilles
Marseilles, Musée Cantini. *Paul Guigou.* November 23–December 31, 1959. Catalogue by J. Latour and M. J.-A. Cartier; preface by G. Bazin.

1959, Milan
Milan, Palazzo Reale. *Celebrazioni centenarie di 1859.* 1959.

1959, Montpellier
Montpellier, Musée Fabre. *Frédéric Bazille.* October 13–31, 1959.

1959, Paris, Galerie Daber
Paris, Galerie Daber. *Eva Gonzales.* 1959.

1959, Paris, Musée Jacquemart-André
Paris, Musée Jacquemart-André. *La Vie parisienne au temps de Guys, Nadar, Worth....* November 13–December 31, 1959.

1959, St. Germain en Laye
St. Germain en Laye, Galerie Doves. *Eva Gonzales.* 1959. Catalogue by C. Roger-Marx.

1959–60, Philadelphia, Boston
Philadelphia, Philadelphia Museum of Art. *Gustave Courbet 1819–1877.* December 17, 1959–February 14, 1960. Also shown at Boston, Museum of Fine Arts, February 26–April 14, 1960. Foreword by H. Clifford; preface by R. Huyghe; catalogue by G. Delestre.

1960, Copenhagen
Copenhagen, Ny Carlsberg Glyptotek. *Portraits français de Largillière à Manet.* October 15–November 15, 1960.

1960, Dayton
Dayton, Oh., Dayton Art Institute. *French Paintings 1789–1929 from the Collection of Walter P. Chrysler, Jr.* March 25–May 22, 1960.

1960, New York
New York, Wildenstein & Co., Inc. *Degas: Loan Exhibition for the Benefit of the Citizens' Committee for Children of New York, Inc.* April 7–May 7, 1960.

1960, Nice
Nice. *Centenaire de la réunion du Comte de Nice à la France; le Second Empire.* 1960.

1960, Paris, Galerie Durand-Ruel
Paris, Galerie Durand-Ruel. *Edgar Degas 1834–1917.* June 9–October 1, 1960.

1960, Paris, Louvre
Paris, Musée du Louvre, Cabinet des Dessins. *Dessins de Jean-François Millet.* 1960.

1961, Cambridge, Mass.
Cambridge, Mass., Fogg Art Museum, Harvard University. *Ingres and Degas: Two Classic Draftsmen.* April 24–May 20, 1961.

1961, Paris, Louvre
Paris, Musée du Louvre. *Gustave Moreau.* 1961. Catalogue by R. Von Holten.

1961, Vichy
Vichy. *D'Ingres à Renoir, la vie artistique sous le Second Empire.* June–October 1961.

1962, Besançon
Besançon, Ecole d'Horlogerie. *Centenaire de l'Ecole d'Horlogerie.* 1962. No catalogue.

1962, Le Touquet
Le Touquet. *Les Peintres de la Côte d'Opale.* 1962. No catalogue.

1962, London
Kenwood, London County Council. *An American University Collection.* May–October 1962.

1962, London, Royal Academy
London, Royal Academy of Arts. *Primitives to Picasso: An Exhibition from Municipal and University Collections in Great Brit-*

*ain.* Winter 1962.

1962, London, Victoria and Albert Museum
London, Victoria and Albert Museum. *The International Exhibition of 1862.* 1962.

1962, Paris, Louvre
Paris, Musée du Louvre. *Figures de Corot.* June–September 1972. By G. Bazin.

1962, Paris, Louvre, Cabinet des Dessins
Paris, Musée du Louvre, Cabinet des Dessins. *Dessins de Corot (1796–1875).* 1962. Introduction by J. Bouchot-Saupique; catalogue by M. Servot.

1962, Paris, Louvre, "Joaillerie"
1962, Paris, Musée du Louvre. *Dix Siècles de joaillerie française.* May 3–June 3, 1962.

1962, Versailles
Versailles, Musée National du Château de Versailles. *La Comédie française 1680–1962.* From April 27, 1962.

1962–63, Paris, Louvre
Paris, Musée du Louvre. *Rodin inconnu.* December 1962–January, 1963. Introduction by C. Goldscheider.

1962–63, San Francisco, etc.
San Francisco, California Palace of the Legion of Honor. *Barbizon Revisited.* September 27–November 4, 1962. Also shown at Toledo, Toledo Museum of Art, November 20–December 27, 1962; Cleveland, Cleveland Museum of Art, January 15–February 24, 1963; Boston, Museum of Fine Arts, March 14–April 28, 1963. Essay and catalogue by R.L. Herbert.

1963, Cleveland
Cleveland, The Cleveland Museum of Art. *Style, Truth, and the Portrait.* October 1–November 10, 1963. Catalogue by R.G. Saisselin.

1963, Grasse
Grasse, Musée Fragonard. *Charles Nègre, artiste, peintre, photographe, 1820–1880.* 1963. No catalogue.

1963, Nancy
Nancy, Musée des Beaux-Arts. *Hommage à Roger Marx 1859–1913; de Daumier à Rouault.* November–December 1963.

1963, Oberlin
Oberlin, Oh., Oberlin College, Allen Memorial Art Museum. *Youthful Works by Great Artists.* March 10–30, 1963. Catalogue in *Allen Memorial Art Museum Bulletin,* vol. XX, no. 3 (spring 1963), pp. 169–207.

1963, Paris, Louvre
Paris, Musée du Louvre. *Centenaire d'Eugène Delacroix 1798–1863.* May–September 1963. Introduction by M. Sérullaz. *See also* Sérullaz, 1963.

1963, Philadelphia
Philadelphia, Philadelphia Museum of Art. *A World of Flowers: Paintings and Prints.* May 2–June 9, 1963. Catalogue in *Philadelphia Museum of Art Bulletin,* vol. LVIII, no. 277 (spring 1963).

1964, Carcassonne
Carcassonne, Château Comtal de Carcassonne. *Viollet-le-Duc.* 1964.

1964, Cherbourg
Cherbourg, Musée Thomas Henry. *Cent Cinquantième anniversaire de la naissance de Jean-François Millet, 1814–1875.* July–September 1964. Catalogue by L. Lepoittevin.

1964, Detroit
Detroit, Cobel Hall. *French Masterworks.* 1964. No catalogue.

1964, Edinburgh
Edinburgh, The Arts Council. *Delacroix.* 1964.

1964, Houston
Houston, University of Saint Thomas. *Out of This World.* March 17–April 30, 1964.

1964, Paris, Louvre
Paris, Musée du Louvre, Cabinet des Dessins. *Dessins de Sculpteurs de Pajou à Rodin.* 1964. Catalogue by L. Duclaux (drawings), M. Beaulieu and F. Baron (sculpture).

1964, Paris, Musée des Arts Décoratifs
Paris, Musée des Arts Décoratifs. *Christofle cent ans d'orfèvrerie d'avant garde.* June–October 1964.

1964, Reims
Reims, Musée des Beaux-Arts. *Auguste Ravier: 1814–1895.* October 17–December 13, 1964.

1964, Rennes
Rennes, Musée des Beaux-Arts. *Eugène Boudin en Bretagne.* 1964. Catalogue by R. Schmidt.

1964, Saint Louis
Saint Louis, Mo. City Art Museum. *200 Years of American Painting.* April 1–May 31, 1964.

1964–65, Munich
Munich, Haus der Kunst. *Französische Malerei des 19. Jahrhunderts von David bis Cézanne.* October 7, 1964–January 6, 1965. Introduction by G. Bazin.

1964–65, Tokyo, Fukuoka, Kyoto
Tokyo. *Exhibition of French Art.* 1964–65. Also shown at Fukuoka and Kyoto.

1965, Lisbon

Lisbon, Fondation Gulbenkian. *Un Século de pintura francesa: 1850–1950.* 1965.

1965, New York
New York, Wildenstein & Co., Inc. *Loan Exhibition, C. Pissarro.* March 25–May 1, 1965. Introduction by J. Rewald.

1965, Paris, Bibliothèque Nationale
Paris, Bibliothèque Nationale. *Nadar.* 1965.

1965, Paris, Hôtel de Béthune Sully
Paris, Hôtel de Béthune Sully. *Eugène Viollet-le-Duc, 1814–1879.* Spring 1965. Introduction by P.M. Auzas.

1965, Paris, Louvre
Paris, Musée du Louvre, Cabinet des Dessins. *Boudin, aquarelles et pastels.* 1965.

1965, Paris, Musée des Arts Décoratifs
Paris, Musée des Arts Décoratifs. *Les Trésors des églises de France.* 1965. Introduction by J. Taralon.

1965, Paris, Musée des Arts Décoratifs, "Photographie"
Paris, Musée des Arts Décoratifs. *Un Siècle de photographie de Niépce à Man Ray.* 1965. Introduction by A. Jammes.

1965, Paris, Petit Palais
Paris, Petit Palais. *Trois Millénaires d'art et de marine.* March 4–May 2, 1965.

1965, Rome
Rome, Palazzo Venezia. *Mostra Nazionale Dantesca.* 1965.

1965–66, Essen
Essen, Museum Folkwang. *Die Kalotypie in Frankreich.* 1965–66. Catalogue by O. Steinert and A. Jammes.

1965–66, New York
New York, Finch College Museum of Art. *French Landscape Painters from Four Centuries.* October 20, 1965–January 9, 1966. Catalogue and introduction by R.L. Manning.

1966, Minneapolis
Minneapolis, The Minneapolis Institute of Arts. *Treasures from the Allen Memorial Art Museum.* July 21–September 11, 1966.

1966, Munich
Munich, Staatmuseum. *Charles Nègre, 1820–1880.* September–December 1966.

1966, Paris, Mobilier National
Paris, Mobilier National. *Les Gobelins, trois siècles de tapisserie.* June–October 1966.

1966, South Hadley
South Hadley, Mass., Mount Holyoke College. *Linear Art in the Nineteenth Century.* 1966. No catalogue.

1966, Williamstown
Williamstown, Mass., Sterling and Francine Clark Art Institute. *Exhibit Thirty-Four: French Drawings of the 19th Century.* From August 28, 1966.

1966–67, Philadelphia, Chicago
Philadelphia, Philadelphia Museum of Art. *Edouard Manet 1832–1883.* November 3–December 11, 1966. Also shown at Chicago, The Art Institute of Chicago, January 13–February 19, 1967. Catalogue by A.C. Hanson.

1967, Montauban
Montauban, Musée Ingres. *Ingres et son temps: Exposition organisée pour le centenaire de la mort d'Ingres.* June 24–September 15, 1967. Catalogue by D. Ternois and J. Lacambre.

1967, Montreal
Montreal, Expo 67, International Fine Arts Exhibition (Exposition Internationale des Beaux-Arts). *Man and His World (Terre des Hommes).* April 28–October 27, 1967. Introduction by R. Elie.

1967, Paris, Académie des Beaux-Arts
Paris, Académie des Beaux-Arts. *Evocation de l'Académie de France à Rome à l'occasion de son troisième centenaire.* June–July 1967. Catalogue by A. Caubet and F. Avrilo.

1967, Paris, Hôtel de la Monnaie
Paris, Hôtel de la Monnaie. *La Médaille en France, de Ponscarme à la fin de la belle époque.* June–September 1967. Preface by P. Dehaye and M. Rheims; catalogue by Y. Goldenberg.

1967, Paris, Hôtel Meurice
Paris, Hôtel Meurice. *Hommage à Meissonier.* 1967.

1967, Paris, Musée des Arts Décoratifs
Paris, Musée des Arts Décoratifs. *Trois Siècles de papiers peints.* June 22–October 15, 1967.

1967–68, Nice
Nice, Palais de la Méditerranée. *Rodin et son temps.* December 1967–January 1968. Preface by C. Goldscheider.

1967–68, Paris, Louvre
Paris, Musée du Louvre (Galerie Mollien). *Théodore Rousseau 1812–1867.* November 29, 1967–February 12, 1968. Catalogue by M. Laclotte, H. Toussaint, and M.-T. de Forges.

1967–68, Paris, Orangerie
Paris, Orangerie. *Vingt Ans d'acquisitions au Musée du Louvre: 1947–1967.* December 16, 1967–March 1968.

1967–68, Paris, Petit Palais
Paris, Petit Palais. *Ingres.* October 27, 1967–January 29, 1968. Foreword by M. Laclotte; catalogue by L. Duclaux, J. Foucart, M. Sérullaz and D. Ternois.

1968, Baltimore
Baltimore, Baltimore Museum of Art. *From El Greco to Pollack: Early and Late Works by European and American Artists.* October 22–December 8, 1968.

1968, Berlin
Berlin, Akademie der Künste and Deutsche Gesellschaft für Bildenden Kunst. *Le Salon imaginaire.* October 6–November 24, 1968. Catalogue by P. Hahlbrock, H.E. Killy, and E. Roters.

1968, Bloomington
Bloomington, Indiana University Art Museum. *The Academic Tradition: An Exhibition of Nineteenth Century French Drawings.* June 19–August 11, 1968.

1968, Dijon
Dijon, Musée de Dijon. *Napoléon III et la Côte-d'Or.* 1968.

1968, Providence, Toronto
Providence, Rhode Island School of Design Museum of Art. *James Jacques Joseph Tissot, 1836–1902: A Retrospective Exhibition.* February 28–March 29, 1968. Also shown at Toronto, The Art Gallery of Toronto, April 6–May 5, 1968. Catalogue by H. Zerner, D.S. Brooke, and M. Wentworth.

1968–69, Paris, Petit Palais
Paris, Petit Palais. *Baudelaire.* November 23, 1968–March 17, 1969. Catalogue by A. Calvet et al.

1969, Ambérieu-en-Bugey
Ambérieu-en-Bugey, Château des Allymes. *Un Demi-Siècle de vie poétique à travers Gabriel-Vicaire.* 1969.

1969, Kyoto, Tokyo
Kyoto. *Exposition Delacroix.* 1969. Also shown at Tokyo.

1969, London
London, The Lefevre Gallery. *Claude Monet; The Early Years. [Exhibition] from British Collections in Aid of the Police Dependent's Trust.* May 8–June 7, 1969. By D. Sutton.

1969, Minneapolis
Minneapolis, The Minneapolis Institute of Arts. *The Past Rediscovered: French Painting 1800–1900.* July 3–September 7, 1969.

1969, Paris, Bibliothèque Nationale
Paris, Bibliothèque Nationale. *Berlioz.* 1969.

1969, Philadelphia
Philadelphia, Philadelphia Museum of Art. *French Primitive Photography.* November 17–December 28, 1969. Introduction by M. White; commentaries by A. Jammes and R. Sobieszek.

1969, Sarasota
Sarasota Fla., John and Mable Ringling Museum of Art. *Au Théâtre.* January 6–26, 1969. No catalogue.

1969–70, London, Florence, Paris
London, P. & D. Colnaghi & Co. Ltd. *Master Drawings from the National Gallery Collection [Ottawa].* July 3–31, 1969. Also shown at Florence, Uffizi, Gabinetto dei Disegni, September 15–October 26, 1969; Paris, Musée du Louvre, Cabinet des Dessins, November 15, 1969–February 2, 1970.

1969–70, Rome, Milan
Rome, Villa Medici. *Gustave Courbet 1819–1877.* Also shown at Milan, Palazzo Reale. 1969–70.

1970, Baltimore
Baltimore, The Walters Art Gallery. *Fortuny and His Circle.* 1970.

1970, College Park
College Park, University of Maryland Art Gallery. *Thomas Couture: Paintings and Drawings in American Collections.* February 5–March 15, 1970. Introduction by G. Levitine; essays by A. de Leiris and J. Van Nimmen; catalogue by J. Van Nimmen.

1970, La Rochelle
La Rochelle, Bibliothèque Municipale and Musée des Beaux-Arts. *Fromentin, le peintre et l'écrivain, 1820–1876.* 1970.

1970, London
London, Wildenstein & Co. Ltd. *Pictures from Southampton.* June 11–July 18, 1970. Catalogue by D. Sutton.

1970, New York
New York, Wildenstein & Co., Inc. *A. Loan Exhibition. One Hundred Years of Impressionism. A Tribute to Durand-Ruel: For the Benefit of the New York University Art Collection.* April 2–May 9, 1970.

1970, Paris, Galerie Daber
Paris, Galerie Daber. *Mon Cher Guigou.* May 28–June 27, 1970.

1970, Saint Louis
Saint Louis, Washington University. *Salon de Resserre.* 1970.

1970, Tokyo, Kyoto, Fukuoka
Tokyo, Seiby Department Store Gallery. *Jean-François Millet et ses amis; peintres de Barbizon.* August 15–September 30, 1970. Also shown at Kyoto, Municipal Museum of Kyoto; Fukuoka, November 12–December 6, 1970.

1970, Valenciennes
Valenciennes, Musée des Beaux-Arts. *Henri Harpignies, 1819–1916.* June 20–September 21, 1970.

457

1970–71, Leningrad, Moscow
Leningrad. *Peintures impressionnistes dans les musées français*. 1970–71. Also shown at Moscow. *See* 1971, Madrid.
1971, Bordeaux
Bordeaux, Musée d'Aquitaine. *2000 Ans d'histoire*. February 13–June 30, 1971.
1971, London
London, Wartski Gallery. *A Thousand Years of Enamel*. May 18–June 5, 1971.
1971, Louisville
Louisville, Ky., J.B. Speed Art Museum. *Nineteenth-Century French Sculpture: Monuments for the Middle Class*. November 2–December 5, 1971. Introduction by R. Mirolli; catalogue by J. Von Nimmen and R. Mirolli.
1971, Madrid
Madrid. *Los Impresionistas franceses*. 1971. *See* 1970–71, Leningrad, Moscow.
1971, New York, Philadelphia
New York, Columbia University, Wildenstein. *From Realism to Symbolism; Whistler and His World*. March 4–April 3, 1971. Also shown at Philadelphia, Philadelphia Museum of Art, April 15–May 23, 1971. Essays by A. Staley and T. Reff.
1971, Nottingham
Nottingham, University Art Gallery. *Alfred Sisley (1839–99) Impressionist Landscapes*. February 6–27, 1971.
1971, Paris, Hôtel de la Monnaie
Paris, Hôtel de la Monnaie. *Les Graveurs d'acier et la médaille de l'antiquité à nos jours*. June–October 1971.
1971, Rochester
Rochester, N.Y., International Museum of Photography, George Eastman House. *Figure in Landscape*. 1971. Catalogue by H.H. Jones III. Catalogue unnumbered.
1971, Vannes, Brest
Vannes, Palais des Arts. *Quelques Aspects du paysage français du XIXe siècle*. Tableaux du Musée du Louvre. 1971. Also shown at Brest.
1971–72, Nagoya, etc.
Nagoya. *Exposition des chefs-d'œuvre du Musée des Beaux-Arts de Bordeaux*. 1971–72. Also shown at Kamakura, Osaka, and Fukuoka.
1971–72, Villequier, Paris
Villequier, Musée Victor Hugo. *Dessins de Victor Hugo*. June–October 1971. Also shown at Paris, Maison de Victor Hugo, November 1971–January 1972. Catalogue by P. Georgel.
1972, Darmstadt
Darmstadt, Hessisches Landesmuseum. *Von Ingres bis Renoir. Meisterzeichnungen aus dem Louvre, Paris*. April 22–June 18, 1972. Foreword by M. Sérullaz.
1972, Limoges
Limoges, Musée Adrien-Dubouché. *L'Art de la poterie de 1880 à 1900*. 1972.
1972, Mortagne
Mortagne and Chartres. *Félix Bracquemond 1833–1914: Gravures, dessins, céramiques. Marie Bracquemond 1841–1916 : Tableaux*. May–September 1972. Catalogue by J.-P. Bouillon.
1972, Munich
Munich, Haus der Kunst. *World Cultures and Modern Art: The Encounter of 19th and 20th Century European Art and Music with Asia, Africa, Oceania, Afro- and Indo-America; Exhibition on the Occasion of the Games of the XXth Olympiad Munich 1972*. June 16–September 30, 1972.
1972, New York
New York, Wildenstein & Co., Inc. *Faces from the World of Impressionism and Post-Impressionism*. November 2–December 9, 1972.
1972, Paris, Grand Palais
Paris, Grand Palais. *Peintres de l'imaginaire. Symbolistes et surréalistes belges*. February 4–April 8, 1972.
1972, Paris, Louvre
Paris, Musée du Louvre, Cabinet des Dessins. *Dessins d'architecture du XVe au XIXe siècle dans les collections du Musée du Louvre*. March 20–June 5, 1972. Catalogue by G. Monnier.
1972, Saint-Omer
Saint-Omer, Musée de l'Hôtel Sandelin. *François-Nicolas Chifflart, 1825–1901*. September 16–November 6, 1972.
1972, Seoul
Seoul, Musée du Palais Duksoo. *Jean-François Millet et les peintres de la vie rurale en France au XIXe siècle*. 1972.
1972–73, Dayton, Minneapolis, Baltimore
Dayton, Oh., The Dayton Art Institute. *Jean-Léon Gérôme (1824–1904)*. November 10–December 30, 1972. Also shown at Minneapolis, The Minneapolis Institute of Arts, January 26–March 11, 1973; Baltimore, The Walters Art Gallery, April 6–May 20, 1973. Catalogue and introduction by G.M. Ackerman; essay by R. Ettinghausen.
1973, Besançon, Bourg-en-Bresse, Aix-les-Bains
Besançon. *Le Paysage dans la peinture française du XIXe siècle. Tableaux du Louvre*. 1973. Also shown at Bourg-en-Bresse and Aix-les-Bains.
1973, Boston

Boston, Museum of Fine Arts. *Impressionism: French and American*. June 18–October 14, 1973.
1973, Bourg-en-Bresse
Bourg-en-Bresse, Musée. *Antoine Chintreuil 1814–1873*. 1973.
1973, Brive
Brive, Musée Ernest Rupin. *Napoléon III, 1808–1873; Second Empire, 1852–1870*. May 12–July 12, 1973.
1973, Chicago
Chicago, The Art Institute of Chicago. *Paintings by Renoir*. February 3–April 1, 1973.
1973, New York, Shepherd Gallery
New York, Shepherd Gallery. *Western European Bronzes of the Nineteenth Century: A Survey*. 1973. Catalogue by R. Kashey and M.L.H. Reymert.
1973, Paris, Musée des Arts Décoratifs
Paris, Musée des Arts Décoratifs. *Equivoques: Peintures françaises du XIXe siècle*. March 9–May 14, 1973. Catalogue by O. Lépine.
1973, Paris, Petit Palais
Paris, Petit Palais. *Pompéi*. January–March 1973. Catalogue by G. Cerulli-Irelli et al.
1973, Saint-Omer
Saint-Omer, Musée de Saint-Omer. *L'Art de la céramique de 1880 à 1920*. 1973.
1973, San Francisco
San Francisco, The Fine Arts Museums of San Francisco: California Palace of the Legion of Honor. *Three Centuries of French Art: Selections from the Norton Simon, Inc., Museum of Art and the Norton Simon Foundation*. From May 3, 1973. Introduction by F.L. Graham.
1973, Strasbourg
Strasbourg, Musée des Beaux-Arts. *Jean-Jacques Henner–Henri Zuber*. 1973. Preface by V. Beyer.
1973, Turin
Turin, Musée Civico, Galleria Civica d'Arte Moderna. *Combattimento per un'immagine. Fotografi e pittori*. March–April 1973. Catalogue by D. Palazzoli and L. Carluccio. Catalogue unnumbered.
1973–74, Paris, Légion d'Honneur
Paris, Musée National de la Légion d'Honneur. *Napoléon III raconté par les décorations*. 1973–74.
1973–74, Paris, Louvre
Paris, Musée du Louvre. *Copies, répliques, pastiches*. (Dossier du Département des Peintures, no. 3). 1973–74.
1974, Binghamton, New York, Williamstown
Binghamton, State University of New York at Binghamton. *Strictly Academic: Life Drawing in the Nineteenth Century*. March 30–April 24, 1974. Also shown at New York, Finch College Museum of Art, May 8–June 16, 1974; Williamstown, Sterling and Francine Clark Art Institute, July 2–September 1, 1974.
1974, Castres
Castres, Musée Goya. *Mariano Fortuny et ses amis français*. June 22–September 1974.
1974, Hempstead
Hempstead, N.Y., Hofstra University, The Emily Lowe Gallery. *Art Pompier: Anti-Impressionism: 19th Century French Salon Painting*. October 22–December 15, 1974.
1974, London
London, Royal Academy of Arts, The Diploma Galleries. *Impressionism: Its Masters, Its Precursors, and Its Influence in Britain*. February 9–April 28, 1974. Introduction by J. House.
1974, London, Victoria and Albert Museum
London, Victoria and Albert Museum. *Drawings by Victor Hugo*. 1974. Catalogue by P. Georgel.
1974, Los Angeles
Los Angeles, Los Angeles County Museum of Art. *Gustave Moreau*. July 23–September 1, 1974. Catalogue by J. Kaplan.
1974, Los Angeles, Riverside
Los Angeles, Los Angeles County Museum of Art. *The Impressionists and the Salon (1874–1886) Honoring the Centennial of the First Impressionist Exhibition: California Collections*. April 16–May 12, 1974. Also shown at Riverside, University of California, May 20–June 20, 1974. Introduction by K.H. Mead.
1974, Montrouge
Montrouge, Hôtel de Ville. *Amaury-Duval, 1808–1885*. May 2–June 3, 1974. Preface by B. Foucart; catalogue by V. Noël-Bouton.
1974, Nantes
Nantes, Musée des Beaux-Arts. *Sept Ans d'enrichissements*. May 10–30, 1974.
1974, Paris, Bibliothèque Nationale
Paris, Bibliothèque Nationale. *Ernest Renan*. 1974.
1974, Paris, Bibliothèque Nationale, "Bracquemond"
Paris, Bibliothèque Nationale, Galerie Mansart. *Hommage à Félix Bracquemond*. From September 13, 1974. Catalogue by J.-P. Bouillon, in *Société des Peintres Graveurs Français Reconnue d'Utilité Publique*.
1974, Paris, Grand Palais

Paris, Grand Palais. *Le Musée du Luxembourg en 1874; Peintures*. May 31–November 18, 1974. Catalogue by G. Lacambre with J. de Rohan-Chabat.
1974, Paris, Grand Palais, "Impressionnisme"
Paris, Grand Palais. *Centenaire de l'Impressionnisme*. September 21–November 24, 1974. Also shown at New York, Metropolitan Museum of Art. Essay by R. Huyghe; foreword by H. Adhémar and A.M. Clark; catalogue by A. Dayez, M. Hoog, and C. Moffett.
1974, Paris, Grand Palais, "Paris d'Hier"
Paris, Société des Artistes Français. *Le Salon de 1974. Paris d'hier et d'aujourd'hui*. 1974.
1974, Tours
Tours, Musée des Beaux-Arts. *La Céramique Tourangelle au XIXe siècle*. October 11–November 24, 1974. No catalogue.
1974–75, London, etc.
London, Heim Gallery. *From Poussin to Puvis de Chavannes*. October 11–November 15, 1974. Also shown at Cambridge, Fitzwilliam Museum, November 25, 1974–January 3, 1975; Birmingham, City Museum and Art Gallery, January 10–February 14, 1975; Glasgow, Glasgow Art Gallery and Museum, February 28–March 20, 1975. Introduction by H. Oursel.
1974–75, New York
New York, Fairleigh Dickinson University, New York Cultural Center. *William Adolphe Bouguereau*. December 13, 1974–February 2, 1975. Also shown at San Francisco, The Fine Arts Museums of San Francisco; California Palace of the Legion of Honor. Catalogue by R. Isaacson.
1974–75, Paris, Bibliothèque Forney
Paris, Bibliothèque Forney. *Céramique impressionniste, l'atelier Haviland de Paris–Auteuil 1873–1882*. December, 1974–February 1975.
1974–75, Williamstown
Williamstown, Mass., Sterling and Francine Clark Art Institute. *A Selection of Drawings*. December 17, 1974–March 2, 1975.
1974–75, Winterthur, etc.
Winterthur, Kunstmuseum. *Charles Gleyre ou les illusions perdues*. 1974–75. Also shown at Marseilles, Musée Cantini; Munich, Städtische Galerie im Lenbachhaus Kiel, Kunsthalle; Arau, Aargauer Kunsthaus; Lausanne, Musée Cantonal des Beaux-Arts.
1974–76, France, Musées de Province
France, Musées de Province. *La Comédie française–collections et documents*. 1974–76.
1975, Barbizon
Barbizon, Salle des Fêtes. *Barbizon au temps de J.-F. Millet 1849–1875*. May 3–June 2, 1975.
1975, Charleroi
Charleroi, Palais des Beaux-Arts. *Rétrospective Alfred Stevens*. January 11–February 16, 1975.
1975, Cherbourg
Cherbourg, Musée Thomas Henry. *Jean-François Millet 1814–1875, et le thème du paysan dans la peinture française du XIXe siècle*. July–August 1975.
1975, Chicago
Chicago, The Art Institute of Chicago. *Paintings by Monet*. March 15–May 11, 1975. Foreword by J. Maxon; essays by A. Masson, G. Seiberling, and J. Morandel.
1975, London
London, Bethnal Green Museum. *Jumbo and Other Elephants*. 1975.
1975, Marseilles
Marseilles, Musée Cantini. *L'Orient en question, 1825–1875: de Missolonghi à Suez, ou l'orientalisme de Delacroix à Flaubert*. 1975. Catalogue by M. Latour, et al.
1975, Montpellier
Montpellier, Musée Fabre. *Alexandre Cabanel*. 1975.
1975, New York
New York, The Metropolitan Museum of Art. *Notable Acquisitions 1965–1975*. 1975. Preface by O. Raggio.
1975, New York, Museum of Modern Art
New York, The Museum of Modern Art. *The Architecture of the Ecole des Beaux-Arts*. October 29, 1975–January 4, 1976. Preface by A. Drexler. Catalogue unnumbered.
1975, New York, Shepherd Gallery
New York, Shepherd Gallery. *Ingres and Delacroix through Degas and Puvis de Chavannes: The Figure in French Art 1800–1870*. May–June 1975. Catalogue by M.L.H. Reymert et al.
1975, Paris, Grand Palais
Palais, Grand Palais. *Sur les Traces de Jean-Baptiste Carpeaux*. March 11–May 5, 1975. Catalogue by V. Beyer, A. Braunwald, L. Duclaux, F. Perot, and A. Pingeot.
1975, Paris, Orangerie
Paris, Orangerie. *Hommage à Corot: Peintures et dessins des collections françaises*. June 6–September 29, 1975. Foreword by M. Laclotte; essay by M. Sérullaz; catalogue by H. Toussaint, G. Monnier, and M. Servot.

1975, Providence
Providence, Brown University Department of Art, Rhode Island School of Design Museum. *Rubenism.* January 30–February 23, 1975.
1975, Sèvres
Sèvres, Musée National de Céramique. *Porcelaines de Sèvres au XIX^e siècle.* May 24–November 3, 1975.
1975, Toronto
Toronto, Art Gallery of Ontario. *Puvis de Chavannes and the Modern Tradition.* October 24–November 30, 1975. By R.J. Wattenmaker.
1975, Valenciennes
Valenciennes, Musée des Beaux-Arts. *Dessins de Jean-Baptiste Carpeaux à Valenciennes.* 1975.
1975–76, Cambridge, Mass.
Cambridge, Mass., Harvard University, Fogg Art Museum. *Metamorphoses in Nineteenth-Century Sculpture.* November 19, 1975–January 7, 1976. Catalogue edited by J.L. Wasserman; texts by G.F. Benge, A. Braunwald, A.M. Wagner, et al.
1975–76, Cleveland, etc.
Cleveland, The Cleveland Museum of Art. *Japonisme: Japanese Influence on French Art 1854–1910.* July 9–August 31, 1975. Also shown at New Brunswick, N. J., The Rutgers University Art Gallery, October 4–November 16, 1975; Baltimore, The Walters Art Gallery, December 10, 1975–January 26, 1976. Catalogue by G.P. Weisberg, P.D. Cate, G. Needham, M. Eidelberg, and W.R. Johnston.
1975–76, Frankfurt, Hamburg, The Hague
Frankfurt, Städelsches Kunstinstitut und Städtische Galerie. *Charles Meryon: Paris um 1850: Zeichnungen, Radierungen, Photographien.* October 23, 1975–January 4, 1976. Also shown at Hamburg, Hamburger Kunsthalle, January 30–March 14, 1976; The Hague, Haags Gemeentemuseum, March 27–June 5, 1976. Essay by E.P. Janis; catalogue by M. Stuffman.
1975–76, Paris, Grand Palais
Paris, Grand Palais. *Jean-François Millet.* October 17, 1975–January 5, 1976. Catalogue by R.L. Herbert. *See also* 1976, London, Hayward Gallery.
1975–76, Rome
Rome, Académie de France, Villa Medici. *Corot.* 1975–76.
1976, Chartres
Chartres, Musée. *Les Scènes agricoles dans la peinture française du XIX^e siècle.* June 19–September 12, 1976. No catalogue.
1976, Dijon
Dijon, Musée des Beaux-Arts. *Catalogue des peintures, dessins, estampes, des sculpteurs œuvres.* 1976. Catalogue by S. Lemoine.
1976, Düsseldorf
Düsseldorf, Städtische Kunsthalle. *Nadar karikaturist, fotograf, aeronaut.* 1976. Essay by M. Villette.
1976, London, Colnaghi
London, P. & D. Colnaghi & Co. Ltd. *Photography. The First Eighty Years.* October 27–December 1, 1976. Catalogue by V. Lloyd et al.
1976, London, Hayward Gallery
London, Hayward Gallery. *Jean-François Millet.* January 22–March 7, 1976. Catalogue by R.L. Herbert. *See also* 1975–76, Paris, Grand Palais.
1976, London, Victoria and Albert Museum
London, Victoria and Albert Museum. *Minton 1798–1910.* August–October 1976. By E. Aslin and P. Atterbury.
1976, Nantes
Nantes, Musée des Beaux-Arts. *Insolite et Symbolisme, Tissot, Merson, Maxence.* 1976.
1976, New York

New York, Shepherd Gallery. *The Non-Dissenters.* 1976.
1976, Norton
Norton, Mass., Wheaton College, Watson Gallery. *Process of Perfection.* November 15–December 15, 1976.
1976, Ottawa
Ottawa, National Gallery of Canada. *Charles Nègre 1820–1880.* May 21–June 20, 1976. Catalogue by J. Borcoman.
1976, Paris, Bibliothèque Historique
Paris, Bibliothèque Historique de la Ville de Paris. *Paris, la rue, le mobilier urbain du Second Empire à nos jours.* January–March 1976.
1976, Paris, Bibliothèque Nationale
Paris, Bibliothèque Nationale. *Une Invention du XIX^e siècle, expression et technique: La Photographie; collections de la Société Française de Photographie.* 1976. Introduction by J.J. Trillat; catalogue by B. Marbot et al.
1976, Paris, Grand Palais
Paris, Grand Palais. *En Egypte au temps de Flaubert, 1839–1860, les premiers photographes.* 1976. Catalogue by M.-T. and A. Jammes.
1976, Paris, Hôtel de Béthune Sully
Paris, Hôtel de Béthune Sully. *Henri Labrouste.* 1976. Catalogue in *Les Monuments Historiques de la France*, no. 6 (1975), pp. 28–37.
1976–77, Arras
Arras, Musée. *Jules et Emile Breton, peintres de l'Artois.* November 14, 1976–January 31, 1977. Catalogue forthcoming.
1976–77, Los Angeles, etc.
Los Angeles, Los Angeles County Museum of Art. *Women Artists: 1550–1950.* December 21, 1976–March 13, 1977. Also shown at Austin, The University of Texas at Austin, University Art Museum, April 12–June 12, 1977; Pittsburgh, Carnegie Institute, Museum of Art, July 14–September 4, 1977; Brooklyn, The Brooklyn Museum, October 8–November 27, 1977. Catalogue by A.S. Harris and L. Nochlin.
1976–77, Northampton, Williamstown
Northampton, Mass., Smith College Museum of Art. *Jongkind and the Pre-Impressionists. Painters of the Ecole Saint-Siméon.* October 15–December 5, 1976. Also shown at Williamstown, Mass., Sterling and Francine Clark Art Institute, December 17, 1976–February 13, 1977. By C.C. Cunningham with S.D. Peters and K. Zimmerer.
1976–77, Paris, Archives Nationales
Paris, Archives Nationales. *Le Parisien chez lui au XIX^e siècle.* 1976–77.
1976–77, Paris, Grand Palais
Paris, Grand Palais. *Puvis de Chavannes 1824–1898.* November 26, 1976–February 14, 1977. Catalogue by L. d'Argencourt, J. Foucart, M.-C Boucher-Regnault, and D. Druick. *See also* 1977, Ottawa.
1976–77, Paris, Muséum d'Histoire Naturelle
Paris, Muséum National d'Histoire Naturelle. *L'Animal de Lascaux à Picasso.* June 15, 1976–January 7, 1977.
1976–77, Vienna
Vienna, Graphische Sammlung Albertina. *Von Ingres bis Cézanne, Aquarelle und Zeichnungen aus dem Louvre.* 1976–77.
1977, Chicago
Chicago, The Art Institute of Chicago. *The First Century of Photography, Niepce to Atget, from the Collection of André Jammes.* 1977. Essay by A. and M.-T. Jammes; catalogue by T. Travis.
1977, Chicago, Antiquarian Society
Chicago, The Art Institute of Chicago. *The Antiquarian Society: The First One Hundred Years.* April 23–June 19, 1977.
1977, Hyeres
Hyeres, La Rotonde. *L'Architecture Hyeroise de Napoléon III à*

*1914.* From September 30, 1977.
1977, Le Mans
Le Mans. *Gustave Moreau et J.K. Huysmans.* 1977. Preface by G. Lacambre.
1977, Leningrad
Leningrad, State Hermitage Museum. *Eugène Boudin.* 1977.
1977, London
London, Shepherd Gallery, The Alpine Club Gallery. *French Nineteenth-Century Paintings.* 1977.
1977, New York
New York, The Metropolitan Museum of Art. *Nadar, Portraits from the Collection of Samuel Wagstaff.* 1977. No catalogue.
1977, Ottawa
Ottawa, The National Gallery of Canada. *Puvis de Chavannes 1824–1898.* March 25–May 8, 1977. Catalogue by L. d'Argencourt, M.-C. Boucher, D. Druick, and J. Foucart. *See also* 1976–77, Paris, Grand Palais.
1977, Paris, Musée Hébert
Paris, Musée Hébert. *L'Italie romantique vue par Hébert (1817–1908).* 1977.
1977, Saint-Tropez
Saint-Tropez, Musée de l'Annonciade. *Le Drapeau.* 1977.
1977, Saint-Omer
Saint-Omer, Musée de l'Hôtel Sandelin. *Léon Belly,* 1977.
1977, Santa Barbara
Santa Barbara, Santa Barbara Museum of Art. *Varieties of Nineteenth-Century European Photography: Documents and Expressions.* 1977. No catalogue.
1977, Zurich
Zurich, Kunsthaus. *Malerei und Photographie im Dialog von 1840 bis Heute.* 1977. Catalogue by E. Billeter et al.
1977–78, Ann Arbor, Baltimore, Montreal
Ann Arbor, The University of Michigan Museum of Art. *Alfred Stevens.* September 10–October 16, 1977. Also shown at Baltimore, The Walters Art Gallery, November 20, 1977–January 1, 1978; Montreal, Musée des Beaux-Arts, February 2–March 19, 1978. By W.A. Coles.
1977–78, Paris, Grand Palais
Paris, Grand Palais. *Gustave Courbet (1819–1877).* September 30, 1977–January 2, 1978. Essay by A. Bowness; biography by M.-T. de Forges; catalogue by H. Toussaint. *See also* 1978, London.
1978, Chalon-sur-Saône
Chalon-sur-Saône, Musée Nicéphore Niépce. *Les Albums photographiques édités par Louis-Désiré Blanquart-Evrard, 1851–1855.* February 17–March 17, 1978. Catalogue by I. Jammes.
1978, Chapel Hill
Chapel Hill, University of North Carolina, William Hayes Ackland Memorial Art Center. *French Nineteenth-Century Oil Sketches: David to Degas.* 1978. By J.M. Wisdom.
1978, Chicago
Chicago, The Art Institute of Chicago. *Frédéric Bazille and Early Impressionism.* March 4–April 30, 1978. Essays by J.P. Marandel and F. Daulte; catalogue by J.P. Marandel.
1978, London
London, Arts Council of Great Britain, Royal Academy of Arts. *Gustave Courbet 1819–1877.* January 19–March 19, 1978. Essay by A. Bowness; biography by M.-T. de Forges; catalogue by H. Toussaint. *See also* 1977–78, Paris, Grand Palais.
1978, Peking, Shanghai
Peking. *Paysages et paysans français 1820–1905.* 1978. Also shown at Shanghai.

# Museum Catalogues

Catalogue, Amiens, Musée de Picardie, 1876
Amiens, Musée de Picardie. *Catalogue des objets d'antiquité et de curiosité exposés dans le Musée de Picardie.* Amiens, 1876.
Catalogue, Angers, Musée, 1887
Angers, Musée. *Supplément du 1^er juillet 1887 au livret du Musée d'Angers.* By H. Jouin. Angers, 1887.
Catalogues, Bagnères-de-Bigorre
Bagnères-de-Bigorre, Musée Municipal. *Catalogue.* Bagnères-de-Bigorre, 1857, 1864.
Catalogue, Bayonne, Musée Bonnat, 1952
Bayonne, Musée Bonnat. *Catalogue sommaire.* Paris, 1952.

Catalogue, Besançon, Musées, 1886
Besançon, Musées. *Musées de Besançon: Catalogue des peintures, dessins, sculptures et antiquités.* By A. Castan. 7th ed. Besançon, 1886.
Catalogue, Besançon, Musées, 1955
Besançon, Musées. *Musées de Besançon: Collections d'horlogerie.* By P. Mesnage. Besançon, 1955.
Catalogues, Bordeaux, Musée
Bordeaux, Musée. *Catalogue des tableaux, sculptures, gravures, dessins exposés dans les galeries du Musée de Bordeaux.* By E. Vallet. Bordeaux, 1881, 1894.

Catalogue, Bordeaux, Musée, 1910
Bordeaux, Musée. *Ville de Bordeaux. Musée de peinture.* By D. Alaux. Bordeaux, 1910.
Catalogue, Bordeaux, Musée, 1933
Bordeaux, Musée. *Ville de Bordeaux. Musée de peinture et de sculpture.* Bellegarde, 1933.
Catalogue, Boston, Museum of Fine Arts, 1955
Boston, Museum of Fine Arts. *Summary Catalogue of European Paintings in Oil, Tempera, and Pastel.* Boston, 1955.
Catalogue, Bremen, Kunsthalle, 1925
Bremen, Kunsthalle. *Katalog der Gemälde und Bildhauerwerke*

in der Kunsthalle zu Bremen. Bremen, 1925.

Catalogue, Bremen, Kunsthalle, 1973
Bremen, Kunsthalle. *Katalog der Gemälde des 19. und 20. Jahrhunderts in der Kunsthalle Bremen.* By G. Gerkens and U. Heiderich. 2 vols. Bremen, 1973.

Catalogues, Caen, Musée
Caen, Musée. *Catalogue des tableaux, sculptures, dessins, gravures et aquarelles exposé dans les galeries du Musée de Caen.* By G. Menegoz. Caen, 1913, 1928.

Catalogue, Gray, Musée Baron Martin, 1959
Gray, Musée Baron Martin. *Catalogue du Musée Baron Martin à Gray.* By A.P. de Mirimonde. Gray, 1959.

Catalogue, Le Mée, Musée Chapu, 1977
Le Mée, Musée Chapu. *Henri Chapu au Mée-sur-Seine.* By A.-C. Lussiez. Le Mée, 1977.

Catalogue, Lille, Musée des Beaux-Arts, 1872
Lille, Musée des Beaux-Arts. *Catalogue de tableaux, bas-reliefs et statues.* Lille, 1872.

Catalogue, Lille, Musée des Beaux-Arts, 1893
Lille, Musée des Beaux-Arts. *Catalogue des tableaux du Musée de Lille.* Introduction by J. Lenglart. Lille, 1893.

Catalogue, Lisieux, Musée, 1925
Lisieux, Musée de Lisieux. *Catalogue des œuvres de peinture, aquarelles, dessins et sculptures exposées dans le Musée de Lisieux.* By J. Deville. Lisieux, 1925.

Catalogue, Lyons, Musée Historique des Tissus, 1929
Lyons, Musée Historique des Tissus. *Catalogue des principales pièces exposées.* By H. d'Hennezel. Lyons, 1929.

Catalogue, Marseilles, Musée des Beaux-Arts, 1876
Marseilles, Musée des Beaux-Arts. *Catalogue des objets d'art composant la collection du Musée de Marseilles.* By Bouillon-Landais. Marseilles, 1876.

Catalogue, Mexico City, Museo Nacional de Historia, 1976
Mexico City, Museo Nacional de Historia. *Plata Christofle de Maximiliano de Habsburgo.* By A. Ussel, G. de la Torre, and M.C.S. de Bonfil. Mexico City, 1976.

Catalogue, Minneapolis, Institute of Arts, 1971
Minneapolis, The Minneapolis Institute of Arts. *European Paintings in the Minneapolis Institute of Arts.* Minneapolis, 1971.

Catalogue Oberlin, Allen Memorial Art Museum, 1967
Oberlin, Oh., Allen Memorial Art Museum. *Catalogue of European and American Paintings and Sculpture in the Allen Memorial Art Museum, Oberlin College.* By W. Stechow. Oberlin, 1967.

Catalogue, Oslo, Nasjonalgalleriet, 1973
Oslo, Nasjonalgalleriet. *Katalog over utenlandsk Malerkunst.* Oslo, 1973.

Catalogue, Paris, Conservatoire National des Arts et Métiers, 1908
Paris, Conservatoire National des Arts et Métiers. *Catalogue officiel des collections du Conservatoire National des Arts et Métiers.* Vol. IV: *Arts chimiques, matières colorantes et teinture, céramique et verrerie.* Paris, 1908.

Catalogue, Paris, Jeu de Paume, 1947
Paris, Musée du Jeu de Paume. *Catalogue des peintures et sculptures exposés au Musée de l'Impressionnisme (Jeu de Paume de Tuileries). Les Impressionnistes, leurs précurseurs et leurs contemporains.* Paris, 1947.

Catalogue, Paris, Jeu de Paume, 1973
Paris, Musée du Jeu de Paume. *Catalogue des peintures...* Paris, 1973.

Catalogue, Paris, Louvre, 1903
Paris, Musée National du Louvre. *Catalogue sommaire des peintures exposées dans les Galeries.* Paris, 1903.

Catalogue, Paris, Louvre, Paintings, 1972
Paris, Musée du Louvre. *Catalogue des peintures.* Vol. 1: *Ecole française.* Paris, 1972.

Catalogues, Paris, Luxembourg
Paris, Musée du Luxembourg. *Notice des peintures, sculptures, gravures, et lithographies de l'école moderne de France.* Paris, 1852. Later editions published regularly with slight title variations until 1900, with introductions successively by P. de Chennevières, E. Arago, and L. Bénédite. Subsequently published in 1912, 1924, and 1927.

Catalogues Illustrés, Paris, Luxembourg
Paris, Musée du Luxembourg. *Catalogue illustré d'après les dessins originaux des artistes et divers documents.* Paris. Published regularly from 1884.

Catalogue Raisonné, Paris, Luxembourg, 1896
Paris, Musée du Luxembourg. *Catalogue raisonné et illustré des peintures, sculptures, dessins, gravures en médailles et sur pierres fines et objets d'art divers des écoles contemporaines.* By L. Bénédite. Paris, 1896.

Catalogue, Paris, Musée des Arts Décoratifs, 1934
Paris, Musée des Arts Décoratifs. *Guide illustré du Musée des Arts Décoratifs.* New ed. Paris, 1934.

Catalogue, Paris, Musée des Arts Décoratifs, 1967
Paris, Musée des Arts Décoratifs. *Guide illustré du Musée des Arts Décoratifs.* Paris, 1967.

Catalogue, Paris, Musée des Souverains, 1868
Paris, Musée des Souverains. *Notice des antiquités, objets du moyen âge, de la renaissance et des temps modernes composant le Musée des Souverains.* By H. Barbet de Jouy. 2nd ed. Paris, 1868.

Catalogue, Paris, Musée Monétaire, 1892
Paris, Musée Monétaire de la Monnaie de Paris. *Médailles françaises dont les coins sont conservés au Musée Monétaire.* Paris, 1892.

Catalogue, Philadelphia, John G. Johnson Collection, 1941
Philadelphia, John G. Johnson Collection. *Catalogue of Paintings.* Foreword by H. Marceau. Philadelphia, 1941.

Catalogues, Philadelphia, Museum of Art, Wilstach Collection
Philadelphia, Philadelphia Museum of Art. *The W.P. Wilstach Collection.* Philadelphia, 1900, 1910, 1913, 1922.

Catalogue, Philadelphia, Rodin Museum, 1976
Philadelphia, Rodin Museum. *The Sculpture of Auguste Rodin. The Collection of the Rodin Museum, Philadelphia.* By J.L. Tancock. Philadelphia, 1976.

Catalogue, Quimper, Musée des Beaux-Arts, 1976
Quimper, Musée des Beaux-Arts. *Catalogue.* By P. Quiniou. Quimper, 1976. n.p.

Catalogues, Rouen, Musée de Peinture et de Sculpture
Rouen, Musée de Peinture et de Sculpture. *Catalogue.* Rouen, 1890, 1911, 1967.

Catalogue, Sèvres, Musée Céramique, 1897
Sèvres, Musée Céramique. *Manufacture Nationale de Sèvres. Catalogue du Musée Céramique.* Vol. IV, series D: *Faïences.* By E. Garnier. Paris, 1897.

Catalogue, Troyes, Musée, 1897
Troyes, Musée. *Musée de Troyes. Art décoratif (Musée Piat). Catalogue descriptif et raisonné.* By L. Le Clert. Troyes, 1897.

Catalogue, Troyes, Musée, 1904
Troyes, Musée. *Art décoratif (Musée Piat). Catalogue descriptif et raisonné.* First supplement. (Extract from *Mémoires de la Société Académique de l'Aube*, vol. LXVIII, 1904.) Troyes, 1905.

Catalogue, Troyes, Musée, 1931
Troyes, Musée. *Catalogue des sculptures du Musée de Troyes.* 6th ed. Troyes, 1931.

Catalogue, Versailles, Musée Impérial, 1860
Versailles, Musée Impérial. *Notice du Musée Impérial de Versailles. Première étage.* Paris, 1860.

Catalogue, Washington, D.C., National Gallery of Art, 1968
Washington, D.C., National Gallery of Art. *Summary Catalogue of European Paintings and Sculpture, National Gallery of Art.* 2 vols. Washington, D.C., 1968.

Catalogue, Williamstown, Clark Art Institute, 1964
Williamstown, Mass., Sterling and Francine Clark Art Institute. *Drawings from the Clark Art Institute: A Catalogue Raisonné of the Robert Sterling Clark Collection of European and American Drawings, Sixteenth through Nineteenth Centuries, at the Sterling and Francine Clark Art Institute.* By E. Haverkamp-Begemann, S.D. Lawder, C.W. Talbot. 2 vols. New Haven and London, 1964.

# Index of Artists, Craftsmen, and Manufacturers

463

# Acknowledgments

The American authors wish to thank the following people, who, in addition to the lenders to the exhibition, have most generously shared their information and research, much of it previously unpublished, and offered valuable advice and aid:
Jean d'Albis (who provided material on the porcelain factories of Limoges), Roger Allen, Mrs. Robert André, Maddy Aries, Elizabeth Aslin, Florence Austin, Hugues Autexier, Marie-Hélène Babelon, Katherine Baetjer, Lesley K. Baier, Y. de Beauregard, Geoffrey de Bellaigue, Wendy Belser, M. Beurdeley, Albert Boime (particularly for sharing much unpublished material on Couture), Mme G. Bonté, Michael Botwinick, Henri Bouilhet, Tony Bouilhet, Jean-Paul Bouillon, J. Bourdon, Sophie Boutet de Monvel, François Braunschweig, Marcelle Brunet (who provided archival material from Sèvres), Yvonne Brunhammer, Shirley Bury, Peter Castle, Comte René de Chambrun, R.J. Charleston, Andrew S. Ciechanowiecki, Gérald Collot, Jean Coural, Jacques Damiot, G. Deherre, Msgr Roger Desreumaux, James Draper, Arthur Drexler, Donald Drew Egbert, Ralph Esmerian, Jr., Sarah C. Faunce, Peter Fergusson, Vicomte Fleury, Jacques Foucart, Henri-Pierre Fourest, Marie de Gary, Nadine Gasc, Jean Gaube du Gers, Yvonne Goldenberg, Priscilla Grace, John A. Griswold, Leon de Groer, Marguerite Guillaume, Jean-Pierre Guillen, Sophie Guillot de Suduiraut, Antoinette Hallé, Karl Hammer, June Hargrove, Bunny Harvey, Robert Herbert, David Herwaldt, Hans-Jörgen Heuser, Ulrich Hiesinger, Jack Hillier, Carol Hollman, Gérard Hubert, Gérard Ingold, Jacqueline Jacqué, Annie Jacques, Isabelle Jammes, Martha Jenks, Bertrand Jestaz, Françoise Jestaz, William R. Johnston, Elizabeth Jones, Martine Kahane, Robert Kashey, R.C. Kenedy, David Kindler, Julien Lafargue, Denise Ledoux-Lebard, Olivier LeFuel, François LePage, Msgr A. Lepautre, Neil Levine, Sally Linden, Mme Lotte, Duc de Luynes, Anne McCauley, Wendy MacNeil, J. Patrice Marandel, Bernard Marbet, Marianne Margolis, Katherine Marmoz, Mrs. John Mecom, John Messina, Jean-Marie Meulia, Bruno Meyer, Robert de Micheaux, J. Jefferson Miller, II, Geneviève Monnier, Mme P.-M. Moreau, Maria Morris, Weston Naef, Hervé Oursel, Merribell M. Parsons, Olga Popovitch, Tamara Préaud (who provided archival references for Sèvres), Christian Prevost-Marcilhacy, Margot Raissac, Muriel de Raissac, Hella Robels, Mme Rochat, Christianne Roger, C. Romanet, Naomi Rosenblum, Daniel Rosenfeld, Haavard Rostrup, Baron Guy de Rothschild, Gérard Rousset-Charnys, Mme P. de Sainte Marie, Guy Sarrauste de Menthière, Josiane Sartre, Donald Schneider, Alan Shestack, Susan Siegfried, Robert A. Sobieszek, Alice Stern, J. Stoll, Jim Stone, Max Terrier, Marie de Thézy, Peter Thornton, Nicole Toussaint du Wast, F. Vallet, Ann Van Zanten, Philippe Verdier, Jacqueline Viaux, Geneviève Viollet-le-Duc, Comte de Virieu, Anne Middleton Wagner, Hugh Wakefield, John Walsh, Cary R. Wasserman, Adam Weinberg, Michael Wentworth, Jacques Wilhelm.

The following members of the staff of the Philadelphia Museum of Art have contributed substantially toward the production of this catalogue: Sherry Babbitt, Margot Bartle, Nancy Baxter, Clarisse Carnell, Alice Lefton, Barbara Sevy, Suzanne Wells.

Translations by Frances Frenaye, Christine Garnon-Donoghue, Tom Leighton, Kathleen A. Lynch, Anne Poulet, Catherine Jandine Hill, John Shepley, Emily Toll

Catalogue coordinated and edited by
George H. Marcus with the assistance of Janet M. Iandola

Designed by Bruno Pfäffli, Arcueil, and
printed by Imprimerie Blanchard, Le Plessis-Robinson

The audiovisual program that accompanies the exhibition was sponsored by
IBM France and IBM Europe.

Photographs supplied by the lenders and the following:
A.P.P.A.P. S.A., Paris; G. Baubé, Gisors; Jean Bienaimé, Troyes; E. Irving Blomstrann, New Britain, Conn.; Madeleine Bonnard, Borel, Marseilles; R. Boulhaut, Verdun; Will Brown, Philadelphia; Bulloz, Paris; Chuzeville, Paris; Alain Danvers, Bordeaux; Ellebé, Rouen; S. Faideau, Forges-les-Eaux; Françoise Foliot, Paris; Gérondal, Lomme-Lille; Giraudon, Paris; Hutin, Compiègne; Bruno Jarret, Paris; Lauros-Giraudon, Paris; Clément Ledermann; Leroy, Arras; Wim Molenkamp, Amsterdam; Claude O'Sughrue, Montpellier; R.J. Paté, Caen; Phéliphot S.A., Auxerre; Photorama S.A., Le Havre; Piaget, Saint Louis; Réunion des Musées Nationaux, Paris; *Revue de l'Art*, Paris; Rheinisches Bildarchiv, Cologne; Guy Roumagnac, Montauban; Studio Madec, Nantes